ANNOTATED INSTRUCTOR'S EDITION

Understanding Basic Statistics

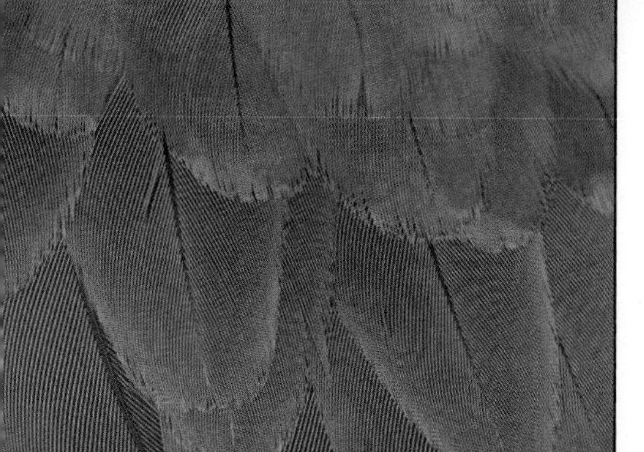

ANNOTATED INSTRUCTOR'S EDITION

FIFTH EDITION

Understanding Basic Statistics

Charles Henry Brase
Regis University

Corrinne Pellillo Brase
Arapahoe Community College

BROOKS/COLE
CENGAGE Learning™

Australia • Brazil • Japan • Korea • Mexico • Singapore • Spain • United Kingdom • United States

***Understanding Basic Statistics,* Fifth Edition**
Charles Henry Brase and Corrinne Pellillo Brase

Senior Acquiring Sponsoring Editor: Molly Taylor
Development Editor: Carl Chudyk
Editorial Associate: Andrew Lipsett
Associate Media Editor: Catie Ronquillo
Senior Marketing Manager: Greta Kleinert
Marketing Coordinator: Angela Kim
Marketing Communications Manager: Mary Anne Payumo
Project Manager, Editorial Production: Paula Kmetz
Art & Design Manager: Jill Haber
Senior Manufacturing Coordinator: Diane Gibbons
Photo Researcher: Lisa Jelly Smith
Copy Editor: Jean Bermingham
Cover Designer: Nina Wishnok
Cover Image: © Roy Toft/Getty Images
Compositor: Nesbitt Graphics, Inc.

A complete list of photo credits appears in the back of the book, immediately following the appendix.

Library of Congress Control Number: 2008934780

Student Edition

ISBN-13: 978-0-547-13249-5

ISBN-10: 0-547-13249-2

Annotated Instructor's Edition

ISBN-13: 978-0-547-18852-2

ISBN-10: 0-547-18852-8

Brooks/Cole
10 Davis Drive
Belmont, CA 94002-3098
USA

Cengage Learning is a leading provider of customized learning solutions with office locations around the globe, including Singapore, the United Kingdom, Australia, Mexico, Brazil, and Japan. Locate your local office at **www.cengage.com/global.**

Cengage Learning products are represented in Canada by Nelson Education, Ltd.

For your course and learning solutions, visit **academic.cengage.com.**

Purchase any of our products at your local college store or at our preferred online store **www.ichapters.com.**

Printed in Canada
2 3 4 5 6 7 12 11 10

This book is dedicated to the memory of
a great teacher, mathematician, and friend

Burton W. Jones

Professor Emeritus, University of Colorado

Contents

4 Correlation and Regression 118

5 Elementary Probability Theory 156

6 The Binomial Probability Distribution and Related Topics 202

7 Normal Curves and Sampling Distributions 242

8 Estimation 306

9 Hypothesis Testing 350

10 Inferences About Differences 404

11 Additional Topics Using Inference 456

Appendix: Tables A1

Students need to develop critical thinking skills in order to understand and evaluate the limitations of statistical methods. *Understanding Basic Statistics* makes students aware of method appropriateness, assumptions, biases, and justifiable conclusions.

CRITICAL THINKING **Bias and Variability**

Whenever we use a sample statistic as an estimate of a population parameter, we need to consider both *bias* and *variability* of the statistic.

A sample statistic is **unbiased** if the mean of its sampling distribution equals the value of the parameter being estimated.

The spread of the sampling distribution indicates the **variability of the statistic.** The spread is affected by the sampling method and the sample size. Statistics from larger random samples have spreads that are smaller.

We see from the central limit theorem that the sample mean $\bar{x}$ is an unbiased estimator of the mean μ when $n \geq 30$. The variability of $\bar{x}$ decreases as the sample size increases.

In Section 8.3, we will see that the sample proportion $\hat{p}$ is an unbiased estimator of the population proportion of successes p in binomial experiments with sufficiently large numbers of trials n. Again, we will see that the variability of $\hat{p}$ decreases with increasing numbers of trials.

The sample variance s^2 is an unbiased estimator for the population variance σ^2.

◀ NEW! Critical Thinking

Critical thinking is an important skill for students to develop in order to avoid reaching misleading conclusions. The Critical Thinking feature provides additional clarification on specific concepts as a safeguard against incorrect evaluation of information.

NEW! Interpretation ▶

Increasingly, calculators and computers are used to generate the numeric results of a statistical process. However, the student still needs to correctly interpret those results in the context of a particular application. The Interpretation feature calls attention to this important step.

(b) Assuming the milk is not contaminated, what is the probability that the average bacteria count $\bar{x}$ for one day is between 2350 and 2650 bacteria per milliliter?

SOLUTION: We convert the interval

$$2350 \leq \bar{x} \leq 2650$$

to a corresponding interval on the standard z axis.

$$z = \frac{\bar{x} - \mu}{\sigma/\sqrt{n}} \approx \frac{\bar{x} - 2500}{46.3}$$

$$\bar{x} = 2350 \quad \text{converts to} \quad z = \frac{2350 - 2500}{46.3} \approx -3.24$$

$$\bar{x} = 2650 \quad \text{converts to} \quad z = \frac{2650 - 2500}{46.3} \approx 3.24$$

Therefore,

$$\begin{aligned} P(2350 \leq \bar{x} \leq 2650) &= P(-3.24 \leq z \leq 3.24) \\ &= 0.9994 - 0.0006 \\ &= 0.9988 \end{aligned}$$

The probability is 0.9988 that $\bar{x}$ is between 2350 and 2650.

(c) INTERPRETATION At the end of each day, the inspector must decide to accept or reject the accumulated milk that has been held in cold storage awaiting shipment. Suppose the 42 samples taken by the inspector have a mean bacteria count $\bar{x}$ that is *not* between 2350 and 2650. If you were the inspector, what would be your comment on this situation?

SOLUTION: The probability that $\bar{x}$ is between 2350 and 2650 is very high. If the inspector finds that the average bacteria count for the 42 samples is not between 2350 and 2650, then it is reasonable to conclude that there is something wrong with the milk. If $\bar{x}$ is less than 2350, you might suspect someone added chemicals to the milk to artificially reduce the bacteria count. If $\bar{x}$ is above 2650, you might suspect some other kind of biologic contamination.

5. *Critical Thinking* Consider the numbers

   2 3 4 5 5

   (a) Compute the mode, median, and mean.
   (b) If the numbers represented codes for the colors of T-shirts ordered from a catalog, which average(s) would make sense?
   (c) If the numbers represented one-way mileages for trails to different lakes, which average(s) would make sense?
   (d) Suppose the numbers represent survey responses from 1 to 5, with 1 = disagree strongly, 2 = disagree, 3 = agree, 4 = agree strongly, and 5 = agree very strongly. Which averages make sense?

6. *Critical Thinking* Consider a data set of 15 distinct measurements with mean A and median B.
   (a) If the highest number were increased, what would be the effect on the median and mean? Explain.
   (b) If the highest number were decreased to a value still larger than B, what would be the effect on the median and mean?
   (c) If the highest number were decreased to a value smaller than B, what would be the effect on the median and mean?

◀ NEW! Critical Thinking Exercises

In every section and chapter problem set, Critical Thinking problems provide students with the opportunity to test their understanding of the application of statistical methods and their interpretation of their results.

No language can be spoken without learning the vocabulary, including statistics. *Understanding Basic Statistics* introduces statistical terms with deliberate care.

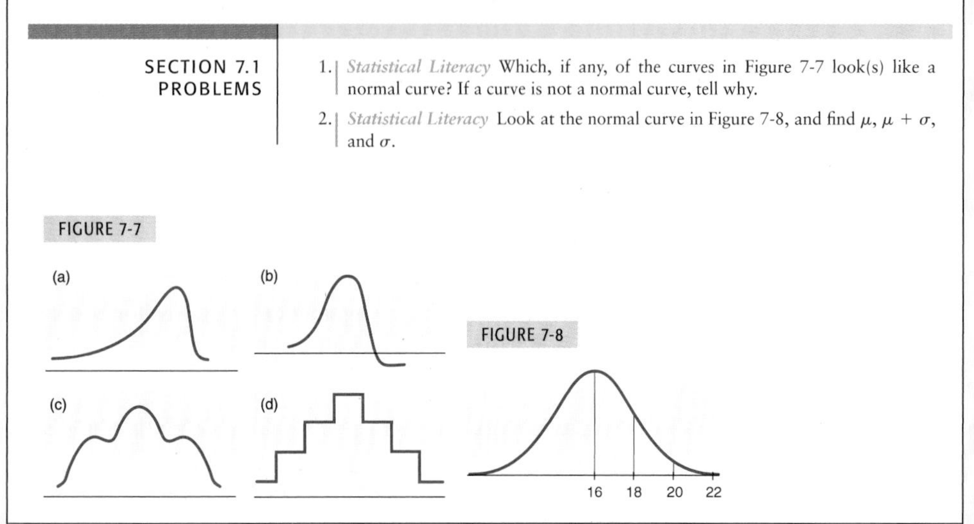

SECTION 7.1 PROBLEMS

1. *Statistical Literacy* Which, if any, of the curves in Figure 7-7 look(s) like a normal curve? If a curve is not a normal curve, tell why.

2. *Statistical Literacy* Look at the normal curve in Figure 7-8, and find μ, $\mu + \sigma$, and σ.

◄ NEW! Statistical Literacy Problems

In every section and chapter problem set, Statistical Literacy problems test student understanding of terminology, statistical methods, and the appropriate conditions for use of the different processes.

Definition Boxes ►

Whenever important terms are introduced in text, yellow definition boxes appear within the discussions. These boxes make it easy to reference or review terms as they are used further.

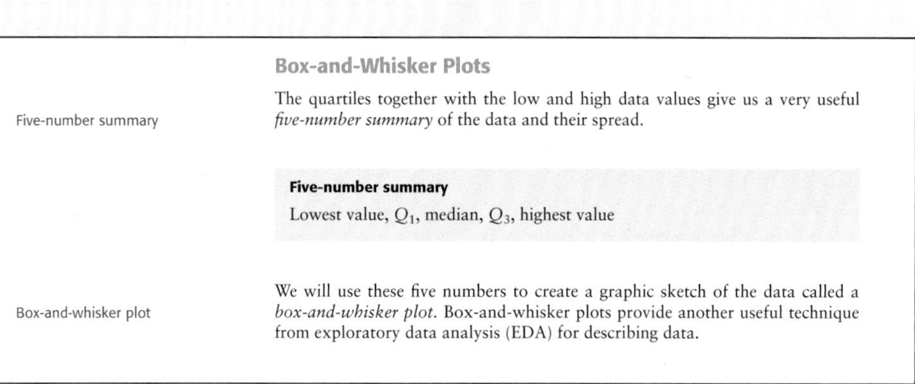

Box-and-Whisker Plots

Five-number summary

The quartiles together with the low and high data values give us a very useful *five-number summary* of the data and their spread.

Five-number summary

Lowest value, Q_1, median, Q_3, highest value

Box-and-whisker plot

We will use these five numbers to create a graphic sketch of the data called a *box-and-whisker plot*. Box-and-whisker plots provide another useful technique from exploratory data analysis (EDA) for describing data.

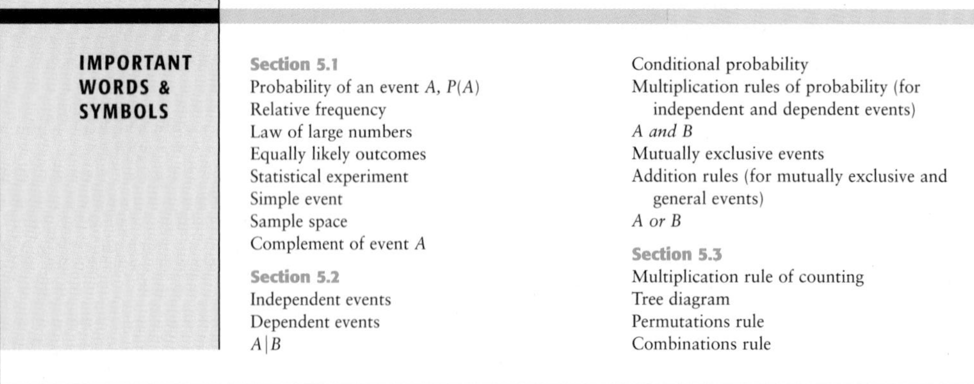

IMPORTANT WORDS & SYMBOLS

Section 5.1
Probability of an event A, $P(A)$
Relative frequency
Law of large numbers
Equally likely outcomes
Statistical experiment
Simple event
Sample space
Complement of event A

Section 5.2
Independent events
Dependent events
$A|B$
Conditional probability
Multiplication rules of probability (for independent and dependent events)
A and B
Mutually exclusive events
Addition rules (for mutually exclusive and general events)
A or B

Section 5.3
Multiplication rule of counting
Tree diagram
Permutations rule
Combinations rule

▲ Important Words & Symbols

The Important Words & Symbols within the Chapter Review feature at the end of each chapter summarizes the terms introduced in the Definition Boxes for student review at a glance.

Linking Concepts: Writing Projects ►

Much of statistical literacy is the ability to communicate concepts effectively. The Linking Concepts: Writing Projects feature at the end of each chapter tests both statistical literacy and critical thinking by asking the student to express their understanding in words.

LINKING CONCEPTS: WRITING PROJECTS

Discuss each of the following topics in class or review the topics on your own. Then write a brief but complete essay in which you summarize the main points. Please include formulas and graphs as appropriate.

1. An average is an attempt to summarize a collection of data into just *one* number. Discuss how the mean, median, and mode all represent averages in this context. Also discuss the differences among these averages. Why is the mean a balance point? Why is the median a midway point? Why is the mode the most common data point? List three areas of daily life in which you think one of the mean, median, or mode would be the best choice to describe an "average."
2. Why do we need to study the variation of a collection of data? Why isn't the average by itself adequate? We have studied three ways to measure variation. The range, the standard deviation, and, to a large extent, a box-and-whisker plot all indicate the variation within a data collection. Discuss similarities and differences among these ways of measuring data variation. Why would it seem reasonable to pair the median with a box-and-whisker plot and to pair the mean with the standard deviation? What are the advantages and disadvantages of each method of describing data spread? Comment on statements such as the following: (a) The range is easy to compute, but it doesn't give much information; (b) although the standard deviation is more complicated to compute, it has some significant applications; (c) the box-and-whisker plot is fairly easy to construct, and it gives a lot of information at a glance.

31. *Expand Your Knowledge: Estimating the Standard Deviation* *Consumer Reports* gave information about the ages at which various household products are replaced. For example, color TVs are replaced at an average age of $\mu = 8$ years after purchase, and the (95% of data) range was from 5 to 11 years. Thus, the range was $11 - 5 = 6$ years. Let x be the age (in years) at which a color TV is replaced. Assume that x has a distribution that is approximately normal.
    (a) The empirical rule (Section 7.1) indicates that for a symmetrical and bell-shaped distribution, approximately 95% of the data lies within two standard deviations of the mean. Therefore, a 95% range of data values extending from $\mu - 2\sigma$ to $\mu + 2\sigma$ is often used for "commonly occurring" data values. Note that the interval from $\mu - 2\sigma$ to $\mu + 2\sigma$ is 4σ in length. This leads to a "rule of thumb" for estimating the standard deviation from a 95% range of data values.

◄ Expand Your Knowledge Problems

Expand Your Knowledge problems present optional enrichment topics that go beyond the material introduced in a section. Vocabulary and concepts needed to solve the problems are included at point-of-use, expanding students' statistical literacy.

NEW! Expand Your Knowledge: Foreshadowing ►

The Foreshadowing feature alerts students to additional material presented in Expand Your Knowledge problems. Students can skip ahead to learn more, or investigate later.

Empirical rule

Problems 31 through 35 of Section 7.3 show how to use the empirical rule to estimate the standard deviation when we know the low and high values of sample data drawn from a distribution that is approximately normal.

mal distributions, we can get a much more precise result, which is given by the *empirical rule.*

Empirical rule

For a distribution that is symmetrical and bell-shaped (in particular, for a normal distribution):

Approximately 68% of the data values will lie within 1 standard deviation on each side of the mean.

Approximately 95% of the data values will lie within 2 standard deviations on each side of the mean.

Approximately 99.7% (or almost all) of the data values will lie within 3 standard deviations on each side of the mean.

Real knowledge is delivered through direction, not just facts. *Understanding Basic Statistics* ensures the student knows what is being covered and why at every step along the way to statistical literacy.

Chapter Preview ► Questions

Preview Questions at the beginning of each chapter give the student a taste of what types of questions can be answered with an understanding of the knowledge to come.

ESTIMATION

PREVIEW QUESTIONS

How do you estimate the expected value of a random variable? What assumptions are needed? How much confidence should be placed in such estimates? (SECTION 8.1)

At the beginning design stage of a statistical project, how large a sample size should you plan to get? (SECTION 8.1)

What famous statistician worked for Guinness brewing company in Ireland? What has this to do with constructing estimates from sample data? (SECTION 8.2)

How do you estimate the proportion p *of successes in a binomial experiment? How does the normal approximation fit into this process?* (SECTION 8.3)

FOCUS PROBLEM

Trick or Treat!!!

About 28% of U.S. households turn out the lights and pretend not to be at home on Halloween (*Source: Are You Normal About Money?* by Bernice Kanner, Bloomberg Press).

Alice is a sociology student who is studying the affluent Cherry Creek neighborhood in Denver. As part of a larger survey, Alice interviewed a random sample of 35 households. One of the questions she asked was whether the resident turned out the lights and pretended not to be at home on Halloween. It was found that 11 of the 35 residents actually did this practice.

(a) Compute a 90% confidence interval for p, the proportion of all households in Cherry Creek that pretend not to be at home on Halloween.

(b) What assumptions are necessary to calculate the confidence interval of part (a)? Do you think these assumptions are met in this case? Explain.

(c) The national proportion is about 0.28. Is 0.28 in the confidence interval you computed? Based on your answer, does it seem that the Cherry Creek neighborhood is much different (either higher or lower proportion) from the population of all U.S. households? Explain.

(See Problem 12 of Section 8.3.)

12. *Focus Problem: Trick or Treat* In a survey of a random sample of 35 households in the Cherry Creek neighborhood of Denver, it was found that 11 households turned out the lights and pretended not to be home on Halloween.
    (a) Compute a 90% confidence interval for p, the proportion of all households in Cherry Creek that pretend not to be home on Halloween.
    (b) What assumptions are necessary to calculate the confidence interval of part (a)?
    (c) *Interpretation:* The national proportion of all households in the United States that turn out the lights and pretend not to be home on Halloween is 0.28. Is 0.28 in the confidence interval you computed? Based on your answer, does it seem that the Cherry Creek neighborhood is much different (either higher or lower proportion) from the population of all U.S. households? Explain.

▲ Chapter Focus Problems

The Preview Questions in each chapter are followed by Focus Problems, which serve as more specific examples of what questions the student will soon be able to answer. The Focus Problems are set within appropriate applications and are incorporated into the end-of-section exercises, giving students the opportunity to test their understanding.

Focus Points ►

Each section opens with bulleted Focus Points describing the primary learning objectives of the section.

SECTION 3.1

Measures of Central Tendency: Mode, Median, and Mean

FOCUS POINTS

- Compute mean, median, and mode from raw data.
- Interpret what mean, median, and mode tell you.
- Explain how mean, median, and mode can be affected by extreme data values.
- What is a trimmed mean? How do you compute it?
- Compute a weighted average.

The average price of an ounce of gold is $920. The Zippy car averages 39 miles per gallon on the highway. A survey showed the average shoe size for women is size 8.

In each of the preceding statements, *one* number is used to describe the entire sample or population. Such a number is called an *average*. There are many ways to compute averages, but we will study only three of the major ones.

The easiest average to compute is the *mode*.

The **mode** of a data set is the value that occurs most frequently.

EXAMPLE 1 MODE

Count the letters in each word of this sentence and give the mode. The numbers of letters in the words of the sentence are

5 3 7 2 4 4 2 4 8 3 4 3 4

Scanning the data, we see that 4 is the mode because more words have 4 letters than any other number. For larger data sets, it is useful to order—or sort—the data before scanning them for the mode.

Chapter Review

SUMMARY

Organizing and presenting data are the main purposes of the branch of statistics called descriptive statistics. Graphs provide an important way to show how the data are distributed.

- Frequency tables show how the data are distributed within set classes. The classes are chosen so that they cover all data values and so that each data value falls within only one class. The number of classes and the class width determine the class limits and class boundaries. The number of data values falling within a class is the class frequency.
- A histogram is a graphical display of the information in a frequency table. Classes are shown on the horizontal axis, with corresponding frequencies on the vertical axis. Relative-frequency histograms show relative frequencies on the vertical axis. Dotplots are like histograms except that the classes are individual data values.
- Bar graphs, Pareto charts, and pie charts are useful for showing how quantitative or qualitative data are distributed over chosen categories.
- Time-series graphs show how data change over set intervals of time.
- Stem-and-leaf displays are an effective means of ordering data and showing important features of the distribution.

Graphs aren't just pretty pictures. They help reveal important properties of the data distribution, including the shape and whether or not there are any outliers.

▲ REVISED! Chapter Summaries

The Summary within each Chapter Review feature now also appears in bulleted form, so students can see what they need to know at a glance.

Statistics is not done in a vacuum. *Understanding Basic Statistics* gives students valuable skills for the real world with technology instruction, genuine applications, actual data, and group projects.

Tech Notes ▶

Tech Notes appearing throughout the text give students helpful hints on using TI-84 Plus and TI-83 Plus calculators, Microsoft Excel, and Minitab to solve a problem. They include display screens to help students visualize and better understand the solution.

TECH NOTES *Stem-and-leaf display*

TI-84Plus/TI-83Plus Does not support stem-and-leaf displays. You can sort the data by using keys **Stat** ➤ **Edit** ➤ **2:SortA.**

Excel Does not support stem-and-leaf displays. You can sort the data by using the menu choices **Data** ➤ **Sort.**

Minitab Use the menu selections **Graph** ➤ **Stem-and-Leaf** and fill in the dialogue box.

Minitab Release 14 Stem-and-Leaf Display (for Data in Guided Exercise 4)

```
Stem-and-Leaf of Scores     N=35
Leaf Unit=1.0

   1      8   3
   5      9   2789
  14     10   123455669
 (11)    11   01222267789
  10     12   045568
   4     13   125
   1     14   3
```

The values shown in the left column represent depth. Numbers above the value in parentheses show the cumulative number of values from the top to the stem of the middle value. Numbers below the value in parentheses show the cumulative number of values from the bottom to the stem of the middle value. The number in parentheses shows how many values are on the same line as the middle value.

USING TECHNOLOGY

Binomial Distributions

Although tables of binomial probabilities can be found in most libraries, such tables are often inadequate. Either the value of p (the probability of success on a trial) you are looking for is not in the table, or the value of n (the number of trials) you are looking for is too large for the table. In Chapter 7, we will study the normal approximation to the binomial. This approximation is a great help in many practical applications. Even so, we sometimes use the formula for the binomial probability distribution on a computer or graphing calculator to compute the probability we want.

Applications

The following percentages were obtained over many years of observation by the U.S. Weather Bureau. All data listed are for the month of December.

Location	Long-Term Mean % of Clear Days in Dec.
Juneau, Alaska	18%
Seattle, Washington	24%
Hilo, Hawaii	36%
Honolulu, Hawaii	60%
Las Vegas, Nevada	75%
Phoenix, Arizona	77%

Adapted from *Local Climatological Data*, U.S. Weather Bureau publication, "Normals, Means, and Extremes" Table.

In the locations listed, the month of December is a relatively stable month with respect to weather. Since weather patterns from one day to the next are more or less the same, it is reasonable to use a binomial probability model.

1. Let r be the number of clear days in December. Since December has 31 days, $0 \le r \le 31$. Using appropriate computer software or calculators available to you, find the probability $P(r)$ for each of the listed locations when $r = 0, 1, 2, \ldots, 31$.
2. For each location, what is the expected value of the probability distribution? What is the standard deviation?

You may find that the use of cumulative probabilities and appropriate subtraction of probabilities, rather than adding probabilities, will make finding the solutions to Applications 3 to 7 easier.

3. Estimate the probability that Juneau will have at most 7 clear days in December.
4. Estimate the probability that Seattle will have from 5 to 10 (including 5 and 10) clear days in December.
5. Estimate the probability that Hilo will have at least 12 clear days in December.
6. Estimate the probability that Phoenix will have 20 or more clear days in December.
7. Estimate the probability that Las Vegas will have from 20 to 25 (including 20 and 25) clear days in December.

Technology Hints

TI-84Plus/TI-83Plus, Excel, Minitab

The Tech Notes in Section 6.2 give specific instructions for binomial distribution functions on the TI-84Plus and TI-83Plus calculators, Excel, and Minitab.

SPSS

In SPSS, the function **PDF.BINOM(q,n,p)** gives the probability of q successes out of n trials, where p is the probability of success on a single trial. In the data editor, name a variable r and enter values 0 through n. Name another variable Prob_r. Then use the menu choices **Transform** ➤ **Compute.** In the dialogue box, use Prob_r for the target variable. In the function box, select **PDF.BINOM(q,n,p).** Use the variable r for q and appropriate values for n and p. Note that the function **CDF.BINOM(q,n,p)** gives the cumulative probability of 0 through q successes.

◀ REVISED!

Using Technology

Further technology instruction is available at the end of each chapter in the Using Technology section. Problems are presented with real-world data from a variety of disciplines that can be solved by using TI-84 Plus and TI-83 Plus calculators, Microsoft Excel, Minitab, and SPSS.

EXAMPLE 11 CENTRAL LIMIT THEOREM

A certain strain of bacteria occurs in all raw milk. Let x be the bacteria count per milliliter of milk. The health department has found that if the milk is not contaminated, then x has a distribution that is more or less mound-shaped and symmetrical. The mean of the x distribution is $\mu = 2500$, and the standard deviation is $\sigma = 300$. In a large commercial dairy, the health inspector takes 42 random samples of the milk produced each day. At the end of the day, the bacteria count in each of the 42 samples is averaged to obtain the sample mean bacteria count $\bar{x}$.

(a) Assuming the milk is not contaminated, what is the distribution of $\bar{x}$?

SOLUTION: The sample size is $n = 42$. Since this value exceeds 30, the central limit theorem applies, and we know that $\bar{x}$ will be approximately normal with mean and standard deviation

$$\mu_{\bar{x}} = \mu = 2500$$

$$\sigma_{\bar{x}} = \sigma/\sqrt{n} = 300/\sqrt{42} \approx 46.3$$

◀ UPDATED! **Applications**

Real-world applications are used from the beginning to introduce each statistical process. Rather than just crunching numbers, students come to appreciate the value of statistics through relevant examples.

of years centered about the mean in which about 68% of
g dates) will be found.
of years centered about the mean in which about 95% of
g dates) will be found.
(c) estimate a range of years centered about the mean in which almost all the data (tree-ring dates) will be found.

10. *Vending Machine: Soft Drinks* A vending machine automatically pours soft drinks into cups. The amount of soft drink dispensed into a cup is normally distributed with a mean of 7.6 ounces and standard deviation of 0.4 ounce. Examine Figure 7-3 and answer the following questions.
(a) Estimate the probability that the machine will overflow an 8-ounce cup.
(b) Estimate the probability that the machine will not overflow an 8-ounce cup.
(c) The machine has just been loaded with 850 cups. How many of these do you expect will overflow when served?

11. *Pain Management: Laser Therapy* "Effect of Helium-Neon Laser Auriculotherapy on Experimental Pain Threshold" is the title of an article in the journal *Physical Therapy* (Vol. 70, No. 1, pp. 24–30). In this article, laser therapy was discussed as a useful alternative to drugs in pain management of chronically ill patients. To

Most exercises in each section ▶ are applications problems.

are 2 for
value of sales, and 3 for reports. What would the overall rating be for a sales representative with ratings of 5 for new contacts, 8 for successful contacts, 7 for total contacts, 9 for dollar volume of sales, and 7 for reports?

DATA HIGHLIGHTS: GROUP PROJECTS

Break into small groups and discuss the following topics. Organize a brief outline in which you summarize the main points of your group discussion.

1. *The Story of Old Faithful* is a short book written by George Marler and published by the Yellowstone Association. Chapter 7 of this interesting book talks about the effect of the 1959 earthquake on eruption intervals for Old Faithful Geyser. Dr. John Rinehart (a senior research scientist with the National Oceanic and Atmospheric Administration) has done extensive studies of the eruption intervals before and after the 1959 earthquake. Examine Figure 3-11. Notice the general shape. Is the graph more or less symmetrical? Does it have a single mode frequency? The mean interval between eruptions has remained steady at about 65 minutes for the past 100 years. Therefore, the 1959 earthquake did not significantly change the mean, but it did change the distribution of eruption intervals. Examine Figure 3-12. Would you say there are really two frequency modes, one shorter and the other longer? Explain. The overall mean is about the same for both graphs, but one graph has a much larger standard deviation (for eruption intervals) than the other. Do no calculations, just look at both graphs, and then explain which graph has the smaller and which has the larger standard deviation. Which distribution will have the larger coefficient of variation? In everyday terms, what would this mean if you were actually at Yellowstone waiting to see the next eruption of Old Faithful? Explain your answer.

Old Faithful Geyser, Yellowstone National Park

FIGURE 3-11

Typical Behavior of Old Faithful Geyser Before 1959 Quake

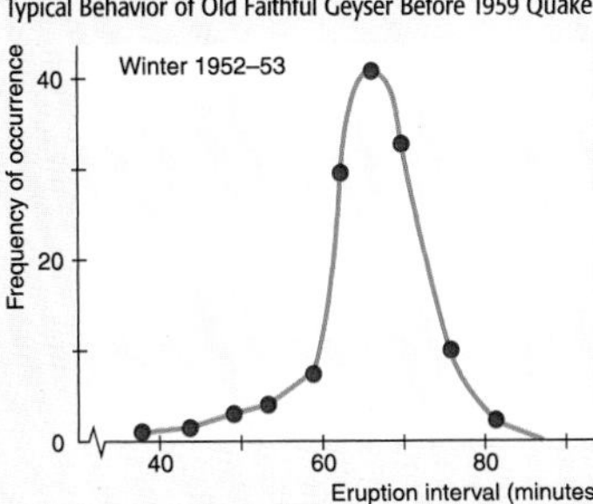

FIGURE 3-12

Typical Behavior of Old Faithful Geyser After 1959 Quake

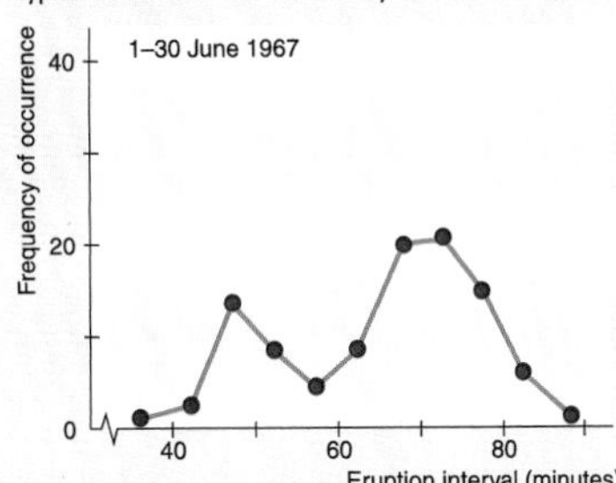

◀ **Data Highlights: Group Projects**

Using Group Projects, students gain experience working with others by discussing a topic, analyzing data, and collaborating to formulate their response to the questions posed in the exercise.

Get to the "Aha!" moment faster. *Understanding Basic Statistics* provides the push students need to get there through guidance and example.

PROCEDURE

HOW TO COMPUTE QUARTILES

1. Order the data from smallest to largest.
2. Find the median. This is the second quartile.
3. The first quartile Q_1 is then the median of the lower half of the data; that is, it is the median of the data falling *below* the Q_2 position (and not including Q_2).
4. The third quartile Q_3 is the median of the upper half of the data; that is, it is the median of the data falling *above* the Q_2 position (and not including Q_2).

In short, all we do to find the quartiles is find three medians.

Interquartile range

The median, or second quartile, is a popular measure of the center utilizing relative position. A useful measure of data spread utilizing relative position is the *interquartile range (IQR)*. It is simply the difference between the third and first quartiles.

Interquartile range $= Q_3 - Q_1$

The interc
look at an

◀ Procedures

Procedure display boxes summarize simple step-by-step strategies for carrying out statistical procedures and methods as they are introduced. Students can refer back to these boxes as they practice using the procedures.

Guided Exercises ▶

Students gain experience with new procedures and methods through Guided Exercises. Beside each problem in a Guided Exercise, a completely worked-out solution appears for immediate reinforcement.

GUIDED EXERCISE 10 **Probability regarding $\bar{x}$**

In mountain country, major highways sometimes use tunnels instead of long, winding roads over high passes. However, too many vehicles in a tunnel at the same time can cause a hazardous situation. Traffic engineers are studying a long tunnel in Colorado. If x represents the time for a vehicle to go through the tunnel, it is known that the x distribution has mean $\mu = 12.1$ minutes and standard deviation $\sigma = 3.8$ minutes under ordinary traffic conditions. From a histogram of x values, it was found that the x distribution is mound-shaped with some symmetry about the mean.

Engineers have calculated that, *on average*, vehicles should spend from 11 to 13 minutes in the tunnel. If the time is less than 11 minutes, traffic is moving too fast for safe travel in the tunnel. If the time is more than 13 minutes, there is a problem of bad air quality (too much carbon monoxide and other pollutants).

Under ordinary conditions, there are about 50 vehicles in the tunnel at one time. What is the probability that the mean time for 50 vehicles in the tunnel will be from 11 to 13 minutes?

We will answer this question in steps.

(a) Let $\bar{x}$ represent the sample mean based on samples of size 50. Describe the $\bar{x}$ distribution.

➡ From the central limit theorem, we expect the $\bar{x}$ distribution to be approximately normal with mean and standard deviation

$$\mu_{\bar{x}} = \mu = 12.1 \qquad \sigma_{\bar{x}} = \frac{\sigma}{\sqrt{n}} = \frac{3.8}{\sqrt{50}} \approx 0.54$$

(b) Find $P(11 < \bar{x} < 13)$.

➡ We convert the interval

$11 < \bar{x} < 13$

to a standard z interval and use the standard normal probability table to find our answer. Since

$$z = \frac{\bar{x} - \mu}{\sigma/\sqrt{n}} \approx \frac{\bar{x} - 12.1}{0.54}$$

$\bar{x} = 11$ converts to $z \approx \frac{11 - 12.1}{0.54} = -2.04$

and $\bar{x} = 13$ converts to $z \approx \frac{13 - 12.1}{0.54} = 1.67$

Therefore,

$$\begin{aligned} P(11 < \bar{x} < 13) &= P(-2.04 < z < 1.67) \\ &= 0.9525 - 0.0207 \\ &= 0.9318 \end{aligned}$$

(c) Interpret your answer to part (b).

➡ It seems that about 93% of the time there should be no safety hazard for average traffic flow.

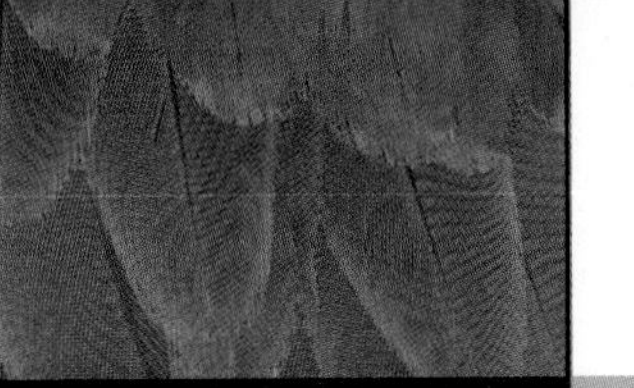

Preface

Welcome to the exciting world of statistics! We have written this text to make statistics accessible to everyone, including those with a limited mathematics background. Statistics affects all aspects of our lives. Whether we are testing new medical devices or determining what will entertain us, applications of statistics are so numerous that, in a sense, we are limited only by our own imagination in discovering new uses for statistics.

Overview

The fifth edition of *Understanding Basic Statistics* continues to emphasize concepts of statistics. Statistical methods are carefully presented with a focus on understanding both the *suitability of the method* and the *meaning of the result*. Statistical methods and measurements are developed in the context of applications.

We have retained and expanded features that made the first four editions of the text very readable. Definition boxes highlight important terms. Procedure displays summarize steps for analyzing data. Examples, exercises, and problems touch on applications appropriate to a broad range of interests.

New with the fifth edition is the Online Study Center, encompassing all interactive online products and services with this text. Online homework powered by Web-Assign® is now available through Cengage Learning's course management system. Also available in the Online Study Center are over 100 data sets (in Microsoft Excel, Minitab, SPSS, and TI-84Plus/TI-83Plus ASCII file formats), lecture aids, a glossary, statistical tables, intructional video (also available on DVDs), an Online Multimedia eBook, and interactive tutorials.

Understanding Basic Statistics, Fifth Edition, is carefully designed to present *core topics* of an introductory course in statistics. Our other text, *Understandable Statistics*, Ninth Edition, is a more comprehensive text with additional topics. Both books feature the same effective pedagogy and instructional design.

Major Changes in the Fifth Edition

With each new edition, the authors reevaluate the scope, appropriateness, and effectiveness of the text's presentation and reflect on extensive user feedback. Revisions have been made throughout the text to clarify explanations of important concepts and to update problems.

Critical Thinking and Statistical Literacy

Critical thinking is essential in understanding and evaluating information. There are more than a few situations in statistics in which the lack of critical thinking can lead to conclusions that are misleading or incorrect. Throughout the text, critical thinking is emphasized and highlighted. In each section and chapter problem set students are asked to apply their critical thinking abilities.

Statistical literacy is fundamental for applying and interpreting statistical results. Students need to know correct statistical terminology. The knowledge of correct terminology helps students focus on correct analysis and processes. Each section and chapter problem set has questions designed to reinforce statistical literacy.

More Emphasis on Interpretation

Calculators and computers are very good at providing the numerical results of statistical processes. It is up to the user of statistics to interpret the results in the context of an application. Were the correct processes used to analyze the data? What do the results mean? Students are asked these questions throughout the text.

New Content

In Chapter 1 there is more emphasis on experimental design.

Tests of homogeneity are discussed with chi-square tests of independence in Section 11.1

Other Changes

In general, the material on descriptive statistics has been streamlined, so that a professor can move more quickly to topics of inferential statistics.

Chapter 2, Organizing Data, has been rearranged so that the section on frequency distributions and histograms is the first section. The second section discusses other types of graphs.

In Chapter 3, the discussion of grouped data has been incorporated in Expand Your Knowledge problems.

In Chapter 8, Estimation, discussion of sample size for a specified error of estimate is now incorporated into the sections that introduce confidence intervals for the mean and for a proportion.

Continuing Content

Introduction of Hypothesis Testing Using *P*-Values

In keeping with the use of computer technology and standard practice in research, hypothesis testing is introduced using *P*-values. The critical region method is still supported, but not given primary emphasis.

Use of Student's *t* Distribution in Confidence Intervals and Testing of Means

If the normal distribution is used in confidence intervals and testing of means, then the *population standard deviation must be known.* If the population standard deviation is not known, then under conditions described in the text, the Student's *t* distribution is used. This is the most commonly used procedure in statistical research. It is also used in statistical software packages such as Microsoft Excel, Minitab, SPSS, and TI-84Plus/TI-83Plus calculators.

Confidence Intervals and Hypothesis Tests of Difference of Means

If the normal distribution is used, then both population standard deviations must be known. When this is not the case, the Student's *t* distribution incorporates an approximation for *t*, with a commonly used conservative choice for the degrees of freedom. Satterthwaite's approximation for the degrees of freedom as used in computer software is also discussed. The pooled standard deviation is presented for appropriate applications ($\sigma_1 \approx \sigma_2$).

Features in the Fifth Edition

Chapter and Section Lead-ins

- *Preview Questions* at the beginning of each chapter are keyed to the sections.
- *Focus Problems* at the beginning of each chapter demonstrate types of questions students can answer once they master the concepts and skills presented in the chapter.
- *Focus Points* at the beginning of each section describe the primary learning objectives of the section.

Carefully Developed Pedagogy

- *Examples* show students how to select and use appropriate procedures.
- *Guided Exercises* within the sections give students an opportunity to work with a new concept. Completely worked-out solutions appear beside each exercise to give immediate reinforcement.
- *Definition boxes* highlight important definitions throughout the text.
- *Procedure displays* summarize appropriate conditions and key strategies for carrying out statistical procedures and methods.
- *Labels* for each example or guided exercise highlight the technique, concept, or process illustrated by the example or guided exercise. In addition, labels for section and chapter problems describe the field of application and show the wide variety of subjects in which statistics is used.
- *Section and chapter problems* require the student to use all the new concepts mastered in the section or chapter. Problem sets include a variety of real-world applications with data or settings from identifiable sources. Key steps and solutions to odd-numbered problems appear at the end of the book.
- NEW! *Statistical Literacy problems* ask students to focus on correct terminology and processes of appropriate statistical methods. Such problems occur in every section and chapter problem set.
- NEW! *Critical Thinking problems* ask students to analyze and comment on various issues that arise in the application of statistical methods and in the interpretation of results. These problems occur in every section and chapter problem set.
- *Expand Your Knowledge problems* present enrichment topics such as dot plots; grouped data; estimation of standard deviation from a range of data values; residual plots; relationship between confidence intervals and two-tailed hypothesis tests; and more.
- NEW! *Expand Your Knowledge Foreshadowing* alerts students to optional material presented in the exercise sets.
- *Cumulative review problem sets* occur after every third chapter and include key topics from previous chapters. Answers to *all* cumulative review problems are given at the end of the book.
- *Data Highlights and Linking Concepts* provide group projects and writing projects.
- *Viewpoints* are brief essays presenting diverse situations in which statistics is used.

Technology within the Text

- *Tech Notes* within sections provide brief point-of-use instructions for the TI-84Plus and TI-83Plus calculators, Microsoft Excel, and Minitab.
- *Using Technology* sections have been revised to show the use of SPSS as well as the TI-84Plus and TI-83Plus calculators, Microsoft Excel, and Minitab.

Alternate Routes Through the Text

Understanding Basic Statistics, Fifth Edition, is designed to be flexible. It offers the professor a choice of teaching possibilities. In most one-semester courses, it is not practical to cover all the material in depth. However, depending on the emphasis of the course, the professor may choose to cover various topics. For help in topic selection, refer to the Table of Prerequisite Material on page 1.

- *Linear regression.* Chapter 4, Correlation and Regression, may be delayed until after Chapter 9. The descriptive topics of linear regression may then be followed immediately by the inferential topics of linear regression presented in Chapter 11.
- *Probability.* For courses requiring minimal probability, Section 5.1 (What Is Probability?) and the first part of Section 5.2 (Some Probability Rules—Compound Events) will be sufficient.

Acknowledgments

It is our pleasure to acknowledge the prepublication reviewers of this text. All of their insights and comments have been very valuable to us. Reviewers of this text include:

Reza Abbasian, Texas Lutheran University
Paul Ache, Kutztown University
Kathleen Almy, Rock Valley College
Polly Amstutz, University of Nebraska at Kearney
Delores Anderson, Truett-McConnell College
Robert J. Astalos, Feather River College
Lynda L. Ballou, Kansas State University
Mary Benson, Pensacola Junior College
Larry Bernett, Benedictine University
Kiran Bhutani, The Catholic University of America
Kristy E. Bland, Valdosta State University
John Bray, Broward Community College
Bill Burgin, Gaston College
Ferry Butar, Sam Houston State University
Toni Carroll, Siena Heights University
Coskun Cetin, Sacramento State University
Pinyuen Chen, Syracuse University
David Cochener, Austin Peay University
Jennifer M. Dollar, Grand Rapids Community College
Larry E. Dunham, Wor-Wic Community College
Andrew Ellett, Indiana University
Mary Fine, Moberly Area Community College
Rene Garcia, Miami-Dade Community College
Larry Green, Lake Tahoe Community College
Mary Hartz, Mohawk Valley Community College
Jane Keller, Metropolitan Community College
Raja Khoury, Collin County Community College
Diane Koenig, Rock Valley College
Charles G. Laws, Cleveland State Community College
Marc Loizeaux, University of Tennessee at Chattanooga
Michael R. Lloyd, Henderson State University
Beth Long, Pellissippi State Technical and Community College
Lewis Lum, University of Portland

Darcy P. Mays, Virginia Commonwealth University
Charles C. Okeke, College of Southern Nevada, Las Vegas
Bernard Omolo, University of South Carolina Upstate
Peg Pankowski, Community College of Allegheny County
Mazbahur Rahman, Minnesota State University, Mankato
Azar Raiszadeh, Chattanooga State Technical Community College
Michael L. Russo, Suffolk County Community College
Janel Schultz, Saint Mary's University of Minnesota
Sankara Sethuraman, Augusta State University
Winson Taam, Oakland University
Jennifer L. Taggart, Rockford College
Janis Todd, Campbell University
William Truman, University of North Carolina at Pembroke
Karen Watson, Fort Valley State University
Bill White, University of South Carolina Upstate
Jim Wienckowski, State University of New York at Buffalo
Stephen M. Wilkerson, Susquehanna University
Hongkai Zhang, East Central University
Shunpu Zhang, University of Alaska, Fairbanks
Cathy Zuccoteveloff, Trinity College

We would especially like to thank George Pasles for his careful accuracy review of this text. We are especially appreciative of the excellent work by the editorial and production professionals at Cengage Learning. In particular, we thank Molly Taylor, Andrew Lipsett, Katherine Greig, Erin Timm, Rachel D'Angelo Wimberly, Joanna Carter-O'Connell, and Carl Chudyk. Without their creative insight and attention to detail, a project of this quality and magnitude would not be possible. Finally, we acknowledge the cooperation of Minitab, Inc., SPSS, Texas Instruments, and Microsoft Excel.

Charles Henry Brase

Corrinne Pellillo Brase

Additional Resources—Get More from Your Textbook!

Instructor Resources

Instructor's Annotated Edition (IAE) Answers to all exercises, teaching comments, and pedagogical suggestions appear in the margin, or at the end of the text in the case of large graphs.

Instructor's Resource Guide with Complete Solutions Contains complete solutions to all exercises, sample tests for each chapter, Teaching Hints, and Transparency Masters for the tables and frequently used formulas in the text.

Diploma Testing Provides instructors with a wide array of new algorithmic exercises along with improved functionality and ease of use. Instructors can create, author/edit algorithmic questions, customize, and deliver multiple types of tests.

Student Resources

Student Solutions Manual Provides solutions to the odd-numbered section and chapter exercises and to all the Cumulative Review exercises in the student textbook.

Technology Guides Separate Guides exist with information and examples for each of four technology tools. Guides are available for the TI-84Plus and TI-83Plus graphing calculators, Minitab software (version 15) Microsoft Excel (2003/2007), and SPSS software (version 16).

Instructional DVDs Hosted by Dana Mosely, these text-specific DVDs cover all sections of the text and provide explanations of key concepts, examples, exercises, and applications in a lecture-based format. DVDs are close-captioned for the hearing-impaired.

MINITAB (Release 15) and SPSS (Release 16) CD-ROMs These statistical software packages manipulate and interpret data to produce textual, graphical, and tabular results. MINITAB and/or SPSS may be packaged with the textbook. Student versions are available.

The Online Study Center encompasses the interactive online products and services integrated with Cengage Learning textbook programs. The Online Study Center is available via Cengage Learning's online course management system. The Online Study Center now includes homework powered by **WebAssign®**; a new **Multimedia eBook**, videos, tutorials, and **SMARTHINKING®**.

- **NEW! Online Multimedia eBook** Integrates numerous assets such as video explanations and tutorials to expand upon and reinforce concepts as they appear in the text.

- **SMARTHINKING® Live, Online Tutoring** Provides an easy-to-use and effective online, text-specific tutoring service. A dynamic **Whiteboard** and a **Graphing Calculator** function enable students and e-structors to collaborate easily.
- **The Online Teaching Center** Students can continue their learning with a new Multimedia eBook, ACE practice tests, glossary flash cards, online data sets, statistical tables and formulae, and more.
- **The Online Teaching Center** Instructors can download transparencies, chapter tests, instructor's solutions, course sequences, a printed test bank, lecture aids (PowerPoint®), and digital art and figures.

Online Course Management Content for Blackboard®, WebCT®, and eCollege® Deliver program- or text-specific Cengage Learning content online using your institution's local course management system. Cengage Learning offers homework, tutorials, videos, and other resources formatted for Blackboard, WebCT, eCollege, and other course management systems. Add to an existing online course or create a new one by selecting from a wide range of powerful learning and instructional materials.

For more information, visit **www.cengage.com/statistics/Brase/UBS5e** or contact your local Cengage Learning sales representative.

Annotated Instructor's Edition

Understanding Basic Statistics

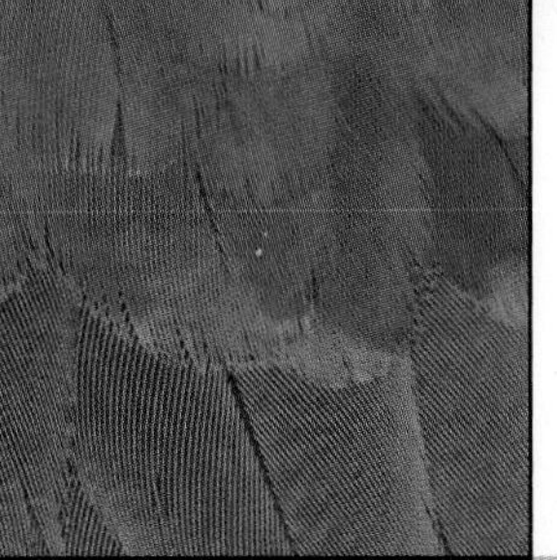

Table of Prerequisite Material

Chapter		Prerequisite Sections
1	Getting Started	None
2	Organizing Data	1.1, 1.2
3	Averages and Variation	1.1, 1.2, 2.1
4	Correlation and Regression	1.1, 1.2, 3.1, 3.2
5	Elementary Probability Theory	1.1, 1.2, 2.1
6	The Binomial Probability Distribution and Related Topics	1.1, 1.2, 2.1, 3.1, 3.2, 5.1, 5.2 5.3 useful but not essential
7	Normal Curves and Sampling Distributions	
	(omit 7.6)	1.1, 1.2, 2.1, 3.1, 3.2, 5.1, 5.2, 6.1
	(include 7.6)	also 6.2, 6.3
8	Estimation	
	(omit 8.3)	1.1, 1.2, 2.1, 3.1, 3.2, 5.1, 5.2, 6.1, 7.1, 7.2, 7.3, 7.4, 7.5
	(include 8.3)	also 6.2, 6.3, 7.6
9	Hypothesis Testing	
	(omit 9.3)	1.1, 1.2, 2.1, 3.1, 3.2, 5.1, 5.2, 6.1, 7.1, 7.2, 7.3, 7.4, 7.5
	(include 9.3)	also 6.2, 6.3, 7.6
10	Inferences About Differences	
	(omit 10.3)	1.1, 1.2, 2.1, 3.1, 3.2, 5.1, 5.2, 6.1, 7.1, 7.2, 7.3, 7.4, 7.5, 8.1, 8.2, 9.1, 9.2
	(include 10.3)	also 6.2, 6.3, 7.6, 9.3
11	Additional Topics Using Inference	
	(Part I: 11.1, 11.2, 11.3)	1.1, 1.2, 2.1, 3.1, 3.2, 5.1, 5.2, 6.1, 7.1, 7.2, 7.3, 7.4, 7.5, 9.1
	(Part II: 11.4)	Chapter 4, 8.1, 8.2 also

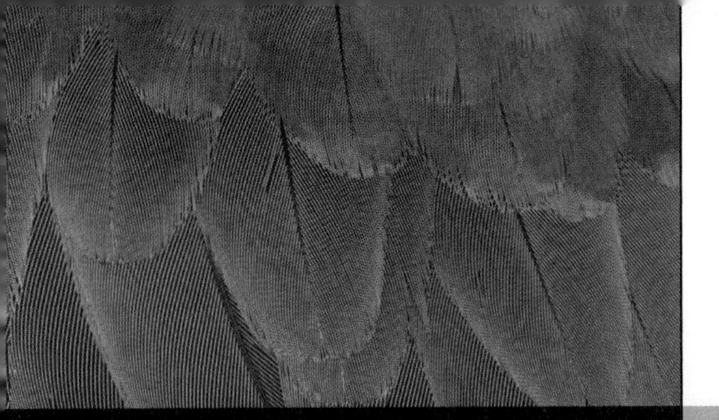

1

Chance favors the prepared mind.

—Louis Pasteur

Statistical techniques are tools of thought . . . not substitutes for thought.

—Abrahm Kaplan

Louis Pasteur (1822–1895) is the founder of modern bacteriology. When studying cholera, he accidentally left some bacillus culture unattended over the summer. In the fall, he injected laboratory animals with this bacilli. To his surprise, the animals did not die—in fact, they had become vaccinated against cholera!

As the first quote at the left reminds us, our chances of success are greatly improved if we have a "prepared mind." The statistical methods you will learn in this book will help you achieve a prepared mind for the study of many different fields. The second quote reminds us that statistics is an important tool, but it is not a replacement for an in-depth knowledge of the field to which it is being applied.

The authors of this book want you to understand and enjoy statistics. The reading material will *tell you* about the subject. The examples will *show you* how it works. To understand, however, you must *get involved*. Guided exercises, calculator and computer applications, section and chapter problems, and writing exercises are all designed to get you involved in the subject. As you grow in your understanding of statistics, we believe you will enjoy learning a subject that has a world full of interesting applications.

For on-line student resources, visit the Brase/Brase, *Understanding Basic Statistics,* 5th edition web site at **www.cengage.com/statistics/Brase/UBS5e.**

GETTING STARTED

PREVIEW QUESTIONS

Why is statistics important? (SECTION 1.1)

What is the nature of data? (SECTION 1.1)

How can you draw a random sample? (SECTION 1.2)

What are other sampling techniques? (SECTION 1.2)

How can you design ways to collect data? (SECTION 1.3)

FOCUS PROBLEM

Where Have All the Fireflies Gone?

A feature article in *The Wall Street Journal* discusses the disappearance of fireflies. In the article, Professor Sara Lewis of Tufts University and other scholars express concern about the decline in the worldwide population of fireflies.

There are a number of possible explanations for the decline, including habitat reduction of woodlands, wetlands, and open fields; pesticides; and pollution. Artificial nighttime lighting might interfere with the Morse-code-like mating ritual of the fireflies. Some chemical companies pay a bounty for fireflies because the insects contain two rare chemicals used in medical research and electronic detection systems in spacecraft.

What does any of this have to do with statistics?

The truth, at this time, is that no one really knows (a) how much the world firefly population has declined or (b) how to explain the decline. The population of all fireflies is simply too large to study in its entirety.

In any study of fireflies, we must rely on incomplete information from samples. Furthermore, from these samples we must draw realistic conclusions that have statistical integrity. This is the kind of work that makes use of statistical methods to determine ways to collect, analyze, and investigate data.

Adapted from Ohio State University Firefly Files logo

Suppose you are conducting a study to compare firefly populations exposed to normal daylight/darkness conditions with firefly populations exposed to continuous light (24 hours a day). You set up two firefly colonies in a laboratory environment. The two colonies are identical except that one colony is exposed to normal daylight/darkness conditions and the other is exposed to continuous light. Each colony is populated with the same number of mature fireflies. After 72 hours, you count the number of living fireflies in each colony.

After completing this chapter, you will be able to answer the following questions.

(a) Is this an experiment or an observation study? Explain.

(b) Is there a control group? Is there a treatment group?

(c) What is the variable in this study?

(d) What is the level of measurement (nominal, interval, ordinal, or ratio) of the variable?

(See Problem 9 of the Chapter 1 Review Problems.)

SECTION 1.1

What Is Statistics?

FOCUS POINTS

- Identify variables in a statistical study.
- Distinguish between quantitative and qualitative variables.
- Identify populations and samples.
- Distinguish between parameters and statistics.
- Determine the level of measurement.
- Compare descriptive and inferential statistics.

Introduction

Decision making is an important aspect of our lives. We make decisions based on the information we have, our attitudes, and our values. Statistical methods help us examine information. Moreover, statistics can be used for making decisions when we are faced with uncertainties. For instance, if we wish to estimate the proportion of people who will have a severe reaction to a flu shot without giving the shot to everyone who wants it, statistics provides appropriate methods. Statistical methods enable us to look at information from a small collection of people or items and make inferences about a larger collection of people or items.

Procedures for analyzing data, together with rules of inference, are central topics in the study of statistics.

Statistics

> **Statistics** is the study of how to collect, organize, analyze, and interpret numerical information from data.

The statistical procedures you will learn in this book should supplement your built-in system of inference—that is, the results of statistical procedures and good sense should dovetail. Of course, statistical methods themselves have no power to work miracles. These methods can help us make some decisions, but not all conceivable decisions. Remember, a properly applied statistical procedure is no more accurate than the data, or facts, on which it is based. Finally, statistical results should be interpreted by one who understands not only the methods, but also the subject matter to which they have been applied.

The general prerequisite for statistical decision making is the gathering of data. First, we need to identify the individuals or objects to be included in the study and the characteristics or features of the individuals that are of interest.

Individuals
Variable

Individuals are the people or objects included in the study.
A **variable** is a characteristic of the individual to be measured or observed.

This is a good time to remind students that individuals and variables are conceptually different.

For instance, if we want to conduct a study about the people who have climbed Mt. Everest, then the individuals in the study are all people who have actually made it to the summit. One variable might be the height of such individuals. Other variables might be age, weight, gender, nationality, income, and so on. Regardless of the variables we use, we would not include measurements or observations from people who have not climbed the mountain.

Quantitative variable
Qualitative variable

The variables in a study may be *quantitative* or *qualitative* in nature.

A **quantitative variable** has a value or numerical measurement for which operations such as addition or averaging make sense. A **qualitative variable** describes an individual by placing the individual into a category or group, such as male or female.

For the Mt. Everest climbers, variables such as height, weight, age, or income are *quantitative* variables. *Qualitative variables* involve nonnumerical observations such as gender or nationality. Sometimes qualitative variables are referred to as *categorical variables*.

Another important issue regarding data is their source. Do the data comprise information from *all* individuals of interest, or from just *some* of the individuals?

Population data
Sample data

In **population data,** the data are from *every* individual of interest.
In **sample data,** the data are from *only some* of the individuals of interest.

It is important to know whether the data are population data or sample data. Data from a specific population are fixed and complete. Data from a sample may vary from sample to sample and are *not* complete.

Parameter
Statistic

A **parameter** is a numerical measure that describes an aspect of a population.
A **statistic** is a numerical measure that describes an aspect of a sample.

For instance, if we have data from *all* the individuals who have climbed Mt. Everest, then we have population data. The proportion of males in the *population* of all climbers who have conquered Mt. Everest is an example of a *parameter.*

On the other hand, if our data come from just some of the climbers, we have sample data. The proportion of male climbers in the *sample* is an example of a *statistic.* Note that different samples may have different values for the proportion of male climbers. One of the important features of sample statistics is that they can vary from sample to sample, whereas population parameters are fixed for a given population.

EXAMPLE 1 Using basic terminology

The Hawaii Department of Tropical Agriculture is conducting a study of ready-to-harvest pineapples in an experimental field.

(a) The pineapples are the *objects* (individuals) of the study. If the researchers are interested in the individual weights of pineapples in the field, then the *variable* consists of weights. At this point, it is important to specify units of measurement and degree of accuracy of measurement. The weights could be

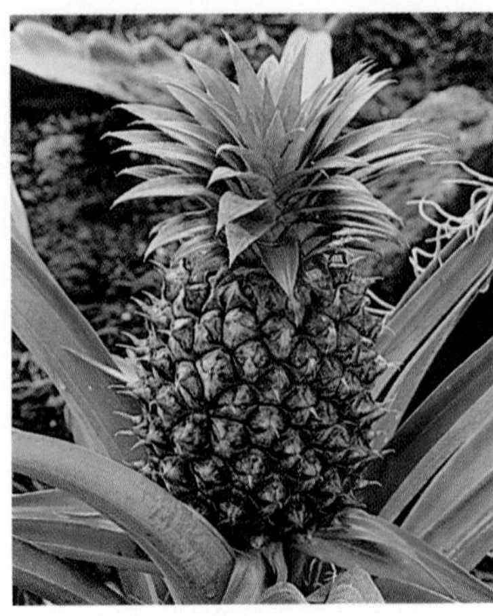

measured to the nearest ounce or gram. Weight is a *quantitative* variable because it is a numerical measure. If the weights of *all* the ready-to-harvest pineapples in the field are included in the data, then we have a *population*. The average weight of all ready-to-harvest pineapples in the field is a *parameter.*

(b) Suppose the researchers also want data on taste. A panel of tasters rates the pineapples according to the categories "poor," "acceptable," and "good." Only some of the pineapples are included in the taste test. In this case, the *variable* is taste. This is a *qualitative* or *categorical* variable. Because only some of the pineapples in the field are included in the study, we have a *sample*. The proportion of pineapples in the sample with a taste rating of "good" is a *statistic.*

Throughout this text, you will encounter *guided exercises* embedded in the reading material. These exercises are included to give you an opportunity to work immediately with new ideas. The questions guide you through appropriate analysis. Cover the answers on the right side (an index card will fit this purpose). After you have thought about or written down *your own response*, check the answers. If there are several parts to an exercise, check each part before you continue. You should be able to answer most of these exercise questions, but don't skip them—they are important.

GUIDED EXERCISE 1 | ***Using basic terminology***

Television station QUE wants to know the proportion of TV owners in Virginia who watch the station's new program at least once a week. The station asked a group of 1000 TV owners in Virginia if they watch the program at least once a week.

(a) Identify the individuals of the study and the variable.
➡ The individuals are the 1000 TV owners surveyed. The variable is the response does, or does not, watch the new program at least once a week.

(b) Do the data comprise a sample? If so, what is the underlying population?
➡ The data comprise a sample of the population of responses from all TV owners in Virginia.

(c) Is the variable qualitative or quantitative?
➡ Qualitative—the categories are the two possible responses, does or does not watch the program.

(d) Identify a quantitative variable that might be of interest.
➡ Age or income might be of interest.

(e) Is the proportion of viewers in the sample who watch the new program at least once a week a statistic or a parameter?
➡ Statistic—the proportion is computed from sample data.

Levels of Measurement: Nominal, Ordinal, Interval, Ratio

The topic "Levels of Measurement" will require some explanation. Most students will pick up the material quickly by studying examples.

We have categorized data as either qualitative or quantitative. Another way to classify data is according to one of the four *levels of measurement*. These levels indicate the type of arithmetic that is appropriate for the data, such as ordering, taking differences, or taking ratios.

Levels of measurement

Nominal level

The **nominal level of measurement** applies to data that consist of names, labels, or categories. There are no implied criteria by which the data can be ordered from smallest to largest.

Ordinal level

The **ordinal level of measurement** applies to data that can be arranged in order. However, differences between data values either cannot be determined or are meaningless.

Interval level

The **interval level of measurement** applies to data that can be arranged in order. In addition, differences between data values are meaningful.

Ratio level

The **ratio level of measurement** applies to data that can be arranged in order. In addition, both differences between data values and ratios of data values are meaningful. Data at the ratio level have a true zero.

EXAMPLE 2 LEVELS OF MEASUREMENT

Identify the type of data.

(a) Taos, Acoma, Zuni, and Cochiti are the names of four Native American pueblos from the population of names of all Native American pueblos in Arizona and New Mexico.

SOLUTION: These data are at the *nominal* level. Notice that these data values are simply names. By looking at the name alone, we cannot determine if one name is "greater than or less than" another. Any ordering of the names would be numerically meaningless.

(b) In a high school graduating class of 319 students, Jim ranked 25th, June ranked 19th, Walter ranked 10th, and Julia ranked 4th, where 1 is the highest rank.

SOLUTION: These data are at the *ordinal* level. Ordering the data clearly makes sense. Walter ranked higher than June. Jim had the lowest rank, and Julia the highest. However, numerical differences in ranks do not have meaning. The difference between June's and Jim's rank is 6, and this is the same difference that exists between Walter's and Julia's rank. However, this difference doesn't really mean anything significant. For instance, if you looked at grade point average, Walter and Julia may have had a large gap between their grade point averages, whereas June and Jim may have had closer grade point averages. In any ranking system, it is only the relative standing that matters. Differences between ranks are meaningless.

(c) Body temperatures (in degrees Celsius) of trout in the Yellowstone River.

SOLUTION: These data are at the *interval* level. We can certainly order the data, and we can compute meaningful differences. However, for Celsius-scale temperatures, there is not an inherent starting point. The value 0°C may seem to be a starting point, but this value does not indicate the state of "no heat." Furthermore, it is not correct to say that 20°C is twice as hot as 10°C.

(d) Length of trout swimming in the Yellowstone River.

SOLUTION: These data are at the *ratio* level. An 18-inch trout is three times as long as a 6-inch trout. Observe that we can divide 6 into 18 to determine a meaningful *ratio* of trout lengths.

In summary, there are four levels of measurement. The nominal level is considered the lowest, and in ascending order we have the ordinal, interval, and ratio levels. In general, calculations based on a particular level of measurement may not be appropriate for a lower level.

PROCEDURE

HOW TO DETERMINE THE LEVEL OF MEASUREMENT

The levels of measurement, listed from lowest to highest, are nominal, ordinal, interval, and ratio. To determine the level of measurement of a set of data, state the *highest level* that can be justified for the entire collection of data. Consider which calculations are suitable for the data.

It is useful to tell students to categorize the level of measurement by the *highest level* appropriate for the data. Asking students to justify their choice for the level of measurement is also helpful.

Level of Measurement	Suitable Calculation
Nominal	We can put the data into categories.
Ordinal	We can order the data from smallest to largest or "worst" to "best." Each data value can be *compared* with another data value.
Interval	We can order the data and also take the differences between data values. At this level, it makes sense to compare the differences between data values. For instance, we can say that one data value is 5 more than or 12 less than another data value.
Ratio	We can order the data, take differences, and also find the ratio between data values. For instance, it makes sense to say that one data value is twice as large as another.

GUIDED EXERCISE 2 | *Levels of measurement*

The following describe different data associated with a state senator. For each data entry, indicate the corresponding *level of measurement*.

(a) The senator's name is Sam Wilson. ➡ Nominal level

(b) The senator is 58 years old. ➡ Ratio level. Notice that age has a meaningful zero. It makes sense to give age ratios. For instance, Sam is twice as old as someone who is 29.

(c) The years in which the senator was elected to the Senate are 1992, 1998, and 2004. ➡ Interval level. Dates can be ordered, and the difference between dates has meaning. For instance, 2004 is six years later than 1998. However, ratios do not make sense. The year 2000 is not twice as large as the year 1000. In addition, the year 0 does not mean "no time."

(d) The senator's total taxable income last year was $878,314. ➡ Ratio level. It makes sense to say that the senator's income is 10 times that of someone earning $87,831.40.

Continued

GUIDED EXERCISE 2 *continued*

(e) The senator surveyed his constituents regarding his proposed water protection bill. The choices for response were strong support, support, neutral, against, or strongly against.	Ordinal level. The choices can be ordered, but there is no meaningful numerical difference between two choices.
(f) The senator's marital status is "married."	Nominal level
(g) A leading news magazine claims the senator is ranked seventh for his voting record on bills regarding public education.	Ordinal level. Ranks can be ordered, but differences between ranks may vary in meaning.

CRITICAL THINKING

"Data! Data! Data!" he cried impatiently. "I can't make bricks without clay." Sherlock Holmes said these words in *The Adventure of the Copper Beeches* by Sir Arthur Conan Doyle.

Reliable statistical conclusions require reliable data. This section has provided some of the vocabulary used in discussing data. As you read a statistical study or conduct one, pay attention to the nature of the data and the ways they were collected.

When you select a variable to measure, be sure to specify the process and requirements for measurement. For example, if the variable is the weight of ready-to-harvest pineapples, specify the unit of weight, the accuracy of measurement, and maybe even the particular scale to be used. If some weights are in ounces and others in grams, the data are fairly useless.

Another concern is whether or not your measurement instrument truly measures the variable. Just asking people if they know the geographic location of the island nation of Fiji may not provide accurate results. The answers may reflect the fact that the respondents want you to think they are knowledgeable. Asking people to locate Fiji on a map may give more reliable results.

The level of measurement is also an issue. You can put numbers into a calculator or computer and do all kinds of arithmetic. However, you need to judge whether the operations are meaningful. For ordinal data such as restaurant rankings, you can't conclude that a 4-star restaurant is "twice as good" as a 2-star restaurant, even though the number 4 is twice 2.

Are the data from a sample, or do they comprise the entire population? Sample data can vary from one sample to another! This means that if you are studying the same statistic from two different samples of the same size, the data values may be different. In fact, the ways in which sample statistics vary among different samples of the same size will be the focus of our study from Chapter 7 on.

Looking Ahead

The purpose of collecting and analyzing data is to obtain information. Statistical methods provide us tools with which we can obtain information from data. These methods break into two branches.

Descriptive statistics

Descriptive statistics involves methods of organizing, picturing, and summarizing information from samples or populations.

Inferential statistics

Inferential statistics involves methods of using information from a sample to draw conclusions regarding the population.

We will look at methods of descriptive statistics in Chapters 2, 3, and 4. These methods may be applied to data from samples or populations.

Sometimes we do not have access to an entire population. At other times, the difficulties or expense of working with the entire population is prohibitive. In such cases, we will use inferential statistics together with probability. These are the topics of Chapters 5 through 11.

VIEWPOINT The First Measured Century

The twentieth century saw measurements of aspects of American life that never had been systematically studied before. Social conditions involving crime, sex, food, fun, religion, and work were numerically investigated. The measurements and survey responses taken over the entire century reveal unsuspected statistical trends. The First Measured Century *is a book by Caplow, Hicks, and Wattenberg. It is also a PBS documentary available on video. For more information, visit the Online Study Center at* **www.cengage.com/statistics/Brase/UBS5e** *and find the link to the PBS* First Measured Century *documentary.*

SECTION 1.1 PROBLEMS

Tables and art to accompany margin answers may be found in the back of the book.

1. An individual is a member of the population of interest. A variable is an aspect of an individual to be measured or observed.
2. Qualitative.
3. A parameter is a numerical measurement describing data from a population. A statistic is a numerical measurement describing data from a sample.
4. A parameter from a given population never changes. Data from samples may vary from sample to sample, and so corresponding sample statistics may vary from sample to sample.
5. (a) Response regarding frequency of eating at fast-food restaurants.
   (b) Qualitative.
   (c) Responses for *all* adults in the U.S.
6. (a) Miles per gallon.
   (b) Quantitative.
   (c) Gasoline mileage for *all* new cars.
7. (a) Nitrogen concentration (mg nitrogen/l water).
   (b) Quantitative.
   (c) Nitrogen concentration (mg nitrogen/l water) in the entire lake.

1. *Statistical Literacy* What is the difference between an individual and a variable?

2. *Statistical Literacy* Are data at the nominal level of measurement quantitative or qualitative?

3. *Statistical Literacy* What is the difference between a parameter and a statistic?

4. *Statistical Literacy* For a set population, does a parameter ever change? If there are three different samples of the same size from a set population, is it possible to get three different values for the same statistic?

5. *Marketing: Fast Food* A nationwide survey of adults asks, "How many times per week do you eat in a fast-food restaurant?" Possible answers: 0, 1–3, 4 or more.
   (a) Identify the variable.
   (b) Is the variable quantitative or qualitative?
   (c) What is the implied population?

6. *Advertising: Auto Mileage* What is the average miles per gallon (mpg) for all new cars? Using *Consumer Reports*, a random sample of 35 new cars gave an average of 21.1 mpg.
   (a) Identify the variable.
   (b) Is the variable quantitative or qualitative?
   (c) What is the implied population?

7. *Ecology: Wetlands* Government agencies carefully monitor water quality and its effect on wetlands (Reference: *Environmental Protection Agency Wetland Report* EPA 832-R-93-005). Of particular concern is the concentration of nitrogen in water draining from fertilized lands. Too much nitrogen can kill fish and wildlife. Twenty-eight samples of water were taken at random from a lake. The nitrogen concentration (milligrams of nitrogen per liter of water) was determined for each sample.
   (a) Identify the variable.
   (b) Is the variable quantitative or qualitative?
   (c) What is the implied population?

8. (a) Number of ferromagnetic artifacts per 100 square meters.
   (b) Quantitative.
   (c) Number of ferromagnetic artifacts per each distinct 100-square-meter plot in the Tara region.

8. *Archaeology: Ireland* The archaeological site of Tara is more than 4000 years old. Tradition states that Tara was the seat of the high kings of Ireland. Because of its archaeological importance, Tara has received extensive study (Reference: *Tara: An Archaeological Survey* by Conor Newman, Royal Irish Academy, Dublin). Suppose an archaeologist wants to estimate the density of ferromagnetic artifacts in the Tara region. For this purpose, a random sample of 55 plots, each of size 100 square meters, is used. The number of ferromagnetic artifacts for each plot is determined.
   (a) Identify the variable.
   (b) Is the variable quantitative or qualitative?
   (c) What is the implied population?

9. (a) Ratio.
   (b) Interval.
   (c) Nominal.
   (d) Ordinal.
   (e) Ratio.
   (f) Ratio.

9. *Student Life: Levels of Measurement* Categorize these measurements associated with student life according to level: nominal, ordinal, interval, or ratio.
   (a) Length of time to complete an exam
   (b) Time of first class
   (c) Major field of study
   (d) Course evaluation scale: poor, acceptable, good
   (e) Score on last exam (based on 100 possible points)
   (f) Age of student

10. (a) Ordinal.
    (b) Ratio.
    (c) Nominal.
    (d) Interval.
    (e) Ratio.
    (f) Nominal.

10. *Business: Levels of Measurement* Categorize these measurements associated with a robotics company according to level: nominal, ordinal, interval, or ratio.
    (a) Salesperson's performance: below average, average, above average
    (b) Price of company's stock
    (c) Names of new products
    (d) Temperature (°F) in CEO's private office
    (e) Gross income for each of the past 5 years
    (f) Color of product packaging

11. (a) Nominal.
    (b) Ratio.
    (c) Interval.
    (d) Ordinal.
    (e) Ratio.
    (f) Interval.

11. *Fishing: Levels of Measurement* Categorize these measurements associated with fishing according to level: nominal, ordinal, interval, or ratio.
    (a) Species of fish caught: perch, bass, pike, trout
    (b) Cost of rod and reel
    (c) Time of return home
    (d) Guidebook rating of fishing area: poor, fair, good
    (e) Number of fish caught
    (f) Temperature of water in degrees Fahrenheit

12. Form B.

12. *Education: Teacher Evaluation* If you were going to apply *statistical methods* to analyze teacher evaluations, which question form, A or B, would be better?
    Form A: In your own words, tell how this teacher compares with other teachers you have had.
    Form B: Use the following scale to rank your teacher as compared with other teachers you have had.

1	2	3	4	5
worst	**below average**	**average**	**above average**	**best**

13. Answers vary.
    (a) For example: Use pounds. Round weights to the nearest pound. Since backpacks might weigh as much as 30 pounds, you might use a high-quality bathroom scale.
    (b) Some students may not allow you to weigh their backpacks for privacy reasons, etc.
    (c) Possibly. Some students may want to impress you with the heaviness of their backpacks, or they may be embarrassed about the "junk" they have stowed inside and thus may clean out their backpacks.

13. ***Critical Thinking*** You are interested in the weights of backpacks students carry to class and decide to conduct a study using the backpacks carried by 30 students.
    (a) Give some instructions for weighing the backpacks. Include unit of measure, accuracy of measure, and type of scale.
    (b) Do you think each student asked will allow you to weigh his or her backpack?
    (c) Do you think telling students ahead of time that you are going to weigh their backpacks will make a difference in the weights?

SECTION 1.2

Random Samples

FOCUS POINTS

- Explain the importance of random samples.
- Construct a simple random sample using random numbers.
- Simulate a random process.
- Describe stratified sampling, cluster sampling, systematic sampling, multistage sampling, and convenience sampling.

Simple Random Samples

This is a conceptually important section on which it is worth spending a little extra time in class discussion. See Linking Concepts and Using Technology.

Eat lamb—20,000 coyotes can't be wrong!

This slogan is sometimes found on bumper stickers in the western United States. The slogan indicates the trouble that ranchers have experienced in protecting their flocks from predators. Based on their experience with this sample of the coyote population, the ranchers concluded that *all* coyotes are dangerous to their flocks and should be eliminated! The ranchers used a special poison bait to get rid of the coyotes. Not only was this poison distributed on ranch land, but with government cooperation it also was distributed widely on public lands.

The ranchers found that the results of the widespread poisoning were not very beneficial. The sheep-eating coyotes continued to thrive while the general population of coyotes and other predators declined. What was the problem? The sheep-eating coyotes the ranchers had observed were not a representative sample of all coyotes. Modern methods of predator control target the sheep-eating coyotes. To a certain extent, the new methods have come about through a closer examination of the sampling techniques used.

Simple random sample

In this section, we will examine several widely used sampling techniques. One of the most important sampling techniques is a *simple random sample.*

A **simple random sample** of n measurements from a population is a subset of the population selected in a manner such that every sample of size n from the population has an equal chance of being selected.

In a simple random sample, not only does every sample of the specified size have an equal chance of being selected, but also every individual of the population has an equal chance of being selected. However, the fact that each individual has an equal chance of being selected does not necessarily imply a simple random sample. Remember, for a simple random sample, every sample of the given size must also have an equal chance of being selected.

GUIDED EXERCISE 3

Simple random sample

Is open space around metropolitan areas important? Players of the Colorado Lottery might think so, since some of the proceeds of the game are used to fund open space and outdoor recreational space. To play the game, you pay 1 dollar and choose any six different numbers from the group of numbers 1 through 42. If your group of six numbers matches the winning group of six numbers selected by simple random sampling, then you are a winner of a grand prize of at least 1.5 million dollars.

(a) Is the number 25 as likely to be selected in the winning group of six numbers as the number 5?

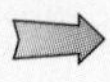

Yes. Because the winning numbers constitute a simple random sample, each number from 1 through 42 has an equal chance of being selected.

Continued

GUIDED EXERCISE 3 *continued*

(b) Could all the winning numbers be even?

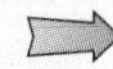 Yes, since six even numbers is one of the possible groups of six numbers.

(c) Your friend always plays the numbers

1 2 3 4 5 6

Could she ever win?

 Yes. In a simple random sample, the listed group of six numbers is *as likely as any* of the 5,245,786 possible groups of six numbers to be selected as the winner. (See Section 5.3 to learn how to compute the number of possible groups of six numbers that can be selected from 42 numbers.)

How do we get random samples? Suppose you need to know if the emission systems of the latest shipment of Toyotas satisfy pollution-control standards. You want to pick a random sample of 30 cars from this shipment of 500 cars and test them. One way to pick a random sample is to number the cars 1 through 500, write these numbers on cards, mix up the cards, and then draw 30 numbers. The sample will consist of the cars with the chosen numbers. If you mix the cards sufficiently, this procedure produces a random sample.

Random-number table

Most calculators have random-number generators. A short discussion about calculator- or computer-generated random numbers could be useful here. See the reference in Using Technology.

An easier way to select the numbers is to use a *random-number table*. You can make one yourself by writing the digits 0 through 9 on separate cards and mixing up these cards in a hat. Then draw a card, record the digit, return the card, and mix up the cards again. Draw another card, record the digit, and so on. Table 1 in the Appendix is a ready-made random-number table (adapted from Rand Corporation, *A Million Random Digits with 100,000 Normal Deviates*). Let's see how to pick our random sample of 30 Toyotas by using this random-number table.

EXAMPLE 3 RANDOM-NUMBER TABLE

Use a random-number table to pick a random sample of 30 cars from a population of 500 cars.

SOLUTION: Again, we assign each car a different number between 1 and 500, inclusive. Then we use the random-number table to choose the sample. Table 1 in the Appendix has 35 rows and 10 blocks of five digits each; it can be thought of as a solid mass of digits that has been broken up into rows and blocks for user convenience.

You read the digits by beginning anywhere in the table. We dropped a pin on the table, and the head of the pin landed in row 15, block 5. We'll begin there and list all the digits in that row. If we need more digits, we'll move on to row 16, and so on. The digits we begin with are

99281 59640 15221 96079 09961 05371

Since the highest number assigned to a car is 500, and this number has three digits, we regroup our digits into blocks of 3:

992 815 964 015 221 960 790 996 105 371

To construct our random sample, we use the first 30 car numbers we encounter in the random-number table when we start at row 15, block 5. We skip the first three groups—992, 815, and 964—because these numbers are all too large. The next group of three digits is 015, which corresponds to 15. Car number 15 is the first car included in our sample, and the next is car number 221. We skip the next three groups and then include car numbers 105 and 371. To get the rest of the cars in the sample, we continue to the next line and use the random-number table in the same fashion. If we encounter a number we've used before, we skip it.

This is a good time for a class discussion about why a random sample can be thought of as a kind of miniature population. A good discussion topic is how bias could be introduced into a sample that is not random.

COMMENT When we use the term *(simple) random sample,* we have very specific criteria in mind for selecting the sample. One proper method for selecting a simple random sample is to use a computer- or calculator-based random-number generator or a table of random numbers as we have done in the example. The term *random* should not be confused with *haphazard!*

PROCEDURE

HOW TO DRAW A RANDOM SAMPLE

1. Number all members of the population sequentially.
2. Use a table, calculator, or computer to select random numbers from the numbers assigned to the population members.
3. Create the sample by using population members with numbers corresponding to those randomly selected.

Simulation

Another important use of random-number tables is in *simulation.* We use the word *simulation* to refer to the process of providing numerical imitations of "real" phenomena. Simulation methods have been productive in studying a diverse array of subjects such as nuclear reactors, cloud formation, cardiology (and medical science in general), highway design, production control, shipbuilding, airplane design, war games, economics, and electronics. A complete list would probably include something from every aspect of modern life. In Guided Exercise 4 we'll perform a brief simulation.

A **simulation** is a numerical facsimile or representation of a real-world phenomenon.

GUIDED EXERCISE 4 Simulation

Use a random-number table to simulate the outcomes of tossing a balanced (that is, fair) penny 10 times.

(a) How many outcomes are possible when you toss a coin once?

→ Two—heads or tails

(b) There are several ways to assign numbers to the two outcomes. Because we assume a fair coin, we can assign an even digit to the outcome "heads" and an odd digit to the outcome "tails." Then, starting at block 3 of row 2 of Table 1 in the Appendix, list the first 10 single digits.

→ 7 1 5 4 9 4 4 8 4 3

(c) What are the outcomes associated with the 10 digits?

→ T T T H T H H H H T

(d) If you start in a different block and row of Table 1 in the Appendix, will you get the same sequence of outcomes?

→ It is possible, but not very likely. (In Section 5.3 you will learn how to determine that there are 1024 possible sequences of outcomes for 10 tosses of a coin.)

TECH NOTES

Sampling with replacement

This is a good time to bring up the concepts of sampling with or without replacement. Simulations often use sampling with replacement.

Most statistical software packages, spreadsheet programs, and statistical calculators generate random numbers. In general, these devices sample with replacement. *Sampling with replacement* means that although a number has been selected for the sample, it is *not removed* from the population. Therefore, the same number may be selected for the sample more than once. If you need to sample without replacement, generate more items than you need for the sample. Then sort the sample and remove duplicate values. Specific procedures for generating random samples using the TI-84Plus/TI-83Plus calculator, Excel, Minitab, and SPSS are shown in Using Technology at the end of this chapter. More details are given in the separate Technology Guides for each of these technologies.

Other Sampling Techniques

Although we will assume throughout this text that (simple) random samples are used, other methods of sampling also are widely used. Appropriate statistical techniques exist for these sampling methods, but they are beyond the scope of this text.

Stratified sampling

One of these alternative sampling methods is called *stratified sampling*. Groups or classes inside a population that share a common characteristic are called *strata* (plural of *stratum*). For example, in the population of all undergraduate college students, some strata might be freshmen, sophomores, juniors, or seniors. Other strata might be men or women, in-state students or out-of-state students, and so on. In the method of stratified sampling, the population is divided into at least two distinct strata. Then a (simple) random sample of a certain size is drawn from each stratum, and the information obtained is carefully adjusted or weighted in all resulting calculations.

The groups or strata are often sampled in proportion to their actual percentages of occurrence in the overall population. However, other (more sophisticated) ways of determining the optimal sample size in each stratum may give the best results. In general, statistical analysis and tests based on data obtained from stratified samples are somewhat different from techniques discussed in an introductory course in statistics. Such methods for stratified sampling will not be discussed in this text.

Systematic sampling

Another popular method of sampling is called *systematic sampling*. In this method, it is assumed that the elements of the population are arranged in some natural sequential order. We select a (random) starting point and then select every kth element for our sample. For example, people lining up to buy rock concert tickets are "in order." To generate a systematic sample of these people (and ask questions regarding topics such as age, smoking habits, income level, etc.), we could include every fifth person in line. The "starting" person is selected at random from the first five.

The advantage of a systematic sample is that it is easy to select. However, there are dangers in using systematic sampling. When the population is repetitive or cyclic in nature, systematic sampling should not be used. For example, consider a fabric mill that produces dress material. Suppose the loom that produces the material makes a mistake every 17th yard, but we check only every 16th yard with an automated electronic scanner. In this case, a random starting point may or may not result in detection of fabric flaws before a large amount of fabric is produced.

Cluster sampling

Cluster sampling is a method used extensively by government agencies and certain private research organizations. In cluster sampling, we begin by dividing the demographic area into sections. Then we randomly select sections or clusters. Every member of the cluster is included in the sample. For example, in conducting a survey of school children in a large city, we could first randomly select five schools and then include all the children from each selected school.

Multistage samples

Often a population is very large or geographically spread out. In such cases, samples are constructed through a *multistage sample design* of several stages, with the final stage consisting of clusters. For instance, the government Current

Population Survey interviews about 60,000 households across the United States each month by means of a multistage sample design.

For the Current Population Survey, the first stage consists of selecting samples of large geographic areas that do not cross state lines. These areas are further broken down into smaller blocks, which are stratified according to ethnic and other factors. Stratified samples of the blocks are then taken. Finally, housing units in each chosen block are broken into clusters of nearby housing units. A random sample of these clusters of housing units is selected, and each household in the final cluster is interviewed.

Convenience sampling

Convenience sampling simply uses results or data that are conveniently and readily obtained. In some cases, this data may be all that is available, and in many cases, it is better than no information at all. However, convenience sampling does run the risk of being severely biased. For instance, consider a newsperson who wishes to get the "opinions of the people" about a proposed seat tax to be imposed on tickets to all sporting events. The revenues from the seat tax will then be used to support the local symphony. The newsperson stands in front of a classical music store at noon and surveys the first five people coming out of the store who will cooperate. This method of choosing a sample will produce some opinions, and perhaps some human interest stories, but it certainly has bias. It is hoped that the city council will not use these opinions as the sole basis for a decision about the proposed tax. It is good advice to be very cautious indeed when the data come from the method of convenience sampling.

Sampling techniques

Random sampling: Use a simple random sample from the entire population.

Stratified sampling: Divide the entire population into distinct subgroups called strata. The strata are based on a specific characteristic such as age, income, education level, and so on. All members of a stratum share the specific characteristic. Draw random samples from each stratum.

Systematic sampling: Number all members of the population sequentially. Then, from a starting point selected at random, include every *k*th member of the population in the sample.

Cluster sampling: Divide the entire population into pre-existing segments or clusters. The clusters are often geographic. Make a random selection of clusters. Include every member of each selected cluster in the sample.

Multistage sampling: Use a variety of sampling methods to create successively smaller groups at each stage. The final sample consists of clusters.

Convenience sampling: Create a sample by using data from population members that are readily available.

CRITICAL THINKING

Sampling frame

We call the list of individuals from which a sample is actually selected the *sampling frame*. Ideally, the sampling frame is the entire population. However, from a practical perspective, not all members of a population may be accessible. For instance, a telephone directory used as the sample frame for residential telephone contacts would not include unlisted numbers.

Undercoverage

When the sample frame does not match the population, we have what is called *undercoverage*. In demographic studies, undercoverage could result if the homeless, fugitives from the law, and so forth were not included in the study.

A **sampling frame** is a list of individuals from which a sample is actually selected.

Undercoverage results when population members are omitted from the sample frame.

Sampling error

In general, even when the sampling frame and the population match, a sample is not a perfect representation of a population. Therefore, information drawn from a sample may not exactly match corresponding information from the population. To the extent that sample information does not match the corresponding population information, we have an error, called a *sampling error.*

A **sampling error** is the difference between measurements from a sample and corresponding measurements from the respective population. It is caused by the fact that the sample does not perfectly represent the population.

A **nonsampling error** is the result of poor sample design, sloppy data collection, faulty measuring instruments, bias in questionnaires, and so on.

Sampling errors do not represent mistakes! They are simply the consequences of using samples instead of populations. However, be alert to nonsampling errors, which may sometimes occur inadvertently.

VIEWPOINT **Extraterrestrial Life?**

Do you believe intelligent life exists on other planets? Using methods of random sampling, a Fox News opinion poll found that about 54% of all U.S. men do believe in intelligent life on other planets, whereas only 47% of U.S. women believe there is such life. How could you conduct a random survey of students on your campus regarding belief in extraterrestrial life?

SECTION 1.2 PROBLEMS

Tables and art to accompany margin answers may be found in the back of the book.

1. In a stratified sample, random samples from each strata are included. In a cluster sample, the clusters to be included are selected at random and then all members of each selected cluster are included.
2. In a simple random sample, every sample of size n has an equal chance of being included. In a systematic sample, the only samples possible are those including every kth item from the random starting position.
3. The advice is wrong. A sampling error only accounts for the difference in results based on the use of a sample rather than the entire population.
4. (a) Yes. (b) No. No.
   (c) Assign each of the students a distinct number from 1 through 40. Then use a random-number table or software to select a sample of size 20.

1. *Statistical Literacy* Explain the difference between a stratified sample and a cluster sample.
2. *Statistical Literacy* Explain the difference between a simple random sample and a systematic sample.
3. *Statistical Literacy* Marcie conducted a study of the cost of breakfast cereal. She recorded the costs of several boxes of cereal. However, she neglected to take into account the number of servings in each box. Someone told her not to worry because she just had some sampling error. Comment on that advice.
4. ***Critical Thinking*** Consider the students in your statistics class as the population and suppose they are seated in four rows of 10 students each. To select a sample, you toss a coin. If it comes up heads, you use the 20 students sitting in the first two rows as your sample. If it comes up tails, you use the 20 students sitting in the last two rows as your sample.
   (a) Does every student have an equal chance of being selected for the sample? Explain.
   (b) Is it possible to include students sitting in row 3 with students sitting in row 2 in your sample? Is your sample a simple random sample? Explain.
   (c) Describe a process you could use to get a simple random sample of size 20 from a class of size 40.

5. Answers vary. This is a good problem to use to discuss ways in which a sample could be biased.

5. *Critical Thinking* Suppose you are assigned the number 1, and the other students in your statistics class call out consecutive numbers until each person in the class has his or her own number. Explain how you could get a random sample of four students from your statistics class.
   (a) Explain why the first four students walking into the classroom would not necessarily form a random sample.
   (b) Explain why four students coming in late would not necessarily form a random sample.
   (c) Explain why four students sitting in the back row would not necessarily form a random sample.
   (d) Explain why the four tallest students would not necessarily form a random sample.

6. Answers vary.
   (a) Not all 250 students are likely to be in class on Monday. The absent students do not have a chance of being included in the sample.
   (b) Students being home-schooled or attending a private school do not have a chance of being included in the sample.

6. *Critical Thinking* In each of the following situations, the sampling frame does not match the population, resulting in undercoverage. Give examples of population members that might have been omitted.
   (a) The population consists of all 250 students in your large statistics class. You plan to obtain a simple random sample of 30 students by using the sampling frame of students present next Monday.
   (b) The population consists of all 15-year-olds living in the attendance district of a local high school. You plan to obtain a simple random sample of 200 such residents by using the student roster of the high school as the sampling frame.

7. Answers vary. Use groups of two digits.

7. *Sampling: Random* Use a random-number table to generate a list of 10 random numbers between 1 and 99. Explain your work.

8. Answers vary. Use groups of three digits.

8. *Sampling: Random* Use a random-number table to generate a list of eight random numbers from 1 to 976. Explain your work.

9. Answers vary. Use groups of four digits.

9. *Sampling: Random* Use a random-number table to generate a list of six random numbers from 1 to 8615. Explain your work.

10. Answers vary. Use single digits with odd corresponding to heads and even to tails.

10. *Simulation: Coin Toss* Use a random-number table to simulate the outcomes of tossing a quarter 25 times. Assume that the quarter is balanced (i.e., fair).

11. (a) Yes; outcome of die roll can repeat; 2.
    (b) No; process is random.

11. *Computer Simulation: Roll of a Die* A die is a cube with dots on each face. The faces have 1, 2, 3, 4, 5, or 6 dots. The table below is a computer simulation (from the software package Minitab) of the results of rolling a fair die 20 times.

DATA DISPLAY

ROW	C1	C2	C3	C4	C5	C6	C7	C8	C9	C10
1	5	2	2	2	5	3	2	3	1	4
2	3	2	4	5	4	5	3	5	3	4

   (a) Assume that each number in the table corresponds to the number of dots on the upward face of the die. Is it appropriate that the same number appears more than once? Why? What is the outcome of the fourth roll?
   (b) If we simulate more rolls of the die, do you expect to get the same sequence of outcomes? Why or why not?

12. Answers vary. Use groups of three digits.

12. *Simulation: Birthday Problem* Suppose there are 30 people at a party. Do you think any two share the same birthday? Let's use the random-number table to simulate the birthdays of the 30 people at the party. Ignoring leap year, let's assume that the year has 365 days. Number the days, with 1 representing January 1, 2 representing January 2, and so forth, with 365 representing December 31. Draw a random sample of 30 days (with replacement). These days represent the birthdays of the people at the party. Were any two of the birthdays the same? Compare your results with those obtained by other students in the class. Would you expect the results to be the same or different?

13. Answers vary. Use single digits with correct answer placed in corresponding position.

13. *Education: Test Construction* Professor Gill is designing a multiple-choice test. There are to be 10 questions. Each question is to have five choices for answers. The choices are to be designated by the letters *a, b, c, d,* and *e*. Professor Gill wishes to use a random-number table to determine which letter choice should correspond to the correct answer for a question. Using the number correspondence 1 for *a*, 2 for *b*, 3 for *c*, 4 for *d*, and 5 for *e*, use a random-number table to determine the letter choice for the correct answer for each of the 10 questions.

14. Answers vary. Use single digits with even corresponding to true and odd to false.

14. *Education: Test Construction* Professor Gill uses true–false questions. She wishes to place 20 such questions on the next test. To decide whether to place a true statement or a false statement in each of the 20 questions, she uses a random-number table. She selects 20 digits from the table. An even digit tells her to use a true statement. An odd digit tells her to use a false statement. Use a random-number table to pick a sequence of 20 digits, and describe the corresponding sequence of 20 true–false questions. What would the test key for your sequence look like?

15. (a) Simple random.
(b) Cluster.
(c) Convenience.
(d) Systematic.
(e) Stratified.

15. *Sampling Methods: Benefits Package* An important part of employee compensation is a benefits package, which might include health insurance, life insurance, child care, vacation days, retirement plan, parental leave, bonuses, etc. Suppose you want to conduct a survey of benefits packages available in private businesses in Hawaii. You want a sample size of 100. Some sampling techniques are described below. Categorize each technique as *simple random sample, stratified sample, systematic sample, cluster sample,* or *convenience sample.*
   (a) Assign each business in the Island Business Directory a number, and then use a random-number table to select the businesses to be included in the sample.
   (b) Use postal ZIP Codes to divide the state into regions. Pick a random sample of 10 ZIP Code areas and then include all the businesses in each selected ZIP Code area.
   (c) Send a team of five research assistants to Bishop Street in downtown Honolulu. Let each assistant select a block or building and interview an employee from each business found. Each researcher can have the rest of the day off after getting responses from 20 different businesses.
   (d) Use the Island Business Directory. Number all the businesses. Select a starting place at random, and then use every 50th business listed until you have 100 businesses.
   (e) Group the businesses according to type: medical, shipping, retail, manufacturing, financial, construction, restaurant, hotel, tourism, other. Then select a random sample of 10 businesses from each business type.

16. (a) Stratified.
(b) Simple random.
(c) Cluster.
(d) Systematic.
(e) Convenience.

16. *Sampling Methods: Health Care* Modern Managed Hospitals (MMH) is a national for-profit chain of hospitals. Management wants to survey patients discharged this past year to obtain patient satisfaction profiles. They wish to use a sample of such patients. Several sampling techniques are described below. Categorize each technique as *simple random sample, stratified sample, systematic sample, cluster sample,* or *convenience sample.*
   (a) Obtain a list of patients discharged from all MMH facilities. Divide the patients according to length of hospital stay (2 days or less, 3–7 days, 8–14 days, more than 14 days). Draw simple random samples from each group.
   (b) Obtain lists of patients discharged from all MMH facilities. Number these patients, and then use a random-number table to obtain the sample.
   (c) Randomly select some MMH facilities from each of five geographic regions, and then include all the patients on the discharge lists of the selected hospitals.
   (d) At the beginning of the year, instruct each MMH facility to survey every 500th patient discharged.
   (e) Instruct each MMH facility to survey 10 discharged patients this week and send in the results.

SECTION 1.3

Introduction to Experimental Design

FOCUS POINTS

- Discuss what it means to take a census.
- Describe simulations, observational studies, and experiments.
- Identify control groups, placebo effects, completely randomized experiments, and randomized block experiments.
- Discuss potential pitfalls that might make your data unreliable.

Planning a Statistical Study

Planning a statistical study and gathering data are essential components of obtaining reliable information. Depending on the nature of the statistical study, a great deal of expertise and resources may be required during the planning stage. In this section, we look at some of the basics of planning a statistical study.

PROCEDURE

Topics presented under the heading "Planning a Statistical Study" can be used for a good class discussion.

BASIC GUIDELINES FOR PLANNING A STATISTICAL STUDY

1. First, identify the individuals or objects of interest.
2. Specify the variables as well as protocols for taking measurements or making observations.
3. Determine if you will use an entire population or a representative sample. If using a sample, decide on a viable sampling method.
4. In your data collection plan, address issues of ethics, subject confidentiality, and privacy. If you are collecting data at a business, store, college, or other institution, be sure to be courteous and to obtain permission as necessary.
5. Collect the data.
6. Use appropriate descriptive statistics methods (Chapters 2, 3, and 4) and make decisions using appropriate inferential statistics methods (Chapters 8–11).
7. Finally, note any concerns you might have about your data collection methods and list any recommendations for future studies.

Census

One issue to consider is whether to use the entire population in a study or a representative sample. If we use data from the entire population, we have a *census*.

In a **census**, measurements or observations from the *entire* population are used.

When the population is small and easily accessible, a census is very useful because it gives complete information about the population. However, obtaining a census can be both expensive and difficult. Every 10 years, the U.S. Department of Commerce Census Bureau is required to conduct a census of the United States. However, contacting some members of the population—such as the homeless—is almost impossible. Sometimes members of the population will not respond. In such cases, statistical estimates for the missing responses are often supplied.

Sample

If we use data from only part of the population of interest, we have a *sample*.

In a **sample**, measurements or observations from *part* of the population are used.

In the previous section, we examined several sampling strategies: simple random, stratified, cluster, systematic, multistage, and convenience. In this text, we will study methods of inferential statistics based on simple random samples.

Simulation

As discussed in Section 1.2, a *simulation* is a numerical facsimile of a real-world phenomenon. Sometimes simulation is called a "dry lab" approach, in the sense that it is a mathematical imitation of a real situation. Advantages of simulation are that numerical and statistical simulations can fit real-world problems extremely well. The researcher can explore procedures through simulation that might be very dangerous in real life.

Experiments and Observation

When gathering data for a statistical study, we want to distinguish between observational studies and experiments.

This is a good time to remind students that an experiment is conceptually different from an observational study.

In an **observational study,** observations and measurements of individuals are conducted in a way that doesn't change the response or the variable being measured.

In an **experiment,** a *treatment* is deliberately imposed on the individuals in order to observe a possible change in the response or variable being measured.

EXAMPLE 4 EXPERIMENT

In 1778, Captain James Cook landed in what we now call the Hawaiian Islands. He gave the islanders a present of several goats, and over the years these animals multiplied into wild herds totaling several thousand. They eat almost anything, including the famous silver sword plant, which was once unique to Hawaii. At one time, the silver sword grew abundantly on the island of Maui (in Haleakala, a national park on that island, the silver sword can still be found), but each year there seemed to be fewer and fewer plants. Biologists suspected that the goats were partially responsible for the decline in the number of plants and conducted a statistical study that verified their theory.

Silver sword plant, Haleakala National Park

(a) To test the theory, park biologists set up stations in remote areas of Haleakala. At each station, two plots of land similar in soil conditions, climate, and plant count were selected. One plot was fenced to keep out the goats, while the other was not. At regular intervals a plant count was made in each plot. This study involves an *experiment* because a *treatment* (the fence) was imposed on one plot.

(b) The experiment involved two plots at each station. The plot that was not fenced represents the *control* plot. This is the plot on which a treatment was specifically not imposed, although the plot was similar to the fenced plot in every other way.

Placebo effect

Statistical experiments are commonly used to determine the effect of a treatment. However, the design of the experiment needs to *control* for other possible causes of the effect. For instance, in medical experiments, the *placebo effect* is the improvement or change that is the result of patients just believing in the treatment, whether or not the treatment itself is effective.

The **placebo effect** occurs when a subject receives no treatment but (incorrectly) believes he or she is, in fact, receiving treatment and responds favorably.

This could be a good time to have a class discussion about the placebo effect (see the Viewpoint at the end of this section).

To account for the placebo effect, patients are divided into two groups. One group receives the prescribed treatment. The other group, called the *control group*, receives a dummy or placebo treatment that is disguised to look like the real treatment. Finally, after the treatment cycle, the medical condition of the patients in the *treatment group* is compared to that of the patients in the control group.

Completely randomized experiment

A common way to assign patients to treatment and control groups is by using a random process. This is the essence of a *completely randomized experiment.*

A **completely randomized experiment** is one in which a random process is used to assign each individual to one of the treatments.

EXAMPLE 5 COMPLETELY RANDOMIZED EXPERIMENT

Can chest pain be relieved by drilling holes in the heart? For more than a decade, surgeons have been using a laser procedure to drill holes in the heart. Many patients report a lasting and dramatic decrease in angina (chest pain) symptoms. Is the relief due to the procedure, or is it a placebo effect? A recent research project at Lenox Hill Hospital in New York City provided some information about this issue by using a completely randomized experiment. The laser treatment was applied through a less invasive (catheter laser) process. A group of 298 volunteers with severe, untreatable chest pain were randomly assigned to get the laser treatment or not. The patients were sedated but awake. They could hear the doctors discuss the laser process. Each patient thought he or she was receiving the treatment.

The experimental design can be pictured as

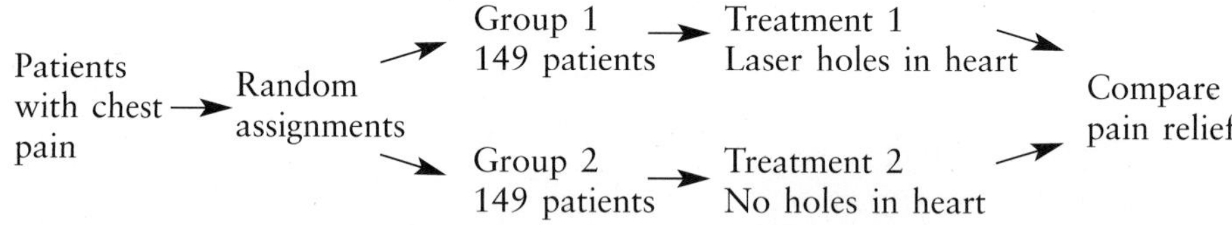

The laser patients did well. But shockingly, the placebo group showed more improvement in pain relief. The medical impacts of this study are still being investigated.

It is difficult to control all the variables that might influence the response to a treatment. One way to control some of the variables is through *blocking.*

Randomized block design

A **block** is a group of individuals sharing some common features that might affect the treatment.

In a **randomized block experiment,** individuals are first sorted into blocks, and then a random process is used to assign each individual in the block to one of the treatments.

A randomized block design utilizing gender for blocks in the experiment involving laser holes in the heart would be

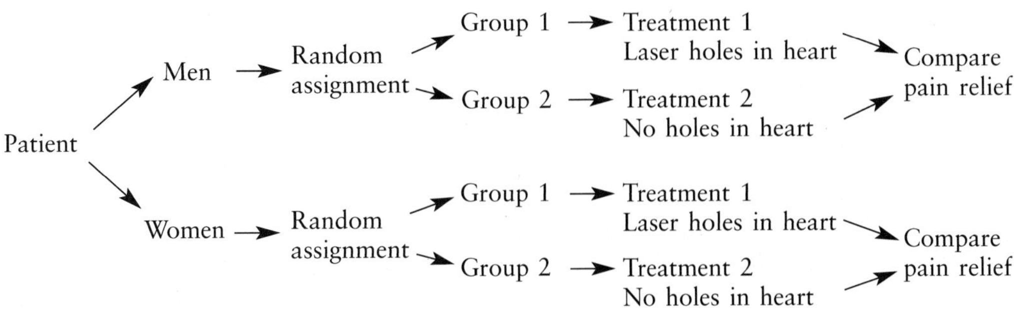

The study cited in Example 5 has many features of good experimental design.

There is a **control group.** This group received a dummy treatment, enabling the researchers to control for the placebo effect. In general, a control group is used to account for the influence of other known or unknown variables that might be an underlying cause of a change in response in the experimental group. Such variables are called **lurking** or **confounding variables.**

Randomization is used to assign individuals to the two treatment groups. This helps prevent bias in selecting members for each group.

Replication of the experiment on many patients reduces the possibility that the differences in pain relief for the two groups occurred by chance alone.

Double-blind experiment

Many experiments are also *double-blind.* This means that neither the individuals in the study nor the observers know which subjects are receiving the treatment. Double-blind experiments help control for subtle biases that a doctor might pass on to a patient.

GUIDED EXERCISE 5 | Collecting data

Which technique for gathering data (sampling, experiment, simulation, or census) do you think might be the most appropriate for the following studies?

(a) Study of the effect of stopping the cooling process of a nuclear reactor.

→ Simulation, since you probably do not want to risk a nuclear meltdown.

(b) Study of the amount of time college students taking a full course load spend watching television.

→ Sampling and using an observational study would work well. Notice that obtaining the information from a student probably will not change the amount of time the student spends watching television.

(c) Study of the effect on bone mass of a calcium supplement given to young girls.

→ Experimentation. A study by Tom Lloyd reported in the *Journal of the American Medical Association* utilized 94 young girls. Half were randomly selected and given a placebo. The other half were given calcium supplements to bring their daily calcium intake up to about 1400 milligrams per day. The group getting the experimental treatment of calcium gained 1.3% more bone mass in a year than the girls getting the placebo.

(d) Study of the credit hours load of *each* student enrolled at your college at the end of the drop/add period this semester.

→ Census. The registrar can obtain records for *every* student.

Surveys

Once you decide whether you are going to use sampling, census, observation, or experiments, a common means to gather data about people is to ask them questions. This process is the essence of *surveying*. Sometimes the possible responses are simply yes or no. Other times the respondents choose a number on a scale that represents their feelings from, say, strongly disagree to strongly agree. Such a scale is called a *Likert scale*. In the case of an open-ended, discussion-type response, the researcher must determine a way to convert the response to a category or number.

A number of issues can arise when using a survey.

Some potential pitfalls of a survey

Nonresponse: Individuals either cannot be contacted or refuse to participate. Nonresponse can result in significant undercoverage of a population.

Truthfulness of response: Respondents may lie intentionally or inadvertently.

Faulty recall: Respondents may not accurately remember when or whether an event took place.

Hidden bias: The question may be worded in such a way as to elicit a specific response. The order of questions might lead to biased responses. Also, the number of responses on a Likert scale may force responses that do not reflect the respondent's feelings or experience.

Vague wording: Words such as "often," "seldom," and "occasionally" mean different things to different people.

Interviewer influence: Factors such as tone of voice, body language, dress, gender, authority, and ethnicity of the interviewer might influence responses.

Voluntary response: Individuals with strong feelings about a subject are more likely than others to respond. Such a study is interesting but not reflective of the population.

Lurking and confounding variables

Sometimes our goal is to understand the cause-and-effect relationships between two or more variables. Such studies can be complicated by *lurking variables* or *confounding variables*.

A **lurking variable** is one for which no data have been collected but that nevertheless has influence on other variables in the study.

Two variables are **confounded** when the effects of one cannot be distinguished from the effects of the other. Confounding variables may be part of the study, or they may be outside lurking variables.

For instance, consider a study involving just two variables, amount of gasoline used to commute to work and time to commute to work. Level of traffic congestion is a likely lurking variable that increases both of the study variables. In a study involving several variables such as grade point average, difficulty of courses, IQ, and available study time, some of the variables might be confounded. For instance, students with less study time might opt for easier courses.

Generalizing results

Some researchers want to generalize their findings to a situation of wider scope than that of the actual data setting. The true scope of a new discovery must be determined by repeated studies in various real-world settings. Statistical experiments showing that a drug had a certain effect on a collection of laboratory rats do not guarantee that the drug will have a similar effect on a herd of wild horses in Montana.

Study sponsor

This is a good opportunity for an in-class summary of topics presented so far.

The sponsorship of a study is another area of concern. Subtle bias may be introduced. For instance, if a pharmaceutical company is paying freelance researchers to work on a study, the researchers may dismiss rare negative findings about a drug or treatment.

GUIDED EXERCISE 6 Cautions about data

Comment on the usefulness of the data collected as described.

(a) A uniformed police officer interviews a group of 20 college freshmen. She asks each one his or her name and then if he or she has used an illegal drug in the last month.

→ Respondents may not answer truthfully. Some may refuse to participate.

(b) Jessica saw some data that show that cities with more low-income housing have more homeless people. Does building low-income housing cause homelessness?

→ There may be some confounding or lurking variables, such as the size of the city. Larger cities may have more low-income housing and more homeless.

(c) A survey about quality of food in the student cafeteria was conducted by having forms available for customers to pick up at the cash register. A drop box for completed forms was available outside the cafeteria.

→ The voluntary response likely will produce more negative comments.

(d) Extensive studies on coronary problems were conducted using men over age 50 as the subjects.

→ Conclusions for men over age 50 may or may not generalize to other age and gender groups. These results may be useful for women or younger people, but studies specifically involving these groups may need to be performed.

Choosing Data Collection Techniques

We've briefly discussed three common techniques for gathering data: observational studies, experiments, and surveys. Which technique is best? The answer depends on the number of variables of interest and the level of confidence needed regarding statements of relationships among the variables.

- Surveys may be the best choice for gathering information across a wide range of many variables. Many questions can be included in a survey. However, great care must be taken in the construction of the survey instrument and in the administration of the survey. Nonresponse and other issues discussed earlier can introduce bias.
- Observational studies are the next most convenient technique for gathering information on many variables. Protocols for taking measurements or recording observations need to be specified carefully.
- Experiments are the most stringent and restrictive data-gathering technique. They can be time-consuming, expensive, and difficult to administer. In experiments, the goal is often to study the effects of changing only one variable at a time. Because of the requirements, the number of variables may be more limited. Experiments must be designed carefully to ensure that the resulting data are relevant to the research questions.

COMMENT An experiment is the best technique for reaching valid conclusions. By carefully controlling for other variables, the effect of changing one variable on a treatment group and comparing it to a control group yields results carrying high confidence.

The next most effective technique for obtaining results that have high confidence is the use of observational studies. Care must be taken that the act of observation does not change the behavior being measured or observed.

The least effective technique for drawing conclusions is the survey. Surveys have many pitfalls and by their nature cannot give exceedingly precise results. A medical survey asking patients if they feel better after taking a specific drug gives some information, but not precise information about the drug's effects. However, surveys are widely used to gauge attitudes, gather demographic information, study social and political trends, and so on.

VIEWPOINT Is the Placebo Effect a Myth?

Henry Beecher, former Chief of Anesthesiology at Massachusetts General Hospital, published a paper in the Journal of the American Medical Association *(1955) in which he claimed that the placebo effect is so powerful that about 35% of patients would improve simply if they believed a dummy treatment (placebo) was real. However, two Danish medical researchers refuted this widely accepted claim in the* New England Journal of Medicine. *They said the placebo effect is nothing more than a "regression effect," referring to a well-known statistical observation that patients who feel especially bad one day will almost always feel better the next day, no matter what is done for them. However, other respected statisticians question the findings of the Danish researchers. Regardless of the new controversy surrounding the placebo effect, medical researchers agree that placebos are still needed in clinical research. Double-blind research using placebos prevents the researchers from inadvertently biasing results.*

SECTION 1.3 PROBLEMS

Tables and art to accompany margin answers may be found in the back of the book.

1. Answers vary. People with higher incomes are more likely to have high-speed Internet access and to spend more time on-line. People with high-speed Internet access might spend less time watching TV news or programming. People with higher incomes might spend less time watching TV because of access to other entertainment venues.

1. *Statistical Literacy* A study involves three variables: income level, hours spent watching TV per week, and hours spent at home on the Internet per week. List some ways the variables might be confounded.

2. *Statistical Literacy* Consider a completely randomized experiment in which a control group is given a placebo for congestion relief and a treatment group is given a new drug for congestion relief. Describe a double-blind procedure for this experiment and discuss some benefits of such a procedure.

3. *Ecology: Gathering Data* Which technique for gathering data (observational study or experiment) do you think was used in the following studies?
   (a) The Colorado Division of Wildlife netted and released 774 fish at Quincy Reservoir. There were 219 perch, 315 blue gill, 83 pike, and 157 rainbow trout.
   (b) The Colorado Division of Wildlife caught 41 bighorn sheep on Mt. Evans and gave each one an injection to prevent heartworm. A year later, 38 of these sheep did not have heartworm, while the other three did.
   (c) The Colorado Division of Wildlife imposed special fishing regulations on the Deckers section of the South Platte River. All trout under 15 inches had to be released. A study of trout before and after the regulation went into effect showed that the average length of a trout increased by 4.2 inches after the new regulation.
   (d) An ecology class used binoculars to watch 23 turtles at Lowell Ponds. It was found that 18 were box turtles and 5 were snapping turtles.

4. *General: Gathering Data* Which technique for gathering data (sampling, experiment, simulation, or census) do you think was used in the following studies?
   (a) An analysis of a sample of 31,000 patients from New York hospitals suggests that the poor and the elderly sue for malpractice at one-fifth the rate of wealthier patients (*Journal of the American Medical Association*).
   (b) The effects of wind shear on airplanes during both landing and takeoff were studied by using complex computer programs that mimic actual flight.
   (c) A study of all league football scores attained through touchdowns and field goals was conducted by the National Football League to determine whether field goals account for more scoring events than touchdowns (*USA Today*).
   (d) An Australian study included 588 men and women who already had some precancerous skin lesions. Half got a skin cream containing a sunscreen with a sun protection factor of 17; half got an inactive cream. After 7 months, those using the sunscreen with the sun protection had fewer new precancerous skin lesions (*New England Journal of Medicine*).

5. *General: Completely Randomized Experiment* How would you use a completely randomized experiment in each of the following settings? Is a placebo being used or not? Be specific and give details.
   (a) A veterinarian wants to test a strain of antibiotic on calves to determine their resistance to common infection. In a pasture are 22 newborn calves. There is enough vaccine for 10 calves. However, blood tests to determine resistance to infection can be done on all calves.
   (b) The Denver Police Department wants to improve its image with teenagers. A uniformed officer is sent to a school one day a week for 10 weeks. Each day the officer visits with students, eats lunch with students, attends pep rallies, and so on. There are 18 schools, but the police department can visit only half of these schools this semester. A survey regarding how teenagers view police is sent to all 18 schools at the end of the semester.
   (c) A skin patch contains a new drug to help people quit smoking. A group of 75 cigarette smokers have volunteered as subjects to test the new skin patch. For one month, 40 of the volunteers receive skin patches with the new drug. The other volunteers receive skin patches with no drugs. At the end of two months, each subject is surveyed regarding his or her current smoking habits.

6. *Surveys: Manipulation* The *New York Times* did a special report on polling that was carried in papers across the nation. The article pointed out how readily the results of a survey can be manipulated. Some features that can influence the results of a poll include the following: the number of possible responses, the phrasing of the question, the sampling techniques used (voluntary response or sample designed to be representative), the fact that words may mean different things to different people, the questions that precede the question of interest, and finally, the fact that respondents can offer opinions on issues they know nothing about.
   (a) Consider the expression "over the last few years." Do you think that this expression means the same time span to everyone? What would be a more precise phrase?
   (b) Consider this question: "Do you think fines for running stop signs should be doubled?" Do you think the response would be different if the question "Have you ever run a stop sign?" preceded the question about fines?
   (c) Consider this question: "Do you watch too much television?" What do you think the responses would be if the only responses possible were yes or no? What do you think the responses would be if the possible responses were rarely, sometimes, or frequently?

7. ***Critical Thinking*** An agricultural study is conducted to compare the harvest volumes of two types of barley. The site for the experiment is bordered by a river. The field is divided into eight plots of approximately the same size. The experiment calls for the plots to be blocked into four plots per block. Then, two plots of each block will be randomly assigned to one of the two barley types.

2. For a double-blind procedure, neither the people administering the treatments nor the patients receiving the treatments know whether a placebo or the new drug is being given. The process eliminates possible bias resulting from administrator influence on patients or from patient psychology regarding the benefits of the drug.

3. (a) Observational study.
   (b) Experiment.
   (c) Experiment.
   (d) Observational study.

4. (a) Sampling.
   (b) Simulation.
   (c) Census.
   (d) Experiment.

5. (a) Use random selection to pick 10 calves to inoculate; test all calves; no placebo.
   (b) Use random selection to pick 9 schools to visit; survey all schools; no placebo.
   (c) Use random selection to pick 40 volunteers for skin patch with drug; survey all volunteers; placebo used.

6. (a) No. Answers vary.
   (b) Yes.
   (c) Answers vary.

7. Based on the information given, Scheme A is better because it blocks all plots bordering the river together and all plots away from the river together. The blocks of Scheme B do not seem to differ from each other.

Two blocking schemes are shown below, with one block indicated by the white region and the other by the grey region. Which blocking scheme, A or B, would be better? Explain.

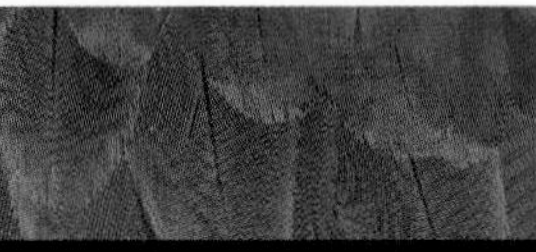

Chapter Review

SUMMARY

In this chapter, you've seen that statistics is the study of how to collect, organize, analyze, and interpret numerical information from populations or samples. This chapter discussed some of the features of data and ways to collect data. In particular, the chapter discussed

- Individuals or subjects of a study and the variables associated with those individuals
- Data classification as qualitative or quantitative, and levels of measurement of data
- Sample and population data. Summary measurements from sample data are called statistics, and those from population data are called parameters.
- Sampling strategies, including simple random, stratified, systematic, multistage, and convenience. Inferential techniques presented in this text are based on simple random samples.
- Methods of obtaining data: Use of a census, simulation, observational studies, experiments, and surveys
- Concerns: Undercoverage of a population, nonresponse, bias in data from surveys and other factors, effects of confounding or lurking variables on other variables, generalization of study results beyond the population of the study, and study sponsorship

IMPORTANT WORDS & SYMBOLS

Section 1.1*
Statistics
Individual
Variable
Quantitative variable
Qualitative variable
Population data
Sample data
Parameter
Statistic
Levels of measurement
  Nominal
  Ordinal
  Interval
  Ratio
Descriptive statistics
Inferential statistics

Section 1.2
Simple random sample
Random-number table
Simulation
Sampling with replacement
Stratified sample
Systematic sample
Cluster sample
Multistage sample
Convenience sample
Sampling frame
Undercoverage
Sample error
Nonsample error

Section 1.3
Census
Observational study
Experiment
Placebo effect
Completely randomized experiment
Block
Randomized block experiment
Double-blind experiment

*Indicates section of first appearance.

Control group	Replication
Treatment group	Survey
Confounding variable	Nonresponse
Lurking variable	Voluntary response
Randomization	Hidden bias

VIEWPOINT Is Chocolate Good for Your Heart?

A study of 7841 Harvard alumni showed that the death rate was 30% lower in those who ate candy compared with those who abstained. It turns out that candy, especially chocolate, contains antioxidants that help slow the aging process. Also, chocolate, like aspirin, reduces the activity of blood platelets that contribute to plaque and blood clotting. Furthermore, chocolate seems to raise levels of high-density lipoprotein (HDL), the good cholesterol. However, these results are all preliminary. The investigation is far from complete. A wealth of information on this topic was published in the August 2000 issue of the Journal of Nutrition. *Statistical studies and reliable experimental design are indispensable in this type of research.*

CHAPTER REVIEW PROBLEMS

Tables and art to accompany margin answers may be found in the back of the book.

1. (a) Stratified.
   (b) Students on your campus with work-study jobs.
   (c) Hours scheduled; quantitative; ratio.
   (d) Rating of applicability of work experience to future employment; qualitative; ordinal.
   (e) Statistic.
   (f) 60%; the people choosing not to respond may have certain characteristics, such as not working many hours, that would bias the study.
   (g) No. The sample frame is restricted to one campus.

1. *Statistical Literacy* You are conducting a study of students doing work-study jobs on your campus. Among the questions on the survey instrument are:

   A. How many hours are you scheduled to work each week? Answer to the nearest hour.

   B. How applicable is this work experience to your future employment goals?

   Respond using the following scale: 1 = not at all, 2 = somewhat, 3 = very

   (a) Suppose you take random samples from the following groups: freshmen, sophomores, juniors, and seniors. What kind of sampling technique are you using (simple random, stratified, systematic, cluster, multistage, convenience)?
   (b) Describe the individuals of this study.
   (c) What is the variable for question A? Classify the variable as qualitative or quantitative. What is the level of the measurement?
   (d) What is the variable for question B? Classify the variable as qualitative or quantitative. What is the level of the measurement?
   (e) Is the proportion of responses "3 = very" to question B a statistic or a parameter?
   (f) Suppose only 40% of the students you selected for the sample respond. What is the nonresponse rate? Do you think the nonresponse rate might introduce bias into the study? Explain.
   (g) Would it be appropriate to generalize the results of your study to all work-study students in the nation? Explain.

2. Population: opinions of all listeners; variable: opinion of a caller; yes, voluntary response.

2. *Radio Talk Show: Sample Bias* A radio talk show host asked listeners to respond either yes or no to the question, Is the candidate who spends the most on a campaign the most likely to win? Fifteen people called in and nine said yes. What is the implied population? What is the variable? Can you detect any bias in the selection of the sample?

3. Assign digits so that 3 out of the 10 digits 0 through 9 correspond to the answer "Yes" and 7 of the digits correspond to the answer "No." One assignment is digits 0, 1, and 2 correspond to "Yes" while digits 3, 4, 5, 6, 7, 8, and 9 correspond to "No." Starting with line 1, block 1 of Table 1, this assignment of digits gives the sequence No, Yes, No, No, Yes, No, No.

3. *Simulation: TV Habits* One cable station knows that approximately 30% of its viewers have TIVO and can easily skip over advertising breaks. You are to design a simulation of how a random sample of seven station viewers would respond to the question, "Do you have TIVO?" How would you assign the random digits 0 through 9 to the responses "Yes" and "No" to the TIVO question? Use your random digit assignment and the random-number table to generate the responses from a random sample of seven station viewers.

4. (a) Cluster.
(b) Convenience.
(c) Systematic.
(d) Simple random.
(e) Stratified.

4. *General: Type of Sampling* Categorize the type of sampling (simple random, stratified, systematic, cluster, or convenience) used in each of the following situations.
(a) To conduct a preelection opinion poll on a proposed amendment to the state constitution, a random sample of 10 telephone prefixes (first three digits of the phone number) was selected, and all households from the phone prefixes selected were called.
(b) To conduct a study on depression among the elderly, a sample of 30 patients in one nursing home was used.
(c) To maintain quality control in a brewery, every 20th bottle of beer coming off the production line was opened and tested.
(d) Subscribers to the magazine *Sound Alive* were assigned numbers. Then a sample of 30 subscribers was selected by using a random-number table. The subscribers in the sample were invited to rate new compact disc players for a "What the Subscribers Think" column.
(e) To judge the appeal of a proposed television sitcom, a random sample of 10 people from each of three different age categories was selected and those chosen were asked to rate a pilot show.

5. (a) Observational study.
(b) Experiment.

5. *General: Gathering Data* Which technique for gathering data (observational study or experiment) do you think was used in the following studies? Explain.
(a) The U.S. Census Bureau tracks population age. In 1900, the percentage of the population that was 19 years old or younger was 44.4%. In 1930, the percentage was 38.8%; in 1970, the percentage was 37.9%; and in 2000, the percentage in the age group was down to 28.5% (*The First Measured Century,* T. Caplow, L. Hicks, B. J. Wattenberg).
(b) After receiving the same lessons, a class of 100 students was randomly divided into two groups of 50 each. One group was given a multiple-choice exam covering the material in the lessons. The other group was given an essay exam. The average test scores for the two groups were then compared.

6. (a) Use random selection to pick half to solicit by mail; compute percentage of donors in each group; compare results; no placebo.
(b) Use random selection to pick 43 volunteers to be given whitening gel; evaluate tooth whiteness for all participants; compare results; placebo used. For a double-blind experiment, neither the subjects nor researchers who interact with the subjects or who evaluate the tooth whiteness should know which subjects received the whitening gel.
(c) First assign individuals to the three blocks based on age. Use random selection to assign half the individuals in each block to mail solicitation and the other half to phone. Compute percentages of donors in each group for each block. Compare results within each block.

6. *General: Experiment* How would you use a completely randomized experiment in each of the following settings? Is a placebo being used or not? Be specific and give details.
(a) A charitable nonprofit organization wants to test two methods of fundraising. From a list of 1000 past donors, half will be sent literature about the successful activities of the charity and asked to make another donation. The other 500 donors will be contacted by phone and asked to make another donation. The percentage of people from each group who make a new donation will be compared.
(b) A tooth-whitening gel is to be tested for effectiveness. A group of 85 adults have volunteered to participate in the study. Of these, 43 are to be given a gel that contains the tooth-whitening chemicals. The remaining 42 are to be given a similar-looking package of gel that does not contain the tooth-whitening chemicals. A standard method will be used to evaluate the whiteness of teeth for all participants. Then the results for the two groups will be compared. How could this experiment be designed to be double-blind?
(c) Consider the experiment described in part (a). Describe how you would use a randomized block experiment with blocks based on age. Use three blocks: donors under 30 years old, donors 30 to 59 years old, donors 60 and over.

7. This is a good problem for class discussion. Some items, such as age and grade point average, might be sensitive information. You could ask the class to design a data form that can be filled out anonymously. Other issues to discuss involve the accuracy and honesty of the responses.

7. *Student Life: Data Collection Project* Make a statistical profile of your own statistics class. Items of interest might be
(a) Height, age, gender, pulse, number of siblings, marital status
(b) Number of college credit hours completed (as of beginning of term); grade point average
(c) Major; number of credit hours enrolled in this term
(d) Number of scheduled hours working per week
(e) Distance from residence to first class; time it takes to travel from residence to first class
(f) Year, make, and color of car usually driven

What directions would you give to people answering these questions? For instance, how accurate should the measurements be? Should age be recorded as of last birthday?

8. Students may easily spend several hours at this web site.

8. *Census: Web Site* *Census and You*, a publication of the Census Bureau, indicates that "Wherever your Web journey ends up, it should start at the Census Bureau's site." Visit the Online Study Center at **www.cengage.com/statistics/Brase/UBS5e** and find a link to the Census Bureau's site, as well as to Fedstats, another extensive site offering links to federal data. The Census Bureau site touts itself as the source of "official statistics." But it is willing to share the spotlight. The web site now has links to other "official" sources: other federal agencies, foreign statistical agencies, and state data centers. If you have access to the Internet, check out the Census Bureau's site.

9. (a) Experiment, since a treatment is imposed on one colony.
(b) The control group receives normal daylight/darkness conditions. The treatment group has light 24 hours per day.
(c) The number of fireflies living at the end of 72 hours.
(d) Ratio.

9. *Focus Problem: Fireflies* Suppose you are conducting a study to compare firefly populations exposed to normal daylight/darkness conditions with firefly populations exposed to continuous light (24 hours a day). You set up two firefly colonies in a laboratory environment. The two colonies are identical except that one colony is exposed to normal daylight/darkness conditions and the other is exposed to continuous light. Each colony is populated with the same number of mature fireflies. After 72 hours, you count the number of living fireflies in each colony.
(a) Is this an experiment or an observation study? Explain.
(b) Is there a control group? Is there a treatment group?
(c) What is the variable in this study?
(d) What is the level of measurement (nominal, interval, ordinal, or ratio) of the variable?

DATA HIGHLIGHTS: GROUP PROJECTS

1. Use a random-number table or random-number generator to simulate tossing a fair coin 10 times. Generate 20 such simulations of 10 coin tosses. Compare the simulations. Are there any strings of 10 heads? of 4 heads? Does it seem that in most of the simulations half the outcomes are heads? half are tails? In Chapter 6, we will study the probabilities of getting from 0 to 10 heads in such a simulation.

2. Use a random-number table or random-number generator to generate a random sample of 30 distinct values from the set of integers from 1 to 100. Instructions for doing this using the TI-84Plus/TI-83Plus, Excel, Minitab, or SPSS are given in Using Technology at the end of this chapter. Generate five such samples. How many of the samples include the number 1? the number 100? Comment about the differences among the samples. How well do the samples seem to represent the numbers between 1 and 100?

LINKING CONCEPTS: WRITING PROJECTS

Discuss each of the following topics in class or review the topics on your own. Then write a brief but complete essay in which you summarize the main points. Please include formulas and graphs as appropriate.

1. What does it mean when we say that we are going to use a sample to draw an inference about a population? Why is a random sample so important to this process? If we wanted a random sample of students in the cafeteria, why couldn't we just take the students who order Diet Pepsi with their lunch? Comment on the statement, "A random sample is like a miniature population, whereas samples that are not random are likely to be biased." Why would the students who order Diet Pepsi with lunch not be a random sample of students in the cafeteria?

2. In your own words, explain the differences among the following sampling techniques: simple random sample, stratified sample, systematic sample, cluster sample, multistage sample, and convenience sample. Describe situations in which each type might be useful.

USING TECHNOLOGY

General spreadsheet programs such as Microsoft Excel, specific statistical software packages such as Minitab or SPSS, and graphing calculators such as the TI-84Plus and TI-83Plus all offer computing support for statistical methods. Applications in this section may be completed using software or calculators with statistical functions. Select keystroke or menu choices are shown for the TI-84Plus and TI-83Plus calculators, Minitab, Excel, and SPSS in the Technology Hints portion of this section. More details can be found in the software-specific Technology Guide that accompanies this text.

Applications

Most software packages sample *with replacement.* That is, the same number may be used more than once in the sample. If your applications require sampling without replacement, draw more items than you need. Then use sort commands in the software to put the data in order, and delete repeated data.

1. Simulate the results of tossing a fair die 18 times. Repeat the simulation. Are the results the same? Did you expect them to be the same? Why or why not? Do there appear to be equal numbers of outcomes 1 through 6 in each simulation? In Chapter 5, we will encounter the law of large numbers, which tells us that we would expect equal numbers of particular outcomes only when the simulation is very large.

2. A college has 5000 students, and the registrar wishes to use a random sample of 50 students to examine credit hour enrollment for this semester. Write a brief description of how a random sample can be drawn. Draw a random sample of 50 students. Are you sampling with or without replacement?

Technology Hints: Random Numbers

TI-84Plus/TI-83Plus

To select a random set of integers between two specified values, press the **MATH** key and highlight **PRB** with **5:randInt** (low value, high value, sample size). Press Enter and fill in the low value, high value, and sample size. To store the sample in list L1, press the **STO➡** key and then L1. The screen display shows two random samples of size 5 drawn from the integers between 1 and 100.

```
randInt(1,100,5)
{63 89 13 46 47}
randInt(1,100,5)
{29 82 99 50 41}
```

Excel

To select a random number between two specified values, type the command**=Randbetween(low value, high value)** in the formula bar. Alternatively, access a dialogue box for the command by clicking on the **paste function** (f_x) key on the menu bar. Then choose **All** in the left drop-down menu and **RANDBETWEEN** in the right menu. Fill in the dialogue box.

A5 = =RANDBETWEEN(1,100)

	A	B	C	D	E
1	99				
2	58				
3	69				
4	86				
5	13				

Minitab

To generate random integers between specified values, use the menu selection **Calc ➤ Random Data ➤ Integer.** Fill in the dialogue box to get five random numbers between 1 and 100.

Worksheet 2 ***

↓	C1
1	8
2	35
3	33
4	9
5	15

SPSS

SPSS is a research statistical package for the social sciences. Data are entered in the data editor, which has a spreadsheet format. In the data editor window, you have a choice of data view (default) or variable view. In the variable view, you name variables, declare type (numeric for measurements, string for category), determine format, and declare measurement type. The choices for measurement type are scale (for ratio or interval data), ordinal, or nominal. Once you have entered data, you can use the menu bar at the top of the screen to select activities, graphs, or analysis appropriate to the data.

SPSS supports several random sample activities. In particular, you can select a random sample from an existing data set or from a variety of probability distributions.

Selecting a random integer between two specified values involves several steps. First, in the data editor, enter the sample numbers in the first column. For instance, to generate five random numbers, list the values 1 through 5 in the first column. Notice that the label for the first column is now var00001. SPSS does not have a direct function for selecting a random sample of integers. However, there is a function for sampling values from the uniform distribution of all real numbers between two specified values. We will use that function and then truncate the values to obtain a random sample of integers between two specified values.

Use the menu options **Transform ➤ Compute.** In the dialog box, type in var00002 as the target variable. Then, in the function box, select the function **RV.UNIFORM(min, max).** Use 1 as the minimum and 101 as the maximum. The maximum is 101 because numbers between 100 and 101 truncate to 100.

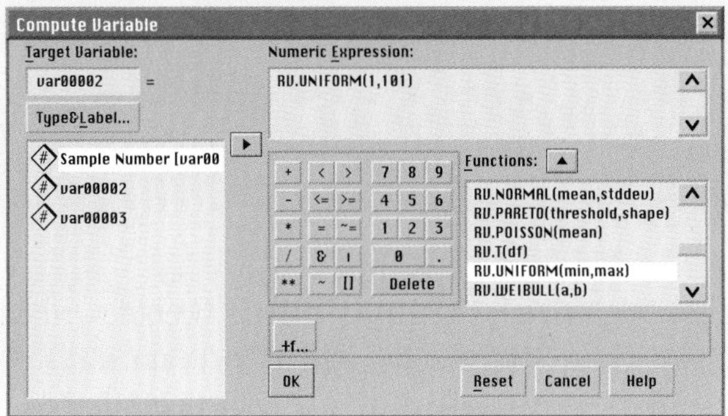

The random numbers from the uniform distribution now appear in the second column under var00002. You can visually truncate the values to obtain random integers. However, if you want SPSS to truncate the values for you, you can again use the menu choices **Transform ➤ Compute.** In the dialogue box, enter var00003 for the target variable. From the functions box, select **TRUNC(numexpr).** Use var00002 in place of numexpr. The random integers between 1 and 100 appear in the third column under var00003.

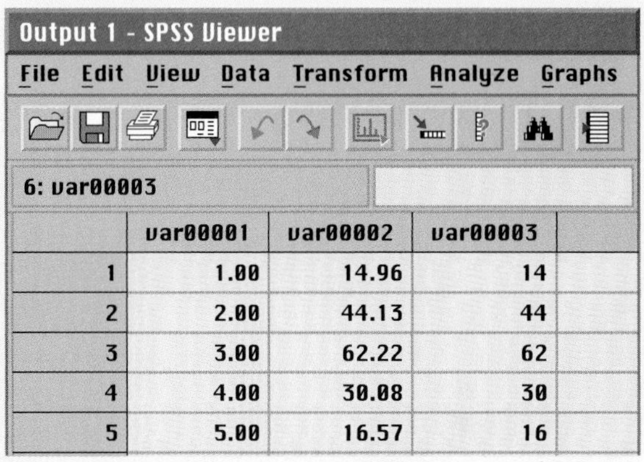

	var00001	var00002	var00003
1	1.00	14.96	14
2	2.00	44.13	44
3	3.00	62.22	62
4	4.00	30.08	30
5	5.00	16.57	16

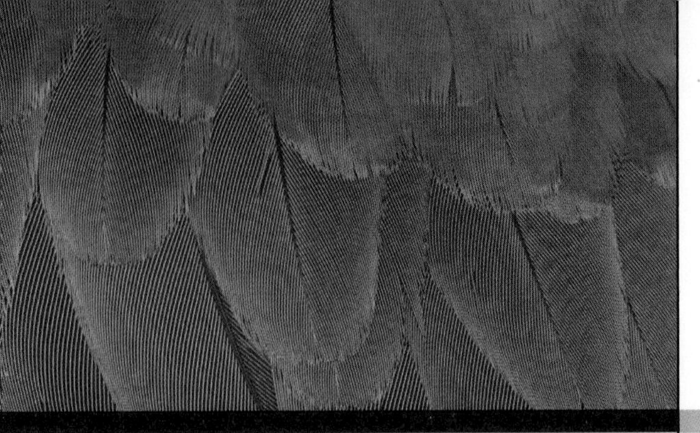

2

In dwelling upon the vital importance of sound observation, it must never be lost sight of what observation is for. It is not for the sake of piling up miscellaneous information or curious facts, but for the sake of saving life and increasing health and comfort.

—Florence Nightingale,
Notes on Nursing

Florence Nightingale (1820–1910) has been described as a "passionate statistician" and a "relevant statistician." She viewed statistics as a science that allowed one to transcend his or her narrow individual experience and aspire to the broader service of humanity. She was one of the first nurses to use graphic representation of statistics, illustrating with charts and diagrams how improved sanitation decreased the rate of mortality. Her statistical reports about the appalling sanitary conditions at Scutari (the main British hospital during the Crimean War) were taken very seriously by the English Secretary at War, Sidney Herbert. When sanitary reforms recommended by Nightingale were instituted in military hospitals, the mortality rate dropped from an incredible 42.7% to only 2.2%.

For on-line student resources, visit the Brase/Brase, *Understanding Basic Statistics,* 5th edition web site at **www.cengage.com/statistics/Brase/UBS5e.**

ORGANIZING DATA

PREVIEW QUESTIONS

What are histograms? When are they used? (SECTION 2.1)

What are common distribution shapes? (SECTION 2.1)

How can you select graphs appropriate for given data sets? (SECTION 2.2)

How can you quickly order data and, at the same time, reveal the distribution shape? (SECTION 2.3)

FOCUS PROBLEM

Say It with Pictures

Edward R. Tufte, in his book *The Visual Display of Quantitative Information,* presents a number of guidelines for producing good graphics. According to the criteria, a graphical display should

- show the data;
- induce the viewer to think about the substance of the graphic rather than about the methodology, the design, the technology, or other production devices;
- avoid distorting what the data have to say.

As an example of a graph that violates some of the criteria, Tufte includes a graphic that appeared in a well-known newspaper. Figure 2-1(a), on the next page, shows a facsimile of the problem graphic, whereas part (b) of the figure shows a better rendition of the data display.

After completing this chapter, you will be able to answer the following questions.

(a) Look at the graph in Figure 2-1(a). Is it essentially a bar graph? Explain. What are some of the flaws of Figure 2-1(a) as a bar graph?

(b) Examine Figure 2-1(b), which shows the same information. Is it essentially a time-series graph? Explain. In what ways does the second graph seem to display the information in a clearer manner?

(See Problem 5 of the Chapter 2 Review Problems.)

FIGURE 2-1

(a) Fuel Economy Standards for Autos

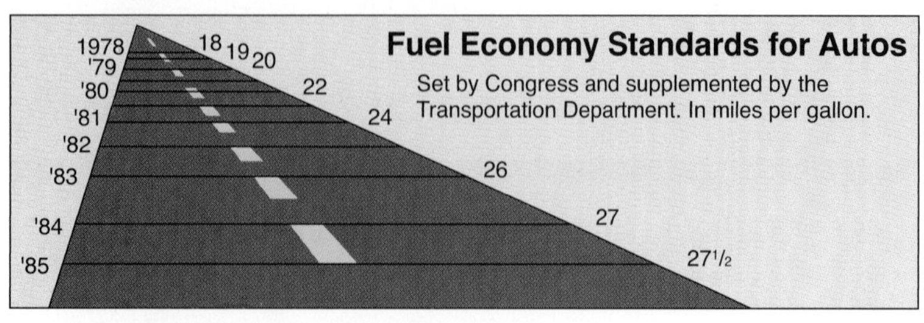

Source: Copyright © 1978 by The New York Times Company. Reprinted by permission.

(b) REQUIRED FUEL ECONOMY STANDARDS: NEW CARS BUILT FROM 1978 TO 1985

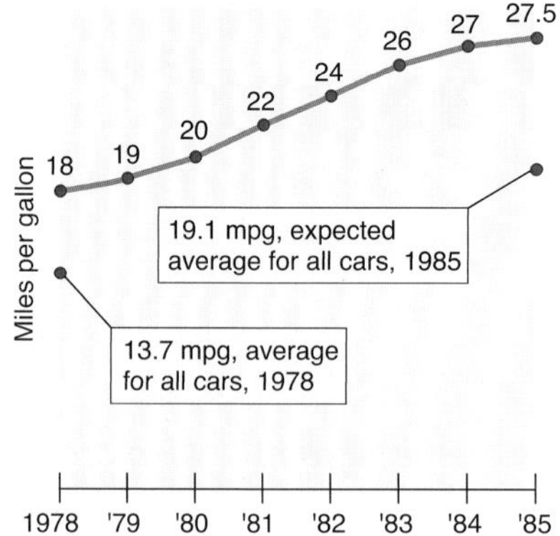

Source: The Visual Display of Quantitative Information by Edward R. Tufte, p. 57. Copyright © 1983. Reprinted by permission of Graphics Press.

SECTION 2.1 Frequency Distributions, Histograms, and Related Topics

FOCUS POINTS

- Organize raw data using a frequency table.
- Construct histograms and relative-frequency histograms.
- Recognize basic distribution shapes: uniform, symmetric, skewed, and bimodal.
- Interpret graphs in the context of the data setting.

Frequency Tables

When we have a large set of quantitative data, it's useful to organize it into smaller intervals or *classes* and count how many data values fall into each class. A frequency table does just that.

A **frequency table** partitions data into classes or intervals and shows how many data values are in each class. The classes or intervals are constructed so that each data value falls into exactly one class.

Although this section is not conceptually difficult, it may require a little more time.

Constructing a frequency table involves a number of steps. Example 1 demonstrates the steps.

EXAMPLE 1 FREQUENCY TABLE

A task force to encourage car pooling conducted a study of one-way commuting distances of workers in the downtown Dallas area. A random sample of 60 of these workers was taken. The commuting distances of the workers in the sample are given in Table 2-1. Make a frequency table for these data.

SOLUTION:

(a) First decide how many classes you want. Five to 15 classes usually are used. If you use fewer than five classes, you risk losing too much information. If you use more than 15 classes, the data may not be sufficiently summarized. Let the

TABLE 2-1 One-Way Commuting Distances (in Miles) for 60 Workers in Downtown Dallas

13	47	10	3	16	20	17	40	4	2
7	25	8	21	19	15	3	17	14	6
12	45	1	8	4	16	11	18	23	12
6	2	14	13	7	15	46	12	9	18
34	13	41	28	36	17	24	27	29	9
14	26	10	24	37	31	8	16	12	16

spread of the data and the purpose of the frequency table be your guide when selecting the number of classes. In the case of the commuting data, let's use *six* classes.

Class width

(b) Next, find the *class width* for the six classes.

PROCEDURE

How to find the class width

1. Compute $\dfrac{\text{Largest data value} - \text{smallest data value}}{\text{Desired number of classes}}$
2. Increase the computed value to the next highest whole number.

Note: To ensure that all the classes taken together cover the data, we need to increase the result of step 1 to the *next whole number,* even if step 1 produced a whole number. For instance, if the calculation in step 1 produces the value 4, we make the class width 5.

To find the class width for the commuting data, we observe that the largest distance commuted is 47 miles and the smallest is 1 mile. Using six classes, the class width is 8, since

$$\text{Class width} = \frac{47 - 1}{6} \approx 7.7 \quad \text{(increase to 8)}$$

(c) Now we determine the data range for each class.

Class limits

The **lower class limit** is the lowest data value that can fit in a class. The **upper class limit** is the highest data value that can fit in a class. The **class width** is the difference between the *lower* class limit of one class and the *lower* class limit of the next class.

The smallest commuting distance in our sample is 1 mile. We use this *smallest* data value as the lower class limit of the *first* class. Since the class width is 8, we add 8 to 1 to find that the *lower* class limit for the *second* class is 9. Following this pattern, we establish *all* the *lower class limits.* Then we fill in the *upper class limits* so that the classes span the entire range of data. Table 2-2, on the next page, shows the upper and lower class limits for the commuting distance data.

(d) Now we are ready to tally the commuting distance data into the six classes and find the frequency for each class.

It is useful to point out that the difference between consecutive lower class limits is the class width, 8. This is also true of consecutive upper class limits.

TABLE 2-2 **Frequency Table of One-Way Commuting Distances for 60 Downtown Dallas Workers (data in miles)**

Class Limits	Class Boundaries			
Lower–Upper	Lower–Upper	Tally	Frequency	Class Midpoint
1–8	0.5–8.5	卌 卌 ||||	14	4.5
9–16	8.5–16.5	卌 卌 卌 卌 |	21	12.5
17–24	16.5–24.5	卌 卌 |	11	20.5
25–32	24.5–32.5	卌 |	6	28.5
33–40	32.5–40.5	||||	4	36.5
41–48	40.5–48.5	||||	4	44.5

Problems 15, 16, and 17 introduce dotplots, which are diagrams that show the frequency with which each data value occurs.

PROCEDURE

HOW TO TALLY DATA

Tallying data is a method for counting data values that fall into a particular class or category.

To tally data into classes for a frequency table, examine each data value. Determine which class contains the data value and make a tally mark or vertical stroke (|) beside that class. For ease of counting, each fifth tally mark of a class is placed diagonally across the prior four marks (卌).

Class frequency

The *class frequency* for a class is the number of tally marks corresponding to that class.

Table 2-2 shows the tally and frequency of each class.

Class midpoint or class mark

(e) The center of each class is called the *midpoint* (or *class mark*). The midpoint is often used as a representative value of the entire class. The midpoint is found by adding the lower and upper class limits of one class and dividing by 2.

$$\textbf{Midpoint} = \frac{\text{Lower class limit} + \text{upper class limit}}{2}$$

Table 2-2 shows the class midpoints.

Class boundaries

(f) There is a space between the upper limit of one class and the lower limit of the next class. The halfway points of these intervals are called *class boundaries*. These are shown in Table 2-2.

PROCEDURE

HOW TO FIND CLASS BOUNDARIES (INTEGER DATA)

To find **upper class boundaries,** add 0.5 unit to the upper class limits.
To find **lower class boundaries,** subtract 0.5 unit from the lower class limits.

Relative frequency

Basic frequency tables show how many data values fall into each class. It's also useful to know the *relative frequency* of a class. The relative frequency of a class is the proportion of all data values that fall into that class. To find the relative frequency of a particular class, divide the class frequency f by the total of all frequencies n (sample size).

TABLE 2-3 Relative Frequencies of One-Way Commuting Distances

Class	Frequency f	Relative Frequency f/n
1–8	14	$14/60 \approx 0.23$
9–16	21	$21/60 \approx 0.35$
17–24	11	$11/60 \approx 0.18$
25–32	6	$6/60 \approx 0.10$
33–40	4	$4/60 \approx 0.07$
41–48	4	$4/60 \approx 0.07$

$$\textbf{Relative frequency} = \frac{f}{n} = \frac{\text{Class frequency}}{\text{Total of all frequencies}}$$

Table 2-3 shows the relative frequencies for the commuter data of Table 2-1. Since we already have the frequency table (Table 2-2), the relative-frequency table is obtained easily. The sample size is $n = 60$. Notice that the sample size is the total of all the frequencies. Therefore, the relative frequency for the first class (the class from 1 to 8) is

$$\text{Relative frequency} = \frac{f}{n} = \frac{14}{60} \approx 0.23$$

The symbol $\approx$ means "approximately equal to." We use the symbol because we rounded the relative frequency. Relative frequencies for the other classes are computed in a similar way.

The total of the relative frequencies should be 1. However, rounded results may make the total slightly higher or lower than 1.

Let's summarize the procedure for making a frequency table that includes relative frequencies.

PROCEDURE

Use this summary as a kind of flow chart to help students organize their work.

How to make a frequency table

1. Determine the number of classes and the corresponding class width.
2. Create the distinct classes. We use the convention that the *lower class limit* of the first class is the smallest data value. Add the class width to this number to get the *lower class limit* of the next class.
3. Fill in *upper class limits* to create distinct classes that accommodate all possible data values from the data set.
4. Tally the data into classes. Each data value should fall into exactly one class. Total the tallies to obtain each *class frequency.*
5. Compute the *midpoint* (class mark) for each class.
6. Determine the *class boundaries.*

Problems 13 and 14 show the procedure for making a frequency table with decimal data.

PROCEDURE

How to make a relative-frequency table

First make a frequency table. Then, for each class, compute the *relative frequency* f/n, where f is the class frequency and n is the total sample size.

Histograms and Relative-Frequency Histograms

Relative-frequency tables and relative-frequency histograms are useful extensions of frequency tables and histograms.

Histograms and relative-frequency histograms provide effective visual displays of data that have been organized into frequency tables. In these graphs, we use bars to represent each class, where the width of the bar is the class width. For histograms, the height of the bar is the class frequency, whereas for relative-frequency histograms, the height of the bar is the relative frequency of that class.

PROCEDURE

HOW TO MAKE A HISTOGRAM OR A RELATIVE-FREQUENCY HISTOGRAM

1. Make a frequency table (including relative frequencies) with the designated number of classes.
2. Place class boundaries on the horizontal axis and frequencies or relative frequencies on the vertical axis.
3. For each class of the frequency table, draw a bar whose width extends between corresponding class boundaries. For histograms, the height of each bar is the corresponding class frequency. For relative-frequency histograms, the height of each bar is the corresponding class relative frequency.

EXAMPLE 2 HISTOGRAM AND RELATIVE-FREQUENCY HISTOGRAM

Make a histogram and a relative-frequency histogram with six bars for the data in Table 2-1 showing one-way commuting distances.

Once you have a histogram, a quick way of creating a relative-frequency diagram is to use the same graph, but change the vertical axis of f values to f/n values. In other words, simply divide the tick mark labels on the f axis by n to create the corresponding f/n axis. This is how the answers to the Section 2.1 problems were generated.

SOLUTION: The first step is to make a frequency table and a relative-frequency table with six classes. We'll use Table 2-2 and Table 2-3. Figures 2-2 and 2-3 show the histogram and relative-frequency histogram. In both graphs, class boundaries are marked on the horizontal axis. For each class of the frequency table, make a corresponding bar with horizontal width extending from the lower boundary to the upper boundary of the respective class. For a histogram, the height of each bar is the corresponding class frequency. For a relative-frequency histogram, the height of each bar is the corresponding relative frequency. Notice that the basic shapes of the graphs are the same. The only difference involves the vertical axis. The vertical axis of the histogram shows frequencies, whereas that of the relative-frequency histogram shows relative frequencies.

FIGURE 2-2

Histogram for Dallas Commuters: One-Way Commuting Distances

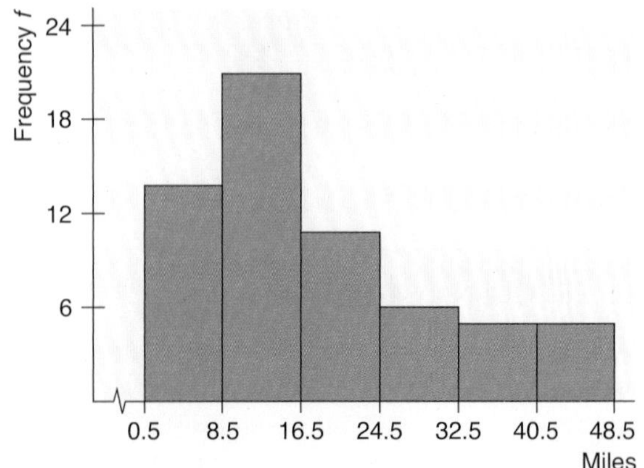

FIGURE 2-3

Relative-Frequency Histogram for Dallas Commuters: One-Way Commuting Distances

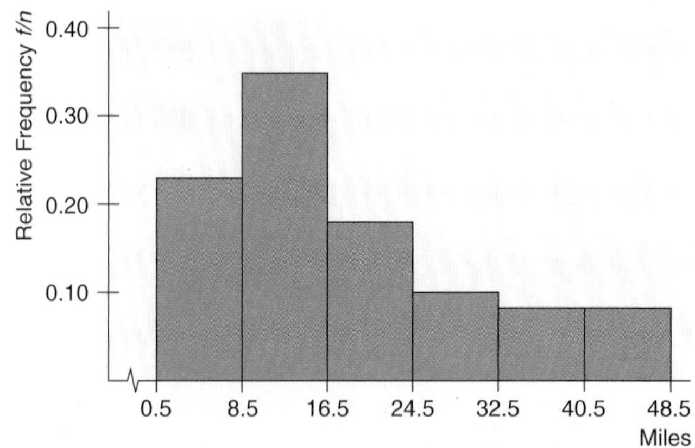

COMMENT The use of class boundaries in histograms assures us that the bars of the histogram touch and that no data fall on the boundaries. Both of these features are important. But a histogram displaying class boundaries may look awkward. For instance, the mileage range of 8.5 to 16.5 miles shown in Figure 2-2 isn't as natural a choice as a mileage range of 8 to 16 miles. For this reason, many magazines and newspapers do not use class boundaries as labels on a histogram. Instead, some use lower class limits as labels, with the convention that *a data value falling on the class limit is included in the next higher class (class to the right of the limit)*. Another convention is to label midpoints instead of class boundaries. Determine the convention being used before creating frequency tables and histograms on a computer.

GUIDED EXERCISE 1 Histogram and relative-frequency histogram

An irate customer called Dollar Day Mail Order Company 40 times during the last two weeks to see why his order had not arrived. Each time he called, he recorded the length of time he was put "on hold" before being allowed to talk to a customer service representative. See Table 2-4.

TABLE 2-4 **Length of Time on Hold, in Minutes**

1	5	5	6	7	4	8	7	6	5
5	6	7	6	6	5	8	9	9	10
7	8	11	2	4	6	5	12	13	6
3	7	8	8	9	9	10	9	8	9

(a) What are the largest and smallest values in Table 2-4? If we want five classes in a frequency table, what should the class width be?

➡ The largest value is 13; the smallest value is 1. The class width is

$$\frac{13-1}{5} = 2.4 \approx 3$$ *Note: Increase* the value to 3.

(b) Complete the following frequency table.

TABLE 2-5 **Time on Hold**

Class Limits Lower–Upper	Tally	Frequency	Midpoint
1–3	____	____	____
4–____	____	____	____
____–9	____	____	____
____–____	____	____	____
____–____	____	____	____

➡ TABLE 2-6 **Completion of Table 2-5**

Class Limits Lower–Upper	Tally	Frequency	Midpoint
1–3	III	3	2
4–6	~~IIII~~ ~~IIII~~ ~~IIII~~	15	5
7–9	~~IIII~~ ~~IIII~~ ~~IIII~~ II	17	8
10–12	IIII	4	11
13–15	I	1	14

(c) Recall that the class boundary is halfway between the upper limit of one class and the lower limit of the next. Use this fact to find the class boundaries in Table 2-7 and to complete the partial histogram in Figure 2-4.

TABLE 2-7 **Class Boundaries**

Class Limits	Class Boundaries
1–3	0.5–3.5
4–6	3.5–6.5
7–9	6.5–____
10–12	____–____
13–15	____–____

➡ TABLE 2-8 **Completion of Table 2-7**

Class Limits	Class Boundaries
1–3	0.5–3.5
4–6	3.5–6.5
7–9	6.5–9.5
10–12	9.5–12.5
13–15	12.5–15.5

Continued

GUIDED EXERCISE 1 *continued*

FIGURE 2-4

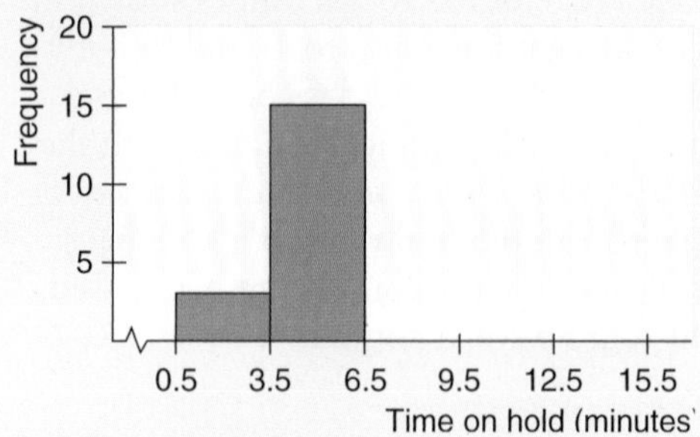

FIGURE 2-5 Completion of Figure 2-4

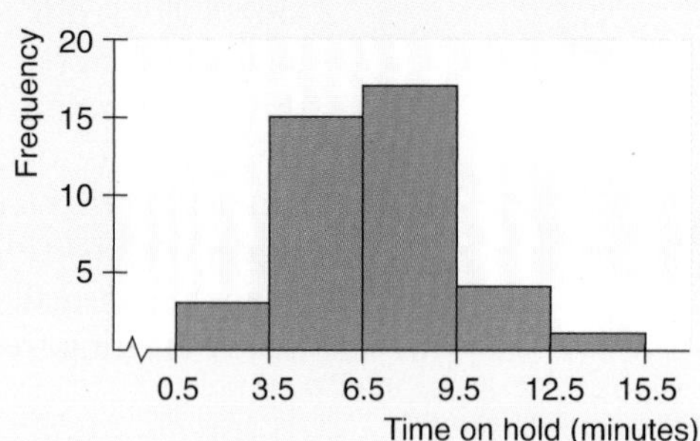

(d) Compute the relative class frequency f/n for each class in Table 2-9 and complete the partial relative-frequency histogram in Figure 2-6.

TABLE 2-9 **Relative Class Frequency**

Class	f/n
1–3	3/40 = 0.075
4–6	15/40 = 0.375
7–9	____
10–12	____
13–15	____

TABLE 2-10 **Completion of Table 2-9**

Class	f/n
1–3	0.075
4–6	0.375
7–9	0.425
10–12	0.100
13–15	0.025

FIGURE 2-6

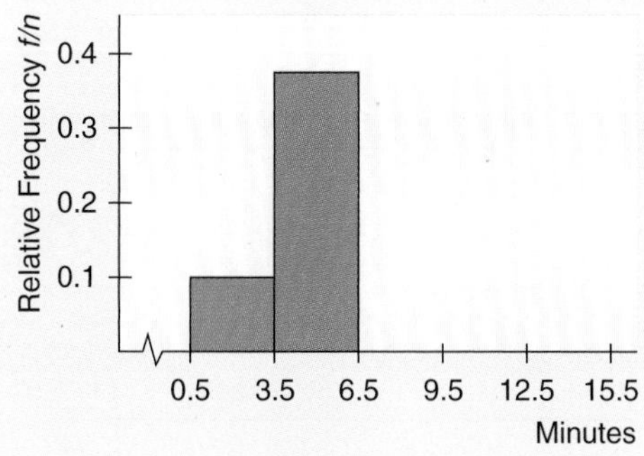

FIGURE 2-7 Completion of Figure 2-6

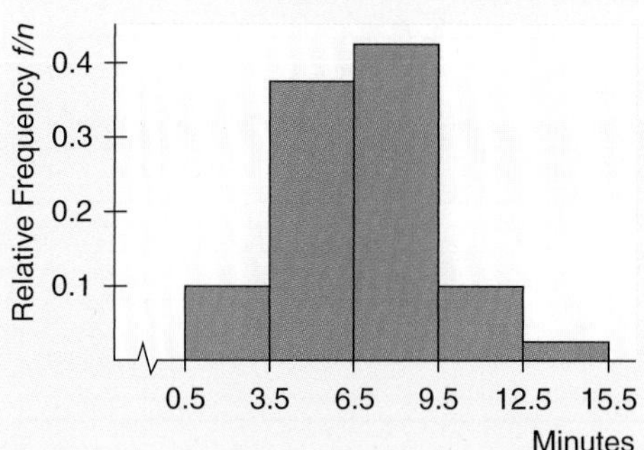

We will see relative-frequency distributions again when we study probability in Chapter 5. There we will see that if a random sample is large enough, then we can estimate the probability of an event by the relative frequency of the event. The relative-frequency distribution then can be interpreted as a *probability distribution*. Such distributions will form the basis of our work in inferential statistics.

Distribution Shapes

Histograms are valuable and useful tools. If the raw data came from a random sample of population values, the histogram constructed from the sample values should have a distribution shape that is reasonably similar to that of the population.

FIGURE 2-8

Types of Histograms

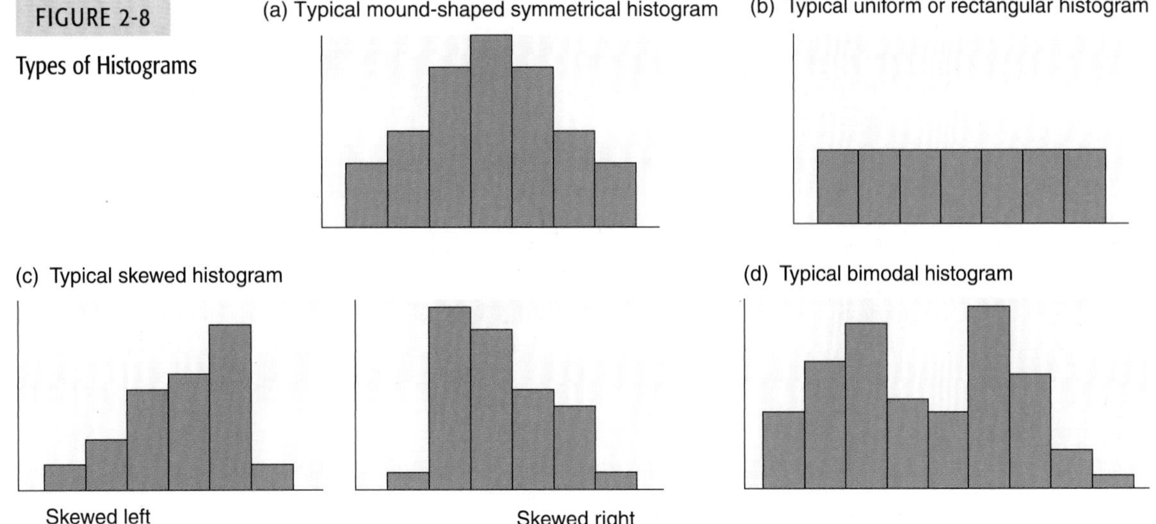

Several terms are commonly used to describe histograms and their associated population distributions.

Mound-shaped symmetrical distributions will be especially important in later work.

(a) ***Mound-shaped symmetrical:*** This term refers to a histogram in which both sides are (more or less) the same when the graph is folded vertically down the middle. Figure 2-8(a) shows a typical mound-shaped symmetrical histogram.

(b) ***Uniform or rectangular:*** These terms refer to a histogram in which every class has equal frequency. From one point of view, a uniform distribution is symmetrical with the added property that the bars are of the same height. Figure 2-8(b) illustrates a typical histogram with a uniform shape.

(c) ***Skewed left or skewed right:*** These terms refer to a histogram in which one tail is stretched out longer than the other. The direction of skewness is on the side of the *longer* tail. So, if the longer tail is on the left, we say the histogram is skewed to the left. Figure 2-8(c) shows a typical histogram skewed to the left and another skewed to the right.

(d) ***Bimodal:*** This term refers to a histogram in which the two classes with the largest frequencies are separated by at least one class. The top two frequencies of these classes may have slightly different values. This type of situation sometimes indicates that we are sampling from two different populations. Figure 2-8(d) illustrates a typical histogram with a bimodal shape.

CRITICAL THINKING

A bimodal distribution shape might indicate that the data are from two different populations. For instance, a histogram showing the heights of a random sample of adults is likely to be bimodal because two populations, male and female, were combined.

If there are gaps in the histogram between bars at either end of the graph, the data set might include *outliers*.

Outliers in a data set are data values that are very different from other measurements in the data set.

Outliers may indicate data recording errors. Valid outliers may be so unusual that they should be examined separately from the rest of the data. For instance, in a study of salaries of employees at one company, the chief CEO salary may be so high and unique for the company that it should be considered separately from the other salaries. Decisions about outliers that are not recording errors need to be made by people familiar with both the field and the purpose of the study.

TECH NOTES The TI-84Plus/TI-83Plus calculators, Excel, and Minitab all create histograms. However, each technology automatically selects the number of classes to use. In Using Technology at the end of this chapter, you will see instructions for specifying the number of classes yourself and for generating histograms such as those we create "by hand."

VIEWPOINT Mush, You Huskies!

In 1925, the village of Nome, Alaska, had a terrible diphtheria epidemic. Serum was available in Anchorage but had to be brought to Nome by dogsled over the 1161-mile Iditarod Trail. Since 1973, the Iditarod Dog Sled Race from Anchorage to Nome has been an annual sporting event with a current purse of more than $600,000. Winning times range from more than 20 days to a little over 9 days.

To collect data on winning times, visit the Online Study Center at **www.cengage.com/statistics/Brase/UBS5e** *and find the link to the Iditarod. Make a frequency distribution for these times.*

SECTION 2.1 PROBLEMS

Tables and art to accompany margin answers may be found in the back of the book.

1. Class limits are possible data values. Class limits specify the span of data values that fall within a class. Class boundaries are not possible data values. They are values halfway between the upper class limit of one class and the lower class limit of the next.

2. Each data value must fall into one class. The data values of 50 and above do not have a class.

3. The classes overlap so that some data values, such as 20, fall within two classes.

1. *Statistical Literacy* What is the difference between a class boundary and a class limit?
2. *Statistical Literacy* A data set has values ranging from a low of 10 to a high of 52. What's wrong with using the class limits 10–19, 20–29, 30–39, 40–49 for a frequency table?
3. *Statistical Literacy* A data set has values ranging from a low of 10 to a high of 50. What's wrong with using the class limits 10–20, 20–30, 30–40, 40–50 for a frequency table?
4. *Statistical Literacy* A data set has values ranging from a low of 10 to a high of 50. The class width is to be 10. What's wrong with using the class limits 10–20, 21–31, 32–42, 43–53 for a frequency table with a class width of 10?
5. ***Critical Thinking*** Look at the histogram in Figure 2-9(a), which shows mileage, in miles per gallon (mpg), for a random selection of passenger cars (Reference: *Consumer Reports*).
   (a) Is the shape of the histogram essentially bimodal?
   (b) Jose looked at the raw data and discovered that the 54 data values included both the city and highway mileages for 27 cars. He used the city mileages for the

FIGURE 2-9 (a) Histogram of mpg

(b)

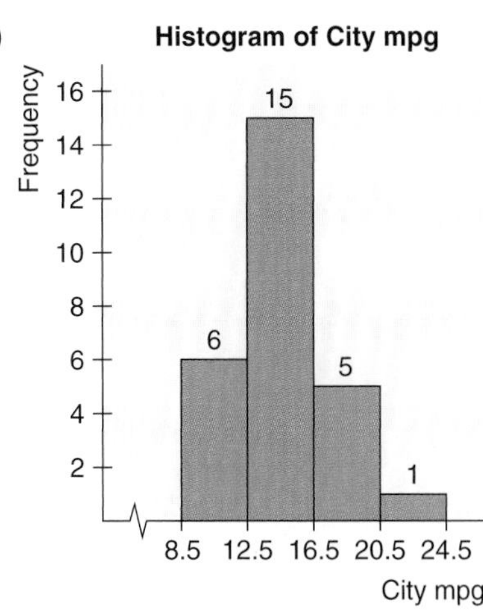

4. The class width is the difference between the lower class limit of one class and the lower class limit of the next class. The classes listed have a class width of 11.

5. (a) Yes.
(b)

Class	f
16.5–20.5	2
20.5–24.5	3
24.5–28.5	3
28.5–32.5	12
32.5–36.5	6
36.5–40.5	1

6. (a)

Class	f
23.5–69.5	35
69.5–115.5	0
115.5–161.5	0
161.5–207.5	0
207.5–253.5	1

(b) Yes. Yes.
(c)

Class	f
23.5–32.5	7
32.5–41.5	11
41.5–50.5	5
50.5–59.5	6
59.5–68.5	6

Yes.

7. (a) Class width = 25.
(b)

Class	f
236–260	4
261–285	9
286–310	25
311–335	16
336–360	3

(e) Approximately mound-shaped symmetrical.

27 cars to make the histogram in Figure 2-9(b). Using this information and Figure 2-9, parts (a) and (b), construct a histogram for the highway mileages of the same cars. Use class boundaries 16.5, 20.5, 24.5, 28.5, 32.5, 36.5, and 40.5.

6. *Critical Thinking* The following data represent salaries, in thousands of dollars, for employees of a small company. Notice that the data have been sorted in increasing order.

24	25	25	27	27	29	30	35	35	35	36	38	38
39	39	40	40	40	45	45	45	45	47	52	52	52
58	59	59	61	61	67	68	68	68	250			

(a) Make a histogram using the class boundaries 23.5, 69.5, 115.5, 161.5, 207.5, 253.5.
(b) Look at the last data value. Does it appear to be an outlier? Could this be the owner's salary?
(c) Eliminate the high salary of 250 thousand dollars. Make a new histogram using the class boundaries 23.5, 32.5, 41.5, 50.5, 59.5, 68.5. Does this histogram reflect the salary distribution of most of the employees better than the histogram in part (a)?

For Problems 7–12, use the specified number of classes to do the following.
(a) Find the class width.
(b) Make a frequency table showing class limits, class boundaries, midpoints, frequencies, and relative frequencies.
(c) Draw a histogram.
(d) Draw a relative-frequency histogram.
(e) Categorize the basic distribution shape as uniform, mound-shaped symmetrical, bimodal, skewed left, or skewed right.

7. *Sports: Dog Sled Racing* How long does it take to finish the 1161-mile Iditarod Dog Sled Race from Anchorage to Nome, Alaska (*see* Viewpoint)? Finish times (to the nearest hour) for 57 dogsled teams are shown below.

261	271	236	244	279	296	284	299	288	288	247	256
338	360	341	333	261	266	287	296	313	311	307	307
299	303	277	283	304	305	288	290	288	289	297	299
332	330	309	328	307	328	285	291	295	298	306	315
310	318	318	320	333	321	323	324	327			

Use five classes.

8. (a) Class width = 11.
(b)

Class	f
45–55	3
56–66	7
67–77	22
78–88	26
89–99	9
100–110	3

(e) Approximately mound-shaped symmetrical.

8. *Medical: Glucose Testing* The following data represent glucose blood levels (mg/100 ml) after a 12-hour fast for a random sample of 70 women (Reference: *American Journal of Clinical Nutrition*, Vol. 19, pp. 345–351). *Note:* These data are also available for download at the Online Study Center.

45	66	83	71	76	64	59	59
76	82	80	81	85	77	82	90
87	72	79	69	83	71	87	69
81	76	96	83	67	94	101	94
89	94	73	99	93	85	83	80
78	80	85	83	84	74	81	70
65	89	70	80	84	77	65	46
80	70	75	45	101	71	109	73
73	80	72	81	63	74		

Use six classes.

9. (a) Class width = 12.
(b)

Class	f
1–12	6
13–24	10
25–36	5
37–48	13
49–60	8

(e) Somewhat bimodal.

9. *Medical: Tumor Recurrence* Certain kinds of tumors tend to recur. The following data represent the lengths of time, in months, for a tumor to recur after chemotherapy (Reference: D. P. Byar, *Journal of Urology*, Vol. 10, pp. 556–561). *Note:* These data are also available for download at the Online Study Center.

19	18	17	1	21	22	54	46	25	49
50	1	59	39	43	39	5	9	38	18
14	45	54	59	46	50	29	12	19	36
38	40	43	41	10	50	41	25	19	39
27	20								

Use five classes.

10. (a) Class width = 28.
(b)

Class	f
10–37	7
38–65	25
66–93	26
94–121	9
122–149	5
150–177	0
178–205	1

(e) Skewed slightly right, with possible outlier.

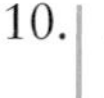

10. *Archaeology: New Mexico* The Wind Mountain excavation site in New Mexico is an important archaeological location of the ancient Native American Anasazi culture. The following data represent depths (in cm) below surface grade at which significant artifacts were discovered at this site (Reference: A. I. Woosley and A. J. McIntyre, *Mimbres Mogollon Archaeology*, University of New Mexico Press). *Note:* These data are also available for download at the Online Study Center.

85	45	75	60	90	90	115	30	55	58
78	120	80	65	65	140	65	50	30	125
75	137	80	120	15	45	70	65	50	45
95	70	70	28	40	125	105	75	80	70
90	68	73	75	55	70	95	65	200	75
15	90	46	33	100	65	60	55	85	50
10	68	99	145	45	75	45	95	85	65
65	52	82							

Use seven classes.

11. (a) Class width = 9.
(b)

Class	f
10–18	6
19–27	26
28–36	20
37–45	1
46–54	2

(e) Skewed slightly right.

11. *Environment: Gasoline Consumption* The following data represent highway fuel consumption in miles per gallon (mpg) for a random sample of 55 models of passenger cars (Source: Environmental Protection Agency). *Note:* These data are also available for download at the Online Study Center.

30	27	22	25	24	25	24	15
35	35	33	52	49	10	27	18
20	23	24	25	30	24	24	24
18	20	25	27	24	32	29	27
24	27	26	25	24	28	33	30
13	13	21	28	37	35	32	33
29	31	28	28	25	29	31	

Use five classes.

12. (a) Class width = 6.
(b)

Class	f
0–5	13
6–11	15
12–17	11
18–23	3
24–29	6
30–35	4
36–41	2
42–47	1

(e) Skewed right.

12. *Advertising: Readability* "Readability Levels of Magazine Ads," by F. K. Shuptrine and D. D. McVicker, is an article in the *Journal of Advertising Research*. (For more information, visit the Online Study Center at **www.cengage.com/statistics/Brase/UBS5e** and find the link to DASL, the Carnegie Mellon University Data and Story Library. Look in Data Subjects under Consumer and then Magazine Ads Readability file.) The following is a list of the number of three-syllable (or longer) words in advertising copy of randomly selected magazine advertisements.

34	21	37	31	10	24	39	10	17	18	32
17	3	10	6	5	6	6	13	22	25	3
5	2	9	3	0	4	29	26	5	5	24
15	3	8	16	9	10	3	12	10	10	10
11	12	13	1	9	43	13	14	32	24	15

Use eight classes.

The method for finding the class width as described in this section is valid for integer data. Problem 13 and Problem 14 show how to find the class width for data containing decimals. Remind students to "clear" the decimals, make the frequency table, and then "restore" the decimals.

13. (b) Class width = 0.40.

Class	f
0.46–0.85	4
0.86–1.25	5
1.26–1.65	10
1.66–2.05	5
2.06–2.45	5
2.46–2.85	3

13. *Expand Your Knowledge: Decimal Data* The following data represent tonnes of wheat harvested each year (1894–1925) from Plot 19 at the Rothamsted Agricultural Experiment Stations, England.

2.71	1.62	2.60	1.64	2.20	2.02	1.67	1.99	2.34	1.26	1.31
1.80	2.82	2.15	2.07	1.62	1.47	2.19	0.59	1.48	0.77	2.04
1.32	0.89	1.35	0.95	0.94	1.39	1.19	1.18	0.46	0.70	

(a) Multiply each data value by 100 to "clear" the decimals.
(b) Use the standard procedures of this section to make a frequency table and histogram with your whole-number data. Use six classes.
(c) Divide class limits, class boundaries, and class midpoints by 100 to get back to your original data values.

14. (b) Class width = 0.043.

Class	f
0.107–0.149	3
0.150–0.192	4
0.193–0.235	3
0.236–0.278	10
0.279–0.321	6

14. *Decimal Data: Batting Averages* The following data represent baseball batting averages for a random sample of National League players near the end of the baseball season. The data are from the baseball statistics section of *The Denver Post*.

0.194	0.258	0.190	0.291	0.158	0.295	0.261	0.250	0.181
0.125	0.107	0.260	0.309	0.309	0.276	0.287	0.317	0.252
0.215	0.250	0.246	0.260	0.265	0.182	0.113	0.200	

(a) Multiply each data value by 1000 to "clear" the decimals.
(b) Use the standard procedures of this section to make a frequency table and histogram with your whole-number data. Use five classes.
(c) Divide class limits, class boundaries, and class midpoints by 1000 to get back to your original data.

15. *Expand Your Knowledge: Dotplot* Another display technique that is somewhat similar to a histogram is a *dotplot*. In a dotplot, the data values are displayed along the horizontal axis. A dot is then plotted over each data value in the data set.

PROCEDURE

HOW TO MAKE A DOTPLOT

Display the data along a horizontal axis. Then plot each data value with a dot or point above the corresponding value on the horizontal axis. For repeated data values, stack the dots.

The next display shows a dotplot generated by Minitab (➤Graph ➤Dotplot) for the number of licensed drivers per 1000 residents by state, including the District of Columbia (Source: U.S. Department of Transportation).

Dotplot for Licensed Drivers per 1000 Residents

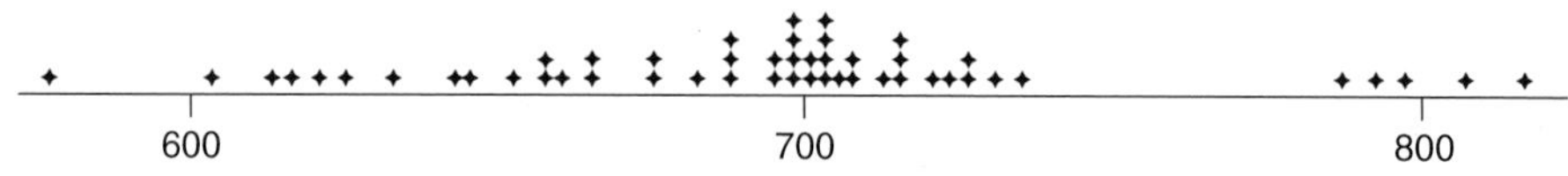

Licensed drivers

15. (a) One.
(b) 5/51 or 9.8%.
(c) 650 to 750.

(a) From the dotplot, how many states have 600 or fewer licensed drivers per 1000 residents?
(b) About what percentage of the states (out of 51) seem to have close to 800 licensed drivers per 1000 residents?
(c) Consider the intervals 550 to 650, 650 to 750, and 750 to 850 licensed drivers per 1000 residents. In which interval do most of the states fall?

Point out that dotplots show the frequency of individual data values. The raw data can be retrieved from the dotplot.

16. See even answer section.

17. See odd answer section.

16. *Dotplot: Dog Sled Racing* Make a dotplot for the data in Problem 7 regarding the finish time (number of hours) for the Iditarod Dog Sled Race. Compare the dotplot to the histogram of Problem 7.

17. *Dotplot: Tumor Recurrence* Make a dotplot for the data in Problem 9 regarding the recurrence of tumors after chemotherapy. Compare the dotplot to the histogram of Problem 9.

SECTION 2.2 Bar Graphs, Circle Graphs, and Time-Series Graphs

FOCUS POINTS

- Determine types of graphs appropriate for specific data.
- Construct bar graphs, Pareto charts, circle graphs, and time-series graphs.
- Interpret information displayed in graphs.

Histograms provide a useful visual display of the distribution of data. However, the data must be quantitative. In this section, we examine other types of graphs, some of which are suitable for qualitative or category data as well.

Let's start with *bar graphs*. These are graphs that can be used to display quantitative or qualitative data.

Although the material in this section is important, it can be covered quickly. These are the types of graphs often presented in newspaper and magazine articles. See Data Highlights.

Features of a bar graph

1. Bars can be vertical or horizontal.
2. Bars are of uniform width and uniformly spaced.
3. The lengths of the bars represent values of the variable being displayed, the frequency of occurrence, or the percentage of occurrence. The same measurement scale is used for the length of each bar.
4. The graph is well annotated with title, labels for each bar, and vertical scale or actual value for the length of each bar.

EXAMPLE 3 **BAR GRAPH**

Figure 2-10 shows two bar graphs depicting the life expectancies for men and women born in the designated year. Let's analyze the features of these graphs.

SOLUTION: The graphs are called *clustered bar graphs* because there are two bars for each year of birth. One bar represents the life expectancy for men, and the other represents the life expectancy for women. The height of each bar represents the life expectancy (in years).

Changing scales

An important feature illustrated in Figure 2-10(b) is that of a *changing scale.* Notice that the scale between 0 and 65 is compressed. The changing scale amplifies the apparent difference between life spans for men and women, as well as the increase in projected life span from those born in 1980 to those born in 2010.

Changing scale

Whenever you use a changing scale in a graphic, warn the viewer by using a squiggle -√- on the changed axis. Sometimes, if a single bar is unusually long, the bar length is compressed with a squiggle in the bar itself.

Quality control is an important aspect of today's production and service industries. Dr. W. Edwards Deming was one of the developers of total quality management (TQM). In his book *Out of Crisis,* he outlines many strategies for monitoring and improving service and production industries. In particular, Dr. Deming recommends the use of some statistical methods to organize and analyze data from industries so that sources of problems can be identified and then corrected. *Pareto* (pronounced "Pah-rāy-tō") *charts* are among the many techniques used in quality-control programs.

Pareto charts

Pareto charts are easy to create and have practical value in highlighting major effects (either good or bad). See Data Highlights, Problem 1 (Slobs Make the Worst Roommates) and Linking Concepts, Problem 1.

A **Pareto chart** is a bar graph in which the bar height represents frequency of an event. In addition, the bars are arranged from left to right according to decreasing height.

FIGURE 2-10

Life Expectancy

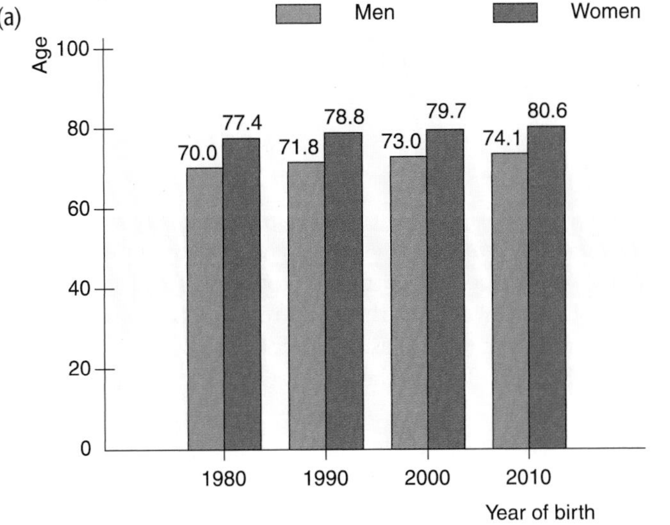

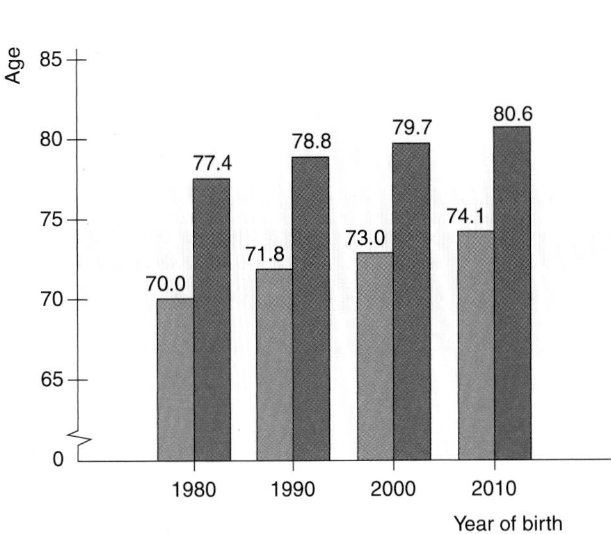

Source: U.S. Census Bureau

GUIDED EXERCISE 2 Pareto charts

This exercise is adapted from *The Deming Management Method* by Mary Walton. Suppose you want to arrive at college 15 minutes before your first class so that you can feel relaxed when you walk into class. An early arrival time also allows room for unexpected delays. However, you always find yourself arriving "just in time" or slightly late. What causes you to be late? Charlotte made a list of possible causes and then kept a checklist for 2 months (Table 2-11). On some days more than one item was checked because several events occurred that caused her to be late.

TABLE 2-11 **Causes for Lateness** (September–October)

Cause	Frequency
Snoozing after alarm goes off	15
Car trouble	5
Too long over breakfast	13
Last-minute studying	20
Finding something to wear	8
Talking too long with roommate	9
Other	3

(a) Make a Pareto chart showing the causes for lateness. Be sure to label the causes, and draw the bars using the same vertical scale.

FIGURE 2-11 Pareto Chart: Conditions That Might Cause Lateness

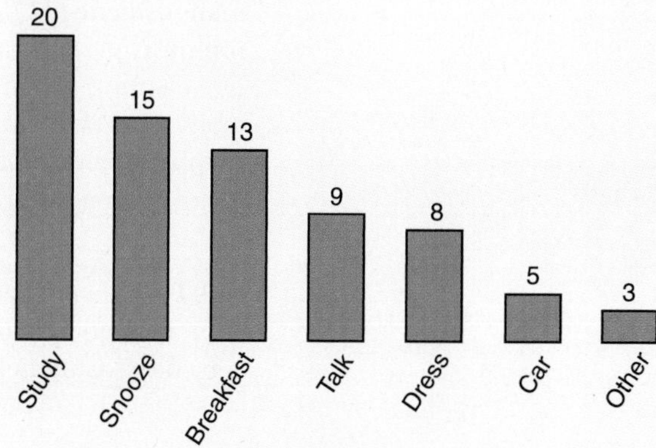

(b) Looking at the Pareto chart, what recommendations do you have for Charlotte?

According to the chart, rearranging study time, or getting up earlier to allow for studying, would cure Charlotte's most frequent cause for lateness. Repairing the car might be important, but for getting to campus early, it would not be as effective as adjusting study time.

Circle graphs or pie charts

Another popular pictorial representation of data is the *circle graph* or *pie chart.* It is relatively safe from misinterpretation and is especially useful for showing the division of a total quantity into its component parts. The total quantity, or 100%, is represented by the entire circle. Each wedge of the circle represents a component part of the total. These proportional segments are usually labeled with corresponding percentages of the total. Guided Exercise 3 shows how to make a circle graph.

In a **circle graph** or **pie chart,** wedges of a circle visually display proportional parts of the total population that share a common characteristic.

GUIDED EXERCISE 3 Circle graph

How long do we spend talking on the telephone in the evening (at home after 5 P.M.)? The results from a recent survey of 500 people (as reported in *USA Today*) are shown in Table 2-12. We'll make a circle graph to display these data.

TABLE 2-12 **Time Spent on Home Telephone After 5 P.M.**

Time	Number	Fractional Part	Percentage	Number of Degrees
Less than ½ hour	296	296/500	59.2	59.2% × 360° ≈ 213°
½ hour to 1 hour	83	83/500	16.6	16.6% × 360° ≈ 60°
More than 1 hour	121	____	____	____
Total	____		____	____

(a) Fill in the missing information in Table 2-12 for "More than 1 hour." Remember that the central angle of a circle is 360°. Round to the nearest degree.

→ For "More than 1 hour," Fractional Part = 121/500; Percentage = 24.2%, Number of Degrees = 24.2% × 360° ≈ 87°. The symbol ≈ means "approximately equal."

(b) Fill in the totals. What is the total number of responses? Do the percentages total 100% (within rounding error)? Do the numbers of degrees total 360° (within rounding error)?

→ The total number of responses is 500. The percentages total 100%. You must have such a total in order to create a circle graph. The numbers of degrees total 360°.

(c) Draw a circle graph. Divide the circle into pieces with the designated numbers of degrees. Label each piece, and show the percentage corresponding to each piece. The numbers of degrees are usually omitted from pie charts shown in newspapers, magazines, journals, and reports.

→ 

FIGURE 2-12 Hours on Home Telephone After 5 P.M

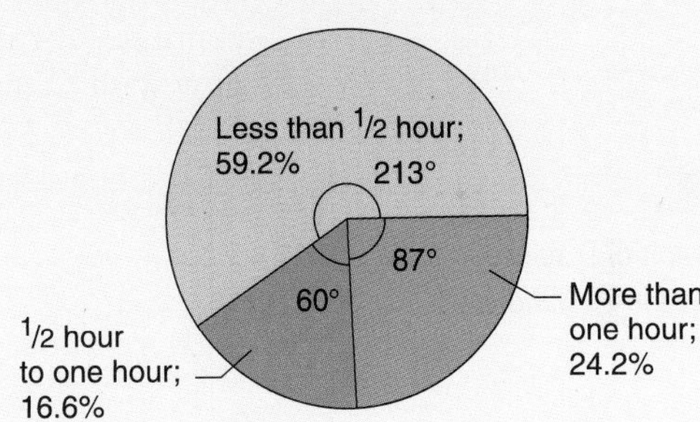

Suppose you begin an exercise program that involves walking or jogging for 30 minutes a day. You exercise several times a week but monitor yourself by logging the distance you cover in 30 minutes each Saturday. How do you display these data in a meaningful way? Making a bar chart showing the frequency of distances you cover might be interesting, but it does not really show how the distance you cover in 30 minutes has changed over time. A graph showing the distance covered on each date will let you track your performance over time.

Time-series graph

We will use a *time-series graph*. A time-series graph is a graph showing data measurements in chronological order. To make a time-series graph, we put time on the horizontal scale and the variable being measured on the vertical scale. In a basic time-series graph, we connect the data points by line segments.

In a **time-series graph,** data are plotted in order of occurrence at regular intervals over a period of time.

EXAMPLE 4 **TIME-SERIES GRAPH**

Suppose you have been in the walking/jogging exercise program for 20 weeks, and for each week you have recorded the distance you covered in 30 minutes. Your data log is shown in Table 2-13.

(a) Make a time-series graph.

SOLUTION: The data are appropriate for a time-series graph because they represent the same measurement (distance covered in a 30-minute period) taken at different times. The measurements are also recorded at equal time intervals (every week). To make our time-series graph, we list the weeks in order on the horizontal scale. Above each week, plot the distance covered that week on the vertical scale. Then connect the dots. Figure 2-13 shows the time-series graph. Be sure the scales are labeled.

TABLE 2-13 **Distance (in Miles) Walked/Jogged in 30 Minutes**

Week	1	2	3	4	5	6	7	8	9	10
Distance	1.5	1.4	1.7	1.6	1.9	2.0	1.8	2.0	1.9	2.0
Week	11	12	13	14	15	16	17	18	19	20
Distance	2.1	2.1	2.3	2.3	2.2	2.4	2.5	2.6	2.4	2.7

(b) From looking at Figure 2-13, can you detect any patterns?

SOLUTION: There seems to be an upward trend in distance covered. The distances covered in the last few weeks are about a mile farther than those for the first few weeks. However, we cannot conclude that this trend will continue. Perhaps you have reached your goal for this training activity and now wish to maintain a distance of about 2.5 miles in 30 minutes.

FIGURE 2-13

Time-Series Graph of Distance (in miles) Jogged in 30 Minutes

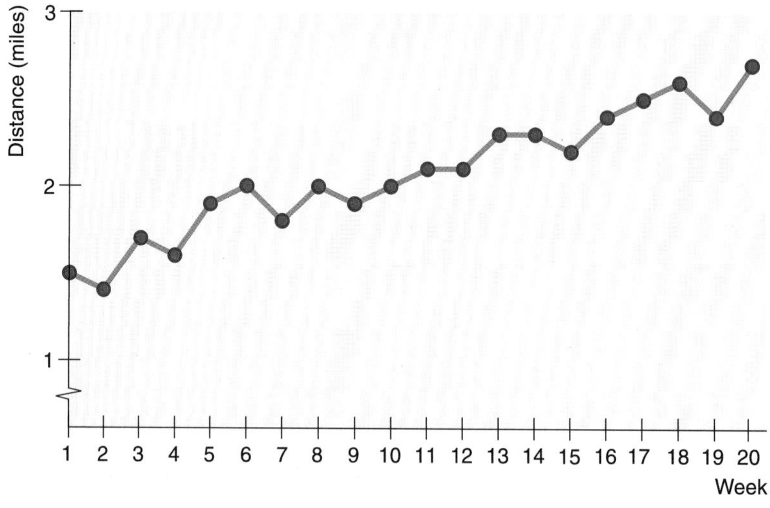

Time series

Data sets composed of similar measurements taken at regular intervals over time are called *time series.* Time series are often used in economics, finance, sociology, medicine, and any situation in which we want to study or monitor a similar measurement over a period of time. A time-series graph can reveal some of the main features of a time series.

Time-series data consist of measurements of the same variable for the same subject taken at regular intervals over a period of time.

CRITICAL THINKING We've seen several styles of graphs. Which kinds are suitable for a specific data collection?

PROCEDURE

This is a good time for a class discussion about the types of graphs appropriate for given data sets.

HOW TO DECIDE WHICH TYPE OF GRAPH TO USE

Bar graphs are useful for quantitative or qualitative data. With qualitative data, the frequency or percentage of occurrence can be displayed. With quantitative data, the measurement itself can be displayed, as was done in the bar graph showing life expectancy. Watch that the measurement scale is consistent, and notice whether a jump scale squiggle is used.

Pareto charts identify the frequency of events or categories in decreasing order of frequency of occurrence.

Circle graphs display how a *total* is dispersed into several categories. The circle graph is very appropriate for qualitative data, or any data for which percentage of occurrence makes sense. Circle graphs are most effective when the number of categories or wedges is 10 or fewer.

Time-series graphs display how data change over time. It is best if the units of time are consistent in a given graph. For instance, measurements taken every day should not be mixed on the same graph with data taken every week.

For any graph: Provide a title, label the axes, and identify units of measure. As Edward Tufte suggests in his book *The Visual Display of Quantitative Information,* don't let artwork or skewed perspective cloud the clarity of the information displayed.

TECH NOTES *Bar graphs, circle graphs, and time-series graphs*

TI-84Plus/TI-83Plus Only time-series. Place consecutive values 1 through the number of time segments in list L1 and corresponding data in L2. Press **Stat Plot** and highlight an *xy* line plot.

Excel Use the chart wizard on the toolbar. Select the desired option and follow the instructions in the dialogue boxes.

Minitab Use the menu selection **Graph.** Select the desired option and follow the instructions in the dialogue boxes.

VIEWPOINT Do Ethical Standards Vary by Situation?

The Lutheran Brotherhood did a national survey and found that nearly 60% of all U.S. adults claim that ethical standards vary by situation; 33% claim that there is only one ethical standard; and 7% were not sure. How could you draw a circle graph to make a visual impression of Americans' views on ethical standards?

SECTION 2.2 PROBLEMS

Tables and art to accompany margin notes may be found in the back of the book.

1. Pareto chart, because it shows the items in order of importance to the greatest number of employees.

2. Time-series graph, since the pattern of stock prices over time is more relevant than just the frequency of a specific range of closing prices.

1. *Critical Thinking* A personnel office is gathering data regarding working conditions. Employees are given a list of five conditions that they might want to see improved. They are asked to select the one item that is most critical to them. Which type of graph, circle graph or Pareto chart, would be most useful for displaying the results of the survey? Why?

2. *Critical Thinking* Your friend is thinking about buying shares of stock in a company. You have been tracking the closing prices of the stock shares for the past 90 trading days. Which type of graph for the data, histogram or time-series, would be best to show your friend? Why?

3. *Education: Does College Pay Off?* It is costly in both time and money to go to college. Does it pay off? According to the Bureau of Census, the answer is yes. The average annual income (in thousands of dollars) of a *household* headed by a person with the stated education level is as follows: 16.1 if ninth grade is the highest level achieved, 34.3 for high school graduates, 48.6 for those holding associate degrees, 62.1 for those with bachelor's degrees, 71.0 for those with master's degrees, and 84.1 for those with doctoral degrees. Make a bar graph showing household income for each education level.

4. *Accidents: Child Deaths* How safe is the world for kids? Unfortunately, some children between the ages of 1 and 14 die of injuries every year. United Nations data show that by nation, the annual numbers of deaths from injuries per 100,000 children are as follows: Australia, 9.5; Canada, 9.7; Denmark, 8.1; France, 9.1; Germany, 8.3; Hungary, 10.8; Ireland, 8.3; Italy, 6.1; Japan, 8.4; Korea, 25.6; Mexico, 19.8; New Zealand, 13.7; Netherlands, 6.6; Poland, 13.4; Portugal, 17.8; Spain, 8.1; Sweden, 5.2; Switzerland, 9.6; U.K., 6.1; United States, 14.1. Display these data in a Pareto chart.

5. *Commercial Fishing: Gulf of Alaska* It's not an easy life, but it's a good life! Suppose you decide to take the summer off and sign on as a deck hand for a commercial fishing boat in Alaska that specializes in deep-water fishing for groundfish. What kind of fish can you expect to catch? One way to answer this question is to examine government reports on groundfish caught in the Gulf of Alaska. The following list indicates the types of fish caught annually in thousands of metric tons (Source: *Report on the Status of U.S. Living Marine Resources,* National Oceanic and Atmospheric Administration): flatfish, 36.3; Pacific cod, 68.6; sablefish, 16.0; Walleye pollock, 71.2; rockfish, 18.9. Make a Pareto chart showing the annual harvest for commercial fishing in the Gulf of Alaska.

6. *Archaeology: Ireland* Commercial dredging operations in ancient rivers occasionally uncover archaeological artifacts of great importance. One such artifact is Bronze Age spearheads recovered from ancient rivers in Ireland. A recent study gave the following information regarding discoveries of ancient bronze spearheads in Irish rivers.

River	Bann	Blackwater	Erne	Shannon	Barrow
No. of spearheads	19	8	15	33	14

(Based on information from *Crossing the Rubicon, Bronze Age Studies 5,* Lorraine Bourke, Department of Archaeology, National University of Ireland, Galway.)
(a) Make a Pareto chart for these data.
(b) Make a circle graph for these data.

7. *Lifestyle: Hide the Mess!* A survey of 1000 adults (reported in *USA Today*) uncovered some interesting housekeeping secrets. When unexpected company comes, where do we hide the mess? The survey showed that 68% of the respondents toss their mess in the closet, 23% shove things under the bed, 6% put things in the bathtub, and 3% put the mess in the freezer. Make a circle graph to display this information.

8. *Education: College Professors' Time* How do college professors spend their time? *The National Education Association Almanac of Higher Education* gives the following average allocation of professional time: teaching, 51%; research, 16%; professional growth, 5%; community service, 11%; service to the college, 11%; and consulting outside the college, 6%. Make a pie chart showing the allocation of professional time for college professors.

9. *FBI Report: Hawaii* In the Aloha state, you are very unlikely to be murdered! However, it is considerably more likely that your house might be burgled, your car might be stolen, or you might be punched in the nose. That said, Hawaii is still a great place for a vacation or, if you are very lucky, to live. The following numbers represent the crime rates per 100,000 population in Hawaii: murder, 2.6; rape, 33.4; robbery, 93.3; house burglary, 911.6; motor vehicle theft, 550.7; assault, 125.3 (Source: *Crime in the United States,* U.S. Department of Justice, Federal Bureau of Investigation).
   (a) Display this information in a Pareto chart, showing the crime rate for each category.
   (b) Could the information as reported be displayed as a circle graph? Explain. *Hint:* Other forms of crime, such as arson, are not included in the information. In addition, some crimes might occur together.

10. *Driving: Bad Habits* Driving would be more pleasant if we didn't have to put up with the bad habits of other drivers. *USA Today* reported the results of a Valvoline Oil Company survey of 500 drivers in which the drivers marked their complaints about other drivers. The top complaints turned out to be tailgating, marked by 22% of the respondents; not using turn signals, marked by 19%; being cut off, marked by 16%; other drivers driving too slowly, marked by 11%; and other drivers being inconsiderate, marked by 8%. Make a Pareto chart showing percentage of drivers listing each stated complaint. Could this information as reported be put in a circle graph? Why or why not?

11. *Ecology: Lakes* Pyramid Lake, Nevada, is described as the pride of the Paiute Indian Nation. It is a beautiful desert lake famous for very large trout. The elevation of the lake surface (feet above sea level) varies according to the annual flow of the Truckee River from Lake Tahoe. The U.S. Geological Survey provided the following data:

Year	Elevation	Year	Elevation	Year	Elevation
1986	3817	1992	3798	1998	3811
1987	3815	1993	3797	1999	3816
1988	3810	1994	3795	2000	3817
1989	3812	1995	3797		
1990	3808	1996	3802		
1991	3803	1997	3807		

Make a time-series graph displaying the data. For more information, visit the Online Study Center at **www.cengage.com/statistics/Brase/UBS5e** and find the link to the Pyramid Lake Fisheries.

12. *Vital Statistics: Height* How does average height for boys change as boys get older? According to *Physician's Handbook*, the average heights at different ages are as follows:

Age (years)	0.5	1	2	3	4	5	6	7
Height (inches)	26	29	33	36	39	42	45	47

Age (years)	8	9	10	11	12	13	14
Height (inches)	50	52	54	56	58	60	62

Make a time-series graph of average height for ages 0.5 through 14 years.

SECTION 2.3

Stem-and-Leaf Displays

FOCUS POINTS

- Construct a stem-and-leaf display from raw data.
- Use a stem-and-leaf display to visualize data distribution.
- Compare a stem-and-leaf display to a histogram.

Exploratory Data Analysis

Together with histograms and other graphing techniques, the stem-and-leaf display is one of many useful ways of studying data in a field called *exploratory data analysis* (often abbreviated as *EDA*). John W. Tukey wrote one of the definitive books on the subject, *Exploratory Data Analysis* (Addison-Wesley). Another very useful reference for EDA techniques is the book *Applications, Basics, and Computing of Exploratory Data Analysis* by Paul F. Velleman and David C. Hoaglin (Duxbury Press). Exploratory data analysis techniques are particularly useful for detecting patterns and extreme data values. They are designed to help us explore a data set, ask questions we had not thought of before, or pursue leads in many directions.

Emphasize that these methods are good initial steps in the analysis of new data. See Linking Concepts, Problem 3.

EDA techniques are similar to those of an explorer. An explorer has a general idea of destination but is always alert to the unexpected. An explorer needs to assess situations quickly and often simplify and clarify them. An explorer makes pictures—that is, maps showing the relationships of landscape features. The aspects of rapid implementation, visual displays such as graphs and charts, data simplification, and robustness (that is, analysis that is not influenced much by extreme data values) are key ingredients of EDA techniques. In addition, these techniques are good for exploration because they require very few prior assumptions about the data.

EDA methods are especially useful when our data have been gathered for general interest and observation of subjects. For example, we may have data regarding the ages of applicants to graduate programs. We don't have a specific question in mind; we want to see what the data reveal. Are the ages fairly uniform or spread out? Are there exceptionally young or old applicants? If there are, we might look at other characteristics of these applicants, such as field of study. EDA methods help us to quickly absorb some aspects of the data that then may lead us to ask specific questions to which we might apply methods of traditional statistics.

In contrast, when we design an experiment to produce data aimed at answering a specific question, we focus on particular aspects of the data that are useful to us. If we want to determine the average highway gas mileage of a specific sports car, we use that model car in well-designed tests. We don't need to worry about unexpected road conditions, poorly trained drivers, different fuel grades, sudden stops and starts, etc. Our experiment is designed to control outside factors. Consequently, we do not need to "explore" our data as much. We can often make valid assumptions about the data. Methods of traditional statistics will be very useful in analyzing such data and answering our specific questions.

Stem-and-Leaf Display

In this text, we will introduce two EDA techniques: stem-and-leaf displays and, in Section 3.3, box-and-whisker plots. Let's first look at a stem-and-leaf display.

A **stem-and-leaf display** is a method of exploratory data analysis that is used to rank-order and arrange data into groups.

We know that frequency distributions and histograms provide a useful organization and summary of data. However, in a histogram, we lose most of the specific data values. A stem-and-leaf display is a device that organizes and groups data but allows us to recover the original data if desired. In the next example, we will make a stem-and-leaf display.

EXAMPLE 5 STEM-AND-LEAF DISPLAY

Many airline passengers seem weighted down by their carry-on luggage. Just how much weight are they carrying? The carry-on luggage weights in pounds for a random sample of 40 passengers returning from a vacation to Hawaii were recorded (see Table 2-14).

TABLE 2-14 **Weights of Carry-On Luggage in Pounds**

30	27	12	42	35	47	38	36	27	35
22	17	29	3	21	0	38	32	41	33
26	45	18	43	18	32	31	32	19	21
33	31	28	29	51	12	32	18	21	26

To make a stem-and-leaf display, we break the digits of each data value into *two parts*. The left group of digits is called the *stem*, and the remaining group of digits on the right is called the *leaf*. We are free to choose the number of digits to be included in the stem.

The weights in our example consist of two-digit numbers. For a two-digit number, the stem selection is obviously the left digit. In our case, the tens digits will form the stems, and the units digits will form the leaves. For example, for the weight 12, the stem is 1 and the leaf is 2. For the weight 18, the stem is again 1, but the leaf is 8. In the stem-and-leaf display, we list each possible stem once on the left and all its leaves in the same row on the right, as in Figure 2-14(a) on the next page. Finally, we order the leaves as shown in Figure 2-14(b).

Figure 2-14 shows a stem-and-leaf display for the weights of carry-on luggage. From the stem-and-leaf display in Figure 2-14, we see that two bags weighed 27 lb, one weighed 3 lb, one weighed 51 lb, and so on. We see that most of the weights were in the 30-lb range, only two were less than 10 lb, and six were over 40 lb. Note that the lengths of the lines containing the leaves give the visual impression that a sideways histogram would present.

As a final step, we need to indicate the scale. This is usually done by indicating the value represented by the stem and one leaf.

FIGURE 2-14

Stem-and-Leaf Displays of Airline Carry-On Luggage Weights

(a) Leaves Not Ordered

3 | 2 represents 32 lb

Stem	Leaves
0	3 0
1	2 7 8 8 9 2 8
2	7 7 2 9 1 6 1 8 9 1 6
3	0 5 8 6 5 8 2 3 2 1 2 3 1 2
4	2 7 1 5 3
5	1

(b) Final Display with Leaves Ordered

3 | 2 represents 32 lb

Stem	Leaves
0	0 3
1	2 2 7 8 8 8 9
2	1 1 1 2 6 6 7 7 8 9 9
3	0 1 1 2 2 2 2 3 3 5 5 6 8 8
4	1 2 3 5 7
5	1

There are no firm rules for selecting the group of digits for the stem. But whichever group you select, you must list all the possible stems from smallest to largest in the data collection.

PROCEDURE

A stem-and-leaf display organizes numbers in much the same way alphabetization organizes words. If you wanted to alphabetize 100 papers by name, you would probably begin by sorting the names according to the first letter. You would put all the papers with names beginning with the letter A in one stack, those beginning with the letter B in another stack, and so forth. A basic stem-and-leaf display is analogous to such a process. You put all the numbers beginning with the same stem on one line.

HOW TO MAKE A STEM-AND-LEAF DISPLAY

1. Divide the digits of each data value into two parts. The leftmost part is called the *stem* and the rightmost part is called the *leaf*.
2. Align all the stems in a vertical column from smallest to largest. Draw a vertical line to the right of all the stems.
3. Place all leaves having the same stem in the same row as the stem, and arrange the leaves in increasing order.
4. Use a label to indicate the magnitude of the numbers in the display. We include the decimal position in the label rather than with the stems or leaves.

GUIDED EXERCISE 4 Stem-and-leaf display

What does it take to win at sports? If you're talking about basketball, one sports writer gave the answer. He listed the winning scores of the conference championship games over the last 35 years. The scores for those games follow below.

132	118	124	109	104	101	125	83	99
131	98	125	97	106	112	92	120	103
111	117	135	143	112	112	116	106	117
119	110	105	128	112	126	105	102	

To make a stem-and-leaf display, we'll use the first *two* digits as the stems (see Figure 2-15). Notice that the distribution of scores is fairly symmetrical.

Continued

GUIDED EXERCISE 4 *continued*

(a) Use the first *two* digits as the stem. Then order the leaves. Provide a label that shows the meaning and units of the first stem and first leaf.

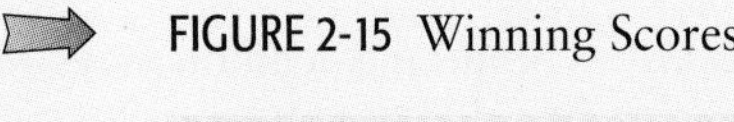

FIGURE 2-15 Winning Scores

08 | 3 represents 083 or 83 points

Stem	Leaves
08	3
09	2 7 8 9
10	1 2 3 4 5 5 6 6 9
11	0 1 2 2 2 2 6 7 7 8 9
12	0 4 5 5 6 8
13	1 2 5
14	3

(b) Looking at the distribution, would you say that it is fairly symmetrical?

Yes. Notice that stem 11 has the most data.

To finish alphabetizing the papers, you would then look at the second letter of each name in a stack, and order all the papers in the A stack, the B stack, etc. To order the numbers in a data set, you would then simply look at the leaves for each stem, and arrange them in ascending order. This is done in Example 5 and Guided Exercise 4.

COMMENT Stem-and-leaf displays organize the data, let the data analyst spot extreme values, and are easy to create. In fact, they can be used to organize data so that frequency tables are easier to make. However, at this time, histograms are used more often in formal data presentations, whereas stem-and-leaf displays are used by data analysts to gain initial insights about the data.

TECH NOTES *Stem-and-leaf display*

TI-84Plus/TI-83Plus Does not support stem-and-leaf displays. You can sort the data by using keys **Stat ➤ Edit ➤ 2:SortA.**

Excel Does not support stem-and-leaf displays. You can sort the data by using the menu choices **Data ➤ Sort.**

Minitab Use the menu selections **Graph ➤ Stem-and-Leaf** and fill in the dialogue box.

Minitab Release 14 Stem-and-Leaf Display (for Data in Guided Exercise 4)

```
Stem-and-Leaf of Scores      N=35
Leaf Unit=1.0

   1                     8    3
   5                     9    2789
  14                    10    123455669
 (11)                   11    01222267789
  10                    12    045568
   4                    13    125
   1                    14    3
```

The values shown in the left column represent depth. Numbers above the value in parentheses show the cumulative number of values from the top to the stem of the middle value. Numbers below the value in parentheses show the cumulative number of values from the bottom to the stem of the middle value. The number in parentheses shows how many values are on the same line as the middle value.

CRITICAL THINKING

Stem-and-leaf displays show each of the original or truncated data values. By looking at the display "sideways," you can see the distribution shape of the data. If there are large gaps between stems containing leaves, especially at the top or bottom of the display, the data values in the first or last lines may be outliers. Outliers should be examined carefully to see if they are data errors or simply unusual data values. Someone very familiar with the field of study as well as the purpose of the study should decide how to treat outliers.

Problems 5 and 6 show how to split a stem.

Problem 10 discusses back-to-back stem-and-leaf displays.

VIEWPOINT What Does It Take to Win?

Scores for NFL Super Bowl games can be found at the NFL web site. Visit the Online Study Center at **www.cengage.com/statistics/Brase/UBS5e** *and find the link to the NFL. Once at the NFL web site, follow the links to the Super Bowl. Of special interest in football statistics is the spread, or difference, between scores of the winning and losing teams. If the spread is too large, the game may seem one-sided, and TV viewers become less interested in the game (and accompanying commercial ads). Make a stem-and-leaf display of the spread for all NFL Super Bowl games and analyze the results.*

SECTION 2.3 PROBLEMS

Tables and art to accompany margin answers may be found in the back of the book.

1. (a) 4 | 7 = 47 years

4	7
5	2 7 8 8
6	1 6 6 8 8
7	0 2 2 3 3 5 6 7
8	4 4 4 5 6 6 7 9
9	0 1 1 2 3 7

(b) Yes.

2. 4 | 0 = 40%

0	9
1	
2	0 3 4 7 7 8
3	0 1 3 5 5 5 6 7 8 8 9
4	2 2 6 6 6 8 9 9
5	0 0 0 2 2 4 6 6 9 9
6	0 7
7	2 3 4
8	1 5 7 7 9
9	0 1

1. *Cowboys: Longevity* How long did *real* cowboys live? One answer may be found in the book *The Last Cowboys* by Connie Brooks (University of New Mexico Press). This delightful book presents a thoughtful sociological study of cowboys in West Texas and Southeastern New Mexico around the year 1890. A sample of 32 cowboys gave the following years of longevity:

58	52	68	86	72	66	97	89	84	91	91
92	66	68	87	86	73	61	70	75	72	73
85	84	90	57	77	76	84	93	58	47	

   (a) Make a stem-and-leaf display for these data.
   (b) Consider the following quote from Baron von Richthofen in his *Cattle Raising on the Plains of North America:* "Cowboys are to be found among the sons of the best families. The truth is probably that most were not a drunken, gambling lot, quick to draw and fire their pistols." Does the data distribution of longevity lend credence to this quote?

2. *Ecology: Habitat* Wetlands offer a diversity of ecological benefits. They provide a habitat for wildlife, spawning grounds for U.S. commercial fish, and renewable timber resources. In the last 200 years, the United States has lost more than half its wetlands. *Environmental Almanac* gives the percentage of wetlands lost in each state in the last 200 years. For the lower 48 states, the percentage loss of wetlands per state is as follows:

46	37	36	42	81	20	73	59	35	50
87	52	24	27	38	56	39	74	56	31
27	91	46	9	54	52	30	33	28	35
35	23	90	72	85	42	59	50	49	
48	38	60	46	87	50	89	49	67	

Make a stem-and-leaf display of these data. Be sure to indicate the scale. How are the percentages distributed? Is the distribution skewed? Are there any gaps?

3. *Health Care: Hospitals* The American Medical Association Center for Health Policy Research included data, by state, on the number of community hospitals and the average patient stay (in days) in its publication *State Health Care Data: Utilization, Spending, and Characteristics*. The data (by state) are shown in the table. Make a stem-and-leaf display of the data for the average length of stay in days. Comment about the general shape of the distribution.

3. 5 | 2 = 5.2 days

Stem	Leaves
5	2 3 5 5 6 7
6	0 2 4 6 6 7 7 8 8 8 8 9 9
7	0 0 0 0 0 0 1 1 1 2 2 2 3 3 3 3 4 4 5 5 6 6 8
8	4 5 7
9	4 6 9
10	0 3
11	1

The distribution is skewed right.

State	No. of Hospitals	Average Length of Stay	State	No. of Hospitals	Average Length of Stay	State	No. of Hospitals	Average Length of Stay
Alabama	119	7.0	Kentucky	107	6.9	N. Dakota	47	11.1
Alaska	16	5.7	Louisiana	136	6.7	Ohio	193	6.6
Arizona	61	5.5	Maine	38	7.2	Oklahoma	113	6.7
Arkansas	88	7.0	Maryland	51	6.8	Oregon	66	5.3
California	440	6.0	Massachusetts	101	7.0	Pennsylvania	236	7.5
Colorado	71	6.8	Michigan	175	7.3	Rhode Island	12	6.9
Connecticut	35	7.4	Minnesota	148	8.7	S. Carolina	68	7.1
Delaware	8	6.8	Mississippi	102	7.2	S. Dakota	52	10.3
Dist. of Columbia	11	7.5	Missouri	133	7.4	Tennessee	122	6.8
Florida	227	7.0	Montana	53	10.0	Texas	421	6.2
Georgia	162	7.2	Nebraska	90	9.6	Utah	42	5.2
Hawaii	19	9.4	Nevada	21	6.4	Vermont	15	7.6
Idaho	41	7.1	New Hampshire	27	7.0	Virginia	98	7.0
Illinois	209	7.3	New Jersey	96	7.6	Washington	92	5.6
Indiana	113	6.6	New Mexico	37	5.5	W. Virginia	59	7.1
Iowa	123	8.4	New York	231	9.9	Wisconsin	129	7.3
Kansas	133	7.8	N. Carolina	117	7.3	Wyoming	27	8.5

4. *Health Care: Hospitals* Using the number of hospitals per state listed in the table in Problem 3, make a stem-and-leaf display for the number of community hospitals per state. Which states have an unusually high number of hospitals?

4. 0 | 8 = 8 hospitals

Stem	Leaves	Stem	Leaves
0	8	15	
1	1 2 5 6 9	16	2
2	1 7 7	17	5
3	5 7 8	18	
4	1 2 7	19	3
5	1 2 3 9	20	9
6	1 6 8	21	
7	1	22	7
8	8	23	1 6
9	0 2 6 8		
10	1 2 7	42	1
11	3 3 7 9	43	
12	2 3 9	44	0
13	3 3 6		
14	8		

California and Texas.

When a data set has a small range of numbers resulting in few stems and many leaves per stem, the stems are sometimes divided into two lines, with leaf digits 0–4 on one line and digits 5–9 on the next. This process is described in Problem 5 and used in Problems 6 and 9.

5. *Expand Your Knowledge: Split Stem* The Boston Marathon is the oldest and best known U.S. marathon. It covers a route from Hopkinton, Massachusetts, to downtown Boston. The distance is approximately 26 miles. Visit the Online Study Center at **www.cengage.com/statistics/Brase/UBS5e** and find the link to the Boston Marathon. Search the marathon site to find a wealth of information about the history of the race. In particular, the site gives the winning times for the Boston Marathon. They are all over 2 hours. The following data are the minutes over 2 hours for the winning male runners:

1961–1980

23	23	18	19	16	17	15	22	13	10
18	15	16	13	9	20	14	10	9	12

1981–2000

9	8	9	10	14	7	11	8	9	8
11	8	9	7	9	9	10	7	9	9

(a) Make a stem-and-leaf display for the minutes over 2 hours of the winning times for the years 1961 to 1980. Use two lines per stem.

PROCEDURE

HOW TO SPLIT A STEM

When a stem has many leaves, it is useful to split the stem into two lines or more. For two lines per stem, place leaves 0 to 4 on the first line and leaves 5 to 9 on the next line.

5. (a) 0 | 9 = 9 minutes past 2 hours
0 | 9 9
1 | 0 0 2 3 3 4
1 | 5 5 6 6 7 8 8 9
2 | 0 2 3 3
(b) 0 | 7 = 7 minutes past 2 hours
0 | 7 7 7 8 8 8 8 8 9 9 9 9 9 9 9
1 | 0 0 1 1 4
(c) 1961–1980: 8 times under 15 minutes. 1981–2000: All times under 15 minutes.

6. (a) 6 | 5 = score of 65
6 | 5 6 7 7
7 | 0 1 1 1 1 1 1 1 1 1 1 1 2 2 2 3 3 3 3 4 4 4
7 | 5 5 5 5 5 5 5
(b) 6 | 8 = score of 68
6 | 8 9 9 9 9 9
7 | 0 0 0 0 1 1 1 1 1 1 1 1 1 2 2 2 2 2 2 3 3 3 3 3 3 4 4 4
(c) Scores are lower in the fourth round. In the first round, both low and high scores are more extreme.

(b) Make a stem-and-leaf display for the minutes over 2 hours of the winning times for the years 1981 to 2000. Use two lines per stem.

(c) Compare the two distributions. How many times under 15 minutes are in each distribution?

6. *Split Stem: Golf* The U.S. Open Golf Tournament was played at Congressional Country Club, Bethesda, Maryland, with prizes ranging from $465,000 for first place to $5000. Par for the course is 70. The tournament consists of four rounds played on different days. The scores for each round of the 32 players who placed in the money (more than $17,000) were given on a web site. For more information, visit the Online Study Center at **www.cengage.com/statistics/Brase/UBS5e** and find the link to golf. The scores for the first round were as follows:

71	65	67	73	74	73	71	71	74	73	71
70	75	71	72	71	75	75	71	71	74	75
66	75	75	75	71	72	72	73	71	67	

The scores for the fourth round for these same players were as follows:

69	69	73	74	72	72	70	71	71	70	72
73	73	72	71	71	71	69	70	71	72	73
74	72	71	68	69	70	69	71	73	74	

(a) Make a stem-and-leaf display for the first-round scores. Use two lines per stem. (See Problem 5.)

(b) Make a stem-and-leaf display for the fourth-round scores. Use two lines per stem.

(c) Compare the two distributions. How do the highest scores compare? How do the lowest scores compare?

Are cigarettes bad for our health? Cigarette smoking involves tar, carbon monoxide, and nicotine. The first two are definitely not good for a person's health, and the last ingredient can cause addiction. Problems 7, 8, and 9 refer to Table 2-15, which was taken from the web site maintained by the *Journal of Statistics Education.* For more information, visit the Online Study Center at **www.cengage.com/statistics/Brase/UBS5e** and find the link to the *Journal of Statistics Education.* Follow the links to the cigarette data.

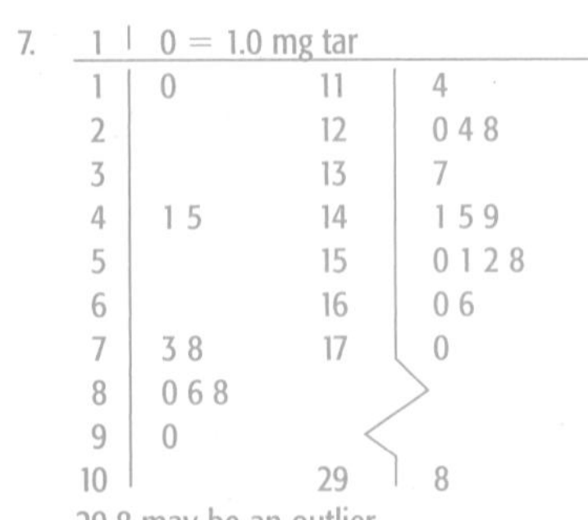

7. 1 | 0 = 1.0 mg tar
1 | 0
2 |
3 |
4 | 1 5
5 |
6 |
7 | 3 8
8 | 0 6 8
9 | 0
10 |
11 | 4
12 | 0 4 8
13 | 7
14 | 1 5 9
15 | 0 1 2 8
16 | 0 6
17 | 0
29 | 8
29.8 may be an outlier.

7. *Health: Cigarette Smoke* Use the data in Table 2-15 to make a stem-and-leaf display for milligrams of tar per cigarette smoked. Are there any outliers?

8. *Health: Cigarette Smoke* Use the data in Table 2-15 to make a stem-and-leaf display for milligrams of carbon monoxide per cigarette smoked. Are there any outliers?

9. *Health: Cigarette Smoke* Use the data in Table 2-15 to make a stem-and-leaf display for milligrams of nicotine per cigarette smoked. In this case, truncate the measurements at the tenths position and use two lines per stem (see Problem 5, part a).

TABLE 2-15 Milligrams of Tar, Nicotine, and Carbon Monoxide (CO) per One Cigarette

Brand	Tar	Nicotine	CO	Brand	Tar	Nicotine	CO
Alpine	14.1	0.86	13.6	MultiFilter	11.4	0.78	10.2
Benson & Hedges	16.0	1.06	16.6	Newport Lights	9.0	0.74	9.5
Bull Durham	29.8	2.03	23.5	Now	1.0	0.13	1.5
Camel Lights	8.0	0.67	10.2	Old Gold	17.0	1.26	18.5
Carlton	4.1	0.40	5.4	Pall Mall Lights	12.8	1.08	12.6
Chesterfield	15.0	1.04	15.0	Raleigh	15.8	0.96	17.5
Golden Lights	8.8	0.76	9.0	Salem Ultra	4.5	0.42	4.9
Kent	12.4	0.95	12.3	Tareyton	14.5	1.01	15.9
Kool	16.6	1.12	16.3	True	7.3	0.61	8.5
L&M	14.9	1.02	15.4	Viceroy Rich Light	8.6	0.69	10.6
Lark Lights	13.7	1.01	13.0	Virginia Slims	15.2	1.02	13.9
Marlboro	15.1	0.90	14.4	Winston Lights	12.0	0.82	14.9
Merit	7.8	0.57	10.0				

Source: Journal of Statistics Education web site at **http://www.amstat.org/publications/jse.** Reprinted with permission.

8. 1 | 5 = 1.5 mg CO

Stem	Leaves	Stem	Leaves
1	5	11	
2		12	3 6
3		13	0 6 9
4	9	14	4 9
5	4	15	0 4 9
6		16	3 6
7		17	5
8	5	18	5
9	0 5		
10	0 2 2 6	23	5

23.5 mg may be an outlier.

9. 0 | 1 = 0.1 milligram

Stem	Leaves
0	1 4 4
0	5 6 6 6 7 7 7 8 8 9 9 9
1	0 0 0 0 0 0 0 1 2
1	
2	0

For Problem 10, explain that the leaves are ordered *outward* from the stem on both the left and right sides.

10. (a) 25 cm to 110 cm for Site 1; 20 cm to 125 cm for Site II.
 (b) Site 1 distribution is somewhat symmetrical; Site II distribution has two distinct parts.
 (c) Possibly.

10. *Expand Your Knowledge: Back-to-Back Stem Plot* In archaeology, the depth (below surface grade) at which artifacts are found is very important. Greater depths sometimes indicate older artifacts, perhaps from a different archaeological period. Figure 2-16 is a *back-to-back stem plot* showing the depths of artifact locations at two different archaeological sites. These sites are from similar geographic locations. Notice that the stems are in the center of the diagram. The leaves for Site I artifact depths are shown to the left of the stems, while the leaves for Site II are to the right of the stems (see *Mimbres Mogollon Archaeology* by A. I. Woosley and A. J. McIntyre, University of New Mexico Press).
 (a) What are the least and greatest depths of artifact finds at Site I? at Site II?
 (b) Describe the data distribution of depths of artifact finds at Site I and at Site II.
 (c) At Site II, there is a gap in the depths at which artifacts were found. Does the Site II data distribution suggest that there might have been a period of no occupation?

FIGURE 2-16

Depth (in cm) of Artifact Location

5 | 2 | 0 = 25 cm at Site I and 20 cm at Site II

Site I		Site II
5	2	0 5 5
5 0	3	0 0 0 0 5 5
5 5 5 5	4	0 0 0 5
5 0	5	0 0 5 5
5 5 5 5 5 0	6	0 0 0 5 5 5
5 5 5 5 5 5 0 0	7	
5 5 0 0 0	8	
5 5 0 0	9	
5 5	10	
0	11	0 0 5 5 5 5
	12	0 0 0 0 5

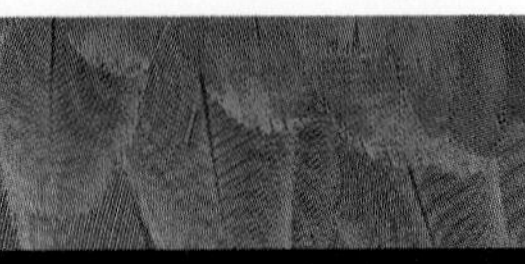

Chapter Review

SUMMARY

Organizing and presenting data are the main purposes of the branch of statistics called descriptive statistics. Graphs provide an important way to show how the data are distributed.

- Frequency tables show how the data are distributed within set classes. The classes are chosen so that they cover all data values and so that each data value falls within only one class. The number of classes and the class width determine the class limits and class boundaries. The number of data values falling within a class is the class frequency.
- A histogram is a graphical display of the information in a frequency table. Classes are shown on the horizontal axis, with corresponding frequencies on the vertical axis. Relative-frequency histograms show relative frequencies on the vertical axis. Dotplots are like histograms except that the classes are individual data values.
- Bar graphs, Pareto charts, and pie charts are useful for showing how quantitative or qualitative data are distributed over chosen categories.
- Time-series graphs show how data change over set intervals of time.
- Stem-and-leaf displays are an effective means of ordering data and showing important features of the distribution.

Graphs aren't just pretty pictures. They help reveal important properties of the data distribution, including the shape and whether or not there are any outliers.

IMPORTANT WORDS & SYMBOLS

Section 2.1
Frequency
Frequency distribution
Class width
Class, lower limit, upper limit
Class frequency
Class midpoint or mark
Frequency table
Class boundaries
Histogram
Relative-frequency table
Relative-frequency histogram
Mound-shaped symmetrical distribution
Uniform distribution
Skewed left
Skewed right
Bimodal distribution
Outlier
Dotplot

Section 2.2
Bar graph
Pareto chart
Pie chart or circle graph
Time-series graph
Time series

Section 2.3
EDA
Stem
Leaf
Stem-and-leaf display
Back-to-back stem plot

VIEWPOINT Personality Clash!

Karl Pearson and Sir Ronald Fisher are two very famous mathematicians who contributed a great deal to the understanding and practice of modern statistics. Each was an outstanding person in his own right; however, the men had a terrific personality clash in the world of statistics. In Chapter 4 we will study the Pearson product moment correlation coefficient. Fisher's F-distribution *is the central probability distribution in the field known as* analysis of variance*. In Chapter 9 we will examine two interpretations of statistical testing: the classical method of critical regions, favored by Karl Pearson, and the P-value method, favored by Sir Ronald Fisher. For a fixed level of significance, both methods can be shown to be equivalent. The P-value method is favored strongly by research and technology and is therefore emphasized in this text. The personality battles of Pearson and Fisher are chronicled in the popular book* The Lady Tasting Tea: How Statistics Revolutionized Science in the Twentieth Century *by David Salsburg.*

CHAPTER REVIEW PROBLEMS

Tables and art to accompany margin answers may be found in the back of the book.

1. (a) Bar graph, Pareto chart, pie chart.
   (b) All.
2. Time-series graph, because the change in data over time is the most relevant issue.
3. Any large gaps between bars or between stems with leaves at the beginning or end of the data set might indicate that the extreme data values are outliers.
4. Dotplots and stem-and-leaf displays both show all the data values. Stem-and-leaf displays group all data values having the same stem, whereas dotplots group only data values that are exactly the same.
5. (a) Yes, with lines used instead of bars. However, because of the perspective nature of the drawing, the lengths of the bars do not represent the mileages. The scale for each bar changes.
   (b) Yes. The scale does not change and the viewer is not distracted by the graphic of the highway.
6. (a) 140; 440.
   (b) Increasing.
   (c) 1,183,589; 1,437,335.

1. *Critical Thinking* Consider these types of graphs: histogram, bar graph, Pareto chart, pie chart, stem-and-leaf display.
   (a) Which are suitable for qualitative data?
   (b) Which are suitable for quantitative data?

2. *Critical Thinking* A consumer interest group is tracking the percentage of household income spent on gasoline over the past 30 years. Which graphical display would be more useful, a histogram or a time-series graph? Why?

3. *Critical Thinking* Describe how data outliers might be revealed in histograms and stem-and-leaf plots.

4. *Expand Your Knowledge* How are dotplots and stem-and-leaf displays similar? How are they different?

5. *Focus Problem: Fuel Economy* Solve the focus problem at the beginning of this chapter.

6. *Criminal Justice: Prisoners* The time plot in Figure 2-17 gives the number of state and federal prisoners per 100,000 population (Source: *Statistical Abstract of the United States*, 120th Edition).
   (a) Estimate the number of prisoners per 100,000 people for 1980 and for 1997.
   (b) During the time period shown, there was increased prosecution of drug offenses, longer sentences for common crimes, and reduced access to parole. What does the time-series graph say about the prison population change per 100,000 people?
   (c) In 1997, the U.S. population was approximately 266,574,000 people. At the rate of 444 prisoners per 100,000 population, about how many prisoners were in the system? The projected U.S. population for the year 2020 is 323,724,000. If the rate of prisoners per 100,000 stays the same as it was in 1997, about how many prisoners do you expect will be in the system in 2020? To obtain the most recent information, visit the Online Study Center at **www.cengage.com/statistics/Brase/UBS5e** and find the link to the Census Bureau.

FIGURE 2-17

Number of State and Federal Prisoners per 100,000 Population

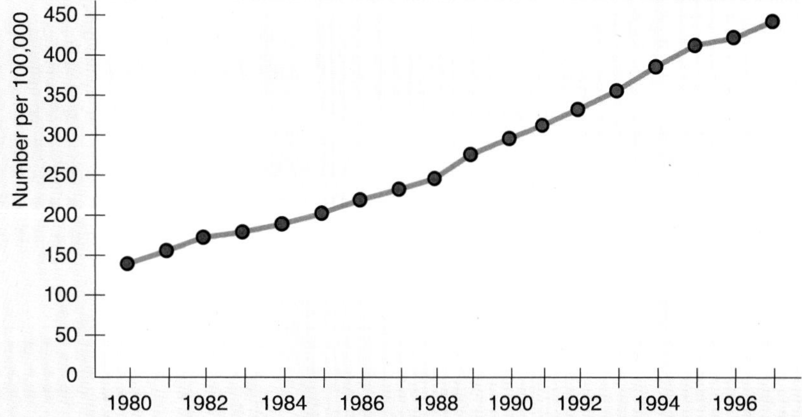

7. *IRS: Tax Returns* Almost everyone files (or sometime will file) a federal income tax return. A research poll for Turbo Tax (a computer software package designed to aid in tax-return preparation) asked what aspect of filing a return people thought to be the most difficult. The results showed that 43% of the respondents said understanding the IRS jargon, 28% said knowing deductions, 10% said getting the right form, 8% said calculating the numbers, and 10% didn't know. Make a circle graph to display this information. *Note:* Percentages will not total 100% because of rounding.

8. (b) Class width = 7.

Class	f
16–22	8
23–29	11
30–36	11
37–43	7
44–50	6
51–57	4
58–64	3

(d) Skewed slightly right.

8. *Law Enforcement: DUI* Driving under the influence of alcohol (DUI) is a serious offense. The following data give the ages of a random sample of 50 drivers arrested while driving under the influence of alcohol. This distribution is based on the age distribution of DUI arrests given in the *Statistical Abstract of the United States* (112th Edition).

46	16	41	26	22	33	30	22	36	34
63	21	26	18	27	24	31	38	26	55
31	47	27	43	35	22	64	40	58	20
49	37	53	25	29	32	23	49	39	40
24	56	30	51	21	45	27	34	47	35

(a) Make a stem-and-leaf display of the age distribution.
(b) Make a frequency table using seven classes.
(c) Make a histogram showing class boundaries.
(d) Identify the shape of the distribution.

9. (a) Class width = 11.

Class	f
69–79	2
80–90	3
91–101	8
102–112	19
113–123	22
124–134	3
135–145	3

(d) Skewed slightly left.

9. *Agriculture: Apple Trees* The following data represent trunk circumferences (in mm) for a random sample of 60 four-year-old apple trees at East Malling Agriculture Research Station in England (Reference: S. C. Pearce, University of Kent at Canterbury). *Note:* These data are also available for download at the Online Study Center.

108	99	106	102	115	120	120	117	122	142
106	111	119	109	125	108	116	105	117	123
103	114	101	99	112	120	108	91	115	109
114	105	99	122	106	113	114	75	96	124
91	102	108	110	83	90	69	117	84	142
122	113	105	112	117	122	129	100	138	117

(a) Make a frequency table with seven classes showing class limits, class boundaries, midpoints, frequencies, and relative frequencies.
(b) Draw a histogram.
(c) Draw a relative-frequency histogram.
(d) Identify the shape of the distribution.

10. *Law: Corporation Lawsuits* Many people say the civil justice system is overburdened. Many cases center on suits involving businesses. The following data are based on a *Wall Street Journal* report. Researchers conducted a study of lawsuits involving 1908 businesses ranked in the Fortune 1000 over a 20-year period. They found the following distribution of civil justice caseloads brought before the federal courts:

Case Type	Number of Filings (in thousands)
Contracts	107
General torts (personal injury)	191
Asbestos liability	49
Other product liability	38
All other	21

Note: Contracts cases involve disputes over contracts between businesses.

(a) Make a Pareto chart of the caseloads. Which types of cases occur most frequently?

(b) Make a pie chart showing the percentage of cases of each type.

11. (a) 1240s.
(b) 75.
(c) From 1204 to 1211, inclusive.

11. *Archaeology: Tree-Ring Data* *The Sand Canyon Archaeological Project*, edited by W. D. Lipe and published by Crow Canyon Archaeological Center, contains the stem-and-leaf diagram shown in Figure 2-18. The study uses tree rings to accurately determine the year in which a tree was cut. The figure gives the tree-ring-cutting dates for samples of timbers found in the architectural units at Sand Canyon Pueblo. The text referring to the figure says, "The three-digit numbers in the left column represent centuries and decades A.D. The numbers to the right represent individual years, with each number derived from an individual sample. Thus, **124 2 2 2** represents three samples dated to A.D. 1242." Use Figure 2-18 and the verbal description to answer the following questions.

(a) Which decade contained the most samples?

(b) How many samples had a tree-ring-cutting date between 1200 A.D. and 1239 A.D., inclusive?

(c) What are the dates of the longest interval during which no tree-cutting samples occurred? What might this indicate about new construction or renovation of the pueblo structures during this period?

FIGURE 2-18

Tree-Ring-Cutting Dates from Architectural Units of Sand Canyon Pueblo: *The Sand Canyon Archaeological Project*

Stem	Leaves
119	5 6
120	0 0 1 2 3 3 3 3 3 3 3 3 3 3 3 3 3 3 3 3 3 3 3 3 3 3 3 3
120	
121	2
121	5 5
122	0 0 1 1 1 1 2 2 3 4 4 4 4 4 4 4
122	5 8 9
123	0 1 2 3 3 4
123	5 5 5 5 5 5 5 5 5 5 5 5 5 5 5 6 8 8 9
124	1 2 2 2 2 2 2 2 2 2 2 2 2 2 2 2 2 2 2 2 2 2 2 2 3 4 4
124	5 6 8 9 9 9 9 9 9 9 9 9 9
125	0 0 0 0 0 0 0 0 0 0 0 0 0 0 0 1 1 1 1 1 1 2 2 2
125	
126	0 0 0 1 2 2 2 2 2 2 2 2 2 2 2 2 2 4 4 4 4 4 4 4
126	5 5 5 6 6 7
127	0 1 1 1 1 4 4

DATA HIGHLIGHTS: GROUP PROJECTS

Break into small groups and discuss the following topics. Organize a brief outline in which you summarize the main points of your group discussion.

1. Examine Figure 2-19, "Everyone Agrees: Slobs Make Worst Roommates." This is a clustered bar graph because two percentages are given for each response category: responses from men and responses from women. Comment on how the artistic rendition has slightly changed the format of a bar graph. Do the bars seem to have lengths that accurately reflect the relative percentages of the responses? In your own opinion, does the artistic rendition enhance or confuse the information? Explain. Which characteristic of "worst roommates" does the graphic seem to illustrate? Can this graph be considered a Pareto chart for men? for women? Why or why not? From the information given in the figure, do you

think the survey listed just the four given annoying characteristics? Do you think a respondent could choose more than one characteristic? Explain your answer in terms of the percentages given and in terms of the explanation given in the graphic. Could this information also be displayed in one circle graph for men and another for women? Explain.

2. Examine Figure 2-20, "Global Teen Worries." How many countries were contained in the sample? The graph contains bars and a circle. Which bar is the longest? Which bar represents the greatest percentage? Is this a bar graph or not? If not, what changes would need to be made to put the information into a bar graph? Could the graph be made into a Pareto chart? Could it be made into a circle graph? Explain.

FIGURE 2-19

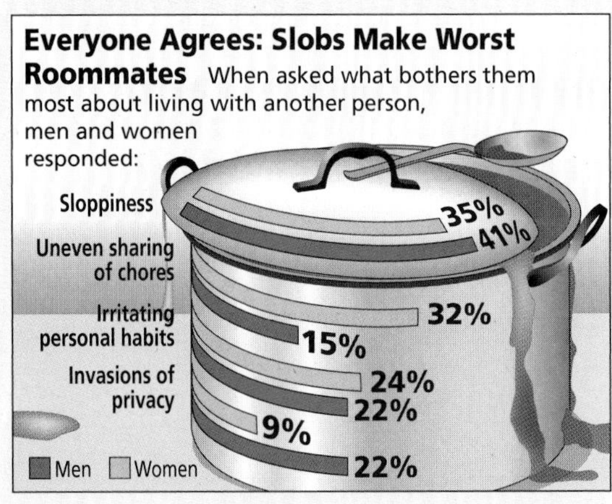

Source: Advantage Business Research for Mattel *Compatibility*

FIGURE 2-20

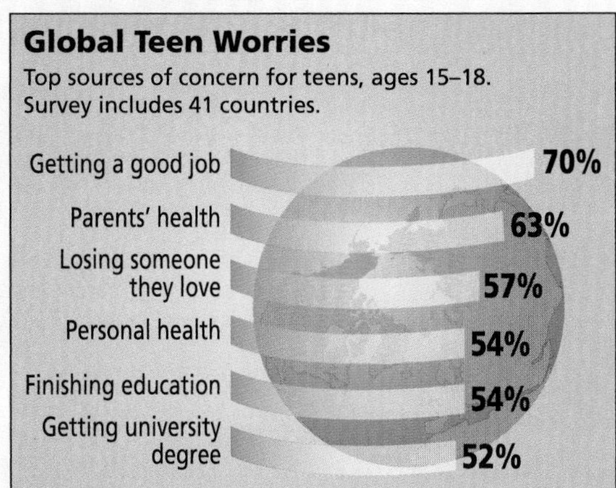

Source: BrainWaves Group's New World Teen Study

LINKING CONCEPTS: WRITING PROJECTS

Discuss each of the following topics in class or review the topics on your own. Then write a brief but complete essay in which you summarize the main points. Please include formulas and graphs as appropriate.

1. In your own words, explain the differences among histograms, relative-frequency histograms, bar graphs, circle graphs, time-series graphs, Pareto charts, and stem-and-leaf displays. If you have nominal data, which graphic displays might be useful? What if you have ordinal, interval, or ratio data?

2. What do we mean when we say that a histogram is skewed to the left? to the right? What is a bimodal histogram? Discuss the following statement: "A bimodal histogram usually results if we draw a sample from two populations at once." Suppose you took a sample of weights of college football players and with this sample you included weights of cheerleaders. Do you think a histogram made from the combined weights would be bimodal? Explain.

3. Discuss the statement that stem-and-leaf displays are quick and easy to construct. How can we use a stem-and-leaf display to make the construction of a frequency table easier? How does a stem-and-leaf display help you spot extreme values quickly?

4. Go to the library and pick up a current issue of *The Wall Street Journal, Newsweek, Time, USA Today,* or other news media. Examine each newspaper or magazine for graphs of the types discussed in this chapter. List the variables used, method of data collection, and general types of conclusion drawn from the graphs. Another source for information is the Internet. Explore several web sites, and categorize the graphs you find as you did for the print media. For interesting web sites, visit the Online Study Center at **www.cengage.com/statistics/Brase/UBS5e** and find links to the Social Statistics Briefing Room, to law enforcement, and to golf.

USING TECHNOLOGY

Applications

The following tables show the first-round winning scores for the NCAA men's and women's basketball teams.

TABLE 2-16 **Men's Winning First-Round NCAA Tournament Scores**

95	70	79	99	83	72	79	101
69	82	86	70	79	69	69	70
95	70	77	61	69	68	69	72
89	66	84	77	50	83	63	58

TABLE 2-17 **Women's Winning First-Round NCAA Tournament Scores**

80	68	51	80	83	75	77	100
96	68	89	80	67	84	76	70
98	81	79	89	98	83	72	100
101	83	66	76	77	84	71	77

1. Use the software or method of your choice to construct separate histograms for the men's and women's winning scores. Try 5, 7, and 10 classes for each. Which number of classes seems to be the best choice? Why?
2. Use the same class boundaries for the histograms of men's and of women's scores. How do the scores for the two groups compare? What general shape do the histograms follow?
3. Use the software or method of your choice to make stem-and-leaf displays for each set of scores. If your software does not make stem-and-leaf displays, sort the data first and then make a back-to-back display by hand. Do there seem to be any extreme values in either set? How do the data sets compare?

Technology Hints: Creating Histograms

The default histograms produced by the TI-84Plus/TI-83Plus calculators, Minitab, and Excel all determine automatically the number of classes to be used. To control the number of classes the technology uses, follow the key steps as indicated. The display screens are generated for data found in Table 2-1—One-Way Commuting Distances (in Miles) for 60 Workers in Downtown Dallas.

TI-84Plus/TI-83Plus

Determine the class width for the number of classes you want and the lower class boundary for the first class. Enter the data in list L1.

Press **STATPLOT** and highlight On and the histogram plot.

Press **WINDOW** and set Xmin = lowest class boundary, Xscl = class width. Use appropriate values for the other settings.

Press **GRAPH. TRACE** gives boundaries and frequency.

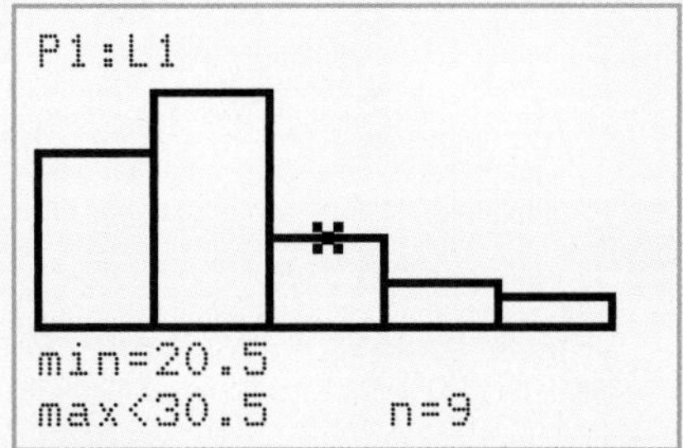

Excel

Determine the upper class boundaries for the five classes. Enter the data. In a separate column, enter the upper class boundaries. Use the menu selection **Tools ➤ Data Analysis ➤ Histogram.**

Put the data range in the Input Range. Put the upper class boundaries range in the Bin Range.

To make bars touch, right click on a bar and select **Format Data Series ➤ Options tab.** Set the **gap width** to 0.

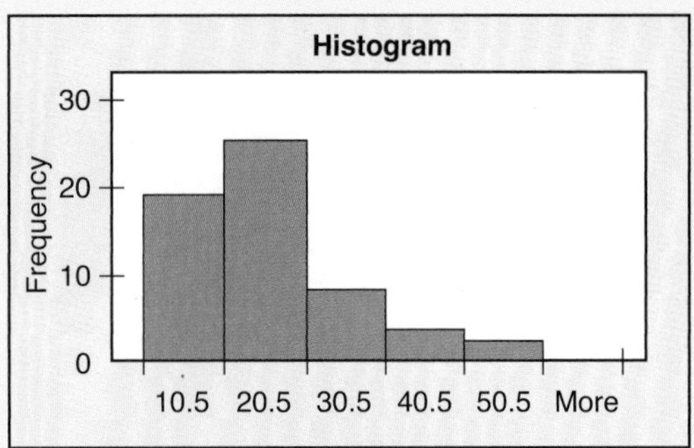

Minitab

Determine the class boundaries. Enter the data. Use the menu selection **Graph ➤ Histogram.**

Choose **Simple** and click **OK.** Select the graph variable and click **OK** to obtain a histogram with automatically selected classes. To set your own class boundaries, double-click the displayed histogram. In the dialogue box, select **Binning.** Then choose **Cutpoint** and enter the class boundaries as cutpoint positions.

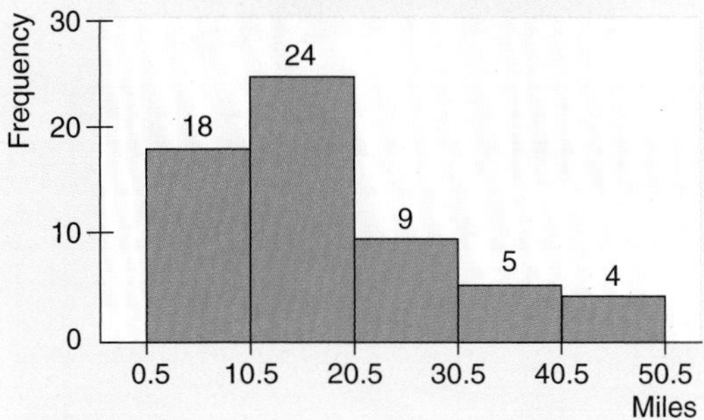

SPSS

The SPSS screen shot shows the default histogram created by the menu choices **Analyze ➤ Descriptive Statistics ➤ Frequencies.** In the dialogue box, move the variable containing the data into the variables window. Click **Charts** and select **Histograms.** Click the Continue button and then the OK button. In SPSS version 12, there are procedures to control the boundaries (cutpoints) of the histogram.

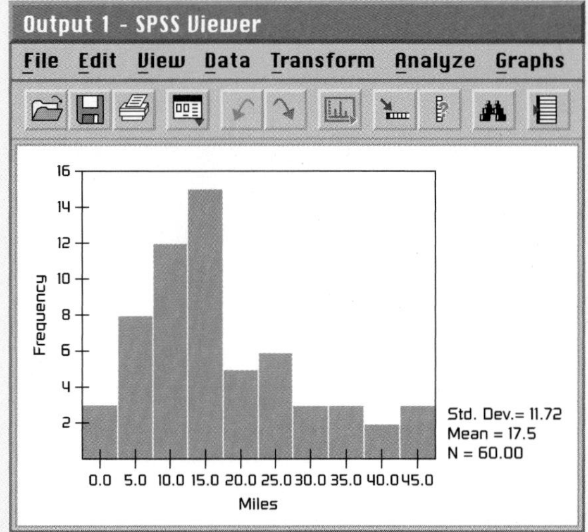

Specific instructions for setting class boundaries (cutpoints) of a histogram are provided in the Technology Guide that accompanies this text.

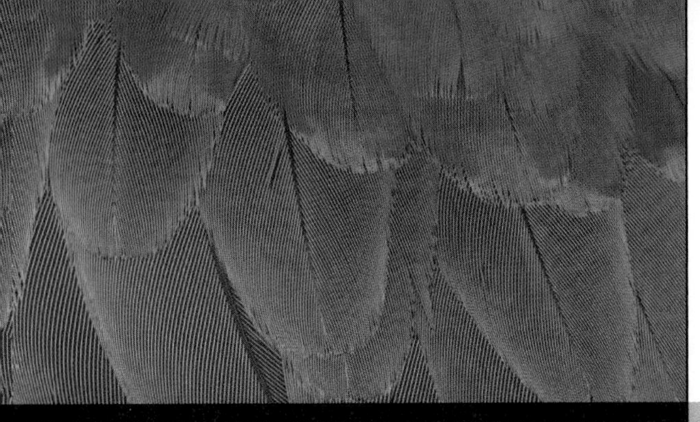

3

While the individual man is an insolvable puzzle, in the aggregate he becomes a mathematical certainty. You can, for example, never foretell what any one man will do, but you can say with precision what an average number will be up to.

—Arthur Conan Doyle,
The Sign of Four

Sherlock Holmes spoke the words quoted at the left to his colleague Dr. Watson as the two were unraveling a mystery. The detective was implying that if a single member is drawn at random from a population, we cannot predict *exactly* what that member will look like. However, there are some "average" features of the entire population that an individual is likely to possess. The degree of certainty with which we would expect to observe such average features in any individual depends on our knowledge of the variation among individuals in the population. Sherlock Holmes has led us to two of the most important statistical concepts: average and variation.

For on-line student resources, visit the Brase/Brase, *Understanding Basic Statistics,* 5th edition web site at **www.cengage.com/statistics/Brase/UBS5e.**

AVERAGES AND VARIATION

PREVIEW QUESTIONS

What are commonly used measures of central tendency? What do they tell you? (SECTION 3.1)

How do variance and standard deviation measure data spread? Why is this important? (SECTION 3.2)

How do you make a box-and-whisker plot, and what does it tell you about the spread of the data? (SECTION 3.3)

FOCUS PROBLEM

The Educational Advantage

Is it really worth all the effort to get a college degree? From a philosophical point of view, the love of learning is sufficient reason to get a college degree. However, the U.S. Census Bureau makes another relevant point. Annually, college graduates (bachelor's degree) earn on average $23,291 more than high school graduates. This means college graduates earn about 83.4% more than high school graduates, and according to "Education Pays" on the next page, the gap in earnings is increasing. Furthermore, as the College Board indicates, for most Americans college remains relatively affordable.

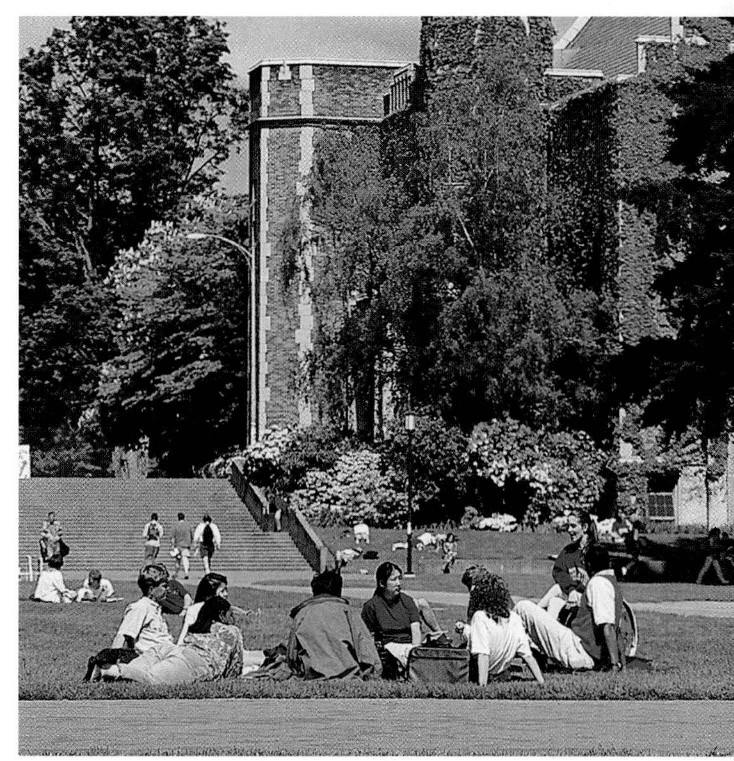

After completing this chapter, you will be able to answer the following questions.

(a) Does a college degree *guarantee* someone an 83.4% increase in earnings over a high school degree? Remember, we are using only *averages* from census data.

(b) Using census data (not shown in "Education Pays"), it is estimated that the standard deviation of college-graduate earnings is about $8,500. Compute a 75% Chebyshev confidence interval centered on the mean ($51,206) for bachelor's degree earnings.

(c) How much does college tuition cost? That depends, of course, on where you go to college. Construct a weighted average. Using the data from "College Affordable for Most," estimate midpoints for the cost intervals. Say 46% of tuitions cost about \$4,500; 21% cost about \$7,500; 7% cost about \$12,000; 8% cost about \$18,000; 9% cost about \$24,000; and 9% cost about \$31,000. Compute the weighted average of college tuition charged at all colleges. (See Problem 9 in the Chapter Review Problems.)

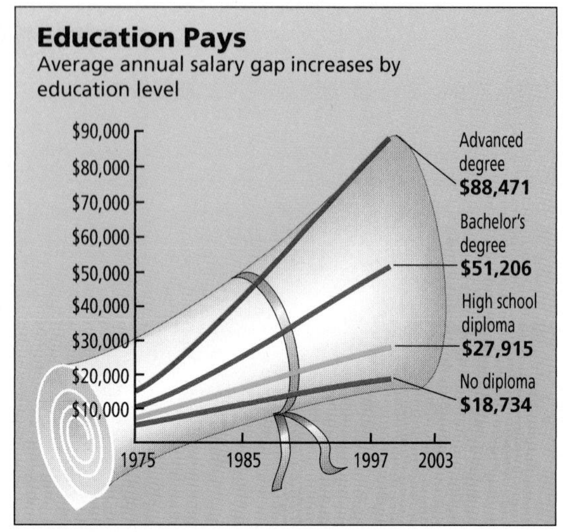

Source: Census Bureau

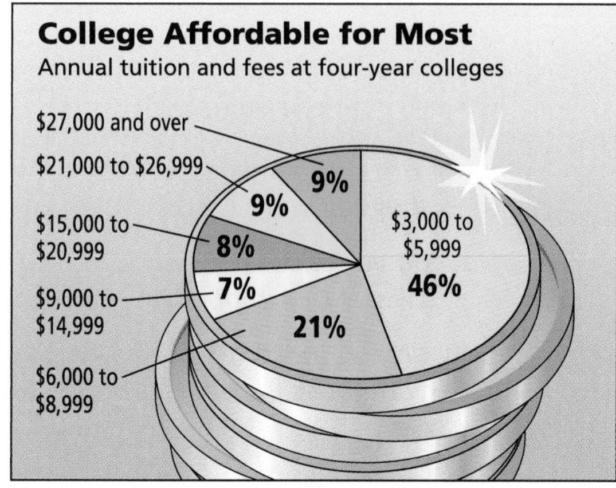

Source: The College Board

SECTION 3.1 Measures of Central Tendency: Mode, Median, and Mean

FOCUS POINTS

- Compute mean, median, and mode from raw data.
- Interpret what mean, median, and mode tell you.
- Explain how mean, median, and mode can be affected by extreme data values.
- What is a trimmed mean? How do you compute it?
- Compute a weighted average.

This section can be covered quickly. Good discussion topics include *The Story of Old Faithful* in Data Highlights, Problem 1; Linking Concepts, Problem 1; and the trade winds of Hawaii (Using Technology).

The average price of an ounce of gold is \$920. The Zippy car averages 39 miles per gallon on the highway. A survey showed the average shoe size for women is size 8.

In each of the preceding statements, *one* number is used to describe the entire sample or population. Such a number is called an *average*. There are many ways to compute averages, but we will study only three of the major ones.

The easiest average to compute is the *mode*.

The **mode** of a data set is the value that occurs most frequently.

EXAMPLE 1 MODE

Count the letters in each word of this sentence and give the mode. The numbers of letters in the words of the sentence are

5 3 7 2 4 4 2 4 8 3 4 3 4

Scanning the data, we see that 4 is the mode because more words have 4 letters than any other number. For larger data sets, it is useful to order—or sort—the data before scanning them for the mode.

Not every data set has a mode. For example, if Professor Fair gives equal numbers of A's, B's, C's, D's, and F's, then there is no modal grade. In addition, the mode is not very stable. Changing just one number in a data set can change the mode dramatically. However, the mode is a useful average when we want to know the most frequently occurring data value, such as the most frequently requested shoe size.

Median

Another average that is useful is the *median,* or central value, of an ordered distribution. When you are given the median, you know there are an equal number of data values in the ordered distribution that are above it and below it.

The notation $\tilde{x}$ (read "x tilde") is sometimes used to designate the median of a data set.

PROCEDURE

How to find the median

The **median** is the central value of an ordered distribution. To find it,

1. Order the data from smallest to largest.
2. For an *odd* number of data values in the distribution,

$$\text{Median} = \text{Middle data value}$$

3. For an *even* number of data values in the distribution,

$$\text{Median} = \frac{\text{Sum of middle two values}}{2}$$

EXAMPLE 2

Median

What do barbecue-flavored potato chips cost? According to *Consumer Reports,* Volume 66, No. 5, the prices per ounce in cents of the rated chips are

19 19 27 28 18 35

(a) To find the median, we first order the data, and then note that there are an even number of entries. So the median is constructed using the two middle values.

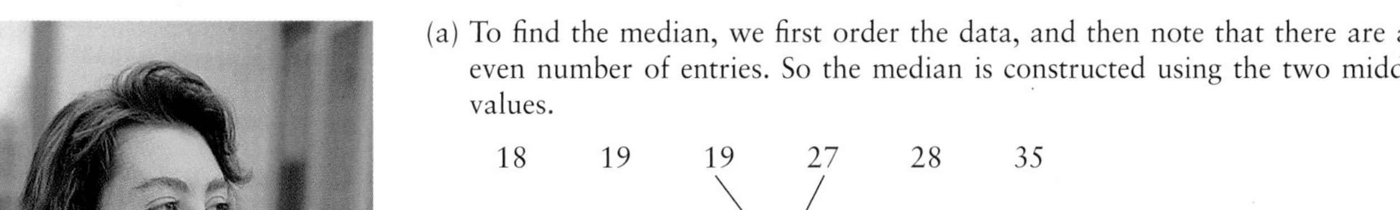

18 19 19 27 28 35

middle values

$$\text{Median} = \frac{19 + 27}{2} = 23 \text{ cents}$$

(b) According to *Consumer Reports,* the brand with the lowest overall taste rating costs 35 cents per ounce. Eliminate that brand, and find the median price per ounce for the remaining barbecue-flavored chips. Again order the data. Note that there are an odd number of entries, so the median is simply the middle value.

18 19 19 27 28

↑

middle value

$$\text{Median} = \text{middle value} = 19 \text{ cents}$$

(c) One ounce of potato chips is considered a small serving. Is it reasonable to budget about $10.45 to serve the barbecue-flavored chips to 55 people?

Yes, since the median price of the chips is 19 cents per small serving. This budget for chips assumes that there is plenty of other food!

The median uses the *position* rather than the specific value of each data entry. If the extreme values of a data set change, the median usually does not change. This is why the median is often used as the average for house prices. If one mansion costing several million dollars sells in a community of much-lower-priced homes, the median selling price for houses in the community would be affected very little, if at all.

GUIDED EXERCISE 1 Median and mode

Belleview College must make a report to the budget committee about the average credit hour load a full-time student carries. (A 12-credit-hour load is the minimum requirement for full-time status. For the same tuition, students may take up to 20 credit hours.) A random sample of 40 students yielded the following information (in credit hours):

17	12	14	17	13	16	18	20	13	12
12	17	16	15	14	12	12	13	17	14
15	12	15	16	12	18	20	19	12	15
18	14	16	17	15	19	12	13	12	15

(a) Organize the data from smallest to largest number of credit hours.

→

12	12	12	12	12	12	12	12	12	12
13	13	13	13	14	14	14	14	15	(15)
(15)	15	15	15	16	16	16	16	17	17
17	17	17	18	18	18	19	19	20	20

(b) Since there are an ________ (odd, even) number of values, we add the two middle values and divide by 2 to get the median. What is the median credit hour load?

→ There are an even number of entries. The two middle values are circled in part (a).

$$\text{Median} = \frac{15 + 15}{2} = 15$$

(c) What is the mode of this distribution? Is it different from the median? If the budget committee is going to fund the school according to the average student credit hour load (more money for higher loads), which of these two averages do you think the college will use?

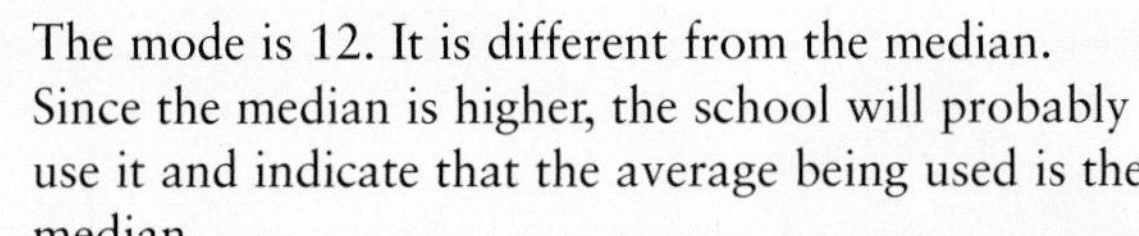

→ The mode is 12. It is different from the median. Since the median is higher, the school will probably use it and indicate that the average being used is the median.

Note: For small ordered data sets, we can easily scan the set to find the *location* of the median. However, for large ordered data sets of size n, it is convenient to have a formula to find the middle of the data set.

For an ordered data set of size n,

$$\textbf{Position of the middle value} = \frac{n + 1}{2}$$

For instance, if $n = 99$, then the middle value is the $(99 + 1)/2$ or 50th data value in the ordered data. If $n = 100$, then $(100 + 1)/2 = 50.5$ tells us that the two middle values are in the 50th and 51st positions.

Mean

Most students will recognize the computation procedure for the mean as the process they follow to compute a simple average of test grades.

An average that uses the exact value of each entry is the *mean* (sometimes called the *arithmetic mean*). To compute the mean, we add the values of all the entries and then divide by the number of entries.

$$\textbf{Mean} = \frac{\text{Sum of all entries}}{\text{Number of entries}}$$

The mean is the average usually used to compute a test average.

EXAMPLE 3 MEAN

To graduate, Linda needs at least a B in biology. She did not do very well on her first three tests; however, she did well on the last four. Here are her scores:

58 67 60 84 93 98 100

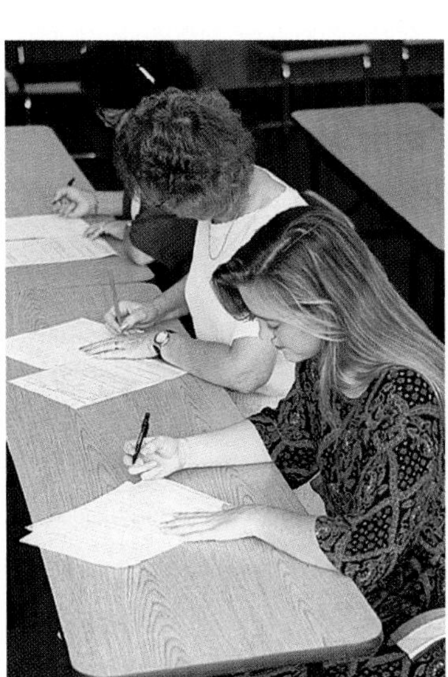

Compute the mean and determine if Linda's grade will be a B (80 to 89 average) or a C (70 to 79 average).

SOLUTION:

$$\text{Mean} = \frac{\text{Sum of scores}}{\text{Number of scores}} = \frac{58 + 67 + 60 + 84 + 93 + 98 + 100}{7}$$

$$= \frac{560}{7} = 80$$

Since the average is 80, Linda will get the needed B.

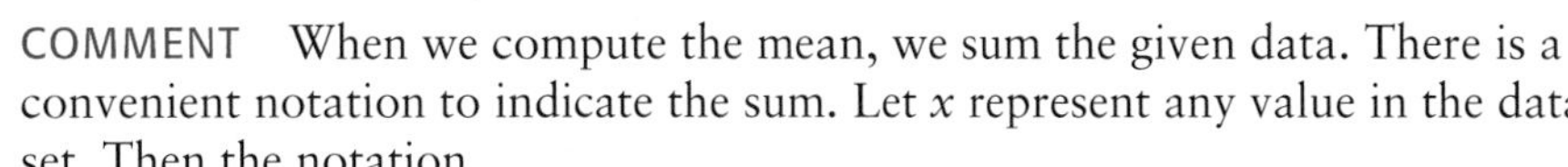

COMMENT When we compute the mean, we sum the given data. There is a convenient notation to indicate the sum. Let x represent any value in the data set. Then the notation

Σx (read "the sum of all given x values")

means that we are to sum all the data values. In other words, we are to sum all the entries in the distribution. The *summation symbol* Σ means *sum the following* and is capital sigma, the S of the Greek alphabet.

Formulas for the mean

The symbol for the mean of a *sample* distribution of x values is denoted by $\bar{x}$ (read "x bar"). If your data comprise the entire *population*, we use the symbol μ (lowercase Greek letter mu, pronounced "mew") to represent the mean.

PROCEDURE

HOW TO FIND THE MEAN

1. Compute Σx; that is, find the sum of all the data values.
2. Divide the sum total by the number of data values.

Sample statistic $\bar{x}$ Population parameter μ

$$\bar{x} = \frac{\Sigma x}{n} \qquad \mu = \frac{\Sigma x}{N}$$

where n = number of data values in the sample

N = number of data values in the population

This is a good time to review calculator procedures with students, with particular emphasis on order of operations.

CALCULATOR NOTE It is very easy to compute the mean on *any* calculator: Simply add the data values and divide the total by the number of data. However, on calculators with a statistics mode, you place the calculator in that mode, *enter* the data, and then press the key for the mean. The key is usually designated $\bar{x}$. Because the formula for the population mean is the same as that for the sample mean, the same key gives the value for μ.

We have seen three averages: the mode, the median, and the mean. For later work, the mean is the most important. A disadvantage of the mean, however, is that it can be affected by exceptional values.

Resistant measure

A *resistant measure* is one that is not influenced by extremely high or low data values. The mean is not a resistant measure of center because we can make the mean as large as we want by changing the size of only one data value. The median, on the other hand, is more resistant. However, a disadvantage of the median is that it is not sensitive to the specific size of a data value.

Trimmed mean

A measure of center that is more resistant than the mean but still sensitive to specific data values is the *trimmed mean*. A trimmed mean is the mean of the data values left after "trimming" a specified percentage of the smallest and largest data values from the data set. Usually a 5% trimmed mean is used. This implies that we trim the lowest 5% of the data as well as the highest 5% of the data. A similar procedure is used for a 10% trimmed mean.

PROCEDURE

HOW TO COMPUTE A 5% TRIMMED MEAN

1. Order the data from smallest to largest.
2. Delete the bottom 5% of the data and the top 5% of the data. *Note:* If the calculation of 5% of the number of data values does not produce a whole number, *round* to the nearest integer.
3. Compute the mean of the remaining 90% of the data.

GUIDED EXERCISE 2 Mean and trimmed mean

Barron's Profiles of American Colleges, 19th Edition, lists average class size for introductory lecture courses at each of the profiled institutions. A sample of 20 colleges and universities in California showed class sizes for introductory lecture courses to be

(14)	20	20	20	20	23	25	30	30	30
35	35	35	40	40	42	50	50	80	(80)

(a) Compute the mean for the entire sample.

→ Add all the values and divide by 20:

$$\bar{x} = \frac{\Sigma x}{n} = \frac{719}{20} \approx 36.0$$

(b) Compute a 5% trimmed mean for the sample.

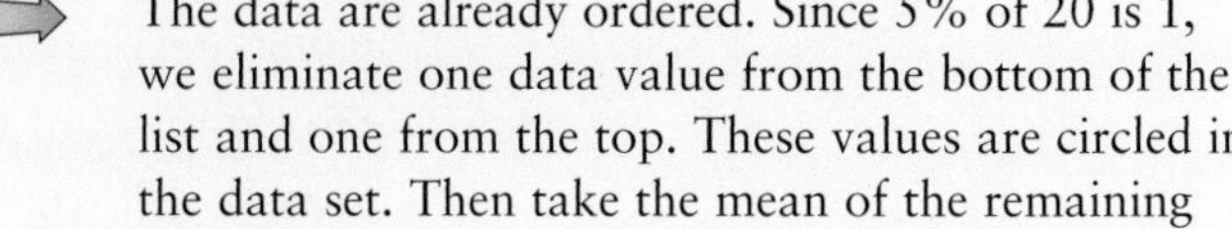

→ The data are already ordered. Since 5% of 20 is 1, we eliminate one data value from the bottom of the list and one from the top. These values are circled in the data set. Then take the mean of the remaining 18 entries.

$$5\% \text{ trimmed mean} = \frac{\Sigma x}{n} = \frac{625}{18} \approx 34.7$$

Continued

GUIDED EXERCISE 2 *continued*

(c) Find the median of the original data set. ➡ Note that the data are already ordered.

$$\text{Median} = \frac{30 + 35}{2} = 32.5$$

(d) Find the median of the 5% trimmed data set. Does the median change when you trim the data? ➡ The median is still 32.5. Notice that trimming the same number of entries from both ends leaves the middle position of the data set unchanged.

(e) Is the trimmed mean or the original mean closer to the median? ➡ The trimmed mean is closer to the median.

TECH NOTES

Minitab, Excel, and TI-84Plus/TI-83Plus calculators all provide the mean and median of a data set. Minitab and Excel also provide the mode. The TI-84Plus/TI-83Plus calculators sort data, so you can easily scan the sorted data for the mode. Minitab provides the 5% trimmed mean, as does Excel.

All this technology is a wonderful aid for analyzing data. However, *a measurement has no meaning if you do not know what it represents or how a change in data values might affect the measurement.* The defining formulas and procedures for computing the measures tell you a great deal about the measures. Even if you use a calculator to evaluate all the statistical measures, pay attention to the information the formulas and procedures give you about the components or features of the measurement.

CRITICAL THINKING

The ideas at the right can be used to review levels of measurement and link some of those concepts to the material in this section.

In Chapter 1, we examined four levels of data: nominal, ordinal, interval, and ratio. The mode (if it exists) can be used with all four levels, including nominal. For instance, the modal color of all passenger cars sold last year might be blue. The median may be used with data at the ordinal level or above. If we ranked the passenger cars in order of customer satisfaction level, we could identify the median satisfaction level. For the mean, our data need to be at the interval or ratio level (although there are exceptions in which the mean of ordinal-level data is computed). We can certainly find the mean model year of used passenger cars sold or the mean price of new passenger cars.

Data types and averages

Another issue of concern is that of taking the average of averages. For instance, if the values \$520, \$640, \$730, \$890, and \$920 represent the mean monthly rents for five different apartment complexes, we can't say that \$740 (the mean of the five numbers) is the mean monthly rent of all the apartments. We need to know the number of apartments in each complex before we can determine an average based on the number of apartments renting at each designated amount.

Distribution shapes and averages

In general, when a data distribution is mound-shaped symmetrical, the values for the mean, median, and mode are the same or almost the same. For skewed-left distributions, the mean is less than the median and the median is less than the mode. For skewed-right distributions, the mode is the smallest value, the median is the next largest, and the mean is the largest. Figure 3-1, on the next page, shows the general relationships among the mean, median, and mode for different types of distributions.

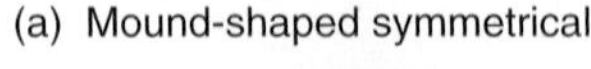

Distribution Types and Averages

(a) Mound-shaped symmetrical

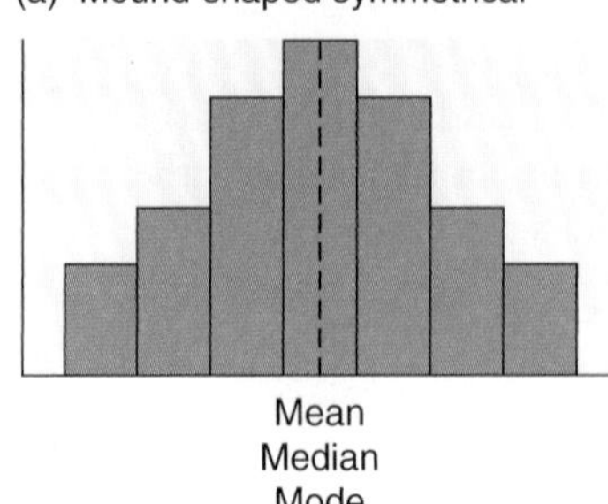

(b) Skewed left

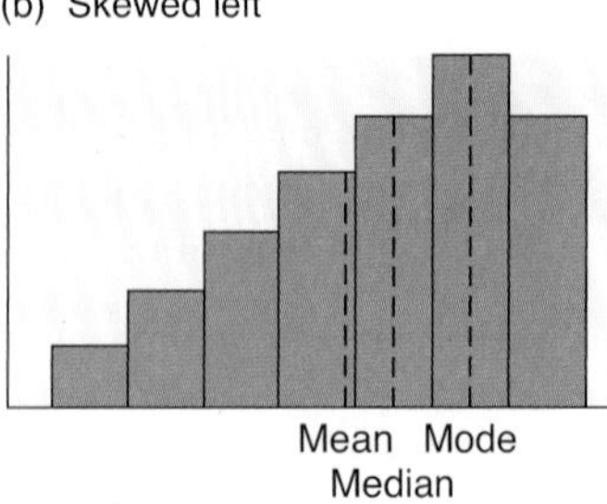

(c) Skewed right

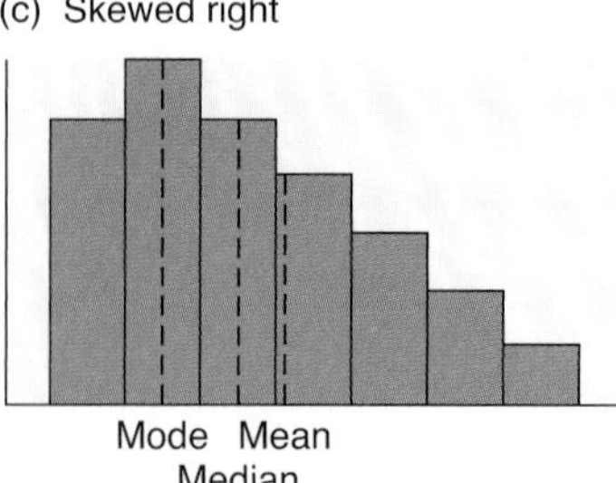

Weighted Average

Weighted average

Sometimes we wish to average numbers, but we want to assign more importance, or weight, to some of the numbers. For instance, suppose your professor tells you that your grade will be based on a midterm and a final exam, each of which is based on 100 possible points. However, the final exam will be worth 60% of the grade and the midterm only 40%. How could you determine an average score that would reflect these different weights? The average you need is the *weighted average*.

Weighted averages have many real-world applications. This is a good time to mention that the sum of the weights may or may not be 1, depending on the application.

$$\textbf{Weighted average} = \frac{\Sigma xw}{\Sigma w}$$

where x is a data value and w is the weight assigned to that data value. The sum is taken over all data values.

EXAMPLE 4 WEIGHTED AVERAGE

Suppose your midterm test score is 83 and your final exam score is 95. Using weights of 40% for the midterm and 60% for the final exam, compute the weighted average of your scores. If the minimum average for an A is 90, will you earn an A?

SOLUTION: By the formula, we multiply each score by its weight and add the results together. Then we divide by the sum of all the weights. Converting the percentages to decimal notation, we get

$$\text{Weighted average} = \frac{83(0.40) + 95(0.60)}{0.40 + 0.60}$$

$$= \frac{33.2 + 57}{1} = 90.2$$

Your average is high enough to earn an A.

TECH NOTES The TI-84Plus/TI-83Plus calculators directly support weighted averages. Both Excel and Minitab can be programmed to provide the averages.

TI-84Plus/TI-83Plus Enter the data into one list, such as L1, and the corresponding weights into another list, such as L2. Then press **Stat ➤ Calc ➤ 1: 1-Var Stats**. Enter the list containing the data, followed by a comma and the list containing the weights.

VIEWPOINT What's Wrong with Pitching Today?

One way to answer this question is to look at averages. *Batting averages and average hits per game are shown for selected years from 1901 to 2000 (Source:* The Wall Street Journal*).*

Year	1901	1920	1930	1941	1951	1961	1968	1976	1986	2000
B.A.	0.277	0.284	0.288	0.267	0.263	0.256	0.231	0.256	0.262	0.276
Hits	19.2	19.2	20.0	18.4	17.9	17.3	15.2	17.3	17.8	19.1

A quick scan of the averages shows that batting averages and average hits per game are virtually the same as almost 100 years ago. It seems there is nothing *wrong with today's pitching! So what's changed? For one thing, the rules have changed! The strike zone is considerably smaller than it once was, and the pitching mound is lower. Both give the hitter an advantage over the pitcher. Even so, pitchers don't give up hits with any greater frequency than they did a century ago (look at the averages). However, modern hits go much farther, which is something a pitcher can't control.*

SECTION 3.1 PROBLEMS

Tables and art to accompany margin answers may be found in the back of the book.

1. Median; mode; mean.
2. Statistic, $\bar{x}$; parameter, μ.
3. Mean, median, and mode are approximately equal.
4. (a) Mean, median, and mode if it exists.
 (b) Mode if it exists.
 (c) Mean, median, and mode if it exists.
5. (a) Mode = 5; median = 4; mean = 3.8.
 (b) Mode.
 (c) Mean, median, and mode.
 (d) Mode, median.
6. (a) Mean increases; median remains the same.
 (b) Mean decreases; median remains the same.
 (c) Both decrease.

Problem 6 helps students understand how specific data values enter into computations of the mean, median, and mode.

1. *Statistical Literacy* Consider the mode, median, and mean. Which average represents the middle value of a data distribution? Which average represents the most frequent value of a distribution? Which average takes all the specific values into account?

2. *Statistical Literacy* What symbol is used for the arithmetic mean when it is a sample statistic? What symbol is used when the arithmetic mean is a population parameter?

3. *Critical Thinking* When a distribution is mound-shaped symmetrical, what is the general relationship among the values of the mean, median, and mode?

4. *Critical Thinking* Consider the following types of data that were obtained from a random sample of 49 credit card accounts. Identify all the averages (mean, median, or mode) that can be used to summarize the data.
 (a) Outstanding balance on each account
 (b) Name of credit card (e.g., MasterCard, Visa, American Express, etc.)
 (c) Dollar amount due on next payment

5. *Critical Thinking* Consider the numbers

 2 3 4 5 5

 (a) Compute the mode, median, and mean.
 (b) If the numbers represented codes for the colors of T-shirts ordered from a catalog, which average(s) would make sense?
 (c) If the numbers represented one-way mileages for trails to different lakes, which average(s) would make sense?
 (d) Suppose the numbers represent survey responses from 1 to 5, with 1 = disagree strongly, 2 = disagree, 3 = agree, 4 = agree strongly, and 5 = agree very strongly. Which averages make sense?

6. *Critical Thinking* Consider a data set of 15 distinct measurements with mean A and median B.
 (a) If the highest number were increased, what would be the effect on the median and mean? Explain.
 (b) If the highest number were decreased to a value still larger than B, what would be the effect on the median and mean?
 (c) If the highest number were decreased to a value smaller than B, what would be the effect on the median and mean?

7. Mean ≈ 167.3°F; median = 171°F; mode = 178°F.

7. *Environmental Studies: Death Valley* How hot does it get in Death Valley? The following data are taken from a study conducted by the National Park System, of which Death Valley is a unit. The ground temperatures (°F) were taken from May to November in the vicinity of Furnace Creek.

146	152	168	174	180	178	179
180	178	178	168	165	152	144

Compute the mean, median, and mode for these ground temperatures.

8. $\bar{x} \approx 6.2$; median = 6; mode = 7.

8. *Ecology: Wolf Packs* How large is a wolf pack? The following information is from a random sample of winter wolf packs in regions of Alaska, Minnesota, Michigan, Wisconsin, Canada, and Finland (Source: *The Wolf*, by L. D. Mech, University of Minnesota Press). Winter pack size:

13	10	7	5	7	7	2	4	3
2	3	15	4	4	2	8	7	8

Compute the mean, median, and mode for the size of winter wolf packs.

9. (a) $\bar{x} \approx 3.27$; median = 3; mode = 3.
(b) $\bar{x} \approx 4.21$; median = 2; mode = 1.
(c) Lower Canyon mean is greater; median and mode are less.
(d) Trimmed mean = 3.75 and is closer to Upper Canyon mean.

9. *Medical: Injuries* The Grand Canyon and the Colorado River are beautiful, rugged, and sometimes dangerous. Thomas Myers is a physician at the park clinic in Grand Canyon Village. Dr. Myers has recorded (for a 5-year period) the number of visitor injuries at different landing points for commercial boat trips down the Colorado River in both the Upper and Lower Grand Canyon (Source: *Fateful Journey* by Myers, Becker, Stevens).

Upper Canyon: Number of Injuries per Landing Point Between North Canyon and Phantom Ranch

2 3 1 1 3 4 6 9 3 1 3

Lower Canyon: Number of Injuries per Landing Point Between Bright Angel and Lava Falls

8 1 1 0 6 7 2 14 3 0 1 13 2 1

(a) Compute the mean, median, and mode for injuries per landing point in the Upper Canyon.
(b) Compute the mean, median, and mode for injuries per landing point in the Lower Canyon.
(c) Compare the results of parts (a) and (b).
(d) The Lower Canyon stretch had some extreme data values. Compute a 5% trimmed mean for this region, and compare this result to the mean for the Upper Canyon computed in part (a).

10. (a) $\bar{x} \approx 26.3$ yr; median = 25.5 yr; mode = 25 yr.
(b) Median; answers are very close.

10. *Football: Age of Professional Players* How old are professional football players? The 11th Edition of *The Pro Football Encyclopedia* gave the following information. Random sample of pro football player ages in years:

24	23	25	23	30	29	28	26	33	29
24	37	25	23	22	27	28	25	31	29
25	22	31	29	22	28	27	26	23	21
25	21	25	24	22	26	25	32	26	29

(a) Compute the mean, median, and mode of the ages.
(b) Compare the averages. Does one seem to represent the age of the pro football players most accurately? Explain.

11. (a) $\bar{x} = \$136.15$; median = \$66.50; mode = \$60.
(b) Trimmed mean ≈ \$121.28; yes.
(c) Median, as well as low and high price.

11. *Leisure: Maui Vacation* How expensive is Maui? If you want a vacation rental condominium (up to four people), visit the Online Study Center at **www.cengage.com/statistics/Brase/UBS5e**, find the link to Maui, and then search for accom-

modations. The *Maui News* gave the following costs in dollars per day for a random sample of condominiums located throughout the island of Maui.

89	50	68	60	375	55	500	71	40	350
60	50	250	45	45	125	235	65	60	130

(a) Compute the mean, median, and mode for the data.
(b) Compute a 5% trimmed mean for the data, and compare it with the mean computed in part (a). Does the trimmed mean more accurately reflect the general level of the daily rental costs?
(c) If you were a travel agent and a client asked about the daily cost of renting a condominium on Maui, what average would you use? Explain. Is there any other information about the costs that you think might be useful, such as the spread of the costs?

12. 87.65.

12. *Grades: Weighted Average* In your biology class, your final grade is based on several things: a lab score, scores on two major tests, and your score on the final exam. There are 100 points available for each score. However, the lab score is worth 25% of your total grade, each major test is worth 22.5%, and the final exam is worth 30%. Compute the weighted average for the following scores: 92 on the lab, 81 on the first major test, 93 on the second major test, and 85 on the final exam.

13. 8.5.

13. *Merit Pay Scale: Weighted Average* At General Hospital, nurses are given performance evaluations to determine eligibility for merit pay raises. The supervisor rates the nurses on a scale of 1 to 10 (10 being the highest rating) for several activities: promptness, record keeping, appearance, and bedside manner with patients. Then an average is determined by giving a weight of 2 for promptness, 3 for record keeping, 1 for appearance, and 4 for bedside manner with patients. What is the average rating for a nurse with ratings of 9 for promptness, 7 for record keeping, 6 for appearance, and 10 for bedside manner?

14. (a) 67.1 mg/l.
(b) No; the average chlorine compound concentration (mg/l) seems a bit too high.

14. *EPA: Wetlands* Where does all the water go? According to the Environmental Protection Agency (EPA), in a typical wetland environment, 38% of the water is outflow; 47% is seepage; 7% evaporates; and 8% remains as water volume in the ecosystem (Reference: United States Environmental Protection Agency Case Studies Report 832-R-93-005). Chloride compounds as residuals from residential areas are a problem for wetlands. Suppose that in a particular wetland environment the following concentrations (mg/l) of chloride compounds were found: outflow, 64.1; seepage, 75.8; remaining due to evaporation, 23.9; in the water volume, 68.2.
(a) Compute the weighted average of chlorine compound concentration (mg/l) for this ecological system.
(b) Suppose the EPA has established an average chlorine compound concentration target of no more than 58 (mg/l). Comment on whether this wetlands system meets the target standard for chlorine compound concentration.

SECTION 3.2 Measures of Variation

FOCUS POINTS

- Find the range, variance, and standard deviation.
- Compute the coefficient of variation from raw data. Why is the coefficient of variation important?
- Apply Chebyshev's theorem to raw data. What does a Chebyshev interval tell us?

An average is an attempt to summarize a set of data using just one number. As some of our examples have shown, an average taken by itself may not always be very meaningful. We need a statistical cross-reference that measures the spread of the data.

The range is one such measure of variation.

The **range** is the difference between the largest and smallest values of a data distribution.

EXAMPLE 5

RANGE

Most professors find that this section contains concepts that are new to many students. A little more class time may be needed.

A large bakery regularly orders cartons of Maine blueberries. The average weight of the cartons is supposed to be 22 ounces. Random samples of cartons from two suppliers were weighed. The weights in ounces of the cartons were

Supplier I:	17	22	22	22	27
Supplier II:	17	19	20	27	27

Blueberry patch

(a) Compute the range of carton weights from each supplier.

$$\text{Range} = \text{Largest value} - \text{Smallest value}$$
$$\text{Supplier I range} = 27 - 17 = 10 \text{ ounces}$$
$$\text{Supplier II range} = 27 - 17 = 10 \text{ ounces}$$

(b) Compute the mean weight of cartons from each supplier.
In both cases the mean is 22 ounces.

(c) Look at the two samples again. The samples have the same range and mean. How do they differ? The bakery uses one carton of blueberries in each blueberry muffin recipe. It is important that the cartons be of consistent weight so that the muffins turn out right.

Supplier I provides more cartons that have weights closer to the mean. Or, put another way, the weights of cartons from Supplier I are more clustered around the mean. The bakery might find Supplier I more satisfactory.

As we see in Example 5, although the range tells the difference between the largest and smallest values in a distribution, it does not tell us how much other values vary from one another or from the mean.

Variance and Standard Deviation

Variance and standard deviation

There are many ways to measure data spread, and s is only one way (the range is another way). However, just as *standard* time is the time to which most people refer, *standard* deviation is the measure of data spread to which most people refer.

We need a measure of the distribution or spread of data around an expected value (either $\bar{x}$ or μ). The *variance* and *standard deviation* provide such measures. Formulas and rationale for these measures are described in the next Procedure display. Then, examples and guided exercises show how to compute and interpret these measures.

As we will see later, the formulas for variance and standard deviation differ slightly depending on whether we are using a sample or the entire population.

PROCEDURE

HOW TO COMPUTE THE SAMPLE VARIANCE AND SAMPLE STANDARD DEVIATION

Quantity	Description
x	The variable x represents a **data value** or outcome.
Mean $\bar{x} = \dfrac{\Sigma x}{n}$	This is the **average of the data values,** or what you "expect" to happen the next time you conduct the statistical experiment. Note that n is the sample size.

Continued

$x - \bar{x}$	This is the **difference** between what happened and what you expected to happen. This represents a "deviation" away from what you "expect" and is a measure of risk.
$\Sigma(x - \bar{x})^2$	The expression $\Sigma(x - \bar{x})^2$ is called the **sum of squares.** The $(x - \bar{x})$ quantity is squared to make it nonnegative. The sum is over all the data. If you don't square $(x - \bar{x})$, then the sum $\Sigma(x - \bar{x})$ is equal to 0 because the negative values cancel the positive values. This occurs even if some $(x - \bar{x})$ values are large, indicating a large deviation or risk.
Sum of squares $\Sigma(x - \bar{x})^2$ or $\Sigma x^2 - \frac{(\Sigma x)^2}{n}$	This is an **algebraic simplification of the sum of squares** that is easier to compute. The **defining formula** for the sum of squares is the upper one. The **computation formula** for the sum of squares is the lower one. Both formulas give the same result.
Sample variance $s^2 = \frac{\Sigma(x - \bar{x})^2}{n - 1}$ or $s^2 = \frac{\Sigma x^2 - (\Sigma x)^2/n}{n - 1}$	The **sample variance** is $\mathbf{s^2}$. The variance can be thought of as a kind of average of the $(x - \bar{x})^2$ values. However, for technical reasons, we divide the sum by the quantity $n - 1$ rather than n. This gives us the best mathematical estimate for the sample variance. The **defining formula** for the variance is the upper one. The **computation formula** for the variance is the lower one. Both formulas give the same result.
Sample standard deviation $s = \sqrt{\frac{\Sigma(x - \bar{x})^2}{n - 1}}$ or $s = \sqrt{\frac{\Sigma x^2 - (\Sigma x)^2/n}{n - 1}}$	This is the **sample standard deviation, *s*.** Why do we take the square root? Well, if the original x units were, say, days or dollars, then the s^2 units would be days squared or dollars squared (wow, what's that?). We take the square root to return to the original units of the data measurements. The standard deviation can be thought of as a measure of variability or risk. Larger values of s imply greater variability in the data. The **defining formula** for the standard deviation is the upper one. The **computation formula** for the standard deviation is the lower one. Both formulas give the same result.

COMMENT Why is s called a *sample standard* deviation? First, it is computed from sample data. Then why do we use the word *standard* in the name? We know s is a measure of deviation or risk. You should be aware that there are other statistical measures of risk that we have not yet mentioned. However, s is the one that everyone uses, so it is called the "standard" (like standard time).

Some students have trouble comprehending the information contained in a formula. It may be useful to verbalize the formula for s. It says to compare each data value to the mean, square the difference, sum the squares of the differences, then divide by the quantity $(n - 1)$ and, finally, take the square root of the result.

In statistics, the sample standard deviation and sample variance are used to describe the spread of data about the mean $\bar{x}$. The next example shows how to find these quantities by using the defining formulas. Guided Exercise 3 shows how to use the computation formulas.

As you will discover, for "hand" calculations, the computation formulas for s^2 and s are much easier to use. However, the defining formulas for s^2 and s emphasize the fact that the variance and standard deviation are based on the differences between each data value and the mean.

Defining formulas (sample statistic)

$$\text{Sample variance} = s^2 = \frac{\Sigma(x - \bar{x})^2}{n - 1} \quad (1)$$

$$\text{Sample standard deviation} = s = \sqrt{\frac{\Sigma(x - \bar{x})^2}{n - 1}} \quad (2)$$

where x is a member of the data set, $\bar{x}$ is the mean, and n is the number of data values. The sum is taken over all data values.

Computation formulas (sample statistic)

$$\text{Sample variance} = s^2 = \frac{\Sigma x^2 - (\Sigma x)^2/n}{n - 1} \qquad (3)$$

$$\text{Sample standard deviation} = s = \sqrt{\frac{\Sigma x^2 - (\Sigma x)^2/n}{n - 1}} \qquad (4)$$

where x is a member of the data set, $\bar{x}$ is the mean, and n is the number of data values. The sum is taken over all data values.

EXAMPLE 6 SAMPLE STANDARD DEVIATION (DEFINING FORMULA)

Big Blossom Greenhouse was commissioned to develop an extra large rose for the Rose Bowl Parade. A random sample of blossoms from Hybrid A bushes yielded the following diameters (in inches) for mature peak blooms.

2 3 3 8 10 10

Use the defining formula to find the sample variance and standard deviation.

SOLUTION: Several steps are involved in computing the variance and standard deviation. A table will be helpful (see Table 3-1). Since $n = 6$, we take the sum of the entries in the first column of Table 3-1 and divide by 6 to find the mean $\bar{x}$.

$$\bar{x} = \frac{\Sigma x}{n} = \frac{36}{6} = 6.0 \text{ inches}$$

TABLE 3-1 **Diameters of Rose Blossoms (in inches)**

Column I x	Column II $x - \bar{x}$	Column III $(x - \bar{x})^2$
2	$2 - 6 = -4$	$(-4)^2 = 16$
3	$3 - 6 = -3$	$(-3)^2 = 9$
3	$3 - 6 = -3$	$(-3)^2 = 9$
8	$8 - 6 = 2$	$(2)^2 = 4$
10	$10 - 6 = 4$	$(4)^2 = 16$
10	$10 - 6 = 4$	$(4)^2 = 16$
$\Sigma x = 36$		$\Sigma(x - \bar{x})^2 = 70$

Using this value for $\bar{x}$, we obtain Column II. Square each value in the second column to obtain Column III, and then add the values in Column III. To get the sample variance, divide the sum of Column III by $n - 1$. Since $n = 6, n - 1 = 5$.

$$s^2 = \frac{\Sigma(x - \bar{x})^2}{n - 1} = \frac{70}{5} = 14$$

Now obtain the sample standard deviation by taking the square root of the variance.

$$s = \sqrt{s^2} = \sqrt{14} \approx 3.74$$

(Use a calculator to compute the square root. Because of rounding, we use the approximately equal symbol, $\approx$.)

GUIDED EXERCISE 3 — Sample standard deviation (computation formula)

Big Blossom Greenhouse gathered another random sample of mature peak blooms from Hybrid B. The six blossoms had the following widths (in inches):

5 5 5 6 7 8

(a) Again, we will construct a table so that we can find the mean, variance, and standard deviation more easily. In this case, what is the value of n? Find the sum of Column I in Table 3-2, and compute the mean.

$n = 6$. The sum of Column I is $\Sigma x = 36$, so the mean is

$$\bar{x} = \frac{36}{6} = 6 \text{ inches}$$

TABLE 3-2 Complete Columns I and II

I x	II x^2
5	____
5	____
5	____
6	____
7	____
8	____
$\Sigma x =$ ____	$\Sigma x^2 =$ ____

TABLE 3-3 Completion of Table 3-2

I x	II x^2
5	25
5	25
5	25
6	36
7	49
8	64
$\Sigma x = 36$	$\Sigma x^2 = 224$

(b) What is the value of n? of $n - 1$? Use the computation formula to find the sample variance s^2. *Note:* Be sure to distinguish between Σx^2 and $(\Sigma x)^2$. For Σx^2, you square the x values first and then sum them. For $(\Sigma x)^2$, you sum the x values first and then square the result.

$n = 6$; $n - 1 = 5$.

$$s^2 = \frac{\Sigma x^2 - (\Sigma x)^2/n}{n - 1} = \frac{224 - (36)^2/6}{5} = \frac{8}{5} = 1.6$$

(c) Use a calculator to find the square root of the variance. Is this the standard deviation?

$s = \sqrt{s^2} = \sqrt{1.6} \approx 1.26$

Yes.

Let's summarize and compare the results of Guided Exercise 3 and Example 6. The greenhouse found the following blossom diameters for Hybrid A and Hybrid B:

Hybrid A: Mean, 6.0 inches; standard deviation, 3.74 inches

Hybrid B: Mean, 6.0 inches; standard deviation, 1.26 inches

In both cases, the means are the same: 6 inches. But the first hybrid has a larger standard deviation. This means that the blossoms of Hybrid A are less consistent than those of Hybrid B. If you want a rosebush that occasionally has 10-inch blooms and 2-inch blooms, use the first hybrid. But if you want a bush that consistently produces roses close to 6 inches across, use Hybrid B.

This is a good time to discuss rounding of calculated answers.

ROUNDING NOTE Rounding errors cannot be completely eliminated, even if a computer or calculator does all the computations. However, software and calculator routines are designed to minimize the error. If the mean is rounded, the value of the standard deviation will change slightly depending on how much the mean is rounded. If you do your calculations "by hand" or reenter intermediate values into a calculator, try to carry one or two more digits than occur in the original data. If your resulting answers vary slightly from those in this text, do not be overly concerned. The text answers are computer- or calculator-generated.

Population mean, variance, and standard deviation

In most applications of statistics, we work with a random sample of data rather than the entire population of *all* possible data values. However, if we have data for the entire population, we can compute the *population mean* μ, *population variance* σ^2, and *population standard deviation* σ (lowercase Greek letter sigma) using the following formulas:

This is a good time once again to stress the difference between sample data and population data. It is interesting to note that the concept of population variance σ^2 was borrowed from classical mechanics. If you check a college physics textbook, you will find that the formula for σ^2 is essentially the same formula physicists use for the second moment.

Population parameters

$$\text{Population mean} = \mu = \frac{\Sigma x}{N}$$

$$\text{Population variance} = \sigma^2 = \frac{\Sigma(x - \mu)^2}{N}$$

$$\text{Population standard deviation} = \sigma = \sqrt{\frac{\Sigma(x - \mu)^2}{N}}$$

where N is the number of data values in the population and x represents the individual data values of the population.

Problems 13 through 17 discuss the mean and standard deviation for *grouped data.*

We note that the formula for μ is the same as the formula for $\bar{x}$ (the sample mean) and the formulas for σ^2 and σ are the same as those for s^2 and s (sample variance and sample standard deviation), except that the population size N is used instead of $n - 1$. Also, μ is used instead of $\bar{x}$ in the formulas for σ^2 and σ.

In the formulas for s and σ we use $n - 1$ to compute s, and N to compute σ. Why? The reason is that N (capital letter) represents the *population size,* whereas n (lowercase letter) represents the sample size. Since a random sample usually will not contain extreme data values (large or small), we divide by $n - 1$ in the formula for s to make s a little larger than it would have been had we divided by n. Courses in advanced theoretical statistics show that this procedure will give us the best possible estimate for the standard deviation σ. In fact, s is called the *unbiased estimate* for σ. If we have the population of all data values, then extreme data values are, of course, present, so we divide by N instead of $N - 1$.

COMMENT The computation formula for the population standard deviation is

$$\sigma = \sqrt{\frac{\Sigma x^2 - (\Sigma x)^2/N}{N}}$$

We've seen that the standard deviation (sample or population) is a measure of data spread. We will use the standard deviation extensively in later chapters.

TECH NOTES Most scientific or business calculators have a statistics mode and provide the mean and sample standard deviation directly. The TI-84Plus/TI-83Plus calculators, Excel, and Minitab provide the median and several other measures as well.

In Chapter 7 we will use the standard deviation to study standard z values and areas under normal curves. In Chapters 8 and 9 we will use it to study the inferential statistics topics of estimation and testing. The standard deviation will appear again in our study of regression and correlation.

Many technologies display only the sample standard deviation s. You can quickly compute σ if you know s by using the formula

$$\sigma = s\sqrt{\frac{n-1}{n}}$$

The mean given in displays can be interpreted as the sample mean $\overline{x}$ or the population mean μ as appropriate.

The three displays show output for the hybrid rose data of Guided Exercise 3.

TI-84Plus/TI-83Plus Display Press **STAT ➤ CALC ➤ 1:1-Var Stats.** S_x is the sample standard deviation. σ_x is the population standard deviation.

```
1-Var Stats
 x̄=6
 Σx=36
 Σx²=224
 Sx=1.264911064
 σx=1.154700538
↓n=6
```

Excel Display Menu choices: **Tools ➤ Data Analysis ➤ Descriptive Statistics.** Check the summary statistics box. The standard deviation is the sample standard deviation.

Column 1	
Mean	6
Standard Error	0.516398
Median	5.5
Mode	5
Standard Deviation	1.264911
Sample Variance	1.6
Kurtosis	–0.78125
Skewness	0.889391
Range	3
Minimum	5
Maximum	8
Sum	36
Count	6

Minitab Display Menu choices: **Stat ➤ Basic Statistics ➤ Display Descriptive Statistics.** StDev is the sample standard deviation. TrMean is a 5% trimmed mean.

```
N          Mean      Median     TrMean      StDev     SE Mean
6          6.000     5.500      6.000       1.265     0.516
Minimum         Maximum      Q1          Q3
5.000           8.000        5.000       7.250
```

Now let's look at two immediate applications of the standard deviation. The first is the coefficient of variation, and the second is Chebyshev's theorem.

Coefficient of Variation

Coefficient of variation

A disadvantage of the standard deviation as a comparative measure of variation is that it depends on the units of measurement. This means that it is difficult to use the standard deviation to compare measurements from different populations. For this reason, statisticians have defined the *coefficient of variation,* which expresses the standard deviation as a percentage of the sample or population mean.

A good class discussion topic about *CV* can be found in Linking Concepts, Problem 3 (robin eggs and elephants). See also Data Highlights, Problem 1 (Old Faithful).

If $\bar{x}$ and s represent the sample mean and sample standard deviation, respectively, then the sample **coefficient of variation** CV is defined to be

$$CV = \frac{s}{\bar{x}} \cdot 100$$

If μ and σ represent the population mean and population standard deviation, respectively, then the population coefficient of variation CV is defined to be

$$CV = \frac{\sigma}{\mu} \cdot 100$$

Notice that the numerator and denominator in the definition of CV have the same units, so CV itself has no units of measurement. This gives us the advantage of being able to directly compare the variability of two different populations using the coefficient of variation.

In the next example and guided exercise, we will compute the CV of a population and of a sample and then compare the results.

EXAMPLE 7 COEFFICIENT OF VARIATION

The Trading Post on Grand Mesa is a small, family-run store in a remote part of Colorado. The Grand Mesa region contains many good fishing lakes, so the Trading Post sells spinners (a type of fishing lure). The store has a very limited selection of spinners. In fact, the Trading Post has only eight different types of spinners for sale. The prices (in dollars) are

2.10 1.95 2.60 2.00 1.85 2.25 2.15 2.25

Since the Trading Post has only eight different kinds of spinners for sale, we consider the eight data values to be the *population.*

(a) Use a calculator with appropriate statistics keys to verify that for the Trading Post data, $\mu \approx \$2.14$ and $\sigma \approx \$0.22$.

SOLUTION: Since the computation formulas for $\bar{x}$ and μ are identical, most calculators provide the value of $\bar{x}$ only. Use the output of this key for μ. The computation formulas for the sample standard deviation s and the population standard deviation σ are slightly different. Be sure that you use the key for σ (sometimes designated as σ_n or σ_x).

(b) Compute the CV of prices for the Trading Post and comment on the meaning of the result.

SOLUTION:

$$CV = \frac{\sigma}{\mu} \times 100 = \frac{0.22}{2.14} \times 100 = 10.28\%$$

The coefficient of variation can be thought of as a measure of the spread of the data relative to the average of the data. Since the Trading Post is very small, it carries a small selection of spinners that are all priced similarly. The CV tells us that the standard deviation of the spinner prices is only 10.28% of the mean.

GUIDED EXERCISE 4 Coefficient of variation

Cabela's in Sidney, Nebraska, is a very large outfitter that carries a broad selection of fishing tackle. It markets its products nationwide through a catalog service. A random sample of 10 spinners from Cabela's extensive spring catalog gave the following prices (in dollars):

1.69 1.49 3.09 1.79 1.39 2.89 1.49 1.39 1.49 1.99

(a) Use a calculator with sample mean and sample standard deviation keys to compute $\bar{x}$ and s.

→ $\bar{x} = \$1.87$ and $s \approx \$0.62$.

(b) Compute the CV for the spinner prices at Cabela's.

→ $CV = \frac{s}{\bar{x}} \times 100 = \frac{0.62}{1.87} \times 100 = 33.16\%$

(c) Compare the mean, standard deviation, and CV for the spinner prices at the Grand Mesa Trading Post (Example 7) and Cabela's. Comment on the differences.

→ The CV for Cabela's is more than three times the CV for the Trading Post. Why? First, because of the remote location, the Trading Post tends to have somewhat higher prices (larger μ). Second, the Trading Post is very small, so it has a rather limited selection of spinners with a smaller variation in price.

Chebyshev's Theorem

Chebyshev's theorem is a little abstract and may require some extra class time. Stress the completely general nature of Chebyshev's theorem. A good class discussion topic can be found in Linking Concepts, Problem 4 (butterflies and the orbits of the planets).

From our earlier discussion about standard deviation, we recall that the spread or dispersion of a set of data about the mean will be small if the standard deviation is small, and it will be large if the standard deviation is large. If we are dealing with a symmetrical bell-shaped distribution, then we can make very definite statements about the proportion of the data that must lie within a certain number of standard deviations on either side of the mean. This will be discussed in detail in Chapter 7 when we talk about normal distributions.

However, the concept of data spread about the mean can be expressed quite generally for *all data distributions* (skewed, symmetric, or other shape) by using the remarkable theorem of Chebyshev.

Chebyshev's theorem

For *any* set of data (either population or sample) and for any constant k greater than 1, the proportion of the data that must lie within k standard deviations on either side of the mean is *at least*

$$1 - \frac{1}{k^2}$$

Results of Chebyshev's theorem

For *any* set of data:

- *at least* 75% of the data fall in the interval from $\mu - 2\sigma$ to $\mu + 2\sigma$.
- *at least* 88.9% of the data fall in the interval from $\mu - 3\sigma$ to $\mu + 3\sigma$.
- *at least* 93.8% of the data fall in the interval from $\mu - 4\sigma$ to $\mu + 4\sigma$.

The results of Chebyshev's theorem can be derived by using the theorem and a little arithmetic. For instance, if we create an interval $k = 2$ standard deviations on either side of the mean, Chebyshev's theorem tells us that

$$1 - \frac{1}{2^2} = 1 - \frac{1}{4} = \frac{3}{4} \text{ or } 75\%$$

is the minimum percentage of data in the $\mu - 2\sigma$ to $\mu + 2\mu$ interval.

Notice that Chebyshev's theorem refers to the *minimum* percentage of data that must fall within the specified number of standard deviations of the mean. If the distribution is mound-shaped, an even *greater* percentage of data will fall into the specified intervals (see the Empirical Rule in Section 7.1).

EXAMPLE 8 CHEBYSHEV'S THEOREM

Students Who Care is a student volunteer program in which college students donate work time to various community projects such as planting trees. Professor Gill is the faculty sponsor for this student volunteer program. For several years, Dr. Gill has kept a careful record of x = total number of work hours volunteered by a student in the program each semester. For a random sample of students in the program, the mean number of hours was $\bar{x} = 29.1$ hours each semester, with a standard deviation of $s = 1.7$ hours each semester. Find an interval A to B for the number of hours volunteered into which at least 75% of the students in this program would fall.

SOLUTION: According to results of Chebyshev's theorem, at least 75% of the data must fall within 2 standard deviations of the mean. Because the mean is $\bar{x} = 29.1$ and the standard deviation is $s = 1.7$, the interval is

$$\bar{x} - 2s \text{ to } \bar{x} + 2s$$
$$29.1 - 2(1.7) \text{ to } 29.1 + 2(1.7)$$
$$25.7 \text{ to } 32.5$$

At least 75% of the students would fall into the group that volunteered from 25.7 to 32.5 hours each semester.

GUIDED EXERCISE 5 **Chebyshev interval**

The *East Coast Independent News* periodically runs ads in its own classified section offering a month's free subscription to those who respond. In this way, management can get a sense of the number of subscribers who read the classified section each day. Over a period of 2 years, careful records have been kept. The mean number of responses per ad is $\bar{x} = 525$, with standard deviation $s = 30$.

Determine a Chebyshev interval about the mean in which at least 88.9% of the data fall.

By Chebyshev's theorem, at least 88.9% of the data fall into the interval

$\bar{x} - 3s$ to $\bar{x} + 3s$

Because $\bar{x} = 525$ and $s = 30$, the interval is

$525 - 3(30)$ to $525 + 3(30)$

or from 435 to 615 responses per ad.

CRITICAL THINKING

Averages such as the mean are often referred to in the media. However, an average by itself does not tell much about the way data are distributed about the mean. Knowledge about the standard deviation or variance, along with the mean, gives a much better picture of the data distribution.

Chebyshev's theorem tells us that no matter what the data distribution looks like, at least 75% of the data will fall within 2 standard deviations of the mean. As we will see in Chapter 7, when the distribution is mound-shaped and symmetrical, about 95% of the data are within 2 standard deviations of the mean. Data values beyond 2 standard deviations from the mean are less common than those closer to the mean.

In fact, one indicator that a data value might be an *outlier* is that it is more than 2.5 standard deviations from the mean (*Oxford Dictionary of Statistics*, Oxford University Press).

VIEWPOINT Socially Responsible Investing

Make a difference and *make money! Socially responsible mutual funds tend to screen out corporations that sell tobacco, weapons, and alcohol, as well as companies that are environmentally unfriendly. In addition, these funds screen out companies that use child labor in sweatshops. There are 68 socially responsible funds tracked by the Social Investment Forum. For more information, visit the Online Study Center at* **www.cengage.com/statistics/Brase/UBS5e** *and find the link to social investing.*

How do these funds rate compared to other funds? One way to answer this question is to study the annual percent returns of the funds using both the mean and standard deviation. (See Problem 12 of this section.)

SECTION 3.2 PROBLEMS

Tables and art to accompany margin answers may be found in the back of the book.

1. Mean.
2. The standard deviation s is the square root of the variance s^2.
3. Yes. For the sample standard deviation s, the sum $\Sigma(x - \bar{x})^2$ is divided by $n - 1$, where n is the sample size. For the population standard deviation σ, the sum $\Sigma(x - \mu)^2$ is divided by N, where N is the population size.
4. Sample statistic: s. Population parameter: σ.
5. (a) (i), (ii), (iii).
   (b) The data change between data sets (i) and (ii) increased the squared difference $\Sigma(x - \bar{x})^2$ by 10, whereas the data change between data sets (ii) and (iii) increased the squared difference $\Sigma(x - \bar{x})^2$ by only 6.

1. *Statistical Literacy* Which average—mean, median, or mode—is associated with the standard deviation?

2. *Statistical Literacy* What is the relationship between the variance and the standard deviation for a sample data set?

3. *Statistical Literacy* When computing the standard deviation, does it matter whether the data are sample data or data comprising the entire population? Explain.

4. *Statistical Literacy* What symbol is used for the standard deviation when it is a sample statistic? What symbol is used for the standard deviation when it is a population parameter?

5. ***Critical Thinking*** Each of the following data sets has a mean of $\bar{x} = 10$.

   (i) 8 9 10 11 12 (ii) 7 9 10 11 13 (iii) 7 8 10 12 13

   (a) Without doing any computations, order the data sets according to increasing value of standard deviations.
   (b) Why do you expect the difference in standard deviations between data sets (i) and (ii) to be greater than the difference in standard deviations between data sets (ii) and (iii)? *Hint:* Consider how much the data in the respective sets differ from the mean.

6. (a) No.
(b) Yes, since 80 is more than 2.5 standard deviations above the mean.

7. (a) 15.
(b) Use a calculator.
(c) 37; 6.08.
(d) 37; 6.08.
(e) $\sigma^2 \approx 29.59$; $\sigma \approx 5.44$.

8. (a) $\Sigma x = 103$; $\Sigma x^2 = 4607$; $\Sigma y = 90$; $\Sigma y^2 = 2258$.
(b) For total stock: $\bar{x} = 10.3$; $s^2 \approx 394.0$; $s \approx 19.85$. For balanced: $\bar{y} = 9$; $s^2 \approx 160.8$; $s \approx 12.68$.
(c) For total stock x, -29.4 to 50; for balanced y, -16.36 to 34.36; 75% of the returns for the balanced fund fall within a narrower range than those of the stock fund. In particular, the low returns for the balanced fund are not as low as those of the stock fund. However, the stock fund returns range to higher values than the balanced fund returns.
(d) For the stock fund, $CV \approx 192.7\%$; for the balanced fund, $CV \approx 140.9\%$. For each unit of return, the balanced fund has lower risk.

9. (a) 7.87.
(b) Use a calculator.
(c) $\bar{x} \approx 1.24$; $s^2 \approx 1.78$; $s \approx 1.33$.
(d) $CV \approx 107\%$. The standard deviation of the time to failure is just slightly larger than the average time.

6. *Critical Thinking: Outliers* One indicator of an outlier is that an observation is more than 2.5 standard deviations from the mean. Consider the data value 80.
(a) If a data set has mean 70 and standard deviation 5, is 80 a suspect outlier?
(b) If a data set has mean 70 and standard deviation 3, is 80 a suspect outlier?

7. *General Concepts: Variance, Standard Deviation* Given the sample data

x:	23	17	15	30	25

(a) Find the range.
(b) Verify that $\Sigma x = 110$ and $\Sigma x^2 = 2568$.
(c) Use the results of part (b) and appropriate computation formulas to compute the sample variance s^2 and sample standard deviation s.
(d) Use the defining formulas to compute the sample variance s^2 and sample standard deviation s.
(e) Suppose the given data comprise the entire population of all x values. Compute the population variance σ^2 and population standard deviation σ.

8. *Investing: Stocks and Bonds* Do bonds reduce the overall risk of an investment portfolio? Let x be a random variable representing annual percent return for Vanguard Total Stock Index (all stocks). Let y be a random variable representing annual return for Vanguard Balanced Index (60% stock and 40% bond). For the past several years, we have the following data (Reference: Morningstar Research Group, Chicago).

x:	11	0	36	21	31	23	24	−11	−11	−21
y:	10	−2	29	14	22	18	14	−2	−3	−10

(a) Compute Σx, Σx^2, Σy, and Σy^2.
(b) Use the results of part (a) to compute the sample mean, variance, and standard deviation for x and for y.
(c) Compute a 75% Chebyshev interval about the mean for x values and also for y values. Use the intervals to compare the two funds.
(d) Compute the coefficient of variation for each fund. Use the coefficients of variation to compare the two funds. If s represents risk and $\bar{x}$ represents expected return, then $s/\bar{x}$ can be thought of as a measure of risk per unit of expected return. In this case, why is a smaller CV better? Explain.

9. *Space Shuttle: Epoxy* Kevlar epoxy is a material used on the NASA Space Shuttle. Strands of this epoxy were tested at the 90% breaking strength. The following data represent time to failure (in hours) for a random sample of 50 epoxy strands (Reference: R. E. Barlow, University of California, Berkeley). Let x be a random variable representing time to failure (in hours) at 90% breaking strength. *Note:* These data are also available for download at the Online Study Center.

0.54	1.80	1.52	2.05	1.03	1.18	0.80	1.33	1.29	1.11
3.34	1.54	0.08	0.12	0.60	0.72	0.92	1.05	1.43	3.03
1.81	2.17	0.63	0.56	0.03	0.09	0.18	0.34	1.51	1.45
1.52	0.19	1.55	0.02	0.07	0.65	0.40	0.24	1.51	1.45
1.60	1.80	4.69	0.08	7.89	1.58	1.64	0.03	0.23	0.72

(a) Find the range.
(b) Use a calculator to verify that $\Sigma x = 62.11$ and $\Sigma x^2 \approx 164.23$.
(c) Use the results of part (b) to compute the sample mean, variance, and standard deviation for the time to failure.
(d) Use the results of part (c) to compute the coefficient of variation. What does this number say about time to failure? Why does a small CV indicate more consistent data, whereas a larger CV indicates less consistent data? Explain.

10. (a) $\Sigma x = 284.95$; $\Sigma x^2 \approx 7046.80$; $\Sigma y = 421.5$; $\Sigma y^2 \approx 14{,}562.29$.
(b) For Grid E, $\bar{x} \approx 20.35$; $s^2 \approx 96$; $s \approx 9.79$; for Grid H, $\bar{y} = 28.1$; $s^2 \approx 194$; $s \approx 13.93$.
(c) For Grid E, 0.77 to 39.93; for Grid H, 0.24 to 55.96. Grid H shows a wider 75% range of values.
(d) For Grid E, $CV \approx 48\%$; for Grid H, $CV \approx 50\%$. Grid H demonstrates slightly greater variability per expected signal. The *CV*, together with the Chebyshev interval, indicates that Grid H might have more buried artifacts.

11. (a) Use a calculator.
(b) $\bar{x} = 49$; $s^2 \approx 687.49$; $s \approx 26.22$.
(c) $\bar{y} = 44.8$; $s^2 \approx 508.50$; $s \approx 22.55$.
(d) Mallard nest $CV \approx 53.5\%$; Canada goose nest $CV \approx 50.3\%$. The *CV* gives the ratio of the standard deviation to the mean; the *CV* for mallard nests is slightly higher.

10. *Archaeology: Ireland* The Hill of Tara in Ireland is a place of great archaeological importance. This region has been occupied by people for more than 4,000 years. Geomagnetic surveys detect subsurface anomalies in the earth's magnetic field. These surveys have led to many significant archaeological discoveries. After collecting data, the next step is to begin a statistical study. The following data measure magnetic susceptibility (centimeter-gram-second $\times 10^{-6}$) on two of the main grids of the Hill of Tara (Reference: *Tara: An Archaeological Survey* by Conor Newman, Royal Irish Academy, Dublin).

Grid E: *x* variable

13.20	5.60	19.80	15.05	21.40	17.25	27.45
16.95	23.90	32.40	40.75	5.10	17.75	28.35

Grid H: *y* variable

11.85	15.25	21.30	17.30	27.50	10.35	14.90
48.70	25.40	25.95	57.60	34.35	38.80	41.00
31.25						

(a) Compute Σx, Σx^2, Σy, and Σy^2.
(b) Use the results of part (a) to compute the sample mean, variance, and standard deviation for *x* and for *y*.
(c) Compute a 75% Chebyshev interval about the mean for *x* values and also for *y* values. Use the intervals to compare the magnetic susceptibility on the two grids. Higher numbers indicate higher magnetic susceptibility. However, extreme values, high or low, could mean an anomaly and possible archaeological treasure.
(d) Compute the sample coefficient of variation for each grid. Use the *CV*s to compare the two grids. If *s* represents variability in the signal (magnetic susceptibility) and $\bar{x}$ represents the expected level of the signal, then $s/\bar{x}$ can be thought of as a measure of the variability per unit of expected signal. Remember, a considerable variability in the signal (above or below average) might indicate buried artifacts. Why, in this case, would a large *CV* be better, or at least more exciting? Explain.

11. *Wildlife: Mallard Ducks and Canada Geese* For mallard ducks and Canada geese, what percentage of nests are successful (at least one offspring survives)? Studies in Montana, Illinois, Wyoming, Utah, and California gave the following percentages of successful nests (Reference: *The Wildlife Society Press*, Washington, D.C.).

***x*: Percentage success for mallard duck nests**

56	85	52	13	39

***y*: Percentage success for Canada goose nests**

24	53	60	69	18

(a) Use a calculator to verify that $\Sigma x = 245$; $\Sigma x^2 = 14{,}755$; $\Sigma y = 224$; and $\Sigma y^2 = 12{,}070$.
(b) Use the results of part (a) to compute the sample mean, variance, and standard deviation for *x*, the percent of successful mallard nests.
(c) Use the results of part (a) to compute the sample mean, variance, and standard deviation for *y*, the percent of successful Canada goose nests.
(d) Use the results of parts (b) and (c) to compute the coefficient of variation for successful mallard nests and Canada goose nests. Write a brief explanation of the meaning of these numbers. What do these results say about the nesting success rates for mallards compared to Canada geese? Would you say one group of data is more or less consistent than the other? Explain.

12. (a) Pax, $CV \approx 146.7\%$; Vanguard, $CV \approx 138.6\%$. Vanguard fund has slightly less risk per unit of return.
(b) Pax, -18.52% to 37.68%; Vanguard, -15.98% to 34.02%. Vanguard has a narrower range of returns, with less downside but also less upside.

12. *Investing: Socially Responsible Mutual Funds* Pax World Balanced is a highly respected, socially responsible mutual fund of stocks and bonds (see Viewpoint). Vanguard Balanced Index is another highly regarded fund that represents the entire U.S. stock and bond market (an index fund). The mean and standard deviation of annualized percent returns are shown below. The annualized mean and standard deviation are based on the years 1993 through 2002 (Source: Morningstar).

Pax World Balanced: $\bar{x} = 9.58\%$; $s = 14.05\%$

Vanguard Balanced Index: $\bar{x} = 9.02\%$; $s = 12.50\%$

(a) Compute the coefficient of variation for each fund. If $\bar{x}$ represents return and s represents risk, then explain why the coefficient of variation can be taken to represent risk per unit of return. From this point of view, which fund appears to be better? Explain.

(b) Compute a 75% Chebyshev interval about the mean for each fund. Use the intervals to compare the two funds. As usual, past performance does not guarantee future performance.

13. Since $CV = s/\bar{x}$, then $s = CV(\bar{x})$. $s = 0.033$.

13. *Medical: Physician Visits* In some reports, the mean and coefficient of variation are given. For instance, in *Statistical Abstract of the United States*, 116th Edition, one report gives the average number of physician visits by males per year. The average reported is 2.2, and the reported coefficient of variation is 1.5%. Use this information to determine the standard deviation of the annual number of visits to physicians made by males.

Grouped data

Expand your knowledge: Grouped data

When data are grouped, such as in a frequency table or histogram, we can estimate the mean and standard deviation by using the following formulas. Notice that all data values in a given class are treated as though each of them equals the midpoint x of the class.

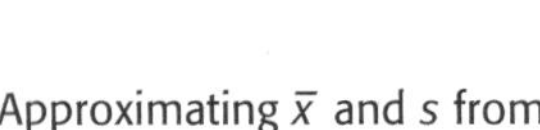

Approximating $\bar{x}$ and s from grouped data

Sample mean for a frequency distribution

$$\bar{x} = \frac{\Sigma xf}{n} \tag{5}$$

Sometimes grouped data are the only data we can get our hands on. In other situations, it is easier first to group the data and then to estimate the mean and standard deviation.

Sample standard deviation for a frequency distribution

$$s = \sqrt{\frac{\Sigma(x - \bar{x})^2 f}{n - 1}} \tag{6}$$

Computation formula for the sample standard deviation

$$s = \sqrt{\frac{\Sigma x^2 f - (\Sigma xf)^2/n}{n - 1}} \tag{7}$$

where

x is the midpoint of a class,

f is the number of entries in that class,

n is the total number of entries in the distribution, and $n = \Sigma f$.

The summation Σ is over all classes in the distribution.

Use formulas (5) and (6) or (5) and (7) to solve Problems 14–17. To use formulas (5) and (6) to evaluate the sample mean and standard deviation, use the following column heads:

Midpoint x	Frequency f	xf	$(x - \bar{x})$	$(x - \bar{x})^2$	$(x - \bar{x})^2 f$

For formulas (5) and (7), use these column heads:

Midpoint x	Frequency f	xf	x^2	$x^2 f$

Note: On the TI-84Plus/TI-83Plus calculators, enter the midpoints in column L_1 and the frequencies in column L_2. Then use **1-VarStats L_1, L_2**.

14. $\bar{x} \approx 16.1$; $s^2 \approx 119.9$; $s \approx 10.95$.

14. *Grouped Data: Anthropology* What was the age distribution of prehistoric Native Americans? Extensive anthropologic studies in the southwestern United States gave the following information about a prehistoric extended family group of 80 members who lived on what is now the Navajo Reservation in northwestern New Mexico. (Source: Based on information taken from *Prehistory in the Navajo Reservation District*, by F. W. Eddy, Museum of New Mexico Press.)

Age range (years)	1–10*	11–20	21–30	31 and over
Number of individuals	34	18	17	11

* Includes infants.

For this community, estimate the mean age expressed in years, the sample variance, and the sample standard deviation. For the class 31 and over, use 35.5 as the class midpoint.

15. $\bar{x} \approx 35.8$; $s^2 \approx 61.1$; $s \approx 7.82$.

15. *Grouped Data: Shoplifting* What is the age distribution of adult shoplifters (21 years of age or older) in supermarkets? The following is based on information taken from the National Retail Federation. A random sample of 895 incidents of shoplifting gave the following age distribution:

Age range (years)	21–30	31–40	41 and over
Number of shoplifters	260	348	287

Estimate the mean age, sample variance, and sample standard deviation for the shoplifters. For the class 41 and over, use 45.5 as the class midpoint.

16. $\bar{x} \approx 7.9$ hours; $s \approx 1.05$ hours; $CV \approx 13.29\%$.

16. *Grouped Data: Hours of Sleep per Day* Alexander Borbely is a professor at the University of Zurich Medical School, where he is director of the sleep laboratory. The histogram in Figure 3-2 is based on information from his book *Secrets of Sleep*. The histogram displays hours of sleep per day for a random sample of 200 subjects. Estimate the mean hours of sleep, standard deviation of hours of sleep, and coefficient of variation.

FIGURE 3-2 Hours of Sleep Each Day (24-hour period)

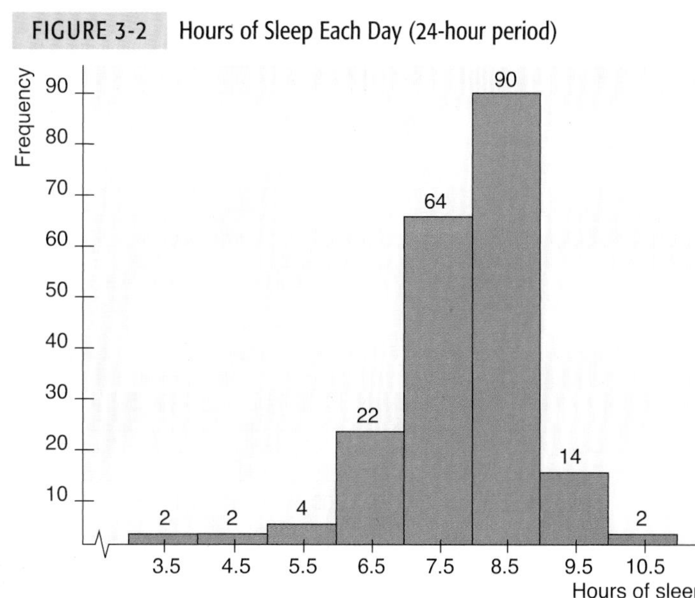

17. $\bar{x} \approx 15.6$; $s^2 \approx 23.4$; $s \approx 4.8$.

17. *Grouped Data: Business Administration* What are the big corporations doing with their wealth? One way to answer this question is to examine profits as percentage of assets. A random sample of 50 *Fortune 500* companies gave the following information. (*Source*: Based on information from *Fortune 500*, Vol. 135, No. 8.)

Profit as percentage of assets	8.6–12.5	12.6–16.5	16.6–20.5	20.6–24.5	24.6–28.5
Number of companies	15	20	5	7	3

Estimate the sample mean, sample variance, and sample standard deviation for profit as percentage of assets.

SECTION 3.3

Percentiles and Box-and-Whisker Plots

FOCUS POINTS

- Interpret the meaning of percentile scores.
- Compute the median, quartiles, and five-number summary from raw data.
- Make a box-and-whisker plot. Interpret the results.
- Describe how a box-and-whisker plot indicates spread of data about the median.

We've seen measures of central tendency and spread for a set of data. The arithmetic mean $\bar{x}$ and the standard deviation s will be very useful in later work. However, because they each utilize every data value, they can be heavily influenced by one or two extreme data values. In cases where our data distributions are heavily skewed or even bimodal, we often get a better summary of the distribution by utilizing relative position of data rather than exact values.

Recall that the median is an average computed by using relative position of the data. If we are told that 81 is the median score on a biology test, we know that after the data have been ordered, 50% of the data fall at or below the median value of 81. The median is an example of a *percentile;* in fact, it is the 50th percentile. The general definition of the Pth percentile follows.

Percentile

For whole numbers P (where $1 \le P \le 99$), the Pth **percentile** of a distribution is a value such that P% of the data fall at or below it and $(100 - P)$% of the data fall at or above it.

In Figure 3-3, we see the 60th percentile marked on a histogram. We see that 60% of the data lie below the mark and 40% lie above it.

FIGURE 3-3

A Histogram with the 60th Percentile Shown

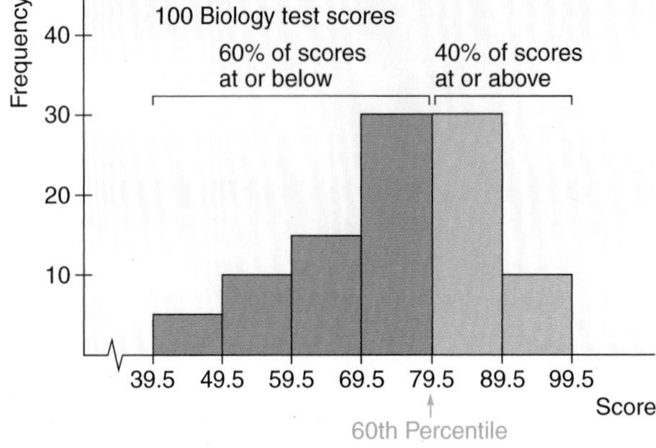

GUIDED EXERCISE 6 Percentiles

You took the English achievement test to obtain college credit in freshman English by examination.

(a) If your score is at the 89th percentile, what percentage of scores are at or below yours?

→ The percentile means that 89% of the scores are at or below yours.

(b) If the scores ranged from 1 to 100 and your raw score is 95, does this necessarily mean that your score is at the 95th percentile?

→ No, the percentile gives an indication of relative position of the scores. The determination of your percentile has to do with the number of scores at or below yours. If everyone did very well and only 80% of the scores fell at or below yours, you would be at the 80th percentile even though you got 95 out of 100 points on the exam.

There are 99 percentiles, and in an ideal situation, the 99 percentiles divide the data set into 100 equal parts. (See Figure 3-4.) However, if the number of data elements is not exactly divisible by 100, the percentiles will not divide the data into equal parts.

FIGURE 3-4

Percentiles

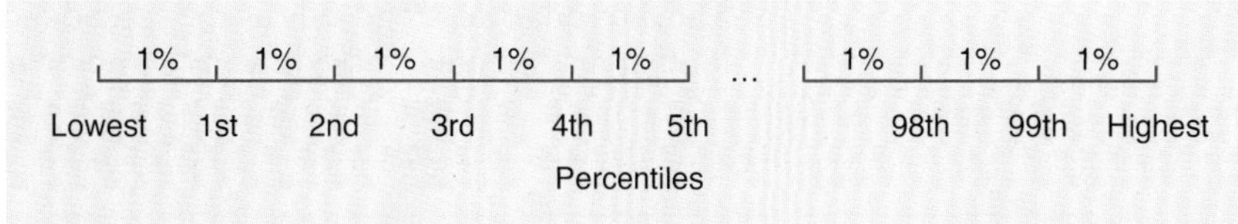

There are several widely used conventions for finding percentiles. They lead to slightly different values for different situations, but these values are close together. For all conventions, the data are first *ranked* or ordered from smallest to largest. A natural way to find the Pth percentile is to then find a value such that P% of the data fall at or below it. This will not always be possible, so we take the nearest value satisfying the criterion. It is at this point that there are a variety of processes to determine the exact value of the percentile.

Quartiles

We will not be very concerned about exact procedures for evaluating percentiles in general. However, *quartiles* are special percentiles used so frequently that we want to adopt a specific procedure for their computation.

Quartiles are those percentiles that divide the data into fourths. The *first quartile* Q_1 is the 25th percentile, the *second quartile* Q_2 is the median, and the *third quartile* Q_3 is the 75th percentile. (See Figure 3-5.)

FIGURE 3-5

Quartiles

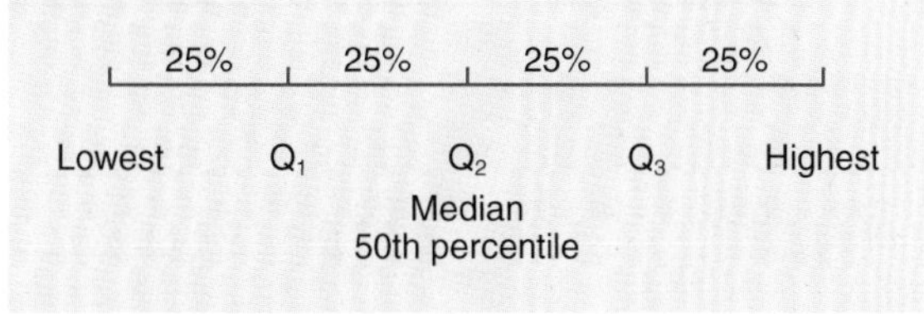

Again, several conventions are used for computing quartiles, but the following convention utilizes the median and is widely adopted.

PROCEDURE

It is helpful to remind students that the median itself does not fall into either the lower or upper half of the data. In the case of an even number of data, however, the two values used to compute the median are included in the lower and upper halves of the data, respectively.

HOW TO COMPUTE QUARTILES

1. Order the data from smallest to largest.
2. Find the median. This is the second quartile.
3. The first quartile Q_1 is then the median of the lower half of the data; that is, it is the median of the data falling *below* the Q_2 position (and not including Q_2).
4. The third quartile Q_3 is the median of the upper half of the data; that is, it is the median of the data falling *above* the Q_2 position (and not including Q_2).

In short, all we do to find the quartiles is find three medians.

Interquartile range

The median, or second quartile, is a popular measure of the center utilizing relative position. A useful measure of data spread utilizing relative position is the *interquartile range (IQR)*. It is simply the difference between the third and first quartiles.

$$\textbf{Interquartile range} = Q_3 - Q_1$$

The interquartile range tells us the spread of the middle half of the data. Now let's look at an example to see how to compute all of these quantities.

EXAMPLE 9 QUARTILES

In a hurry? On the run? Hungry as well? How about an ice cream bar as a snack? Ice cream bars are popular among all age groups. *Consumer Reports* did a study of ice cream bars. Twenty-seven bars with taste ratings of at least "fair" were listed, and cost per bar was included in the report. Just how much will an ice cream bar cost? The data, expressed in dollars, appear in Table 3-4. As you can see, the cost varies quite a bit, partly because the bars are not of uniform size.

TABLE 3-4 **Cost of Ice Cream Bars** (in dollars)

0.99	1.07	1.00	0.50	0.37	1.03	1.07	1.07
0.97	0.63	0.33	0.50	0.97	1.08	0.47	0.84
1.23	0.25	0.50	0.40	0.33	0.35	0.17	0.38
0.20	0.18	0.16					

TABLE 3-5 **Ordered Cost of Ice Cream Bars** (in dollars)

0.16	0.17	0.18	0.20	0.25	0.33	0.33	0.35
0.37	0.38	0.40	0.47	0.50	0.50	0.50	0.63
0.84	0.97	0.97	0.99	1.00	1.03	1.07	1.07
1.07	1.08	1.23					

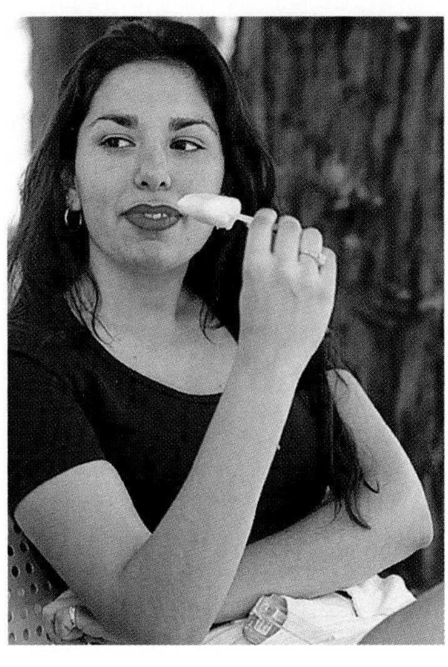

(a) Find the quartiles.

SOLUTION: We first order the data from smallest to largest. Table 3-5 shows the data in order. Next, we find the median. Since the number of data values is 27, there are an odd number of data, and the median is simply the center or 14th value. The value is shown boxed in Table 3-5.

$$\text{Median} = Q_2 = 0.50$$

There are 13 values below the median position, and Q_1 is the median of these values. It is the middle or seventh value and is shaded in Table 3-5.

$$\text{First quartile} = Q_1 = 0.33$$

There are also 13 values above the median position. The median of these is the seventh value from the right end. This value is also shaded in Table 3-5.

$$\text{Third quartile} = Q_3 = 1.00$$

(b) Find the interquartile range.

SOLUTION:

$$\begin{aligned} IQR &= Q_3 - Q_1 \\ &= 1.00 - 0.33 \\ &= 0.67 \end{aligned}$$

This means that the middle half of the data has a cost spread of 67¢.

GUIDED EXERCISE 7 Quartiles

Many people consider the number of calories in an ice cream bar as important as, if not more important than, the cost. The *Consumer Reports* article also included the calorie count of the rated ice cream bars (Table 3-6). There were 22 vanilla-flavored bars rated. Again, the bars varied in size, and some of the smaller bars had fewer calories. The calorie counts for the vanilla bars follow.

TABLE 3-6 Calories in Vanilla-Flavored Ice Cream Bars

342	377	319	353	295
234	294	286	377	182
310	439	111	201	182
197	209	147	190	151
131	151			

(a) Our first step is to order the data. See Table 3-7. 

TABLE 3-7 Ordered Data

111	131	147	151	151	182
182	190	197	201	209	234
286	294	295	310	319	342
353	377	377	439		

(b) There are 22 data values. Find the median. 

Average the 11th and 12th data values boxed together in Table 3-7.

$$\begin{aligned} \text{Median} &= \frac{209 + 234}{2} \\ &= 221.5 \end{aligned}$$

Continued

GUIDED EXERCISE 7 *continued*

(c) How many values are below the median position? Find Q_1.

Since the median lies halfway between the 11th and 12th values, there are 11 values below the median position. Q_1 is the median of these values.

$Q_1 = 182$

(d) There are the same number of data above as below the median. Use this fact to find Q_3.

Q_3 is the median of the upper half of the data. There are 11 values in the upper portion.

$Q_3 = 319$

(e) Find the interquartile range and comment on its meaning.

$$IQR = Q_3 - Q_1 = 319 - 182 = 137$$

The middle portion of the data has a spread of 137 calories.

Box-and-Whisker Plots

Five-number summary

The quartiles together with the low and high data values give us a very useful *five-number summary* of the data and their spread.

A good class discussion topic can be found in Linking Concepts, Problem 2. This problem compares earlier concepts of this chapter with the box-and-whisker plot. It is good to emphasize that the box-and-whisker plot is easy to construct and contains a lot of information at a glance.

Five-number summary

Lowest value, Q_1, median, Q_3, highest value

Box-and-whisker plot

We will use these five numbers to create a graphic sketch of the data called a *box-and-whisker plot.* Box-and-whisker plots provide another useful technique from exploratory data analysis (EDA) for describing data.

PROCEDURE

Use the five-number summary and steps 1 to 4 for making a box-and-whisker plot as a kind of mental flowchart to help students organize their work.

It is helpful to point out that a box-and-whisker plot serves the function of a description of data spread about the median, while the standard deviation is a measure of spread about the mean.

HOW TO MAKE A BOX-AND-WHISKER PLOT

1. Draw a vertical scale to include the lowest and highest data values.
2. To the right of the scale, draw a box from Q_1 to Q_3.
3. Include a solid line through the box at the median level.
4. Draw vertical lines, called *whiskers,* from Q_1 to the lowest value and from Q_3 to the highest value.

FIGURE 3-6

Box-and-Whisker Plot

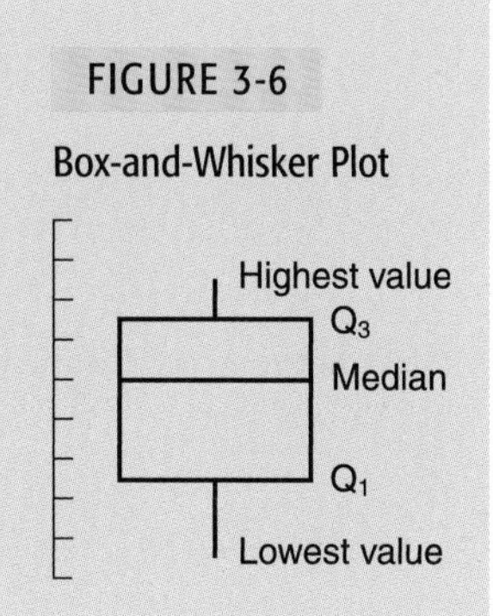

The next example demonstrates the process of making a box-and-whisker plot.

EXAMPLE 10 BOX-AND-WHISKER PLOT

Using the data from Guided Exercise 7, make a box-and-whisker plot showing the calories in vanilla-flavored ice cream bars. Use the plot to make observations about the distribution of calories.

(a) In Guided Exercise 7, we ordered the data (see Table 3-7) and found the values of the median, Q_1, and Q_3. From this previous work we have the following five-number summary:

low value = 111; Q_1 = 182; median = 221.5; Q_3 = 319; high value = 439

(b) We select an appropriate vertical scale and make the plot (Figure 3-7).

(c) A quick glance at the box-and-whisker plot reveals the following:

(i) The box tells us where the middle half of the data lies, so we see that half of the ice cream bars have between 182 and 319 calories, with an interquartile range of 137 calories.

(ii) The median is slightly closer to the lower part of the box. This means that the lower calorie counts are more concentrated. The calorie counts above the median are more spread out, indicating that the distribution is slightly skewed toward the higher values.

(iii) The upper whisker is longer than the lower, which again emphasizes skewness toward the higher values.

FIGURE 3-7

Box-and-Whisker Plot for Calories in Vanilla-Flavored Ice Cream Bars

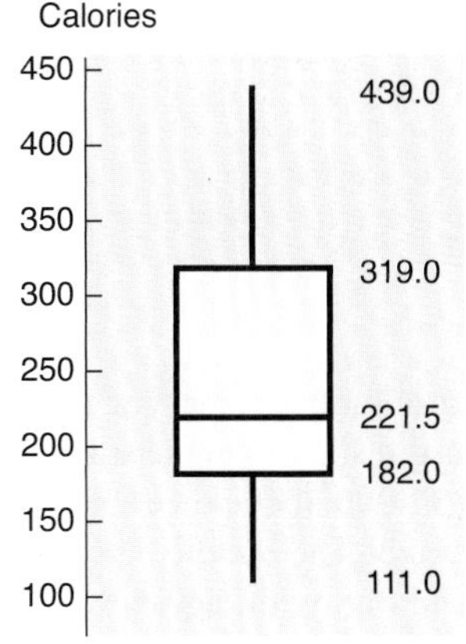

COMMENT In exploratory data analysis, *hinges* rather than quartiles are used to create the box. Hinges are computed in a manner similar to the method used to compute quartiles. However, in the case of an odd number of data values, include the median itself in both the lower and upper halves of the data (see *Applications, Basics, and Computing of Exploratory Data Analysis*, by Paul Velleman and David Hoaglin, Duxbury Press). This has the effect of shrinking the box and moving the ends of the box slightly toward the median. For an even number of data, the quartiles as we computed them equal the hinges.

GUIDED EXERCISE 8 Box-and-whisker plot

The Renata College Development Office sent salary surveys to alumni who graduated 2 and 5 years ago. The voluntary responses received are summarized in the box-and-whisker plots shown in Figure 3-8 on the next page.

(a) From Figure 3-8, estimate the median and extreme values of salaries of alumni graduating 2 years ago. In what range are the middle half of the salaries?

The median seems to be about $44,000. The extremes are about $33,000 and $54,000. The middle half of the salaries fall between $40,000 and $47,000.

(b) From Figure 3-8, estimate the median and the extreme values of salaries of alumni graduating 5 years ago. What is the location of the middle half of the salaries?

The median seems to be $47,000. The extremes are $34,000 and $58,000. The middle half of the data are enclosed by the box with low side at $41,000 and high side at $50,000.

Continued

GUIDED EXERCISE 8 *continued*

FIGURE 3-8

Box-and-Whisker Plots for Alumni Salaries (in thousands of dollars)

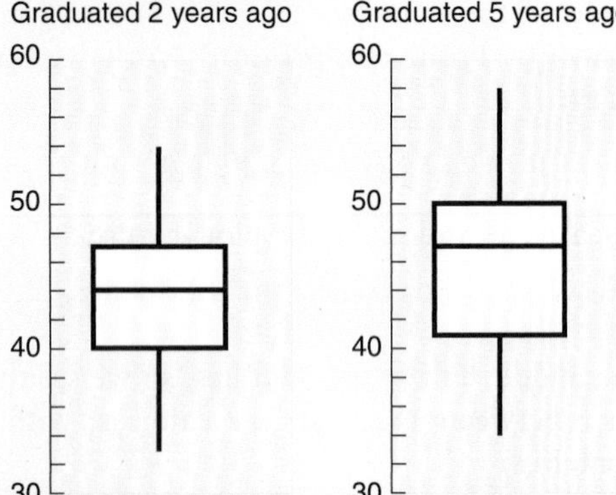

(c) Compare the two box plots and make comments about the salaries of alumni graduating 2 and 5 years ago.

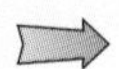

The salaries of the alumni graduating 5 years ago have a larger range. They begin slightly higher than and extend to levels about $4,000 above the salaries of those graduating 2 years ago. The middle half of the data are also more spread out, with higher boundaries and a higher median.

CRITICAL THINKING

Box-and-whisker plots provide a graphic display of the spread of data about the median. The box shows the location of the middle half of the data. One quarter of the data are located along each whisker.

To the extent that the median is centered in the box and the whiskers are about the same length, the data distribution is symmetric around the median. If the median line is near one end of the box, the data are skewed toward the other side of the box.

We have developed the skeletal box-and-whisker display. Other variations include *fences,* which are marks placed on either side of the box to represent various portions of data. Values that lie beyond the fences are *outliers*. Problem 10 of this section discusses some criteria for locating fences and identifying outliers.

Problem 10 discusses how to identify possible outliers on a box-and-whisker plot.

TECH NOTES

Box-and-Whisker Plot

Both Minitab and the TI-84Plus/TI-83Plus calculators support box-and-whisker plots. On the TI-84Plus/TI-83Plus, the quartiles Q_1 and Q_3 are calculated as we calculate them in this text. In Minitab and Excel, they are calculated using a slightly different process.

TI-84Plus/TI-83Plus Press STATPLOT ➤ **On.** Highlight box plot. Use **Trace** and the arrow keys to display the values of the five-number summary. The display shows the plot for calories in ice cream bars.

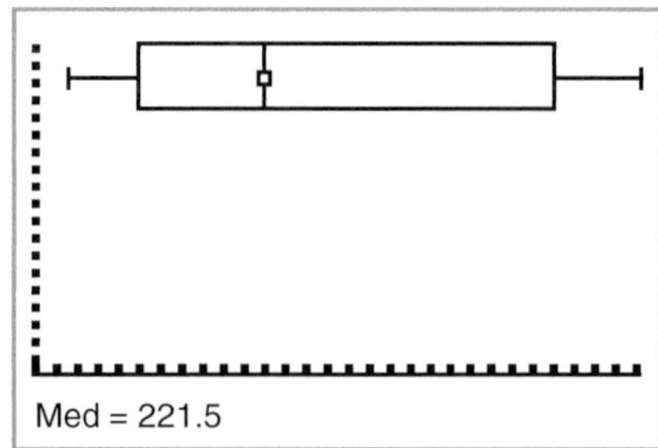

Excel Does not produce plot. **Paste Function** (fx) ➤ **Statistics** ➤ **Quartiles** gives the five-number summary.

Minitab Press **Graph** ➤ **Boxplot.** In the dialogue box, set Display to IQRange Box.

VIEWPOINT Is Shorter Higher?

Can you estimate a person's height *from the* pitch *of his or her voice? Is a soprano shorter than an alto? Is a bass taller than a tenor? A statistical study of singers in the New York Choral Society provided information. For more information, visit the Online Study Center at* **www.cengage.com/statistics/Brase/UBS5e** *and find the link to DASL, the Carnegie Mellon University Data and Story Library. From Data Subjects, select music and then singers. Methods of this chapter can be used with new methods we will learn in Chapters 8 and 9 to examine such questions from a statistical point of view.*

SECTION 3.3 PROBLEMS

Tables and art to accompany margin answers may be found in the back of the book.

1. 82% at or below; 18% above.
2. 75th percentile.
3. No, it might have a percentile rank of less than 70.
4. Timothy; Timothy's percentile score is higher.
5. Low = 2; Q_1 = 9.5; median = 23; Q_3 = 28.5; high = 42; IQR = 19.

1. *Statistical Literacy* Angela took a general aptitude test and scored in the 82nd percentile for aptitude in accounting. What percentage of the scores were at or below her score? What percentage were above?

2. *Statistical Literacy* One standard for admission to Redfield College is that the student must rank in the upper quartile of his or her graduating high school class. What is the minimal percentile rank of a successful applicant?

3. ***Critical Thinking*** The town of Butler, Nebraska, decided to give a teacher-competency exam and defined the passing scores to be those in the 70th percentile or higher. The raw test scores ranged from 0 to 100. Was a raw score of 82 necessarily a passing score? Explain.

4. ***Critical Thinking*** Clayton and Timothy took different sections of Introduction to Economics. Each section had a different final exam. Timothy scored 83 out of 100 and had a percentile rank in his class of 72. Clayton scored 85 out of 100 but his percentile rank in his class was 70. Who performed better with respect to the rest of the students in the class, Clayton or Timothy? Explain your answer.

5. *Health Care: Nurses* At Center Hospital there is some concern about the high turnover of nurses. A survey was done to determine how long (in months) nurses had been in their current positions. The responses (in months) of 20 nurses were

23	2	5	14	25	36	27	42	12	8
7	23	29	26	28	11	20	31	8	36

Make a box-and-whisker plot of the data. Find the interquartile range.

6. (a) Low = 3; Q_1 = 16; median = 23; Q_3 = 30; high = 72; *IQR* = 14.
(b) Compare to Problem 5.

6. *Health Care: Staff* Another survey was done at Center Hospital to determine how long (in months) clerical staff had been in their current positions. The responses (in months) of 20 clerical staff members were

25	22	7	24	26	31	18	14	17	20
31	42	6	25	22	3	29	32	15	72

(a) Make a box-and-whisker plot. Find the interquartile range.
(b) Compare this plot with the one in Problem 5. Discuss the locations of the medians, the locations of the middle halves of the data banks, and the distances from Q_1 and Q_3 to the extreme values.

7. (a) Low = 17; Q_1 = 22; median = 24; Q_3 = 27; high = 38; *IQR* = 5.
(b) Third quartile, since it is between the median and Q_3.

7. *Sociology: College Graduates* What percentage of the general U.S. population have bachelor's degrees? The *Statistical Abstract of the United States,* 120th Edition, gives the percentage of bachelor's degrees by state. For convenience, the data are sorted in increasing order.

17	18	18	18	19	20	20	20	21	21
21	21	22	22	22	22	22	22	23	23
24	24	24	24	24	24	24	24	25	26
26	26	26	26	26	27	27	27	27	27
28	28	29	31	31	32	32	34	35	38

(a) Make a box-and-whisker plot and find the interquartile range.
(b) Illinois has a bachelor's degree percentage rate of about 26%. Into what quartile does this rate fall?

8. (a) Low = 5; Q_1 = 9; median = 10; Q_3 = 12; high = 15; *IQR* = 3.
(b) First quartile, since it is below Q_1.

8. *Sociology: High-school Dropouts* What percentage of the general U.S. population are high-school dropouts? The *Statistical Abstract of the United States,* 120th Edition, gives the percentage of high-school dropouts by state. For convenience, the data are sorted in increasing order.

5	6	7	7	7	7	8	8	8	8
8	9	9	9	9	9	9	9	10	10
10	10	10	10	10	10	11	11	11	11
11	11	11	11	12	12	12	12	13	13
13	13	13	13	14	14	14	14	14	15

(a) Make a box-and-whisker plot and find the interquartile range.
(b) Wyoming has a dropout rate of about 7%. Into what quartile does this rate fall?

9. (a) Lowest, California; highest, Pennsylvania.
(b) Pennsylvania.
(c) Smallest range, California; smallest *IQR*, Texas.
(d) Part (a), Texas; part (b), Pennsylvania; part (c), California.

9. *Auto Insurance: Interpret Graphs* *Consumer Reports* rated automobile insurance companies and gave annual premiums for top-rated companies in several states. Figure 3-9 shows box plots for annual premiums for urban customers (married couple with one 17-year-old son) in three states. The box plots in Figure 3-9 were all drawn using the same scale on a TI-84Plus/TI-83Plus calculator.

FIGURE 3-9

Insurance Premium (annual, urban)

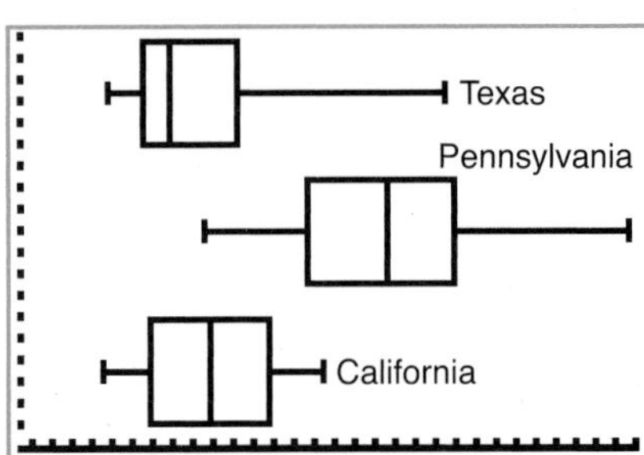

FIGURE 3-10

Five-Number Summaries for Insurance Premiums

(a)	(b)	(c)
1-Var Stats	1-Var Stats	1-Var Stats
↑n=10	↑n=10	↑n=10
minX=2382	minX=3314	minX=2323
Q1=2758	Q1=4326	Q1=2801
Med=2991	Med=5116.5	Med=3377.5
Q3=3652	Q3=5801	Q3=3966
maxX=5715	maxX=7527	maxX=4482

(a) Which state has the lowest premium? the highest?
(b) Which state has the highest median premium?
(c) Which state has the smallest range of premiums? the smallest interquartile range?
(d) Figure 3-10 gives the five-number summaries generated on the TI-84Plus/TI-83Plus calculators for the box plots of Figure 3-9. Match the five-number summaries to the appropriate box plots.

This problem gives one criterion sometimes used to identify outliers in a data set.

10. *Expand Your Knowledge: Outliers* Some data sets include values so high or so low that they seem to stand apart from the rest of the data. These data are called *outliers*. Outliers may represent data collection errors, data entry errors, or simply valid but unusual data values. It is important to identify outliers in the data set and examine the outliers carefully to determine if they are in error. One way to detect outliers is to use a box-and-whisker plot. Data values that fall beyond the limits

Lower limit: $Q_1 - 1.5 \times (IQR)$
Upper limit: $Q_3 + 1.5 \times (IQR)$

where IQR is the interquartile range, are suspected outliers. In the computer software package Minitab, values beyond these limits are plotted with asterisks (*).

Students from a statistics class were asked to record their heights in inches. The heights (as recorded) were

65	72	68	64	60	55	73	71	52	63	61	74
69	67	74	50	4	75	67	62	66	80	64	65

(a) Make a box-and-whisker plot of the data.
(b) Find the value of the interquartile range (IQR).
(c) Multiply the IQR by 1.5 and find the lower and upper limits.
(d) Are there any data values below the lower limit? above the upper limit? List any suspected outliers. What might be some explanations for the outliers?

10. (a) Low = 4; Q_1 = 61.5; median = 65.5; Q_3 = 71.5; high = 80.
(b) IQR = 10.
(c) Lower limit, 46.5; upper, 86.5.
(d) Yes, 4 is below the lower limit and is probably an error.

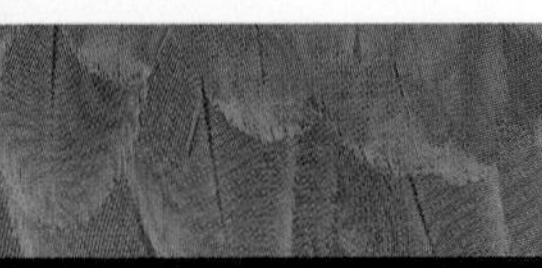

Chapter Review

SUMMARY

To characterize numerical data, we use both measures of center and of spread.

- Commonly used measures of center are the arithmetic mean, the median, and the mode. The weighted average and trimmed mean are also used as appropriate.
- Commonly used measures of spread are the variance, the standard deviation, and the range. The variance and standard deviation are measures of spread about the mean.
- Chebyshev's theorem enables us to estimate the data spread about the mean.
- The coefficient of variation lets us compare the relative spreads of different data sets.
- Other measures of data spread include percentiles, which indicate the percentage of data falling at or below the specified percentile value.
- Box-and-whisker plots show how the data are distributed about the median and the location of the middle half of the data distribution.

In later work, the average we will use most often is the mean; the measure of variation we will use most often is the standard deviation.

IMPORTANT WORDS & SYMBOLS

Section 3.1

Average
Mode
Median
Mean
Sample mean, $\bar{x}$
Population mean, μ
Summation symbol, Σ
Resistant measure
Trimmed mean
Weighted average

Section 3.2

Range
Sum of squares, $\Sigma(x - \bar{x})^2$
Sample standard deviation, s
Sample variance, s^2
Population standard deviation, σ
Population size, N
Coefficient of variation, CV
Chebyshev's theorem
Mean of grouped data
Standard deviation of grouped data

Section 3.3

Percentile
Quartile
Interquartile range, IQR
Five-number summary
Box-and-whisker plot
Whisker
Outlier

VIEWPOINT The Fujita Scale

How do you measure a tornado? Professor Fujita and Allen Pearson (Director of the National Severe Storm Forecast Center) developed a measure based on wind speed and type of damage done by a tornado. The result is an excellent example of both descriptive and inferential statistical methods. For more information, visit the Online Study Center at **www.cengage.com/statistics/Brase/UBS5e** *and find the link to the tornado project. Then look up Fujita scale. If we group the data a little, the scale becomes*

FS	*WS*	%
F0 & F1	40–112	67
F2 & F3	113–206	29
F4 & F5	207–318	4

where FS represents Fujita scale; WS, wind speed in miles per hour; and %, percentage of all tornados. For 100 tornados, what would be your estimate for the mean and standard deviation of wind speed?

CHAPTER REVIEW PROBLEMS

Tables and art to accompany margin answers may be found in the back of the book.

1. (a) Variance and standard deviation.
   (b) Box-and-whisker plot.

1. *Statistical Literacy*
   (a) Which measures of variation indicate spread about the mean?
   (b) Which graphic display shows the median and data spread about the median?

2. *Critical Thinking* Look at the two histograms below. Each involves the same number of data. The data are all whole numbers, so the height of each bar represents the number of values equal to the corresponding midpoint shown on the horizontal axis. Notice that both distributions are symmetric.

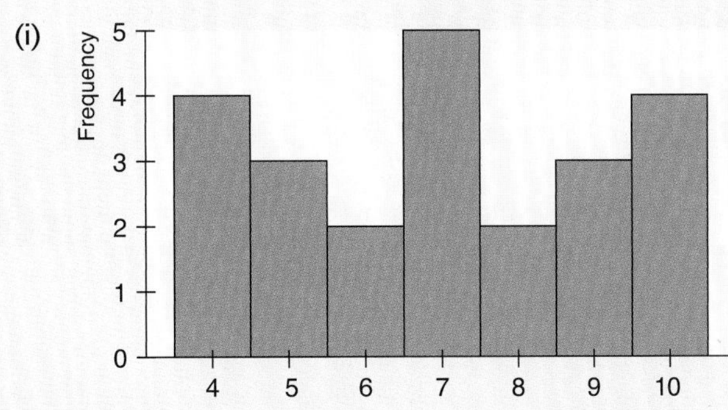

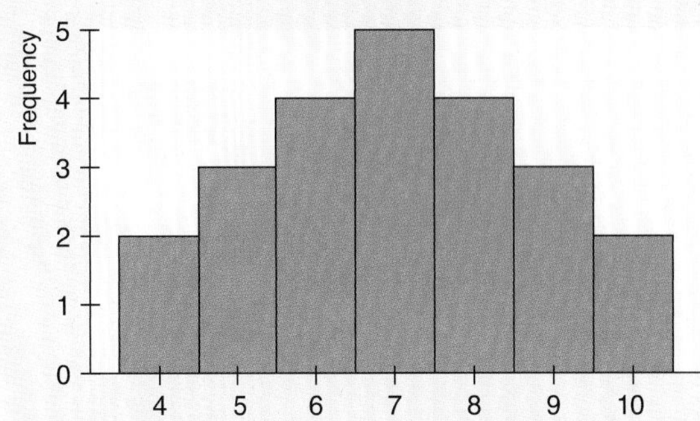

2. (a) For both histograms, mode = 7; median = 7; mean = 7.
   (b) Distribution (i), because more of the data are farther from the mean.
3. (a) For both data sets, mean = 20 and range = 24.
   (b) The C1 distribution seems more symmetric because the mean and median are equal, and the median is in the center of the interquartile range. In the C2 distribution, the mean is less than the median.
   (c) The C1 distribution has a larger interquartile range that is symmetric about the median. The C2 distribution has a very compressed interquartile range with the median equal to Q_3.
4. (a) $\bar{x} \approx 4.53$; median = 4.05; mode = 1.9.
   (b) $s \approx 2.46$; $CV \approx 54.4\%$; range = 6.7.

   (a) Estimate the mode, median, and mean for each histogram.
   (b) Which distribution has the larger standard deviation? Why?

3. *Critical Thinking* Consider the following Minitab display of two data sets.

Variable	N	Mean	SE Mean	StDev	Minimum	Q1	Median	Q3	Maximum
C1	20	20.00	1.62	7.26	7.00	15.00	20.00	25.00	31.00
C2	20	20.00	1.30	5.79	7.00	20.00	22.00	22.00	31.00

   (a) What are the respective means? the respective ranges?
   (b) Which data set seems more symmetric? Why?
   (c) Compare the interquartile ranges of the two sets. How do the middle halves of the data sets compare?

4. *Consumer: Radon Gas* "Radon: The Problem No One Wants to Face" is the title of an article appearing in *Consumer Reports*. Radon is a gas emitted from the ground that can collect in houses and buildings. At certain levels it can cause lung cancer. Radon concentrations are measured in picocuries per liter (pCi/L). A radon level of 4 pCi/L is considered "acceptable." Radon levels in a house vary from week to week. In one house, a sample of 8 weeks had the following readings for radon level (in pCi/L):

   1.9 2.8 5.7 4.2 1.9 8.6 3.9 7.2

   (a) Find the mean, median, and mode.
   (b) Find the sample standard deviation, coefficient of variation, and range.

5. (a) Low = 31; Q_1 = 40; median = 45; Q_3 = 52.5; high = 68; IQR = 12.5.
   (b) Class width = 8.

Class	Midpoint	f
31–38	34.5	11
39–46	42.5	24
47–54	50.5	15
55–62	58.5	7
63–70	66.5	3

   $\bar{x} \approx 46.1$; $s \approx 8.64$; 28.82 to 63.38.
   (c) $\bar{x} = 46.15$; $s \approx 8.63$.

5. *Political Science: Georgia Democrats* How Democratic is Georgia? County-by-county results are shown for a recent election. For your convenience, the data have been sorted in increasing order (Source: *County and City Data Book*, 12th edition, U.S. Census Bureau).

Percentage of Democratic Vote by Counties in Georgia

31	33	34	34	35	35	35	36	38	38	38	39	40	40	40	40
41	41	41	41	41	41	41	42	42	43	44	44	44	45	45	46
46	46	46	47	48	49	49	49	49	50	51	52	52	53	53	53
53	53	55	56	56	57	57	59	62	66	66	68				

(a) Make a box-and-whisker plot of the data. Find the interquartile range.
(b) *Grouped Data:* Make a frequency table using five classes. Then estimate the mean and sample standard deviation using the frequency table. Compute a 75% Chebyshev interval centered about the mean.
(c) If you have a statistical calculator or computer, use it to find the actual sample mean and sample standard deviation. Otherwise, use the values $\Sigma x = 2769$ and $\Sigma x^2 = 132{,}179$ to compute the sample mean and sample standard deviation.

6. (a) 85.77.
(b) 82.17.

6. *Grades: Weighted Average* Professor Cramer determines a final grade based on attendance, two papers, three major tests, and a final exam. Each of these activities is worth a total of 100 possible points. However, the activities carry different weights. Attendance is worth 5%, each paper is worth 8%, each test is worth 15%, and the final is worth 34%.
(a) What is the average for a student with 92 on attendance, 73 on the first paper, 81 on the second paper, 85 on test 1, 87 on test 2, 83 on test 3, and 90 on the final exam?
(b) Compute the average for a student with the above scores on the papers, tests, and final exam, but with a score of only 20 on attendance.

7. 156.25 pounds.

7. *General: Average Weight* An elevator is loaded with 16 people and is at its load limit of 2500 pounds. What is the mean weight of these people?

8. (a) Low = 7.8; Q_1 = 14.2; median = 20.25; Q_3 = 23.8; high = 29.5.
(b) *IQR* = 9.6 kilograms.
(d) Yes, the lower half shows slightly more spread.

8. *Agriculture: Harvest Weight of Maize* The following data represent weights in kilograms of maize harvest from a random sample of 72 experimental plots on St. Vincent, an island in the Caribbean (Reference: B. G. F. Springer, *Proceedings, Caribbean Food Corps. Soc.*, Vol. 10, pp. 147–152). *Note:* These data are also available for download at the Online Study Center. For convenience, the data are presented in increasing order.

7.8	9.1	9.5	10.0	10.2	10.5	11.1	11.5	11.7	11.8
12.2	12.2	12.5	13.1	13.5	13.7	13.7	14.0	14.4	14.5
14.6	15.2	15.5	16.0	16.0	16.1	16.5	17.2	17.8	18.2
19.0	19.1	19.3	19.8	20.0	20.2	20.3	20.5	20.9	21.1
21.4	21.8	22.0	22.0	22.4	22.5	22.5	22.8	22.8	23.1
23.1	23.2	23.7	23.8	23.8	23.8	23.8	24.0	24.1	24.1
24.5	24.5	24.9	25.1	25.2	25.5	26.1	26.4	26.5	26.7
27.1	29.5								

(a) Compute the five-number summary.
(b) Compute the interquartile range.
(c) Make a box-and-whisker plot.
(d) Discuss the distribution. Does the lower half of the distribution show more data spread than the upper half?

9. (a) No.
(b) \$34,206 to \$68,206.
(c) \$10,875.

9. *Focus Problem: The Educational Advantage* Solve the focus problem at the beginning of this chapter.

10. (a) Low = 6; Q_1 = 10; median = 11; Q_3 = 13; high = 16; *IQR* = 3.
(b) Class width = 3.

Class	Midpoint	*f*
6–8	7	4
9–11	10	24
12–14	13	15
15–17	16	7

$\bar{x} \approx 11.5$; $s \approx 2.52$; 6.46 to 16.54.
(c) $\bar{x} \approx 11.48$; $s \approx 2.44$.

10. *Agriculture: Bell Peppers* The pathogen *Phytophthora capsici* causes bell pepper plants to wilt and die. A research project was designed to study the effect of soil water content and the spread of the disease in fields of bell peppers (Source: *Journal of Agricultural, Biological, and Environmental Statistics*, Vol. 2, No. 2). It is thought that too much water helps spread the disease. The fields were divided into rows and quadrants. The soil water content (percent of water by volume of soil) was determined for each plot. An important first step in such a research project is to give a statistical description of the data.

Soil Water Content for Bell Pepper Study

15	14	14	14	13	12	11	11	11	11	10	11	13	16	10
9	15	12	9	10	7	14	13	14	8	9	8	11	13	13
15	12	9	10	9	9	16	16	12	10	11	11	12	15	6
10	10	10	11	9										

(a) Make a box-and-whisker plot of the data. Find the interquartile range.
(b) *Grouped Data:* Make a frequency table using four classes. Then estimate the mean and sample standard deviation using the frequency table. Compute a 75% Chebyshev interval centered about the mean.
(c) If you have a statistical calculator or computer, use it to find the actual sample mean and sample standard deviation.

11. 7.56.

11. *Performance Rating: Weighted Average* A performance evaluation for new sales representatives at Office Automation Incorporated involves several ratings done on a scale of 1 to 10, with 10 the highest rating. The activities rated include new contacts, successful contacts, total contacts, dollar volume of sales, and reports. Then an overall rating is determined by using a weighted average. The weights are 2 for new contacts, 3 for successful contacts, 3 for total contacts, 5 for dollar value of sales, and 3 for reports. What would the overall rating be for a sales representative with ratings of 5 for new contacts, 8 for successful contacts, 7 for total contacts, 9 for dollar volume of sales, and 7 for reports?

DATA HIGHLIGHTS: GROUP PROJECTS

Old Faithful Geyser, Yellowstone National Park

Break into small groups and discuss the following topics. Organize a brief outline in which you summarize the main points of your group discussion.

1. *The Story of Old Faithful* is a short book written by George Marler and published by the Yellowstone Association. Chapter 7 of this interesting book talks about the effect of the 1959 earthquake on eruption intervals for Old Faithful Geyser. Dr. John Rinehart (a senior research scientist with the National Oceanic and Atmospheric Administration) has done extensive studies of the eruption intervals before and after the 1959 earthquake. Examine Figure 3-11. Notice the general shape. Is the graph more or less symmetrical? Does it have a single mode frequency? The mean interval between eruptions has remained steady at about 65 minutes for the past 100 years. Therefore, the 1959 earthquake did not significantly change the mean, but it did change the distribution of eruption intervals. Examine Figure 3-12. Would you say there are really two frequency modes, one shorter and the other longer? Explain. The overall mean is about the same for both graphs, but one graph has a much larger standard deviation (for eruption intervals) than the other. Do no calculations, just look at both graphs, and then explain which graph has the smaller and which has the larger standard deviation. Which distribution will have the larger coefficient of variation? In everyday terms, what would this mean if you were actually at Yellowstone waiting to see the next eruption of Old Faithful? Explain your answer.

FIGURE 3-11

Typical Behavior of Old Faithful Geyser Before 1959 Quake

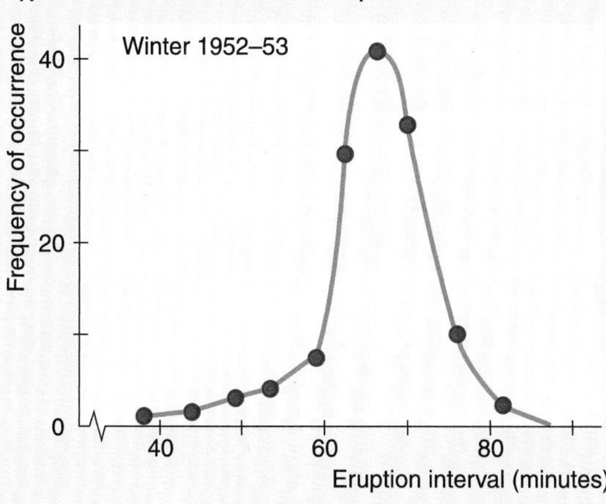

FIGURE 3-12

Typical Behavior of Old Faithful Geyser After 1959 Quake

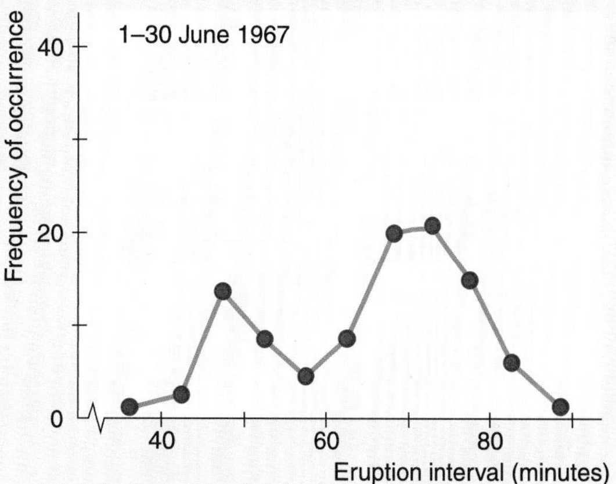

FIGURE 3-13

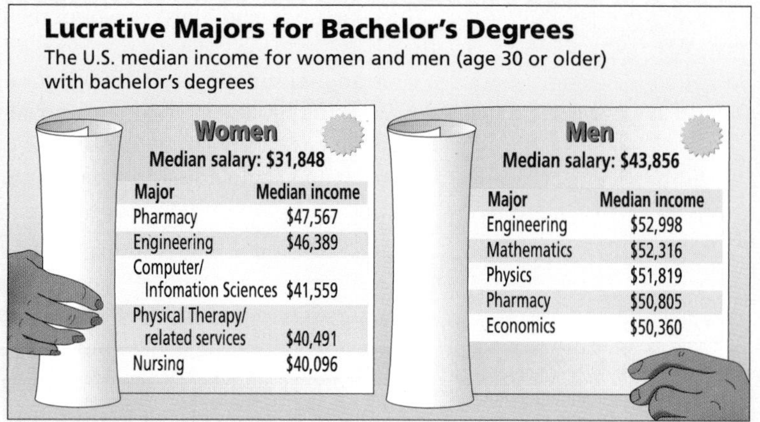

Lucrative Majors for Bachelor's Degrees
The U.S. median income for women and men (age 30 or older) with bachelor's degrees
Women
Median salary: $31,848
Major Median income
Pharmacy $47,567
Engineering $46,389
Computer/ Infomation Sciences $41,559
Physical Therapy/ related services $40,491
Nursing $40,096
Men
Median salary: $43,856
Major Median income
Engineering $52,998
Mathematics $52,316
Physics $51,819
Pharmacy $50,805
Economics $50,360

Source: Bureau of Labor Statistics

2. Most academic advisors tell students to major in a field the student really loves. After all, it is true that money cannot buy happiness! Nevertheless, it is interesting to at least look at some of the higher-paying fields of study. After all, a field like mathematics can be a lot of fun, once you get into it. We see that women's salaries tend to be less than men's salaries. However, women's salaries are rapidly catching up, and this benefits the entire work force in different ways. Figure 3-13 shows the median incomes for college graduates with different majors. The employees in the sample are all at least 30 years old. Does it seem reasonable to assume that many of the employees are in jobs beyond the entry level? Explain. Compare the median incomes shown for all women aged 30 or older holding bachelor's degrees with the median incomes for men of similar age holding bachelor's degrees. Look at the particular majors listed. What percentage of men holding bachelor's degrees in mathematics make $52,316 or more? What percentage of women holding computer/information science degrees make $41,559 or more? How do median incomes for men and women holding engineering degrees compare? What about pharmacy degrees?

LINKING CONCEPTS: WRITING PROJECTS

Discuss each of the following topics in class or review the topics on your own. Then write a brief but complete essay in which you summarize the main points. Please include formulas and graphs as appropriate.

1. An average is an attempt to summarize a collection of data into just *one* number. Discuss how the mean, median, and mode all represent averages in this context. Also discuss the differences among these averages. Why is the mean a balance point? Why is the median a midway point? Why is the mode the most common data point? List three areas of daily life in which you think one of the mean, median, or mode would be the best choice to describe an "average."

2. Why do we need to study the variation of a collection of data? Why isn't the average by itself adequate? We have studied three ways to measure variation. The range, the standard deviation, and, to a large extent, a box-and-whisker plot all indicate the variation within a data collection. Discuss similarities and differences among these ways of measuring data variation. Why would it seem reasonable to pair the median with a box-and-whisker plot and to pair the mean with the standard deviation? What are the advantages and disadvantages of each method of describing data spread? Comment on statements such as the following: (a) The range is easy to compute, but it doesn't give much information; (b) although the standard deviation is more complicated to compute, it has some significant applications; (c) the box-and-whisker plot is fairly easy to construct, and it gives a lot of information at a glance.

3. Why is the coefficient of variation important? What do we mean when we say that the coefficient of variation has no units? What advantage can there be in having no units? Why is *relative size* important?

   Consider robin eggs; the mean weight of a collection of robin eggs is 0.72 ounce and the standard deviation is 0.12 ounce. Now consider elephants; the mean weight of elephants in a zoo is 6.42 tons, with a standard deviation 1.07 tons. The units of measurement are different and there is a great deal of difference between the size of an elephant and that of a robin's egg. Yet the coefficient of variation is about the same for both. Comment on this from the viewpoint of the size of the standard deviation relative to the mean.

4. What is Chebyshev's theorem? Suppose you have a friend who knows very little about statistics. Write a paragraph or two in which you describe Chebyshev's theorem for your friend. Keep the discussion as simple as possible, but be sure to get the main ideas across to your friend. Suppose he or she asks, "What is this stuff good for?" and suppose you respond (a little sarcastically) that Chebyshev's theorem applies to everything from butterflies to the orbits of the planets! Would you be correct? Explain.

USING TECHNOLOGY

Raw Data

Application

Using the software or calculator available to you, do the following.

1. Trade winds are one of the beautiful features of island life in Hawaii. The following data represent total air movement in miles per day over a weather station in Hawaii as determined by a continuous anemometer recorder. The period of observation is January 1 to February 15, 1971.

26	14	18	14
113	50	13	22
27	57	28	50
72	52	105	138
16	33	18	16
32	26	11	16
17	14	57	100
35	20	21	34
18	13	18	28
21	13	25	19
11	19	22	19
15	20		

Source: United States Department of Commerce, National Oceanic and Atmospheric Administration, Environmental Data Service. *Climatological Data, Annual Summary, Hawaii,* Vol. 67, No. 13. Asheville: National Climatic Center, 1971, pp. 11, 24.

(a) Use the computer to find the sample mean, median, and (if it exists) mode. Also, find the range, sample variance, and sample standard deviation.

(b) Use the five-number summary provided by the computer to make a box-and-whisker plot of total air movement over the weather station.

(c) Four data values are exceptionally high: 113, 105, 138, and 100. The strong winds of January 5 (113 reading) brought in a cold front that dropped snow on Haleakala National Park (at the 8000 ft elevation). The residents were so excited that they drove up to see the snow and caused such a massive traffic jam that the Park Service had to close the road. The winds of January 15, 16, and 28 (readings 105, 138, and 100) accompanied a storm with funnel clouds that did much damage. Eliminate these values (i.e., 100, 105, 113, and 138) from the data bank and redo parts (a) and (b). Compare your results with those previously obtained. Which average is most affected? What happens to the standard deviation? How do the two box-and-whisker plots compare?

Technology Hints: Raw Data

TI-84Plus/TI-83Plus, Excel, Minitab

The Tech Notes of Section 3.2 give brief instructions for finding summary statistics for raw data using the TI-84Plus/TI-83Plus calculators, Excel, and Minitab. The Tech Notes of Section 3.3 give brief instructions for constructing box plots using the TI-84Plus/TI-83Plus calculators and Minitab.

SPSS

Many commands in SPSS provide an option to display various summary statistics. A direct way to display summary statistics is to use the menu choices **Analyze ➤ Descriptive Statistics ➤ Descriptives.** In the dialogue box, move the variable containing your data into the variables box. Click **Options...** and then check the summary statistics you wish to display. Click Continue and then OK. Notice that the median is not available. A more complete list of summary statistics is available with the menu choices **Analyze ➤ Descriptive Statistics ➤ Frequencies.** Click the **Statistics** button and check the summary statistics you wish to display.

For box-and-whisker plots, use the menu options **Graphs ➤ Interactive ➤ Boxplot.** In the dialogue box, place the variable containing your data in the box along the vertical axis. After selecting the options you want, click OK.

Cumulative Review Problems

CHAPTERS 1–3

Critical Thinking and Literacy

1. Consider the following measures: mean, median, variance, standard deviation, percentile.
   (a) Which measures utilize relative position of the data values?
   (b) Which measures utilize actual data values regardless of relative position?
2. Describe how the presence of possible outliers might be identified on
   (a) histograms.
   (b) dotplots.
   (c) stem-and-leaf displays.
   (d) box-and-whisker plots.
3. Consider two data sets A and B. The sets are identical except that the high value of data set B is three times greater than the high value of data set A.
   (a) How do the medians of the two data sets compare?
   (b) How do the means of the two data sets compare?
   (c) How do the standard deviations of the two data sets compare?
   (d) How do the box-and-whisker plots of the two data sets compare?
4. You are examining two data sets involving test scores, set A and set B. The score 86 appears in both data sets. In which of the following data sets does 86 represent a higher score? Explain.
   (a) The percentile rank of 86 is higher in set A than in set B.
   (b) The mean is 80 in both data sets, but set A has a higher standard deviation.

Applications

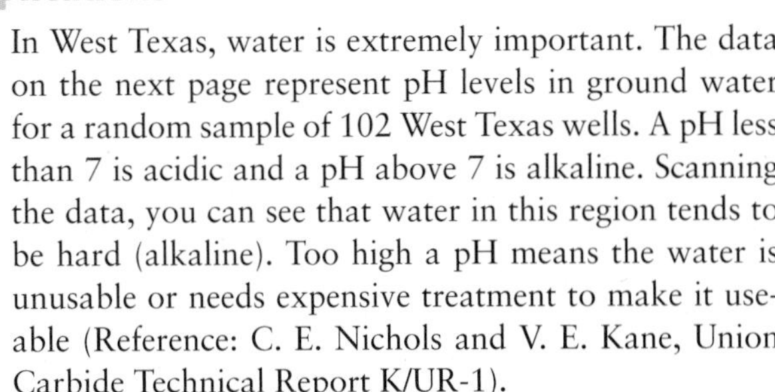

In West Texas, water is extremely important. The data on the next page represent pH levels in ground water for a random sample of 102 West Texas wells. A pH less than 7 is acidic and a pH above 7 is alkaline. Scanning the data, you can see that water in this region tends to be hard (alkaline). Too high a pH means the water is unusable or needs expensive treatment to make it useable (Reference: C. E. Nichols and V. E. Kane, Union Carbide Technical Report K/UR-1).

Tables and art to accompany margin answers may be found in the back of the book.

1. (a) Median, percentile.
   (b) Mean, variance, standard deviation.
2. (a) Gap between first bar and rest of bars or between last bar and rest of bars.
   (b) Large gap between data on far-left or far-right side and rest of data.
   (c) Several empty stems above stem including lowest values or before stem including highest values.
   (d) Data beyond fences placed at $Q_1 - 1.5(IQR)$ and $Q_3 + 1.5(IQR)$.
3. (a) Same.
   (b) Set B has a higher mean.
   (c) Set B has a higher standard deviation.
   (d) Set B has a much longer whisker beyond Q_3.
4. (a) Set A because 86 is the relatively higher score, since a larger percentage of scores fall below it.
   (b) Set B because 86 is more standard deviations above the mean.

These data are also available for download at the Online Study Center. For convenience, the data are presented in increasing order.

***x*: pH of Ground Water in 102 West Texas Wells**

7.0	7.0	7.0	7.0	7.0	7.0	7.0	7.0	7.1	7.1	7.1	7.1
7.1	7.1	7.1	7.1	7.1	7.1	7.2	7.2	7.2	7.2	7.2	7.2
7.2	7.2	7.2	7.2	7.3	7.3	7.3	7.3	7.3	7.3	7.3	7.3
7.3	7.3	7.3	7.4	7.4	7.4	7.4	7.4	7.4	7.4	7.4	7.4
7.5	7.5	7.5	7.5	7.5	7.5	7.5	7.5	7.6	7.6	7.6	7.6
7.6	7.6	7.6	7.6	7.6	7.7	7.7	7.7	7.7	7.7	7.7	7.8
7.8	7.8	7.8	7.8	7.9	7.9	7.9	7.9	7.9	8.0	8.1	8.1
8.1	8.1	8.1	8.1	8.1	8.2	8.2	8.2	8.2	8.2	8.2	8.2
8.4	8.5	8.6	8.7	8.8	8.8						

5. Write a brief description in which you outline how you would obtain a random sample of 102 West Texas water wells. Explain how random numbers would be used in the selection process.
6. Is the given data nominal, ordinal, interval, or ratio? Explain.
7. Make a stem-and-leaf display. Use five lines per stem so that leaf values 0 and 1 are on one line, 2 and 3 are on the next line, 4 and 5 are on the next, 6 and 7 are on the next, and 8 and 9 are on the last line of the stem.
8. Make a frequency table, histogram, and relative-frequency histogram using five classes. Recall that for decimal data, we "clear the decimal" to determine classes for whole number data and then reinsert the decimal to obtain the classes for the frequency table of the original data.
9. Compute the range, mean, median, and mode for the given data.
10. (a) Verify that $\Sigma x = 772.9$ and $\Sigma x^2 = 5876.65$.
    (b) Compute the sample variance, sample standard deviation, and coefficient of variation for the given data. Is the sample standard deviation small relative to the mean pH?
11. Compute a 75% Chebyshev interval centered on the mean.
12. Make a box-and-whisker plot. Find the interquartile range.

Summary

Wow! In Problems 5–12 you constructed a lot of information regarding the pH of West Texas ground water based on sample data. Let's continue the investigation.

13. Look at the histogram you created in Problem 8. Is the pH distribution for these wells symmetric or skewed? Are lower or higher values more common?
14. Look at the stem-and-leaf plot you created in Problem 7. Are there any unusually high or low pH levels in this sample of wells? How many wells are neutral (pH of 7)?

5. Assign consecutive numbers to all the wells in the study region. Then use a random number table, computer, or calculator to select 102 values that are less than or equal to the highest number assigned to a well in the study region. The sample consists of the wells with numbers corresponding to those selected.
6. Ratio.
7. 7 | 0 represents a pH level of 7.0

7	0 0 0 0 0 0 0 0 1 1 1 1 1 1 1 1 1 1
7	2 2 2 2 2 2 2 2 2 2 3 3 3 3 3 3 3 3 3 3 3
7	4 4 4 4 4 4 4 4 4 5 5 5 5 5 5 5 5
7	6 6 6 6 6 6 6 6 6 7 7 7 7 7 7
7	8 8 8 8 8 9 9 9 9 9
8	0 1 1 1 1 1 1 1
8	2 2 2 2 2 2 2
8	4 5
8	6 7
8	8 8

8. Clear the decimals. Then the highest value is 88 and the lowest is 70. The class width for the whole numbers is 4. For the actual data, the class width is 0.4.
9. Range = 1.8; $\bar{x} \approx 7.58$; median = 7.5; mode = 7.3.
10. (a) Use a calculator or computer.
    (b) $s^2 \approx 0.20$; $s \approx 0.45$; $CV \approx 5.9\%$.
11. 6.68 to 8.48.
12. $IQR = 0.7$.
13. Skewed right. Lower values are more common.
14. No, there are no gaps in the plot, but only 6 out of 102, or about 6%, have pH levels at or above 8.4. Eight wells are neutral.

15. Use the box-and-whisker plot from Problem 12 to describe how the data are spread about the median. Are the pH values above the median more spread out than those below? Is this observation consistent with the skew of the histogram?

16. Suppose you are working for the regional water commissioner. You have been asked to submit a brief report on the pH level of ground water in the West Texas region. Write such a report and include appropriate graphs.

15. Half the wells have pH levels between 7.2 and 7.9. The data are skewed toward the high values, with the upper half of the pH levels spread out more than the lower half. The upper half ranges between 7.5 and 8.8, while the lower half is clustered between 7 and 7.5.

16. The report should emphasize the relatively low mean, median, and mode, and the fact that half the wells have a pH level of less than 7.5. The data are clustered at the low end of the range.

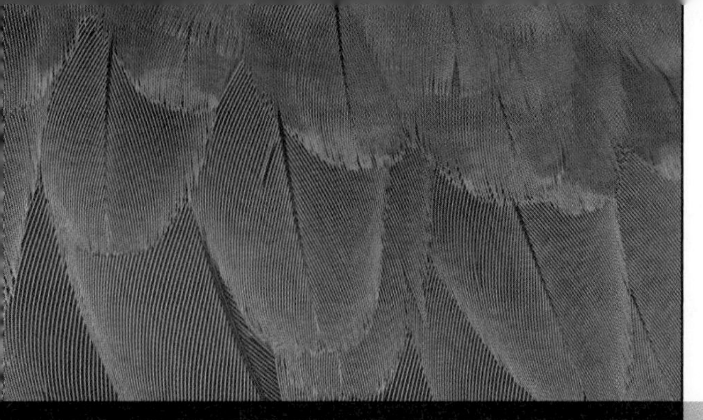

4

When it is not in our power to determine what is true, we ought to follow what is most probable.

—René Descartes

It is important to realize that statistics and probability do not deal in the realm of certainty. If there is any realm of human knowledge in which genuine certainty exists, you may be sure that our statistical methods are not needed there. In most human endeavors, and in almost all of the natural world around us, the element of chance happenings cannot be avoided. When we cannot expect something with true certainty, we must rely on probability to be our guide. In this chapter, we will study regression, correlation, and forecasting. One of the tools we will use is a scatter plot. René Descartes (1596–1650) was the first mathematician to systematically use rectangular coordinate plots. For this reason, such a coordinate axis is called a Cartesian axis.

For on-line student resources, visit the Brase/Brase, *Understanding Basic Statistics,* 5th edition web site at **www.cengage.com/statistics/Brase/UBS5e.**

Correlation and Regression

PREVIEW QUESTIONS

How can you use a scatter diagram to visually estimate the degree of linear correlation of two random variables? (SECTION 4.1)

How do you compute the correlation coefficient and what does it tell you about the strength of the linear relationship between two random variables? (SECTION 4.1)

What is the least-squares criterion? How do you find the equation of the least-squares line? (SECTION 4.2)

What is the coefficient of determination, and what does it tell you about the explained variation of y *in a random sample of data pairs* (x, y)*?* (SECTION 4.2)

FOCUS PROBLEM

Changing Populations and Crime Rate

Is the crime rate higher in neighborhoods in which people do not know each other very well? Is there a relationship between crime rate and population change? If so, can we make predictions based on such a relationship? Is the relationship statistically significant? Is it possible to predict crime rate from population changes?

Denver is a city that has had a lot of growth and consequently a lot of population change in recent years. Sociologists studying population changes and crime rate could find a wealth of information in Denver statistics. Let x be a random variable representing percentage change in neighborhood population in the past few years, and let y be a random variable representing crime rate (crimes per 1000 population). A random sample of six Denver neighborhoods gave the following information (Source: *Neighborhood Facts,* The Piton Foundation). To find out more about the Piton Foundation, visit the Online Study Center at **www.cengage.com/statistics/Brase/UBS5e** and find the link to the Piton Foundation.

x	29	2	11	17	7	6
y	173	35	132	127	69	53

Using information presented in this chapter, you will be able to analyze the relationship between the variables x and y using the following tools.

- Scatter diagram
- Sample correlation coefficient and coefficient of determination
- Least-squares line equation
- Predictions for y using the least-squares line

(See Problem 10 in the Chapter Review Problems.)

SECTION 4.1

Scatter Diagrams and Linear Correlation

FOCUS POINTS

- Make a scatter diagram.
- Visually estimate the location of the "best-fitting" line for a scatter diagram.
- Use sample data to compute the sample correlation coefficient r.
- Investigate the meaning of the correlation coefficient r.

Studies of correlation and regression of two variables usually begin with a graph of *paired data values* (x, y). We call such a graph a *scatter diagram.*

Scatter diagram

A **scatter diagram** is a graph in which data pairs (x, y) are plotted as individual points on a grid with horizontal axis x and vertical axis y. We call x the **explanatory** variable and y the **response** variable.

By looking at a scatter diagram of data pairs, you can observe whether there seems to be a linear relationship between the x and y values.

EXAMPLE 1 SCATTER DIAGRAM

Phosphorous is a chemical used in many household and industrial cleaning compounds. Unfortunately, phosphorous tends to find its way into surface water, where it can kill fish, plants, and other wetland creatures. Phosphorous reduction programs are required by law and are monitored by the Environmental Protection Agency (EPA). (Reference: *EPA Case Study 832-R-93-005.*)

A random sample of eight sites in a California wetlands study gave the following information about phosphorous reduction in drainage water. In this study, x is a random variable that represents phosphorous concentration (in 100 mg/l) at the inlet of a passive biotreatment facility, and y is a random variable that represents total phosphorous concentration (in 100 mg/l) at the outlet of the passive biotreatment facility.

x	5.2	7.3	6.7	5.9	6.1	8.3	5.5	7.0
y	3.3	5.9	4.8	4.5	4.0	7.1	3.6	6.1

(a) Make a scatter diagram for these data.

SOLUTION: Figure 4-1 shows points corresponding to the given data pairs. These plotted points constitute the scatter diagram. To make the diagram, first

Problem 17 explores the effect on a scatter diagram of different choices of scales on the axes.

FIGURE 4-1

Phosphorous Reduction (100 mg/l)

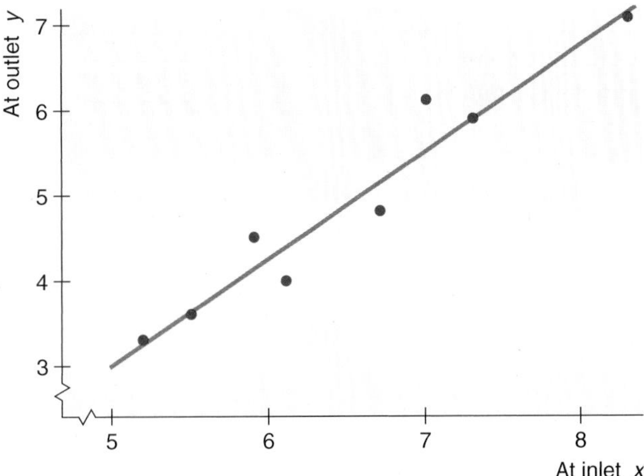

scan the data and decide on an appropriate scale for each axis. Figure 4-1 shows the scatter diagram (points) along with a line segment showing the basic trend. Notice a "jump scale" on both axes.

(b) Comment on the relationship between x and y shown in Figure 4-1.

SOLUTION: By inspecting the figure, we see that smaller values of x are associated with smaller values of y, and larger values of x tend to be associated with larger values of y. Roughly speaking, the general trend seems to be reasonably well represented by an upward-sloping line segment, as shown in the diagram.

Of course, it is possible to draw many curves close to the points in Figure 4-1, but a straight line is the simplest and most widely used for elementary studies of paired data. We can draw many lines in Figure 4-1, but in some sense, the "best" line should be the one that comes closest to each of the points of the scatter diagram. To single out one line as the "best-fitting line," we must find a mathematical criterion for this line and a formula representing the line. This will be done in Section 4.2 using the *method of least squares*.

Introduction to linear correlation

Another problem precedes that of finding the "best-fitting line." That is the problem of determining how well the points of the scatter diagram are suited for fitting *any* line. Certainly, if the points are a very poor fit to *any* line, there is little use in trying to find the "best" line.

If the points of a scatter diagram are located so that *no* line is realistically a "good" fit, we then say that the points possess *no linear correlation*. We see some examples of scatter diagrams for which there is no linear correlation in Figure 4-2.

FIGURE 4-2

Scatter Diagrams with No Linear Correlation

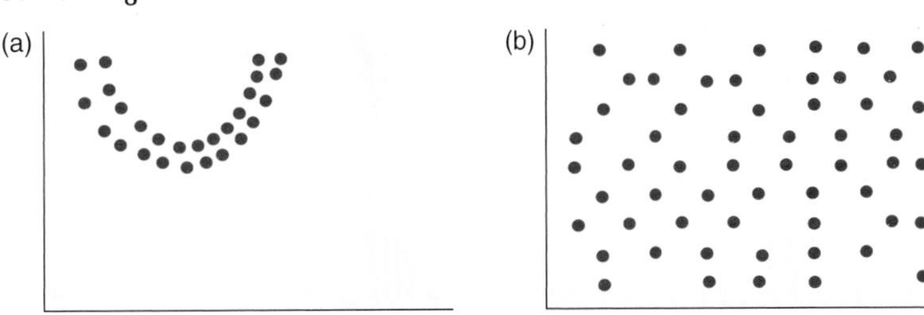

GUIDED EXERCISE 1 Scatter diagram

A large industrial plant has seven divisions that do the same type of work. A safety inspector visits each division of 20 workers quarterly. The number x of work-hours devoted to safety training and the number y of work-hours lost due to industry-related accidents are recorded for each separate division in Table 4-1.

TABLE 4-1 **Safety Report**

Division	x	y
1	10.0	80
2	19.5	65
3	30.0	68
4	45.0	55
5	50.0	35
6	65.0	10
7	80.0	12

(a) Make a scatter diagram for these pairs. Place the x values on the horizontal axis and the y values on the vertical axis.

→ FIGURE 4-3 Scatter Diagram for Safety Report

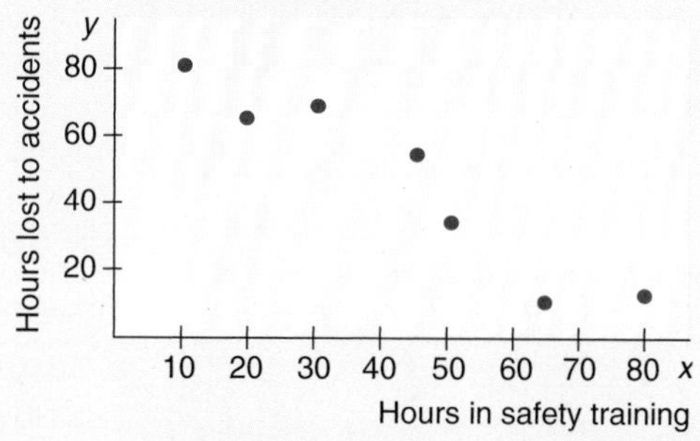

(b) As the number of hours spent on safety training increases, what happens to the number of hours lost due to industry-related accidents?

→ In general, as the number of hours in safety training goes up, the number of hours lost due to accidents goes down.

(c) Does a line fit the data reasonably well?

→ A line fits reasonably well.

(d) Draw a line that you think "fits best."

→ Use a downward-sloping line that lies close to the points. Later, you will find the equation of the line that is a "best fit."

TECH NOTES The TI-84Plus and TI-83Plus calculators, Excel, and Minitab all produce scatter plots. For each technology, enter the x values in one column and the corresponding y values in another column. The displays show the data from Guided Exercise 1 regarding safety training and hours lost because of accidents. Notice that the scatter plots do not necessarily show the origin.

TI-84Plus/TI-83Plus Enter the data into two columns. Use **Stat Plot** and choose the first type. Use option **9: ZoomStat** under **Zoom.** To check the scale, look at the settings displayed under **Window.**

Excel Enter the data into two columns. Use the menu choices **Chart wizard ➤ Scatter Diagram.** Dialogue box choices permit you to label the axes and title the chart. Changing the size of the diagram box changes the scale on the axes.

Minitab Enter the data into two columns. Use the menu selections **Stat ➤ Regression ➤ Fitted Line Plot.** The best-fit line is automatically plotted on the scatter diagram.

TI-84Plus/TI-83Plus Display

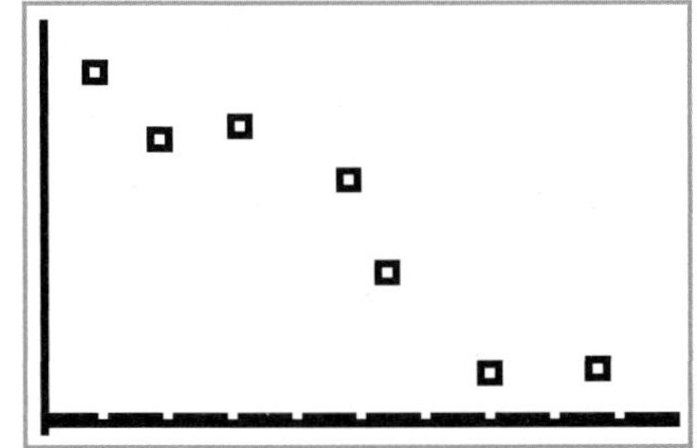

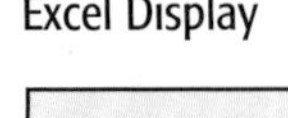

Excel Display

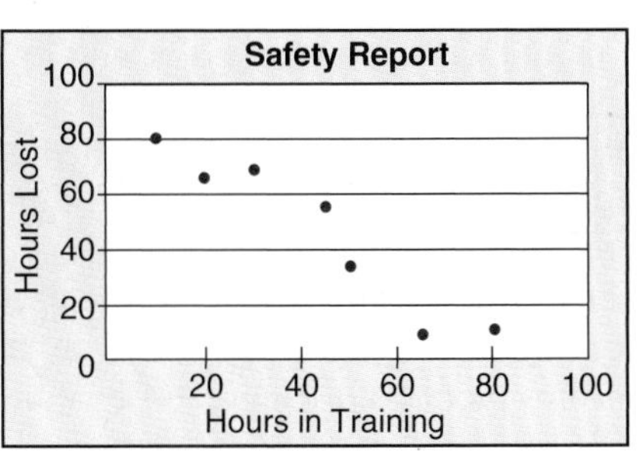

Minitab Display

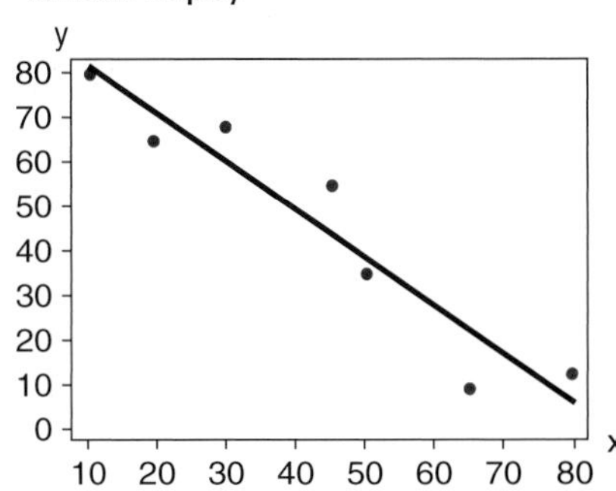

This section contains conceptually important material and is worth some extra class time. Good topics for class discussion can be found in Data Highlights, Linking Concepts (Problem 1), and Using Technology (physical geography).

Sample Correlation Coefficient r

Looking at a scatter diagram to see whether a line best describes the relationship between the values of data pairs is useful. In fact, whenever you are looking for a relationship between two variables, making a scatter diagram is a good first step.

There is a mathematical measurement that describes the strength of the linear association between two variables. This measure is the *sample correlation coefficient r*. The full name for r is the *Pearson product-moment correlation coefficient*, named in honor of the English statistician Karl Pearson (1857–1936), who is credited with formulating r.

The **correlation coefficient** r is a numerical measurement that assesses the strength of a *linear* relationship between two variables x and y.

1. r is a unitless measurement between -1 and 1. In symbols, $-1 \leq r \leq 1$. If $r = 1$, there is perfect positive linear correlation. If $r = -1$, there is perfect negative linear correlation. If $r = 0$, there is no linear correlation. The closer r is to 1 or -1, the better a line describes the relationship between the two variables x and y.

Positive correlation

Negative correlation

2. Positive values of r imply that as x increases, y tends to increase. Positive r values indicate *positive* correlation. Negative values of r imply that as x increases, y tends to decrease. Negative r values indicate *negative* correlation.

3. The value of r is the same regardless of which variable is the explanatory variable and which is the response variable. In other words, the value of r is the same for the pairs (x, y) and the corresponding pairs (y, x).

4. The value of r does not change when either variable is converted to different units.

Problem 18 demonstrates that the value of r does not change when x and y values are exchanged in the data pairs.

We'll develop the defining formula for r and then give a more convenient computation formula.

Development of Formula for *r*

If there is a *positive* linear relation between variables x and y, then high values of x are paired with high values of y, and low values of x are paired with low values of y. [See Figure 4-4(a).] In the case of *negative* linear correlation, high values of x are paired with low values of y, and low values of x are paired with high values of y. This relation is pictured in Figure 4-4(b). If there is *little or no linear correlation* between x and y, however, then we will find both high and low x values sometimes paired with high y values and sometimes paired with low y values. This relation is shown in Figure 4-4(c).

These observations lead us to the development of the formula for the correlation coefficient r. Taking *high* to mean "above the mean," we can express the relationships pictured in Figure 4-4 by considering the products

$$(x - \bar{x})(y - \bar{y})$$

If both x and y are high, both factors will be positive, and the product will be positive as well. The sign of this product will depend on the relative values of x and y compared with their respective means.

$$(x - \bar{x})(y - \bar{y}) \begin{cases} \text{is positive if } x \text{ and } y \text{ are both "high"} \\ \text{is positive if } x \text{ and } y \text{ are both "low"} \\ \text{is negative if } x \text{ is "low," but } y \text{ is "high"} \\ \text{is negative if } x \text{ is "high," but } y \text{ is "low"} \end{cases}$$

In the case of positive linear correlation, most of the products $(x - \bar{x})(y - \bar{y})$ will be positive, and so will the sum over all the data pairs,

$$\Sigma(x - \bar{x})(y - \bar{y})$$

If your students obtain the value of r directly from a calculator or computer, you may omit the computation formula for r. However, it is useful to discuss the defining formula for r and the motivation for the formula. In Example 2, direct the students to do part (b) by calculator. In Guided Exercise 2, have students omit part (c).

For negative linear correlation, the products will tend to be negative, so the sum also will be negative. On the other hand, in the case of little, if any, linear correlation, the sum will tend to be zero.

One trouble with the preceding sum is that it will be larger or smaller depending on the units of x and y. Because we want r to be unitless, we standardize both x and y of a data pair by dividing each factor $(x - \bar{x})$ by the sample standard deviation s_x and each factor $(y - \bar{y})$ by s_y. Finally, we take an average of all the

FIGURE 4-4

Patterns for Linear Correlation

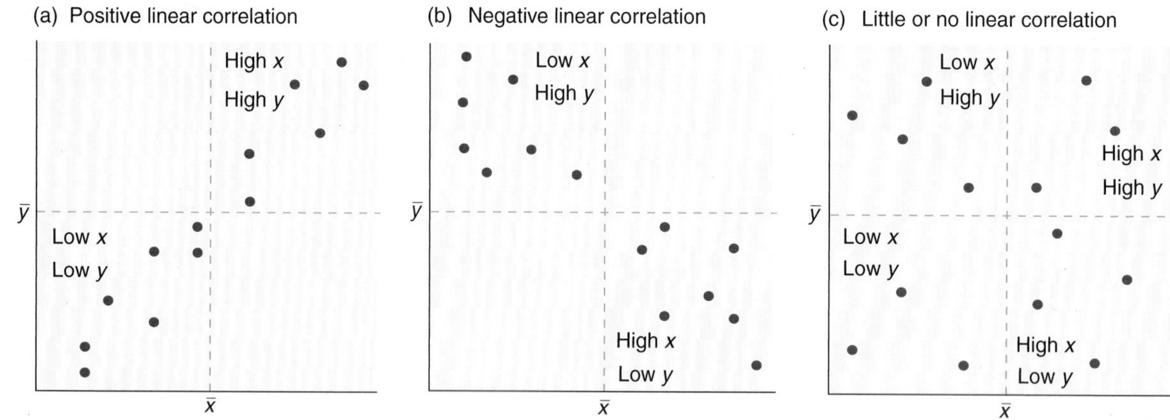

products. For technical reasons, we take the average by dividing by $n - 1$ instead of by n. This process leads us to the desired measurement, r.

$$r = \frac{1}{n-1} \Sigma \frac{(y - \bar{y})}{s_y} \cdot \frac{(x - \bar{x})}{s_x} \qquad (1)$$

Computation Formula for r

The defining formula for r shows how the mean and standard deviation of each variable in the data pair enter into the formulation of r. However, the defining formula is technically difficult to work with because of all the subtractions and products. A computation formula for r uses the raw data values of x and y directly.

PROCEDURE

The quantity $s_x s_y r = \frac{\Sigma(x - \bar{x})(y - \bar{y})}{n - 1}$ is called the sample covariance of x and y. Covariance is used in the study of linear combinations of dependent random variables.

How to compute the sample correlation coefficient r

Obtain a random sample of n data pairs (x, y).

1. Using the data pairs, compute Σx, Σy, Σx^2, Σy^2, and Σxy.
2. With n = sample size, Σx, Σy, Σx^2, Σy^2, and Σxy, you are ready to compute the sample correlation coefficient r using the computation formula

$$r = \frac{n\Sigma xy - (\Sigma x)(\Sigma y)}{\sqrt{n\Sigma x^2 - (\Sigma x)^2}\sqrt{n\Sigma y^2 - (\Sigma y)^2}} \qquad (2)$$

Be careful! The notation Σx^2 means first square x and then calculate the sum, whereas $(\Sigma x)^2$ means first sum the x values, then square the result.

Note: For inferences (Section 11.4), the data pairs should have a *bivariate normal variation*. That is, for a fixed value of x, the y values should have a normal distribution and vice versa for a fixed y value. Chapter 7 discusses normal distributions.

It can be shown mathematically that r is always a number between $+1$ and -1 $(-1 \le r \le +1)$. Table 4-2 gives a quick summary of some basic facts about r.

For most applications, you will use a calculator or computer software to compute r directly. However, to build some familiarity with the structure of the correlation coefficient, it is useful to do some calculations for yourself. Example 2 and Guided Exercise 2 show how to use the computation formula to compute r.

EXAMPLE 2 **Computing r**

Sand driven by wind creates large beautiful dunes at the Great Sand Dunes National Monument, Colorado. Of course, the same natural forces also create large dunes in the Great Sahara and Arabia. Is there a linear correlation between wind velocity and sand drift rate? Let x be a random variable representing wind velocity (in 10 cm/sec) and let y be a random variable representing drift rate of sand (in 100 g/cm/sec). A test site at the Great Sand Dunes National Monument gave the following information about x and y. (Reference: *Hydrologic, Geologic, and Biologic Research at Great Sand Dunes National Monument*, Proceedings of the National Park Service Research Symposium.)

TABLE 4-2 **Some Facts About the Correlation Coefficient**

If r Is	Then	The Scatter Diagram Might Look Something Like
0	There is no linear relation among the points of the scatter diagram.	
1 or -1	There is a perfect linear relation between x and y values; all points lie on the least-squares line.	$r = -1$ $r = 1$
Between 0 and 1 ($0 < r < 1$)	The x and y values have a *positive correlation.* By this, we mean that *large* x values are associated with *large* y values, and *small* x values are associated with *small* y values.	As we go from left to right, the least-squares line goes *up.*
Between -1 and 0 ($-1 < r < 0$)	The x and y values have a *negative correlation.* By this, we mean that *large* x values are associated with *small* y values, and *small* x values are associated with *large* y values.	As we go from left to right, the least-squares line goes *down.*

x	70	115	105	82	93	125	88
y	3	45	21	7	16	62	12

(a) Construct a scatter diagram. Do you expect r to be positive?

SOLUTION: Figure 4-5 displays the scatter diagram. From the scatter diagram, it appears that as x values increase, y values also tend to increase. Therefore, r should be positive.

FIGURE 4-5

Wind Velocity (10 cm/sec) and Drift Rate of Sand (100 g/cm/sec)

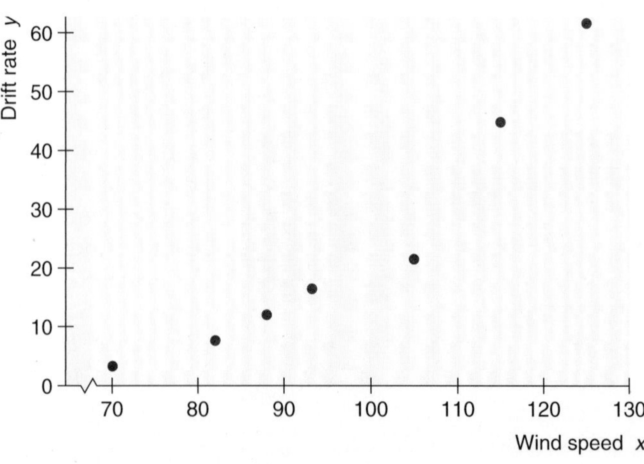

TABLE 4-3 Computation Table

x	y	x^2	y^2	xy
70	3	4900	9	210
115	45	13,225	2025	5175
105	21	11,025	441	2205
82	7	6724	49	574
93	16	8649	256	1488
125	62	15,625	3844	7750
88	12	7744	144	1056
$\Sigma x = 678$	$\Sigma y = 166$	$\Sigma x^2 = 67{,}892$	$\Sigma y^2 = 6768$	$\Sigma xy = 18{,}458$

(b) Compute r using the computation formula (Formula 2).

SOLUTION: To find r, we need to compute Σx, Σx^2, Σy, Σy^2, and Σxy. It is convenient to organize the data in a table of five columns (Table 4-3) and then sum the entries in each column. Of course, many calculators give these sums directly. Using the computation formula for r, the sums from Table 4-3, and $n = 7$, we have

$$r = \frac{n\Sigma xy - (\Sigma x)(\Sigma y)}{\sqrt{n\Sigma x^2 - (\Sigma x)^2}\sqrt{n\Sigma y^2 - (\Sigma y)^2}} \qquad (2)$$

$$= \frac{7(18{,}458) - (678)(166)}{\sqrt{7(67{,}892) - (678)^2}\sqrt{7(6768) - (166)^2}} \approx \frac{16{,}658}{(124.74)(140.78)} \approx 0.949$$

Note: Using a calculator to compute r directly gives 0.949, to three places after the decimal.

(c) What does the value of r tell you?

SOLUTION: Since r is very close to 1, we have an indication of a strong positive linear correlation between wind velocity and drift rate of sand. In other words, we expect that higher wind speeds tend to mean greater drift rates. Because r is so close to 1, the association between the variables appears to be linear.

It is quite a task to compute r for even seven data pairs. The use of columns as in Example 2 is extremely helpful. Your value for r should always be between -1 and 1, inclusive. Use a scatter diagram to get a rough idea of the value of r. If your computed value of r is outside the allowable range, or if it disagrees quite a bit with the scatter diagram, recheck your calculations. Be sure you distinguish between expressions such as (Σx^2) and $(\Sigma x)^2$. Negligible rounding errors may occur, depending on how you (or your calculator) round.

GUIDED EXERCISE 2 Computing r

In one of the Boston city parks, there has been a problem with muggings in the summer months. A police cadet took a random sample of 10 days (out of the 90-day summer) and compiled the following data. For each day, x represents the number of police officers on duty in the park and y represents the number of reported muggings on that day.

x	10	15	16	1	4	6	18	12	14	7
y	5	2	1	9	7	8	1	5	3	6

Continued

GUIDED EXERCISE 2 *continued*

(a) Construct a scatter diagram of x and y values.

Figure 4-6 shows the scatter diagram.

FIGURE 4-6 Scatter Diagram for Number of Police Officers versus Number of Muggings

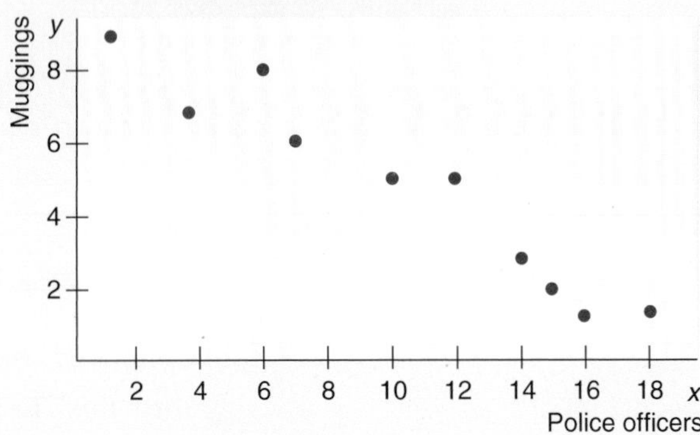

(b) From the scatter diagram, do you think the computed value of r will be positive, negative, or zero? Explain.

r will be negative. The general trend is that large x values are associated with small y values, and vice versa. From left to right, the least-squares line goes down.

(c) Verify that $\Sigma x = 103$, $\Sigma y = 47$, $\Sigma x^2 = 1347$, $\Sigma y^2 = 295$, and $\Sigma xy = 343$.

Use a calculator.

(d) Compute r. Alternatively, find the value of r directly by using a calculator or computer software.

$$r = \frac{n\Sigma xy - (\Sigma x)(\Sigma y)}{\sqrt{n\Sigma x^2 - (\Sigma x)^2}\sqrt{n\Sigma y^2 - (\Sigma y)^2}}$$

$$= \frac{10(343) - (103)(47)}{\sqrt{10(1347) - (103)^2}\sqrt{10(295) - (47)^2}}$$

$$\approx \frac{-1411}{(53.49)(27.22)} \approx -0.969$$

TECH NOTES Most calculators that support two-variable statistics provide the value of the correlation coefficient r directly. Statistical software provides r, r^2, or both.

TI-84Plus/TI-83Plus First use **CATALOG**, find **DiagnosticOn**, and press **Enter** twice. Then, when you use **STAT**, **CALC**, option **8:LinReg(a+bx)**, the value of r will be given (data from Example 2). In the next section, we will discuss the line $y = a + bx$ and the meaning of r^2.

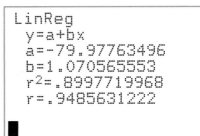

```
LinReg
 y=a+bx
 a=-79.97763496
 b=1.070565553
 r²=.8997719968
 r=.9485631222
```

Excel Use the menu selection **Paste function** (fx) ➤ **Statistical** ➤ **Correl.**

Minitab Use the menu selection **Stat** ➤ **Basic Statistics** ➤ **Correlation.**

CRITICAL THINKING

Sample correlation compared to population correlation

In Section 11.4, we use a Student's t distribution to test ρ for significance. However, Problem 19 of this section includes a table for testing ρ using levels of significance $\alpha = 0.01$ or $\alpha = 0.05$. To test for significance using the table in Problem 19, students simply compare the value of r to a value in the table.

Problem 19 shows an informal process for determining whether or not r is significant.

Cautions About Correlation

The correlation coefficient can be thought of as a measure of how well a linear model fits the data points on a scatter diagram. The closer r is to $+1$ or -1, the better a line "fits" the data. Values of r close to 0 indicate a poor fit to any line.

Usually, a scatter diagram does not contain *all* possible data points that could be gathered. Most scatter diagrams represent only a *random sample* of data pairs taken from a very large population of all possible pairs. Because r is computed on the basis of a random sample of (x, y) pairs, we expect the values of r to vary from one sample to the next (much as the sample mean $\bar{x}$ varies from sample to sample). This brings up the question of the *significance* of r. Or, put another way, what are the chances that our random sample of data pairs indicates a high correlation when, in fact, the population x and y values are not so strongly correlated? Right now, let's just say that the significance of r is a separate issue that will be treated in Section 11.4, where we test the *population correlation coefficient* ρ (Greek letter *rho*, pronounced "row").

r = **sample correlation coefficient** computed from a random sample of (x, y) data pairs

ρ = **population correlation coefficient** computed from all population data pairs (x, y)

Causation

The correlation coefficient is a mathematical tool for measuring the strength of a linear relationship between two variables. As such, it makes no implication about cause or effect. The fact that two variables tend to increase or decrease together does not mean a change in one is *causing* a change in the other. A strong correlation between x and y is sometimes due to other (either known or unknown) variables. Such variables are called *lurking variables.*

It is good to emphasize that the concept of *strength of relationship* between random variables x and y should not be confused with the concept of a *cause-and-effect* relation between the variables. Example 3 and Problems 7 to 10 can be used for a good class discussion regarding this point.

In ordered pairs (x, y), x is called the **explanatory** variable and y is called the **response** variable. When r indicates a linear correlation between x and y, changes in values of y tend to respond to changes in values of x according to a linear model. A **lurking variable** is a variable that is neither an explanatory nor a response variable. Yet, a lurking variable may be responsible for changes in both x and y.

EXAMPLE 3 CAUSATION AND LURKING VARIABLES

Over a period of years, the population of a certain town increased. It was observed that during this period the correlation between x, the number of people attending church, and y, the number of people in the city jail, was $r = 0.90$. Does going to church *cause* people to go to jail? Is there a *lurking variable* that might cause both variables x and y to increase?

SOLUTION: We hope church attendance does not cause people to go to jail! During this period, there was an increase in population. Therefore, it is not too surprising that both the number of people attending church and the number of people in jail increased. The high correlation between x and y is likely due to the lurking variable of population increase.

VIEWPOINT Low on Credit, High on Cost!!!

How do you measure automobile insurance risk? One way is to use a little statistics and customer credit rating. Insurers say statistics show that drivers who have a history of bad credit are more likely to be in serious car accidents. According to a high-level executive at Allstate Insurance Company, financial instability is an extremely powerful predictor of future insurance losses. In short, there seems to be a strong correlation between bad credit ratings and auto insurance claims. Consequently, insurance companies want to charge higher premiums to customers with bad credit ratings. Consumer advocates object strongly because they say bad credit does not cause *automobile accidents. More than 20 states prohibit or restrict the use of credit ratings in determining auto insurance premiums. Insurance companies respond by saying that your best defense is to pay your bills on time!*

SECTION 4.1 PROBLEMS

Tables and art to accompany margin answers may be found in the back of the book.

1. Explanatory variable is placed along horizontal axis, usually x axis. Response variable is placed along vertical axis, usually y axis.
2. Increases.
3. Decreases.
4. (a) Strong negative linear correlation.
   (b) No or weak linear correlation.
   (c) Strong positive linear correlation.
5. (a) Moderate.
   (b) None.
   (c) High.
6. (a) Moderate.
   (b) High.
   (c) None.

Note: Answers may vary due to rounding.

1. *Statistical Literacy* When drawing a scatter diagram, along which axis is the explanatory variable placed? Along which axis is the response variable placed?

2. *Statistical Literacy* Suppose two variables are positively correlated. Does the response variable increase or decrease as the explanatory variable increases?

3. *Statistical Literacy* Suppose two variables are negatively correlated. Does the response variable increase or decrease as the explanatory variable increases?

4. *Statistical Literacy* Describe the relationship between two variables when the correlation coefficient r is
   (a) near -1
   (b) near 0
   (c) near 1

5. *Critical Thinking: Linear Correlation* Look at the following diagrams. Does each diagram show high linear correlation, moderate or low linear correlation, or no linear correlation?

(a)
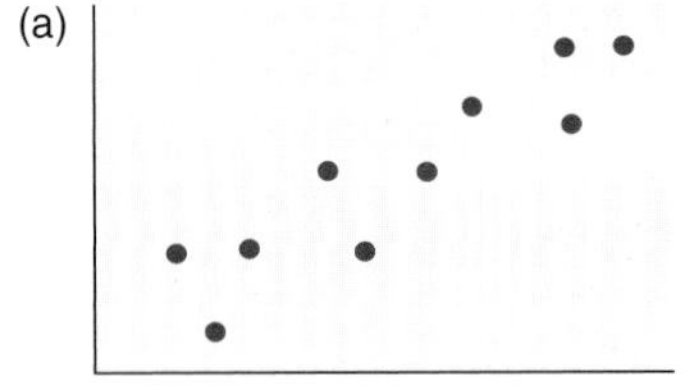
(b)
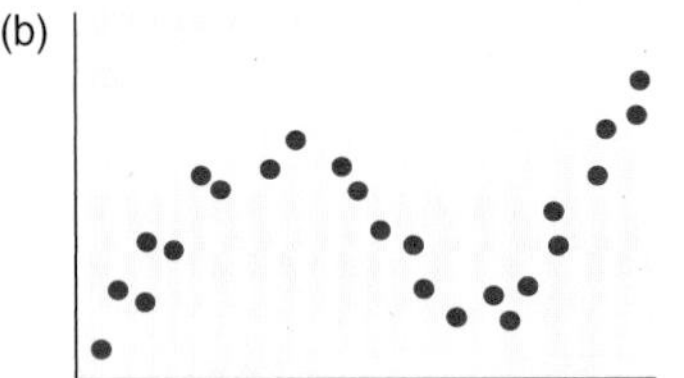
(c)
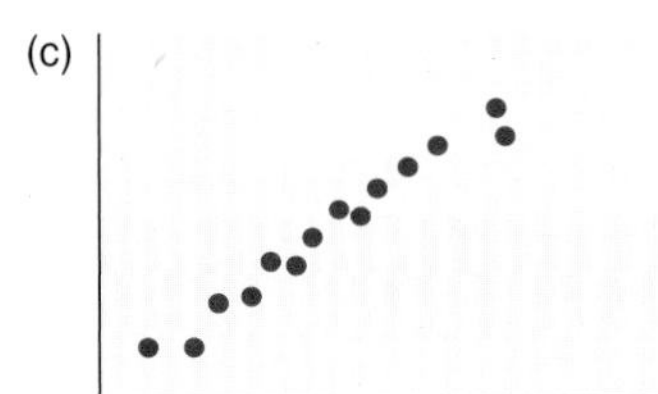

6. *Critical Thinking: Linear Correlation* Look at the following diagrams. Does each diagram show high linear correlation, moderate or low linear correlation, or no linear correlation?

(a)
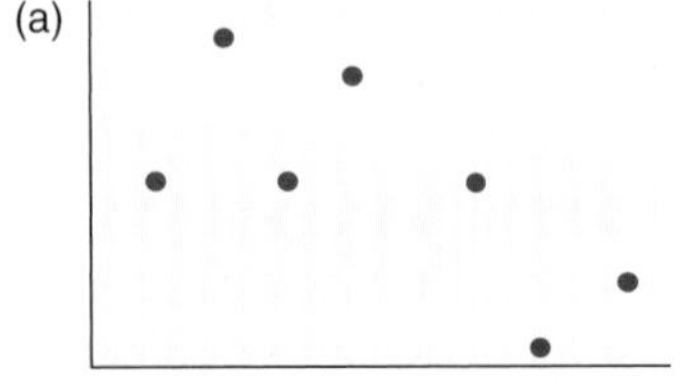
(b)
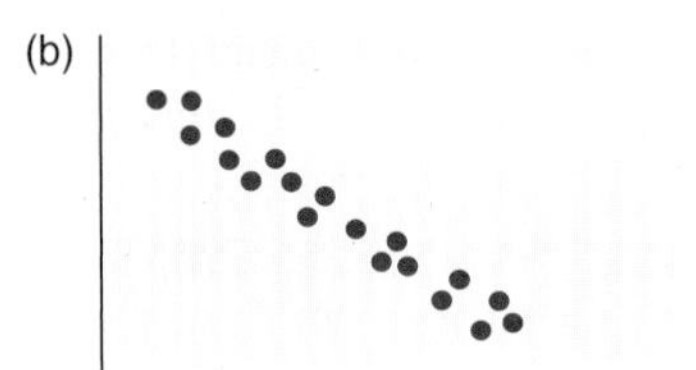
(c)
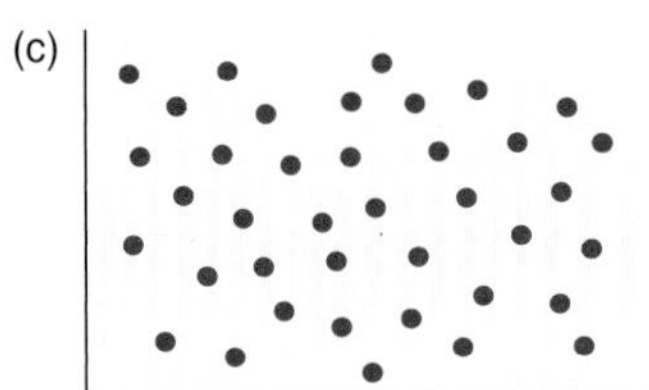

7. (a) No.
(b) Increasing population might be a lurking variable causing both variables to increase.

7. *Critical Thinking: Lurking Variables* Over the past few years, there has been a strong positive correlation between the annual consumption of diet soda drinks and the number of traffic accidents.
   (a) Do you think increasing consumption of diet soda drinks causes traffic accidents? Explain.
   (b) What lurking variables might be causing the increase in one or both of the variables? Explain.

8. (a) No.
(b) Rising cost of living might be a lurking variable causing both variables to increase.

8. *Critical Thinking: Lurking Variables* Over the past decade, there has been a strong positive correlation between teacher salaries and prescription drug costs.
   (a) Do you think paying teachers more causes prescription drugs to cost more? Explain.
   (b) What lurking variables might be causing the increase in one or both of the variables? Explain.

9. (a) No.
(b) One lurking variable responsible for average annual income increases is inflation. Better training might be a lurking variable responsible for shorter times to run the mile.

9. *Critical Thinking: Lurking Variables* Over the past 50 years, there has been a strong negative correlation between average annual income and the record time to run 1 mile. In other words, average annual incomes have been rising while the record time to run 1 mile has been decreasing.
   (a) Do you think increasing incomes cause decreasing times to run the mile? Explain.
   (b) What lurking variables might be causing the increase in one or both of the variables? Explain.

10. (a) No.
(b) A lurking variable might be better health care and treatments.

10. *Critical Thinking: Lurking Variables* Over the past 30 years in the United States, there has been a strong negative correlation between the number of infant deaths at birth and the number of people over age 65.
   (a) Is the fact that people are living longer causing a decrease in infant mortalities at birth?
   (b) What lurking variables might be causing the increase in one or both of the variables? Explain.

11. (a) Line slopes upward (method to find equation is given in Section 4.2).
(b) Strong; positive.
(c) $r \approx 0.972$; increase.

11. *Veterinary Science: Shetland Ponies* How much should a healthy Shetland pony weigh? Let x be the age of the pony (in months), and let y be the average weight of the pony (in kilograms). The following information is based on data taken from *The Merck Veterinary Manual* (a reference used in most veterinary colleges).

x	3	6	12	18	24
y	60	95	140	170	185

   (a) Make a scatter diagram and draw the line you think best fits the data.
   (b) Would you say the correlation is low, moderate, or strong? positive or negative?
   (c) Use a calculator to verify that $\Sigma x = 63$, $\Sigma x^2 = 1089$, $\Sigma y = 650$, $\Sigma y^2 = 95{,}350$, and $\Sigma xy = 9930$. Compute r. As x increases, does the value of r imply that y should tend to increase or decrease? Explain.

12. (a) Line slopes downward (method to find equation is given in Section 4.2).
(b) Moderate; negative.
(c) $r \approx -0.945$; decrease.

12. *Health Insurance: Administrative Cost* The following data are based on information from *Domestic Affairs*. Let x be the average number of employees in a group health insurance plan, and let y be the average administrative cost as a percentage of claims.

x	3	7	15	35	75
y	40	35	30	25	18

   (a) Make a scatter diagram and draw the line you think best fits the data.

(b) Would you say the correlation is low, moderate, or strong? positive or negative?
(c) Use a calculator to verify that $\Sigma x = 135$, $\Sigma x^2 = 7133$, $\Sigma y = 148$, $\Sigma y^2 = 4674$, and $\Sigma xy = 3040$. Compute r. As x increases, does the value of r imply that y should tend to increase or decrease? Explain.

13. (a) Line slopes downward (method to find equation is given in Section 4.2).
(b) Strong; negative.
(c) $r \approx -0.990$; decrease.

13. *Meteorology: Cyclones* Can a low barometer reading be used to predict maximum wind speed of an approaching tropical cyclone? Data for this problem are based on information taken from *Weatherwise* (Vol. 46, No. 1), a publication of the American Meteorological Society. For a random sample of tropical cyclones, let x be the lowest pressure (in millibars) as a cyclone approaches, and let y be the maximum wind speed (in miles per hour) of the cyclone.

x	1004	975	992	935	985	932
y	40	100	65	145	80	150

(a) Make a scatter diagram and draw the line you think best fits the data.
(b) Would you say the correlation is low, moderate, or strong? positive or negative?
(c) Use a calculator to verify that $\Sigma x = 5823$, $\Sigma x^2 = 5{,}655{,}779$, $\Sigma y = 580$, $\Sigma y^2 = 65{,}750$, and $\Sigma xy = 556{,}315$. Compute r. As x increases, does the value of r imply that y should tend to increase or decrease? Explain.

14. (a) Line slopes upward (method to find equation is given in Section 4.2).
(b) Low; positive.
(c) $r \approx 0.511$; increase.

14. *Geology: Earthquakes* Is the magnitude of an earthquake related to the depth below the surface at which the quake occurs? Let x be the magnitude of an earthquake (on the Richter scale), and let y be the depth (in kilometers) of the quake below the surface at the epicenter. The following is based on information taken from the National Earthquake Information Service of the U.S. Geological Survey. Additional data may be found by visiting the Online Study Center at **www.cengage.com/statistics/Brase/UBS5e** and finding the link to earthquakes.

x	2.9	4.2	3.3	4.5	2.6	3.2	3.4
y	5.0	10.0	11.2	10.0	7.9	3.9	5.5

(a) Make a scatter diagram and draw the line you think best fits the data.
(b) Would you say the correlation is low, moderate, or strong? positive or negative?
(c) Use a calculator to verify that $\Sigma x = 24.1$, $\Sigma x^2 = 85.75$, $\Sigma y = 53.5$, $\Sigma y^2 = 458.31$, and $\Sigma xy = 190.18$. Compute r. As x increases, does the value of r imply that y should tend to increase or decrease? Explain.

15. (a) Line slopes upward (method to find equation is given in Section 4.2).
(b) High; positive.
(c) $r \approx 0.948$; increase.

15. *Baseball: Batting Averages and Home Runs* In baseball, is there a linear correlation between batting average and home run percentage? Let x represent the batting average of a professional baseball player, and let y represent the player's home run percentage (number of home runs per 100 times at bat). A random sample of $n = 7$ professional baseball players gave the following information. (Reference: *The Baseball Encyclopedia,* Macmillan Publishing Company.)

x	0.243	0.259	0.286	0.263	0.268	0.339	0.299
y	1.4	3.6	5.5	3.8	3.5	7.3	5.0

(a) Make a scatter diagram and draw the line you think best fits the data.
(b) Would you say the correlation is low, moderate, or high? positive or negative?
(c) Use a calculator to verify that $\Sigma x = 1.957$, $\Sigma x^2 \approx 0.553$, $\Sigma y = 30.1$, $\Sigma y^2 = 150.15$, and $\Sigma xy \approx 8.753$. Compute r. As x increases, does the value of r imply that y should tend to increase or decrease? Explain.

16. (a) Line slopes upward (method to find equation is given in Section 4.2).
(b) Moderate; positive.
(c) $r \approx 0.765$; increase.

16. *University Crime: FBI Report* Do larger universities tend to have more property crime? University crime statistics are affected by a variety of factors. The surrounding community, accessibility given to outside visitors, and many other factors influence crime rate. Let x be a variable that represents student enrollment (in thousands) on a university campus, and let y be a variable that represents the number of burglaries in a year on the university campus. A random sample of $n = 8$ universities in California gave the following information about enrollments and annual burglary incidents. (Reference: *Crime in the United States*, Federal Bureau of Investigation.)

x	12.5	30.0	24.5	14.3	7.5	27.7	16.2	20.1
y	26	73	39	23	15	30	15	25

(a) Make a scatter diagram and draw the line you think best fits the data.
(b) Would you say the correlation is low, moderate, or high? positive or negative?
(c) Using a calculator, verify that $\Sigma x = 152.8$, $\Sigma x^2 = 3350.98$, $\Sigma y = 246$, $\Sigma y^2 = 10{,}030$, and $\Sigma xy = 5488.4$. Compute r. As x increases, does the value of r imply that y should tend to increase or decrease? Explain.

This problem can generate a good class discussion about ways to (accidentally or intentionally) misrepresent data.

17. (d) Stretching the scale on the y axis makes the line appear steeper. Shrinking the scale on the y axis makes the line appear flatter. The slope of the line does not change. Only the appearance (visual impression) of the slope changes as the scale of the y axis changes.

17. *Expand Your Knowledge: Effect of Scale on Scatter Diagram* The initial visual impact of a scatter diagram depends on the scales used on the x and y axes. Consider the following data:

x	1	2	3	4	5	6
y	1	4	6	3	6	7

(a) Make a scatter diagram using the same scale on both the x and y axes (i.e., make sure the unit lengths on the two axes are equal).
(b) Make a scatter diagram using a scale on the y axis that is twice as long as that on the x axis.
(c) Make a scatter diagram using a scale on the y axis that is half as long as that on the x axis.
(d) On each of the three graphs, draw the straight line that you think best fits the data points. How do the slopes (or directions) of the three lines appear to change? (*Note:* The actual slopes are the same; they just appear different because of the choice of scale factors.)

18. (a) Same.
(b) Same.
(c) $r \approx 0.61859$ in both cases.

18. *Expand Your Knowledge: Effect on r of Exchanging x and y Values* Examine the computation formula for r, the sample correlation coefficient [Formulas (1) and (2) of this section].
(a) In the formula for r, if we exchange the symbols x and y, do we get a different result or do we get the same (equivalent) result? Explain.
(b) If we have a set of x and y data values and we exchange corresponding x and y values to get a new data set, should the sample correlation coefficient be the same for both sets of data? Explain.
(c) Compute the sample correlation coefficient r for each of the following data sets and show that r is the same for both.

x	1	3	4
y	2	1	6

x	2	1	6
y	1	3	4

19. (a) $r \approx 0.972$ with $n = 5$ is significant for $\alpha = 0.05$. For this α, we conclude that age and weight of Shetland ponies are correlated.
(b) $r \approx -0.990$ with $n = 6$ is significant for $\alpha = 0.01$. For this α, we conclude that lowest barometric pressure reading and maximum wind speed for cyclones are correlated.

19. *Expand Your Knowledge: Using a Table to Test ρ* The correlation coefficient r is a *sample* statistic. What does it tell us about the value of the population correlation coefficient ρ (Greek letter rho)? We will build the formal structure of hypothesis tests of ρ in Section 11.4. However, there is a quick way to determine if the sample evidence based on r is strong enough to conclude that there is some population correlation between the variables. In other words, we can use the

TABLE 4-4 Critical Values for Correlation Coefficient r

n	$\alpha = 0.05$	$\alpha = 0.01$	n	$\alpha = 0.05$	$\alpha = 0.01$	n	$\alpha = 0.05$	$\alpha = 0.01$
3	1.00	1.00	13	0.53	0.68	23	0.41	0.53
4	0.95	0.99	14	0.53	0.66	24	0.40	0.52
5	0.88	0.96	15	0.51	0.64	25	0.40	0.51
6	0.81	0.92	16	0.50	0.61	26	0.39	0.50
7	0.75	0.87	17	0.48	0.61	27	0.38	0.49
8	0.71	0.83	18	0.47	0.59	28	0.37	0.48
9	0.67	0.80	19	0.46	0.58	29	0.37	0.47
10	0.63	0.76	20	0.44	0.56	30	0.36	0.46
11	0.60	0.73	21	0.43	0.55			
12	0.58	0.71	22	0.42	0.54			

value of r to determine if $\rho \neq 0$. We do this by comparing the value $|r|$ to an entry in Table 4-4. The value of α in the table gives us the probability of concluding that $\rho \neq 0$ when, in fact, $\rho = 0$ and there is no population correlation. We have two choices for α: $\alpha = 0.05$ or $\alpha = 0.01$.

PROCEDURE

HOW TO USE TABLE 4-4 TO TEST ρ

1. First compute r from a random sample of n data pairs (x, y).
2. Find the table entry in the row headed by n and the column headed by your choice of α. Your choice of α is the risk you are willing to take of mistakenly concluding that $\rho \neq 0$ when, in fact, $\rho = 0$.
3. Compare $|r|$ to the table entry.
   (a) If $|r| \geq$ table entry, then there is sufficient evidence to conclude that $\rho \neq 0$, and we say that r is **significant.** In other words, we conclude that there is some population correlation between the two variables x and y.
   (b) If $|r| <$ table entry, then the evidence is insufficient to conclude that $\rho \neq 0$, and we say that r is **not significant.** We do not have enough evidence to conclude that there is any correlation between the two variables x and y.

(a) Look at Problem 11 regarding the variables x = age of a Shetland pony and y = weight of that pony. Is the value of $|r|$ large enough to conclude that weight and age of Shetland ponies are correlated? Use $\alpha = 0.05$.
(b) Look at Problem 13 regarding the variables x = lowest barometric pressure as a cyclone approaches and y = maximum wind speed of the cyclone. Is the value of $|r|$ large enough to conclude that lowest barometric pressure and wind speed of a cyclone are correlated? Use $\alpha = 0.01$.

20. (a) No; yes.
(b) No; yes.
(c) No; no; no; A larger sample size means that a smaller $|r|$ might be significant.

20. *Expand Your Knowledge: Sample Size and Significance of Correlation* In this problem, we use Table 4-4 to explore the significance of r based on different sample sizes. See Problem 19.
(a) Is a sample correlation coefficient $r = 0.820$ significant at the $\alpha = 0.01$ level based on a sample size of $n = 7$ data pairs? What about $n = 9$ data pairs?
(b) Is a sample correlation coefficient $r = 0.40$ significant at the $\alpha = 0.05$ level based on a sample size of $n = 20$ data pairs? What about $n = 27$ data pairs?
(c) Is it true that in order to be significant, an r value must be larger than 0.90? larger than 0.70? larger than 0.50? What does sample size have to do with the significance of r? Explain.

SECTION 4.2 Linear Regression and the Coefficient of Determination

FOCUS POINTS

- State the least-squares criterion.
- Use sample data to find the equation of the least-squares line. Graph the least-squares line.
- Use the least-squares line to predict a value of the response variable y for a specified value of the explanatory variable x.
- Explain the difference between interpolation and extrapolation.
- Explain why extrapolation beyond the sample data range might give results that are misleading or meaningless.
- Use r^2 to determine *explained* and *unexplained* variation of the response variable y.

In this section, emphasize concepts, examples, and procedures. Tell students not to rush through calculations. Hurried work usually results in errors.

In Denali National Park, Alaska, the wolf population is dependent on a large, strong caribou population. In this wild setting, caribou are found in very large herds. The well-being of an entire caribou herd is not threatened by wolves. In fact, it is thought that wolves keep caribou herds strong by helping prevent overpopulation. Can the caribou population be used to predict the size of the wolf population?

Let x be a random variable that represents the fall caribou population (in hundreds) in Denali National Park, and let y be a random variable that represents the late-winter wolf population in the park. A random sample of recent years gave the following information. (Reference: U.S. Department of the Interior, National Biological Service.)

x	30	34	27	25	17	23	20
y	66	79	70	60	48	55	60

Looking at the scatter diagram in Figure 4-7 on page 136, we can ask some questions.

1. Do the data indicate a linear relationship between x and y?
2. Can you find an equation for the best-fitting line relating x and y? Can you use this relationship to predict the size of the wolf population when you know the size of the caribou population?
3. What fractional part of the variability in y can be associated with the variability in x? What fractional part of the variability in y is not associated with a corresponding variability in x?

The first step in answering these questions is to try to express the relationship as a mathematical equation. There are many possible equations, but the simplest and most widely used is the linear equation, or the equation of a straight line. Because we will be using this line to predict the y values from the x values, we call x the *explanatory variable* and y the *response variable.*

Explanatory variable

Response variable

Least-squares criterion

Our job is to find the "best" linear equation representing the points of the scatter diagram. For our criterion of best-fitting line, we use the *least-squares criterion,* which states that the line we fit to the data points must be such that *the sum of the squares of the vertical distances from the points to the line be made as small as possible.* The least-squares criterion is illustrated in Figure 4-8.

Least-squares criterion

The sum of the squares of the vertical distances from the data points (x, y) to the line is made as small as possible.

FIGURE 4-7

Caribou and Wolf Populations

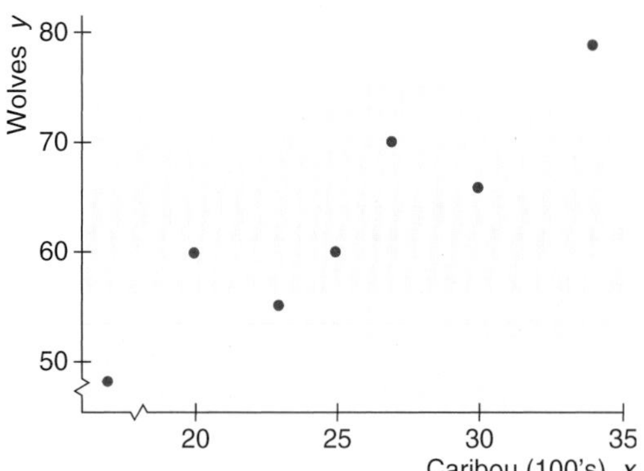

FIGURE 4-8

Least-Squares Criterion

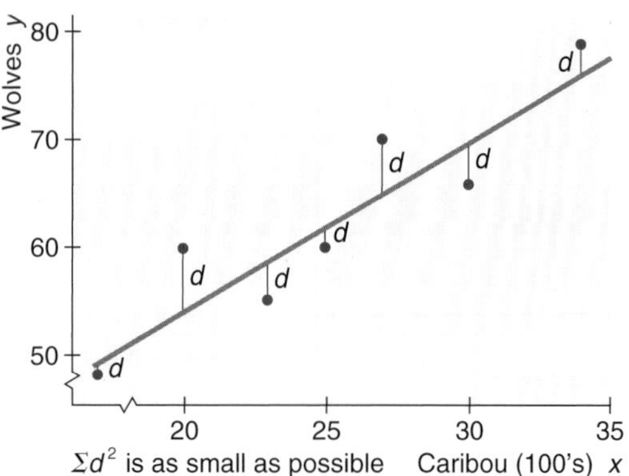

In Figure 4-8, d represents the difference between the y coordinate of the data point and the corresponding y coordinate on the line. Thus, if the data point lies above the line, d is positive, but if the data point is below the line, d is negative. As a result, the sum of the d values can be small even if the points are widely spread in the scatter diagram. However, the squares d^2 cannot be negative. By minimizing the sum of the squares, we are, in effect, not allowing positive and negative d values to "cancel out" one another in the sum. It is in this way that we can meet the least-squares criterion of minimizing the sum of the squares of the vertical distances between the points and the line over *all* points in the scatter diagram.

Least-squares line

This is a good time to emphasize notation and how to organize work using a table.

We use the notation $\hat{y} = a + bx$ for the least-squares line. A little algebra tells us that b is the slope and a is the intercept of the line. In this context, $\hat{y}$ (read "y hat") represents the value of the response variable y estimated using the least-squares line and a given value of the explanatory variable x.

Techniques of calculus can be applied to show that a and b may be computed using the following procedure.

PROCEDURE

HOW TO FIND THE EQUATION OF THE LEAST-SQUARES LINE $\hat{y} = a + bx$

Obtain a random sample of n data pairs (x, y), where x is the *explanatory variable* and y is the *response variable.*

1. Using the data pairs, compute Σx, Σy, Σx^2, Σy^2, and Σxy. Then compute the sample means $\bar{x}$ and $\bar{y}$.
2. With n = sample size, Σx, Σy, Σx^2, Σy^2, Σxy, $\bar{x}$, and $\bar{y}$, you are ready to compute the slope b and intercept a using the computation formulas

$$\text{Slope:} \quad b = \frac{n\Sigma xy - (\Sigma x)(\Sigma y)}{n\Sigma x^2 - (\Sigma x)^2} \tag{3}$$

$$\text{Intercept:} \quad a = \bar{y} - b\bar{x} \tag{4}$$

Be careful! The notation Σx^2 means first square x and then calculate the sum, whereas $(\Sigma x)^2$ means first sum the x values, then square the result.

Continued

3. The equation of the least-squares line computed from your sample data is

$$\hat{y} = a + bx \tag{5}$$

Note: For inferences (Section 11.4), the data pairs should have a *bivariate normal variation.* That is, for a fixed value of x, the y values should have a normal distribution and vice versa for a fixed y value. Chapter 7 discusses normal distributions.

COMMENT The computation formulas for the slope of the least-squares line, the correlation coefficient r, and the standard deviations s_x and s_y use many of the same sums. There is, in fact, a relationship between the correlation coefficient r and the slope b of the least-squares line. In instances where we know r, s_x, and s_y, we can use the following formula to compute b.

This formula clarifies the interrelations among the values of b, r, and the sample standard deviations of the variables x and y.

$$b = r\left(\frac{s_y}{s_x}\right) \tag{6}$$

COMMENT In other mathematics courses, the slope-intercept form of the equation of a line is usually given as $y = mx + b$, where m refers to the slope of the line and b to the y-coordinate of the y-intercept. In statistics, when there is only one explanatory variable, it is common practice to use the letter b to designate the slope of the least-squares line and the letter a to designate the y-coordinate of the intercept. For example, these are the symbols used on the TI-84Plus and TI-83Plus calculators as well as many other calculators.

Using the formulas to find the values of a and b

If your students are finding the values of a and b directly from a calculator, have them omit the computation discussions and go to the margin header "Using the values of a and b to construct the equation of the least-squares line." In Guided Exercise 3, do part (a) and then parts (e) through (g).

For most applications, you can use a calculator or computer software to compute a and b directly. However, to build some familiarity with the structure of the computation formulas, it is useful to do some calculations for yourself. Example 4 shows how to use the computation formulas to find the values of a and b and the equation of the least-squares line $\hat{y} = a + bx$.

Note: If you are using your calculator to find the values of a and b directly, then you may omit the discussion regarding use of the formulas. Go to the margin header "Using the values of a and b to construct the equation of the least-squares line."

EXAMPLE 4 **LEAST-SQUARES LINE**

Let's find the least-squares equation relating the variables x = size of caribou population (in hundreds) and y = size of wolf population in Denali National Park. Use x as the explanatory variable and y as the response variable.

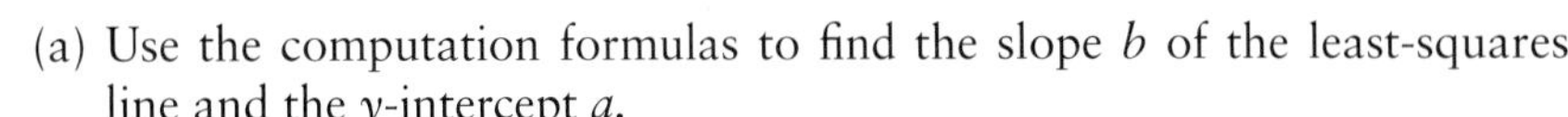

(a) Use the computation formulas to find the slope b of the least-squares line and the y-intercept a.

SOLUTION: Table 4-5 on the next page gives the data values x and y along with the values x^2, y^2, and xy. First compute the sample means.

$$\bar{x} = \frac{\Sigma x}{n} = \frac{176}{7} \approx 25.14 \quad \text{and} \quad \bar{y} = \frac{\Sigma y}{n} = \frac{438}{7} \approx 62.57$$

Next compute the slope b.

$$b = \frac{n\Sigma xy - (\Sigma x)(\Sigma y)}{n\Sigma x^2 - (\Sigma x)^2} = \frac{7(11{,}337) - (176)(438)}{7(4628) - (176)^2} = \frac{2271}{1420} \approx 1.60$$

TABLE 4-5 Sums for Computing b, $\bar{x}$, and $\bar{y}$

x	y	x^2	y^2	xy
30	66	900	4356	1980
34	79	1156	6241	2686
27	70	729	4900	1890
25	60	625	3600	1500
17	48	289	2304	816
23	55	529	3025	1265
20	60	400	3600	1200
$\Sigma x = 176$	$\Sigma y = 438$	$\Sigma x^2 = 4628$	$\Sigma y^2 = 28{,}026$	$\Sigma xy = 11{,}337$

Use the values of b, $\bar{x}$, and $\bar{y}$ to compute the y-intercept a.

$$a = \bar{y} - b\bar{x} \approx 62.57 - 1.60(25.14) \approx 22.35$$

Note that calculators give the values $b \approx 1.599$ and $a \approx 22.36$. These values differ slightly from those you computed using the formulas because of rounding.

Using the values of a and b to construct the equation of the least-squares line

(b) Use the values of a and b (either computed or obtained from a calculator) to find the equation of the least-squares line.

SOLUTION:

$$\hat{y} = a + bx$$

$$\hat{y} \approx 22.35 + 1.60x \quad \text{since} \quad a \approx 22.35 \quad \text{and} \quad b \approx 1.60$$

Graphing the least-squares line

(c) Graph the equation of the least-squares line on a scatter diagram.

SOLUTION: To graph the least-squares line, we have several options available. The slope-intercept method of algebra is probably the quickest, but may not always be convenient if the intercept is not within the range of the sample data values. It is just as easy to select two x values in the range of the x data values and then use the least-squares line to compute two corresponding $\hat{y}$ values.

In fact, we already have the coordinates of one point on the least-squares line. By the formula for the intercept [Equation (4)], the point $(\bar{x}, \bar{y})$ is always on the least-squares line. For our example, $(\bar{x}, \bar{y}) = (25.14, 62.57)$.

It is good to emphasize that the point $(\bar{x}, \bar{y})$ is always on the least-squares line.

The point $(\bar{x}, \bar{y})$ is always on the least-squares line.

Another x value within the data range is $x = 34$. Using the least-squares line to compute the corresponding $\hat{y}$ value gives

$$\hat{y} \approx 22.35 + 1.60(34) \approx 76.75$$

We place the two points (25.14, 62.57) and (34, 76.75) on the scatter diagram (using a different symbol than that used for the sample data points) and connect the points with a line segment (Figure 4-9).

Meaning of slope

In the equation $\hat{y} = a + bx$, the slope b tells us how many units $\hat{y}$ changes for each unit change in x. In Example 4 regarding size of wolf and caribou populations,

$$\hat{y} \approx 22.35 + 1.60x$$

FIGURE 4-9

Caribou and Wolf Populations

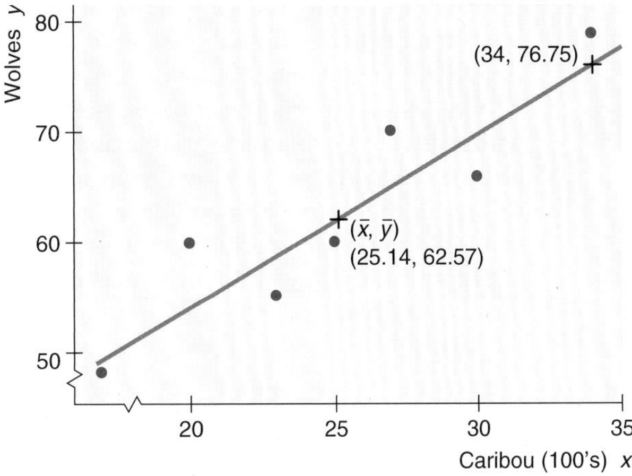

The slope 1.60 tells us that if the number of caribou (in hundreds) changes by 1 (hundred), then we expect the sustainable wolf population to change by 1.60. In other words, our model says that an increase of 100 caribou will increase the predicted wolf population by 1.60. If the caribou population decreases by 400, we predict the sustainable wolf population to decrease by 6.4.

In business, finance, and other applications, the slope of the least-squares line is called the *marginal change*. That is, the marginal change is the change in the response variable for each unit change in the explanatory variable.

The slope of the least-squares line tells us how many units the response variable is expected to change for each unit change in the explanatory variable. The number of units change in the response variable for each unit change in the explanatory variable is called the **marginal change** of the response variable.

CRITICAL THINKING

Using the Least-Squares Line for Prediction

Predicting y for a specified x

Making predictions is one of the main applications of linear regression. In other words, you use the equation of the least-squares line to predict the $\hat{y}$ value for a specified x value. Of course, the accuracy of the prediction depends on how well the least-squares line fits the original raw data points. It is a good idea to check that the correlation coefficient indicates a strong linear correlation.

Interpolation, extrapolation

Another issue that affects the validity of predictions is whether you are *interpolating* or *extrapolating*.

Predicting $\hat{y}$ values for x values that are **between** observed x values in the data set is called **interpolation.**

Predicting $\hat{y}$ values for x values that are **beyond** observed x values in the data set is called **extrapolation.** Extrapolation may produce unrealistic forecasts.

Emphasize that there is a real conceptual difference between *interpolation* and *extrapolation*. We are not studying methods of extrapolation in this text. Predicting y values for x values far beyond the range of given data may result in unrealistic forecasts.

The least-squares line is developed from sample data pairs (x, y). The least-squares line may not reflect the relationship between x and y for values of x outside the data range. For example, there is a fairly high correlation between height and age for boys ages 1 year to 10 years. In general, the older the boy, the taller the boy. A least-squares line based on such data would give good predictions

This is an important point to emphasize. If you want to predict x values from y values, you must find a completely new least-squares line.

Problem 17 demonstrates that for the same data set, the least-squares lines for predicting y or for predicting x are essentially different.

of height for ages between 1 and 10. However, it would be fairly meaningless to use the same linear regression line to predict the height of a 20-year-old or 50-year-old man.

Another consideration when working with predictions is the fact that the least-squares line is based on sample data. Each different sample will produce a slightly different equation for the least-squares line.

One more important fact about predictions: The least-squares line is developed with x as the explanatory variable and y as the response variable. This model can be used only to predict y values from specified x values. If you wish to begin with y values and predict corresponding x values, you must start all over and compute a new equation. Such an equation would be developed using a model with x as the response variable and y as the explanatory variable. See Problem 17 at the end of this section. Note that the equation for predicting x values *cannot* be derived from the least-squares line predicting y simply by solving the equation for x.

The least-squares line developed with x as the explanatory variable and y as the response variable can be used only to predict y values from specified x values.

The next example shows how to use the least-squares line for predictions.

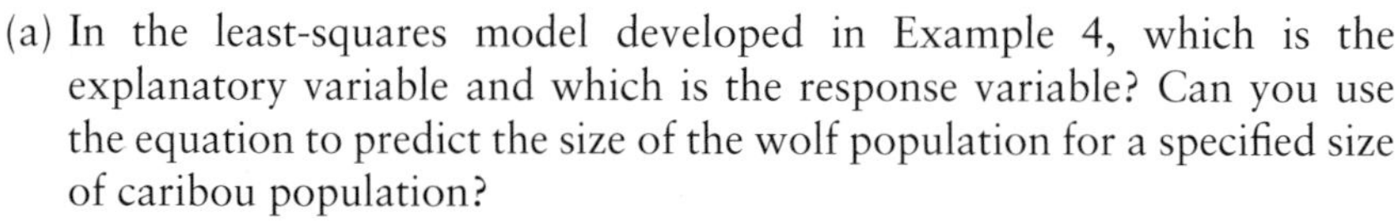

EXAMPLE 5 PREDICTIONS

We continue with Example 4 regarding size of the wolf population as it relates to size of the caribou population. Suppose you want to predict the size of the wolf population when the size of the caribou population is 21 (hundred).

(a) In the least-squares model developed in Example 4, which is the explanatory variable and which is the response variable? Can you use the equation to predict the size of the wolf population for a specified size of caribou population?

SOLUTION: The least-squares line $\hat{y} \approx 22.35 + 1.60x$ was developed using x = size of caribou population (in hundreds) as the explanatory variable and y = size of wolf population as the response variable. We can use the equation to predict the y value for a specified x value.

(b) The sample data pairs have x values ranging from 17 (hundred) to 34 (hundred) for the size of the caribou population. To predict the size of the wolf population when the size of the caribou population is 21 (hundred), will you be interpolating or extrapolating?

SOLUTION: Interpolating, since 21 (hundred) falls within the range of sample x values.

(c) Predict the size of the wolf population when the caribou population is 21 (hundred).

SOLUTION: Using the least-squares line from Example 4 and the value 21 in place of x gives

$$\hat{y} \approx 22.35 + 1.60x \approx 22.35 + 1.60(21) \approx 55.95$$

Rounding up to a whole number gives a prediction of 56 for the size of the wolf population.

GUIDED EXERCISE 3 Least-squares line

The Quick Sell car dealership has been using 1-minute spot ads on a local TV station. The ads always occur during the evening hours and advertise the different models and price ranges of cars on the lot that week. During a 10-week period, the Quick Sell dealer kept a weekly record of the number x of TV ads versus the number y of cars sold. The results are given in Table 4-6.

The manager decided that Quick Sell can afford only 12 ads per week. At that level of advertisement, how many cars can Quick Sell expect to sell each week? We'll answer this question in several steps.

TABLE 4-6

x	y
6	15
20	31
0	10
14	16
25	28
16	20
28	40
18	25
10	12
8	15

(a) Draw a scatter diagram for the data.

➡ The scatter diagram is shown in Figure 4-10. The plain red dots in Figure 4-10 are the points of the scatter diagram. Notice that the least-squares line is also shown with two extra points used to position the line.

FIGURE 4-10 Scatter Diagram and Least-Squares Line for Table 4-6

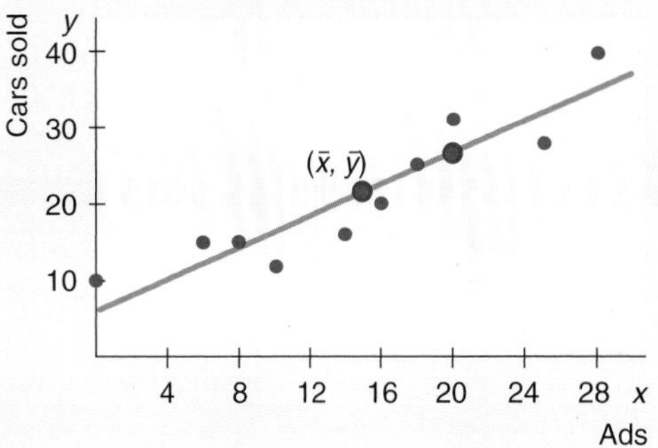

(b) Verify that $\Sigma x = 145$, $\Sigma y = 212$, $\Sigma x^2 = 2785$, and $\Sigma xy = 3764$.

➡ Use a calculator.

(c) Compute the sample means $\bar{x}$ and $\bar{y}$.

➡ $$\bar{x} = \frac{\Sigma x}{n} = \frac{145}{10} = 14.5$$

$$\bar{y} = \frac{\Sigma y}{n} = \frac{212}{10} = 21.2$$

(d) Compute a and b for the equation $\hat{y} = a + bx$ of the least-squares line.

➡ $$b = \frac{n\Sigma xy - (\Sigma x)(\Sigma y)}{n\Sigma x^2 - (\Sigma x)^2}$$

$$= \frac{10(3764) - (145)(212)}{10(2785) - (145)^2} = \frac{6900}{6825} \approx 1.01$$

$$a = \bar{y} - b\bar{x}$$

$$\approx 21.2 - 1.01(14.5) \approx 6.56$$

Continued

GUIDED EXERCISE 3 *continued*

(e) What is the equation of the least-squares line $\hat{y} = a + bx$?

➡ Using the values of a and b computed in part (d) or values of a and b obtained directly from a calculator,

$$\hat{y} \approx 6.56 + 1.01x$$

(f) Plot the least-squares line on your scatter diagram.

➡ The least-squares line goes through the point $(\bar{x}, \bar{y}) = (14.5, 21.2)$. To get another point on the line, select a value for x and compute the corresponding y value using the equation $y = 6.56 + 1.01x$. For $x = 20$, we get $y = 6.56 + 1.01(20) = 26.8$, so the point (20, 26.8) is also on the line. The least-squares line is shown in Figure 4-10.

(g) Read the y value for $x = 12$ from your graph. Then use the equation of the least-squares line to calculate y when $x = 12$. How many cars can the manager expect to sell if 12 ads per week are aired on TV?

➡ The graph gives $y \approx 19$. From the equation, we get

$$\begin{aligned} y &= 6.56 + 1.01x \\ &= 6.56 + 1.01(12) \quad \text{using 12 in place of } x \\ &= 18.68 \end{aligned}$$

To the nearest whole number, the manager can expect to sell 19 cars when 12 ads are aired on TV each week.

TECH NOTES

When we have more data pairs, it is convenient to use a technology tool such as the TI-84Plus and TI-83Plus calculators, Excel, or Minitab to find the equation of the least-squares line. The displays show results for the data of Guided Exercise 3 regarding car sales and ads.

Many calculators support two-variable statistics and produce the equation of the least-squares line. Such calculators often have a function key that gives the predicted *y* value for a given *x* value. It is worthwhile to spend some time acquainting students with these calculator functions.

TI-84Plus/TI-83Plus Press STAT, choose **Calculate,** and use option **8:LinReg(a+bx).** For a graph showing the scatter plot and the least-squares line, press the **STAT PLOT** key, turn on a plot, and highlight the first type. Then press the **Y=** key. To enter the equation of the least-squares line, press **VARS,** select **5:Statistics,** highlight **EQ,** and then highlight **1:RegEQ.** Press **ENTER.** Finally, press **ZOOM** and choose **9:ZoomStat.**

Excel There are several ways to find the equation of the least-squares line in Excel. One way is to make a scatter plot using the menu choices **Chart wizard ➤ Scatter Diagram.** When the diagram is complete, **right click** on one of the points on the diagram, select **trendline,** and under Options check to display equation of line.

TI-84Plus/TI-83Plus Display

```
LinReg
 y=a+bx
 a=6.5407
 b=1.0110
 r²=.8449
 r=.9192
```

Excel Display

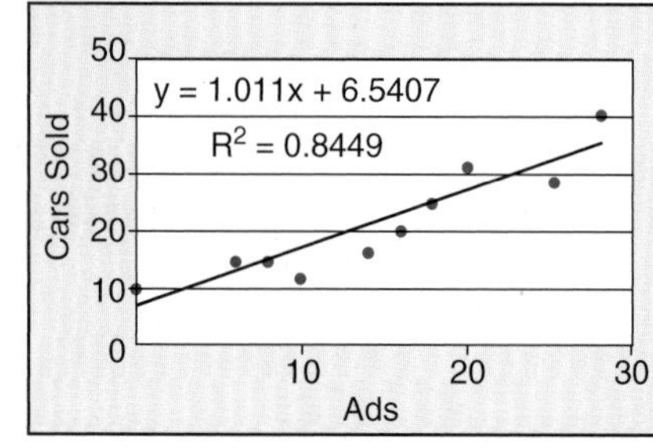

Minitab There are a number of ways to generate the least-squares line. One way is to use the menu selection **Stat ➤ Regression ➤ Fitted Line Plot.** The least-squares equation is shown with the diagram.

Coefficient of Determination

There is another way to answer the question, How good is the least-squares line as an instrument of regression? The *coefficient of determination* r^2 is the square of the sample correlation coefficient r.

Emphasize that once we have computed r from Equation (2) on page 125, it is easy to get r^2. Also, comment 2 in the box is a good point to emphasize.

Coefficient of determination r^2

1. Compute the sample correlation coefficient r using the procedure of Section 4.1. Then simply compute r^2, the sample coefficient of determination.
2. The value r^2 is the ratio of explained variation over total variation. That is, r^2 is the fractional amount of total variation in y that can be explained by using the linear model $\hat{y} = a + bx$.
3. Furthermore, $1 - r^2$ is the fractional amount of total variation in y that is due to random chance or to the possibility of lurking variables that influence y.

Problems 15 and 16 present *residual plots*. A residual plot provides another visual way of determining whether linear regression is appropriate.

In other words, the coefficient of determination r^2 is a measure of the proportion of variation in y that is explained by the regression line, using x as the explanatory variable. If $r = 0.90$, then $r^2 = 0.81$ is the coefficient of determination. We can say that about 81% of the (variation) behavior of the y variable can be explained by the corresponding (variation) behavior of the x variable if we use the equation of the least-squares line. The remaining 19% of the (variation) behavior of the y variable is due to random chance or to the possibility of lurking variables that influence y.

GUIDED EXERCISE 4 Coefficient of determination r^2

In Guided Exercise 3, we looked at the relationship between x = number of 1-minute spot ads on TV advertising different models of cars and y = number of cars sold each week by the sponsoring car dealership.

(a) Using the sums found in Guided Exercise 3, compute the correlation coefficient r. $n = 10$, $\Sigma x = 145$, $\Sigma y = 212$, $\Sigma x^2 = 2785$, and $\Sigma xy = 3764$. You also need $\Sigma y^2 = 5320$.

$$r = \frac{n\Sigma xy - (\Sigma x)(\Sigma y)}{\sqrt{n\Sigma x^2 - (\Sigma x)^2}\sqrt{n\Sigma y^2 - (\Sigma y)^2}}$$

→ $$r = \frac{10(3764) - (145)(212)}{\sqrt{10(2785) - (145)^2}\sqrt{10(5320) - (212)^2}}$$
$$\approx \frac{6900}{(82.61)(90.86)}$$
$$\approx 0.919$$

(b) Compute the coefficient of determination r^2.

→ $r^2 \approx 0.845$

(c) What percentage of the variation in the number of car sales can be explained by the ads and the least-squares line?

→ 84.5%

(d) What percentage of the variation in the number of car sales is not explained by the ads and the least-squares line?

→ 100% − 84.5%, or 15.5%

VIEWPOINT It's Freezing!

Can you use average temperatures in January to predict how bad the rest of the winter will be? Can you predict the number of days with freezing temperatures for the entire calendar year using conditions in January? How good would such a forecast be for predicting growing season or number of frost-free days? Methods of this section can help you answer such questions. For more information, visit the Online Study Center at **www.cengage.com/statistics/Brase/UBS5e** *and find the link to temperatures.*

SECTION 4.2 PROBLEMS

Tables and art to accompany margin answers may be found in the back of the book.

1. $b = -2$. When x changes by 1 unit, y decreases by 2 units.
2. Marginal change is slope; 3 units.
3. Extrapolation. Extrapolation beyond the range of the data is dangerous because the relationship pattern might change.
4. Negative.
5. (a) $\hat{y} \approx 318.16 - 30.878x$.
   (b) About 31 fewer frost-free days.
   (c) $r \approx -0.981$. Note that if the slope is negative, r is also negative.

6. (a) $\hat{y} \approx 0.8565 + 0.40248x$.
   (b) About 40.25 kcal/24 hr.
   (c) $r \approx 0.984$.

1. *Statistical Literacy* For the least-squares line $\hat{y} = 5 - 2x$, what is the value of the slope? When x changes by 1 unit, by how much does $\hat{y}$ change?

2. *Statistical Literacy* For the least squares line $\hat{y} = 5 + 3x$, what is the marginal change in $\hat{y}$ for each unit change in x?

3. *Critical Thinking* When we use a least-squares line to predict y values for x values beyond the range of x values found in the data, are we extrapolating or interpolating? Are there any concerns about such predictions?

4. *Critical Thinking* If two variables have a negative linear correlation, is the slope of the least-squares line positive or negative?

5. *Critical Thinking: Interpreting Computer Printouts* We use the form $\hat{y} = a + bx$ for the least-squares line. In some computer printouts, the least-squares equation is not given directly. Instead, the value of the constant a is given, and the coefficient b of the explanatory or predictor variable is displayed. Sometimes a is referred to as the constant, and sometimes as the intercept. Data from *Climatology Report No. 77-3* of the Department of Atmospheric Science, Colorado State University, showed the following relationship between elevation (in thousands of feet) and average number of frost-free days per year in Colorado locations.

   A Minitab printout provides

```
Predictor        Coef     SE Coef       T         P
Constant       318.16      28.31      11.24     0.002
Elevation     -30.878      3.511      -8.79     0.003

S = 11.8603      R-Sq = 96.3%
```

   Notice that "Elevation" is listed under "Predictor." This means that elevation is the explanatory variable x. Its coefficient is the slope b. "Constant" refers to a in the equation $\hat{y} = a + bx$.
   (a) Use the printout to write the least-squares equation.
   (b) For each 1000-foot increase in elevation, how many fewer frost-free days are predicted?
   (c) The printout gives the value of the coefficient of determination r^2. What is the value of r? Be sure to give the correct sign for r based on the sign of b.

6. *Critical Thinking: Interpreting Computer Printouts* Refer to the description of a computer display for regression described in Problem 5. The following Minitab display gives information regarding the relationship between the body weight of a child (in kilograms) and the metabolic rate of the child (in 100 kcal/24 hr). The data is based on information from *The Merck Manual* (a commonly used reference in medical schools and nursing programs).

```
Predictor      Coef      SE Coef       T        P
Constant      0.8565     0.4148      2.06    0.084
Weight        0.40248    0.02978    13.52    0.000

S = 0.517508       R-Sq = 96.8%
```

(a) Write out the least-squares equation.
(b) For each 1-kilogram increase in weight, by how much does the metabolic rate of a child increase?
(c) What is the value of the correlation coefficient r?

For Problems 7–14, please do the following.
(a) Draw a scatter diagram displaying the data.
(b) Verify the given sums Σx, Σy, Σx^2, Σy^2, and Σxy and the value of the sample correlation coefficient r.
(c) Find $\bar{x}$, $\bar{y}$, a, and b. Then find the equation of the least-squares line $\hat{y} = a + bx$.
(d) Graph the least-squares line on your scatter diagram. Be sure to use the point $(\bar{x}, \bar{y})$ as one of the points on the line.
(e) Find the value of the coefficient of determination r^2. What percentage of the variation in y can be *explained* by the corresponding variation in x and the least-squares line? What percentage is *unexplained*?

Answers may vary slightly due to rounding.

7. (b) Use a calculator.
(c) $\bar{x} \approx 33.67$ (in hundreds) jobs; $\bar{y} \approx 4.67$ (in hundreds) entry-level jobs; $a \approx -0.748$; $b \approx 0.161$; $\hat{y} \approx -0.748 + 0.161x$.
(e) $r^2 \approx 0.740$; 74.0% of variation explained and 26.0% unexplained.
(f) 5.69 jobs.

7. *Economics: Entry-Level Jobs* An economist is studying the job market in Denver area neighborhoods. Let x represent the total number of jobs in a given neighborhood, and let y represent the number of entry-level jobs in the same neighborhood. A sample of six Denver neighborhoods gave the following information (units in hundreds of jobs).

x	16	33	50	28	50	25
y	2	3	6	5	9	3

Source: Neighborhood Facts, The Piton Foundation. To fiind out more, visit the Online Study Center at **www.cengage.com/statistics/Brase/UBS5e** and fiind the link to the Piton Foundation.

Complete parts (a) through (e), given $\Sigma x = 202$, $\Sigma y = 28$, $\Sigma x^2 = 7754$, $\Sigma y^2 = 164$, $\Sigma xy = 1096$, and $r \approx 0.860$.
(f) For a neighborhood with $x = 40$ jobs, how many are predicted to be entry-level jobs?

8. (b) Use a calculator.
(c) $\bar{x} \approx 6.386\%$; $\bar{y} \approx -2.486\%$; $a \approx -3.311$; $b \approx 0.129$; $\hat{y} \approx -3.311 + 0.129x$.
(e) $r^2 \approx 0.007$; 0.7% of variation explained, 99.3% unexplained.
(f) The correlation between the variables is so low that it does not make sense to use the least-squares line for prediction.

8. *Violent Crimes: Prisons* Does prison really deter violent crime? Let x represent percent change in the rate of violent crime and y represent percent change in the rate of imprisonment in the general U.S. population. For 7 recent years, the following data have been obtained (Source: *The Crime Drop in America,* edited by Blumstein and Wallman, Cambridge University Press).

x	6.1	5.7	3.9	5.2	6.2	6.5	11.1
y	−1.4	−4.1	−7.0	−4.0	3.6	−0.1	−4.4

Complete parts (a) through (e), given $\Sigma x = 44.7$, $\Sigma y = -17.4$, $\Sigma x^2 = 315.85$, $\Sigma y^2 = 116.1$, $\Sigma xy = -107.18$, and $r \approx 0.084$.
(f) *Critical Thinking:* Considering the values of r and r^2, does it make sense to use the least-squares line for prediction? Explain.

9. (b) Use a calculator.
(c) $\bar{x} = 37.375$; $\bar{y} = 20.875$ mpg; $a \approx 43.326$; $b \approx -0.6007$; $\hat{y} \approx 43.326 - 0.6007x$.
(e) $r^2 \approx 0.895$; 89.5% of variation explained and 10.5% unexplained.
(f) 20.5 mpg.

9. *Weight of Car: Miles per Gallon* Do heavier cars really use more gasoline? Suppose a car is chosen at random. Let x be the weight of the car (in hundreds of pounds), and let y be the miles per gallon (mpg). The following information is based on data taken from *Consumer Reports* (Vol. 62, No. 4).

x	27	44	32	47	23	40	34	52
y	30	19	24	13	29	17	21	14

Complete parts (a) through (e), given $\Sigma x = 299$, $\Sigma y = 167$, $\Sigma x^2 = 11{,}887$, $\Sigma y^2 = 3773$, $\Sigma xy = 5814$, and $r \approx -0.946$.

(f) Suppose a car weighs $x = 38$ (hundred pounds). What does the least-squares line forecast for $y =$ miles per gallon?

10. (b) Use a calculator.
(c) $\bar{x} = 3.25$; $\bar{y} = 38.5$; $a \approx 51.286$; $b \approx -3.934$; $\hat{y} \approx 51.29 - 3.934x$.
(e) $r^2 \approx 0.975$; 97.5% of variation explained and 2.5% unexplained.
(f) 35.55%.

10. *Basketball: Fouls* Data for this problem are based on information from *STATS Basketball Scoreboard*. It is thought that basketball teams that make too many fouls in a game tend to lose the game even if they otherwise play well. Let x be the number of fouls more than (i.e., over and above) the opposing team. Let y be the percentage of times the team with the larger number of fouls wins the game.

x	0	2	5	6
y	50	45	33	26

Complete parts (a) through (e), given $\Sigma x = 13$, $\Sigma y = 154$, $\Sigma x^2 = 65$, $\Sigma y^2 = 6290$, $\Sigma xy = 411$, and $r \approx -0.988$.

(f) If a team had $x = 4$ fouls over and above the opposing team, what does the least-squares equation forecast for y?

11. (b) Use a calculator.
(c) $\bar{x} = 47$ years; $\bar{y} \approx 16.43\%$; $a \approx 39.761$; $b \approx -0.496$; $\hat{y} \approx 39.761 - 0.496x$.
(e) $r^2 \approx 0.920$; 92.0% of variation explained, 8.0% unexplained.
(f) 27.36%.

11. *Auto Accidents: Age* Data for this problem are based on information taken from *The Wall Street Journal*. Let x be the age in years of a licensed automobile driver. Let y be the percentage of all fatal accidents (for a given age) due to speeding. For example, the first data pair indicates that 36% of all fatal accidents involving 17-year-olds are due to speeding.

x	17	27	37	47	57	67	77
y	36	25	20	12	10	7	5

Complete parts (a) through (e), given $\Sigma x = 329$, $\Sigma y = 115$, $\Sigma x^2 = 18{,}263$, $\Sigma y^2 = 2639$, $\Sigma xy = 4015$, and $r \approx -0.959$.

(f) Predict the percentage of all fatal accidents due to speeding for 25-year-olds.

12. (b) Use a calculator.
(c) $\bar{x} = 62$ years; $\bar{y} \approx 18.67\%$; $a \approx -27.745$; $b \approx 0.749$; $\hat{y} \approx -27.75 + 0.75x$.
(e) $r^2 \approx 0.889$; 88.9% of variation explained, 11.1% unexplained.
(f) 24.75%.

12. *Auto Accidents: Age* Let x be the age of a licensed driver in years. Let y be the percentage of all fatal accidents (for a given age) due to failure to yield the right of way. For example, the first data pair states that 5% of all fatal accidents involving 37-year-olds are due to failure to yield the right of way. *The Wall Street Journal* article referenced in Problem 11 reported the following data:

x	37	47	57	67	77	87
y	5	8	10	16	30	43

Complete parts (a) through (e), given $\Sigma x = 372$, $\Sigma y = 112$, $\Sigma x^2 = 24{,}814$, $\Sigma y^2 = 3194$, $\Sigma xy = 8254$, and $r \approx 0.943$.

(f) Predict the percentage of all fatal accidents due to failing to yield the right of way for 70-year-olds.

13. (b) Use a calculator.
(c) $\bar{x} = 6.25$; $\bar{y} = 32.8$; $a = -104.7$; $b = 22$; $\hat{y} = -104.7 + 22x$.
(e) $r^2 \approx 0.833$; 83.3% of variation explained, 16.7% unexplained.
(f) 38.3.

13. *Archaeology: Artifacts* Data for this problem are based on information taken from *Prehistoric New Mexico: Background for Survey* (by D. E. Stuart and R. P. Gauthier, University of New Mexico Press). It is thought that prehistoric Indians did not take their best tools, pottery, and household items when they visited higher elevations for their summer camps. It is hypothesized that archaeological sites tend to lose their cultural identity and specific cultural affiliation as the elevation of the site increases. Let x be the elevation (in thousands of feet) of an archaeological site in the southwestern United States. Let y be the percentage of unidentified artifacts (no specific cultural affiliation) at a given elevation. The following data were obtained for a collection of archaeological sites in New Mexico:

x	5.25	5.75	6.25	6.75	7.25
y	19	13	33	37	62

Complete parts (a) through (e), given $\Sigma x = 31.25$, $\Sigma y = 164$, $\Sigma x^2 \approx 197.813$, $\Sigma y^2 = 6832$, $\Sigma xy = 1080$, and $r \approx 0.913$.

(f) At an archaeological site with elevation 6.5 (thousand feet), what does the least-squares equation forecast for y = percentage of culturally unidentified artifacts?

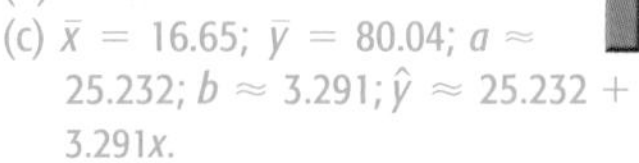

14. (b) Use a calculator.
(c) $\bar{x} = 16.65$; $\bar{y} = 80.04$; $a \approx 25.232$; $b \approx 3.291$; $\hat{y} \approx 25.232 + 3.291x$.
(e) $r^2 \approx 0.697$; 69.7% of variation explained, 30.3% unexplained.
(f) 87.8°F.

14. *Cricket Chirps: Temperature* Anyone who has been outdoors on a summer evening has probably heard crickets. Did you know that it is possible to use the cricket as a thermometer? Crickets tend to chirp more frequently as temperatures increase. This phenomenon was studied in detail by George W. Pierce, a physics professor at Harvard. In the following data, x is a random variable representing chirps per second and y is a random variable representing temperature (°F). These data are also available for download at the Online Study Center.

x	20.0	16.0	19.8	18.4	17.1	15.5	14.7	17.1
y	88.6	71.6	93.3	84.3	80.6	75.2	69.7	82.0

x	15.4	16.2	15.0	17.2	16.0	17.0	14.4
y	69.4	83.3	79.6	82.6	80.6	83.5	76.3

Source: Reprinted by permission of the publisher from *The Songs of Insects* by George W. Pierce, p. 20, Cambridge, Mass.: Harvard University Press, Copyright © 1948 by the President and Fellows of Harvard College.

Complete parts (a) through (e), given $\Sigma x = 249.8$, $\Sigma y = 1200.6$, $\Sigma x^2 = 4200.56$, $\Sigma y^2 = 96{,}725.86$, $\Sigma xy = 20{,}127.47$, and $r \approx 0.835$.

(f) What is the predicted temperature when $x = 19$ chirps per second?

15. (a) Yes. The pattern of residuals appears randomly scattered about the horizontal line at 0.
(b) No. There do not appear to be any outliers.

Refer students to the Data Highlights section for a discussion of influential points.

15. *Expand Your Knowledge: Residual Plot* The least-squares line usually does not go through all the sample data points (x, y). In fact, for a specified x value from a data pair (x, y), there is usually a difference between the predicted value $\hat{y}$ and the y value paired with x. This difference is called the *residual*.

The **residual** is the difference between the y value in a specified data pair (x, y) and the value $\hat{y} = a + bx$ predicted by the least-squares line for the same x.

$y - \hat{y}$ is the **residual.**

One way to assess how well a least-squares line serves as a model for the data is to create a **residual plot.** To make a residual plot, we put the x values in order on the horizontal axis and plot the corresponding residuals $y - \hat{y}$ in the vertical direction. Because the mean of the residuals is always zero for a least-squares model, we place a horizontal line at zero. The accompanying figure shows a residual plot for the data of Guided Exercise 3, in which the relationship between the number of ads run per week and the number of cars sold that week was explored. To make the residual plot, first compute all the residuals. Remember that x and y are the given data values, and $\hat{y}$ is computed from the least-squares line $\hat{y} \approx 6.56 + 1.01x$.

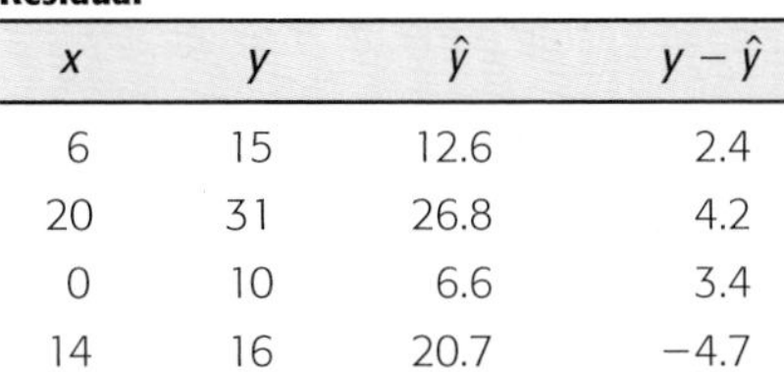

Residual

x	y	$\hat{y}$	$y - \hat{y}$
6	15	12.6	2.4
20	31	26.8	4.2
0	10	6.6	3.4
14	16	20.7	−4.7
25	28	31.8	−3.8

Residual

x	y	$\hat{y}$	$y - \hat{y}$
16	20	22.7	−2.7
28	40	34.8	5.2
18	25	24.7	0.3
10	12	16.7	−4.7
8	15	14.6	0.4

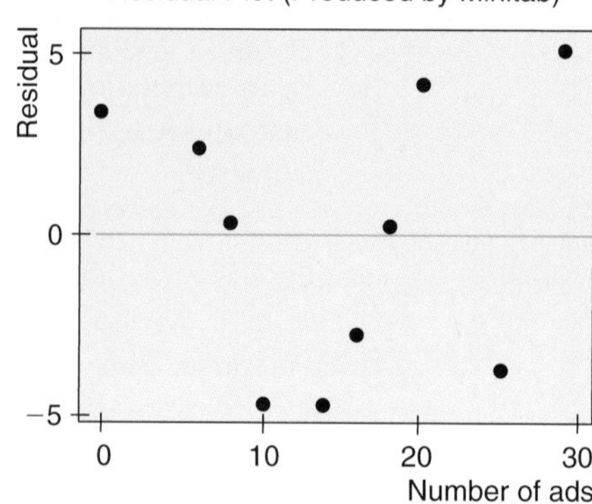

(a) If the least-squares line provides a reasonable model for the data, the pattern of points in the plot will seem random and unstructured about the horizontal line at 0. Is this the case for the residual plot?

(b) If a point on the residual plot seems far outside the pattern of other points, it might reflect an unusual data point (x, y), called an *outlier*. Such points may have quite an influence on the least-squares model. Do there appear to be any outliers in the data for the residual plot?

16. (b) Residuals seem to be scattered randomly about the horizontal line at 0. No outliers.

16. *Residual Plot: Miles per Gallon* Consider the data of Problem 9.
(a) Make a residual plot for the least-squares model.
(b) Use the residual plot to comment on the appropriateness of the least-squares model for these data. See Problem 15.

This can be a good class discussion problem.

17. (a) Result checks.
(b) Result checks.
(c) Yes.
(d) The equation $x = 0.9337y - 0.1335$ does not match part (b).
(e) In general, switching x and y values produces a *different* least-squares equation. When you perform a linear regression, it is important that you know which variable is the explanatory variable and which is the response variable.

17. *Critical Thinking: Exchange x and y in Least-Squares Equation*
(a) Suppose you are given the following x, y data pairs:

x	1	3	4
y	2	1	6

Show that the least-squares equation for these data is $y = 1.071x + 0.143$ (rounded to three digits after the decimal).

(b) Now suppose you are given these x, y data pairs:

x	2	1	6
y	1	3	4

Show that the least-squares equation for these data is $y = 0.357x + 1.595$ (rounded to three digits after the decimal).

(c) In the data for parts (a) and (b), did we simply exchange the x and y values of each data pair?

(d) Solve $y = 0.143 + 1.071x$ for x. Do you get the least-squares equation of part (b) with the symbols x and y exchanged?

(e) In general, suppose we have the least-squares equation $y = a + bx$ for a set of data pairs x, y. If we solve this equation for x, will we *necessarily* get the least-squares equation for the set of data pairs y, x (with x and y exchanged)? Explain using parts (a) through (d).

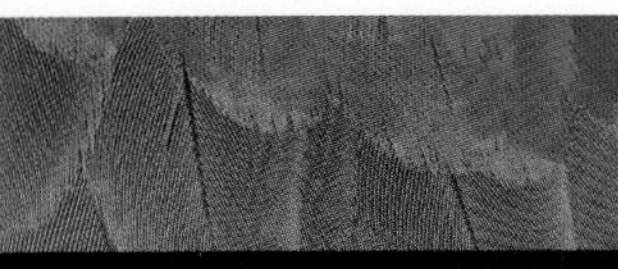

Chapter Review

SUMMARY

This chapter discusses linear regression models and inferences related to these models.

- A scatter diagram of data pairs (x, y) gives a graphical display of the relationship (if any) between x and y data. We are looking for a linear relationship.
- For data pairs (x, y), x is called the *explanatory variable* and is plotted along the horizontal axis. The *response variable* y is plotted along the vertical axis.
- The Pearson product-moment *correlation coefficient* r gives a numerical measurement assessing the strength of a linear relationship between x and y. It is based on a random sample of (x, y) data pairs.
- The value of r ranges from -1 to 1, with 1 indicating perfect positive linear correlation, -1 indicating perfect negative linear correlation, and 0 indicating no linear correlation.
- If the scatter diagram and correlation coefficient r indicate a linear relationship between x and y values of the data pairs, we use the least-squares criterion to develop the equation of the least-squares line

$$\hat{y} = a + bx$$

where $\hat{y}$ is the value of y predicted by the least-squares line for a given x value, a is the y-intercept, and b is the slope.
- The *coefficient of determination* r^2 is a value that measures the proportion of variation in y explained by the least-squares line, the linear regression model, and the variation in the explanatory variable x.
- The difference $y - \hat{y}$ between the y value in the data pair (x, y) and the corresponding predicted value $\hat{y}$ for the same x is called the *residual*.

IMPORTANT WORDS & SYMBOLS

Section 4.1
Paired data values
Explanatory variable
Response variable
Scatter diagram
Sample correlation coefficient r
Perfect linear correlation
No linear correlation
Lurking variable

Section 4.2
Least-squares criterion
Least-squares line $\hat{y} = a + bx$
Meaning of slope
Interpolation
Extrapolation
Explained variation
Unexplained variation
Coefficient of determination r^2
Residual
Residual plot

VIEWPOINT Living Arrangements

Male, female, married, single, living alone, living with friends or relatives—all these categories are of interest to the U.S. Census Bureau. In addition to these categories, there are others, such as age, income, and health needs. How strongly correlated are these variables? Can we use one or more of these variables to predict the others? How good is such a prediction? Methods of this chapter can help you answer such questions. For more information regarding such data, visit the Online Study Center at **www.cengage.com/statistics/Brase/UBS5e** *and find the link to Census Bureau.*

CHAPTER REVIEW PROBLEMS

Tables and art to accompany margin answers may be found in the back of the book.

1. r will be close to 0.
2. No. Different samples from the same population may give different results, leading to different values for the sample statistic r.
3. Results are more reliable for interpolation.
4. Residual $= y - \hat{y} = 2$.

1. *Statistical Literacy* Suppose the scatter diagram of a random sample of data pairs (x, y) shows no linear relationship between x and y. Do you expect the value of the sample correlation coefficient r to be close to 1, -1, or 0?

2. ***Critical Thinking*** Suppose you and a friend each take different random samples of data pairs (x, y) from the same population. Assume the samples are the same size. Based on your sample, you compute $r = 0.83$. Based on her sample, your friend computes $r = 0.79$. Is your friend's value for r wrong? Explain.

3. *Statistical Literacy* When using the least-squares line for prediction, are results more reliable for extrapolation or interpolation?

4. *Statistical Literacy* Suppose that for $x = 3$, the predicted value is $\hat{y} = 6$. The data pair (3, 8) is part of the sample data. What is the value of the residual for $x = 3$?

In Problems 5–10,

(a) Draw a scatter diagram for the data.

(b) Find $\bar{x}$, $\bar{y}$, b, and the equation of the least-squares line. Plot the line on the scatter diagram of part (a).

(c) Find the sample correlation coefficient r and the coefficient of determination. What percentage of variation in y is explained by the least-squares model?

5. (b) $\bar{x} = 3$; $\bar{y} \approx 17.38$; $b \approx 1.27$; $\hat{y} \approx 13.57 + 1.27x$.
(c) $r \approx 0.685$; $r^2 \approx 0.469$; 46.9% explained.

5. *Desert Ecology: Wildlife* Bighorn sheep are beautiful wild animals found throughout the western United States. Data for this problem are based on information taken from *The Desert Bighorn*, edited by Monson and Sumner (University of Arizona Press). Let x be the age of a bighorn sheep (in years), and let y be the mortality rate (percent that die) for this age group. For example, $x = 1$, $y = 14$ means that 14% of the bighorn sheep between 1 and 2 years old died. A random sample of Arizona bighorn sheep gave the following information:

x	1	2	3	4	5
y	14	18.9	14.4	19.6	20.0

Complete parts (a) through (c), given $\Sigma x = 15$, $\Sigma y = 86.9$, $\Sigma x^2 = 55$, $\Sigma y^2 = 1544.73$, and $\Sigma xy = 273.4$.

6. (b) $\bar{x} = 6.0$; $\bar{y} = 35.9$; $b \approx 0.9390$; $\hat{y} \approx 30.266 + 0.939x$.
(c) $r \approx 0.761$; $r^2 \approx 0.579$; 57.9% explained.
(d) 32.14 (thousand dollars).

6. *Sociology: Job Changes* A sociologist is interested in the relation between $x =$ number of job changes and $y =$ annual salary (in thousands of dollars) for people living in the Nashville area. A random sample of 10 people employed in Nashville provided the following information:

x (Number of job changes)	4	7	5	6	1	5	9	10	10	3
y (Salary in $1000)	33	37	34	32	32	38	43	37	40	33

Complete parts (a) through (c), given $\Sigma x = 60$, $\Sigma y = 359$, $\Sigma x^2 = 442$, $\Sigma y^2 = 13{,}013$, and $\Sigma xy = 2231$.

(d) If someone had $x = 2$ job changes, what does the least-squares line predict for y, the annual salary?

7. (b) $\bar{x} \approx 21.43$; $\bar{y} \approx 126.79$; $b \approx 1.285$; $\hat{y} \approx 99.25 + 1.285x$.
(c) $r \approx 0.468$; $r^2 \approx 0.219$; 21.9% explained.
(d) 124.95 pounds.

7. *Medical: Fat Babies* Modern medical practice tells us not to encourage babies to become too fat. Is there a positive correlation between the weight x of a 1-year-old baby and the weight y of the mature adult (30 years old)? A random sample of medical files produced the following information for 14 females:

x (lb)	21	25	23	24	20	15	25	21	17	24	26	22	18	19
y (lb)	125	125	120	125	130	120	145	130	130	130	130	140	110	115

Complete parts (a) through (c), given $\Sigma x = 300$, $\Sigma y = 1775$, $\Sigma x^2 = 6572$, $\Sigma y^2 = 226{,}125$, and $\Sigma xy = 38{,}220$.

(d) If a female baby weighs 20 pounds at 1 year, what do you predict she will weigh at 30 years of age?

8. (b) $\bar{x} \approx 16.53$; $\bar{y} \approx 6.47$; $b \approx 0.2928$; $\hat{y} \approx 1.626 + 0.293x$.
(c) $r \approx 0.790$; $r^2 \approx 0.624$; 62.4% explained.
(d) 7.

8. *Sales: Insurance* Dorothy Kelly sells life insurance for the Prudence Insurance Company. She sells insurance by making visits to her clients' homes. Dorothy believes that the number of sales should depend, to some degree, on the number of visits made. For the past several years, she kept careful records of the number of visits (x) she made each week and the number of people (y) who bought insurance that week. For a random sample of 15 such weeks, the x and y values follow:

x	11	19	16	13	28	5	20	14	22	7	15	29	8	25	16
y	3	11	8	5	8	2	5	6	8	3	5	10	6	10	7

Complete parts (a) through (c), given $\Sigma x = 248$, $\Sigma y = 97$, $\Sigma x^2 = 4856$, $\Sigma y^2 = 731$, and $\Sigma xy = 1825$.

(d) In a week during which Dorothy makes 18 visits, how many people do you predict will buy insurance from her?

9. (b) $\bar{x} \approx 16.38$; $\bar{y} \approx 10.13$; $b \approx 0.554$; $\hat{y} \approx 1.051 + 0.554x$.
(c) $r \approx 0.913$; $r^2 \approx 0.833$; 83.3% explained.
(d) 9.36.

9. *Marketing: Coupons* Each box of Healthy Crunch breakfast cereal contains a coupon entitling the buyer to a free package of garden seeds. At the Healthy Crunch home office, they use the weight of incoming mail to determine how many of their employees are to be assigned to collecting coupons and mailing out seed packages on a given day. (Healthy Crunch has a policy of answering all its mail on the day it is received.)

Let x = weight of incoming mail and y = number of employees required to process the mail in one working day. A random sample of 8 days gave the following data:

x (lb)	11	20	16	6	12	18	23	25
y (Number of employees)	6	10	9	5	8	14	13	16

Complete parts (a) through (c), given $\Sigma x = 131$, $\Sigma y = 81$, $\Sigma x^2 = 2435$, $\Sigma y^2 = 927$, and $\Sigma xy = 1487$.

(d) If Healthy Crunch receives 15 pounds of mail, how many employees should be assigned to mail duty that day?

10. (b) $\bar{x} = 12$; $\bar{y} \approx 98.167$; $b \approx 5.107$; $\hat{y} \approx 36.88 + 5.107x$.
(c) $r \approx 0.927$; $r^2 \approx 0.859$; 85.9% explained.
(d) 98.176.

10. *Focus Problem: Changing Population and Crime Rate* Let x be a random variable representing percentage change in neighborhood population in the past few years, and let y be a random variable representing crime rate (crimes per 1000 population). A random sample of six Denver neighborhoods gave the following information (Source: *Neighborhood Facts*, The Piton Foundation).

x	29	2	11	17	7	6
y	173	35	132	127	69	53

Complete parts (a) through (c), given $\Sigma x = 72$, $\Sigma y = 589$, $\Sigma x^2 = 1340$, $\Sigma y^2 = 72{,}277$, and $\Sigma xy = 9499$.

(d) For a neighborhood with x = 12% change in population in the past few years, predict the change in the crime rate (per 1000 residents).

DATA HIGHLIGHTS: GROUP PROJECTS

Break into small groups and discuss the following topics. Organize a brief outline in which you summarize the main points of your group discussion.

Scatter diagrams! Are they really useful? Scatter diagrams give a first impression of a data relationship and help us assess whether a linear relation provides a reasonable model for the data. In addition, we can spot *influential points*. A data point with an extreme x value can heavily influence the position of the least-squares line. In this project, we look at data sets with an influential point.

x	1	4	5	9	10	15
y	3	7	6	10	12	4

(a) Compute r and b, the slope of the least-squares line. Find the equation of the least-squares line, and sketch the line on the scatter diagram.

(b) Notice the point boxed in blue in Figure 4-11. Does it seem to lie away from the linear pattern determined by the other points? The coordinates of that point are (15, 4). Is it an influential point? Remove that point from the model and recompute r, b, and the equation of the least-squares line. Sketch this least-squares line on the diagram. How does the removal of the influential point affect the values of r and b and the position of the least-squares line?

(c) Consider the scatter diagram of Figure 4-12. Is there an influential point? If you remove the influential point, will the slope of the new least-squares line be larger or smaller than the slope of the line calculated using the original data? Will the correlation coefficient be larger or smaller?

FIGURE 4-11

Scatter Diagram

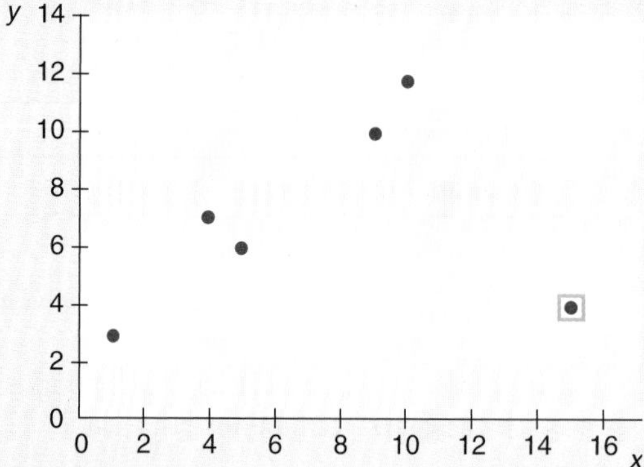

FIGURE 4-12

Scatter Diagram

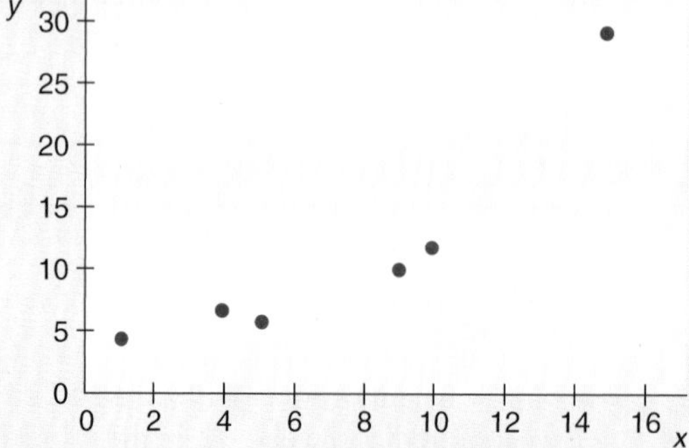

LINKING CONCEPTS: WRITING PROJECTS

Discuss each of the following topics in class or review the topics on your own. Then write a brief but complete essay in which you summarize the main points. Please include formulas and graphs as appropriate.

1. What do we mean when we say that two variables have a strong positive (or negative) linear correlation? What would a scatter diagram for these variables look like? Is it possible that two variables could be strongly related somehow but have a low *linear* correlation? Explain and draw a scatter diagram to demonstrate your point.
2. What do we mean by the least-squares criterion? Give a very general description of how the least-squares criterion is involved in the construction of the least-squares line. Why do we say the least-squares line is the "best-fitting" line for the data set?
3. Use the Internet or go to the library and find a magazine or journal article in your field of major interest to which the content of this chapter could be applied. List the variables used, method of data collection, and general type of information and conclusions drawn.

USING TECHNOLOGY

Simple Linear Regression (one explanatory variable)

The data in this section are taken from this reference:

> King, Cuchlaine A. M. *Physical Geography.* Oxford: Basil Blackwell, 1980, 77–86, 196–206. Reprinted with permission of the publishers.

Throughout the world, natural ocean beaches are beautiful sights to see. If you have visited natural beaches, you may have noticed that when the gradient or dropoff is steep, the grains of sand tend to be larger. In fact, a man-made beach with the "wrong" size granules of sand tends to be washed away and eventually replaced when the proper size grain is selected by the action of the ocean and the gradient of the bottom. Since manmade beaches are expensive, grain size is an important consideration.

In the data that follow, x = median diameter (in millimeters) of granules of sand, and y = gradient of beach slope in degrees on natural ocean beaches.

x	y
0.17	0.63
0.19	0.70
0.22	0.82
0.235	0.88
0.235	1.15
0.30	1.50
0.35	4.40
0.42	7.30
0.85	11.30

1. Find the sample mean and standard deviation for x and y.
2. Make a scatter plot. Would you expect a moderately high correlation and a good fit for the least-squares line?
3. Find the equation of the least-squares line, and graph the line on the scatter plot.
4. Find the correlation coefficient r and the coefficient of determination r^2. Is r significant at the 1% level of significance?
5. Suppose you have a truckload of sifted sand in which the median size of granules is 0.38 mm. If you want to put this sand on a beach and you don't want the sand to wash away, then what does the least-squares line predict for the angle of the beach? *Note:* Heavy storms that produce abnormal waves may also wash out the sand. However, in the long run, the size of sand granules that remain on the beach or that are brought back to the beach by long-term wave action are determined to a large extent by the angle at which the beach drops off.
6. Suppose we now have a truckload of sifted sand in which the median size of the granules is 0.45 mm. Repeat Problem 5.

Technology Hints (Simple Regression)

TI-84Plus/TI-83Plus

Be sure to set **DiagnosticOn** (under **Catalog**).

(a) Scatter diagram: Use **STAT PLOT**, select the first type, use **ZOOM** option **9:ZoomStat.**

(b) Least-squares line and r: Use **STAT, CALC,** option **8:LinReg(a + bx).**

(c) Graph least-squares line and predict: Press **Y=.** Then, under **VARS**, select **5:Statistics,** then select **EQ,** and finally select item **1:RegEQ.** Press **ENTER.** This sequence of steps will automatically set Y_1 = your regression equation. Press **GRAPH.** To find a predicted value, when the graph is showing, press the **CALC** key and select item **1:Value.** Enter the x value and the corresponding y value will appear.

Excel

(a) Scatter plot, least-squares **line**, r^2: Use **Chart wizard.** Select **scatter plot.** Once plot is displayed, *right* click on any data point. Select **trend line.** Under options, check display line and display r^2.

(b) Prediction: Use paste function (f_x) ➤ **Statistical** ➤ **Forecast.**

(c) Coefficient r: Use (f_x) ➤ **Statistical** ➤ **Correl.**

Minitab

(a) Scatter plot, least-squares line, r^2: Use menu selection **Stat** ➤ **Regression** ➤ **Fitted line plot.**

(b) Coefficient r: Use menu selection **Stat** ➤ **Basic Statistics** ➤ **Correlation.**

SPSS

SPSS offers several options for finding the correlation coefficient r and the equation of the least-squares line. First enter the data in the data editor and label the variables appropriately in the variable view window. Use the menu choices **Analyze ➤ Regression ➤ Linear** and select dependent and independent variables. The output includes the correlation coefficient, the constant, and the coefficient of the dependent variable.

SPSS Display

Model Summary

Model	R	R Square	Adjusted R Square	Std. Error of the Estimate
1	.927[a]	.859	.823	22.59076

a. Predictors: (Constant), % change in population

Coefficients[a]

Model		Unstandardized Coefficients B	Unstandardized Coefficients Std. Error	Standardized Coefficients Beta	t	Sig.
1	(Constant)	36.881	15.474		2.383	.076
	% change in population	5.107	1.035	.927	4.932	.008

a. Dependent Variable: Crime rate per 1,000

With the menu choices **Graph ➤ Interactive ➤ Scatterplot,** SPSS produces a scatter diagram with the least-squares line, least-squares equation, coefficient of determination r^2, and optional prediction bands. In the dialogue box, move the dependent variable to the box along the vertical axis and the independent variable to the box along the horizontal axis. Click the "fit" tab, highlight **Regression,** and check the box to include the constant in the equation. For optional prediction band, check individual, enter the confidence level, and check total. The following display shows a scatter diagram for the data in this chapter's Focus Problem regarding crime rate and percentage change in population.

SPSS Display for Focus Problem

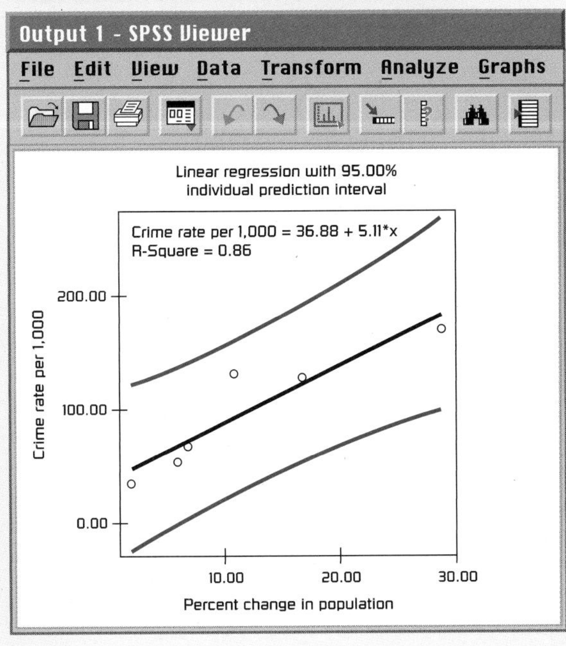

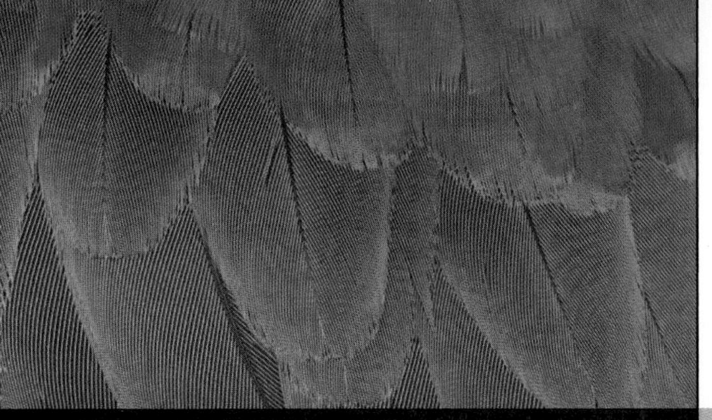

5

We see that the theory of probabilities is at bottom only common sense reduced to calculation; it makes us appreciate with exactitude what reasonable minds feel by a sort of instinct, often without being able to account for it.

—PIERRE-SIMON LAPLACE

For on-line student resources, visit the Brase/Brase, *Understanding Basic Statistics,* 5th edition web site at **www.cengage.com/statistics/Brase/UBS5e.**

The quote to the left explains how the great mathematician Pierre-Simon Laplace (1749–1827) described the theory of mathematical probability. The discovery of the mathematical theory of probability was shared by two Frenchmen: Blaise Pascal and Pierre Fermat. These seventeenth-century scholars were attracted to the subject by the inquiries of the Chevalier de Méré, a gentleman gambler.

Although the first applications of probability were to games of chance and gambling, today the subject seems to pervade almost every aspect of modern life. Everything from the orbits of spacecraft to the social behavior of woodchucks is described in terms of probabilities.

Elementary Probability Theory

PREVIEW QUESTIONS

Why would anyone study probability? Hint: *Most big issues in life involve uncertainty.* (SECTION 5.1)

What are the basic definitions and rules of probability? (SECTION 5.2)

What are counting techniques, trees, permutations, and combinations? (SECTION 5.3)

FOCUS PROBLEM

How Often Do Lie Detectors Lie?

James Burke is an educator who is known for his interesting science-related radio and television shows aired by the British Broadcasting Corporation. His book *Chances: Risk and Odds in Everyday Life* (Virginia Books, London) contains a great wealth of fascinating information about probabilities. The following quote is from Professor Burke's book:

> *If I take a polygraph test and lie, what is the risk I will be detected?* According to some studies, there's about a 72 percent chance you will be caught by the machine.
>
> *What is the risk that if I take a polygraph test it will incorrectly say that I lied?* At least 1 in 15 will be thus falsely accused.

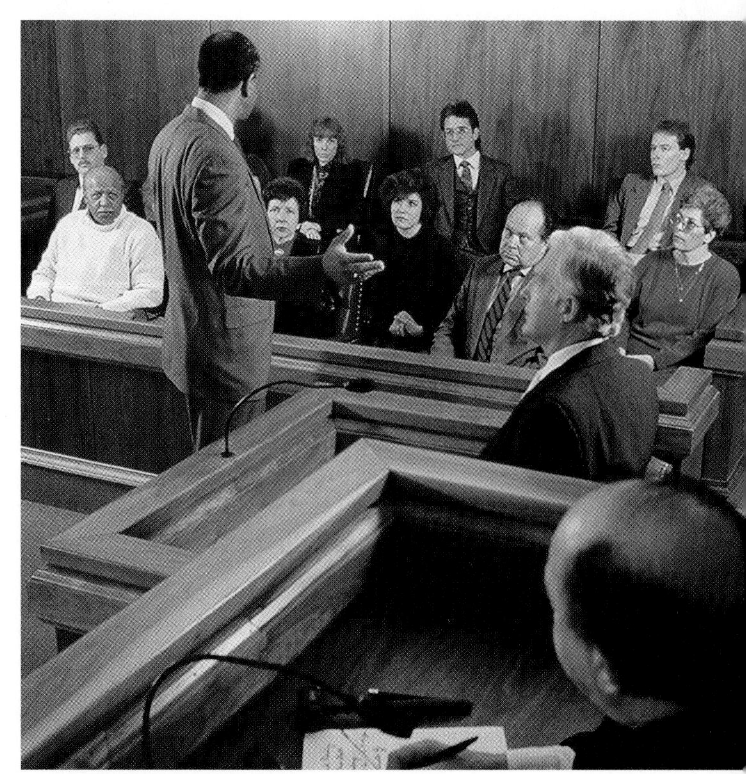

Both of these statements contain conditional probabilities, which we will study in Section 5.2. Information from that section will enable us to answer the following:

Suppose a person answers 10% of a long battery of questions with lies. Assume that the remaining 90% of the questions are answered truthfully.

1. Estimate the percentage of answers the polygraph will *wrongly* indicate as lies.
2. Estimate the percentage of answers the polygraph will *correctly* indicate as lies.

(See Problem 19 of Section 5.2.)

SECTION 5.1 What Is Probability?

FOCUS POINTS

- Assign probabilities to events.
- Explain how the law of large numbers relates to relative frequencies.
- Apply basic rules of probability to everyday life.
- Explain the relationship between statistics and probability.

We encounter statements given in terms of probability all the time. An excited sports announcer claims that Sheila has a 90% chance of breaking the world record in the upcoming 100-yard dash. Henry figures that if he guesses on a true–false question, the probability of getting it right is 1/2. The Right to Health Lobby claims the probability is 0.40 of getting an erroneous report from a medical laboratory at one low-cost health center. It is consequently lobbying for a federal agency to license and monitor all medical laboratories.

When we use probability in a statement, we're using a *number between 0 and 1* to indicate the likelihood of an event.

Basic concepts

This section is a general introduction to probability. Most students pick up the basic ideas quickly.

Probability is a numerical measure between 0 and 1 that describes the likelihood that an event will occur. Probabilities closer to 1 indicate that the event is more likely to occur. Probabilities closer to 0 indicate that the event is less likely to occur.

$P(A)$, read "P of A," denotes the **probability of event A.**

If $P(A) = 1$, the event A is certain to occur.

If $P(A) = 0$, the event A is certain not to occur.

It is important to know what probability statements mean and how to determine probabilities of events, because probability is the language of inferential statistics.

Probability assignments

1. A probability assignment based on **intuition** incorporates past experience, judgment, or opinion to estimate the likelihood of an event.
2. A probability assignment based on **relative frequency** uses the formula

   $$\text{Probability of event} = \text{relative frequency} = \frac{f}{n} \qquad (1)$$

   where f is the frequency of the event occurrence in a sample of n observations.
3. A probability assignment based on **equally likely outcomes** uses the formula

   $$\text{Probability of event} = \frac{\text{Number of outcomes favorable to event}}{\text{Total number of outcomes}} \qquad (2)$$

EXAMPLE 1 PROBABILITY ASSIGNMENT

Consider each of the following events, and determine how the probability is assigned.

(a) A sports announcer claims that Sheila has a 90% chance of breaking the world record in the 100-yard dash.

SOLUTION: It is likely the sports announcer used intuition based on Sheila's past performance.

(b) Henry figures that if he guesses on a true–false question, the probability of getting it right is 0.50.

SOLUTION: In this case there are two possible outcomes: Henry's answer is either correct or incorrect. Since Henry is guessing, we assume the outcomes are equally likely. There are $n = 2$ equally likely outcomes, and only one is correct. By Formula (2),

$$P(\text{correct answer}) = \frac{\text{Number of favorable outcomes}}{\text{Total number of outcomes}} = \frac{1}{2} = 0.50$$

(c) The Right to Health Lobby claims that the probability of getting an erroneous medical laboratory report is 0.40, based on a random sample of 200 laboratory reports, of which 80 were erroneous.

SOLUTION: Formula (1) for relative frequency gives the probability, with sample size $n = 200$ and number of errors $f = 80$.

$$P(\text{error}) = \text{relative frequency} = \frac{f}{n} = \frac{80}{200} = 0.40$$

We've seen three ways to assign probabilities: intuition, relative frequency, and—when outcomes are equally likely—a formula. Which do we use? Most of the time it depends on the information that is at hand or that can be feasibly obtained. Our choice of methods also depends on the particular problem. In Guided Exercise 1, you will see three different situations, and you will decide the best way to assign the probabilities. *Remember, probabilities are numbers between 0 and 1, so don't assign probabilities outside this range.*

GUIDED EXERCISE 1 **Determine a probability**

Assign a probability to the indicated event on the basis of the information provided. Indicate the technique you used: intuition, relative frequency, or the formula for equally likely outcomes.

(a) A random sample of 500 students at Hudson College were surveyed, and it was determined that 375 wore glasses or contact lenses. Estimate the probability that a Hudson College student selected at random wears corrective lenses.

In this case we are given a sample size of 500, and we are told that 375 of these students wear corrective lenses. It is appropriate to use a relative frequency for the desired probability:

$$P(\text{student needs corrective lenses}) = \frac{f}{n} = \frac{375}{500} = 0.75$$

Continued

GUIDED EXERCISE 1 *continued*

(b) The Friends of the Library host a fund-raising barbecue. George is on the cleanup committee. There are four members on this committee, and they draw lots to see who will clean the grills. Assuming that each member is equally likely to be drawn, what is the probability that George will be assigned the grill-cleaning job?

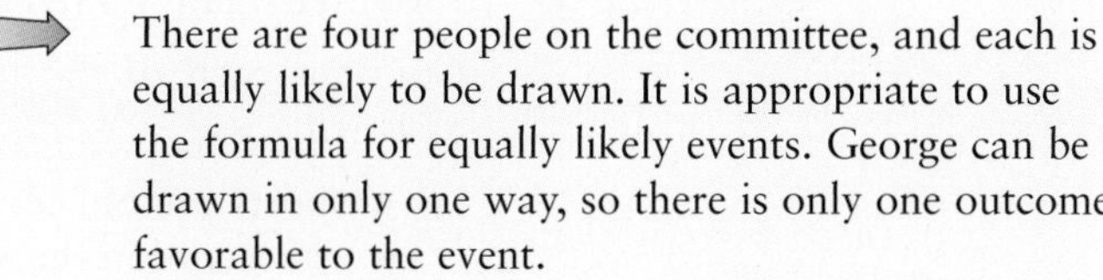

→ There are four people on the committee, and each is equally likely to be drawn. It is appropriate to use the formula for equally likely events. George can be drawn in only one way, so there is only one outcome favorable to the event.

$$P(\text{George}) = \frac{\text{No. of favorable outcomes}}{\text{Total no. of outcomes}} = \frac{1}{4} = 0.25$$

(c) Joanna photographs whales for Sea Life Adventure Films. On her next expedition, she is to film blue whales feeding. Based on her knowledge of the habits of blue whales, she is almost certain she will be successful. What specific number do you suppose she estimates for the probability of success?

→ Since Joanna is almost certain of success, she should make the probability close to 1. We could say $P(\text{success})$ is above 0.90 but less than 1. This probability assignment is based on intuition.

The technique of using the relative frequency of an event as the probability of that event is a common way of assigning probabilities and will be used a great deal in later chapters. The underlying assumption we make is that if an event occurred a certain percentage of times in the past, it will occur about the same percentage of times in the future. In fact, this assumption can be strengthened to a very general statement called the *law of large numbers*.

Law of large numbers

Law of large numbers

In the long run, as the sample size increases and increases, the relative frequencies of outcomes get closer and closer to the theoretical (or actual) probability value.

The law of large numbers is the reason such businesses as health insurance, automobile insurance, and gambling casinos can exist and make a profit.

No matter how we compute probabilities, it is useful to know what outcomes are possible in a given setting. For instance, if you are going to decide the probability that Hardscrabble will win the Kentucky Derby, you need to know which other horses will be running.

To determine the possible outcomes for a given setting, we need to define a *statistical experiment*.

Statistical experiment

Since the terms *statistical experiment* and *sample space* are very important, they should be given some extra emphasis.

A **statistical experiment** or **statistical observation** can be thought of as any random activity that results in a definite outcome.

Event

An **event** is a collection of one or more outcomes of a statistical experiment or observation.

Simple event

A **simple event** is one particular outcome of a statistical experiment.

Sample space

The set of all simple events constitutes the **sample space** of an experiment.

EXAMPLE 2 USING A SAMPLE SPACE

Human eye color is controlled by a single pair of genes (one from the father and one from the mother) called a *genotype*. Brown eye color, B, is dominant over blue eye color, ℓ. Therefore, in the genotype $B\ell$, consisting of one brown gene B and one blue gene ℓ, the brown gene dominates. A person with a $B\ell$ genotype has brown eyes.

If both parents have brown eyes and have genotype $B\ell$, what is the probability that their child will have blue eyes? What is the probability the child will have brown eyes?

SOLUTION: To answer these questions, we need to look at the sample space of all possible eye-color genotypes for the child. They are given in Table 5-1.

TABLE 5-1 Eye Color Genotypes for Child

	Mother	
Father	B	ℓ
B	BB	$B\ell$
ℓ	ℓB	$\ell\ell$

According to genetics theory, the four possible genotypes for the child are equally likely. Therefore, we can use Formula (2) to compute probabilities. Blue eyes can occur only with the $\ell\ell$ genotype, so there is only one outcome favorable to blue eyes. By Formula (2),

$$P(\text{blue eyes}) = \frac{\text{Number of favorable outcomes}}{\text{Total number of outcomes}} = \frac{1}{4}$$

Brown eyes occur with the three remaining genotypes: BB, $B\ell$, and ℓB. By Formula (2),

$$P(\text{brown eyes}) = \frac{\text{Number of favorable outcomes}}{\text{Total number of outcomes}} = \frac{3}{4}$$

GUIDED EXERCISE 2 Using a sample space

Professor Gutierrez is making up a final exam for a course in literature of the Southwest. He wants the last three questions to be of the true–false type. To guarantee that the answers do not follow his favorite pattern, he lists all possible true–false combinations for three questions on slips of paper and then picks one at random from a hat.

(a) Finish listing the outcomes in the given sample space.

TTT	FTT	TFT	______
TTF	FTF	TFF	______

→ The missing outcomes are FFT and FFF.

(b) What is the probability that all three items will be false? Use the formula

$$P(\text{all F}) = \frac{\text{No. of favorable outcomes}}{\text{Total no. of outcomes}}$$

→ There is only one outcome, FFF, favorable to all false, so

$$P(\text{all F}) = \frac{1}{8}$$

(c) What is the probability that exactly two items will be true?

→ There are three outcomes that have exactly two true items: TTF, TFT, and FTT. Thus,

$$P(\text{two T}) = \frac{\text{No. of favorable outcomes}}{\text{Total no. of outcomes}} = \frac{3}{8}$$

There is another important point about probability assignments of simple events.

The **sum** of the probabilities of all simple events in a sample space must equal 1.

We can use this fact to determine the probability that an event will *not* occur. For instance, if you think the probability is 0.65 that you will win a tennis match, you assume the probability is 0.35 that your opponent will win.

Complement of an event

The *complement* of an event A is the event that A *does not occur.* We use the notation A^c to designate the complement of event A. Figure 5-1 shows the event A and its complement A^c.

Notice that the two distinct events A and A^c make up the entire sample space. Therefore, the sum of their probabilities is 1.

The **complement of event A** is the event that A *does not occur.* A^c designates the complement of event A. Furthermore,

1. $P(A) + P(A^c) = 1$
2. $P(\text{event } A \text{ does } not \text{ occur}) = P(A^c) = 1 - P(A)$ (3)

EXAMPLE 3 COMPLEMENT OF AN EVENT

The probability that a college student who has not received a flu shot will get the flu is 0.45. What is the probability that a college student will *not* get the flu if the student has not had the flu shot?

SOLUTION: In this case, we have

$P(\text{will get flu}) = 0.45$

$P(\text{will } not \text{ get flu}) = 1 - P(\text{will get flu}) = 1 - 0.45 = 0.55$

FIGURE 5-1

The Event A and Its Complement A^c

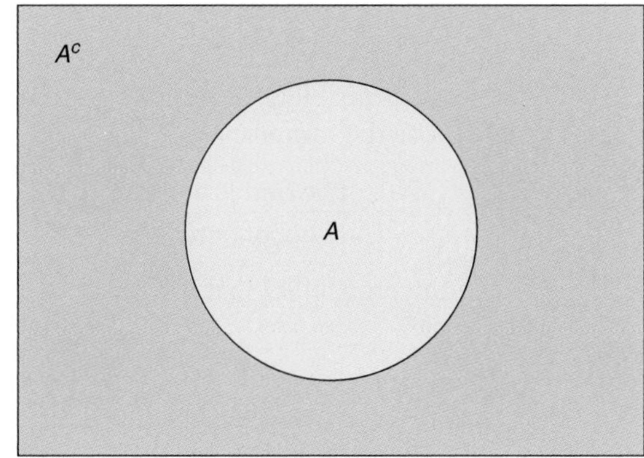

GUIDED EXERCISE 3 Complement of an event

A veterinarian tells you that if you breed two cream-colored guinea pigs, the probability that an offspring will be pure white is 0.25. What is the probability that an offspring will not be pure white?

(a) P(pure white) + P(*not* pure white) = _______ → 1

(b) P(*not* pure white) = _______ → 1 − 0.25, or 0.75

Summary: Some important facts about probability

1. A **statistical experiment** or **statistical observation** is any random activity that results in a definite outcome. A **simple event** consists of one and only one outcome of the experiment. The **sample space** is the set of all simple events. An **event** A is any subset of the sample space.
2. The probability of an event A is denoted by $P(A)$.
3. The probability of an event is a number between 0 and 1. The closer to 1 the probability is, the more likely it is the event will occur. The closer to 0 the probability is, the less likely it is the event will occur.
4. The sum of the probabilities of all simple events in a sample space is 1.
5. Probabilities can be assigned by using intuition, relative frequencies, or the formula for equally likely outcomes. Additional ways to assign probabilities will be introduced in later chapters.
6. The **complement** of an event A is denoted by A^c. So, A^c is the event that A does not occur.
7. $P(A) + P(A^c) = 1$

Probability Related to Statistics

We conclude this section with a few comments on the nature of statistics versus probability. Although statistics and probability are closely related fields of mathematics, they are nevertheless separate fields. It can be said that probability is the medium through which statistical work is done. In fact, if it were not for probability theory, inferential statistics would not be possible.

Put very briefly, probability is the field of study that makes statements about what will occur when samples are drawn from a *known population.* Statistics is the field of study that describes how samples are to be obtained and how inferences are to be made about *unknown populations.*

A simple but effective illustration of the difference between these two subjects can be made by considering how we treat the following examples.

Example of a probability application

Condition: We *know* the exact makeup of the *entire* population.

Example: Given 3 green marbles, 5 red marbles, and 4 white marbles in a bag, draw 6 marbles at random from the bag. What is the probability that none of the marbles drawn is red?

Example of a statistical application

Condition: We have only *samples* from an otherwise *unknown* population.

Example: Draw a random sample of 6 marbles from the (unknown) population of all marbles in a bag and observe the colors. Based on the sample results, make a conjecture about the colors and numbers of marbles in the entire population of all marbles in the bag.

In another sense, probability and statistics are like flip sides of the same coin. On the probability side, you know the overall description of the population. The central problem is to compute the likelihood that a specific outcome will happen. On the statistics side, you know only the results of a sample drawn from the population. The central problem is to describe the sample (descriptive statistic) and to draw conclusions about the population based on the sample results (inferential statistics).

In statistical work, the inferences we draw about an unknown population are not claimed to be absolutely correct. Since the population remains unknown (in a theoretical sense), we must accept a "best guess" for our conclusions and act using the most probable answer rather than absolute certainty.

Linking Concepts, Problem 1, can be used to help students summarize in a class discussion (or in homework) what they have learned about probability so far.

Probability is the topic of this chapter. However, we will not study probability just for its own sake. Probability is a wonderful field of mathematics, but we will study mainly the ideas from probability that are needed for a proper understanding of statistics.

VIEWPOINT What Makes a Good Teacher?

A survey of 735 students at nine colleges in the United States was taken to determine instructor behaviors that help students succeed. Data from this survey can be found by visiting the Online Study Center at **www.cengage.com/statistics/Brase/UBS5e** *and finding the link to DASL, the Carnegie Mellon University Data and Story Library. Once at the DASL site, select Data Subjects, then Psychology, and then Instructor Behavior. You can estimate the probability of a particular student response (very positive, neutral, very negative) to different instructor behaviors. For example, more than 90% of the students responded "very positive" to the instructor's use of real-world examples in the classroom.*

SECTION 5.1 PROBLEMS

Tables and art to accompany margin answers may be found in the back of the book.

1. Equally likely outcomes, relative frequency, intuition.
2. A^c is "no rain today." 0.70.
3. (a) 1.
   (b) 0.

1. *Statistical Literacy* List three methods of assigning probabilities.
2. *Statistical Literacy* Suppose the newspaper states that the probability of rain today is 30%. What is the complement of the event "rain today"? What is the probability of the complement?
3. *Statistical Literacy* What is the probability of
   (a) an event A that is certain to occur?
   (b) an event B that is impossible?
4. *Statistical Literacy* What is the law of large numbers? If you were using the relative frequency of an event to estimate the probability of the event, would it be better to use 100 trials or 500 trials? Explain.

4. The law of large numbers states that in the long run, as the sample size or number of trials increases, the relative frequency of outcomes gets closer to the theoretical probability of the outcome. Better to use 500 trials.
5. No. The probability of tails on the second toss is 0.50 regardless of the outcome on the first toss.
6. (a) Cannot be negative.
   (b) Must be ≤ 1.
   (c) 120% = 1.20 is too large.
   (d) Yes; it is a number between 0 and 1.
7. Answers vary. Probability as relative frequency.
8. Answers vary. Probability as relative frequency.
9. (a) $P(0) = 15/375$; $P(1) = 71/375$; $P(2) = 124/375$; $P(3) = 131/375$; $P(4) = 34/375$.
   (b) Yes.
10. (a) Values 1, 2, 3, 4, 5, 6; equally likely.
   (b) 1/6 for each outcome; yes; yes.
   (c) 2/3.
   (d) 1/3.

5. *Critical Thinking* On a single toss of a fair coin, the probability of heads is 0.5 and the probability of tails is 0.5. If you toss a coin twice and get heads on the first toss, are you guaranteed to get tails on the second toss? Explain.

6. *Critical Thinking*
   (a) Explain why -0.41 cannot be the probability of some event.
   (b) Explain why 1.21 cannot be the probability of some event.
   (c) Explain why 120% cannot be the probability of some event.
   (d) Can the number 0.56 be the probability of an event? Explain.

7. *Probability Estimate: Wiggle Your Ears* Can you wiggle your ears? Use the students in your statistics class (or a group of friends) to estimate the percentage of people who can wiggle their ears. How can your result be thought of as an estimate for the probability that a person chosen at random can wiggle his or her ears? *Comment:* National statistics indicate that about 13% of Americans can wiggle their ears (Source: Bernice Kanner, *Are You Normal?*, St. Martin's Press, New York).

8. *Probability Estimate: Raise One Eyebrow* Can you raise one eyebrow at a time? Use the students in your statistics class (or a group of friends) to estimate the percentage of people who can raise one eyebrow at a time. How can your result be thought of as an estimate for the probability that a person chosen at random can raise one eyebrow at a time? *Comment:* National statistics indicate that about 30% of Americans can raise one eyebrow at a time (see source in Problem 7).

9. *Myers–Briggs: Personality Types* Isabel Briggs Myers was a pioneer in the study of personality types. The personality types are broadly defined according to four main preferences. Do married couples choose similar or different personality types in their mates? The following data give an indication (Source: I. B. Myers and M. H. McCaulley, *A Guide to the Development and Use of the Myers–Briggs Type Indicators*).

Similarities and Differences in a Random Sample of 375 Married Couples

Number of Similar Preferences	Number of Married Couples
All four	34
Three	131
Two	124
One	71
None	15

Suppose that a married couple is selected at random.
   (a) Use the data to estimate the probability that they will have 0, 1, 2, 3, or 4 personality preferences in common.
   (b) Do the probabilities add up to 1? Why should they? What is the sample space in this problem?

10. *General: Roll a Die*
   (a) If you roll a single die and count the number of dots on top, what is the sample space of all possible outcomes? Are the outcomes equally likely?
   (b) Assign probabilities to the outcomes of the sample space of part (a). Do the probabilities add up to 1? Should they add up to 1? Explain.
   (c) What is the probability of getting a number less than 5 on a single throw?
   (d) What is the probability of getting 5 or 6 on a single throw?

11. (a) P(6 A.M.–noon) = 290/966;
P(noon–6 P.M.) = 135/966;
P(6 P.M.–midnight) = 319/966;
P(midnight–6 A.M.) = 222/966.
(b) Yes.

11. *Psychology: Creativity* When do creative people get their *best* ideas? *USA Today* did a survey of 966 inventors (who hold U.S. patents) and obtained the following information:

Time of Day When Best Ideas Occur

Time	Number of Inventors
6 A.M.–12 noon	290
12 noon–6 P.M.	135
6 P.M.–12 midnight	319
12 midnight–6 A.M.	222

(a) Assuming that the time interval includes the left limit and all the times up to but not including the right limit, estimate the probability that an inventor has a best idea during each time interval: from 6 A.M. to 12 noon, from 12 noon to 6 P.M., from 6 P.M. to 12 midnight, from 12 midnight to 6 A.M.
(b) Do the probabilities of part (a) add up to 1? Why should they? What is the sample space in this problem?

12. (a) 0.81.
(b) 0.19.
(c) Germinate or not germinate; yes; yes.
(d) No.

12. *Agriculture: Cotton* A botanist has developed a new hybrid cotton plant that can withstand insects better than other cotton plants. However, there is some concern about the germination of seeds from the new plant. To estimate the probability that a seed from the new plant will germinate, a random sample of 3000 seeds was planted in warm, moist soil. Of these seeds, 2430 germinated.
(a) Use relative frequencies to estimate the probability that a seed will germinate. What is your estimate?
(b) Use relative frequencies to estimate the probability that a seed will *not* germinate. What is your estimate?
(c) Either a seed germinates or it does not. What is the sample space in this problem? Do the probabilities assigned to the sample space add up to 1? Should they add up to 1? Explain.
(d) Are the outcomes in the sample space of part (c) equally likely?

13. (a) 0.46.
(b) 0.43.
(c) 0.20.
(d) 0.57.

13. *Business: Customers* John runs a computer software store. Yesterday he counted 127 people who walked by his store, 58 of whom came into the store. Of the 58, only 25 bought something in the store.
(a) Estimate the probability that a person who walks by the store will enter the store.
(b) Estimate the probability that a person who walks into the store will buy something.
(c) Estimate the probability that a person who walks by the store will come in *and* buy something.
(d) Estimate the probability that a person who comes into the store will buy nothing.

SECTION 5.2 Some Probability Rules—Compound Events

FOCUS POINTS

- Compute probabilities of general compound events.
- Compute probabilities involving independent events or mutually exclusive events.
- Use survey results to compute conditional probabilities.

Conditional Probability and Multiplication Rules

You roll two dice. What is the probability that you will get a 5 on each die? You draw two cards from a well-shuffled, standard deck without replacing the first card before drawing the second. What is the probability that both will be aces?

This section might require a little extra class time. Stress examples with attention to basic definitions and formulas.

It seems that these two problems are nearly alike. They are alike in the sense that in each case you are to find the probability of two events occurring *together.* In the first problem, you are to find

$P(5 \text{ on 1st die } \textit{and } 5 \text{ on 2nd die})$

In the second, you want

$P(\text{ace on 1st card } \textit{and} \text{ ace on 2nd card})$

Independent events

The two problems differ in one important aspect, however. In the dice problem, the outcome of a 5 on the first die does not have any effect on the probability of getting a 5 on the second die. Because of this, the events are *independent.*

Two events are **independent** if the occurrence or nonoccurrence of one does *not* change the probability that the other will occur.

In the card problem, the probability of an ace on the first card is 4/52, since there are 52 cards in the deck and 4 of them are aces. If you get an ace on the first card, then the probability of an ace on the second is changed to 3/51, because one ace has already been drawn and only 51 cards remain in the deck. Therefore, the two events in the card-draw problem are *not* independent. They are, in fact, *dependent,* since the outcome of the first draw changes the probability of getting an ace on the second draw.

Probability of *A* and *B*

Why does the *independence* or *dependence* of two events matter? The types of events determine the way we compute the probability of the two events happening together. If two events *A* and *B* are *independent,* then we use Formula (4) to compute the probability of the event *A and B*:

Multiplication rule for independent events

$$P(A \textit{ and } B) = P(A) \cdot P(B) \tag{4}$$

Conditional probability

If the events are *dependent,* then we must take into account the changes in the probability of one event caused by the occurrence of the other event. The notation $P(A, \textit{given } B)$ denotes the probability that event *A* will occur *given* that event *B* has occurred. This is called a *conditional probability.* We read $P(A, \textit{given } B)$ as "probability of *A* given *B*." If *A* and *B* are dependent events, then $P(A) \neq P(A, \textit{given } B)$ because the occurrence of event *B* has changed the probability that event *A* will occur. A standard notation for **$P(A, \textit{given } B)$ is $P(A|B)$.**

General multiplication rule for any events

$$P(A \text{ and } B) = P(A) \cdot P(B|A) \quad (5)$$

$$P(A \text{ and } B) = P(B) \cdot P(A|B) \quad (6)$$

We will use either Formula (5) or Formula (6) according to the information available.

Formulas (4), (5), and (6) constitute the *multiplication rules* of probability. They help us compute the probability of events happening together when the sample space is too large for convenient reference or when it is not completely known.

Note: For conditional probability, observe that the multiplication rule

$$P(A \text{ and } B) = P(B) \cdot P(A|B)$$

can be solved for $P(A|B)$, leading to

Conditional probability (when $P(B) \neq 0$)

$$P(A|B) = \frac{P(A \text{ and } B)}{P(B)}$$

We will see some applications of this formula in later chapters.

Let's use the multiplication rules to complete the dice and card problems. We'll compare the results with those obtained by using the sample space directly.

EXAMPLE 4

Stress that the outcomes, such as (1 on 1st die, 5 on 2nd die) and (5 on 1st die, 1 on 2nd die), are *different* outcomes. However, by the multiplication rule, the probabilities of the two outcomes are the same.

MULTIPLICATION RULE, INDEPENDENT EVENTS

Suppose you are going to throw two fair dice. What is the probability of getting a 5 on each die?

SOLUTION USING THE MULTIPLICATION RULE: The two events are independent, so we should use Formula (4). $P(5 \text{ on 1st die } \textit{and } 5 \text{ on 2nd die}) = P(5 \text{ on 1st}) \cdot P(5 \text{ on 2nd})$. To finish the problem, we need to compute the probability of getting a 5 when we throw one die.

There are six faces on a die, and on a fair die each is equally likely to come up when you throw the die. Only one face has five dots, so by Formula (2) for equally likely outcomes,

$$P(5 \text{ on die}) = \frac{1}{6}$$

Now we can complete the calculation.

$$P(5 \text{ on 1st die } \textit{and } 5 \text{ on 2nd die}) = P(5 \text{ on 1st}) \cdot P(5 \text{ on 2nd})$$

$$= \frac{1}{6} \cdot \frac{1}{6} = \frac{1}{36}$$

SOLUTION USING SAMPLE SPACE: The first task is to write down the sample space. Each die has six equally likely outcomes, and each outcome of the second die can be paired with each of the first. The sample space is shown in Figure 5-2. The total number of outcomes is 36, and only one is favorable to a 5 on the first die

FIGURE 5-2

Sample Space for Two Dice

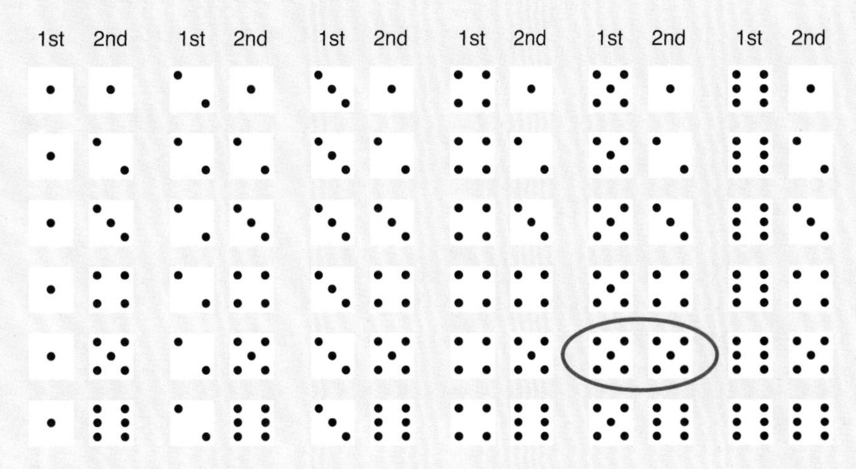

and a 5 on the second. The 36 outcomes are equally likely, so by Formula (2) for equally likely outcomes,

$$P(5 \text{ on 1st } \textit{and} \text{ on 2nd}) = \frac{1}{36}$$

The two methods yield the same result. The multiplication rule was easier to use because we did not need to look at all 36 outcomes in the sample space for tossing two dice.

EXAMPLE 5 MULTIPLICATION RULE, DEPENDENT EVENTS

Compute the probability of drawing two aces from a well-shuffled deck of 52 cards if the first card is not replaced before the second card is drawn.

MULTIPLICATION RULE METHOD: These events are *dependent*. The probability of an ace on the first draw is 4/52, but on the second draw the probability of an ace is only 3/51 if an ace was drawn for the first card. An ace on the first draw changes the probability of an ace on the second draw. By the multiplication rule for dependent events,

$$P(\text{ace on 1st } \textit{and} \text{ ace on 2nd}) = P(\text{ace on 1st}) \cdot P(\text{ace on 2nd} \mid \text{ace on 1st})$$

$$= \frac{4}{52} \cdot \frac{3}{51} = \frac{12}{2652} \approx 0.0045$$

SAMPLE SPACE METHOD: We won't actually look at the sample space because each of the 51 possible outcomes for the second card must be paired with each of the 52 possible outcomes for the first card. This gives us a total of 2652 outcomes in the sample space! We'll just think about the sample space and try to list all the outcomes favorable to the event of aces on both cards. The 12 favorable outcomes are shown in Figure 5-3 on the next page. By the formula for equally likely outcomes,

$$P(\text{ace on 1st card } \textit{and} \text{ ace on 2nd card}) = \frac{12}{2652} \approx 0.0045$$

Again, the two methods agree.

FIGURE 5-3

Outcomes Favorable to Drawing Two Aces

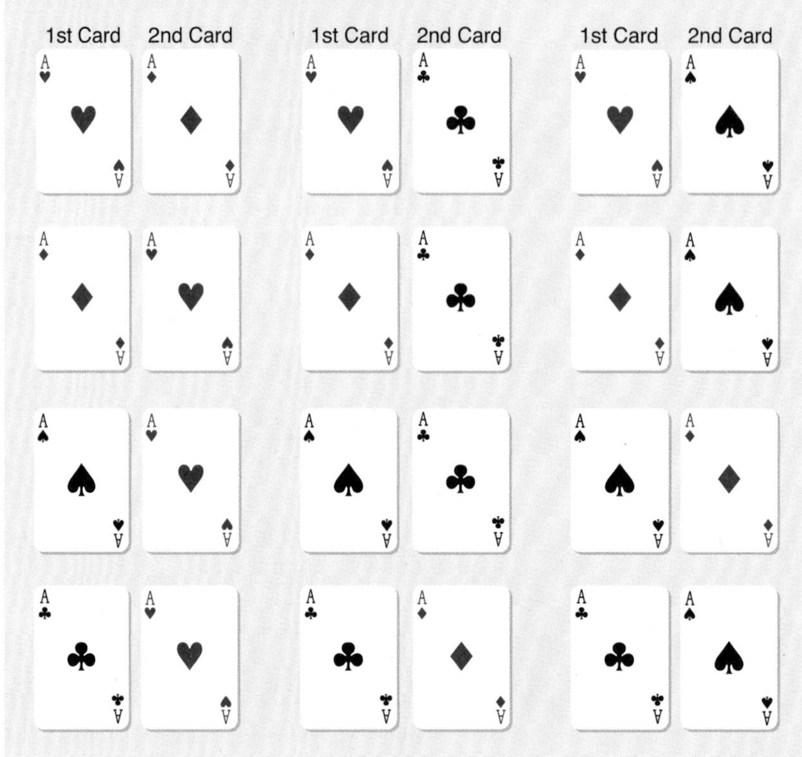

The multiplication rules apply whenever we wish to determine the probability of two events happening *together.* To indicate "together," we use *and* between the events. But before you use a multiplication rule to compute the probability of *A and B*, you must determine if *A* and *B* are independent or dependent events.

PROCEDURE

HOW TO USE THE MULTIPLICATION RULES

1. First determine whether A and B are independent events. If $P(A) = P(A|B)$, then the events are independent.
2. If A and B are independent events,

$$P(A \text{ and } B) = P(A) \cdot (B) \quad (4)$$

3. If A and B are any events,

$$P(A \text{ and } B) = P(A) \cdot P(B|A) \quad (5)$$

$$\text{or } P(A \text{ and } B) = P(B) \cdot P(A|B) \quad (6)$$

Let's practice using the multiplication rule.

GUIDED EXERCISE 4 Multiplication rule

Andrew is 55, and the probability that he will be alive in 10 years is 0.72. Ellen is 35, and the probability that she will be alive in 10 years is 0.92. Assuming that the life span of one will have no effect on the life span of the other, what is the probability they both will be alive in 10 years?

(a) Are these events dependent or independent?

→ Since the life span of one does not affect the life span of the other, the events are independent.

(b) Use the appropriate multiplication rule to find *P*(Andrew alive in 10 years *and* Ellen alive in 10 years).

→ We use the rule for independent events:

$$P(A \text{ and } B) = P(A) \cdot P(B)$$

P(Andrew alive *and* Ellen alive)

$= P(\text{Andrew alive}) \cdot P(\text{Ellen alive})$

$= (0.72)(0.92) \approx 0.66$

GUIDED EXERCISE 5 Dependent events

A quality-control procedure for testing Ready-Flash disposable cameras consists of drawing two cameras at random from each lot of 100 without replacing the first camera before drawing the second. If both are defective, the entire lot is rejected. Find the probability that both cameras are defective if the lot contains 10 defective cameras. Since we are drawing the cameras at random, assume that each camera in the lot has an equal chance of being drawn.

(a) What is the probability of getting a defective camera on the first draw?

→ The sample space consists of all 100 cameras. Since each is equally likely to be drawn and there are 10 defective ones,

$$P(\text{defective camera}) = \frac{10}{100} = \frac{1}{10}$$

(b) The first camera drawn is not replaced, so there are only 99 cameras for the second draw. What is the probability of getting a defective camera on the second draw if the first camera was defective?

→ If the first camera was defective, then there are only 9 defective cameras left among the 99 remaining cameras in the lot.

P(def. camera on 2nd draw | def. camera on 1st)

$$= \frac{9}{99} = \frac{1}{11}$$

(c) Are the probabilities computed in parts (a) and (b) different? Does drawing a defective camera on the first draw change the probability of getting a defective camera on the second draw? Are the events dependent?

→ The answer to all these questions is yes.

(d) Use the formula for dependent events,

$$P(A \text{ and } B) = P(A) \cdot P(B \mid A)$$

to compute *P*(1st camera defective *and* 2nd camera defective).

→
$$P(\text{1st defective and 2nd defective}) = \frac{1}{10} \cdot \frac{1}{11} = \frac{1}{110} \approx 0.009$$

More than two independent events

The multiplication rule for independent events extends to more than two independent events. If you toss a fair coin, then roll a fair die, and finally draw a card from a standard deck of bridge cards, the three events are independent. To compute the probability of the outcome heads on the coin *and* 5 on the die *and* an ace for the card, we use the extended multiplication rule for independent events together with the facts

$$P(\text{head}) = \frac{1}{2}, P(5) = \frac{1}{6}, P(\text{ace}) = \frac{4}{52} = \frac{1}{13}$$

Then

$$P(\text{head } \textit{and } 5 \textit{ and } \text{ace}) = \frac{1}{2} \cdot \frac{1}{6} \cdot \frac{1}{13}$$

$$= \frac{1}{156}$$

Addition Rules

One of the multiplication rules can be used any time we are trying to find the probability of two events happening *together*. Pictorially, we are looking for the probability of the shaded region in Figure 5-4(a).

Probability of *A or B*

Another way to combine events is to consider the possibility of one event *or* another occurring. For instance, if a sports car saleswoman gets an extra bonus if she sells a convertible or a car with leather upholstery, she is interested in the probability that you will buy a car that is a convertible *or* has leather upholstery. Of course, if you bought a convertible with leather upholstery, that would be fine, too. Pictorially, the shaded portion of Figure 5-4(b) represents the outcomes satisfying the *or* condition. Notice that the condition *A or B* is satisfied by any one of the following conditions:

1. Any outcome in *A* occurs.
2. Any outcome in *B* occurs.
3. Any outcome in both *A* and *B* occurs.

It is important to distinguish between the *or* combinations and the *and* combinations because we apply different rules to compute their probabilities.

FIGURE 5-4

(a) The Event *A and B*

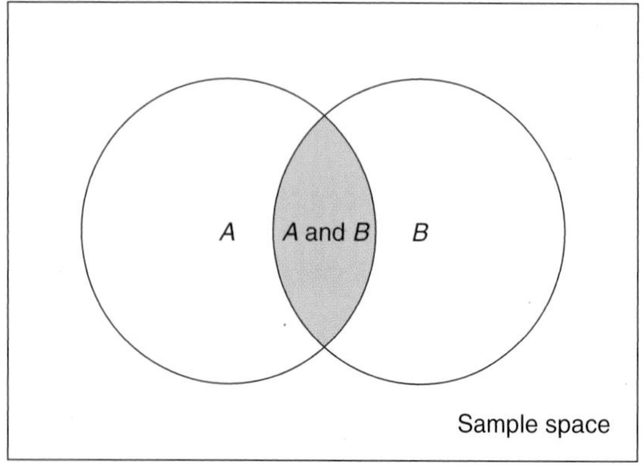

(b) The Event *A or B*

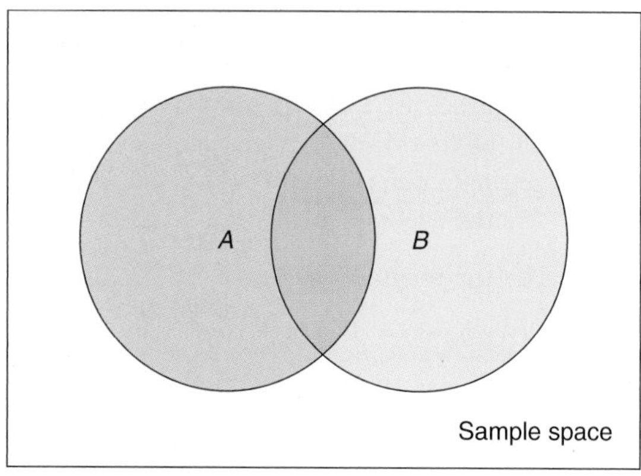

GUIDED EXERCISE 6 Combining events

Indicate how each of the following pairs of events are combined. Use either the *and* combination or the *or* combination.

(a) Satisfying the humanities requirement by taking a course in the history of Japan or by taking a course in classical literature → Use the *or* combination.

(b) Buying new tires and aligning the tires → Use the *and* combination.

(c) Getting an A not only in psychology but also in biology → Use the *and* combination.

(d) Having at least one of these pets: cat, dog, bird, rabbit → Use the *or* combination.

Once you decide that you are to find the probability of an *or* combination rather than an *and* combination, what formula do you use? Again, it depends on the situation. If you want to compute the probability of drawing either a jack or a king on a single draw from a well-shuffled deck of cards, the formula is simple:

$$P(\text{jack } or \text{ king}) = P(\text{jack}) + P(\text{king}) = \frac{4}{52} + \frac{4}{52} = \frac{8}{52} = \frac{2}{13}$$

since there are 4 jacks and 4 kings in a deck of 52 cards.

If you want to compute the probability of drawing a king or a diamond on a single draw, the formula is a bit more complicated. We have to take the overlap of the two events into account so that we do not count the outcomes twice. We can see the overlap of the two events in Figure 5-5.

$$P(\text{king}) = \frac{4}{52} \quad P(\text{diamond}) = \frac{13}{52} \quad P(\text{king } and \text{ diamond}) = \frac{1}{52}$$

FIGURE 5-5

Drawing a King or a Diamond from a Standard Deck

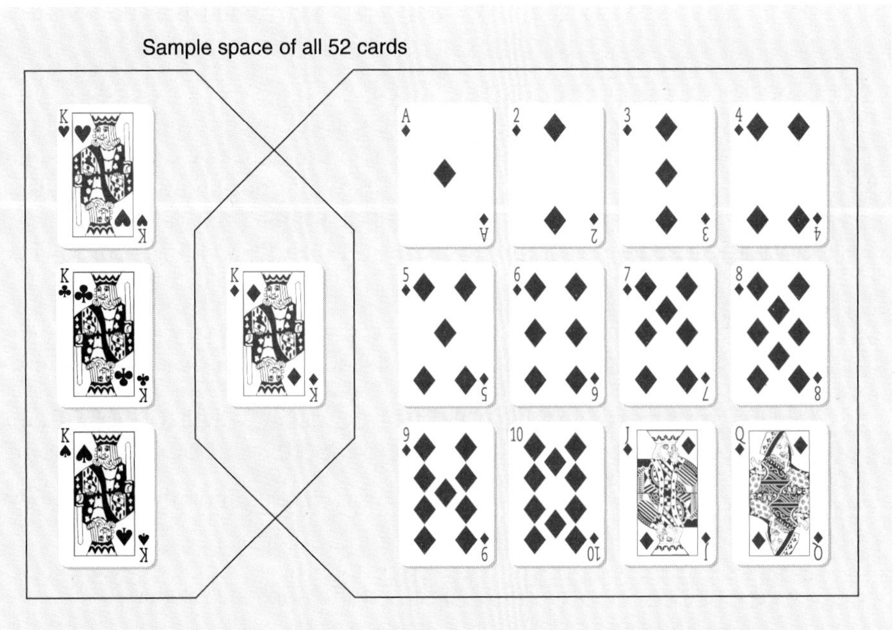

If we simply add *P*(king) and *P*(diamond), we're including *P*(king *and* diamond) twice in the sum. To compensate for this double summing, we simply subtract *P*(king *and* diamond) from the sum. Therefore,

$$\begin{aligned} P(\text{king } or \text{ diamond}) &= P(\text{king}) + P(\text{diamond}) - P(\text{king } and \text{ diamond}) \\ &= \frac{4}{52} + \frac{13}{52} - \frac{1}{52} \\ &= \frac{16}{52} = \frac{4}{13} \end{aligned}$$

Mutually exclusive events

We say the events *A* and *B* are *mutually exclusive* or *disjoint* if they cannot occur together. This means that *A* and *B* have no outcomes in common or, put another way, that $P(A \text{ and } B) = 0$.

Two events are **mutually exclusive** or **disjoint** if they cannot occur together. In particular, events *A* and *B* are mutually exclusive if $P(A \text{ and } B) = 0$.

Formula (7) is the *addition rule for mutually exclusive events A* and *B*.

Addition rule for *mutually exclusive* events *A* and *B*

$$P(A \text{ or } B) = P(A) + P(B) \tag{7}$$

If the events are not mutually exclusive, we must use the more general Formula (8), which is the *general addition rule for any events A* and *B*.

General addition rule for any events *A* and *B*

$$P(A \text{ or } B) = P(A) + P(B) - P(A \text{ and } B) \tag{8}$$

Again, this is a good point to emphasize. Remind students about the difference between mutually exclusive events and events that are not mutually exclusive. Linking Concepts, Problem 2, can be used for a class discussion about the relationship between the concepts of independent events and mutually exclusive events.

You may ask: Which formula should we use? The answer is: Use Formula (7) only if you know that *A* and *B* are mutually exclusive (i.e., cannot occur together); if you do not know whether *A* and *B* are mutually exclusive, then use Formula (8). Formula (8) is valid either way. Notice that when *A* and *B* are mutually exclusive, then $P(A \text{ and } B) = 0$, so Formula (8) reduces to Formula (7).

PROCEDURE

HOW TO USE THE ADDITION RULES

1. First determine whether *A* and *B* are mutually exclusive events. If $P(A \text{ and } B) = 0$, then the events are mutually exclusive.
2. If *A* and *B* are mutually exclusive events,

   $$P(A \text{ or } B) = P(A) + P(B) \tag{7}$$

3. If *A* and *B* are any events,

   $$P(A \text{ or } B) = P(A) + P(B) - P(A \text{ and } B) \tag{8}$$

GUIDED EXERCISE 7 Mutually exclusive events

The Cost Less Clothing Store carries seconds in slacks. If you buy a pair of slacks in your regular waist size without trying them on, the probability that the waist will be too tight is 0.30 and the probability that it will be too loose is 0.10.

(a) Are the events "too tight" and "too loose" mutually exclusive?

→ The waist cannot be both too tight and too loose at the same time, so the events are mutually exclusive.

(b) If you choose a pair of slacks at random in your regular waist size, what is the probability that the waist will be too tight or too loose?

→ Since the events are mutually exclusive,

P(too tight *or* too loose)
= P(too tight) + P(too loose)
= 0.30 + 0.10
= 0.40

GUIDED EXERCISE 8 General addition rule

Professor Jackson is in charge of a program to prepare students for a high school equivalency exam. Records show that 80% of the students need work in math, 70% need work in English, and 55% need work in both areas.

(a) Are the events "needs math" and "needs English" mutually exclusive?

→ These events are not mutually exclusive, since some students need both. In fact,

P(needs math *and* needs English) = 0.55

(b) Use the appropriate formula to compute the probability that a student selected at random needs math *or* needs English.

→ Since the events are not mutually exclusive, we use Formula (8):

P(needs math *or* needs English)
= P(needs math) + P(needs English)
− P(needs math *and* English)
= 0.80 + 0.70 − 0.55
= 0.95

More than two mutually exclusive events

The addition rule for mutually exclusive events can be extended to apply to the situation in which we have more than two events, all of which are mutually exclusive to all the other events.

EXAMPLE 6 Mutually exclusive events

Laura is playing Monopoly. On her next move she needs to throw a sum bigger than 8 on the two dice in order to land on her own property and pass Go. What is the probability that Laura will roll a sum bigger than 8?

SOLUTION: When two dice are thrown, the largest sum that can come up is 12. Consequently, the only sums larger than 8 are 9, 10, 11, and 12. These outcomes

The addition rule extends to more than two events that are *not* mutually exclusive, and the multiplication rule extends to more than two events that are *not* independent as well. However, the formulas for these extensions are more complicated than the formulas given in the text for the restricted conditions of mutually exclusive or independent.

are mutually exclusive, since only one of these sums can possibly occur on one throw of the dice. The probability of throwing more than 8 is the same as

$$P(9 \text{ or } 10 \text{ or } 11 \text{ or } 12)$$

Since the events are mutually exclusive,

$$\begin{aligned} P(9 \text{ or } 10 \text{ or } 11 \text{ or } 12) &= P(9) + P(10) + P(11) + P(12) \\ &= \frac{4}{36} + \frac{3}{36} + \frac{2}{36} + \frac{1}{36} \\ &= \frac{10}{36} = \frac{5}{18} \end{aligned}$$

To get the specific values of $P(9)$, $P(10)$, $P(11)$, and $P(12)$, we used the sample space for throwing two dice (see Figure 5-2 on page 169). There are 36 equally likely outcomes—for example, those favorable to 9 are 6, 3; 3, 6; 5, 4; and 4, 5. So $P(9) = 4/36$. The other values can be computed in a similar way.

Further Examples

Surveys are very popular with students. Surveys are something they can relate to, and the problem solutions are relatively straightforward.

Most of us have been asked to participate in a survey. Schools, retail stores, news media, and government offices all conduct surveys. There are many types of surveys, and it is not our intention to give a general discussion of this topic. Let us study a very popular method called the *simple tally survey.* Such a survey consists of questions to which the responses can be recorded in the rows and columns of a table called a *contingency table.* These questions are appropriate to the information you want and are designed to cover the *entire* population of interest. In addition, the questions should be designed so that you can partition the sample space of responses into distinct (that is, mutually exclusive) sectors.

If the survey includes responses from a reasonably large random sample, then the results should be representative of the population. In this case, you can estimate simple probabilities, conditional probabilities, and the probabilities of some combinations of events directly from the results of the survey.

EXAMPLE 7 SURVEY

At Hopewell Electronics, all 140 employees were asked about their political affiliations. The employees were grouped by type of work, as executives or production workers. The results with row and column totals are shown in Table 5-2.

TABLE 5-2 Employee Type and Political Affiliation

	Political Affiliation			
Employee Type	Democrat (*D*)	Republican (*R*)	Independent (*I*)	Row Total
Executive (*E*)	5	34	9	48
Production worker (*PW*)	63	21	8	92
Column Total	68	55	17	140 Grand Total

Suppose an employee is selected at random from the 140 Hopewell employees. Let us use the following notation to represent different events of choosing: E = executive; PW = production worker; D = Democrat; R = Republican; I = Independent.

(a) Compute $P(D)$ and $P(E)$.

SOLUTION: To find these probabilities, we look at the *entire* sample space.

$$P(D) = \frac{\text{Number of Democrats}}{\text{Number of employees}} = \frac{68}{140} \approx 0.486$$

$$P(E) = \frac{\text{Number of executives}}{\text{Number of employees}} = \frac{48}{140} \approx 0.343$$

(b) Compute $P(D|E)$.

SOLUTION: For the conditional probability, we restrict our attention to the portion of the sample space satisfying the condition of being an executive.

$$P(D|E) = \frac{\text{Number of executives who are Democrats}}{\text{Number of executives}} = \frac{5}{48} \approx 0.104$$

(c) Are the events D and E independent?

SOLUTION: One way to determine if the events D and E are independent is to see if $P(D) = P(D|E)$ [or equivalently, if $P(E) = P(E|D)$]. Since $P(D) \approx 0.486$ and $P(D|E) \approx 0.104$, we see that $P(D) \neq P(D|E)$. This means that the events D and E are *not* independent. The probability of event D "depends on" whether or not event E has occurred.

(d) Compute $P(D \textit{ and } E)$.

SOLUTION: This probability is not conditional, so we must look at the entire sample space.

$$P(D \textit{ and } E) = \frac{\text{Number of executives who are Democrats}}{\text{Total number of employees}} = \frac{5}{140} \approx 0.036$$

Let's recompute this probability using the rules of probability for dependent events.

$$P(D \textit{ and } E) = P(E) \cdot P(D|E) = \frac{48}{140} \cdot \frac{5}{48} = \frac{5}{140} \approx 0.036$$

The results using the rules are consistent with those using the sample space.

(e) Compute $P(D \textit{ or } E)$.

SOLUTION: From part (d), we know that the events Democrat or executive are not mutually exclusive, because $P(D \textit{ and } E) \neq 0$. Therefore,

$$P(D \textit{ or } E) = P(D) + P(E) - P(D \textit{ and } E)$$

$$= \frac{68}{140} + \frac{48}{140} - \frac{5}{140} = \frac{111}{140} \approx 0.793$$

GUIDED EXERCISE 9 Survey

Using Table 5-2 on page 176, let's consider other probabilities regarding the types of employees at Hopewell and their political affiliations. This time let's consider the production worker and the affiliation of Independent. Suppose an employee is selected at random from the group of 140.

(a) Compute $P(I)$ and $P(PW)$.

$$P(I) = \frac{\text{No. of Independents}}{\text{Total no. of employees}} = \frac{17}{140} \approx 0.121$$

$$P(PW) = \frac{\text{No. of production workers}}{\text{Total no. of employees}} = \frac{92}{140} \approx 0.657$$

(b) Compute $P(I|PW)$. This is a conditional probability. Be sure to restrict your attention to production workers, since that is the condition given.

$$P(I|PW) = \frac{\text{No. of Independent production workers}}{\text{No. of production workers}} = \frac{8}{92} \approx 0.087$$

(c) Compute $P(I \text{ and } PW)$. In this case, look at the entire sample space and the number of employees who are both Independent and in production.

$$P(I \text{ and } PW) = \frac{\text{No. of Independent production workers}}{\text{Total no. employees}} = \frac{8}{140} \approx 0.057$$

(d) Use the multiplication rule for dependent events to calculate $P(I \text{ and } PW)$. Is the result the same as that of part (c)?

By the multiplication rule,

$$P(I \text{ and } PW) = P(PW) \cdot P(I|PW) = \frac{92}{140} \cdot \frac{8}{92} = \frac{8}{140} \approx 0.057$$

The results are the same.

(e) Compute $P(I \text{ or } PW)$. Are the events mutually exclusive?

Since the events are not mutully exclusive,

$$P(I \text{ or } PW) = P(I) + P(PW) - P(I \text{ and } PW) = \frac{17}{140} + \frac{92}{140} - \frac{8}{140} = \frac{101}{140} \approx 0.721$$

Basic probability rules

As you apply probability to various settings, keep the following rules in mind.

Summary of basic probability rules

A statistical experiment or statistical observation is any random activity that results in a recordable outcome. The sample space is the set of all simple events that are the outcomes of the statistical experiment and cannot be broken into other "simpler" events. A general event is any subset of the sample space. The notation $P(A)$ designates the probability of event A.

1. $P(\text{entire sample space}) = 1$
2. For any event A: $0 \leq P(A) \leq 1$
3. A^c designates the **complement** of A: $P(A^c) = 1 - P(A)$.
4. Events A and B are **independent events** if $P(A) = P(A|B)$.
5. Multiplication Rules

   General: $P(A \text{ and } B) = P(A) \cdot P(B|A)$

   Independent events: $P(A \text{ and } B) = P(A) \cdot P(B)$
6. Conditional Probability: $P(A|B) = \dfrac{P(A \text{ and } B)}{P(B)}$ when $P(B) \neq 0$
7. Events A and B are **mutually exclusive** if $P(A \text{ and } B) = 0$.
8. Addition Rules

   General: $P(A \text{ or } B) = P(A) + P(B) - P(A \text{ and } B)$

   Mutually exclusive events: $P(A \text{ or } B) = P(A) + P(B)$

CRITICAL THINKING

Translating events described by common English phrases into events described using *and, or, complement*, or *given* takes a bit of care. Table 5-3 shows some common phrases and their corresponding translations into symbols.

In this section, we have studied some important rules that are valid in all probability spaces. The rules and definitions of probability not only are interesting, but they also have extensive *applications* in our everyday lives.

TABLE 5-3 English Phrases and Corresponding Symbolic Translations

Consider the following events for a person selected at random from the general population:

A = person is taking college classes

B = person is under 30 years old

Phrase	Symbolic Expression
1. The probability that a person is under 30 years old and is taking college classes is 40%.	$P(B \text{ and } A) = 0.40$ or $P(A \text{ and } B) = 0.40$
2. The probability that a person under 30 years old is taking college classes is 45%.	$P(A\|B) = 0.45$
3. The probability is 45% that a person is taking college classes if the person is under 30.	$P(A\|B) = 0.45$
4. The probability that a person taking college classes is under 30 is 0.60.	$P(B\|A) = 0.60$
5. The probability that a person is not taking college classes or is under 30 years old is 0.75.	$P(A^c \text{ or } B) = 0.75$

VIEWPOINT The Psychology of Odors

The Smell and Taste Treatment Research Foundation of Chicago collected data on the time required to complete a maze while subjects were smelling different scents. Data for this survey can be found by visiting the Online Study Center at **www.cengage.com/statistics/Brase/UBS5e** *and finding the link to DASL, the Carnegie Mellon University Data and Story Library. Once at the DASL site, select Data Subjects, then Psychology, and then Scents. You can estimate conditional probabilities regarding response times for smokers, nonsmokers, and types of scents.*

SECTION 5.2 PROBLEMS

Tables and art to accompany margin answers may be found in the back of the book.

1. No. By definition, mutually exclusive events cannot occur together.
2. 0.3.
3. (a) Because the events are mutually exclusive, A cannot occur if B has occurred. $P(A|B) = 0$.
   (b) Because $P(A|B) \neq P(A)$, the events A and B are not independent.
4. (a) $P(A \text{ and } B) = P(A) \cdot P(B)$, since events A and B are independent. Because both $P(A)$ and $P(B)$ are not equal to zero, $P(A \text{ and } B) \neq 0$.
   (b) A and B are not mutually exclusive because $P(A \text{ and } B) \neq 0$.
5. (a) $P(A \text{ and } B)$.
   (b) $P(B|A)$.
   (c) $P(A^c|B)$.
   (d) $P(A \text{ or } B)$.
   (e) $P(B^c \text{ or } A)$.
6. (a) $P(A^c \text{ or } B)$.
   (b) $P(B|A)$.
   (c) $P(A|B)$.
   (d) $P(A \text{ and } B^c)$.
   (e) $P(A \text{ and } B)$.

1. *Statistical Literacy* If two events are mutually exclusive, can they occur concurrently? Explain.

2. *Statistical Literacy* If two events A and B are independent and you know that $P(A) = 0.3$, what is the value of $P(A|B)$?

3. ***Critical Thinking*** Suppose two events A and B are mutually exclusive, with $P(A) \neq 0$ and $P(B) \neq 0$. By working through the following steps, you'll see why two mutually exclusive events are not independent.
   (a) For mutually exclusive events, can event A occur if event B has occurred? What is the value of $P(A|B)$?
   (b) Using the information from part (a), can you conclude that events A and B are *not* independent if they are mutually exclusive? Explain.

4. ***Critical Thinking*** Suppose two events A and B are independent, with $P(A) \neq 0$ and $P(B) \neq 0$. By working through the following steps, you'll see why two independent events are not mutually exclusive.
   (a) What formula is used to compute $P(A \text{ and } B)$? Is $P(A \text{ and } B) \neq 0$? Explain.
   (b) Using the information from part (a), can you conclude that events A and B are *not* mutually exclusive?

5. ***Critical Thinking*** Consider the following events for a driver selected at random from the general population:

   A = driver is under 25 years old

   B = driver has received a speeding ticket

   Translate each of the following phrases into symbols.
   (a) The probability the driver has received a speeding ticket and is under 25 years old
   (b) The probability a driver who is under 25 years old has received a speeding ticket
   (c) The probability a driver who has received a speeding ticket is 25 years old or older
   (d) The probability the driver is under 25 years old or has received a speeding ticket
   (e) The probability the driver has not received a speeding ticket or is under 25 years old

6. ***Critical Thinking*** Consider the following events for a college student selected at random:

   A = student is female

   B = student is majoring in business

   Translate each of the following phrases into symbols.
   (a) The probability the student is male or is majoring in business
   (b) The probability a female student is majoring in business

(c) The probability a business major is female
(d) The probability the student is female and is not majoring in business
(e) The probability the student is female and is majoring in business

7. (a) 0.2; yes.
(b) 0.4; yes.
(c) 0.8.

7. *General: Candy Colors* M&M plain candies come in various colors. According to the M&M/Mars Department of Consumer Affairs (link to the Mars company web site from the Online Study Center at **www.cengage.com/statistics/Brase/UBS5e**), the distribution of colors for plain M&M candies is

Color	Purple	Yellow	Red	Orange	Green	Blue	Brown
Percentage	20%	20%	20%	10%	10%	10%	10%

Suppose you have a large bag of plain M&M candies and you choose one candy at random. Find
(a) *P*(green candy *or* blue candy). Are these outcomes mutually exclusive? Why?
(b) *P*(yellow candy *or* red candy). Are these outcomes mutually exclusive? Why?
(c) *P*(*not* purple candy)

8. (a) 111/288.
(b) 81/288.
(c) 237/288.
(d) 159/288.
(e) 18/288.

8. *Environmental: Land Formations* Arches National Park is located in southern Utah. The park is famous for its beautiful desert landscape and its many natural sandstone arches. Park Ranger Edward McCarrick started an inventory (not yet complete) of natural arches within the park that have an opening of at least 3 feet. The following table is based on information taken from the book *Canyon Country Arches and Bridges,* by F. A. Barnes. The height of the arch opening is rounded to the nearest foot.

Height of arch, feet	3–9	10–29	30–49	50–74	75 and higher
Number of arches in park	111	96	30	33	18

For an arch chosen at random in Arches National Park, use the preceding information to estimate the probability that the height of the arch opening is
(a) 3 to 9 feet
(b) 30 feet or taller
(c) 3 to 49 feet
(d) 10 to 74 feet
(e) 75 feet or taller

9. (a) Yes.
(b) 0.028.
(c) 0.028.
(d) 0.056.

9. *General: Roll Two Dice* You roll two fair dice, one green and one red.
(a) Are the outcomes on the dice independent?
(b) Find *P*(5 on green die *and* 3 on red die).
(c) Find *P*(3 on green die *and* 5 on red die).
(d) Find *P*((5 on green die *and* 3 on red die) *or* (3 on green die *and* 5 on red die)).

10. (a) Yes.
(b) 1/36.
(c) 1/36.
(d) 1/18.

10. *General: Roll Two Dice* You roll two fair dice, one green and one red.
(a) Are the outcomes on the dice independent?
(b) Find *P*(1 on green die *and* 2 on red die).
(c) Find *P*(2 on green die *and* 1 on red die).
(d) Find *P*((1 on green die *and* 2 on red die) *or* (2 on green die *and* 1 on red die)).

11. (a) 5/36.
(b) 1/12.
(c) 2/9; yes.

11. *General: Roll Two Dice* You roll two fair dice, one green and one red.
(a) What is the probability of getting a sum of 6?
(b) What is the probability of getting a sum of 4?
(c) What is the probability of getting a sum of 6 *or* 4? Are these outcomes mutually exclusive?

12. (a) 1/6.
(b) 1/18.
(c) 2/9; yes.

12. *General: Roll Two Dice* You roll two fair dice, one green and one red.
(a) What is the probability of getting a sum of 7?
(b) What is the probability of getting a sum of 11?
(c) What is the probability of getting a sum of 7 *or* 11? Are these outcomes mutually exclusive?

13. (a) No.
(b) 4/663.
(c) 4/663.
(d) 8/663.

13. *General: Deck of Cards* You draw two cards from a standard deck of 52 cards without replacing the first one before drawing the second.
(a) Are the outcomes on the two cards independent? Why?
(b) Find P(ace on 1st card *and* king on 2nd).
(c) Find P(king on 1st card *and* ace on 2nd).
(d) Find the probability of drawing an ace *and* a king in either order.

14. (a) No.
(b) 0.006.
(c) 0.006.
(d) 0.012.

14. *General: Deck of Cards* You draw two cards from a standard deck of 52 cards without replacing the first one before drawing the second.
(a) Are the outcomes on the two cards independent? Why?
(b) Find P(3 on 1st card *and* 10 on 2nd).
(c) Find P(10 on 1st card *and* 3 on 2nd).
(d) Find the probability of drawing a 10 *and* a 3 in either order.

15. (a) Yes.
(b) 1/169.
(c) 1/169.
(d) 2/169.

15. *General: Deck of Cards* You draw two cards from a standard deck of 52 cards, but before you draw the second card, you put the first one back and reshuffle the deck.
(a) Are the outcomes on the two cards independent? Why?
(b) Find P(ace on 1st card *and* king on 2nd).
(c) Find P(king on 1st card *and* ace on 2nd).
(d) Find the probability of drawing an ace *and* a king in either order.

16. (a) Yes.
(b) 0.0059.
(c) 0.0059.
(d) 0.0118.

16. *General: Deck of Cards* You draw two cards from a standard deck of 52 cards, but before you draw the second card, you put the first one back and reshuffle the deck.
(a) Are the outcomes on the two cards independent? Why?
(b) Find P(3 on 1st card *and* 10 on 2nd).
(c) Find P(10 on 1st card *and* 3 on 2nd).
(d) Find the probability of drawing a 10 *and* a 3 in either order.

17. (a) 0.63.
(b) 0.78.
(c) 0.41.
(d) 0.49.

17. *Marketing: Toys* *USA Today* gave the information shown in the table about ages of children receiving toys. The percentages represent all toys sold.

Age (years)	Percentage of Toys
2 and under	15%
3–5	22%
6–9	27%
10–12	14%
13 and over	22%

What is the probability that a toy is purchased for someone
(a) 6 years old or older?
(b) 12 years old or younger?
(c) between 6 and 12 years old?
(d) between 3 and 9 years old?

A child between 10 and 12 years old looks at this probability distribution and asks, "Why are people more likely to buy toys for kids older than I am (13 and over) than for kids in my age group (10–12)?" How would you respond?

18. (a) 0.0175.
(b) 0.21.
(c) 0.133; 0.012.
(d) 0.07; 0.12.

18. *Health Care: Flu* Based on data from the *Statistical Abstract of the United States*, 112th Edition, only about 14% of senior citizens (65 years old or older) get the flu each year. However, about 24% of people under 65 years old get the flu each year. The general population consists of 12.5% senior citizens (65 years old or older).
(a) What is the probability that a person selected at random from the general population is a senior citizen who will get the flu this year?
(b) What is the probability that a person selected at random from the general population is a person under age 65 who will get the flu this year?
(c) Answer parts (a) and (b) for a community that has 95% senior citizens.
(d) Answer parts (a) and (b) for a community that has 50% senior citizens.

Problem 19 is a little tricky. However, most students enjoy the challenge.

19. *Focus Problem: Lie Detector Test* In this problem, you are asked to solve part of the Focus Problem at the beginning of this chapter. In his book *Chances: Risk and Odds in Everyday Life*, James Burke states that there is a 72% chance a polygraph test (lie detector test) will catch a person who is, in fact,

19. (a) 6.3%.
(b) 7.2%.
(c) 3.5%; 36%.
(d) 1.05%; 61.2%.

lying. Furthermore, there is approximately a 7% chance that the polygraph will falsely accuse someone of lying.

(a) Suppose a person answers 90% of a long battery of questions truthfully. What percentage of the answers will the polygraph *wrongly* indicate are lies?
(b) Suppose a person answers 10% of a long battery of questions with lies. What percentage of the answers will the polygraph *correctly* indicate are lies?
(c) Repeat parts (a) and (b) if 50% of the questions are answered truthfully and 50% are answered with lies.
(d) Repeat parts (a) and (b) if 15% of the questions are answered truthfully and the rest are answered with lies.

Most students enjoy survey problems of this type.

20. (a) 110/130.
(b) 20/130.
(c) 50/70.
(d) 20/70.
(e) 110/200.
(f) 20/200.

20. *Survey: Medical Tests* Diagnostic tests of medical conditions can have several types of results. The test result can be positive or negative, whether or not a patient has the condition. A positive test (+) indicates that the patient has the condition. A negative test (−) indicates that the patient does not have the condition. Remember, a positive test does not prove that the patient has the condition. Additional medical work may be required. Consider a random sample of 200 patients, some of whom have a medical condition and some of whom do not. Results of a new diagnostic test for the condition are shown.

	Condition Present	Condition Absent	Row Total
Test Result +	110	20	130
Test Result −	20	50	70
Column Total	130	70	200

Assume the sample is representative of the entire population. For a person selected at random, compute the following probabilities:

(a) $P(+|\text{condition present})$; this is known as the *sensitivity* of a test.
(b) $P(-|\text{condition present})$; this is known as the *false-negative rate*.
(c) $P(-|\text{condition absent})$; this is known as the *specificity* of a test.
(d) $P(+|\text{condition absent})$; this is known as the *false-positive rate*.
(e) $P(\text{condition present } and\ +)$; this is the *predictive value* of the test.
(f) $P(\text{condition present } and\ -)$.

21. (a) 72/154.
(b) 82/154.
(c) 79/116.
(d) 37/116.
(e) 72/270.
(f) 82/270.

21. *Survey: Lung/Heart* In an article entitled "Diagnostic accuracy of fever as a measure of postoperative pulmonary complications" (*Heart Lung* 10, No. 1:61), J. Roberts and colleagues discuss using a fever of 38°C or higher as a diagnostic indicator of postoperative atelectasis (collapse of the lung) as evidenced by x-ray observation. For fever $\geq$ 38°C as the diagnostic test, the results for postoperative patients are

	Condition Present	Condition Absent	Row Total
Test Result +	72	37	109
Test Result −	82	79	161
Column Total	154	116	270

For the meaning of + and −, see Problem 20. Complete parts (a) through (f) from Problem 20.

22. *Survey: Customer Loyalty* Are customers more loyal in the East or in the West? The following table is based on information from *Trends in the United States,* published by the Food Marketing Institute, Washington, D.C. The columns represent length of customer loyalty (in years) at a primary supermarket. The rows represent regions of the United States.

22. (a) 291/2008.
(b) 77/452.
(c) 826/2008.
(d) 131/373.
(e) 41/157.
(f) 53/157.
(g) 420/452.
(h) 332/373.
(i) No. $P(15+ \text{ year}) = 535/2008 \neq P(15+ \text{ year} | \text{East}) = 118/452$.

	Less Than 1 Year	1–2 Years	3–4 Years	5–9 Years	10–14 Years	15 or More Years	Row Total
East	32	54	59	112	77	118	452
Midwest	31	68	68	120	63	173	523
South	53	92	93	158	106	158	660
West	41	56	67	78	45	86	373
Column Total	157	270	287	468	291	535	2008

What is the probability that a customer chosen at random
(a) has been loyal 10 to 14 years?
(b) has been loyal 10 to 14 years, given that he or she is from the East?
(c) has been loyal *at least* 10 years?
(d) has been loyal *at least* 10 years, given that he or she is from the West?
(e) is from the West, given that he or she has been loyal less than 1 year?
(f) is from the South, given that he or she has been loyal less than 1 year?
(g) has been loyal *1 or more years,* given that he or she is from the East?
(h) has been loyal *1 or more years,* given that he or she is from the West?
(i) Are the events "from the East" and "loyal 15 or more years" independent? Explain.

23. (a) 686/1160; 270/580; 416/580.
(b) No.
(c) 270/1160; 416/1160.
(d) 474/1160; 310/580.
(e) No.
(f) 996/1160.

23. *Survey: Sales Approach* In a sales effectiveness seminar, a group of sales representatives tried two approaches to selling a customer a new automobile: the aggressive approach and the passive approach. For 1160 customers, the following record was kept:

	Sale	No Sale	Row Total
Aggressive	270	310	580
Passive	416	164	580
Column Total	686	474	1160

Suppose a customer is selected at random from the 1160 participating customers. Let us use the following notation for events: A = aggressive approach, Pa = passive approach, S = sale, N = no sale. So, $P(A)$ is the probability that an aggressive approach was used, and so on.
(a) Compute $P(S)$, $P(S|A)$, and $P(S|Pa)$.
(b) Are the events S = sale and Pa = passive approach independent? Explain.
(c) Compute $P(A \textit{ and } S)$ and $P(Pa \textit{ and } S)$.
(d) Compute $P(N)$ and $P(N|A)$.
(e) Are the events N = no sale and A = aggressive approach independent? Explain.
(f) Compute $P(A \textit{ or } S)$.

SECTION 5.3 Tree Diagrams and Counting Techniques

FOCUS POINTS

- Organize outcomes in a sample space using tree diagrams.
- Compute number of ordered arrangements of outcomes using permutations.
- Compute number of (nonordered) groupings of outcomes using combinations.
- Explain how counting techniques relate to probability in everyday life.

When outcomes are equally likely, we compute the probability of an event by using the formula

$$P(A) = \frac{\text{Number of outcomes favorable to the event } A}{\text{Number of outcomes in the sample space}}$$

Although this section contains valuable material, it can be omitted if time is limited. However, time spent on this section gives students a stronger understanding of probability.

The probability formula requires that we be able to determine the number of outcomes in the sample space. In the problems we have done in previous sections, this task has not been difficult because the number of outcomes was small or the sample space consisted of fairly straightforward events. The tools we present in this section will help you count the number of possible outcomes in larger sample spaces or those formed by more complicated events.

Multiplication rule of counting

When an outcome of an experiment is composed of a series of events, the multiplication rule gives us the *total number* of outcomes.

Multiplication rule of counting

Consider the series of events E_1 through E_m, where n_1 is the number of possible outcomes for event E_1, n_2 is the number of possible outcomes for event E_2, and n_m designates the number of possible outcomes for event E_m. Then the product

$$n_1 \times n_2 \times \cdots \times n_m$$

gives the total number of possible outcomes for the series of events E_1, followed by E_2, up through event E_m.

The multiplication rule of counting is best explained by using a few examples.

EXAMPLE 8 MULTIPLICATION RULE

Jacqueline is in a nursing program and is required to take a course in psychology and one in physiology (A and P) next semester. She also wants to take Spanish II. If there are two sections of psychology, two of A and P, and three of Spanish II, how many different class schedules can Jacqueline choose from? (Assume that the times of the sections do not conflict.)

SOLUTION: Creating a class schedule can be considered an experiment with a series of three events. There are two possible outcomes for the psychology section, two for the A and P section, and three for the Spanish II section. By the multiplication rule, the total number of class schedules possible is

$$2 \times 2 \times 3 = 12$$

Tree diagram

A *tree diagram* gives a visual display of the total number of outcomes of an experiment consisting of a series of events. From a tree diagram, we can determine not only the total number of outcomes, but also the individual outcomes.

EXAMPLE 9 TREE DIAGRAM

Tree diagrams are a good way to visualize a sample space involving several stages. Most students pick up this material quickly.

Using the information from Example 8, let's make a tree diagram that shows all the possible course schedules for Jacqueline.

SOLUTION: Figure 5-6 on the next page shows the tree diagram. Let's study the diagram. There are two branches from Start. These branches indicate the two possible choices for psychology sections. No matter which section of psychology Jacqueline chooses, she can choose from the two available A and P sections. Therefore, we have two branches leading from *each* psychology branch. Finally, after the psychology and A and P sections are selected, there are three choices for Spanish II. That is why there are three branches from *each* A and P section.

The tree ends with a total of 12 branches. The number of end branches tells us the number of possible schedules. The outcomes themselves can be listed from the tree by following each series of branches from Start to End. For instance, the top branch from Start generates the schedules shown in Table 5-4. The other six schedules can be listed in a similar manner, except they begin with the second section of psychology.

FIGURE 5-6

Tree Diagram for Selecting Class Schedules

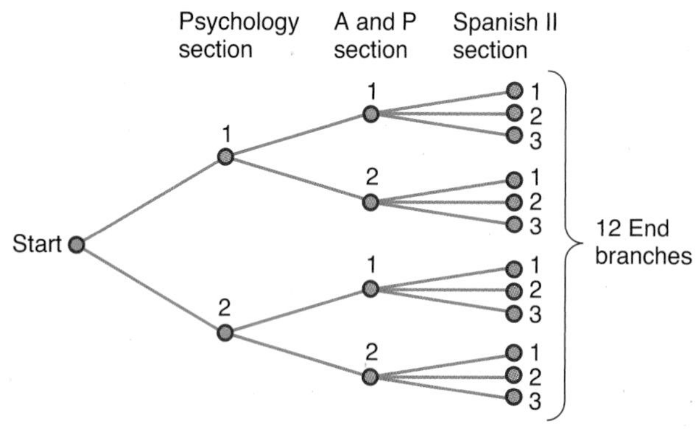

TABLE 5-4 **Schedules Utilizing Section 1 of Psychology**

Psychology Section	A and P Section	Spanish II Section
1	1	1
1	1	2
1	1	3
1	2	1
1	2	2
1	2	3

GUIDED EXERCISE 10 Tree diagram and multiplication rule

Louis plays three tennis matches. Use a tree diagram to list the possible win and loss sequences Louis can experience for the set of three matches.

(a) On the first match Louis can win or lose. From Start, indicate these two branches.

FIGURE 5-7 W = Win, L = Lose

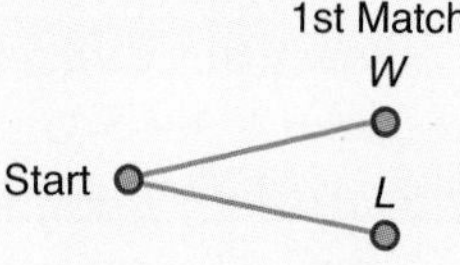

(b) Regardless of whether Louis wins or loses the first match, he plays the second and can again win or lose. Attach branches representing these two outcomes to *each* of the first match results.

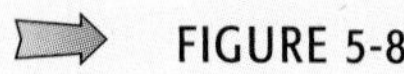

FIGURE 5-8

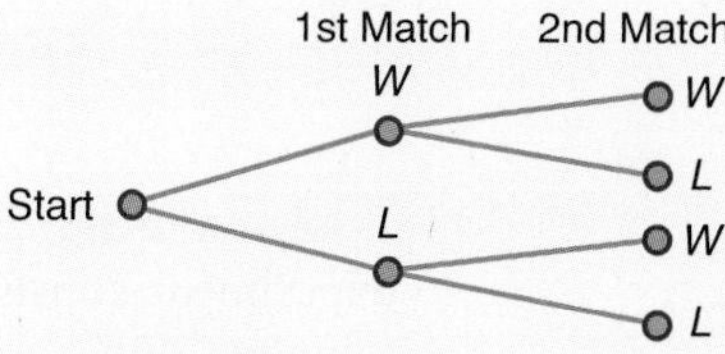

(c) Louis may win or lose the third match. Attach branches representing these two outcomes to *each* of the second match results.

FIGURE 5-9

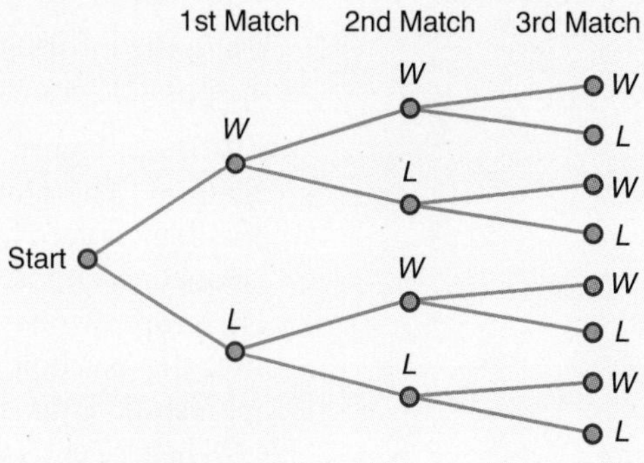

Continued

GUIDED EXERCISE 10 *continued*

(d) How many possible win–lose sequences are there for the three matches?

➡ Since there are eight branches at the end, there are eight sequences.

(e) Complete this list of win–lose sequences.

1st	2nd	3rd
W	W	W
W	W	L
W	L	W
W	L	L
____	____	____
____	____	____
____	____	____
____	____	____

➡ The last four sequences all involve a loss on Match 1.

1st	2nd	3rd
L	W	W
L	W	L
L	L	W
L	L	L

(f) Use the multiplication rule to compute the total number of outcomes for the three matches.

➡ The number of outcomes for a series of three events, each with two outcomes, is

$$2 \times 2 \times 2 = 8$$

Tree diagrams help us display the outcomes of an experiment involving several stages. If we label each branch of the tree with an appropriate probability, we can use the tree diagram to help us compute the probability of an outcome displayed on the tree. One of the easiest ways to illustrate this feature of tree diagrams is to use the experiment of drawing balls out of an urn. We do this in the next example.

EXAMPLE 10 TREE DIAGRAM AND PROBABILITY

Suppose there are five balls in an urn. They are identical except for color. Three of the balls are red and two are blue. You are instructed to draw out one ball, note its color, and set it aside. Then you are to draw out another ball and note its color. What are the outcomes of the experiment? What is the probability of each outcome?

SOLUTION: The tree diagram in Figure 5-10 will help us answer these questions. Notice that since you did not replace the first ball before drawing the second one, the two stages of the experiment are dependent. The probability associated with

FIGURE 5-10

Tree Diagram for Urn Experiment

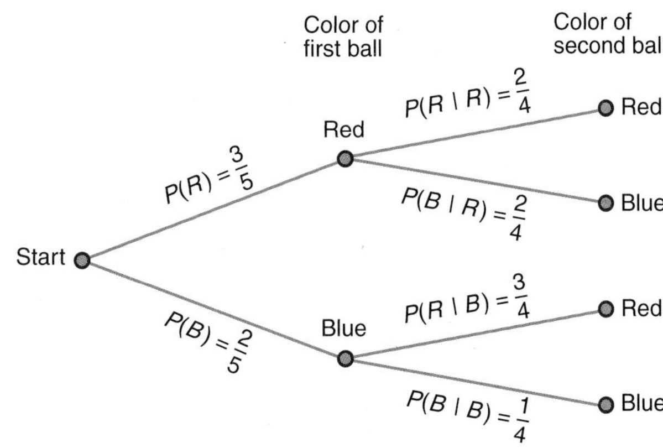

the color of the second ball depends on the color of the first ball. For instance, on the top branches, the color of the first ball drawn is red, so we compute the probabilities of the colors on the second ball accordingly. The tree diagram helps us organize the probabilities.

From the diagram, we see that there are four possible outcomes to the experiment. They are

RR = red on 1st *and* red on 2nd

RB = red on 1st *and* blue on 2nd

BR = blue on 1st *and* red on 2nd

BB = blue on 1st *and* blue on 2nd

To compute the probability of each outcome, we will use the multiplication rule for dependent events. As we follow the branches for each outcome, we will find the necessary probabilities.

$$P(R \text{ on 1st } \textit{and } R \text{ on 2nd}) = P(R) \cdot P(R|R) = \frac{3}{5} \cdot \frac{2}{4} = \frac{3}{10}$$

$$P(R \text{ on 1st } \textit{and } B \text{ on 2nd}) = P(R) \cdot P(B|R) = \frac{3}{5} \cdot \frac{2}{4} = \frac{3}{10}$$

$$P(B \text{ on 1st } \textit{and } R \text{ on 2nd}) = P(B) \cdot P(R|B) = \frac{2}{5} \cdot \frac{3}{4} = \frac{3}{10}$$

$$P(B \text{ on 1st } \textit{and } B \text{ on 2nd}) = P(B) \cdot P(B|B) = \frac{2}{5} \cdot \frac{1}{4} = \frac{1}{10}$$

Notice that the probabilities of the outcomes in the sample space add to 1, as they should.

Sometimes when we consider n items, we need to know the number of different *ordered arrangements* of the n items that are possible. The multiplication rules can help us find the number of possible ordered arrangements. Let's consider the classic example of determining the number of different ways in which eight people can be seated at a dinner table. For the first chair at the head of the table, there are eight choices. For the second chair, there are seven choices, since one person is already seated. For the third chair, there are six choices, since two people are already seated. By the time we get to the last chair, there is only one person left for that seat. We can view each arrangement as an outcome of a series of eight events. Event 1 is *fill the first chair,* event 2 is *fill the second chair,* and so forth. The multiplication rule will tell us the number of different outcomes.

Choices for	1st	2nd	3rd	4th	5th	6th	7th	8th	Chair position
	↓	↓	↓	↓	↓	↓	↓	↓	
	(8)	(7)	(6)	(5)	(4)	(3)	(2)	(1)	= 40,320

In all, there are 40,320 different seating arrangements for eight people. It is no wonder that it takes a little time to seat guests at a dinner table!

The multiplication pattern shown above is not unusual. In fact, it is an example of the multiplication indicated by the factorial notation 8!.

Factorial notation

! is read "factorial"

8! is read "8 factorial"

$8! = 8 \cdot 7 \cdot 6 \cdot 5 \cdot 4 \cdot 3 \cdot 2 \cdot 1$

In general, $n!$ indicates the product of n with each of the positive counting numbers less than n. *By special definition,* $0! = 1$.

Factorial notation

For a counting number n,

$$0! = 1$$

$$1! = 1$$

$$n! = n(n-1)(n-2)\cdots 1$$

GUIDED EXERCISE 11 Factorial

(a) Evaluate 3!.

→ $3! = 3 \cdot 2 \cdot 1 = 6$

(b) In how many different ways can three objects be arranged in order? How many choices do you have for the first position? for the second position? for the third position?

→ You have three choices for the first position, two for the second position, and one for the third position. By the multiplication rule, you have

$(3)(2)(1) = 3! = 6$ arrangements

Permutations

We have considered the number of ordered arrangements of n objects taken as an entire group. But what if we don't arrange the entire group? Specifically, we considered a dinner party for eight and found the number of ordered seating arrangements for all eight people. However, suppose you have an open house and have only five chairs. How many ways can five of the eight people seat themselves in the chairs? The formula we use to compute this number is called the *permutation formula.* As we see in the next example, the *permutations rule* is really another version of the multiplication rule.

Counting rule for permutations

The number of permutations (*ordered arrangements*) of n distinct objects taken r at a time is

$$P_{n,r} = \frac{n!}{(n-r)!} \qquad (9)$$

where n and r are whole numbers and $n \geq r$. Another commonly used notation for permutations is nPr.

EXAMPLE 11 PERMUTATIONS RULE

Let's compute the number of possible ordered seating arrangements for eight people in five chairs.

SOLUTION: In this case, we are considering a total of $n = 8$ different people, and we wish to arrange $r = 5$ of these people. Substituting into Formula (9), we have

$$P_{n,r} = \frac{n!}{(n-r)!}$$

$$P_{8,5} = \frac{8!}{(8-5)!} = \frac{8!}{3!} = \frac{40{,}320}{6} = 6720$$

Using the multiplication rule, we get the same results

Chair	1		2		3		4		5		
Choices for	8	×	7	×	6	×	5	×	4	=	6720

The permutations rule has the advantage of using factorials. Most scientific calculators have a factorial key (!) as well as a permutations key (nPr) (see Tech Notes).

TECH NOTES Most scientific calculators have a factorial key, often designated **x!** or **n!**. Many of these same calculators have the permutation function built in, often labeled nPr. They also have the combination function, which is discussed next. The combination function is often labeled nCr.

TI-84Plus/TI-83Plus The factorial, permutation, and combination functions are all under **MATH**, then **PRB.**

Excel Use the **paste function** (fx), then select **all. Fact** gives factorials, **Permut** gives permutations, and **Combin** gives combinations.

Combinations

In each of our previous counting formulas, we have taken the *order* of the objects or people into account. For instance, suppose that in your political science class you are given a list of 10 books. You are to select 4 to read during the semester. The order in which you read the books is not important. We are interested in the *different groupings* or *combinations* of 4 books from among the 10 on the list. The next formula tells us how to compute the number of different combinations.

This is a good time to stress that in permutations, the *order* of occurrence is important, whereas in combinations it is not even taken into consideration.

Counting rule for combinations

The number of *combinations* of n objects taken r at a time is

$$C_{n,r} = \frac{n!}{r!(n - r)!} \tag{10}$$

where n and r are whole numbers and $n \geq r$. Other commonly used notations for combinations include nCr and $\binom{n}{r}$.

Notice the difference between the concepts of permutations and combinations. When we consider permutations, we are considering groupings *and order*. When we consider combinations, we are considering only the number of different groupings. For combinations, order within the groupings is not considered. As a result, the number of combinations of n objects taken r at a time is generally smaller than the number of permutations of the same n objects taken r at a time. In fact, the combinations formula is simply the permutations formula with the number of permutations of each distinct group divided out. In the formula for combinations, notice the factor of $r!$ in the denominator.

Now let's look at an example in which we use the *combinations rule* to compute the number of *combinations* of 10 books taken 4 at a time.

EXAMPLE 12 **COMBINATIONS**

In your political science class, you are assigned to read any 4 books from a list of 10 books. How many different groups of 4 are available from the list of 10?

SOLUTION: In this case, we are interested in *combinations,* rather than permutations, of 10 books taken 4 at a time. Using $n = 10$ and $r = 4$, we have

$$C_{n,r} = \frac{n!}{r!(n-r)!} = \frac{10!}{4!(10-4)!} = 210$$

There are 210 different groups of 4 books that can be selected from the list of 10. An alternate solution method is to use the combinations key (often nCr or $C_{n,r}$) on a calculator.

PROCEDURE

HOW TO DETERMINE THE NUMBER OF OUTCOMES OF AN EXPERIMENT

1. If the experiment consists of a series of stages with various outcomes, use the multiplication rule or a tree diagram.
2. If the outcomes consist of *ordered* subgroups of r items taken from a group of n items, use the permutations rule, $P_{n,r}$.

$$P_{n,r} = \frac{n!}{(n-r)!} \tag{9}$$

3. If the outcomes consist of *non-ordered* subgroups of r items taken from a group of n items, use the combinations rule, $C_{n,r}$.

$$C_{n,r} = \frac{n!}{r!(n-r)!} \tag{10}$$

GUIDED EXERCISE 12 **Permutations and combinations**

The board of directors at Belford Community Hospital has 12 members.

(i) Three officers—president, vice president, and treasurer—must be elected from the members. How many different slates of officers are possible? We will view a slate of officers as a list of three people, with the president listed first, the vice president listed second, and the treasurer listed third. For instance, if Mr. Acosta, Ms. Hill, and Mr. Smith wish to be on a slate together, there are several different slates possible, depending on the person listed for each office. Not only are we asking for the number of different groups of three names for a slate, we are also concerned about order.

(a) Do we use the permutations rule or the combinations rule? What is the value of n? What is the value of r?

We use the permutations rule, since order is important. The size of the group from which the slates of officers are to be selected is n. The size of each slate is r.

$n = 12$ and $r = 3$

Continued

GUIDED EXERCISE 12 *continued*

(b) Use the permutations rule with $n = 12$ and $r = 3$ to compute $P_{12,3}$.

→ $P_{n,r} = \frac{n!}{(n-r)!} = \frac{12!}{(12-3)!} = 1320$

An alternative method is to use the permutations key on a calculator.

(ii) Three members from the group of 12 on the board of directors at Belford Community Hospital will be selected to go to a convention (all expenses paid) in Hawaii. How many different groups of 3 are possible?

(c) Do we use the permutations rule or the combinations rule? What is the value of n? What is the value of r?

→ We use the combinations rule, because order is not important. The size of the board is $n = 12$ and the size of each group going to the convention is $r = 3$.

(d) Use the combinations rule with $n = 12$ and $r = 3$ to compute $C_{12,3}$.

→ $C_{n,r} = \frac{n!}{r!(n-r)!} = \frac{12!}{3!(12-3)!} = 220$

An alternative method is to use the combinations key on a calculator.

VIEWPOINT Powerball

Powerball is a multistate lottery game that consists of drawing five distinct whole numbers from the numbers 1 through 55. Then one more number from the numbers 1 through 42 is selected as the Powerball number (this number can be one of the original five). Powerball numbers are drawn every Wednesday and Saturday. If you match all six numbers, you win the jackpot, which is worth at least 10 million dollars. Use methods of this section to show that there are 146,107,962 possible Powerball plays. For more information about the game of Powerball and the probability of winning different prizes, visit the Online Study Center at **www.cengage.com/statistics/Brase/UBS5e** *and find the link to the Multi-State Lottery Association. Then select Powerball.*

SECTION 5.3 PROBLEMS

Tables and art to accompany margin answers may be found in the back of the book.

1. The permutations rule counts the number of different *arrangements* of r items out of n distinct items, whereas the combinations rule counts only the *number* of groups of r items out of n distinct items. The number of permutations is greater than or equal to the number of combinations.

1. *Statistical Literacy* What is the main difference between a situation in which the use of the permutations rule is appropriate and one in which the use of the combinations rule is appropriate?

2. *Statistical Literacy* Consider a series of events. How does a tree diagram help you list all the possible outcomes of a series of events? How can you use a tree diagram to determine the total number of outcomes of a series of events?

3. ***Critical Thinking*** For each of the following situations, explain why the combinations rule or the permutations rule should be used.
   (a) Determine the number of different groups of 5 items that can be selected from 12 distinct items.
   (b) Determine the number of different arrangements of 5 items that can be selected from 12 distinct items.

4. ***Critical Thinking*** You need to know the number of different arrangements possible for five distinct letters. You decide to use the permutations rule, but your friend tells you to use 5!. Who is correct? Explain.

2. From "Start," the first branches show all possible outcomes of the first event. Beginning at the end of each first-event branch, all possible outcomes of the second event are shown as branches, and so on. All the possible outcomes are shown as distinct paths from "Start" to the end of each last branch. Counting the number of final branches gives the total number of outcomes.
3. (a) Use the combinations rule, since only the items in the group and not their arrangement is of concern.
   (b) Use the permutations rule, since the number of arrangements within each group is of interest.
4. Both methods are correct, since you are counting all possible arrangements of 5 items taken 5 at a time.
5. (b) 3.
   (c) 3/8.
6. (b) 2.
   (c) 1/6.
7. (b) RR, 1/15; RB, 1/5; RY, 1/15; BR, 1/5; BB, 1/5; BY, 1/10; YR, 1/15; YB, 1/10.
8. (b) 1/64.
9. 24.
10. 24.
11. 36.
12. (a) 36.
    (b) 9.
    (c) 0.25.

5. *Tree Diagram*
   (a) Draw a tree diagram to display all the possible head–tail sequences that can occur when you flip a coin three times.
   (b) How many sequences contain exactly two heads?
   (c) *Probability extension:* Assuming the sequences are all equally likely, what is the probability that you will get exactly two heads when you toss a coin three times?

6. *Tree Diagram*
   (a) Draw a tree diagram to display all the possible outcomes that can occur when you flip a coin and then toss a die.
   (b) How many outcomes contain a head and a number greater than 4?
   (c) *Probability extension:* Assuming the outcomes displayed in the tree diagram are all equally likely, what is the probability that you will get a head *and* a number greater than 4 when you flip a coin and toss a die?

7. *Tree Diagram* There are six balls in an urn. They are identical except for color. Two are red, three are blue, and one is yellow. You are to draw a ball from the urn, note its color, and set it aside. Then you are to draw another ball from the urn and note its color.
   (a) Make a tree diagram to show all possible outcomes of the experiment. Label the probability associated with each stage of the experiment on the appropriate branch.
   (b) *Probability extension:* Compute the probability for each outcome of the experiment.

8. *Tree Diagram*
   (a) Make a tree diagram to show all the possible sequences of answers for three multiple-choice questions, each with four possible responses.
   (b) *Probability extension:* Assuming that you are guessing the answers so that all outcomes listed in the tree are equally likely, what is the probability that you will guess the one sequence that contains all three correct answers?

9. *Multiplication Rule* Four wires (red, green, blue, and yellow) need to be attached to a circuit board. A robotic device will attach the wires. The wires can be attached in any order, and the production manager wishes to determine which order would be fastest for the robot to use. Use the multiplication rule of counting to determine the number of possible sequences of assembly that must be tested. (*Hint:* There are four choices for the first wire, three for the second, two for the third, and only one for the fourth.)

10. *Multiplication Rule* A sales representative must visit four cities: Omaha, Dallas, Wichita, and Oklahoma City. There are direct air connections between each of the cities. Use the multiplication rule of counting to determine the number of different choices the sales representative has for the order in which to visit the cities. How is this problem similar to Problem 9?

11. *Counting: Agriculture* Barbara is a research biologist for Green Carpet Lawns. She is studying the effects of fertilizer type, temperature at time of application, and water treatment after application. She has four fertilizer types, three temperature zones, and three water treatments to test. Determine the number of different lawn plots she needs in order to test each fertilizer type, temperature range, and water treatment configuration.

12. *Counting: Outcomes* You toss a pair of dice.
    (a) Determine the number of possible pairs of outcomes. (Recall that there are six possible outcomes for each die.)
    (b) There are three even numbers on each die. How many outcomes are possible with even numbers appearing on each die?
    (c) *Probability extension:* What is the probability that both dice will show an even number?

13. 20.
14. 336.
15. 5040.
16. 362,880.
17. 10.
18. 56.
19. 1.
20. 1.
21. $P_{15,3} = 2730$.

13. Compute $P_{5,2}$.

14. Compute $P_{8,3}$.

15. Compute $P_{7,7}$.

16. Compute $P_{9,9}$.

17. Compute $C_{5,2}$.

18. Compute $C_{8,3}$.

19. Compute $C_{7,7}$.

20. Compute $C_{8,8}$.

21. *Counting: Hiring* There are three nursing positions to be filled at Lilly Hospital. Position 1 is the day nursing supervisor; position 2 is the night nursing supervisor; and position 3 is the nursing coordinator position. There are 15 candidates qualified for all three of the positions. Determine the number of different ways the positions can be filled by these applicants.

22. $P_{10,3} = 720$.

22. *Counting: Lottery* In the Cash Now lottery game, there are 10 finalists who submitted entry tickets on time. From these 10 tickets, three grand prize winners will be drawn. The first prize is one million dollars, the second prize is one hundred thousand dollars, and the third prize is ten thousand dollars. Determine the total number of different ways in which the winners can be drawn. (Assume that the tickets are not replaced after they are drawn.)

23. $P_{5,3} = 60$.

23. *Counting: Sports* The University of Montana ski team has five entrants in a men's downhill ski event. The coach would like the first, second, and third places to go to the team members. In how many ways can the five team entrants achieve first, second, and third places?

24. $C_{10,3} = 120$.

24. *Counting: Sales* During the Computer Daze special promotion, a customer purchasing a computer and printer is given a choice of three free software packages. There are 10 different software packages from which to select. How many different groups of software packages can be selected?

25. $C_{15,5} = 3003$.

25. *Counting: Hiring* There are 15 qualified applicants for 5 trainee positions in a fast-food management program. How many different groups of trainees can be selected?

26. (a) $C_{12,5} = 792$.
(b) 0.001.
(c) 21; 0.027.

26. *Counting: Grading* One professor grades homework by randomly choosing 5 out of 12 homework problems to grade.
   (a) How many different groups of 5 problems can be chosen from the 12 problems?
   (b) *Probability extension:* Jerry did only 5 problems of one assignment. What is the probability that the problems he did comprised the group that was selected to be graded?
   (c) Silvia did 7 problems. How many different groups of 5 did she complete? What is the probability that one of the groups of 5 she completed comprised the group selected to be graded?

27. (a) $C_{12,6} = 924$.
(b) $C_{7,6} = 7$.
(c) 0.008.

27. *Counting: Hiring* The qualified applicant pool for six management trainee positions consists of seven women and five men.
   (a) How many different groups of applicants can be selected for the positions?
   (b) How many different groups of trainees would consist entirely of women?
   (c) *Probability extension:* If the applicants are equally qualified and the trainee positions are selected by drawing the names at random so that all groups of six are equally likely, what is the probability that the trainee class will consist entirely of women?

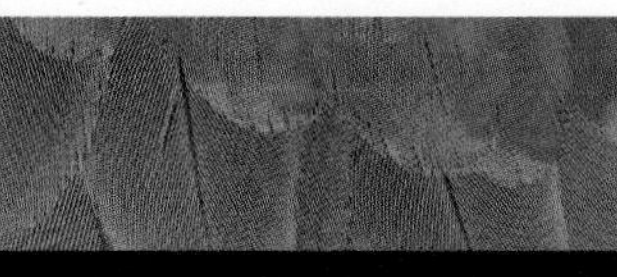

Chapter Review

SUMMARY

In this chapter, we explored basic features of probability.

- The probability of an event A is a number between 0 and 1, inclusive. The more likely the event, the closer the probability of the event is to 1.
- There are three main ways to determine the probability of an event: the method of relative frequency, the method of equally likely outcomes, and intuition.
- The law of large numbers indicates that as the number of trials of a statistical experiment or observation increases, the relative frequency of a designated event becomes closer to the theoretical probability of that event.
- Events are mutually exclusive if they cannot occur together. Events are independent if the occurrence of one event does not change the probability of the occurrence of the other.
- Conditional probability is the probability that one event will occur, given that another event has occurred.
- The complement rule gives the probability that an event will not occur. The addition rule gives the probability that at least one of two specified events will occur. The multiplication rule gives the probability that two events will occur together.
- To determine the probability of equally likely events, we need to know how many outcomes are possible. Devices such as tree diagrams, and counting rules such as the multiplication rule of counting, the permutations rule, and the combinations rule, help us determine the total number of possible outcomes of a statistical experiment or observation.

In most of the statistical applications of later chapters, we will use the addition rule for mutually exclusive events and the multiplication rule for independent events.

IMPORTANT WORDS & SYMBOLS

Section 5.1

Probability of an event A, $P(A)$
Relative frequency
Law of large numbers
Equally likely outcomes
Statistical experiment
Simple event
Sample space
Complement of event A

Section 5.2

Independent events
Dependent events
$A|B$
Conditional probability
Multiplication rules of probability (for independent and dependent events)
A and B
Mutually exclusive events
Addition rules (for mutually exclusive and general events)
A or B

Section 5.3

Multiplication rule of counting
Tree diagram
Permutations rule
Combinations rule

VIEWPOINT Deathday and Birthday

Can people really postpone death? If so, how much can the timing of death be influenced by psychological, social, or other influential factors? One special event is a birthday. Do famous people try to postpone their deaths until an important birthday? Both Thomas Jefferson and John Adams died on July 4, 1826, when the United States was celebrating its 50th birthday. Is this only a strange coincidence, or is there an unexpected connection between birthdays and deathdays? The probability associated with a decline in death rate of famous people just before important birthdays has been studied by Professor D. P. Phillips of the State University of New York and is presented in the book Statistics, A Guide to the Unknown, *edited by J. M. Tanur.*

CHAPTER REVIEW PROBLEMS

Tables and art to accompany margin answers may be found in the back of the book.

1. (a) The individual does not own a cell phone.
   (b) The individual owns a cell phone as well as a laptop computer.
   (c) The individual owns either a cell phone or a laptop computer, and maybe both.
   (d) The individual owns a cell phone, given he or she owns a laptop computer.
   (e) The individual owns a laptop computer, given he or she owns a cell phone.
2. (a) No. You need to know the value of $P(A \text{ and } B)$.
   (b) Yes. Because the events are mutually exclusive, $P(A \text{ and } B) = 0$ and $P(A \text{ or } B) = P(A) + P(B)$.
3. (a) No. You need to know that the events are independent or you need to know the value of $P(A|B)$ or $P(B|A)$.
   (b) Yes. For independent events, $P(A \text{ and } B) = P(A) \cdot P(B)$.
4. The information supplied yields the result $P(B|A) = 2$. Probabilities must be between 0 and 1, inclusive. The value of $P(A \text{ and } B)$ cannot be greater than $P(A)$ or $P(B)$ individually.
5. 24%; 45%; 10.8%.
6. 20%; 59%; 11.8%.
7. (a) Probability is ratio of number of times tack lands point up to number of times dropped.
   (b) Up, down.
   (c) $P(\text{up}) = 0.32$; $P(\text{down}) = 0.68$.
8. (a) 0.470; 0.390; 0.140.
   (b) 0.840; 0.040.
   (c) 0.100; 0.240.
   (d) 0.420; 0.060.
   (e) 0.860; yes.
   (f) No.

1. *Statistical Literacy* Consider the following two events for an individual:

   A = owns a cell phone $\quad B$ = owns a laptop computer

   Translate each event into words.
   (a) A^c
   (b) A *and* B
   (c) A *or* B
   (d) $A|B$
   (e) $B|A$

2. *Critical Thinking* You are given the information that $P(A) = 0.30$ and $P(B) = 0.40$.
   (a) Do you have enough information to compute $P(A \text{ or } B)$? Explain.
   (b) If you know that events A and B are mutually exclusive, do you have enough information to compute $P(A \text{ or } B)$? Explain.

3. *Critical Thinking* You are given the information that $P(A) = 0.30$ and $P(B) = 0.40$.
   (a) Do you have enough information to compute $P(A \text{ and } B)$? Explain.
   (b) If you know that events A and B are independent, do you have enough information to compute $P(A \text{ and } B)$? Explain.

4. *Critical Thinking* For a class activity, your group has been assigned the task of generating a quiz question that requires use of the formula for conditional probability to compute $P(B|A)$. Your group comes up with the following question: "If $P(A \text{ and } B) = 0.40$ and $P(A) = 0.20$, what is the value of $P(B|A)$?" What is wrong with this question? *Hint:* Consider the answer you get when using the correct formula, $P(B|A) = P(A \text{ and } B)/P(A)$.

5. *Salary Raise: Women* Does it pay to ask for a raise? A national survey of heads of households showed the percentage of those who asked for a raise and the percentage who got one (*USA Today*). According to the survey, of the women interviewed, 24% had asked for a raise, and of those women who had asked for a raise, 45% received the raise. If a woman is selected at random from the survey population of women, find the following probabilities: P(woman asked for a raise); P(woman received raise, *given* she asked for one); P(woman asked for raise *and* received raise).

6. *Salary Raise: Men* According to the same survey quoted in Problem 5, of the men interviewed, 20% had asked for a raise and 59% of the men who had asked for a raise received the raise. If a man is selected at random from the survey population of men, find the following probabilities: P(man asked for a raise); P(man received raise, *given* he asked for one); P(man asked for raise *and* received raise).

7. *General: Thumbtack* Drop a thumbtack and observe how it lands.
   (a) Describe how you could use a relative frequency to estimate the probability that a thumbtack will land with its flat side down.
   (b) What is the sample space of outcomes for the thumbtack?
   (c) How would you make a probability assignment to this sample space if, when you drop 500 tacks, 340 land flat side down?

8. *Survey: Reaction to Poison Ivy* Allergic reactions to poison ivy can cause much misery. Plant oils cause the reaction. Researchers at Allergy Institute did a study to determine the effects of washing the oil off within 5 minutes of exposure. A random sample of 1000 people with known allergies to poison ivy participated in the study. Oil from the poison ivy plant was rubbed on a patch of skin. For 500 of the subjects, it was washed off *within* 5 minutes. For the other 500 subjects, the oil was washed off *after* 5 minutes. The results are summarized in Table 5-5.

TABLE 5-5 Time Within Which Oil Was Washed Off

Reaction	Within 5 Minutes	After 5 Minutes	Row Total
None	420	50	470
Mild	60	330	390
Strong	20	120	140
Column Total	500	500	1000

Let's use the following notation for the various events: W = washing oil off within 5 minutes, A = washing oil off after 5 minutes, N = no reaction, M = mild reaction, S = strong reaction. Find the following probabilities for a person selected at random from this sample of 1000 subjects.

(a) $P(N)$, $P(M)$, $P(S)$

(b) $P(N|W)$, $P(S|W)$

(c) $P(N|A)$, $P(S|A)$

(d) $P(N \text{ and } W)$, $P(M \text{ and } W)$

(e) $P(N \text{ or } M)$. Are the events N = no reaction and M = mild reaction mutually exclusive? Explain.

(f) Are the events N = no reaction and W = washing oil off within 5 minutes independent? Explain.

9. 2, 0.028; 3, 0.056; 4, 0.083; 5, 0.111; 6, 0.139; 7, 0.167; 8, 0.139; 9, 0.111; 10, 0.083; 11, 0.056; 12, 0.028.

9. *General: Two Dice* In a game of craps, you roll two fair dice. Whether you win or lose depends on the sum of the numbers occurring on the tops of the dice. Let x be the random variable that represents the sum of the numbers on the tops of the dice.

(a) What values can x take on?

(b) What is the probability distribution of these x values (that is, what is the probability that x = 2, 3, etc.)?

10. 0.693.

10. *Academic: Passing French* Class records at Rockwood College indicate that a student selected at random has probability 0.77 of passing French 101. For the student who passes French 101, the probability is 0.90 that he or she will pass French 102. What is the probability that a student selected at random will pass both French 101 and French 102?

11. $C_{8,2} = 28$.

11. *Combination: City Council* There is money to send two of eight city council members to a conference in Honolulu. All want to go, so they decide to choose the members who will go to the conference by a random process. How many different combinations of two council members can be selected from the eight who want to go to the conference?

12. (a) 42, (b) 21, (c) 6, (d) 1.

12. Compute. (a) $P_{7,2}$ (b) $C_{7,2}$ (c) $P_{3,3}$ (d) $C_{4,4}$

13. 1024; 0.00098.

13. *Counting: Exam Answers* There are five multiple-choice questions on an exam, each with four possible answers. Determine the number of possible answer sequences for the five questions. Only one of the sequences can contain all five correct answers. If you are guessing, so that you are as likely to choose one sequence of answers as another, what is the probability of getting all five answers correct?

14. *Scheduling: College Courses* A student must satisfy the literature, social science, and philosophy requirements this semester. There are four literature courses to select from, three social science courses, and two philosophy courses. Make a tree diagram showing all the possible sequences of literature, social science, and philosophy courses.

15. 1000.

15. *General: Combination Lock* To open a combination lock, you turn the dial to the right and stop at a number; then you turn it to the left and stop at a second number. Finally, you turn the dial back to the right and stop at a third number. If you use the correct sequence of numbers, the lock opens. If the dial of the lock contains 10 numbers, 0 through 9, determine the number of different combinations possible for the lock. (*Note:* The same number can be reused.)

16. $P_{3,3} = 6$.

16. *General: Combination Lock* You have a combination lock. Again, to open it, you turn the dial to the right and stop at a first number; then you turn it to the left and stop at a second number. Finally, you turn the dial to the right and stop at a third number. Suppose you remember that the three numbers for your lock are 2, 9, and 5, but you don't remember the order in which the numbers must occur. How many sequences of these three numbers are possible?

DATA HIGHLIGHTS: GROUP PROJECTS

Break into small groups and discuss the following topics. Organize a brief outline in which you summarize the main points of your group discussion.

1. Look at Figure 5-11, "Who's Cracking the Books?"
   (a) Does the figure show the probability distribution of grade records for male students? for female students? Describe all the grade-record probability distributions shown in Figure 5-11. Find the probability that a male student selected at random has a grade record showing mostly A's.
   (b) Is the probability distribution shown for all students making mostly A's? Explain your answer. *Hint:* Do the percentages shown for mostly A's add up to 1? Can Figure 5-11 be used to determine the probability that a student selected at random has mostly A's? Can it be used to determine the probability that a female student selected at random has mostly A's? What is the probability?
   (c) Can we use the information shown in the figure to determine the probability that a graduating senior has grades consisting of mostly B's or higher? What is the probability?
   (d) Does Figure 5-11 give sufficient information to determine the probability that a student selected at random is in the age range 19 to 23 *and* has grades that are mostly B's? What is the probability that a student selected at random has grades that are mostly B's, *given* he or she is in the age range 19 to 23?
   (e) Suppose that 65% of the students at State University are between 19 and 23 years of age. What is the probability that a student selected at random is in this age range *and* has grades that are mostly B's?

FIGURE 5-11

Who's Cracking the Books?

Undergraduate Grade Record by Student Characteristic

Student characteristic		C's and D's or lower	B's and C's	Mostly B's	A's and B's	Mostly A's
Gender:	Men	38.8 %	16.6 %	22.6 %	9.6 %	12.4 %
	Women	29.4	16.2	26.2	12.0	16.2
Class level:	Graduating senior	15.8 %	21.9 %	34.5 %	14.7 %	13.0 %
	All other class levels	35.4	15.8	23.6	10.5	14.7
Age:	18 or younger	42.6 %	14.7 %	23.4 %	9.4 %	10.0 %
	19 to 23	38.1	19.0	25.1	9.4	8.3
	24 to 29	33.3	16.9	24.7	10.3	14.9
	30 to 39	23.1	13.2	25.9	14.8	23.0
	40 and older	20.1	10.1	22.0	14.8	33.0

Source: U.S. Department of Education

2. Consider the information given in Figure 5-12, "Vulnerable Knees." What is the probability that an orthopedic case selected at random involves knee problems? For such cases, estimate the probability that the case requires full knee replacement. Compute the probability that an orthopedic case selected at random involves a knee problem *and* requires a full knee replacement. Next, look at the probability distribution for ages of patients requiring full knee replacements. Medicare insurance coverage begins when a person reaches age 65. What is the probability that the age of a person receiving a knee replacement is 65 or older?

FIGURE 5-12

Vulnerable Knees

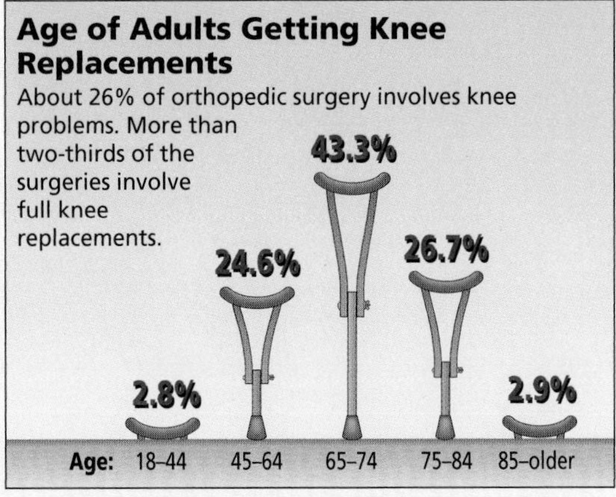
Age of Adults Getting Knee Replacements
About 26% of orthopedic surgery involves knee problems. More than two-thirds of the surgeries involve full knee replacements.
2.8%
24.6%
43.3%
26.7%
2.9%
Age: 18–44 45–64 65–74 75–84 85–older

Source: American Academy of Orthopedic Surgeons

LINKING CONCEPTS: WRITING PROJECTS

Discuss each of the following topics in class or review the topics on your own. Then write a brief but complete essay in which you summarize the main points. Please include formulas as appropriate.

1. Discuss the following concepts and give examples from everyday life in which you might encounter each concept. *Hint:* For instance, consider the "experiment" of arriving for class. Some possible outcomes are not arriving (that is, missing class), arriving on time, and arriving late.
   (a) Sample space.
   (b) Probability assignment to a sample space. In your discussion, be sure to include answers to the following questions.
      (i) Is there more than one valid way to assign probabilities to a sample space? Explain and give an example.
      (ii) How can probabilities be estimated by relative frequencies? How can probabilities be computed if events are equally likely?
2. Discuss the concepts of mutually exclusive events and independent events. List several examples of each type of event from everyday life.
   (a) If A and B are mutually exclusive events, does it follow that A and B *cannot* be independent events? Give an example to demonstrate your answer. *Hint:* Discuss an election in which only one person can win the election. Let A be the event that party A's candidate wins, and let B be the event that party B's candidate wins. Does the outcome of one event determine the outcome of the other event? Are A and B mutually exclusive events?
   (b) Discuss the conditions under which $P(A \text{ and } B) = P(A) \cdot P(B)$ is true. Under what conditions is this statement not true?

(c) Discuss the conditions under which $P(A \text{ or } B) = P(A) + P(B)$ is true. Under what conditions is this statement not true?

3. Although we learn a good deal about probability in this course, the main emphasis is on statistics. Write a few paragraphs in which you talk about the distinction between probability and statistics. In what types of problems would probability be the main tool? In what types of problems would statistics be the main tool? Give some examples of both types of problems. What kinds of outcomes or conclusions do we expect from each type of problem?

USING TECHNOLOGY

Demonstration of the Law of Large Numbers

Computers can be used to simulate experiments. With packages such as Excel, Minitab, and SPSS, programs using random-number generators can be designed (see the *Technology Guide*) to simulate activities such as tossing a die.

The following printouts show the results of the simulations for tossing a die 6, 500, 50,000, 500,000, and 1,000,000 times. Notice how the relative frequencies of the outcomes approach the theoretical probabilities of 1/6 or 0.16667 for each outcome. Do you expect the same results every time the simulation is done? Why or why not?

Results of tossing one die 6 times

Outcome	Number of Occurrences	Relative Frequency
⚀	0	.00000
⚁	1	.16667
⚂	2	.33333
⚃	0	.00000
⚄	1	.16667
⚅	2	.33333

Results of tossing one die 500 times

Outcome	Number of Occurrences	Relative Frequency
⚀	87	.17400
⚁	83	.16600
⚂	91	.18200
⚃	69	.13800
⚄	87	.17400
⚅	83	.16600

Results of tossing one die 50,000 times

Outcome	Number of Occurrences	Relative Frequency
⚀	8528	.17056
⚁	8354	.16708
⚂	8246	.16492
⚃	8414	.16828
⚄	8178	.16356
⚅	8280	.16560

Results of tossing one die 500,000 times

Outcome	Number of Occurrences	Relative Frequency
⚀	83644	.16729
⚁	83368	.16674
⚂	83398	.16680
⚃	83095	.16619
⚄	83268	.16654
⚅	83227	.16645

Results of tossing one die 1,000,000 times

Outcome	Number of Occurrences	Relative Frequency
⚀	166643	.16664
⚁	166168	.16617
⚂	167391	.16739
⚃	165790	.16579
⚄	167243	.16724
⚅	166765	.16677

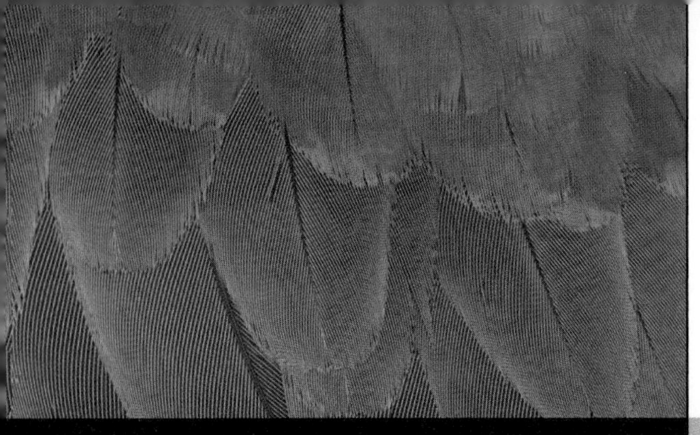

6

Education is the key to unlock the golden door of freedom.

—George Washington Carver

George Washington Carver (1859–1943) won international fame for agricultural research. After graduating from Iowa State College, he was appointed a faculty member in the Iowa State Botany Department. Carver took charge of the greenhouse and started a fungus collection that later included more than 20,000 species. This collection brought him professional acclaim in the field of botany.

At the invitation of his friend Booker T. Washington, Carver joined the faculty of the Tuskegee Institute, where he spent the rest of his long and distinguished career. Carver's creative genius accounted for more than 300 inventions from peanuts, 118 inventions from sweet potatoes, and 75 inventions from pecans.

Gathering and analyzing data were important components of Carver's work. Methods you will learn in this course are widely used in research in every field, including agriculture.

For on-line student resources, visit the Brase/Brase, *Understanding Basic Statistics,* 5th edition web site at **www.cengage.com/statistics/Brase/UBS5e.**

The Binomial Probability Distribution and Related Topics

PREVIEW QUESTIONS

What is a random variable? How do you compute μ and σ for a discrete random variable? (SECTION 6.1)

Many of life's experiences consist of some successes together with some failures. Suppose you make n *attempts to succeed at a certain project. How can you use the binomial probability distribution to compute the probability of* r *successes?* (SECTION 6.2)

How do you compute μ and σ for the binomial distribution? (SECTION 6.3)

FOCUS PROBLEM

Personality Preference Types: Introvert or Extrovert?

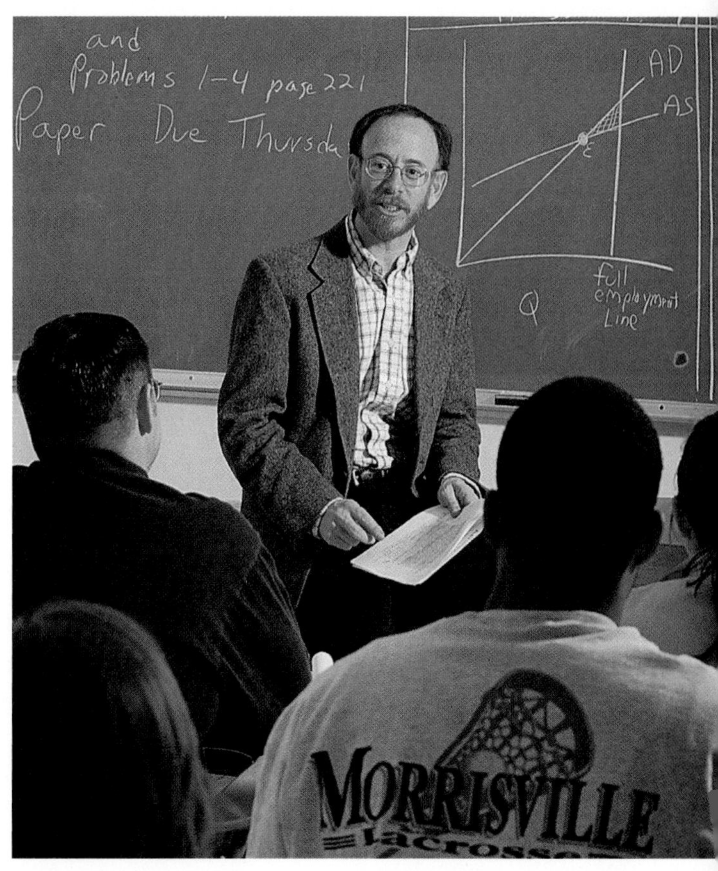

Isabel Briggs Myers was a pioneer in the study of personality types. Her work has been used successfully in counseling, educational, and industrial settings. In the book *A Guide to the Development and Use of the Myers-Briggs Type Indicators*, by Myers and McCaully, it was reported that based on a very large sample (2282 professors), approximately 45% of all university professors are extroverted.

After completing this chapter, you will be able to answer the following questions. Suppose you have classes with six different professors.

(a) What is the probability that all six are extroverts?

(b) What is the probability that none of your professors is an extrovert?

(c) What is the probability that at least two of your professors are extroverts?

(d) In a group of six professors selected at random, what is the *expected number* of extroverts? What is the *standard deviation* of the distribution?

(See Problem 14 of Section 6.3.)

COMMENT Both extroverted and introverted professors can be excellent teachers.

SECTION 6.1 Introduction to Random Variables and Probability Distributions

FOCUS POINTS

- Distinguish between discrete and continuous random variables.
- Graph discrete probability distributions.
- Compute μ and σ for a discrete probability distribution.

Random Variables

This is a conceptually important section. Most students find the material easy to pick up. However, it is still a good idea to emphasize the importance of these concepts for later work. Problem 1 of Data Highlights contains good material for a class discussion.

For our purposes, we say that a *statistical experiment* or *observation* is any process by which measurements are obtained. For instance, you might count the number of eggs in a robin's nest or measure daily rainfall in inches. It is common practice to use the letter x to represent the quantitative result of an experiment or observation. As such, we call x a variable.

A quantitative variable x is a **random variable** if the value that x takes on in a given experiment or observation is a chance or random outcome.

A **discrete random variable** can take on only a finite number of values or a countable number of values.

A **continuous random variable** can take on any of the countless number of values in a line interval.

The distinction between discrete and continuous random variables is important because of the different mathematical techniques associated with the two kinds of random variables.

In most of the cases we will consider, a *discrete random variable* will be the result of a count. The number of students in a statistics class is a discrete random variable. Values such as 15, 25, 50, and 250 are all possible. However, 25.5 students is not a possible value for the number of students.

Most of the *continuous random variables* we will see will occur as the result of a measurement on a continuous scale. For example, the air pressure in an automobile tire represents a continuous random variable. The air pressure could, in theory, take on any value from 0 lb/in^2 (psi) to the bursting pressure of the tire. Values such as 20.126 psi, 20.12678 psi, and so forth are possible.

GUIDED EXERCISE 1 Discrete or continuous random variables

Which of the following random variables are discrete and which are continuous?

(a) *Measure* the time it takes a student selected at random to register for the fall term.

→ Time can take on any value, so this is a continuous random variable.

(b) *Count* the number of bad checks drawn on Upright Bank on a day selected at random.

→ The number of bad checks can be only a whole number such as 0, 1, 2, 3, etc. This is a discrete variable.

Continued

GUIDED EXERCISE 1 *continued*

(c) *Measure* the amount of gasoline needed to drive your car 200 miles. → We are measuring volume, which can assume any value, so this is a continuous random variable.

(d) Pick a random sample of 50 registered voters in a district and find the number who voted in the last county election. → This is a count, so the variable is discrete.

Probability Distribution of a Discrete Random Variable

A random variable has a probability distribution whether it is discrete or continuous.

Probability distribution

A **probability distribution** is an assignment of probabilities to each distinct value of a discrete random variable or to each interval of values of a continuous random variable.

In this chapter we discuss discrete probability distributions. In Chapter 7 we begin our discussion of continuous probability distributions.

Features of the probability distribution of a discrete random variable

1. The probability distribution has a probability assigned to *each* distinct value of the random variable.
2. The sum of all the assigned probabilities must be 1.

EXAMPLE 1 DISCRETE PROBABILITY DISTRIBUTION

Dr. Mendoza developed a test to measure boredom tolerance. He administered it to a group of 20,000 adults between the ages of 25 and 35. The possible scores were 0, 1, 2, 3, 4, 5, and 6, with 6 indicating the highest tolerance for boredom. The test results for this group are shown in Table 6-1.

(a) If a subject is chosen at random from this group, the probability that he or she will have a score of 3 is 6000/20,000, or 0.30. In a similar way, we can use relative frequencies to compute the probabilities for the other scores (Table 6-2). These probability assignments make up the probability distribution. Notice that the scores are mutually exclusive: No one subject has two scores. The sum of the probabilities of all the scores is 1.

TABLE 6-1 **Boredom Tolerance Test Scores for 20,000 Subjects**

Score	Number of Subjects
0	1400
1	2600
2	3600
3	6000
4	4400
5	1600
6	400

TABLE 6-2 **Probability Distribution of Scores on Boredom Tolerance Test**

Score x	Probability $P(x)$
0	0.07
1	0.13
2	0.18
3	0.30
4	0.22
5	0.08
6	0.02
	$\Sigma P(x) = 1$

FIGURE 6-1

Graph of the Probability Distribution of Test Scores

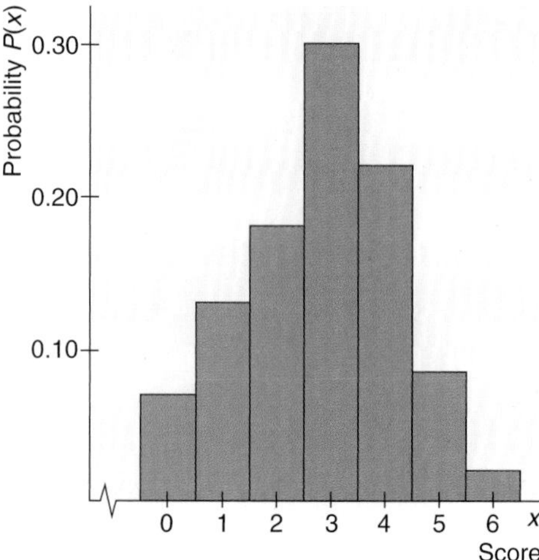

(b) The graph of this distribution is simply a relative-frequency histogram (see Figure 6-1) in which the height of the bar over a score represents the probability of that score. Since each bar is 1 unit wide, the area of the bar over a score equals the height and thus represents the probability of that score. Since the sum of the probabilities is 1, the area under the graph is also 1.

(c) The Topnotch Clothing Company needs to hire someone with a score on the boredom tolerance test of 5 or 6 to operate the fabric press machine. Since the scores 5 and 6 are mutually exclusive, the probability that someone in the group who took the boredom tolerance test made either a 5 or a 6 is the sum

$$P(5 \text{ } or \text{ } 6) = P(5) + P(6)$$
$$= 0.08 + 0.02 = 0.10$$

Notice that to find $P(5 \text{ } or \text{ } 6)$, we could have simply added the *areas* of the bars over 5 and over 6. One out of 10 of the group who took the boredom tolerance test would qualify for the position at Topnotch Clothing.

GUIDED EXERCISE 2 **Discrete probability distribution**

One of the elementary tools of cryptanalysis (the science of code breaking) is to use relative frequencies of occurrence of different letters in the alphabet to break standard English alphabet codes. Large samples of plain text such as newspaper stories generally yield about the same relative frequencies for letters. A sample 1000 letters long yielded the information in Table 6-3.

(a) Use the relative frequencies to compute the omitted probabilities in Table 6-3.

→ Table 6-4 shows the completion of Table 6-3.

Continued

GUIDED EXERCISE 2 *continued*

TABLE 6-3 Frequencies of Letters in a 1000-Letter Sample

Letter	Freq.	Prob.	Letter	Freq.	Prob.
A	73	_____	N	78	0.078
B	9	0.009	O	74	_____
C	30	0.030	P	27	0.027
D	44	0.044	Q	3	0.003
E	130	_____	R	77	0.077
F	28	0.028	S	63	0.063
G	16	0.016	T	93	0.093
H	35	0.035	U	27	_____
I	74	_____	V	13	0.013
J	2	0.002	W	16	0.016
K	3	0.003	X	5	0.005
L	35	0.035	Y	19	0.019
M	25	0.025	Z	1	0.001

Source: From *Elementary Cryptanalysis: A Mathematical Approach,* by Abraham Sinkov. Copyright © 1968 by Yale University. Reprinted by permission of Random House, Inc.

TABLE 6-4 Entries for Table 6-3

Letter	Relative Frequency	Probability
A	$\frac{73}{1000}$	0.073
E	$\frac{130}{1000}$	0.130
I	$\frac{74}{1000}$	0.074
O	$\frac{74}{1000}$	0.074
U	$\frac{27}{1000}$	0.027

(b) Do the probabilities of all the individual letters add up to 1?

→ Yes.

(c) If a letter is selected at random from a newspaper story, what is the probability that the letter will be a vowel?

→ If a letter is selected at random,

$$\begin{aligned} P(a, e, i, o, \text{ or } u) &= P(a) + P(e) + P(i) + P(o) + P(u) \\ &= 0.073 + 0.130 + 0.074 + 0.074 + 0.027 \\ &= 0.378 \end{aligned}$$

Mean and standard deviation of a discrete probability distribution

A probability distribution can be thought of as a relative-frequency distribution based on a very large n. As such, it has a mean and standard deviation. If we are referring to the probability distribution of a *population,* then we use the Greek letters μ for the mean and σ for the standard deviation. When we see the Greek letters used, we know the information given is from the *entire population* rather than just a sample. If we have a sample probability distribution, we use $\bar{x}$ (x bar) and s, respectively, for the mean and standard deviation.

This is a good time to emphasize that we are shifting gears from a discussion of the mean and standard deviation of raw data to a discussion of the mean and standard deviation of a probability distribution.

The **mean** and the **standard deviation of a discrete population probability distribution** are found by using these formulas:

$\mu = \Sigma xP(x)$; μ is called the **expected value** of x.

$\sigma = \sqrt{\Sigma(x - \mu)^2 P(x)}$; σ is called the **standard deviation** of x.

where x is the value of a random variable,
$P(x)$ is the probability of that variable, and
the sum Σ is taken for all the values of the random variable.

Note: μ is the *population mean* and σ is the underlying *population standard deviation* because the sum Σ is taken over *all* values of the random variable (i.e., the entire sample space).

Expected value

The mean of a probability distribution is often called the *expected value* of the distribution. This terminology reflects the idea that the mean represents a "central point" or "cluster point" for the entire distribution. Of course, the mean or expected value is an average value, and as such, it *need not be a point of the sample space.*

The standard deviation is often represented as a measure of *risk*. A larger standard deviation implies a greater likelihood that the random variable x is different from the expected value μ.

EXAMPLE 2

EXPECTED VALUE, STANDARD DEVIATION

Are we influenced to buy a product by an ad we saw on TV? The National Infomercial Marketing Association determined the number of times *buyers* of a product watched a TV infomercial *before* purchasing the product. The results are shown here:

Number of times buyers saw infomercial	1	2	3	4	5*
Percentage of buyers	27%	31%	18%	9%	15%

*This category was 5 or more, but will be treated as 5 in this example.

We can treat the information shown as an estimate of the probability distribution because the events are mutually exclusive and the sum of the percentages is 100%. Compute the mean and standard deviation of the distribution.

SOLUTION: We put the data into the first two columns of a computation table and then fill in the other entries (see Table 6-5). The average number of times a buyer views the infomercial before purchase is

$$\mu = \Sigma xP(x) = 2.54 \text{ (sum of column 3)}$$

To find the standard deviation, we take the square root of the sum of column 6:

$$\sigma = \sqrt{\Sigma(x - \mu)^2 P(x)} \approx \sqrt{1.869} \approx 1.37$$

TABLE 6-5 Number of Times Buyers View Infomercial Before Making Purchase

x (number of viewings)	$P(x)$	$xP(x)$	$x - \mu$	$(x - \mu)^2$	$(x - \mu)^2 P(x)$
1	0.27	0.27	−1.54	2.372	0.640
2	0.31	0.62	−0.54	0.292	0.091
3	0.18	0.54	0.46	0.212	0.038
4	0.09	0.36	1.46	2.132	0.192
5	0.15	0.75	2.46	6.052	0.908
	$\mu = \Sigma xP(x) = 2.54$				$\Sigma(x - \mu)^2 P(x) = 1.869$

You might point out that the formulas for μ and σ of a discrete probability distribution are equivalent to the formulas for μ and σ for grouped data. Ask students to replace $P(x)$ in the formulas of this section with the relative frequency f/n and then, using a little algebra, show that the formulas of this section are equivalent to those for grouped data.

CALCULATOR NOTE Some calculators, including the TI-84Plus/TI-83Plus models, accept fractional frequencies. If yours does, you can get μ and σ directly by using techniques for grouped data and the calculator's STAT mode.

GUIDED EXERCISE 3 Expected value

At a carnival, you pay \$2.00 to play a coin-flipping game with three fair coins. On each coin, one side has the number 0 and the other side has the number 1. You flip the three coins at one time, and you win \$1.00 for every 1 that appears on top. Are your expected earnings equal to the cost to play? We'll answer this question in several steps.

(a) In this game, the random variable of interest counts the number of 1s that show. What is the sample space for the values of this random variable?

→ The sample space is {0, 1, 2, 3}, since any of these numbers of 1s can appear.

(b) There are eight equally likely outcomes for throwing three coins. They are 000, 001, 010, 011, 100, 101, ______, and ______.

→ 110 and 111.

(c) Complete Table 6-6.

TABLE 6-6

Number of 1s, x	Frequency	$P(x)$	$xP(x)$
0	1	0.125	0
1	3	0.375	____
2	3	____	____
3	____	____	____

→ TABLE 6-7 **Completion of Table 6-6**

Number of 1s, x	Frequency	$P(x)$	$xP(x)$
0	1	0.125	0
1	3	0.375	0.375
2	3	0.375	0.750
3	1	0.125	0.375

(d) The expected value is the sum

$\mu = \Sigma xP(x)$

Sum the appropriate column of Table 6-6 to find this value.

Interpretation: Are your expected earnings less than, equal to, or more than the cost of the game?

→ The expected value can be found by summing the last column of Table 6-7. The expected value is \$1.50. It cost \$2.00 to play the game; the expected value is less than the cost. The carnival is making money. In the long run, the carnival can expect to make an average of about 50 cents per player.

We have seen probability distributions of discrete variables and the formulas to compute the mean and standard deviation of a discrete population probability distribution. Probability distributions of continuous random variables are similar except that the probability assignments are made to intervals of values rather than to specific values of the random variable. We will see an important example of a discrete probability distribution, the binomial distribution, in the next section, and one of a continuous probability distribution in Chapter 7 when we study the normal distribution.

VIEWPOINT The Rosetta Project

Around 196 B.C., Egyptian priests inscribed a decree on a granite slab affirming the rule of 13-year-old Ptolemy V. The proclamation was in Egyptian hieroglyphics with another translation in a form of ancient Greek. By 1799, the meaning of Egyptian hieroglyphics had been lost for many centuries. However, Napoleon's troops discovered the granite slab (Rosetta Stone). Linguists used the Rosetta Stone and their knowledge of ancient Greek to unlock the meaning of the Egyptian hieroglyphics.

Linguistic experts say that because of industrialization and globalization, by the year 2100 as many as 90% of the world's languages may be extinct. To help preserve some of these languages for future generations, 1000 translations of the first three chapters of Genesis have been inscribed in tiny text onto 3-inch nickel disks and encased in hardened glass balls that are expected to last at least 1000 years. Why Genesis? Because it is the most translated text in the world. The Rosetta Project is sending the disks to libraries and universities all over the world. It is very difficult to send information into the future. However, if in the year 2500 linguists are using the "Rosetta Disks" to unlock the meaning of a lost language, you may be sure they will use statistical methods of cryptanalysis (see Guided Exercise 2). To find out more about the Rosetta Project, visit the Online Study Center at **www.cengage.com/statistics/Brase/UBS5e** *and find the link to the Rosetta Project site.*

SECTION 6.1 PROBLEMS

Tables and art to accompany margin answers may be found in the back of the book.

1. (a) Discrete.
   (b) Continuous.
   (c) Continuous.
   (d) Discrete.
   (e) Continuous.
2. (a) Continuous.
   (b) Continuous.
   (c) Discrete.
   (d) Continuous.
   (e) Discrete.
3. (a) Yes.
   (b) No, probabilities total to more than 1.
4. No. Look at Guided Exercise 3. The possible outcomes are 0, 1, 2, and 3, but the expected value is 1.5.
5. (a) Yes, 7 of the 10 digits represent "making a basket."
   (b) Let *S* represent "making a basket" and *F* represent "missing the shot." *F, F, S, S, S, F, F, F, S, S.*
   (c) Yes. Again, 7 of the 10 digits represent "making a basket." *S, S, S, S, S, S, S, S, S, S.*

1. *Statistical Literacy* Which of the following are continuous variables, and which are discrete?
   (a) Number of traffic fatalities per year in the state of Florida
   (b) Distance a golf ball travels after being hit with a driver
   (c) Time required to drive from home to college on any given day
   (d) Number of ships in Pearl Harbor on any given day
   (e) Your weight before breakfast each morning

2. *Statistical Literacy* Which of the following are continuous variables, and which are discrete?
   (a) Speed of an airplane
   (b) Age of a college professor chosen at random
   (c) Number of books in the college bookstore
   (d) Weight of a football player chosen at random
   (e) Number of lightning strikes in Rocky Mountain National Park on a given day

3. *Statistical Literacy* Consider each distribution. Determine if it is a valid probability distribution or not, and explain your answer.

(a)

x	0	1	2
$P(x)$	0.25	0.60	0.15

(b)

x	0	1	2
$P(x)$	0.25	0.60	0.20

4. *Statistical Literacy* Consider the probability distribution of a random variable x. Is the expected value of the distribution necessarily one of the possible values of x? Explain or give an example.

5. *Critical Thinking: Simulation* We can use the random number table to simulate outcomes from a given discrete probability distribution. Jose plays basketball and has probability 0.7 of making a free-throw shot. Let x be the random variable that counts the number of successful shots out of 10 attempts. Consider the digits 0 through 9 of the random number table. Since Jose has a 70% chance of

making a shot, assign the digits 0 through 6 to "making a basket from the free-throw line" and the digits 7 through 9 to "missing the shot."

(a) Do 70% of the possible digits 0 through 9 represent "making a basket"?

(b) Start at line 2, column 1 of the random number table. Going across the row, determine the results of 10 "trials." How many free-throw shots are successful in this simulation?

(c) Your friend decides to assign the digits 0 through 2 to "missing the shot" and the digits 3 through 9 to "making the basket." Is this assignment valid? Explain. Using this assignment, repeat part (b).

6. (a) Yes. Events are distinct; probabilities total to 1.
(c) 42.58.
(d) 12.31.

6. *Marketing: Age* What is the age distribution of promotion-sensitive shoppers? A *supermarket super shopper* is defined as a shopper for whom at least 70% of the items purchased were on sale or purchased with a coupon. The following table is based on information taken from *Trends in the United States* (Food Marketing Institute, Washington, D.C.).

Age range, years	18–28	29–39	40–50	51–61	62 and over
Midpoint x	23	34	45	56	67
Percent of super shoppers	7%	44%	24%	14%	11%

For the 62-and-over group, use the midpoint 67 years.

(a) Using the age midpoints x and the percentage of super shoppers, do we have a valid probability distribution? Explain.

(b) Use a histogram to graph the probability distribution of part (a).

(c) Compute the expected age μ of a super shopper.

(d) Compute the standard deviation σ for ages of super shoppers.

7. (a) Yes, events are distinct and probabilities total to 1.
(c) $\mu = 32.3$.
(d) $\sigma \approx 16.12$.

7. *Marketing: Income* What is the income distribution of super shoppers (see Problem 6)? In the following table, income units are in thousands of dollars, and each interval goes up to but does not include the given high value. The midpoints are given to the nearest thousand dollars.

Income range	5–15	15–25	25–35	35–45	45–55	55 or more
Midpoint x	10	20	30	40	50	60
Percent of super shoppers	21%	14%	22%	15%	20%	8%

(a) Using the income midpoints x and the percent of super shoppers, do we have a valid probability distribution? Explain.

(b) Use a histogram to graph the probability distribution of part (a).

(c) Compute the expected income μ of a super shopper.

(d) Compute the standard deviation σ for the income of super shoppers.

8. *History: Florence Nightingale* What was the age distribution of nurses in Great Britain at the time of Florence Nightingale? Thanks to Florence Nightingale and the British census of 1851, we have the following information (based on data from the classic text *Notes on Nursing*, by Florence Nightingale). *Note:* In 1851, there were 25,466 nurses in Great Britain. Furthermore, Nightingale made a strict distinction between nurses and domestic servants.

Age range (yr)	20–29	30–39	40–49	50–59	60–69	70–79	80+
Midpoint x	24.5	34.5	44.5	54.5	64.5	74.5	84.5
Percent of nurses	5.7%	9.7%	19.5%	29.2%	25.0%	9.1%	1.8%

8. (a) Yes, outcomes are distinct and probabilities total to 1.
(c) 0.359.
(d) 53.76.
(e) 13.66.

(a) Using the age midpoints x and the percent of nurses, do we have a valid probability distribution? Explain.
(b) Use a histogram to graph the probability distribution of part (a).
(c) Find the probability that a British nurse selected at random in 1851 would be 60 years of age or older.
(d) Compute the expected age μ of a British nurse contemporary to Florence Nightingale.
(e) Compute the standard deviation σ for ages of nurses shown in the distribution.

9. (b) 0.56.
(c) 0.20.
(d) 0.82.
(e) 0.899.

9. *Fishing: Trout* The following data are based on information taken from *Daily Creel Summary,* published by the Paiute Indian Nation, Pyramid Lake, Nevada. Movie stars and U.S. presidents have fished Pyramid Lake. It is one of the best places in the lower 48 states to catch trophy cutthroat trout. In this table, x = number of fish caught in a 6-hour period. The percentage data are the percentages of fishermen who caught x fish in a 6-hour period while fishing from shore.

x	0	1	2	3	4 or more
%	44%	36%	15%	4%	1%

(a) Convert the percentages to probabilities and make a histogram of the probability distribution.
(b) Find the probability that a fisherman selected at random fishing from shore catches one or more fish in a 6-hour period.
(c) Find the probability that a fisherman selected at random fishing from shore catches two or more fish in a 6-hour period.
(d) Compute μ, the expected value of the number of fish caught per fisherman in a 6-hour period (round 4 or more to 4).
(e) Compute σ, the standard deviation of the number of fish caught per fisherman in a 6-hour period (round 4 or more to 4).

10. (a) 0.763; complement.
(b) 0.368.
(c) 0.016.
(d) 1.25.
(e) 0.97.

10. *Criminal Justice: Parole* *USA Today* reported that approximately 25% of all state prison inmates released on parole become repeat offenders while on parole. Suppose the parole board is examining five prisoners up for parole. Let x = number of prisoners out of five on parole who become repeat offenders. The methods of Section 6.2 can be used to compute the probability assignments for the x distribution.

x	0	1	2	3	4	5
P(x)	0.237	0.396	0.264	0.088	0.015	0.001

(a) Find the probability that one or more of the five parolees will be repeat offenders. How does this number relate to the probability that none of the parolees will be repeat offenders?
(b) Find the probability that two or more of the five parolees will be repeat offenders.
(c) Find the probability that four or more of the five parolees will be repeat offenders.
(d) Compute μ, the expected number of repeat offenders out of five.
(e) Compute σ, the standard deviation of the number of repeat offenders out of five.

11. (a) 15/719; 704/719.
(b) $0.73; $14.27.

11. *Fund Raiser: Hiking Club* The college hiking club is having a fund raiser to buy new equipment for fall and winter outings. The club is selling Chinese fortune cookies at a price of $1 per cookie. Each cookie contains a piece of paper with a different number written on it. A random drawing will determine which number is the winner of a dinner for two at a local Chinese restaurant. The dinner is valued at $35. Since the fortune cookies were donated to the club, we can ignore the cost of the cookies. The club sold 719 cookies before the drawing.

(a) Lisa bought 15 cookies. What is the probability she will win the dinner for two? What is the probability she will not win?

(b) Lisa's expected earnings can be found by multiplying the value of the dinner by the probability that she will win. What are Lisa's expected earnings? How much did she effectively contribute to the hiking club?

12. (a) 0.0021; 0.9979.
(b) $4.20; less; $25.80.

12. *Spring Break: Caribbean Cruise* The college student senate is sponsoring a spring break Caribbean cruise raffle. The proceeds are to be donated to the Samaritan Center for the Homeless. A local travel agency donated the cruise, valued at $2000. The students sold 2852 raffle tickets at $5 per ticket.

(a) Kevin bought six tickets. What is the probability that Kevin will win the spring break cruise to the Caribbean? What is the probability that Kevin will not win the cruise?

(b) Kevin's expected earnings can be found by multiplying the value of the cruise by the probability that Kevin will win. What are Kevin's expected earnings? Is this more or less than the amount Kevin paid for the six tickets? How much did Kevin effectively contribute to the Samaritan Center for the Homeless?

13. (a) 0.01191; $595.50.
(b) $646; $698; $751.50; $806.50; $3497.50 total.
(c) $4197.50.
(d) $1502.50.

13. *Expected Value: Life Insurance* Jim is a 60-year-old Anglo male in reasonably good health. He wants to take out a $50,000 term (that is, straight death benefit) life insurance policy until he is 65. The policy will expire on his 65th birthday. The probability of death in a given year is provided by the Vital Statistics Section of the *Statistical Abstract of the United States* (116th Edition).

x = age	60	61	62	63	64
P(death at this age)	0.01191	0.01292	0.01396	0.01503	0.01613

Jim is applying to Big Rock Insurance Company for his term insurance policy.

(a) What is the probability that Jim will die in his 60th year? Using this probability and the $50,000 death benefit, what is the expected cost to Big Rock Insurance?

(b) Repeat part (a) for years 61, 62, 63, and 64. What would be the total expected cost to Big Rock Insurance over the years 60 through 64?

(c) If Big Rock Insurance wants to make a profit of $700 above the expected total cost paid out for Jim's death, how much should it charge for the policy?

(d) If Big Rock Insurance Company charges $5000 for the policy, how much profit does the company expect to make?

14. (a) 0.00756; $378.
(b) $412.50; $448; $482.50; $517.50; $2238.50 total.
(c) $2938.50.
(d) $2761.50.

14. *Expected Value: Life Insurance* Sara is a 60-year-old Anglo female in reasonably good health. She wants to take out a $50,000 term (that is, straight death benefit) life insurance policy until she is 65. The policy will expire on her 65th birthday. The probability of death in a given year is provided by the Vital Statistics Section of the *Statistical Abstract of the United States* (116th Edition).

x = age	60	61	62	63	64
P(death at this age)	0.00756	0.00825	0.00896	0.00965	0.01035

Sara is applying to Big Rock Insurance Company for her term insurance policy.

(a) What is the probability that Sara will die in her 60th year? Using this probability and the $50,000 death benefit, what is the expected cost to Big Rock Insurance?

(b) Repeat part (a) for years 61, 62, 63, and 64. What would be the total expected cost to Big Rock Insurance over the years 60 through 64?

(c) If Big Rock Insurance wants to make a profit of $700 above the expected total cost paid out for Sara's death, how much should it charge for the policy?

(d) If Big Rock Insurance Company charges $5000 for the policy, how much profit does the company expect to make?

SECTION 6.2

Binomial Probabilities

FOCUS POINTS

- List the defining features of a binomial experiment.
- Compute binomial probabilities using the formula $P(r) = C_{n,r}p^r q^{n-r}$.
- Use the binomial table to find $P(r)$.
- Use the binomial probability distribution to solve real-world applications.

Binomial Experiment

On a TV quiz show, each contestant has a try at the wheel of fortune. The wheel of fortune is a roulette wheel with 36 slots, one of which is gold. If the ball lands in the gold slot, the contestant wins $50,000. No other slot pays. What is the probability that the quiz show will have to pay the fortune to 3 contestants out of 100?

In this problem, the contestant and the quiz show sponsors are concerned about only two outcomes from the wheel of fortune: The ball lands on the gold, or the ball does not land on the gold. This problem is typical of an entire class of problems that are characterized by the feature that there are exactly two possible outcomes (for each trial) of interest. These problems are called *binomial experiments,* or *Bernoulli experiments,* after the Swiss mathematician Jacob Bernoulli, who studied them extensively in the late 1600s.

Features of a binomial experiment

The binomial distribution is a probability distribution of a discrete random variable. We use the random variable r to *count* the number of successes out of n trials.

Features of a binomial experiment

1. There are a *fixed number of trials.* We denote this number by the letter n.
2. The n trials are *independent* and repeated under identical conditions.
3. Each trial has only *two outcomes:* success, denoted by S, and failure, denoted by F.
4. For each individual trial, the *probability of success is the same.* We denote the probability of success by p and that of failure by q. Since each trial results in either success or failure, $p + q = 1$ and $q = 1 - p$.
5. The central problem of a binomial experiment is to find the *probability of r successes out of n trials.*

EXAMPLE 3 BINOMIAL EXPERIMENT

Let's see how the wheel of fortune problem meets the criteria of a binomial experiment. We'll take the criteria one at a time.

SOLUTION:

1. Each of the 100 contestants has a trial at the wheel, so there are $n = 100$ trials in this problem.
2. Assuming that the wheel is fair, the *trials are independent,* since the result of one spin of the wheel has no effect on the results of other spins.
3. We are interested in only two outcomes on each spin of the wheel: The ball either lands on the gold, or it does not. Let's call landing on the gold *success* (S) and not landing on the gold *failure* (F). In general, the assignment of the terms *success* and *failure* to outcomes does not imply good or bad results. These terms are assigned simply for the user's convenience.

4. On each trial, the probability p of success (landing on the gold) is 1/36, since there are 36 slots and only one of them is gold. Consequently, the probability of failure is

$$q = 1 - p = 1 - \frac{1}{36} = \frac{35}{36}$$

on each trial.

5. We want to know the probability of 3 successes out of 100 trials, so $r = 3$ in this example. It turns out that the probability the quiz show will have to pay the fortune to 3 contestants out of 100 is about 0.23. Later in this section we'll see how this probability was computed.

Sampling without replacement

Any time we make selections from a population *without replacement, we do not have independent trials.* However, replacement is often not practical. If the number of trials is quite small with respect to the population, we *almost* have independent trials, and we can say the situation is *closely approximated* by a binomial experiment. For instance, suppose we select 20 tuition bills at random from a collection of 10,000 bills issued at one college and observe if each bill is in error or not. If 600 of the 10,000 bills are in error, then the probability that the first one selected is in error is 600/10,000, or 0.0600. If the first is in error, then the probability that the second is in error is 599/9999, or 0.0599. Even if the first 19 bills selected are in error, the probability that the 20th is also in error is 581/9981, or 0.0582. All these probabilities round to 0.06, and we can say that the independence condition is approximately satisfied.

GUIDED EXERCISE 4 Binomial experiment

Let's analyze the following binomial experiment to determine p, q, n, and r:

According to the *Textbook of Medical Physiology,* 5th Edition, by Arthur Guyton, 9% of the population has blood type B. Suppose we choose 18 people at random from the population and test the blood type of each. What is the probability that three of these people have blood type B? (*Note:* Independence is approximated because 18 people is an extremely small sample with respect to the entire population.)

(a) In this experiment, we are observing whether or not a person has type B blood. We will say we have a success if the person has type B blood. What is failure?

→ Failure occurs if a person does not have type B blood.

(b) The probability of success is 0.09, since 9% of the population has type B blood. What is the probability of failure, q?

→ The probability of failure is

$$q = 1 - p$$
$$= 1 - 0.09 = 0.91$$

(c) In this experiment, there are $n =$ ______ trials.

→ In this experiment, $n = 18$.

(d) We wish to compute the probability of 3 successes out of 18 trials. In this case, $r =$ ______.

→ In this case, $r = 3$.

Next, we will see how to compute the probability of r successes out of n trials when we have a binomial experiment.

Computing Probabilities for a Binomial Experiment Using the Binomial Distribution Formula

The central problem of a binomial experiment is to find the probability of r successes out of n trials. Now we'll see how to find these probabilities.

A model with three trials

This part will probably require extra class time. Good class discussion topics can be found in Data Highlights, Problem 2 (final frontier); Linking Concepts, Problem 2; and Using Technology (U.S. Weather Bureau example).

Suppose you are taking a timed final exam. You have three multiple-choice questions left to do. Each question has four suggested answers, and only one of the answers is correct. You have only 5 seconds left to do these three questions, so you decide to mark answers on the answer sheet without even reading the questions. Assuming that your answers are randomly selected, what is the probability that you get zero, one, two, or all three questions correct?

This is a binomial experiment. Each question can be thought of as a trial, so there are $n = 3$ trials. The possible outcomes on each trial are success S, indicating a correct response, or failure F, meaning a wrong answer. The trials are independent—the outcome of any one trial does not affect the outcome of the others.

What is the probability of success on any question? Since you are guessing and there are four answers from which to select, the probability of a correct answer is 0.25. The probability q of a wrong answer is then 0.75. In short, we have a binomial experiment with $n = 3$, $p = 0.25$, and $q = 0.75$.

Now, what are the possible outcomes in terms of success or failure for these three trials? Let's use the notation SSF to mean success on the first question, success on the second, and failure on the third. There are eight possible combinations of S's and F's. They are

SSS *SSF* *SFS* *FSS* *SFF* *FSF* *FFS* *FFF*

To compute the probability of each outcome, we use the multiplication law for independent events. For instance, the probability of success on the first two questions and failure on the last is

$$P(SSF) = P(S) \cdot P(S) \cdot P(F) = p \cdot p \cdot q = p^2q = (0.25)^2(0.75) \approx 0.047$$

In a similar fashion, we can compute the probability of each of the eight outcomes. These are shown in Table 6-8, along with the number of successes r associated with each outcome.

TABLE 6-8 Outcomes for a Binomial Experiment with $n = 3$ Trials

Outcome	Probability of Outcome	r (number of successes)
SSS	$P(SSS) = P(S)P(S)P(S) = p^3 = (0.25)^3 \approx 0.016$	3
SSF	$P(SSF) = P(S)P(S)P(F) = p^2q = (0.25)^2(0.75) \approx 0.047$	2
SFS	$P(SFS) = P(S)P(F)P(S) = p^2q = (0.25)^2(0.75) \approx 0.047$	2
FSS	$P(FSS) = P(F)P(S)P(S) = p^2q = (0.25)^2(0.75) \approx 0.047$	2
SFF	$P(SFF) = P(S)P(F)P(F) = pq^2 = (0.25)(0.75)^2 \approx 0.141$	1
FSF	$P(FSF) = P(F)P(S)P(F) = pq^2 = (0.25)(0.75)^2 \approx 0.141$	1
FFS	$P(FFS) = P(F)P(F)P(S) = pq^2 = (0.25)(0.75)^2 \approx 0.141$	1
FFF	$P(FFF) = P(F)P(F)P(F) = q^3 = (0.75)^3 \approx 0.422$	0

Now we can compute the probability of r successes out of three trials for $r = 0, 1, 2$, or 3. Let's compute $P(1)$. The notation $P(1)$ stands for the probability of one success. For three trials, there are three different outcomes that show exactly one success. They are the outcomes *SFF*, *FSF*, and *FFS*. Since the outcomes are mutually exclusive, we can add the probabilities. So,

This is a good time to remind students of the concept of mutually exclusive events from Chapter 5 and of the addition rule for mutually exclusive events.

$$\begin{aligned} P(1) = P(SFF \text{ or } FSF \text{ or } FFS) &= P(SFF) + P(FSF) + P(FFS) \\ &= pq^2 + pq^2 + pq^2 \\ &= 3pq^2 \\ &= 3(0.25)(0.75)^2 \\ &= 0.422 \end{aligned}$$

In the same way, we can find $P(0)$, $P(2)$, and $P(3)$. These values are shown in Table 6-9.

TABLE 6-9 $P(r)$ **for** $n = 3$ **Trials,** $p = 0.25$

r (number of successes)	$P(r)$ (probability of r successes in 3 trials)		$P(r)$ for $p = 0.25$
0	$P(0) = P(FFF)$	$= q^3$	0.422
1	$P(1) = P(SFF) + P(FSF) + P(FFS)$	$= 3pq^2$	0.422
2	$P(2) = P(SSF) + P(SFS) + P(FSS)$	$= 3p^2q$	0.141
3	$P(3) = P(SSS)$	$= p^3$	0.016

We have done quite a bit of work to determine your chances of $r = 0, 1, 2$, or 3 successes on three multiple-choice questions if you are just guessing. Now we see that there is only a small chance (about 0.016) that you will get them all correct.

For most applications in this text, we will be able to use Table 2 of the Appendix. However, for many other applications, the formula itself must be used. Stress that it is important to be able to use both tables and formulas.

Table 6-9 can be used as a model for computing the probability of r successes out of only *three* trials. How can we compute the probability of 7 successes out of 10 trials? We can develop a table for $n = 10$, but this would be a tremendous task because there are 1024 possible combinations of successes and failures on 10 trials. Fortunately, mathematicians have given us a direct formula to compute the probability of r successes for any number of trials.

General formula for binomial probability distribution

Many calculators have a built-in combinations key (binomial coefficient). See the calculator display in the next example.

Formula for the binomial probability distribution

$$P(r) = \frac{n!}{r!(n-r)!}p^r q^{n-r} = C_{n,r}p^r q^{n-r}$$

where n = number of trials

p = probability of success on each trial

$q = 1 - p$ = probability of failure on each trial

r = random variable representing the number of successes out of n trials $(0 \le r \le n)$

! = factorial notation. Recall from Section 5.3 that the factorial symbol $n!$ designates the product of all the integers between 1 and n. For instance, $4! = 4 \cdot 3 \cdot 2 \cdot 1 = 24$. Special cases are $1! = 1$ and $0! = 1$.

$C_{n,r} = \dfrac{n!}{r!(n-r)!}$ is the binomial coefficient. Many calculators have a key designated nCr that gives the value of $C_{n,r}$ directly.

Note: The binomial coefficient $C_{n,r}$ represents the number of combinations of n distinct objects (n = number of trials in this case) taken r at a time (r = number of successes). For more information about $C_{n,r}$, see Section 5.3.

Let's look more carefully at the formula for $P(r)$. There are two main parts. The expression $p^r q^{n-r}$ is the probability of getting one outcome with r successes and $n - r$ failures. The binomial coefficient $C_{n,r}$ counts the number of outcomes that have r successes and $n - r$ failures. For instance, in the case of $n = 3$ trials, we saw in Table 6-8 that the probability of getting an outcome with one success and two failures was pq^2. This is the value of $p^r q^{n-r}$ when $r = 1$ and $n = 3$. We also observed that there were three outcomes with one success and two failures, so $C_{3,1}$ is 3.

Now let's take a look at an application of the binomial distribution formula in Example 4.

EXAMPLE 4 COMPUTE $P(r)$ USING THE BINOMIAL DISTRIBUTION FORMULA

Privacy is a concern for many users of the Internet. One survey showed that 59% of Internet users are somewhat concerned about the confidentiality of their e-mail. Based on this information, what is the probability that for a random sample of 10 Internet users, 6 are concerned about the privacy of their e-mail?

SOLUTION:

(a) This is a binomial experiment with 10 trials. If we assign success to an Internet user being concerned about the privacy of e-mail, the probability of success is 59%. We are interested in the probability of 6 successes. We have

$$n = 10 \qquad p = 0.59 \qquad q = 0.41 \qquad r = 6$$

By the formula,

$$P(6) = C_{10,6}(0.59)^6(0.41)^{10-6}$$

$$= 210(0.59)^6(0.41)^4 \quad \text{Use a calculator or the formula for } C_{n,r}.$$

$$\approx 210(0.0422)(0.0283) \quad \text{Use a calculator.}$$

$$\approx 0.25$$

There is a 25% chance that *exactly* 6 of the 10 Internet users are concerned about the privacy of e-mail.

FIGURE 6-2

TI-84Plus/TI-83Plus Display

```
10 nCr 6*.59^6*.
41^(10-6)
        .2503034245
```

(b) Many calculators have a built-in combinations function. On the TI-84Plus and TI-83Plus calculators, press the **MATH** key and select **PRB**. The combinations function is designated nCr. Figure 6-2 displays the process for computing $P(6)$ directly on these calculators.

Using a Binomial Distribution Table

In many cases, we will be interested in the probability of a range of successes. In such cases, we need to use the addition rule for mutually exclusive events. For instance, for $n = 6$ and $p = 0.50$,

$$P(4 \text{ or } \textit{fewer} \text{ successes}) = P(r \leq 4)$$

$$= P(r = 4 \text{ or } 3 \text{ or } 2 \text{ or } 1 \text{ or } 0)$$

$$= P(4) + P(3) + P(2) + P(1) + P(0)$$

It would be a bit of a chore to use the binomial distribution formula to compute all the required probabilities. Table 2 of the Appendix gives values of $P(r)$ for selected p values and values of n through 20. To use the table, find the appropriate section for n, and then use the entries in the columns headed by the p values and the rows headed by the r values.

Table 6-10 is an excerpt from Table 2 of the Appendix showing the section for $n = 6$. Notice that all possible r values between 0 and 6 are given as row headers. The value $p = 0.50$ is one of the column headers. For $n = 6$ and $p = 0.50$, you can find the value of $P(4)$ by looking at the entry in the row headed by 4 and the column headed by 0.50. Notice that $P(4) = 0.234$.

TABLE 6-10 Excerpt from Table 2 of the Appendix for $n = 6$

						p				
n	*r*	.01	.05	.10 ...	.30 ...	.50 ...	.70 ...	.85	.90	.95
⋮										
6	0	.941	.735	.531 ...	.118 ...	.016 ...	.001 ...	.000	.000	.000
	1	.057	.232	.354 ...	.303 ...	.094 ...	.010 ...	.000	.000	.000
	2	.001	.031	.098 ...	.324 ...	.234 ...	.060 ...	.006	.001	.000
	3	.000	.002	.015 ...	.185 ...	.312 ...	.185 ...	.042	.015	.002
	4	.000	.000	.001 ...	.060 ...	.234 ...	.324	.176	.098	.031
	5	.000	.000	.000 ...	.010 ...	.094 ...	.303 ...	.399	.354	.232
	6	.000	.000	.000 ...	.001 ...	.016 ...	.118 ...	.377	.531	.735

Likewise, you can find other values of $P(r)$ from the table. In fact, for $n = 6$ and $p = 0.50$,

$$P(r \le 4) = P(4) + P(3) + P(2) + P(1) + P(0)$$
$$= 0.234 + 0.312 + 0.234 + 0.094 + 0.016 = 0.890$$

Alternatively, to compute $P(r \le 4)$ for $n = 6$, you can use the fact that the total of all $P(r)$ values for r between 0 and 6 is 1. Then

$$P(r \le 4) = 1 - P(5) - P(6)$$
$$= 1 - 0.094 - 0.016 = 0.890$$

Note: In Table 2 of the Appendix, probability entries of 0.000 do not mean the probability is exactly zero. Rather, to three digits after the decimal, the probability rounds to 0.000.

EXAMPLE 5

USING THE BINOMIAL DISTRIBUTION TABLE TO FIND $P(r)$

A biologist is studying a new hybrid tomato. It is known that the seeds of this hybrid tomato have probability 0.70 of germinating. The biologist plants six seeds.

(a) What is the probability that *exactly* four seeds will germinate?

SOLUTION: This is a binomial experiment with $n = 6$ trials. Each seed planted represents an independent trial. We'll say germination is success, so the probability for success on each trial is 0.70.

$$n = 6 \qquad p = 0.70 \qquad q = 0.30 \qquad r = 4$$

We wish to find P(4), the probability of exactly four successes.

In Table 2 of the Appendix, find the section with $n = 6$ (excerpt is given in Table 6-10). Then find the entry in the column headed by $p = 0.70$ and the row headed by $r = 4$. This entry is 0.324.

$$P(4) = 0.324$$

(b) What is the probability that *at least* four seeds will germinate?

SOLUTION: In this case, we are interested in the probability of four or more seeds germinating. This means we are to compute $P(r \geq 4)$. Since the events are mutually exclusive, we can use the addition rule.

$$P(r \geq 4) = P(r = 4 \quad or \quad r = 5 \quad or \quad r = 6) = P(4) + P(5) + P(6)$$

We already know the value of $P(4)$. We need to find $P(5)$ and $P(6)$.

Use the same part of the table but find the entries in the row headed by the r value 5 and then the r value 6. Be sure to use the column headed by the value of p, 0.70.

$$P(5) = 0.303 \quad \text{and} \quad P(6) = 0.118$$

Now we have all the parts necessary to compute $P(r \geq 4)$.

$$\begin{aligned} P(r \geq 4) &= P(4) + P(5) + P(6) \\ &= 0.324 + 0.303 + 0.118 \\ &= 0.745 \end{aligned}$$

In Guided Exercise 5, you'll practice using the formula for $P(r)$ in one part, and then in the second part you'll use Table 2 of the Appendix for $P(r)$ values.

GUIDED EXERCISE 5 *Find P(r)*

A rarely performed and somewhat risky eye operation is known to be successful in restoring the eyesight of 30% of the patients who undergo the operation. A team of surgeons has developed a new technique for this operation that has been successful in four of six operations. Does it seem likely that the new technique is much better than the old? We'll use the binomial probability distribution to answer this question. We'll compute the probability of at least four successes in six trials for the old technique.

(a) Each operation is a binomial trial. In this case, $n =$ ____, $p =$ ____, $q =$ ____, $r =$ ____.

→ $n = 6, p = 0.30, q = 1 - 0.30 = 0.70, r = 4$

(b) Use your values of n, p, and q, as well as your calculator to compute $P(4)$ from the formula:

$$P(r) = C_{n,r}p^r q^{n-r}$$

→
$$\begin{aligned} P(4) &= C_{6,4}(0.30)^4(0.70)^2 \\ &= 15(0.0081)(0.490) \\ &\approx 0.060 \end{aligned}$$

(c) Compute the probability of *at least* four successes out of the six trials.

$$\begin{aligned} P(r \geq 4) &= P(r = 4 \text{ or } r = 5 \text{ or } r = 6) \\ &= P(4) + P(5) + P(6) \end{aligned}$$

Use Table 2 of the Appendix to find values of $P(4)$, $P(5)$, and $P(6)$. Then use these values to compute $P(r \geq 4)$.

→ To find $P(4)$, $P(5)$, and $P(6)$ in Table 2, we look in the section labeled $n = 6$. Then we find the column headed by $p = 0.30$. To find $P(4)$, we use the row labeled $r = 4$. For the values of $P(5)$ and $P(6)$, use the same column but change the row headers to $r = 5$ and $r = 6$, respectively.

$$\begin{aligned} P(r \geq 4) &= P(4) + P(5) + P(6) \\ &= 0.060 + 0.010 + 0.001 = 0.071 \end{aligned}$$

(d) *Interpretation:* Under the older operation technique, the probability that at least four patients out of six regain their eyesight is ______. Does it

→ It seems the new technique is better than the old since, by pure chance, the probability of four or more successes out of six trials is only 0.071 for the

Continued

GUIDED EXERCISE 5 *continued*

seem that the new technique is better than the old? Would you encourage the surgeon team to do more work on the new technique?

old technique. This means one of the following two things may be happening:

(i) The new method is no better than the old method, and our surgeons have encountered a rare event (probability 0.071), or

(ii) The new method is in fact better. We think it is worth encouraging the surgeons to do more work on the new technique.

Using Technology to Compute Binomial Probabilities

Some calculators and computer software packages support the binomial distribution. In general, these technologies will provide both the probability $P(r)$ for an exact number of successes r and the cumulative probability $P(r \leq k)$, where k is a specified value less than or equal to the number of trials n. Note that most of the technologies use the letter x instead of r for the random variable denoting the number of successes out of n trials.

TECH NOTES

The software packages Minitab and Excel, as well as the TI-84Plus and TI-83Plus calculators, include built-in binomial probability distribution options. These options give the probability $P(r)$ of a specific number of successes r as well as the cumulative total probability for r or fewer successes.

TI-84Plus/TI-83Plus Press the **DISTR** key and scroll to **binompdf**(n, p, r). Enter the number of trials n, the probability of success on a single trial p, and the number of successes r. This gives $P(r)$. For the cumulative probability that there are r or fewer successes, use **binomcdf**(n, p, r).

```
binompdf(6,.3,4)
                .059535
binomcdf(6,.3,4)
                .989065
```

$P(r = 4)$ = .059535

$P(r \leq 4)$ = .989065

Excel Menu Choice: **Paste Function** (f_x) ➤ **Statistical** ➤ **Binomdist.** In the dialogue box, fill in the values r, n, and p. For $P(r)$, use false; for P(at least r successes), use true.

Minitab First, enter the r values $0, 1, 2, \ldots, n$ in a column. Then use menu choice **Calc** ➤ **Probability Distribution** ➤ **Binomial.** In the dialogue box, select Probability for $P(r)$ or Cumulative for P(at least r successes). Enter the number of trials n, the probability of success p, and the column containing the r values. A sample printout is shown in Problem 17 at the end of this section.

Common expressions and corresponding inequalities

Many times we are asked to compute the probability of a range of successes. For instance, in a binomial experiment with n trials, we may be asked to compute the probability of four or more successes. Table 6-11 shows how common English expressions such as "four or more successes" translate to inequalities involving r.

TABLE 6-11 Common English Expressions and Corresponding Inequalities (Consider a binomial experiment with *n* trials and *r* successes.)

Expression	Inequality
Four or more successes At least four successes No fewer than four successes Not less than four successes	$r \geq 4$ That is, $r = 4, 5, 6, \ldots, n$
Four or fewer successes At most four successes No more than four successes The number of successes does not exceed four	$r \leq 4$ That is, $r = 0, 1, 2, 3,$ or 4
More than four successes The number of successes exceeds four	$r > 4$ That is, $r = 5, 6, 7, \ldots, n$
Fewer than four successes The number of successes is not as large as four	$r < 4$ That is, $r = 0, 1, 2, 3$

VIEWPOINT *Lies! Lies!! Lies!!! The Psychology of Deceit*

This is the title of an intriguing book by C. V. Ford, professor of psychiatry. The book recounts the true story of Floyd "Buzz" Fay, who was falsely convicted of murder on the basis of a failed polygraph examination. During his $2\frac{1}{2}$ years of wrongful imprisonment, Buzz became a polygraph expert. He taught inmates, who freely confessed guilt, how to pass a polygraph examination. (For more information on this topic, see Problem 15.)

SECTION 6.2 PROBLEMS

Tables and art to accompany margin answers may be found in the back of the book.

1. The random variable measures the number of successes out of *n* trials. This text uses the letter *r* for the random variable.
2. Trials are independent if the outcome of one trial does not affect the probability of success on any other trial.
3. Two outcomes, success or failure.
4. No. A binomial experiment requires that the probability of success be the same for each trial.
5. (a) No. A binomial probability model applies to only two outcomes per trial.
   (b) Yes. Assign outcome A to "success" and outcomes B and C to "failure." $p = 0.40$.
6. Yes. The five trials are independent, are repeated under the same conditions, have only two outcomes, and have the same probability of success. $n = 5$, $r = 2$, $p = 0.20$.

1. *Statistical Literacy* What does the random variable for a binomial experiment of *n* trials measure?

2. *Statistical Literacy* What does it mean to say that the trials of an experiment are independent?

3. *Statistical Literacy* For a binomial experiment, how many outcomes are possible for each trial? What are the possible outcomes?

4. *Statistical Literacy* In a binomial experiment, is it possible for the probability of success to change from one trial to the next? Explain.

5. ***Critical Thinking*** In an experiment, there are *n* independent trials. For each trial, there are three outcomes, A, B, and C. For each trial, the probability of outcome A is 0.40; the probability of outcome B is 0.50; and the probability of outcome C is 0.10. Suppose there are 10 trials.
   (a) Can we use the binomial experiment model to determine the probability of four outcomes of type A, five of type B, and one of type C? Explain.
   (b) Can we use the binomial experiment model to determine the probability of four outcomes of type A and six outcomes that are not of type A? Explain. What is the probability of success on each trial?

6. ***Critical Thinking*** In a carnival game, there are six identical boxes, one of which contains a prize. A contestant wins the prize by selecting the box containing it. Before each game, the old prize is removed and another prize is placed at random in one of the six boxes. Is it appropriate to use the binomial probability

distribution to find the probability that a contestant who plays the game five times wins exactly twice? Check each of the criteria for a binomial experiment and give the values of n, r, and p.

7. (a) A trial consists of looking at the class status of a student enrolled in introductory statistics. Two outcomes are "freshman" and "not freshman." Success is freshman status; failure is any other class status. $P(\text{success}) = 0.40$.
(b) Trials are not independent. With a population of only 30 students, in 5 trials without replacement, the probability of success rounded to the nearest hundredth changes for the later trials.

8. (a) Yes.
(b) *S, F, S, S, S, S, S, S, S, S, S, S, S, S, F.*
(c) Yes. All successes.

7. *Critical Thinking* According to the college registrar's office, 40% of students enrolled in an introductory statistics class this semester are freshmen, 25% are sophomores, 15% are juniors, and 20% are seniors. You want to determine the probability that, in a random sample of five students enrolled in introductory statistics this semester, exactly two are freshmen.
(a) Describe a trial. Can we model a trial as having only two outcomes? If so, what is success? What is failure? What is the probability of success?
(b) We are sampling without replacement. If only 30 students are enrolled in introductory statistics this semester, is it appropriate to model 5 trials as independent, with the same probability of success on each trial? Explain.

8. *Critical Thinking: Simulation* Central Eye Clinic advertises that 90% of its patients approved for LASIK surgery to correct vision problems have successful surgeries.
(a) In the random number table, assign the digits 0 through 8 to the event "successful surgery" and the digit 9 to the event "unsuccessful surgery." Does this assignment of digits simulate 90% successful outcomes?
(b) Use the random digit assignment model of part (a) to simulate the outcomes of 15 trials. Begin at column 1, line 2.
(c) Your friend assigned the digits 1 through 9 to the event "successful surgery" and the digit 0 to the event "unsuccessful surgery." Does this assignment of digits simulate 90% successful outcomes? Using this digit assignment, repeat part (b).

In each of the following problems, the binomial distribution will be used. Answers may vary slightly depending on whether the binomial distribution formula, the binomial distribution table, or distribution results from a calculator or computer are used. Please answer the following questions and then complete the problem.

What makes up a trial? What is a success? What is a failure?
What are the values of n, p, and q?

9. $n = 3$; $p = 0.5$.
(a) 0.125.
(b) 0.375.
(c) 0.500.
(d) 0.125.

9. *Binomial Probabilities: Coin Flip* A fair quarter is flipped three times. For each of the following probabilities, use the formula for the binomial distribution and a calculator to compute the requested probability. Next, look up the probability in Table 2 of the Appendix and compare the table result with the computed result.
(a) Find the probability of getting exactly three heads.
(b) Find the probability of getting exactly two heads.
(c) Find the probability of getting two or more heads.
(d) Find the probability of getting exactly three tails.

10. $n = 10$; $p = 0.2$.
(a) 0.000 (to three digits).
(b) 0.107.
(c) 0.892; 0.893; they should be equal, but because of rounding error they differ slightly.
(d) $P(r \geq 5) = 0.033$.

10. *Binomial Probabilities: Multiple-Choice Quiz* Richard has just been given a 10-question multiple-choice quiz in his history class. Each question has five answers, of which only one is correct. Since Richard has not attended class recently, he doesn't know any of the answers. Assuming that Richard guesses on all 10 questions, find the indicated probabilities.
(a) What is the probability that he will answer all questions correctly?
(b) What is the probability that he will answer all questions incorrectly?
(c) What is the probability that he will answer at least one of the questions correctly? Compute this probability two ways. First, use the rule for mutually exclusive events and the probabilities shown in Table 2 of the Appendix. Then use the fact that $P(r \geq 1) = 1 - P(r = 0)$. Compare the two results. Should they be equal? Are they equal? If not, how do you account for the difference?
(d) What is the probability that Richard will answer at least half the questions correctly?

11. (a) $n = 12$; $p = 0.55$ for male; 0.740; 0.473; 0.135.
(b) $n = 12$; $p = 0.70$ for male; 0.961; 0.117; 0.493.

11. *Ecology: Wolves* The following is based on information taken from *The Wolf in the Southwest: The Making of an Endangered Species*, edited by David Brown (University of Arizona Press). Before 1918, approximately 55% of the wolves in the New Mexico and Arizona region were male, and 45% were female. However, cattle ranchers in this area have made a determined effort to exterminate wolves. From 1918 to the present, approximately 70% of wolves in the region are male, and 30% are female. Biologists suspect that male wolves are more likely than females to return to an area where the population has been greatly reduced.
(a) Before 1918, in a random sample of 12 wolves spotted in the region, what is the probability that 6 or more were male? What is the probability that 6 or more were female? What is the probability that fewer than 4 were female?
(b) Answer part (a) for the period from 1918 to the present.

12. $n = 7$; $p = 0.10$.
(a) 0.478.
(b) 0.522.
(c) 0.974.

12. *Sociology: Ethics* The one-time fling! Have you ever purchased an article of clothing (dress, sports jacket, etc.), worn the item *once* to a party, and then returned the purchase? This is called a *one-time fling*. About 10% of all adults deliberately do a one-time fling and feel no guilt about it! (Source: *Are You Normal?*, by Bernice Kanner, St. Martin's Press) In a group of seven adult friends, what is the probability that
(a) no one has done a one-time fling?
(b) at least one person has done a one-time fling?
(c) no more than two people have done a one-time fling?

13. $n = 6$; $p = 0.90$.
(a) 0.531.
(b) 0.000 (to three digits).
(c) 0.983.
(d) 0.017 as complement of part (c); 0.016 directly from table.

13. *Sociology: Mother-in-Law* Sociologists say that 90% of married women claim that their husband's mother is the biggest bone of contention in their marriages (sex and money are lower-rated areas of contention). (See the source in Problem 12.) Suppose that six married women are having coffee together one morning. What is the probability that
(a) all of them dislike their mother-in-law?
(b) none of them dislike their mother-in-law?
(c) at least four of them dislike their mother-in-law?
(d) no more than three of them dislike their mother-in-law?

14. $n = 20$; $p = 0.10$.
(a) 0.878.
(b) 0.323.
(c) 0.122.
(d) 0.677.

14. *Sociology: Dress Habits* A research team at Cornell University conducted a study showing that approximately 10% of all businessmen who wear ties wear them so tightly that they actually reduce blood flow to the brain, diminishing cerebral functions (Source: *Chances: Risk and Odds in Everyday Life*, by James Burke). At a board meeting of 20 businessmen, all of whom wear ties, what is the probability that
(a) at least one tie is too tight?
(b) more than two ties are too tight?
(c) no tie is too tight?
(d) at least 18 ties are *not* too tight?

15. $n = 9$; $p = 0.85$.
(a) 0.232.
(b) 0.995.
(c) 0.005 as complement of part (b); 0.006 directly from table.
(d) 0.000 (to three digits).

15. *Psychology: Deceit* Aldrich Ames is a convicted traitor who leaked American secrets to a foreign power. Yet Ames took routine lie detector tests and each time passed them. How can this be done? Recognizing control questions, employing unusual breathing patterns, biting one's tongue at the right time, pressing one's toes hard to the floor, and counting backwards by 7 are countermeasures that are difficult to detect but can change the results of a polygraph examination (Source: *Lies! Lies!! Lies!!! The Psychology of Deceit*, by C. V. Ford, professor of psychiatry, University of Alabama). In fact, it is reported in Professor Ford's book that after only 20 minutes of instruction by "Buzz" Fay (a prison inmate), 85% of those trained were able to pass the polygraph examination even when guilty of a crime. Suppose that a random sample of nine students (in a psychology laboratory) are told a "secret" and then given instructions on how to pass the polygraph examination without revealing their knowledge of the secret. What is the probability that
(a) all the students are able to pass the polygraph examination?
(b) more than half the students are able to pass the polygraph examination?

(c) no more than four of the students are able to pass the polygraph examination?
(d) all the students fail the polygraph examination?

16. Parts (d) and (e) can be used for class discussion and are a good motivation for later topics in testing (Chapter 9). $p = 0.60$.
(a) 0.683.
(b) 0.633.
(c) 0.166.
(d) 0.001.
(e) 0.003.

16. *Hardware Store: Income* Trevor is interested in purchasing the local hardware/sporting goods store in the small town of Dove Creek, Montana. After examining accounting records for the past several years, he found that the store has been grossing over \$850 per day about 60% of the business days it is open. Estimate the probability that the store will gross over \$850
(a) at least 3 out of 5 business days.
(b) at least 6 out of 10 business days.
(c) fewer than 5 out of 10 business days.
(d) fewer than 6 out of the next 20 business days. *Interpretation:* If this actually happened, might it shake your confidence in the statement $p = 0.60$? Might it make you suspect that p is less than 0.60? Explain.
(e) more than 17 out of the next 20 business days. *Interpretation:* If this actually happened, might you suspect that p is greater than 0.60? Explain.

17. $n = 8$; $p = 0.53$.
(a) 0.812515; yes, truncated at five digits.
(b) 0.187486; 0.18749; yes, rounded to five digits.

17. *Business Ethics: Privacy* A survey conducted by Peter D. Hart Research Associates for the Shell Poll was reported in *USA Today.* According to the survey, 53% of adults are concerned that Social Security numbers are used for general identification. For a group of eight adults selected at random, we used Minitab to generate the binomial probability distribution and the cumulative binomial probability distribution (menu selections ➤ **Calc** ➤ **Probability Distributions** ➤ **Binomial**).

Number	r	P(r)	P(<=r)
	0	0.002381	0.00238
	1	0.021481	0.02386
	2	0.084781	0.10864
	3	0.191208	0.29985
	4	0.269521	0.56937
	5	0.243143	0.81251
	6	0.137091	0.94960
	7	0.044169	0.99377
	8	0.006226	1.00000

Find the probability that out of eight adults selected at random,
(a) at most five are concerned about Social Security numbers being used for identification. Do the problem by adding the probabilities $P(r = 0)$ through $P(r = 5)$. Is this the same as the cumulative probability $P(r \leq 5)$?
(b) more than five are concerned about Social Security numbers being used for identification. First, do the problem by adding the probabilities $P(r = 6)$ through $P(r = 8)$. Then do the problem by subtracting the cumulative probability $P(r \leq 5)$ from 1. Do you get the same results?

18. (a) Same.
(b) Same.
(c) $r = 1$.
(d) Column headed by $p = 0.80$.

18. *Binomial Distribution Table: Symmetry* Study the binomial distribution table (Table 2 of the Appendix). Notice that the probability of success on a single trial p ranges from 0.01 to 0.95. Some binomial distribution tables stop at 0.50 because of the symmetry in the table. Let's look for that symmetry. Consider the section of the table for which $n = 5$. Look at the numbers in the columns headed by $p = 0.30$ and $p = 0.70$. Do you detect any similarities? Consider the following probabilities for a binomial experiment with five trials.
(a) Compare P(3 successes), where $p = 0.30$, with P(2 successes), where $p = 0.70$.
(b) Compare P(3 or more successes), where $p = 0.30$, with P(2 or fewer successes), where $p = 0.70$.
(c) Find the value of P(4 successes), where $p = 0.30$. For what value of r is P(r successes) the same using $p = 0.70$?
(d) What column is symmetrical with the one headed by $p = 0.20$?

SECTION 6.3

Additional Properties of the Binomial Distribution

FOCUS POINTS

- Make histograms for binomial distributions.
- Compute μ and σ for a binomial distribution.

Graphing a Binomial Distribution

Any probability distribution may be represented in graphic form. How should we graph the binomial distribution? Remember, the binomial distribution tells us the probability of r successes out of n trials. Therefore, we'll place values of r along the horizontal axis and values of $P(r)$ on the vertical axis. The binomial distribution is a *discrete* probability distribution because r can assume only whole-number values such as 0, 1, 2, 3, . . . Therefore, a histogram is an appropriate graph of a binomial distribution.

PROCEDURE

HOW TO GRAPH A BINOMIAL DISTRIBUTION

1. Place r values on the horizontal axis.
2. Place $P(r)$ values on the vertical axis.
3. Construct a bar over each r value extending from $r - 0.5$ to $r + 0.5$. The height of the corresponding bar is $P(r)$.

Let's look at an example to see exactly how we'll make these histograms.

EXAMPLE 6 GRAPH OF A BINOMIAL DISTRIBUTION

This is a good time to emphasize a geometric approach to probability using histograms. Recall for the students Section 2.1 and the relative-frequency discussion. Data Highlights, Problem 1 (Powerball) and Problem 2 (final frontier); Linking Concepts, Problems 3 and 4; and Using Technology (U.S. Weather Bureau example) can be used for class discussion.

A waiter at the Green Spot Restaurant has learned from long experience that the probability that a lone diner will leave a tip is only 0.7. During one lunch hour, the waiter serves six people who are dining by themselves. Make a graph of the binomial probability distribution that shows the probabilities that 0, 1, 2, 3, 4, 5, or all 6 lone diners leave tips.

SOLUTION: This is a binomial experiment with $n = 6$ trials. Success is achieved when the lone diner leaves a tip, so the probability of success is 0.7 and that of failure is 0.3:

$$n = 6 \qquad p = 0.7 \qquad q = 0.3$$

We want to make a histogram showing the probability of r successes when $r = 0, 1, 2, 3, 4, 5$, or 6. It is easier to make the histogram if we first make a table of r values and the corresponding $P(r)$ values (Table 6-12). We'll use Table 2 of the Appendix to find the $P(r)$ values for $n = 6$ and $p = 0.70$.

To construct the histogram, we'll put r values on the horizontal axis and $P(r)$ values on the vertical axis. Our bars will be 1 unit wide and will be centered over the appropriate r value. The height of the bar over a particular r value tells the probability of that r (see Figure 6-3).

The probability of a particular value of r is given not only by the height of the bar over that r value but also by the *area* of the bar. Each bar is only 1 unit wide, so its area (area = height times width) equals its height. Since the area of each bar represents the probability of the r value

FIGURE 6-3

Graph of the Binomial Distribution for $n = 6$ and $p = 0.7$

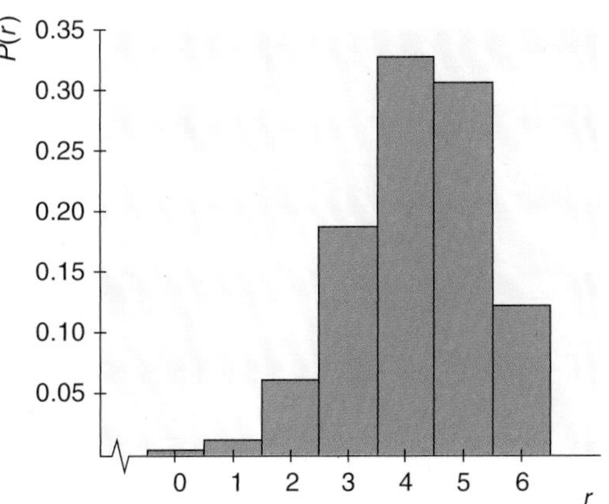

TABLE 6-12 **Binomial Distribution for $n = 6$ and $p = 0.70$**

r	$P(r)$
0	0.001
1	0.010
2	0.060
3	0.185
4	0.324
5	0.303
6	0.118

under it, the sum of the areas of the bars must be 1. In this example, the sum turns out to be 1.001. It is not exactly equal to 1 because of rounding error.

Guided Exercise 6 illustrates another binomial distribution with $n = 6$ trials. The graph will be different from that of Figure 6-3 because the probability of success p is different.

GUIDED EXERCISE 6 Graph of a binomial distribution

Jim enjoys playing basketball. He figures that he makes about 50% of the field goals he attempts during a game. Make a histogram showing the probability that Jim will make 0, 1, 2, 3, 4, 5, or 6 shots out of six attempted field goals.

(a) This is a binomial experiment with $n =$ _______ trials. In this situation, we'll say success occurs when Jim makes an attempted field goal. What is the value of p?

→ In this example, $n = 6$ and $p = 0.5$.

(b) Use Table 2 of the Appendix to complete Table 6-13 of $P(r)$ values for $n = 6$ and $p = 0.5$.

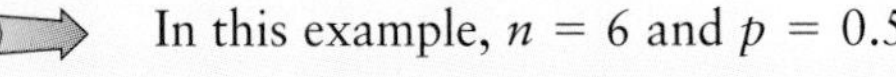

TABLE 6-13

r	$P(r)$
0	0.016
1	0.094
2	0.234
3	_____
4	_____
5	_____
6	_____

→ TABLE 6-14 **Completion of Table 6-13**

r	$P(r)$
.	.
.	.
.	.
3	0.312
4	0.234
5	0.094
6	0.016

Continued

GUIDED EXERCISE 6 *continued*

(c) Use the values of $P(r)$ given in Table 6-14 to complete the histogram in Figure 6-4.

Figure 6-4 Beginning of Graph of Binomial Distribution for $n = 6$ and $p = 0.5$

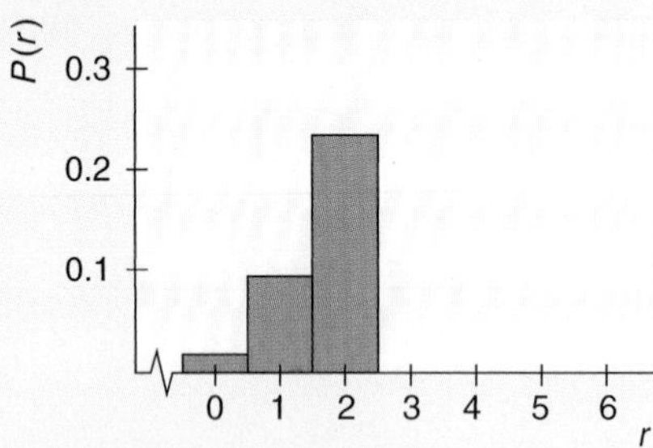

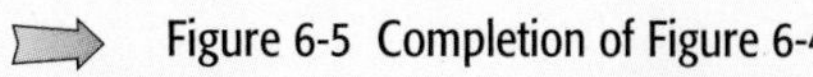

Figure 6-5 Completion of Figure 6-4

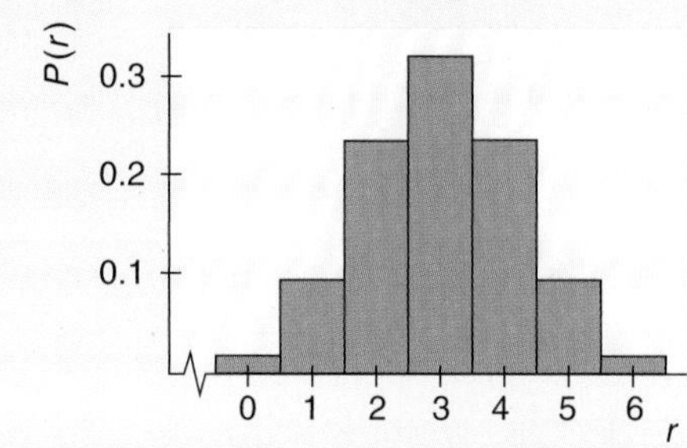

(d) The area of the bar over $r = 2$ is 0.234. What is the area of the bar over $r = 4$? How does the probability that Jim makes exactly two field goals out of six compare with the probability that he makes exactly four field goals out of six?

The area of the bar over $r = 4$ is also 0.234. Jim is as likely to make two out of six field goals attempted as he is to make four out of six.

In Example 6 and Guided Exercise 6, we see the graphs of two binomial distributions associated with $n = 6$ trials. The two graphs are different because the probability of success p is different in the two cases. In Example 6, $p = 0.7$ and the graph is skewed to the left—that is, the left tail is longer. In Guided Exercise 6, p is equal to 0.5 and the graph is symmetrical—that is, if we fold it in half, the two halves coincide exactly. Whenever *p equals 0.5, the graph of the binomial distribution will be symmetrical no matter how many trials we have.* In Chapter 7, we will see that if the number of trials n is quite large, the binomial distribution is almost symmetrical even when p is not close to 0.5.

Mean and Standard Deviation of a Binomial Distribution

Mean and standard deviation of binomial probability distributions

Two other features that help describe the graph of any distribution are the balance point of the distribution and the spread of the distribution about that balance point. The *balance point* is the mean μ of the distribution, and the *measure of spread* that is most commonly used is the standard deviation σ. The mean μ is the *expected value* of the number of successes.

For the binomial distribution, we can use two special formulas to compute the mean μ and the standard deviation σ. These are easier to use than the general formulas in Section 6.1 for μ and σ of any discrete probability distribution.

PROCEDURE

This is a good place to emphasize μ as the geometric balance point and σ as a measure of spread for the probability histogram.

HOW TO COMPUTE μ AND σ FOR A BINOMIAL DISTRIBUTION

$\mu = np$ is the **expected number of successes** for the random variable r

$\sigma = \sqrt{npq}$ is the **standard deviation** for the random variable r

where

r is a random variable representing the number of successes in a binomial distribution,

Continued

n is the number of trials,
p is the probability of success on a single trial, and
$q = 1 - p$ is the probability of failure on a single trial.

EXAMPLE 7 **COMPUTE μ AND σ**

Let's compute the mean and standard deviation for the distribution of Example 6 that describes that probabilities of lone diners leaving tips at the Green Spot Restaurant.

SOLUTION: In Example 6,

$$n = 6 \qquad p = 0.7 \qquad q = 0.3$$

For the binomial distribution,

$$\mu = np = 6(0.7) = 4.2$$

The balance point of the distribution is at $\mu = 4.2$. The standard deviation is given by

$$\sigma = \sqrt{npq} = \sqrt{6(0.7)(0.3)} = \sqrt{1.26} \approx 1.12$$

The mean μ is not only the balance point of the distribution; it is also the *expected value* of r. Specifically, in Example 6, the waiter can expect 4.2 lone diners out of 6 to leave a tip. (The waiter would probably round the expected value to 4 tippers out of 6.)

GUIDED EXERCISE 7 **Expected value and standard deviation**

When Jim (of Guided Exercise 6) shoots field goals in basketball games, the probability that he makes a shot is only 0.5.

(a) The mean of the binomial distribution is the expected value of r successes out of n trials. Out of six throws, what is the expected number of goals Jim will make?

→ The expected value is the mean μ:

$$\mu = np = 6(0.5) = 3$$

Jim can expect to make three goals out of six tries.

(b) For six trials, what is the standard deviation of the binomial distribution of the number of successful field goals Jim makes?

→ $\sigma = \sqrt{npq} = \sqrt{6(0.5)(0.5)} = \sqrt{1.5} \approx 1.22$

CRITICAL THINKING **Unusual Values**

Chebyshev's Theorem tells us that no matter what the data distribution looks like, at least 75% of the data will fall within 2 standard deviations of the mean. As we will see in Chapter 7, when the distribution is mound-shaped and symmetrical, about 95% of the data are within 2 standard deviations of the mean.

Data values beyond 2 standard deviations from the mean are less common than those closer to the mean.

In fact, one indicator that a data value might be an outlier is that it is more than 2.5 standard deviations from the mean (Source: *Statistics,* by G. Upton and I. Cook, Oxford University Press).

Unusual values

For a binomial distribution, it is unusual for the number of successes r to be higher than $\mu + 2.5\sigma$ or lower than $\mu - 2.5\sigma$.

We can use this indicator to determine whether a specified number of successes out of n trials in a binomial experiment is unusual.

For instance, consider a binomial experiment with 20 trials for which probability of success on a single trial is $p = 0.70$. The expected number of successes is $\mu = 14$, with a standard deviation of $\sigma \approx 2$. A number of successes above 19 or below 9 would be considered unusual. However, such numbers of successes are possible.

VIEWPOINT

Kodiak Island, Alaska

Kodiak Island is famous for its giant brown bears. The sea surrounding the island is also famous for its king crab. The state of Alaska, Department of Fish and Game, has collected a huge amount of data regarding ocean latitude, ocean longitude, and size of king crab. Of special interest to commercial fishing skippers is the size of crab. Those too small must be returned to the sea. To find locations and sizes of king crab catches near Kodiak Island, visit the Online Study Center at **www.cengage.com/statistics/Brase/UBS5e** *and find the link to the StatLib site hosted by the Department of Statistics at Carnegie Mellon University. Once at StatLib, go to crab data. From this information, it is possible to use methods of this chapter and Chapter 8 to estimate the proportion of legal crab in a sea skipper's catch.*

SECTION 6.3 PROBLEMS

Tables and art to accompany margin answers may be found in the back of the book.

1. The average number of successes.
2. The expected value is higher for the first distribution.
3. (a) Yes, 120 is more than 2.5 standard deviations above the expected value.
   (b) Yes, 40 is less than 2.5 standard deviations below the expected value.
   (c) No, 70 to 90 successes is within 2.5 standard deviations of the expected value.

1. *Statistical Literacy* What does the expected value of a binomial distribution with n trials tell you?

2. *Statistical Literacy* Consider two binomial distributions, with n trials each. The first distribution has a higher probability of success on each trial than the second. How does the expected value of the first distribution compare to that of the second?

3. ***Critical Thinking*** Consider a binomial distribution of 200 trials with expected value 80 and standard deviation of about 6.9. Use the criterion that it is unusual to have data values more than 2.5 standard deviations above the mean or 2.5 standard deviations below the mean to answer the following questions.
   (a) Would it be unusual to have more than 120 successes out of 200 trials? Explain.
   (b) Would it be unusual to have fewer than 40 successes out of 200 trials? Explain.
   (c) Would it be unusual to have from 70 to 90 successes out of 200 trials? Explain.

4. (a) $p = 0.5$; $\mu = 5$; yes.
(b) Right.
(c) Left.

4. *Critical Thinking* Consider a binomial distribution with 10 trials. Look at Table 2 (Appendix) showing binomial probabilities for various values of p, the probability of success on a single trial.
(a) For what value of p is the distribution symmetric? What is the expected value of this distribution? Is the distribution centered over this value?
(b) For small values of p, is the distribution skewed right or left?
(c) For large values of p, is the distribution skewed right or left?

5. (a) Symmetrical.
(b) Skewed right.
(c) Skewed left.
(d) Mirror images.
(e) Skewed left.

5. *Binomial Distribution: Histograms* Consider a binomial distribution with $n = 5$ trials. Use the probabilities given in Table 2 of the Appendix to make histograms showing the probabilities of $r = 0, 1, 2, 3, 4,$ and 5 successes for each of the following. Comment on the skewness of each distribution.
(a) The probability of success is $p = 0.50$.
(b) The probability of success is $p = 0.25$.
(c) The probability of success is $p = 0.75$.
(d) What is the relationship between the distributions shown in parts (b) and (c)?
(e) If the probability of success is $p = 0.73$, do you expect the distribution to be skewed to the right or to the left? Why?

6. (b) $\mu = 0.08$.
(c) 0.998.
(d) $\sigma = 0.281$.

6. *Quality Control: Syringes* The quality-control inspector of a production plant will reject a batch of syringes if two or more defective syringes are found in a random sample of eight syringes taken from the batch. Suppose the batch contains 1% defective syringes.
(a) Make a histogram showing the probabilities of $r = 0, 1, 2, 3, 4, 5, 6, 7,$ and 8 defective syringes in a random sample of eight syringes.
(b) Find μ. What is the expected number of defective syringes the inspector will find?
(c) What is the probability that the batch will be accepted?
(d) Find σ.

7. (b) $\mu = 1.4$; $\sigma \approx 1.058$.

7. *Education: Illiteracy* *USA Today* reported that about 20% of all people in the United States are illiterate. Suppose you take seven people at random off a city street.
(a) Make a histogram showing the probability distribution of the number of illiterate people out of the seven people in the sample.
(b) Find the mean and standard deviation of this probability distribution. Find the expected number of people in this sample who are illiterate.

8. (b) $\mu = 4.25$; $\sigma \approx 0.798$; expected number is about 4.

8. *Insurance: Auto* The Mountain States Office of State Farm Insurance Company reports that approximately 85% of all automobile damage liability claims were made by people under 25 years of age. A random sample of five automobile insurance liability claims is under study.
(a) Make a histogram showing the probability that $r = 0$ to 5 claims are made by people under 25 years of age.
(b) Find the mean and standard deviation of this probability distribution. For samples of size 5, what is the expected number of claims made by people under 25 years of age?

9. (b) $\mu = 2$; $\sigma \approx 1.225$.

9. *Hype: Improved Products* *The Wall Street Journal* reported that approximately 25% of the people who are told a product is *improved* will believe that it is, in fact, improved. The remaining 75% believe that this is just hype (the same old thing with no real improvement). Suppose a marketing study consists of a random sample of eight people who are given a sales talk about a new, *improved* product.
(a) Make a histogram showing the probability that $r = 0$ to 8 people believe the product is, in fact, improved.
(b) Compute the mean and standard deviation of this probability distribution.

10. (a) $P(0) = 0.004$; $P(1) = 0.047$; $P(2) = 0.211$; $P(3) = 0.422$; $P(4) = 0.316$.
(c) $\mu = 3$; $\sigma \approx 0.866$.

10. *Criminal Justice: Parole* *USA Today* reports that about 25% of all prison parolees become repeat offenders. Alice is a social worker whose job is to counsel people on parole. Let us say success means a person does not become a repeat offender. Alice has been given a group of four parolees.

(a) Find the probability $P(r)$ of r successes ranging from 0 to 4.
(b) Make a histogram for the probability distribution of part (a).
(c) What is the expected number of parolees in Alice's group who will not be repeat offenders? What is the standard deviation?

11. (a) 0.032.
(b) 0.053.
(c) $\mu = 9$; $\sigma = 1.5$.

11. *Criminal Justice: Jury Duty* Have you ever tried to get out of jury duty? About 25% of those called will find an excuse (work, poor health, travel out of town, etc.) to avoid jury duty (Source: Bernice Kanner, *Are You Normal?*, St. Martin's Press, New York). If 12 people are called for jury duty,
(a) what is the probability that all 12 will be available to serve on the jury?
(b) what is the probability that 6 or more will *not* be available to serve on the jury?
(c) Find the expected number of those available to serve on the jury. What is the standard deviation?

12. (a) 0.262.
(b) 0.738.
(c) $\mu = 1.2$; $\sigma \approx 0.98$.

12. *Law Enforcement: Property Crime* Does crime pay? The *FBI Standard Survey of Crimes* showed that for about 80% of all property crimes (burglary, larceny, car theft, etc.), the criminals are never found and the case is never solved (Source: *True Odds*, by James Walsh, Merrit Publishing). Suppose a neighborhood district in a large city suffers repeated property crimes, not always perpetuated by the same criminals. The police are investigating six property crime cases in this district.
(a) What is the probability that none of the crimes will ever be solved?
(b) What is the probability that at least one crime will be solved?
(c) What is the expected number of crimes that will be solved? What is the standard deviation?

13. (a) 0.698; 0.028.
(b) Japan, $\mu = 6.65$, $\sigma \approx 0.58$; U.S., $\mu = 4.2$, $\sigma \approx 1.30$.

13. *Criminal Justice: Convictions* Innocent until proven guilty? In Japanese criminal trials, about 95% of the defendants are found guilty. In the United States, about 60% of the defendants are found guilty in criminal trials (Source: *The Book of Risks*, by Larry Laudan, John Wiley and Sons). Suppose you are a news reporter following seven criminal trials.
(a) If the trials were in Japan, what is the probability that all the defendants would be found guilty? What is this probability if the trials were in the United States?
(b) Of the seven trials, what is the expected number of guilty verdicts in Japan? What is the expected number in the United States? What is the standard deviation in each case?

14. (a) 0.008.
(b) 0.028.
(c) 0.836.
(d) $\mu = 2.7$; $\sigma = 1.219$.

14. *Focus Problem: Personality Types* We now have the tools to solve the Chapter Focus Problem. In the book *A Guide to the Development and Use of the Myers-Briggs Type Indicators* by Myers and McCaully, it was reported that approximately 45% of all university professors are extroverted. Suppose you have classes with six different professors.
(a) What is the probability that all six are extroverts?
(b) What is the probability that none of your professors is an extrovert?
(c) What is the probability that at least two of your professors are extroverts?
(d) In a group of six professors selected at random, what is the *expected number* of extroverts? What is the *standard deviation* of the distribution?

15. (a) Out of n trials, there can be 0 through n successes. The sum of the probabilities for all members of the sample space must be 1.
(b) $r \geq 1$ consists of all members of the sample space except $r = 0$.
(c) $r \geq 2$ consists of all members of the sample space except $r = 0$ and $r = 1$.
(d) $r \geq m$ consists of all members of the sample space except for r values between 0 and $m - 1$.

15. ***Critical Thinking*** Let r be a binomial random variable representing the number of successes out of n trials.
(a) Explain why the sample space for r consists of the set $\{0, 1, 2, \ldots, n\}$ and why the sum of the probabilities of all the entries in the entire sample space must be 1.
(b) Explain why $P(r \geq 1) = 1 - P(0)$.
(c) Explain why $P(r \geq 2) = 1 - P(0) - P(1)$.
(d) Explain why $P(r \geq m) = 1 - P(0) - P(1) - \cdots - P(m - 1)$ for $1 \leq m \leq n$.

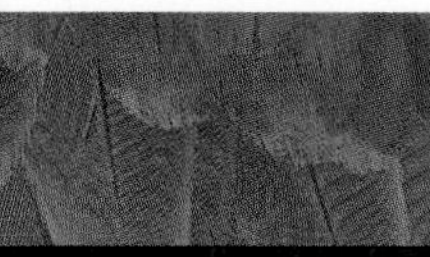

Chapter Review

SUMMARY

This chapter discusses random variables and important probability distributions associated with discrete random variables.

- The value of a *random variable* is determined by chance.
- Random variables are either *discrete* or *continuous*.
- A probability distribution of a discrete random variable x consists of all distinct values of x and the corresponding probabilities $P(x)$. For each x, $0 \le P(x) \le 1$ and $\Sigma P(x) = 1$.
- A discrete probability distribution can be displayed visually by a *probability histogram* in which the values of the random variable x are displayed on the horizontal axis, the height of each bar is $P(x)$, and each bar is 1 unit wide.
- For discrete probability distributions,

  $$\mu = \Sigma xP(x) \quad \text{and} \quad \sigma = \sqrt{\Sigma(x - \mu)^2 P(x)}$$

- The mean μ is called the *expected value* of the probability distribution.
- A *binomial experiment* consists of a fixed number n of independent trials repeated under identical conditions. There are two outcomes for each trial, called *success* and *failure*. The probability p of success on each trial is the same.
- The number of successes r in a binomial experiment is the random variable for the binomial probability distribution. Probabilities can be computed using a formula or using probability distribution outputs from a computer or calculator. Some probabilities can be found in Table 2 of the Appendix.
- For a binomial distribution,

  $$\mu = np \quad \text{and} \quad \sigma = \sqrt{npq}$$

  where $q = 1 - p$.
- For a binomial experiment, the number of successes is usually within the interval from $\mu - 2.5\sigma$ to $\mu + 2.5\sigma$. A number of successes outside this range of values is unusual but can occur.

IMPORTANT WORDS & SYMBOLS

Section 6.1

Random variable
  Discrete
  Continuous
Population parameters
Mean μ of a probability distribution
Standard deviation σ of a probability distribution
Expected value μ

Section 6.2

Binomial experiment
Independent trials
Successes and failures in a binomial experiment
Probability of success $P(S) = p$
Probability of failure $P(F) = q = 1 - p$
Binomial coefficient $C_{n,r}$
Binomial probability distribution
  $P(r) = C_{n,r}p^r q^{n-r}$

Section 6.3

Mean for the binomial distribution $\mu = np$
Standard deviation for the binomial distribution $\sigma = \sqrt{npq}$

VIEWPOINT What's Your Type?

Are students and professors really *compatible? One way of answering this question is to look at Myers-Briggs Type Indicators for personality preferences. What is the probability that your professor is introverted and judgmental? What is the probability that you are extroverted and perceptive? Are most of the leaders in student government extroverted and judgmental? Is it true that members of Phi Beta Kappa have personality types more like the professors'? We will consider questions such as these in more detail in Chapter 8 (estimation) and Chapter 9 (hypothesis testing), where we will continue our work with binomial probabilities. In the meantime, you can find many answers regarding careers, probability, and personality types in* Applications of the Myers-Briggs Type Indicator in Higher Education, *edited by J. Provost and S. Anchors.*

CHAPTER REVIEW PROBLEMS

Tables and art to accompany margin answers may be found in the back of the book.

1. A description of all distinct possible values of a random variable x, with a probability assignment $P(x)$ for each value or range of values. $0 \le P(x) \le 1$ and $\Sigma P(x) = 1$.
2. A fixed number of trials n that are repeated under identical conditions. The trials are independent and have only two outcomes, called success or failure. The probability of success on each trial is the same. The random variable is the number of successes r out of n trials.
3. (a) Yes. $\mu = 2$ and $\sigma \approx 1.3$. Numbers of successes above 5.25 are unusual.
   (b) No. It would be unusual to get more than five questions correct.
4. As the number of trials increases, both μ and σ increase.
5. (a) 38 months; 11.6.
6. (a) 0.378; 0.179; 0.247; 0.189; 0.007.
   (b) 5.28 yr; 4.88 yr.

1. *Statistical Literacy* What are the requirements for a probability distribution?

2. *Statistical Literacy* List the criteria for a binomial experiment. What does the random variable of a binomial experiment measure?

3. *Critical Thinking* For a binomial probability distribution, it is unusual for the number of successes to be less than $\mu - 2.5\sigma$ or greater than $\mu + 2.5\sigma$.
   (a) For a binomial experiment with 10 trials for which the probability of success on a single trial is 0.2, is it unusual to have more than five successes? Explain.
   (b) If you were simply guessing on a multiple-choice exam consisting of 10 questions with 5 possible responses for each question, would you be likely to get more than half of the questions correct? Explain.

4. *Critical Thinking* Consider a binomial experiment. If the number of trials is increased, what happens to the expected value? to the standard deviation? Explain.

5. *Probability Distribution: Auto Leases* Consumer Banker Association released a report showing the lengths of automobile leases for new automobiles. The results are as follows.

Lease Length in Months	Percent of Leases
13–24	12.7%
25–36	37.1%
37–48	28.5%
49–60	21.5%
More than 60	0.2%

   (a) Use the midpoint of each class, and call the midpoint of the last class 66.5 months, for purposes of computing the expected lease term. Also find the standard deviation of the distribution.
   (b) Sketch a graph of the probability distribution for the duration of new auto leases.

6. *Ecology: Predator and Prey* Isle Royale, an island in Lake Superior, has provided an important study site of wolves and their prey. In the National Park Service Scientific Monograph Series 11, *Wolf Ecology and Prey Relationships on Isle Royale,* Peterson gives the results of many wolf–moose studies. Of special interest is the study of the number of moose killed by wolves. In the period from 1958 to

1974, there were 296 moose deaths identified as wolf kills. The age distribution of the kills is as follows.

Age of Moose in Years	Number Killed by Wolves
Calf (0.5 yr)	112
1–5	53
6–10	73
11–15	56
16–20	2

(a) For each age group, compute the probability that a moose in that age group is killed by a wolf.
(b) Consider all ages in a class equal to the class midpoint. Find the expected age of a moose killed by a wolf and the standard deviation of the ages.

7. (b) 0.504.
(c) $\mu = 5.5$; $\sigma \approx 1.57$.

7. *Insurance: Auto* State Farm Insurance studies show that in Colorado, 55% of the auto insurance claims submitted for property damage were submitted by males under 25 years of age. Suppose 10 property damage claims involving automobiles are selected at random.
(a) Let r be the number of claims made by males under age 25. Make a histogram for the r-distribution probabilities.
(b) What is the probability that six or more claims are made by males under age 25?
(c) What is the expected number of claims made by males under age 25? What is the standard deviation of the r probability distribution?

8. (a) 0.924.
(b) 0.595.

8. *Quality Control: Pens* A stationery store has decided to accept a large shipment of ball-point pens if an inspection of 20 randomly selected pens yields no more than two defective pens.
(a) Find the probability that this shipment is accepted if 5% of the total shipment is defective.
(b) Find the probability that this shipment is not accepted if 15% of the total shipment is defective.

9. (a) 0.039.
(b) 0.403.
(c) 8.

9. *Criminal Justice: Inmates* According to *Harper's Index*, 50% of all federal inmates are serving time for drug dealing. A random sample of 16 federal inmates is selected.
(a) What is the probability that 12 or more are serving time for drug dealing?
(b) What is the probability that 7 or fewer are serving time for drug dealing?
(c) What is the expected number of inmates serving time for drug dealing?

10. 160 flights; 5.66 flights.

10. *Airlines: On-Time Arrivals* *Consumer Reports* rated airlines and found that 80% of the flights involved in the study arrived on time (that is, within 15 minutes of scheduled arrival time). Assuming that the on-time arrival rate is representative of the entire commercial airline industry, consider a random sample of 200 flights. What is the expected number that will arrive on time? What is the standard deviation of this distribution?

11. (b) 0.244; 0.999.
(c) 7.5.
(d) 1.37.

11. *Agriculture: Grapefruit* It is estimated that 75% of a grapefruit crop is good; the other 25% have rotten centers that cannot be detected unless the grapefruit are cut open. The grapefruit are sold in sacks of 10. Let r be the number of good grapefruit in a sack.
(a) Make a histogram of the probability distribution of r.
(b) What is the probability of getting no more than one bad grapefruit in a sack? What is the probability of getting at least one good grapefruit in a sack?
(c) What is the expected number of good grapefruit in a sack?
(d) What is the standard deviation of the r probability distribution?

12. 77.9; 1.97.

12. *Restaurants: Reservations* The Orchard Café has found that about 5% of the diners who make reservations don't show up. If 82 reservations have been

made, how many diners can be expected to show up? Find the standard deviation of this distribution.

13. 0.000 (to three digits).

13. *College Life: Student Government* The student government claims that 85% of all students favor an increase in student fees to buy indoor potted plants for the classrooms. A random sample of 12 students produced 2 in favor of the project. What is the probability that 2 or fewer in the sample will favor the project, assuming the student government's claim is correct? *Interpretation:* Do the data support the student government's claim, or does it seem that the percentage favoring the increase in fees is less than 85%?

DATA HIGHLIGHTS: GROUP PROJECTS

Break into small groups and discuss the following topics. Organize a brief outline in which you summarize the main points of your group discussion.

1. Powerball! Imagine, you could win a jackpot worth at least $10 million. Some jackpots have been worth more than $250 million! Powerball is a multistate lottery. To play Powerball, you purchase a $1 ticket. On the ticket you select five distinct white balls (numbered 1 through 55) and then one red Powerball (numbered 1 through 42). The red Powerball number may be any of the numbers 1 through 42, including any of the numbers you selected for the white balls. Every Wednesday and Saturday there is a drawing. If your chosen numbers match those drawn, you win! Figure 6-6 shows all the prizes and the probability of winning each prize, and specifies how many numbers on your ticket must match those drawn to win the prize. The Multi-State Lottery Association maintains a web site that displays the results of each drawing, as well as a history of the results of previous

FIGURE 6-6

Match	Approximate Probability	Prize
5 white balls + Powerball	0.0000000068	Jackpot*
5 white balls	0.000000281	$200,000
4 white balls + Powerball	0.00000171	$10,000
4 white balls	0.0000701	$100
3 white balls + Powerball	0.0000838	$100
3 white balls	0.0034	$7
2 white balls + Powerball	0.0013	$7
1 white ball + Powerball	0.0079	$4
0 white balls + Powerball	0.0145	$3
Overall chance of winning	0.0273 (one play)	

*The Jackpot will be divided equally (if necessary) among multiple winners and is paid in 30 annual installments or in a reduced lump sum.

drawings. To update Powerball data, visit the Online Study Center at **www.cengage.com/statistics/BraseUBS5e** and find the link to the Multi-State Lottery Association.

(a) Assume the jackpot is \$10 million and there will be only one jackpot winner. Figure 6-6 lists the prizes and the probability of winning each prize. What is the probability of *not winning* any prize? Consider all the prizes and their respective probabilities, and the prize of \$0 (no win) and its probability. Use all these values to estimate your expected winnings μ if you play one ticket. How much do you effectively contribute to the state in which you purchased the ticket (ignoring the overhead cost of operating Powerball)?

(b) Suppose the jackpot increased to \$25 million (and there was to be only one winner). Compute your expected winnings if you buy one ticket. Does the probability of winning the jackpot change because the jackpot is higher?

(c) Pretend that you are going to buy 10 Powerball tickets when the jackpot is \$10 million. Use the random-number table to select your numbers. Check the Multi-State Lottery Association web site (or any other Powerball site) for the most recent drawing results to see if you would have won a prize.

(d) The probability of winning *any* prize is about 0.0273. Suppose you decide to buy five tickets. Use the binomial distribution to compute the probability of winning (any prize) at least once. *Note:* You will need to use the binomial formula. Carry at least three digits after the decimal.

2. Would you like to travel in space, if given a chance? According to Opinion Research for Space Day Partners, if your answer is yes, you are not alone. Forty-four percent of adults surveyed agreed that they would travel in space if given a chance. Look at Figure 6-7, and use the information presented to answer the following questions.

(a) According to Figure 6-7, the probability that an adult selected at random agrees with the statement that humanity should explore planets is 64%. Round this probability to 65%, and use this estimate with the binomial distribution table to determine the probability that of 10 adults selected at random, at least half agree that humanity should explore planets.

(b) Does space exploration have an impact on daily life? Find the probability that of 10 adults selected at random, at least 9 agree that space exploration does have an impact on daily life. *Hint:* Use the formula for the binomial distribution.

(c) In a room of 35 adults, what is the expected number who would travel in space, given a chance? What is the standard deviation?

FIGURE 6-7

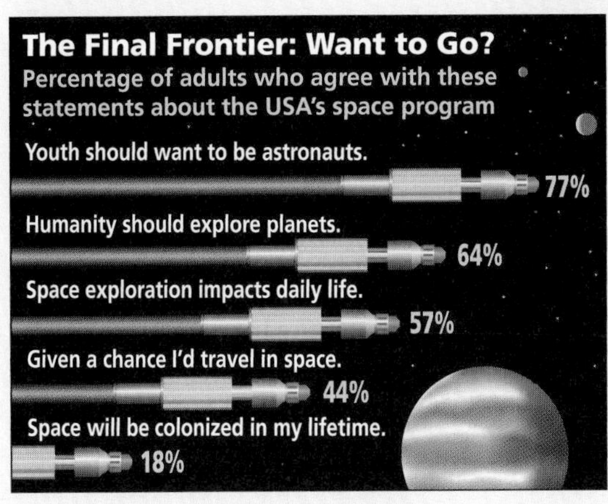
The Final Frontier: Want to Go?
Percentage of adults who agree with these statements about the USA's space program
Youth should want to be astronauts.
77%
Humanity should explore planets.
64%
Space exploration impacts daily life.
57%
Given a chance I'd travel in space.
44%
Space will be colonized in my lifetime.
18%

Source: Opinion Research for Space Day Partners

LINKING CONCEPTS: WRITING PROJECTS

Discuss each of the following topics in class or review the topics on your own. Then write a brief but complete essay in which you summarize the main points. Please include formulas and graphs as appropriate.

1. Discuss what we mean by a binomial experiment. As you can see, a binomial process or binomial experiment involves a lot of assumptions! For example, all the trials are supposed to be independent and repeated under identical conditions. Is this always true? Can we always be completely certain that the probability of success does not change from one trial to the next? In the real world, there is almost nothing we can be absolutely sure about, so the *theoretical* assumptions of the binomial probability distribution often will not be completely satisfied. Does that mean we cannot use the binomial distribution to solve practical problems? Looking at this chapter, the answer seems to be that we can indeed use the binomial distribution even if not all the assumptions are *exactly* met. We find in practice that the conclusions are sufficiently accurate for our intended application. List three applications of the binomial distribution for which you think,

although some of the assumptions are not exactly met, there is adequate reason to apply the binomial distribution anyhow.

2. Why do we need to learn the formula for the binomial probability distribution? Using the formula repeatedly can be very tedious. To cut down on tedious calculations, most people will use a binomial table such as the one found in the Appendix of this book.
   (a) However, there are many applications for which a table in the back of *any* book is not adequate. For instance, compute

   $$P(r = 3) \quad \text{where } n = 5 \text{ and } p = 0.735$$

   Can you find the result in the table? Do the calculation by using the formula. List some other situations in which a table might not be adequate to solve a particular binomial distribution problem.
   (b) The formula itself also has limitations. For instance, consider the difficulty of computing

   $$P(r \geq 285) \quad \text{where } n = 500 \text{ and } p = 0.6$$

   What are some of the difficulties you run into? Consider the calculation of $P(r = 285)$. You will be raising 0.6 and 0.4 to very high powers; this will give you very, very small numbers. Then you need to compute $C_{500,285}$, which is a very, very large number. When combining extremely large and extremely small numbers in the same calculation, most accuracy is lost unless you carry a huge number of significant digits. If this isn't tedious enough, consider the steps you need to compute

   $$P(r \geq 285) = P(r = 285) + P(r = 286) + \cdots + P(r = 500)$$

   Does it seem clear that we need a better way to estimate $P(r \geq 285)$? In Chapter 7, you will learn a much better way to estimate binomial probabilities when the number of trials is large.

3. In Chapter 3, we learned about means and standard deviations. In Section 6.1, we learned that probability distributions also can have a mean and standard deviation. Discuss what is meant by the expected value and standard deviation of a binomial distribution. How does this relate back to the material we learned in Chapter 3 and Section 6.1?

4. In Chapter 2, we looked at the shapes of distributions. Review the concepts of skewness and symmetry; then categorize the following distributions as to skewness or symmetry:
   (a) A binomial distribution with $n = 11$ trials and $p = 0.50$
   (b) A binomial distribution with $n = 11$ trials and $p = 0.10$
   (c) A binomial distribution with $n = 11$ trials and $p = 0.90$

   In general, does it seem true that binomial probability distributions in which the probability of success is close to 0 are skewed right, whereas those with probability of success close to 1 are skewed left?

USING TECHNOLOGY

Binomial Distributions

Although tables of binomial probabilities can be found in most libraries, such tables are often inadequate. Either the value of p (the probability of success on a trial) you are looking for is not in the table, or the value of n (the number of trials) you are looking for is too large for the table. In Chapter 7, we will study the normal approximation to the binomial. This approximation is a great help in many practical applications. Even so, we sometimes use the formula for the binomial probability distribution on a computer or graphing calculator to compute the probability we want.

Applications

The following percentages were obtained over many years of observation by the U.S. Weather Bureau. All data listed are for the month of December.

Location	Long-Term Mean % of Clear Days in Dec.
Juneau, Alaska	18%
Seattle, Washington	24%
Hilo, Hawaii	36%
Honolulu, Hawaii	60%
Las Vegas, Nevada	75%
Phoenix, Arizona	77%

Adapted from *Local Climatological Data,* U.S. Weather Bureau publication, "Normals, Means, and Extremes" Table.

In the locations listed, the month of December is a relatively stable month with respect to weather. Since weather patterns from one day to the next are more or less the same, it is reasonable to use a binomial probability model.

1. Let r be the number of clear days in December. Since December has 31 days, $0 \le r \le 31$. Using appropriate computer software or calculators available to you, find the probability $P(r)$ for each of the listed locations when $r = 0, 1, 2, \ldots, 31$.
2. For each location, what is the expected value of the probability distribution? What is the standard deviation?

You may find that the use of cumulative probabilities and appropriate subtraction of probabilities, rather than adding probabilities, will make finding the solutions to Applications 3 to 7 easier.

3. Estimate the probability that Juneau will have at most 7 clear days in December.
4. Estimate the probability that Seattle will have from 5 to 10 (including 5 and 10) clear days in December.
5. Estimate the probability that Hilo will have at least 12 clear days in December.
6. Estimate the probability that Phoenix will have 20 or more clear days in December.
7. Estimate the probability that Las Vegas will have from 20 to 25 (including 20 and 25) clear days in December.

Technology Hints

TI-84Plus/TI-83Plus, Excel, Minitab

The Tech Notes in Section 6.2 give specific instructions for binomial distribution functions on the TI-84Plus and TI-83Plus calculators, Excel, and Minitab.

SPSS

In SPSS, the function **PDF.BINOM(q,n,p)** gives the probability of q successes out of n trials, where p is the probability of success on a single trial. In the data editor, name a variable r and enter values 0 through n. Name another variable Prob_r. Then use the menu choices **Transform ➤ Compute.** In the dialogue box, use Prob_r for the target variable. In the function box, select **PDF.BINOM(q,n,p).** Use the variable r for q and appropriate values for n and p. Note that the function **CDF.BINOM(q,n,p)** gives the cumulative probability of 0 through q successes.

Cumulative Review Problems

CHAPTERS 4–6

The Hill of Tara is located in south central Meath, not far from Dublin, Ireland. Tara is of great cultural and archaeological importance, since it is by legend the seat of the ancient high kings of Ireland. For more information, see *Tara: An Archaeological Survey*, by Conor Newman, Royal Irish Academy, Dublin.

Magnetic surveying is one technique used by archaeologists to determine anomalies arising from variations in magnetic susceptibility. Unusual changes in magnetic susceptibility might (or might not) indicate an important archaeological discovery. Let x be a random variable that represents a magnetic susceptibility (MS) reading for a randomly chosen site on the Hill of Tara. A random sample of 120 sites gave the readings shown in Table A below.

TABLE A Magnetic Susceptibility Readings, centimeter-gram-second $\times 10^{-6}$ (cmg $\times 10^{-6}$)

Comment	Magnetic Susceptibility	Number of Readings	Estimated Probability
"cool"	$0 \le x < 10$	30	$30/120 = 0.25$
"neutral"	$10 \le x < 20$	54	$54/120 = 0.45$
"warm"	$20 \le x < 30$	18	$18/120 = 0.15$
"very interesting"	$30 \le x < 40$	12	$12/120 = 0.10$
"hot spot"	$40 \le x$	6	$6/120 = 0.05$

1. *Statistical Literacy: Sample Space* What is a statistical experiment? How could the magnetic susceptibility intervals $0 \le x < 10$, $10 \le x < 20$, and so on be considered events in the sample space of all possible readings?

2. *Statistical Literacy: Probability* What is probability? What do we mean by relative frequency as a probability estimate for events? What is the law of large numbers? How would the law of large numbers apply in this context?

3. *Statistical Literacy: Probability Distribution* Do the probabilities shown in Table A add up to 1? Why should they total to 1?

4. *Probability Rules* For a site chosen at random, estimate the following probabilities.
   (a) $P(0 \le x < 30)$ (b) $P(10 \le x < 40)$
   (c) $P(x < 20)$ (d) $P(x \ge 20)$
   (e) $P(30 \le x)$ (f) $P(x$ *not* less than $10)$
   (g) $P(0 \le x < 10$ *or* $40 \le x)$
   (h) $P(40 \le x$ *and* $20 \le x)$

5. *Discrete Probability Distribution* Consider the midpoint of each interval. Assign the value 45 as the midpoint for the interval $40 \le x$. The midpoints constitute the sample space for a discrete random variable. Using Table A, compute the expected value μ and the standard deviation σ.

Midpoint x	5	15	25	35	45
$P(x)$					

6. *Binomial Distribution* Suppose a reading between 30 and 40 is called "very interesting" from an archaeological point of view. Let us say you take readings at $n = 12$ sites chosen at random. Let r be a binomial random variable that represents the number of "very interesting" readings from these 12 sites.
   (a) Let us call "very interesting" a binomial success. Use Table A to find p, the probability of success on a single trial, where $p = P(\text{success}) = P(30 \le x < 40)$.

Tables and art to accompany margin answers may be found in the back of the book.

1. The specified ranges of readings are disjoint and cover all possible readings.
2. Essay.
3. Yes; the events constitute the entire sample space.
4. (a) 0.85. (b) 0.70. (c) 0.70. (d) 0.30. (e) 0.15. (f) 0.75. (g) 0.30. (h) 0.05.
5.

x	5	15	25	35	45
$P(x)$	0.25	0.45	0.15	0.10	0.05

$\mu \approx 17.5$; $\sigma \approx 10.9$.

6. (a) $p = 0.10$. (b) $\mu = 1.2$; $\sigma \approx 1.04$. (c) 0.718. (d) 0.889.

(b) What is the expected value μ and standard deviation σ for the random variable r?
(c) What is the probability that you will find *at least* one "very interesting" reading in the 12 sites?
(d) What is the probability that you will find *fewer than* three "very interesting" readings in the 12 sites?

7. *Linear Regression: Blood Glucose* Let x be a random variable that represents blood glucose level after a 12-hour fast. Let y be a random variable representing blood glucose level 1 hour after drinking sugar water (after the 12-hour fast). Units are in mg/10 ml. A random sample of eight adults gave the following information. (Reference: *American Journal of Clinical Nutrition*, Vol. 19, pp. 345–351.)

$$\Sigma x = 63.8; \Sigma x^2 = 521.56; \Sigma y = 90.7;$$
$$\Sigma y^2 = 1070.87; \Sigma xy = 739.65$$

x	6.2	8.4	7.0	7.5	8.1	6.9	10.0	9.7
y	9.8	10.7	10.3	11.9	14.2	7.0	14.6	12.2

(a) Draw a scatter diagram for the data.
(b) Find the equation of the least-squares line and graph it on the scatter diagram.
(c) Find the sample correlation coefficient r and the sample coefficient of determination r^2. Explain the meaning of r^2 in the context of the application.
(d) If $x = 9.0$, use the least-squares line to predict y.

7. (a) Scatter diagram.
(b) $\hat{y} \approx 1.135 + 1.279x$.
(c) $r \approx 0.700$; $r^2 \approx 0.490$; 49% of the variance in y is explained by the model and the variance in x.
(d) 12.65.

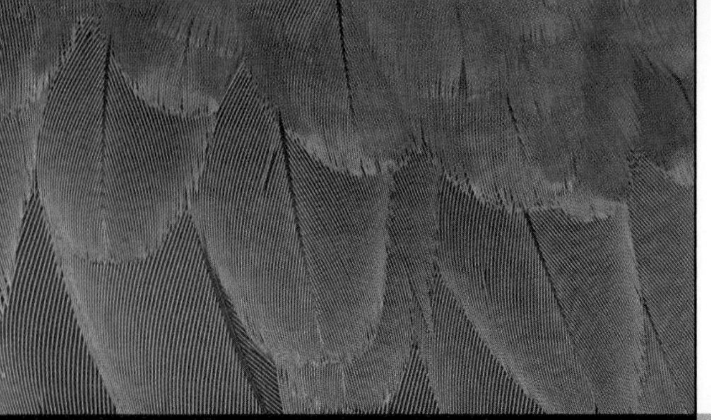

7

One cannot escape the feeling that these mathematical formulas have an independent existence and an intelligence of their own, that they are wiser than we are, wiser even than their discoverers, that we get more out of them than was originally put into them.

—Heinrich Hertz

How can it be that mathematics, a product of human thought independent of experience, is so admirably adapted to the objects of reality?

—Albert Einstein

Heinrich Hertz (1857–1894) was a pioneer in the study of radio waves. His work and the later work of Maxwell and Marconi led the way to modern radio, television, and radar. Albert Einstein is world renowned for his great discoveries in relativity and nuclear physics. Everyone who has worked in both mathematics and real-world applications cannot help but marvel at how the "pure thought" of the mathematical sciences can predict and explain events in other realms. In this chapter, we will study the most important type of probability distribution in all of mathematical statistics: the normal distribution. Why is the normal distribution so important? Two of the reasons are that it applies to a wide variety of situations and that other distributions tend to become normal under certain conditions.

For on-line student resources, visit the Brase/Brase, *Understanding Basic Statistics,* 5th edition web site at **www.cengage.com/statistics/Brase/UBS5e.**

Normal Curves and Sampling Distributions

PREVIEW QUESTIONS

What are some characteristics of a normal distribution? What does the empirical rule tell you about data spread about the mean? (SECTION 7.1)

Can you compare apples and oranges, or maybe elephants and butterflies? In most cases, the answer is no—unless you first standardize *your measurements. What are a* standard normal distribution *and a* standard z score*?* (SECTION 7.2)

How do you convert any normal distribution to a standard normal distribution? How do you find probabilities of "standardized events"? (SECTION 7.3)

As humans, our experiences are finite and limited. Consequently, most of the important decisions in our lives are based on sample (incomplete) information. What is a probability sampling distribution? How do sampling distributions help us make good decisions based on incomplete information? (SECTION 7.4)

There is an old saying: All roads lead to Rome. In statistics, we could recast this saying: All probability distributions average out to be normal distributions (as the sample size increases). How can we take advantage of this in our study of sampling distributions? (SECTION 7.5)

The binomial and normal distributions are two of the most important probability distributions in statistics. Under certain limiting conditions, the binomial can be thought to evolve (or envelope) into the normal distribution. How can you apply this concept in the real world? (SECTION 7.6)

FOCUS PROBLEM

Impulse Buying

The Food Marketing Institute, Progressive Grocer, New Products News, and Point of Purchaser Advertising Institute are organizations that analyze supermarket sales. One of the interesting discoveries was that the average amount of impulse buying in a grocery store was very time-dependent. As reported in the *Denver Post,* "when you dilly dally in a store for 10 unplanned minutes, you can kiss nearly $20 goodbye." For this reason, it is in the best interest of the supermarket to keep you in the store longer. In the *Post* article, it was pointed out that long checkout lines (near end-aisle displays), "samplefest" events of tasting free samples, video kiosks, magazine and book sections, and so on help keep customers in the store longer. On average, a single customer who strays from his or her grocery list can plan on impulse spending of \$20 for every 10 minutes spent wandering about in the supermarket.

Let x represent the dollar amount spent on supermarket impulse buying in a 10-minute (unplanned) shopping interval. Based on the *Post* article, the mean of the x distribution is about \$20 and the (estimated) standard deviation is about \$7.

(a) Consider a random sample of $n = 100$ customers, each of whom has 10 minutes of unplanned shopping time in a supermarket. From the central limit theorem, what can you say about the probability distribution of $\bar{x}$, the *average* amount spent by these customers due to impulse buying? Is the $\bar{x}$ distribution approximately normal? What are the mean and standard deviation of the $\bar{x}$ distribution? Is it necessary to make any assumption about the x distribution? Explain.

(b) What is the probability that $\bar{x}$ is between \$18 and \$22?

(c) Let us assume that x has a distribution that is approximately normal. What is the probability that x is between \$18 and \$22?

(d) In part (b), we used $\bar{x}$, the *average* amount spent, computed for 100 customers. In part (c), we used x, the amount spent by only *one* individual customer. The answers to parts (b) and (c) are very different. Why would this happen? In this example, $\bar{x}$ is a much more predictable or reliable statistic than x. Consider that almost all marketing strategies and sales pitches are designed for the *average* customer and *not* the *individual* customer. How does the central limit theorem tell us that the average customer is much more predictable than the individual customer? (See Problem 16 of Section 7.5.)

SECTION 7.1 Graphs of Normal Probability Distributions

FOCUS POINTS

- Graph a normal curve and summarize its important properties.
- Apply the empirical rule to solve real-world problems.

One of the most important examples of a continuous probability distribution is the *normal distribution.* This distribution was studied by the French mathematician Abraham de Moivre (1667–1754) and later by the German mathematician Carl Friedrich Gauss (1777–1855), whose work is so important that the normal distribution is sometimes called *Gaussian.* The work of these mathematicians provided a foundation on which much of the theory of statistical inference is based.

Applications of a normal probability distribution are so numerous that some mathematicians refer to it as "a veritable Boy Scout knife of statistics." However, before we can apply it, we must examine some of the properties of a normal distribution.

A rather complicated formula, presented later in this section, defines a normal distribution in terms of μ and σ, the mean and standard deviation of the population distribution. It is only through this formula that we can verify if a distribution is normal. However, we can look at the graph of a normal distribution and get a good pictorial idea of some of the essential features of any normal distribution.

Normal curve

The graph of a normal distribution is called a *normal curve.* It possesses a shape very much like the cross section of a pile of dry sand. Because of its shape, blacksmiths would sometimes use a pile of dry sand in the construction of a mold for a bell. Thus the normal curve is also called a *bell-shaped curve* (see Figure 7-1).

We see that a general normal curve is smooth and symmetrical about the vertical line extending upward from the mean μ. Notice that the highest point of

FIGURE 7-1

A Normal Curve

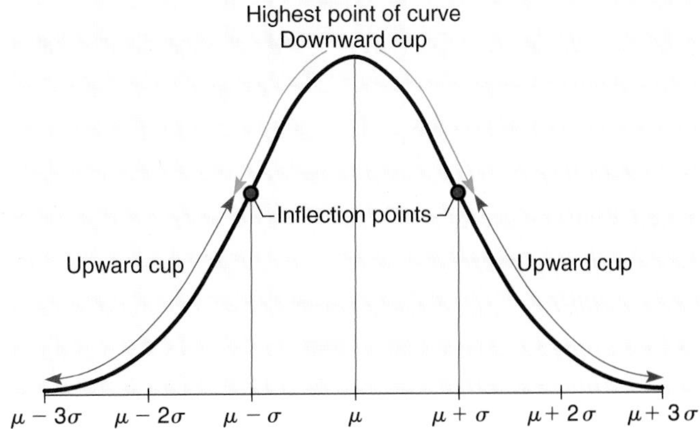

the curve occurs over μ. If the distribution were graphed on a piece of sheet metal, cut out, and placed on a knife edge, the balance point would be at μ. We also see that the curve tends to level out and approach the horizontal (x axis) like a glider making a landing. However, in mathematical theory, such a glider would never quite finish its landing because a normal curve never touches the horizontal axis.

The parameter σ controls the spread of the curve. The curve is quite close to the horizontal axis at $\mu + 3\sigma$ and $\mu - 3\sigma$. Thus, if the standard deviation σ is large, the curve will be more spread out; if it is small, the curve will be more peaked. Figure 7-1 shows the normal curve cupped downward for an interval on either side of the mean μ. Then it begins to cup upward as we go to the lower part of the bell. The exact places where the *transition* between the upward and downward cupping occurs are above the points $\mu + \sigma$ and $\mu - \sigma$. In the terminology of calculus, transition points such as these are called *inflection points*.

Important properties of a normal curve

1. The curve is bell-shaped, with the highest point over the mean μ.
2. The curve is symmetrical about a vertical line through μ.
3. The curve approaches the horizontal axis but never touches or crosses it.
4. The inflection (transition) points between cupping upward and downward occur above $\mu + \sigma$ and $\mu - \sigma$.

The parameters that control the shape of a normal curve are the mean μ and the standard deviation σ. When both μ and σ are specified, a specific normal curve is determined. In brief, μ locates the balance point and σ determines the extent of the spread.

GUIDED EXERCISE 1 Identify μ and σ on a normal curve

Look at the normal curves in Figure 7-2.

FIGURE 7-2

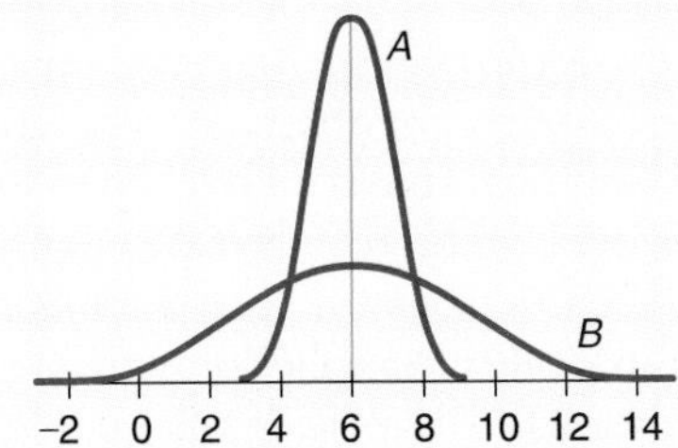

Continued

GUIDED EXERCISE 1 *continued*

(a) Do these distributions have the same mean? If so, what is it?

→ The means are the same, since both graphs have the high point over 6. $\mu = 6$.

(b) One of the curves corresponds to a normal distribution with $\sigma = 3$ and the other to one with $\sigma = 1$. Which curve has which σ?

→ Curve A has $\sigma = 1$ and curve B has $\sigma = 3$. (Since curve B is more spread out, it has the larger σ value.)

COMMENT The normal distribution curve is always above the horizontal axis. The area beneath the curve and above the axis is exactly 1. As such, the normal distribution curve is an example of a *density curve*. The formula used to generate the shape of the normal distribution curve is called the *normal density function*. If x is a normal random variable with mean μ and standard deviation σ, the formula for the normal density function is

If your students are intimidated by this formula, assure them that they will not need to use the formula directly. Instead, they will be using tables (that are based on the formula and additional mathematics). Graphing technology tools have built-in functions for graphing normal distributions.

$$f(x) = \frac{e^{(-1/2)((x-\mu)/\sigma)^2}}{\sigma\sqrt{2\pi}}$$

In this text, we will not use this formula explicitly. However, we will use tables of areas based on the normal density function.

The total area under any normal curve studied in this book will *always* be 1. The graph of the normal distribution is important because the portion of the *area* under the curve above a given interval represents the *probability* that a measurement will lie in that interval.

Empirical rule

In Section 3.2, we studied Chebyshev's theorem. This theorem gives us information about the *smallest* proportion of data that lies within 2, 3, or k standard deviations of the mean. This result applies to *any* distribution. However, for normal distributions, we can get a much more precise result, which is given by the *empirical rule*.

Problems 31 through 35 of Section 7.3 show how to use the empirical rule to estimate the standard deviation when we know the low and high values of sample data drawn from a distribution that is approximately normal.

Empirical rule

For a distribution that is symmetrical and bell-shaped (in particular, for a normal distribution):

Approximately 68% of the data values will lie within 1 standard deviation on each side of the mean.

Approximately 95% of the data values will lie within 2 standard deviations on each side of the mean.

Approximately 99.7% (or almost all) of the data values will lie within 3 standard deviations on each side of the mean.

Linking Concepts, Problem 1, provides a good topic for class discussion. This is a good place to link our study of Chebyshev's theorem, the empirical rule, and a (very brief) mention of Chapter 8 (theory of estimation).

The preceding statement is called the *empirical rule* because, for symmetrical, bell-shaped distributions, the given percentages are observed in practice. Furthermore, for the normal distribution, the empirical rule is a direct consequence of the very nature of the distribution (see Figure 7-3). Notice that the empirical rule is a stronger statement than Chebyshev's theorem in that it gives *definite percentages*, not just lower limits. Of course, the empirical rule applies only to normal or symmetrical, bell-shaped distributions, whereas Chebyshev's theorem applies to all distributions.

FIGURE 7-3

Area Under a Normal Curve

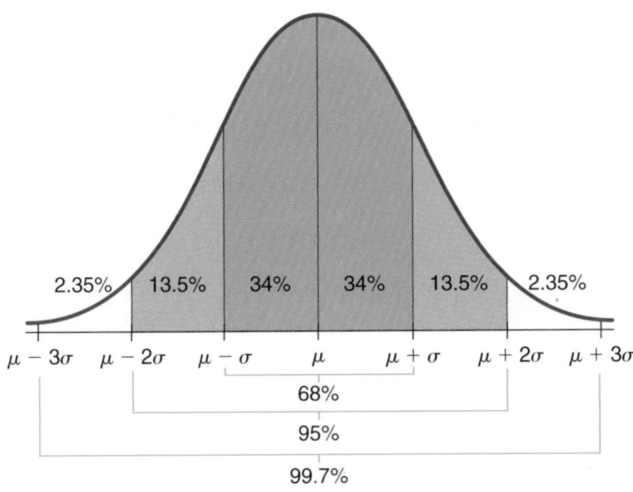

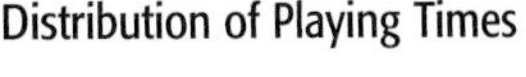

FIGURE 7-4

Distribution of Playing Times

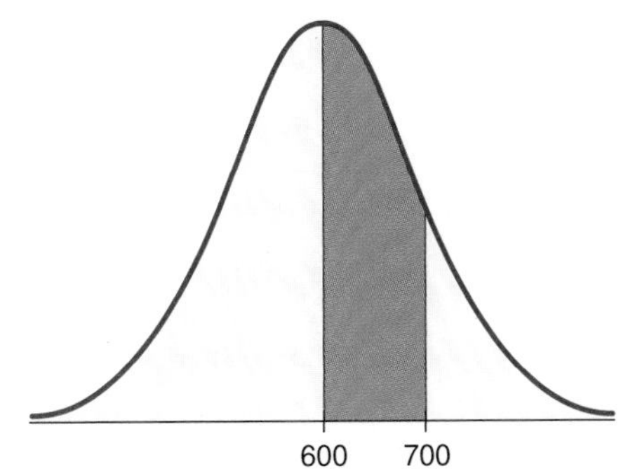

EXAMPLE 1 EMPIRICAL RULE

The playing life of a Sunshine radio is normally distributed with mean $\mu = 600$ hours and standard deviation $\sigma = 100$ hours. What is the probability that a radio selected at random will last from 600 to 700 hours?

SOLUTION: The probability that the playing life will be between 600 and 700 hours is equal to the percentage of the total area under the curve that is shaded in Figure 7-4. Since $\mu = 600$ and $\mu + \sigma = 600 + 100 = 700$, we see that the shaded area is simply the area between μ and $\mu + \sigma$. The area from μ to $\mu + \sigma$ is 34% of the total area. This tells us that the probability a Sunshine radio will last between 600 and 700 playing hours is about 0.34.

GUIDED EXERCISE 2 Empirical rule

The yearly wheat yield per acre on a particular farm is normally distributed with mean $\mu = 35$ bushels and standard deviation $\sigma = 8$ bushels.

(a) Shade the area under the curve in Figure 7-5 that represents the probability that an acre will yield between 19 and 35 bushels.

→ See Figure 7-6.

(b) Is the area the same as the area between $\mu - 2\sigma$ and μ?

→ Yes, since $\mu = 35$ and $\mu - 2\sigma = 35 - 2(8) = 19$.

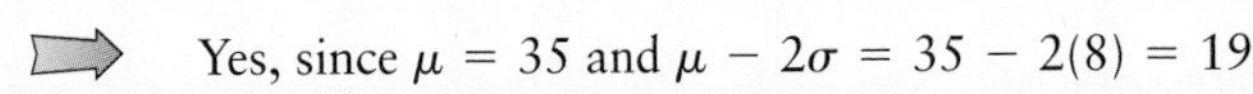

FIGURE 7-5

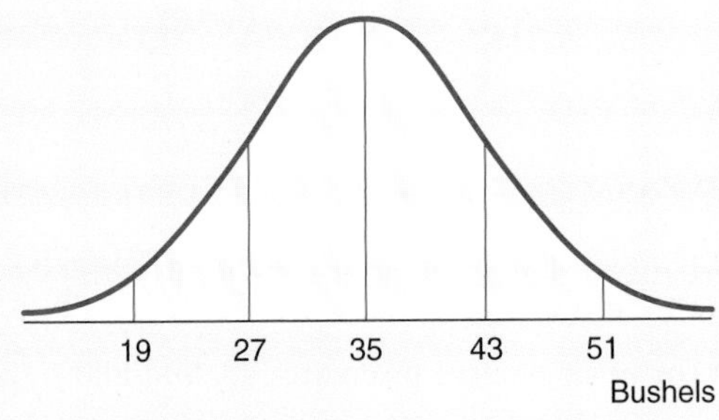

FIGURE 7-6 Completion of Figure 7-5

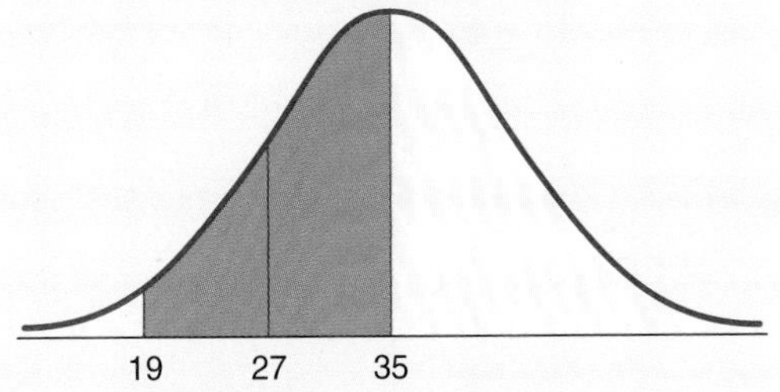

Continued

GUIDED EXERCISE 2 *continued*

(c) Use Figure 7-3 to find the percentage of area over the interval between 19 and 35.

→ The area between the values $\mu - 2\sigma$ and μ is 47.5% of the total area.

(d) *Interpretation:* What is the probability that the yield will be between 19 and 35 bushels per acre?

→ It is 47.5% of the total area, which is 1. Therefore, the probability is 0.475 that the yield will be between 19 and 35 bushels.

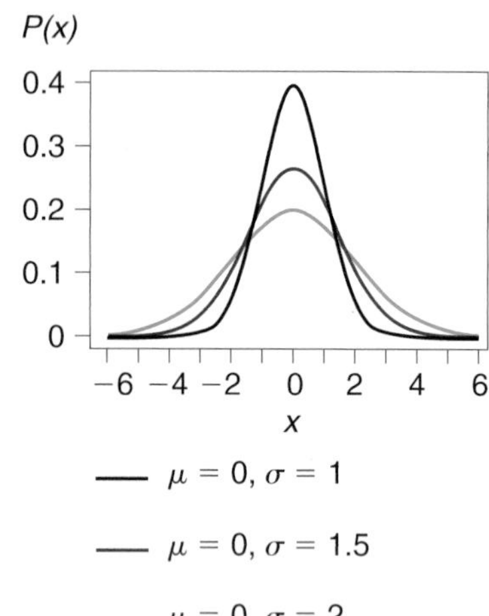

TECH NOTES We can graph normal distributions using the TI-84Plus and TI-83Plus calculators, Excel, and Minitab. In each technology, set the range of x values between -3.5σ and 3.5σ. Then use the built-in normal density functions to generate the corresponding y values.

TI-84Plus/TI-83Plus Press the Y= key. Then, under **DISTR**, select **1:normalpdf** (x,μ,σ) and fill in desired μ and σ values. Press the **WINDOW** key. Set **Xmin** to $\mu - 3\sigma$ and **Xmax** to $\mu + 3\sigma$. Finally, press the **ZOOM** key and select option **0:ZoomFit.**

Excel In one column, enter x values from -3.5σ to 3.5σ in increments of 0.2σ. In the next column, enter y values by using the menu choices **Paste function** (f_x) ➤ **Statistical** ➤ **NORMDIST**(x, μ, σ, false). Next, use the chart wizard, and select **XY(scatter)**. Choose the first picture with the dots connected and fill in the dialogue boxes.

Minitab In one column, enter x values from -3.5σ to 3.5σ in increments of 0.2σ. In the next column, enter y values by using the menu choices **Calc** ➤ **Probability Distribution** ➤ **Normal.** Fill in the dialogue box. Next, use menu choices **Graph** ➤ **Plot.** Fill in the dialogue box. Under Display, select connect.

VIEWPOINT In Control? Out of Control?

If you care about quality, you also must care about control! Dr. Walter Shewhart invented control charts when he was working for Bell Laboratories. A control chart plots data values around a central value, such as the mean. The great contribution of control charts is that they separate variation into two sources: (1) random or chance causes (in control) and (2) special or assignable causes (out of control). A process is said to be in statistical control *when it is no longer afflicted with special or assignable causes. The performance of a process that is in statistical control is predictable. Predictability and quality control tend to be closely associated.*

(Source: Adapted from the classic text *Statistical Methods from the Viewpoint of Quality Control,* by W. A. Shewhart, with foreword by W. E. Deming, Dover Publications.)

SECTION 7.1 PROBLEMS

1. *Statistical Literacy* Which, if any, of the curves in Figure 7-7 look(s) like a normal curve? If a curve is not a normal curve, tell why.

2. *Statistical Literacy* Look at the normal curve in Figure 7-8, and find μ, $\mu + \sigma$, and σ.

Tables and art to accompany margin answers may be found in the back of the book.

1. (a) No, it's skewed.
   (b) No, it crosses the horizontal axis.
   (c) No, it has three peaks.
   (d) No, the curve is not smooth.
2. $\mu = 16$; $\mu + \sigma = 18$; $\sigma = 2$.

FIGURE 7-7

FIGURE 7-8

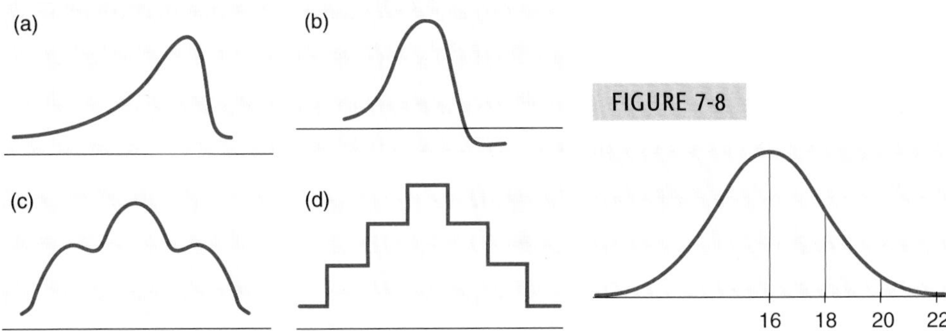

3. Figure 7-9 has larger standard deviation; 10; 4.

3. *Critical Thinking* Look at the two normal curves in Figures 7-9 and 7-10. Which has the larger standard deviation? What is the mean of the curve in Figure 7-9? What is the mean of the curve in Figure 7-10?

FIGURE 7-10

FIGURE 7-9

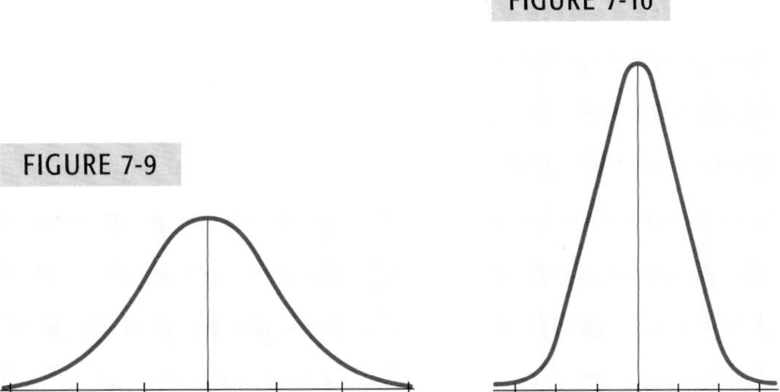

4. (e) No. The values of μ and σ are independent in this case.

4. *Critical Thinking* Sketch a normal curve
   (a) with mean 15 and standard deviation 2.
   (b) with mean 15 and standard deviation 3.
   (c) with mean 12 and standard deviation 2.
   (d) with mean 12 and standard deviation 3.
   (e) Consider two normal curves. If the first one has a larger mean than the second one, must it have a larger standard deviation as well? Explain your answer.

5. (a) 50%.
   (b) 68%.
   (c) 99.7%.

5. *Critical Thinking* What percentage of the area under the normal curve lies
   (a) to the left of μ?
   (b) between $\mu - \sigma$ and $\mu + \sigma$?
   (c) between $\mu - 3\sigma$ and $\mu + 3\sigma$?

6. (a) 50%.
   (b) 95%.
   (c) 0.15%.

6. *Critical Thinking* What percentage of the area under the normal curve lies
   (a) to the right of μ?
   (b) between $\mu - 2\sigma$ and $\mu + 2\sigma$?
   (c) to the right of $\mu + 3\sigma$?

7. (a) 50%.
   (b) 50%.
   (c) 68%.
   (d) 95%.

7. *Distribution: Heights of Coeds* Assuming that the heights of college women are normally distributed with mean 65 inches and standard deviation 2.5 inches (based on information from *Statistical Abstract of the United States,* 112th Edition), answer the following questions. (*Hint:* Use Problems 5 and 6 and Figure 7-3.)
   (a) What percentage of women are taller than 65 inches?
   (b) What percentage of women are shorter than 65 inches?
   (c) What percentage of women are between 62.5 inches and 67.5 inches?
   (d) What percentage of women are between 60 inches and 70 inches?

8. (a) 95% or 950 chicks.
(b) 68% or 680 chicks.
(c) 50% or 500 chicks.
(d) 99.7% or 997 chicks.

8. *Distribution: Rhode Island Red Chicks* The incubation time for Rhode Island Red chicks is normally distributed with a mean of 21 days and standard deviation of approximately 1 day (based on information from *World Book Encyclopedia*). Look at Figure 7-3 and answer the following questions. If 1000 eggs are being incubated, how many chicks do we expect will hatch
(a) in 19 to 23 days?
(b) in 20 to 22 days?
(c) in 21 days or fewer?
(d) in 18 to 24 days? (Assume all eggs eventually hatch.)
(*Note:* In this problem, let us agree to think of a single day or a succession of days as a continuous interval of time.)

9. (a) From 1207 to 1279.
(b) From 1171 to 1315.
(c) From 1135 to 1351.

9. *Archaeology: Tree Rings* At Burnt Mesa Pueblo, archaeological studies have used the method of tree-ring dating in an effort to determine when prehistoric people lived in the pueblo. Wood from several excavations gave a mean of (year) 1243 with a standard deviation of 36 years (*Bandelier Archaeological Excavation Project: Summer 1989 Excavations at Burnt Mesa Pueblo,* edited by Kohler, Washington State University Department of Anthropology). The distribution of dates was more or less mound-shaped and symmetrical about the mean. Use the empirical rule to
(a) estimate a range of years centered about the mean in which about 68% of the data (tree-ring dates) will be found.
(b) estimate a range of years centered about the mean in which about 95% of the data (tree-ring dates) will be found.
(c) estimate a range of years centered about the mean in which almost all the data (tree-ring dates) will be found.

10. (a) 0.16.
(b) 0.84.
(c) About 136 cups.

10. *Vending Machine: Soft Drinks* A vending machine automatically pours soft drinks into cups. The amount of soft drink dispensed into a cup is normally distributed with a mean of 7.6 ounces and standard deviation of 0.4 ounce. Examine Figure 7-3 and answer the following questions.
(a) Estimate the probability that the machine will overflow an 8-ounce cup.
(b) Estimate the probability that the machine will not overflow an 8-ounce cup.
(c) The machine has just been loaded with 850 cups. How many of these do you expect will overflow when served?

11. (a) From 1.70 mA to 4.60 mA.
(b) From 0.25 mA to 6.05 mA.

11. *Pain Management: Laser Therapy* "Effect of Helium-Neon Laser Auriculotherapy on Experimental Pain Threshold" is the title of an article in the journal *Physical Therapy* (Vol. 70, No. 1, pp. 24–30). In this article, laser therapy was discussed as a useful alternative to drugs in pain management of chronically ill patients. To measure pain threshold, a machine was used that delivered low-voltage direct current to different parts of the body (wrist, neck, and back). The machine measured current in milliamperes (mA). The pretreatment experimental group in the study had an average threshold of pain (pain was first detectable) at $\mu = 3.15$ mA with standard deviation $\sigma = 1.45$ mA. Assume that the distribution of threshold pain, measured in milliamperes, is symmetrical and more or less mound-shaped. Use the empirical rule to
(a) estimate a range of milliamperes centered about the mean in which about 68% of the experimental group will have a threshold of pain.
(b) estimate a range of milliamperes centered about the mean in which about 95% of the experimental group will have a threshold of pain.

SECTION 7.2

Standard Units and Areas Under the Standard Normal Distribution

FOCUS POINTS

- Given μ and σ, convert raw data to z scores.
- Given μ and σ, convert z scores to raw data.
- Graph the standard normal distribution, and find areas under the standard normal curve.

z Scores and Raw Scores

Normal distributions vary from one another in two ways: The mean μ may be located anywhere on the x axis, and the bell shape may be more or less spread according to the size of the standard deviation σ. The differences among the normal distributions cause difficulties when we try to compute the area under the curve in a specified interval of x values and, hence, the probability that a measurement will fall into that interval.

It would be a futile task to try to set up a table of areas under the normal curve for each different μ and σ combination. We need a way to standardize the distributions so that we can use *one* table of areas for *all* normal distributions. We achieve this standardization by considering how many standard deviations a measurement lies from the mean. In this way, we can compare a value in one normal distribution with a value in another, different normal distribution. The next situation shows how this is done.

Suppose Tina and Jack are in two different sections of the same course. Each section is quite large, and the scores on the midterm exams of each section follow a normal distribution. In Tina's section, the average (mean) was 64 and her score was 74. In Jack's section, the mean was 72 and his score was 82. Both Tina and Jack were pleased that their scores were each 10 points above the average of each respective section. However, the fact that each was 10 points above average does not really tell us how each did *with respect to the other students in the section.* In Figure 7-11, we see the normal distribution of grades for each section.

Tina's 74 was higher than most of the other scores in her section, while Jack's 82 is only an upper-middle score in his section. Tina's score is far better with respect to her class than Jack's score with respect to his class.

Standard score

The preceding situation demonstrates that it is not sufficient to know the difference between a measurement (x value) and the mean of a distribution. We need also to consider the spread of the curve, or the standard deviation. What we really want to know is the number of standard deviations between a measurement and the mean. This "distance" takes both μ and σ into account.

FIGURE 7-11

Distributions of Midterm Scores

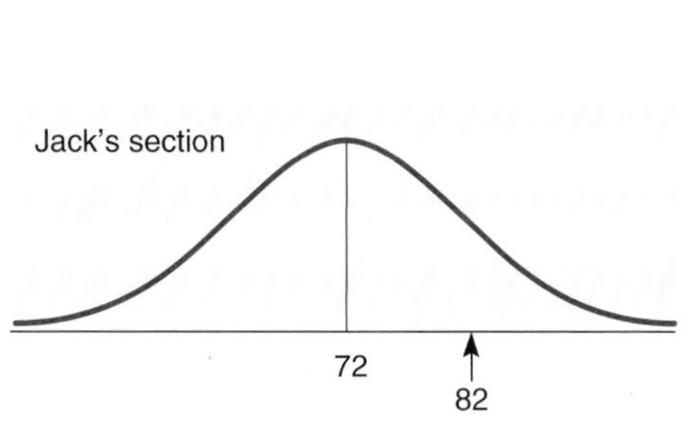

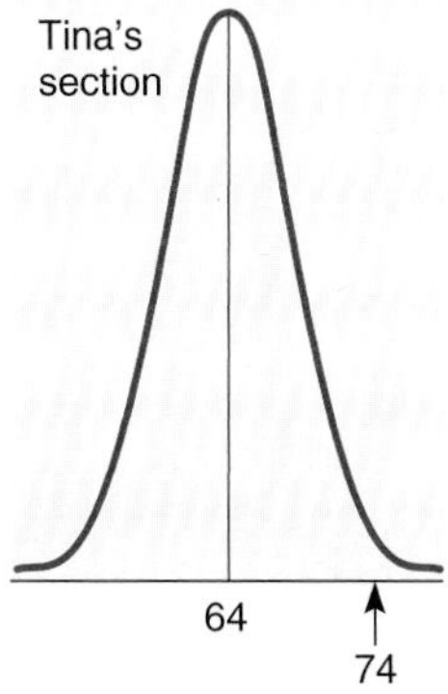

This is a good opportunity to use ordinary English to describe a formula. Emphasize that z is the number of "σ units" that the raw data value x differs (either way) from the mean μ. Positive z values are above the mean, and negative z values are below the mean. Linking Concepts, Problem 2 provides a good class discussion topic.

We can use a simple formula to compute the number z of standard deviations between a measurement x and the mean μ of a normal distribution with standard deviation σ:

$$\left(\begin{array}{c}\text{Number of standard deviations}\\ \text{between the measurement and}\\ \text{the mean}\end{array}\right) = \left(\frac{\text{Difference between the measurement and the mean}}{\text{Standard deviation}}\right)$$

z score

The z **value** or z **score** gives the number of standard deviations between the original measurement x and the mean μ of the x distribution.

$$z = \frac{x - \mu}{\sigma}$$

TABLE 7-1

***x* Values and Corresponding *z* Values**

x Value in Original Distribution	Corresponding z Value or Standard Unit
$x = \mu$	$z = 0$
$x > \mu$	$z > 0$
$x < \mu$	$z < 0$

The mean is a special value of a distribution. Let's see what happens when we convert $x = \mu$ to a z value:

$$z = \frac{x - \mu}{\sigma} = \frac{\mu - \mu}{\sigma} = 0$$

The mean of the original distribution is always zero, in standard units. This makes sense because the mean is zero standard variations from itself.

An x value in the original distribution that is *above* the mean μ has a corresponding z value that is *positive*. Again, this makes sense because a measurement above the mean would be a positive number of standard deviations from the mean. Likewise, an x value *below* the mean has a *negative* z value. (See Table 7-1.)

Although our applications using z scores will relate to normal distributions, z scores can be computed for raw scores from any distribution.

Note

Unless otherwise stated, in the remainder of the book we will take the word *average* to be either the sample arithmetic mean $\bar{x}$ or the population mean μ.

EXAMPLE 2 STANDARD SCORE

A pizza parlor franchise specifies that the average (mean) amount of cheese on a large pizza should be 8 ounces and the standard deviation only 0.5 ounce. An inspector picks out a large pizza at random in one of the pizza parlors and finds that it is made with 6.9 ounces of cheese. Assume that the amount of cheese on a pizza follows a normal distribution. If the amount of cheese is below the mean by more than *three* standard deviations, the parlor will be in danger of losing its franchise.

How many standard deviations from the mean is 6.9? Is the pizza parlor in danger of losing its franchise?

SOLUTION: Since we want to know the number of standard deviations from the mean, we want to convert 6.9 to standard z units.

$$z = \frac{x - \mu}{\sigma} = \frac{6.9 - 8}{0.5} = -2.20$$

Therefore, the amount of cheese on the selected pizza is only 2.20 standard deviations below the mean. The fact that z is negative indicates that the amount of cheese is 2.20 standard deviations *below* the mean. The parlor will not lose its franchise based on this sample.

Raw score

We have seen how to convert an original *raw score* x to a standard score z. If we know the standard score z, we can solve the z formula for the corresponding raw score x.

This is a good time to remind students that the formulas $z = (x - \mu)/\sigma$ and $x = z\sigma + \mu$ are logically (i.e., algebraically) equivalent. Both formulas are important and have many useful applications.

Given an x distribution with mean μ and standard deviation σ, the **raw score x** corresponding to a z score is

$$x = z\sigma + \mu$$

GUIDED EXERCISE 3 Standard score and raw score

Rod figures that it takes an average (mean) of 17 minutes with a standard deviation of 3 minutes to drive from home, park the car, and walk to an early-morning class.

(a) One day it took Rod 21 minutes to get to class. How many standard deviations from the average is that? Is the z value positive or negative? Explain why it should be either positive or negative.

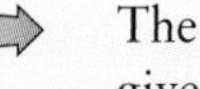

The number of standard deviations from the mean is given by the z value:

$$z = \frac{x - \mu}{\sigma} = \frac{21 - 17}{3} \approx 1.33$$

The z value is positive. We should expect a positive z value, since 21 minutes is *more* than the mean of 17.

(b) What commuting time corresponds to a standard score of $z = -2.5$? *Interpretation:* Could Rod count on making it to class in this amount of time or less?

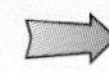

$x = z\sigma + \mu = (-2.5)(3) + 17 = 9.5$ minutes

No, commute times at or less than 2.5 standard deviations below the mean are rare.

Standard Normal Distribution

If the original distribution of x *values is normal,* then the corresponding z *values have a normal distribution as well.* The z distribution has a mean of 0 and a standard deviation of 1. The normal curve with these properties has a special name.

Standard normal distribution

The **standard normal distribution** is a normal distribution with mean $\mu = 0$ and standard deviation $\sigma = 1$ (Figure 7-12).

Any normal distribution of x values can be converted to the standard normal distribution by converting all x values to their corresponding z values. The resulting standard distribution will always have mean $\mu = 0$ and standard deviation $\sigma = 1$.

FIGURE 7-12

The Standard Normal Distribution ($\mu = 0, \sigma = 1$)

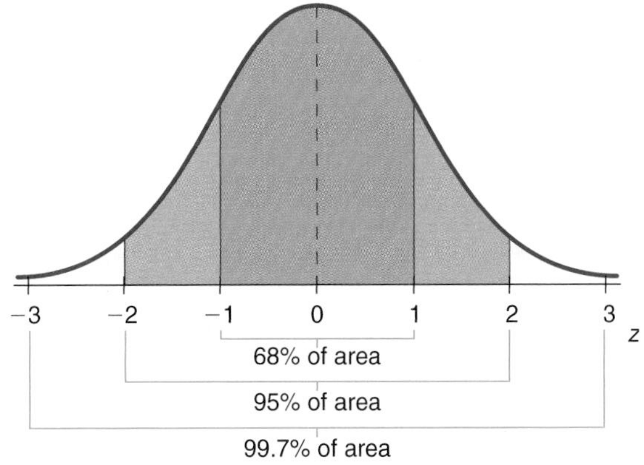

Areas Under the Standard Normal Curve

We have seen how to convert *any* normal distribution to the *standard* normal distribution. We can change any x value to a z value and back again. But what is the advantage of all this work? The advantage is that there are extensive tables that show the *area under the standard normal curve* for almost any interval along the z axis. The areas are important because each area is equal to the *probability* that the measurement of an item selected at random falls in this interval. Thus, the *standard* normal distribution can be a tremendously helpful tool.

Using a Standard Normal Distribution Table

Using a table to find areas and probabilities associated with the standard normal distribution is a fairly straightforward activity. However, it is important to first observe the range of z values for which areas are given. This range is usually depicted in a picture that accompanies the table.

Left-tail style table

In this text, *we will use the left-tail style table*. This style table gives cumulative areas to the left of a specified z. Determining other areas under the curve utilizes the fact that the area under the entire curve is 1. Taking advantage of the symmetry of the normal distribution is also useful. The procedures you learn for using the left-tail style normal distribution table apply directly to cumulative normal distribution areas found on calculators and in computer software packages such as Excel and Minitab.

EXAMPLE 3 STANDARD NORMAL DISTRIBUTION TABLE

Use Table 3 of the Appendix to find the described areas under the standard normal curve.

(a) Find the area under the standard normal curve to the left of $z = -1.00$.

SOLUTION: First, shade the area to be found on the standard normal distribution curve, as shown in Figure 7-13. Notice that the z value we are using is negative. This means that we will look at the portion of Table 3 of the Appendix for which the z values are negative. In the upper-left corner of the table, we see the letter z. The column under z gives us the units value and tenths value for z. The other column headings indicate the hundredths value of z. Table entries give areas under the standard normal curve to the left of the listed z values. To find the area to the left of $z = -1.00$, we use the row headed by -1.0 and then move to the column headed by the hundredths position .00. This entry is shaded in Table 7-2. We see that the area is 0.1587.

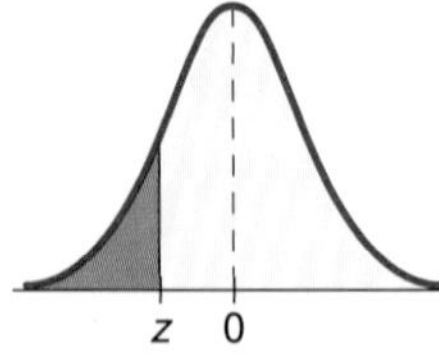

TABLE 7-2 **Excerpt from Table 3 of the Appendix Showing Negative z Values**

z	.00	.01	...	.07	.08	.09
−3.4	.0003	.0003	...	.0003	.0003	.0002
⋮						
−1.1	.1357	.1335	...	.1210	.1190	.1170
−1.0	.1587	.1562	...	.1423	.1401	.1379
−0.9	.1841	.1814	...	.1660	.1635	.1611
⋮						
−0.0	.5000	.4960	...	.4721	.4681	.4641

(b) Find the area to the left of $z = 1.18$, as illustrated in Figure 7-14.

FIGURE 7-13

Area to the Left of $z = -1.00$

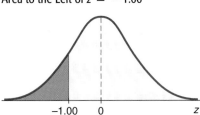

FIGURE 7-14

Area to the Left of $z = 1.18$

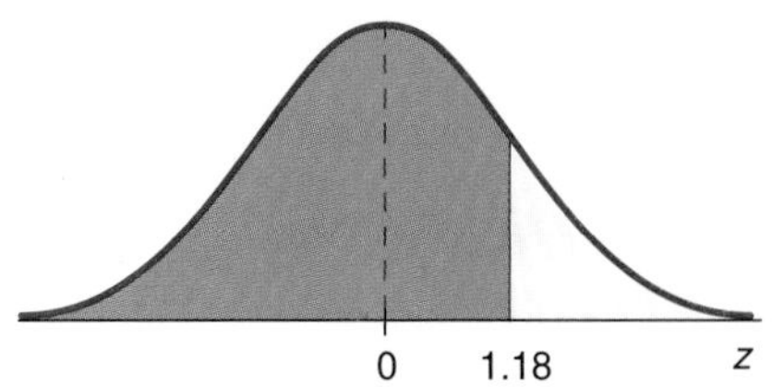

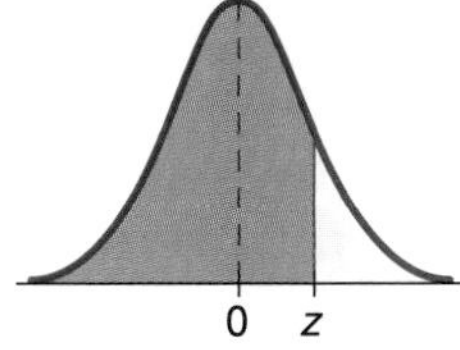

TABLE 7-3 Excerpt from Table 3 of the Appendix Showing Positive *z* Values

z	.00	.01	.02	...	.08	.09
0.0	.5000	.5040	.5080	...	.5319	.5359
:						
0.9	.8159	.8186	.8212	...	.8365	.8359
1.0	.8413	.8438	.8461	...	.8599	.8621
1.1	.8643	.8665	.8686	...	.8810	.8830
:						
3.4	.9997	.9997	.9997	...	.9997	.9998

SOLUTION: In this case, we are looking for an area to the left of a positive z value, so we look in the portion of Table 3 that shows positive z values. Again, we first sketch the area to be found on a standard normal curve, as shown in Figure 7-14. Look in the row headed by 1.1 and move to the column headed by .08. The desired area is shaded (see Table 7-3). We see that the area to the left of 1.18 is 0.8810.

GUIDED EXERCISE 4 *Using the standard normal distribution table*

Table 3, Areas of a Standard Normal Distribution, is located in the Appendix as well as in the endpapers of the text. Spend a little time studying the table, and then answer these questions.

(a) As z values increase, do the areas to the left of z increase?

Yes. As z values increase, we move to the right on the normal curve, and the areas increase.

(b) If a z value is negative, is the area to the left of z less than 0.5000?

Yes. Remember that a negative z value is on the left side of the standard normal distribution. The entire left half of the normal distribution has area 0.5, so any area to the left of $z = 0$ will be less than 0.5.

(c) If a z value is positive, is the area to the left of z greater than 0.5000? 

Yes. Positive z values are on the right side of the standard normal distribution, and any area to the left of a positive z value includes the entire left half of the normal distribution.

Using Table 3 to find other areas

Table 3 gives areas under the standard normal distribution that are to the *left of a z value.* How do we find other areas under the standard normal curve?

PROCEDURE

HOW TO USE A LEFT-TAIL STYLE STANDARD NORMAL DISTRIBUTION TABLE

1. For areas to the left of a specified z value, use the table entry directly.
2. For areas to the right of a specified z value, look up the table entry for z and subtract the area from 1.
   Note: Another way to find the same area is to use the symmetry of the normal curve and look up the table entry for $-z$.
3. For areas between two z values, z_1 and z_2 (where $z_2 > z_1$), *subtract* the table area for z_1 from the table area for z_2.

It may be useful to point out that students can always use the operation of subtraction to find areas under the standard normal curve that are not in a left tail.

Figure 7-15 illustrates the procedure for using Table 3, Areas of a Standard Normal Distribution, to find any specified area under the standard normal distribution. Again, it is useful to sketch the area in question before you use Table 3.

It is useful to point out to students that we use z values formatted to two places after the decimal and areas formatted to four places after the decimal.

This is a good comment to point out to students. By using tables, we must necessarily round answers to the level of accuracy found in the table. By treating areas to the left of a z value smaller than -3.49 as zero, the corresponding probability error will be less than 0.0002, or less than 2 out of 10,000. Likewise, by treating areas to the right of a z value greater than 3.49 as zero, the corresponding probability error will be less than 2 out of 10,000 as well.

COMMENT Notice that the z values shown in Table 3 of the Appendix are formatted to the hundredths position. It is convenient to *round or format z values to the hundredths position* before using the table. The areas are all given to four places after the decimal, so give your answers to four places after the decimal.

COMMENT The smallest z value shown in Table 3 is -3.49, while the largest value is 3.49. These values are, respectively, far to the left and far to the right on the standard normal distribution, with very little area beyond either value. We will follow the common convention of treating any area to the left of a z value smaller than -3.49 as 0.000. Similarly, we will consider any area to the right of a z value greater than 3.49 as 0.000. We understand that there is some area in these extreme tails. However, these areas are each less than 0.0002. Now let's get real about this! Some very specialized applications, beyond the

FIGURE 7-15

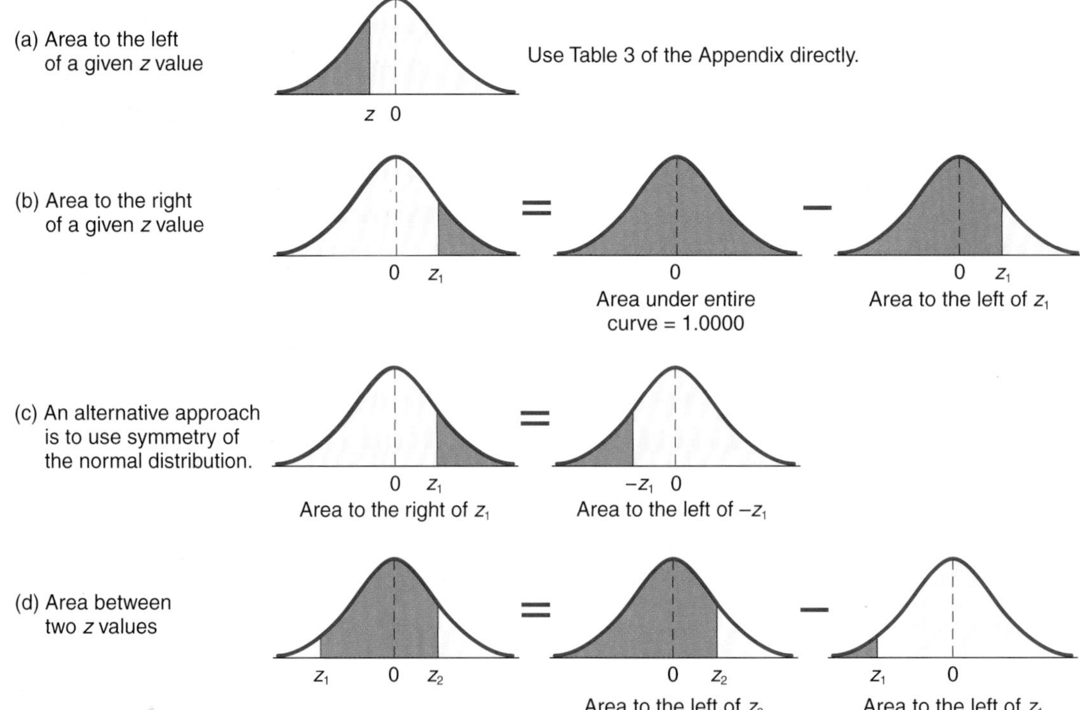

scope of this book, do need to measure areas and corresponding probabilities in these extreme tails. But in most practical applications, *we follow the convention of treating the areas in the extreme tails as zero.*

Convention for using Table 3 of the Appendix

1. Treat any area to the left of a z value smaller than -3.49 as 0.000.
2. Treat any area to the left of a z value greater than 3.49 as 1.000.

EXAMPLE 4 USING TABLE TO FIND AREAS

Use Table 3 of the Appendix to find the specified areas.

(a) Find the area between $z = 1.00$ and $z = 2.70$.

SOLUTION: First, sketch a diagram showing the area (see Figure 7-16). Because we are finding the area between two z values, we subtract corresponding table entries.

Since Table 3 uses z values rounded to the hundredths position, it is a good idea to round z values to the nearest hundredth.

$$\begin{aligned}(\text{Area between 1.00 and 2.70}) &= (\text{Area left of 2.70}) - (\text{Area left of 1.00})\\ &= 0.9965 - 0.8413\\ &= 0.1552\end{aligned}$$

(b) Find the area to the right of $z = 0.94$.

SOLUTION: First, sketch the area to be found (see Figure 7-17).

$$\begin{aligned}(\text{Area to right of 0.94}) &= (\text{Area under entire curve}) - (\text{Area to left of 0.94})\\ &= 1.000 - 0.8264\\ &= 0.1736\end{aligned}$$

Alternatively,

$$\begin{aligned}(\text{Area to right of 0.94}) &= (\text{Area to left of } -0.94)\\ &= 0.1736\end{aligned}$$

FIGURE 7-16

Area from $z = 1.00$ to $z = 2.70$

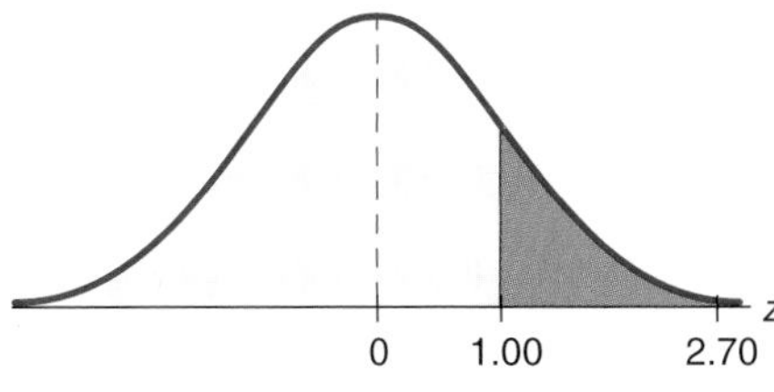

FIGURE 7-17

Area to the Right of $z = 0.94$

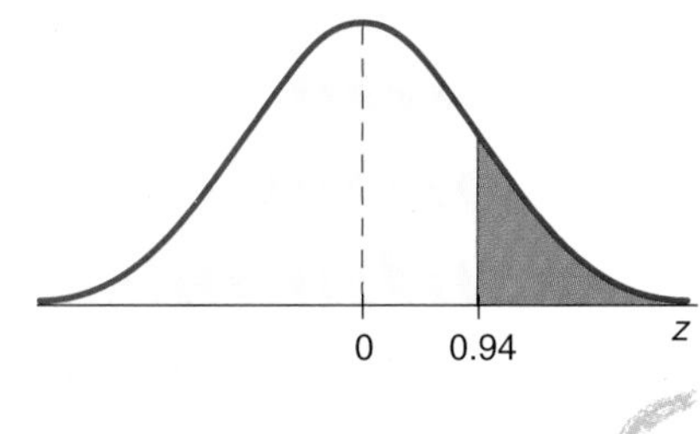

Probabilities associated with the standard normal distribution

We have practiced the skill of finding areas under the standard normal curve for various intervals along the z axis. This skill is important because *the probability* that z lies in an interval *is given by the area* under the standard normal curve above that interval.

Because the normal distribution is continuous, there is no area under the curve exactly over a specific z. Therefore, probabilities such as $P(z \geq z_1)$ are the same as $P(z > z_1)$. When dealing with probabilities or areas under a normal curve that are specified with inequalities, *strict inequality* symbols can be used *interchangeably* with *inequality-or-equal* symbols.

GUIDED EXERCISE 5 **Probabilities associated with the standard normal distribution**

Let z be a random variable with a standard normal distribution.

(a) $P(z \geq 1.15)$ refers to the probability that z values lie to the right of 1.15. Shade the corresponding area under the standard normal curve (Figure 7-18) and find $P(z \geq 1.15)$.

FIGURE 7-18 Area to Be Found

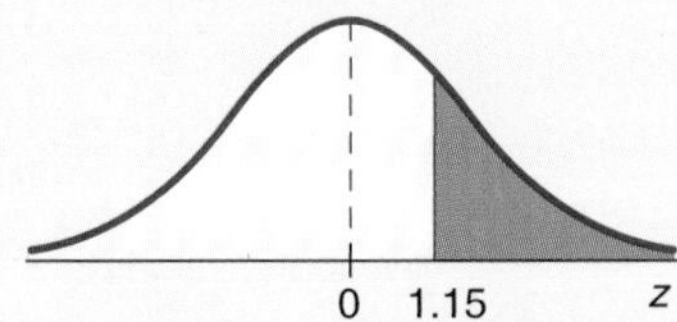

$P(z \geq 1.15) = 1.000 - P(z \leq 1.15) = 1.000 - 0.8749 = 0.1251$

Alternatively,

$P(z \geq 1.15) = P(z \leq -1.15) = 0.1251$

(b) Find $P(-1.78 \leq z \leq 0.35)$. First, sketch the area under the standard normal curve corresponding to the area (Figure 7-19).

FIGURE 7-19 Area to Be Found

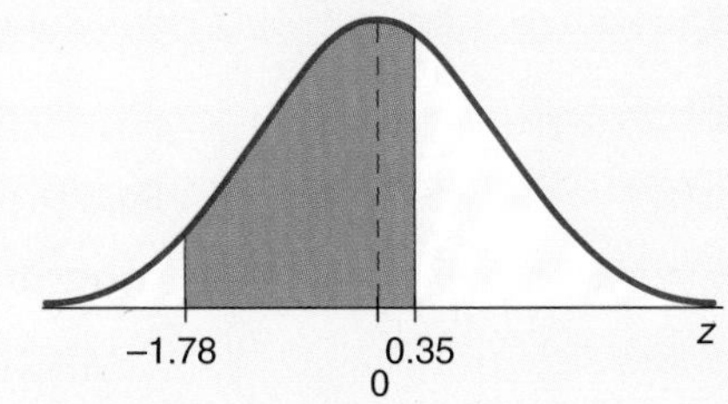

$$P(-1.78 \leq z \leq 0.35) = P(z \leq 0.35) - P(z \leq -1.78)$$
$$= 0.6368 - 0.0375 = 0.5993$$

TECH NOTES The TI-84Plus and TI-83Plus calculators, Excel, and Minitab all provide cumulative areas under any normal distribution, including the standard normal. The Tech Notes of Section 7.3 show examples.

VIEWPOINT Mighty Oaks from Little Acorns Grow!

Just how big is that acorn? What if we compare it with other acorns? Is that oak tree taller than an average oak tree? How does it compare with other oak trees? What do you mean, this oak tree has a larger geographic range? Compared with what? Answers to questions such as these can be given only if we resort to standardized statistical units. *Can you compare a single oak tree with an entire forest of oak trees? The answer is yes, if you use* standardized z scores. *For more information about sizes of acorns, oak trees, and geographic locations, visit the Online Study Center at* **www.cengage.com/statistics/Brase/UBS5e** *and find the link to DASL, the Carnegie Mellon University Data and Story Library. From the DASL site, find Biology under Data Subjects, and select Acorns. Follow the links to Data Subjects, Biology, and Acorns.*

SECTION 7.2 PROBLEMS

Tables and art to accompany margin answers may be found in the back of the book.

In these problems, assume that all distributions are *normal*. In all problems in Chapter 7, *average* is always taken to be the arithmetic mean $\bar{x}$ or μ.

1. *Statistical Literacy* What does a standard score measure?

2. *Statistical Literacy* Does a raw score less than the mean correspond to a positive or negative standard score? What about a raw score greater than the mean?

3. *Statistical Literacy* What is the value of the standard score for the mean of a distribution?

4. *Statistical Literacy* What are the values of the mean and standard deviation of a standard normal distribution?

5. *Critical Thinking* Consider the following scores:
   (i) Score of 40 from a distribution with mean 50 and standard deviation 10
   (ii) Score of 45 from a distribution with mean 50 and standard deviation 5

   How do the two scores compare relative to their respective distributions?

6. *Critical Thinking* Raul received a score of 80 on a history test for which the class mean was 70 with standard deviation 10. He received a score of 75 on a biology test for which the class mean was 70 with standard deviation 2.5. On which test did he do better relative to the rest of the class?

7. *z Scores: First Aid Course* The college Physical Education Department offered an Advanced First Aid course last semester. The scores on the comprehensive final exam were normally distributed, and the z scores for some of the students are shown below:

Robert, 1.10	Juan, 1.70	Susan, −2.00
Joel, 0.00	Jan, −0.80	Linda, 1.60

   (a) Which of these students scored above the mean?
   (b) Which of these students scored on the mean?
   (c) Which of these students scored below the mean?
   (d) If the mean score was $\mu = 150$ with standard deviation $\sigma = 20$, what was the final exam score for each student?

8. *z Scores: Fawns* Fawns between 1 and 5 months old in Mesa Verde National Park have a body weight that is approximately normally distributed with mean $\mu = 27.2$ kilograms and standard deviation $\sigma = 4.3$ kilograms (based on information from *The Mule Deer of Mesa Verde National Park*, by G. W. Mierau and J. L. Schmidt, Mesa Verde Museum Association). Let x be the weight of a fawn in kilograms. Convert the following x intervals to z intervals.
   (a) $x < 30$ (b) $19 < x$ (c) $32 < x < 35$

   Convert the following z intervals to x intervals.
   (d) $-2.17 < z$ (e) $z < 1.28$ (f) $-1.99 < z < 1.44$
   (g) *Interpretation:* If a fawn weighs 14 kilograms, would you say it is an unusually small animal? Explain using z values and Figure 7-12.
   (h) *Interpretation:* If a fawn is unusually large, would you say that the z value for the weight of the fawn will be close to 0, −2, or 3? Explain.

9. *z Scores: Red Blood Cell Count* Let x = red blood cell (RBC) count in millions per cubic millimeter of whole blood. For healthy females, x has an approximately normal distribution with mean $\mu = 4.8$ and standard deviation $\sigma = 0.3$ (based on information from *Diagnostic Tests with Nursing Implications*, edited by S. Loeb, Springhouse Press). Convert the following x intervals to z intervals.
   (a) $4.5 < x$ (b) $x < 4.2$ (c) $4.0 < x < 5.5$

Margin answers:

1. The number of standard deviations from the mean.
2. Raw score less than the mean corresponds to a negative standard score; raw score greater than the mean corresponds to a positive standard score.
3. 0.
4. $\mu = 0$; $\sigma = 1$.
5. They are the same, since both are 1 standard deviation below the mean.
6. The biology test, since his score is 2 standard deviations above the mean. His history score is only 1 standard deviation above the mean.
7. (a) Robert, Juan, Linda.
   (b) Joel.
   (c) Susan, Jan.
   (d) Robert, 172; Juan, 184; Susan, 110; Joel, 150; Jan, 134; Linda, 182.
8. (a) $z < 0.65$.
   (b) $-1.91 < z$.
   (c) $1.12 < z < 1.81$.
   (d) $17.9 < x$.
   (e) $x < 32.7$.
   (f) $18.6 < x < 33.4$.
   (g) $z = -3.07$; this fawn is very small.
   (h) $z = 3$ for a very large fawn.
9. (a) $-1.00 < z$.
   (b) $z < -2.00$.
   (c) $-2.67 < z < 2.33$.
   (d) $x < 4.4$.
   (e) $5.2 < x$.
   (f) $4.1 < x < 4.5$.
   (g) Yes, $z = 3.67$.

Convert the following z intervals to x intervals.
(d) $z < -1.44$ (e) $1.28 < z$ (f) $-2.25 < z < -1.00$
(g) *Interpretation:* If a female had an RBC count of 5.9 or higher, would that be considered unusually high? Explain using z values and Figure 7-12.

10. (a) Site 1, $z = -0.63$; site 2, $z = 2.80$. (b) The item from site 2 is more unusual.

10. *Normal Curve: Tree Rings* Tree-ring dates were used extensively in archaeological studies at Burnt Mesa Pueblo (*Bandelier Archaeological Excavation Project: Summer 1989 Excavations at Burnt Mesa Pueblo*, edited by Kohler, Washington State University Department of Anthropology). At one site on the mesa, tree-ring dates (for many samples) gave a mean date of μ_1 = year 1272 with standard deviation σ_1 = 35 years. At a second, removed site, the tree-ring dates gave a mean of μ_2 = year 1122 with standard deviation σ_2 = 40 years. Assume that both sites had dates that were approximately normally distributed. In the first area, an object was found and dated as x_1 = year 1250. In the second area, another object was found and dated as x_2 = year 1234.
(a) Convert both x_1 and x_2 to z values, and locate both of these values under the standard normal curve of Figure 7-12.
(b) *Interpretation:* Which of these two items is the more unusual as an archaeological find in its location?

In Problems 11–28, sketch the areas under the standard normal curve over the indicated intervals, and find the specified areas.

11. 0.5000. 12. 0.5000.
13. 0.0934. 14. 0.3192.
15. 0.6736. 16. 0.7642.
17. 0.0643. 18. 0.4404.
19. 0.8888. 20. 0.9850.
21. 0.4993. 22. 0.4732.
23. 0.8953. 24. 0.8980.
25. 0.3471. 26. 0.0628.
27. 0.0306. 28. 0.4641.

11. To the right of $z = 0$
12. To the left of $z = 0$
13. To the left of $z = -1.32$
14. To the left of $z = -0.47$
15. To the left of $z = 0.45$
16. To the left of $z = 0.72$
17. To the right of $z = 1.52$
18. To the right of $z = 0.15$
19. To the right of $z = -1.22$
20. To the right of $z = -2.17$
21. Between $z = 0$ and $z = 3.18$
22. Between $z = 0$ and $z = -1.93$
23. Between $z = -2.18$ and $z = 1.34$
24. Between $z = -1.40$ and $z = 2.03$
25. Between $z = 0.32$ and $z = 1.92$
26. Between $z = 1.42$ and $z = 2.17$
27. Between $z = -2.42$ and $z = -1.77$
28. Between $z = -1.98$ and $z = -0.03$

In Problems 29–48, let z be a random variable with a standard normal distribution. Find the indicated probability, and shade the corresponding area under the standard normal curve.

29. 0.5000. 30. 0.5000.
31. 0.4483. 32. 0.0158.
33. 0.8849. 34. 0.9993.
35. 0.0885. 36. 0.0150.
37. 0.8849. 38. 0.9332.
39. 0.8808. 40. 0.8369.
41. 0.3226. 42. 0.0718.
43. 0.4474. 44. 0.2054.
45. 0.2939. 46. 0.4911.
47. 0.6704. 48. 0.7664.

29. $P(z \le 0)$
30. $P(z \ge 0)$
31. $P(z \le -0.13)$
32. $P(z \le -2.15)$
33. $P(z \le 1.20)$
34. $P(z \le 3.20)$
35. $P(z \ge 1.35)$
36. $P(z \ge 2.17)$
37. $P(z \ge -1.20)$
38. $P(z \ge -1.50)$
39. $P(-1.20 \le z \le 2.64)$
40. $P(-2.20 \le z \le 1.04)$
41. $P(-2.18 \le z \le -0.42)$
42. $P(-1.78 \le z \le -1.23)$
43. $P(0 \le z \le 1.62)$
44. $P(0 \le z \le 0.54)$
45. $P(-0.82 \le z \le 0)$
46. $P(-2.37 \le z \le 0)$
47. $P(-0.45 \le z \le 2.73)$
48. $P(-0.73 \le z \le 3.12)$

SECTION 7.3

Areas Under Any Normal Curve

FOCUS POINTS

- Compute the probability of "standardized events."
- Find a z score from a given normal probability (inverse normal).
- Use the inverse normal to solve guarantee problems.

Normal Distribution Areas

In many applied situations, the original normal curve is not the standard normal curve. Generally, there will not be a table of areas available for the original normal curve. This does not mean that we cannot find the probability that a measurement x will fall into an interval from a to b. What we must do is *convert* the original measurements x, a, and b to z values.

PROCEDURE

HOW TO WORK WITH NORMAL DISTRIBUTIONS

To find areas and probabilities for a random variable x that follows a normal distribution with mean μ and standard deviation σ, convert x values to z values using the formula

$$z = \frac{x - \mu}{\sigma}$$

Then use Table 3 of the Appendix to find corresponding areas and probabilities.

EXAMPLE 5 **NORMAL DISTRIBUTION PROBABILITY**

Let x have a normal distribution with $\mu = 10$ and $\sigma = 2$. Find the probability that an x value selected at random from this distribution is between 11 and 14. In symbols, find $P(11 \le x \le 14)$.

SOLUTION: Since probabilities correspond to areas under the distribution curve, we want to find the area under the x curve above the interval from $x = 11$ to $x = 14$. To do so, we will convert the x values to standard z values and then use Table 3 of the Appendix to find the corresponding area under the standard curve.

We use the formula

$$z = \frac{x - \mu}{\sigma}$$

to convert the given x interval to a z interval.

Since Table 3 uses z values rounded to the hundredths position, it is a good idea to round z values to the nearest hundredth.

$$z_1 = \frac{11 - 10}{2} = 0.50 \qquad \text{(Use } x = 11, \mu = 10, \sigma = 2.)$$

$$z_2 = \frac{14 - 10}{2} = 2.00 \qquad \text{(Use } x = 14, \mu = 10, \sigma = 2.)$$

The corresponding areas under the x and z curves are shown in Figure 7-20 on the next page. From Figure 7-20, we see that

$$\begin{aligned} P(11 \le x \le 14) &= P(0.50 \le z \le 2.00) \\ &= P(z \le 2.00) - P(z \le 0.50) \\ &= 0.9772 - 0.6915 \qquad \text{(from Table 3 of the Appendix)} \\ &= 0.2857 \end{aligned}$$

The probability is 0.2857 that an x value selected at random from a normal distribution with mean 10 and standard deviation 2 lies between 11 and 14.

FIGURE 7-20

Corresponding Areas Under the x Curve and z Curve

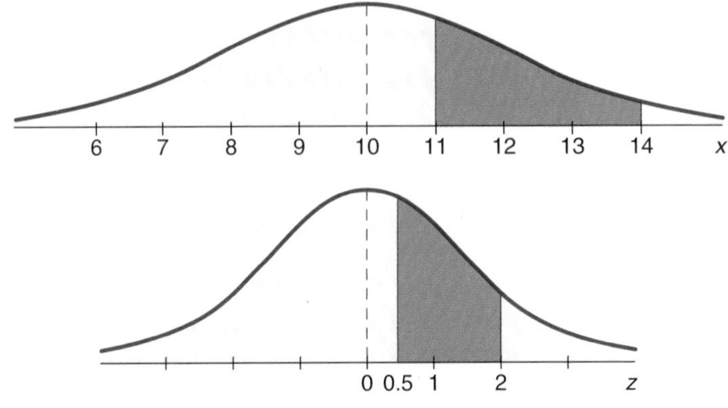

GUIDED EXERCISE 6 Normal distribution probability

Sunshine Stereo cassette decks have a deck life that is normally distributed with a mean of 2.3 years and a standard deviation of 0.4 year. What is the probability that a cassette deck will break down during the guarantee period of 2 years?

(a) Let x represent the life of a cassette deck. The statement that the cassette deck breaks during the 2-year guarantee period means the life is less than 2 years, or $x \leq 2$. Convert this to a statement about z.

$$z = \frac{x - \mu}{\sigma} = \frac{2 - 2.3}{0.4} = -0.75$$

So, $x \leq 2$ means $z \leq -0.75$.

(b) Indicate the area to be found in Figure 7-21. Does this area correspond to the probability that $z \leq -0.75$?

See Figure 7-22.
Yes, the shaded area does correspond to the probability that $z \leq -0.75$.

FIGURE 7-21

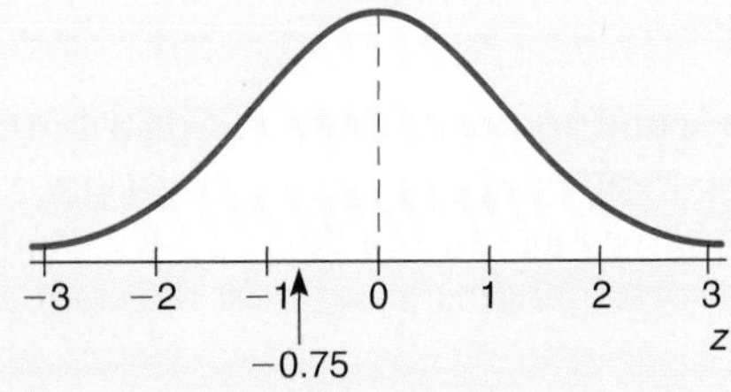

FIGURE 7-22 $z \leq -0.75$

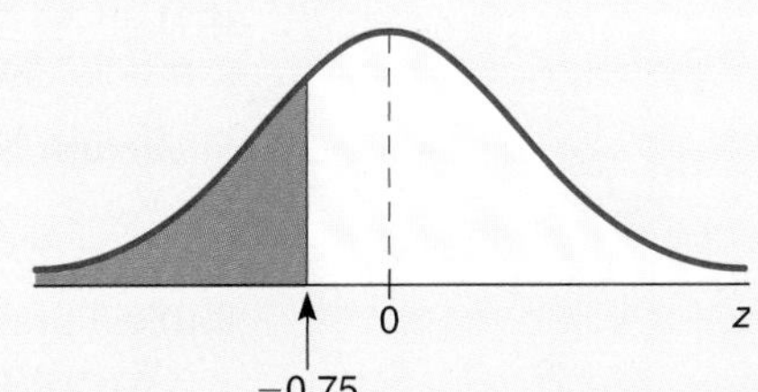

(c) Use Table 3 of the Appendix to find $P(z \leq -0.75)$.

0.2266

(d) What is the probability that the cassette deck will break before the end of the guarantee period? [*Hint:* $P(x \leq 2) = P(z \leq -0.75)$.] *Interpretation:* About what percentage of decks might the company have to repair or replace?

The probability is

$$P(x \leq 2) = P(z \leq -0.75) = 0.2266$$

This means that the company will repair or replace about 23% of the cassette decks.

TECH NOTES The TI-84Plus and TI-83Plus calculators, Excel, and Minitab all provide areas under any normal distribution. Excel and Minitab give the left-tail area to the left of a specified x value. The TI-84Plus/TI-83Plus has you specify an interval from a lower bound to an upper bound and provides the area under the normal curve for that interval. For example, to solve Guided Exercise 6 regarding the probability that a cassette deck will break during the guarantee period, we find $P(x \leq 2)$ for a normal distribution with $\mu = 2.3$ and $\sigma = 0.4$.

TI-84Plus/TI-83Plus Press the DISTR key, select **2:normalcdf (lower bound, upper bound, μ, σ)** and press Enter. Type in the specified values. For a left-tail area, use a lower bound setting at about 4 standard deviations below the mean. Likewise, for a right-tail area, use an upper bound setting about 4 standard deviations above the mean. For our example, use a lower bound of $\mu - 4\sigma = 2.3 - 4(0.4) = 0.7$.

```
normalcdf(.7,2,2.3,
.4)
           .2265955934
```

Excel Select **Paste Function** (fx) ➤ **Statistical** ➤ NORMDIST. Fill in the dialogue box, using True for cumulative.

=	=NORMDIST(2,2.3,0.4, TRUE)	
C	D	E
0.226627		

Minitab Use the menu selection **Calc** ➤ **Probability Distribution** ➤ **Normal.** Fill in the dialogue box, marking cumulative.

```
Cumulative Distribution Function
Normal with mean = 2.3 and
standard deviation = 0.4
        x      P(X <= x)
      2.0        0.2266
```

Inverse Normal Distribution

Finding z or x, given a probability

Sometimes we need to find z or x values that correspond to a given area under the normal curve. This situation arises when we want to specify a guarantee period such that a given percentage of the total products produced by a company last at least as long as the duration of the guarantee period. In such cases, we use the standard normal distribution table "in reverse." When we look up an area and find the corresponding z value, we are using the *inverse normal probability distribution*.

EXAMPLE 6 FIND x, GIVEN PROBABILITY

Magic Video Games, Inc., sells an expensive video games package. Because the package is so expensive, the company wants to advertise an impressive guarantee for the life expectancy of its computer control system. The guarantee policy will refund the full purchase price if the computer fails during the guarantee period. The research department has done tests that show that the mean life for the computer is 30 months, with standard deviation of 4 months. The computer life is normally distributed. How long can the guarantee period be if management does not want to refund the purchase price on more than 7% of the Magic Video packages?

This is a good time to point out to students that Guided Exercise 6 and Example 6 are like flip sides of the same coin. They are similar in that they both involve the normal distribution, but the end conclusions are quite different.

SOLUTION: Let us look at the distribution of lifetimes for the computer control system, and shade the portion of the distribution in which the computer lasts fewer months than the guarantee period. (See Figure 7-23.)

FIGURE 7-23

7% of the Computers Have a Lifetime Less Than the Guarantee Period

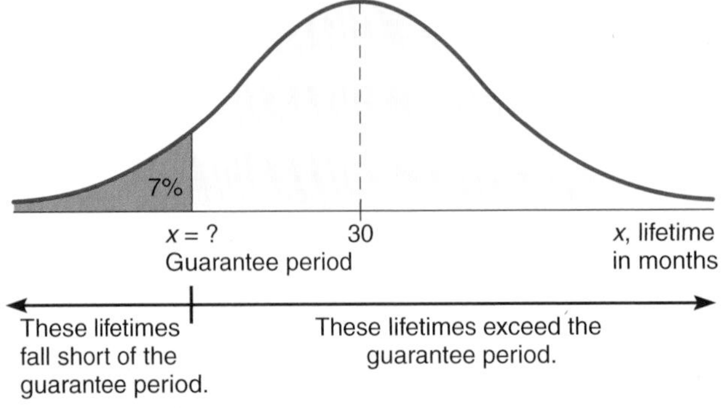

TABLE 7-4 **Excerpt from Table 3 of the Appendix**

z	.00	...	.07		.08	.09
⋮						
−1.4	.0808		.0708	↑ 0.0700	.0694	.0681

If a computer system lasts fewer months than the guarantee period, a full-price refund will have to be made. The lifetimes requiring a refund are in the shaded region in Figure 7-23. This region represents 7% of the total area under the curve.

We can use Table 3 of the Appendix to find the z value such that 7% of the total area under the *standard* normal curve lies to the left of the z value. Then we convert the z value to its corresponding x value to find the guarantee period.

We want to find the z value with 7% of the area under the standard normal curve to the left of z. Since we are given the area in a left tail, we can use Table 3 of the Appendix directly to find z. The area value is 0.0700. However, this area is not in our table, so we use the closest area, which is 0.0694, and the corresponding z value of $z = -1.48$ (see Table 7-4).

To translate this value back to an x value (in months), we use the formula

$$
\begin{aligned}
x &= z\sigma + \mu \\
&= -1.48(4) + 30 \qquad \text{(Use } \sigma = 4 \text{ months and } \mu = 30 \text{ months.)} \\
&= 24.08 \text{ months}
\end{aligned}
$$

The company can guarantee the Magic Video Games package for $x = 24$ months. For this guarantee period, they expect to refund the purchase price of no more than 7% of the video games packages.

Example 6 had us find a z value corresponding to a given area to the left of z. What if the specified area is to the right of z or between $-z$ and z? Figure 7-24 shows us how to proceed.

When discussing interpolation conventions, remind students that areas change very slowly in the tails of the normal distribution. It is useful to look at the normal distribution table (Table 3 of the Appendix) and study the areas for z values between −2.00 and −3.49.

COMMENT When we use Table 3 of the Appendix to find a z value corresponding to a given area, we usually use the nearest area value rather than interpolating between values. However, when the area value given is exactly halfway between two area values of the table, we use the z value halfway between the z values of the corresponding table areas. Example 7

FIGURE 7-24

Inverse Normal: Use Table 3 of the Appendix to Find z Corresponding to a Given Area A ($0 < A < 1$)

(a) **Left-tail case:** The given area A is to the left of z.

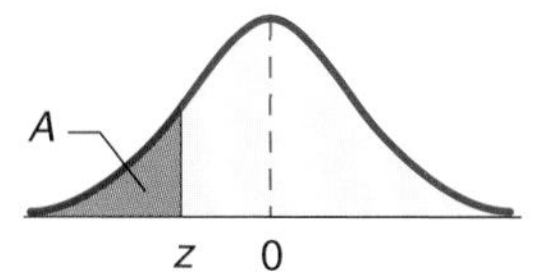

or

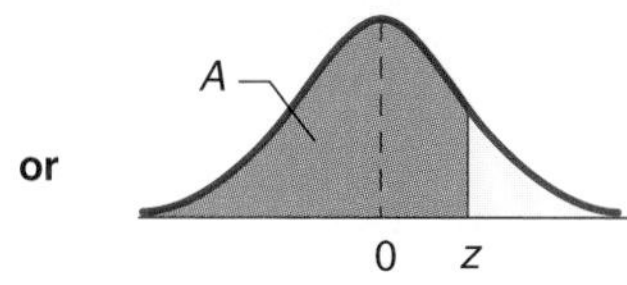

For the left-tail case, look up the number A in the body of the table and use the corresponding z value.

(b) **Right-tail case:** The given area A is to the right of z.

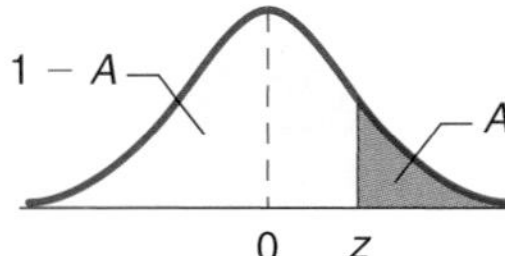

or

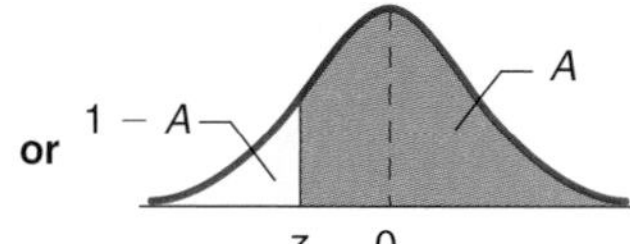

For the right-tail case, look up the number $1 - A$ in the body of the table and use the corresponding z value.

(c) **Center case:** The given area A is symmetric and centered above $z = 0$. Half of A lies to the left and half lies to the right of $z = 0$.

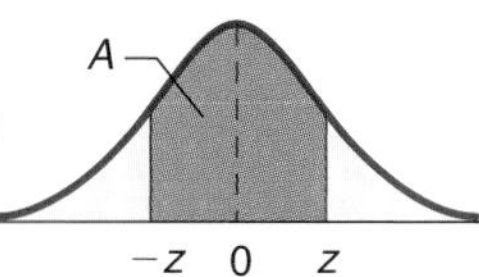

For the center case, look up the number $\frac{1 - A}{2}$ in the body of the table and use the corresponding $\pm z$ value.

demonstrates this procedure. However, this interpolation convention is not always used, especially if the area is changing slowly, as it does in the tail ends of the distribution. *When the z value corresponding to an area is smaller than -2, the standard convention is to use the z value corresponding to the smaller area. Likewise, when the z value is larger than 2, the standard convention is to use the z value corresponding to the larger area.* We will see an example of this special case in Example 1 of Section 8.1.

EXAMPLE 7 FIND z

Find the z value such that 90% of the area under the standard normal curve lies between $-z$ and z.

SOLUTION: Sketch a picture showing the described area (see Figure 7-25).

FIGURE 7-25

Area Between $-z$ and z Is 90%

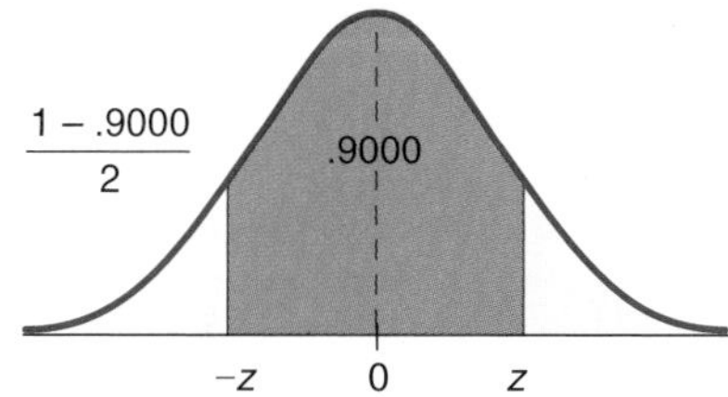

We find the corresponding area in the left tail.

$$\text{(Area left of } -z) = \frac{1 - 0.9000}{2}$$
$$= 0.0500$$

Looking in Table 7-5, we see that 0.0500 lies exactly between areas 0.0495 and 0.0505. The halfway value between $z = -1.65$ and $z = -1.64$ is $z = -1.645$. Therefore, we conclude that 90% of the area under the standard normal curve lies between the z values -1.645 and 1.645.

TABLE 7-5 **Excerpt from Table 3 of the Appendix**

z	...	.04		.05
⋮				
−1.6		.0505	↑ 0.0500	.0495

GUIDED EXERCISE 7 **Find z**

Find the z value such that 3% of the area under the standard normal curve lies to the right of z.

(a) Draw a sketch of the standard normal distribution showing the described area (Figure 7-26).

FIGURE 7-26 3% of Total Area Lies to the Right of z

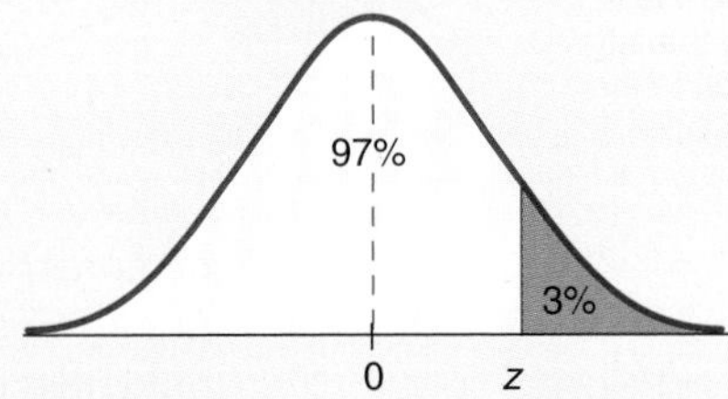

(b) Find the area to the left of z.

Area to the left of $z = 1 - 0.0300 = 0.9700$.

(c) Look up the area in Table 7-6 and find the corresponding z.

The closest area is 0.9699. This area is to the left of $z = 1.88$.

TABLE 7-6 **Excerpt from Table 3 of the Appendix**

z	.00	.01	.02	.03	.04	.05	.06	.07	.08	.09
1.8	.9641	.9649	.9656	.9664	.9671	.9678	.9686	.9693	.9699	.9706
1.9	.9713	.9719	.9726	.9732	.9738	.9744	.9750	.9756	.9761	.9767

(d) Suppose the time to complete a test is normally distributed with $\mu = 40$ minutes and $\sigma = 5$ minutes. After how many minutes can we expect all but about 3% of the tests to be completed?

We are looking for an x value such that 3% of the normal distribution lies to the right of x. In part (c), we found that 3% of the standard normal curve lies to the right of $z = 1.88$. We convert $z = 1.88$ to an x value.

$$x = z\sigma + \mu$$
$$= 1.88(5) + 40 = 49.4 \text{ minutes}$$

All but about 3% of the tests will be complete after 50 minutes.

(e) Use Table 7-7 to find a z value such that 3% of the area under the standard normal curve lies to the left of z.

The closest area is 0.0301. This is the area to the left of $z = -1.88$.

TABLE 7-7 **Excerpt from Table 3 of the Appendix**

z	.00	.01	.02	.03	.04	.05	.06	.07	.08	.09
−1.9	.0287	.0281	.0274	.0268	.0262	.0256	.0250	.0244	.0239	.0233
−1.8	.0359	.0351	.0344	.0336	.0329	.0322	.0314	.0307	.0301	.0294

(f) Compare the z value of part (c) with the z value of part (e). Is there any relationship between the z values?

One z value is the negative of the other. This result is expected because of the symmetry of the normal distribution.

TECH NOTES

When we are given a z value and we find an area to the left of z, we are using a normal distribution function. When we are given an area to the left of z and we find the corresponding z, we are using an inverse normal distribution function. The TI-84Plus and TI-83Plus calculators, Excel, and Minitab all have inverse normal distribution functions for any normal distribution. For instance, to find an x value from a normal distribution with mean 40 and standard deviation 5 such that 97% of the area lies to the left of x, use the described instructions.

TI-84Plus/TI-83Plus Press the **DISTR** key and select **3:invNorm(area,μ,σ)**.

```
invNorm(.97,40,5)
             49.40396805
```

Excel Select **Paste Function** (fx) ➤ **Statistical** ➤ **NORMINV**. Fill in the dialogue box.

```
= =NORMINV(0.97,40,5)
      C          D
 49.40395
```

Minitab Use the menu selection **Calc** ➤ **Probability Distribution** ➤ **Normal.** Fill in the dialogue box, marking Inverse Cumulative.

```
Inverse Cumulative Distribution Function
Normal with mean = 40.000 and
  standard deviation = 5.00000
       P(X <= x)        x
          0.9700    49.4040
```

CRITICAL THINKING

Checking for Normality

How can we tell if data follow a normal distribution? There are several checks we can make. The following procedure lists some guidelines.

PROCEDURE

HOW TO DETERMINE WHETHER DATA HAVE A NORMAL DISTRIBUTION

The following guidelines represent some useful devices for determining whether or not data follow a normal distribution.

1. **Histogram:** Make a histogram. For a normal distribution, the histogram should be roughly bell-shaped.
2. **Outliers:** For a normal distribution, there should not be more than one outlier. One way to check for outliers is to use a box-and-whisker plot. Recall that outliers are those data values that are

   above Q_3 by an amount greater than 1.5 × interquartile range

   below Q_1 by an amount greater than 1.5 × interquartile range

Continued

3. **Skewness:** Normal distributions are symmetric. One measure of skewness for sample data is given by Pearson's index:

$$\text{Pearson's index} = \frac{3(\bar{x} - \text{median})}{s}$$

An index value greater than 1 or less than −1 indicates skewness. Skewed distributions are not normal.

4. **Normal quantile plot (or normal probability plot):** This plot is provided through statistical software on a computer or graphing calculator. The Using Technology feature at the end of this chapter gives a brief description of how such plots are constructed. The section also gives commands for producing such plots on the TI-84Plus calculator, Minitab, or SPSS.

   Examine a normal quantile plot of the data.

   If the points lie close to a straight line, the data come from a distribution that is approximately normal.

   If the points do not lie close to a straight line or if they show a pattern that is not a straight line, the data are likely to come from a distribution that is not normal.

EXAMPLE 8 ASSESSING NORMALITY

Consider the following data, which are rounded to the nearest integer.

19	19	19	16	21	14	23	17	19	20	18	24	20	13	16
17	19	18	19	17	21	24	18	23	19	21	22	20	20	20
24	17	20	22	19	22	21	18	20	22	16	15	21	23	21
18	18	20	15	25										

(a) Look at the histogram and box-and-whisker plot generated by Minitab in Figure 7-27 and comment about normality of the data from these indicators.

FIGURE 7-27

Histogram and Box-and-Whisker Plot

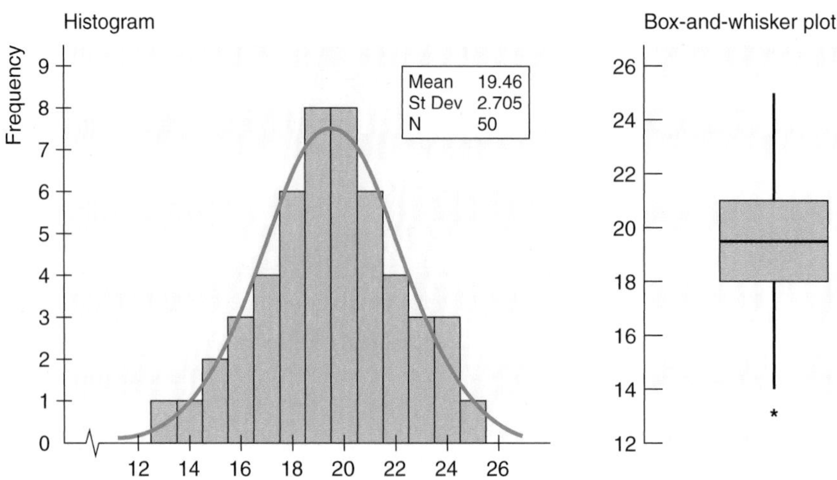

SOLUTION: Note that the histogram is approximately normal. The box-and-whisker plot shows just one outlier. Both of these graphs indicate normality.

(b) Use Pearson's index to check for skewness.

SOLUTION: Summary statistics from Minitab:

```
Variable   N  N*   Mean  Se Mean  StDev  Minimum      Q1  Median      Q3
C2        50   0  19.460   0.382  2.705   13.000  18.000  19.500  21.000
Variable   Maximum
C2          25.000
```

We see that $\bar{x} = 19.46$, median $= 19.5$, and $s = 2.705$.

$$\text{Pearson's index} = \frac{3(19.46 - 19.5)}{2.705} \approx -0.04$$

Since the index is between -1 and 1, we detect no skewness. The data appear to be symmetric.

(c) Look at the normal quantile plot in Figure 7-28 and comment on normality.

FIGURE 7-28

Normal Quantile Plot

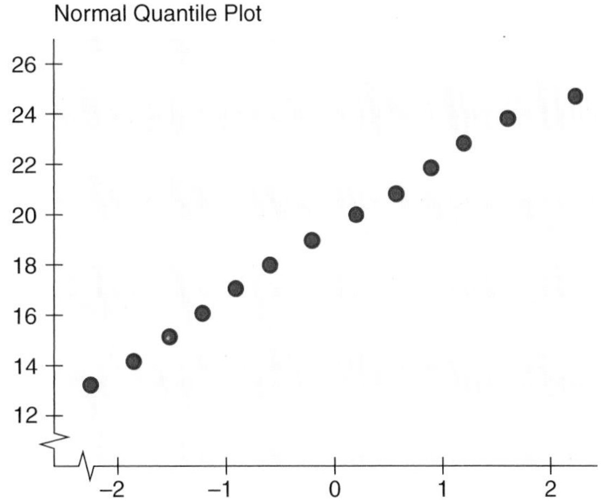

SOLUTION: The data fall close to a straight line, so the data appear to come from a normal distribution.

(d) Interpret the results.

SOLUTION: The histogram is roughly bell-shaped, there is only one outlier, Pearson's index does not indicate skewness, and the points on the normal quantile plot lie fairly close to a straight line. It appears that the data are likely from a distribution that is approximately normal.

VIEWPOINT Want to Be an Archaeologist?

Each year about 4500 students work with professional archaeologists in scientific research at the Crow Canyon Archaeological Center, Cortez, Colorado. In fact, Crow Canyon was included in The Princeton Review Guide to America's Top 100 Internships. *The nonprofit, multidisciplinary program at Crow Canyon enables students and laypeople with little or no background to get started in archaeological research. The only requirement is that you be interested in Native American culture and history. By the way, a knowledge of introductory statistics could come in handy for this internship. For more information about the program, visit the Online Study Center at* **www.cengage.com/statistics/Brase/UBS5e** *and find the link to Crow Canyon.*

SECTION 7.3 PROBLEMS

Tables and art to accompany margin answers may be found in the back of the book.

1. 0.50.
2. Positive.
3. Negative.
4. (a) Yes.
   (b) Yes, the points are close to a straight line.
   (c) $IQR = 2$; values above 34 or below 26 are outliers.
   (d) Pearson's index ≈ 0.265.
   (e) The data appear to be from a normal distribution. The outliers are not extreme, and other indicators support the assumption that the data are from a normal distribution.

1. *Statistical Literacy* Consider a normal distribution with mean 30 and standard deviation 2. What is the probability that a value selected at random from this distribution is greater than 30?

2. *Statistical Literacy* Suppose 5% of the area under the standard normal curve lies to the right of z. Is z positive or negative?

3. *Statistical Literacy* Suppose 5% of the area under the standard normal curve lies to the left of z. Is z positive or negative?

4. *Critical Thinking: Normality* Consider the following data. The summary statistics, histogram, and normal quantile plot were generated by Minitab.

27	27	27	28	28	28	28	28	28	29	29	29	29	29	29
29	29	29	29	30	30	30	30	30	30	30	30	30	30	30
30	31	31	31	31	31	31	31	31	32	32	32	32	33	33
33	33	33	34	34										

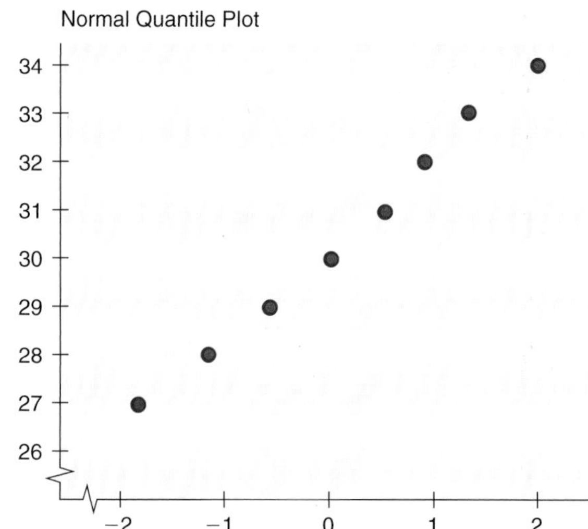

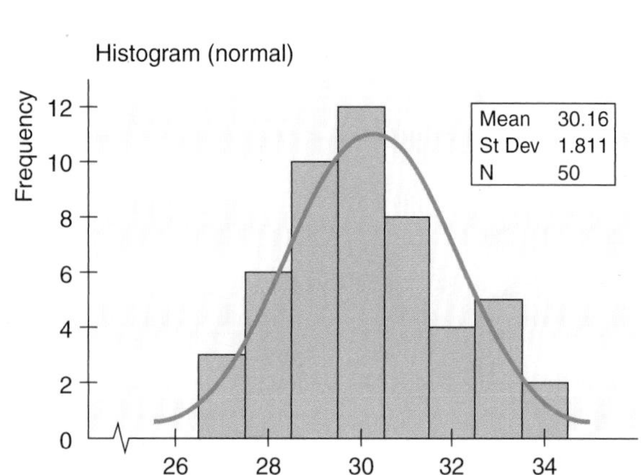


```
Variable  N  N*  Mean    SE Mean  StDev  Minimum  Q1      Median  Q3
Data      50  0  30.160  0.256    1.811  27.000   29.000  30.000  31.000
Variable  Maximum
Data       34.000
```

(a) Does the histogram indicate normality for the data distribution? Explain.
(b) Does the normal quantile plot indicate normality for the data distribution? Explain.
(c) Compute the interquartile range and check for outliers.
(d) Compute Pearson's index. Does the index value indicate skewness?
(e) Using parts (a) through (d), would you say the data are from a normal distribution?

In Problems 5–14, assume that x has a normal distribution with the specified mean and standard deviation. Find the indicated probabilities.

5. 0.5328. 6. 0.8914.
7. 0.2286. 8. 0.0471.
9. 0.1593. 10. 0.1693.
11. 0.0016. 12. 0.0918.
13. 0.7486. 14. About 1.

5. $P(3 \le x \le 6)$; $\mu = 4$; $\sigma = 2$
6. $P(10 \le x \le 26)$; $\mu = 15$; $\sigma = 4$
7. $P(50 \le x \le 70)$; $\mu = 40$; $\sigma = 15$
8. $P(7 \le x \le 9)$; $\mu = 5$; $\sigma = 1.2$
9. $P(8 \le x \le 12)$; $\mu = 15$; $\sigma = 3.2$
10. $P(40 \le x \le 47)$; $\mu = 50$; $\sigma = 15$
11. $P(x \ge 30)$; $\mu = 20$; $\sigma = 3.4$
12. $P(x \ge 120)$; $\mu = 100$; $\sigma = 15$
13. $P(x \ge 90)$; $\mu = 100$; $\sigma = 15$
14. $P(x \ge 2)$; $\mu = 3$; $\sigma = 0.25$

In Problems 15–24, find the z value described and sketch the area described.

15. Find z such that 6% of the standard normal curve lies to the left of z.

16. Find z such that 5.2% of the standard normal curve lies to the left of z.

17. Find z such that 55% of the standard normal curve lies to the left of z.

18. Find z such that 97.5% of the standard normal curve lies to the left of z.

19. Find z such that 8% of the standard normal curve lies to the right of z.

20. Find z such that 5% of the standard normal curve lies to the right of z.

21. Find z such that 82% of the standard normal curve lies to the right of z.

22. Find z such that 95% of the standard normal curve lies to the right of z.

23. Find the z value such that 98% of the standard normal curve lies between $-z$ and z.

24. Find the z value such that 95% of the standard normal curve lies between $-z$ and z.

25. *Medical: Blood Glucose* A person's blood glucose level and diabetes are closely related. Let x be a random variable measured in milligrams of glucose per deciliter (1/10 of a liter) of blood. After a 12-hour fast, the random variable x will have a distribution that is approximately normal with mean $\mu = 85$ and standard deviation $\sigma = 25$ (*Diagnostic Tests with Nursing Implications*, edited by S. Loeb, Springhouse Press). *Note:* After 50 years of age, both the mean and standard deviation tend to increase. What is the probability that, for an adult (under 50 years old) after a 12-hour fast,
(a) x is more than 60?
(b) x is less than 110?
(c) x is between 60 and 110?
(d) x is greater than 140 (borderline diabetes starts at 140)?

26. *Medical: Blood Protoplasm* Porphyrin is a pigment in blood protoplasm and other body fluids that is significant in body energy and storage. Let x be a random variable that represents the number of milligrams of porphyrin per deciliter of blood. In healthy adults, x is approximately normally distributed with mean $\mu = 38$ and standard deviation $\sigma = 12$ (see reference in Problem 25). What is the probability that
(a) x is less than 60?
(b) x is greater than 16?
(c) x is between 16 and 60?
(d) x is more than 60? (This may indicate an infection, anemia, or another type of illness.)

27. *Archaeology: Hopi Village* Thickness measurements of ancient prehistoric Native American pot shards discovered in a Hopi village are approximately normally distributed, with a mean of 5.1 millimeters (mm) and a standard deviation of 0.9 mm (Source: *Homol'ovi II: Archaeology of an Ancestral Hopi Village, Arizona*, edited by E. C. Adams and K. A. Hays, University of Arizona Press). For a randomly found shard, what is the probability that the thickness is
(a) less than 3.0 mm?
(b) more than 7.0 mm?
(c) between 3.0 mm and 7.0 mm?

28. *Law Enforcement: Police Response Time* Police response time to an emergency call is the difference between the time the call is first received by the dispatcher and the time a patrol car radios that it has arrived at the scene (based on information from the *Denver Post*). Over a long period of time, it has been determined that the police response time has a normal distribution with a mean of 8.4 minutes and a standard deviation of 1.7 minutes. For a randomly received emergency call, what is the probability that the response time will be

15. −1.555.
16. −1.63.
17. 0.13.
18. 1.96.
19. 1.41.
20. 1.645.
21. −0.92.
22. −1.645.
23. ±2.33.
24. ±1.96.
25. (a) 0.8413. (b) 0.8413. (c) 0.6826. (d) 0.0139.
26. (a) 0.9664. (b) 0.9664. (c) 0.9328. (d) 0.0336.
27. (a) 0.0099. (b) 0.0174. (c) 0.9727.
28. (a) 0.8036. (b) 0.0228. (c) 0.1736.

(a) between 5 and 10 minutes?
(b) less than 5 minutes?
(c) more than 10 minutes?

29. (a) 0.1292; replace 13%.
(b) 34.76; guarantee for 35 months.

29. *Guarantee: Batteries* Quick Start Company makes 12-volt car batteries. After many years of product testing, the company knows that the average life of a Quick Start battery is normally distributed, with a mean of 45 months and a standard deviation of 8 months.
(a) If Quick Start guarantees a full refund on any battery that fails within the 36-month period after purchase, what percentage of its batteries will the company expect to replace?
(b) *Inverse Normal Distribution* If Quick Start does not want to make refunds for more than 10% of its batteries under the full-refund guarantee policy, for how long should the company guarantee the batteries (to the nearest month)?

30. (a) About 21.2%.
(b) 22 months.

30. *Guarantee: Watches* Accrotime is a manufacturer of quartz crystal watches. Accrotime researchers have shown that the watches have an average life of 28 months before certain electronic components deteriorate, causing the watch to become unreliable. The standard deviation of watch lifetimes is 5 months, and the distribution of lifetimes is normal.
(a) If Accrotime guarantees a full refund on any defective watch for 2 years after purchase, what percentage of total production will the company expect to replace?
(b) *Inverse Normal Distribution* If Accrotime does not want to make refunds on more than 12% of the watches it makes, how long should the guarantee period be (to the nearest month)?

Part (a) of Problems 31–34 presents good conceptual links back to the empirical rule. In many practical applications, a 95% of data estimate of the range can give us a good working estimate of the standard deviation.

31. (a) $\sigma \approx 1.5$ years.
(b) 0.9772.
(c) 0.9082.
(d) About 6.1 years.

31. *Expand Your Knowledge: Estimating the Standard Deviation* *Consumer Reports* gave information about the ages at which various household products are replaced. For example, color TVs are replaced at an average age of $\mu = 8$ years after purchase, and the (95% of data) range was from 5 to 11 years. Thus, the range was $11 - 5 = 6$ years. Let x be the age (in years) at which a color TV is replaced. Assume that x has a distribution that is approximately normal.
(a) The empirical rule (Section 7.1) indicates that for a symmetrical and bell-shaped distribution, approximately 95% of the data lies within two standard deviations of the mean. Therefore, a 95% range of data values extending from $\mu - 2\sigma$ to $\mu + 2\sigma$ is often used for "commonly occurring" data values. Note that the interval from $\mu - 2\sigma$ to $\mu + 2\sigma$ is 4σ in length. This leads to a "rule of thumb" for estimating the standard deviation from a 95% range of data values.

95%
$\mu - 2\sigma$ μ $\mu + 2\sigma$

Estimating the standard deviation

For a symmetric, bell-shaped distribution,

$$\textbf{standard deviation} \approx \frac{\text{range}}{4} \approx \frac{\text{high value} - \text{low value}}{4}$$

where it is estimated that about 95% of the commonly occurring data values fall into this range.

Use this "rule of thumb" to approximate the standard deviation of x values, where x is the age (in years) at which a color TV is replaced.
(b) What is the probability that someone will keep a color TV more than 5 years before replacing it?
(c) What is the probability that someone will keep a color TV fewer than 10 years before replacing it?
(d) *Inverse Normal Distribution* Assume that the average life of a color TV is 8 years with a standard deviation of 1.5 years before it breaks. Suppose that a

company guarantees color TVs and will replace a TV that breaks while under guarantee with a new one. However, the company does not want to replace more than 10% of the TVs under guarantee. For how long should the guarantee be made (rounded to the nearest tenth of a year)?

32. (a) $\sigma \approx 2.5$ years.
(b) 0.1151.
(c) 0.0548.
(d) About 9.9 years.

32. *Estimating the Standard Deviation: Refrigerator Replacement* *Consumer Reports* indicated that the average life of a refrigerator before replacement is $\mu = 14$ years with a (95% of data) range from 9 to 19 years. Let x = age at which a refrigerator is replaced. Assume that x has a distribution that is approximately normal.
(a) Find a good approximation for the standard deviation of x values. *Hint:* See Problem 31.
(b) What is the probability that someone will keep a refrigerator fewer than 11 years before replacing it?
(c) What is the probability that someone will keep a refrigerator more than 18 years before replacing it?
(d) *Inverse Normal Distribution* Assume that the average life of a refrigerator is 14 years, with the standard deviation given in part (a) before it breaks. Suppose that a company guarantees refrigerators and will replace a refrigerator that breaks while under guarantee with a new one. However, the company does not want to replace more than 5% of the refrigerators under guarantee. For how long should the guarantee be made (rounded to the nearest tenth of a year)?

33. (a) $\sigma \approx 12$ beats/minute.
(b) 0.0401.
(c) 0.1210.
(d) 0.8389.
(e) 61 beats/minute.

33. *Estimating the Standard Deviation: Veterinary Science* The resting heart rate for an adult horse should average about $\mu = 46$ beats per minute with a (95% of data) range from 22 to 70 beats per minute, based on information from *The Merck Veterinary Manual* (a classic reference used in most veterinary colleges). Let x be a random variable that represents the resting heart rate for an adult horse. Assume that x has a distribution that is approximately normal.
(a) Estimate the standard deviation of the x distribution. *Hint:* See Problem 31.
(b) What is the probability that the heart rate is less than 25 beats per minute?
(c) What is the probability that the heart rate is greater than 60 beats per minute?
(d) What is the probability that the heart rate is between 25 and 60 beats per minute?
(e) *Inverse Normal Distribution* A horse whose resting heart rate is in the upper 10% of the probability distribution of heart rates may have a secondary infection or illness that needs to be treated. What is the heart rate corresponding to the upper 10% cutoff point of the probability distribution?

34. (a) $\sigma \approx 5.25$ ounces.
(b) 0.0228.
(c) 0.0526.
(d) 0.9246.
(e) About 17.8 ounces.

34. *Estimating the Standard Deviation: Veterinary Science* How much should a healthy kitten weigh? A healthy 10-week-old (domestic) kitten should weigh an average of $\mu = 24.5$ ounces with a (95% of data) range from 14 to 35 ounces. (See reference in Problem 33.) Let x be a random variable that represents the weight (in ounces) of a healthy 10-week-old kitten. Assume that x has a distribution that is approximately normal.
(a) Estimate the standard deviation of the x distribution. *Hint:* See Problem 31.
(b) What is the probability that a healthy 10-week-old kitten will weigh less than 14 ounces?
(c) What is the probability that a healthy 10-week-old kitten will weigh more than 33 ounces?
(d) What is the probability that a healthy 10-week-old kitten will weigh between 14 and 33 ounces?
(e) *Inverse Normal Distribution* A kitten whose weight is in the bottom 10% of the probability distribution of weights is called *undernourished*. What is the cutoff point for the weight of an undernourished kitten?

35. (a) About 81 months.
(b) 0.0526.
(c) $2,630,000.
(d) $370,000.

35. *Insurance: Satellites* A relay microchip in a telecommunications satellite has a life expectancy that follows a normal distribution with a mean of 90 months and a

standard deviation of 3.7 months. When this computer-relay microchip malfunctions, the entire satellite is useless. A large London insurance company is going to insure the satellite for 50 million dollars. Assume that the only part of the satellite in question is the microchip. All other components will work indefinitely.

(a) *Inverse Normal Distribution* For how many months should the satellite be insured to be 99% confident that it will last beyond the insurance date?

(b) If the satellite is insured for 84 months, what is the probability that it will malfunction before the insurance coverage ends?

(c) If the satellite is insured for 84 months, what is the expected loss to the insurance company?

(d) If the insurance company charges \$3 million for 84 months of insurance, how much profit does the company expect to make?

SECTION 7.4 Sampling Distributions

FOCUS POINTS

- Review such commonly used terms as *random sample, relative frequency, parameter, statistic,* and *sampling distribution.*
- From raw data, construct a relative frequency distribution for $\bar{x}$ values and compare the result to a theoretical sampling distribution.

Let us begin with some common statistical terms. Most of these have been discussed before, but this is a good time to review them.

From a statistical point of view, a *population* can be thought of as a set of measurements (or counts), either existing or conceptual. We discussed populations at some length in Chapter 1. A *sample* is a subset of measurements from the population. For our purposes, the most important samples are *random samples,* which were discussed in Section 1.2.

When we compute a descriptive measure such as an average, it makes a difference whether it was computed from a population or from a sample.

Statistic
Parameter

A **statistic** is a numerical descriptive measure of a *sample.*
A **parameter** is a numerical descriptive measure of a *population.*

For students wanting a memory device, point out that *population* and *parameter* both begin with the letter *p,* while *sample* and *statistic* both begin with the letter *s.*

It is important to notice that for a given population, a specified parameter is a fixed quantity. On the other hand, the value of a statistic might vary depending on which sample has been selected.

This section emphasizes some important statistical terminology. Students should realize we are "shifting gears" from a raw data distribution to a sampling distribution.

Some commonly used statistics and corresponding parameters

Measure	*Statistic*	*Parameter*
Mean	$\bar{x}$ (x bar)	μ (mu)
Variance	s^2	σ^2 (sigma squared)
Standard deviation	s	σ (sigma)
Proportion	$\hat{p}$ (p hat)	p

Often we do not have access to all the measurements of an entire population because of constraints on time, money, or effort. So, we must use measurements from a sample instead. In such cases, we will use a statistic (such as $\bar{x}$, s, or $\hat{p}$) to make *inferences* about a corresponding population parameter (e.g., μ, σ, or p). The principal types of inferences we will make are the following.

Types of inferences

1. **Estimation:** In this type of inference, we estimate the *value* of a population parameter.
2. **Testing:** In this type of inference, we formulate a *decision* about the value of a population parameter.
3. **Regression:** In this type of inference, we make *predictions* or *forecasts* about the value of a statistical variable.

Sampling distribution

To evaluate the reliability of our inferences, we will need to know the probability distribution for the statistic we are using. Such a probability distribution is called a *sampling distribution.* Perhaps Example 9 below will help clarify this discussion.

A **sampling distribution** is a probability distribution of a sample statistic based on all possible simple random samples of the *same size* from the same population.

EXAMPLE 9 SAMPLING DISTRIBUTION FOR $\bar{x}$

Pinedale, Wisconsin, is a rural community with a children's fishing pond. Posted rules state that all fish under 6 inches must be returned to the pond, only children under 12 years old may fish, and a limit of five fish may be kept per day. Susan is a college student who was hired by the community last summer to make sure the rules were obeyed and to see that the children were safe from accidents. The pond contains only rainbow trout and has been well stocked for many years. Each child has no difficulty catching his or her limit of five trout.

As a project for her biometrics class, Susan kept a record of the lengths (to the nearest inch) of all trout caught last summer. Hundreds of children visited the pond and caught their limit of five trout, so Susan has a lot of data. To make Table 7-8, Susan selected 100 children at random and listed the lengths of each of the five trout caught by a child in the sample. Then, for each child, she listed the mean length of the five trout that child caught.

Now let us turn our attention to the following question: What is the average (mean) length of a trout taken from the Pinedale children's pond last summer?

SOLUTION: We can get an idea of the average length by looking at the far-right column of Table 7-8. But just looking at 100 of the $\bar{x}$ values doesn't tell us much. Let's organize our $\bar{x}$ values into a frequency table. We used a class width of 0.38 to make Table 7-9.

Note: Techniques of Section 2.1 dictate a class width of 0.4. However, this choice results in the tenth class being beyond the data. Consequently, we shortened the class width slightly and also started the first class with a value slightly smaller than the smallest data value.

The far-right column of Table 7-9 contains relative frequencies $f/100$. Recall that the relative frequencies may be thought of as probabilities, so we effectively have a probability distribution. Because $\bar{x}$ represents the mean length of a trout (based on samples of five trout caught by each child), we estimate the probability of $\bar{x}$ falling into each class by using the relative frequencies. Figure 7-29 is a relative-frequency or probability distribution of the $\bar{x}$ values.

TABLE 7-8 Length Measurements of Trout Caught by a Random Sample of 100 Children at the Pinedale Children's Pond

Sample	Length (to nearest inch)					$\bar{x}$ = Sample Mean	Sample	Length (to nearest inch)					$\bar{x}$ = Sample Mean
1	11	10	10	12	11	10.8	51	9	10	12	10	9	10.0
2	11	11	9	9	9	9.8	52	7	11	10	11	10	9.8
3	12	9	10	11	10	10.4	53	9	11	9	11	12	10.4
4	11	10	13	11	8	10.6	54	12	9	8	10	11	10.0
5	10	10	13	11	12	11.2	55	8	11	10	9	10	9.6
6	12	7	10	9	11	9.8	56	10	10	9	9	13	10.2
7	7	10	13	10	10	10.0	57	9	8	10	10	12	9.8
8	10	9	9	9	10	9.4	58	10	11	9	8	9	9.4
9	10	10	11	12	8	10.2	59	10	8	9	10	12	9.8
10	10	11	10	7	9	9.4	60	11	9	9	11	11	10.2
11	12	11	11	11	13	11.6	61	11	10	11	10	11	10.6
12	10	11	10	12	13	11.2	62	12	10	10	9	11	10.4
13	11	10	10	9	11	10.2	63	10	10	9	11	7	9.4
14	10	10	13	8	11	10.4	64	11	11	12	10	11	11.0
15	9	11	9	10	10	9.8	65	10	10	11	10	9	10.0
16	13	9	11	12	10	11.0	66	8	9	10	11	11	9.8
17	8	9	7	10	11	9.0	67	9	11	11	9	8	9.6
18	12	12	8	12	12	11.2	68	10	9	10	9	11	9.8
19	10	8	9	10	10	9.4	69	9	9	11	11	11	10.2
20	10	11	10	10	10	10.2	70	13	11	11	9	11	11.0
21	11	10	11	9	12	10.6	71	12	10	8	8	9	9.4
22	9	12	9	10	9	9.8	72	13	7	12	9	10	10.2
23	8	11	10	11	10	10.0	73	9	10	9	8	9	9.0
24	9	12	10	9	11	10.2	74	11	11	10	9	10	10.2
25	9	9	8	9	10	9.0	75	9	11	14	9	11	10.8
26	11	11	12	11	11	11.2	76	14	10	11	12	12	11.8
27	10	10	10	11	13	10.8	77	8	12	10	10	9	9.8
28	8	7	9	10	8	8.4	78	8	10	13	9	8	9.6
29	11	11	8	10	11	10.2	79	11	11	11	13	10	11.2
30	8	11	11	9	12	10.2	80	12	10	11	12	9	10.8
31	11	9	12	10	10	10.4	81	10	9	10	10	13	10.4
32	10	11	10	11	12	10.8	82	11	10	9	9	12	10.2
33	12	11	8	8	11	10.0	83	11	11	10	10	10	10.4
34	8	10	10	9	10	9.4	84	11	10	11	9	9	10.0
35	10	10	10	10	11	10.2	85	10	11	10	9	7	9.4
36	10	8	10	11	13	10.4	86	7	11	10	9	11	9.6
37	11	10	11	11	10	10.6	87	10	11	10	10	10	10.2
38	7	13	9	12	11	10.4	88	9	8	11	10	12	10.0
39	11	11	8	11	11	10.4	89	14	9	12	10	9	10.8
40	11	10	11	12	9	10.6	90	9	12	9	10	10	10.0
41	11	10	9	11	12	10.6	91	10	10	8	6	11	9.0
42	11	13	10	12	9	11.0	92	8	9	11	9	10	9.4
43	10	9	11	10	11	10.2	93	8	10	9	9	11	9.4
44	10	9	11	10	9	9.8	94	12	11	12	13	10	11.6
45	12	11	9	11	12	11.0	95	11	11	9	9	9	9.8
46	13	9	11	8	8	9.8	96	8	12	8	11	10	9.8
47	10	11	11	11	10	10.6	97	13	11	11	12	8	11.0
48	9	9	10	11	11	10.0	98	10	11	8	10	11	10.0
49	10	9	9	10	10	9.6	99	13	10	7	11	9	10.0
50	10	10	6	9	10	9.0	100	9	9	10	12	12	10.4

TABLE 7-9 Frequency Table for 100 Values of $\bar{x}$

Class	Class Limits Lower	Class Limits Upper	f = Frequency	$f/100$ = Relative Frequency
1	8.39	8.76	1	0.01
2	8.77	9.14	5	0.05
3	9.15	9.52	10	0.10
4	9.53	9.90	19	0.19
5	9.91	10.28	27	0.27
6	10.29	10.66	18	0.18
7	10.67	11.04	12	0.12
8	11.05	11.42	5	0.05
9	11.43	11.80	3	0.03

The bars of Figure 7-29 represent our estimated probabilities of $\bar{x}$ values based on the data of Table 7-8. The bell-shaped curve represents the theoretical probability distribution that would be obtained if the number of children (i.e., number of $\bar{x}$ values) were much larger.

FIGURE 7-29

Estimates of Probabilities of $\bar{x}$ Values

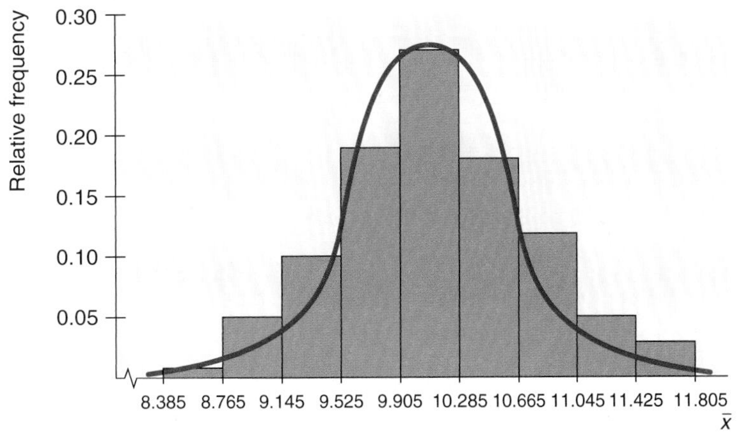

Figure 7-29 represents a *probability sampling distribution* for the sample mean $\bar{x}$ of trout lengths based on random samples of size 5. We see that the distribution is mound-shaped and even somewhat bell-shaped. Irregularities are due to the small number of samples used (only 100 sample means) and the rather small sample size (five trout per child). These irregularities would become less obvious and even disappear if the sample of children became much larger, if we used a larger number of classes in Figure 7-29, and if the number of trout in each sample became larger. In fact, the curve would eventually become a perfect bell-shaped curve. We will discuss this property at some length in the next section, which introduces the *central limit theorem*.

It is useful to remind students that in a sampling distribution, all samples must be of the *same size*.

GUIDED EXERCISE 8 Terminology

(a) What is a population parameter? Give an example.

➡ A population parameter is a numerical descriptive measure of a population. Examples are μ, σ, and p. (There are many others.)

(b) What is a sample statistic? Give an example.

➡ A sample statistic or statistic is a numerical descriptive measure of a sample. Examples are $\bar{x}$, s, and $\hat{p}$.

Continued

GUIDED EXERCISE 8 *continued*

(c) What is a sampling distribution?

A sampling distribution is a probability distribution for the sample statistic we are using.

(d) In Table 7-8, what makes up the members of the sample? What is the sample statistic corresponding to each sample? What is the sampling distribution? To which population parameter does this sampling distribution correspond?

There are 100 samples, each of which comprises five trout lengths. In the first sample, the five trout have lengths 11, 10, 10, 12, and 11. The sample statistic is the sample mean $\bar{x} = 10.8$. The sampling distribution is shown in Figure 7-29. This sampling distribution relates to the population mean μ of all lengths of trout taken from the Pinedale children's pond (i.e., trout over 6 inches long).

(e) Where will sampling distributions be used in our study of statistics?

Sampling distributions will be used for statistical inference. (Chapter 8 will concentrate on a method of inference called *estimation*. Chapter 9 will concentrate on a method of inference called *testing*.)

VIEWPOINT "Chance Favors the Prepared Mind"

—Louis Pasteur

It also has been said that a discovery is nothing more than an accident that meets a prepared mind. Sampling can be one of the best forms of preparation. In fact, sampling may be the primary way we humans venture into the unknown. Probability sampling distributions can provide new information for the sociologist, scientist, or economist. In addition, ordinary human sampling of life can help writers and artists develop preferences, style, and insight. Ansel Adams became famous for photographing lyrical, unforgettable landscapes such as "Moonrise, Hernandez, New Mexico." Adams claimed that he was a strong believer in the quote by Pasteur. In fact, he claims that the Hernandez photograph was just such a favored chance happening that his prepared mind readily grasped. During his lifetime, Adams made over $25 million from sales and royalties on the Hernandez photograph.

SECTION 7.4 PROBLEMS

These problems provide good topics for an in-class discussion of basic terminology.

1. Answers vary. Remind students to identify the individuals (subjects) and variable involved.
2. See Section 1.2.
3. A numerical descriptive measure of a population. Examples include μ, σ^2, σ, p, and ρ (rho) for those who have already studied linear regression from Chapter 4.
4. A numerical descriptive measure of a sample. Examples: $\bar{x}$, s, s^2, $\hat{p}$, and so forth.

This is a good time to review several important concepts, some of which we have studied earlier. Please write out a careful but brief answer to each of the following questions.

1. *Statistical Literacy* What is a population? Give three examples.
2. *Statistical Literacy* What is a random sample from a population? (*Hint:* See Section 1.2.)
3. *Statistical Literacy* What is a population parameter? Give three examples.
4. *Statistical Literacy* What is a sample statistic? Give three examples.
5. *Statistical Literacy* What is the meaning of the term *statistical inference*? What types of inferences will we make about population parameters?
6. *Statistical Literacy* What is a sampling distribution?
7. *Critical Thinking* How do frequency tables, relative frequencies, and histograms showing relative frequencies help us understand sampling distributions?

5. A statistical inference is a conclusion about the value of a population parameter based on information about the corresponding sample statistic and probability. We will do both estimation and testing.
6. A probability distribution for a sample statistic.
7. They help us visualize the sampling distribution through tables and graphs that approximately represent the sampling distribution.

8. *Critical Thinking* How can relative frequencies be used to help us estimate probabilities occurring in sampling distributions?

9. *Critical Thinking* Give an example of a specific sampling distribution we studied in this section. Outline other possible examples of sampling distributions from areas such as business administration, economics, finance, psychology, political science, sociology, biology, medical science, sports, engineering, chemistry, linguistics, and so on.

8. A relative frequency can be thought of as a measure or estimate of the likelihood of a certain statistic falling within the class bounds.

9. We studied the sampling distribution of mean trout lengths based on samples of size 5.

SECTION 7.5 The Central Limit Theorem

FOCUS POINTS

- For a normal distribution, use μ and σ to construct the theoretical sampling distribution for the statistic $\bar{x}$.
- For large samples, use sample estimates to construct a good approximate sampling distribution for the statistic $\bar{x}$.
- Learn the statement and underlying meaning of the central limit theorem well enough to explain it to a friend who is intelligent but (unfortunately) doesn't know much about statistics.

The $\bar{x}$ Distribution, Given x Is Normal

In Section 7.4, we began a study of the distribution of $\bar{x}$ values, where $\bar{x}$ was the (sample) mean length of five trout caught by children at the Pinedale children's fishing pond. Let's consider this example again in the light of a very important theorem of mathematical statistics.

THEOREM 7.1 **For a Normal Probability Distribution** Let x be a random variable with a *normal distribution* whose mean is μ and whose standard deviation is σ. Let $\bar{x}$ be the sample mean corresponding to random samples of size n taken from the x distribution. Then the following statements are true:

(a) The $\bar{x}$ distribution is a *normal distribution*.

(b) The mean of the $\bar{x}$ distribution is μ.

(c) The standard deviation of the $\bar{x}$ distribution is $\sigma/\sqrt{n}$.

Linking Concepts, Problem 3, provides material for a class discussion of Theorem 7.1 and a discussion of why sampling distributions are important in statistical work.

We conclude from Theorem 7.1 that when x has a normal distribution, the $\bar{x}$ distribution will be normal *for any sample size n*. Furthermore, we can convert the $\bar{x}$ distribution to the standard normal z distribution using the following formulas.

Some students may need to be reminded to use parentheses in the numerator and denominator when they compute z on their calculators.

$$\mu_{\bar{x}} = \mu$$

$$\sigma_{\bar{x}} = \frac{\sigma}{\sqrt{n}}$$

$$z = \frac{\bar{x} - \mu_{\bar{x}}}{\sigma_{\bar{x}}} = \frac{\bar{x} - \mu}{\sigma/\sqrt{n}}$$

where n is the sample size,
μ is the mean of the $\bar{x}$ distribution, and
σ is the standard deviation of the x distribution.

Some students might prefer to use the equivalent formula

$$z = \frac{(\bar{x} - \mu)\sqrt{n}}{\sigma}$$

Theorem 7.1 is a wonderful theorem! It states that the $\bar{x}$ distribution will be normal provided the x distribution is normal. The sample size n could be 2, 3, 4, or any (fixed) sample size we wish. Furthermore, the mean of the $\bar{x}$ distribution is μ (same as for the x distribution), but the standard deviation is $\sigma/\sqrt{n}$ (which is, of course, smaller than σ). The next example illustrates Theorem 7.1.

EXAMPLE 10 PROBABILITY REGARDING x AND $\bar{x}$

Suppose a team of biologists has been studying the Pinedale children's fishing pond. Let x represent the length of a single trout taken at random from the pond. This group of biologists has determined that x has a normal distribution with mean $\mu = 10.2$ inches and standard deviation $\sigma = 1.4$ inches.

(a) What is the probability that a *single trout* taken at random from the pond is between 8 and 12 inches long?

SOLUTION: We use the methods of Section 7.3, with $\mu = 10.2$ and $\sigma = 1.4$, to get

$$z = \frac{x - \mu}{\sigma} = \frac{x - 10.2}{1.4}$$

Therefore,

$$\begin{aligned} P(8 < x < 12) &= P\left(\frac{8 - 10.2}{1.4} < z < \frac{12 - 10.2}{1.4}\right) \\ &= P(-1.57 < z < 1.29) \\ &= 0.9015 - 0.0582 = 0.8433 \end{aligned}$$

Therefore, the probability is about 0.8433 that a *single* trout taken at random is between 8 and 12 inches long.

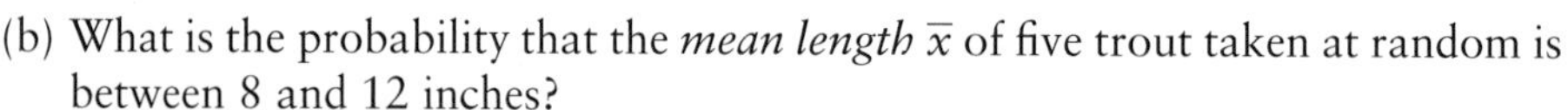

(b) What is the probability that the *mean length* $\bar{x}$ of five trout taken at random is between 8 and 12 inches?

SOLUTION: If we let $\mu_{\bar{x}}$ represent the mean of the distribution, then Theorem 7.1, part (b), tells us that

$$\mu_{\bar{x}} = \mu = 10.2$$

If $\sigma_{\bar{x}}$ represents the standard deviation of the $\bar{x}$ distribution, then Theorem 7.1, part (c), tells us that

$$\sigma_{\bar{x}} = \sigma/\sqrt{n} = 1.4/\sqrt{5} \approx 0.63$$

To create a standard z variable from $\bar{x}$, we subtract $\mu_{\bar{x}}$ and divide by $\sigma_{\bar{x}}$:

$$z = \frac{\bar{x} - \mu_{\bar{x}}}{\sigma_{\bar{x}}} = \frac{\bar{x} - \mu}{\sigma/\sqrt{n}} \approx \frac{\bar{x} - 10.2}{0.63}$$

To standardize the interval $8 < \bar{x} < 12$, we use 8 and then 12 in place of $\bar{x}$ in the preceding formula for z.

$$8 < \bar{x} < 12$$

$$\frac{8 - 10.2}{0.63} < z < \frac{12 - 10.2}{0.63}$$

$$-3.49 < z < 2.86$$

Theorem 7.1, part (a), tells us that $\bar{x}$ has a normal distribution. Therefore,

$$P(8 < \bar{x} < 12) = P(-3.49 < z < 2.86) = 0.9979 - 0.0002 = 0.9977$$

The probability is about 0.9977 that the mean length based on a sample size of 5 is between 8 and 12 inches.

(c) Looking at the results of parts (a) and (b), we see that the probabilities (0.8433 and 0.9977) are quite different. Why is this the case?

SOLUTION: According to Theorem 7.1, both x and $\bar{x}$ have a normal distribution, and both have the same mean of 10.2 inches. The difference is in the standard deviations for x and $\bar{x}$. The standard deviation of the x distribution is $\sigma = 1.4$. The standard deviation of the $\bar{x}$ distribution is

$$\sigma_{\bar{x}} = \sigma/\sqrt{n} = 1.4/\sqrt{5} \approx 0.63$$

The standard deviation of the $\bar{x}$ distribution is less than half the standard deviation of the x distribution. Figure 7-30 shows the distributions of x and $\bar{x}$.

FIGURE 7-30

General Shapes of the x and $\bar{x}$ Distributions

(a) The x distribution with $\mu = 10.2$ and $\sigma = 1.4$

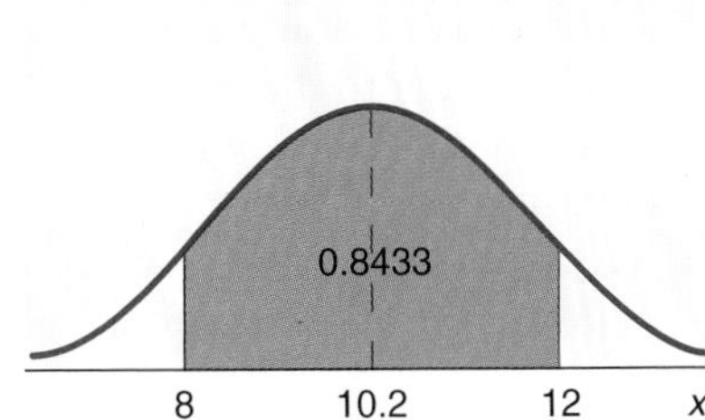

(b) The $\bar{x}$ distribution with $\mu_{\bar{x}} = 10.2$ and $\sigma_{\bar{x}} = 0.63$ for samples of size $n = 5$

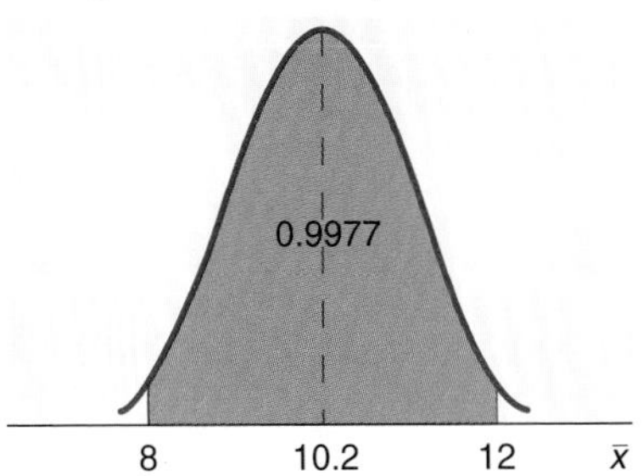

Looking at Figure 7-30(a) and (b), we see that both curves use the same scale on the horizontal axis. The means are the same, and the shaded area is above the interval from 8 to 12 on each graph. It becomes clear that the smaller standard deviation of the $\bar{x}$ distribution has the effect of gathering together much more of the total probability into the region over its mean. Therefore, the region from 8 to 12 has a much higher probability for the $\bar{x}$ distribution.

Standard error of the mean

Theorem 7.1 describes the distribution of a particular statistic: namely, the distribution of sample mean $\bar{x}$. The standard deviation of a statistic is referred to as the *standard error* of that statistic.

It is good to point out that the term *standard error* is very widely used in statistical literature.

The **standard error** is the standard deviation of a sampling distribution. For the $\bar{x}$ sampling distribution,

$$\textbf{standard error} = \sigma_{\bar{x}} = \sigma/\sqrt{n}$$

Statistical software

The expression *standard error* appears commonly on printouts and refers to the standard deviation of the sampling distribution being used. (In Minitab, the expression SE MEAN refers to the standard error of the mean.)

The $\bar{x}$ Distribution, Given x Follows Any Distribution

Central limit theorem

Theorem 7.1 gives complete information about the $\bar{x}$ distribution, provided the original x distribution is known to be normal. What happens if we don't have information about the shape of the original x distribution? The *central limit theorem* tells us what to expect.

The central limit theorem is a generalization of the DeMoivre-Laplace theorem.

THEOREM 7.2 **The Central Limit Theorem for Any Probability Distribution** If x possesses *any* distribution with mean μ and standard deviation σ, then the sample mean $\overline{x}$ based on a random sample of size n will have a distribution that approaches the distribution of a normal random variable with mean μ and standard deviation $\sigma/\sqrt{n}$ as n increases without limit.

Using Technology has students use a random-number table as a tool for demonstrating the central limit theorem.

The central limit theorem is indeed surprising! It says that x can have *any* distribution whatsoever, but as the sample size gets larger and larger, the distribution of $\overline{x}$ will approach a *normal* distribution. From this relation, we begin to appreciate the scope and significance of the normal distribution.

Large sample

In the central limit theorem, the degree to which the distribution of $\overline{x}$ values fits a normal distribution depends on both the selected value of n and the original distribution of x values. A natural question is: How large should the sample size be if we want to apply the central limit theorem? After a great deal of theoretical as well as empirical study, statisticians agree that if n is 30 or larger, the $\overline{x}$ distribution will appear to be normal and the central limit theorem will apply. However, this rule should not be applied blindly. If the x distribution is definitely not symmetrical about its mean, then the $\overline{x}$ distribution also will display a lack of symmetry. In such a case, a sample size larger than 30 may be required to get a reasonable approximation to the normal.

In practice, it is a good idea, when possible, to make a histogram of sample x values. If the histogram is approximately mound-shaped, and if it is more or less symmetrical, then we may be assured that, for all practical purposes, the $\overline{x}$ distribution will be well approximated by a normal distribution and the central limit theorem will apply when the sample size is 30 or larger. The main thing to remember is that in almost all practical applications, a sample size of 30 or more is adequate for the central limit theorem to hold. However, in a few rare applications, you may need a sample size larger than 30 to get reliable results.

Let's summarize this information for convenient reference: For almost all x distributions, if we use a random sample of size 30 or larger, the $\overline{x}$ distribution will be approximately normal. The larger the sample size becomes, the closer the $\overline{x}$ distribution gets to the normal. Furthermore, we may convert the $\overline{x}$ distribution to a standard normal distribution using the following formulas.

Data Highlights (*Iris setosa*) provides a good topic for a class discussion or in-class demonstration of the central limit theorem.

Using the central limit theorem to convert the $\overline{x}$ distribution to the standard normal distribution

$$\mu_{\overline{x}} = \mu$$

$$\sigma_{\overline{x}} = \frac{\sigma}{\sqrt{n}}$$

$$z = \frac{\overline{x} - \mu_{\overline{x}}}{\sigma_{\overline{x}}} = \frac{\overline{x} - \mu}{\sigma/\sqrt{n}}$$

where n is the sample size ($n \geq 30$),
μ is the mean of the x distribution, and
σ is the standard deviation of the x distribution.

Guided Exercise 9 shows how to standardize $\overline{x}$ when appropriate. Then, Example 11 demonstrates the use of the central limit theorem in a decision-making process.

GUIDED EXERCISE 9 **Central limit theorem**

(a) Suppose x has a *normal* distribution with mean $\mu = 18$ and standard deviation $\sigma = 3$. If you draw random samples of size 5 from the x distribution and $\bar{x}$ represents the sample mean, what can you say about the $\bar{x}$ distribution? How could you standardize the $\bar{x}$ distribution?

→ Since the x distribution is given to be *normal*, the $\bar{x}$ distribution also will be normal even though the sample size is much less than 30. The mean is $\mu_{\bar{x}} = \mu = 18$. The standard deviation is

$\sigma_{\bar{x}} = \sigma/\sqrt{n} = 3/\sqrt{5} \approx 1.3$

We could standardize $\bar{x}$ as follows:

$$z = \frac{\bar{x} - \mu}{\sigma/\sqrt{n}} \approx \frac{\bar{x} - 18}{1.3}$$

(b) Suppose you know that the x distribution has mean $\mu = 75$ and standard deviation $\sigma = 12$, but you have no information as to whether or not the x distribution is normal. If you draw samples of size 30 from the x distribution and $\bar{x}$ represents the sample mean, what can you say about the $\bar{x}$ distribution? How could you standardize the $\bar{x}$ distribution?

→ Since the sample size is large enough, the $\bar{x}$ distribution will be an approximately normal distribution. The mean of the $\bar{x}$ distribution is

$\mu_{\bar{x}} = \mu = 75$

The standard deviation of the $\bar{x}$ distribution is

$\sigma_{\bar{x}} = \sigma/\sqrt{n} = 12/\sqrt{30} \approx 2.2$

We could standardize $\bar{x}$ as follows:

$$z = \frac{\bar{x} - \mu}{\sigma/\sqrt{n}} \approx \frac{\bar{x} - 75}{2.2}$$

(c) Suppose you did not know that x had a normal distribution. Would you be justified in saying that the $\bar{x}$ distribution is approximately normal if the sample size were $n = 8$?

→ No, the sample size should be 30 or larger if we don't know that x has a normal distribution.

EXAMPLE 11 CENTRAL LIMIT THEOREM

A certain strain of bacteria occurs in all raw milk. Let x be the bacteria count per milliliter of milk. The health department has found that if the milk is not contaminated, then x has a distribution that is more or less mound-shaped and symmetrical. The mean of the x distribution is $\mu = 2500$, and the standard deviation is $\sigma = 300$. In a large commercial dairy, the health inspector takes 42 random samples of the milk produced each day. At the end of the day, the bacteria count in each of the 42 samples is averaged to obtain the sample mean bacteria count $\bar{x}$.

(a) Assuming the milk is not contaminated, what is the distribution of $\bar{x}$?

SOLUTION: The sample size is $n = 42$. Since this value exceeds 30, the central limit theorem applies, and we know that $\bar{x}$ will be approximately normal with mean and standard deviation

$$\mu_{\bar{x}} = \mu = 2500$$
$$\sigma_{\bar{x}} = \sigma/\sqrt{n} = 300/\sqrt{42} \approx 46.3$$

(b) Assuming the milk is not contaminated, what is the probability that the average bacteria count $\bar{x}$ for one day is between 2350 and 2650 bacteria per milliliter?

SOLUTION: We convert the interval

$$2350 \le \bar{x} \le 2650$$

to a corresponding interval on the standard z axis.

$$z = \frac{\bar{x} - \mu}{\sigma/\sqrt{n}} \approx \frac{\bar{x} - 2500}{46.3}$$

$$\bar{x} = 2350 \quad \text{converts to} \quad z = \frac{2350 - 2500}{46.3} \approx -3.24$$

$$\bar{x} = 2650 \quad \text{converts to} \quad z = \frac{2650 - 2500}{46.3} \approx 3.24$$

Therefore,

$$\begin{aligned} P(2350 \le \bar{x} \le 2650) &= P(-3.24 \le z \le 3.24) \\ &= 0.9994 - 0.0006 \\ &= 0.9988 \end{aligned}$$

The probability is 0.9988 that $\bar{x}$ is between 2350 and 2650.

(c) INTERPRETATION At the end of each day, the inspector must decide to accept or reject the accumulated milk that has been held in cold storage awaiting shipment. Suppose the 42 samples taken by the inspector have a mean bacteria count $\bar{x}$ that is *not* between 2350 and 2650. If you were the inspector, what would be your comment on this situation?

SOLUTION: The probability that $\bar{x}$ is between 2350 and 2650 is very high. If the inspector finds that the average bacteria count for the 42 samples is not between 2350 and 2650, then it is reasonable to conclude that there is something wrong with the milk. If $\bar{x}$ is less than 2350, you might suspect someone added chemicals to the milk to artificially reduce the bacteria count. If $\bar{x}$ is above 2650, you might suspect some other kind of biologic contamination.

PROCEDURE

HOW TO FIND PROBABILITIES REGARDING $\bar{x}$

Given a probability distribution of x values where

n = sample size
μ = mean of the x distribution
σ = standard deviation of the x distribution

1. If the x distribution is *normal*, then the $\bar{x}$ distribution is *normal*.
2. Even if the x distribution is *not* normal, if the *sample size* $n \ge 30$, then, by the central limit theorem, the $\bar{x}$ distribution is *approximately normal*.
3. Convert $\bar{x}$ to z using the formula

$$z = \frac{\bar{x} - \mu_{\bar{x}}}{\sigma_{\bar{x}}} = \frac{\bar{x} - \mu}{\sigma/\sqrt{n}}$$

4. Use the standard normal distribution to find the corresponding probabilities of events regarding $\bar{x}$.

GUIDED EXERCISE 10 Probability regarding $\bar{x}$

In mountain country, major highways sometimes use tunnels instead of long, winding roads over high passes. However, too many vehicles in a tunnel at the same time can cause a hazardous situation. Traffic engineers are studying a long tunnel in Colorado. If x represents the time for a vehicle to go through the tunnel, it is known that the x distribution has mean $\mu = 12.1$ minutes and standard deviation $\sigma = 3.8$ minutes under ordinary traffic conditions. From a histogram of x values, it was found that the x distribution is mound-shaped with some symmetry about the mean.

Engineers have calculated that, *on average,* vehicles should spend from 11 to 13 minutes in the tunnel. If the time is less than 11 minutes, traffic is moving too fast for safe travel in the tunnel. If the time is more than 13 minutes, there is a problem of bad air quality (too much carbon monoxide and other pollutants).

Under ordinary conditions, there are about 50 vehicles in the tunnel at one time. What is the probability that the mean time for 50 vehicles in the tunnel will be from 11 to 13 minutes?

We will answer this question in steps.

(a) Let $\bar{x}$ represent the sample mean based on samples of size 50. Describe the $\bar{x}$ distribution.

→ From the central limit theorem, we expect the $\bar{x}$ distribution to be approximately normal with mean and standard deviation

$$\mu_{\bar{x}} = \mu = 12.1 \qquad \sigma_{\bar{x}} = \frac{\sigma}{\sqrt{n}} = \frac{3.8}{\sqrt{50}} \approx 0.54$$

(b) Find $P(11 < \bar{x} < 13)$.

→ We convert the interval

$$11 < \bar{x} < 13$$

to a standard z interval and use the standard normal probability table to find our answer. Since

$$z = \frac{\bar{x} - \mu}{\sigma/\sqrt{n}} \approx \frac{\bar{x} - 12.1}{0.54}$$

$$\bar{x} = 11 \text{ converts to } z \approx \frac{11 - 12.1}{0.54} = -2.04$$

$$\text{and } \bar{x} = 13 \text{ converts to } z \approx \frac{13 - 12.1}{0.54} = 1.67$$

Therefore,

$$\begin{aligned} P(11 < \bar{x} < 13) &= P(-2.04 < z < 1.67) \\ &= 0.9525 - 0.0207 \\ &= 0.9318 \end{aligned}$$

(c) Interpret your answer to part (b).

→ It seems that about 93% of the time there should be no safety hazard for average traffic flow.

CRITICAL THINKING

Bias and Variability

Whenever we use a sample statistic as an estimate of a population parameter, we need to consider both *bias* and *variability* of the statistic.

A sample statistic is **unbiased** if the mean of its sampling distribution equals the value of the parameter being estimated.

The spread of the sampling distribution indicates the **variability of the statistic.** The spread is affected by the sampling method and the sample size. Statistics from larger random samples have spreads that are smaller.

We see from the central limit theorem that the sample mean $\overline{x}$ is an unbiased estimator of the mean μ when $n \geq 30$. The variability of $\overline{x}$ decreases as the sample size increases.

In Section 8.3, we will see that the sample proportion $\hat{p}$ is an unbiased estimator of the population proportion of successes p in binomial experiments with sufficiently large numbers of trials n. Again, we will see that the variability of $\hat{p}$ decreases with increasing numbers of trials.

The sample variance s^2 is an unbiased estimator for the population variance σ^2.

VIEWPOINT Chaos!

Is there a different side to random sampling? Can sampling be used as a weapon? According to The Wall Street Journal, *the answer could be yes! The acronym for* Create Havoc Around Our System *is* CHAOS. *The Association of Flight Attendants (AFA) is a union that successfully used CHAOS against Alaska Airlines in 1994 as a negotiation tool.* **CHAOS** *involves a small sample of random strikes—a few flights at a time—instead of a mass walkout. The president of the AFA claims that by striking randomly, "we take control of the schedule." The entire schedule becomes unreliable, and that is something management cannot tolerate. In 1986, TWA flight attendants struck in a mass walkout, and all were permanently replaced! Using* **CHAOS**, *only a few jobs are put at risk, and these are usually not lost. It appears that random sampling can be used as a weapon.*

SECTION 7.5 PROBLEMS

Note: Answers may differ slightly depending on how many digits are carried in the standard deviation.

1. The standard deviation.
2. The standard error.
3. $\overline{x}$ is an unbiased estimator for μ; $\hat{p}$ is an unbiased estimator for p.
4. As the sample size increases, the variability decreases.
5. (a) 30 or more.
   (b) No.

In these problems, the word *average* refers to the arithmetic mean $\overline{x}$ or μ, as appropriate.

1. *Statistical Literacy* What is the standard error of a sampling distribution?

2. *Statistical Literacy* What is the standard deviation of a sampling distribution called?

3. *Statistical Literacy* List two unbiased estimators and their corresponding parameters.

4. *Statistical Literacy* Describe how the variability of the $\overline{x}$ distribution changes as the sample size increases.

5. *Statistical Literacy*
   (a) If we have a distribution of x values that is more or less mound-shaped and somewhat symmetrical, what is the sample size needed to claim that the distribution of sample means $\overline{x}$ from random samples of that size is approximately normal?

(b) If the original distribution of x values is known to be normal, do we need to make any restriction about sample size in order to claim that the distribution of sample means $\overline{x}$ taken from random samples of a given size is normal?

6. *Critical Thinking* Suppose x has a distribution with $\mu = 72$ and $\sigma = 8$.
(a) If random samples of size $n = 16$ are selected, can we say anything about the $\overline{x}$ distribution of sample means?
(b) If the original x distribution is *normal,* can we say anything about the $\overline{x}$ distribution of random samples of size 16? Find $P(68 \le \overline{x} \le 73)$.

6. (a) No, sample size is too small.
(b) Normal with mean 72 and standard deviation 2; 0.6687.

7. *Critical Thinking* Consider two $\overline{x}$ distributions corresponding to the same x distribution. The first $\overline{x}$ distribution is based on samples of size $n = 100$ and the second is based on samples of size $n = 225$. Which $\overline{x}$ distribution has the smaller standard error? Explain.

7. The second. The standard error of the first is $\sigma/10$, while that of the second is $\sigma/15$, where σ is the standard deviation of the original x distribution.

8. *Critical Thinking* Consider an x distribution with standard deviation $\sigma = 12$.
(a) If specifications for a research project require the standard error of the corresponding $\overline{x}$ distribution to be 2, how large does the sample size need to be?
(b) If specifications for a research project require the standard error of the corresponding $\overline{x}$ distribution to be 1, how large does the sample size need to be?

8. (a) $n = 36$, since $\sigma/\sqrt{n} = 12/\sqrt{36} = 2$.
(b) $n = 144$, since $\sigma/\sqrt{n} = 12/\sqrt{144} = 1$.

9. *Critical Thinking* Suppose x has a distribution with $\mu = 15$ and $\sigma = 14$.
(a) If a random sample of size $n = 49$ is drawn, find $\mu_{\overline{x}}$, $\sigma_{\overline{x}}$, and $P(15 \le \overline{x} \le 17)$.
(b) If a random sample of size $n = 64$ is drawn, find $\mu_{\overline{x}}$, $\sigma_{\overline{x}}$, and $P(15 \le \overline{x} \le 17)$.
(c) Why should you expect the probability of part (b) to be higher than that of part (a)? (*Hint:* Consider the standard deviations in parts (a) and (b).)

9. (a) $\mu_{\overline{x}} = 15$; $\sigma_{\overline{x}} = 2.0$; 0.3413.
(b) $\mu_{\overline{x}} = 15$; $\sigma_{\overline{x}} = 1.75$; 0.3729.
(c) The standard deviation of part (b) is smaller, resulting in a narrower distribution.

10. *Critical Thinking* Suppose an x distribution has mean $\mu = 5$. Consider two corresponding $\overline{x}$ distributions, the first based on samples of size $n = 49$ and the second based on samples of size $n = 81$.
(a) What is the value of the mean of each of the two $\overline{x}$ distributions?
(b) For which $\overline{x}$ distribution is $P(\overline{x} > 6)$ smaller? Explain.
(c) For which $\overline{x}$ distribution is $P(4 < \overline{x} < 6)$ greater? Explain.

10. (a) $\mu_{\overline{x}} = 5$.
(b) Distribution with $n = 81$, since the standard deviation is smaller, resulting in a distribution that is less spread out about the mean.
(c) Distribution with $n = 81$, since the standard deviation is smaller, resulting in a distribution that is less spread out about the mean.

11. *Coal: Automatic Loader* Coal is carried from a mine in West Virginia to a power plant in New York in hopper cars on a long train. The automatic hopper car loader is set to put 75 tons of coal into each car. The actual weights of coal loaded into each car are *normally distributed,* with mean $\mu = 75$ tons and standard deviation $\sigma = 0.8$ ton.
(a) What is the probability that one car chosen at random will have less than 74.5 tons of coal?
(b) What is the probability that 20 cars chosen at random will have a mean load weight $\overline{x}$ of less than 74.5 tons of coal?
(c) *Interpretation:* Suppose the weight of coal in one car was less than 74.5 tons. Would that fact make you suspect that the loader had slipped out of adjustment? Suppose the weight of coal in 20 cars selected at random had an average $\overline{x}$ of less than 74.5 tons. Would that fact make you suspect that the loader had slipped out of adjustment? Why?

11. (a) 0.2643.
(b) 0.0026.
(c) No; yes.

12. *Vital Statistics: Heights of Men* The heights of 18-year-old men are approximately *normally distributed,* with mean 68 inches and standard deviation 3 inches (based on information from *Statistical Abstract of the United States,* 112th Edition).
(a) What is the probability that an 18-year-old man selected at random is between 67 and 69 inches tall?
(b) If a random sample of nine 18-year-old men is selected, what is the probability that the mean height $\overline{x}$ is between 67 and 69 inches?
(c) *Interpretation:* Compare your answers to parts (a) and (b). Is the probability in part (b) much higher? Why would you expect this?

12. (a) 0.2586.
(b) 0.6826.
(c) Yes; the standard deviation is smaller for the $\overline{x}$ distribution.

13. *Medical: Blood Glucose* Let x be a random variable that represents the level of glucose in the blood (milligrams per deciliter of blood) after a 12-hour fast.

13. (a) 0.0359.
(b) 0.0054.
(c) 0.0009.
(d) Less than 0.0002.
(e) Yes.

Assume that for people under 50 years old, x has a distribution that is approximately normal, with mean $\mu = 85$ and estimated standard deviation $\sigma = 25$ (based on information from *Diagnostic Tests with Nursing Applications*, edited by S. Loeb, Springhouse). A test result of $x < 40$ is an indication of severe excess insulin, and medication is usually prescribed.

(a) What is the probability that, on a single test, $x < 40$?
(b) Suppose a doctor uses the average $\bar{x}$ for two tests taken about a week apart. What can we say about the probability distribution of $\bar{x}$? *Hint:* See Theorem 7.1. What is the probability that $\bar{x} < 40$?
(c) Repeat part (b) for $n = 3$ tests taken a week apart.
(d) Repeat part (b) for $n = 5$ tests taken a week apart.
(e) *Interpretation:* Compare your answers to parts (a), (b), (c), and (d). Did the probabilities decrease as n increased? Explain what this might imply if you were a doctor or a nurse. If a patient had a test result of $\bar{x} < 40$ based on five tests, explain why either you are looking at an extremely rare event or (more likely) the person has a case of excess insulin.

14. (a) 0.0110.
(b) 0.0006.
(c) Less than 0.0002.
(d) The probabilities decreased as n increased. It would be an extremely rare event for a person to have two or three tests below 3500 purely by chance.

14. *Medical: White Blood Cells* Let x be a random variable that represents white blood cell count per cubic milliliter of whole blood. Assume that x has a distribution that is approximately normal, with mean $\mu = 7500$ and estimated standard deviation $\sigma = 1750$ (see reference in Problem 13). A test result of $x < 3500$ is an indication of leukopenia. This indicates bone marrow depression that may be the result of a viral infection.

(a) What is the probability that, on a single test, x is less than 3500?
(b) Suppose a doctor uses the average $\bar{x}$ for two tests taken about a week apart. What can we say about the probability distribution of $\bar{x}$? What is the probability of $\bar{x} < 3500$?
(c) Repeat part (b) for $n = 3$ tests taken a week apart.
(d) *Interpretation:* Compare your answers to parts (a), (b), and (c). How did the probabilities change as n increased? If a person had $\bar{x} < 3500$ based on three tests, what conclusion would you draw as a doctor or a nurse?

15. (a) 0.1020.
(b) 224.
(c) 0.0014.
(d) 0.8849. Unlikely.

15. *Wildlife: Deer* Let x be a random variable that represents the weights in kilograms (kg) of healthy adult female deer (does) in December in Mesa Verde National Park. Then x has a distribution that is approximately normal with mean $\mu = 63.0$ kg and standard deviation $\sigma = 7.1$ kg (Source: *The Mule Deer of Mesa Verde National Park,* by G. W. Mierau and J. L. Schmidt, Mesa Verde Museum Association). Suppose a doe that weighs less than 54 kg is considered undernourished.

(a) What is the probability that a single doe captured (weighed and released) at random in December is undernourished?
(b) If the park has about 2200 does, what number do you expect to be undernourished in December?
(c) *Interpretation:* To estimate the health of the December doe population, park rangers use the rule that the average weight of $n = 50$ does should be more than 60 kg. If the average weight is less than 60 kg, it is thought that the entire population of does might be undernourished. What is the probability that the average weight $\bar{x}$ for a random sample of 50 does is less than 60 kg (assuming a healthy population)?
(d) *Interpretation:* Compute the probability that $\bar{x} < 64.2$ kg for 50 does (assuming a healthy population). Suppose park rangers captured, weighed, and released 50 does in December, and the average weight was $\bar{x} = 64.2$ kg. Do you think the doe population is undernourished or not? Explain.

16. (a) Approximately normal, with mean \$20 and standard deviation \$0.70.
(b) 0.9958.
(c) 0.2282.
(d) Essay.

16. *Focus Problem: Impulse Buying* Let x represent the dollar amount spent on supermarket impulse buying in a 10-minute (unplanned) shopping interval. Based on a *Denver Post* article, the mean of the x distribution is about \$20 and the estimated standard deviation is about \$7.

(a) Consider a random sample of $n = 100$ customers, each of whom has 10 minutes of unplanned shopping time in a supermarket. From the central limit theorem, what can you say about the probability distribution of $\bar{x}$, the average amount spent by these customers due to impulse buying? What are the mean and standard deviation of the $\bar{x}$ distribution? Is it necessary to make any assumption about the x distribution? Explain.
(b) What is the probability that $\bar{x}$ is between \$18 and \$22?
(c) Let us assume that x has a distribution that is approximately normal. What is the probability that x is between \$18 and \$22?
(d) *Interpretation:* In part (b), we used $\bar{x}$, the *average* amount spent, computed for 100 customers. In part (c), we used x, the amount spent by only *one* customer. The answers to parts (b) and (c) are very different. Why would this happen? In this example, $\bar{x}$ is a much more predictable or reliable statistic than x. Consider that almost all marketing strategies and sales pitches are designed for the *average* customer and *not the individual* customer. How does the central limit theorem tell us that the average customer is much more predictable than the individual customer?

Problem 17 requires a little extra attention to detail. Discussing this problem in class would be useful. In particular, point out that in part (a), the random variable x is itself an average based on the number of stocks or bonds in the fund. In part (b), the random variable is $\bar{x}$, an average based on the specified number of months or years. For part (b), point out that n = number of specified months or years.

17. (a) x is a mean of a sample of size $n = 250$. By the central limit theorem, the x distribution is approximately normal.
(b) 0.8105.
(c) 0.9849.
(d) Yes.
(e) 0.0005. Unlikely.

17. *Finance: Templeton Funds* Templeton World is a mutual fund that invests in both U.S. and foreign markets. Let x be a random variable that represents the monthly percentage return for the Templeton World fund. Based on information from the *Morningstar Guide to Mutual Funds* (available in most libraries), x has mean $\mu = 1.6\%$ and standard deviation $\sigma = 0.9\%$.
(a) Templeton World fund has over 250 stocks that combine together to give the overall monthly percentage return x. We can consider the monthly return of the stocks in the fund to be a sample from the population of monthly returns of all world stocks. Then we see that the overall monthly return x for Templeton World fund is itself an average return computed using all 250 stocks in the fund. Why would this indicate that x has an approximately normal distribution? Explain. *Hint:* See the discussion after Theorem 7.2.
(b) After 6 months, what is the probability that the *average* monthly percentage return $\bar{x}$ will be between 1% and 2%? *Hint:* See Theorem 7.1, and assume that x has a normal distribution as based on part (a).
(c) After 2 years, what is the probability that $\bar{x}$ will be between 1% and 2%?
(d) Compare your answers to parts (b) and (c). Did the probability increase as n (number of months) increased? Why would this happen?
(e) *Interpretation:* If after 2 years the average monthly percentage return $\bar{x}$ was less than 1%, would that tend to shake your confidence in the statement that $\mu = 1.6\%$? Might you suspect that μ has slipped below 1.6%? Explain.

SECTION 7.6 Normal Approximation to the Binomial Distribution

FOCUS POINTS

- State the assumptions needed to use the normal approximation to the binomial distribution.
- Compute μ and σ for the normal approximation.
- Use the continuity correction to convert a range of r values to a corresponding range of normal x values.
- Convert the x values to a range of standardized z scores and find desired probabilities.

The probability that a new vaccine will protect adults from cholera is known to be 0.85. The vaccine is administered to 300 adults who must enter an area where the disease is prevalent. What is the probability that more than 280 of these adults will be protected from cholera by the vaccine?

This question falls into the category of a binomial experiment with the number of trials n equal to 300, the probability of success p equal to 0.85, and the number of successes r greater than 280. It is possible to use the formula for the binomial distribution to compute the probability that r is greater than 280. However, this approach would involve a number of tedious and long calculations. There is an easier way to do this problem, for under the conditions stated below, the normal distribution can be used to approximate the binomial distribution.

Criteria $np > 5$ and $nq > 5$

Section 7.6 provides another application of the normal distribution. In this section, we present the normal approximation to the binomial distribution. In Chapter 8, the normal approximation to the related probability distribution of $\hat{p} = r/n$ will be presented.

Normal approximation to the binomial distribution

Consider a binomial distribution where

n = number of trials

r = number of successes

p = probability of success on a single trial

$q = 1 - p$ = probability of failure on a single trial

If $np > 5$ and $nq > 5$, then r has a binomial distribution that is approximated by a normal distribution with

$$\mu = np \quad \text{and} \quad \sigma = \sqrt{npq}$$

Note: As n increases, the approximation becomes better.

Example 12 demonstrates that as n increases, the normal approximation to the binomial distribution improves.

EXAMPLE 12 BINOMIAL DISTRIBUTION GRAPHS

Graph the binomial distributions for which $p = 0.25$, $q = 0.75$, and the number of trials is first $n = 3$, then $n = 10$, then $n = 25$, and finally $n = 50$.

SOLUTION: The authors used a computer program to obtain the binomial distributions for the given values of p, q, and n. The results have been organized and graphed in Figures 7-31, 7-32, 7-33, and 7-34.

When $n = 3$, the outline of the histogram does not even begin to take the shape of a normal curve. But when $n = 10$, 25, or 50, it does begin to take a normal shape, indicated by the red curve. From a theoretical point of view, the histograms in Figures 7-32, 7-33, and 7-34 would have bars for all values of r from $r = 0$ to $r = n$. However, in the construction of these histograms, the bars of height less than 0.001 unit have been omitted—that is, in this example, probabilities less than 0.001 have been rounded to 0.

FIGURE 7-31

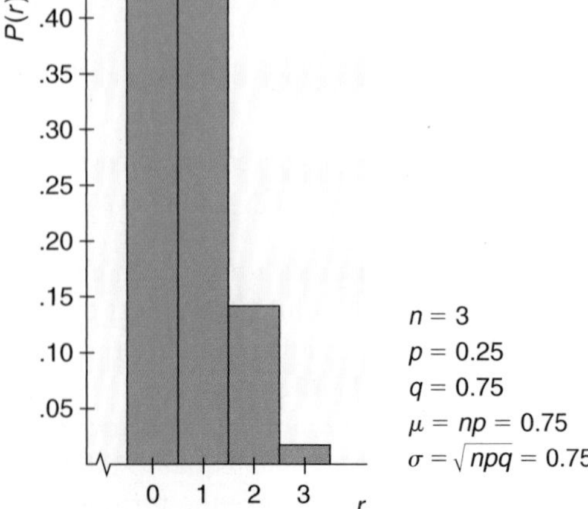

FIGURE 7-32

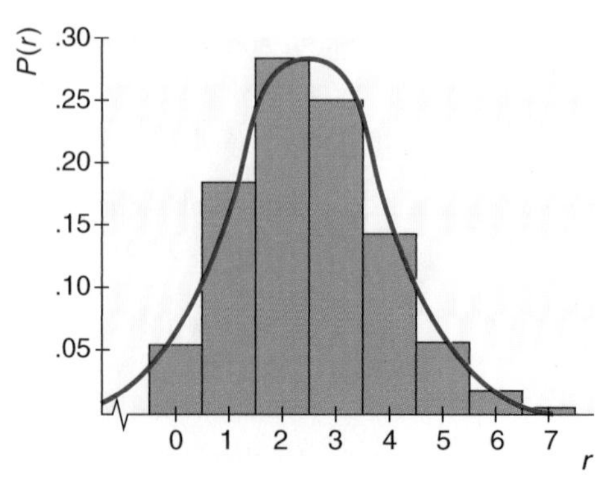

FIGURE 7-33 Good Normal Approximation; $np > 5$ and $nq > 5$

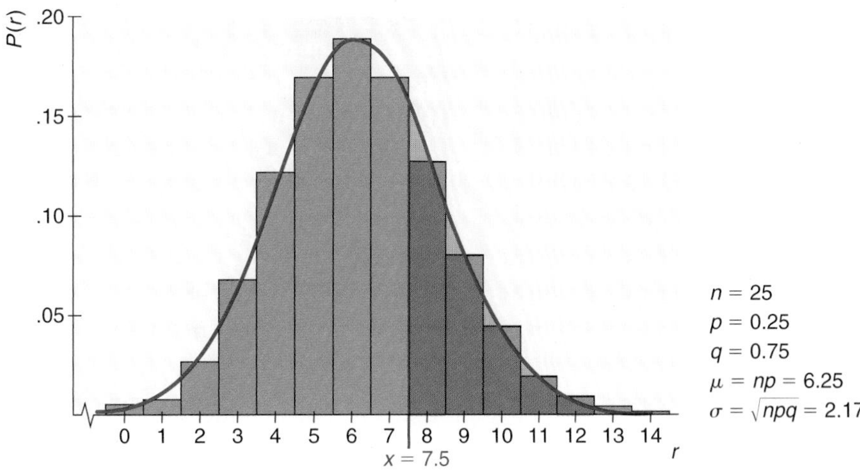

FIGURE 7-34 Good Normal Approximation; $np > 5$ and $nq > 5$

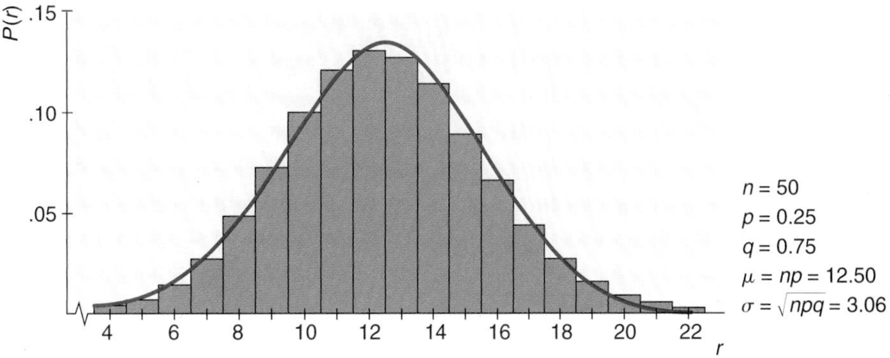

EXAMPLE 13 NORMAL APPROXIMATION

The owner of a new apartment building must install 25 water heaters. From past experience in other apartment buildings, she knows that Quick Hot is a good brand. A Quick Hot heater is guaranteed for 5 years only, but from the owner's past experience, she knows that the probability it will last 10 years is 0.25.

(a) What is the probability that 8 or more of the 25 water heaters will last at least 10 years? Define success to mean a water heater lasts at least 10 years.

SOLUTION: In this example, $n = 25$ and $p = 0.25$, so Figure 7-33 represents the probability distribution we will use. Let r be the binomial random variable corresponding to the number of successes out of $n = 25$ trials. We want to find $P(r \geq 8)$ by using the normal approximation. This probability is represented graphically (Figure 7-33) by the area of the bar over $r = 8$ plus the areas of all bars to the right of the bar over $r = 8$.

The process of treating the area of the bar over r as an area from $r - 0.5$ to $r + 0.5$ is often referred to as the *continuity correction* to the normal approximation.

Let x be a normal random variable corresponding to a normal distribution with $\mu = np = 25(0.25) = 6.25$ and $\sigma = \sqrt{npq} = \sqrt{25(0.25)(0.75)} \approx 2.17$. This normal curve is represented by the red line in Figure 7-33. The area under the normal curve from $x = 7.5$ to the right is approximately the same as the areas of the bars from the bar over $r = 8$ to the right. It is important to notice that we start with $x = 7.5$ because the bar over $r = 8$ really starts at $x = 7.5$.

The areas of the bars and the area under the corresponding red (normal) curve are approximately equal, so we conclude that $P(r \geq 8)$ is approximately equal to $P(x \geq 7.5)$.

When we convert $x = 7.5$ to standard units, we get

$$z = \frac{x - \mu}{\sigma} = \frac{7.5 - 6.25}{2.17} \qquad \text{(Use } \mu = 6.25 \text{ and } \sigma = 2.17.\text{)}$$
$$\approx 0.58$$

The probability we want is

$$P(x \geq 7.5) = P(z \geq 0.58) = 1 - P(z \leq 0.58) = 1 - 0.7190 = 0.2810$$

(b) How does this result compare with the result we can obtain by using the formula for the binomial probability distribution with $n = 25$ and $p = 0.25$?

SOLUTION: Using the binomial distribution function on the TI-84Plus/ TI-83Plus model calculators, the authors computed that $P(r \geq 8) \approx 0.2735$. This means that the probability is approximately 0.27 that 8 or more water heaters will last at least 10 years.

(c) How do the results of parts (a) and (b) compare?

SOLUTION: The error of approximation is the difference between the approximate normal value (0.2810) and the binomial value (0.2735). The error is only $0.2810 - 0.2735 = 0.0075$, which is negligible for most practical purposes.

We knew in advance that the normal approximation to the binomial probability would be good, since $np = 25(0.25) = 6.25$ and $nq = 25(0.75) = 18.75$ are both greater than 5. These are the conditions that assure us that the normal approximation will be sufficiently close to the binomial probability for most practical purposes.

Continuity correction: converting r values to x values

Remember that when we use the normal distribution to approximate the binomial, we are computing the areas under bars. The bar over the discrete variable r extends from $r - 0.5$ to $r + 0.5$. This means that the corresponding continuous normal variable x extends from $r - 0.5$ to $r + 0.5$. Adjusting the values of discrete random variables to obtain a corresponding range for a continuous random variable is called making a *continuity correction*.

PROCEDURE

HOW TO MAKE THE CONTINUITY CORRECTION

Convert the discrete random variable r (number of successes) to the continuous normal random variable x by doing the following:

1. If r is a **left point** of an interval, subtract 0.5 to obtain the corresponding normal variable x; that is, $x = r - 0.5$.
2. If r is a **right point** of an interval, add 0.5 to obtain the corresponding normal variable x: that is, $x = r + 0.5$.

For instance, $P(6 \leq r \leq 10)$, where r is a binomial random variable, is approximated by $P(5.5 \leq x \leq 10.5)$, where x is the corresponding normal random variable (see Figure 7-35).

FIGURE 7-35

$P(6 \leq r \leq 10)$ Is Approximately Equal to $P(5.5 \leq x \leq 10.5)$

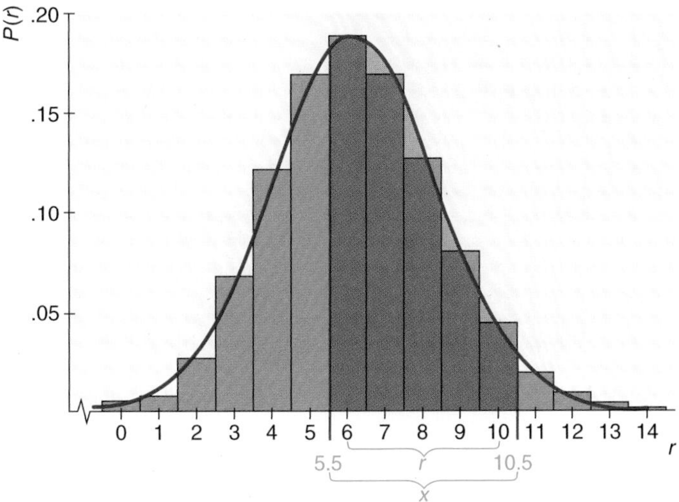

GUIDED EXERCISE 11 Continuity correction

From many years of observation, a biologist knows that the probability is only 0.65 that any given Arctic tern will survive the migration from its summer nesting area to its winter feeding grounds. A random sample of 500 Arctic terns were banded at their summer nesting area. Use the normal approximation to the binomial and the following steps to find the probability that between 310 and 340 of the banded Arctic terns will survive the migration. Let r be the number of surviving terns.

Arctic tern

(a) To approximate $P(310 \leq r \leq 340)$, we use the normal curve with $\mu =$ _______ and $\sigma =$ _______.

→ We use the normal curve with

$\mu = np = 500(0.65) = 325$ and

$\sigma = \sqrt{npq} = \sqrt{500(0.65)(0.35)} \approx 10.67$

(b) $P(310 \leq r \leq 340)$ is approximately equal to $P($_______$\leq x \leq$_______$)$, where x is a variable from the normal distribution described in part (a).

→ Since 310 is the left endpoint, we subtract 0.5, and since 340 is the right endpoint, we add 0.5. Consequently,

$P(310 \leq r \leq 340) \approx P(309.5 \leq x \leq 340.5)$

(c) Convert the condition $309.5 \leq x \leq 340.5$ to a condition in standard units.

→ Since $\mu = 325$ and $\sigma \approx 10.67$, the condition $309.5 \leq x \leq 340.5$ becomes

$$\frac{309.5 - 325}{10.67} \leq z \leq \frac{340.5 - 325}{10.67}$$

or

$-1.45 \leq z \leq 1.45$

(d) $P(310 \leq r \leq 340) = P(309.5 \leq x \leq 340.5)$
$= P(-1.45 \leq z \leq 1.45)$
$=$ _______

→ $P(-1.45 \leq z \leq 1.45) = P(z \leq 1.45) - P(z \leq -1.45)$
$= 0.9265 - 0.0735$
$= 0.8530$

Continued

GUIDED EXERCISE 11 *continued*

(e) Will the normal distribution make a good approximation to the binomial for this problem? Explain your answer.

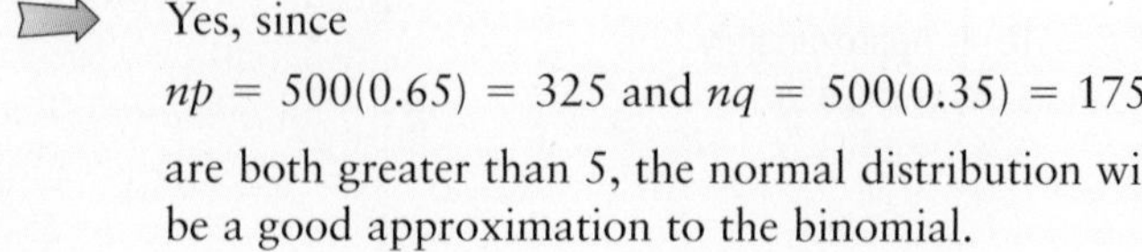

Yes, since

$np = 500(0.65) = 325$ and $nq = 500(0.35) = 175$

are both greater than 5, the normal distribution will be a good approximation to the binomial.

VIEWPOINT | Sunspots, Tree Rings, and Statistics

Ancient Chinese astronomers recorded extreme sunspot activity, with a peak around 1200 A.D. Mesa Verde tree rings in the period between 1276 and 1299 were unusually narrow, indicating a drought and/or a severe cold spell in the region at that time. A cooling trend could have narrowed the window of frost-free days below the approximately 80 days needed for cultivation of aboriginal corn and beans. Is this the reason the ancient Anasazi dwellings in Mesa Verde were abandoned? Is there a connection to the extreme sunspot activity? Much research and statistical work continues to be done on this topic.

Reference: *Prehistoric Astronomy in the Southwest,* by J. McKim Malville and C. Putnam, Department of Astronomy, University of Colorado.

SECTION 7.6 PROBLEMS

Tables and art to accompany margin answers may be found in the back of the book.

1. $np > 5$ and $nq > 5$, where $q = 1 - p$.
2. The binomial distribution is a probability of a discrete random variable, whereas the normal distribution is a probability of a continuous random variable.
3. No, $np = 4.3$ and does not satisfy the criterion that $np > 5$.
4. (a) 0.159 (from Table 2 of the Appendix). (b) $\mu = 9$; $\sigma \approx 2.225$; 0.1615. (c) Difference of about 0.003.
5. $np > 5$; $nq > 5$. (a) Approximately 1, or almost certain. (b) Approximately 0, or almost impossible.
6. $np > 5$; $nq > 5$. (a) 0.0132. (b) 0.1131. (c) 0.9744. (d) 0.2514.

Note: When we say *between a* and *b,* we mean every value from *a* to *b, including a* and *b*. Due to rounding, your answers might vary slightly from answers given in the text.

1. *Statistical Literacy* Binomial probability distributions depend on the number of trials n of a binomial experiment and the probability of success p on each trial. Under what conditions is it appropriate to use a normal approximation to the binomial?

2. *Statistical Literacy* When we use a normal distribution to approximate a binomial distribution, why do we make a continuity correction?

3. *Critical Thinking* You need to compute the probability of 5 or fewer successes for a binomial experiment with 10 trials. The probability of success on a single trial is 0.43. Since this probability of success is not in the table, you decide to use the normal approximation to the binomial. Is this an appropriate strategy? Explain.

4. *Critical Thinking* Consider a binomial experiment with 20 trials and probability 0.45 of success on a single trial.
   (a) Use the binomial distribution to find the probability of exactly 10 successes.
   (b) Use the normal distribution to approximate the probability of exactly 10 successes.
   (c) Compare the results of parts (a) and (b).

In the following problems, check that it is appropriate to use the normal approximation to the binomial. Then use the normal distribution to estimate the requested probabilities.

5. *Health: Lead Contamination* More than a decade ago, high levels of lead in the blood put 88% of children at risk. A concerted effort was made to remove lead from the environment. Now, according to the *Third National Health and Nutrition Examination Survey (NHANES III)* conducted by the Centers for Disease Control, only 9% of children in the United States are at risk of high blood-lead levels.
   (a) In a random sample of 200 children taken more than a decade ago, what is the probability that 50 or more had high blood-lead levels?
   (b) In a random sample of 200 children taken now, what is the probability that 50 or more have high blood-lead levels?

6. *Insurance: Claims* Do you try to *pad* an insurance claim to cover your deductible? About 40% of all U.S. adults will try to pad their insurance claims! (Source: *Are*

You Normal?, by Bernice Kanner, St. Martin's Press.) Suppose that you are the director of an insurance adjustment office. Your office has just received 128 insurance claims to be processed in the next few days. What is the probability that
(a) half or more of the claims have been padded?
(b) fewer than 45 of the claims have been padded?
(c) from 40 to 64 of the claims have been padded?
(d) more than 80 of the claims have *not* been padded?

7. $np > 5$; $nq > 5$.
(a) 0.9906.
(b) 0.2676.
(c) 0.6092.
(d) 0.0026.

7. *Longevity: 90th Birthday* It is estimated that 3.5% of the general population will live past their 90th birthday (*Statistical Abstract of the United States*, 112th Edition). In a graduating class of 753 high school seniors, what is the probability that
(a) 15 or more will live beyond their 90th birthday?
(b) 30 or more will live beyond their 90th birthday?
(c) between 25 and 35 will live beyond their 90th birthday?
(d) more than 40 will live beyond their 90th birthday?

8. $np > 5$; $nq > 5$.
(a) 0.7881.
(b) 0.9936.
(c) 0.7817.

8. *Fishing: Billfish* Ocean fishing for billfish is very popular in the Cozumel region of Mexico. In *World Record Game Fishes* (published by the International Game Fish Association), it was stated that in the Cozumel region about 44% of strikes (while trolling) resulted in a catch. Suppose that on a given day a fleet of fishing boats got a total of 24 strikes. What is the probability that the number of fish caught was
(a) 12 or fewer?
(b) 5 or more?
(c) between 5 and 12?

9. $np > 5$; $nq > 5$.
(a) 0.9738.
(b) 0.9599.
(c) 0.3446.
(d) 0.1271.

9. *Grocery Stores: New Products* The *Denver Post* stated that 80% of all new products introduced in grocery stores fail (are taken off the market) within 2 years. If a grocery store chain introduces 66 new products, what is the probability that within 2 years
(a) 47 or more fail?
(b) 58 or fewer fail?
(c) 15 or more succeed?
(d) fewer than 10 succeed?

10. $np > 5$; $nq > 5$.
(a) 0.9370.
(b) 0.9842.
(c) 0.9633.
(d) 0.7157.

10. *Crime: Murder* What are the chances that a person who is murdered actually knew the murderer? The answer to this question explains why a lot of police detective work begins with relatives and friends of the victim! About 64% of people who are murdered actually knew the person who committed the murder (*Chances: Risk and Odds in Everyday Life*, by James Burke). Suppose that a detective file in New Orleans has 63 current unsolved murders. What is the probability that
(a) at least 35 of the victims knew their murderers?
(b) at most 48 of the victims knew their murderers?
(c) fewer than 30 victims did *not* know their murderers?
(d) more than 20 victims did *not* know their murderers?

Problems 11 and 12 ask students to recall some probability rules from Section 5.2.

11. $np > 5$; $nq > 5$.
(a) 0.8665.
(b) 0.8577.
(c) 0.222.
(d) 0.8439.

11. *Supermarkets: Free Samples* Do you take the free samples offered in supermarkets? About 60% of all customers will take free samples. Furthermore, of those who take the free samples, about 37% will buy what they have sampled. (See reference in Problem 6.) Suppose you set up a counter in a supermarket offering free samples of a new product. The day you were offering free samples, 317 customers passed by your counter.
(a) What is the probability that more than 180 will take your free sample?
(b) What is the probability that fewer than 200 will take your free sample?
(c) What is the probability that a customer will take a free sample *and* buy the product? *Hint:* Use the multiplication rule for *dependent* events. Notice that we are given the conditional probability $P(\text{buy}|\text{sample}) = 0.37$, while $P(\text{sample}) = 0.60$.
(d) What is the probability that between 60 and 80 customers will take the free sample *and* buy the product? *Hint:* Use the probability of success calculated in part (c).

12. $np > 5$; $nq > 5$.
(a) 0.1587.
(b) 0.8686.
(c) 0.3175.
(d) 0.6246.

12. *Ice Cream: Flavors* What's your favorite ice cream flavor? For people who buy ice cream, the all-time favorite is still vanilla. About 25% of ice cream sales are vanilla. Chocolate accounts for only 9% of ice cream sales. (See reference in Problem 6.) Suppose that 175 customers go to a grocery store in Cheyenne, Wyoming, today to buy ice cream.
(a) What is the probability that 50 or more will buy vanilla?
(b) What is the probability that 12 or more will buy chocolate?
(c) A customer who buys ice cream is not limited to one container or one flavor. What is the probability that someone who is buying ice cream will buy chocolate or vanilla? *Hint:* Chocolate flavor and vanilla flavor are not mutually exclusive events. Assume that the choice to buy one flavor is independent of the choice to buy another flavor. Then use the multiplication rule for independent events, together with the addition rule for events that are not mutually exclusive, to compute the requested probability. (See Section 5.2.)
(d) What is the probability that between 50 and 60 customers will buy chocolate or vanilla ice cream? *Hint:* Use the probability of success computed in part (c).

In this problem, note that the normal approximation to the binomial is based on $n = 267$ reservations with $p = 0.94$.

13. $np > 5$; $nq > 5$.
(a) 0.94.
(b) $P(r \leq 255)$.
(c) 0.8770.

13. *Airline Flights: No-Shows* Based on long experience, an airline found that about 6% of the people making reservations on a flight from Miami to Denver do not show up for the flight. Suppose the airline overbooks this flight by selling 267 ticket reservations for an airplane with only 255 seats.
(a) What is the probability that a person holding a reservation will show up for the flight?
(b) Let $n = 267$ represent the number of ticket reservations. Let r represent the number of people with reservations who show up for the flight. Which expression represents the probability that a seat will be available for everyone who shows up holding a reservation?

$$P(255 \leq r); \quad P(r \leq 255); \quad P(r \leq 267); \quad P(r = 255)$$

(c) Use the normal approximation to the binomial distribution and part (b) to answer the following question: What is the probability that a seat will be available for every person who shows up holding a reservation?

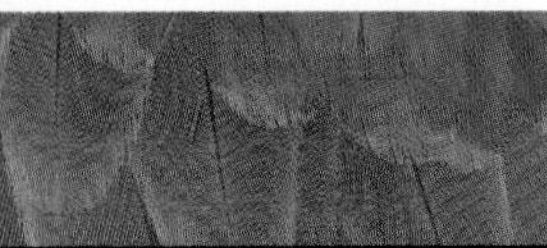

Chapter Review

SUMMARY

In this chapter, we examined properties and applications of the normal probability distribution.

- A normal probability distribution is a distribution of a continuous random variable. Normal distributions are bell-shaped and symmetric around the mean. The high point occurs over the mean, and most of the area occurs within 3 standard deviations of the mean. The mean and median are equal.
- The empirical rule for normal distributions gives areas within 1, 2, and 3 standard deviations of the mean. Approximately

  68% of the data lie within the interval $\mu \pm \sigma$

  95% of the data lie within the interval $\mu \pm 2\sigma$

  99.7% of the data lie within the interval $\mu \pm 3\sigma$
- For symmetric, bell-shaped distributions,

$$\text{standard deviation} \approx \frac{\text{range of data}}{4}$$

- A z-score measures the number of standard deviations a raw score x lies from the mean.

$$z = \frac{x - \mu}{\sigma} \quad \text{and} \quad x = z\sigma + \mu$$

- For the standard normal distribution, $\mu = 0$ and $\sigma = 1$.
- Table 3 of the Appendix gives areas under a standard normal distribution that are to the left of a specified value of z.
- After raw scores x have been converted to z scores, the standard normal distribution table can be used to find probabilities associated with intervals of x values from any normal distribution.

- The inverse normal distribution is used to find z values associated with areas to the left of z. Table 3 of the Appendix can be used to find approximate z values associated with specific probabilities.
- Tools for assessing the normality of a data distribution include:

  Histogram of the data. A roughly bell-shaped histogram indicates normality.

  Presence of outliers. A limited number indicates normality.

  Skewness. For normality, Pearson's index is between -1 and 1.

  Normal quantile plot. For normality, points lie close to a straight line.

Sampling distributions give us the basis for inferential statistics. By studying the distribution of a sample statistic, we can learn about the corresponding population parameter.

- For random samples of size n, the $\bar{x}$ distribution is the sampling distribution for the sample mean of an x distribution with population mean μ and population standard deviation σ. If the x distribution is normal, then the corresponding $\bar{x}$ distribution is normal.

  By the central limit theorem, when n is sufficiently large ($n \geq 30$), the $\bar{x}$ distribution is approximately normal even if the original x distribution is not normal.

  In both cases,

$$\mu_{\bar{x}} = \mu$$

$$\sigma_{\bar{x}} = \frac{\sigma}{\sqrt{n}}$$

- The binomial distribution can be approximated by a normal distribution with $\mu = np$ and $\sigma = \sqrt{npq}$ provided

  $np > 5$ and $nq > 5$, with $q = 1 - p$

  and a continuity correction is made.

Data from many applications follow distributions that are approximately normal. We will see normal distributions used extensively in later chapters.

IMPORTANT WORDS & SYMBOLS

Section 7.1
Normal distribution
Normal curve
Upward cup and downward cup on normal curve
Symmetry of normal curve
Empirical rule

Section 7.2
z value or z score
Standard units
Standard normal distribution ($\mu = 0$ and $\sigma = 1$)
Raw score, x
Area under the standard normal curve

Section 7.3
Areas under any normal curve
Normality indicators

Section 7.4
Population parameter
Statistic
Sampling distribution

Section 7.5
$\mu_{\bar{x}}$
$\sigma_{\bar{x}}$
Standard error of the mean
Central limit theorem

Section 7.6
Normal approximation to the binomial distribution
Continuity correction

VIEWPOINT Nenana Ice Classic

The Nenana Ice Classic is a betting pool offering a large cash prize to the lucky winner who can guess the time, to the nearest minute, of the ice breakup on the Tanana River in the town of Nenana, Alaska. Official breakup time is defined as the time when the surging river dislodges a tripod on the ice. This breaks an attached line and stops a clock set to Yukon Standard Time. The event is so popular that the first state legislature of Alaska (1959) made the Nenana Ice Classic an official statewide lottery. Since 1918, the earliest breakup was April 20, 1940, at 3:27 P.M., and the latest recorded breakup was May 20, 1964, at 11:41 A.M. Want to make a statistical guess predicting when the ice will break up? Breakup times from 1918 to 1996 are recorded in The Alaska Almanac, *published by Alaska Northwest Books, Anchorage.*

CHAPTER REVIEW PROBLEMS

Tables and art to accompany margin answers may be found in the back of the book.

1. Normal probability distributions are distributions of continuous random variables. They are symmetric about the mean and bell-shaped. Most of the data fall within 3 standard deviations of the mean. The mean and median are the same.
2. 68% within 1 standard deviation of μ; 95% within 2 standard deviations of μ; 99.7% within 3 standard deviations of μ.
3. No, the probability is only about 2.5%.
4. No, np and nq must both be greater than 5.
5. (a) A normal distribution.
   (b) The mean μ of the x distribution.
   (c) $\sigma/\sqrt{n}$, where σ is the standard deviation of the x distribution.
   (d) Approximately normal with the same mean, but the standard deviations will be $\sigma/\sqrt{50}$ and $\sigma/\sqrt{100}$, respectively.
6. All the $\bar{x}$ distributions will be normal with mean 15. The standard deviations will be 3/2, 3/4, and 3/10, respectively.
7. (a) 0.9821.
   (b) 0.3156.
   (c) 0.2977.
8. (a) 0.7967.
   (b) 0.9938.
   (c) 0.2865.
9. 1.645.
10. ± 2.58.
11. (a) 0.89.
    (b) 0.
    (c) 0.2514.
12. (a) 336.5.
    (b) 261.25.
    (c) 0.9544.
13. (a) 0.0166.
    (b) 0.9750.

1. *Statistical Literacy* Describe a normal probability distribution.

2. *Statistical Literacy* According to the empirical rule, approximately what percentage of the area under a normal distribution lies within 1 standard deviation of the mean? within 2 standard deviations? within 3 standard deviations?

3. *Statistical Literacy* For a normal distribution, is it likely that a data value selected at random is more than 2 standard deviations above the mean?

4. *Statistical Literacy* Can a normal distribution always be used to approximate a binomial distribution? Explain.

5. ***Critical Thinking*** Let x be a random variable representing the amount of sleep each adult in New York City got last night. Consider a sampling distribution of sample means $\bar{x}$.
   (a) As the sample size becomes increasingly large, what distribution does the $\bar{x}$ distribution approach?
   (b) As the sample size becomes increasingly large, what value will the mean $\mu_{\bar{x}}$ of the $\bar{x}$ distribution approach?
   (c) What value will the standard deviation $\sigma_{\bar{x}}$ of the sampling distribution approach?
   (d) How do the two $\bar{x}$ distributions for sample size $n = 50$ and $n = 100$ compare?

6. ***Critical Thinking*** If x has a normal distribution with mean $\mu = 15$ and standard deviation $\sigma = 3$, describe the distribution of $\bar{x}$ values for sample size n, where $n = 4$, $n = 16$, and $n = 100$. How do the $\bar{x}$ distributions compare for the various sample sizes?

7. Given that x is a normal variable with mean $\mu = 47$ and standard deviation $\sigma = 6.2$, find
   (a) $P(x \leq 60)$ (b) $P(x \geq 50)$ (c) $P(50 \leq x \leq 60)$

8. Given that x is a normal variable with mean $\mu = 110$ and standard deviation $\sigma = 12$, find
   (a) $P(x \leq 120)$ (b) $P(x \geq 80)$ (c) $P(108 \leq x \leq 117)$

9. Find z such that 5% of the area under the standard normal curve lies to the right of z.

10. Find z such that 99% of the area under the standard normal curve lies between $-z$ and z.

11. *Nursing: Exams* On a practical nursing licensing exam, the mean score is 79 and the standard deviation is 9 points.
    (a) What is the standardized score of a student with a raw score of 87?
    (b) What is the standardized score of a student with a raw score of 79?
    (c) Assuming the scores follow a normal distribution, what is the probability that a score selected at random is above 85?

12. *Aptitude Tests: Mechanical* On an auto mechanic aptitude test, the mean score is 270 points and the standard deviation is 35 points.
    (a) If a student has a standardized score of 1.9, how many points is that?
    (b) If a student has a standardized score of -0.25, how many points is that?
    (c) Assuming the scores follow a normal distribution, what is the probability that a student will get between 200 and 340 points?

13. *Recycling: Aluminum Cans* One environmental group did a study of recycling habits in a California community. It found that 70% of the aluminum cans sold in the area were recycled.
    (a) If 400 cans are sold today, what is the probability that 300 or more will be recycled?

(b) Of the 400 cans sold, what is the probability that between 260 and 300 will be recycled?

14. (a) 0.5000.
(b) 4260 hours.

14. *Guarantee: Disc Players* Future Electronics makes compact disc players. Its research department found that the life of the laser beam device is normally distributed, with mean 5000 hours and standard deviation 450 hours.
(a) Find the probability that the laser beam device will wear out in 5000 hours or less.
(b) *Inverse Normal Distribution* Future Electronics wants to place a guarantee on the players so that no more than 5% fail during the guarantee period. Because the laser pickup is the part most likely to wear out first, the guarantee period will be based on the life of the laser beam device. How many playing hours should the guarantee cover? (Round to the next playing hour.)

15. (a) 0.9772.
(b) 17.3 hours.

15. *Guarantee: Package Delivery* Express Courier Service has found that the delivery time for packages is normally distributed, with mean 14 hours and standard deviation 2 hours.
(a) For a package selected at random, what is the probability that it will be delivered in 18 hours or less?
(b) *Inverse Normal Distribution* What should be the guaranteed delivery time on all packages in order to be 95% sure that the package will be delivered before this time? (*Hint:* Note that 5% of the packages will be delivered at a time beyond the guaranteed time period.)

16. (a) 0.8665.
(b) 0.7330.

16. *Medical: Blood Type* Blood type AB is found in only 3% of the population (*Textbook of Medical Physiology,* by A. Guyton, M.D.). If 250 people are chosen at random, what is the probability that
(a) 5 or more will have this blood type?
(b) between 5 and 10 will have this blood type?

17. (a) 0.2389.
(b) 0.0162.

17. *Job Interview: Length* The personnel office at a large electronics firm regularly schedules job interviews and maintains records of the interviews. From the past records, they have found that the length of a first interview is normally distributed, with mean $\mu = 35$ minutes and standard deviation $\sigma = 7$ minutes.
(a) What is the probability that a first interview will last 40 minutes or longer?
(b) Nine first interviews are usually scheduled per day. What is the probability that the average length of time for the nine interviews will be 40 minutes or longer?

18. (a) 0.2743.
(b) 0.0287.
(c) The standard deviation of $\bar{x}$ is smaller.

18. *Drugs: Effects* A new muscle relaxant is available. Researchers from the firm developing the relaxant have done studies that indicate that the time lapse between administration of the drug and beginning effects of the drug is normally distributed, with mean $\mu = 38$ minutes and standard deviation $\sigma = 5$ minutes.
(a) The drug is administered to one patient selected at random. What is the probability that the time it takes to go into effect is 35 minutes or less?
(b) The drug is administered to a random sample of 10 patients. What is the probability that the average time before it is effective for all 10 patients is 35 minutes or less?
(c) Comment on the differences of the results in parts (a) and (b).

19. 0.8164.

19. *Psychology: IQ Scores* Assume that IQ scores are normally distributed, with a standard deviation of 15 points and a mean of 100 points. If 100 people are chosen at random, what is the probability that the sample mean of IQ scores will not differ from the population mean by more than 2 points?

20. 0.8664.

20. *Hatchery Fish: Length* A large tank of fish from a hatchery is being delivered to a lake. The hatchery claims that the mean length of fish in the tank is 15 inches, and the standard deviation is 2 inches. A random sample of 36 fish is taken from the tank. Let $\bar{x}$ be the mean sample length of these fish. What is the probability that $\bar{x}$ is within 0.5 inch of the claimed population mean?

DATA HIGHLIGHTS: GROUP PROJECTS

Break into small groups and discuss the following topics. Organize a brief outline in which you summarize the main points of your group discussion.

Iris setosa is a beautiful wildflower that is found in such diverse places as Alaska, the Gulf of St. Lawrence, much of North America, and even in English meadows and parks. R. A. Fisher, with his colleague Dr. Edgar Anderson, studied these flowers extensively. Dr. Anderson described how he collected information on irises:

Wild iris

> I have studied such irises as I could get to see, in as great detail as possible, measuring iris standard after iris standard and iris fall after iris fall, sitting squat-legged with record book and ruler in mountain meadows, in cypress swamps, on lake beaches, and in English parks. [Anderson, E., "The Irises of the Gaspé Peninsula," *Bulletin, American Iris Society*, 59:2–5, 1935.]

The data in Table 7-10 were collected by Dr. Anderson and were published by his friend and colleague R. A. Fisher in a paper entitled "The Use of Multiple Measurements in Taxonomic Problems" (*Annals of Eugenics*, part II, 179–188, 1936). To find these data, visit the Online Study Center at **www.cengage.com/statistics/Brase/UBS5e** and find the link to DASL, the Carnegie Mellon University Data and Story Library. From the DASL site, look under famous data sets.

Let x be a random variable representing petal length. Using a TI-84Plus/TI-83Plus calculator, it was found that the sample mean is $\overline{x} = 1.46$ centimeters (cm) and the sample standard deviation is $s = 0.17$ cm. Figure 7-36 shows a histogram for the given data generated on a TI-84Plus/TI-83Plus calculator.

(a) Examine the histogram for petal lengths. Would you say that the distribution is approximately mound-shaped and symmetrical? Our sample has only 50 irises; if many thousands of irises had been used, do you think the distribution would look even more like a normal curve? Let x be the petal length of *Iris setosa*. Research has shown that x has an approximately normal distribution, with mean $\mu = 1.5$ cm and standard deviation $\sigma = 0.2$ cm.

(b) Use the empirical rule with $\mu = 1.5$ and $\sigma = 0.2$ to get an interval in which approximately 68% of the petal lengths will fall. Repeat this for 95% and 99.7%. Examine the raw data and compute the percentage of the raw data that actually falls into each of these intervals (the 68% interval, the 95% interval, and the 99.7% interval). Compare your computed percentages with those given by the empirical rule.

(c) Compute the probability that a petal length is between 1.3 and 1.6 cm. Compute the probability that a petal length is greater than 1.6 cm.

(d) Suppose that a random sample of 30 irises is obtained. Compute the probability that the average petal length for this sample is between 1.3 and 1.6 cm. Compute the probability that the average petal length is greater than 1.6 cm.

(e) Compare your answers to parts (c) and (d). Do you notice any differences? Why would these differences occur?

TABLE 7-10 Petal Length in Centimeters for *Iris setosa*

1.4	1.4	1.3	1.5	1.4
1.7	1.4	1.5	1.4	1.5
1.5	1.6	1.4	1.1	1.2
1.5	1.3	1.4	1.7	1.5
1.7	1.5	1	1.7	1.9
1.6	1.6	1.5	1.4	1.6
1.6	1.5	1.5	1.4	1.5
1.2	1.3	1.4	1.3	1.5
1.3	1.3	1.3	1.6	1.9
1.4	1.6	1.4	1.5	1.4

FIGURE 7-36

Petal Length (cm) for *Iris setosa* (TI-84Plus/TI-83Plus)

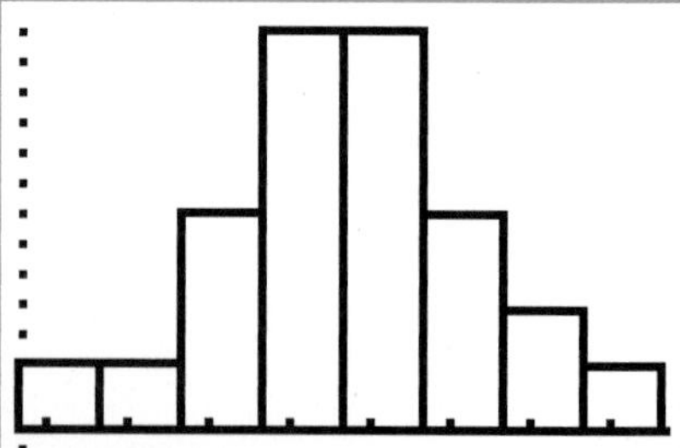

LINKING CONCEPTS: WRITING PROJECTS

Discuss each of the following topics in class or review the topics on your own. Then write a brief but complete essay in which you summarize the main points. Please include formulas and graphs as appropriate.

1. If you look up the word *empirical* in a dictionary, you will find that it means "relying on experiment and observation rather than on theory." Discuss the empirical rule in this context. The empirical rule certainly applies to the normal distribution, but does it also apply to a wide variety of other distributions that are not *exactly* (theoretically) normal? Discuss the terms *mound-shaped* and *symmetrical.* Draw several sketches of distributions that are mound-shaped *and* symmetrical. Draw sketches of distributions that are not mound-shaped or symmetrical. To which distributions will the empirical rule apply?

2. Why are standard z values so important? Is it true that z values have no units of measurement? Why would this be desirable for comparing data sets with *different* units of measurement? How can we assess differences in quality or performance by simply comparing z values under a standard normal curve? Examine the formula for computing standard z values. Notice that it involves *both* the mean and standard deviation. Recall that in Chapter 3 we commented that the mean of a data collection is not entirely adequate to describe the data; you need the standard deviation as well. Discuss this topic again in light of what you now know about normal distributions and standard z values.

3. Most people would agree that increased information should give better predictions. Discuss how sampling distributions actually enable better predictions by providing more information. Examine Theorem 7.1 again. Suppose that x is a random variable with a *normal* distribution. Then $\bar{x}$, the sample mean based on random samples of size n, also will have a normal distribution for *any* value of $n = 1, 2, 3, \ldots$

   What happens to the standard deviation of the $\bar{x}$ distribution as n (the sample size) increases? Consider the following table for different values of n.

n	1	2	3	4	10	50	100
$\sigma/\sqrt{n}$	1σ	0.71σ	0.58σ	0.50σ	0.32σ	0.14σ	0.10σ

   In this case, "increased information" means a larger sample size n. Give a brief explanation as to why a *large* standard deviation will usually result in poor statistical predictions, whereas a *small* standard deviation usually results in much better predictions. Since the standard deviation of the sampling distribution $\bar{x}$ is $\sigma/\sqrt{n}$, we can decrease the standard deviation by increasing n. In fact, if we look at the preceding table, we see that if we use a sample size of only $n = 4$, we cut the standard deviation of $\bar{x}$ by 50% of the standard deviation σ of x. If we were to use a sample of size $n = 100$, we would cut the standard deviation of $\bar{x}$ to 10% of the standard deviation σ of x.

   Give the preceding discussion some thought and explain why you should get much better predictions for μ by using $\bar{x}$ from a sample of size n rather than by just using x. Write a brief essay in which you explain why sampling distributions are an important tool in statistics.

Using Technology

Normal Quantile Plot

How can we determine if data originated from a normal distribution? We can look at a stem-and-leaf plot or histogram of the data to check for general symmetry, skewness, clusters of data, or outliers. However, a more sensitive way to check that a distribution is normal is to look at a special graph called a *normal quantile plot* (or a variation of this plot called a *normal probability plot* in some software packages). It really is not feasible to make a normal quantile plot by hand, but statistical software packages provide such plots. A simple version of the basic idea behind normal quantile plots involves the following process:

(a) Arrange the observed data values in order from smallest to largest, and determine the percentile occupied by each value. For instance, if there are 20 data values, the smallest datum is at the 5% point, the next smallest is at the 10% point, and so on.

(b) Find the z values that correspond to the percentile points. For instance, the z value that corresponds to the percentile 5% (i.e., percent in the left tail of the distribution) is $z = -1.645$.

(c) Plot each data value x against the corresponding percentile z score. If the data are close to a normal distribution, the plotted points will lie close to a straight line. (If the data are close to a standard normal distribution, the points will lie close to the line $x = z$.)

The actual process that statistical software packages use to produce the z scores for the data is more complicated.

Interpreting normal quantile plots

If the points of a normal quantile plot lie close to a straight line, the plot indicates that the data follow a normal distribution. Systematic deviations from a straight line or bulges in the plot indicate that the data distribution is not normal. Individual points off the line may be outliers.

Consider Figure 7-37. This figure shows Minitab-generated quantile plots for two data sets. The black dots show the normal quantile plot for the salary data of government employees. The red dots show the normal quantile plot for a random sample of 42 data values drawn from a theoretical normal distribution with the same mean and standard deviation as the salary data ($\mu \approx 3421$, $\sigma \approx 709$).

FIGURE 7-37 Normal Quantile Plots

- Salary data for (city) government employees
- A random sample of 42 values from a theoretical normal distribution with the same mean and standard deviation as the salary data

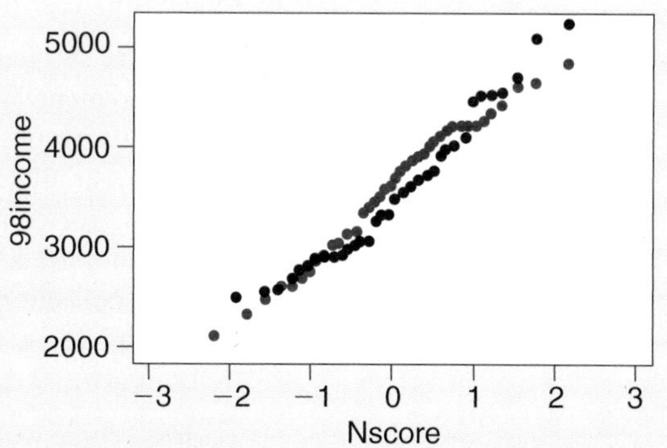

(a) Do the black dots lie close to a straight line? Do the salaries appear to follow a normal distribution? Are there any outliers on the low or high side? Would you say that any of the salaries are "out of line" for a normal distribution?

(b) Do the red dots lie close to a straight line? We know the red dots represent a sample drawn from a normal distribution. Is the normal quantile plot for the red dots consistent with this fact? Are there any outliers shown?

Technology Hints

TI-84Plus/TI-83Plus

Enter the data. Press **STATPLOT** and select one of the plots. Highlight **ON**. Then highlight the sixth plot option. To get a plot similar to that of Figure 7-37, choose Y as the data axis. Next press **GRAPH**.

Minitab

Minitab has several types of normal quantile plots that use different types of scales. To create a normal quantile plot similar to that of Figure 7-37, enter the data in column C1. Then use the menu choices **Calc ➤ Calculator.** In the dialogue box listing the functions, scroll to **Normal Scores.** Use **NSCOR(C1)** and store the results in column C2. Finally, use the menu choices **Graph ➤ Plot.** In the dialogue box, use C1 for variable y and C2 for variable x.

SPSS

Enter the data. Use the menu choices **Analyze ➤ Descriptive Statistics ➤ Explore.** In the dialogue box, move your data variable to the dependent list. Check **Plots. . . .** Check "Normality plots with tests." The graph appears in the output window.

Project Illustrating the Central Limit Theorem

As we have seen in this chapter, the value of a sample statistic such as $\bar{x}$ varies from one sample to another. The central limit theorem describes the distribution of the sample statistic $\bar{x}$ when samples are sufficiently large.

We can use technology tools to generate samples of the same size from the same population. Then we can look at the statistic $\bar{x}$ for each sample and the resulting $\bar{x}$ distribution.

Step 1: Generate random samples of specified size n from a population.

The random-number table enables us to sample from the uniform distribution of digits 0 through 9. Use either the random-number table or a random-number generator to generate 30 samples of size 10.

Step 2: Compute the sample mean $\bar{x}$ of the digits in each sample.

Step 3: Compute the sample mean of the means (i.e., $\bar{x}_{\bar{x}}$) as well as the standard deviation $s_{\bar{x}}$ of the sample means.

The population mean of the uniform distribution of digits from 0 through 9 is 4.5. How does $\bar{x}_{\bar{x}}$ compare to this value?

Step 4: Compare the sample distribution of $\bar{x}$ values to a normal distribution having the mean and standard deviation computed in Step 3.

(a) Use the values of $\bar{x}_{\bar{x}}$ and $s_{\bar{x}}$ computed in Step 3 to create the intervals shown in column 1 of Table 7-11.

(b) Tally the sample means computed in Step 2 to determine how many fall into each interval of column 2. Then compute the percent of data in each interval and record the results in column 3.

(c) The percentages listed in column 4 are those from a normal distribution (see Figure 7-3 showing the empirical rule). Compare the percentages in column 3 to those in column 4. How do the sample percentages compare with the hypothetical normal distribution?

Step 5: Create a histogram showing the sample means computed in Step 2.

Look at the histogram and compare it to a normal distribution with the mean and standard deviation of the $\bar{x}$s (as computed in Step 3).

Step 6: Compare the results of this project to the central limit theorem.

Increase the sample size of Step 1 to 20, 30, and 40, and repeat Steps 1 to 5.

Technology Hints

The TI-84Plus and TI-83Plus calculators, Excel, Minitab, and SPSS all support the process of drawing random samples from a variety of distributions. Macros can be written in Excel, Minitab, and the professional version of SPSS to

TABLE 7-11 **Frequency Table of Sample Means**

1. Interval	2. Frequency	3. Percent	4. Hypothetical Normal Distribution
$\bar{x} - 3s$ to $\bar{x} - 2s$	Tally the sample means computed in step 2 and place here.	Compute percents from column 2 and place here.	2% or 3%
$\bar{x} - 2s$ to $\bar{x} - s$			13% or 14%
$\bar{x} - s$ to $\bar{x}$			About 34%
$\bar{x}$ to $\bar{x} + s$			About 34%
$\bar{x} + s$ to $\bar{x} + 2s$			13% or 14%
$\bar{x} + 2s$ to $\bar{x} + 3s$			2% or 3%

repeat the six steps of the project. Figure 7-38 shows histograms generated by SPSS for random samples of size 30 and size 100. The samples are taken from a uniform probability distribution.

FIGURE 7-38

SPSS-Generated Histograms for Samples of Size 30 and Size 100

(a) $n = 30$

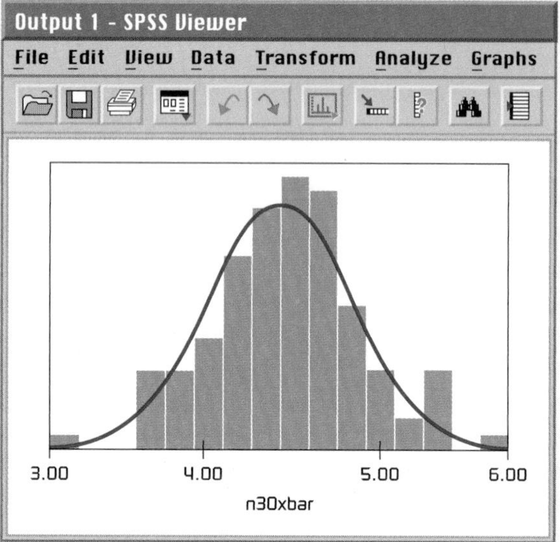

(b) $n = 100$

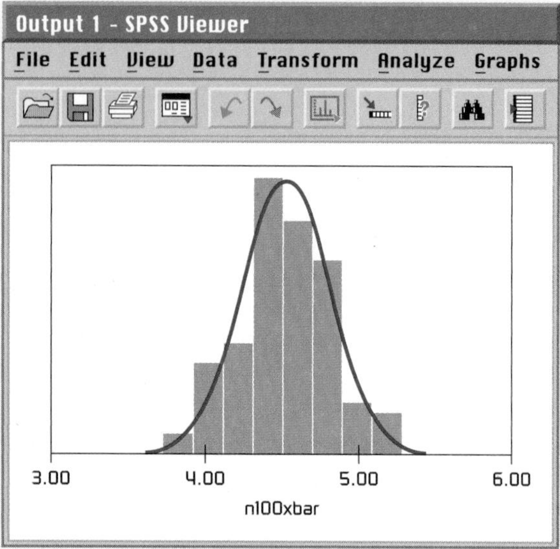

TI-84Plus/TI-83Plus

You can generate random samples from uniform, normal, and binomial distributions. Press **MATH** and select **PRB.** Selection **5:randInt(lower, upper, sample size m)** generates *m* random integers from the specified interval. Selection **6:randNorm(μ, σ, sample size m)** generates *m* random numbers from a normal distribution with mean μ and standard deviation σ. Selection **7:randBin(number of trials n, p, sample size m)** generates *m* random values (number of successes out of *n* trials) for a binomial distribution with probability of success *p* on each trial. You can put these values in lists by using **Edit** under **Stat.** Highlight the list header, press Enter, and then select one of the options discussed.

Excel

Use the menu selection **Tools ➤ Data Analysis ➤ Random Number Generator.** The dialogue box provides choices for the population distribution, including uniform, binomial, and normal distributions. Fill in the required parameters and designate the location for the output.

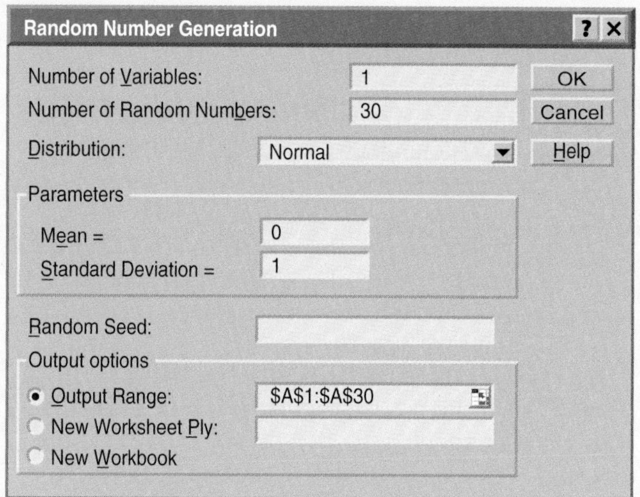

Minitab

Use the menu selections **Calc ➤ Random Data.** Then select the population distribution. The choices include uniform, binomial, and normal distributions. Fill in the dialogue box, where the number of rows indicates the number of data in the sample.

SPSS

SPSS supports random samples from a variety of distributions, including binomial, normal, and uniform. In data view, generate a column of consecutive integers from 1 to *n*, where *n* is the sample size. In variable view, name the variables sample1, sample2, and so on, through sample30. These variables head the columns containing each of the 30 samples of size *n*. Then use the menu choices **Transform ➤ Compute.** In the dialogue box, use sample1 as the target variable for the first sample, and so forth. In the function box, select

RV.UNIFORM(min,max) for samples from a uniform distribution. Functions **RV.NORMAL(mean,stddev)** and **RV.BINOM(n,p)** provide random samples from normal and binomial distributions, respectively.

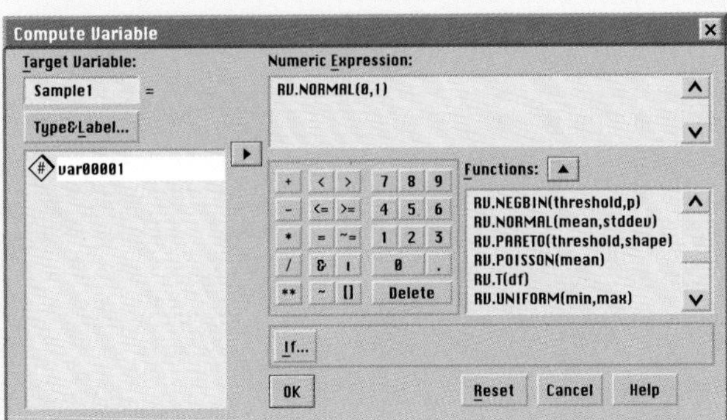

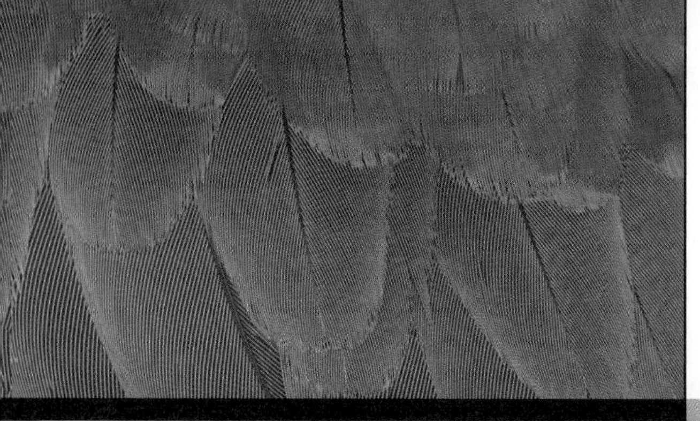

*We dance round in a ring
and suppose,
But the Secret sits in the
middle and knows.*

—Robert Frost,
"The Secret Sits"*

In Chapter 1, we said that statistics is the study of how to collect, organize, analyze, and interpret numerical data. That part of statistics concerned with analysis, interpretation, and forming conclusions about the source of the data is called *statistical inference*. Problems of statistical inference require us to draw a *sample* of observations from a larger *population*. A sample usually contains incomplete information, so in a sense we must "dance round in a ring and suppose," to quote the words of the celebrated American poet Robert Lee Frost (1874–1963). Nevertheless, conclusions about the population can be obtained from sample data by the use of statistical estimates. This chapter introduces you to several widely used methods of estimation.

For on-line student resources, visit the Brase/Brase, *Understanding Basic Statistics,* 5th edition web site at **www.cengage.com/statistics/Brase/UBS5e.**

ESTIMATION

PREVIEW QUESTIONS

How do you estimate the expected value of a random variable? What assumptions are needed? How much confidence should be placed in such estimates? (SECTION 8.1)

At the beginning design stage of a statistical project, how large a sample size should you plan to get? (SECTION 8.1)

What famous statistician worked for Guinness brewing company in Ireland? What has this to do with constructing estimates from sample data? (SECTION 8.2)

How do you estimate the proportion p *of successes in a binomial experiment? How does the normal approximation fit into this process?* (SECTION 8.3)

FOCUS PROBLEM

Trick or Treat!!!

About 28% of U.S. households turn out the lights and pretend not to be at home on Halloween (*Source: Are You Normal About Money?* by Bernice Kanner, Bloomberg Press).

Alice is a sociology student who is studying the affluent Cherry Creek neighborhood in Denver. As part of a larger survey, Alice interviewed a random sample of 35 households. One of the questions she asked was whether the resident turned out the lights and pretended not to be at home on Halloween. It was found that 11 of the 35 residents actually did this practice.

(a) Compute a 90% confidence interval for p, the proportion of all households in Cherry Creek that pretend not to be at home on Halloween.

(b) What assumptions are necessary to calculate the confidence interval of part (a)? Do you think these assumptions are met in this case? Explain.

(c) The national proportion is about 0.28. Is 0.28 in the confidence interval you computed? Based on your answer, does it seem that the Cherry Creek neighborhood is much different (either higher or lower proportion) from the population of all U.S. households? Explain.

(See Problem 12 of Section 8.3.)

SECTION 8.1

Estimating μ When σ Is Known

FOCUS POINTS

- Explain the meaning of confidence level, error of estimate, and critical value.
- Find the critical value corresponding to a given confidence level.
- Compute confidence intervals for μ when σ is known. Interpret the results.
- Compute the sample size to be used for estimating a mean μ.

Because of time and money constraints, difficulty in finding population members, and so forth, we usually do not have access to *all* measurements of an *entire* population. Instead we rely on information from a sample.

In this section, we develop techniques for estimating the population mean μ using sample data. We assume the population standard deviation σ is known.

Let's begin by listing some basic assumptions used in the development of our formulas for estimating μ when σ is known.

This section contains conceptually important material. It may be a good idea to spend a little extra class time here before moving on. Problem 1 in Linking Concepts contains good material for a class discussion about the meaning of confidence intervals.

Assumptions about the random variable *x*

1. We have a *simple random sample* of size n drawn from a population of x values.
2. The value of σ, the population standard deviation of x, *is known.*
3. If the *x distribution is normal,* then our methods work for *any sample size n.*
4. If x has an unknown distribution, then we require a *sample size $n \geq 30$.* However, if the x distribution is distinctly skewed and definitely not mound-shaped, a sample of size 50 or even 100 or higher may be necessary.

Point estimate

An estimate of a population parameter given by a single number is called a *point estimate* for that parameter. It will come as no great surprise that we use $\bar{x}$ (the sample mean) as the point estimate for μ (the population mean).

A **point estimate** of a population parameter is an estimate of the parameter using a single number.

$\bar{x}$ is the **point estimate** for μ.

Margin of error

Even with a large random sample, the value of $\bar{x}$ usually is not *exactly* equal to the population mean μ. The *margin of error* is the magnitude of the difference between the sample point estimate and the true population parameter value.

When using $\bar{x}$ as a point estimate for μ, the **margin of error** is the magnitude of $\bar{x} - \mu$ or $|\bar{x} - \mu|$.

We cannot say exactly how close $\bar{x}$ is to μ when μ is unknown. Therefore, the exact margin of error is unknown when the population parameter is unknown.

FIGURE 8-1

Confidence Level c and Corresponding Critical Value z_c Shown on the Standard Normal Curve

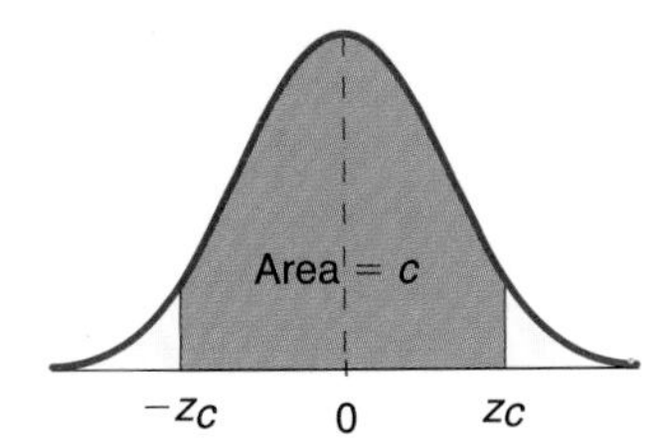

Finding the critical value

Of course, μ is usually not known or there would be no need to estimate it. In this section, we will use the language of probability to give us an idea of the size of the margin of error when we use $\bar{x}$ as a point estimate for μ.

First, we need to learn about *confidence levels*. The reliability of an estimate will be measured by the confidence level.

Suppose we want a confidence level of c (see Figure 8-1). Theoretically, you can choose c to be any value between 0 and 1, but usually c is equal to a number such as 0.90, 0.95, or 0.99. In each case, the value z_c is the number such that the area under the standard normal curve falling between $-z_c$ and z_c is equal to c. The value z_c is called the *critical value* for a confidence level of c.

For a confidence level c, the **critical value** z_c is the number such that the area under the standard normal curve between $-z_c$ and z_c equals c.

The area under the normal curve from $-z_c$ to z_c is the probability that the standardized normal variable z lies in that interval. This means that

$$P(-z_c < z < z_c) = c$$

EXAMPLE 1 FIND A CRITICAL VALUE (NORMAL DISTRIBUTION)

Let us use Table 3 of the Appendix to find a number $z_{0.99}$ such that 99% of the area under the standard normal curve lies between $-z_{0.99}$ and $z_{0.99}$. That is, we will find $z_{0.99}$ such that

$$P(-z_{0.99} < z < z_{0.99}) = 0.99$$

SOLUTION: In Section 7.3, we saw how to find the z value when we were given an area between $-z$ and z. The first thing we did was to find the corresponding area to the left of $-z$. If A is the area between $-z$ and z, then $(1 - A)/2$ is the area to the left of z. In our case, the area between $-z$ and z is 0.99. The corresponding area in the left tail is $(1 - 0.99)/2 = 0.005$ (see Figure 8-2).

Next, we use Table 3 of the Appendix to find the z value corresponding to a left-tail area of 0.0050. Table 8-1 shows an excerpt from Table 3 of the Appendix.

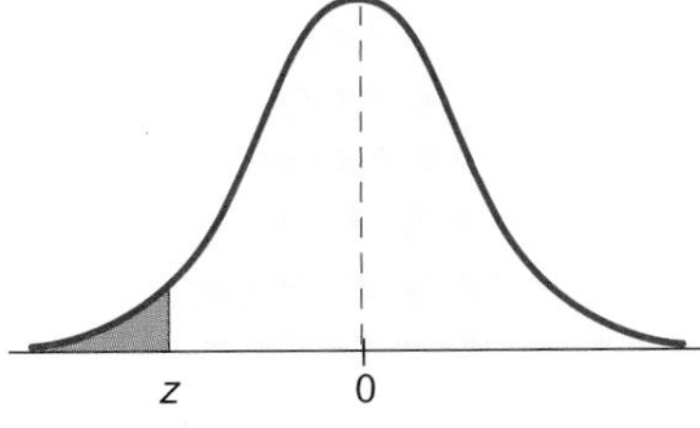

TABLE 8-1 **Excerpt from Table 3 of the Appendix**

z	.00	...	.07	.08	.09
−3.4	.0003		.0003	.0003	.0002
⋮					
−2.5	.0062		.0051	.0049	.0048
			↑ .0050		

FIGURE 8-2

Area Between $-z$ and z Is 0.99

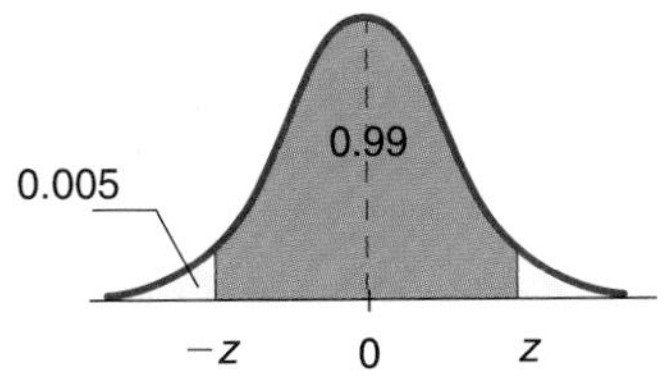

From Table 8-1, we see that the desired area, 0.0050, is exactly halfway between the areas corresponding to $z = -2.58$ and $z = -2.57$. Because the two area values are so close together, we use the more conservative z value -2.58 rather than interpolate. In fact, $z_{0.99} \approx 2.576$. However, to two decimal places, we use $z_{0.99} = 2.58$ as the critical value for a confidence level of $c = 0.99$. We have

$$P(-2.58 < z < 2.58) \approx 0.99$$

Remind students that Table 8-2 will be a convenient reference for commonly used critical values from the normal distribution in this section and later sections. This content also occurs in Table 3(b) of the Appendix.

TABLE 8-2 Some Levels of Confidence and Their Corresponding Critical Values

Level of Confidence c	Critical Value z_c
0.70, or 70%	1.04
0.75, or 75%	1.15
0.80, or 80%	1.28
0.85, or 85%	1.44
0.90, or 90%	1.645
0.95, or 95%	1.96
0.98, or 98%	2.33
0.99, or 99%	2.58

The results of Example 1 will be used a great deal in our later work. For convenience, Table 8-2 gives some levels of confidence and corresponding critical values z_c. The same information is provided in Table 3(b) of the Appendix.

An estimate is not very valuable unless we have some kind of measure of how "good" it is. The language of probability can give us an idea of the size of the margin of error caused by using the sample mean $\bar{x}$ as an estimate for the population mean.

Remember that $\bar{x}$ is a random variable. Each time we draw a sample of size n from a population, we can get a different value for $\bar{x}$. According to the central limit theorem, if the sample size is large, then $\bar{x}$ has a distribution that is approximately normal with mean $\mu_{\bar{x}} = \mu$, the population mean we are trying to estimate. The standard deviation is $\sigma_{\bar{x}} = \sigma/\sqrt{n}$. If x has a normal distribution, these results are true *for any sample size.* (See Theorem 7.1.)

This information, together with our work on confidence levels, leads us (as shown in the comment that follows) to the probability statement

$$P\left(-z_c \frac{\sigma}{\sqrt{n}} < \bar{x} - \mu < z_c \frac{\sigma}{\sqrt{n}}\right) = c \tag{1}$$

Equation (1) uses the language of probability to give us an idea of the size of the margin of error for the corresponding confidence level c. In words, Equation (1) states that the probability is c that our point estimate $\bar{x}$ is within a distance $\pm z_c(\sigma/\sqrt{n})$ of the population mean μ. This relationship is shown in Figure 8-3.

COMMENT To derive Equation (1), we start with the probability statement $P(-z_c < z < z_c) = c$. Since $n \geq 30$, we can use the central limit theorem and replace z by $(\bar{x} - \mu)/(\sigma/\sqrt{n})$. Finally, we multiply all parts of the inequality by $(\sigma/\sqrt{n})$ to obtain Equation (1).

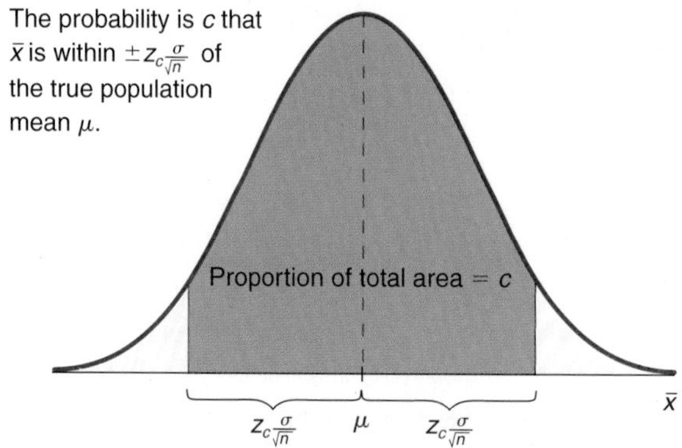

FIGURE 8-3

Distribution of Sample Means $\bar{x}$

The *margin of error* (or absolute error) using $\overline{x}$ as a point estimate for μ is $|\overline{x} - \mu|$. In most practical problems, μ is unknown, so the margin of error is also unknown. However, Equation (1) allows us to compute an *error tolerance* E that serves as a bound on the margin of error. Using a $c\%$ level of confidence, we can say that the point estimate $\overline{x}$ differs from the population mean μ by a *maximal margin of error*

Maximal margin of error, E

$$E = z_c \frac{\sigma}{\sqrt{n}} \tag{2}$$

Note: Formula (2) for E is based on the fact that the sampling distribution for $\overline{x}$ is exactly normal, with mean μ and standard deviation $\sigma/\sqrt{n}$. This occurs whenever the x distribution is normal with mean μ and standard deviation σ. If the x distribution is not normal, then according to the central limit theorem, large samples ($n \geq 30$) produce an $\overline{x}$ distribution that is approximately normal, with mean μ and standard deviation $\sigma/\sqrt{n}$.

Using Equations (1) and (2), we conclude that

Confidence interval for μ with σ known

$$P(-E < \overline{x} - \mu < E) = c \tag{3}$$

Applying a little algebra to Equation (3) produces

$$P(\overline{x} - E < \mu < \overline{x} + E) = c \tag{4}$$

Equation (4) states that there is a chance c that the interval from $\overline{x} - E$ to $\overline{x} + E$ contains the population mean μ. We call this interval a *c confidence interval for μ*.

Data Highlights, Problem 1a through 1e (clam digging), contains interesting material for class examples and/or discussion.

A ***c* confidence interval for μ** is an interval computed from sample data in such a way that c is the probability of generating an interval containing the actual value of μ. In other words, c is the proportion of confidence intervals, based on random samples of size n, that actually contain μ.

We may get a different confidence interval for each different sample that is taken. Some intervals will contain the population mean μ and others will not. However, in the long run, the proportion of confidence intervals that contain μ is c.

PROCEDURE

HOW TO FIND A CONFIDENCE INTERVAL FOR μ WHEN σ IS KNOWN

Let x be a random variable appropriate to your application. Obtain a simple random sample (of size n) of x values from which you compute the sample mean $\overline{x}$. The value of σ is already known (perhaps from a previous study).

If you can assume that x has a normal distribution, then any sample size n will work. If you cannot assume this, then use a sample size of $n \geq 30$.

Confidence interval for μ when σ is known

$$\overline{x} - E < \mu < \overline{x} + E \tag{5}$$

where $\overline{x}$ = sample mean of a simple random sample

$$E = z_c \frac{\sigma}{\sqrt{n}}$$

c = confidence level ($0 < c < 1$)

z_c = critical value for confidence level c based on the standard normal distribution (See Table 3(b) of the Appendix for frequently used values.)

EXAMPLE 2 **CONFIDENCE INTERVAL FOR μ WITH σ KNOWN**

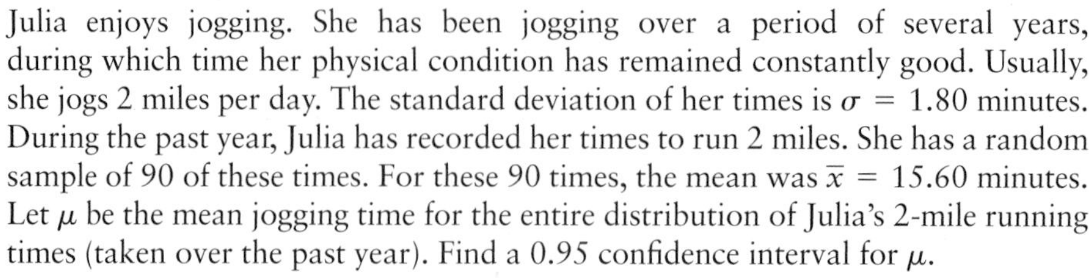

Julia enjoys jogging. She has been jogging over a period of several years, during which time her physical condition has remained constantly good. Usually, she jogs 2 miles per day. The standard deviation of her times is $\sigma = 1.80$ minutes. During the past year, Julia has recorded her times to run 2 miles. She has a random sample of 90 of these times. For these 90 times, the mean was $\bar{x} = 15.60$ minutes. Let μ be the mean jogging time for the entire distribution of Julia's 2-mile running times (taken over the past year). Find a 0.95 confidence interval for μ.

SOLUTION: The interval from $\bar{x} - E$ to $\bar{x} + E$ will be a 95% confidence interval for μ. In this case, $c = 0.95$, so $z_c = 1.96$ (see Table 8-2). The sample size $n = 90$ is large enough for the $\bar{x}$ distribution to be approximately normal, with mean μ and standard deviation $\sigma/\sqrt{n}$. Therefore,

$$E = z_c \frac{\sigma}{\sqrt{n}}$$

$$E = 1.96\left(\frac{1.80}{\sqrt{90}}\right)$$

$$E \approx 0.37$$

Using Equation (5), the given value of $\bar{x}$, and our computed value for E, we get the 95% confidence interval for μ.

$$\bar{x} - E < \mu < \bar{x} + E$$

$$15.60 - 0.37 < \mu < 15.60 + 0.37$$

$$15.23 < \mu < 15.97$$

INTERPRETATION We conclude with 95% confidence that the interval from 15.23 minutes to 15.97 minutes is one that contains the population mean μ of jogging times for Julia.

CRITICAL THINKING

Interpreting Confidence Intervals

A few comments are in order about the general meaning of the term *confidence interval.*

See Linking Projects, project 1 for a further discussion about probabilities associated with confidence intervals.

- Since $\bar{x}$ is a random variable, the endpoints $\bar{x} \pm E$ are also random variables. Equation (4) states that we have a chance c of obtaining a sample such that the interval, once it is computed, will contain the parameter μ.
- After the confidence interval is numerically fixed for a specific sample, it either does or does not contain μ. So, the probability is 1 or 0 that the interval, when it is fixed, will contain μ.

A nontrivial probability statement can be made only about variables, not constants.

- Equation (4), $P(\bar{x} - E < \mu < \bar{x} + E) = c$, really states that if we draw many random samples of size n and get lots of confidence intervals, then the proportion of all intervals that will turn out to contain the mean μ is c.

  For example, in Figure 8-4, the horizontal lines represent 0.90 confidence intervals for various samples of the same size from an x distribution. Some of these intervals contain μ and others do not. Since the intervals are 0.90 confidence intervals, about 90% of all such intervals should contain μ. For each sample, the interval goes from $\bar{x} - E$ to $\bar{x} + E$.

Using Technology has an SPSS simulation of confidence intervals using random numbers. The output could make a good class demonstration.

FIGURE 8-4

0.90 Confidence Intervals for Samples of the Same Size

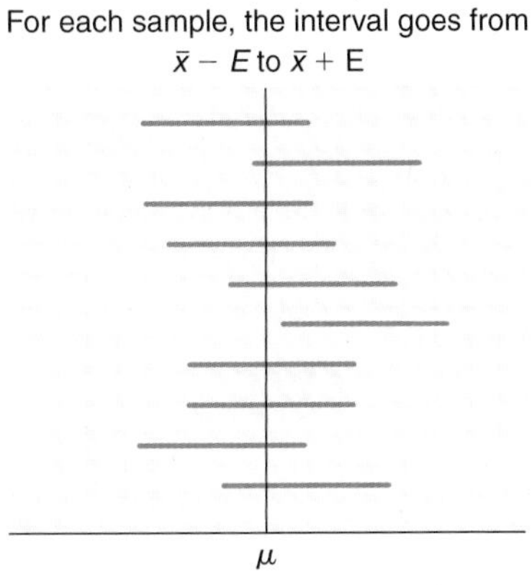

For each sample, the interval goes from $\bar{x} - E$ to $\bar{x} + E$

μ

- Once we have a *specific* confidence interval for μ, such as $3 < \mu < 5$, all we can say is that we are $c\%$ confident that we have one of the intervals that actually contains μ. Another appropriate statement is that at the c confidence level, our interval contains μ.

COMMENT Please see Using Technology at the end of this chapter for a computer demonstration of this discussion about confidence intervals.

GUIDED EXERCISE 1 Confidence interval for μ with σ known

Walter usually meets Julia at the track. He prefers to jog 3 miles. From long experience, he knows that $\sigma = 2.40$ minutes for his jogging times. For a random sample of 90 jogging sessions, Walter's mean time was $\bar{x} = 22.50$ minutes. Let μ be the mean jogging time for the entire distribution of Walter's 3-mile running times over the past several years. Find a 0.99 confidence interval for μ.

(a) What is the value of $z_{0.99}$? (See Table 8-2.) → $z_{0.99} = 2.58$

(b) Is the $\bar{x}$ distribution approximately normal? → Yes; we know this from the central limit theorem.

(c) What is the value of E? → $E = z_c\frac{\sigma}{\sqrt{n}} = 2.58\left(\frac{2.40}{\sqrt{90}}\right) \approx 0.65$

(d) What are the endpoints for a 0.99 confidence interval for μ? → The endpoints are given by

$\bar{x} - E \approx 22.50 - 0.65 = 21.85$

$\bar{x} + E \approx 22.50 + 0.65 = 23.15$

(e) Interpret the confidence interval. → We are 99% certain that the interval from 21.85 to 23.15 is an interval that contains the population mean time μ.

When we use samples to estimate the mean of a population, we generate a small error. However, samples are useful even when it is possible to survey the entire population because the use of a sample may yield savings of time or effort in collecting data.

TECH NOTES The TI-84Plus and TI-83Plus calculators, Excel, and Minitab all support confidence intervals for μ when σ is known. The level of support varies according to the technology. When a confidence interval is given, the standard mathematical notation (lower value, upper value) is used. For instance, the notation (15.23, 15.97) means the interval from 15.23 to 15.97.

TI-84Plus/TI-83Plus This calculator gives the most extensive support. The user can opt to enter raw data or just summary statistics. In each case, the value of σ must be specified. Press the **STAT** key, then select **TESTS,** and use **7:ZInterval.** The TI-84Plus/TI-83Plus output shows the results for Example 2.

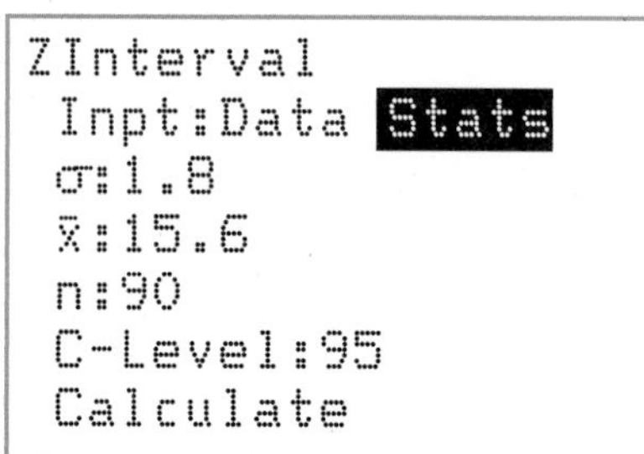


```
ZInterval
 (15.228, 15.972)
 x̄=15.6
 n=90
```

Excel Excel gives only the value of the maximal error of estimate E. Use the menu choice **Paste Function** (fx) ➤ **Statistics** ➤ **Confidence(alpha, σ, n).** In the dialogue box, the value of alpha is 1 − confidence level. The Excel output shows the value of E for Example 2.

= =CONFIDENCE(0.05,1.8,90)

C	D	E
0.371876		

An alternate approach incorporating raw data (using the Student's t distribution presented in the next section) uses the menu choices **Tools** ➤ **Data Analysis** ➤ **Describe Statistics.** Again, the value of E for the interval is given.

Minitab Raw data are required. Use the menu choices **Stat** ➤ **Basic Statistics** ➤ **1-SampleZ.**

Sample Size for Estimating the Mean μ

In the design stages of statistical research projects, it is a good idea to decide in advance on the confidence level you wish to use and to select the *maximum* margin of error E you want for your project. How you choose to make these decisions depends on the requirements of the project and the practical nature of the problem.

Whatever specifications you make, the next step is to determine the sample size. Solving the formula that gives the maximal margin of error E for n enables us to determine the minimum sample size.

PROCEDURE

HOW TO FIND THE SAMPLE SIZE n FOR ESTIMATING μ WHEN σ IS KNOWN

Assuming the distribution of sample means $\bar{x}$ is approximately normal, then

$$n = \left(\frac{z_c \sigma}{E}\right)^2 \qquad (6)$$

Continued

where E = specified maximal error of estimate
σ = population standard deviation
z_c = critical value from the normal distribution for the desired confidence level c. Commonly used values of z_c can be found in Table 3(b) of the Appendix.

If n is not a whole number, increase n to the next higher whole number. Note that n is the minimal sample size for a specified confidence level and maximal error of estimate E.

COMMENT If you have a *preliminary study* involving a sample size of 30 or larger, then for most practical purposes it is safe to approximate σ with the sample standard deviation s in the formula for sample size.

EXAMPLE 3 SAMPLE SIZE FOR ESTIMATING μ

A wildlife study is designed to find the mean weight of salmon caught by an Alaskan fishing company. A preliminary study of a random sample of 50 salmon showed $s \approx 2.15$ pounds. How large a sample should be taken to be 99% confident that the sample mean $\bar{x}$ is within 0.20 pound of the true mean weight μ?

Salmon moving upstream

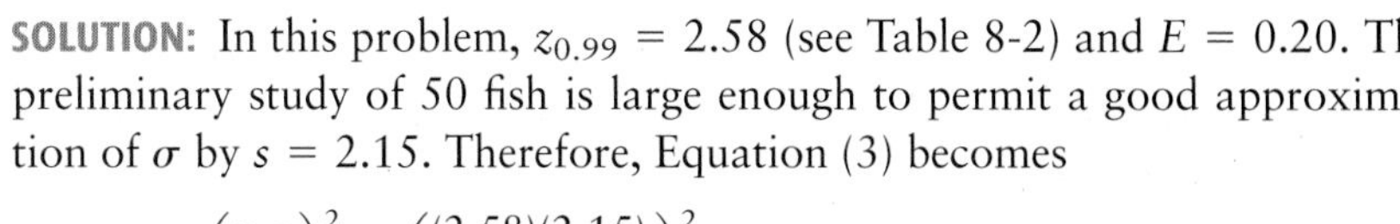
SOLUTION: In this problem, $z_{0.99} = 2.58$ (see Table 8-2) and $E = 0.20$. The preliminary study of 50 fish is large enough to permit a good approximation of σ by $s = 2.15$. Therefore, Equation (3) becomes

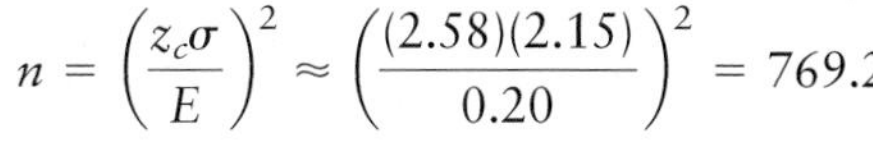
$$n = \left(\frac{z_c\sigma}{E}\right)^2 \approx \left(\frac{(2.58)(2.15)}{0.20}\right)^2 = 769.2$$

Note: In determining sample size, any fractional value of n is always rounded to the *next higher whole number.* We conclude that a sample size of 770 will be large enough to satisfy the specifications. Of course, a sample size larger than 770 also works.

VIEWPOINT Music and Techno Theft

Performing rights organizations ASCAP (American Society of Composers, Authors, and Publishers) and BMI (Broadcast Music, Inc.) collect royalties for songwriters and music publishers. Radio, television, cable, nightclubs, restaurants, elevators, and even beauty parlors play music that is copyrighted by a composer or publisher. The royalty payment for this music turns out to be more than a billion dollars a year (Source: The Wall Street Journal*). How do ASCAP and BMI know who is playing what music? The answer is, they don't know! Instead of tracking* exactly *what gets played, they use random sampling and* confidence intervals*. For example, each radio station (there are more than 10,000 in the U.S.) has randomly chosen days of programming analyzed every year. The results are used to assess royalty fees. In fact, Deloitte & Touche (a financial services company) administers the sampling process.*

Although the system is not perfect, it helps bring order into an otherwise chaotic accounting system. Such methods of "copyright policing" help prevent techno theft, ensuring that many songwriters and recording artists get a reasonable return for their creative work.

SECTION 8.1 PROBLEMS

Tables and art to accompany margin answers may be found in the back of the book.

1. True. By definition, critical values z_c are values such that $c\%$ of the area under the normal curve falls between $-z_c$ and z_c.
2. True. Because the mean of the $\bar{x}$ distribution equals the mean of the x distribution and the standard error of the $\bar{x}$ distribution decreases as n increases, $\bar{x}$ is the point estimate for μ.
3. True. By definition, the margin of error is the magnitude of the difference between $\bar{x}$ and μ.
4. False. Different random samples may give different values for $\bar{x}$, resulting in different values for the bounds of the confidence interval $\bar{x} \pm E$.
5. False. The maximum error of estimate is $E = z_c \frac{\sigma}{\sqrt{n}}$. As the sample size n increases, the maximal error decreases, resulting in a shorter confidence interval for μ.
6. True. The maximum error of estimate is $E = z_c \frac{\sigma}{\sqrt{n}}$. As σ decreases, E decreases, resulting in a shorter confidence interval for μ.
7. False. The maximal error of estimate E controls the length of the confidence interval regardless of the value of $\bar{x}$.
8. True. The critical value z_c decreases as the confidence level decreases. Therefore, the maximal error of estimate $E = z_c \frac{\sigma}{\sqrt{n}}$ decreases as well.
9. μ is either in the interval 10.1 to 12.2 or not. Therefore, the probability that μ is in this interval is either 0 or 1, not 0.95.
10. Yes. The proportion of all confidence intervals based on random samples of size n that actually contain μ is 0.90.
11. (a) 3.04 gm to 3.26 gm; 0.11 gm.
    (b) Distribution of weights is normal with known σ.
    (c) There is an 80% chance that the confidence interval is one of the intervals containing the population average weight of Allen's hummingbirds in this region.
    (d) $n = 28$.
12. (a) 4.07 mg/dl to 6.63 mg/dl; 1.28 mg/dl.
    (b) Distribution of acid concentration is normal with known σ.
    (c) There is a 95% chance that the confidence interval is one of the intervals containing the population average uric acid level for this patient.
    (d) $n = 11$.

In Problems 1–8, answer true or false. Explain your answer.

1. *Statistical Literacy* The value z_c is a value from the standard normal distribution such that $P(-z_c < z < z_c) = c$.

2. *Statistical Literacy* The point estimate for the population mean μ of an x distribution is $\bar{x}$, computed from a random sample of the x distribution.

3. *Statistical Literacy* Consider a random sample of size n from an x distribution. For such a sample, the margin of error for estimating μ is the magnitude of the difference between $\bar{x}$ and μ.

4. *Statistical Literacy* Every random sample of the same size from a given population will produce exactly the same confidence interval for μ.

5. *Statistical Literacy* A larger sample size produces a longer confidence interval for μ.

6. *Statistical Literacy* If the standard deviation for an x distribution decreases, c confidence intervals based on the same sample size will become shorter.

7. *Statistical Literacy* If the sample mean $\bar{x}$ of a random sample from an x distribution is relatively small, then the confidence interval for μ will be relatively short.

8. *Statistical Literacy* For the same random sample, when the confidence level c is reduced, the confidence interval for μ becomes shorter.

9. ***Critical Thinking*** Sam computed a 95% confidence interval for μ from a specific random sample. His confidence interval was $10.1 < \mu < 12.2$. He claims that the probability that μ is in this interval is 0.95. What is wrong with his claim?

10. ***Critical Thinking*** Sam computed a 90% confidence interval for μ from a specific random sample of size n. He claims that at the 90% confidence level, his confidence interval contains μ. Is this claim correct? Explain.

Answers may vary slightly due to rounding.

11. *Zoology: Hummingbirds* Allen's hummingbird (*Selasphorus sasin*) has been studied by zoologist Bill Alther (Reference: *Hummingbirds*, K. Long and W. Alther). A small group of 15 Allen's hummingbirds has been under study in Arizona. The average weight for these birds is $\bar{x} = 3.15$ grams. Based on previous studies, we can assume that the weights of Allen's hummingbirds have a normal distribution, with $\sigma = 0.33$ gram.
    (a) Find an 80% confidence interval for the average weights of Allen's hummingbirds in the study region. What is the margin of error?
    (b) What conditions are necessary for your calculations?
    (c) Give a brief interpretation of your results in the context of this problem.
    (d) *Sample Size:* Find the sample size necessary for an 80% confidence level with a maximal error of estimate $E = 0.08$ for the mean weights of the hummingbirds.

12. *Diagnostic Tests: Uric Acid* Overproduction of uric acid in the body can be an indication of cell breakdown. This may be an advance indication of illness such as gout, leukemia, or lymphoma (Reference: *Manual of Laboratory and Diagnostic Tests*, F. Fischbach). Over a period of months, an adult male patient has taken eight blood tests for uric acid. The mean concentration was $\bar{x} = 5.35$ mg/dl. The distribution of uric acid in healthy adult males can be assumed to be normal, with $\sigma = 1.85$ mg/dl.
    (a) Find a 95% confidence interval for the population mean concentration of uric acid in this patient's blood. What is the margin of error?
    (b) What conditions are necessary for your calculations?
    (c) Give a brief interpretation of your results in the context of this problem.
    (d) *Sample Size:* Find the sample size necessary for a 95% confidence level with maximal error of estimate $E = 1.10$ for the mean concentration of uric acid in this patient's blood.

13. (a) 34.62 ml/kg to 40.38 ml/kg; 2.88 ml/kg.
(b) The sample size is large (30 or more) and σ is known.
(c) There is a 99% chance that the confidence interval is one of the intervals containing the population average blood plasma level for male firefighters.
(d) $n = 60$.

13. *Diagnostic Tests: Plasma Volume* Total plasma volume is important in determining the required plasma component in blood replacement therapy for a person undergoing surgery. Plasma volume is influenced by the overall health and physical activity of an individual. (Reference: See Problem 12.) Suppose that a random sample of 45 male firefighters are tested and that they have a plasma volume sample mean of $\bar{x} = 37.5$ ml/kg (milliliters plasma per kilogram body weight). Assume that $\sigma = 7.50$ ml/kg for the distribution of blood plasma.
(a) Find a 99% confidence interval for the population mean blood plasma volume in male firefighters. What is the margin of error?
(b) What conditions are necessary for your calculations?
(c) Give a brief interpretation of your results in the context of this problem.
(d) *Sample Size:* Find the sample size necessary for a 99% confidence level with maximal error of estimate $E = 2.50$ for the mean plasma volume in male firefighters.

14. (a) \$6.38 to \$7.38 per 100 pounds; \$0.50 per 100 pounds.
(b) $n = 111$.
(c) \$1914 to \$2214; \$150.

14. *Agriculture: Watermelon* What price do farmers get for their watermelon crops? In the third week of July, a random sample of 40 farming regions gave a sample mean of $\bar{x} = \$6.88$ per 100 pounds of watermelon. Assume that σ is known to be \$1.92 per 100 pounds (Reference: *Agricultural Statistics*, U.S. Department of Agriculture).
(a) Find a 90% confidence interval for the population mean price (per 100 pounds) that farmers in this region get for their watermelon crop. What is the margin of error?
(b) *Sample Size:* Find the sample size necessary for a 90% confidence level with maximal error of estimate $E = 0.3$ for the mean price per 100 pounds of watermelon.
(c) A farm brings 15 tons of watermelon to market. Find a 90% confidence interval for the population mean cash value of this crop. What is the margin of error? *Hint:* 1 ton is 2000 pounds.

Generally speaking, shorter confidence intervals are more useful. Problems 15, 16, and 17 explore how changes in the confidence level, σ, and sample size n affect the lengths of the intervals.

15. (a) 125.7 to 151.3 larceny cases; 12.8 larceny cases.
(b) 123.3 to 153.7 larceny cases; 15.2 larceny cases.
(c) 118.4 to 158.6 larceny cases; 20.1 larceny cases.
(d) Yes.
(e) Yes.

15. *FBI Report: Larceny* Thirty small communities in Connecticut (population near 10,000 each) gave an average of $\bar{x} = 138.5$ reported cases of larceny per year. Assume that σ is known to be 42.6 cases per year (Reference: *Crime in the United States*, Federal Bureau of Investigation).
(a) Find a 90% confidence interval for the population mean annual number of reported larceny cases in such communities. What is the margin of error?
(b) Find a 95% confidence interval for the population mean annual number of reported larceny cases in such communities. What is the margin of error?
(c) Find a 99% confidence interval for the population mean annual number of reported larceny cases in such communities. What is the margin of error?
(d) Compare the margins of error for parts (a) through (c). As the confidence levels increase, do the margins of error increase?
(e) *Critical Thinking:* Compare the lengths of the confidence intervals for parts (a) through (c). As the confidence levels increase, do the confidence intervals increase in length?

It is usually difficult to change σ. However, in some scientific experiments, the researcher may be able to control variables such as measuring technique or laboratory conditions to decrease σ.

16. (a) \$46,191 to \$54,489; \$4149.
(b) \$47,697 to \$52,983; \$2643.
(c) \$49,156 to \$51,524; \$1184.
(d) Yes.
(e) Yes.

16. *Salaries: Student Services* Consider college officials in admissions, registration, counseling, financial aid, campus ministry, food services, and so on. How much money do these people make each year? Suppose you read in your local newspaper that 45 officials in student services earned an average of $\bar{x} = \$50,340$ each year (Reference: *Chronicle of Higher Education*).
(a) Assume that $\sigma = \$16,920$ for salaries of college officials in student services. Find a 90% confidence interval for the population mean salaries of such personnel. What is the margin of error?
(b) Assume that $\sigma = \$10,780$ for salaries of college officials in student services. Find a 90% confidence interval for the population mean salaries of such personnel. What is the margin of error?
(c) Assume that $\sigma = \$4830$ for salaries of college officials in student services. Find a 90% confidence interval for the population mean salaries of such personnel. What is the margin of error?

(d) Compare the margins of error for parts (a) through (c). As the standard deviation decreases, does the margin of error decrease?

(e) *Critical Thinking:* Compare the lengths of the confidence intervals for parts (a) through (c). As the standard deviation decreases, does the length of a 90% confidence interval decrease?

17. (a) \$53,871 to \$64,009; \$5069.
(b) \$55,138 to \$62,742; \$3802.
(c) \$56,175 to \$61,705; \$2765.
(d) Yes.
(e) Yes.

17. *Salaries: College Administrators* How much do college administrators (not teachers or service personnel) make each year? Suppose you read the local newspaper and find that the average annual salary of administrators in the local college is $\bar{x}$ = \$58,940. Assume that σ is known to be \$18,490 for college administrator salaries (Reference: *The Chronicle of Higher Education*).

(a) Suppose that $\bar{x}$ = \$58,940 is based on a random sample of $n = 36$ administrators. Find a 90% confidence interval for the population mean annual salary of local college administrators. What is the margin of error?

(b) Suppose that $\bar{x}$ = \$58,940 is based on a random sample of $n = 64$ administrators. Find a 90% confidence interval for the population mean annual salary of local college administrators. What is the margin of error?

(c) Suppose that $\bar{x}$ = \$58,940 is based on a random sample of $n = 121$ administrators. Find a 90% confidence interval for the population mean annual salary of local college administrators. What is the margin of error?

(d) Compare the margins of error for parts (a) through (c). As the sample size increases, does the margin of error decrease?

(e) *Critical Thinking:* Compare the lengths of the confidence intervals for parts (a) through (c). As the sample size increases, does the length of a 90% confidence interval decrease?

18. (a) 1008 to 1142 cm/sec.
(b) There is a 95% chance that this is a confidence interval that contains the population mean wind speed. Notice that all values in the interval exceed 1000 cm/sec. This indicates that at this site, the population average wind speed is such that the sand is always moving.

18. *Ecology: Sand Dunes* At wind speeds above 1000 centimeters per second (cm/sec), significant sand-moving events begin to occur. Wind speeds below 1000 cm/sec deposit sand and wind speeds above 1000 cm/sec move sand to new locations. The cyclic nature of wind and moving sand determines the shape and location of large dunes (Reference: *Hydraulic, Geologic, and Biologic Research at Great Sand Dunes National Monument and Vicinity, Colorado,* Proceedings of the National Park Service Research Symposium). At a test site, the prevailing direction of the wind did not change noticeably. However, the velocity did change. Sixty wind speed readings gave an average velocity of $\bar{x}$ = 1075 cm/sec. Based on long-term experience, σ can be assumed to be 265 cm/sec.

(a) Find a 95% confidence interval for the population mean wind speed at this site.

(b) *Interpretation:* Does the confidence interval indicate that the population mean wind speed is such that the sand is always moving at this site? Explain.

19. (a) The mean rounds to the given value.
(b) 34.19 thousand to 37.81 thousand.
(c) Yes. \$30,000 is below the lower bound of the confidence interval.
(d) Yes. \$40,000 is above the upper bound of the confidence interval.
(e) 33.41 thousand to 38.59 thousand. Yes. Yes.

19. *Profits: Banks* Jobs and productivity! How do banks rate? One way to answer this question is to examine annual profits per employee. *Forbes Top Companies,* edited by J. T. Davis (John Wiley & Sons), gave the following data about annual profits per employee (in units of one thousand dollars per employee) for representative companies in financial services. Companies such as Wells Fargo, First Bank System, and Key Banks were included. Assume $\sigma \approx 10.2$ thousand dollars.

42.9	43.8	48.2	60.6	54.9	55.1	52.9	54.9	42.5	33.0	33.6
36.9	27.0	47.1	33.8	28.1	28.5	29.1	36.5	36.1	26.9	27.8
28.8	29.3	31.5	31.7	31.1	38.0	32.0	31.7	32.9	23.1	54.9
43.8	36.9	31.9	25.5	23.2	29.8	22.3	26.5	26.7		

(a) Use a calculator or appropriate computer software to verify that, for the preceding data, $\bar{x} \approx 36.0$.

(b) Let us say that the preceding data are representative of the entire sector of (successful) financial services corporations. Find a 75% confidence interval for μ, the average annual profit per employee for all successful banks.

Problem 19(c) contains a good topic for a class discussion about statistical inference and can be used as an early motivation for later work in testing (Chapter 9). Problem 20 contains a similar question.

(c) *Interpretation:* Let us say that you are the manager of a local bank with a large number of employees. Suppose the annual profits per employee are less than 30 thousand dollars per employee. Do you think this might be somewhat low compared with other successful financial institutions? Explain by referring to the confidence interval you computed in part (b).
(d) *Interpretation:* Suppose the annual profits are more than 40 thousand dollars per employee. As manager of the bank, would you feel somewhat better? Explain by referring to the confidence interval you computed in part (b).
(e) Repeat parts (b), (c), and (d) for a 90% confidence level.

20. (a) The mean rounds to the given value.
(b) 4.28 thousand to 5.92 thousand.
(c) Yes.
(d) Yes.
(e) 3.84 thousand to 6.36 thousand; 3 thousand is below; 6.5 thousand is above.

20. *Profits: Retail* Jobs and productivity! How do retail stores rate? One way to answer this question is to examine annual profits per employee. The following data give annual profits per employee (in units of one thousand dollars per employee) for companies in retail sales. See reference in Problem 19. Companies such as Gap, Nordstrom, Circuit City, Dillards, JCPenney, Sears, Wal-Mart, Office Depot, and Toys 'Я' Us are included. Assume $\sigma \approx 3.8$ thousand dollars.

4.4	6.5	4.2	8.9	8.7	8.1	6.1	6.0	2.6	2.9	8.1	−1.9
11.9	8.2	6.4	4.7	5.5	4.8	3.0	4.3	−6.0	1.5	2.9	4.8
−1.7	9.4	5.5	5.8	4.7	6.2	15.0	4.1	3.7	5.1	4.2	

(a) Use a calculator or appropriate computer software to verify that, for the preceding data, $\bar{x} \approx 5.1$.
(b) Let us say that the preceding data are representative of the entire sector of retail sales companies. Find an 80% confidence interval for μ, the average annual profit per employee for retail sales.
(c) *Interpretation:* Let us say that you are the manager of a retail store with a large number of employees. Suppose the annual profits per employee are less than 3 thousand dollars per employee. Do you think this might be low compared with other retail stores? Explain by referring to the confidence interval you computed in part (b).
(d) *Interpretation:* Suppose the annual profits are more than 6.5 thousand dollars per employee. As store manager, would you feel somewhat better? Explain by referring to the confidence interval you computed in part (b).
(e) Repeat parts (b), (c), and (d) for a 95% confidence interval.

SECTION 8.2

Estimating μ When σ Is Unknown

FOCUS POINTS

- Learn about degrees of freedom and Student's t distributions.
- Find critical values using degrees of freedom and confidence levels.
- Compute confidence intervals for μ when σ is unknown. What does this information tell you?

In order to use the normal distribution to find confidence intervals for a population mean μ, we need to know the value of σ, the population standard deviation. However, much of the time, when μ is unknown, σ is unknown as well. In such cases, we use the sample standard deviation s to approximate σ. When we use s to approximate σ, the sampling distribution for $\bar{x}$ follows a new distribution called a *Student's t distribution.*

Student's t Distributions

Student's t distributions were discovered in 1908 by W. S. Gosset. He was employed as a statistician by Guinness brewing company, a company that discouraged publication of research by its employees. As a result, Gosset published his research under the pseudonym *Student*. Gosset was the first to recognize the importance of developing statistical methods for obtaining reliable information from samples of populations with unknown σ. Gosset used the variable t when he introduced the distribution in 1908. To this day and in his honor, it is still called a Student's t distribution. It might be more fitting to call this distribution *Gosset's t distribution;* however, in the literature of mathematical statistics, it is known as a *Student's t distribution.*

The variable t is defined as follows. A Student's t distribution depends on sample size n.

This section contains our first introduction to the Student's t distribution. A little extra class time would be well invested.

Assume that x has a normal distribution with mean μ. For samples of size n with sample mean $\bar{x}$ and sample standard deviation s, the **t variable**

$$t = \frac{\bar{x} - \mu}{\frac{s}{\sqrt{n}}} \qquad (7)$$

has a **Student's t distribution** with **degrees of freedom $d.f.$** $= n - 1$.

Chi-square goodness-of-fit tests in Section 11.2 can be used to help us determine if a distribution is normal. See Problems 9 and 10 of Section 11.2.

If many random samples of size n are drawn, then we get many t values from Equation (7). These t values can be organized into a frequency table, and a histogram can be drawn, thereby giving us an idea of the shape of the t distribution (for a given n).

Fortunately, all this work is not necessary because mathematical theorems can be used to obtain a formula for the t distribution. However, it is important to observe that these theorems state that the shape of the t distribution depends only on n, provided the basic variable x has a normal distribution. So, *when we use a t distribution, we will assume that the x distribution is normal.*

Degrees of freedom

A simplistic explanation of degrees of freedom is that it is the number of variables free to change when a statistic or parameter is fixed. In this application of the Student's t distribution, the number of degrees of freedom is based on the number of variables free to change when we use the formula for the sample standard deviation. The sample mean $\bar{x}$ is included in the formula for s. This means that only $n - 1$ of the original n data values are free to vary when $\bar{x}$ is fixed. Students grasp this idea when they see a test average example. For instance, if a student needs a 90 average based on three tests, and the first two scores are 82 and 95, then the last score is fixed. It must be a 93. In other words, only the first two scores were "free to vary."

Table 4 of the Appendix gives values of the variable t corresponding to what we call the number of *degrees of freedom*, abbreviated *d.f.* For the methods used in this section, the number of degrees of freedom is given by the formula

$$d.f. = n - 1 \qquad (8)$$

where *d.f.* stands for the degrees of freedom and n is the sample size. Each choice for *d.f.* gives a different t distribution.

The graph of a t distribution is always symmetrical about its mean, which (as for the z distribution) is 0. The main observable difference between a t distribution and the standard normal z distribution is that a t distribution has somewhat thicker tails.

Figure 8-5 shows a standard normal z distribution and Student's t distribution with $d.f. = 3$ and $d.f. = 5$.

FIGURE 8-5

A Standard Normal Distribution and Student's t Distribution with $d.f. = 3$ and $d.f. = 5$

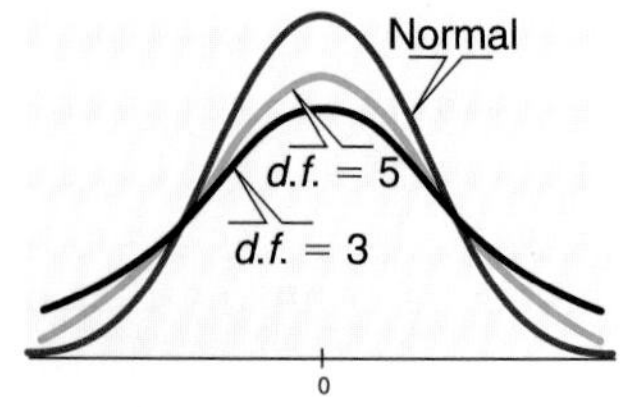

Properties of a Student's t distribution

1. The distribution is *symmetric* about the mean 0.
2. The distribution depends on the *degrees of freedom, d.f.* ($d.f. = n - 1$ for μ confidence intervals).
3. The distribution is *bell-shaped*, but has thicker tails than the standard normal distribution.
4. As the degrees of freedom increase, the t distribution *approaches* the standard normal distribution.

FIGURE 8-6

Area Under the t Curve Between $-t_c$ and t_c

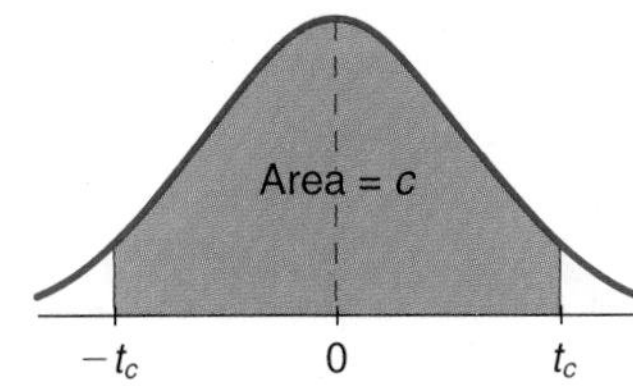

Using Table 4 to Find Critical Values for Confidence Intervals

Table 4 of the Appendix gives various t values for different degrees of freedom *d.f.* We will use this table to find *critical values* t_c for a c confidence level. In other words, we want to find t_c such that an area equal to c under the t distribution for a given number of degrees of freedom falls between $-t_c$ and t_c. In the language of probability, we want to find t_c such that

$$P(-t_c < t < t_c) = c$$

This probability corresponds to the shaded area in Figure 8-6.

Table 4 of the Appendix has been arranged so that c is one of the column headings, and the degrees of freedom *d.f.* are the row headings. To find t_c for any specific c, we find the column headed by that c value and read down until we reach the row headed by the appropriate number of degrees of freedom *d.f.* (You will notice two other column headings: one-tail area and two-tail area. We will use these later, but for the time being, ignore them.)

Convention for using a Student's *t* distribution table

If the degrees of freedom *d.f.* you need are not in the table, use the closest *d.f.* in the table that is *smaller.* This procedure results in a critical value t_c that is more conservative in the sense that it is larger. The resulting confidence interval will be longer and have a probability that is slightly higher than c.

EXAMPLE 4 STUDENT'S t DISTRIBUTION

Use Table 8-3 (an excerpt from Table 4 of the Appendix) to find the critical value t_c for a 0.99 confidence level for a t distribution with sample size $n = 5$.

SOLUTION:

(a) First, we find the column with c heading 0.990.

(b) Next, we compute the number of degrees of freedom: $d.f. = n - 1 = 5 - 1 = 4$.

(c) We read down the column under the heading $c = 0.99$ until we reach the row headed by 4 (under *d.f.*). The entry is 4.604. Therefore, $t_{0.99} = 4.604$.

TABLE 8-3 **Student's *t* Distribution Critical Values (Excerpt from Table 4 of the Appendix)**

one-tail area	–	–	–	–
two-tail area	–	–	–	–
d.f. \ ***c***	**... 0.900**	**0.950**	**0.980**	**0.990 ...**
⋮				
3	... 2.353	3.182	4.541	5.841 ...
4	... 2.132	2.776	3.747	4.604 ...
⋮				
7	... 1.895	2.365	2.998	3.449 ...
8	... 1.860	2.306	2.896	3.355 ...

GUIDED EXERCISE 2 | ***Student's t distribution table***

Use Table 4 of the Appendix (or Table 8-3 showing an excerpt from the table) to find t_c for a 0.90 confidence level for a t distribution with sample size $n = 9$.

(a) We find the column headed by $c =$ ________.

➡ $c = 0.900$.

(b) The degrees of freedom are given by $d.f. = n - 1 =$ ________.

➡ $d.f. = n - 1 = 9 - 1 = 8$.

(c) Read down the column found in part (a) until you reach the entry in the row headed by $d.f. = 8$. The value of $t_{0.90}$ is ________ for a sample of size 9.

➡ $t_{0.90} = 1.860$ for a sample of size $n = 9$.

(d) Find t_c for a 0.95 confidence level for a t distribution with sample size $n = 9$.

➡ $t_{0.95} = 2.306$ for a sample of size $n = 9$.

Maximal margin of error, E

In Section 8.1, we found bounds $\pm E$ on the margin of error for a c confidence level. Using the same basic approach, we arrive at the conclusion that

$$E = t_c \frac{s}{\sqrt{n}} \tag{9}$$

is the maximal margin of error for a c confidence level when σ is unknown (i.e., $|\bar{x} - \mu| < E$ with probability c). The analogue of Equation (1) in Section 8.1 is

$$P\left(-t_c \frac{s}{\sqrt{n}} < \bar{x} - \mu < t_c \frac{s}{\sqrt{n}}\right) = c \tag{10}$$

COMMENT Comparing Equation (10) with Equation (1) in Section 8.1, it becomes evident that we are using the same basic method on the t distribution that we did on the z distribution.

Likewise, for samples from normal populations with unknown σ, Equation (4) of Section 8.1 becomes

$$P(\bar{x} - E < \mu < \bar{x} + E) = c \tag{11}$$

where $E = t_c(s/\sqrt{n})$. Let us organize what we have been doing in a convenient summary.

PROCEDURE

Confidence interval for μ with σ unknown

This is a good time to point out the strong similarities and the differences between methods when σ is known and σ is unknown.

HOW TO FIND A CONFIDENCE INTERVAL FOR μ WHEN σ IS UNKNOWN

Let x be a random variable appropriate to your application. Obtain a simple random sample (of size n) of x values from which you compute the sample mean $\bar{x}$ and the sample standard deviation s.

If you can assume that x has a normal distribution or simply a mound-shaped symmetric distribution, then any sample size n will work. If you cannot assume this, then use a sample size of $n \geq 30$.

Continued

Confidence interval for μ when σ is unknown

$$\bar{x} - E < \mu < \bar{x} + E \quad (12)$$

where $\bar{x}$ = sample mean of a simple random sample

$$E = t_c \frac{s}{\sqrt{n}}$$

c = confidence level ($0 < c < 1$)

t_c = critical value for confidence level c and degrees of freedom $d.f. = n - 1$
(See Table 4 of the Appendix.)

COMMENT In our applications of Student's t distributions, we have made the basic assumption that x has a normal distribution. However, the same methods apply even if x is only approximately normal. In fact, the main requirement for using a Student's t distribution is that the distribution of x values be reasonably symmetrical and mound-shaped. If this is the case, then the methods we employ with the t distribution can be considered valid for most practical applications.

EXAMPLE 5 CONFIDENCE INTERVAL FOR μ, σ UNKNOWN

Suppose an archaeologist discovers only seven fossil skeletons from a previously unknown species of miniature horse. Reconstructions of the skeletons of these seven miniature horses show the shoulder heights (in centimeters) to be

45.3 47.1 44.2 46.8 46.5 45.5 47.6

For these sample data, the mean is $\bar{x} \approx 46.14$ and the sample standard deviation is $s \approx 1.19$. Let μ be the mean shoulder height (in centimeters) for this entire species of miniature horse, and assume that the population of shoulder heights is approximately normal.

Find a 99% confidence interval for μ, the mean shoulder height of the entire population of such horses.

SOLUTION: In this case, $n = 7$, so $d.f. = n - 1 = 7 - 1 = 6$. For $c = 0.990$, Table 4 of the Appendix gives $t_{0.99} = 3.707$ (for $d.f. = 6$). The sample standard deviation is $s \approx 1.19$.

$$E = t_c \frac{s}{\sqrt{n}} = (3.707)\frac{1.19}{\sqrt{7}} \approx 1.67$$

The 99% confidence interval is

$$\bar{x} - E < \mu < \bar{x} + E$$
$$46.14 - 1.67 < \mu < 46.14 + 1.67$$
$$44.5 < \mu < 47.8$$

INTERPRETATION The archaeologist can be 99% confident that the interval from 44.5 cm to 47.8 cm is an interval that contains the population mean μ for shoulder height of this species of miniature horse.

GUIDED EXERCISE 3 **Confidence interval for μ, σ unknown**

A company has a new process for manufacturing large artificial sapphires. In a trial run, 37 sapphires are produced. The mean weight for these 37 gems is $\bar{x} = 6.75$ carats, and the sample standard deviation is $s = 0.33$ carat. Let μ be the mean weight for the distribution of all sapphires produced by the new process.

(a) What is *d.f.* for this setting?

→ $d.f. = n - 1$, where n is the sample size. Since $n = 37$, $d.f. = 37 - 1 = 36$.

(b) Use Table 4 of the Appendix to find $t_{0.95}$. Note that $d.f. = 36$ is not in the table. Use the *d.f.* closest to 36 that is *smaller* than 36.

→ $d.f. = 35$ is the closest *d.f.* in the table that is *smaller* than 36. Using $d.f. = 35$ and $c = 0.95$, we find $t_{0.95} = 2.030$.

(c) Find E.

→ $$E = t_{0.95}\frac{s}{\sqrt{n}}$$

$$\approx 2.030\frac{0.33}{\sqrt{37}} \approx 0.11 \text{ carat}$$

(d) Find a 95% confidence interval for μ.

→ $$\bar{x} - E < \mu < \bar{x} + E$$

$$6.75 - 0.11 < \mu < 6.75 + 0.11$$

$$6.64 \text{ carats} < \mu < 6.86 \text{ carats}$$

(e) Interpret the confidence interval in the context of the problem.

→ The company can be 95% confident that the interval from 6.64 to 6.86 is an interval that contains the population mean weight of sapphires produced by the new process.

We have several formulas for confidence intervals for the population mean μ. How do we choose an appropriate one? We need to look at the sample size, the distribution of the original population, and whether or not the population standard deviation σ is known.

Point out to students that this summary can be used as a kind of mental flowchart to help them organize their work in chapter problems and exams.

Summary: Confidence intervals for the mean

Assume that you have a random sample of size n from an x distribution and that you have computed $\bar{x}$ and s. A confidence interval for μ is

$$\bar{x} - E < \mu < \bar{x} + E$$

where E is the margin of error. How do you find E? It depends on how much you know about the x distribution.

Situation I (most common)

You don't know the population standard deviation σ. In this situation, you use the t distribution with margin of error

$$E = t_c\frac{s}{\sqrt{n}}$$

where degrees of freedom

$$d.f. = n - 1$$

Continued

Although a t distribution can be used in many situations, you need to observe some guidelines. If n is less than 30, x should have a distribution that is mound-shaped and approximately symmetric. It's even better if the x distribution is normal. If n is 30 or more, the central limit theorem (Chapter 7) implies that these restrictions can be relaxed.

Situation II (almost never happens!)

You actually know the population value of σ. In addition, you know that x has a normal distribution. If you don't know that the x distribution is normal, then your sample size n must be 30 or larger. In this situation, you use the standard normal z distribution with margin of error

$$E = z_c \frac{\sigma}{\sqrt{n}}$$

Which distribution should you use for $\bar{x}$?

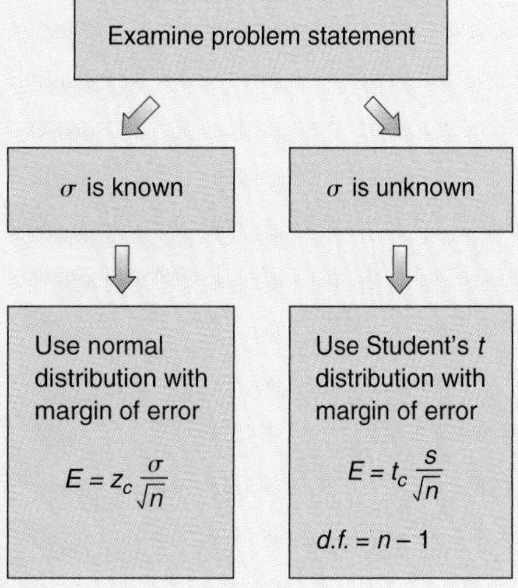
Examine problem statement
σ is known
σ is unknown
Use normal distribution with margin of error
E = z_c σ/√n
Use Student's t distribution with margin of error
E = t_c s/√n
d.f. = n − 1

Problem 21 shows a common alternate method of computing confidence intervals for large samples if s is not known. This method uses the normal distribution when $n \geq 30$ and s is not known.

COMMENT To find confidence intervals for μ based on small samples, we need to know that the population distribution is approximately normal. What if this is not the case? A procedure called *bootstrap* utilizes computer power to generate an approximation for the $\bar{x}$ sampling distribution. Essentially, the bootstrap method treats the sample as if it were the population. Then, using repetition, it takes many samples (often thousands) from the original sample. This process is called *resampling*. The sample mean $\bar{x}$ is computed for each resample and a distribution of sample means is created. For example, a 95% confidence interval reflects the range for the middle 95% of the bootstrap $\bar{x}$ distribution.

TECH NOTES

The TI-84Plus and TI-83Plus calculators, Excel, and Minitab support confidence intervals using the Student's t distribution.

TI-84Plus/TI-83Plus Press the STAT key, select TESTS, and choose the option **8:TInterval.** You may use either raw data in a list or summary statistics.

Excel Excel gives only the value of the maximal margin of error E. You can easily construct the confidence interval by computing $\bar{x} - E$ and $\bar{x} + E$. Use the menu choices **Tools ➤ Data Analysis ➤ Describe Statistics.** In the dialogue box, check summary statistics and check confidence level for mean. Then set the desired confidence level. Under these menu choices, Excel uses the Student's t distribution.

Minitab Use the menu choices **Stat ➤ Basic Statistics ➤ 1-Sample t.** In the dialogue box, indicate the column that contains the raw data. The Minitab output shows the confidence interval for Example 5.

```
T Confidence Intervals
Variable    N      Mean     StDev    SE Mean       99.0 % CI
C1          7    46.143     1.190      0.450    (44.475, 47.810)
```

VIEWPOINT Earthquakes!

California, Washington, Nevada, and even Yellowstone National Park all have earthquakes. Some earthquakes are severe! Earthquakes often bring fear and anxiety to people living near the quake. Is San Francisco due for a really big quake like the 1906 major earthquake? How big are the sizes of recent earthquakes compared with really big earthquakes? What is the duration of an earthquake? How long is the time span between major earthquakes? One way to answer questions such as these is to use existing data to estimate confidence intervals for the average size, duration, and time interval between quakes. Recent data sets for computing such confidence intervals can be found at the National Earthquake Information Service of the U.S. Geological Survey web site. To access the site, visit the Online Study Center at **www.cengage.com/statistics/Brase/UBS5e** *and find the link to National Earthquake Information Service.*

SECTION 8.2 PROBLEMS

Tables and art to accompany margin answers may be found in the back of the book.

1. 2.110.
2. 5.841.
3. 1.721.
4. 2.201.
5. $t = 0$.
6. Standard normal distribution.
7. $n = 10$, with *d.f.* $= 9$.
8. $n = 10$, with *d.f.* $= 9$.
9. Shorter. For *d.f.* $= 40$, z_c is less than t_c, and the resulting margin of error E is smaller.
10. Shorter. As the degrees of freedom increase, values of t_c decrease, and the corresponding margin of error E decreases.

1. Use Table 4 of the Appendix to find t_c for a 0.95 confidence level when the sample size is 18.

2. Use Table 4 of the Appendix to find t_c for a 0.99 confidence level when the sample size is 4.

3. Use Table 4 of the Appendix to find t_c for a 0.90 confidence level when the sample size is 22.

4. Use Table 4 of the Appendix to find t_c for a 0.95 confidence level when the sample size is 12.

5. *Statistical Literacy* Student's t distributions are symmetric about a value of t. What is that t value?

6. *Statistical Literacy* As the degrees of freedom increase, what distribution does the Student's t distribution become more like?

7. *Critical Thinking* Consider a 90% confidence interval for μ. Assume σ is not known. For which sample size, $n = 10$ or $n = 20$, is the critical value t_c larger?

8. *Critical Thinking* Consider a 90% confidence interval for μ. Assume σ is not known. For which sample size, $n = 10$ or $n = 20$, is the confidence interval longer?

9. *Critical Thinking* Lorraine computed a confidence interval for μ based on a sample of size 41. Since she did not know σ, she used s in her calculations. Lorraine used the normal distribution for the confidence interval instead of a Student's t distribution. Will her interval be longer or shorter than one obtained by using an appropriate Student's t distribution? Explain.

10. *Critical Thinking* Lorraine was in a hurry when she computed a confidence interval for μ. Because σ was not known, she used a Student's t distribution. However, she accidentally used degrees of freedom n instead of $n - 1$. Will her confidence interval be longer or shorter than one found using the correct degrees of freedom $n - 1$? Explain.

In Problems 11–17, assume that the population of x values has an approximately normal distribution. Answers may vary slightly due to rounding.

11. (a) The mean and standard deviation round to the values given.
(b) 1249 to 1295.

11. *Archaeology: Tree Rings* At Burnt Mesa Pueblo, the method of tree ring dating gave the following years A.D. for an archaeological excavation site (*Bandelier Archaeological Excavation Project: Summer 1990 Excavations at Burnt Mesa Pueblo*, edited by Kohler, Washington State University):

1189	1271	1267	1272	1268	1316	1275	1317	1275

(a) Use a calculator with mean and standard deviation keys to verify that the sample mean year is $\bar{x} \approx 1272$, with sample standard deviation $s \approx 37$ years.
(b) Find a 90% confidence interval for the mean of all tree ring dates from this archaeological site.

12. (a) Use a calculator.
(b) \$72.55 to \$94.95.

12. *Camping: Cost of a Sleeping Bag* How much does a sleeping bag cost? Let's say you want a sleeping bag that should keep you warm in temperatures from 20°F to 45°F. A random sample of prices (\$) for sleeping bags in this temperature range was taken from *Backpacker Magazine: Gear Guide* (Vol. 25, Issue 157, No. 2). Brand names include American Camper, Cabela's, Camp 7, Caribou, Cascade, and Coleman.

80	90	100	120	75	37	30	23	100	110
105	95	105	60	110	120	95	90	60	70

(a) Use a calculator with mean and sample standard deviation keys to verify that $\bar{x} \approx \$83.75$ and $s \approx \$28.97$.
(b) Using the given data as representative of the population of prices of all summer sleeping bags, find a 90% confidence interval for the mean price μ of all summer sleeping bags.

13. (a) Use a calculator.
(b) 74.7 lb to 107.3 lb.

13. *Wildlife: Mountain Lions* How much do wild mountain lions weigh? *The 77th Annual Report of the New Mexico Department of Game and Fish*, edited by Bill Montoya, gave the following information. Adult wild mountain lions (18 months or older) captured and released for the first time in the San Andres Mountains gave the following weights (pounds):

68	104	128	122	60	64

(a) Use a calculator with mean and sample standard deviation keys to verify that $\bar{x} = 91.0$ pounds and $s \approx 30.7$ pounds.
(b) Find a 75% confidence interval for the population average weight μ of all adult mountain lions in the specified region.

14. Use a calculator; 88.7 thousand to 125.1 thousand dollars.

14. *Franchise: Candy Store* Do you want to own your own candy store? Wow! With some interest in running your own business and a decent credit rating, you can probably get a bank loan on startup costs for franchises such as Candy Express, The Fudge Company, Karmel Corn, and Rocky Mountain Chocolate Factory. Startup costs (in thousands of dollars) for a random sample of candy stores are given below (Source: *Entrepreneur Magazine*, Vol. 23, No. 10).

95	173	129	95	75	94	116	100	85

Use a calculator with mean and sample standard deviation keys to verify that $\bar{x} \approx 106.9$ thousand dollars and $s \approx 29.4$ thousand dollars. Find a 90% confidence interval for the population average startup costs μ for candy store franchises.

15. (a) The mean and standard deviation round to the given values.
(b) 8.41 to 11.49.
(c) Since all values in the 99.9% confidence interval are above 6, we can be almost certain that this patient no longer has a calcium deficiency.

15. *Diagnostic Tests: Total Calcium* Over the past several months, an adult patient has been treated for tetany (severe muscle spasms). This condition is associated with an average total calcium level below 6 mg/dl (Reference: *Manual of Laboratory and Diagnostic Tests*, F. Fischbach). Recently, the patient's total calcium tests gave the following readings (in mg/dl).

9.3	8.8	10.1	8.9	9.4	9.8	10.0
9.9	11.2	12.1				

(a) Use a calculator to verify that $\bar{x} = 9.95$ and $s \approx 1.02$.
(b) Find a 99.9% confidence interval for the population mean of total calcium in this patient's blood.
(c) *Interpretation:* Based on your results in part (b), do you think this patient still has a calcium deficiency? Explain.

16. Use a calculator; 57.7% to 66.9%.

16. *Hospitals: Charity Care* What percentage of hospitals provide at least some charity care? The following problem is based on information taken from *State Health Care Data: Utilization, Spending, and Characteristics* (American Medical Association). Based on a random sample of hospital reports from eastern states, the following information was obtained (units in percentage of hospitals providing at least some charity care):

57.1 56.2 53.0 66.1 59.0 64.7 70.1 64.7 53.5 78.2

Use a calculator with mean and sample standard deviation keys to verify that $\bar{x} \approx 62.3\%$ and $s \approx 8.0\%$. Find a 90% confidence interval for the population average μ of the percentage of hospitals providing at least some charity care.

17. (a) Boxplots differ in length of interquartile box, location of median, and length of whiskers. The boxplots come from different samples.
(b) Yes; no; for 95% confidence intervals, we expect about 95% of the samples to generate intervals that contain the mean of the population.

17. *Critical Thinking: Boxplots and Confidence Intervals* The distribution of heights of 18-year-old men in the United States is approximately normal, with mean 68 inches and standard deviation 3 inches (U.S. Census Bureau). In Minitab, we can simulate the drawing of random samples of size 20 from this population (➤ **Calc** ➤ **Random Data** ➤ **Normal,** with 20 rows from a distribution with mean 68 and standard deviation 3). Then we can have Minitab compute a 95% confidence interval and draw a boxplot of the data (➤ **Stat** ➤ **Basic Statistics** ➤ **1—Sample t,** with boxplot selected in the graphs). The boxplots and confidence intervals for four different samples are shown in the accompanying figures. The four confidence intervals are

VARIABLE	N	MEAN	STDEV	SEMEAN	95.0 % CI
Sample 1	20	68.050	2.901	0.649	(66.692 , 69.407)
Sample 2	20	67.958	3.137	0.702	(66.490 , 69.426)
Sample 3	20	67.976	2.639	0.590	(66.741 , 69.211)
Sample 4	20	66.908	2.440	0.546	(65.766 , 68.050)

(a) Examine the figure [parts (a) to (d)]. How do the boxplots for the four samples differ? Why should you expect the boxplots to differ?

95% Confidence Intervals for Mean Height of 18-Year-Old Men (Sample size 20)

(a) Boxplot of Sample 1
(with 95% *t*-confidence interval for the mean)

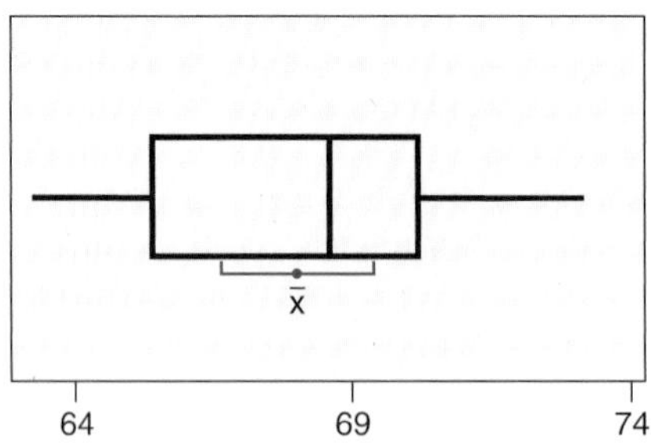

(b) Boxplot of Sample 2
(with 95% *t*-confidence interval for the mean)

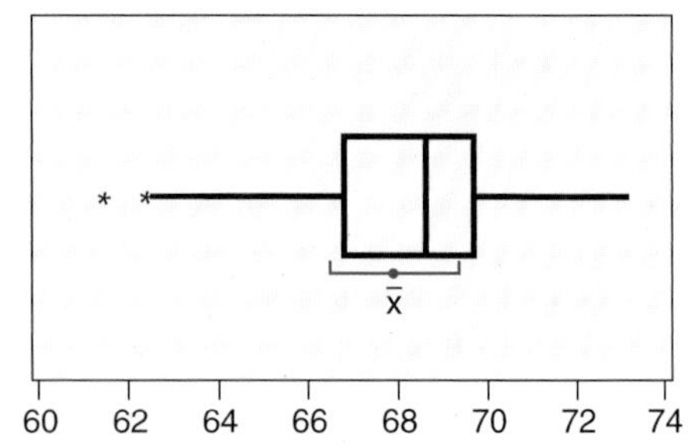

(c) Boxplot of Sample 3
(with 95% *t*-confidence interval for the mean)

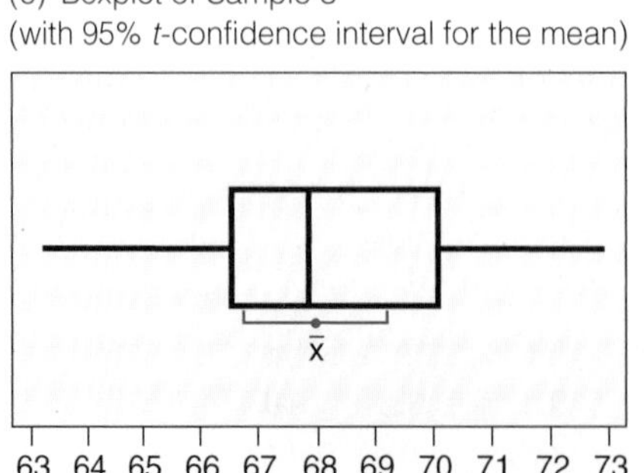

(d) Boxplot of Sample 4
(with 95% *t*-confidence interval for the mean)

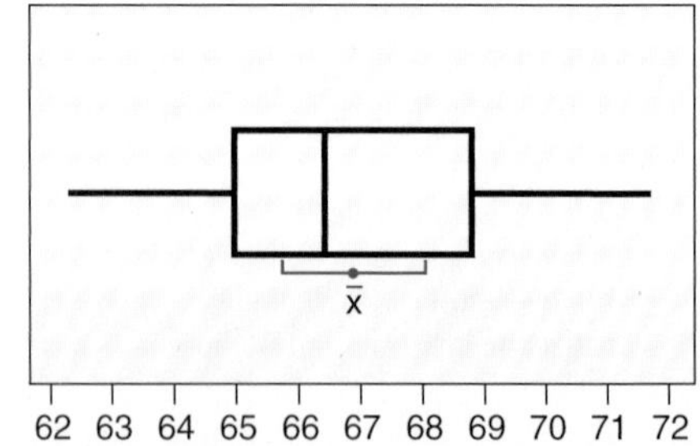

(b) Examine the 95% confidence intervals for the four samples shown in the printout. Do the intervals differ in length? Do the intervals all contain the expected population mean of 68 inches? If we draw more samples, do you expect all of the resulting 95% confidence intervals to contain $\mu = 68$? Why or why not?

18. (a) The mean and standard deviation round to the given values.
(b) 58.8 to 69.6 crimes per 1000 population.
(c) Maybe. 57 is just slightly below the lower bound of the confidence interval.
(d) Yes. 75 is higher than the upper bound of the confidence interval.
(e) 55.9 to 72.5 crimes per 1000 population. No; 57 is within the interval, so it may not be below average. Since 75 is still above the upper limit of the confidence interval, it seems that more patrols in this neighborhood are justified.
(f) By the central limit theorem, when n is large, the $\bar{x}$ distribution is approximately normal. In general, $n \geq 30$ is considered large.

18. *Crime Rate: Denver* The following data represent crime rates per 1000 population for a random sample of 46 Denver neighborhoods (Reference: *The Piton Foundation*, Denver, Colorado).

63.2	36.3	26.2	53.2	65.3	32.0	65.0
66.3	68.9	35.2	25.1	32.5	54.0	42.4
77.5	123.2	66.3	92.7	56.9	77.1	27.5
69.2	73.8	71.5	58.5	67.2	78.6	33.2
74.9	45.1	132.1	104.7	63.2	59.6	75.7
39.2	69.9	87.5	56.0	154.2	85.5	77.5
84.7	24.2	37.5	41.1			

(a) Use a calculator with mean and sample standard deviation keys to verify that $\bar{x} \approx 64.2$ and $s \approx 27.9$ crimes per 1000 population.
(b) Let us say the preceding data are representative of the population crime rates in Denver neighborhoods. Compute an 80% confidence interval for μ, the population mean crime rate for all Denver neighborhoods.
(c) *Interpretation:* Suppose you are advising the police department about police patrol assignments. One neighborhood has a crime rate of 57 crimes per 1000 population. Do you think that this rate is below the average population crime rate and that fewer patrols could safely be assigned to this neighborhood? Use the confidence interval to justify your answer.
(d) *Interpretation:* Another neighborhood has a crime rate of 75 crimes per 1000 population. Does this crime rate seem to be higher than the population average? Would you recommend assigning more patrols to this neighborhood? Use the confidence interval to justify your answer.
(e) Repeat parts (b), (c), and (d) for a 95% confidence interval.
(f) In previous problems, we assumed the x distribution was normal or approximately normal. Do we need to make such an assumption in this problem? Why or why not? *Hint:* See the central limit theorem in Section 7.5.

19. (a) The mean and standard deviation round to the given values.
(b) 21.6 to 28.8.
(c) 19.4 to 31.0.
(d) Using both confidence intervals, we can say that the P/E for Bank One is well below the population average. The P/E for AT&T Wireless is well above the population average. The P/E for Disney is within both confidence intervals. It appears that the P/E for Disney is close to the population average P/E.
(e) By the central limit theorem, when n is large, the $\bar{x}$ distribution is approximately normal. In general, $n \geq 30$ is considered large.

19. *Finance: P/E Ratio* The price of a share of stock divided by the company's estimated future earnings per share is called the P/E ratio. High P/E ratios usually indicate "growth" stocks, or maybe stocks that are simply overpriced. Low P/E ratios indicate "value" stocks or bargain stocks. A random sample of 51 of the largest companies in the United States gave the following P/E ratios (Reference: *Forbes*).

11	35	19	13	15	21	40	18	60	72	9	20
29	53	16	26	21	14	21	27	10	12	47	14
33	14	18	17	20	19	13	25	23	27	5	16
8	49	44	20	27	8	19	12	31	67	51	26
19	18	32									

(a) Use a calculator with mean and sample standard deviation keys to verify that $\bar{x} \approx 25.2$ and $s \approx 15.5$.
(b) Find a 90% confidence interval for the P/E population mean μ of all large U.S. companies.
(c) Find a 99% confidence interval for the P/E population mean μ of all large U.S. companies.
(d) *Interpretation:* Bank One (now merged with J. P. Morgan) had a P/E of 12, AT&T Wireless had a P/E of 72, and Disney had a P/E of 24. Examine the confidence intervals in parts (b) and (c). How would you describe these stocks at the time the sample was taken?

(e) In previous problems, we assumed the x distribution was normal or approximately normal. Do we need to make such an assumption in this problem? Why or why not? *Hint:* See the central limit theorem in Section 7.5.

20. (a) The mean and standard deviation round to the given values.
(b) Use $d.f. = 40$ in the table; 1.93 to 2.65.
(c) Use $d.f. = 40$ in the table; 1.71 to 2.87.
(d) Both Tim Huelett and Herb Hunter have home run percentages that are in the confidence intervals. This means that there is a high probability they are both close to average. Jackie Jensen has a home run percentage that is above the upper limits of both confidence intervals. We can be 99% sure that his home run percentage is above the population average.
(e) By the central limit theorem, when n is large, the $\bar{x}$ distribution is approximately normal. In general, $n \geq 30$ is considered large.

20. *Baseball: Home Run Percentage* The home run percentage is the number of home runs per 100 times at bat. A random sample of 43 professional baseball players gave the following data for home run percentages (Reference: *The Baseball Encyclopedia*, Macmillan).

1.6	2.4	1.2	6.6	2.3	0.0	1.8	2.5	6.5	1.8
2.7	2.0	1.9	1.3	2.7	1.7	1.3	2.1	2.8	1.4
3.8	2.1	3.4	1.3	1.5	2.9	2.6	0.0	4.1	2.9
1.9	2.4	0.0	1.8	3.1	3.8	3.2	1.6	4.2	0.0
1.2	1.8	2.4							

(a) Use a calculator with mean and standard deviation keys to verify that $\bar{x} \approx 2.29$ and $s \approx 1.40$.
(b) Compute a 90% confidence interval for the population mean μ of home run percentages for all professional baseball players. *Hint:* If you use Table 4 of the Appendix, be sure to use the closest $d.f.$ that is *smaller.*
(c) Compute a 99% confidence interval for the population mean μ of home run percentages for all professional baseball players.
(d) *Interpretation:* The home run percentages for three professional players are

Tim Huelett, 2.5 Herb Hunter, 2.0 Jackie Jensen, 3.8

Examine your confidence intervals and describe how the home run percentages for these players compare to the population average.
(e) In previous problems, we assumed the x distribution was normal or approximately normal. Do we need to make such an assumption in this problem? Why or why not? *Hint:* See the central limit theorem in Section 7.5.

This exercise may be used to introduce students to Method 2 as an alternate method for computing confidence intervals for μ when $n \geq 30$. Method 2 is used in many textbooks, and in fact was used in earlier editions of this text. However, Method 1 is used in this text and is used in most statistical research and statistical software.

21. (a) $d.f. = 30$; 43.58 to 46.82; 43.26 to 47.14; 42.58 to 47.82.
(b) 43.63 to 46.77; 43.33 to 47.07; 42.74 to 47.66.
(c) Yes; the respective intervals based on the Student's t distribution are slightly longer.
(d) For Student's t, $d.f. = 80$; 44.22 to 46.18; 44.03 to 46.37; 43.65 to 46.75. For standard normal, 44.23 to 46.17; 44.05 to 46.35; 43.68 to 46.72. The intervals using the t distribution are still slightly longer than the corresponding intervals using the standard normal distribution. However, with a larger sample size, the differences between the two methods is less pronounced.

21. *Expand Your Knowledge: Alternate Method for Confidence Intervals* When σ is unknown and the sample is of size $n \geq 30$, there are two methods for computing confidence intervals for μ.

Method 1: Use the Student's t distribution with $d.f. = n - 1$.
This is the method used in the text. It is widely employed in statistical studies. Also, most statistical software packages use this method.

Method 2: When $n \geq 30$, use the sample standard deviation s as an estimate for σ, and then use the standard normal distribution.
This method is based on the fact that for large samples, s is a fairly good approximation for σ. Also, for large n, the critical values for the Student's t distribution approach those of the standard normal distribution.

Consider a random sample of size $n = 31$, with sample mean $\bar{x} = 45.2$ and sample standard deviation $s = 5.3$.
(a) Compute 90%, 95%, and 99% confidence intervals for μ using Method 1 with a Student's t distribution. Round endpoints to two digits after the decimal.
(b) Compute 90%, 95%, and 99% confidence intervals for μ using Method 2 with the standard normal distribution. Use s as an estimate for σ. Round endpoints to two digits after the decimal.
(c) Compare intervals for the two methods. Would you say that confidence intervals using a Student's t distribution are more conservative in the sense that they tend to be longer than intervals based on the standard normal distribution?
(d) Repeat parts (a) through (c) for a sample of size $n = 81$. With increased sample size, do the two methods give respective confidence intervals that are more similar?

SECTION 8.3

Estimating p in the Binomial Distribution

FOCUS POINTS

- Compute the maximal margin of error for proportions using a given level of confidence.
- Compute confidence intervals for p and interpret the results.
- Interpret poll results.
- Compute the sample size to be used for estimating a proportion p when we have an estimate for p.
- Compute the sample size to be used for estimating a proportion p when we have no estimate for p.

The binomial distribution is completely determined by the number of trials n and the probability p of success on a single trial. For most experiments, the number of trials is chosen in advance. Then the distribution is completely determined by p. In this section, we will consider the problem of estimating p under the assumption that n has already been selected.

We are employing what are called *large-sample methods*. We will assume that the normal curve is a good approximation to the binomial distribution, and when necessary, we will use sample estimates for the standard deviation. Empirical studies have shown that these methods are quite good provided *both*

Basic criteria

$$np > 5 \quad \text{and} \quad nq > 5, \qquad \text{where } q = 1 - p$$

Let r be the number of successes out of n trials in a binomial experiment. We will take the sample proportion of successes $\hat{p}$ (read "p hat") $= r/n$ as our *point estimate for* p, the population proportion of successes.

This is a good time to link back to the normal approximation to the binomial as presented in Section 7.6. Good topics for class discussion can be found in Data Highlights, Problem 2 (daylight saving time) and Problem 3 (percent of coupons that are redeemed).

The **point estimates for p and q** are

$$\hat{p} = \frac{r}{n}$$

$$\hat{q} = 1 - \hat{p}$$

where n = number of trials and r = number of successes.

For example, suppose that 800 students are selected at random from a student body of 20,000 and that they are each given a shot to prevent a certain type of flu. These 800 students are then exposed to the flu, and 600 of them do not get the flu. What is the probability p that the shot will be successful for any single student selected at random from the entire population of 20,000 students? We estimate p for the entire student body by computing r/n from the sample of 800 students. The value $\hat{p} = r/n$ is 600/800, or 0.75. The value $\hat{p} = 0.75$ is then the *point estimate* for p.

The difference between the actual value of p and the estimate $\hat{p}$ is the size of our error caused by using $\hat{p}$ as a point estimate for p. The magnitude of $\hat{p} - p$ is called the *margin of error* for using $\hat{p} = r/n$ as a point estimate for p. In absolute value notation, the margin of error is $|\hat{p} - p|$.

Margin of error

To compute the bounds for the margin of error, we need some information about the distribution of $\hat{p} = r/n$ values for different samples of the same size n. It turns out that, for large samples, the distribution of $\hat{p}$ values is well approximated by a *normal curve* with

$$\text{mean } \mu = p \qquad \text{and} \qquad \text{standard error } \sigma = \sqrt{pq/n}$$

Since the distribution of $\hat{p} = r/n$ is approximately normal, we use features of the standard normal distribution to find the bounds for the difference $\hat{p} - p$. Recall that z_c is the number such that an area equal to c under the standard normal curve falls between $-z_c$ and z_c. Then, in terms of the language of probability,

$$P\left(-z_c\sqrt{\frac{pq}{n}} < \hat{p} - p < z_c\sqrt{\frac{pq}{n}}\right) = c \qquad (13)^*$$

Equation (13) states that the chance is c that the numerical difference between $\hat{p}$ and p is between $-z_c\sqrt{pq/n}$ and $z_c\sqrt{pq/n}$. With the c confidence level, our estimate $\hat{p}$ differs from p by no more than

Maximal margin of error, E

$$E = z_c\sqrt{pq/n}$$

As in Section 8.1, we call E the *maximal margin of error.*

Confidence interval for p

To find a c confidence interval for p, we will use E in place of the expression $z_c\sqrt{pq/n}$ in Equation (13). Then we get

$$P(-E < \hat{p} - p < E) = c \qquad (14)$$

Some algebraic manipulation produces the mathematically equivalent statement

$$P(\hat{p} - E < p < \hat{p} + E) = c \qquad (15)$$

Equation (15) states that the probability is c that p lies in the interval from $\hat{p} - E$ to $\hat{p} + E$. Therefore, the interval from $\hat{p} - E$ to $\hat{p} + E$ is the c confidence interval for p that we wanted to find.

There is one technical difficulty in computing the c confidence interval for p. The expression $E = z_c\sqrt{pq/n}$ requires that we know the values of p and q. In most situations, we will not know the actual values of p or q, so we will use our point estimates

$$p \approx \hat{p} \quad \text{and} \quad q = 1 - p \approx 1 - \hat{p}$$

to estimate E. These estimates are safe for most practical purposes, since we are dealing with large-sample theory (that is, cases where $np > 5$ and $nq > 5$).

For convenient reference, we'll summarize the information about c confidence intervals for p, the probability of success in a binomial distribution.

PROCEDURE

This is a good time to focus student attention on key points that have been presented so far.

HOW TO FIND A CONFIDENCE INTERVAL FOR A PROPORTION p

Consider a binomial experiment with n trials, where p represents the population probability of success and $q = 1 - p$ represents the population probability of failure. Let r be a random variable that represents the number of successes out of the n binomial trials.

The point estimates for p and q are

$$\hat{p} = \frac{r}{n} \quad \text{and} \quad \hat{q} = 1 - \hat{p}$$

The number of trials n should be sufficiently large so that both $n\hat{p} > 5$ and $n\hat{q} > 5$.

Confidence interval for p

$$\hat{p} - E < p < \hat{p} + E$$

Continued

*Recall from Section 7.6 that when n is large, the binomial distribution of the number of successes r is approximately normal, with mean $\mu = np$ and standard deviation $\sigma = \sqrt{npq}$. Therefore, $z = (r - np)/\sqrt{npq}$. Dividing the numerator and denominator by n shows that $\hat{p} = r/n$ has a normal distribution with mean $\mu = p$ and standard deviation $\sigma = \sqrt{pq/n}$. Beginning with the equation $P(-z_c < z < z_c) = c$, replacing z by $(\hat{p} - p)/\sqrt{pq/n}$, and multiplying all parts of the inequality by $\sqrt{pq/n}$, we obtain Equation (13).

where $E \approx z_c\sqrt{\frac{\hat{p}\hat{q}}{n}} = z_c\sqrt{\frac{\hat{p}(1-\hat{p})}{n}}$

c = confidence level ($0 < c < 1$)

z_c = critical value for confidence level c based on the standard normal distribution (See Table 3(b) of the Appendix for frequently used values.)

EXAMPLE 6 CONFIDENCE INTERVAL FOR p

Let's return to our flu shot experiment described at the beginning of this section. Suppose that 800 students were selected at random from a student body of 20,000 and given shots to prevent a certain type of flu. All 800 students were exposed to the flu, and 600 of them did not get the flu. Let p represent the probability that the shot will be successful for any single student selected at random from the entire population of 20,000. Let q be the probability that the shot is not successful.

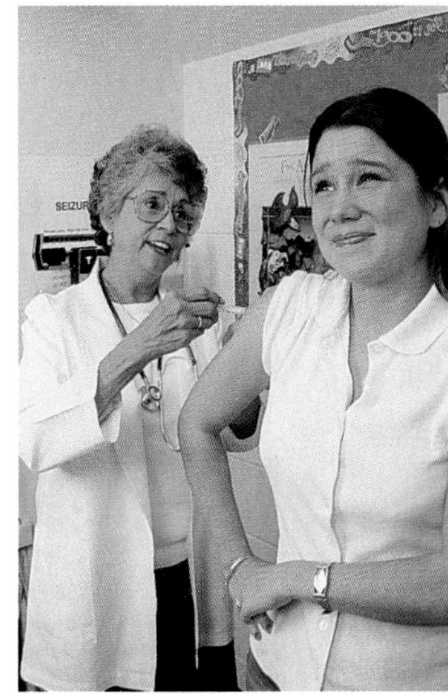

(a) What is the number of trials n? What is the value of r?

SOLUTION: Since each of the 800 students receiving the shot may be thought of as a trial, then $n = 800$, and $r = 600$ is the number of successful trials.

(b) What are the point estimates for p and q?

SOLUTION: We estimate p by the sample point estimate

$$\hat{p} = \frac{r}{n} = \frac{600}{800} = 0.75$$

We estimate q by

$$\hat{q} = 1 - \hat{p} = 1 - 0.75 = 0.25$$

(c) Would it seem that the number of trials is large enough to justify a normal approximation to the binomial?

SOLUTION: Since $n = 800$, $p \approx 0.75$, and $q \approx 0.25$, then

$$np \approx (800)(0.75) = 600 > 5 \quad \text{and} \quad nq \approx (800)(0.25) = 200 > 5$$

A normal approximation is certainly justified.

(d) Find a 99% confidence interval for p.

SOLUTION:

$$z_{0.99} = 2.58 \text{ (see Table 8-2 or Table 3(b) of the Appendix)}$$

$$E \approx z_{0.99}\sqrt{\frac{\hat{p}(1-\hat{p})}{n}} \approx 2.58\sqrt{\frac{(0.75)(0.25)}{800}} \approx 0.0395$$

The 99% confidence interval is then

$$\hat{p} - E < p < \hat{p} + E$$
$$0.75 - 0.0395 < p < 0.75 + 0.0395$$
$$0.71 < p < 0.79$$

INTERPRETATION We are 99% confident that the probability a flu shot will be effective for a student selected at random is between 0.71 and 0.79.

GUIDED EXERCISE 4 *Confidence interval for p*

A random sample of 188 books purchased at a local bookstore showed that 66 of the books were murder mysteries. Let p represent the proportion of books sold by this store that are murder mysteries.

(a) What is a point estimate for p?

$$\hat{p} = \frac{r}{n} = \frac{66}{188} = 0.35$$

(b) Find a 90% confidence interval for p.

$$E \approx z_c\sqrt{\frac{\hat{p}(1-\hat{p})}{n}}$$

$$= 1.645\sqrt{\frac{(0.35)(1-0.35)}{188}} \approx 0.0572$$

The confidence interval is

$$\hat{p} - E < p < \hat{p} + E$$

$$0.35 - 0.0572 < p < 0.35 + 0.0572$$

$$0.29 < p < 0.41$$

(c) Interpret the confidence interval you just computed.

If we had computed the interval for many different sets of 188 books, we would have found that about 90% of the intervals actually contained p, the population proportion of mysteries. Consequently, we can be 90% confident that our interval is one of the intervals that contains the unknown value p.

(d) To compute the confidence interval, we used a normal approximation. Does this seem justified?

$n = 188$; $p \approx 0.35$; $q \approx 0.65$

Since $np \approx 65.8 > 5$ and $nq \approx 122.2 > 5$, the approximation is justified.

It is interesting to note that our sample point estimate $\hat{p} = r/n$ and the confidence interval for the population proportion p do not depend on the size of the population. In our bookstore example, it made no difference how many books the store sold. On the other hand, the size of the sample does affect the accuracy of a statistical estimate. At the end of this section, we will study the effect of sample size on the reliability of our estimate.

TECH NOTES The TI-84Plus and TI-83Plus calculators and Minitab provide confidence intervals for proportions.

TI-84Plus/TI-83Plus Press the **STAT** key, select **TESTS,** and choose option **A:1-PropZInt.** The letter x represents the number of successes r. The TI-84Plus/TI-83Plus output shows the results for Guided Exercise 4.

```
1-PropZInt
 (.29381,.40832)
 p̂=.3510638298
 n=188
```

Minitab Use the menu selections **Stat ➤ Basic Statistics ➤ 1 Proportion.** In the dialogue box, select Summarized Data and fill in the number of trials and the number of successes. Under Options, select a confidence interval. Minitab uses the binomial distribution directly unless Normal is checked. The Minitab output shows the results for Guided Exercise 4. Information from Chapter 9 material is also shown.

```
Test and Confidence Interval for One Proportion (Using Binomial)
Test of p = 0.5 vs p not = 0.5
                                                             Exact
Sample     X      N      Sample p          90.0 % CI        P-Value
  1       66    188      0.351064    (0.293222, 0.412466)    0.000
```

```
Test and Confidence Interval for One Proportion (Using Normal)
Test of p = 0.5 vs p not = 0.5
Sample    X    N   Sample p        90.0 % CI          Z-Value  P-Value
  1      66  188   0.351064  (0.293805, 0.408323)     -4.08     0.000
```

Interpreting Results from a Poll

Newspapers frequently report the results of an opinion poll. In articles that give more information, a statement about the margin of error accompanies the poll results. In most polls, the margin of error is given for a *95% confidence interval.*

Margin of error is widely referred to in the literature of statistics and in the media. See Linking Concepts, Problem 3, for more about the margin of error.

General interpretation of poll results

1. When a poll states the results of a survey, the proportion reported to respond in the designated manner is $\hat{p}$, the sample estimate of the population proportion.
2. The *margin of error* is the maximal error E of a 95% confidence interval for p.
3. A 95% confidence interval for the population proportion p is

   poll report $\hat{p}$ − margin of error $E < p <$ poll report $\hat{p}$ + margin of error E

COMMENT Leslie Kish, a statistician at the University of Michigan, was the first to apply the term *margin of error*. He was a pioneer in the study of population sampling techniques. His book *Survey Sampling* is still widely used all around the world.

Some articles clarify the meaning of the margin of error further by stating that it is an error due to sampling. For instance, the following comments accompany results of a political poll reported in an issue of *The Wall Street Journal.*

How Poll Was Conducted

The Wall Street Journal/NBC News poll was based on nationwide telephone interviews of 1508 adults conducted last Friday through Tuesday by the polling organizations of Peter Hart and Robert Teeter.

The sample was drawn from 315 randomly selected geographic points in the continental U.S. Each region was represented in proportion to its population. Households were selected by a method that gave all telephone numbers . . . an equal chance of being included.

One adult, 18 years or older, was selected from each household by a procedure to provide the correct number of male and female respondents.

Chances are 19 of 20 that if all adults with telephones in the U.S. had been surveyed, the findings would differ from these poll results by no more than 2.6 percentage points in either direction.

GUIDED EXERCISE 5 Reading a poll

Read the last paragraph of the article excerpt, "How Poll Was Conducted."

(a) What confidence level corresponds to the phrase "chances are 19 of 20 that if . . ."

$$\frac{19}{20} = 0.95$$

A 95% confidence interval is being discussed.

(b) The complete article indicates that everyone in the sample was asked the question, "Which party, the Democratic Party or the Republican Party, do you think would do a better job handling . . . education?" Possible responses were Democrats, neither, both, or Republicans. The poll reported that 32% of the respondents said "Democrats." Does 32% represent the sample statistic $\hat{p}$ or the population parameter p for the proportion of adults responding "Democrat"?

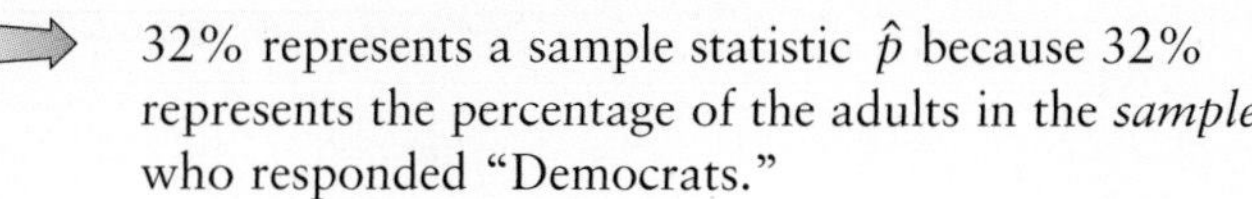

32% represents a sample statistic $\hat{p}$ because 32% represents the percentage of the adults in the *sample* who responded "Democrats."

(c) Continue reading the last paragraph of the article. It goes on to state, ". . . if all adults with telephones in the U.S. had been surveyed, the findings would differ from these poll results by no more than 2.6 percentage points in either direction." Use this information, together with parts (a) and (b), to find a 95% confidence interval for the proportion p of the specified population who would respond "Democrat" to the question.

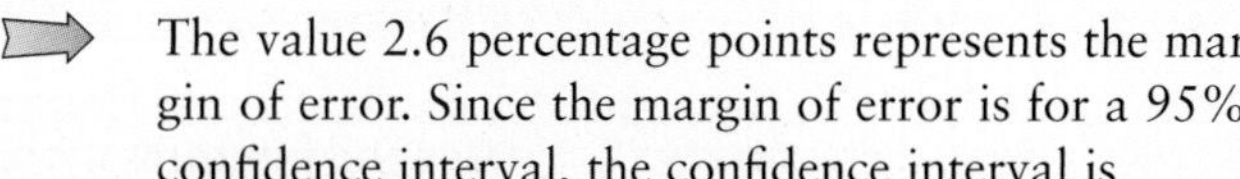

The value 2.6 percentage points represents the margin of error. Since the margin of error is for a 95% confidence interval, the confidence interval is

$$32\% - 2.6\% < p < 32\% + 2.6\%$$
$$29.4\% < p < 34.6\%$$

The poll indicates that at the time of the poll, between 29.4% and 34.6% of the specified population thought Democrats would do a better job handling education.

Sample Size for Estimating p

Suppose you want to specify the maximal margin of error in advance for a confidence interval for p at a given confidence level c. What sample size do you need? The answer depends on whether or not you have a preliminary estimate for the population probability of success p in a binomial distribution.

PROCEDURE

HOW TO FIND THE SAMPLE SIZE n FOR ESTIMATING A PROPORTION p

$$n = p(1 - p)\left(\frac{z_c}{E}\right)^2 \quad \text{if you have a preliminary estimate for } p \qquad (16)$$

$$n = \frac{1}{4}\left(\frac{z_c}{E}\right)^2 \quad \text{if you do } \textit{not} \text{ have a preliminary estimate for } p \qquad (17)$$

where E = specified maximal error of estimate

z_c = critical value from the normal distribution for the desired confidence level c. Commonly used values of z_c can be found in Table 3(b) of the Appendix.

Continued

If n is not a whole number, increase n to the next higher whole number. Also, if necessary, increase the sample size n to ensure that both $np > 5$ and $nq > 5$. Note that n is the minimal sample size for a specified confidence level and maximal error of estimate.

COMMENT To obtain Equation (16), simply solve the formula that gives the maximal error of estimate E of p for the sample size n. When you don't have an estimate for p, a little algebra can be used to show that the maximum value of $p(1 - p)$ is 1/4.

EXAMPLE 7 Sample size for estimating p

A company is in the business of selling wholesale popcorn to grocery stores. The company buys directly from farmers. A buyer for the company is examining a large amount of corn from a certain farmer. Before the purchase is made, the buyer wants to estimate p, the probability that a kernel will pop.

Suppose a random sample of n kernels is taken and r of these kernels pop. The buyer wants to be 95% sure that the point estimate $\hat{p} = r/n$ for p will be in error either way by less than 0.01.

(a) If no preliminary study is made to estimate p, how large a sample should the buyer use?

SOLUTION: In this case, we use Equation (17) with $z_{0.95} = 1.96$ (see Table 8-2) and $E = 0.01$.

$$n = \frac{1}{4}\left(\frac{z_c}{E}\right)^2 = \frac{1}{4}\left(\frac{1.96}{0.01}\right)^2 = 0.25(38{,}416) = 9604$$

The buyer would need a sample of $n = 9604$ kernels.

(b) A preliminary study showed that p was approximately 0.86. If the buyer uses the results of the preliminary study, how large a sample should be used?

SOLUTION: In this case, we use Equation (16) with $p \approx 0.86$. Again, from Table 8-2, $z_{0.95} = 1.96$, and from the problem, $E = 0.01$.

$$n = p(1 - p)\left(\frac{z_c}{E}\right)^2 = (0.86)(0.14)\left(\frac{1.96}{0.01}\right)^2 = 4625.29$$

The sample size should be at least $n = 4626$ kernels. This sample is less than half the sample size necessary without the preliminary study.

VIEWPOINT "Band-Aid Surgery"

Faster recovery time and less pain! Sounds great. An alternate surgical technique called laparoscopic *("Band-Aid")* surgery *involves small incisions in which tiny video cameras and long surgical instruments are maneuvered. Instead of a 10-inch incision, surgeons might use four little stabs of about $\frac{1}{2}$-inch in length. However, not every such surgery is successful. An article in the Health Section of* The Wall Street Journal *recommends using a surgeon who has done at least 50 such surgeries. Then the prospective patient should ask about the* rate of conversion*—that is, the proportion* p *of times the surgeon has been forced by complications to switch in midoperation to conventional surgery. A confidence interval for the proportion* p *would be useful patient information!*

SECTION 8.3 PROBLEMS

Tables and art to accompany margin answers may be found in the back of the book.

For all these problems, carry at least four digits after the decimal in your calculations. Answers may vary slightly due to rounding.

1. *Statistical Literacy* For a binomial experiment with r successes out of n trials, what value do we use as a point estimate for the probability of success p on a single trial?

   1. $\hat{p} = r/n$.

2. *Statistical Literacy* In order to use a normal distribution to compute confidence intervals for p, what conditions on np and nq need to be satisfied?

   2. $np > 5$ and $nq > 5$, where $p \approx \hat{p}$ and $q \approx 1 - \hat{p}$.

3. *Critical Thinking* Results of a poll of a random sample of 3003 American adults showed that 20% do not know that caffeine contributes to dehydration. The poll was conducted for the Nutrition Information Center and had a margin of error of ±1.4%.
   (a) Does the margin of error take into account any problems with the wording of the survey question, interviewer errors, bias from sequence of questions, and so forth?
   (b) What does the margin of error reflect?

   3. (a) No.
   (b) The difference between $\hat{p}$ and p. In other words, the margin of error is the difference between results based on a random sample and results based on a population.

4. *Critical Thinking* You want to conduct a survey to determine the proportion of people who favor a proposed tax policy. How does increasing the sample size affect the size of the margin of error?

   4. Increasing n decreases E.

5. *Myers-Briggs: Actors* Isabel Myers was a pioneer in the study of personality types. The following information is taken from *A Guide to the Development and Use of the Myers-Briggs Type Indicator,* by Myers and McCaulley (Consulting Psychologists Press). In a random sample of 62 professional actors, it was found that 39 were extroverts.
   (a) Let p represent the proportion of all actors who are extroverts. Find a point estimate for p.
   (b) Find a 95% confidence interval for p. Give a brief interpretation of the meaning of the confidence interval you have found.
   (c) Do you think the conditions $np > 5$ and $nq > 5$ are satisfied in this problem? Explain why this would be an important consideration.

   5. (a) $\hat{p} = 0.6290$.
   (b) 0.51 to 0.75.
   (c) Yes.

6. *Myers-Briggs: Judges* In a random sample of 519 judges, it was found that 285 were introverts (see reference of Problem 5).
   (a) Let p represent the proportion of all judges who are introverts. Find a point estimate for p.
   (b) Find a 99% confidence interval for p. Give a brief interpretation of the meaning of the confidence interval you have found.
   (c) Do you think the conditions $np > 5$ and $nq > 5$ are satisfied in this problem? Explain why this would be an important consideration.

   6. (a) $\hat{p} = 0.5491$.
   (b) 0.49 to 0.61.
   (c) Yes.

7. *Navajo Lifestyle: Traditional Hogans* A random sample of 5222 permanent dwellings on the entire Navajo Indian Reservation showed that 1619 were traditional Navajo hogans (*Navajo Architecture: Forms, History, Distributions,* by Jett and Spencer, University of Arizona Press).
   (a) Let p be the proportion of all permanent dwellings on the entire Navajo Reservation that are traditional hogans. Find a point estimate for p.
   (b) Find a 99% confidence interval for p. Give a brief interpretation of the confidence interval.
   (c) Do you think that $np > 5$ and $nq > 5$ are satisfied for this problem? Explain why this would be an important consideration.

   7. (a) $\hat{p} = 0.3100$.
   (b) 0.29 to 0.33.
   (c) Yes.

8. *Archaeology: Pottery* Santa Fe black-on-white is a type of pottery commonly found at archaeological excavations in Bandelier National Monument. At one excavation site, a sample of 592 potsherds was found, of which 360 were identified as Santa Fe black-on-white (*Bandelier Archaeological Excavation Project: Summer 1990 Excavations at Burnt Mesa Pueblo and Casa del Rito,* edited by Kohler and Root, Washington State University).

   8. (a) $\hat{p} = 0.6081$.
   (b) 0.57 to 0.65.
   (c) Yes.

(a) Let p represent the population proportion of Santa Fe black-on-white potsherds at the excavation site. Find a point estimate for p.
(b) Find a 95% confidence interval for p. Give a brief statement of the meaning of the confidence interval.
(c) Do you think the conditions $np > 5$ and $nq > 5$ are satisfied in this problem? Why would this be important?

9. (a) $\hat{p} = 0.5420$.
(b) 0.53 to 0.56.
(c) Yes.

9. *Health Care: Colorado Physicians* A random sample of 5792 physicians in Colorado showed that 3139 provided at least some charity care (i.e., treated poor people at no cost). These data are based on information from *State Health Care Data: Utilization, Spending, and Characteristics* (American Medical Association).
(a) Let p represent the proportion of all Colorado physicians who provide some charity care. Find a point estimate for p.
(b) Find a 99% confidence interval for p. Give a brief explanation of the meaning of your answer in the context of this problem.
(c) Is the normal approximation to the binomial justified in this problem? Explain.

10. (a) $\hat{p} = 0.7600$.
(b) 0.75 to 0.77.
(c) Yes.

10. *Law Enforcement: Escaped Convicts* Case studies showed that out of 10,351 convicts who escaped from U.S. prisons, only 7867 were recaptured (*The Book of Odds*, by Shook and Shook, Signet).
(a) Let p represent the proportion of all escaped convicts who eventually will be recaptured. Find a point estimate for p.
(b) Find a 99% confidence interval for p. Give a brief statement of the meaning of the confidence interval.
(c) Is use of the normal approximation to the binomial justified in this problem? Explain.

11. (a) $\hat{p} = 0.0304$.
(b) 0.02 to 0.05.
(c) Yes.

11. *Fishing: Barbless Hooks* In a combined study of northern pike, cutthroat trout, rainbow trout, and lake trout, it was found that 26 out of 855 fish died when caught and released using barbless hooks on flies or lures. All hooks were removed from the fish. (Source: *A National Symposium on Catch and Release Fishing*, Humboldt State University Press.)
(a) Let p represent the proportion of all pike and trout that die (i.e., p is the mortality rate) when caught and released using barbless hooks. Find a point estimate for p.
(b) Find a 99% confidence interval for p, and give a brief explanation of the meaning of the interval.
(c) Is the normal approximation to the binomial justified in this problem? Explain.

12. (a) $\hat{p} \approx 0.3143$; 0.185 to 0.443.
(b) np and nq both exceed 5.
(c) It seems that the Cherry Creek neighborhood is not different from the rest of the U.S.

12. *Focus Problem: Trick or Treat* In a survey of a random sample of 35 households in the Cherry Creek neighborhood of Denver, it was found that 11 households turned out the lights and pretended not to be home on Halloween.
(a) Compute a 90% confidence interval for p, the proportion of all households in Cherry Creek that pretend not to be home on Halloween.
(b) What assumptions are necessary to calculate the confidence interval of part (a)?
(c) *Interpretation:* The national proportion of all households in the United States that turn out the lights and pretend not to be home on Halloween is 0.28. Is 0.28 in the confidence interval you computed? Based on your answer, does it seem that the Cherry Creek neighborhood is much different (either higher or lower proportion) from the population of all U.S. households? Explain.

13. (a) $\hat{p} = 0.8603$.
(b) 0.84 to 0.89.
(c) A recent study shows that 86% of women shoppers remained loyal to their favorite supermarket last year. The margin of error was 2.5 percentage points.

13. *Marketing: Customer Loyalty* In a marketing survey, a random sample of 730 women shoppers revealed that 628 remained loyal to their favorite supermarket during the past year (i.e., did not switch stores). (Source: *Trends in the United States: Consumer Attitudes and the Supermarket*, The Research Department, Food Marketing Institute.)
(a) Let p represent the proportion of all women shoppers who remain loyal to their favorite supermarket. Find a point estimate for p.

(b) Find a 95% confidence interval for p. Give a brief explanation of the meaning of the interval.
(c) *Interpretation:* As a news writer, how would you report the survey results regarding the percentage of women supermarket shoppers who remained loyal to their favorite supermarket during the past year? What is the margin of error based on a 95% confidence interval?

14. (a) $\hat{p} = 0.2727$.
(b) 0.25 to 0.30.
(c) A recent study shows that 27.3% of all shoppers stock up on a real supermarket bargain, with margin of error 2.8 percent.

14. *Marketing: Bargain Hunters* In a marketing survey, a random sample of 1001 supermarket shoppers revealed that 273 always stock up on an item when they find that item at a real bargain price. See reference in Problem 13.
(a) Let p represent the proportion of all supermarket shoppers who always stock up on an item when they find a real bargain. Find a point estimate for p.
(b) Find a 95% confidence interval for p. Give a brief explanation of the meaning of the interval.
(c) As a news writer, how would you report the survey results on the percentage of supermarket shoppers who stock up on items when they find the item is a real bargain? What is the margin of error based on a 95% confidence interval?

15. (a) $\hat{p} = 0.25$.
(b) 0.22 to 0.28.
(c) A survey of 1000 large corporations has shown that 25% will choose a nonsmoking job candidate over an equally qualified smoker. The margin of error was 2.7%.

15. *Lifestyle: Smoking* In a survey of 1000 large corporations, 250 said that, given a choice between a job candidate who smokes and an equally qualified nonsmoker, the nonsmoker would get the job (*USA Today*).
(a) Let p represent the proportion of all corporations preferring a nonsmoking candidate. Find a point estimate for p.
(b) Find a 0.95 confidence interval for p.
(c) As a news writer, how would you report the survey results regarding the proportion of corporations that would hire the equally qualified nonsmoker? What is the margin of error based on a 95% confidence interval?

16. $\hat{p} = 0.19$; $E = 0.03$; 0.16 to 0.22.

16. *Opinion Poll: Crime and Violence* A *New York Times*/CBS poll asked the question, "What do you think is the most important problem facing this country today?" Nineteen percent of the respondents answered "crime and violence." The margin of sampling error was plus or minus 3 percentage points. Following the convention that the margin of error is based on a 95% confidence interval, find a 95% confidence interval for the percentage of the population that would respond "crime and violence" to the question asked by the pollsters.

17. (a) 208.
(b) 68.

17. *Medical: Blood Type* A random sample of medical files is used to estimate the proportion p of all people who have blood type B.
(a) If you have no preliminary estimate for p, how many medical files should you include in a random sample in order to be 85% sure that the point estimate $\hat{p}$ will be within a distance of 0.05 from p?
(b) Answer part (a) if you use the preliminary estimate that about 8 out of 90 people have blood type B. (Reference: *Manual of Laboratory and Diagnostic Tests,* F. Fischbach.)

18. (a) 456.
(b) 257.

18. *Business: Phone Contact* How hard is it to reach a businessperson by phone? Let p be the proportion of calls to businesspeople for which the caller reaches the person being called on the *first* try.
(a) If you have no preliminary estimate for p, how many business phone calls should you include in a random sample to be 80% sure that the point estimate $\hat{p}$ will be within a distance of 0.03 from p?
(b) The *Book of Odds,* by Shook and Shook (Signet), reports that businesspeople can be reached by a single phone call approximately 17% of the time. Using this (national) estimate for p, answer part (a).

19. (a) 666.
(b) 662.

19. *Campus Life: Coeds* What percentage of your campus student body is female? Let p be the proportion of women students on your campus.
(a) If no preliminary study is made to estimate p, how large a sample is needed to be 99% sure that a point estimate $\hat{p}$ will be within a distance of 0.05 from p?

(b) The *Statistical Abstract of the United States*, 112th Edition, indicates that approximately 54% of college students are females. Answer part (a) using this estimate for p.

20. (a) 97.
(b) 52 total, or 14 more.

20. *Small Business: Bankruptcy* The National Council of Small Businesses is interested in the proportion of small businesses that declared Chapter 11 bankruptcy last year. Since there are so many small businesses, the National Council intends to estimate the proportion from a random sample. Let p be the proportion of small businesses that declared Chapter 11 bankruptcy last year.
(a) If no preliminary sample is taken to estimate p, how large a sample is necessary to be 95% sure that a point estimate $\hat{p}$ will be within a distance of 0.10 from p?
(b) In a preliminary random sample of 38 small businesses, it was found that six had declared Chapter 11 bankruptcy. How many *more* small businesses should be included in the sample to be 95% sure that a point estimate $\hat{p}$ will be within a distance of 0.10 from p?

Chapter Review

SUMMARY

How do you get information about a population by looking at a random sample? One way is to use point estimates and confidence intervals.

- Point estimates and their corresponding parameters are

  $\bar{x}$ for μ

  $\hat{p}$ for p

- Confidence intervals are of the form

  point estimate $- E <$ parameter $<$ point estimate $+ E$

- E is the maximal margin of error. Specific values of E depend on the parameter, level of confidence, whether population standard deviations are known, sample size, and the shapes of the original population distributions.

  For μ: $E = z_c \dfrac{\sigma}{\sqrt{n}}$ when σ is known;

  $E = t_c \dfrac{s}{\sqrt{n}}$ with $d.f. = n - 1$ when σ is unknown

  For p: $E = z_c \sqrt{\dfrac{\hat{p}(1 - \hat{p})}{n}}$ when $n\hat{p} > 5$ and $n\hat{q} > 5$

- Confidence intervals have an associated probability c called the confidence level. For a given sample size, the proportion of all corresponding confidence intervals that contain the parameter in question is c.

IMPORTANT WORDS & SYMBOLS

Section 8.1
Maximal margin of error E
Confidence level c
Critical values z_c
Point estimate for μ
Confidence interval for μ
c confidence interval
Sample size for specified E

Section 8.2
Student's t variable
Degrees of freedom ($d.f.$)
Critical values t_c

Section 8.3
Point estimate for p, $\hat{p}$
Confidence interval for p
Margin of error for polls
Sample size for specified E

VIEWPOINT — All Systems Go?

On January 28, 1986, the Space Shuttle Challenger *caught fire and blew up only seconds after launch. A great deal of good engineering went into the design of the* Challenger. *However, when a system has several confidence levels operating at once, it can happen, in rare cases, that risks will increase rather than cancel out. Diane Vaughn is a professor of sociology at Boston College and author of the book* The Challenger Launch Decision *(University of Chicago Press). Her book contains an excellent discussion of risks, the normalization of deviants, and cost/safety tradeoffs. Vaughn's book is described as "a remarkable and important analysis of how social structures can induce consequential errors in a decision process" (Robert K. Merton, Columbia University).*

CHAPTER REVIEW PROBLEMS

1. See text.
2. $\bar{x}$ = mean of the confidence interval endpoints = \$4.30; E = \$0.15.
3. (a) No, the probability that μ is in the interval is either 0 or 1.
   (b) Yes, 99% confidence intervals are constructed in such a way that 99% of all such confidence intervals based on random samples of the designated size will contain μ.
4. Interval for a mean; \$1549 to \$1591; \$1536 to \$1604.
5. Interval for a mean; 176.91 to 180.49.
6. Sample size for a mean; 102.

1. *Statistical Literacy* In your own words, carefully explain the meanings of the following terms: point estimate, critical value, maximal margin of error, confidence level, and confidence interval.

2. ***Critical Thinking*** Suppose you are told that a 95% confidence interval for the average price of a gallon of regular gasoline in your state is from \$4.15 to \$4.45. Use the fact that the confidence interval for the mean is in the form $\bar{x} - E$ to $\bar{x} + E$ to compute the sample mean and the maximal margin of error E.

3. ***Critical Thinking*** If you have a 99% confidence interval for μ based on a simple random sample,
   (a) is it correct to say that the *probability* that μ is in the specified interval is 99%? Explain.
   (b) is it correct to say that in the long run, if you computed many, many confidence intervals using the prescribed method, about 99% of such intervals would contain μ? Explain.

For Problems 4–12, categorize each problem according to parameter being estimated, proportion p or mean μ. Then solve the problem.

4. *Auto Insurance: Claims* Anystate Auto Insurance Company took a random sample of 370 insurance claims paid out during a 1-year period. The average claim paid was \$1570. Assume σ = \$250. Find 0.90 and 0.99 confidence intervals for the mean claim payment.

5. *Psychology: Closure* Three experiments investigating the relation between need for cognitive closure and persuasion were reported in "Motivated Resistance and Openness to Persuasion in the Presence or Absence of Prior Information," by A. W. Kruglanski (*Journal of Personality and Social Psychology*, Vol. 65, No. 5, pp. 861–874). Part of the study involved administering a "need for closure scale" to a group of students enrolled in an introductory psychology course. The "need for closure scale" has scores ranging from 101 to 201. For the 73 students in the highest quartile of the distribution, the mean score was $\bar{x} = 178.70$. Assume a population standard deviation of $\sigma = 7.81$. These students were all classified as high on their need for closure. Assume that the 73 students represent a random sample of all students who are classified as high on their need for closure. Find a 95% confidence interval for the population mean score μ on the "need for closure scale" for all students with a high need for closure.

6. *Psychology: Closure* How large a sample is needed in Problem 5 if we wish to be 99% confident that the sample mean score is within 2 points of the population mean score for students who are high on the need for closure?

7. Interval for a mean.
(a) Use a calculator.
(b) 64.1 to 84.3.

7. *Archaeology: Excavations* The Wind Mountain archaeological site is located in southwestern New Mexico. Wind Mountain was home to an ancient culture of prehistoric Native Americans called Anasazi. A random sample of excavations at Wind Mountain gave the following depths (in centimeters) from present-day surface grade to the location of significant archaeological artifacts (Source: *Mimbres Mogollon Archaeology*, by A. Woosley and A. McIntyre, University of New Mexico Press).

85	45	120	80	75	55	65	60
65	95	90	70	75	65	68	

(a) Use a calculator with mean and sample standard deviation keys to verify that $\bar{x} \approx 74.2$ cm and $s \approx 18.3$ cm.
(b) Compute a 95% confidence interval for the mean depth μ at which archaeological artifacts from the Wind Mountain excavation site can be found.

8. Interval for a mean.
(a) Use a calculator.
(b) 14.27 to 17.33.

8. *Archaeology: Pottery* Sherds of clay vessels were put together to reconstruct rim diameters of the original ceramic vessels at the Wind Mountain archaeological site (see source in Problem 7). A random sample of ceramic vessels gave the following rim diameters (in centimeters):

15.9	13.4	22.1	12.7	13.1	19.6	11.7	13.5	17.7	18.1

(a) Use a calculator with mean and sample standard deviation keys to verify that $\bar{x} \approx 15.8$ cm and $s \approx 3.5$ cm.
(b) Compute an 80% confidence interval for the population mean μ of rim diameters for such ceramic vessels found at the Wind Mountain archaeological site.

9. Interval for a proportion; 0.50 to 0.54.

9. *Telephone Interviews: Survey* The National Study of the Changing Work Force conducted an extensive survey of 2958 wage and salaried workers on issues ranging from relationships with their bosses to household chores. The data were gathered through hour-long telephone interviews with a nationally representative sample (*The Wall Street Journal*). In response to the question, "What does success mean to you?" 1538 responded, "Personal satisfaction from doing a good job." Let p be the population proportion of all wage and salaried workers who would respond the same way to the stated question. Find a 90% confidence interval for p.

10. Sample size for a proportion; 9589.

10. *Telephone Interviews: Survey* How large a sample is needed in Problem 9 if we wish to be 95% confident that the sample percentage of those equating success with personal satisfaction is within 1% of the population percentage? (*Hint:* Use $p \approx 0.52$ as a preliminary estimate.)

11. Interval for a proportion.
(a) $\hat{p} = 0.4072$.
(b) 0.333 to 0.482.

11. *Archaeology: Pottery* Three-circle, red-on-white is one distinctive pattern painted on ceramic vessels of the Anasazi period found at the Wind Mountain archaeological site (see source for Problem 7). At one excavation, a sample of 167 potsherds indicated that 68 were of the three-circle, red-on-white pattern.
(a) Find a point estimate $\hat{p}$ for the proportion of all ceramic potsherds at this site that are of the three-circle, red-on-white pattern.
(b) Compute a 95% confidence interval for the population proportion p of all ceramic potsherds with this distinctive pattern found at the site.

12. Sample size for a proportion;
$n = 258$ total, or 91 more.

12. *Archaeology: Pottery* Consider the three-circle, red-on-white pattern discussed in Problem 11. How many ceramic potsherds must be found and identified if we are to be 95% confident that the sample proportion $\hat{p}$ of such potsherds is within 6% of the population proportion of three-circle, red-on-white patterns found at this excavation site? (*Hint:* Use the results of Problem 11 as a preliminary estimate.)

DATA HIGHLIGHTS: GROUP PROJECTS

Digging clams

Break into small groups and discuss the following topics. Organize a brief outline in which you summarize the main points of your group discussion.

1. Garrison Bay is a small bay in Washington state. A popular recreational activity in the bay is clam digging. For several years, this harvest has been monitored and the size distribution of clams recorded. Data for lengths and widths of little neck clams (*Protothaca staminea*) were recorded by a method of systematic sampling in a study done by S. Scherba and V. F. Gallucci ("The Application of Systematic Sampling to a Study of Infaunal Variation in a Soft Substrate Intertidal Environment," *Fishery Bulletin* 74:937–948). The data in Tables 8-4 and 8-5 give lengths and widths for 35 little neck clams.
   (a) Use a calculator to compute the sample mean and sample standard deviation for the lengths and widths. Compute the coefficient of variation for each.
   (b) Compute a 95% confidence interval for the population mean length of all Garrison Bay little neck clams.
   (c) How many more little neck clams would be needed in a sample if you wanted to be 95% sure that the sample mean length is within a maximal margin of error of 10 mm of the population mean length?

TABLE 8-4 **Lengths of Little Neck Clams (mm)**

530	517	505	512	487	481	485	479	452	468
459	449	472	471	455	394	475	335	508	486
474	465	420	402	410	393	389	330	305	169
91	537	519	509	511					

TABLE 8-5 **Widths of Little Neck Clams (mm)**

494	477	471	413	407	427	408	430	395	417
394	397	402	401	385	338	422	288	464	436
414	402	383	340	349	333	356	268	264	141
77	498	456	433	447					

   (d) Compute a 95% confidence interval for the population mean width of all Garrison Bay little neck clams.
   (e) How many more little neck clams would be needed in a sample if you wanted to be 95% sure that the sample mean width is within a maximal margin of error of 10 mm of the population mean width?

2. Examine Figure 8-7, "Fall Back."
   (a) Of the 1024 adults surveyed, 66% were reported to favor daylight saving time. How many people in the sample preferred daylight saving time? Using the statistic $\hat{p} = 0.66$ and sample size $n = 1024$, find a 95% confidence interval for the proportion of people p who favor daylight saving time. How could you report this information in terms of a margin of error?
   (b) Look at Figure 8-7 to find the sample statistic $\hat{p}$ for the proportion of people preferring standard time. Find a 95% confidence interval for the population proportion p of people who favor standard time. Report the same information in terms of a margin of error.

3. Examine Figure 8-8, "Coupons: Limited Use."
   (a) Use Figure 8-8 to estimate the percentage of merchandise coupons that were redeemed. Also estimate the percentage dollar value of the coupons that were redeemed. Are these numbers approximately equal?

FIGURE 8-7

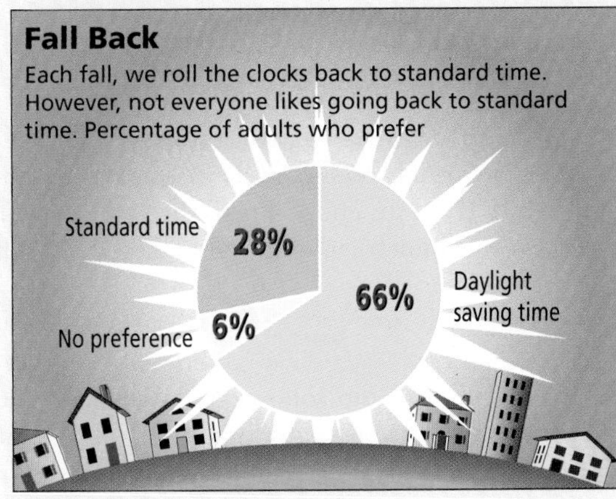

Source: Hilton Time Survey of 1024 adults

FIGURE 8-8 Coupons: Limited Use

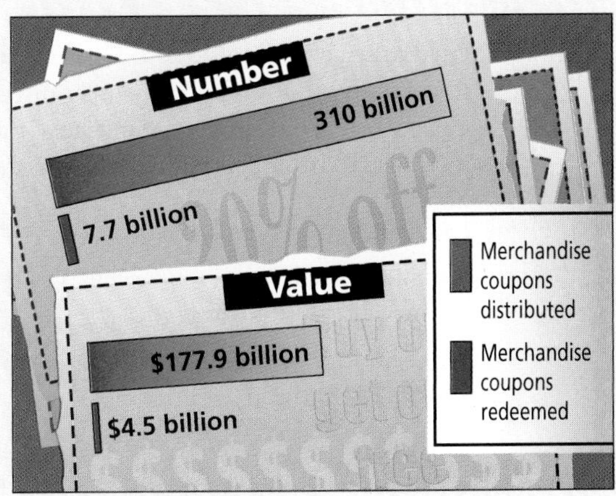

Source: NCH Promotional Services

(b) Suppose you are a marketing executive working for a national chain of toy stores. You wish to estimate the percentage of coupons that will be redeemed for the toy stores. How many coupons should you check to be 95% sure that the percentage of coupons redeemed is within 1% of the population proportion of all coupons redeemed for the toy store?

(c) Use the results of part (a) as a preliminary estimate for p, the percentage of coupons that are redeemed, and redo part (b).

(d) Suppose you sent out 937 coupons and found that 27 were redeemed. Explain why you could be 95% confident that the proportion of such coupons redeemed in the future would be between 1.9% and 3.9%.

(e) Suppose the dollar value of a collection of coupons was \$10,000. Use the data in Figure 8-8 to find the expected value and standard deviation of the dollar value of the redeemed coupons. What is the probability that between \$225 and \$275 (out of the \$10,000) is redeemed?

LINKING CONCEPTS: WRITING PROJECTS

Discuss each of the following topics in class or review the topics on your own. Then write a brief but complete essay in which you summarize the main points. Please include formulas and graphs as appropriate.

1. In this chapter, we have studied confidence intervals. Carefully read the following statements about confidence intervals:
   (a) Once the endpoints of the confidence interval are numerically fixed, then the parameter in question (either μ or p) does or does not fall inside the "fixed" interval.
   (b) A given fixed interval either does or does not contain the parameter μ or p; therefore, the probability is 1 or 0 that the parameter is in the interval.

   Next, read the following statements. Then discuss all four statements in the context of what we actually mean by a confidence interval.
   (c) Nontrivial probability statements can be made only about variables, not constants.
   (d) The confidence level c represents the proportion of all (fixed) intervals that would contain the parameter if we repeated the process many, many times.
2. Throughout Chapter 8, we have used the normal distribution, the central limit theorem, or the Student's t distribution.
   (a) Give a brief outline describing how confidence intervals for means use the normal distribution or Student's t distribution in their basic construction.
   (b) Give a brief outline describing how the normal approximation to the binomial distribution is used in the construction of confidence intervals for a proportion p.
   (c) Give a brief outline describing how the sample size for a predetermined error tolerance and level of confidence is determined from the normal distribution or the central limit theorem.
3. When the results of a survey or a poll are published, the sample size is usually given, as well as the margin of error. For example, suppose the *Honolulu Star Bulletin* reported that it surveyed 385 Honolulu residents and 78% said they favor mandatory jail sentences for people convicted of driving under the influence of drugs or alcohol (with margin of error of 3 percentage points in either direction). Usually the confidence level of the interval is not given, but it is standard practice to use the margin of error for a 95% confidence interval when no other confidence level is given.
   (a) The paper reported a point estimate of 78%, with margin of error of $\pm 3\%$. Write this information in the form of a confidence interval for p, the population proportion of residents favoring mandatory jail sentences for people convicted of driving under the influence. What is the assumed confidence level?
   (b) The margin of error is simply the error due to using a sample instead of the entire population. It does not take into account the bias that might be introduced by the wording of the question, by the truthfulness of the respondents, or by other factors. Suppose the question was asked in this fashion: "Considering the devastating injuries suffered by innocent victims in auto accidents caused by drunken or drugged drivers, do you favor a mandatory jail sentence for those convicted of driving under the influence of drugs or alcohol?" Do you think the wording of the question would influence the respondents? Do you think the population proportion of those favoring mandatory jail sentences is accurately represented by a confidence interval based on responses to such a question? Explain your answer.

If the question had been: "Considering existing overcrowding of our prisons, do you favor a mandatory jail sentence for people convicted of driving under the influence of drugs or alcohol?" Do you think the population proportion of those favoring mandatory sentences is accurately represented by a confidence interval based on responses to such a question? Explain.

Using Technology

Confidence Interval Demonstration

When we generate different random samples of the same size from a population, we discover that $\bar{x}$ varies from sample to sample. Likewise, different samples produce different confidence intervals for μ. The endpoints $\bar{x} \pm E$ of a confidence interval are statistical variables. A 90% confidence interval tells us that if we obtain lots of confidence intervals (for the same sample size), then the proportion of all intervals that will turn out to contain μ is 90%.

(a) Use the technology of your choice to generate 10 large random samples from a population with a known mean μ.

(b) Construct a 90% confidence interval for the mean for each sample.

(c) Examine the confidence intervals and note the percentage of the intervals that contain the population mean μ. We have 10 confidence intervals. Will exactly 90% of 10 intervals always contain μ? Explain. What if we have 1000 intervals?

Technology Hints for Confidence Interval Demonstration

TI-84Plus/TI-83Plus

The TI-84Plus/TI-83Plus generates random samples from uniform, normal, and binomial distributions. Press the **MATH** key and select **PRB**. Choice **5:randInt(lower, upper, sample size *n*)** generates random samples of size n from the integers between the specified lower and upper values. Choice **6:randNorm(μ, σ, sample size *n*)** generates random samples of size n from a normal distribution with specified mean and standard deviation. Choice **7:randBin(number of trials, *p*, sample size)** generates samples of the specified size from the designated binomial distribution. Under **STAT**, select **EDIT** and highlight the list name, such as L1. At the = sign, use the **MATH** key to access the desired population distribution. Finally, use **Zinterval** under the **TESTS** option of the **STAT** key to generate 90% confidence intervals.

Excel

Use the menu choices **Tools ➤ Data Analysis ➤ Random Number Generator.** In the dialogue box, the number of variables refers to the number of samples. The number of random numbers refers to the number of data in each sample. Select the population distribution (uniform, normal, binomial). The command **Paste function** (fx) ➤ **Statistical ➤ Confidence(1 − confidence level, σ, sample size)** gives the maximal margin of error E. To find a 90% confidence interval for each sample, use **Confidence(0.10, σ, sample size)** to find the maximal margin of error E. Note that if you use the population standard deviation σ in the function, the value of E will be the same for all samples of the same size. Next, find the sample mean $\bar{x}$ for each sample (use **Paste function** (fx) ➤ **Statistical ➤ Average**). Finally, construct the endpoints $\bar{x} \pm E$ of the confidence interval for each sample.

Minitab

Minitab provides options for sampling from a variety of distributions. To generate random samples from a specific distribution, use the menu selection **Calc ➤ Random Data ➤** and then select the population distribution. In the dialogue box, the *number of rows of data* represents the *sample size*. The *number of samples* corresponds to the number of columns selected for data storage. For example, C1−C10 in data storage produces 10 different random samples of the specified size. Use the menu selection **Stat ➤ Basic Statistics ➤ 1 sample *z*** to generate confidence intervals for the mean μ from each sample. In the variables box, list all the columns containing your samples. For instance, using C1−C10 in the variables list will produce confidence intervals for each of the 10 samples stored in columns C1 through C10.

The Minitab display shows 90% confidence intervals for 10 different random samples of size 50 taken from a normal distribution with $\mu = 30$ and $\sigma = 4$. Notice that, as expected, 9 out of 10 of the intervals contain $\mu = 30$.

Minitab Display

Z Confidence Intervals (Samples from a Normal Population with $\mu = 30$ and $\sigma = 4$)

The assumed sigma = 4.00

Variable	N	Mean	StDev	SE Mean	90.0 % CI
C1	50	30.265	4.300	0.566	(29.334, 31.195)
C2	50	31.040	3.957	0.566	(30.109, 31.971)
C3	50	29.940	4.195	0.566	(29.010, 30.871)
C4	50	30.753	3.842	0.566	(29.823, 31.684)
C5	50	30.047	4.174	0.566	(29.116, 30.977)
C6	50	29.254	4.423	0.566	(28.324, 30.185)
C7	50	29.062	4.532	0.566	(28.131, 29.992)
C8	50	29.344	4.487	0.566	(28.414, 30.275)
C9	50	30.062	4.199	0.566	(29.131, 30.992)
C10	50	29.989	3.451	0.566	(29.058, 30.919)

SPSS

SPSS uses a Student's t distribution to generate confidence intervals for the mean and difference of means. Use the menu choices **Analyze ➤ Compare Means** and then **One-Sample T Test** for confidence intervals for a single mean. In the dialogue box, use 0 for the test value. Click **Options...** to provide the confidence level.

To generate 10 random samples of size $n = 30$ from a normal distribution with $\mu = 30$ and $\sigma = 4$, first enter consecutive integers from 1 to 30 in a column of the data editor. Then, under variable view, enter the variable names Sample1 through Sample10. Use the menu choices **Transform ➤ Compute.** In the dialogue box, use Sample1 for the target variable, then select the function **RV.Normal(mean, stddev).** Use 30 for the mean and 4 for the standard deviation. Continue until you have 10 samples. To sample from other distributions, use appropriate functions in the Compute dialogue box.

The SPSS display shows 90% confidence intervals for 10 different random samples of size 30 taken from a normal distribution with $\mu = 30$ and $\sigma = 4$. Notice that, as expected, 9 of the 10 intervals contain the population mean $\mu = 30$.

SPSS Display

90% t-confidence intervals for random samples of size $n = 30$ from a normal distribution with $\mu = 30$ and $\sigma = 4$.

	t	df	Sig(2-tail)	Mean	Lower	Upper
SAMPLE1	42.304	29	.000	29.7149	28.5214	30.9084
SAMPLE2	43.374	29	.000	30.1552	28.9739	31.3365
SAMPLE3	53.606	29	.000	31.2743	30.2830	32.2656
SAMPLE4	35.648	29	.000	30.1490	28.7120	31.5860
SAMPLE5	47.964	29	.000	31.0161	29.9173	32.1148
SAMPLE6	34.718	29	.000	30.3519	28.8665	31.8374
SAMPLE7	34.698	29	.000	30.7665	29.2599	32.2731
SAMPLE8	39.731	29	.000	30.2388	28.9456	31.5320
SAMPLE9	44.206	29	.000	29.7256	28.5831	30.8681
SAMPLE10	49.981	29	.000	29.7273	28.7167	30.7379

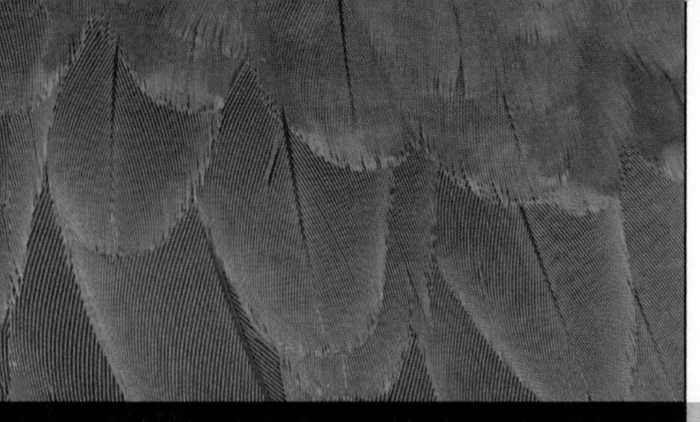

9

"Would you tell me, please, which way I ought to go from here?"

"That depends a good deal on where you want to get to," said the Cat.

"I don't much care where—" said Alice.

"Then it doesn't matter which way you go," said the Cat.

—Lewis Carroll
Alice's Adventures in Wonderland

Charles Lutwidge Dodgson (1832–1898) was an English mathematician who loved to write children's stories in his free time. The dialogue between Alice and the Cheshire Cat occurs in the masterpiece *Alice's Adventures in Wonderland,* written by Dodgson under the pen name Lewis Carroll. These lines relate to our study of hypothesis testing. Statistical tests cannot answer all of life's questions. They cannot always tell us "where to go," but after this decision is made on other grounds, they can help us find the best way to get there.

For on-line student resources, visit the Brase/Brase, *Understanding Basic Statistics,* 5th edition web site at **www.cengage.com/statistics/Brase/UBS5e.**

HYPOTHESIS TESTING

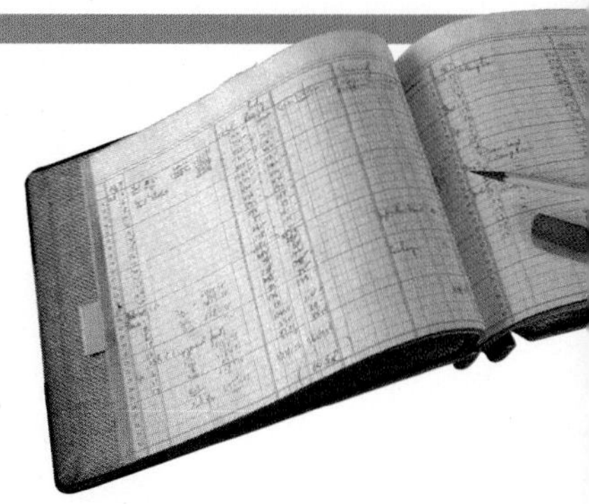

PREVIEW QUESTIONS

Many of life's questions require a yes or no answer. When you must act on incomplete (sample) information, how do you decide whether to accept or reject a proposal? (SECTION 9.1)

What is the P-value of a statistical test? What does this measurement have to do with performance reliability? (SECTION 9.1)

How do you construct statistical tests for μ? Does it make a difference whether σ is known or unknown? (SECTION 9.2)

How do you construct statistical tests for the proportion p of successes in a binomial experiment? (SECTION 9.3)

FOCUS PROBLEM

Benford's Law: The Importance of Being Number 1

Benford's Law states that in a wide variety of circumstances, numbers have "1" as their first nonzero digit disproportionately often. Benford's Law applies to such diverse topics as the drainage areas of rivers; properties of chemicals; populations of towns; figures in newspapers, magazines, and government reports; and the half-lives of radioactive atoms!

Specifically, such diverse measurements begin with "1" about 30% of the time, with "2" about 18% of time, and with "3" about 12.5% of the time. Larger digits occur less often. For example, less than 5% of the numbers in circumstances such as these begin with the digit 9. This is in dramatic contrast to a random sampling situation, in which each of the digits 1 through 9 has an equal chance of appearing.

The first nonzero digits of numbers taken from large bodies of numerical records such as tax returns, population studies, government records, and so forth show the probabilities of occurrence as displayed in the table on the next page.

More than 100 years ago, the astronomer Simon Newcomb noticed that books of logarithm tables were much dirtier near the fronts of the tables. It seemed that people were more frequently looking up numbers with

First nonzero digit	1	2	3	4	5	6	7	8	9
Probability	0.301	0.176	0.125	0.097	0.079	0.067	0.058	0.051	0.046

a low first digit. This was regarded as an odd phenomenon and a strange curiosity. The phenomenon was rediscovered in 1938 by physicist Frank Benford (hence the name *Benford's Law*).

More recently, Ted Hill, a mathematician at the Georgia Institute of Technology, studied situations that might demonstrate Benford's Law. Professor Hill showed that such probability distributions are likely to occur when we have a "distribution of distributions." Put another way, large random collections of random samples tend to follow Benford's Law. This seems to be especially true for samples taken from large government data banks, accounting reports for large corporations, large collections of astronomical observations, and so forth. For more information, see *American Scientist,* Vol. 86, pp. 358–363, and *Chance,* American Statistical Association, Vol. 12, No. 3, pp. 27–31.

Can Benford's Law be applied to help solve a real-world problem? Well, one application might be accounting fraud! Suppose the first nonzero digits of the entries in the accounting records of a large corporation (such as Enron or WorldCom) did not follow Benford's Law. Should this set off an accounting alarm for the FBI or the stockholders? How "significant" would this be? Such questions are the subject of statistics.

In Section 9.3, you will see how to use sample data to test whether the proportion of first nonzero digits of the entries in a large accounting report follows Benford's Law. Problems 5 and 6 of Section 9.3 relate to Benford's Law and accounting discrepancies. In one problem, you are asked to use sample data to determine if accounting books have been "cooked" by "pumping numbers up" to make the company look more attractive or perhaps to provide a cover for money laundering. In the other problem, you are asked to determine if accounting books have been "cooked" by artificially lowered numbers, perhaps to hide profits from the Internal Revenue Service or to divert company profits to unscrupulous employees. (See Problems 5 and 6 of Section 9.3.)

SECTION 9.1 Introduction to Statistical Tests

FOCUS POINTS

- Understand the rationale for statistical tests.
- Identify the null and alternate hypotheses in a statistical test.
- Identify right-tailed, left-tailed, and two-tailed tests.
- Use a test statistic to compute a *P*-value.
- Recognize types of errors, level of significance, and power of a test.
- Understand the meaning and risks of rejecting or not rejecting the null hypothesis.

In Chapter 1, we emphasized the fact that one of a statistician's most important jobs is to draw inferences about populations based on samples taken from the populations. Most statistical inference centers around the parameters of a population (often the mean or probability of success in a binomial trial). Methods for drawing inferences about parameters are of two types: Either we make decisions concerning the value of the parameter, or we actually estimate the value of the parameter. When we estimate the value (or location) of a parameter, we are using methods of estimation such as those studied in Chapter 8. Decisions concerning the value of a parameter are obtained by *hypothesis testing*, the topic we shall study in this chapter.

Students often ask which method should be used on a particular problem—that is, should the parameter be estimated, or should we test a *hypothesis* involving the parameter? The answer lies in the practical nature of the problem and the questions posed about it. Some people prefer to test theories concerning the parameters. Others prefer to express their inferences as estimates. Both estimation and hypothesis testing are found extensively in the literature of statistical applications.

Stating Hypotheses

Null hypothesis

This section contains much important terminology. Data Highlights and Linking Concepts provide some good material for class discussion.

Our first step is to establish a working hypothesis about the population parameter in question. This hypothesis is called the *null hypothesis*, denoted by the symbol H_0. The value specified in the null hypothesis is often a historical value, a claim, or a production specification. For instance, if the average height of a professional male basketball player was 6.5 feet 10 years ago, we might use a null hypothesis H_0: $\mu = 6.5$ feet for a study involving the average height of this year's professional male basketball players. If television networks claim that the average length of time devoted to commercials in a 60-minute program is 12 minutes, we would use H_0: $\mu = 12$ minutes as our null hypothesis in a study regarding the average length of time devoted to commercials. Finally, if a repair shop claims that it should take an average of 25 minutes to install a new muffler on a passenger automobile, we would use H_0: $\mu = 25$ minutes as the null hypothesis for a study of how well the repair shop is conforming to specified average times for a muffler installation.

Alternate hypothesis

Any hypothesis that differs from the null hypothesis is called an *alternate hypothesis*. An alternate hypothesis is constructed in such a way that it is the one to be accepted when the null hypothesis must be rejected. The alternate hypothesis is denoted by the symbol H_1. For instance, if we believe the average height of professional male basketball players is taller than it was 10 years ago, we would use an alternate hypothesis H_1: $\mu > 6.5$ feet with the null hypothesis H_0: $\mu = 6.5$ feet.

Null hypothesis H_0: This is the statement that is under investigation or being tested. Usually the null hypothesis represents a statement of "no effect," "no difference," or, put another way, "things haven't changed."

Alternate hypothesis H_1: This is the statement you will adopt in the situation in which the evidence (data) is so strong that you reject H_0. A statistical test is designed to assess the strength of the evidence (data) against the null hypothesis.

EXAMPLE 1 NULL AND ALTERNATE HYPOTHESES

A car manufacturer advertises that its new subcompact models get 47 miles per gallon (mpg). Let μ be the mean of the mileage distribution for these cars. You assume that the manufacturer will not underrate the car, but you suspect that the mileage might be overrated.

(a) What shall we use for H_0?

SOLUTION: We want to see if the manufacturer's claim that $\mu = 47$ mpg can be rejected. Therefore, our null hypothesis is simply that $\mu = 47$ mpg. We denote the null hypothesis as

$$H_0: \mu = 47 \text{ mpg}$$

(b) What shall we use for H_1?

SOLUTION: From experience with this manufacturer, we have every reason to believe that the advertised mileage is too high. If μ is not 47 mpg, we are sure it is less than 47 mpg. Therefore, the alternate hypothesis is

H_1: $\mu < 47$ mpg

GUIDED EXERCISE 1 **Null and alternate hypotheses**

A company manufactures ball bearings for precision machines. The average diameter of a certain type of ball bearing should be 6.0 mm. To check that the average diameter is correct, the company formulates a statistical test.

(a) What should be used for H_0? (*Hint:* What is the company trying to test?)

→ If μ is the mean diameter of the ball bearings, the company wants to test whether $\mu = 6.0$ mm. Therefore, H_0: $\mu = 6.0$ mm.

(b) What should be used for H_1? (*Hint:* An error either way, too small or too large, would be serious.)

→ An error either way could occur, and it would be serious. Therefore, H_1: $\mu \neq 6.0$ mm (μ is either smaller than or larger than 6.0 mm).

COMMENT: NOTATION REGARDING THE NULL HYPOTHESIS In statistical testing, the null hypothesis H_0 always contains the equals symbol. However, in the null hypothesis, some statistical software packages and texts also include the inequality symbol that is opposite that shown in the alternate hypothesis. For instance, if the alternate hypothesis is "μ is less than 3" ($\mu < 3$), then the corresponding null hypothesis is sometimes written as "μ is greater than or equal to 3" ($\mu \geq 3$). The mathematical construction of a statistical test uses the null hypothesis to assign a specific number (rather than a range of numbers) to the parameter μ in question. The null hypothesis establishes a single fixed value for μ, so we are working with a single distribution having a specific mean. In this case, H_0 assigns $\mu = 3$. So, when H_1: $\mu < 3$ is the alternate hypothesis, we follow the commonly used convention of writing the null hypothesis simply as H_0: $\mu = 3$.

Types of Tests

The null hypothesis H_0 always states that the parameter of interest *equals* a specified value. The alternate hypothesis H_1 states that the parameter is *less than, greater than,* or simply *not equal to* the same value. We categorize a statistical test as *left-tailed, right-tailed,* or *two-tailed* according to the alternate hypothesis.

Types of statistical tests

A statistical test is:

left-tailed if H_1 states that the parameter is less than the value claimed in H_0

right-tailed if H_1 states that the parameter is greater than the value claimed in H_0

two-tailed if H_1 states that the parameter is different from (or not equal to) the value claimed in H_0

TABLE 9-1 The Null and Alternate Hypotheses for Tests of the Mean μ

Null Hypothesis	Alternate Hypotheses and Type of Test		
Claim about μ or historical value of μ	You believe that μ is less than value stated in H_0.	You believe that μ is more than value stated in H_0.	You believe that μ is different from value stated in H_0.
H_0: $\mu = k$	H_1: $\mu < k$	H_1: $\mu > k$	H_1: $\mu \neq k$
	Left-tailed test	Right-tailed test	Two-tailed test

In this introduction to statistical tests, we discuss tests involving a population mean μ. However, you should keep an open mind and be aware that the methods outlined apply to testing other parameters as well (e.g., p, σ, $\mu_1 - \mu_2$, $p_1 - p_2$, and so on). Table 9-1 shows how tests of the mean μ are categorized.

Hypothesis Tests of μ, Given x Is Normal and σ Is Known

Once you have selected the null and alternate hypotheses, how do you decide which hypothesis is likely to be valid? Data from a simple random sample and the sample test statistic, together with the corresponding sampling distribution of the test statistic, will help you decide. Example 2 leads you through the decision process.

First, a quick review of Section 7.4 is in order. Recall that a population *parameter* is a numerical descriptive measurement of the entire population. Examples of population parameters are μ, p, and σ. It is important to remember that for a given population, the parameters are *fixed* values. They do not vary! The null hypothesis H_0 makes a statement about a population parameter.

A *statistic* is a numerical descriptive measurement of a sample. Examples of statistics are $\bar{x}$, $\hat{p}$, and s. Statistics usually *vary* from one sample to the next. The probability distribution of the statistic we are using is called a *sampling distribution.*

Test statistic for μ, given x normal and σ known

For hypothesis testing, we take a simple random sample and compute a *test statistic* corresponding to the parameter in H_0. Based on the sampling distribution of the statistic, we can assess how compatible the test statistic is with H_0.

In this section, we use hypothesis tests about the mean to introduce the concepts and vocabulary of hypothesis testing. In particular, let's suppose that x has a *normal distribution* with mean μ and standard deviation σ. Then, Theorem 7.1 tells us that $\bar{x}$ has a *normal distribution* with mean μ and standard deviation $\sigma/\sqrt{n}$.

Given that x has a *normal distribution* with known standard deviation σ, then

$$\textbf{test statistic} = z = \frac{\bar{x} - \mu}{\sigma/\sqrt{n}}$$

where $\bar{x}$ = mean of a simple random sample

μ = value stated in H_0

n = sample size

EXAMPLE 2 STATISTICAL TESTING PREVIEW

Rosie is an aging sheep dog in Montana who gets regular check-ups from her owner, the local veterinarian. Let x be a random variable that represents Rosie's resting heart rate (in beats per minute). From past experience, the vet knows that x has a normal distribution with $\sigma = 12$. The vet checked the *Merck Veterinary Manual* and found that for dogs of this breed, $\mu = 115$ beats per minute.

Over the past six weeks, Rosie's heart rate (beats/min) measured

93	109	110	89	112	117

The sample mean is $\bar{x} = 105.0$. The vet is concerned that Rosie's heart rate may be slowing. Do the data indicate that this is the case?

SOLUTION:

(a) Establish the null and alternate hypotheses.
If "nothing has changed" from Rosie's earlier life, then her heart rate should be nearly average. This point of view is represented by the null hypothesis

$$H_0: \mu = 115$$

However, the vet is concerned about Rosie's heart rate slowing. This point of view is represented by the alternate hypothesis

$$H_1: \mu < 115$$

(b) Are the observed sample data compatible with the null hypothesis?
Are the six observations of Rosie's heart rate compatible with the null hypothesis $H_0: \mu = 115$? To answer this question, you need to know the *probability* of obtaining a sample mean of 105.0 or less from a population with true mean $\mu = 115$. If this probability is small, we conclude that $H_0: \mu = 115$ is not the case. Rather, $H_1: \mu < 115$ and Rosie's heart rate is slowing.

(c) How do you compute the probability in part (b)?
Well, you probably guessed it! We use the sampling distribution for $\bar{x}$ and compute $P(\bar{x} < 105.0)$. Figure 9-1 shows the $\bar{x}$ distribution and the corresponding standard normal distribution with the desired probability shaded.

Since x has a normal distribution, $\bar{x}$ also will have a normal distribution for any sample size n and given σ (see Theorem 7.1). Note that using $\mu = 115$ from H_0, $\sigma = 12$, and $n = 6$, the sample $\bar{x} = 105.0$ converts to

$$\text{test statistic} = z = \frac{\bar{x} - \mu}{\sigma/\sqrt{n}} = \frac{105.0 - 115}{12/\sqrt{6}} \approx -2.04$$

Using the standard normal distribution table, we find that

$$P(\bar{x} < 105.0) = P(z < -2.04) = 0.0207$$

P-value

The area in the left tail that is more extreme than $\bar{x} = 105.0$ is called the *P-value* of the test. In this example, P-value $= 0.0207$. We will learn more about P-values later.

FIGURE 9-1

Sampling Distribution for $\bar{x}$ and Corresponding z Distribution

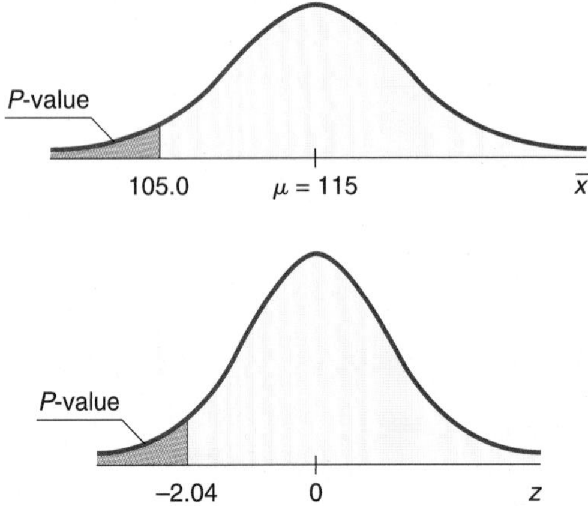

(d) INTERPRETATION What conclusion can be drawn about Rosie's average heart rate?
If H_0: $\mu = 115$ is in fact true, the probability of getting a sample mean of $\bar{x} \leq 105.0$ is only about 2%. Because this probability is small, we reject H_0: $\mu = 115$ and conclude that H_1: $\mu < 115$. Rosie's average heart rate seems to be slowing.

(e) Have we proved H_0: $\mu = 115$ to be false and H_1: $\mu < 115$ to be true?
No! The sample data do not prove H_0 to be false and H_1 to be true! We do say that H_0 has been "discredited" by a small *P*-value of 0.0207. Therefore, we abandon the claim H_0: $\mu = 115$ and adopt the claim H_1: $\mu < 115$.

The *P*-value of a Statistical Test

Rosie the sheep dog has helped us to "sniff out" an important statistical concept.

P-value

Assuming H_0 is true, the *probability* that the test statistic will take on values as extreme as or more extreme than the observed test statistic (computed from sample data) is called the ***P*-value** of the test. The smaller the *P*-value computed from sample data, the stronger the evidence against H_0.

The *P*-value is sometimes called the *probability of chance*. The *P*-value can be thought of as the probability that the results of a statistical experiment are due only to chance. The lower the *P*-value, the greater the likelihood of obtaining the same results (or very similar results) in a repetition of the statistical experiment. Thus a low *P*-value is a good indication that your results are not due to random chance alone.

The *P*-value associated with the observed test statistic takes on different values depending on the alternate hypothesis and the type of test. Let's look at *P*-values and types of tests when the test involves the mean and standard normal distribution. Notice that in Example 2, part (c), we computed a *P*-value for a left-tailed test. Guided Exercise 3 asks you to compute a *P*-value for a two-tailed test.

P-values and types of tests

Let $z_{\bar{x}}$ represent the standardized sample test statistic for testing a mean μ using the standard normal distribution. That is, $z_{\bar{x}} = (\bar{x} - \mu)/(\sigma/\sqrt{n})$.

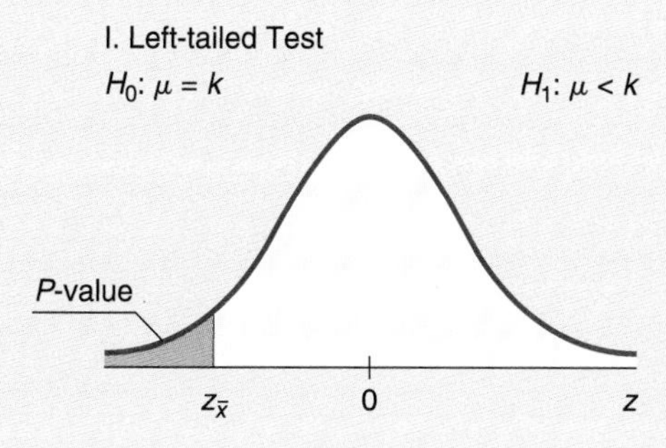

P-value $= P(z < z_{\bar{x}})$
This is the probability of getting a test statistic as low as or lower than $z_{\bar{x}}$.

Continued

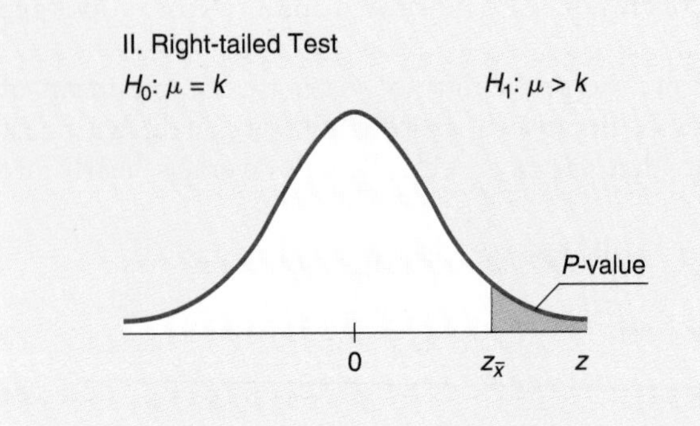

P-value $= P(z > z_{\bar{x}})$
This is the probability of getting a test statistic as high as or higher than $z_{\bar{x}}$.

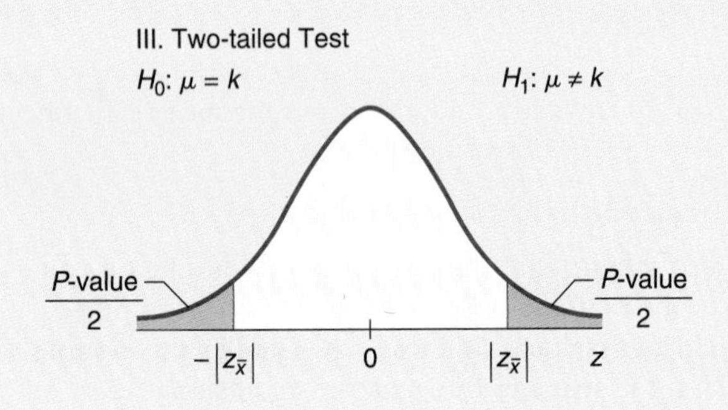

$$\frac{P\text{-value}}{2} = P(z > |z_{\bar{x}}|)\text{; therefore,}$$

$$P\text{-value} = 2P(z > |z_{\bar{x}}|)$$

This is the probability of getting a test statistic either lower than $-|z_{\bar{x}}|$ or higher than $|z_{\bar{x}}|$.

Types of Errors

If we *reject the null hypothesis when it is,* in fact, *true,* we have made an error that is called a *type I error.* On the other hand, if we *accept the null hypothesis when it is,* in fact, *false,* we have made an error that is called a *type II error.* Table 9-2 indicates how these errors occur.

For tests of hypotheses to be well constructed, they must be designed to minimize possible errors of decision. (Usually, we do not know if an error has been made, and therefore, we can talk only about the probability of making an error.) Usually, for a given sample size, an attempt to reduce the probability of one type of error results in an increase in the probability of the other type of error. In practical applications, one type of error may be more serious than another. In such a case, careful attention is given to the more serious error. If we increase the sample size, it is possible to reduce both types of errors, but increasing the sample size may not be possible.

Level of significance

Good statistical practice requires that we announce in advance how much evidence against H_0 will be required to reject H_0. The probability with which we are willing to risk a type I error is called the *level of significance* of a test. The level of significance is denoted by the Greek letter α (pronounced "alpha").

The **level of significance α** is the probability of rejecting H_0 when it is true. This is the probability of a type I error.

TABLE 9-2 Type I and Type II Errors

	Our Decision	
Truth of H_0	And if we do not reject H_0	And if we reject H_0
If H_0 is true	Correct decision; no error	Type I error
If H_0 is false	Type II error	Correct decision; no error

TABLE 9-3 Probabilities Associated with a Statistical Test

	Our Decision	
Truth of H_0	And if we accept H_0 as true	And if we reject H_0 as false
H_0 is true	Correct decision, with corresponding probability $1 - \alpha$	Type I error, with corresponding probability α, called the *level of significance of the test*
H_0 is false	Type II error, with corresponding probability β	Correct decision, with corresponding probability $1 - \beta$, called the *power of the test*

The *probability of making a type II error* is denoted by the Greek letter β (pronounced "beta"). Methods of hypothesis testing require us to choose α and β values to be as small as possible. In elementary statistical applications, we usually choose α first.

Power of a test

The quantity $1 - \beta$ is called the *power of the test* and represents the probability of rejecting H_0 when it is, in fact, false. For a given level of significance, how much power can we expect from a test? The actual value of the power is usually difficult (and sometimes impossible) to obtain, since it requires us to know the H_1 distribution. However, we can make the following general comments:

1. The power of a statistical test increases as the level of significance α increases. A test performed at the $\alpha = 0.05$ level has more power than one performed at $\alpha = 0.01$. This means that the less stringent we make our significance level α, the more likely we will reject the null hypothesis when it is false.
2. Using a larger value of α will increase the power, but it also will increase the probability of a type I error. Despite this fact, most business executives, administrators, social scientists, and scientists use *small* α values. This choice reflects the conservative nature of administrators and scientists, who are usually more willing to make an error by failing to reject a claim (i.e., H_0) than to make an error by accepting another claim (i.e., H_1) that is false. Table 9-3 summarizes the probabilities of errors associated with a statistical test.

COMMENT Since the calculation of the probability of a type II error is treated in advanced statistics courses, we will restrict our attention to the probability of a type I error.

GUIDED EXERCISE 2 Types of errors

Let's reconsider Guided Exercise 1, in which we were considering the manufacturing specifications for the diameter of ball bearings. The hypotheses were

H_0: $\mu = 6.0$ mm (manufacturer's specification) H_1: $\mu \neq 6.0$ mm (cause for adjusting process)

(a) Suppose the manufacturer requires a 1% level of significance. Describe a type I error, its consequence, and its probability.

A type I error is caused when sample evidence indicates that we should reject H_0 when, in fact, the average diameter of the ball bearings being produced is 6.0 mm. A type I error will cause a needless adjustment and delay of the manufacturing process. The probability of such an error is 1% because $\alpha = 0.01$.

Continued

GUIDED EXERCISE 2 *continued*

(b) Discuss a type II error and its consequences.  A type II error occurs if the sample evidence tells us not to reject the null hypothesis H_0: $\mu = 6.0$ mm when, in fact, the average diameter of the ball bearing is either too large or too small to meet specifications. Such an error would mean that the production process would not be adjusted when it really needed to be adjusted. This could possibly result in a large production of ball bearings that do not meet specifications.

Concluding a Statistical Test

Usually, α is specified in advance before any samples are drawn so that results will not influence the choice for the level of significance. To conclude a statistical test, we compare our α value with the P-value computed using sample data and the sampling distribution.

PROCEDURE

HOW TO CONCLUDE A TEST USING THE P-VALUE AND LEVEL OF SIGNIFICANCE α

If P-value $\leq \alpha$, we **reject** the null hypothesis and say the data are **statistically significant** at the level α.

If P-value $> \alpha$, we **do not reject** the null hypothesis.

Statistical significance

The term *statistically significant* is widely used in the literature of statistics and is definitely worth emphasizing. It is a good idea to distinguish between statistical significance and significance with respect to the importance of a result.

In what sense are we using the word *significant*? *Webster's Dictionary* gives two interpretations of *significance:* (1) having or signifying *meaning;* or (2) important or momentous.

In statistical work, significance does not necessarily imply momentous importance. For us, "significant" at the α level has a special *meaning*. It says that at the α level of risk, the evidence (sample data) against the null hypothesis H_0 is sufficient to discredit H_0, so we adopt the alternate hypothesis H_1.

In any case, we do not claim that we have "proved" or "disproved" the null hypothesis H_0. We can say that the probability of a type I error (rejecting H_0 when it is, in fact, true) is α.

Basic components of a statistical test

A statistical test can be thought of as a package of five basic ingredients.

1. **Null hypothesis H_0, alternate hypothesis H_1, and preset level of significance α**

   If the evidence (sample data) against H_0 is strong enough, we reject H_0 and adopt H_1. The level of significance α is the probability of rejecting H_0 when it is, in fact, true.

2. **Test statistic and sampling distribution**

   These are mathematical tools used to measure compatibility of sample data and the null hypothesis.

3. ***P*-value**

   This is the probability of obtaining a test statistic from the sampling distribution that is as extreme as, or more extreme (as specified by H_1) than, the sample test statistic computed from the data under the assumption that H_0 is true.

4. **Test conclusion**

   If P-value $\leq \alpha$, we reject H_0 and say that the data are significant at level α. If P-value $> \alpha$, we do not reject H_0.

5. **Interpretation of the test results**

   Give a simple explanation of your conclusions in the context of the application.

GUIDED EXERCISE 3 Constructing a statistical test for μ (normal distribution)

The Environmental Protection Agency has been studying Miller Creek regarding ammonia nitrogen concentration. For many years, the concentration has been 2.3 mg/l. However, a new golf course and housing developments are raising concern that the concentration may have changed because of lawn fertilizer. Any change (either an increase or a decrease) in the ammonia nitrogen concentration can affect plant and animal life in and around the creek (Reference: *EPA Report* 832-R-93-005). Let x be a random variable representing ammonia nitrogen concentration (in mg/l). Based on recent studies of Miller Creek, we may assume that x has a normal distribution with $\sigma = 0.30$. Recently, a random sample of eight water tests from the creek gave the following x values.

2.1 2.5 2.2 2.8 3.0 2.2 2.4 2.9

The sample mean is $\bar{x} \approx 2.51$.

Let us construct a statistical test to examine the claim that the concentration of ammonia nitrogen has changed from 2.3 mg/l. Use level of significance $\alpha = 0.01$.

(a) What is the null hypothesis? What is the alternate hypothesis? What is the level of significance α?

→ H_0: $\mu = 2.3$

H_1: $\mu \neq 2.3$

$\alpha = 0.01$

(b) Is this a right-tailed, left-tailed, or two-tailed test?

→ Since H_1: $\mu \neq 2.3$, this is a two-tailed test.

(c) What sampling distribution shall we use? Note that the value of μ is given in the null hypothesis, H_0.

→ Since the x distribution is normal and σ is known, use the standard normal distribution with

$$z = \frac{\bar{x} - \mu}{\frac{\sigma}{\sqrt{n}}} = \frac{\bar{x} - 2.3}{\frac{0.3}{\sqrt{8}}}$$

(d) What is the sample test statistic? Convert the sample mean $\bar{x}$ to a standard z value.

→ The sample of eight measurements has mean $\bar{x} = 2.51$. Converting this measurement to z, we have

$$\text{test statistic} = z = \frac{2.51 - 2.3}{\frac{0.3}{\sqrt{8}}} \approx 1.98$$

Continued

GUIDED EXERCISE 3 *continued*

(e) Draw a sketch showing the *P*-value area on the standard normal distribution. Find the *P*-value.

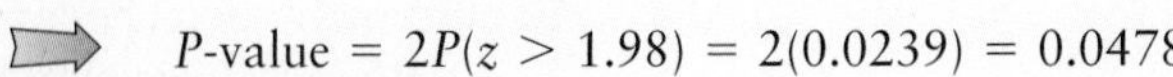

P-value $= 2P(z > 1.98) = 2(0.0239) = 0.0478$

FIGURE 9-2 *P*-value

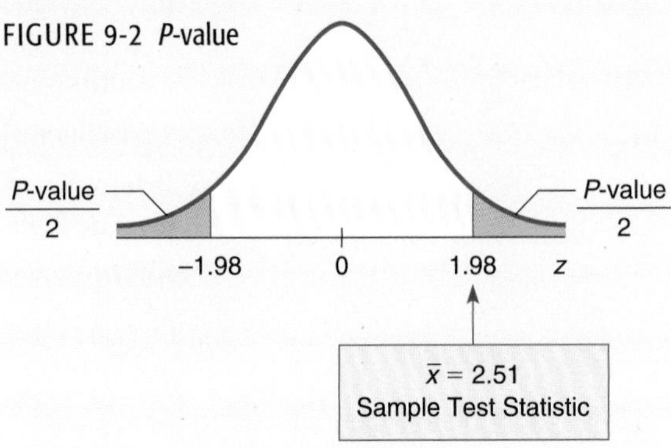

(f) Compare the level of significance α and the *P*-value. What is your conclusion?

Since *P*-value $0.0478 \geq 0.01$, we see that

P-value $> \alpha$. We fail to reject H_0.

(g) Interpret your results in the context of this problem.

The sample data are not significant at the $\alpha = 1\%$ level. At this point in time, there is not enough evidence to conclude that the ammonia nitrogen concentration has changed in Miller Creek.

Meaning of accepting H_0

In most statistical applications, the level of significance is specified to be $\alpha = 0.05$ or $\alpha = 0.01$, although other values can be used. If $\alpha = 0.05$, then we say we are using a 5% level of significance. This means that in 100 similar situations, H_0 will be rejected 5 times, on average, when it should not have been rejected. Using Technology at the end of this chapter shows a simulation of this phenomenon.

Students may oversimplify the meaning of "*accept* or *reject* the null hypothesis." Therefore, it is a good idea to emphasize that accepting the null hypothesis does not mean we have *proven* it to be true, and rejecting it does not mean we have *proven* it to be false beyond all doubt.

When we accept (or fail to reject) the null hypothesis, we should understand that we are *not proving the null hypothesis.* We are saying only that the sample evidence (data) is not strong enough to justify rejection of the null hypothesis. The word *accept* sometimes has a stronger meaning in common English usage than we are willing to give it in our application of statistics. Therefore, we often use the expression *fail to reject* H_0 instead of *accept* H_0. "*Fail to reject* the null hypothesis" simply means that the evidence in favor of rejection was not strong enough (see Table 9-4). Often, in the case that H_0 cannot be rejected, a confidence interval is used to estimate the parameter in question. The confidence interval gives the statistician a range of possible values for the parameter.

TABLE 9-4 **Meaning of the Terms *Fail to Reject* H_0 and *Reject* H_0**

Term	Meaning
Fail to reject H_0	There is not enough evidence in the data (and the test being used) to justify a rejection of H_0. This means that we retain H_0 with the understanding that we have not proved it to be true beyond all doubt.
Reject H_0	There is enough evidence in the data (and the test employed) to justify rejection of H_0. This means that we choose the alternate hypothesis H_1 with the understanding that we have not proved H_1 to be true beyond all doubt.

COMMENT Some comments about P-values and level of significance α should be made. The level of significance α should be a fixed, pre-specified value. Usually, α is chosen before any samples are drawn. The level of significance α is the probability of a type I error. So, α is the probability of rejecting H_0 when, in fact, H_0 is true.

The P-value should *not* be interpreted as the probability of a type I error. The level of significance (in theory) is set in advance before any samples are drawn. The P-value cannot be set in advance, since it is determined from the random sample. The P-value, together with α, should be regarded as tools used to conclude the test. If P-value $\leq \alpha$, then reject H_0, and if P-value $> \alpha$, then do not reject H_0.

In most computer applications and journal articles, only the P-value is given. It is understood that the person using this information will supply an appropriate level of significance α. From an historical point of view, the English statistician F. Y. Edgeworth (1845–1926) was one of the first to use the term *significant* to imply that the sample data indicated a "meaningful" difference from a previously held view.

In this book, we are using the most popular method of testing, which is called the *P-value method.* At the end of the next section, you will learn about another (equivalent) method of testing called the *critical region method.* An extensive discussion regarding the P-value method of testing versus the critical region method can be found in *The American Statistician,* Vol. 57, No. 3, pp. 171–178, American Statistical Association.

VIEWPOINT Lovers Take Heed!!!

If you are going to whisper sweet nothings to your sweetheart, be sure to whisper in the left ear. Professor Sim of Sam Houston State University (Huntsville, Texas) found that emotionally loaded words had a higher recall rate when spoken into a person's left ear, not the right. Professor Sim presented his findings at the British Psychology Society European Congress. He told the Congress that his findings are consistent with the hypothesis that the brain's right hemisphere has more influence in the processing of emotional stimuli. The left ear is controlled by the right side of the brain. Sim's research involved statistical tests like the ones you will study in this chapter.

SECTION 9.1 PROBLEMS

1. *Statistical Literacy* Discuss each of the following topics in class or review the topics on your own. Then write a brief but complete essay in which you answer the following questions.
   (a) What is a null hypothesis H_0?
   (b) What is an alternate hypothesis H_1?
   (c) What is a type I error? a type II error?
   (d) What is the level of significance of a test? What is the probability of a type II error?

   1. See text.

2. *Statistical Literacy* In a statistical test, we have a choice of a left-tailed test, a right-tailed test, or a two-tailed test. Is it the null hypothesis or the alternate hypothesis that determines which type of test is used? Explain your answer.

   2. The alternate hypothesis.

3. *Statistical Literacy* If we fail to reject (i.e., "accept") the null hypothesis, does this mean that we have *proved* it to be true beyond *all* doubt? Explain your answer.

   3. No, we have not proved H_0. The evidence is not sufficient to merit rejecting H_0.

4. No.

5. (a) H_0: $\mu = 60$ kg.
(b) H_1: $\mu < 60$ kg.
(c) H_1: $\mu > 60$ kg.
(d) H_1: $\mu \neq 60$ kg.
(e) Left; right; both sides.

6. (a) H_0: $\mu = 8.3$; H_1: $\mu < 8.3$; left.
(b) H_0: $\mu = 8.3$; H_1: $\mu \neq 8.3$; two-tailed.
(c) H_0: $\mu = 4.5$; H_1: $\mu > 4.5$; right.
(d) H_0: $\mu = 4.5$; H_1: $\mu \neq 4.5$; two-tailed.

7. (a) H_0: $\mu = 16.4$ feet.
(b) H_1: $\mu > 16.4$ feet.
(c) H_1: $\mu < 16.4$ feet.
(d) H_1: $\mu \neq 16.4$ feet.
(e) Right; left; both sides.

4. *Statistical Literacy* If we reject the null hypothesis, does this mean that we have *proved* it to be false beyond *all* doubt? Explain your answer.

5. *Veterinary Science: Colts* The body weight of a healthy 3-month-old colt should be about $\mu = 60$ kg. (Source: *The Merck Veterinary Manual*, a standard reference manual used in most veterinary colleges.)
   (a) If you want to set up a statistical test to challenge the claim that $\mu = 60$ kg, what would you use for the null hypothesis H_0?
   (b) In Nevada, there are many herds of wild horses. Suppose you want to test the claim that the average weight of a wild Nevada colt (3 months old) is less than 60 kg. What would you use for the alternate hypothesis H_1?
   (c) Suppose you want to test the claim that the average weight of such a wild colt is greater than 60 kg. What would you use for the alternate hypothesis?
   (d) Suppose you want to test the claim that the average weight of such a wild colt is *different* from 60 kg. What would you use for the alternate hypothesis?
   (e) For each of the tests in parts (b), (c), and (d), would the area corresponding to the P-value be on the left, on the right, or on both sides of the mean? Explain your answer in each case.

6. *Marketing: Shopping Time* How much customers buy is a direct result of how much time they spend in the store. A study of average shopping times in a large national houseware store gave the following information (Source: *Why We Buy: The Science of Shopping* by P. Underhill):

   Women with female companion: 8.3 min.
   Women with male companion: 4.5 min.

   Suppose you want to set up a statistical test to challenge the claim that a woman with a female friend spends an average of 8.3 minutes shopping in such a store.
   (a) What would you use for the null and alternate hypotheses if you believe the average shopping time is less than 8.3 minutes? Is this a right-tailed, left-tailed, or two-tailed test?
   (b) What would you use for the null and alternate hypotheses if you believe the average shopping time is different from 8.3 minutes? Is this a right-tailed, left-tailed, or two-tailed test?

   Stores that sell mainly to women should figure out a way to engage the interest of men! Perhaps comfortable seats and a big TV with sports programs. Suppose such an entertainment center was installed and you now wish to challenge the claim that a woman with a male friend spends only 4.5 minutes shopping in a houseware store.
   (c) What would you use for the null and alternate hypotheses if you believe the average shopping time is more than 4.5 minutes? Is this a right-tailed, left-tailed, or two-tailed test?
   (d) What would you use for the null and alternate hypotheses if you believe the average shopping time is different from 4.5 minutes? Is this a right-tailed, left-tailed, or two-tailed test?

7. *Meteorology: Storms* *Weatherwise* magazine is published in association with the American Meteorological Society. Volume 46, Number 6 has a rating system to classify Nor'easter storms that frequently hit New England states and can cause much damage near the ocean coast. A *severe* storm has an average peak wave height of 16.4 feet for waves hitting the shore. Suppose that a Nor'easter is in progress at the severe storm class rating.
   (a) Let us say that we want to set up a statistical test to see if the wave action (i.e., height) is dying down or getting worse. What would be the null hypothesis regarding average wave height?
   (b) If you wanted to test the hypothesis that the storm is getting worse, what would you use for the alternate hypothesis?

(c) If you wanted to test the hypothesis that the waves are dying down, what would you use for the alternate hypothesis?

(d) Suppose you do not know if the storm is getting worse or dying out. You just want to test the hypothesis that the average wave height is *different* (either higher or lower) from the severe storm class rating. What would you use for the alternate hypothesis?

(e) For each of the tests in parts (b), (c), and (d), would the area corresponding to the P-value be on the left, on the right, or on both sides of the mean? Explain your answer in each case.

8. (a) H_0: $\mu = 8.7$ sec.
(b) H_1: $\mu > 8.7$ sec.
(c) H_1: $\mu < 8.7$ sec.
(d) Right; left.

8. *Chrysler Concorde: Acceleration* *Consumer Reports* stated that the mean time for a Chrysler Concorde to go from 0 to 60 miles per hour was 8.7 seconds.

(a) If you want to set up a statistical test to challenge the claim of 8.7 seconds, what would you use for the null hypothesis?

(b) The town of Leadville, Colorado, has an elevation over 10,000 feet. Suppose you wanted to test the claim that the average time to accelerate from 0 to 60 miles per hour is longer in Leadville (because of less oxygen). What would you use for the alternate hypothesis?

(c) Suppose you made an engine modification and you think the average time to accelerate from 0 to 60 miles per hour is reduced. What would you use for the alternate hypothesis?

(d) For each of the tests in parts (b) and (c), would the P-value area be on the left, on the right, or on both sides of the mean? Explain your answer in each case.

For Problems 9–14, please provide the following information.

(a) What is the level of significance? State the null and alternate hypotheses. Will you use a left-tailed, right-tailed, or two-tailed test?

(b) What sampling distribution will you use? Explain the rationale for your choice of sampling distribution. What is the value of the sample test statistic?

(c) Find (or estimate) the P-value. Sketch the sampling distribution and show the area corresponding to the P-value.

(d) Based on your answers in parts (a) to (c), will you reject or fail to reject the null hypothesis? Are the data statistically significant at level α?

(e) State your conclusion in the context of the application.

9. (a) $\alpha = 0.01$; H_0: $\mu = 4.7\%$; H_1: $\mu > 4.7\%$; right-tailed.
(b) Normal; $\bar{x} = 5.38$; $z \approx 0.90$.
(c) P-value ≈ 0.1841; on standard normal curve, shade area to the right of 0.90.
(d) P-value of $0.1841 > 0.01$ for α; fail to reject H_0.
(e) Insufficient evidence at the 0.01 level to reject claim that average yield for bank stocks equals average yield for all stocks.

9. *Dividend Yield: Australian Bank Stocks* Let x be a random variable representing dividend yield of Australian bank stocks. We may assume that x has a normal distribution with $\sigma = 2.4\%$. A random sample of 10 Australian bank stocks gave the following yields (in percents).

5.7	4.8	6.0	4.9	4.0	3.4	6.5	7.1	5.3	6.1

The sample mean is $\bar{x} = 5.38\%$. For the entire Australian stock market, the mean dividend yield is $\mu = 4.7\%$ (Reference: *Forbes*). Do these data indicate that the dividend yield of all Australian bank stocks is higher than 4.7%? Use $\alpha = 0.01$.

10. (a) $\alpha = 0.05$; H_0: $\mu = 85$ mg/100 ml; H_1: $\mu > 85$ mg/100 ml; right-tailed.
(b) Normal; $\bar{x} \approx 93.8$; $z \approx 1.99$.
(c) P-value ≈ 0.0233; on standard normal curve, shade area to the right of 1.99.
(d) P-value of $0.0233 \leq 0.05$ for α; reject H_0.
(e) The sample evidence is sufficient at the 0.05 level to justify rejecting H_0. It seems that Gentle Ben's average glucose level is higher than average.

10. *Glucose Level: Horses* Gentle Ben is a Morgan horse at a Colorado dude ranch. Over the past 8 weeks, a veterinarian took the following glucose readings from this horse (in mg/100 ml).

93	88	82	105	99	110	84	89

The sample mean is $\bar{x} \approx 93.8$. Let x be a random variable representing glucose readings taken from Gentle Ben. We may assume that x has a normal distribution, and we know from past experience that $\sigma = 12.5$. The mean glucose level for horses should be $\mu = 85$ mg/100 ml (Reference: *Merck Veterinary Manual*). Do these data indicate that Gentle Ben has an overall average glucose level higher than 85? Use $\alpha = 0.05$.

11. (a) $\alpha = 0.01$; H_0: $\mu = 4.55$ gm; H_1: $\mu < 4.55$ gm; left-tailed.
(b) Normal; $\bar{x} = 3.75$ gm; $z \approx -2.80$.
(c) P-value ≈ 0.0026; on standard normal curve, shade area to the left of -2.80.
(d) P-value of $0.0026 \leq 0.01$ for α; reject H_0.
(e) The sample evidence is sufficient at the 0.01 level to justify rejecting H_0. It seems that the hummingbirds in the Grand Canyon region have a lower average weight.

12. (a) $\alpha = 0.05$; H_0: $\mu = 19$; H_1: $\mu < 19$; left-tailed.
(b) Normal; $\bar{x} \approx 17.1$; $z \approx -1.58$.
(c) P-value ≈ 0.0571; on standard normal curve, shade area to the left of -1.58.
(d) P-value of $0.0571 > 0.05$ for α; fail to reject H_0.
(e) There is insufficient evidence at the 0.05 level to reject H_0. It seems that the average P/E for large banks is not less than that of the S&P 500 index.

13. (a) $\alpha = 0.01$; H_0: $\mu = 11\%$; H_1: $\mu \neq 11\%$; two-tailed.
(b) Normal; $\bar{x} = 12.5\%$; $z = 1.20$.
(c) P-value $= 2(0.1151) = 0.2302$; on standard normal curve, shade area to the right of 1.20 and to the left of -1.20.
(d) P-value of $0.2302 > 0.01$ for α; fail to reject H_0.
(e) There is insufficient evidence at the 0.01 level to reject H_0. It seems that the average hail damage to wheat crops in Weld County matches the national average.

14. (a) $\alpha = 0.01$; H_0: $\mu = 28$ ml/kg; H_1: $\mu \neq 28$ ml/kg; two-tailed.
(b) Normal; $\bar{x} \approx 32.7$ ml/kg; $z \approx 2.62$.
(c) P-value $= 2(0.0044) = 0.0088$; on standard normal curve, shade area to the right of 2.62 and to the left of -2.62.
(d) P-value of $0.0088 < 0.01$ for α; reject H_0.
(e) At the 1% level of significance, the sample average is sufficiently different from $\mu = 28$ that we reject H_0. It seems that Roger's average red blood cell volume is different from the average for healthy adults.

11. *Ecology: Hummingbirds* Bill Alther is a zoologist who studies Anna's hummingbird (*Calypte anna*). (Reference: *Hummingbirds,* K. Long, W. Alther.) Suppose that in a remote part of the Grand Canyon, a random sample of six of these birds was caught, weighed, and released. The weights (in grams) were

3.7	2.9	3.8	4.2	4.8	3.1

The sample mean is $\bar{x} = 3.75$ grams. Let x be a random variable representing weights of Anna's hummingbirds in this part of the Grand Canyon. We assume that x has a normal distribution and $\sigma = 0.70$ gram. It is known that for the population of all Anna's hummingbirds, the mean weight is $\mu = 4.55$ grams. Do the data indicate that the mean weight of these birds in this part of the Grand Canyon is less than 4.55 grams? Use $\alpha = 0.01$.

12. *Finance: P/E of Stocks* The price to earnings ratio (P/E) is an important tool in financial work. A random sample of 14 large U.S. banks (J. P. Morgan, Bank of America, and others) gave the following P/E ratios (Reference: *Forbes*).

24	16	22	14	12	13	17
22	15	19	23	13	11	18

The sample mean is $\bar{x} \approx 17.1$. Generally speaking, a low P/E ratio indicates a "value" or bargain stock. A recent copy of *The Wall Street Journal* indicated that the P/E ratio of the entire S&P 500 stock index is $\mu = 19$. Let x be a random variable representing the P/E ratio of all large U.S. bank stocks. We assume that x has a normal distribution and $\sigma = 4.5$. Do these data indicate that the P/E ratio of all U.S. bank stocks is less than 19? Use $\alpha = 0.05$.

13. *Insurance: Hail Damage* Nationally, about 11% of the total U.S. wheat crop is destroyed each year by hail (Reference: *Agricultural Statistics,* U.S. Department of Agriculture). An insurance company is studying wheat hail damage claims in Weld County, Colorado. A random sample of 16 claims in Weld County gave the following data (% wheat crop lost to hail).

15	8	9	11	12	20	14	11
7	10	24	20	13	9	12	5

The sample mean is $\bar{x} = 12.5\%$. Let x be a random variable that represents the percentage of wheat crop in Weld County lost to hail. Assume that x has a normal distribution and $\sigma = 5.0\%$. Do these data indicate that the percentage of wheat crop lost to hail in Weld County is different (either way) from the national mean of 11%? Use $\alpha = 0.01$.

14. *Medical: Red Blood Cell Volume* Total blood volume (in ml) per body weight (in kg) is important in medical research. For healthy adults, the red blood cell volume mean is about $\mu = 28$ ml/kg (Reference: *Laboratory and Diagnostic Tests,* F. Fischbach). Red blood cell volume that is too low or too high can indicate a medical problem (see reference). Suppose that Roger has had seven blood tests, and the red blood cell volumes were

32	25	41	35	30	37	29

The sample mean is $\bar{x} \approx 32.7$ ml/kg. Let x be a random variable that represents Roger's red blood cell volume. Assume that x has a normal distribution and $\sigma = 4.75$. Do the data indicate that Roger's red blood cell volume is different (either way) from $\mu = 28$ ml/kg? Use a 0.01 level of significance.

SECTION 9.2

Testing the Mean μ

FOCUS POINTS

- Review the general procedure for testing using *P*-values.
- Test μ when σ is known using the normal distribution.
- Test μ when σ is unknown using a Student's *t* distribution.
- Understand the "traditional" method of testing that uses critical regions and critical values instead of *P*-values.

In this section, we continue our study of testing the mean μ. The method we are using is called the *P*-value method. It was used extensively by the famous statistician R. A. Fisher and is the most popular method of testing in use today. At the end of this section, we present another method of testing called the *critical region method* (or *traditional method*). The critical region method was used extensively by the statisticians J. Neyman and E. Pearson. In recent years, the use of this method has been declining. It is important to realize that for a fixed, preset level of significance α, both methods are logically equivalent.

In Section 9.1, we discussed the vocabulary and method of hypothesis testing using *P*-values. Let's quickly review the basic process.

1. We first state a proposed value for a population parameter in the null hypothesis H_0. The alternate hypothesis H_1 states alternative values of the parameter, either $<$, $>$, or $\neq$ the value proposed in H_0. We also set the level of significance α. This is the risk we are willing to take of committing a type I error. That is, α is the probability of rejecting H_0 when it is, in fact, true.

2. We use a corresponding sample statistic from a simple random sample to challenge the statement made in H_0. We convert the sample statistic to a test statistic, which is the corresponding value of the appropriate sampling distribution.

3. We use the sampling distribution of the test statistic and the type of test to compute the *P*-value of this statistic. Under the assumption that the null hypothesis is true, the *P*-value is the probability of getting a sample statistic as extreme as or more extreme than the observed statistic from our random sample.

4. Next, we conclude the test. If the *P*-value is very small, we have evidence to reject H_0 and adopt H_1. What do we mean by "very small"? We compare the *P*-value to the preset level of significance α. If the *P*-value $\leq \alpha$, then we say we have evidence to reject H_0 and adopt H_1. Otherwise, we say that the sample evidence is insufficient to reject H_0.

5. Finally, we interpret the results in the context of the application.

Knowing the sampling distribution of the sample test statistic is an essential part of the hypothesis testing process. For tests of μ, we use one of two sampling distributions for $\bar{x}$: the standard normal distribution or a Student's *t* distribution. As discussed in Chapters 7 and 8, the appropriate distribution depends upon our knowledge of the population standard deviation σ, the nature of the *x* distribution, and the sample size.

Part I: Testing μ When σ Is Known

In most real-world situations, σ is simply not known. However, in some cases a preliminary study or other information can be used to get a realistic and accurate value for σ.

PROCEDURE

HOW TO TEST μ WHEN σ IS KNOWN

Let x be a random variable appropriate to your application. Obtain a simple random sample (of size n) of x values from which you compute the sample mean $\bar{x}$. The value of σ is already known (perhaps from a previous study).

1. In the context of the application, state the *null and alternate hypotheses* and set the *level of significance* α.
2. If you can assume that x has a normal distribution, then any sample size n will work. If you cannot assume this, then use a sample size $n \geq 30$. Use the known σ, the sample size n, the value of $\bar{x}$ from the sample, and μ from the null hypothesis to compute the standardized sample *test statistic*.

$$z = \frac{\bar{x} - \mu}{\frac{\sigma}{\sqrt{n}}}$$

3. Use the standard normal distribution and the type of test, one-tailed or two-tailed, to find the *P-value* corresponding to the test statistic.
4. *Conclude* the test. If P-value $\leq \alpha$, then reject H_0. If P-value $> \alpha$, then do not reject H_0.
5. *Interpret your conclusion* in the context of the application.

In Section 9.1, we examined P-value tests for normal distributions with relatively small sample size ($n < 30$). The next example does not assume a normal distribution, but has a large sample size ($n \geq 30$).

EXAMPLE 3

TESTING μ, σ KNOWN

Sunspots have been observed for many centuries. Records of sunspots from ancient Persian and Chinese astronomers go back thousands of years. Some archaeologists think sunspot activity may somehow be related to prolonged periods of drought in the southwestern United States. Let x be a random variable representing the number of sunspots observed in a four-week period. A random sample of 40 such periods from Spanish colonial times gave the following data (Reference: M. Waldmeir, *Sun Spot Activity*, International Astronomical Union Bulletin).

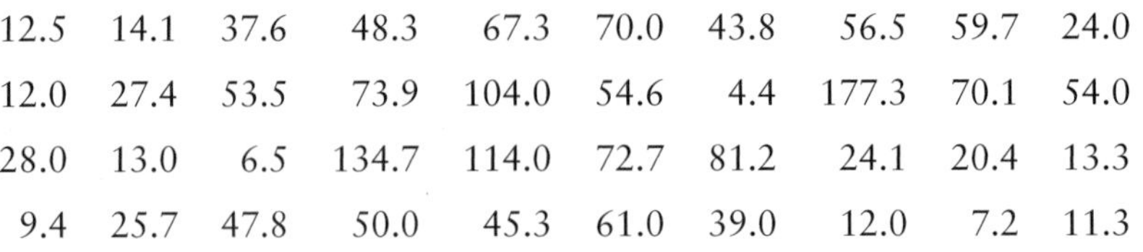

12.5	14.1	37.6	48.3	67.3	70.0	43.8	56.5	59.7	24.0
12.0	27.4	53.5	73.9	104.0	54.6	4.4	177.3	70.1	54.0
28.0	13.0	6.5	134.7	114.0	72.7	81.2	24.1	20.4	13.3
9.4	25.7	47.8	50.0	45.3	61.0	39.0	12.0	7.2	11.3

The sample mean is $\bar{x} \approx 47.0$. Previous studies of sunspot activity during this period indicate that $\sigma = 35$. It is thought that for thousands of years, the mean number of sunspots per four-week period was about $\mu = 41$. Sunspot activity above this level may (or may not) be linked to gradual climate change. Do the data indicate that the mean sunspot activity during the Spanish colonial period was higher than 41? Use $\alpha = 0.05$.

SOLUTION:

(a) Establish the null and alternate hypotheses.
Since we want to know whether the average sunspot activity during the Spanish colonial period was higher than the long-term average of $\mu = 41$,

$$H_0: \mu = 41 \quad \text{and} \quad H_1: \mu > 41$$

(b) Compute the test statistic from the sample data.
Since $n \geq 30$ and we know σ, we use the standard normal distribution. Using $\bar{x} = 47$ from the sample, $\sigma = 35$, $\mu = 41$ from H_0, and $n = 40$,

$$z = \frac{\bar{x} - \mu}{\sigma/\sqrt{n}} \approx \frac{47 - 41}{35/\sqrt{40}} \approx 1.08$$

(c) Find the P-value of the test statistic.
Figure 9-3 shows the P-value. Since we have a right-tailed test, the P-value is the area to the right of $z = 1.08$ shown in Figure 9-3. Using Table 3 of the Appendix, we find that

$$P\text{-value} = P(z > 1.08) \approx 0.1401$$

FIGURE 9-3

P-value Area

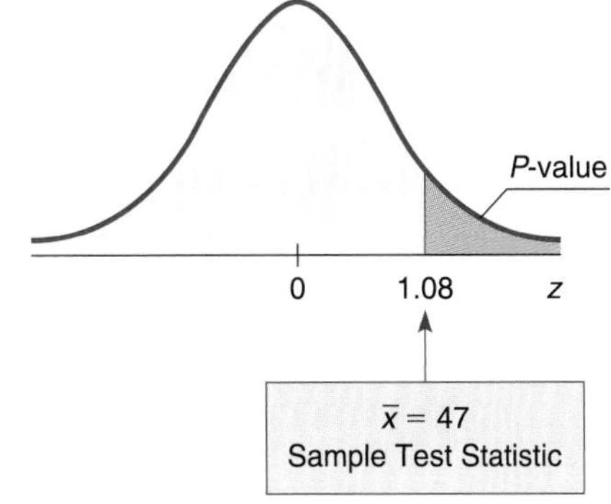

(d) Conclude the test.
Since the P-value of $0.1401 > 0.05$ for α, we do not reject H_0.

(e) Interpret the results.
At the 5% level of significance, the evidence is not sufficient to reject H_0. Based on the sample data, we do not think the average sunspot activity during the Spanish colonial period was higher than the long-term mean.

Part II: Testing μ When σ Is Unknown

In many real-world situations, you have only a random sample of data values. In addition, you may have some limited information about the probability distribution of your data values. Can you still test μ under these circumstances? In most cases, the answer is yes!

PROCEDURE

HOW TO TEST μ WHEN σ IS UNKNOWN

Let x be a random variable appropriate to your application. Obtain a simple random sample (of size n) of x values from which you compute the sample mean $\bar{x}$ and the sample standard deviation s.

1. In the context of the application, state the *null and alternate hypotheses* and set the *level of significance* α.

Continued

2. If you can assume that x has a normal distribution or simply has a mound-shaped symmetric distribution, then any sample size n will work. If you cannot assume this, then use a sample size $n \geq 30$. Use $\bar{x}$, s, and n from the sample, with μ from H_0, to compute the sample *test statistic.*

$$t = \frac{\bar{x} - \mu}{\frac{s}{\sqrt{n}}} \quad \text{with degrees of freedom } d.f. = n - 1$$

3. Use the Student's t distribution and the type of test, one-tailed or two-tailed, to find (or estimate) the *P-value* corresponding to the test statistic.
4. *Conclude* the test. If P-value $\leq \alpha$, then reject H_0. If P-value $> \alpha$, then do not reject H_0.
5. *Interpret your conclusion* in the context of the application.

Using the Student's t table to estimate P-values

When sample sizes are large ($n \geq 30$), it is not uncommon to estimate the population standard deviation σ by the sample standard deviation s and then use the normal distribution for the test statistic $\bar{x}$. For the same data, use of the normal distribution instead of a Student's t distribution results in slightly smaller P-values. In other words, using a Student's t distribution whenever σ is unknown is slightly more conservative in the sense that P-values from a Student's t distribution are slightly larger. In this edition, we follow the more common convention of using a Student's t distribution whenever σ is unknown (and other criteria for the use of a Student's t distribution are met).

In Section 8.2, we used Table 4 of the Appendix, Student's t Distribution, to find critical values t_c for confidence intervals. The critical values are in the body of the table. We find P-values in the *rows* headed by "one-tail area" and "two-tail area," depending on whether we have a one-tailed or two-tailed test. If the test statistic t for the sample statistic $\bar{x}$ is negative, look up the P-value for the corresponding *positive* value of t (i.e., look up the P-value for $|t|$).

Note: In Table 4, areas are given in *one tail* beyond positive t on the right or negative t on the left, and in *two tails* beyond $\pm t$. Notice that in each column, two-tail area = 2(one-tail area). Consequently, we use *one-tail areas* as endpoints of the interval containing the P-value for *one-tailed tests.* We use *two-tail areas* as endpoints of the interval containing the P-value for *two-tailed tests.* (See Figure 9-4.)

Example 4 and Guided Exercise 4 show how to use Table 4 of the Appendix to find an interval containing the P-value corresponding to a test statistic t.

FIGURE 9-4

P-value for One-Tailed Tests and for Two-Tailed Tests

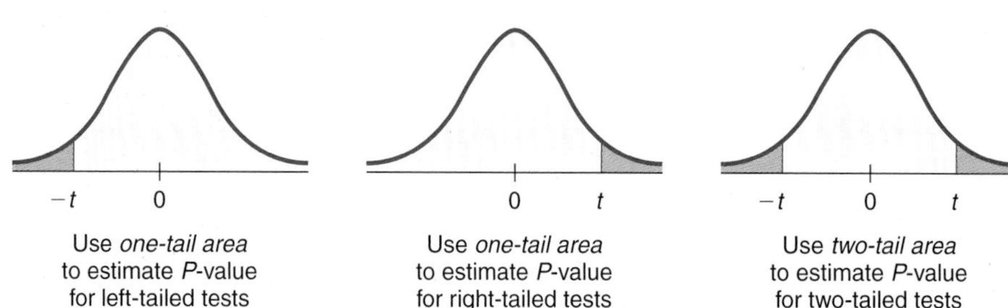
−t
0
Use one-tail area to estimate P-value for left-tailed tests
0
t
Use one-tail area to estimate P-value for right-tailed tests
−t
0
t
Use two-tail area to estimate P-value for two-tailed tests

EXAMPLE 4 TESTING μ, σ UNKNOWN

The drug 6-mP (6-mercaptopurine) is used to treat leukemia. The following data represent the remission times (in weeks) for a random sample of 21 patients using 6-mP (Reference: E. A. Gehan, University of Texas Cancer Center).

10	7	32	23	22	6	16	34	32	25	11
20	19	6	17	35	6	13	9	6	10	

The sample mean is $\bar{x} \approx 17.1$ weeks, with sample standard deviation $s \approx 10.0$. Let x be a random variable representing the remission time (in weeks) for all patients using 6-mP. Assume the x distribution is mound-shaped and symmetric. A previously used drug treatment had a mean remission time of $\mu = 12.5$ weeks.

Do the data indicate that the mean remission time using the drug 6-mP is different (either way) from 12.5 weeks? Use $\alpha = 0.01$.

SOLUTION:

(a) Establish the null and alternate hypotheses.
Since we want to determine if the drug 6-mP provides a mean remission time that is different from that provided by a previously used drug having $\mu = 12.5$ weeks,

$$H_0: \mu = 12.5 \text{ weeks} \qquad \text{and} \qquad H_1: \mu \neq 12.5 \text{ weeks}$$

(b) Compute the test statistic from the sample data.
Since the x distribution is assumed to be mound-shaped and symmetric, we use the Student's t distribution. Using $\bar{x} \approx 17.1$ and $s \approx 10.0$ from the sample data, $\mu = 12.5$ from H_0, and $n = 21$,

$$t \approx \frac{\bar{x} - \mu}{s/\sqrt{n}} \approx \frac{17.1 - 12.5}{10.0/\sqrt{21}} \approx 2.108$$

(c) Find the P-value or the interval containing the P-value.
Figure 9-5 shows the P-value. Using Table 4 of the Appendix, we find an interval containing the P-value. Since this is a two-tailed test, we use entries from the row headed by *two-tail area*. Look up the t value in the row headed by $d.f. = n - 1 = 21 - 1 = 20$. The sample statistic $t = 2.108$ falls between 2.086 and 2.528. The P-value for the sample t falls between the corresponding two-tail areas 0.050 and 0.020. (See Table 9-5, Excerpt from Table 4.)

$$0.020 < P\text{-value} < 0.050$$

FIGURE 9-5

P-value

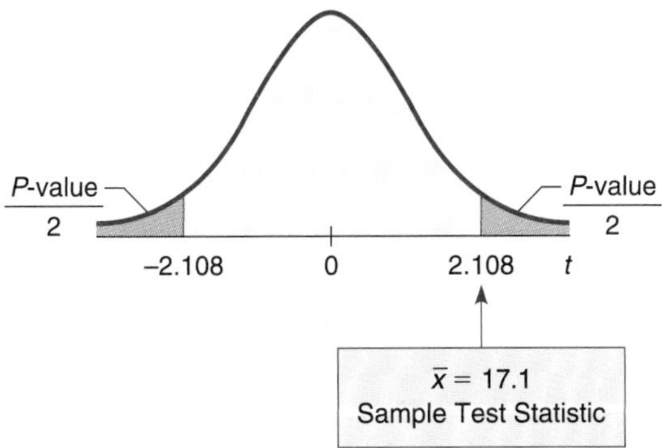

TABLE 9-5 Excerpt from Student's *t* Distribution (Table 4 of the Appendix)

one-tail area	...	...
✓two-tail area	0.050	0.020
d.f. = 20	2.086	2.528
	↑ Sample t = 2.108	

It is useful to stress that the *P*-value corresponding to the test statistic is a *single* value. The interval found in Table 4 of the Appendix contains the specific *P*-value, but the *P*-value itself is not a range of numbers.

(d) Conclude the test.
The following diagram shows the interval that contains the single P-value corresponding to the test statistic. Note that there is just one P-value corresponding to the test statistic. Table 4 of the Appendix does not give that specific value, but it does give a range that contains the specific P-value. As the diagram shows, the entire range is greater than α. This means the specific P-value is greater than α, so we cannot reject H_0.

α
0.01 0.020 0.050

Note: Using the raw data, computer software gives P-value ≈ 0.048. This value is in the interval we estimated. It is larger than the α value of 0.01, so we do not reject H_0.

(e) Interpret the results.
At the 1% level of significance, the evidence is not sufficient to reject H_0. Based on the sample data, we cannot say that the drug 6-mP provides a different average remission time than the previous drug.

GUIDED EXERCISE 4 Testing μ, σ unknown

Archaeologists become excited when they find an anomaly in discovered artifacts. The anomaly may (or may not) indicate a new trading region or a new method of craftsmanship. Suppose the lengths of projectile points (arrowheads) at a certain archaeological site have mean length $\mu = 2.6$ cm. A random sample of 61 recently discovered projectile points in an adjacent cliff dwelling gave the following lengths (in cm) (Reference: A. Woosley and A. McIntyre, *Mimbres Mogollon Archaeology,* University of New Mexico Press).

3.1	4.1	1.8	2.1	2.2	1.3	1.7	3.0	3.7	2.3	2.6	2.2	2.8	3.0
3.2	3.3	2.4	2.8	2.8	2.9	2.9	2.2	2.4	2.1	3.4	3.1	1.6	3.1
3.5	2.3	3.1	2.7	2.1	2.0	4.8	1.9	3.9	2.0	5.2	2.2	2.6	1.9
4.0	3.0	3.4	4.2	2.4	3.5	3.1	3.7	3.7	2.9	2.6	3.6	3.9	3.5
1.9	4.0	4.0	4.6	1.9									

The sample mean is $\bar{x} \approx 2.92$ cm and the sample standard deviation is $s \approx 0.85$, where x is a random variable that represents the lengths (in cm) of all projectile points found at the adjacent cliff dwelling site. Do these data indicate that the mean length of projectile points in the adjacent cliff dwelling is longer than 2.6 cm? Use a 1% level of significance.

(a) State H_0, H_1, and α.

H_0: $\mu = 2.6$ cm; H_1: $\mu > 2.6$ cm; $\alpha = 0.01$

(b) What sampling distribution should you use? What is the t value of the sample test statistic?

Because $n \geq 30$ and σ is unknown, use the Student's t distribution with $d.f. = n - 1 = 61 - 1 = 60$. Using $\bar{x} \approx 2.92$, $s \approx 0.85$, $\mu = 2.6$ from H_0, and $n = 61$,

$$t = \frac{\bar{x} - \mu}{\sigma/\sqrt{n}} \approx \frac{2.92 - 2.6}{0.85/\sqrt{61}} \approx 2.940$$

(c) When you use Table 4 of the Appendix to find an interval containing the P-value, do you use one-tail or two-tail areas? Why? Sketch a figure showing the P-value. Find an interval for the P-value.

This is a right-tailed test, so use a one-tail area.

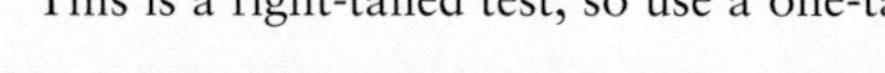

FIGURE 9-6 *P*-value

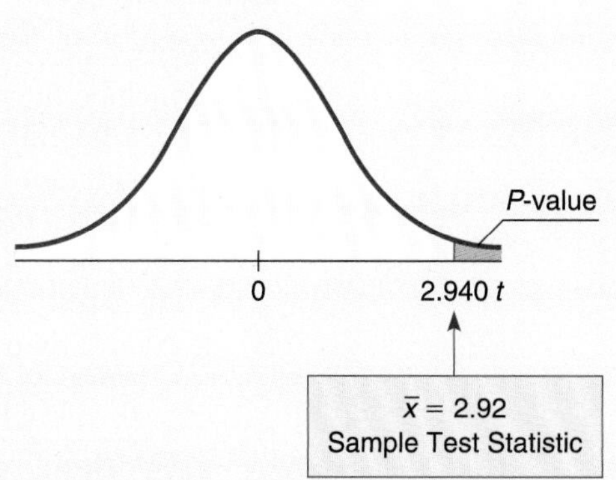

TABLE 9-6 **Excerpt from Student's *t* Table**

✓ one-tail area	...0.005	0.0005
two-tail area	...0.010	0.0010
d.f. = 60	...2.660	3.460
	↑ Sample t = 2.940	

Continued

GUIDED EXERCISE 4 *continued*

Using *d.f.* = 60, we find that the sample $t = 2.940$ is between the critical values 2.660 and 3.460. The sample *P*-value is then between the one-tail areas 0.005 and 0.0005.

$0.0005 < P\text{-value} < 0.005$

(d) Do we reject or fail to reject H_0?

Since the interval containing the *P*-value lies to the left of $\alpha = 0.01$, we reject H_0.

α

0.0005 0.005 0.01

Note: Using the raw data, computer software gives *P*-value ≈ 0.0022. This value is in our estimated range and is less than $\alpha = 0.01$, so we reject H_0.

(e) Interpret your results in the context of the application.

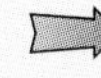

At the 1% level of significance, sample evidence is sufficiently strong to reject H_0 and conclude that the average projectile point length at the adjacent cliff dwelling site is longer than 2.6 cm.

TECH NOTES The TI-84Plus and TI-83Plus calculators, Excel, and Minitab all support testing of μ using the standard normal distribution. The TI-84Plus/TI-83Plus and Minitab support testing of μ using a Student's t distribution. All the technologies return a *P*-value for the test.

TI-84Plus/TI-83Plus You can select to enter raw data (**Data**) or summary statistics (**Stats**). Enter the value of $\boldsymbol{\mu_0}$ used in the null hypothesis $\boldsymbol{H_0: \mu = \mu_0}$. Select the symbol used in the alternate hypothesis ($\boldsymbol{\neq\mu_0, <\mu_0, >\mu_0}$). To test μ using the standard normal distribution, press **Stat,** select **Tests,** and use option **1:Z-Test.** The value for σ is required. To test μ using a Student's t distribution, use option **2:T-Test.** Using data from Example 4 regarding remission times, we have the following displays. The *P*-value is given as p.

```
T-Test
 Inpt:Data Stats
 μ0 :12.5
 List:L1
 Freq:1
 μ:≠μ0 <μ0 >μ0
 Calculate Draw
```

```
T-Tests
 μ≠12.5
 t=2.105902924
 p=.0480466063
 x̄=17.0952381
 Sx=9.999523798
 n=21
```

Excel In Excel, the **ZTEST** function finds the *P*-values for a right-tailed test. (*Note:* Ignore the Excel documentation that mistakenly says ZTEST gives the *P*-value for a two-tailed test.) Use the menu choice **Paste Function** (fx) ➤ **ZTEST.** In the dialogue box, give the cell range containing your data for the array. Use the value of μ stated in H_0 for x. Provide σ. Otherwise, Excel uses the sample standard deviation computed from the data.

Minitab Enter the raw data from a sample. Use the menu selections **Stat ➤ Basic Stat ➤ 1-Sample z** for tests using the standard normal distribution. For tests of μ using a Student's t distribution, select **1-Sample t.**

Part III: Testing μ Using Critical Regions (Traditional Method)

Critical region method

The critical region method for hypothesis testing is convenient when distribution tables are available for finding critical values. However, most statistical software and research journal articles give *P*-values rather than critical values. Most fields of study that require statistics also require that students be able to use *P*-values.

The most popular method of statistical testing is the *P*-value method. For that reason, the *P*-value method is emphasized in this book. Another method of testing is called the *critical region method* or *traditional method.*

For a fixed preset value of the level of significance α, both methods are logically equivalent. Because of this, we treat the traditional method as an "optional" topic and consider only the case of testing μ when σ is known.

Consider the null hypothesis H_0: $\mu = k$. We use information from a random sample, together with the sampling distribution for $\bar{x}$ and the level of significance α, to determine whether or not we should reject the null hypothesis. The essential question is, "How much can $\bar{x}$ vary from $\mu = k$ before we suspect that H_0: $\mu = k$ is false and reject it?"

The answer to the question regarding the relative sizes of $\bar{x}$ and μ, as stated in the null hypothesis, depends on the sampling distribution of $\bar{x}$, the alternate hypothesis H_1, and the level of significance α. If the sample test statistic $\bar{x}$ is sufficiently different from the claim about μ made in the null hypothesis, we reject the null hypothesis.

The values of $\bar{x}$ for which we reject H_0 are called the *critical region* of the $\bar{x}$ distribution. Depending on the alternate hypothesis, the critical region is located on the left side, the right side, or both sides of the $\bar{x}$ distribution. Figure 9-7 shows the relationship of the critical region to the alternate hypothesis and the level of significance α.

Notice that the total area in the critical region is preset to be the level of significance α. This is *not* the *P*-value discussed earlier! In fact, you cannot set the *P*-value in advance because it is determined from a random sample. Recall that the level of significance α should (in theory) be a fixed, preset number assigned before drawing any samples.

The most commonly used levels of significance are $\alpha = 0.05$ and $\alpha = 0.01$. Critical regions of a standard normal distribution are shown for these levels of significance in Figure 9-8. *Critical values* are the boundaries of the critical region. Critical values designated as z_0 for the standard normal distribution are shown in Figure 9-8. For easy reference, they are also included in Table 3 of the Appendix, Areas of a Standard Normal Distribution.

The procedure for hypothesis testing using critical regions follows the same first two steps as the procedure using *P*-values. However, instead of finding a *P*-value for the sample test statistic, we check if the sample test statistic falls in the critical region. If it does, we reject H_0. Otherwise, we do not reject H_0.

FIGURE 9-7

Critical Regions for H_0: $\mu = k$

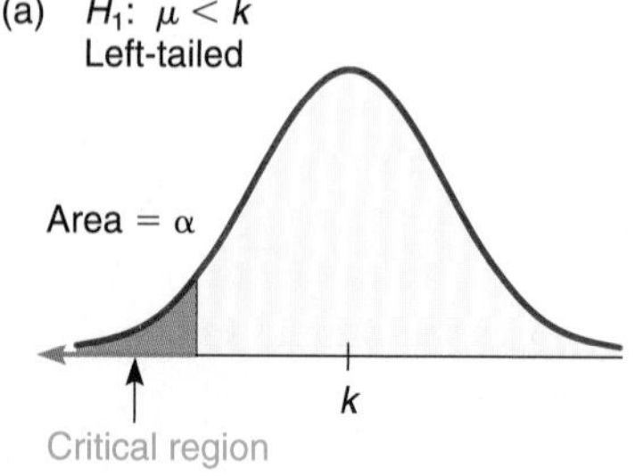

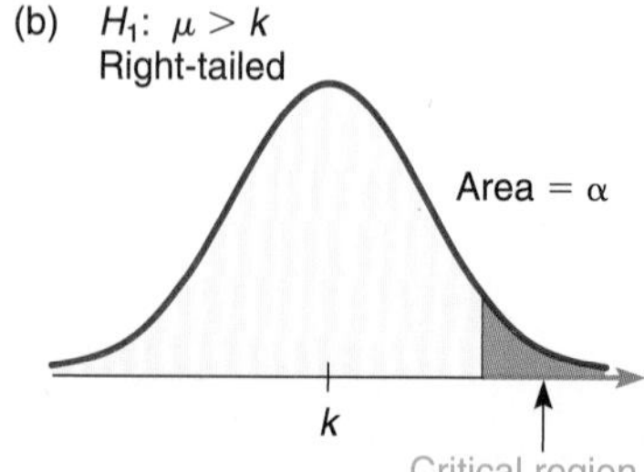

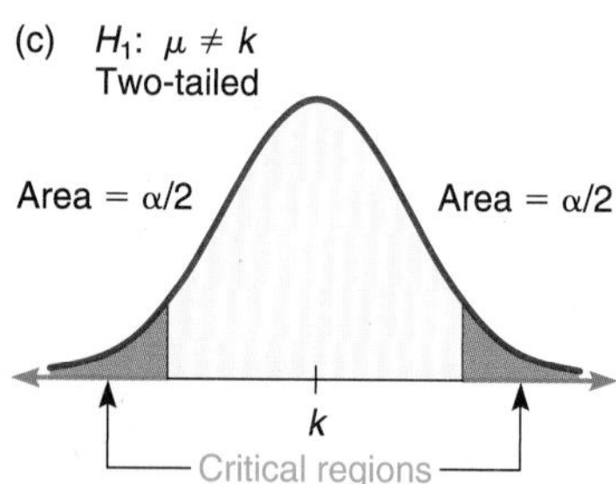

FIGURE 9-8

Critical Values z_0 for Tests Involving a Mean (Large Samples)

Level of significance $\alpha = 0.05$ $\alpha = 0.01$

For a left-tailed test
$H_1: \mu < k$
Critical value z_0
Critical region:
all $z < z_0$

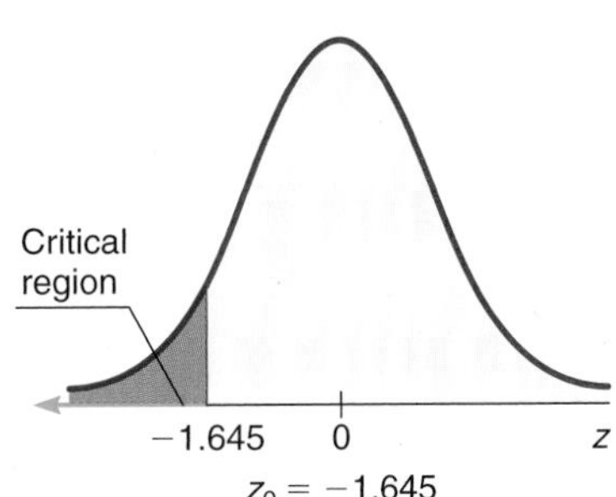

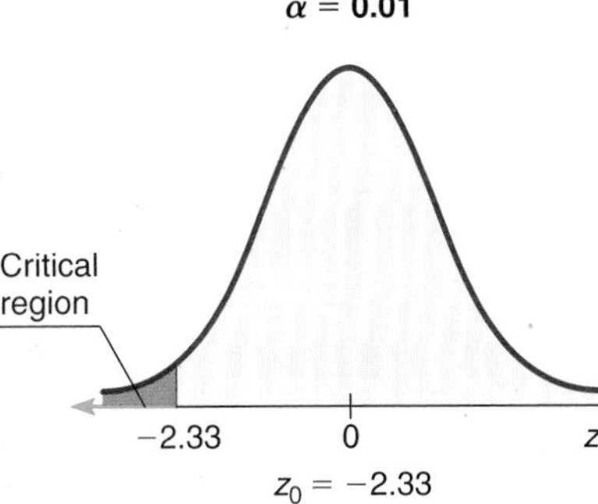

For a right-tailed test
$H_1: \mu > k$
Critical value z_0
Critical region:
all $z > z_0$

Critical region
0 1.645 z
$z_0 = 1.645$

Critical region
0 2.33 z
$z_0 = 2.33$

For a two-tailed test
$H_1: \mu \neq k$
Critical value $\pm z_0$
Critical regions:
all $z < -z_0$ together
with all $z > +z_0$

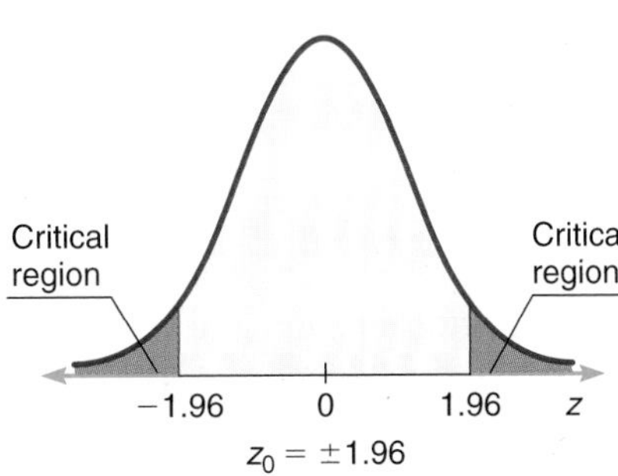

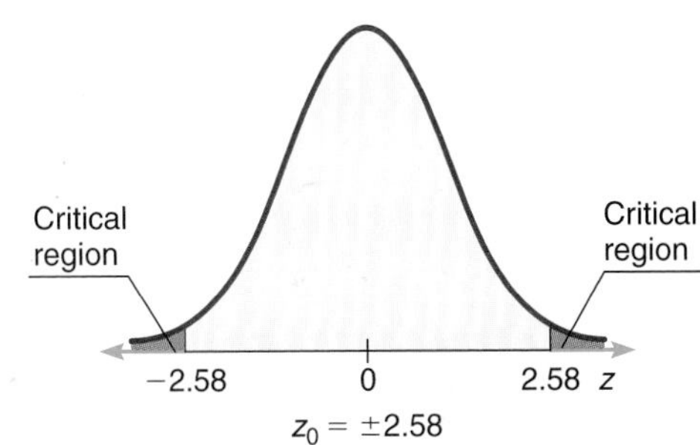

PROCEDURE

How to test μ when σ is known (critical region method)

Let x be a random variable appropriate to your application. Obtain a simple random sample (of size n) of x values from which you compute the sample mean $\bar{x}$. The value of σ is already known (perhaps from a previous study).

1. In the context of the application, state the *null and alternate hypotheses* and set the *level of significance* α. We use the most popular choices, $\alpha = 0.05$ or $\alpha = 0.01$.
2. If you can assume that x has a normal distribution, then any sample size n will work. If you cannot assume this, then use a sample size $n \geq 30$. Use the known σ, the sample size n, the value of $\bar{x}$ from the sample, and μ from the null hypothesis to compute the standardized sample *test statistic.*

$$z = \frac{\bar{x} - \mu}{\frac{\sigma}{\sqrt{n}}}$$

3. Show the *critical region and critical value(s)* on a graph of the sampling distribution. The level of significance α and the alternate hypothesis determine the locations of critical regions and critical values.

Continued

4. *Conclude* the test. If the test statistic z computed in Step 2 is in the critical region, then reject H_0. If the test statistic z is not in the critical region, then do not reject H_0.
5. *Interpret your conclusion* in the context of the application.

EXAMPLE 5 CRITICAL REGION METHOD OF TESTING μ

Consider Example 3 regarding sunspots. Let x be a random variable representing the number of sunspots observed in a four-week period. A random sample of 40 such periods from Spanish colonial times gave the number of sunspots per period. The raw data are given in Example 3. The sample mean is $\bar{x} \approx 47.0$. Previous studies indicate that for this period, $\sigma = 35$. It is thought that for thousands of years, the mean number of sunspots per four-week period was about $\mu = 41$. Do the data indicate that the mean sunspot activity during the Spanish colonial period was higher than 41? Use $\alpha = 0.05$.

SOLUTION:

(a) Set the null and alternate hypotheses.
As in Example 3, we use H_0: $\mu = 41$ and H_1: $\mu > 41$.

(b) Compute the sample test statistic.
As in Example 3, we use the standard normal distribution with $\bar{x} = 47$, $\sigma = 35$, $\mu = 41$ from H_0, and $n = 40$.

$$z = \frac{\bar{x} - \mu}{\sigma/\sqrt{n}} \approx \frac{47 - 41}{35/\sqrt{40}} \approx 1.08$$

(c) Determine the critical region and critical value based on H_1 and $\alpha = 0.05$.
Since we have a right-tailed test, the critical region is the rightmost 5% of the standard normal distribution. According to Figure 9-8, the critical value is $z_0 = 1.645$.

(d) Conclude the test.
We conclude the test by showing the critical region, critical value, and sample test statistic $z = 1.08$ on the standard normal curve. For a right-tailed test with $\alpha = 0.05$, the critical value is $z_0 = 1.645$. Figure 9-9 shows the critical region. As we can see, the sample test statistic does not fall in the critical region. Therefore, we fail to reject H_0.

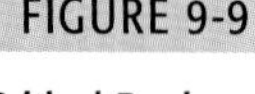

FIGURE 9-9

Critical Region, $\alpha = 0.05$

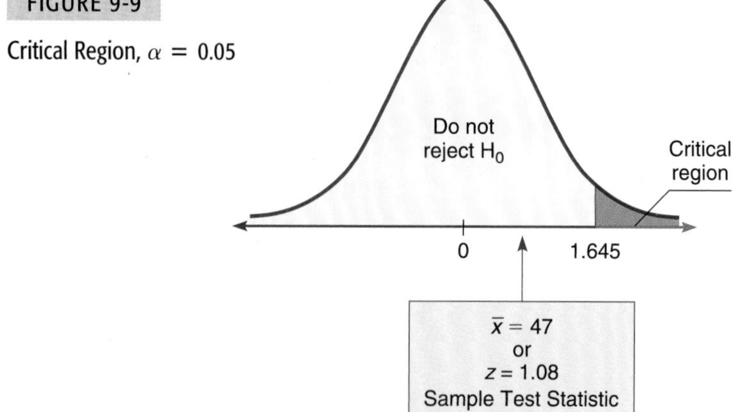

(e) Interpret the results.
At the 5% level of significance, the sample evidence is insufficient to justify rejecting H_0. It seems that the average sunspot activity during the Spanish colonial period was the same as the historical average.

Problems 23 and 24 show how to use confidence intervals to conclude two-tailed tests.

(f) How do the results of the critical region method compare to the results of the P-value method for a 5% level of significance?
The results, as expected, are the same. In both cases, we fail to reject H_0.

The critical region method of testing as outlined applies to tests of other parameters. As with the P-value method, you need to know the sampling distribution of the sample test statistic. Critical values for distributions are usually found in tables rather than in computer software output. For example, Table 4 of the Appendix provides critical values for Student t distributions.

The critical region method of hypothesis testing is very general. The following procedure box outlines the process of concluding a hypothesis test using the critical region method.

PROCEDURE

How to conclude tests using the critical region method

1. Compute the sample test statistic using an appropriate sampling distribution.
2. Using the same sampling distribution, find the critical value(s) as determined by the level of significance α and the nature of the test: right-tailed, left-tailed, or two-tailed.
3. Compare the sample test statistic to the critical value(s).
   (a) For a right-tailed test,
      i. if sample test statistic $\geq$ critical value, reject H_0.
      ii. if sample test statistic $<$ critical value, fail to reject H_0.
   (b) For a left-tailed test,
      i. if sample test statistic $\leq$ critical value, reject H_0.
      ii. if sample test statistic $>$ critical value, fail to reject H_0.
   (c) For a two-tailed test,
      i. if sample test statistic lies beyond critical values, reject H_0.
      ii. if sample test statistic lies between critical values, fail to reject H_0.

VIEWPOINT | Predator or Prey?

Consider animals such as the arctic fox, gray wolf, desert lion, and South American jaguar. Each animal is a predator. What are the total sleep time (hours per day), maximum life span (years), and overall danger index from other animals? Now consider prey such as rabbits, deer, wild horses, and the Brazilian tapir (a wild pig). Is there a statistically significant difference in average sleep time, life span, and danger index? What about other variables such as the ratio of brain weight to body weight or the sleep exposure index (sleeping in a well-protected den or out in the open)? How did prehistoric humans fit into this picture? Scientists have collected a lot of data, and a great deal of statistical work has been done regarding such questions. For more information, see the web site **<http://lib.stat.cmu.edu/>** *and follow the links to Datasets and then Sleep.*

SECTION 9.2 PROBLEMS

Tables and art to accompany margin answers may be found in the back of the book.

1. The P-value for a two-tailed test of μ is twice that for a one-tailed test, based on the same sample data and null hypothesis.
2. If σ is known, use the normal distribution. If σ is not known, use the Student's t distribution with $d.f. = n - 1$.
3. $d.f. = n - 1$.
4. No. When P-value < 0.05, it may not be true that P-value < 0.01, so we may not be able to reject H_0 at the 1% level.
5. Yes. When P-value < 0.01, it is also true that P-value < 0.05.
6. No. The P-value for a two-tailed test is twice the P-value for a one-tailed test, using the same sample data and null hypothesis. Even if P-value < 0.01, it is not necessarily true that $2(P\text{-value}) < 0.01$.

7. (a) $\alpha = 0.01$; H_0: $\mu = 16.4$ ft; H_1: $\mu > 16.4$ ft.
(b) Standard normal; $z \approx 1.54$.
(c) P-value ≈ 0.0618; on standard normal curve, shade area to the right of $z \approx 1.54$.
(d) P-value of $0.0618 > 0.01$ for α; fail to reject H_0.
(e) At the 1% level, there is insufficient evidence to say that the average storm level is increasing.

8. (a) $\alpha = 0.01$; H_0: $\mu = 38$ hr; H_1: $\mu < 38$ hr.
(b) Standard normal; $z \approx -2.86$; on standard normal curve, shade area to the left of -2.86.
(c) P-value ≈ 0.0021.
(d) P-value of $0.0021 \leq 0.01$ for α; reject H_0.
(e) At the 1% level, evidence shows that the average assembly time is less than 38 hr.

1. *Statistical Literacy* For the same sample data and null hypothesis, how does the P-value for a two-tailed test of μ compare to that for a one-tailed test?

2. *Statistical Literacy* To test μ for an x distribution that is mound-shaped using sample size $n \geq 30$, how do you decide whether to use the normal or Student's t distribution?

3. *Statistical Literacy* When using the Student's t distribution to test μ, what value do you use for the degrees of freedom?

4. *Critical Thinking* Consider a test for μ. If the P-value is such that you can reject H_0 at the 5% level of significance, can you always reject H_0 at the 1% level of significance? Explain.

5. *Critical Thinking* Consider a test for μ. If the P-value is such that you can reject H_0 for $\alpha = 0.01$, can you always reject H_0 for $\alpha = 0.05$? Explain.

6. *Critical Thinking* If sample data is such that for a one-tailed test of μ you can reject H_0 at the 1% level of significance, can you always reject H_0 for a two-tailed test at the same level of significance? Explain.

Please provide the following information for Problems 7–20.

(a) What is the level of significance? State the null and alternate hypotheses.
(b) What sampling distribution will you use? Explain the rationale for your choice of sampling distribution. What is the value of the sample test statistic?
(c) Find (or estimate) the P-value. Sketch the sampling distribution and show the area corresponding to the P-value.
(d) Based on your answers in parts (a) to (c), will you reject or fail to reject the null hypothesis? Are the data statistically significant at level α?
(e) Interpret your conclusion in the context of the application.

Note: For degrees of freedom $d.f.$ not given in the Student's t table, use the closest $d.f.$ that is *smaller*. In some situations, this choice of $d.f.$ may increase the P-value by a small amount and therefore produce a slightly more "conservative" answer.

7. *Meteorology: Storms* *Weatherwise* is a magazine published by the American Meteorological Society. One issue gives a rating system used to classify Nor'easter storms that frequently hit New England and can cause much damage near the ocean. A severe storm has an average peak wave height of $\mu = 16.4$ feet for waves hitting the shore. Suppose that a Nor'easter is in progress at the severe storm class rating. Peak wave heights are usually measured from land (using binoculars) off fixed cement piers. Suppose that a reading of 36 waves showed an average wave height of $\bar{x} = 17.3$ feet. Previous studies of severe storms indicate that $\sigma = 3.5$ feet. Does this information suggest that the storm is (perhaps temporarily) increasing above the severe rating? Use $\alpha = 0.01$.

8. *Ford Taurus: Assembly Time* Let x be a random variable that represents assembly times for the Ford Taurus. *The Wall Street Journal* reported that the average assembly time is $\mu = 38$ hours. A modification to the assembly procedure has been made. Experience with this new method indicates that $\sigma = 1.2$ hours. It is thought that the average assembly time may be reduced by this modification. A random sample of 47 new Ford Taurus automobiles coming off the assembly line showed the average assembly time of the new method to be $\bar{x} = 37.5$ hours. Does this indicate that the average assembly time has been reduced? Use $\alpha = 0.01$.

9. *E-mails: Priority Lists* Message mania! A professional employee in a large corporation receives an average of $\mu = 41.7$ e-mails per day. Most of these e-mails are from other employees in the company. Because of the large number of e-mails, employees find themselves distracted and are unable to concentrate when they return to their tasks (Reference: *The Wall Street Journal*). In an effort to reduce distraction caused by such interruptions, one company established a

9. (a) $\alpha = 0.05$; H_0: $\mu = 41.7$; H_1: $\mu \neq 41.7$.
   (b) Standard normal; $z \approx -1.99$.
   (c) *P*-value $\approx 2(0.0233) \approx 0.0466$; on standard normal curve, shade area to the right of 1.99 and to the left of -1.99.
   (d) *P*-value of $0.0466 \leq 0.05$ for α; reject H_0.
   (e) At the 5% level, there is sufficient evidence to say that the average number of e-mails is different with the new priority system.
10. (a) $\alpha = 0.05$; H_0: $\mu = 7.4$; H_1: $\mu \neq 7.4$.
   (b) Student's *t*, *d.f.* $= 30$; $t \approx 2.051$.
   (c) $0.020 < P\text{-value} < 0.050$; on *t* graph, shade area to the left of -2.051 and to the right of 2.051. From TI-84, *P*-value ≈ 0.0491.
   (d) Entire *P*-value interval ≤ 0.05 for α; reject H_0.
   (e) At the 5% level, the evidence is sufficient to say that the drug has changed the mean pH level.
11. (a) $\alpha = 0.01$; H_0: $\mu = 1.75$ yr; H_1: $\mu > 1.75$ yr.
   (b) Student's *t*, *d.f.* $= 45$; $t \approx 2.481$.
   (c) $0.005 < P\text{-value} < 0.010$; on *t* graph, shade area to the right of 2.481. From TI-84, *P*-value ≈ 0.0084.
   (d) Entire *P*-interval ≤ 0.01 for α; reject H_0.
   (e) At the 1% level of significance, the sample data indicate that the average age of the Minnesota region coyotes is greater than 1.75 years.
12. (a) $\alpha = 0.05$; H_0: $\mu = 19$ in.; H_1: $\mu < 19$ in.
   (b) Student's *t* with *d.f.* $= 50$; $t = -1.116$.
   (c) $0.125 < P\text{-value} < 0.250$; on *t* graph, shade area to the left of -1.116. From TI-84, *P*-value $\approx$ 0.1349.
   (d) *P*-value interval > 0.05 for α; fail to reject H_0.
   (e) At the 5% level of significance, the sample data do not indicate that the average trout length is less than 19 inches.
13. (a) $\alpha = 0.05$; H_0: $\mu = 19.4$; H_1: $\mu \neq 19.4$.
   (b) Student's *t*, *d.f.* $= 35$; $t \approx -1.731$.
   (c) $0.050 < P\text{-value} < 0.100$; on *t* graph, shade area to the right of 1.731 and to the left of -1.731. From TI-84, *P*-value $\approx$ 0.0923.
   (d) *P*-value interval > 0.05 for α; fail to reject H_0.
   (e) At the 5% level of significance, the sample evidence does not support rejecting the claim that the average P/E of socially responsible funds is different from that of the S&P stock index.

priority list that all employees were to use before sending an e-mail. One month after the new priority list was put into place, a random sample of 45 employees showed that they were receiving an average of $\bar{x} = 36.2$ e-mails per day. The computer server through which the e-mails are routed showed that $\sigma = 18.5$. Has the new policy had any effect? Use a 5% level of significance to test the claim that there has been a change (either way) in the average number of e-mails received per day per employee.

10. *Medical: Blood Plasma* Let x be a random variable that represents the pH of arterial plasma (i.e., acidity of the blood). For healthy adults, the mean of the x distribution is $\mu = 7.4$ (Reference: *Merck Manual*, a commonly used reference in medical schools and nursing programs). A new drug for arthritis has been developed. However, it is thought that this drug may change blood pH. A random sample of 31 patients with arthritis took the drug for 3 months. Blood tests showed that $\bar{x} = 8.1$ with sample standard deviation $s = 1.9$. Use a 5% level of significance to test the claim that the drug has changed (either way) the mean pH level of the blood.

11. *Wildlife: Coyotes* A random sample of 46 adult coyotes in a region of northern Minnesota showed the average age to be $\bar{x} = 2.05$ years, with sample standard deviation $s = 0.82$ years (based on information from the book *Coyotes: Biology, Behavior and Management* by M. Bekoff, Academic Press). However, it is thought that the overall population mean age of coyotes is $\mu = 1.75$. Do the sample data indicate that coyotes in this region of northern Minnesota tend to live longer than the average of 1.75 years? Use $\alpha = 0.01$.

12. *Fishing: Trout* Pyramid Lake is on the Paiute Indian Reservation in Nevada. The lake is famous for cutthroat trout. Suppose a friend tells you that the average length of trout caught in Pyramid Lake is $\mu = 19$ inches. However, the Creel Survey (published by the Pyramid Lake Paiute Tribe Fisheries Association) reported that of a random sample of 51 fish caught, the mean length was $\bar{x} = 18.5$ inches, with estimated standard deviation $s = 3.2$ inches. Do these data indicate that the average length of a trout caught in Pyramid Lake is less than $\mu = 19$ inches? Use $\alpha = 0.05$.

13. *Investing: Stocks* Socially conscious investors screen out stocks of alcohol and tobacco makers, firms with poor environmental records, and companies with poor labor practices. Some examples of "good," socially conscious companies are Johnson and Johnson, Dell Computers, Bank of America, and Home Depot. The question is, are such stocks overpriced? One measure of value is the P/E, or price-to-earnings ratio. High P/E ratios may indicate a stock is overpriced. For the S&P Stock Index of all major stocks, the mean P/E ratio is $\mu = 19.4$. A random sample of 36 "socially conscious" stocks gave a P/E ratio sample mean of $\bar{x} = 17.9$, with sample standard deviation $s = 5.2$ (Reference: *Morningstar*, a financial analysis company in Chicago). Does this indicate that the mean P/E ratio of all socially conscious stocks is different (either way) from the mean P/E ratio of the S&P Stock Index? Use $\alpha = 0.05$.

14. *Agriculture: Ground Water* Unfortunately, arsenic occurs naturally in some ground water (Reference: *Union Carbide Technical Report K/UR-1*). A mean arsenic level of $\mu = 8.0$ parts per billion (ppb) is considered safe for agricultural use. A well in Texas is used to water cotton crops. This well is tested on a regular basis for arsenic. A random sample of 37 tests gave a sample mean of $\bar{x} = 7.2$ ppb arsenic, with $s = 1.9$ ppb. Does this information indicate that the mean level of arsenic in this well is less than 8 ppb? Use $\alpha = 0.01$.

15. *Medical: Red Blood Cell Count* Let x be a random variable that represents red blood cell count (RBC) in millions of cells per cubic millimeter of whole blood. Then x has a distribution that is approximately normal. For the population of healthy female adults, the mean of the x distribution is about 4.8

14. (a) $\alpha = 0.01$; H_0: $\mu = 8.0$ ppb; H_1: $\mu < 8.0$ ppb.
(b) Student's t, $d.f. = 36$; $t \approx -2.561$.
(c) In Table 4, use the closest $d.f.$ smaller than 36, or $d.f. = 35$; $0.005 < P\text{-value} < 0.010$; on t graph, shade area to the left of -2.561. From TI-84, P-value $\approx$ 0.0074.
(d) P-value interval < 0.01 for α; reject H_0.
(e) At the 1% level of significance, sample data support the claim that the average arsenic content is less than 8.0 ppb.

15. i. Use a calculator. Rounded values are used in part ii.
ii. (a) $\alpha = 0.05$; H_0: $\mu = 4.8$; H_1: $\mu < 4.8$.
(b) Student's t, $d.f. = 5$; $t \approx -3.499$.
(c) $0.005 < P\text{-value} < 0.010$; on t graph, shade the area to the left of -3.499. From TI-84, P-value ≈ 0.0086.
(d) P-value interval ≤ 0.05 for α; reject H_0.
(e) At the 5% level of significance, sample evidence supports the claim that the average RBC count for this patient is less than 4.8.

16. i. Use a calculator. Rounded values are used in part ii.
ii. (a) $\alpha = 0.01$; H_0: $\mu = 14$; H_1: $\mu > 14$.
(b) Student's t, $d.f. = 9$; $t \approx 1.386$.
(c) $0.075 < P\text{-value} < 0.100$; on t graph, shade area to the right of 1.386. From TI-84, P-value $\approx$ 0.0996.
(d) P-value interval > 0.01; fail to reject H_0.
(e) At the 1% level of significance, the sample data do not support the claim that the average HC for this patient is higher than 14.

17. i. Use a calculator. Rounded values are used in part ii.
ii. (a) $\alpha = 0.01$; H_0: $\mu = 67$; H_1: $\mu \neq 67$.
(b) Student's t, $d.f. = 15$; $t \approx -1.962$.
(c) $0.050 < P\text{-value} < 0.100$; on t graph, shade area to the right of 1.962 and to the left of -1.962. From TI-84, P-value $\approx$ 0.0686.
(d) P-value interval > 0.01; fail to reject H_0.
(e) At the 1% level of significance, the sample evidence does not support the claim that the average thickness of slab avalanches in Vail is different from that in Canada.

(based on information from *Diagnostic Tests with Nursing Implications*, Springhouse Corporation). Suppose that a female patient has taken six laboratory blood tests over the past several months and that the RBC count data sent to the patient's doctor are

4.9	4.2	4.5	4.1	4.4	4.3

i. Use a calculator with sample mean and sample standard deviation keys to verify that $\bar{x} = 4.40$ and $s \approx 0.28$.
ii. Do the given data indicate that the population mean RBC count for this patient is lower than 4.8? Use $\alpha = 0.05$.

16. *Medical: Hemoglobin Count* Let x be a random variable that represents hemoglobin count (HC) in grams per 100 milliliters of whole blood. Then x has a distribution that is approximately normal, with population mean of about 14 for healthy adult women (see reference in Problem 15). Suppose that a female patient has taken 10 laboratory blood tests during the past year. The HC data sent to the patient's doctor are

15	18	16	19	14	12	14	17	15	11

i. Use a calculator with sample mean and sample standard deviation keys to verify that $\bar{x} = 15.1$ and $s \approx 2.51$.
ii. Does this information indicate that the population average HC for this patient is higher than 14? Use $\alpha = 0.01$.

17. *Ski Patrol: Avalanches* Snow avalanches can be a real problem for travelers in the western United States and Canada. A very common type of avalanche is called the slab avalanche. These have been studied extensively by David McClung, a professor of civil engineering at the University of British Columbia. Slab avalanches studied in Canada had an average thickness of $\mu = 67$ cm (Source: *Avalanche Handbook*, by D. McClung and P. Schaerer). The ski patrol at Vail, Colorado, is studying slab avalanches in its region. A random sample of avalanches in spring gave the following thicknesses (in cm):

59	51	76	38	65	54	49	62
68	55	64	67	63	74	65	79

i. Use a calculator with mean and standard deviation keys to verify that $\bar{x} \approx 61.8$ cm and $s \approx 10.6$ cm.
ii. Assume the slab thickness has an approximately normal distribution. Use a 1% level of significance to test the claim that the mean slab thickness in the Vail region is different from that in Canada.

18. *Longevity: Honolulu* *USA Today* reported that the state with the longest mean life span is Hawaii, where the population mean life span is 77 years. A random sample of 20 obituary notices in the *Honolulu Advertizer* gave the following information about life span (in years) of Honolulu residents:

72	68	81	93	56	19	78	94	83	84
77	69	85	97	75	71	86	47	66	27

i. Use a calculator with mean and standard deviation keys to verify that $\bar{x} =$ 71.4 years and $s \approx 20.65$ years.
ii. Assuming that life span in Honolulu is approximately normally distributed, does this information indicate that the population mean life span for Honolulu residents is less than 77 years? Use a 5% level of significance.

19. *Fishing: Atlantic Salmon* Homser Lake, Oregon, has an Atlantic salmon catch-and-release program that has been very successful. The average fisherman's catch has been $\mu = 8.8$ Atlantic salmon per day. (Source: *National Symposium on*

18. i. Use a calculator. Rounded values are used in part ii.
ii. (a) $\alpha = 0.05$; H_0: $\mu = 77$ yr; H_1: $\mu < 77$ yr.
(b) Student's t, $d.f. = 19$; $t \approx -1.213$.
(c) $0.100 < P\text{-value} < 0.125$; on t graph, shade area to the left of -1.213. From TI-84, P-value ≈ 0.1200.
(d) P-value interval > 0.05; fail to reject H_0.
(e) At the 5% level of significance, the evidence is not strong enough to conclude that the population mean life span is less than 77 years.

19. i. Use a calculator. Rounded values are used in part ii.
ii. (a) $\alpha = 0.05$; H_0: $\mu = 8.8$; H_1: $\mu \neq 8.8$.
(b) Student's t, $d.f. = 13$; $t \approx -1.337$.
(c) $0.200 < P\text{-value} < 0.250$; on t graph, shade area to the right of 1.337 and to the left of -1.337. From TI-84, P-value ≈ 0.2042.
(d) P-value interval > 0.05; fail to reject H_0.
(e) At the 5% level of significance, we cannot conclude that the average catch is different from 8.8 fish per day.

20. i. Use a calculator. Rounded values are used in part ii.
ii. (a) $\alpha = 0.01$; H_0: $\mu = 1300$; H_1: $\mu \neq 1300$.
(b) Student's t, $d.f. = 9$; $t \approx -2.714$.
(c) $0.020 < P\text{-value} < 0.050$; on t graph, shade region to the right of 2.714 and to the left of -2.714. From TI-84, P-value ≈ 0.0239.
(d) P-value interval > 0.01; fail to reject H_0.
(e) At the 1% level of significance, there is not enough evidence to conclude that the population mean of tree-ring dates is different from that in 1300 A.D.

21. (a) The P-value of a one-tailed test is smaller. For a two-tailed test, the P-value is doubled because it includes the area in both tails.
(b) Yes; the P-value of a one-tailed test is smaller, so it might be smaller than α, whereas the P-value of a two-tailed test may be larger than α.
(c) Yes; if the two-tailed P-value is less than α, the smaller one-tail area is also less than α.
(d) Yes, the conclusions can be different. The conclusion based on the two-tailed test is more conservative in the sense that the sample data must be more extreme (differ more from H_0) in order to reject H_0.

Catch and Release Fishing, Humboldt State University.) Suppose that a new quota system restricting the number of fishermen has been put into effect this season. A random sample of fishermen gave the following catches per day:

12	6	11	12	5	0	2
7	8	7	6	3	12	12

i. Use a calculator with mean and sample standard deviation keys to verify that $\bar{x} \approx 7.36$ and $s \approx 4.03$.

ii. Assuming the catch per day has an approximately normal distribution, use a 5% level of significance to test the claim that the population average catch per day is now different from 8.8.

20. *Archaeology: Tree Rings* Tree-ring dating from archaeological excavation sites is used in conjunction with other chronologic evidence to estimate occupation dates of prehistoric Indian ruins in the southwestern United States. It is thought that Burnt Mesa Pueblo was occupied around 1300 A.D. (based on evidence from potsherds and stone tools). The following data give tree-ring dates (A.D.) from adjacent archaeological sites (*Bandelier Archaeological Excavation Project: Summer 1990 Excavations at Burnt Mesa Pueblo*, edited by T. Kohler, Washington State University Department of Anthropology, 1992):

1189	1267	1268	1275	1275
1271	1272	1316	1317	1230

i. Use a calculator with mean and standard deviation keys to verify that $\bar{x} = 1268$ and $s \approx 37.29$ years.

ii. Assuming the tree-ring dates in this excavation area follow a distribution that is approximately normal, does this information indicate that the population mean of tree-ring dates in the area is different from (either higher or lower than) that in 1300 A.D.? Use a 1% level of significance.

21. *Critical Thinking: One-Tailed versus Two-Tailed Tests*
(a) For the same data and null hypothesis, is the P-value of a one-tailed test (right or left) larger or smaller than that of a two-tailed test? Explain.
(b) For the same data, null hypothesis, and level of significance, is it possible that a one-tailed test results in the conclusion to reject H_0 while a two-tailed test results in the conclusion to fail to reject H_0? Explain.
(c) For the same data, null hypothesis, and level of significance, if the conclusion is to reject H_0 based on a two-tailed test, do you also reject H_0 based on a one-tailed test? Explain.
(d) If a report states that certain data were used to reject a given hypothesis, would it be a good idea to know what type of test (one-tailed or two-tailed) was used? Explain.

22. *Critical Thinking: Comparing Hypothesis Tests with U.S. Courtroom System* Compare statistical testing with legal methods used in a U.S. court setting. Then discuss the following topics in class or consider the topics on your own. Please write a brief but complete essay in which you answer the following questions.
(a) In a court setting, the person charged with a crime is initially considered to be innocent. The claim of innocence is maintained until the jury returns with a decision. Explain how the claim of innocence could be taken to be the null hypothesis. Do we assume that the null hypothesis is true throughout the testing procedure? What would be the alternate hypothesis in a court setting?
(b) The court claims that a person is innocent if the evidence against the person is not adequate to find him or her guilty. This does not mean, however, that the court has necessarily *proved* the person to be innocent. It simply means that the evidence against the person was not adequate for the jury to find him or her guilty. How does this situation compare with a statistical test for

22. Essay or class discussion.

Most students are more or less familiar with the U.S. court system. This can be excellent material for class discussion.

Problems 23 and 24 show the relationship between confidence intervals and two-tailed tests. You may want to spend a little class time discussing these problems.

23. (a) For $\alpha = 0.01$, confidence level $c = 0.99$; interval from 20.28 to 23.72; hypothesized $\mu = 20$ is not in the interval; reject H_0.
(b) H_0: $\mu = 20$; H_1: $\mu \neq 20$; $z = 3.000$; P-value ≈ 0.0026; P-value of $0.0026 \leq 0.01$ for α; reject H_0; conclusions are the same.

24. (a) For $\alpha = 0.01$, confidence level $c = 0.99$; interval from 20.28 to 23.72; hypothesized $\mu = 21$ from H_0 falls in the confidence interval; fail to reject H_0.
(b) H_0: $\mu = 21$; H_1: $\mu \neq 21$; $z = 1.50$; P-value $= 0.1336$; P-value $0.1336 > 0.01$ for α; fail to reject H_0; conclusions are the same.

25. Critical value $z_0 = 2.33$; critical region is values to the right of 2.33; since the sample statistic $z = 1.54$ is not in the critical region, fail to reject H_0. At the 1% level, there is insufficient evidence to say that the average storm level is increasing. Conclusion is same as with P-value method.

26. Critical value $z_0 = -2.33$; critical region is values to the left of -2.33; since the sample statistic $z = -2.86$ is in the critical region, reject H_0. At the 1% level, evidence shows that average assembly time is less than 38 hr. Conclusion is same as with P-value method.

27. Critical values $z_0 = \pm 1.96$; critical regions are values to the left of -1.96 together with values to the right of 1.96. Since the sample test statistic $z = -1.99$ is in the critical region, reject H_0. At the 5% level, there is sufficient evidence to say that the average number of e-mails is different with the new priority system. Conclusion is same as with P-value method.

28. Critical values are $t_0 = \pm 2.042$ for two-tailed test with $d.f. = 30$; critical regions are values to the right of 2.042 together with those to the left of -2.042. Since the sample test statistic $t = 2.051$ is in the critical region, reject H_0. At the 5% level, the evidence is sufficient to say that the drug has changed the mean pH level. Conclusion is same as with P-value method.

which the conclusion is "do not reject" (i.e., accept) the null hypothesis? What would be a type II error in this context?

(c) If the evidence against a person is adequate for the jury to find him or her guilty, then the court claims that the person is guilty. Remember, this does not mean that the court has necessarily *proved* the person to be guilty. It simply means that the evidence against the person was strong enough to find him or her guilty. How does this situation compare with a statistical test for which the conclusion is to "reject" the null hypothesis? What would be a type I error in this context?

(d) In a court setting, the final decision as to whether the person charged is innocent or guilty is made at the end of the trial, usually by a jury of impartial people. In hypothesis testing, the final decision to reject or not reject the null hypothesis is made at the end of the test by using information or data from an (impartial) random sample. Discuss these similarities between statistical hypothesis testing and a court setting.

(e) We hope that you are able to use this discussion to increase your understanding of statistical testing by comparing it with something that is a well-known part of our American way of life. However, all analogies have weak points. It is important not to take the analogy between statistical hypothesis testing and legal court methods too far. For instance, the judge does not set a level of significance and tell the jury to determine a verdict that is wrong only 5% or 1% of the time. Discuss some of these weak points in the analogy between the court setting and hypothesis testing.

23. *Expand Your Knowledge: Confidence Intervals and Two-Tailed Hypothesis Tests* Is there a relationship between confidence intervals and two-tailed hypothesis tests? Let c be the level of confidence used to construct a confidence interval from sample data. Let α be the level of significance for a two-tailed hypothesis test. The following statement applies to hypothesis tests of the mean.

> For a two-tailed hypothesis test with level of significance α and null hypothesis H_0: $\mu = k$, we *reject* H_0 whenever k falls *outside* the $c = 1 - \alpha$ confidence interval for μ based on the sample data. When k falls within the $c = 1 - \alpha$ confidence interval, we do not reject H_0.

(A corresponding relationship between confidence intervals and two-tailed hypothesis tests also is valid for other parameters, such as p, $\mu_1 - \mu_2$, or $p_1 - p_2$, which we will study in Sections 9.3, 10.2, and 10.3.) Whenever the value of k given in the null hypothesis falls *outside* the $c = 1 - \alpha$ confidence interval for the parameter, we *reject* H_0. For example, consider a two-tailed hypothesis test with $\alpha = 0.01$ and

$$H_0: \mu = 20 \qquad H_1: \mu \neq 20$$

A random sample of size 36 has a sample mean $\bar{x} = 22$ from a population with standard deviation $\sigma = 4$.

(a) What is the value of $c = 1 - \alpha$? Using the methods of Chapter 8, construct a $1 - \alpha$ confidence interval for μ from the sample data. What is the value of μ given in the null hypothesis (i.e., what is k)? Is this value in the confidence interval? Do we reject or fail to reject H_0 based on this information?

(b) Using methods of Chapter 9, find the P-value for the hypothesis test. Do we reject or fail to reject H_0? Compare your result to that of part (a).

24. *Confidence Intervals and Two-Tailed Hypothesis Tests* Change the null hypothesis of Problem 23 to H_0: $\mu = 21$. Repeat parts (a) and (b).

25. *Critical Region Method: Standard Normal* Solve Problem 7 using the critical region method of testing (i.e., traditional method). Compare your conclusion with the conclusion obtained by using the P-value method. Are they the same?

29. Critical value is $t_0 = 2.412$ for one-tailed test with *d.f.* = 45; critical region is values to the right of 2.412. Since the sample test statistic $t = 2.481$ is in the critical region, reject H_0. At the 1% level, the sample data indicate that the average age of Minnesota region coyotes is higher than 1.75 yr. Conclusion is same as with *P*-value method.

30. Critical value is $t_0 = -1.676$ for one-tailed test with *d.f.* = 50; critical region is values to the left of -1.676. Since the sample test statistic $t = -1.116$ is not in the critical region, fail to reject H_0. At the 5% level, the sample data do not indicate that the average fish length is less than 19 in. Conclusion is same as with *P*-value method.

26. *Critical Region Method: Standard Normal* Solve Problem 8 using the critical region method of testing. Compare your conclusion with the conclusion obtained by using the *P*-value method. Are they the same?

27. *Critical Region Method: Standard Normal* Solve Problem 9 using the critical region method of testing. Compare your conclusion with the conclusion obtained by using the *P*-value method. Are they the same?

28. *Critical Region Method: Student's t* Table 4 of the Appendix gives critical values for the Student's t distribution. Use an appropriate *d.f.* as the row header. For a *right-tailed* test, the column header is the value of α found in the *one-tail area* row. For a *left-tailed* test, the column header is the value of α found in the *one-tail area* row, but you must change the sign of the critical value t to $-t$. For a *two-tailed* test, the column header is the value of α from the *two-tail area* row. The critical values are the $\pm t$ values shown. Solve Problem 10 using the critical region method of testing. Compare your conclusion with the conclusion obtained by using the *P*-value method. Are they the same?

29. *Critical Region Method: Student's t* Solve Problem 11 using the critical region method of testing. *Hint:* See Problem 28. Compare your conclusion with the conclusion obtained by using the *P*-value method. Are they the same?

30. *Critical Region Method: Student's t* Solve Problem 12 using the critical region method of testing. *Hint:* See Problem 28. Compare your conclusion with the conclusion obtained by using the *P*-value method. Are they the same?

SECTION 9.3 Testing a Proportion *p*

FOCUS POINTS

- Identify the components needed for testing a proportion.
- Compute the sample test statistic.
- Find the *P*-value and conclude the test.

Many situations arise that call for tests of proportions or percentages rather than means. For instance, a college registrar may want to determine if the proportion of students wanting 3-week intensive courses has increased.

How can we make such a test? In this section, we will study tests involving proportions (i.e., percentages or proportions). Such tests are similar to those in Sections 9.1 and 9.2. The main difference is that we are working with a distribution of proportions.

Tests for a single proportion

Data Highlights, Problem 1 ("With Sampling, There Is Too a Free Lunch"), can be used for a lead-in class discussion topic.

Throughout this section, we will assume that the situations we are dealing with satisfy the conditions underlying the binomial distribution. In particular, we will let r be a binomial random variable. This means that r is the number of successes out of n independent binomial trials (for the definition of binomial trial, see Section 6.2). We will use $\hat{p} = r/n$ as our estimate for p, the population probability of success on each trial. The letter q again represents the population probability of failure on each trial, and so $q = 1 - p$. We also assume that the samples are large (i.e., $np > 5$ and $nq > 5$).

For large samples, the distribution of $\hat{p} = r/n$ values is well approximated by a *normal curve* with mean μ and standard deviation σ as follows:

$$\mu = p$$

$$\sigma = \sqrt{\frac{pq}{n}}$$

The null and alternate hypotheses for tests of proportions are

Left-Tailed Test	Right-Tailed Test	Two-Tailed Test
$H_0: p = k$	$H_0: p = k$	$H_0: p = k$
$H_1: p < k$	$H_1: p > k$	$H_1: p \neq k$

depending on what is asked for in the problem. Notice that since p is a probability, the value k must be between 0 and 1.

Sample test statistic

For tests of proportions, we need to convert the sample test statistic $\hat{p}$ to a z value. Then we can find a P-value appropriate for the test. The $\hat{p}$ distribution is approximately normal, with mean p and standard deviation $\sqrt{pq/n}$. Therefore, the conversion of $\hat{p}$ to z follows the formula

When computing z values, be careful with rounding. The expression pq/n usually will need four or more digits after the decimal.

$$z = \frac{\hat{p} - p}{\sqrt{\frac{pq}{n}}}$$

where $\hat{p} = r/n$ is the sample test statistic

n = number of trials

p = proportion specified in H_0

$q = 1 - p$

Using this mathematical information about the sampling distribution for $\hat{p}$, the basic procedure is similar to tests you have conducted before.

PROCEDURE

HOW TO TEST A PROPORTION p

Consider a binomial experiment with n trials, where p represents the population probability of success and $q = 1 - p$ represents the population probability of failure. Let r be a random variable that represents the number of successes out of the n binomial trials.

1. In the context of the application, state the *null and alternate hypotheses* and set the *level of significance* α.
2. The number of trials n should be sufficiently large so that both $np > 5$ and $nq > 5$ (use p from the null hypothesis). In this case, $\hat{p} = r/n$ can be approximated by the normal distribution using the standardized sample *test statistic*

   $$z = \frac{\hat{p} - p}{\sqrt{\frac{pq}{n}}}$$

   where p is the value specified in H_0 and $q = 1 - p$.
3. Use the standard normal distribution and the type of test, one-tailed or two-tailed, to find the *P-value* corresponding to the test statistic.
4. *Conclude* the test. If P-value $\leq \alpha$, then reject H_0. If P-value $> \alpha$, then do not reject H_0.
5. *Interpret your conclusion* in the context of the application.

EXAMPLE 6

TESTING p

A team of eye surgeons has developed a new technique for a risky eye operation to restore the sight of people blinded from a certain disease. Under the old method, it is known that only 30% of the patients who undergo this operation recover their eyesight.

Suppose that surgeons in various hospitals have performed a total of 225 operations using the new method and that 88 have been successful (the patients fully recovered their sight). Can we justify the claim that the new method is better than the old one? (Use a 1% level of significance.)

SOLUTION:

(a) Establish H_0 and H_1 and note the level of significance.
The level of significance is $\alpha = 0.01$. Let p be the probability that a patient fully recovers his or her eyesight. The null hypothesis is that p is still 0.30, even for the new method. The alternate hypothesis is that the new method has improved the chances of a patient recovering his or her eyesight. Therefore,

$$H_0\colon p = 0.30 \quad \text{and} \quad H_1\colon p > 0.30$$

(b) Find the sample test statistic $\hat{p}$ and convert it to a z value, if appropriate.
Using p from H_0, we note that $np = 225(0.3) = 67.5$ is greater than 5 and $nq = 225(0.7) = 157.5$ is also greater than 5, so we can use the normal distribution for the sample statistic $\hat{p}$.

$$\hat{p} = \frac{r}{n} = \frac{88}{225} \approx 0.39$$

The z value corresponding to $\hat{p}$ is

$$z = \frac{\hat{p} - p}{\sqrt{\frac{pq}{n}}} \approx \frac{0.39 - 0.30}{\sqrt{\frac{0.30(0.70)}{225}}} \approx 2.95$$

In the formula, the value for p is from the null hypothesis. H_0 specifies that $p = 0.30$, so $q = 1 - 0.30 = 0.70$.

(c) Find the P-value of the test statistic.
Figure 9-10 shows the P-value. Since we have a right-tailed test, the P-value is the area to the right of $z = 2.95$. Using the normal distribution (Table 3 of the Appendix), we find that P-value $= P(z > 2.95) \approx 0.0016$.

FIGURE 9-10

P-value Area

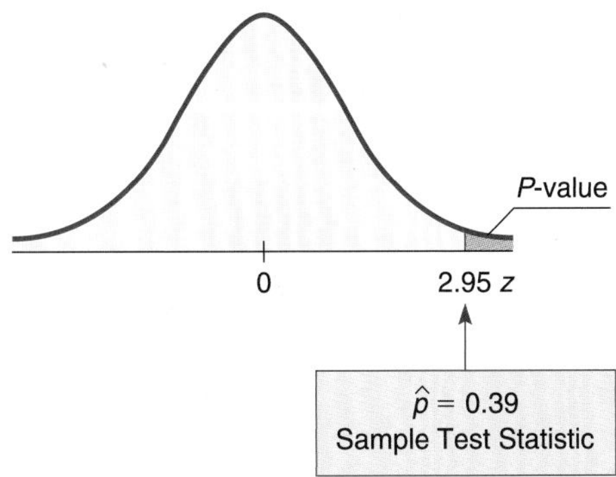

(d) Conclude the test.
Since the P-value of $0.0016 \leq 0.01$ for α, we reject H_0.

(e) Interpret the results.
At the 1% level of significance, the evidence shows that the population probability of success for the new surgery technique is higher than that of the old technique.

GUIDED EXERCISE 5 Testing p

A botanist has produced a new variety of hybrid wheat that is better able to withstand drought than other varieties. The botanist knows that for the parent plants, the proportion of seeds germinating is 80%. The proportion of seeds germinating for the hybrid variety is unknown, but the botanist claims that it is 80%. To test this claim, 400 seeds from the hybrid plant are tested, and it is found that 312 germinate. Use a 5% level of significance to test the claim that the proportion germinating for the hybrid is 80%.

(a) Let p be the proportion of hybrid seeds that will germinate. Notice that we have no prior knowledge about the germination proportion for the hybrid plant. State H_0 and H_1. What is the required level of significance?

H_0: $p = 0.80$; H_1: $p \neq 0.80$; $\alpha = 0.05$

(b) Calculate the sample test statistic $\hat{p}$. Using the value of p in H_0, are both $np > 5$ and $nq > 5$? Can we use the normal distribution for $\hat{p}$?

The number of trials is $n = 400$, and the number of successes is $r = 312$. Thus,

$$\hat{p} = \frac{r}{n} = \frac{312}{400} = 0.78$$

From H_0, $p = 0.80$ and $q = 1 - p = 0.20$.

$$np = 400(0.8) = 320 > 5$$
$$nq = 400(0.2) = 80 > 5$$

So, we can use the normal distribution for $\hat{p}$.

(c) Next, we convert the sample test statistic $\hat{p} = 0.78$ to a z value. Based on our choice for H_0, what value should we use for p in our formula? Since $q = 1 - p$, what value should we use for q? Using these values for p and q, convert $\hat{p}$ to a z value.

According to H_0, $p = 0.80$. Then $q = 1 - p = 0.20$. Using these values in the following formula gives

$$z = \frac{\hat{p} - p}{\sqrt{\dfrac{pq}{n}}} = \frac{0.78 - 0.80}{\sqrt{\dfrac{0.80(0.20)}{400}}} = -1.00$$

CALCULATOR NOTE If you evaluate the denominator separately, be sure to carry at least four digits after the decimal.

(d) Is the test right-tailed, left-tailed, or two-tailed? Find the P-value of the sample test statistic and sketch a standard normal curve showing the P-value.

For a two-tailed test, using the normal distribution (Table 3 of the Appendix), we find that

$$P\text{-value} = 2P(z < -1.00) = 2(0.1587) = 0.3174$$

FIGURE 9-11 *P*-value

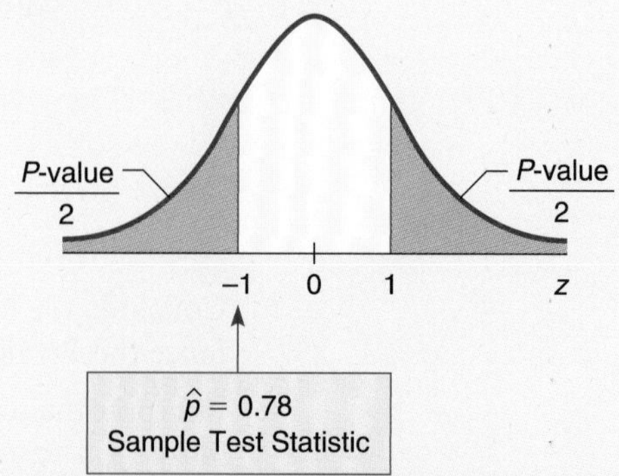

Continued

GUIDED EXERCISE 5 *continued*

(e) Do we reject or fail to reject H_0? Interpret your conclusion in the context of the application.

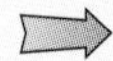

Since

P-value of $0.3174 > 0.05$ for α

we fail to reject H_0. At the 5% level of significance, there is insufficient evidence to conclude that the botanist is wrong.

Critical region method

Since the $\hat{p}$ sampling distribution is approximately normal, we use Table 3, "Areas of a Standard Normal Distribution," in the Appendix to find critical values.

EXAMPLE 7 **CRITICAL REGION METHOD FOR TESTING p**

Let's solve Guided Exercise 5 using the critical region approach. In that problem, 312 of 400 seeds from a hybrid wheat variety germinated. For the parent plants, the proportion of germinating seeds was 80%. Use a 5% level of significance to test the claim that the population proportion of germinating seeds from the hybrid wheat is different from that of the parent plants.

SOLUTION:

(a) As in Guided Exercise 5, we have $\alpha = 0.05$, H_0: $p = 0.80$, and H_1: $p \neq 0.80$. The next step is to find the sample statistic $\hat{p}$ and the corresponding test statistic z. This was done in Guided Exercise 5, where we found that $\hat{p} = 0.78$, with corresponding $z = -1.00$.

(b) Now we find the critical value z_0 for a two-tailed test using $\alpha = 0.05$. This means that we want the total area 0.05 divided between two tails, one to the right of z_0 and one to the left of $-z_0$. As shown in Figure 9-8 of Section 9.2, the critical value(s) are ± 1.96. (See also Table 3, part (c), of the Appendix for critical values of the z distribution.)

(c) Figure 9-12 shows the critical regions and the location of the sample test statistic.

FIGURE 9-12

Critical Regions, $\alpha = 0.05$

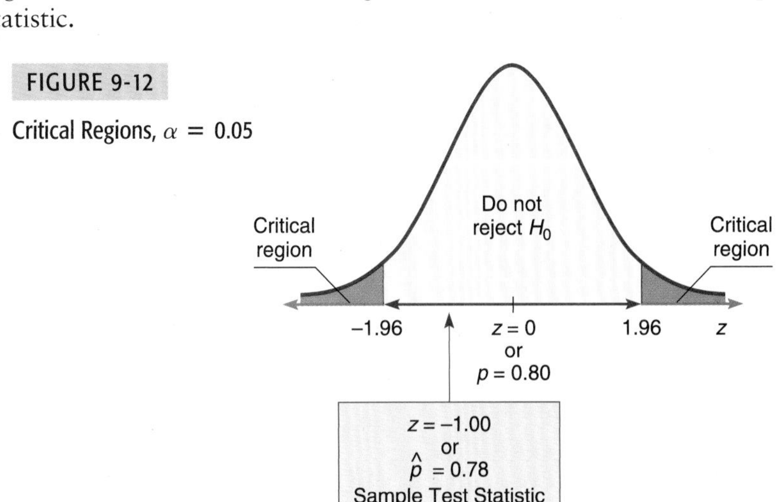

(d) Finally, we conclude the test and compare the results to Guided Exercise 5. Since the sample test statistic does not fall in the critical region, we fail to reject H_0 and conclude that, at the 5% level of significance, the evidence is not strong enough to reject the botanist's claim. This result, as expected, is consistent with the conclusion obtained by using the P-value method.

TECH NOTES

The TI-84Plus/TI-83Plus calculators and Minitab support tests of proportions. The output for both technologies includes the sample proportion $\hat{p}$ and the P-value of $\hat{p}$. Minitab also includes the z value corresponding to $\hat{p}$.

TI-84Plus/TI-83Plus Press STAT, select TESTS, and use option **5:1-PropZTest.** The value of p_0 is from the null hypothesis H_0: $p = p_0$. The number of successes is the value for x.

Minitab Menu selections: **Stat ➤ Basic Statistics ➤ 1 Proportion.** Under options, set the test proportion as the value in H_0. Choose to use the normal distribution.

CRITICAL THINKING

Issues Related to Hypothesis Testing

Through our work with hypothesis tests of μ and p, we've gained experience in setting up, performing, and interpreting results of such tests.

We know that different random samples from the same population are very likely to have sample statistics $\bar{x}$ or $\hat{p}$ that differ from their corresponding parameters μ or p. Some values of a statistic from a random sample will be close to the corresponding parameter. Others may be farther away simply because we happened to draw a random sample of more extreme data values.

The central question in hypothesis testing is whether or not you think the value of the sample test statistic is too far away from the value of the population parameter proposed in H_0 to occur by chance alone.

This is where the P-value of the sample test statistic comes into play. The P-value of the sample test statistic tells you the probability that you would get a sample statistic as far away as, or farther from, the value of the parameter as stated in the null hypothesis H_0.

If the P-value is very small, you reject H_0. But what does "very small" mean? It is customary to define "very small" as smaller than the preset level of significance α.

When you reject H_0, are you absolutely certain that you are making a correct decision? The answer is no! You are simply willing to take a chance that you are making a mistake (a type I error). The level of significance α describes the chance of making a mistake if you reject H_0 when it is, in fact, true.

Several issues come to mind:

1. What if the P-value is so close to α that we "barely" reject or fail to reject H_0? In such cases, researchers might attempt to clarify the results by
   - increasing the sample size.
   - controlling the experiment to reduce the standard deviation.

   Both actions tend to increase the magnitude of the z or t value of the sample test statistic, resulting in a smaller corresponding P-value.
2. How reliable are the study and the measurements in the sample?
   - When reading results of a statistical study, be aware of the source of the data and the reliability of the organization doing the study.
   - Is the study sponsored by an organization that might profit or benefit from the stated conclusions? If so, look at the study carefully to ensure that the measurements, sampling technique, and handling of data are proper and meet professional standards.

VIEWPOINT Who Did What?

Art, music, literature, and science share a common need to classify things: Who painted that picture? Who composed that music? Who wrote that document? Who should get that patent? In statistics, such questions are called classification problems. *For example, the* Federalist Papers *were published anonymously in 1787–1788 by Alexander Hamilton, John Jay, and James Madison. But who wrote what? That question is addressed by F. Mosteller (Harvard University) and D. Wallace (University of Chicago) in the book* Statistics: A Guide to the Unknown, *edited by J. M. Tanur. Other scholars have studied authorship regarding Plato's* Republic *and Plato's* Dialogues, *including the* Symposium. *For more information on this topic, see the source in Problems 13 and 14 of this exercise set.*

SECTION 9.3 PROBLEMS

Answers may vary slightly due to rounding.

1. For the conditions $np > 5$ and $nq > 5$, use the value of p from H_0. Note that $q = 1 - p$.
2. $\hat{p} = r/n$ with corresponding z value.
3. Yes. The corresponding P-value for a one-tailed test is half that for a two-tailed test, so the P-value of the one-tailed test is also less than 0.01.
4. Answers may vary. First, we don't know if the information is based on sample data or population data. If it is based on population data, a hypothesis test is not needed. However, assuming the study is based on sample data, it seems that H_0: $p = 0.15$ and H_1: $p > 0.15$ are appropriate. Without a specific source for the study, we do not know how reliable the information in the sample is. Also, we are not given information about sample size. Level of significance could be one of the common values 0.01 or 0.05. Again, we have no specific information. Finally, if the conclusions are based on sample data, we cannot conclude that they are absolutely true.
5. i. (a) $\alpha = 0.01$; H_0: $p = 0.301$; H_1: $p < 0.301$.
   (b) Standard normal; yes, $np \approx 64.7 > 5$ and $nq \approx 150.3 > 5$; $\hat{p} \approx 0.214$; $z \approx -2.78$.
   (c) P-value ≈ 0.0027; on standard normal curve, shade area to the left of -2.78.
   (d) P-value of $0.0027 \le 0.01$ for α; reject H_0.

1. *Statistical Literacy* To use the normal distribution to test a proportion p, the conditions $np > 5$ and $nq > 5$ must be satisfied. Does the value of p come from H_0, or is it estimated by using $\hat{p}$ from the sample?

2. *Statistical Literacy* Consider a binomial experiment with n trials and r successes. To construct a test for a proportion p, what value do we use for the sample test statistic?

3. ***Critical Thinking*** In general, if sample data are such that the null hypothesis is rejected at the $\alpha = 1\%$ level of significance based on a two-tailed test, is H_0 also rejected at the $\alpha = 1\%$ level of significance for a corresponding one-tailed test? Explain.

4. ***Critical Thinking*** An article in a newspaper states that the proportion of traffic accidents involving road rage is higher this year than it was last year, when it was 15%. Reconstruct the information of the study in terms of a hypothesis test. Discuss possible hypotheses, possible issues about the sample, possible levels of significance, and the "absolute truth" of the conclusion.

For Problems 5–19, please provide the following information.

(a) What is the level of significance? State the null and alternate hypotheses.
(b) What sampling distribution will you use? Do you think the sample size is sufficiently large? Explain. What is the value of the sample test statistic?
(c) Find the P-value of the test statistic. Sketch the sampling distribution and show the area corresponding to the P-value.
(d) Based on your answers in parts (a) to (c), will you reject or fail to reject the null hypothesis? Are the data statistically significant at level α?
(e) Interpret your conclusion in the context of the application.

5. *Focus Problem: Benford's Law* Please read the Focus Problem at the beginning of this chapter. Recall that Benford's Law claims that numbers chosen from very large data files tend to have "1" as the first nonzero digit disproportionately often. In fact, research has shown that if you randomly draw a number from a very large data file, the probability of getting a number with "1" as the leading digit is about 0.301 (see the reference in this chapter's Focus Problem).

   Now suppose you are an auditor for a very large corporation. The revenue report involves millions of numbers in a large computer file. Let us say you took a random sample of $n = 215$ numerical entries from the file and $r = 46$ of the entries had a first nonzero digit of 1. Let p represent the population proportion of all numbers in the corporate file that have a first nonzero digit of 1.

i. Test the claim that p is less than 0.301. Use $\alpha = 0.01$.
ii. If p is in fact less than 0.301, would it make you suspect that there are not enough numbers in the data file with leading 1's? Could this indicate that the books have been "cooked" by "pumping up" or inflating the numbers? Comment from the viewpoint of a stockholder. Comment from the perspective of the Federal Bureau of Investigation as it looks for money laundering in the form of false profits.
iii. Comment on the following statement: If we reject the null hypothesis at level of significance α, we have not *proved* H_0 to be false. We can say that the probability is α that we made a mistake in rejecting H_0. Based on the outcome of the test, would you recommend further investigation before accusing the company of fraud?

6. *Focus Problem: Benford's Law* Again suppose you are the auditor for a very large corporation. The revenue file contains millions of numbers in a large computer data bank (see Problem 5). You draw a random sample of $n = 228$ numbers from this file and $r = 92$ have a first nonzero digit of 1. Let p represent the population proportion of all numbers in the computer file that have a leading digit of 1.
i. Test the claim that p is more than 0.301. Use $\alpha = 0.01$.
ii. If p is in fact larger than 0.301, it would seem there are too many numbers in the file with leading 1's. Could this indicate that the books have been "cooked" by artificially lowering numbers in the file? Comment from the point of view of the Internal Revenue Service. Comment from the perspective of the Federal Bureau of Investigation as it looks for "profit skimming" by unscrupulous employees.
iii. Comment on the following statement: If we reject the null hypothesis at level of significance α, we have not *proved* H_0 to be false. We can say that the probability is α that we made a mistake in rejecting H_0. Based on the outcome of the test, would you recommend further investigation before accusing the company of fraud?

7. *Sociology: Crime Rate* Is the national crime rate really going down? Some sociologists say yes! They say that the reason for the decline in crime rates in the 1980s and 1990s is demographics. It seems that the population is aging, and older people commit fewer crimes. According to the FBI and the Justice Department, 70% of all arrests are of males aged 15 to 34 years. (Source: *True Odds*, by J. Walsh, Merritt Publishing.) Suppose you are a sociologist in Rock Springs, Wyoming, and a random sample of police files showed that of 32 arrests last month, 24 were of males aged 15 to 34 years. Use a 1% level of significance to test the claim that the population proportion of such arrests in Rock Springs is different from 70%.

8. *College Athletics: Graduation Rate* Women athletes at the University of Colorado, Boulder, have a long-term graduation rate of 67% (Source: *The Chronicle of Higher Education*). Over the past several years, a random sample of 38 women athletes at the school showed that 21 eventually graduated. Does this indicate that the population proportion of women athletes who graduate from the University of Colorado, Boulder, is now less than 67%? Use a 5% level of significance.

9. *Highway Accidents: DUI* The U.S. Department of Transportation, National Highway Traffic Safety Administration, reported that 77% of all fatally injured automobile drivers were intoxicated. A random sample of 27 records of automobile driver fatalities in Kit Carson County, Colorado, showed that 15 involved an intoxicated driver. Do these data indicate that the population proportion of driver fatalities related to alcohol is less than 77% in Kit Carson County? Use $\alpha = 0.01$.

(e) At the 1% level of significance, the sample data indicate that the population proportion of numbers with a leading "1" in the revenue file is less than 0.301, predicted by Benford's Law.
ii. Yes; the revenue data file seems to include more numbers with higher first nonzero digits than Benford's Law predicts.
iii. We have not proved H_0 to be false. However, because our sample data led us to reject H_0 and to conclude that there are too few numbers with a leading digit of 1, more investigation is merited.

6. i. (a) $\alpha = 0.01$; H_0: $p = 0.301$; H_1: $p > 0.301$.
(b) Standard normal; yes, $np \approx 68.6 > 5$ and $nq \approx 159.4 > 5$; $\hat{p} \approx 0.404$; $z \approx 3.39$.
(c) P-value ≈ 0.0003; on standard normal curve, shade area to the right of 3.39.
(d) P-value of $0.0003 \le 0.01$ for α; reject H_0.
(e) At the 1% level of significance, the sample data indicate that the proportion of numbers in the revenue file with a leading digit of 1 exceeds 0.301, predicted by Benford's Law.
ii. Yes, there seem to be too many entries with a leading digit of 1.
iii. We have not proved H_0 to be false. However, because our data led us to reject H_0 and to conclude that there are "too many" numbers with a leading digit of 1, more investigation is merited.

7. (a) $\alpha = 0.01$; H_0: $p = 0.70$; H_1: $p \ne 0.70$.
(b) Standard normal; $\hat{p} = 0.75$; $z \approx 0.62$.
(c) P-value $= 2(0.2676) = 0.5352$; on standard normal curve, shade area to the right of 0.62 and to the left of -0.62.
(d) P-value of $0.5352 > 0.01$ for α; fail to reject H_0.
(e) At the 1% level of significance, we cannot say that the population proportion of arrests of males aged 15 to 34 in Rock Springs is different from 70%.

8. (a) $\alpha = 0.05$; H_0: $p = 0.67$; H_1: $p < 0.67$.
(b) Standard normal; $\hat{p} \approx 0.5526$; $z \approx -1.54$.
(c) P-value ≈ 0.0618; on standard normal curve, shade area to the left of -1.54.
(d) P-value of $0.0618 > 0.05$ for α; fail to reject H_0.

10. *Preference: Color* What is your favorite color? A large survey of countries, including the United States, China, Russia, France, Turkey, Kenya, and others, indicated that most people prefer the color blue. In fact, about 24% of the population claim blue as their favorite color. (Reference: Study by J. Bunge and A. Freeman-Gallant, Statistics Center, Cornell University.) Suppose a random sample of $n = 56$ college students were surveyed and $r = 12$ of them said that blue is their favorite color. Does this information imply that the color preference of all college students is different (either way) from that of the general population? Use $\alpha = 0.05$.

11. *Wildlife: Wolves* The following is based on information from *The Wolf in the Southwest: The Making of an Endangered Species,* by David E. Brown (University of Arizona Press). Before 1918, the proportion of female wolves in the general population of all southwestern wolves was about 50%. However, after 1918, southwestern cattle ranchers began a widespread effort to destroy wolves. In a recent sample of 34 wolves, there were only 10 females. One theory is that male wolves tend to return sooner than females to their old territories, where their predecessors were exterminated. Do these data indicate that the population proportion of female wolves is now less than 50% in the region? Use $\alpha = 0.01$.

12. *Fishing: Northern Pike* Athabasca Fishing Lodge is located on Lake Athabasca in northern Canada. In one of its recent brochures, the lodge advertises that 75% of its guests catch northern pike over 20 pounds. Suppose that last summer 64 out of a random sample of 83 guests did, in fact, catch northern pike weighing over 20 pounds. Does this indicate that the population proportion of guests who catch pike over 20 pounds is different from 75% (either higher or lower)? Use $\alpha = 0.05$.

13. *Plato's Republic: Syllable Patterns* Prose rhythm is characterized as the occurrence of five-syllable sequences in long passages of text. This characterization may be used to assess the similarity among passages of text and sometimes the identity of authors. The following information is based on an article by D. Wishart and S. V. Leach appearing in *Computer Studies of the Humanities and Verbal Behavior* (Vol. 3, pp. 90–99). Syllables were categorized as long or short. On analyzing Plato's *Republic,* Wishart and Leach found that about 26.1% of the five-syllable sequences are of the type in which two are short and three are long. Suppose that Greek archaeologists have found an ancient manuscript dating back to Plato's time (about 427–347 B.C.). A random sample of 317 five-syllable sequences from the newly discovered manuscript showed that 61 are of the type two short and three long. Do the data indicate that the population proportion of this type of five-syllable sequence is different (either way) from the text of Plato's *Republic*? Use $\alpha = 0.01$.

14. *Plato's Dialogues: Prose Rhythm* *Symposium* is part of a larger work referred to as Plato's *Dialogues.* Wishart and Leach (see source in Problem 13) found that about 21.4% of five-syllable sequences in *Symposium* are of the type in which four are short and one is long. Suppose an antiquities store in Athens has a very old manuscript that the owner claims is part of Plato's *Dialogues.* A random

(e) At the 5% level of significance, there is insufficient evidence to say that the proportion of women athletes who graduate is less than 67%.

9. (a) $\alpha = 0.01$; H_0: $p = 0.77$; H_1: $p < 0.77$.
(b) Standard normal; $\hat{p} \approx 0.5556$; $z \approx -2.65$.
(c) P-value ≈ 0.004; on standard normal curve, shade area to the left of -2.65.
(d) P-value of $0.004 \leq 0.01$ for α; reject H_0.
(e) At the 1% level of significance, the data show that the population proportion of driver fatalities related to alcohol is less than 77% in Kit Carson County.

10. (a) $\alpha = 0.05$; H_0: $p = 0.24$; H_1: $p \neq 0.24$.
(b) Standard normal; $\hat{p} \approx 0.2143$; $z \approx -0.45$.
(c) P-value $= 2(0.3264) = 0.6528$; on standard normal curve, shade region to the right of 0.45 and to the left of -0.45.
(d) P-value of $0.6528 > 0.05$ for α; fail to reject H_0.
(e) At the 5% level of significance, the data do not indicate that the proportion of college students favoring the color blue is different from 0.24.

11. (a) $\alpha = 0.01$; H_0: $p = 0.50$; H_1: $p < 0.50$.
(b) Standard normal; $\hat{p} \approx 0.2941$; $z \approx -2.40$.
(c) P-value of 0.0082; on standard normal curve, shade region to the left of -2.40.
(d) P-value of $0.0082 \leq 0.01$ for α; reject H_0.
(e) At the 1% level of significance, the data indicate that the population proportion of female wolves in the region is now less than 50%.

12. (a) $\alpha = 0.05$; H_0: $p = 0.75$; H_1: $p \neq 0.75$.
(b) Standard normal; $\hat{p} \approx 0.7711$; $z \approx 0.44$.
(c) P-value $= 2(0.3300) = 0.6600$; on standard normal curve, shade area to the right of 0.44 and to the left of -0.44.
(d) P-value of $0.6600 > 0.05$ for α; do not reject H_0.
(e) At the 5% level of significance, there is insufficient evidence to indicate that the population proportion of guests who catch pike over 20 pounds is different from 75%.

13. (a) $\alpha = 0.01$; H_0: $p = 0.261$; H_1: $p \neq 0.261$.
(b) Standard normal; $\hat{p} \approx 0.1924$; $z \approx -2.78$.
(c) P-value $= 2(0.0027) = 0.0054$; on standard normal curve, shade area to the right of 2.78 and to the left of -2.78.
(d) P-value of $0.0054 \leq 0.01$ for α; reject H_0.
(e) At the 1% level of significance, the sample data indicate that the population proportion of the five-syllable sequence is different from that of Plato's *Republic.*

14. (a) $\alpha = 0.01$; H_0: $p = 0.214$; H_1: $p > 0.214$.
(b) Standard normal; $\hat{p} \approx 0.2759$; $z \approx 3.35$.
(c) P-value $= 0.0004$; on standard normal curve, shade region to the right of 3.35.
(d) P-value of $0.0004 \leq 0.01$ for α; reject H_0.

sample of 493 five-syllable sequences from this manuscript showed that 136 were of the type four short and one long. Do the data indicate that the population proportion of this type of five-syllable sequence is higher than that found in Plato's *Symposium*? Use $\alpha = 0.01$.

15. *Consumers: Product Loyalty* *USA Today* reported that about 47% of the general consumer population in the United States is loyal to the automobile manufacturer of their choice. Suppose Chevrolet did a study of a random sample of 1006 Chevrolet owners and found that 490 said they would buy another Chevrolet. Does this indicate that the population proportion of consumers loyal to Chevrolet is more than 47%? Use $\alpha = 0.01$.

16. *Supermarket: Prices* *Harper's Index* reported that 80% of all supermarket prices end in the digit 9 or 5. Suppose you check a random sample of 115 items in a supermarket and find that 88 have prices that end in 9 or 5. Does this indicate that fewer than 80% of the prices in the store end in the digits 9 or 5? Use $\alpha = 0.05$.

17. *Medical: Hypertension* This problem is based on information taken from *The Merck Manual* (a reference manual used in most medical and nursing schools). Hypertension is defined as a blood pressure reading over 140 mm Hg systolic and/or over 90 mm Hg diastolic. Hypertension, if not corrected, can cause long-term health problems. In the college-age population (18–24 years), about 9.2% have hypertension. Suppose that a blood donor program is taking place in a college dormitory this week (final exams week). Before each student gives blood, the nurse takes a blood pressure reading. Of 196 donors, it is found that 29 have hypertension. Do these data indicate that the population proportion of students with hypertension during final exams week is higher than 9.2%? Use a 5% level of significance.

18. *Medical: Hypertension* Diltiazem is a commonly prescribed drug for hypertension (see source in Problem 17). However, diltiazem causes headaches in about 12% of patients using the drug. It is hypothesized that regular exercise might help reduce the headaches. If a random sample of 209 patients using diltiazem exercised regularly and only 16 had headaches, would this indicate a reduction in the population proportion of patients having headaches? Use a 1% level of significance.

19. *Myers-Briggs: Extroverts* Are most student government leaders extroverts? According to Myers-Briggs estimates, about 82% of college student government leaders are extroverts. (Source: *Myers-Briggs Type Indicator Atlas of Type Tables*.) Suppose that a Myers-Briggs personality preference test was given to a random sample of 73 student government leaders attending a large national leadership conference and that 56 were found to be extroverts. Does this indicate that the population proportion of extroverts among college student government leaders is different (either way) from 82%? Use $\alpha = 0.01$.

20. *Critical Region Method: Testing Proportions* Solve Problem 7 using the critical region method of testing. Since the sampling distribution of $\hat{p}$ is the normal distribution, you can use critical values from the standard normal distribution as shown in Figure 9-8 or part (c) of Table 3 of the Appendix. Compare your

(e) At the 1% level of significance, the sample data indicate that the population proportion of the five-syllable sequence is higher than that found in Plato's *Symposium*.

15. (a) $\alpha = 0.01$; H_0: $p = 0.47$; H_1: $p > 0.47$.
(b) Standard normal; $\hat{p} \approx 0.4871$; $z \approx 1.09$.
(c) P-value $= 0.1379$; on standard normal curve, shade area to the right of 1.09.
(d) P-value of $0.1379 > 0.01$ for α; fail to reject H_0.
(e) At the 1% level of significance, there is insufficient evidence to support the claim that the population proportion of customers loyal to Chevrolet is more than 47%.

16. (a) $\alpha = 0.05$; H_0: $p = 0.80$; H_1: $p < 0.80$.
(b) Standard normal; $\hat{p} \approx 0.7652$; $z \approx -0.93$.
(c) P-value $= 0.1762$; on standard normal curve, shade area to the left of -0.93.
(d) P-value of $0.1762 > 0.05$ for α; fail to reject H_0.
(e) At the 5% level of significance, there is insufficient evidence to claim that the population proportion of prices ending with the digits 9 or 5 is less than 80%.

17. (a) $\alpha = 0.05$; H_0: $p = 0.092$; H_1: $p > 0.092$.
(b) Standard normal; $\hat{p} \approx 0.1480$; $z \approx 2.71$.
(c) P-value $= 0.0034$; on standard normal curve, shade region to the right of 2.71.
(d) P-value of $0.0034 \leq 0.05$ for α; reject H_0.
(e) At the 5% level of significance, the data indicate that the population proportion of students with hypertension during final exams week is higher than 9.2%.

18. (a) $\alpha = 0.01$; H_0: $p = 0.12$; H_1: $p < 0.12$.
(b) Standard normal; $\hat{p} \approx 0.0766$; $z \approx -1.93$.
(c) P-value $= 0.0268$; on standard normal curve, shade region to the left of -1.93.
(d) P-value of $0.0268 > 0.01$ for α; fail to reject H_0.
(e) At the 1% level of significance, the data are insufficient to conclude that the population proportion of patients having headaches is less than 0.12.

19. (a) $\alpha = 0.01$; H_0: $p = 0.82$; H_1: $p \neq 0.82$.
(b) Standard normal; $\hat{p} \approx 0.7671$; $z \approx -1.18$.
(c) P-value $= 2(0.1190) = 0.2380$; on standard normal curve, shade area to the right of 1.18 and to the left of -1.18.
(d) P-value of $0.2380 > 0.01$ for α; fail to reject H_0.
(e) At the 1% level of significance, the evidence is insufficient to indicate that the population proportion of extroverts among college student government leaders is different from 82%.

20. Critical values are $\pm z_0 = \pm 2.58$. The critical regions are values greater than 2.58 together with values less than -2.58. The sample test statistic $z = 0.62$ is not in the critical region, so we do not reject H_0. This result is consistent with the P-value conclusion.

21. Critical value is $z_0 = -2.33$. The critical region consists of values less than -2.33. The sample test statistic $z = -2.65$ is in the critical region, so we reject H_0. This result is consistent with the P-value conclusion.
22. Critical value is $z_0 = 2.33$. The critical region consists of values greater than 2.33. The sample test statistic $z = 1.09$ is not in the critical region, so we fail to reject H_0. This result is consistent with the P-value conclusion.

conclusions with the conclusions obtained by using the P-value method. Are they the same?

21. *Critical Region Method: Testing Proportions* Solve Problem 9 using the critical region method of testing. *Hint:* See Problem 20. Compare your conclusions with the conclusions obtained by using the P-value method. Are they the same?

22. *Critical Region Method: Testing Proportions* Solve Problem 15 using the critical region method of testing. *Hint:* See Problem 20. Compare your conclusions with the conclusions obtained by using the P-value method. Are they the same?

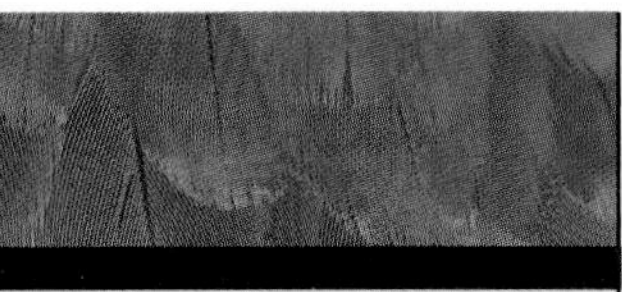

Chapter Review

SUMMARY

Hypothesis testing is a major component of inferential statistics. In hypothesis testing, we propose a specific value for the population parameter in question. Then we use sample data from a random sample and probability to determine whether or not to reject this specific value for the parameter.

Basic components of a hypothesis test:

- The *null hypothesis* H_0 states that a parameter equals a specific value.
- The *alternate hypothesis* H_1 states that the parameter is greater than, less than, or simply not equal to the value specified in H_0.
- The *level of significance* α of the test is the probability of rejecting H_0 when it is true.
- The *sample test statistic* corresponding to the parameter in H_0 is computed from a random sample and appropriate sampling distribution.
- Assuming H_0 is true, the probability that a sample test statistic will take on a value as extreme as, or more extreme than, the observed sample test statistic is the *P-value* of the test. The P-value is computed by using the sample test statistic, the corresponding sampling distribution, H_0, and H_1.
- If P-value $\leq \alpha$, we reject H_0. If P-value $> \alpha$, we fail to reject H_0.
- We say that sample data are *significant* if we can reject H_0.

An alternative way to conclude a test of hypotheses is to use critical regions based on the alternate hypothesis and α. Critical values z_0 are found in Table 3(c) of the Appendix. Critical values t_0 are found in Table 4 of the Appendix. If the sample test statistic falls beyond the critical values—that is, in the critical region—we reject H_0.

The methods of hypothesis testing are very general, and we will see them used again in later chapters. In this chapter, we looked at tests involving

- Parameter μ. Use standard normal or Student's t distribution. See procedure displays in Section 9.2.
- Parameter p. Use standard normal distribution. See procedure displays in Section 9.3.

IMPORTANT WORDS & SYMBOLS

Section 9.1

Hypothesis testing
Hypotheses
Null hypothesis H_0
Alternate hypothesis H_1
right-tailed test
left-tailed test
two-tailed test
sample test statistic
P-value
statistical significance
Type I error
Type II error
α, the level of significance of a test and the probability of a type I error
β, the probability of a type II error
Power of a test $(1 - \beta)$

Section 9.2

d.f. for testing μ when σ is unknown
Critical region
Critical value

Section 9.3

Criteria for using normal approximation to binomial, $np > 5$ and $nq > 5$

VIEWPOINT Will It Rain?

Do cloud seed experiments ever work? If you seed the clouds, will it rain? If it does rain, who will benefit? Who will be displeased by the rain? If you seed the clouds and nothing happens, will taxpayers (who support the effort) complain or rejoice? Maybe this should be studied over a remote island—such as Tasmania (near Australia). Using what you already know about statistical testing, you can conduct your own tests, given the appropriate data. Remember, there are sociological questions (pleased/displeased with result) as well as technical questions (number of inches of rain produced). For data regarding cloud-seeding experiments over Tasmania, visit the Online Study Center at **www.cengage.com/statistics/Brase/UBS5e** *and find the link to DASL, the Carnegie Mellon University Data and Story Library. From the DASL site, look under Datasets for Cloud.*

CHAPTER REVIEW PROBLEMS

1. *Statistical Literacy* When testing μ, how do we decide whether to use the standard normal distribution or a Student's t distribution?

2. *Statistical Literacy* What do we mean when we say a test is *significant*? Does this necessarily mean the results are important?

3. *Critical Thinking* All other conditions being equal, does a larger sample size increase or decrease the corresponding magnitude of the z or t value of the sample test statistic?

4. *Critical Thinking* All other conditions being equal, does a z or t value with larger magnitude have a larger or smaller corresponding P-value?

Before you solve each problem, first categorize it by answering the following question: Are we testing a single mean or a single proportion? Then provide the following information for Problems 5–12.

(a) What is the level of significance? State the null and alternate hypotheses.
(b) What sampling distribution will you use? What assumptions are you making? What is the value of the sample test statistic?
(c) Find (or estimate) the P-value. Sketch the sampling distribution and show the area corresponding to the P-value.
(d) Based on your answers in parts (a) to (c), will you reject or fail to reject the null hypothesis? Are the data statistically significant at level α?
(e) Interpret your conclusion in the context of the application.

Note: For degrees of freedom *d.f.* not in the Student's t table, use the closest *d.f.* that is *smaller*. In some situations, this choice of *d.f.* may increase the P-value by a small amount and therefore produce a slightly more "conservative" answer. Answers may vary due to rounding.

5. *Vehicles: Mileage* Based on information in *Statistical Abstract of the United States* (116th Edition), the average annual miles driven per vehicle in the United States is 11.1 thousand miles, with $\sigma \approx 600$ miles. Suppose that a random sample of 36 vehicles owned by residents of Chicago showed that the average mileage driven last year was 10.8 thousand miles. Does this indicate that the average miles driven per vehicle in Chicago is different from (higher or lower than) the national average? Use a 0.05 level of significance.

6. *Student Life: Employment* Professor Jennings claims that only 35% of the students at Flora College work while attending school. Dean Renata thinks that the professor has underestimated the number of students with part-time or

Answers may vary due to rounding.
1. Look at the original x distribution. If it is normal or $n \geq 30$, and σ is known, use the standard normal distribution. If the x distribution is mound-shaped or $n \geq 30$, and σ is unknown, use the Student's t distribution. The *d.f.* is determined by the application.
2. If a test is significant, we reject H_0. Results may or may not be important.
3. A larger sample size increases the $|z|$ or $|t|$ value of the sample test statistic.
4. A larger $|z|$ or $|t|$ value has a smaller corresponding P-value.
5. Single mean.
(a) $\alpha = 0.05$; H_0: $\mu = 11.1$; H_1: $\mu \neq 11.1$.
(b) Standard normal; $z = -3.00$.
(c) P-value $= 0.0026$; on standard normal curve, shade area to the right of 3.00 and to the left of -3.00.
(d) P-value of $0.0026 \leq 0.05$ for α; reject H_0.
(e) At the 5% level of significance, the evidence is sufficient to say that the miles driven per vehicle in Chicago is different from the national average.
6. Single proportion.
(a) $\alpha = 0.05$; H_0: $p = 0.35$; H_1: $p > 0.35$.
(b) Standard normal; $z = 2.48$.
(c) P-value $= 0.0066$; on standard normal curve, shade area to the right of 2.48.
(d) P-value of $0.0066 \leq 0.05$ for α; reject H_0.
(e) At the 5% level of significance, the evidence indicates that more than 35% of the students have jobs.

full-time jobs. A random sample of 81 students shows that 39 have jobs. Do the data indicate that more than 35% of the students have jobs? (Use a 5% level of significance.)

7. *Toys: Electric Trains* The Toylot Company makes an electric train with a motor that it claims will draw an average of only 0.8 ampere (A) under a normal load. A sample of nine motors was tested, and it was found that the mean current was $\bar{x} = 1.4$ A, with a sample standard deviation of $s = 0.41$ A. Do the data indicate that the Toylot claim of 0.8 A is too low? (Use a 1% level of significance.)

8. *Matches: Number per Box* The Nero Match Company sells matchboxes that are supposed to have an average of 40 matches per box, with $\sigma = 9$. A random sample of 94 Nero matchboxes shows the average number of matches per box to be 43.1. Using a 1% level of significance, can you say that the average number of matches per box is more than 40?

9. *Medical: Plasma Compress* A hospital reported that the normal death rate for patients with extensive burns (more than 40% of skin area) has been significantly reduced by the use of new fluid plasma compresses. Before the new treatment, the mortality rate for extensive burn patients was about 60%. Using the new compresses, the hospital found that only 40 of 90 patients with extensive burns died. Use a 1% level of significance to test the claim that the mortality rate has dropped.

10. *Civil Service: College Degrees* The Congressional Budget Office reports that 36% of federal civilian employees have a bachelor's degree or higher (*The Wall Street Journal*). A random sample of 120 employees in the private sector showed that 33 have a bachelor's degree or higher. Does this indicate that the percentage of employees holding bachelor's degrees or higher in the private sector is less than in the federal civilian sector? Use $\alpha = 0.05$.

11. *Vending Machines: Coffee* A machine in the student lounge dispenses coffee. The average cup of coffee is supposed to contain 7.0 ounces. Eight cups of coffee from this machine show the average content to be 7.3 ounces with a standard deviation of 0.5 ounce. Do you think that the machine has slipped out of adjustment and that the average amount of coffee per cup is different from 7 ounces? Use a 5% level of significance.

12. *Sports Car: Fuel Injection* The manufacturer of a sports car claims that the fuel injection system lasts 48 months before it needs to be replaced. A consumer group tests this claim by surveying a random sample of 10 owners who had the fuel injection system replaced. The ages of the cars at the time of replacement were (in months):

29	42	49	48	53	46	30	51	42	52

i. Use your calculator to verify that the mean age of a car when the fuel injection system fails is $\bar{x} = 44.2$ months, with standard deviation $s \approx 8.61$ months.

ii. Test the claim that the fuel injection system lasts less than an average of 48 months before needing replacement. Use a 5% level of significance.

7. Single mean.
   (a) $\alpha = 0.01$; H_0: $\mu = 0.8$; H_1: $\mu > 0.8$.
   (b) Student's *t*, *d.f.* = 8; $t \approx 4.390$.
   (c) $0.0005 < P\text{-value} < 0.005$; on *t* graph, shade area to the right of 4.390. From TI-84, *P*-value ≈ 0.0012.
   (d) *P*-value interval ≤ 0.01 for α; reject H_0.
   (e) At the 1% level of significance, the evidence is sufficient to say that the Toylot claim of 0.8 A is too low.

8. Single mean.
   (a) $\alpha = 0.01$; H_0: $\mu = 40$; H_1: $\mu > 40$.
   (b) Standard normal; $z = 3.34$.
   (c) *P*-value = 0.0004; on standard normal curve, shade area to the right of 3.34.
   (d) *P*-value of $0.0004 \le 0.01$ for α; reject H_0.
   (e) At the 1% level of significance, the evidence is sufficient to say that the population average number of matches is larger than 40.

9. Single proportion.
   (a) $\alpha = 0.01$; H_0: $p = 0.60$; H_1: $p < 0.60$.
   (b) Standard normal; $z = -3.01$.
   (c) *P*-value = 0.0013; on standard normal curve, shade area to the left of −3.01.
   (d) *P*-value of $0.0013 \le 0.01$ for α; reject H_0.
   (e) At the 1% level of significance, the evidence is sufficient to show that the mortality rate has dropped.

10. Single proportion.
   (a) $\alpha = 0.05$; H_0: $p = 0.36$; H_1: $p < 0.36$.
   (b) Standard normal; $z = -1.94$.
   (c) *P*-value = 0.0262; on standard normal curve, shade area to the left of −1.94.
   (d) *P*-value of $0.0262 \le 0.05$ for α; reject H_0.
   (e) At the 5% level of significance, the evidence is sufficient to show that the population percentage of employees holding bachelor's degrees or higher in the private sector is less than in the federal civilian sector.

11. Single mean.
   (a) $\alpha = 0.05$; H_0: $\mu = 7$ oz; H_1: $\mu \ne 7$ oz.
   (b) Student's *t*, *d.f.* = 7; $t \approx 1.697$.
   (c) $0.100 < P\text{-value} < 0.150$; on *t* graph, shade area to the right of 1.697 and to the left of −1.697. From TI-84, *P*-value ≈ 0.1335.
   (d) *P*-value interval > 0.05 for α; do not reject H_0.
   (e) At the 5% level of significance, the evidence is insufficient to show that the population mean amount of coffee per cup is different from 7 oz.

12. i. Use a calculator.
   ii. Single mean.
   (a) $\alpha = 0.05$; H_0: $\mu = 48$ months; H_1: $\mu < 48$ months.
   (b) Student's *t*, *d.f.* = 9; $t = -1.396$.
   (c) $0.075 < P\text{-value} < 0.100$; on *t* graph, shade area to the left −1.396. From TI-84, *P*-value ≈ 0.0981.
   (d) *P*-value interval > 0.05 for α; do not reject H_0.
   (e) At the 5% level of significance, there is insufficient evidence to claim that the injection system lasts less than an average of 48 months.

DATA HIGHLIGHTS: GROUP PROJECTS

Break into small groups and discuss the following topics. Organize a brief outline in which you summarize the main points of your group discussion.

"With Sampling, There Is Too a Free Lunch"—This is a headline that appeared in *The Wall Street Journal.* The article is about food product samples available at grocery stores. Giving out food samples is expensive and labor-intensive. It clogs supermarket aisles. It is risky. What if a customer tries an item and spits it out on the floor or says the product is awful? It creates litter. Some customers drop toothpicks or small paper cups on the floor or spill the product. However, the budget that companies are willing to spend to have their products sampled is growing. The director of communications for Bigg's "hypermarket" (a combination grocery and general-merchandise store) says that more than 60% of customers sample products and about 37% of those who sample buy the product.

(a) Let's test the hypothesis that 60% of customers sample a particular product. What is the null hypothesis? Do you believe that the percentage of customers who sample products is less than, more than, or just different from 60%? What will you use for the alternate hypothesis?
(b) Choose a level of significance α.
(c) Go to a grocery store when special products are being sampled (not just the usual in-house store samples often available at the deli or bakery). Count the number of customers going by the display when a sample is available and the number of customers who try the sample. Be sure the number of customers n is large enough to use the normal distribution to approximate the binomial.
(d) Using your sample data, conclude the hypothesis test. What is your conclusion?
(e) Do you think different food products might have a higher or lower percentage of customers trying them? For instance, does a higher percentage of customers try samples of pizza than samples of yogurt? How could you use statistics to justify your answer?
(f) Do you want to include young children in your sample? Do they pick up items to include in the customer's basket, or do they just munch the samples?

LINKING CONCEPTS: WRITING PROJECTS

Discuss each of the following topics in class or review the topics on your own. Then write a brief but complete essay in which you summarize the main points. Please include formulas and graphs as appropriate.

The most important questions in life usually cannot be answered with absolute certainty. Many important questions are answered by giving an estimate and a measure of confidence in the estimate. This was the focus of Chapter 8. However, sometimes important questions must be answered in a more straightforward manner by a simple *yes* or *no.* Hypothesis testing is the statistical process of answering questions with a straightforward yes or no *and* providing an estimate of the risk in accepting the answer.

1. Review and discuss type I and type II errors associated with hypothesis testing.
2. Review and discuss the level of significance and power of a statistical test.
3. The following statements are very important. Give them some careful thought and discuss them.
   (a) When we fail to reject the null hypothesis, we do not claim that it is absolutely true. We simply claim that at the given level of significance, the data were not sufficient to reject the null hypothesis.
   (b) When we accept the alternate hypothesis, we do not claim that the null hypothesis is absolutely false. We do claim that at the given level of significance, the data presented enough evidence to reject the null hypothesis.

4. In the text, it is said that a statistical test is a package of five basic ingredients. List these ingredients, discuss them in class, and write a short description of how these ingredients relate to the above discussion questions.
5. As access to computers becomes more and more prevalent, we see the *P*-value reported in hypothesis testing more frequently. Review the use of the *P*-value in hypothesis testing. What is the difference between the level of significance of a test and the *P*-value? Considering both the *P*-value and level of significance, under what conditions do we reject or fail to reject the null hypothesis?

USING TECHNOLOGY

Simulation

Recall that the level of significance α is the probability of mistakenly rejecting a true null hypothesis. If $\alpha = 0.05$, then we expect to mistakenly reject a true null hypothesis about 5% of the time. The following simulation conducted with Minitab demonstrates this phenomenon.

We draw 40 random samples of size 50 from a population that is normally distributed with mean $\mu = 30$ and standard deviation $\sigma = 2.5$. The display shows the results of a hypothesis test with

$$H_0: \mu = 30 \qquad H_1: \mu > 30$$

for each of the 40 samples labeled C1 through C40. Because each of the 40 samples is drawn from a population with mean $\mu = 30$, the null hypothesis H_0: $\mu = 30$ is true for the test based on each sample. However, as the display shows, for some samples we reject the true null hypothesis.

(a) How many of the 40 samples have a sample mean $\bar{x}$ above $\mu = 30$? below $\mu = 30$?

(b) Look at the P-value of the sample statistic $\bar{x}$ in each of the 40 samples. How many P-values are less than or equal to $\alpha = 0.05$? What percent of the P-values are less than or equal to α? What percent of the samples have us reject H_0 when, in fact, each of the samples was drawn from a normal distribution with $\mu = 30$, as hypothesized in the null hypothesis?

(c) If you have access to computer or calculator technology that creates random samples from a normal distribution with a specified mean and standard deviation, repeat this simulation. Do you expect to get the same results? Why or why not?

Minitab Display: Random samples of size 50 from a normal population with $\mu = 30$ and $\sigma = 2.5$

Z-Test

Test of mu = 30.000 vs. mu > 30.000

The assumed sigma = 2.50

Variable	N	Mean	StDev	SE Mean	Z	P
C1	50	30.002	2.776	0.354	0.01	0.50
C2	50	30.120	2.511	0.354	0.34	0.37
C3	50	30.032	2.721	0.354	0.09	0.46
C4	50	30.504	2.138	0.354	1.43	0.077
C5	50	29.901	2.496	0.354	−0.28	0.61
C6	50	30.059	2.836	0.354	0.17	0.43
C7	50	30.443	2.519	0.354	1.25	0.11
C8	50	29.775	2.530	0.354	−0.64	0.74
C9	50	30.188	2.204	0.354	0.53	0.30
C10	50	29.907	2.302	0.354	−0.26	0.60
C11	50	30.036	2.762	0.354	0.10	0.46
C12	50	30.656	2.399	0.354	1.86	0.032
C13	50	30.158	2.884	0.354	0.45	0.33
C14	50	29.830	3.129	0.354	−0.48	0.68
C15	50	30.308	2.241	0.354	0.87	0.19
C16	50	29.751	2.165	0.354	−0.70	0.76
C17	50	29.833	2.358	0.354	−0.47	0.68
C18	50	29.741	2.836	0.354	−0.73	0.77
C19	50	30.441	2.194	0.354	1.25	0.11
C20	50	29.820	2.156	0.354	−0.51	0.69
C21	50	29.611	2.360	0.354	−1.10	0.86
C22	50	30.569	2.659	0.354	1.61	0.054
C23	50	30.294	2.302	0.354	0.83	0.20
C24	50	29.978	2.298	0.354	−0.06	0.53
C25	50	29.836	2.438	0.354	−0.46	0.68
C26	50	30.102	2.322	0.354	0.29	0.39
C27	50	30.066	2.266	0.354	0.19	0.43
C28	50	29.071	2.219	0.354	−2.63	1.00
C29	50	30.597	2.426	0.354	1.69	0.046
C30	50	30.092	2.296	0.354	0.26	0.40
C31	50	29.803	2.495	0.354	−0.56	0.71
C32	50	29.546	2.335	0.354	−1.28	0.90
C33	50	29.702	1.902	0.354	−0.84	0.80
C34	50	29.233	2.657	0.354	−2.17	0.98
C35	50	30.097	2.472	0.354	0.28	0.39
C36	50	29.733	2.588	0.354	−0.76	0.78
C37	50	30.379	2.976	0.354	1.07	0.14
C38	50	29.424	2.827	0.354	−1.63	0.95
C39	50	30.288	2.396	0.354	0.81	0.21
C40	50	30.195	3.051	0.354	0.55	0.29

Technology Hints

TI-84Plus/TI-83Plus

Press **STAT** and select **EDIT.** Highlight the list name, such as L1. Then press **MATH,** select **PRB,** and highlight **6:randNorm(**μ**,** σ**, sample size).** Press enter. Fill in the values of $\mu = 30$, $\sigma = 2.5$, and sample size = 50. Press enter. Now list L1 contains a random sample from the normal distribution specified.

To test the hypothesis H_0: $\mu = 30$ against H_1: $\mu > 30$, press **STAT,** select **TESTS,** and use option **1:Z-Test.** Fill in the value 30 for μ_0, 2.5 for σ, and $> \mu_0$. The output provides the value of the sample statistic $\bar{x}$, its corresponding z value, and the P-value of the sample statistic.

Excel

To draw random samples from a normal distribution with $\mu = 30$ and $\sigma = 2.5$, use the menu choices **Tools ➤ Data Analysis ➤ Random Number Generator.** In the dialogue box below, the number of variables is the number of samples. Fill in the rest of the dialogue box as shown.

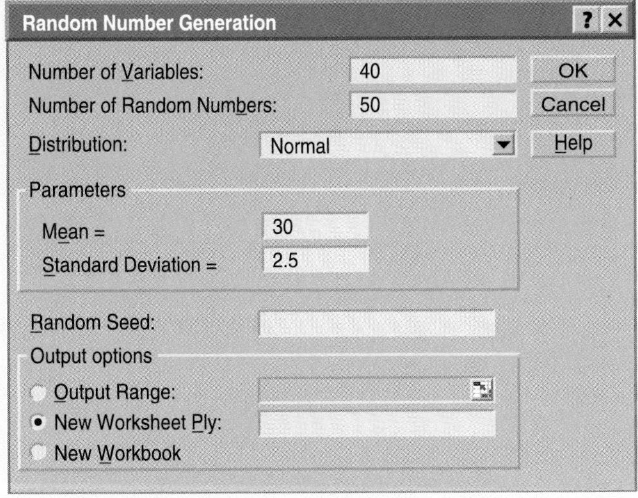

To conduct a hypothesis test of H_0: $\mu = 30$ against H_1: $\mu > 30$, use the command **ZTEST(data range, 30, 2.5).** This command is described as returning the two-tailed P-value of the z test. However, it appears to give the P-value of a right-tailed test. Use the **ZTEST** command with caution and check your results against the table results.

Minitab

To generate random samples from a normal distribution, use the menu choices **Calc ➤ Random Data ➤ Normal.** In the dialogue box, the number of rows refers to the sample size. Use 50 rows. Then designate the columns for the samples. Using C1–C40 will generate 40 random samples and put the samples in columns C1 through C40.

To test the hypothesis H_0: $\mu = 30$ against H_1: $\mu > 30$, use the menu choices **Stat ➤ Basic Statistics ➤ 1-SampleZ.** Use columns C1–C40 as the variables. Fill in 30 for the test mean, use "greater than" for the alternate hypothesis, and use 2.5 for sigma.

SPSS

SPSS uses a Student's t distribution to test the mean and difference of means. SPSS uses the sample standard deviation s even if the population σ is known. Use the menu choices **Analyze ➤ Compare Means** and then **One-Sample T Test** for tests of a single mean. In the dialogue box, fill in the test value of the null hypothesis.

To generate 40 random samples of size $n = 50$ from a normal distribution with $\mu = 30$ and $\sigma = 2.5$, first enter consecutive integers from 1 to 50 in a column of the data editor. Then, under variable view, enter the variable names Sample1 through Sample40. Use the menu choices **Transform ➤ Compute.** In the dialogue box, use Sample1 for the target variable, and then select the function **RV.Normal(mean, stddev).** Use 30 for the mean and 2.5

for the standard deviation. Continue until you have 40 samples. To sample from other distributions, use appropriate functions in the Compute dialogue box.

The SPSS display shows the test results (H_0: $\mu = 30$; H_1: $\mu \neq 30$) for a sample of size $n = 50$ drawn from a normal distribution with $\mu = 30$ and $\sigma = 2.5$. The P-value is given as the significance for a two-tailed test. For a one-tailed test, divide the significance by 2. In the display, the significance is 0.360 for a two-tailed test. So, for a one-tailed test, the P-value is 0.360/2, or 0.180.

SPSS Display

T-Test

One-Sample Statistics

	N	Mean	Std. Deviation	Std. Error Mean
SAMPLE1	50	30.3228	2.46936	.34922

One-Sample Test

	Test Value = 30					
					90% Confidence Interval of the Difference	
	t	df	Sig. (2-tailed)	Mean Difference	Lower	Upper
SAMPLE1	.924	49	.360	.3228	−.2627	.9083

Cumulative Review Problems

CHAPTERS 7–9

Answers may vary due to rounding.

1. *Statistical Literacy* What are the values of the mean and standard deviation of a standard normal distribution?

2. *Statistical Literacy* According to the empirical rule, about what percentage of a normal distribution falls within 2 standard deviations of the mean?

3. *Statistical Literacy* Please give a careful but brief answer to each of the following questions.
   (a) What is a population? How do you get a simple random sample? Give examples.
   (b) What is a sample statistic? What is a sampling distribution? Give examples.
   (c) Give a careful and complete statement of the central limit theorem.
   (d) List at least three areas of everyday life to which the above concepts can be applied. Be specific.

4. *Normal Distribution* *Oxygen demand* is a term biologists use to describe the oxygen needed by fish and other aquatic organisms for survival. The Environmental Protection Agency conducted a study of a wetland area in Marin County, California. In this wetland environment, the mean oxygen demand was $\mu = 9.9$ mg/L with 95% of the data ranging from 6.5 mg/L to 13.3 mg/L (Reference: EPA Report 832-R-93-005). Let x be a random variable that represents oxygen demand in this wetland environment. Assume x has a probability distribution that is approximately normal.
   (a) Use the 95% data range to estimate the standard deviation for oxygen demand. *Hint:* See Problem 31 of Section 7.3.
   (b) An oxygen demand below 8 indicates that some organisms in the wetland environment may be dying. What is the probability that the oxygen demand will fall below 8 mg/L?
   (c) A high oxygen demand can also indicate trouble. An oxygen demand above 12 may indicate an overabundance of organisms that endanger some types of plant life. What is the probability that the oxygen demand will exceed 12 mg/L?

5. *Normal Approximation to the Binomial* The majority of house burglars simply walk into a house that is unlocked! In fact, about 57% of all house burglars gain entrance through an unlocked window or door (Reference: *The Book of Risks* by Larry Laudan). Suppose that $n = 129$ house burglaries will occur tomorrow in Los Angeles. Let r be a binomial random variable that represents the number of burglaries that required no forced entrance.
   (a) We want to approximate the binomial random variable r by a normal random variable x. Is this appropriate? What requirements must be satisfied before we can do this? Do you think these requirements are satisfied in this case? Explain.
   (b) Compute μ and σ for the normal approximation.
   (c) What is the probability that at least 65 of the burglaries required no forced entry?

Patrol car at scene of house robbery

6. *Sampling Distribution $\bar{x}$* Workers at a large toxic cleanup project are concerned that their white blood cell counts may have been reduced. Let x be a random variable that represents white blood cell count per cubic millimeter of whole blood in a healthy adult. Then $\mu = 7500$ and $\sigma \approx 1750$ (Reference: *Diagnostic Tests with Nursing Applications*, S. Loeb). A random sample of $n = 50$ workers from the toxic cleanup site were given a blood test that showed $\bar{x} = 6820$. What is the probability that, for healthy adults, $\bar{x}$ will be this low or lower?
   (a) How does the central limit theorem apply? Explain.
   (b) Compute $P(\bar{x} \le 6820)$.
   (c) *Interpretation:* Based on your answer to part (b), would you recommend that additional facts be obtained, or would you recommend that the workers' claims be dismissed? Explain.

1. $\mu = 0$; $\sigma = 1$.
2. 95%.
3. Essay based on material from Chapter 7 and Section 1.2.
4. (a) $\sigma \approx 1.7$. (b) 0.1314. (c) 0.1075.
5. (a) Yes. Both np and nq are greater than 5.
   (b) $\mu \approx 73.5$ and $\sigma \approx 5.6$.
   (c) $P(r \ge 65) \approx P(x \ge 64.5) \approx P(z \ge -1.61) \approx 0.9463$.
6. (a) Because of the large sample size, the central limit theorem describes the $\bar{x}$ distribution (approximately).
   (b) $P(\bar{x} \le 6820) = P(z \le -2.75) = 0.0030$.
   (c) The probability that the average white blood cell count for 50 healthy adults is as low as or lower than 6820 is very small, 0.0030. Based on this result, it would be reasonable to gather additional facts.

In Problems 7–9, please use the following steps (i) through (v) for all hypothesis tests.

(i) What is the level of significance? State the null and alternate hypotheses.

(ii) What sampling distribution will you use? What assumptions are you making? What is the value of the sample test statistic?

(iii) Find (or estimate) the P-value. Sketch the sampling distribution and show the area corresponding to the P-value.

(iv) Based on your answers in parts (i) to (iii), will you reject or fail to reject the null hypothesis? Are the data statistically significant at level α?

(v) Interpret your conclusion in the context of the application.

Note: For degrees of freedom *d.f.* not in the Student's t table, use the closest *d.f.* that is *smaller.* In some situations, this choice of *d.f.* may increase the P-value by a small amount and thereby produce a slightly more "conservative" answer.

7. *Testing and Estimating μ, σ Known* Let x be a random variable that represents micrograms of lead per liter of water (ug/l). An industrial plant discharges water into a creek. The Environmental Protection Agency has studied the discharged water and found x to have a normal distribution, with $\sigma = 0.7$ ug/l (Reference: *EPA Wetlands Case Studies*).
   (a) The industrial plant says that the population mean value of x is $\mu = 2.0$ ug/l. However, a random sample of $n = 10$ water samples showed that $\bar{x} = 2.56$ ug/l. Does this indicate that the lead concentration population mean is higher than the industrial plant claims? Use $\alpha = 1\%$.
   (b) Find a 95% confidence interval for μ using the sample data and the EPA value for σ.
   (c) How large a sample should be taken to be 95% confident that the sample mean $\bar{x}$ is within a margin of error $E = 0.2$ ug/l of the population mean?

8. *Testing and Estimating μ, σ Unknown* Carboxyhemoglobin is formed when hemoglobin is exposed to carbon monoxide. Heavy smokers tend to have a high percentage of carboxyhemoglobin in their blood (Reference: *Laboratory and Diagnostic Tests,* F. Fishbach). Let x be a random variable representing percentage of carboxyhemoglobin in the blood. For a person who is a regular heavy smoker, x has a distribution that is approximately normal. A random sample of $n = 12$ blood tests given to a heavy smoker gave the following results (percent carboxyhemoglobin in the blood).

9.1	9.5	10.2	9.8	11.3	12.2
11.6	10.3	8.9	9.7	13.4	9.9

   (a) Use a calculator to verify that $\bar{x} \approx 10.49$ and $s \approx 1.36$.
   (b) A long-term population mean $\mu = 10\%$ is considered a health risk. However, a long-term population mean above 10% is considered a clinical alert that the person may be asymptomatic. Do the data indicate that the population mean percentage is higher than 10% for this patient? Use $\alpha = 0.05$.
   (c) Use the given data to find a 99% confidence interval for μ for this patient.

9. *Testing and Estimating a Proportion p* Although older Americans are more afraid of crime, it is young people who are more likely to be the actual victims of crime. It seems that older people are more cautious about the people with whom they associate. A national survey showed that 10% of all people ages 16–19 have been victims of crime (Reference: *Bureau of Justice Statistics*). At Jefferson High School, a random sample of $n = 68$ students (ages 16–19) showed that $r = 10$ had been victims of a crime.
   (a) Do these data indicate that the population proportion of students in this school (ages 16–19) who have been victims of a crime is different (either way) from the national rate for this age group? Use $\alpha = 0.05$. Do you think the conditions $np > 5$

7. (a) i. $\alpha = 0.01$; H_0: $\mu = 2.0$ ug/l; H_1: $\mu > 2.0$ ug/l.
   ii. Standard normal; $z = 2.53$.
   iii. P-value ≈ 0.0057; on standard normal curve, shade area to the right of 2.53.
   iv. P-value of $0.0057 \le 0.01$ for α; reject H_0.
   v. At the 1% level of significance, the evidence is sufficient to say that the population mean discharge level of lead is higher.
   (b) 2.13 ug/l to 2.99 ug/l.
   (c) $n = 48$.
8. (a) Use rounded results to compute t in part (b).
   (b) i. $\alpha = 0.05$; H_0: $\mu = 10\%$; H_1: $\mu > 10\%$.
   ii. Student's t, *d.f.* = 11; $t \approx 1.248$.
   iii. $0.100 < P\text{-value} < 0.125$; on t graph, shade area to the right of 1.248. From TI-84, P-value ≈ 0.1190.
   iv. P-value interval > 0.05 for α; fail to reject H_0.
   v. At the 5% level of significance, the evidence does not indicate that the patient is asymptomatic.
   (c) 9.27% to 11.71%.
9. (a) i. $\alpha = 0.05$; H_0: $p = 0.10$; H_1: $p \neq 0.10$; yes, $np > 5$ and $nq > 5$; necessary to use normal approximation to the binomial.
   ii. Standard normal; $\hat{p} \approx 0.147$; z 5 1.29.
   iii. P-value $= 2P(z > 1.29) \approx 0.1970$; on standard normal curve, shade area to the right of 1.29 and to the left of -1.29.
   iv. P-value of $0.1970 > 0.05$ for α; fail to reject H_0.
   v. At the 5% level of significance, the data do not indicate any difference from the national average for the population proportion of crime victims.
   (b) 0.063 to 0.231.
   (c) From sample, $p \approx \hat{p} \approx 0.147$; $n = 193$.

and $nq > 5$ are satisfied in this setting? Why is this important?

(b) Find a 95% confidence interval for the proportion of students in this school (ages 16–19) who have been victims of a crime.

(c) How large a sample size should be used to be 95% sure that the sample proportion $\hat{p}$ is within a margin of error $E = 0.05$ of the population proportion of all students in this school (ages 16–19) who have been victims of a crime? *Hint:* Use sample data $\hat{p}$ as a preliminary estimate for p.

10. *Essay and Project* In Chapters 7, 8, and 9, you have studied sampling distributions, estimation, and hypothesis testing.

(a) Write a brief essay in which you discuss using information from samples to infer information about populations. Be sure to include methods of estimation and hypothesis testing in your discussion. What two sampling distributions are used in estimation and hypothesis testing of population means or proportions? What are the criteria for determining the appropriate sampling distribution? What is the level of significance of a test? What is the *P*-value? How is the *P*-value related to the alternate hypothesis? How is the null hypothesis related to the sample test statistic? Explain.

(b) Suppose you want to study the length of time devoted to commercial breaks for two different types of television programs. Identify the types of programs you want to study (e.g., sitcoms, sports events, movies, news, children's programs, etc.). Write a brief outline for your study. Discuss how to obtain random samples. How large should the sample be for a specified margin of error? Describe the protocol you will follow to measure the times of the commercial breaks. Determine whether you are going to study the average time devoted to commercials or the proportion of time devoted to commercials. What assumptions will you make regarding population distributions? What graphics might be appropriate? What methods of estimation will you use? What methods of testing will you use?

11. *Critical Thinking* Explain hypothesis testing to a friend, using the following scenario as a model. Describe the hypotheses, the sample statistic, the *P*-value, the meanings of type I and type II errors, and the level of significance. Discuss the significance of the results. Formulas are not required.

A team of research doctors designed a new knee surgery technique utilizing much smaller incisions than the standard method. They believe recovery times are shorter when the new method is used. Under the old method, the average recovery time for full use of the knee is 4.5 months. A random sample of 38 surgeries using the new method showed the average recovery time to be 3.6 months, with sample standard deviation of 1.7 months. The *P*-value for the test is 0.0011. The research team states that the results are statistically significant at the 1% level of significance.

10. (a) Essay.
(b) Outline of study.
11. Essay.

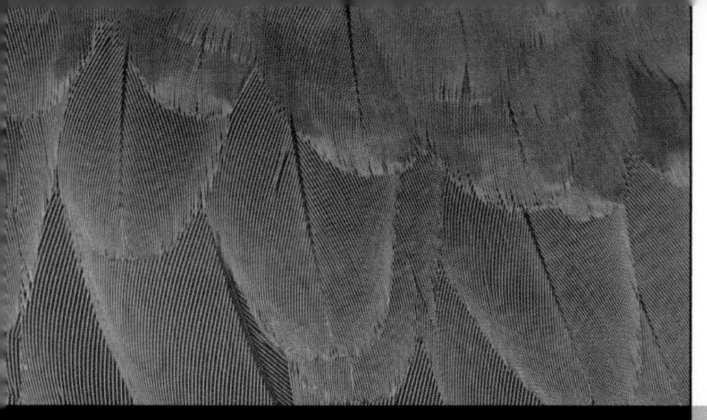

10

- 10.1 Tests Involving Paired Differences (Dependent Samples)
- 10.2 Inferences About the Difference of Two Means $\mu_1 - \mu_2$
- 10.3 Inferences About the Difference of Two Proportions $p_1 - p_2$

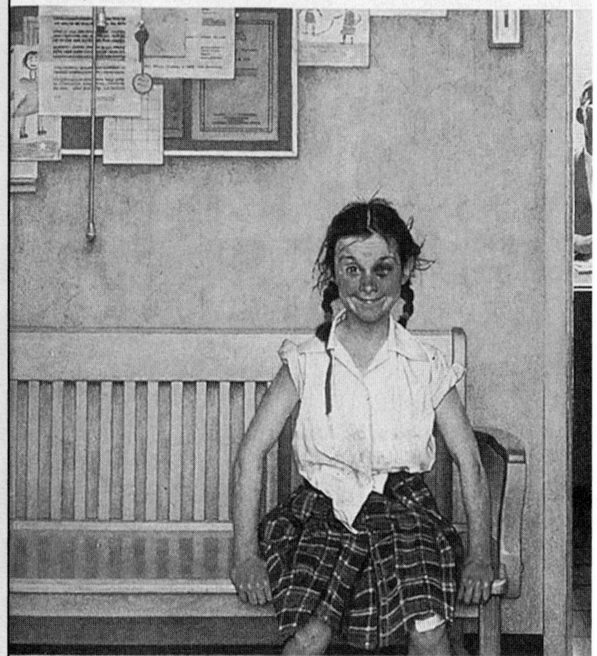

"Girl with Black Eye" by Norman Rockwell (1894–1978)

Norman Rockwell

"So what!"

—Anonymous

Norman Rockwell painted everyday people and situations. In the cover for the *Saturday Evening Post* (May 23, 1953) shown above, a young lady is about to have a conference with her school principal about a schoolyard fight. So what!

Philologists (people who study cultural linguistics) tell us that this expression, "So what!" is a shortened version of "So what is the difference!" They also tell us that there are similar popular or slang expressions about differences in all languages and cultures. It is human nature to challenge the claim that something is better, worse, or just simply different. In this chapter, we will focus on this very human theme by studying a variety of topics regarding questions of whether or not differences exist between two populations.

For on-line student resources, visit the Brase/Brase, *Understanding Basic Statistics,* 5th edition web site at **www.cengage.com/statistics/Brase/UBS5e.**

INFERENCES ABOUT DIFFERENCES

PREVIEW QUESTIONS

What are the statistical advantages of paired data values? How do we construct statistical tests? (SECTION 10.1)

How do we compare means from two independent populations when we know σ for each population? (SECTION 10.2)

What if we want to compare means from two independent populations, but we do not know σ for each population? (SECTION 10.2)

How do we use sample data to compare proportions from two independent populations? (SECTION 10.3)

FOCUS PROBLEM

The Trouble with Wood Ducks

The National Wildlife Federation published an article entitled "The Trouble with Wood Ducks" (*National Wildlife*, Vol. 31, No. 5). In this article, wood ducks are described as beautiful birds living in forested areas such as the Pacific Northwest and Southeast United States. Because of overhunting and habitat destruction, these birds were in danger of extinction. A federal ban on hunting wood ducks in 1918 helped save the species from extinction. Wood ducks like to nest in tree cavities. However, many such trees were disappearing due to heavy timber cutting. For a period of time, it seemed that nesting boxes were the solution to disappearing trees. At first, the wood duck population grew, but after a few seasons, the population declined sharply. Good biology research combined with good statistics provided an answer to this disturbing phenomenon.

Cornell University professors of ecology Paul Sherman and Brad Semel found that the nesting boxes were placed too close to each other. Female wood ducks prefer a secluded nest that is a considerable distance from the next wood duck nest. In fact, female wood duck behavior changed when the nests were too close to each other. Some females would lay their eggs in another female's nest. The result was too many eggs in one nest. The biologists found that if there were too many eggs in a nest, the proportion of eggs that hatched was considerably reduced. In the long run, this meant a decline in the population of wood ducks.

In their study, Sherman and Semel used two placements of nesting boxes. Group I boxes were well separated from each other and well hidden by available brush. Group II boxes were highly visible and grouped closely together.

In group I boxes, there were a total of 474 eggs, of which a field count showed that about 270 hatched. In group II boxes, there were a total of 805 eggs, of which a field count showed that, again, about 270 hatched.

(a) Find a 95% confidence interval for $p_1 - p_2$. Does the interval indicate that the proportion of eggs hatched from group I nest box placements is higher than, lower than, or not different from the proportion of eggs hatched from group II nest boxes?

(b) Use a 5% level of significance to test the hypothesis that the proportion of hatches from group I placements is greater than that from group II placements. Do we reject or fail to reject H_0? Is this result consistent with the information from the 95% confidence interval?

(c) What conclusions about placement of nest boxes can be drawn? In the article, additional concerns are raised about the higher cost of placing and maintaining group I nest boxes. Also at issue is the cost efficiency per successful wood duck hatch. Data in the article do not include information that would help us answer questions of *cost* efficiency. However, the data presented do help us answer questions about the proportions of successful hatches in the two nest box configurations.

(See Problem 18 of Section 10.3.)

SECTION 10.1 Tests Involving Paired Differences (Dependent Samples)

FOCUS POINTS

- Identify paired data and dependent samples.
- Explain the advantages of paired data tests.
- Compute differences and the sample test statistic.
- Estimate the *P*-value and conclude the test.

Creating data pairs

Many statistical applications use *paired data* samples to draw conclusions about the difference between two population means. *Data pairs* occur very naturally in "before and after" situations, where the *same* object or item is measured both before and after a treatment. Applied problems in social science, natural science, and business administration frequently involve a study of matching pairs. Psychological studies of identical twins; biological studies of plant growth on plots of land matched for soil type, moisture, and sun; and business studies on sales of matched inventories are examples of paired data studies.

When working with paired data, it is very important to have a definite and uniform method of creating data pairs that clearly utilizes a natural matching of characteristics. The next example and exercise demonstrate this feature.

Two samples are **dependent** if each data value in one sample can be paired in a meaningful way with a corresponding data value in the other sample.

EXAMPLE 1 PAIRED DATA

A shoe manufacturer claims that among the general population of adults in the United States, the average length of the left foot is longer than that of the right. To compare the average length of the left foot with that of the right, we can take

This is a good time to emphasize that the methods of this section apply only to *dependent* or *paired* differences. The next section (10.2) addresses independent samples.

a random sample of 15 U.S. adults and measure the length of the left foot and then the length of the right foot for each person in the sample. Is there a natural way of pairing the measurements? How many pairs will we have?

SOLUTION: In this case, we can pair each left foot measurement with the same person's right foot measurement. The person serves as the "matching link" between the two distributions. We will have 15 pairs of measurements.

GUIDED EXERCISE 1 Paired data

A psychologist has developed a series of exercises called the Instrumental Enrichment (IE) Program, which he claims is useful in overcoming cognitive deficiencies in mentally retarded children. To test the program, extensive statistical tests are being conducted. In one experiment, a random sample of 10-year-old students with IQ scores below 80 was selected. An IQ test was given to these students before they spent 2 years in an IE Program, and an IQ test was given to the same students after the program.

(a) On what basis can you pair the IQ scores? → Take the "before and after" IQ scores of each individual student.

(b) If there were 20 students in the sample, how many data pairs would you have? → Twenty data pairs. Note that there would be 40 IQ scores, but only 20 pairs.

COMMENT To compare two populations, we cannot always employ paired data tests, but when we can, what are the advantages? Using matched or paired data often can reduce the danger of introducing extraneous or uncontrollable factors into our sample measurements because the matched or paired data have essentially the *same* characteristics except for the *one* characteristic that is being measured. Furthermore, it can be shown that pairing data has the theoretical effect of reducing measurement variability (i.e., variance), which increases the accuracy of statistical conclusions.

When we wish to compare the means of two samples, the first item to be determined is whether or not there is a natural pairing between the data in the two samples. Again, data pairs are created from "before and after" situations, or from matching data by using studies of the same object, or by a process of taking measurements of closely matched items.

Testing the differences d

When testing *paired* data, we take the difference d of the data pairs *first* and look at the mean difference $\bar{d}$. Then we use a test on $\bar{d}$. Theorem 10.1 provides the basis for our work with paired data.

THEOREM 10.1 Consider a random sample of n data pairs. Suppose the differences d between the first and second members of each data pair are (approximately) normally distributed, with population mean μ_d. Then the t values

$$t = \frac{\bar{d} - \mu_d}{s_d/\sqrt{n}}$$

where $\bar{d}$ is the sample mean of the d values, n is the number of data pairs, and

$$s_d = \sqrt{\frac{\Sigma(d - \bar{d})^2}{n - 1}}$$

is the sample standard deviation of the d values, follow a Student's t distribution with degrees of freedom $d.f. = n - 1$.

Hypotheses for testing the mean of paired differences

When testing the mean of the differences of paired data values, the null hypothesis is that there is no difference among the pairs. That is, the mean of the differences μ_d is zero.

$$H_0: \mu_d = 0$$

The alternate hypothesis depends on the problem and can be

$H_1: \mu_d < 0$	$H_1: \mu_d > 0$	$H_1: \mu_d \neq 0$
(left-tailed)	(right-tailed)	(two-tailed)

Sample test statistic

For paired difference tests, we make our decision regarding H_0 according to the evidence of the sample mean $\bar{d}$ of the differences of measurements. By Theorem 10.1, we convert the sample test statistic $\bar{d}$ to a t value using the formula

$$t = \frac{\bar{d} - \mu_d}{(s_d/\sqrt{n})} \text{ with } d.f. = n - 1$$

where s_d = sample standard deviation of the differences d

n = number of data pairs

$\mu_d = 0$, as specified in H_0

P-values from Table 4 of the Appendix

To find the P-value (or an interval containing the P-value) corresponding to the test statistic t computed from $\bar{d}$, we use the Student's t distribution table (Table 4 of the Appendix). Recall from Section 9.2 that we find the test statistic t (or, if t is negative, $|t|$) in the row headed by $d.f. = n - 1$, where n is the number of data pairs. The P-value for the test statistic is the column entry in the *one-tail area* row for one-tailed tests (right or left). For two-tailed tests, the P-value is the column entry in the *two-tail area* row. Usually the exact test statistic t is not in the table, so we obtain an interval that contains the P-value by using adjacent entries in the table. Table 10-1 gives the basic structure for using the Student's t distribution table to find the P-value or an interval containing the P-value.

TABLE 10-1 Using Student's *t* Distribution Table for *P*-values

For one-tailed tests:	one-tail area	*P*-value	*P*-value
For two-tailed tests:	two-tail area	*P*-value	*P*-value
Use row header	$d.f. = n - 1$	↑ Find *t* value	

With the preceding information, you are now ready to test paired differences. First let's summarize the procedure.

PROCEDURE

HOW TO TEST PAIRED DIFFERENCES USING THE STUDENT'S t DISTRIBUTION

Obtain a simple random sample of n matched data pairs A, B. Let d be a random variable representing the difference between the values in a matched data pair. Compute the sample mean $\bar{d}$ and sample standard deviation s_d.

1. Use the *null hypothesis* of *no difference*, $H_0: \mu_d = 0$. In the context of the application, choose the *alternate hypothesis* to be $H_1: \mu_d > 0$, $\mu_d < 0$, or $\mu_d \neq 0$. Set the *level of significance* α.

Continued

2. If you can assume that d has a normal distribution or simply has a mound-shaped symmetric distribution, then any sample size n will work. If you cannot assume this, then use a sample size $n \geq 30$. Use $\bar{d}$, s_d, the sample size n, and $\mu_d = 0$ from the null hypothesis to compute the sample *test statistic*

$$t = \frac{\bar{d} - 0}{\frac{s_d}{\sqrt{n}}} = \frac{\bar{d}\sqrt{n}}{s_d}$$

with degrees of freedom $d.f. = n - 1$.

3. Use the Student's t distribution and the type of test, one-tailed or two-tailed, to find (or estimate) the *P-value* corresponding to the test statistic.
4. *Conclude* the test. If P-value $\leq \alpha$, then reject H_0. If P-value $> \alpha$, then do not reject H_0.
5. *Interpret your conclusion* in the context of the application.

EXAMPLE 2 PAIRED DIFFERENCE TEST

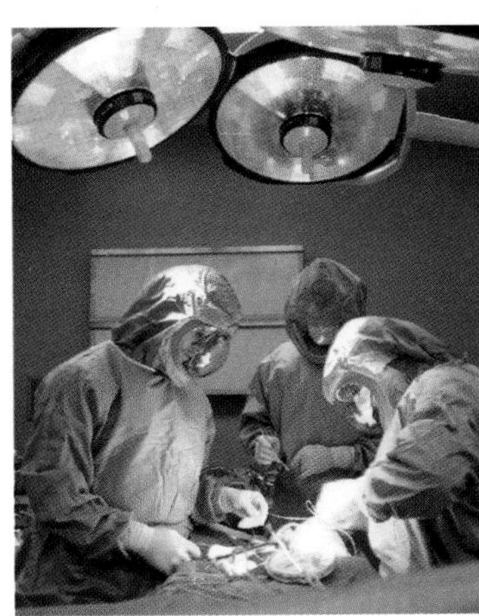

A team of heart surgeons at Saint Ann's Hospital knows that many patients who undergo corrective heart surgery have a dangerous buildup of anxiety before their scheduled operations. The staff psychiatrist at the hospital has started a new counseling program intended to reduce this anxiety. A test of anxiety is given to patients who know they must undergo heart surgery. Then each patient participates in a series of counseling sessions with the staff psychiatrist. At the end of the counseling sessions, each patient is retested to determine anxiety level. Table 10-2 on the next page indicates the results for a random sample of nine patients. Higher scores mean higher levels of anxiety.

From the given data, can we conclude that the counseling sessions reduce anxiety? Use a 0.01 level of significance.

SOLUTION: Before we answer this question, let us notice two important points: (1) we have a *random sample* of nine patients, and (2) we have a *pair* of measurements taken on the same patient before and after counseling sessions. In our problem, the sample size is $n = 9$ pairs (i.e., patients), and the d values are found in the fourth column of Table 10-2.

(a) Note the level of significance and set the hypotheses.
In the problem statement, $\alpha = 0.01$. We want to test the claim that the counseling sessions reduce anxiety. This means that the anxiety level before counseling is expected to be higher than the anxiety level after counseling. In symbols, $d = B - A$ should tend to be positive, and the population mean of differences μ_d also should be positive. Therefore, we have

$$H_0: \mu_d = 0 \quad \text{and} \quad H_1: \mu_d > 0$$

(b) Find the sample test statistic $\bar{d}$ and convert it to a corresponding test statistic t.
First we need to compute $\bar{d}$ and s_d. Using formulas or a calculator and the d values shown in Table 10-2, we find that

$$\bar{d} \approx 33.33 \quad \text{and} \quad s_d \approx 22.92$$

Using these values together with $n = 9$ and $\mu_d = 0$, we have

$$t = \frac{\bar{d} - 0}{(s_d/\sqrt{n})} \approx \frac{33.33}{22.92/\sqrt{9}} \approx 4.363$$

TABLE 10-2

Patient	B Score Before Counseling	A Score After Counseling	$d = B - A$ Difference
Jan	121	76	45
Tom	93	93	0
Diane	105	64	41
Barbara	115	117	−2
Mike	130	82	48
Bill	98	80	18
Frank	142	79	63
Carol	118	67	51
Alice	125	89	36

(c) Find the P-value for the test statistic and sketch the P-value on the t distribution. Since we have a right-tailed test, the P-value is the area to the right of $t = 4.363$, as shown in Figure 10-1. In Table 4 of the Appendix, we find an interval containing the P-value. Use entries from the row headed by $d.f. = n - 1 = 9 - 1 = 8$. The test statistic $t = 4.363$ falls between 3.355 and 5.041. The P-value for the sample t falls between the corresponding one-tail areas 0.005 and 0.0005. (See Table 10-3, Excerpt from Table 4 of the Appendix.)

$$0.0005 < P\text{-value} < 0.005$$

TABLE 10-3 **Excerpt from Student's *t* Distribution Table (Table 4 of the Appendix)**

✓ one-tail area	0.005	0.0005
two-tail area	0.010	0.0010
$d.f. = 8$	3.355 ↑ Sample $t = 4.363$	5.041

FIGURE 10-1

P-value

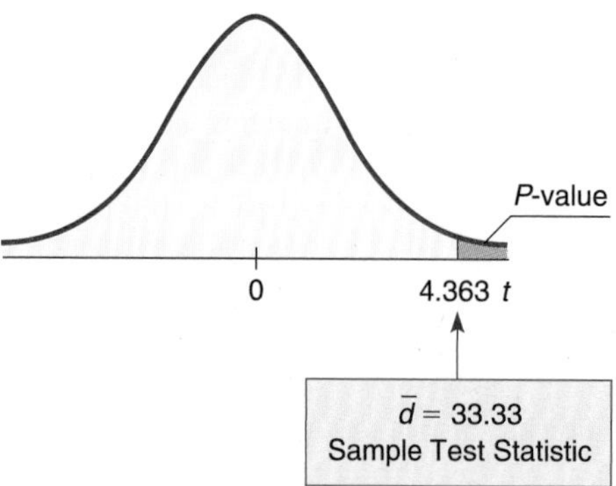

(d) Conclude the test.

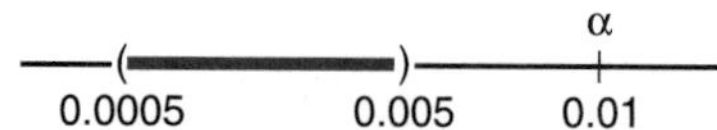

Since the interval containing the P-value lies to the left of $\alpha = 0.01$, we reject H_0. *Note:* Using the raw data and software, P-value ≈ 0.0012.

(e) Interpret the results.
At the 1% level of significance, we conclude that the counseling sessions reduce the average anxiety level of patients about to undergo corrective heart surgery.

The problem we have just solved is a paired difference problem of the "before and after" type. The next guided exercise demonstrates a paired difference problem of the "matched pair" type.

GUIDED EXERCISE 2 | Paired difference test

Do educational toys make a difference in the age at which a child learns to read? To study this question, researchers designed an experiment in which one group of preschool children spent 2 hours each day (for 6 months) in a room well supplied with "educational" toys such as alphabet blocks, puzzles, ABC readers, coloring books featuring letters, and so forth. A control group of children spent 2 hours a day for 6 months in a "noneducational" toy room. It was anticipated that IQ differences and home environment might be uncontrollable factors unless identical twins could be used. Therefore, six pairs of identical twins of preschool age were randomly selected. From each pair, one member was randomly selected to participate in the experimental (i.e., educational toy room) group and the other in the control (i.e., noneducational toy room) group. For each twin, the data item recorded is the age in months at which the child began reading at the primary level (Table 10-4).

TABLE 10-4 **Reading Ages for Identical Twins (in Months)**

Twin Pair	Experimental Group B = Reading Age	Control Group A = Reading Age	Difference $d = B - A$
1	58	60	
2	61	64	
3	53	52	
4	60	65	
5	71	75	
6	62	63	

(a) Compute the entries in the $d = B - A$ column of Table 10-4. Using formulas for the mean and sample standard deviation or a calculator with mean and sample standard deviation keys, compute $\bar{d}$ and s_d.

Pair	$d = B - A$
1	−2
2	−3
3	1
4	−5
5	−4
6	−1

$\bar{d} \approx -2.33$

$s_d \approx 2.16$

(b) What is the null hypothesis?

$H_0: \mu_d = 0$

(c) To test the claim that the experimental group learned to read at a *different age* (either younger or older), what should be the alternate hypothesis?

$H_1: \mu_d \neq 0$

(d) Convert the sample test statistic $\bar{d}$ to a t value. Find the degrees of freedom.

Using $\mu_d = 0$ from H_0, $\bar{d} = -2.33$, $n = 6$, and $s_d = 2.16$, we get

$$t = \frac{\bar{d} - \mu_d}{(s_d/\sqrt{n})} \approx \frac{-2.33 - 0}{(2.16/\sqrt{6})} \approx -2.642$$

$d.f. = n - 1 = 6 - 1 = 5$

Continued

GUIDED EXERCISE 2 *continued*

(e) When we use Table 4 of the Appendix to find an interval containing the P-value, do we use one-tail or two-tail areas? Why? Sketch a figure showing the P-value. Find an interval containing the P-value.

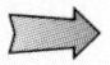

This is a two-tailed test, so we use two-tail areas.

TABLE 10-5 Excerpt from Student's t Table

one-tail area	0.025	0.010
✓two-tail area	0.050	0.020
$d.f.$ = 5	2.571	3.365
	↑ Sample t = 2.642	

FIGURE 10-2 P-value

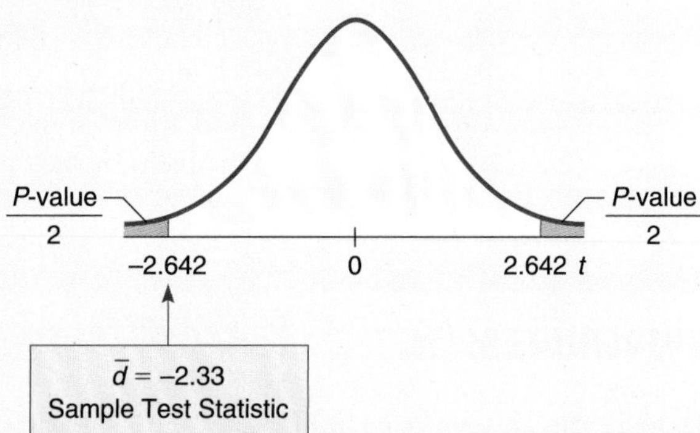

The sample t is between 2.571 and 3.365.

$0.020 < P\text{-value} < 0.050$

(f) Using $\alpha = 0.05$, do we reject or fail to reject H_0? Interpret your results in the context of this application.

Since the interval containing the P-value has values that are all smaller than 0.05, we reject H_0.

α

—(▬▬▬)— 0.020 0.050

At the 5% level of significance, the experiment indicates that educational toys make a difference in the age at which a child learns to read.

Note: Using the raw data and software, P-value ≈ 0.0457.

TECH NOTES Both Excel and Minitab support paired difference tests directly. On the TI-84Plus and TI-83Plus calculators, construct a column of differences and then do a t test on the data in that column. For each technology, be sure to relate the alternate hypothesis to the "before and after" assignments. All the displays show the results for the data of Guided Exercise 2.

TI-84Plus/TI-83Plus Enter the "before" data in column L1 and the "after" data in column L2. Highlight L3, type L1 − L2, and press Enter. The column L3 now contains the $B - A$ differences. To conduct the test, press **STAT**, select **TESTS**, and use option **2:T-Test.** Note that the letter x is used in place of d.

```
L1     L2     L3     3
58     60     -2
61     64     -3
53     52     1
60     65     -5
71     75     -4
62     63     -1
L3(7) =
```

```
T-Test
 μ≠0
 t=-2.645751311
 p=.0456591238
 x̄=-2.333333333
 Sx=2.160246899
 n=6
```

Excel Enter the data in two columns. Use the menu choices **Tools ➤ Data Analysis ➤ t-Test: Paired Two-Sample for Means.** Fill in the dialogue box with the hypothesized mean difference of 0. Set alpha.

B	C	D
t-Test: Paired Two Sample for Means		
	Variable 1	*Variable 2*
Mean	60.83333	63.16666667
Variance	34.96667	55.76666667
Observations	6	6
Pearson Correlation	0.974519	
Hypothesized Mean Difference	0	
df	5	
t Stat	–2.64575	
P(T<=t) one-tail	0.02283	
t Critical one-tail	2.015049	
P(T<=t) two-tail	0.045659	
t Critical two-tail	2.570578	

P-value → P(T<=t) two-tail

Minitab Enter the data in two columns. Use the menu selection **Stat ➤ Basic Statistics ➤ Paired *t*.** Under Options, set the null and alternate hypotheses.

Problem 16 shows how to find confidence intervals for μ_d.

```
Paired T-Test and Confidence Interval
Paired T for B - A
              N      Mean       St Dev SE    Mean
B             6      60.83      5.91         2.41
A             6      63.17      7.47         3.05
Difference    6      -2.333     2.160        0.882
95% CI for mean difference: (-4.601, -0.066)
T-Test of mean difference = 0 (vs not = 0):
    T-Value = -2.65 P-Value = 0.046
```

EXAMPLE 3 CRITICAL REGION METHOD

Let's revisit Guided Exercise 2 regarding educational toys and reading age and conclude the test using the critical region method. Recall that there were six pairs of twins. One twin of each set was given educational toys and the other was not. The difference d in reading ages for each pair of twins was measured, and $\alpha = 0.05$.

SOLUTION: From Guided Exercise 2, we have

$$H_0: \mu_d = 0 \qquad \text{and} \qquad H_1: \mu_d \neq 0$$

We computed the sample test statistic $\bar{d} \approx -2.33$ with corresponding $t \approx -2.642$.

(a) Find the critical values for $\alpha = 0.05$.
Since the number of pairs is $n = 6$, $d.f. = n - 1 = 5$. In the Student's t distribution table (Table 4 of the Appendix), look in the row headed by 5. To find the column, locate $\alpha = 0.05$ in the *two-tail area* row, since we have a two-tailed test. The critical values are $\pm t_0 = \pm 2.571$.

(b) Sketch the critical regions and place the t value of the sample test statistic $\bar{d}$ on the sketch. Conclude the test. Compare the result to the result given by the P-value method of Guided Exercise 2.
Since the sample test statistic falls in the critical region (see Figure 10-3), we reject H_0 at the 5% level of significance. At this level, educational toys seem to make a difference in reading age. Notice that this conclusion is consistent with the conclusion obtained using the P-value.

FIGURE 10-3

Critical Region with $\alpha = 0.05$, $d.f. = 5$

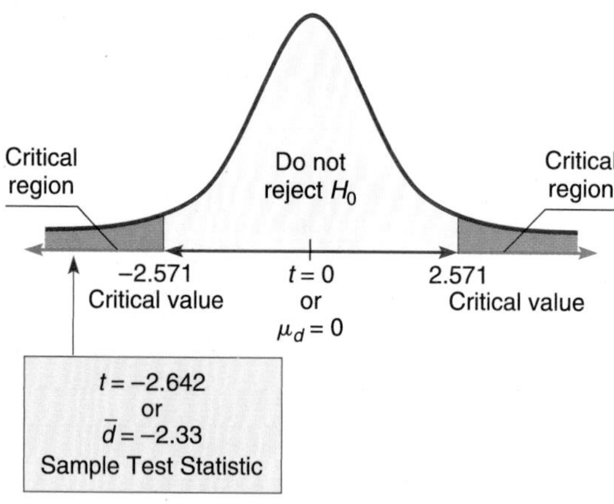

VIEWPOINT DUI

DUI usually means "driving under the influence" of alcohol, *but driving under the influence of* sleep loss *can be just as dangerous. Researchers in Australia have found that after staying awake for 24 hours straight, a person will be about as impaired as if he or she had had enough alcohol to be legally drunk in most U.S. states (Source:* Rocky Mountain News*). Using driver simulation exams and statistical tests (paired difference tests) found in this section, it is possible to show that the null hypothesis H_0: $\mu_d = 0$ cannot be rejected. Or, put another way, the average level of impairment for a given individual from alcohol (at the DUI level) is about the same as the average level of impairment from sleep loss (24 hours without sleep).*

SECTION 10.1 PROBLEMS

Answers may vary slightly due to rounding.

1. Paired data are dependent.
2. Take the difference of corresponding paired data values. The sample test statistic is $\bar{d}$, which is the mean of the differences.
3. H_0: $\mu_d = 0$; that is, the mean of the differences is 0, so there is no difference.
4. n is the number of data pairs.
5. $d.f. = n - 1$.
6. (a) For a right-tailed test, use $d = B - A$.
   (b) For a left-tailed test, use $d = A - B$.

1. *Statistical Literacy* Are data that can be paired independent or dependent?
2. *Statistical Literacy* Consider a set of data pairs. What is the first step in processing the data for a paired differences test? What is the symbol for the sample test statistic? Describe the value of the sample test statistic.
3. *Statistical Literacy* When testing the difference of means for paired data, what is the null hypothesis?
4. *Statistical Literacy* When conducting a paired differences test, what is the value of n?
5. *Statistical Literacy* When using a Student's t distribution for a paired differences test with n data pairs, what value do you use for the degrees of freedom?
6. ***Critical Thinking*** Alisha is conducting a paired differences test for a "before (B score) and after (A score)" situation. She is interested in testing whether the average of the "before" scores is higher than that of the "after" scores.
   (a) To use a right-tailed test, how should Alisha construct the differences between the "before" and "after" scores?
   (b) To use a left-tailed test, how should she construct the differences between the "before" and "after" scores?

Please provide the following information for Problems 7–16.

(a) What is the level of significance? State the null and alternate hypotheses. Will you use a left-tailed, right-tailed, or two-tailed test?

(b) What sampling distribution will you use? What assumptions are you making? What is the value of the sample test statistic?

(c) Find (or estimate) the P-value. Sketch the sampling distribution and show the area corresponding to the P-value.

(d) Based on your answers in parts (a) to (c), will you reject or fail to reject the null hypothesis? Are the data statistically significant at level α?

(e) Interpret your conclusion in the context of the application.

In these problems, assume that the distribution of differences is approximately normal.

Note: For degrees of freedom *d.f.* not in the Student's *t* table, use the closest *d.f.* that is *smaller*. In some situations, this choice of *d.f.* may increase the *P*-value by a small amount and therefore produce a slightly more "conservative" answer.

7. (a) $\alpha = 0.05$; H_0: $\mu_d = 0$; H_1: $\mu_d \neq 0$.
(b) Student's *t*, *d.f.* = 7, $\bar{d} \approx 2.25$; $t \approx 0.818$.
(c) $0.250 < P\text{-value} < 0.500$; on *t* graph, shade area to the left of -0.818 and to the right of 0.818. From TI-84, $P\text{-value} \approx 0.4402$.
(d) *P*-value interval > 0.05 for α; fail to reject H_0.
(e) At the 5% level of significance, the evidence is insufficient to claim a difference in population mean percentage increases between corporate revenue and CEO salary.

7. *Business: CEO Raises* Are America's top chief executive officers (CEOs) really worth all that money? One way to answer this question is to look at row *B*, the annual company percentage increase in revenue, versus row *A*, the CEO's annual percentage salary increase in that same company. (Source: *Forbes*, Vol. 159, No. 10.) A random sample of companies such as John Deere & Co., General Electric, Union Carbide, and Dow Chemical yielded the following data:

B: Percent increase for company	24	23	25	18	6	4	21	37
A: Percent increase for CEO	21	25	20	14	−4	19	15	30

Do these data indicate that the population mean percentage increase in corporate revenue (row *B*) is different from the population mean percentage increase in CEO salary? Use a 5% level of significance.

8. (a) $\alpha = 0.01$; H_0: $\mu_d = 0$; H_1: $\mu_d \neq 0$.
(b) Student's *t*, *d.f.* = 6; $\bar{d} \approx 0.371$; $t \approx 2.08$.
(c) $0.050 < P\text{-value} < 0.100$; on *t* graph, shade area to the left of -2.08 and to the right of 2.08. From TI-84, $P\text{-value} \approx 0.0823$.
(d) *P*-value interval > 0.01 for α; fail to reject H_0.
(e) At the 1% level of significance, the evidence is insufficient to claim that there is a difference in population mean hours per fish caught between boat fishing and shore fishing.

8. *Fishing: Shore or Boat?* Is fishing better from a boat or from the shore? Pyramid Lake is located on the Paiute Indian Reservation in Nevada. Presidents, movie stars, and people who just want to catch fish go to Pyramid Lake for really large cutthroat trout. Let row *B* represent hours per fish caught fishing from the shore, and let row *A* represent hours per fish caught using a boat. The following data are paired by month from October through April. (Source: *Pyramid Lake Fisheries*, Paiute Reservation, Nevada.)

	Oct.	Nov.	Dec.	Jan.	Feb.	March	April
B: Shore	1.6	1.8	2.0	3.2	3.9	3.6	3.3
A: Boat	1.5	1.4	1.6	2.2	3.3	3.0	3.8

Use a 1% level of significance to test if there is a difference in the population mean hours per fish caught using a boat compared with fishing from the shore.

9. (a) $\alpha = 0.01$; H_0: $\mu_d = 0$; H_1: $\mu_d > 0$.
(b) Student's *t*, *d.f.* = 4, $\bar{d} \approx 12.6$; $t \approx 1.243$.
(c) $0.125 < P\text{-value} < 0.250$; on *t* graph, shade area to the right of 1.243. From TI-84, $P\text{-value} \approx 0.1408$.
(d) *P*-value interval > 0.01 for α; fail to reject H_0.
(e) At the 1% level of significance, the evidence is insufficient to claim that average peak wind gusts are higher in January.

9. *Ecology: Rocky Mountain National Park* The following is based on information taken from *Winter Wind Studies in Rocky Mountain National Park*, by D. E. Glidden (Rocky Mountain Nature Association). At five weather stations on Trail Ridge Road in Rocky Mountain National Park, the peak wind gusts (in miles per hour) for January and April are recorded below.

Weather Station	1	2	3	4	5
January	139	122	126	64	78
April	104	113	100	88	61

Does this information indicate that the peak wind gusts are higher in January than in April? Use $\alpha = 0.01$.

10. *Wildlife: Highways* The western United States has a number of four-lane interstate highways that cut through long tracts of wilderness. To prevent car accidents with wild animals, the highways are bordered on both sides with 12-foot-high woven wire fences. Although the fences prevent accidents, they also

disturb the winter migration pattern of many animals. To compensate for this disturbance, the highways have frequent wilderness underpasses designed for exclusive use by deer, elk, and other animals.

In Colorado, there is a large group of deer that spend their summer months in a region on one side of a highway and survive the winter months in a lower region on the other side. To determine if the highway has disturbed deer migration to the winter feeding area, the following data were gathered on a random sample of 10 wilderness districts in the winter feeding area. Row *B* represents the average January deer count for a 5-year period before the highway was built, and row *A* represents the average January deer count for a 5-year period after the highway was built. The highway department claims that the January population has not changed. Test this claim against the claim that the January population has dropped. Use a 5% level of significance. Units used in the table are hundreds of deer.

Wilderness District	1	2	3	4	5	6	7	8	9	10
B: Before highway	10.3	7.2	12.9	5.8	17.4	9.9	20.5	16.2	18.9	11.6
A: After highway	9.1	8.4	10.0	4.1	4.0	7.1	15.2	8.3	12.2	7.3

10. (a) $\alpha = 0.05$; H_0: $\mu_d = 0$; H_1: $\mu_d > 0$.
(b) Student's t, $d.f. = 9$; $\bar{d} \approx 4.50$; $t \approx 3.452$.
(c) $0.0005 < P\text{-value} < 0.005$; on t graph, shade area to the right of 3.452. From TI-84, P-value ≈ 0.0036.
(d) P-value interval ≤ 0.05 for α; reject H_0.
(e) At the 5% level of significance, the evidence is sufficient to claim that the January mean population of deer has dropped. Note that this test does not determine the cause of the drop. Development around the highway, disease, etc. may have affected the deer population.

11. *Wildlife: Wolves* In environmental studies, sex ratios are of great importance. Wolf society, packs, and ecology have been studied extensively at different locations in the U.S. and foreign countries. Sex ratios for eight study sites in northern Europe are shown below (based on *The Wolf* by L. D. Mech, University of Minnesota Press).

Gender Study of Large Wolf Packs

Location of Wolf Pack	% Males (Winter)	% Males (Summer)
Finland	72	53
Finland	47	51
Finland	89	72
Lapland	55	48
Lapland	64	55
Russia	50	50
Russia	41	50
Russia	55	45

It is hypothesized that in winter, "loner" males (not present in summer packs) join the pack to increase survival rate. Use a 5% level of significance to test the claim that the average percentage of males in a wolf pack is higher in winter.

11. (a) $\alpha = 0.05$; H_0: $\mu_d = 0$; H_1: $\mu_d > 0$.
(b) Student's t, $d.f. = 7$; $\bar{d} \approx 6.125$; $t \approx 1.762$.
(c) $0.050 < P\text{-value} < 0.075$; on t graph, shade area to the right of 1.762. From TI-84, P-value ≈ 0.0607.
(d) P-value interval > 0.05 for α; fail to reject H_0.
(e) At the 5% level of significance, the evidence is insufficient to indicate that the population average percentage of male wolves is higher in winter.

12. *Demographics: Birth Rate and Death Rate* In the following data pairs, *A* represents birth rate and *B* represents death rate per 1000 resident population. The data are paired by counties in the Midwest. A random sample of 16 counties gave the following information. (Reference: *County and City Data Book*, U.S. Department of Commerce.)

A:	12.7	13.4	12.8	12.1	11.6	11.1	14.2	15.1
B:	9.8	14.5	10.7	14.2	13.0	12.9	10.9	10.0

A:	12.5	12.3	13.1	15.8	10.3	12.7	11.1	15.7
B:	14.1	13.6	9.1	10.2	17.9	11.8	7.0	9.2

Do the data indicate a difference (either way) between population average birth rate and death rate in this region? Use $\alpha = 0.01$.

12. (a) $\alpha = 0.01$; H_0: $\mu_d = 0$; H_1: $\mu_d \neq 0$.
(b) Student's t, $d.f. = 15$, $\bar{d} \approx 1.1$; $t \approx 1.175$.
(c) $0.250 < P\text{-value} < 0.500$; on t graph, shade area to the left of -1.175 and to the right of 1.175. From TI-84, P-value ≈ 0.2584.
(d) P-value interval > 0.01 for α; fail to reject H_0.
(e) At the 1% level of significance, the evidence is insufficient to claim that the population average birth and death rates are different in this region.

13. (a) $\alpha = 0.05$; H_0: $\mu_d = 0$; H_1: $\mu_d > 0$.
(b) Student's t, $d.f. = 8$; $\bar{d} = 2.0$; $t \approx 1.333$.
(c) $0.100 < P\text{-value} < 0.125$; on t graph, shade area to the right of 1.333. From TI-84, P-value ≈ 0.1096.
(d) P-value interval > 0.05 for α; fail to reject H_0.
(e) At the 5% level of significance, the evidence is insufficient to claim that the population score on the last round is higher than that on the first.

14. (a) $\alpha = 0.05$; H_0: $\mu_d = 0$; H_1: $\mu_1 > 0$.
(b) Student's t, $d.f. = 7$; $\bar{d} \approx 6.125$; $t \approx 2.144$.
(c) $0.025 < P\text{-value} < 0.050$; on t graph, shade area to the right of 2.144. From TI-84, P-value $\approx$ 0.0346.
(d) P-value interval ≤ 0.05 for α; reject H_0.
(e) At the 5% level of significance, the evidence is sufficient to indicate that the population average number of flaked stone tools is higher.

15. i. Use a calculator. Non-rounded results are used in part ii.
ii. (a) $\alpha = 0.05$; H_0: $\mu_d = 0$; H_1: $\mu_d > 0$.
(b) Student's t, $d.f. = 35$; $\bar{d} \approx 2.472$; $t \approx 1.223$.
(c) $0.100 < P\text{-value} < 0.125$; on t graph, shade area to the right of 1.223. From TI-84, P-value $\approx$ 0.1147.
(d) P-value interval > 0.05 for α; fail to reject H_0.
(e) At the 5% level of significance, the evidence is insufficient to claim that the population mean cost of living index for housing is higher than that for groceries.

13. *Golf: Tournaments* Do professional golfers play better in their first round? Let row B represent the score in the fourth (and final) round, and let row A represent the score in the first round of a professional golf tournament. A random sample of finalists in the British Open gave the following data for their first and last rounds in the tournament. (Source: *Golf Almanac*.)

B: Last	73	68	73	71	71	72	68	68	74
A: First	66	70	64	71	65	71	71	71	71

Do the data indicate that the population mean score on the last round is higher than that on the first? Use a 5% level of significance.

14. *Archaeology: Stone Tools* The following is based on information taken from *Bandelier Archaeological Excavation Project: Summer 1990 Excavations at Burnt Mesa Pueblo and Casa del Rito*, edited by T. A. Kohler (Washington State University, Department of Anthropology). The artifact frequency for an excavation of a kiva in Bandelier National Monument gave the following information.

Stratum	Flaked Stone Tools	Nonflaked Stone Tools
1	7	3
2	3	2
3	10	1
4	1	3
5	4	7
6	38	32
7	51	30
8	25	12

Does this information indicate that there tend to be more flaked stone tools than nonflaked stone tools at this excavation site? Use a 5% level of significance.

15. *Economics: Cost of Living Index* In the following data pairs, A represents the cost of living index for housing and B represents the cost of living index for groceries. The data are paired by metropolitan areas in the United States. A random sample of 36 metropolitan areas gave the following information. (Reference: *Statistical Abstract of the United States*, 121st edition.)

A:	132	109	128	122	100	96	100	131	97
B:	125	118	139	104	103	107	109	117	105

A:	120	115	98	111	93	97	111	110	92
B:	110	109	105	109	104	102	100	106	103

A:	85	109	123	115	107	96	108	104	128
B:	98	102	100	95	93	98	93	90	108

A:	121	85	91	115	114	86	115	90	113
B:	102	96	92	108	117	109	107	100	95

i. Let d be the random variable $d = A - B$. Use a calculator to verify that $\bar{d} \approx 2.472$ and $s_d \approx 12.124$.

ii. Do the data indicate that the U.S. population mean cost of living index for housing is higher than that for groceries in these areas? Use $\alpha = 0.05$.

16. (a) $\bar{d} \approx 2.025$; $s_d \approx 7.78$; interval from -4.25 to 8.75.
(b) H_0: $\mu_d = 0$; H_1: $\mu_d \neq 0$; Since $\mu_d = 0$ from the null hypothesis is in the 95% confidence interval, do not reject H_0 at the 5% level of significance. The data do not indicate a difference in population mean percentage increases between company revenue and CEO salaries.

16. *Expand Your Knowledge: Confidence Intervals for μ_d* Using techniques from Section 8.2, we can find a confidence interval for μ_d. Consider a random sample of n matched data pairs A, B. Let $d = B - A$ be a random variable representing the difference between the values in a matched data pair. Compute the sample mean $\bar{d}$ of the differences and the sample standard deviation s_d. If d has a normal distribution or is mound-shaped, or if $n \geq 30$, then a **confidence interval for μ_d** is

$$\bar{d} - E < \mu_d < \bar{d} + E$$

where $E = t_c \dfrac{s_d}{\sqrt{n}}$

c = confidence level $(0 < c < 1)$

t_c = critical value for confidence level c and $d.f. = n - 1$

(a) Using the data of problem 7, find a 95% confidence interval for the mean difference between percentage increase in company revenue and percentage increase in CEO salary.

(b) Use the confidence interval method of hypothesis testing outlined in problem 23 of Section 9.2 to test the hypothesis that population mean percentage increase in company revenue is different from that of CEO salary. Use a 5% level of significance.

17. For a two-tailed test with $\alpha = 0.05$ and $d.f. = 7$, the critical values are $\pm t_0 = \pm 2.365$. The sample test statistic $t = 0.818$ is between -2.365 and 2.365, so we do not reject H_0. This conclusion is the same as that reached by the P-value method.

17. *Critical Region Method: Student's t* Solve Problem 7 using the critical region method of testing. Compare your conclusions with the conclusion obtained by using the P-value method. Are they the same?

18. For a right-tailed test with $\alpha = 0.01$ and $d.f. = 4$, the critical value is $t_0 = 3.747$. The sample test statistic $t = 1.243$ is to the left of t_0, so we do not reject H_0. This conclusion is the same as that reached by the P-value method.

18. *Critical Region Method: Student's t* Solve Problem 9 using the critical region method of testing. Compare your conclusions with the conclusion obtained by using the P-value method. Are they the same?

SECTION 10.2 Inferences About the Difference of Two Means $\mu_1 - \mu_2$

FOCUS POINTS

- Identify independent samples and sampling distributions.
- Compute the sample test statistic and P-value for testing $\mu_1 - \mu_2$.
- Find confidence intervals for $\mu_1 - \mu_2$.

Independent Samples

Many practical applications of statistics involve a comparison of two population means or two population proportions. In Section 10.1, we considered tests of difference of means for *dependent samples*. With dependent samples, we could pair the data and then consider the differences of the data measurements d. In this section, we will turn our attention to inferences regarding differences of means from *independent samples*.

Two samples are **independent** if the selection of sample data from one population is completely unrelated to the selection of sample data from the other population.

Independent samples occur very naturally when we draw *two random samples*, one from the first population and one from the second population. Because *both* samples are random samples, there is no pairing of measurements between the two populations.

GUIDED EXERCISE 3 **Distinguish between independent and dependent samples**

For each experiment, categorize the sampling as independent or dependent, and explain your choice.

(a) In many medical experiments, a sample of subjects is randomly divided into two groups. One group is given a specific treatment, and the other group is given a placebo. After a certain period of time, both groups are measured for the same condition. Do the measurements from these two groups constitute independent or dependent samples?

→ Since the subjects are *randomly assigned* to the two treatment groups (one receives a treatment, the other a placebo), the resulting measurements would form independent samples.

(b) In an accountability study, a group of students in an English composition course is given a pretest. After the course, the same students are given a posttest covering similar material. Are the two groups of scores independent or dependent?

→ Since the pretest scores and the posttest scores are from the same students, the samples are dependent. Each student has both a pretest score and a posttest score, so there is a natural pairing of data values.

Hypothesis Tests and Confidence Intervals for $\mu_1 - \mu_2$ (σ_1 and σ_2 known)

The $\bar{x}_1 - \bar{x}_2$ sampling distribution

In this section, we will use probability distributions that arise from a difference of means. How do we obtain such distributions? Suppose that we have two statistical variables x_1 and x_2, each with its own distribution. We take *independent* random samples of size n_1 from the x_1 distribution and of size n_2 from the x_2 distribution. Then we compute the respective means $\bar{x}_1$ and $\bar{x}_2$. Now consider the difference $\bar{x}_1 - \bar{x}_2$. This expression represents a difference of means. If we repeat this sampling process over and over, we will create lots of $\bar{x}_1 - \bar{x}_2$ values. Figure 10-4 on the next page illustrates the sampling distribution of $\bar{x}_1 - \bar{x}_2$.

The values of $\bar{x}_1 - \bar{x}_2$ that come from repeated (independent) sampling of populations 1 and 2 can be arranged in a relative-frequency table and a relative-frequency histogram (see Section 2.1). This would give us an experimental idea of the theoretical probability distribution of $\bar{x}_1 - \bar{x}_2$.

Fortunately, it is not necessary to carry out this lengthy process for each example. The results have been worked out mathematically. The next theorem presents the main results.

THEOREM 10.2 Let x_1 and x_2 have normal distributions with means μ_1 and μ_2 and standard deviations σ_1 and σ_2, respectively. If we take independent random samples of size n_1 from the x_1 distribution and of size n_2 from the x_2 distribution, then the variable $\bar{x}_1 - \bar{x}_2$ has

1. a normal distribution
2. mean $\mu_1 - \mu_2$
3. standard deviation $\sqrt{\dfrac{\sigma_1^2}{n_1} + \dfrac{\sigma_2^2}{n_2}}$

COMMENT The theorem requires that x_1 and x_2 have *normal* distributions. However, if *both* n_1 and n_2 are 30 or larger, then the central limit theorem (Section 7.5) assures us that $\bar{x}_1$ and $\bar{x}_2$ are approximately normally distributed. In this case, the conclusions of the theorem are again valid even if the original x_1 and x_2 distributions are not exactly normal.

FIGURE 10-4

Sampling Distribution of $\bar{x}_1 - \bar{x}_2$

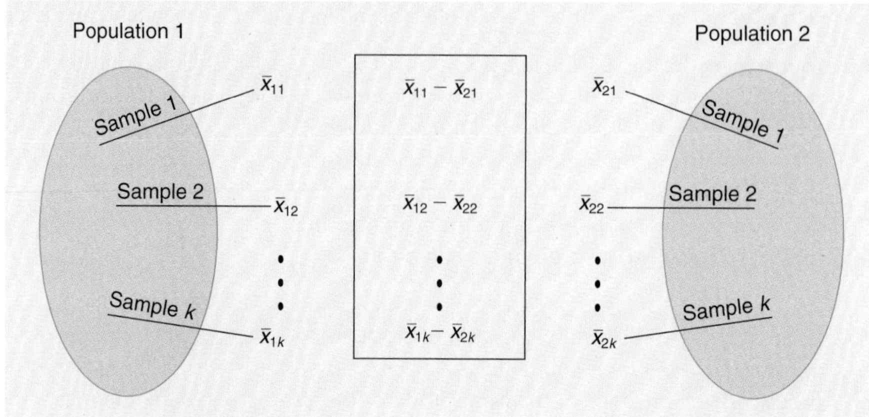

Theorem 10.2 gives us the basis for hypothesis tests and confidence intervals for $\mu_1 - \mu_2$ when σ_1 and σ_2 are both known.

Hypotheses for testing difference of means

When testing the difference of means, it is customary to use the null hypothesis

$$H_0: \mu_1 - \mu_2 = 0 \text{ or, equivalently, } H_0: \mu_1 = \mu_2$$

As mentioned in Section 9.1, the null hypothesis is set up to see if it can be rejected. When testing the difference of means, we first set up the hypothesis H_0 that there is no difference. The alternate hypothesis could then be any of the ones listed in Table 10-6. The alternate hypothesis and consequent type of test used depend on the particular problem. Note that μ_1 is always listed first.

Using Theorem 10.2 and the central limit theorem (Section 7.5), we can summarize the procedure for testing $\mu_1 - \mu_2$ and finding a confidence interval when both σ_1 and σ_2 are known.

TABLE 10-6 Alternate Hypotheses and Type of Test: Difference of Two Means

H_1			Type of Test
$H_1: \mu_1 - \mu_2 < 0$	or equivalently	$H_1: \mu_1 < \mu_2$	Left-tailed test
$H_1: \mu_1 - \mu_2 > 0$	or equivalently	$H_1: \mu_1 > \mu_2$	Right-tailed test
$H_1: \mu_1 - \mu_2 \neq 0$	or equivalently	$H_1: \mu_1 \neq \mu_2$	Two-tailed test

PROCEDURE

HOW TO TEST $\mu_1 - \mu_2$ AND FIND A CONFIDENCE INTERVAL WHEN BOTH σ_1 AND σ_2 ARE KNOWN

Let σ_1 and σ_2 be the population standard deviations of populations 1 and 2. Obtain two independent random samples from populations 1 and 2, where

$\bar{x}_1$ and $\bar{x}_2$ are sample means from populations 1 and 2

n_1 and n_2 are sample sizes from populations 1 and 2

If you can assume that both population distributions 1 and 2 are normal, any sample sizes n_1 and n_2 will work. If you cannot assume this, then use sample sizes $n_1 \geq 30$ and $n_2 \geq 30$.

Continued

Hypothesis test for $\mu_1 - \mu_2$ (σ_1 and σ_2 known)

Testing $\mu_1 - \mu_2$

1. In the context of the application, state the *null and alternate hypotheses* and set the *level of significance* α. It is customary to use H_0: $\mu_1 - \mu_2 = 0$.
2. Use $\mu_1 - \mu_2 = 0$ from the null hypothesis together with $\bar{x}_1$, $\bar{x}_2$, σ_1, σ_2, n_1, and n_2 to compute the sample *test statistic.*

$$z = \frac{(\bar{x}_1 - \bar{x}_2) - (\mu_1 - \mu_2)}{\sqrt{\frac{\sigma_1^2}{n_1} + \frac{\sigma_2^2}{n_2}}} = \frac{\bar{x}_1 - \bar{x}_2}{\sqrt{\frac{\sigma_1^2}{n_1} + \frac{\sigma_2^2}{n_2}}}$$

3. Use the standard normal distribution and the type of test, one-tailed or two-tailed, to find the *P-value* corresponding to the sample test statistic.
4. *Conclude the test.* If P-value $\leq \alpha$, then reject H_0. If P-value $> \alpha$, then do not reject H_0.
5. *Interpret your conclusion* in the context of the application.

Confidence interval for $\mu_1 - \mu_2$ (σ_1 and σ_2 known)

Confidence interval for $\mu_1 - \mu_2$

$$(\bar{x}_1 - \bar{x}_2) - E < \mu_1 - \mu_2 < (\bar{x}_1 - \bar{x}_2) + E$$

where $E = z_c\sqrt{\frac{\sigma_1^2}{n_1} + \frac{\sigma_2^2}{n_2}}$

c = confidence level ($0 < c < 1$)

z_c = critical value for confidence level c based on the standard normal distribution (See Table 3(b) of the Appendix for commonly used values.)

EXAMPLE 4 TESTING THE DIFFERENCE OF MEANS AND FINDING A CONFIDENCE INTERVAL (σ_1 AND σ_2 KNOWN)

A consumer group is testing camp stoves. To test the heating capacity of a stove, it measures the time required to bring 2 quarts of water from 50°F to boiling (at sea level). Two competing models are under consideration. Ten stoves of the first model and 12 stoves of the second model are selected at random and tested. The following results are obtained.

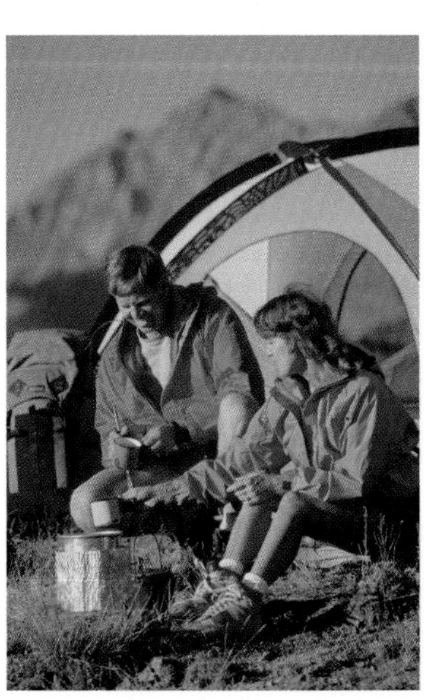

Model 1: Mean time $\bar{x}_1 = 11.4$ min; $\sigma_1 = 2.5$ min; $n_1 = 10$

Model 2: Mean time $\bar{x}_2 = 9.9$ min; $\sigma_2 = 3.0$ min; $n_2 = 12$

Assume that the time required to bring water to a boil is normally distributed for each stove.

Hypothesis test: Is there any difference (either way) between the performances of these two models? Use a 5% level of significance.

SOLUTION:

(a) State the null and alternate hypotheses and note the value of α.
Let μ_1 and μ_2 be the means of the distributions of times for models 1 and 2, respectively. We set up the null hypothesis to state that there is no difference:

$$H_0: \mu_1 = \mu_2 \quad \text{or} \quad H_0: \mu_1 - \mu_2 = 0$$

The alternate hypothesis states that there is a difference:

$$H_1: \mu_1 \neq \mu_2 \quad \text{or} \quad H_1: \mu_1 - \mu_2 \neq 0$$

The level of significance is $\alpha = 0.05$.

(b) Compute the sample test statistic $\bar{x}_1 - \bar{x}_2$ and then convert it to a z value. Note that we use the standard normal distribution because the original distributions are normal and the standard deviations are known.

We are given the values $\bar{x}_1 = 11.4$ and $\bar{x}_2 = 9.9$. Therefore, the sample test statistic is $\bar{x}_1 - \bar{x}_2 = 11.4 - 9.9 = 1.5$. To convert this to a z value, we use the values $\sigma_1 = 2.5$, $\sigma_2 = 3.0$, $n_1 = 10$, and $n_2 = 12$. From the null hypothesis, $\mu_1 - \mu_2 = 0$.

$$z = \frac{(\bar{x}_1 - \bar{x}_2) - (\mu_1 - \mu_2)}{\sqrt{\frac{\sigma_1^2}{n_1} + \frac{\sigma_2^2}{n_2}}} = \frac{1.5}{\sqrt{\frac{2.5^2}{10} + \frac{3.0^2}{12}}} \approx 1.28$$

(c) Find the P-value and sketch the area on the standard normal curve.
Figure 10-5 shows the P-value. Use the standard normal distribution (Table 3 of the Appendix) and the fact that we have a two-tailed test. $P\text{-value} \approx 2(0.1003) = 0.2006$.

FIGURE 10-5

P-value

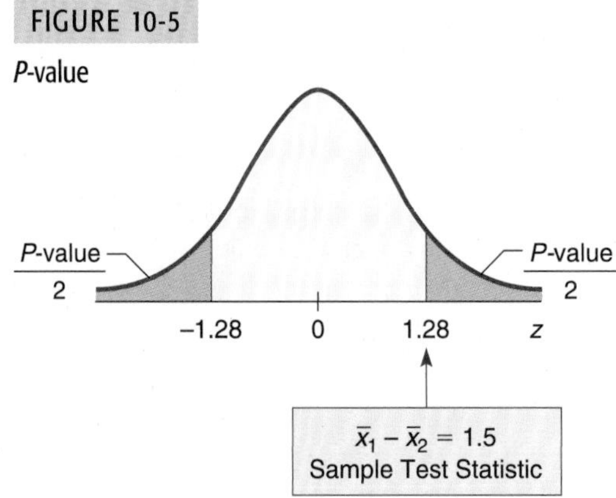

(d) Conclude the test.
The P-value is 0.2006 and $\alpha = 0.05$. Since $P\text{-value} > \alpha$, do not reject H_0.

(e) Interpret the results.
At the 5% level of significance, the sample data do not indicate any difference in the population mean times for boiling water for the two stove models.

Confidence interval: Find a 95% confidence interval for the population difference $\mu_1 - \mu_2$ of mean times to boil water for the two stoves. Interpret the results.

SOLUTION: Note that both σ_1 and σ_2 are known and that the times for each stove to bring 2 quarts of water to a boil are normally distributed. Therefore, by Theorem 10.2, $\bar{x}_1 - \bar{x}_2$ is normal. We use the normal distribution to find the critical value $z_{0.95}$. From Table 3(b) of the Appendix, we see that $z_{0.95} = 1.96$. The confidence interval is

$$(\bar{x}_1 - \bar{x}_2) - E < \mu_1 - \mu_2 < (\bar{x}_1 - \bar{x}_2) + E$$

where $\bar{x}_1 - \bar{x}_2 = 11.4 - 9.9 = 1.5$ min and

$$E = z_c\sqrt{\frac{\sigma_1^2}{n_1} + \frac{\sigma_2^2}{n_2}} = 1.96\sqrt{\frac{2.5^2}{10} + \frac{3.0^2}{12}} \approx 2.30 \text{ min}$$

The confidence interval is

$$-0.8 \text{ min} < \mu_1 - \mu_2 < 3.8 \text{ min}$$

Notice that the confidence interval contains both negative and positive values. At the 95% confidence level, we cannot conclude that μ_1 is either less than or greater than μ_2. This result is consistent with the conclusion of the hypothesis test—that is, at the 5% level, the evidence is not sufficient to conclude that there is a difference in the average times for boiling 2 quarts of water between the two types of stoves.

Meaning of confidence interval for $\mu_1 - \mu_2$

In Example 4, we saw that the confidence interval for $\mu_1 - \mu_2$ contained both positive and negative numbers. At the 95% level of confidence, we could not conclude that there was a difference in value between μ_1 and μ_2. There are two other cases: either all the values in the confidence interval are positive, or they are all negative. The next procedure summarizes the interpretation of all three cases.

PROCEDURE

HOW TO INTERPRET CONFIDENCE INTERVALS FOR DIFFERENCES

Suppose that we construct a $c\%$ confidence interval for $\mu_1 - \mu_2$. Then three cases arise:

1. The $c\%$ confidence interval contains only *negative values*. In this case, we conclude that $\mu_1 - \mu_2 < 0$, and we are therefore $c\%$ confident that $\mu_1 < \mu_2$.
2. The $c\%$ confidence interval contains only *positive values*. In this case, we conclude that $\mu_1 - \mu_2 > 0$, and we can be $c\%$ confident that $\mu_1 > \mu_2$.
3. The $c\%$ confidence interval contains *both positive and negative values*. In this case, we cannot at the $c\%$ confidence level conclude that either μ_1 or μ_2 is larger. However, if we *reduce* the confidence level c to a *smaller value*, then the confidence interval will, in general, be shorter (explain why). A shorter confidence interval *might* put us back into case 1 or case 2 above (again, explain why).

GUIDED EXERCISE 4 **Interpret a confidence interval**

(a) A study reported a 90% confidence interval for the difference of means to be

$$10 < \mu_1 - \mu_2 < 20$$

For this interval, what can you conclude about the respective values of μ_1 and μ_2?

At a 90% level of confidence, we can say that the difference $\mu_1 - \mu_2$ is positive, so $\mu_1 - \mu_2 > 0$ and $\mu_1 > \mu_2$.

(b) A study reported a 95% confidence interval for the difference of means to be

$$-0.32 < \mu_1 - \mu_2 < 0.16$$

From this interval, what can you conclude about the respective values of μ_1 and μ_2?

At the 95% confidence level, we see that the difference of means ranges from negative to positive values. We cannot tell from this interval if μ_1 is greater than μ_2 or μ_1 is less than μ_2.

COMMENT In the case of large samples ($n_1 \geq 30$ and $n_2 \geq 30$), it is not unusual to see σ_1 and σ_2 approximated by s_1 and s_2. Then Theorem 10.2 is used as a basis for approximating confidence intervals for $\mu_1 - \mu_2$. In other words, when samples are large, sample estimates for σ_1 and σ_2 can be used together with the standard normal distribution to test $\mu_1 - \mu_2$ and find confidence intervals. However, in this text, we follow the more common convention of using a Student's t distribution whenever σ_1 and σ_2 are unknown.

Hypothesis Tests and Confidence Intervals for $\mu_1 - \mu_2$ When σ_1 and σ_2 Are Unknown

When σ_1 and σ_2 are unknown, we turn to a Student's t distribution. As before, when we use a Student's t distribution, we require that our populations be normal or approximately normal (mound-shaped and symmetric) when the sample sizes n_1 and n_2 are less than 30. We also replace σ_1 by s_1 and σ_2 by s_2. Then we consider the approximate t value, attributed to Welch (*Biometrika,* Vol. 29, pp. 350–362).

$$t \approx \frac{(\bar{x}_1 - \bar{x}_2) - (\mu_1 - \mu_2)}{\sqrt{\dfrac{s_1^2}{n_1} + \dfrac{s_2^2}{n_2}}}$$

Unfortunately, this approximation is *not* exactly a Student's t distribution. However, it will be a good approximation provided we adjust the degrees of freedom by one of the following methods.

1. The adjustment for the degrees of freedom is calculated from sample data. The formula is called *Satterthwaite's approximation.* It is rather complicated. Satterthwaite's approximation is used in statistical software packages such as Minitab and in the TI-84Plus/TI-83Plus calculators. See Problem 19 for the formula.
2. An alternative method, which is much simpler, is to approximate the degrees of freedom using the *smaller* of $n_1 - 1$ and $n_2 - 1$.

For hypothesis tests and confidence intervals, we take the degrees of freedom *d.f.* to be the smaller of $n_1 - 1$ and $n_2 - 1$. This commonly used choice for the degrees of freedom is more conservative than Satterthwaite's approximation in the sense that it produces a slightly larger P-value for testing or a slightly larger margin of error for confidence intervals.

Applying methods similar to those used for hypothesis tests and confidence intervals for μ when σ is unknown, and using the Welch approximation for t, we obtain the following results.

PROCEDURE

HOW TO TEST $\mu_1 - \mu_2$ AND FIND A CONFIDENCE INTERVAL WHEN σ_1 AND σ_2 ARE UNKNOWN

Obtain two independent random samples from populations 1 and 2, where

$\bar{x}_1$ and $\bar{x}_2$ are sample means from populations 1 and 2

s_1 and s_2 are sample standard deviations from populations 1 and 2

n_1 and n_2 are sample sizes from populations 1 and 2

If you can assume that both population distributions 1 and 2 are normal or at least mound-shaped and symmetric, then any sample sizes n_1 and n_2 will work. If you cannot assume this, then use sample sizes $n_1 \geq 30$ and $n_2 \geq 30$.

Continued

Hypothesis test for $\mu_1 - \mu_2$ (σ_1 and σ_2 unknown)

Testing $\mu_1 - \mu_2$

1. In the context of the application, state the *null and alternate hypotheses* and set the *level of significance* α. It is customary to use H_0: $\mu_1 - \mu_2 = 0$.
2. Use $\mu_1 - \mu_2 = 0$ from the null hypothesis together with $\bar{x}_1$, $\bar{x}_2$, s_1, s_2, n_1, and n_2 to compute the sample *test statistic.*

$$t = \frac{(\bar{x}_1 - \bar{x}_2) - (\mu_1 - \mu_2)}{\sqrt{\dfrac{s_1^2}{n_1} + \dfrac{s_2^2}{n_2}}} = \frac{\bar{x}_1 - \bar{x}_2}{\sqrt{\dfrac{s_1^2}{n_1} + \dfrac{s_2^2}{n_2}}}$$

Problem 19 discusses Satterthwaite's approximation for the degrees of freedom.

The sample test statistic distribution is approximately that of a Student's t with *degrees of freedom d.f.* = *smaller* of $n_1 - 1$ and $n_2 - 1$.

Note that statistical software gives a slightly more accurate and larger *d.f.* based on Satterthwaite's approximation (see Problem 19).

3. Use a Student's t distribution and the type of test, one-tailed or two-tailed, to find the *P-value* corresponding to the sample test statistic.
4. *Conclude the test.* If P-value $\leq \alpha$, then reject H_0. If P-value $> \alpha$, then do not reject H_0.
5. *Interpret your conclusion* in the context of the application.

Confidence interval for $\mu_1 - \mu_2$ (σ_1 and σ_2 unknown)

Confidence interval for $\mu_1 - \mu_2$

$$(\bar{x}_1 - \bar{x}_2) - E < \mu_1 - \mu_2 < (\bar{x}_1 - \bar{x}_2) + E$$

where $E = t_c\sqrt{\dfrac{s_1^2}{n_1} + \dfrac{s_2^2}{n_2}}$

c = confidence level ($0 < c < 1$)

t_c = critical value for confidence level c (See Table 4 of the Appendix.)

d.f. = *smaller* of $n_1 - 1$ and $n_2 - 1$. Note that statistical software gives a slightly more accurate and larger *d.f.* based on Satterthwaite's approximation.

EXAMPLE 5 TESTING THE DIFFERENCE OF MEANS AND FINDING A CONFIDENCE INTERVAL (σ_1 AND σ_2 UNKNOWN)

Two competing headache remedies claim to give fast-acting relief. An experiment was performed to compare the mean lengths of time required for bodily absorption of brand A and brand B headache remedies.

Twelve people were randomly selected and given an oral dosage of brand A. Another 12 were randomly selected and given an equal dosage of brand B. The lengths of time in minutes for the drugs to reach a specified level in the blood were recorded. The means, standard deviations, and sizes of the two samples follow.

Brand A: $\bar{x}_1 = 21.8$ min; $s_1 = 8.7$ min; $n_1 = 12$

Brand B: $\bar{x}_2 = 18.9$ min; $s_2 = 7.2$ min; $n_2 = 12$

Past experience with the drug composition of the two remedies permits researchers to assume that both distributions are approximately normal.

Hypothesis test: Use a 5% level of significance to test the claim that there is no difference in the mean time required for bodily absorption. Also, find or estimate the P-value of the sample test statistic.

SOLUTION:

(a) $\alpha = 0.05$. The null hypothesis is

$$H_0: \mu_1 = \mu_2 \quad \text{or} \quad H_0: \mu_1 - \mu_2 = 0$$

Since we have no prior knowledge about which brand is faster, the alternate hypothesis is

$$H_1: \mu_1 \neq \mu_2 \quad \text{or} \quad H_1: \mu_1 - \mu_2 \neq 0$$

(b) Compute the sample test statistic.
We're given $\bar{x}_1 = 21.8$ and $\bar{x}_2 = 18.9$, so the sample difference is $\bar{x}_1 - \bar{x}_2 = 21.8 - 18.9 = 2.9$. Using $s_1 = 8.7$, $s_2 = 7.5$, $n_1 = 12$, $n_2 = 12$, and $\mu_1 - \mu_2 = 0$ from H_0, we compute the sample test statistic.

$$t = \frac{(\bar{x}_1 - \bar{x}_2) - (\mu_1 - \mu_2)}{\sqrt{\dfrac{s_1^2}{n_1} + \dfrac{s_2^2}{n_2}}} = \frac{2.9}{\sqrt{\dfrac{8.7^2}{12} + \dfrac{7.5^2}{12}}} \approx 0.875$$

(c) Estimate the P-value and sketch the area on a t graph.
Figure 10-6 shows the P-value. The degrees of freedom is $d.f. = 11$ (since both samples are of size 12). Because the test is a two-tailed test, the P-value is the area to the right of 0.875 together with the area to the left of -0.875. In the Student's t distribution table (Table 4 of the Appendix), we find an interval containing the P-value. Find 0.875 in the row headed by $d.f. = 11$. The test statistic 0.875 falls between the entries 0.697 and 1.214. Because this is a two-tailed test, we use the corresponding P-values 0.500 and 0.250 from the *two-tail area* row (see Table 10-7, Excerpt from Table 4). The P-value for the sample t is in the interval

$$0.250 < P\text{-value} < 0.500$$

(d) Conclude the test.

α

0.05 0.250 0.500

Since the interval containing the P-value lies to the right of $\alpha = 0.05$, we fail to reject H_0.
Note: Using Satterthwaite's approximation for the degrees of freedom, $d.f. \approx 21.53$, the P-value ≈ 0.3915. This value is in the interval we computed.

FIGURE 10-6

P-value

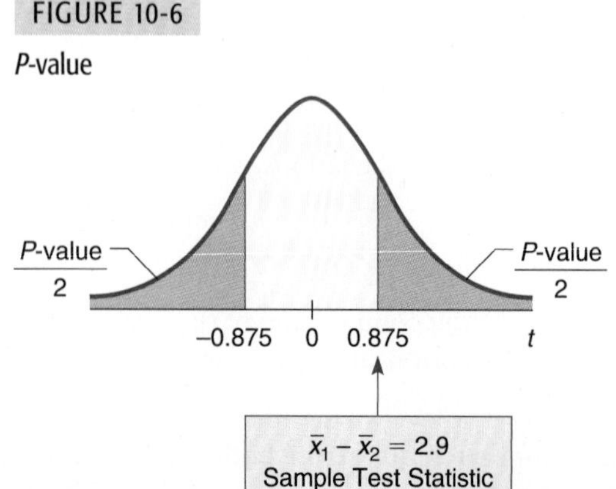

TABLE 10-7 **Excerpt from Table 4 of the Appendix**

one-tail area	0.250	0.125
✓ two-tail area	0.500	0.250
$d.f. = 11$	0.697	1.214
	↑ Sample $t = 0.875$	

(e) Interpret the results.
At the 5% level of significance, there is insufficient evidence to conclude that there is a difference in mean times for the remedies to reach the specified level in the bloodstream.

Confidence interval: Find a 95% confidence interval for the population difference $\mu_1 - \mu_2$ of mean times for the competing drugs to reach a specified level in the blood. Interpret the results.

SOLUTION: Because neither σ_1 nor σ_2 is known and because the distributions of times for each drug to enter the bloodstream are approximately normal, it is appropriate to use a Student's t distribution. We approximate the degrees of freedom by using the smaller of $n_1 - 1$ and $n_2 - 1$. Since n_1 and n_2 are both 12, $d.f. = 12 - 1 = 11$. From Table 4 of the Appendix, we find that $t_{0.95} = 2.201$. The confidence interval is

$$(\bar{x}_1 - \bar{x}_2) - E < \mu_1 - \mu_2 < (\bar{x}_1 - \bar{x}_2) + E$$

with $\bar{x}_1 - \bar{x}_2 = 21.8 - 18.9 = 2.9$ min and

$$E = t_c\sqrt{\frac{s_1^2}{n_1} + \frac{s_2^2}{n_2}} = 2.201\sqrt{\frac{8.7^2}{12} + \frac{7.5^2}{12}} \approx 7.3 \text{ min}$$

The confidence interval is

$$-4.4 \text{ min} < \mu_1 - \mu_2 < 10.2 \text{ min}$$

Note: Using Satterthwaite's formula, $d.f. = 21.53$ and the 95% confidence interval is from -3.99 to 9.79 minutes.

Since the confidence interval contains both negative and positive values, we conclude that at the 95% confidence level, there is no difference in the population mean times for the two drugs to reach the bloodstream. This result is consistent with the two-tailed hypothesis test at the 5% level of significance.

GUIDED EXERCISE 5 Testing the difference of means and finding a confidence interval (σ_1 and σ_2 unknown)

Suppose the experiment to measure the time in minutes for the headache remedies to enter the bloodstream (Example 5) yielded sample means, sample standard deviations, and sample sizes as follows:

Brand A: $\bar{x}_1 = 20.1$ min; $s_1 = 8.7$ min; $n_1 = 12$
Brand B: $\bar{x}_2 = 11.2$ min; $s_2 = 7.5$ min; $n_2 = 8$

Brand B claims to be faster.

Hypothesis test: Is this claim justified at the 5% level of significance? (Use the following steps to obtain the answer.)

(a) What is α? State H_0 and H_1.

→ $\alpha = 0.05$.

$H_0: \mu_1 = \mu_2$ or $H_0: \mu_1 - \mu_2 = 0$

$H_1: \mu_1 > \mu_2$ (or $H_1: \mu_1 - \mu_2 > 0$). This says that the mean time for brand B is less than the mean time for brand A.

Continued

GUIDED EXERCISE 5 *continued*

(b) Compute the sample test statistic $\bar{x}_1 - \bar{x}_2$ and convert it to a t value.

→ $\bar{x}_1 - \bar{x}_2 = 20.1 - 11.2 = 8.9$. Using $s_1 = 8.7$, $s_2 = 7.5$, $n_1 = 12$, $n_2 = 8$, and $\mu_1 - \mu_2 = 0$ from H_0, we have

$$t = \frac{\bar{x}_1 - \bar{x}_2}{\sqrt{\frac{s_1^2}{n_1} + \frac{s_2^2}{n_2}}} = \frac{8.9}{\sqrt{\frac{8.7^2}{12} + \frac{7.5^2}{8}}} \approx 2.437$$

(c) What degrees of freedom do you use? To find an interval containing the P-value, do you use one-tail or two-tail areas of Table 4 of the Appendix? Sketch a figure showing the P-value. Find an interval for the P-value.

→ Since $n_2 < n_1$, $d.f. = n_2 - 1 = 8 - 1 = 7$. Use *one-tail area* of Table 4 of the Appendix.

TABLE 10-8 **Excerpt from Student's *t* Table**

✓ one-tail area	0.025	0.010
two-tail area	0.050	0.020
d.f. = 7	2.365 ↑ Sample t = 2.437	2.998

FIGURE 10-7 *P*-value

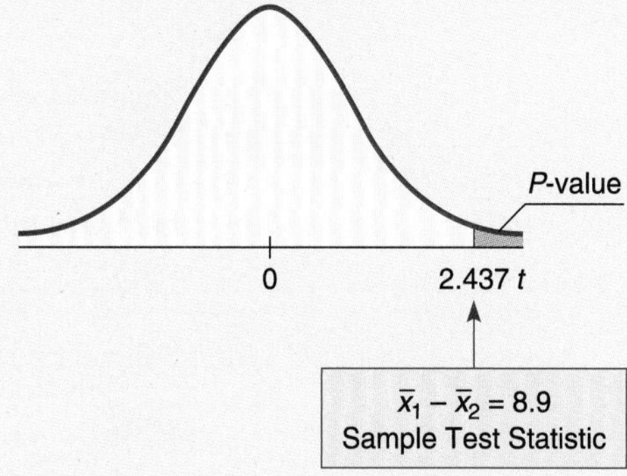

The sample t is between 2.365 and 2.998.

$0.010 < P\text{-value} < 0.025$

(d) Do we reject or fail to reject H_0?

→ Since the interval containing the P-value has values that are all less than 0.05, we reject H_0.

α

0.010 0.025 0.05

Note: On the calculator with Satterthwaite's approximation for *d.f.*, we have *d.f.* = 16.66 and P-value ≈ 0.013.

(e) Interpret the results in the context of the application.

→ At the 5% level of significance, there is evidence that the mean time for brand B to enter the bloodstream is less than the mean time for brand A.

Confidence interval: Find a 90% confidence interval for the difference of population means $\mu_1 - \mu_2$ of times for the two competing headache remedies to enter the bloodstream.

(f) Find the degrees of freedom and the critical value $t_{0.90}$.

→ Since $n_2 < n_1$, $d.f. = n_2 - 1 = 8 - 1 = 7$. From Table 4 of the Appendix, $t_{0.90} = 1.895$.

(g) Find the maximal error of estimate E for a 90% confidence interval.

→ $$E = t_c\sqrt{\frac{s_1^2}{n_1} + \frac{s_2^2}{n_2}} = 1.895\sqrt{\frac{8.7^2}{12} + \frac{7.5^2}{8}} \approx 6.9 \text{ min}$$

Continued

GUIDED EXERCISE 5 *continued*

(h) Find the sample difference $\bar{x}_1 - \bar{x}_2$ and a 90% confidence interval for $\mu_1 - \mu_2$.

→ $\bar{x}_1 - \bar{x}_2 = 20.1 - 11.2 = 8.9$ min

$$(\bar{x}_1 - \bar{x}_2) - E < \mu_1 - \mu_2 < (\bar{x}_1 - \bar{x}_2) + E$$
$$8.9 - 6.9 < \mu_1 - \mu_2 < 8.9 + 6.9$$
$$2 \text{ min} < \mu_1 - \mu_2 < 15.8 \text{ min}$$

With Satterthwaite's formula, $d.f. = 16.66$ and the 90% confidence interval is 2.54 to 15.26 min.

(i) Interpret the results in the context of the application.

→ The confidence interval contains all positive numbers. This indicates that at the 90% confidence level, $\mu_1 > \mu_2$. It seems to take longer for brand A to enter the bloodstream.

COMMENT In Guided Exercise 5, we used a right-tailed test at the 5% level of significance and a 90% confidence interval. With both techniques, we concluded that the time for brand A to enter the bloodstream was longer than the time for brand B. This agreement of results is not an accident. In general, when dealing with the difference of means (and difference of proportions, as discussed in the next section), we will arrive at the same conclusion using either of the following two combinations.

1. Two-tailed hypothesis test at level of significance α and $(1 - \alpha)$ confidence interval
2. One-tailed hypothesis test at level of significance α and $(1 - 2\alpha)$ confidence interval

Alternate method using pooled standard deviation

Problem 20 discusses the use of the pooled standard deviation.

There is another method for testing $\mu_1 - \mu_2$ and finding confidence intervals when σ_1 and σ_2 are unknown. Suppose that the sample values s_1 and s_2 are sufficiently close and that there is reason to believe $\sigma_1 = \sigma_2$ (or that the standard deviations are approximately equal). This situation can happen when you make a slight change or alteration to a known process or method of production. The standard deviation may not change much, but the outputs or means could be very different. When there is reason to believe that $\sigma_1 = \sigma_2$, it is best to use a *pooled standard deviation.* The sample test statistic $\bar{x}_1 - \bar{x}_2$ has a corresponding t variable with an *exact* Student's t distribution and degrees of freedom $d.f. = n_1 + n_2 - 2$. Problem 20 at the end of this section provides the details for using the pooled standard deviation in hypothesis tests of and confidence intervals for $\mu_1 - \mu_2$.

Summary

Depending on the information available, there are several methods for testing and constructing confidence intervals for the difference of means $\mu_1 - \mu_2$ from two independent random samples. To use the normal probability distribution, you need to know σ_1 and σ_2. In addition, you need to know that the original population distributions are both normal or that n_1 and n_2 are both of size at least 30. To use a Student's t distribution, you need to know that the original population distributions are both normal or at least mound-shaped, or that n_1 and n_2 are both at least 30. The decision chart on the next page summarizes the appropriate formulas.

Continued

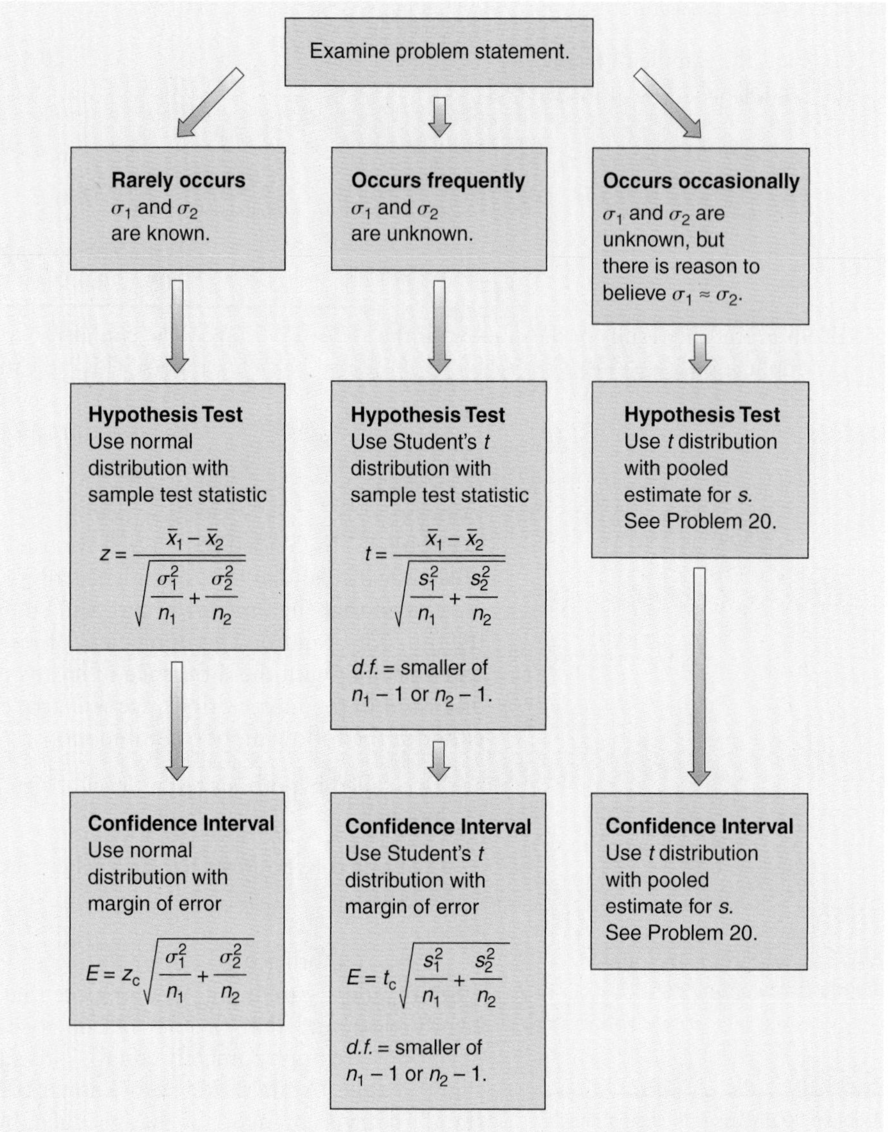

Examine problem statement.
Rarely occurs
σ_1 and σ_2 are known.
Occurs frequently
σ_1 and σ_2 are unknown.
Occurs occasionally
σ_1 and σ_2 are unknown, but there is reason to believe $\sigma_1 \approx \sigma_2$.
Hypothesis Test
Use normal distribution with sample test statistic
$z = \frac{\bar{x}_1 - \bar{x}_2}{\sqrt{\frac{\sigma_1^2}{n_1} + \frac{\sigma_2^2}{n_2}}}$
Hypothesis Test
Use Student's t distribution with sample test statistic
$t = \frac{\bar{x}_1 - \bar{x}_2}{\sqrt{\frac{s_1^2}{n_1} + \frac{s_2^2}{n_2}}}$
$d.f.$ = smaller of $n_1 - 1$ or $n_2 - 1$.
Hypothesis Test
Use t distribution with pooled estimate for s.
See Problem 20.
Confidence Interval
Use normal distribution with margin of error
$E = z_c\sqrt{\frac{\sigma_1^2}{n_1} + \frac{\sigma_2^2}{n_2}}$
Confidence Interval
Use Student's t distribution with margin of error
$E = t_c\sqrt{\frac{s_1^2}{n_1} + \frac{s_2^2}{n_2}}$
$d.f.$ = smaller of $n_1 - 1$ or $n_2 - 1$.
Confidence Interval
Use t distribution with pooled estimate for s.
See Problem 20.

TECH NOTES The TI-84Plus and TI-83Plus calculators, Excel, and Minitab all support testing the difference of means for independent samples. The TI-84Plus/TI-83Plus calculators and Minitab also supply confidence intervals for the difference of means.

TI-84Plus/TI-83Plus Enter either summary statistics or raw data. Press **STAT** and select **TESTS.** Options **3:2-SampZTest** and **4:2-SampTTest** test the difference of means using the normal distribution and a Student's t distribution, respectively. Choice **9:2-SampZInt** finds a confidence interval for a difference of means when σ_1 and σ_2 are known. Choice **0:2-SampTInt** finds a confidence interval for a difference of means when σ_1 and σ_2 are unknown. In general, use **No** for Pooled. Then Satterthwaite's approximation for the degrees of freedom is used. However, if $\sigma_1 \approx \sigma_2$, use **Yes** for Pooled.

Excel Enter the data in two columns. Use the menu choices **Tools ➤ Data Analysis.** The choice **z-Test Two Sample Means** tests the difference of means using the normal distribution. The choice **t-Test: Two-Sample Assuming Unequal Variances** tests the difference of means using a Student's t distribution with Satterthwaite's approximation for the degrees of freedom. The choice **t-Test: Two-Sample Assuming Equal Variances** conducts a test using the pooled standard deviation.

Minitab For differences of means, enter the data into two columns. Use the menu choices **STAT ➤ Basic Statistics ➤ 2 sample t.** Minitab always uses a Student's t distribution for $\mu_1 - \mu_2$. In the dialogue box, leave the box **Assume equal variances** unchecked to use Satterthwaite's approximation for the degrees of freedom. Check the box **Assume equal variances** to use the pooled standard deviation.

Testing $\mu_1 - \mu_2$ Using Critical Regions (Optional)

For a set level of significance, the traditional critical region method yields the same results as the P-value method of hypothesis testing. Critical values z_0 for tests using the standard normal distribution can be found in Table 3(c) of the Appendix. Critical values t_0 for tests using a Student's t distribution are found in Table 4 of the Appendix. Use the row headed by the appropriate degrees of freedom and the column that includes the value of α (level of significance) in the *one-tail area row* for one-tailed tests or the *two-tail area row* for two-tailed tests.

EXAMPLE 6 CRITICAL REGION METHOD

Use the critical region method to solve the application in Example 5 (test $\mu_1 - \mu_2$ when σ_1 and σ_2 are unknown).

SOLUTION: Example 5 involves testing the difference in average times for two headache remedies to reach the bloodstream. For brand A, $\bar{x}_1 = 21.8$ min, $s_1 = 8.7$ min, and $n_1 = 12$; for brand B, $\bar{x}_2 = 18.9$ min, $s_2 = 7.5$ min, and $n_2 = 12$. The level of significance α is 0.05. The Student's t distribution is appropriate because both populations are approximately normal.

(a) To use the critical region method to test for a difference in average times, we use the same hypotheses and the same sample test statistic as in Example 5.

H_0: $\mu_1 = \mu_2$; H_1: $\mu_1 \neq \mu_2$;

sample test statistic: $\bar{x}_1 - \bar{x}_2 = 2.9$ min; sample $t = 0.875$

(b) Instead of finding the P-value of the sample test statistic, we use α and H_1 to find the critical values in Table 4 of the Appendix. We have $d.f. = 11$ (since both samples are of size 12). We find $\alpha = 0.05$ in the *two-tail area* row, since we have a two-tailed test. The critical values are $\pm t_0 = \pm 2.201$.

Next compare the sample test statistic $t = 0.875$ to the critical values. Figure 10-8 shows the critical regions and the sample test statistic. We see that the sample test statistic falls in the "do not reject H_0" region. At the 5% level of significance, the sample evidence does not show a difference in times for the drugs to reach the bloodstream. The result is consistent with the result obtained by the P-value method of Example 5.

FIGURE 10-8

Critical Regions $\alpha = 0.05$; $d.f. = 11$

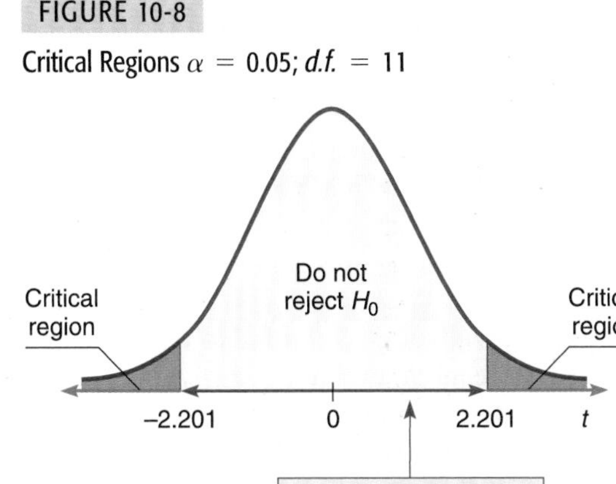

VIEWPOINT Temper! Temper!

In her book Red Ink Behaviors, *Jean Hollands discusses inappropriate, problem behaviors of professional employees in the corporate business world. Temper tantrums, flaming e-mails, omitting essential information, sabotaging fellow workers, and the arrogant opinion that others are "dumb and dispensable" create personnel problems that cost companies a lot in the form of wasted time, reduced productivity, and lost revenues. A study of major industries in the Silicon Valley area gave Hollands data for estimating just how much time and money are wasted by such "red ink behaviors." For more information, see Problems 17 and 18 in this section.*

SECTION 10.2 PROBLEMS

1. *Statistical Literacy* Consider a hypothesis test of difference of means for two independent populations x_1 and x_2. What is the sample test statistic?

2. *Statistical Literacy* Consider a hypothesis test of difference of means for two independent populations x_1 and x_2. Suppose that both sample sizes are greater than 30 and that you know σ_1 but not σ_2. Is it standard practice to use the normal distribution or a Student's t distribution?

3. *Statistical Literacy* Consider a hypothesis test of difference of means for two independent populations x_1 and x_2. What are two ways of expressing the null hypothesis?

4. *Critical Thinking* When conducting a test of the difference of means for two independent populations x_1 and x_2, what alternate hypothesis would indicate that the mean of the x_2 population is larger than that of the x_1 population? Express the alternate hypothesis in two ways.

5. *Critical Thinking* Josh and Kendra each calculated a 90% confidence interval for the difference of means using a Student's t distribution for random samples of size $n_1 = 20$ and $n_2 = 31$. Kendra followed the convention of using the smaller sample size to compute $d.f. = 19$. Josh used his calculator and Satterthwaite's approximation and obtained $d.f. \approx 36.3$. Which confidence interval is shorter? Which confidence interval is more conservative in the sense that the margin of error is larger?

6. *Critical Thinking* If a 90% confidence interval for the difference of means $\mu_1 - \mu_2$ contains all positive values, what can we conclude about the relationship between μ_1 and μ_2 at the 90% confidence level?

Please provide the following information for Problems 7–18, part (a).

(i) What is the level of significance? State the null and alternate hypotheses.
(ii) What sampling distribution will you use? What assumptions are you making? What is the value of the sample test statistic?
(iii) Find (or estimate) the P-value. Sketch the sampling distribution and show the area corresponding to the P-value.
(iv) Based on your answers in parts (i) to (iii), will you reject or fail to reject the null hypothesis? Are the data statistically significant at level α?
(v) Interpret your conclusion in the context of the application.

Note: For degrees of freedom $d.f.$ not in the Student's t table, use the closest $d.f.$ that is *smaller*. In some situations, this choice of $d.f.$ may increase the P-value a small amount, and therefore produce a slightly more "conservative" answer.

Answers may vary due to rounding.

7. *Medical: REM Sleep* REM (rapid eye movement) sleep is sleep during which most dreams occur. Each night a person has both REM and non-REM sleep.

1. $\bar{x}_1 - \bar{x}_2$.
2. Student's t distribution.
3. H_0: $\mu_1 = \mu_2$ or H_0: $\mu_1 - \mu_2 = 0$.
4. H_1: $\mu_1 < \mu_2$; H_1: $\mu_1 - \mu_2 < 0$.
5. Josh's, because the critical value t_c is smaller based on larger $d.f.$; Kendra's, because her value for t_c is larger.
6. $\mu_1 > \mu_2$.
7. (a) (i) $\alpha = 0.01$; H_0: $\mu_1 = \mu_2$; H_1: $\mu_1 > \mu_2$.
(ii) Standard normal; $\bar{x}_1 - \bar{x}_2 = 0.7$; $z \approx 2.57$.
(iii) P-value $= P(z > 2.57) \approx 0.0051$; on standard normal curve, shade area to the right of 2.57.
(iv) P-value of $0.0051 \leq 0.01$ for α; reject H_0.
(v) At the 1% level of significance, the evidence is sufficient to indicate that the population mean REM sleep time for children is more than that for adults.
(b) 0.07 to 1.33.

8. (a) (i) $\alpha = 0.01$; H_0: $\mu_1 = \mu_2$; H_1: $\mu_1 \neq \mu_2$.
(ii) Standard normal; $\bar{x}_1 - \bar{x}_2 = 7$; $z \approx 0.96$.
(iii) *P*-value $= 2P(z > 0.96) = 2(0.1685) = 0.3370$; on standard normal curve, shade area to the right of 0.96 and to the left of -0.96.
(iv) *P*-value of $0.3370 > 0.01$ for α; do not reject H_0.
(v) At the 1% level of significance, the evidence is insufficient to claim that there is a difference in the mean population pollution index between Englewood and Denver.
(b) -11.72 to 25.72.

9. (a) (i) $\alpha = 0.05$; H_0: $\mu_1 = \mu_2$; H_1: $\mu_1 \neq \mu_2$.
(ii) Standard normal; $\bar{x}_1 - \bar{x}_2 = 0.6$; $z \approx 2.16$.
(iii) *P*-value $= 2P(z > 2.16) \approx 2(0.0154) = 0.0308$; on standard normal curve, shade area to the right of 2.16 and to the left of -2.16.
(iv) *P*-value of $0.0308 \leq 0.05$ for α; reject H_0.
(v) At the 5% level of significance, the evidence is sufficient to show that there is a difference between mean responses regarding preference for camping or fishing.
(b) 0.06 to 1.14.

10. (a) (i) $\alpha = 0.05$; H_0: $\mu_1 = \mu_2$; H_1: $\mu_1 < \mu_2$.
(ii) Standard normal; $\bar{x}_1 - \bar{x}_2 = -4.5$; $z \approx -2.91$.
(iii) *P*-value $= P(z < -2.91) \approx 0.0018$; on standard normal curve, shade area to the left of -2.91.
(iv) *P*-value of $0.0018 \leq 0.05$ for α; reject H_0.
(v) At the 5% level of significance, the evidence is sufficient to show that the population mean percentage of young adults who attended college is higher.
(b) -7.044 to -1.956.

11. Use rounded results to compute *t*.
(a) (i) $\alpha = 0.01$; H_0: $\mu_1 = \mu_2$; H_1: $\mu_1 < \mu_2$.
(ii) Student's *t*, *d.f.* = 9; $\bar{x}_1 - \bar{x}_2 = -0.36$; $t \approx -0.965$.
(iii) $0.125 < P\text{-value} < 0.250$; on *t* graph, shade area to the left of -0.965. For TI-84, *d.f.* ≈ 19.96; *P*-value ≈ 0.1731.
(iv) *P*-value interval > 0.01 for α; do not reject H_0.

However, it is thought that children have more REM sleep than adults (Reference: *Secrets of Sleep* by Dr. A. Borbely). Assume that REM sleep time is normally distributed for both children and adults. A random sample of $n_1 = 10$ children (9 years old) showed that they had an average REM sleep time of $\bar{x}_1 = 2.8$ hours per night. From previous studies, it is known that $\sigma_1 = 0.5$ hour. Another random sample of $n_2 = 10$ adults showed that they had an average REM sleep time of $\bar{x}_2 = 2.1$ hours per night. Previous studies show that $\sigma_2 = 0.7$ hour.

(a) Do these data indicate that on average, children tend to have more REM sleep than adults? Use a 1% level of significance.
(b) Find a 98% confidence interval for $\mu_1 - \mu_2$. Explain the meaning of the confidence interval in the context of the problem.

8. *Enviroment: Pollution Index* Based on information from the *Rocky Mountain News*, a random sample of $n_1 = 12$ winter days in Denver gave a sample mean pollution index of $\bar{x}_1 = 43$. Previous studies show that $\sigma_1 = 21$. For Englewood (a suburb of Denver), a random sample of $n_2 = 14$ winter days gave a sample mean pollution index of $\bar{x}_2 = 36$. Previous studies show that $\sigma_2 = 15$. Assume the pollution index is normally distributed in both Englewood and Denver.
(a) Do these data indicate that the mean population pollution index of Englewood is different (either way) from that of Denver in the winter? Use a 1% level of significance.
(b) Find a 99% confidence interval for $\mu_1 - \mu_2$. Explain the meaning of the confidence interval in the context of the problem.

9. *Survey: Outdoor Activities* A Michigan study concerning preference for outdoor activities used a questionnaire with a six-point Likert-type response in which 1 designated "not important" and 6 designated "extremely important." A random sample of $n_1 = 46$ adults were asked about fishing as an outdoor activity. The mean response was $\bar{x}_1 = 4.9$. Another random sample of $n_2 = 51$ adults were asked about camping as an outdoor activity. For this group, the mean response was $\bar{x}_2 = 4.3$. From previous studies, it is known that $\sigma_1 = 1.5$ and $\sigma_2 = 1.2$. *Note:* A *Likert scale* usually has to do with approval of or agreement with a statement in a questionnaire. For example, respondents are asked to indicate whether they "strongly agree," "agree," "disagree," or "strongly disagree" with the statement.
(a) Do these data indicate a difference (either way) regarding preference for camping versus preference for fishing as an outdoor activity? Use a 5% level of significance.
(b) Find a 95% confidence interval for $\mu_1 - \mu_2$. Explain the meaning of the confidence interval in the context of the problem.

10. *Generation Gap: Education* Education influences attitude and lifestyle. Differences in education are a big factor in the "generation gap." Is the younger generation really better educated? Large surveys of people age 65 and older were taken in $n_1 = 32$ U.S. cities. The sample mean for these cities showed that $\bar{x}_1 = 15.2\%$ of the older adults had attended college. Large surveys of young adults (age 25–34) were taken in $n_2 = 35$ U.S. cities. The sample mean for these cities showed that $\bar{x}_2 = 19.7\%$ of the young adults had attended college. From previous studies, it is known that $\sigma_1 = 7.2\%$ and $\sigma_2 = 5.2\%$ (Reference: *American Generations*, S. Mitchell).
(a) Does this information indicate that the population mean percentage of young adults who attended college is higher? Use $\alpha = 0.05$.
(b) Find a 90% confidence interval for $\mu_1 - \mu_2$. Explain the meaning of the confidence interval in the context of the problem.

11. *Crime Rate: FBI* A random sample of $n_1 = 10$ regions in New England gave the following violent crime rates (per million population).

x_1: New England crime rate

3.5	3.7	4.0	3.9	3.3	4.1	1.8	4.8	2.9	3.1

(v) At the 1% level of significance, the evidence is insufficient to indicate that the violent crime rate in the Rocky Mountain region is higher than in New England.
(b) −1.41 to 0.69.
12. Use rounded results to compute t.
(a) (i) $\alpha = 0.05$; H_0: $\mu_1 = \mu_2$; H_1: $\mu_1 > \mu_2$.
(ii) Student's t, $d.f. = 13$; $\bar{x}_1 - \bar{x}_2 = 10.14$; $t \approx 2.053$.
(iii) $0.025 < P\text{-value} < 0.050$; on t graph, shade area to the right of 2.053. For TI-84, $d.f. \approx 27.42$; $P\text{-value} \approx 0.0249$.
(iv) P-value interval ≤ 0.05 for α; reject H_0.
(v) At the 5% level of significance, the evidence is sufficient to indicate that the population mean rate of hay fever is lower for the age group over 50.
(b) 1.39 to 18.89.
13. (a) (i) $\alpha = 0.05$; H_0: $\mu_1 = \mu_2$; H_1: $\mu_1 \neq \mu_2$.
(ii) Student's t, $d.f. = 29$; $\bar{x}_1 - \bar{x}_2 = -9.7$; $t \approx -0.751$.
(iii) $0.250 < P\text{-value} < 0.500$; on t graph, shade area to the right of 0.751 and to the left of −0.751. For TI-84, $d.f. \approx 57.92$; $P\text{-value} \approx 0.4556$.
(iv) P-value interval > 0.05 for α; do not reject H_0.
(v) At the 5% level of significance, the evidence is insufficient to indicate that there is a difference between the control and experimental groups in the mean score on the vocabulary portion of the test.
(b) −36.1 to 16.7.

14. (a) (i) $\alpha = 0.01$; H_0: $\mu_1 = \mu_2$; H_1: $\mu_1 > \mu_2$.
(ii) Student's t, $d.f. = 29$; $\bar{x}_1 - \bar{x}_2 = 19.2$; $t \approx 1.524$.
(iii) $0.050 < P\text{-value} < 0.075$; on t graph, shade area to the right of 1.524. For TI-84, $d.f. \approx 51.83$; $P\text{-value} \approx 0.0668$.
(iv) P-value interval > 0.01 for α; do not reject H_0.
(v) At the 1% level of significance, the evidence is insufficient to claim that the population mean score of the experimental group was higher than that of the control group.
(b) −11.8 to 50.2.

Another random sample of $n_2 = 12$ regions in the Rocky Mountain states gave the following violent crime rates (per million population).

x_2: Rocky Mountain states crime rate

3.7	4.3	4.5	5.3	3.3	4.8	3.5	2.4	3.1	3.5	5.2	2.8

(Reference: *Crime in the United States*, Federal Bureau of Investigation.) Assume that the crime rate distribution is approximately normal in both regions. Use a calculator to verify that $\bar{x}_1 \approx 3.51$, $s_1 \approx 0.81$, $\bar{x}_2 \approx 3.87$, and $s_2 \approx 0.94$.
(a) Do the data indicate that the violent crime rate in the Rocky Mountain region is higher than in New England? Use $\alpha = 0.01$.
(b) Find a 98% confidence interval for $\mu_1 - \mu_2$. Explain the meaning of the confidence interval in the context of the problem.

12. *Medical: Hay Fever* A random sample of $n_1 = 16$ communities in western Kansas gave the following information for people under 25 years of age.

x_1: Rate of hay fever per 1000 population for people under 25

98	90	120	128	92	123	112	93
125	95	125	117	97	122	127	88

A random sample of $n_2 = 14$ regions in western Kansas gave the following information for people over 50 years old.

x_2: Rate of hay fever per 1000 population for people over 50

95	110	101	97	112	88	110
79	115	100	89	114	85	96

(Reference: National Center for Health Statistics.)

Use a calculator to verify that $\bar{x}_1 \approx 109.50$, $s_1 \approx 15.41$, $\bar{x}_2 \approx 99.36$, and $s_2 \approx 11.57$.
(a) Assume that the hay fever rate in each age group has an approximately normal distribution. Do the data indicate that the age group over 50 has a lower rate of hay fever? Use $\alpha = 0.05$.
(b) Find a 90% confidence interval for $\mu_1 - \mu_2$. Explain the meaning of the confidence interval in the context of the problem.

13. *Education: Tutoring* In the journal *Mental Retardation*, an article reported the results of a peer tutoring program to help mildly mentally retarded children learn to read. In the experiment, the mildly retarded children were randomly divided into two groups: the experimental group received peer tutoring along with regular instruction, and the control group received regular instruction with no peer tutoring. There were $n_1 = n_2 = 30$ children in each group. The Gates-MacGintie Reading Test was given to both groups before instruction began. For the experimental group, the mean score on the vocabulary portion of the test was $\bar{x}_1 = 344.5$ with sample standard deviation $s_1 = 49.1$. For the control group, the mean score on the same test was $\bar{x}_2 = 354.2$ with sample standard deviation $s_2 = 50.9$.
(a) Use a 5% level of significance to test the hypothesis that there was no difference in the vocabulary scores of the two groups before the instruction began.
(b) Find a 95% confidence interval for $\mu_1 - \mu_2$. Explain the meaning of the confidence interval in the context of the problem.

14. *Education: Tutoring* In the article cited in Problem 13, the results of the following experiment were reported. Form 2 of the Gates-MacGintie Reading Test was administered to both an experimental group and a control group after 6 weeks of instruction during which the experimental group received peer tutoring and the control group did not. For the experimental group with $n_1 = 30$ children, the mean score on the vocabulary portion of the test was $\bar{x}_1 = 368.4$ with sample standard deviation $s_1 = 39.5$. The average score on the vocabulary portion

of the test for the $n_2 = 30$ subjects in the control group was $\bar{x}_2 = 349.2$, with sample standard deviation $s_2 = 56.6$.

(a) Use a 1% level of significance to test the claim that the experimental group performed better than the control group.

(b) Find a 98% confidence interval for $\mu_1 - \mu_2$. Explain the meaning of the confidence interval in the context of the problem.

15. *Wildlife: Fox Rabies* A study of fox rabies in southern Germany gave the following information about different regions and the occurrence of rabies in each region (Reference: B. Sayers, et al., "A Pattern Analysis Study of a Wildlife Rabies Epizootic," *Medical Informatics* 2:11–34). Based on information from this article, a random sample of $n_1 = 16$ locations in region I gave the following information about the number of cases of fox rabies near that location.

x_1: **Region I data**	1	8	8	8	7	8	8	1
	3	3	3	2	5	1	4	6

A second random sample of $n_2 = 15$ locations in region II gave the following information about the number of cases of fox rabies near that location.

x_2: **Region II data**	1	1	3	1	4	8	5	4
	4	4	2	2	5	6	9	

Use a calculator with sample mean and sample standard deviation keys to verify that $\bar{x}_1 = 4.75$ with $s_1 \approx 2.82$ in region I and $\bar{x}_2 \approx 3.93$ with $s_2 \approx 2.43$ in region II.

(a) Does this information indicate that there is a difference (either way) in the mean number of cases of fox rabies between the two regions? Use a 5% level of significance. (Assume the distribution of rabies cases in both regions is mound-shaped and approximately normal.)

(b) Find a 95% confidence interval for $\mu_1 - \mu_2$. Explain the meaning of the confidence interval in the context of the problem.

16. *Agriculture: Bell Peppers* The pathogen *Phytophthora capsici* causes bell peppers to wilt and die. Because bell peppers are an important commercial crop, this disease has undergone a great deal of agricultural research. It is thought that too much water aids the spread of the pathogen. Two fields are under study. The first step in the research project is to compare the mean soil water content for the two fields (Source: *Journal of Agricultural, Biological, and Environmental Statistics*, Vol. 2, No. 2). Units are percent water by volume of soil.

Field A samples, x_1:

10.2	10.7	15.5	10.4	9.9	10.0	16.6
15.1	15.2	13.8	14.1	11.4	11.5	11.0

Field B samples, x_2:

8.1	8.5	8.4	7.3	8.0	7.1	13.9	12.2
13.4	11.3	12.6	12.6	12.7	12.4	11.3	12.5

Use a calculator with mean and standard deviation keys to verify that $\bar{x}_1 \approx 12.53$, $s_1 \approx 2.39$, $\bar{x}_2 \approx 10.77$, and $s_2 \approx 2.40$.

(a) Assuming the distribution of soil water content in each field is mound-shaped and symmetric, use a 5% level of significance to test the claim that field A has, on average, a higher soil water content than field B.

(b) Find a 90% confidence interval for $\mu_1 - \mu_2$. Explain the meaning of the confidence interval in the context of the problem.

17. *Management: Lost Time* In her book *Red Ink Behaviors*, Jean Hollands reports on the assessment of leading Silicon Valley companies regarding a manager's lost time due to inappropriate behavior of employees. Consider the following independent

15. Use rounded results to compute t.
(a) (i) $\alpha = 0.05$; H_0: $\mu_1 = \mu_2$; H_1: $\mu_1 \neq \mu_2$.
(ii) Student's t, *d.f.* = 14; $\bar{x}_1 - \bar{x}_2 = 0.82$; $t \approx 0.869$.
(iii) $0.250 < P\text{-value} < 0.500$; on t graph, shade area to the right of 0.869 and to the left of -0.869. For TI-84, *d.f.* ≈ 28.81; *P*-value ≈ 0.3940.
(iv) *P*-value interval > 0.05 for α; do not reject H_0.
(v) At the 5% level of significance, the evidence is insufficient to indicate that there is a difference in the mean number of cases of fox rabies between the two regions.
(b) -1.2 to 2.84.

16. Use rounded results to compute t.
(a) (i) $\alpha = 0.05$; H_0: $\mu_1 = \mu_2$; H_1: $\mu_1 > \mu_2$.
(ii) Student's t, *d.f.* = 13; $\bar{x}_1 - \bar{x}_2 = 1.76$; $t \approx 2.008$.
(iii) $0.025 < P\text{-value} < 0.050$; on t graph, shade area to the right of 2.008. For TI-84, *d.f.* ≈ 27.50; *P*-value ≈ 0.0273.
(iv) *P*-value interval ≤ 0.05 for α; reject H_0.
(v) At the 5% level of significance, the evidence is sufficient to indicate that population mean soil water content is higher in field A.
(b) 0.21 to 3.31.

17. Use rounded results to compute t.
(a) (i) $\alpha = 0.05$; H_0: $\mu_1 = \mu_2$; H_1: $\mu_1 \neq \mu_2$.
(ii) Student's t, *d.f.* = 6; $\bar{x}_1 - \bar{x}_2 = -1.64$; $t \approx -1.041$.
(iii) $0.250 < P\text{-value} < 0.500$; on t graph, shade area to the right of 1.041 and to the left of -1.041. For TI-84, *d.f.* ≈ 12.28; *P*-value ≈ 0.3179.
(iv) *P*-value interval > 0.05 for α; do not reject H_0.
(v) At the 5% level of significance, the evidence is insufficient to indicate that the mean time lost due to hot tempers is different from time lost due to technical workers' attitudes.
(b) -5.49 to 2.21.

random variables. The first variable x_1 measures manager's hours per week lost due to hot tempers, flaming e-mails, and general unproductive tensions:

x_1: 1 5 8 4 2 4 10

The variable x_2 measures manager's hours per week lost due to disputes regarding technical workers' superior attitudes that their colleagues are "dumb and dispensable":

x_2: 10 5 4 7 9 4 10 3

Use a calculator with sample mean and standard deviation keys to verify that $\bar{x}_1 \approx 4.86$, $s_1 \approx 3.18$, $\bar{x}_2 = 6.5$, and $s_2 \approx 2.88$.

(a) Does the information indicate that the population mean time lost due to hot tempers is different (either way) from the population mean time lost due to disputes arising from technical workers' superior attitudes? Use $\alpha = 0.05$. Assume that the two lost-time population distributions are mound-shaped and symmetric.

(b) Find a 95% confidence interval for $\mu_1 - \mu_2$. Explain the meaning of the confidence interval in the context of the problem.

18. *Management: Intimidators and Stressors* This problem is based on information regarding productivity in leading Silicon Valley companies (see reference in Problem 17). In large corporations, an "intimidator" is an employee who tries to stop communication, sometimes sabotages others, and, above all, likes to listen to him- or herself talk. Let x_1 be a random variable representing productive hours per week lost by peer employees of an intimidator.

x_1: 8 3 6 2 2 5 2

A "stressor" is an employee with a hot temper that leads to unproductive tantrums in corporate society. Let x_2 be a random variable representing productive hours per week lost by peer employees of a stressor.

x_2: 3 3 10 7 6 2 5 8

Use a calculator with mean and standard deviation keys to verify that $\bar{x}_1 = 4.00$, $s_1 \approx 2.38$, $\bar{x}_2 = 5.5$, and $s_2 \approx 2.78$.

(a) Assuming that the variables x_1 and x_2 are independent, do the data indicate that the population mean time lost due to stressors is greater than the population mean time lost due to intimidators? Use a 5% level of significance. (Assume that the population distributions of time lost due to intimidators and time lost due to stressors are each mound-shaped and symmetric.)

(b) Find a 90% confidence interval for $\mu_1 - \mu_2$. Explain the meaning of the confidence interval in the context of the problem.

> 18. Use rounded results to compute t.
> (a) (i) $\alpha = 0.05$; H_0: $\mu_1 = \mu_2$; H_1: $\mu_1 < \mu_2$.
> (ii) Student's t, $d.f. = 6$; $\bar{x}_1 - \bar{x}_2 = -1.5$; $t \approx -1.126$.
> (iii) $0.125 < P\text{-value} < 0.250$; on t graph, shade area to the left of -1.126. For TI-84, $d.f. \approx 13.00$; P-value ≈ 0.1403.
> (iv) P-value interval > 0.05 for α; do not reject H_0.
> (v) At the 5% level of significance, the evidence is insufficient to indicate that population mean time lost due to stressors is greater than that lost due to intimidators.
> (b) -4.1 to 1.1.

19. *Expand Your Knowledge: Software Approximation for Degrees of Freedom* Given x_1 and x_2 distributions that are normal or approximately normal with unknown σ_1 and σ_2, the value of t corresponding to $\bar{x}_1 - \bar{x}_2$ has a distribution that is approximated by a Student's t distribution. We use the convention that the degrees of freedom is approximately the smaller of $n_1 - 1$ and $n_2 - 1$. However, a more accurate estimate for the appropriate degrees of freedom is given by Satterthwaite's formula:

$$d.f. \approx \frac{\left(\frac{s_1^2}{n_1} + \frac{s_2^2}{n_2}\right)^2}{\frac{1}{n_1 - 1}\left(\frac{s_1^2}{n_1}\right)^2 + \frac{1}{n_2 - 1}\left(\frac{s_2^2}{n_2}\right)^2}$$

where s_1, s_2, n_1, and n_2 are the respective sample standard deviations and sample sizes of independent random samples from the x_1 and x_2 distributions. This is the approximation used by most statistical software. When both n_1 and n_2 are 5 or larger, it is quite accurate. The degrees of freedom computed from this formula are either truncated or not rounded.

> 19. It is useful to point out that for the same sample test statistic t, as the degrees of freedom decrease, the corresponding P-values increase. Smaller degrees of freedom give more conservative results in the sense that a larger P-value may not result in the decision to reject H_0.
> (a) $d.f. = 19.96$ (Some software will truncate this to 19.)
> (b) $d.f. = 9$; the convention of using the smaller of $n_1 - 1$ and $n_2 - 1$ leads to a $d.f.$ that is always less than or equal to that computed by Satterthwaite's formula.

(a) In Problem 11, we tested whether the population average crime rate μ_2 in the Rocky Mountain region is higher than that in New England, μ_1. The data were $n_1 = 10$, $\bar{x}_1 \approx 3.51$, $s_1 \approx 0.81$, $n_2 = 12$, $\bar{x}_2 \approx 3.87$, and $s_2 \approx 0.94$. Use Satterthwaite's formula to compute the degrees of freedom for the Student's t distribution.

(b) When you did Problem 11, you followed the convention that degrees of freedom $d.f. =$ *smaller* of $n_1 - 1$ and $n_2 - 1$. Compare this $d.f.$ with that found by Satterthwaite's formula.

20. The pooled two-sample testing procedure is a commonly used statistical method when it can be assumed that the populations have equal standard deviations. In statistical software, there is usually an option to select equal variances or pooled variances when doing a two-sample t test.
(a) Using pooled standard deviation, $s \approx 2.639$; $t \approx 0.865$; H_0: $\mu_1 = \mu_2$ and H_1: $\mu_1 \neq \mu_2$; $d.f. = 29$; $0.250 < P\text{-value} < 0.500$; P-value interval > 0.05 for α; fail to reject H_0.
(b) -1.12 to 2.76.

20. *Expand Your Knowledge: Pooled Two-Sample Procedure* Consider independent random samples from two populations that are normal or approximately normal, or the case in which both sample sizes are at least 30. Then, if σ_1 and σ_2 are unknown but we have reason to believe that $\sigma_1 = \sigma_2$, we can pool the standard deviations. Using sample sizes n_1 and n_2, the sample test statistic $\bar{x}_1 - \bar{x}_2$ has a Student's t distribution, where

$$t = \frac{\bar{x}_1 - \bar{x}_2}{s\sqrt{\dfrac{1}{n_1} + \dfrac{1}{n_2}}} \text{ with degrees of freedom } d.f. = n_1 + n_2 - 2$$

and the **pooled standard deviation** s is

$$s = \sqrt{\frac{(n_1 - 1)s_1^2 + (n_2 - 1)s_2^2}{n_1 + n_2 - 2}}$$

Hypothesis tests: Use H_0: $\mu_1 = \mu_2$ and an appropriate alternate hypothesis. The test statistic is

$$t = \frac{\bar{x}_1 - \bar{x}_2}{s\sqrt{\dfrac{1}{n_1} + \dfrac{1}{n_2}}} \text{ with } d.f. = n_1 + n_2 - 2$$

A c confidence interval: $(\bar{x}_1 - \bar{x}_2) - E < \mu_1 - \mu_2 < (\bar{x}_1 - \bar{x}_2) + E$

where $E = t_c s\sqrt{\dfrac{1}{n_1} + \dfrac{1}{n_2}}$

$t_c =$ critical value for confidence level c and degrees of freedom $d.f. = n_1 + n_2 - 2$

Note: With statistical software, select the pooled variance or equal variance options.

There are many situations in which we want to compare means from populations having standard deviations that are equal. This method applies even if the standard deviations are known to be only approximately equal. Consider Problem 15 regarding average incidence of fox rabies in two regions. For region I, $n_1 = 16$, $\bar{x}_1 = 4.75$, and $s_1 \approx 2.82$, and for region II, $n_2 = 15$, $\bar{x}_2 \approx 3.93$, and $s_2 \approx 2.43$. The two sample standard deviations are sufficiently close that we can assume $\sigma_1 = \sigma_2$.

(a) Use the method of pooled standard deviation to redo Problem 15(a).

(b) Use the method of pooled standard deviation to redo Problem 15(b).

21. H_0: $\mu_1 = \mu_2$; H_1: $\mu_1 < \mu_2$; for $d.f. = 9$, $\alpha = 0.01$ in the *one-tail area* row, the critical value $t_0 = -2.821$; sample test statistic $t = -0.965$ is not in the critical region; fail to reject H_0. This result is consistent with that obtained by the P-value method.

22. H_0: $\mu_1 = \mu_2$; H_1: $\mu_1 > \mu_2$; for $\alpha = 0.01$ and a right-tailed test, the critical value is $z_0 = 2.33$; sample test statistic $z = 2.57$ is in the critical region; reject H_0. This result is consistent with the result of the P-value method.

21. *Critical Region Method: Testing $\mu_1 - \mu_2$; σ_1, σ_2 Unknown* Redo Problem 11(a) using the critical region method, and compare your results to those obtained using the P-value method.

22. *Critical Region Method: Testing $\mu_1 - \mu_2$; σ_1, σ_2 Known* Redo Problem 7(a) using the critical region method, and compare your results to those obtained using the P-value method.

SECTION 10.3

Inferences About the Difference of Two Proportions $p_1 - p_2$

FOCUS POINTS

- Compute the sample test statistic and *P*-value for testing $p_1 - p_2$.
- Find confidence intervals for $p_1 - p_2$.

Testing a Difference of Proportions $p_1 - p_2$

Is the population proportion of people favoring more wilderness areas different between men and women, between younger people and older people, between ranchers and energy employees, etc.? To answer questions of this type, we explore the sampling distribution $\hat{p}_1 - \hat{p}_2$ from two independent binomial experiments.

THEOREM 10.3 Suppose we have two independent binomial experiments—that is, outcomes from one binomial experiment are in no way paired with outcomes from the other. We use the notation

Binomial Experiment 1	*Binomial Experiment 2*
n_1 = number of trials	n_2 = number of trials
r_1 = number of successes	r_2 = number of successes
p_1 = population probability of success on a single trial	p_2 = population probability of success on a single trial

For *large* values of n_1 and n_2, the distribution of sample differences

$$\hat{p}_1 - \hat{p}_2 = \frac{r_1}{n_1} - \frac{r_2}{n_2}$$

is closely approximated by a *normal distribution* with mean μ and standard deviation σ as shown:

$$\mu = p_1 - p_2 \qquad \sigma = \sqrt{\frac{p_1q_1}{n_1} + \frac{p_2q_2}{n_2}}$$

where $q_1 = 1 - p_1$ and $q_2 = 1 - p_2$.

Pooled estimate $\bar{p}$

For most practical problems involving a comparison of two binomial populations, the experimenters will want to test the null hypothesis $p_1 = p_2$. Consequently, this is the type of test we shall consider. Since the values of p_1 and p_2 are unknown, and since specific values are not assumed under the null hypothesis $p_1 = p_2$, the best estimate for the common value is the total number of successes $(r_1 + r_2)$ divided by the total number of trials $(n_1 + n_2)$. If we denote this *pooled estimate of proportion* by $\bar{p}$ (read "p bar"), then

$$\bar{p} = \frac{r_1 + r_2}{n_1 + n_2}$$

This formula gives the best sample estimate $\bar{p}$ for p_1 and p_2 *under the assumption that* $p_1 = p_2$. Also, $\bar{q} = 1 - \bar{p}$.

Criteria for using the normal approximation to the binomial

COMMENT For most practical applications, the sample sizes n_1 and n_2 are considered large samples if each of the four quantities

$$n_1\bar{p} \qquad n_1\bar{q} \qquad n_2\bar{p} \qquad n_2\bar{q}$$

is larger than 5 (see Section 7.6).

Theorem 10.3 leads to the following procedure for testing $p_1 - p_2$.

PROCEDURE

HOW TO TEST A DIFFERENCE OF PROPORTIONS $p_1 - p_2$

Consider two independent binomial experiments.

Binomial Experiment 1	***Binomial Experiment 2***
n_1 = number of trials	n_2 = number of trials
r_1 = number of successes out of n_1 trials	r_2 = number of successes out of n_2 trials
$\hat{p}_1 = \dfrac{r_1}{n_1}$	$\hat{p}_2 = \dfrac{r_2}{n_2}$
p_1 = population probability of success on a single trial	p_2 = population probability of success on a single trial

1. Use the *null hypothesis* of no difference, H_0: $p_1 - p_2 = 0$. In the context of the application, choose the *alternate hypothesis*. Set the *level of significance* α.
2. The null hypothesis claims that $p_1 = p_2$; therefore, *pooled best estimates* for the population probabilities of success and failure are

$$\bar{p} = \frac{r_1 + r_2}{n_1 + n_2} \quad \text{and} \quad \bar{q} = 1 - \bar{p}$$

The number of trials should be sufficiently large so that all four quantities $n_1\bar{p}$, $n_1\bar{q}$, $n_2\bar{p}$, and $n_2\bar{q}$ are each larger than 5. In this case you compute the sample *test statistic*

$$z = \frac{\hat{p}_1 - \hat{p}_2}{\sqrt{\dfrac{\bar{p}\,\bar{q}}{n_1} + \dfrac{\bar{p}\,\bar{q}}{n_2}}}$$

3. Use the standard normal distribution and a type of test, one-tailed or two-tailed, to find the *P-value* corresponding to the sample test statistic.
4. *Conclude the test.* If *P*-value $\leq \alpha$, then reject H_0. If *P*-value $> \alpha$, then do not reject H_0.
5. *Interpret your conclusion* in the context of the application.

EXAMPLE 7

TESTING THE DIFFERENCE OF PROPORTIONS

The Macek County Clerk wishes to improve voter registration. One method under consideration is to send reminders in the mail to all citizens in the county who are eligible to register. As part of a pilot study to determine if this method will actually improve voter registration, a random sample of 1250 potential voters was taken. This sample was then randomly divided into two groups.

Group 1: There were 625 people in this group. No reminders to register were sent to them. The number of potential voters from this group who registered was 295.

Group 2: This group also contained 625 people. Reminders were sent in the mail to each member in the group, and the number who registered to vote was 350.

The county clerk claims that the proportion of people who registered was significantly greater in group 2. On the basis of this claim, the clerk recommends that the project be funded for the entire population of Macek County. Use a 5% level

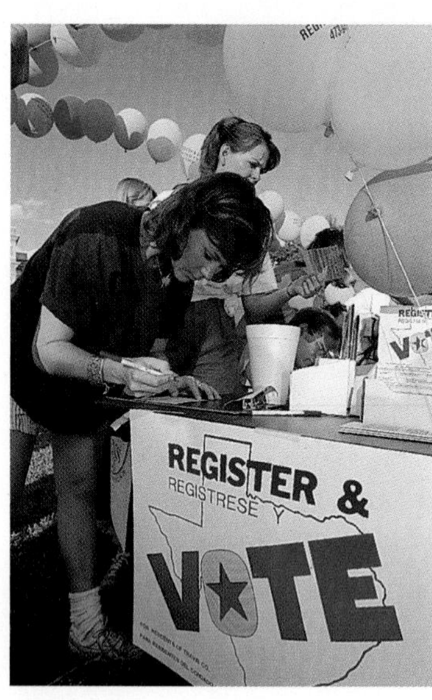

of significance to test the claim that the proportion of potential voters who registered was greater in group 2, the group that received reminders.

SOLUTION:

(a) Note that $\alpha = 0.05$. Let p_1 be the proportion of voters who registered from group 1, and let p_2 be the proportion who registered from group 2. The null hypothesis is that there is no difference in proportions, so

$$H_0: p_1 = p_2 \quad \text{or} \quad H_0: p_1 - p_2 = 0$$

The alternate hypothesis is that the proportion of voters who registered is greater for the group that received reminders.

$$H_1: p_1 < p_2 \quad \text{or} \quad H_1: p_1 - p_2 < 0$$

(b) Compute the sample statistic $\hat{p}_1 - \hat{p}_2$, and convert it to a z value.

CALCULATOR NOTE Carry the values for $\hat{p}_1$, $\hat{p}_2$, and the pooled estimates $\bar{p}$ and $\bar{q}$ to at least three places after the decimal. Then round the z value of the corresponding test statistic to two places after the decimal.

For the first group, the number of successes is $r_1 = 295$ out of $n_1 = 625$ trials. For the second group, there are $r_2 = 350$ successes out of $n_2 = 625$ trials. Since

$$\hat{p}_1 = \frac{r_1}{n_1} = \frac{295}{625} = 0.472 \quad \text{and} \quad \hat{p}_2 = \frac{r_2}{n_2} = \frac{350}{625} = 0.560$$

then

$$\hat{p}_1 - \hat{p}_2 = 0.472 - 0.560 = -0.088$$

To convert this $\hat{p}_1 - \hat{p}_2$ value to a z value, we need to find the *pooled estimate* $\bar{p}$ for the common values of p_1 and p_2, and the corresponding value for $\bar{q}$.

$$\bar{p} = \frac{r_1 + r_2}{n_1 + n_2} = \frac{295 + 350}{625 + 625} = 0.516 \quad \text{and} \quad \bar{q} = 1 - \bar{p} = 0.484$$

Using these values, we find that

$$z = \frac{\hat{p}_1 - \hat{p}_2}{\sqrt{\frac{\bar{p}\,\bar{q}}{n_1} + \frac{\bar{p}\,\bar{q}}{n_2}}} = \frac{-0.088}{\sqrt{\frac{(0.516)(0.484)}{625} + \frac{(0.516)(0.484)}{625}}} \approx -3.11$$

(c) Find the P-value and sketch the area on the standard normal curve.
Figure 10-9 shows the P-value. This is a left-tailed test, so the P-value is the area to the left of -3.11. Using the standard normal distribution (Table 3 of the Appendix), we find P-value $= P(z < -3.11) \approx 0.0009$.

FIGURE 10-9

P-value

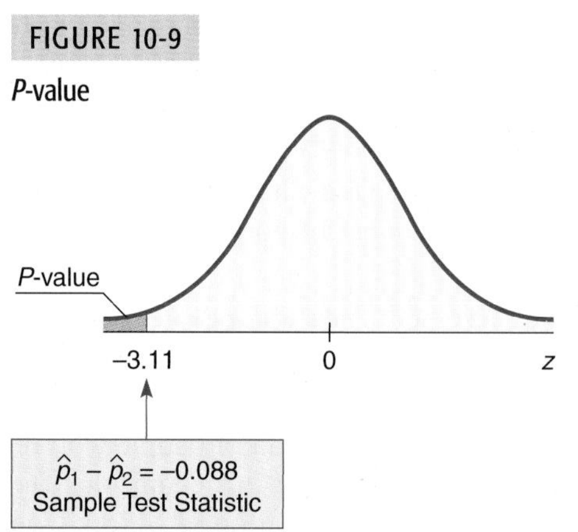

FIGURE 10-10

Critical Region, $\alpha = 0.05$

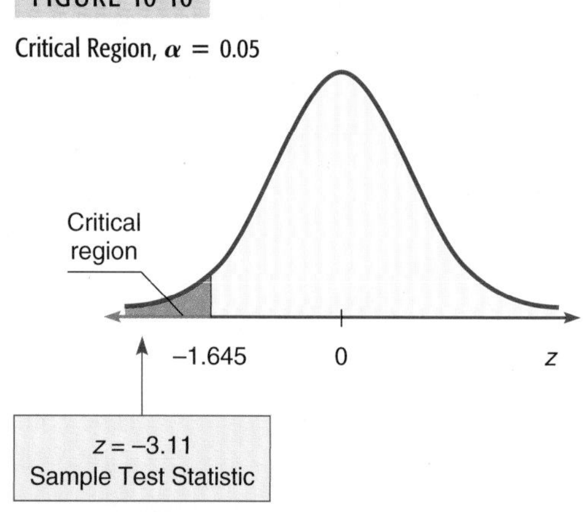

(d) Conclude the test.
Since P-value of $0.0009 \le 0.05$ for α, we reject H_0.

(e) Interpret the results.
At the 5% level of significance, the data indicate that the population proportion of potential voters who registered was greater in group 2, the group that received reminders.

(f) **Critical region method (optional):** Use the critical region method to conclude the test at the 5% level of significance. Compare your results with the P-value method.

In part (b), we found that the sample test statistic is $z = -3.11$. In Table 3(c) of the Appendix, we see that the critical value $z_0 = -1.645$ for a left-tailed test with $\alpha = 0.05$. In Figure 10-10, we see that the sample test statistic falls in the critical region, so we reject H_0. This conclusion is consistent with the conclusion obtained using the P-value method. There is sufficient evidence to conclude that at the 5% level of significance, the population of potential voters who registered was greater in the group receiving reminders.

GUIDED EXERCISE 6 Testing the difference of proportions

In Example 7 about voter registration, suppose that a random sample of 1100 potential voters was randomly divided into two groups.

Group 1: 500 potential voters; no registration reminders sent; 248 registered to vote

Group 2: 600 potential voters; registration reminders sent; 332 registered to vote

Do these data support the claim that the proportion of voters who registered was greater in the group that received reminders than in the group that did not? Use a 1% level of significance.

(a) What is α? State H_0 and H_1.

→ $\alpha = 0.01$. As before, H_0: $p_1 = p_2$ and H_1: $p_1 < p_2$.

(b) Under the null hypothesis $p_1 = p_2$, calculate the *pooled estimates* $\bar{p}$ and $\bar{q}$.

→ $n_1 = 500$, $r_1 = 248$; $n_2 = 600$, $r_2 = 332$

$$\bar{p} = \frac{r_1 + r_2}{n_1 + n_2} = \frac{248 + 332}{500 + 600} \approx 0.527$$

$$\bar{q} = 1 - \bar{p} \approx 1 - 0.527 \approx 0.473$$

(c) What is the value of the sample test statistic $\hat{p}_1 - \hat{p}_2$?

→ $$\hat{p}_1 = \frac{r_1}{n_1} = \frac{248}{500} = 0.496 \qquad \hat{p}_2 = \frac{r_2}{n_2} = \frac{332}{600} \approx 0.553$$

$$\hat{p}_1 - \hat{p}_2 = -0.057$$

(d) Convert the sample test statistic $\hat{p}_1 - \hat{p}_2 = -0.057$ to a z value.

→ $$z = \frac{\hat{p}_1 - \hat{p}_2}{\sqrt{\frac{\bar{p}\,\bar{q}}{n_1} + \frac{\bar{p}\,\bar{q}}{n_2}}} = \frac{-0.057}{\sqrt{\frac{(0.527)(0.473)}{500} + \frac{(0.527)(0.473)}{600}}} \approx -1.89$$

(e) Find the P-value and sketch the area on the standard normal curve.

→ Figure 10-11 on the next page shows the P-value. It is the area to the left of $z = -1.89$. Using Table 3 of the Appendix, we find P-value $= P(z < -1.89) = 0.0294$.

Continued

GUIDED EXERCISE 6 *continued*

FIGURE 10-11 *P*-value

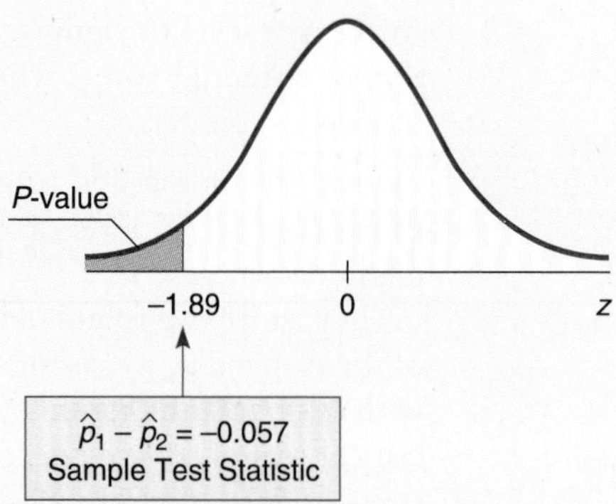

(f) Conclude the test and interpret the results in the context of the application.

Since *P*-value of 0.0294 > 0.01 for α, we cannot reject H_0. At the 1% level of significance, the data do not support the claim that the reminders increase the proportion of registered voters.

Estimating a Difference of Proportions $p_1 - p_2$

We conclude this section with a discussion of confidence intervals for $p_1 - p_2$, the difference of two proportions from two independent binomial probability distributions. Theorem 10.3 gives us the basis for constructing such confidence intervals. Using the notation of Theorem 10.3, recall that for sufficiently large sample sizes n_1 and n_2, the sampling distribution $\hat{p}_1 - \hat{p}_2$ of differences of proportions from two independent binomial probability distributions is approximately normal, with mean $\mu = p_1 - p_2$ and standard deviation $\sigma = \sqrt{p_1q_1/n_1 - p_2q_2/n_2}$.

There is one technical difficulty in computing the standard deviation σ of the $\hat{p}_1 - \hat{p}_2$ distribution. We don't know the values of p_1 or p_2. However, if all four quantities $n_1\hat{p}_1$, $n_1\hat{q}_1$, $n_2\hat{p}_2$, and $n_2\hat{q}_2$ are greater than 5, then a good approximation for the standard deviation σ of the $\hat{p}_1 - \hat{p}_2$ distribution is given by

$$\sigma \approx \hat{\sigma} = \sqrt{\frac{\hat{p}_1\hat{q}_1}{n_1} + \frac{\hat{p}_2\hat{q}_2}{n_2}}$$

This leads to the following procedure for confidence intervals.

PROCEDURE

HOW TO FIND A CONFIDENCE INTERVAL FOR $p_1 - p_2$

Consider two independent binomial experiments.

Binomial Experiment 1	***Binomial Experiment 2***
n_1 = number of trials	n_2 = number of trials
r_1 = number of successes out of n_1 trials	r_2 = number of successes out of n_2 trials
$\hat{p}_1 = \frac{r_1}{n_1}$; $\hat{q}_1 = 1 - \hat{p}_1$	$\hat{p}_2 = \frac{r_2}{n_2}$; $\hat{q}_2 = 1 - \hat{p}_2$
p_1 = population probability of success	p_2 = population probability of success

Continued

The number of trials should be sufficiently large so that all four of the following inequalities are true:

$$n_1\hat{p}_1 > 5; \quad n_1\hat{q}_1 > 5; \quad n_2\hat{p}_2 > 5; \quad n_2\hat{q}_2 > 5$$

Confidence interval for $p_1 - p_2$

$$(\hat{p}_1 - \hat{p}_2) - E \leq p_1 - p_2 \leq (\hat{p}_1 - \hat{p}_2) + E$$

where

$$E \approx z_c\hat{\sigma} = z_c\sqrt{\frac{\hat{p}_1\hat{q}_1}{n_1} + \frac{\hat{p}_2\hat{q}_2}{n_2}}$$

c = confidence level, $0 < c < 1$

z_c = critical value for confidence level c based on the standard normal distribution (See Table 3(b) of the Appendix for commonly used values.)

EXAMPLE 8 CONFIDENCE INTERVAL FOR $p_1 - p_2$

In his book *Secrets of Sleep*, Professor Borbely describes research on dreams in the sleep laboratory at the University of Zurich Medical School. During normal sleep, there is a phase known as *REM* (rapid eye movement). For most people, REM sleep occurs about every 90 minutes or so, and it is thought that dreams occur just before or during the REM phase. Using electronic equipment in the sleep laboratory, it is possible to detect the REM phase in a sleeping person. If a person is wakened immediately after the REM phase, he or she usually can describe a dream that has just taken place. Based on a study of over 650 people in the Zurich sleep laboratory, it was found that about one-third of all dream reports contain feelings of fear, anxiety, or aggression. There is a conjecture that if a person is in a good mood when going to sleep, the proportion of "bad" dreams (fear, anxiety, aggression) might be reduced.

Suppose that two groups of subjects were randomly chosen for a sleep study. In group I, before going to sleep, the subjects spent 1 hour watching a comedy movie. In this group, there were a total of $n_1 = 175$ dreams recorded, of which $r_1 = 49$ were dreams with feelings of anxiety, fear, or aggression. In group II, the subjects did not watch a movie but simply went to sleep. In this group, there were a total of $n_2 = 180$ dreams recorded, of which $r_2 = 63$ were dreams with feelings of anxiety, fear, or aggression.

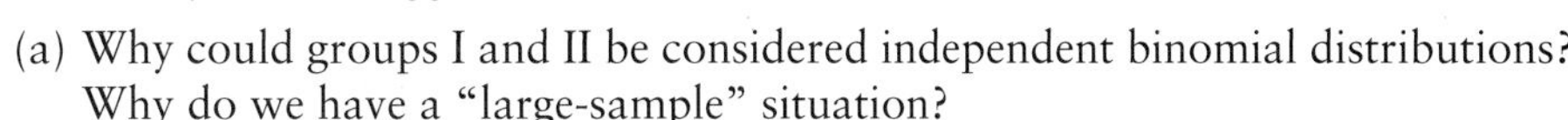

(a) Why could groups I and II be considered independent binomial distributions? Why do we have a "large-sample" situation?

SOLUTION: Since the two groups were chosen randomly, it is reasonable to assume that neither group's response would be related to the other's. In both groups, each recorded dream could be thought of as a trial, with success being a dream with feelings of fear, anxiety, or aggression.

$$\hat{p}_1 = \frac{r_1}{n_1} = \frac{49}{175} = 0.28 \quad \text{and} \quad \hat{q}_1 = 1 - \hat{p}_1 = 0.72$$

$$\hat{p}_2 = \frac{r_2}{n_2} = \frac{63}{180} = 0.35 \quad \text{and} \quad \hat{q}_2 = 1 - \hat{p}_2 = 0.65$$

Since

$$n_1\hat{p}_1 = 49 > 5 \qquad n_1\hat{q}_1 = 126 > 5$$

$$n_2\hat{p}_2 = 63 > 5 \qquad n_2\hat{q}_2 = 117 > 5$$

then large-sample theory is appropriate.

(b) What is $p_1 - p_2$? Compute a 95% confidence interval for $p_1 - p_2$.

SOLUTION: p_1 is the population proportion of successes (bad dreams) for all people who watch comedy movies before bed. Thus, p_1 can be thought of as the percentage of bad dreams for all people who are in a "good mood" when they go to bed. Likewise, p_2 is the percentage of bad dreams for the population of all people who just go to bed (no movie). The difference $p_1 - p_2$ is the population difference.

To find a confidence interval for $p_1 - p_2$, we need the values of z_c, $\hat{\sigma}$, and then E. From Table 3(b) of the Appendix, we see that $z_{0.95} = 1.96$, so

$$\hat{\sigma} = \sqrt{\frac{\hat{p}_1\hat{q}_1}{n_1} + \frac{\hat{p}_2\hat{q}_2}{n_2}} = \sqrt{\frac{(0.28)(0.72)}{175} + \frac{(0.35)(0.65)}{180}}$$

$$\approx \sqrt{0.0024} \approx 0.0492$$

$$E = z_c\hat{\sigma} = 1.96(0.0492) \approx 0.096$$

$$(\hat{p}_1 - \hat{p}_2) - E < p_1 - p_2 < (\hat{p}_1 - \hat{p}_2) + E$$

$$(0.28 - 0.35) - 0.096 < p_1 - p_2 < (0.28 - 0.35) + 0.096$$

$$-0.166 < p_1 - p_2 < 0.026$$

(c) Explain the meaning of the confidence interval that you constructed in part (b).

SOLUTION: We are 95% sure that the interval between −16.6% and 2.6% is one that contains the percentage difference of "bad" dreams for group I and group II. Since the interval −0.166 to 0.026 is not all negative (or all positive), we cannot say that $p_1 - p_2 < 0$ (or $p_1 - p_2 > 0$). Thus, at the 95% confidence level, we *cannot* conclude that $p_1 < p_2$ or $p_1 > p_2$. The comedy movies before bed help some people reduce the percentage of "bad" dreams, but at the 95% confidence level, we cannot say that the *population difference* is reduced.

TECH NOTES The TI-84Plus and TI-83Plus calculators and Minitab support both testing and confidence intervals for the difference of proportions.

TI-84Plus/TI-83Plus Use the STAT key and highlight **TESTS.** The menu choices **B:2-PropZInt** and **6:2-PropZTest** provide confidence intervals and testing, respectively. Note that the symbol x is used to designate the number of successes r.

Minitab Use the menu choices **STAT ➤ Basic Statistics ➤ 2 proportions.** In the dialogue box, under Options, select the null and alternate hypotheses and set the confidence level.

VIEWPOINT What's the difference?

Will two 15-minute piano lessons a week significantly improve a child's analytical reasoning skills? Why piano? Why not computer keyboard instruction or maybe voice lessons? Professor Frances Rauscher, University of Wisconsin, and Professor Gordon Shaw, University of California at Irvine, claim that there is a difference! How could this be measured? A large number of piano students were given complicated tests of mental ability. Independent control groups of other students were given the same tests. Techniques involving the study of differences of means and proportions were used to draw the conclusion that students taking piano lessons did better on tests measuring analytical reasoning skills (Reported in The Denver Post*).*

SECTION 10.3 PROBLEMS

1. *Statistical Literacy* Consider a hypothesis test of difference of proportions for two independent populations. Suppose random samples produce r_1 successes out of n_1 trials for the first population and r_2 successes out of n_2 trials for the second population. What is the sample test statistic for the test?

2. *Statistical Literacy* Consider a hypothesis test of difference of proportions for two independent populations. Suppose random samples produce r_1 successes out of n_1 trials for the first population and r_2 successes out of n_2 trials for the second population. What is the best pooled estimate $\bar{p}$ for the population probability of success using H_0: $p_1 = p_2$?

3. *Critical Thinking* Consider two independent populations for which the proportion of successes in the first population is p_1 and the proportion of successes in the second population is p_2. What alternate hypothesis would indicate that the proportion of successes p_1 in the first population is larger than the proportion of successes p_2 in the second population? Express the alternate hypothesis in two ways.

4. *Critical Thinking* If a 90% confidence interval for the difference of proportions contains some positive and some negative values, what can we conclude about the relationship between p_1 and p_2 at the 90% confidence level?

Please provide the following information for Problems 5–10.

(a) What is the level of significance? State the null and alternate hypotheses.

(b) What sampling distribution will you use? What assumptions are you making? What is the value of the sample test statistic?

(c) Find the *P*-value. Sketch the sampling distribution and show the area corresponding to the *P*-value.

(d) Based on your answers in parts (a) to (c), will you reject or fail to reject the null hypothesis? Are the data statistically significant at level α?

(e) State your conclusion in the context of the application.

Note: Answers may vary due to rounding.

5. *Federal Tax Money: Art Funding* Would you favor spending more federal tax money on the arts? This question was asked by a research group on behalf of *The National Institute* (Reference: *Painting by Numbers*, J. Wypijewski, University of California Press). Of a random sample of $n_1 = 220$ women, $r_1 = 59$ responded yes. Another random sample of $n_2 = 175$ men showed that $r_2 = 56$ responded yes. Does this information indicate a difference (either way) between the population proportion of women and the population proportion of men who favor spending more federal tax dollars on the arts? Use $\alpha = 0.05$.

6. *Art Funding: Politics* Would you favor spending more federal tax money on the arts? This question was asked by a research group on behalf of *The National Institute* (Reference: *Painting by Numbers*, J. Wypijewski, University of California Press). Of a random sample of $n_1 = 93$ politically conservative voters, $r_1 = 21$ responded yes. Another random sample of $n_2 = 83$ politically moderate voters showed that $r_2 = 22$ responded yes. Does this information indicate that the population proportion of conservative voters inclined to spend more federal tax money on funding the arts is less than the proportion of moderate voters so inclined? Use $\alpha = 0.05$.

7. *Sociology: Trusting People* Generally speaking, would you say that most people can be trusted? A random sample of $n_1 = 250$ people in Chicago ages 18–25 showed that $r_1 = 45$ said yes. Another random sample of $n_2 = 280$ people in Chicago ages 35–45 showed that $r_2 = 71$ said yes (based on information from the *National Opinion Research Center*, University of Chicago). Does this indicate that the population proportion of trusting people in Chicago is higher for the older group? Use $\alpha = 0.05$.

1. $\hat{p}_1 - \hat{p}_2$, where $\hat{p}_1 = r_1/n_1$ and $\hat{p}_2 = r_2/n_2$.
2. $\bar{p} = \dfrac{r_1 + r_2}{n_1 + n_2}$.
3. H_1: $p_1 > p_2$; H_1: $p_1 - p_2 > 0$.
4. There is no difference between p_1 and p_2.
4. There is no difference between p_1 and p_2.
5. (a) $\alpha = 0.05$; H_0: $p_1 = p_2$; H_1: $p_1 \neq p_2$.
   (b) Standard normal; $\bar{p} \approx 0.2911$; $\hat{p}_1 - \hat{p}_2 \approx -0.052$; $z \approx -1.13$.
   (c) P-value $= 2P(z < -1.13) \approx 2(0.1292) = 0.2584$; on standard normal curve, shade area to the right of 1.13 and to the left of -1.13.
   (d) P-value of $0.2584 > 0.05$ for α; fail to reject H_0.
   (e) At the 5% level of significance, there is insufficient evidence to conclude that the population proportion of women favoring more tax dollars for the arts is different from the proportion of men.
6. (a) $\alpha = 0.05$; H_0: $p_1 = p_2$; H_1: $p_1 < p_2$.
   (b) Standard normal; $\bar{p} \approx 0.2443$; $\hat{p}_1 - \hat{p}_2 \approx -0.039$; $z \approx -0.61$.
   (c) P-value $\approx P(z < -0.61) \approx 0.2709$; on standard normal curve, shade area to the left of -0.61.
   (d) P-value of $0.2709 > 0.05$ for α; fail to reject H_0.
   (e) At the 5% level of significance, there is insufficient evidence to conclude that the population proportion of conservative voters who favor more tax dollars for the arts is less than the proportion of moderate voters.
7. (a) $\alpha = 0.05$; H_0: $p_1 = p_2$; H_1: $p_1 < p_2$.
   (b) Standard normal; $\bar{p} \approx 0.2189$; $\hat{p}_1 - \hat{p}_2 \approx -0.074$; $z \approx -2.06$.
   (c) P-value $\approx P(z < -2.06) \approx 0.0197$; on standard normal curve, shade area to the left of -2.04.
   (d) P-value of $0.0197 \leq 0.05$ for α; reject H_0.
   (e) At the 5% level of significance, there is sufficient evidence to conclude that the population proportion of trusting people in Chicago is higher for the older group.

8. *Political Science: Voters* This problem is based on information taken from *Life in America's Fifty States,* by G. S. Thomas. A random sample of $n_1 = 288$ voters registered in the state of California showed that 141 voted in the last general election. A random sample of $n_2 = 216$ registered voters in the state of Colorado showed that 125 voted in the most recent general election. Do these data indicate that the population proportion of voter turnout in Colorado is higher than that in California? Use a 5% level of significance.

9. *Extraterrestrials: Believe It?* Based on information from *Harper's Index,* $r_1 = 37$ out of a random sample of $n_1 = 100$ adult Americans who did not attend college believe in extraterrestrials. However, out of a random sample of $n_2 = 100$ adult Americans who did attend college, $r_2 = 47$ claim that they believe in extraterrestrials. Does this indicate that the proportion of people who attended college and who believe in extraterrestrials is higher than the proportion who did not attend college? Use $\alpha = 0.01$.

10. *Art: Politics* Do you prefer paintings in which the people are fully clothed? This question was asked by a professional survey group on behalf of the National Arts Society (see reference in Problem 6). A random sample of $n_1 = 59$ people who are conservative voters showed that $r_1 = 45$ said yes. Another random sample of $n_2 = 62$ people who are liberal voters showed that $r_2 = 36$ said yes. Does this indicate that the population proportion of conservative voters who prefer art with fully clothed people is higher? Use $\alpha = 0.05$.

11. *Critical Region Method: Testing $p_1 - p_2$* Redo Problem 5 using the critical region method, and compare your results to those obtained using the *P*-value method.

12. *Critical Region Method: Testing $p_1 - p_2$* Redo Problem 6 using the critical region method, and compare your results to those obtained using the *P*-value method.

13. *Myers-Briggs: Marriage Counseling* Isabel Myers was a pioneer in the study of personality types. She identified four basic personality preferences that are described at length in the book *A Guide to the Development and Use of the Myers-Briggs Type Indicator,* by Myers and McCaulley (Consulting Psychologists Press). Marriage counselors know that couples who have none of the four preferences in common may have a stormy marriage. Myers took a random sample of 375 married couples and found that 289 had two or more personality preferences in common. In another random sample of 571 married couples, it was found that only 23 had no preferences in common. Let p_1 be the population proportion of all married couples who have two or more personality preferences in common. Let p_2 be the population proportion of all married couples who have no personality preferences in common.
(a) Find a 99% confidence interval for $p_1 - p_2$.
(b) *Interpretation:* Explain the meaning of the confidence interval in part (a) in the context of this problem. Does the confidence interval contain all positive, all negative, or both positive and negative numbers? What does this tell you (at the 99% confidence level) about the proportion of married couples with two or more personality preferences in common compared with the proportion of married couples sharing no personality preferences in common?

14. *Myers-Briggs: Marriage Counseling* Most married couples have two or three personality preferences in common (see reference in Problem 13). Myers used a random sample of 375 married couples and found that 132 had three preferences in common. Another random sample of 571 couples showed that 217 had two personality preferences in common. Let p_1 be the population proportion of all married couples who have three personality preferences in common. Let p_2 be the population proportion of all married couples who have two personality preferences in common.
(a) Find a 90% confidence interval for $p_1 - p_2$.
(b) *Interpretation:* Examine the confidence interval in part (a) and explain what it means in the context of this problem. Does the confidence interval contain

8. (a) $\alpha = 0.05$; H_0: $p_1 = p_2$; H_1: $p_1 < p_2$.
(b) Standard normal; $\bar{p} \approx 0.5278$; $\hat{p}_1 - \hat{p}_2 \approx -0.0891$; $z \approx -1.98$.
(c) *P*-value $\approx P(z < -1.98) \approx 0.0239$; on standard normal curve, shade area to the left of -1.98.
(d) *P*-value of $0.0239 \le 0.05$ for α; reject H_0.
(e) At the 5% level of significance, there is sufficient evidence to conclude that the population proportion of voter turnout in Colorado is greater than that in California.

9. (a) $\alpha = 0.01$; H_0: $p_1 = p_2$; H_1: $p_1 < p_2$.
(b) Standard normal; $\bar{p} = 0.42$; $\hat{p}_1 - \hat{p}_2 \approx -0.10$; $z \approx -1.43$.
(c) *P*-value $\approx P(z < -1.43) \approx 0.0764$; on standard normal curve, shade area to the left of -1.43.
(d) *P*-value of $0.0764 > 0.01$ for α; fail to reject H_0.
(e) At the 1% level of significance, there is insufficient evidence to conclude that the population proportion of adults who believe in extraterrestrials and who attended college is higher than the proportion who did not attend college.

10. (a) $\alpha = 0.05$; H_0: $p_1 = p_2$; H_1: $p_1 > p_2$.
(b) Standard normal; $\bar{p} \approx 0.6694$; $\hat{p}_1 - \hat{p}_2 \approx 0.182$; $z \approx 2.13$.
(c) *P*-value $\approx P(z > 2.13) \approx 0.0166$; on standard normal curve, shade area to the right of 2.13.
(d) *P*-value of $0.0166 \le 0.05$ for α; reject H_0.
(e) At the 5% level of significance, there is sufficient evidence to conclude that the population proportion of conservative voters who prefer art with fully clothed people is higher.

11. H_0: $p_1 = p_2$; H_1: $p_1 \ne p_2$; for $\alpha = 0.05$ and a two-tailed test, the critical values are $\pm z_0 = \pm 1.96$; sample test statistic $z = -1.13$ is not in the critical region; fail to reject H_0. This result is consistent with the result of the *P*-value method.

12. H_0: $p_1 = p_2$; H_1: $p_1 < p_2$; for $\alpha = 0.05$ and a left-tailed test, the critical value is $z_0 = -1.645$; sample test statistic $z = -0.61$ is not in the critical region; fail to reject H_0. This result is consistent with the result of the *P*-value method.

13. (a) $\hat{\sigma} = 0.0232$; $E = 0.0599$; interval from 0.67 to 0.79.
(b) Because the interval contains all positive values, $p_1 > p_2$ at the 99% level.

14. (a) $\hat{p}_1 = 0.3520$; $\hat{p}_2 = 0.3800$; $\hat{\sigma} = 0.032$; -0.08 to 0.02.
(b) No difference.

all positive, all negative, or both positive and negative numbers? What does this tell you about the proportion of married couples with three personality preferences in common compared with the proportion of couples with two preferences in common (at the 90% confidence level)?

15. (a) $\hat{p}_1 = 0.3095$; $\hat{p}_2 = 0.1184$; $\hat{\sigma} = 0.0413$; 0.085 to 0.297.
(b) Interval contains all positive values. At the 99% confidence level, a greater proportion of hogans occur in Fort Defiance.

15. *Navajo Culture: Traditional Hogans* S. C. Jett is a professor of geography at the University of California, Davis. He and a colleague, V. E. Spencer, are experts on modern Navajo culture and geography. The following information is taken from their book *Navajo Architecture: Forms, History, Distributions* (University of Arizona Press). On the Navajo Reservation, a random sample of 210 permanent dwellings in the Fort Defiance region showed that 65 were traditional Navajo hogans. In the Indian Wells region, a random sample of 152 permanent dwellings showed that 18 were traditional hogans. Let p_1 be the population proportion of all traditional hogans in the Fort Defiance region, and let p_2 be the population proportion of all traditional hogans in the Indian Wells region.
(a) Find a 99% confidence interval for $p_1 - p_2$.
(b) *Interpretation:* Examine the confidence interval and comment on its meaning. Does it include numbers that are all positive? all negative? mixed? What if it is hypothesized that Navajo who follow the traditional culture of their people tend to occupy hogans? Comment on the confidence interval for $p_1 - p_2$ in this context.

16. (a) $\hat{p}_1 = 0.6161$; $\hat{p}_2 = 0.1857$; $\hat{\sigma} = 0.05650$; 0.28 to 0.58.
(b) At the 99% confidence level, a greater proportion of artifacts seem to be unidentified at higher elevations.

16. *Archaeology: Cultural Affiliation* "Unknown cultural affiliations and loss of identity at high elevations." These are words used to propose the hypothesis that archaeological sites tend to lose their identity as altitude extremes are reached. This idea is based on the notion that prehistoric people tended *not* to take trade wares to temporary settings and/or isolated areas (Source: *Prehistoric New Mexico: Background for Survey*, by D. E. Stuart and R. P. Gauthier, University of New Mexico Press). As elevation zones of prehistoric people (in what is now the state of New Mexico) increased, there seemed to be a loss of artifact identification. Consider the following information.

Elevation Zone	Number of Artifacts	Number Unidentified
7000–7500 ft	112	69
5000–5500 ft	140	26

Let p_1 be the population proportion of unidentified archaeological artifacts at the elevation zone 7000–7500 ft in the given archaeological area. Let p_2 be the population proportion of unidentified archaeological artifacts at the elevation zone 5000–5500 ft in the given archaeological area.
(a) Find a 99% confidence interval for $p_1 - p_2$.
(b) *Interpretation:* Explain the meaning of the confidence interval in part (a) in the context of this problem. Does the confidence interval contain all positive numbers? all negative numbers? both positive and negative numbers? What does this tell you (at the 99% confidence level) about the population proportion of unidentified artifacts at high elevations (7000–7500 ft) compared with the population proportion of unidentified artifacts at lower elevations (5000–5500 ft)? How does this relate to the stated hypothesis?

Problem 17 contains a good topic for class discussion.

17. (a) Yes; no.
(b) No; yes.

17. *Critical Thinking: Different Confidence Levels*
(a) Suppose that a 95% confidence interval for a difference of proportions contains both positive and negative numbers. Will a 99% confidence interval based on the same data necessarily contain both positive and negative numbers? Explain. What about a 90% confidence interval? Explain.
(b) Suppose that a 95% confidence interval for a difference of proportions contains all positive numbers. Will a 99% confidence interval based on the same data necessarily contain all positive numbers as well? Explain. What about a 90% confidence interval? Explain.

18. (a) $\hat{p}_1 = 0.5696$; 0.53 to 0.61.
(b) $\hat{p}_2 = 0.3354$; 0.30 to 0.37.
(c) $\hat{\sigma} = 0.0282$; 0.18 to 0.29.
(d) At the 95% confidence level, it appears that separated nesting boxes yield more successful hatches.

18. *Focus Problem: Wood Duck Nests* In the Focus Problem at the beginning of this chapter, a study was described comparing the hatch ratios of wood duck nesting boxes. Group I nesting boxes were well separated from each other and well hidden by available brush. There were a total of 474 eggs in group I boxes, of which a field count showed about 270 hatched. Group II nesting boxes were placed in highly visible locations and grouped closely together. There were a total of 805 eggs in group II boxes, of which a field count showed about 270 hatched.
(a) Find a point estimate $\hat{p}_1$ for p_1, the proportion of eggs that hatch in group I nest box placements. Find a 95% confidence interval for p_1.
(b) Find a point estimate $\hat{p}_2$ for p_2, the proportion of eggs that hatch in group II nest box placements. Find a 95% confidence interval for p_2.
(c) Find a 95% confidence interval for $p_1 - p_2$. Does the interval indicate that the proportion of eggs hatched from group I nest boxes is higher than, lower than, or equal to the proportion of eggs hatched from group II nest boxes?
(d) ***Interpretation:*** What conclusions about placement of nest boxes can be drawn? In the article discussed in the Focus Problem, additional concerns are raised about the higher cost of placing and maintaining group I nest boxes. Also at issue is the cost efficiency per successful wood duck hatch.

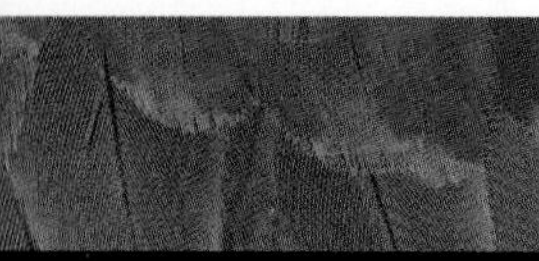

Chapter Review

SUMMARY

In this chapter, we continued the discussion of hypothesis testing and confidence intervals. In particular, we looked at inferences involving paired differences, difference of means and difference of proportions.

- The first task is to determine whether two samples are independent or dependent. Two samples are dependent if each data value in one population can be paired in a meaningful way with a corresponding data value in the other population. Two samples are independent if the selection of data drawn from one population is completely unrelated to the selection of data drawn from the other population.
- Section 10.1 presented the paired difference test for difference of means $\bar{d}$ from dependent samples. The Student's t distribution is used. See procedure displays in Section 10.1 for specific formulas and methods.
- Section 10.2 presented inferences regarding the parameter $\mu_1 - \mu_2$ from independent populations. Both hypothesis tests and confidence intervals were discussed. Depending on our knowledge of population standard deviations, either the normal distribution or the Student's t distribution is used. See procedure displays in Section 10.2.
- Section 10.3 presented inferences regarding the parameter $p_1 - p_2$ from large independent populations. Both hypothesis tests and confidence intervals were discussed. For testing procedures, the pooled estimate for the proportion $\bar{p}$ of successes is used. For sufficiently large numbers of trials, the normal distribution is employed for both confidence intervals and testing. See procedure displays in Section 10.3.

IMPORTANT WORDS & SYMBOLS

Section 10.1
Dependent samples
Data pairs
μ_d, difference of means from data pairs

Section 10.2
Independent samples
d.f. for testing $\mu_1 - \mu_2$ when σ_1 and σ_2 are unknown
Pooled standard deviation

Section 10.3
Pooled estimate of proportion $\bar{p}$

VIEWPOINT Who Watches Cable TV?

Consider the following claim: Average cable TV viewers are, generally speaking, as affluent as newspaper readers and better off than radio or magazine audiences. How do we know that this claim is true? One way to answer such a question is to construct several individual tests of difference of means. One test would compare cable TV viewers with newspaper readers, a second test would compare cable TV viewers with radio audiences, and a third test would compare cable TV viewers with magazine audiences. Another way to handle all three tests at once would be to use techniques of ANOVA (analysis of variance)—a subject often introduced in a second course in statistics. For more information and data, see American Demographics *(Vol. 17, No. 6).*

CHAPTER REVIEW PROBLEMS

1. *Statistical Literacy* When are two random samples independent?

2. *Statistical Literacy* When are two random samples dependent?

For each hypothesis test in Problems 3–10, please provide the following information.

(i) What is the level of significance? State the null and alternate hypotheses.
(ii) What sampling distribution will you use? What assumptions are you making? What is the value of the sample test statistic?
(iii) Find (or estimate) the *P*-value. Sketch the sampling distribution and show the area corresponding to the *P*-value.
(iv) Based on your answers in parts (i) to (iii), will you reject or fail to reject the null hypothesis? Are the data statistically significant at level α?
(v) Interpret your conclusion in the context of the application.

Note: For degrees of freedom *d.f.* not in the Student's *t* table, use the closest *d.f.* that is smaller. In some cases, this choice will increase the *P*-value by a small amount or increase the length of a confidence interval, thereby making the answer slightly more "conservative." Answers may vary due to rounding.

3. *Agriculture: Bell Peppers* The following data represent soil water content (percent water by volume) for independent random samples of soil taken from two experimental fields growing bell peppers (Reference: *Journal of Agricultural, Biological, and Environmental Statistics*). *Note:* These data are also available for download at the Online Study Center.

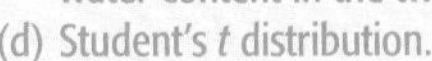

Soil water content from field I: x_1; $n_1 = 72$

15.1	11.2	10.3	10.8	16.6	8.3	9.1	12.3	9.1	14.3
10.7	16.1	10.2	15.2	8.9	9.5	9.6	11.3	14.0	11.3
15.6	11.2	13.8	9.0	8.4	8.2	12.0	13.9	11.6	16.0
9.6	11.4	8.4	8.0	14.1	10.9	13.2	13.8	14.6	10.2
11.5	13.1	14.7	12.5	10.2	11.8	11.0	12.7	10.3	10.8
11.0	12.6	10.8	9.6	11.5	10.6	11.7	10.1	9.7	9.7
11.2	9.8	10.3	11.9	9.7	11.3	10.4	12.0	11.0	10.7
8.8	11.1								

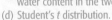

1. Two random samples are independent if the selection of sample data from one population is completely unrelated to the selection of sample data from the other population.
2. Two random samples are dependent if each data value in one sample can be paired in a meaningful way with a corresponding data value in the other sample.
3. Difference of means.
   (a) Use a calculator.
   (b) −0.06 to 1.6.
   (c) We cannot conclude at the 95% confidence level that there is any difference in soil water content in the two fields.
   (d) Student's *t* distribution.
   (e) (i) $\alpha = 0.01$; H_0: $\mu_1 = \mu_2$; H_1: $\mu_1 > \mu_2$.
   (ii) Student's *t*; *d.f.* = 71 (use *d.f.* = 70 in Table 4 of the Appendix); $t \approx 1.841$. For TI-84, *P*-value ≈ 0.034 with *d.f.* ≈ 140.5.
   (iii) 0.025 < *P*-value < 0.050; on *t* graph, shade area to the right of 1.841.
   (iv) *P*-value > 0.01 for α; fail to reject H_0.
   (v) At the 1% level of significance, the evidence does not show that the population mean soil water content of the first field is higher than that of the second.

Soil water content from field II: x_2; $n_2 = 80$

12.1	10.2	13.6	8.1	13.5	7.8	11.8	7.7	8.1	9.2
14.1	8.9	13.9	7.5	12.6	7.3	14.9	12.2	7.6	8.9
13.9	8.4	13.4	7.1	12.4	7.6	9.9	26.0	7.3	7.4
14.3	8.4	13.2	7.3	11.3	7.5	9.7	12.3	6.9	7.6
13.8	7.5	13.3	8.0	11.3	6.8	7.4	11.7	11.8	7.7
12.6	7.7	13.2	13.9	10.4	12.8	7.6	10.7	10.7	10.9
12.5	11.3	10.7	13.2	8.9	12.9	7.7	9.7	9.7	11.4
11.9	13.4	9.2	13.4	8.8	11.9	7.1	8.5	14.0	14.2

(a) Use a calculator with mean and standard deviation keys to verify that $\bar{x}_1 \approx 11.42$, $s_1 \approx 2.08$, $\bar{x}_2 \approx 10.65$, and $s_2 \approx 3.03$.

(b) Let μ_1 be the population mean for x_1 and let μ_2 be the population mean for x_2. Find a 95% confidence interval for $\mu_1 - \mu_2$.

(c) Examine the confidence interval and explain what it means in the context of this problem. Does the interval consist of numbers that are all positive? all negative? of different signs? At the 95% level of confidence, is the population mean soil water content of the first field higher than that of the second field?

(d) Which distribution (standard normal or Student's t) did you use? Why? Do you need information about the soil water content distributions?

(e) Use $\alpha = 0.01$ to test the claim that the population mean soil water content of the first field is higher than that of the second.

4. *Stocks: Retail and Utility* How profitable are different sectors of the stock market? One way to answer such a question is to examine profit as a percentage of stockholder equity. A random sample of 32 retail stocks such as Toys 'Я' Us, Best Buy, and Gap was studied for x_1, profit as a percentage of stockholder equity. The result was $\bar{x}_1 = 13.7$. A random sample of 34 utility (gas and electric) stocks such as Boston Edison, Wisconsin Energy, and Texas Utilities was studied for x_2, profit as a percentage of stockholder equity. The result was $\bar{x}_2 = 10.1$ (Source: *Fortune 500*, Vol. 135, No. 8). Assume $\sigma_1 = 4.1$ and $\sigma_2 = 2.7$.

(a) Let μ_1 represent the population mean profit as a percentage of stockholder equity for retail stocks, and let μ_2 represent the population mean profit as a percentage of stockholder equity for utility stocks. Find a 95% confidence interval for $\mu_1 - \mu_2$.

(b) Examine the confidence interval and explain what it means in the context of this problem. Does the interval consist of numbers that are all positive? all negative? of different signs? At the 95% level of confidence, does it appear that the profit as a percentage of stockholder equity for retail stocks is higher than that for utility stocks?

(c) Test the claim that the profit as a percentage of stockholder equity for retail stocks is higher than that for utility stocks. Use $\alpha = 0.01$.

5. *Wildlife: Wolves* A random sample of 18 adult male wolves from the Canadian Northwest Territories gave an average weight $\bar{x}_1 = 98$ lb with estimated sample standard deviation $s_1 = 6.5$ lb. Another sample of 24 adult male wolves from Alaska gave an average weight $\bar{x}_2 = 90$ lb with estimated sample standard deviation $s_2 = 7.3$ lb (Source: *The Wolf*, by L. D. Mech, University of Minnesota Press).

(a) Let μ_1 represent the population mean weight of adult male wolves from the Northwest Territories, and let μ_2 represent the population mean weight of adult male wolves from Alaska. Find a 75% confidence interval for $\mu_1 - \mu_2$.

(b) Examine the confidence interval and explain what it means in the context of this problem. Does the interval consist of numbers that are all positive? all negative? of different signs? At the 75% level of confidence, does it appear that the average weight of adult male wolves from the Northwest Territories is greater than that of the Alaska wolves?

4. Difference of means.
(a) 1.91% to 5.29%.
(b) Yes. It appears that profit as a percentage of stockholder equity is higher for retail stocks.
(c) (i) $\alpha = 0.01$; H_0: $\mu_1 = \mu_2$; H_1: $\mu_1 > \mu_2$.
(ii) Normal distribution; $z \approx 4.19$.
(iii) P-value ≈ 0.000 (to three decimal places). Shade area to the right of 4.19 on the normal curve.
(iv) P-value $< \alpha = 0.01$; reject H_0.
(v) At the 1% level of significance, there is sufficient evidence to say that the stockholder equity for retail stocks is higher than that for utility stocks.

5. Difference of means.
(a) $d.f. \approx 17$; $E \approx 2.5$; interval from 5.5 to 10.5 lb.
(b) At the 75% level of confidence, it appears that the average weight of adult male wolves from the Northwest Territories is greater.
(c) (i) $\alpha = 0.01$; H_0: $\mu_1 = \mu_2$; H_1: $\mu_1 \neq \mu_2$.
(ii) Student's t; $d.f. = 17$; $t \approx 3.743$.
(iii) $0.001 < P$-value < 0.010; on t graph, shade area to the right of 3.743 and to the left of -3.743.
(iv) P-value ≤ 0.01 for α; reject H_0.
(v) At the 1% level of significance, the evidence is sufficient to conclude that the average weight of adult male wolves in the Northwest Territories is different from that of Alaska wolves.

6. Difference of means.
   (a) $d.f. = 5$; $E \approx 0.9$; interval from 1.2 to 3 pups per den.
   (b) Yes. It appears that the average litter size of wolf pups in Ontario is greater.
   (c) (i) $\alpha = 0.01$; H_0: $\mu_1 = \mu_2$; H_1: $\mu_1 > \mu_2$.
   (ii) Student's t distribution; $d.f. = 5$; $t \approx 3.84$.
   (iii) $0.005 < P\text{-value} < 0.010$. Shade area to the right of 3.84 on the Student's t curve. For TI-84, $d.f. \approx 7.61$; $P\text{-value} \approx 0.003$.
   (iv) $P\text{-value} < \alpha = 0.01$; reject H_0.
   (v) At the 1% level of significance, there is sufficient evidence to say that average litter size of wolf pups in Ontario is greater than the average litter size in Finland.
7. Difference of proportions.
   (a) $\hat{p}_1 = 0.8495$; $\hat{p}_2 = 0.8916$; -0.1409 to 0.0567.
   (b) No. The interval contains both negative and positive numbers. We do not detect a difference in the proportions at the 95% confidence level.
   (c) (i) $\alpha = 0.05$; H_0: $p_1 = p_2$; H_1: $p_1 \neq p_2$.
   (ii) Normal distribution; $z \approx -0.83$.
   (iii) $P\text{-value} = 2(0.2033) = 0.4066$; on the normal graph, shade area to the left of -0.83 and to the right of 0.83.
   (iv) P-value of $0.4066 > \alpha = 0.05$; fail to reject H_0.
   (v) At the 5% level of significance, there is insufficient evidence to conclude that the proportion of accurate responses from face-to-face interviews differs from the proportion for telephone interviews.
8. Difference of two proportions.
   (a) $\hat{p}_1 = 0.533$; $\hat{p}_2 = 0.5435$; -0.2027 to 0.1823.
   (b) No. At the 90% confidence level, we do not detect any differences in the proportions.
   (c) (i) $\alpha = 0.05$; H_0: $p_1 = p_2$; H_1: $p_1 \neq p_2$.
   (ii) Normal distribution; $z \approx -0.09$.
   (iii) $P\text{-value} \approx 0.9282$; shade area to the left of -0.09 together with area to the right of 0.09 on the normal curve.
   (iv) $P\text{-value} > \alpha = 0.05$; fail to reject H_0.
   (v) At the 5% level of significance, there is insufficient evidence to say that there is a difference in the proportion of accurate responses from face-to-face interviews compared with telephone interviews.

(c) Test the claim that the average weight of adult male wolves from the Northwest Territories is different from that of Alaska wolves. Use $\alpha = 0.01$.

6. *Wildlife: Wolves* A random sample of 17 wolf litters in Ontario, Canada, gave an average of $\bar{x}_1 = 4.9$ wolf pups per litter with estimated sample standard deviation $s_1 = 1.0$. Another random sample of 6 wolf litters in Finland gave an average of $\bar{x}_2 = 2.8$ wolf pups per litter with sample standard deviation $s_2 = 1.2$ (see source for Problem 5).
   (a) Find an 85% confidence interval for $\mu_1 - \mu_2$, the difference in population mean litter size between Ontario and Finland.
   (b) Examine the confidence interval and explain what it means in the context of this problem. Does the interval consist of numbers that are all positive? all negative? of different signs? At the 85% level of confidence, does it appear that the average litter size of wolf pups in Ontario is greater than the average litter size in Finland?
   (c) Test the claim that the average litter size of wolf pups in Ontario is greater than the average litter size of wolf pups in Finland. Use $\alpha = 0.01$.

7. *Survey Response: Validity* The book *Survey Responses: An Evaluation of Their Validity*, by E. J. Wentland and K. Smith (Academic Press), includes studies reporting accuracy of answers to questions from surveys. A study by Locander et al. considered the question, "Are you a registered voter?" Accuracy of response was confirmed by a check of city voting records. Two methods of survey were used: a face-to-face interview and a telephone interview. A random sample of 93 people was asked the voter registration question face-to-face. Seventy-nine respondents gave accurate answers (as verified by city records). Another random sample of 83 people was asked the same question during a telephone interview. Seventy-four respondents gave accurate answers. Assume that the samples are representative of the general population.
   (a) Let p_1 be the population proportion of all people who answer the voter registration question accurately during a face-to-face interview. Let p_2 be the population proportion of all people who answer the question accurately during a telephone interview. Find a 95% confidence interval for $p_1 - p_2$.
   (b) Does the interval contain numbers that are all positive? all negative? mixed? Comment on the meaning of the confidence interval in the context of this problem. At the 95% level, do you detect any difference in the proportion of accurate responses from face-to-face interviews compared with the proportion of accurate responses from telephone interviews?
   (c) Test the claim that there is a difference in the proportion of accurate responses from face-to-face interviews compared with telephone interviews. Use $\alpha = 0.05$.

8. *Survey Response: Validity* Locander et al. (see reference in Problem 7) also studied the accuracy of responses on questions involving more sensitive material than voter registration. From public records, individuals were identified as having been charged with drunken driving not less than 6 months or more than 12 months from the starting date of the study. Two random samples from this group were studied. In the first sample of 30 individuals, the respondents were asked in a face-to-face interview if they had been charged with drunken driving in the last 12 months. Of these 30 people interviewed face-to-face, 16 answered the question accurately. The second random sample consisted of 46 people who had been charged with drunken driving. During a telephone interview, 25 of these responded accurately to the question asking if they had been charged with drunken driving during the past 12 months. Assume that the samples are representative of all people recently charged with drunken driving.
   (a) Let p_1 represent the population proportion of all people with recent charges of drunken driving who respond accurately to a face-to-face interview asking if they have been charged with drunken driving during the past 12 months.

Let p_2 represent the population proportion of people who respond accurately to the same question when it is asked in a telephone interview. Find a 90% confidence interval for $p_1 - p_2$.

(b) Does the interval found in part (a) contain numbers that are all positive? all negative? mixed? Comment on the meaning of the confidence interval in the context of this problem. At the 90% level, do you detect any differences in the proportion of accurate responses to the question from face-to-face interviews as compared with the proportion of accurate responses from telephone interviews?

(c) Test the claim that there is a difference in the proportion of accurate responses from face-to-face interviews compared with the proportion of accurate responses from telephone interviews. Use $\alpha = 0.05$.

9. Paired difference test.
(i) $\alpha = 0.05$; H_0: $\mu_d = 0$; H_1: $\mu_d < 0$.
(ii) Student's t, $d.f. = 4$; $\bar{d} \approx -4.94$; $t = -2.832$.
(iii) $0.010 < P\text{-value} < 0.025$; on t graph, shade area to the left of -2.832. From TI-84, P-value ≈ 0.0236.
(iv) P-value ≤ 0.05 for α; reject H_0.
(v) At the 5% level of significance, there is sufficient evidence to claim that the population average net sales improved.

9. *Marketing: Sporting Goods* A marketing consultant was hired to visit a random sample of five sporting goods stores across the state of California. Each store was part of a large franchise of sporting goods stores. The consultant taught the managers of each store better ways to advertise and display their goods. The net sales for 1 month before and 1 month after the consultant's visit were recorded as follows for each store (in thousands of dollars):

Store	1	2	3	4	5
Before visit	57.1	94.6	49.2	77.4	43.2
After visit	63.5	101.8	57.8	81.2	41.9

Do the data indicate that the average net sales improved? (Use $\alpha = 0.05$.)

10. Paired difference test.
(i) $\alpha = 0.01$; H_0: $\mu_d = 0$; H_1: $\mu_d > 0$.
(ii) Student's t, $d.f. = 5$; $\bar{d} \approx 9.833$; $t = 6.066$.
(iii) $0.0005 < P\text{-value} < 0.005$; on t graph, shade area to the right of 6.066. From TI-84, P-value ≈ 0.0009.
(iv) P-value ≤ 0.01 for α; reject H_0.
(v) At the 1% level of significance, there is sufficient evidence to indicate that the program of the experimental group promoted creative problem solving.

10. *Psychology: Creative Thinking* Six sets of identical twins were randomly selected from a population of identical twins. One child was taken at random from each pair to form an experimental group. These children participated in a program designed to promote creative thinking. The other child from each pair was part of the control group that did not participate in the program to promote creative thinking. At the end of the program, a creative problem-solving test was given with the results shown in the following table:

Twin pair	A	B	C	D	E	F
Experimental group	53	35	12	25	33	47
Control group	39	21	5	18	21	42

Higher scores indicate better performance in creative problem solving. Do the data support the claim that the program of the experimental group did promote creative problem solving? (Use $\alpha = 0.01$.)

DATA HIGHLIGHTS: GROUP PROJECTS

Break into small groups and discuss the following topic. Organize a brief outline in which you summarize the main points of your group discussion.

"Sweets May Not Be Culprit in Hyper Kids" was a *USA Today* (February 3, 1994) headline reporting results of a study that appeared in the *New England Journal of Medicine*. In this study, the subjects were 25 normal preschoolers aged 3 to 5, and 23 kids aged 6 to 10, who had been described as "sensitive to sugar." The kids and their families were put on three different diets for 3 weeks each. One diet was high in sugar, one was low in sugar and contained aspartame, and one was low in sugar and contained saccharin. The diets were all free of additives, artificial food coloring, preservatives, and chocolate. All food in the households was removed, and then meals were delivered to the families. Researchers gathered information about the kids' behavior from parents, babysitters, and teachers. In addition, researchers tested the kids for memory, concentration, reading, and math skills. The result: "We couldn't find any difference in terms of their behavior or their learning on any of the three diets," said Mark Wolraich, professor of pediatrics at Vanderbilt University Medical Center, who oversaw the project. In another interview, Dr. Wolraich was quoted as saying, "Our study would say there is no evidence sugar has an adverse effect on children's behavior."

(a) This research involved comparisons of several means, not just two. However, let us take a simplified view of the problem and consider the difference in behavior when children consumed the diet with sugar compared with their behavior when they consumed the diet with aspartame and low sugar. List some variables that might be measured to reflect the behavior of the children.

(b) Let's assume that the general null hypothesis was that there is no difference in children's behavior when they have a diet high in sugar. Was the evidence sufficient to allow the researchers to reject the null hypothesis and conclude that there are differences in children's behavior when they have a diet high in sugar? When we cannot reject H_0, have we *proved* that H_0 is true? In your own words, paraphrase the comments made by Dr. Wolraich.

LINKING CONCEPTS: WRITING PROJECTS

Discuss each of the following topics in class or review the topics on your own. Then write a brief but complete essay in which you summarize the main points. Please include formulas and graphs as appropriate.

Is there a relationship between confidence intervals and two-tailed hypothesis tests? The answer is yes. Let c be the level of confidence used to construct a confidence interval from sample data. Let α be the level of significance for a two-tailed hypothesis test. The following statement applies to hypothesis tests of the mean.

> For a two-tailed hypothesis test with level of significance α and null hypothesis H_0: $\mu = k$, we *reject* H_0 whenever k falls *outside* the $c = 1 - \alpha$ confidence interval for μ based on the sample data. When k falls within the $c = 1 - \alpha$ confidence interval, we do not reject H_0.
>
> For a one-tailed hypothesis test with level of significance α and null hypothesis H_0: $\mu = k$, we *reject* H_0 whenever k falls *outside* the $c = 1 - 2\alpha$ confidence interval for μ based on the sample data. When k falls within the $c = 1 - 2\alpha$ confidence interval, we do not reject H_0.

A corresponding relationship between confidence intervals and two-tailed hypothesis tests is also valid for other parameters such as p, $\mu_1 - \mu_2$, and $p_1 - p_2$.

(a) Consider the hypotheses H_0: $\mu_1 - \mu_2 = 0$ and H_1: $\mu_1 - \mu_2 \neq 0$. Suppose a 95% confidence interval for $\mu_1 - \mu_2$ contains only positive numbers. Should you reject the null hypothesis when $\alpha = 0.05$? Why or why not?

(b) Consider the hypotheses H_0: $p_1 - p_2 = 0$ and H_1: $p_1 - p_2 > 0$. Suppose a 98% confidence interval for $p_1 - p_2$ contains only positive numbers. Should you reject or fail to reject H_0 at the $\alpha = 0.01$ level of significance?

Using Technology

Application

Paired Difference Test

Suppose a random sample of eight nurses' schedules were changed from the day shift to a rotating shift of some night work and some day work. For each of these nurses, the information shown in the table below was recorded about level of tension and anxiety at the end of a day shift and also at the end of a night shift. Higher numbers indicate higher levels of tension.

Data for Nurses Working Both Shifts

Nurse	1	2	3	4	5	6	7	8
Day shift (B)	1.5	3	2	3	2	2	1	2
Night shift (A)	3.5	2	4	4	3.5	2	3.5	3

(a) Explain why the sample data for the day shift cannot be thought of as independent of the sample data for the night shift.

(b) Let us say that A is the random variable representing tension levels of night nurses and B is the random variable representing tension levels of day nurses. If we wanted to test the claim that nurses have a higher level of tension after the night shift, what would we use for the null hypothesis? What would we use for the alternate hypothesis? Choose the appropriate hypotheses and enter your choices on the computer. Use a 2% level of significance. Shall we accept or reject the claim that after a night shift, nurses express more feelings of tension, on average, than they do after a day shift?

(c) What is the smallest level of significance at which these data will allow us to accept the claim that after a night shift, nurses express more feelings of tension?

Technology Hints: Paired Difference Test

TI-84Plus/TI-83Plus

Enter the first number of each data pair in the list L_1 and the corresponding value in the second list L_2. Create the list L_3 by subtracting L_2 from L_1. List L_3 contains the differences d. Our next step is to conduct a t test on the differences in L_3. Press **STAT**, select **TESTS**, and choose **Option 2:T-Test.** Use **Inpt:Data.** The value for μ_0 is 0 because we are testing the hypothesis H_0: $\mu_0 = 0$. Indicate that the data are in list L_3 with **Freq: 1.** Select the appropriate symbol ($\neq$, $<$, or $>$) for the alternate hypothesis, and then choose **Calculate**, which gives the value of the sample test statistic along with its t value and P-value, or **Draw**, which shows the area corresponding to the P-value of the sample test statistic and gives the t value and P-value of the sample test statistic.

Excel

Enter the data in two columns. Then use the menu choices ➤ **Tools** ➤ **Data Analysis** ➤ ***t*-Test: Paired Two-Sample for Means.** The output contains the mean and variance for each data column, the degrees of freedom for the test, the sample t statistic, the P-value for a one-tailed test, the P-value for a two-tailed test, and the critical values t_0 for the specified level of significance for both a one-tailed test and a two-tailed test.

Minitab

Enter the data in two columns. Then use the menu selections ➤ **Stats** ➤ **Basic Statistics** ➤ **Paired-*t*.** The output includes an option for a confidence interval. Other items include the number of data pairs n, the mean, the standard deviation, and the standard error of the mean, for each data set as well as for the differences. The t value of the sample test statistic is given along with the P-value. There is also an option to generate a histogram, dotplot, or boxplot for the differences.

SPSS

Enter the data in two columns in the Data View window. In the Variable View window, name and label the two columns. Be sure the data type is numeric. Use the commands **Analyze** ➤ **Compare Means** ➤ **Paired-Samples T Test.** In the dialogue box, select Options to set the confidence level for a confidence interval. Results for a two-tailed test with H_0: $\mu_d = 0$ and H_1: $\mu_d \neq 0$ are given, with test statistic, standard deviation of the paired differences, standard error, t value of the test statistic, degrees of freedom, and P-value of the test statistic. In the output, **Sig(2-tailed)** is the P-value of the test statistic for a two-tailed test. A confidence interval for the mean of the paired differences is also given, as well as the mean, standard deviation, and standard error for each column of data.

Other Applications

Technology Hints: Inferences for $\mu_1 - \mu_2$

TI-84Plus/TI-83Plus

You have the option of using raw data entered into two separate lists or summary statistics. Press the **STAT** key, select the **TESTS** option, and then use option **3:2-SampZTest** or option **4:2-SampTTest.** The output gives the z ot t value of the sample test statistic and the P-value for the test. For confidence intervals, use option **9:2-SampZInt** or option **0:2-SampTTest** under the Tests option.

Excel

Enter the data in two columns. Then use the menu selection ➤ **Tools** ➤ **Data Analysis** ➤ ***z*-Test Two Sample for Means** if you know σ_1 and σ_2. Otherwise, use **t-Test: Two Sample Assuming Unequal Variances.** The output provides the mean and variance for each variable, the z or t value of the sample test statistic, the P-values for a one-tailed test and a two-tailed test, and the critical z_0 or t_0 values for a one-tailed test and a two-tailed test.

Minitab

When testing the difference of means from independent samples, Minitab always uses the t distribution. The P-value of the sample test statistic will be slightly larger than the P-value generated using the normal distribution.

Enter the data in two columns. Then use the menu selections ➤ **Stat** ➤ **Basic Statistics** ➤ **2-Sample *t*.** Do not check equal variances. The output gives an option for a confidence interval as well as for dotplots or boxplots of the two variables. The output displays the mean, standard deviation, and standard error of the mean for each of the variables. The t value of the sample test statistic and the P-value are based on the Student's t distribution.

SPSS

Enter all the data in one column. In an adjacent column, enter a grouping variable with two values to separate the cases into two independent samples. For instance, use the value 1 to indicate that a data value is from the first sample, and the value 2 to indicate that a data value is from the second sample. Then use the menu choices **Analyze** ➤ **Compare Means** ➤ **Independent-Samples T Test.** In the dialogue box, move the column containing the data into the Test Variable box and the column containing the grouping variables into the Grouping Variable box. Then press Define Groups and enter the grouping values, such as 1 and 2. A confidence interval can be set by using the Options button. The output gives the mean, standard deviation, and standard error for each sample. Test results show the t value, degrees of freedom, and P-value for a two-tailed test for both the case of equal variances and the case of unequal variances. Confidence intervals are also included in the output.

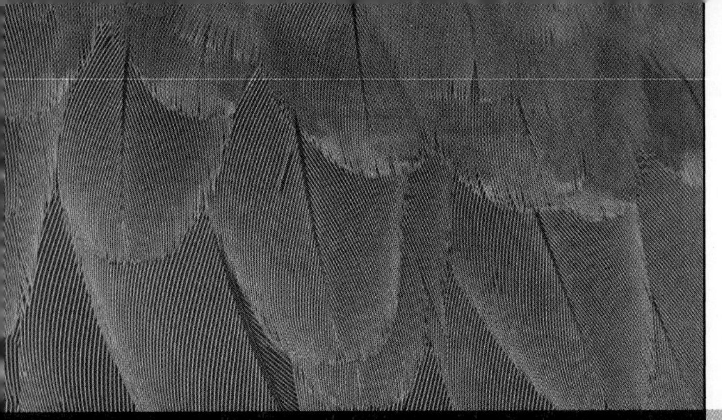

11

Part I: Inferences Using the Chi-Square Distribution

Part II: Inferences Relating to Linear Regression

Make everything as simple as possible, but no simpler.

—Albert Einstein

Today Professor Einstein's theories are well accepted as part of modern physics. However, this was not always the case. When Einstein first discovered relativity and the bending of light in large gravitational fields, his theories were held suspect. Physicists studied starlight as it passed near our sun (a large gravitational field). They discovered that starlight did not travel in a straight line. Instead it bent very slightly, exactly as Einstein had predicted!

Many studies in natural science, medicine, social science, economics, and business require testing one established theory against another new theory. Statistical tests you will learn in this chapter are of great value in such work.

For on-line student resources, visit the Brase/Brase, *Understanding Basic Statistics,* 5th edition web site at **www.cengage.com/statistics/Brase/UBS5e.**

ADDITIONAL TOPICS USING INFERENCE

Mesa Verde National Park

PREVIEW QUESTIONS

How do you decide if random variables are dependent or independent? (SECTION 11.1)

How do you decide if different populations share the same proportions of specified characteristics? (SECTION 11.1)

How do you decide if two distributions are not only dependent, but actually the same distribution? (SECTION 11.2)

How do you construct tests for σ? (SECTION 11.3)

How do you test a correlation coefficient? (SECTION 11.4)

What is the standard error of estimate? How do you compute it, and where is it used? (SECTION 11.4)

How do you compute confidence intervals for a least-squares prediction? (SECTION 11.4)

The slope of the least-squares line represents rate of growth. How can you determine if the rate of growth is statistically significant? (SECTION 11.4)

FOCUS PROBLEM

Archaeology in Bandelier National Monument

Archaeologists at Washington State University did an extensive summer excavation at Burnt Mesa Pueblo in Bandelier National Monument. Their work is published in the book *Bandelier Archaeological Excavation Project: Summer 1990 Excavations at Burnt Mesa Pueblo and Casa del Rito*, edited by T. A. Kohler.

One question the archaeologists asked was: Is raw material used by prehistoric Indians for stone tool manufacture independent of the archaeological excavation site? Two different excavation sites at Burnt Mesa Pueblo gave the information in the table below.

Use a chi-square test with 5% level of significance to test the claim that raw material used for construction of stone tools and excavation site are independent. (See Problem 13 of Section 11.1.)

Archaeological excavation site

Stone Tool Construction Material, Burnt Mesa Pueblo

Material	Site A	Site B	Row Total
Basalt	731	584	1315
Obsidian	102	93	195
Pedernal chert	510	525	1035
Other	85	94	179
Column Total	1428	1296	2724

PART I: INFERENCES USING THE CHI-SQUARE DISTRIBUTION

Overview of the Chi-Square Distribution

This overview of the χ^2 distribution can be presented with any of the Sections 11.1, "Chi-Square: Tests of Independence and of Homogeneity"; 11.2, "Chi-Square: Goodness of Fit"; or 11.3, "Testing a Single Variance or Standard Deviation." By using the overview to present the χ^2 distribution and table, the three sections using the χ^2 distribution can be treated independently and presented in any order.

So far, we have used several probability distributions for hypothesis testing and confidence intervals, with the most frequently used being the normal distribution and the Student's t distribution. In this chapter, we will use another probability distribution, namely, the chi-square distribution (where *chi* is pronounced like the first two letters in the word *kite*). In Part I, we will see applications of the chi-square distribution.

Chi is a Greek letter denoted by the symbol χ, so chi-square is denoted by the symbol χ^2. Because the distribution is of chi-*square* values, the χ^2 values begin at 0 and then are all positive. The graph of the χ^2 distribution is not symmetrical, and like the Student's t distribution, it depends on the number of degrees of freedom. Figure 11-1 shows the χ^2 distribution for several degrees of freedom (*d.f.*).

As the degrees of freedom increase, the graph of the chi-square distribution becomes more bell-like and begins to look more and more symmetric.

Is there a relation between chi-square and normal? Let $z_1, z_2, \ldots, z_n$ be independent standard normal random variables. Then $\chi^2 = z_1^2 + z_2^2 + \cdots + z_n^2$ is a chi-square random variable. In our work, the degrees of freedom are chosen in a theoretical way that is appropriate to the application.

The **mode (high point)** of a chi-square distribution with n degrees of freedom occurs over $n - 2$ (for $n \geq 3$).

Table 5 of the Appendix shows critical values of chi-square distributions for which a designated area falls to the *right* of the critical value. Table 11-1 gives an excerpt from Table 5. Notice that the row headers are degrees of freedom, and the column headers are areas in the *right* tail of the distribution. For instance, according to the table, for a χ^2 distribution with 3 degrees of freedom, the area occurring to the *right* of $\chi^2 = 0.072$ is 0.995. For a χ^2 distribution with 4 degrees of freedom, the area falling to the *right* of $\chi^2 = 13.28$ is 0.010.

In the next three sections, we will see how to apply the chi-square distribution to different applications.

FIGURE 11-1

The χ^2 Distribution

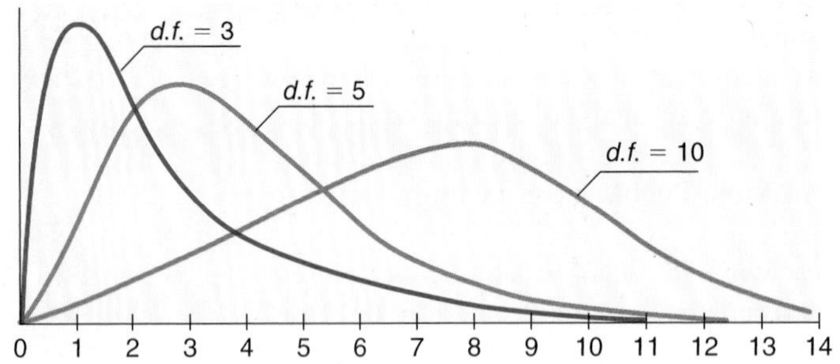

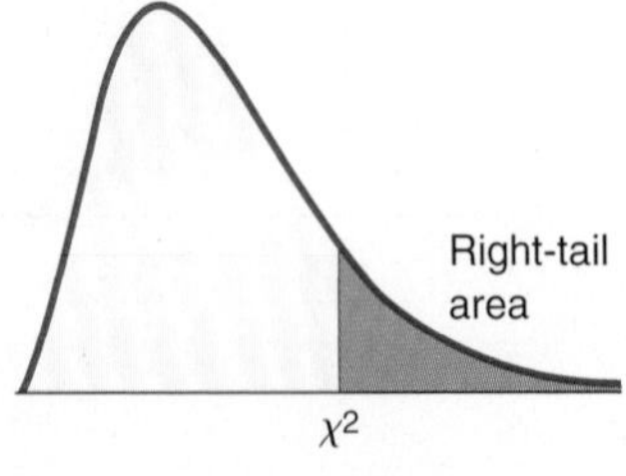

TABLE 11-1 Excerpt from Table 5 (Appendix): The χ^2 Distribution

	Area of the Right Tail					
d.f.	0.995	0.990	0.975	...	0.010	0.005
⋮	⋮	⋮	⋮		⋮	⋮
3	0.072	0.115	0.216		11.34	12.84
4	0.207	0.297	0.484		13.28	14.86

SECTION 11.1

Chi-Square: Tests of Independence and of Homogeneity

FOCUS POINTS

- Set up a test to investigate independence of random variables.
- Use contingency tables to compute the sample χ^2 statistic.
- Find or estimate the *P*-value of the sample χ^2 statistic and complete the test.
- Conduct a test of homogeneity of populations.

Innovative Machines Incorporated has developed two new letter arrangements for computer keyboards. The company wishes to see if there is any relationship between the arrangement of letters on the keyboard and the number of hours it takes a new typing student to learn to type at 20 words per minute. Or, from another point of view, is the time it takes a student to learn to type *independent* of the arrangement of the letters on a keyboard?

To answer questions of this type, we test the hypotheses

Hypotheses

H_0: Keyboard arrangement and learning times *are independent.*

H_1: Keyboard arrangement and learning times *are not independent.*

Chi-square distribution

In problems of this sort, we are testing the *independence* of two factors. The probability distribution we use to make the decision is the *chi-square distribution.* Recall from the overview of the chi-square distribution that *chi* is pronounced like the first two letters of the word *kite* and is a Greek letter denoted by the symbol χ. Thus chi-square is denoted by χ^2.

Innovative Machines' first task is to gather data. Suppose the company took a random sample of 300 beginning typing students and randomly assigned them to learn to type on one of three keyboards. The learning times for this sample are shown in Table 11-2.

Contingency table

Notice that contingency tables could be created from tally surveys such as those discussed in Section 5.2.

Table 11-2 is called a *contingency table.* The *shaded boxes* that contain observed frequencies are called *cells.* The row and column totals are not considered to be cells. This contingency table is of size 3 × 3 (read, "three-by-three") because there are three rows of cells and three columns. When giving the size of a contingency table, we always list the number of *rows first.*

To determine the **size** of a contingency table, count the number of rows containing data and the number of columns containing data. The size is

Number of rows × Number of columns

where the symbol "×" is read "by." The number of rows is always given first.

TABLE 11-2 **Keyboard versus Time to Learn to Type at 20 wpm**

Keyboard	21–40 h	41–60 h	61–80 h	Row Total
A	#1 25	#2 30	#3 25	80
B	#4 30	#5 71	#6 19	120
Standard	#7 35	#8 49	#9 16	100
Column Total	90	150	60	300 Sample size

GUIDED EXERCISE 1 *Size of contingency table*

Give the sizes of the contingency tables in Figures 11-2(a) and (b). Also, count the number of cells in each table. (Remember, each pink shaded box is a cell.)

(a) **FIGURE 11-2(a) Contingency Table**

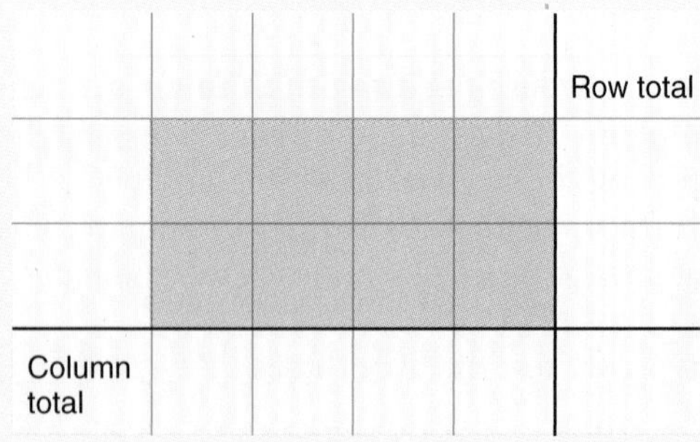

(b) **FIGURE 11-2(b) Contingency Table**

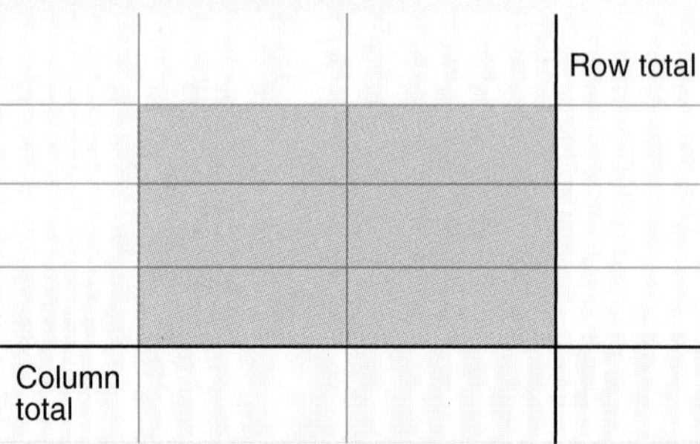

(a) ➡ There are two rows and four columns, so this is a 2 × 4 table. There are eight cells.

(b) ➡ Here we have three rows and two columns, so this is a 3 × 2 table with six cells.

Expected frequency

We are testing the null hypothesis that the keyboard arrangement and the time it takes a student to learn to type are *independent.* We use this hypothesis to determine the *expected frequency* of each cell.

For instance, to compute the expected frequency of cell 1 in Table 11-2, we observe that cell 1 consists of all the students in the sample who learned to type on keyboard A and who mastered the skill at the 20-words-per-minute level in 21 to 40 hours. By the assumption (null hypothesis) that the two events are independent, we use the multiplication law to obtain the probability that a student is in cell 1.

$$P(\text{cell 1}) = P(\text{keyboard A } \textit{and} \text{ skill in 21–40 h})$$
$$= P(\text{keyboard A}) \cdot P(\text{skill in 21–40 h})$$

Because there are 300 students in the sample and 80 used keyboard A,

$$P(\text{keyboard A}) = \frac{80}{300}$$

Also, 90 of the 300 students learned to type in 21–40 hours, so

$$P(\text{skill in 21–40 h}) = \frac{90}{300}$$

Using these two probabilities and the assumption of independence,

$$P(\text{keyboard A } \textit{and} \text{ skill in 21–40 h}) = \frac{80}{300} \cdot \frac{90}{300}$$

Finally, because there are 300 students in the sample, we have the *expected frequency E* for cell 1.

$$E = P(\text{student in cell 1}) \cdot (\text{no. of students in sample})$$
$$= \frac{80}{300} \cdot \frac{90}{300} \cdot 300 = \frac{80 \cdot 90}{300} = 24$$

We can repeat this process for each cell. However, the last step yields an easier formula for the expected frequency *E*.

Formula for expected frequency *E*

$$E = \frac{\text{(Row total)(Column total)}}{\text{Sample size}}$$

It is useful to point out this important note regarding rounding of expected values.

Note: If the expected value is not a whole number, do *not* round it to the nearest whole number.

Let's use this formula in Example 1 to find the expected frequency for cell 2.

EXAMPLE 1 EXPECTED FREQUENCY

Find the expected frequency for cell 2 of contingency Table 11-2.

SOLUTION: Cell 2 is in row 1 and column 2. The *row total* is 80, and the *column total* is 150. The size of the sample is still 300.

$$E = \frac{\text{(Row total)(Column total)}}{\text{Sample size}}$$

$$= \frac{(80)(150)}{300} = 40$$

GUIDED EXERCISE 2 Expected frequency

Table 11-3 contains the *observed frequencies* O and *expected frequencies* E for the contingency table giving keyboard arrangement and number of hours it takes a student to learn to type at 20 words per minute. Fill in the missing expected frequencies.

TABLE 11-3 **Complete Contingency Table of Keyboard Arrangement and Time to Learn to Type**

Keyboard	21–40 h	41–60 h	61–80 h	Row Total
A	#1 $O = 25$ $E = 24$	#2 $O = 30$ $E = 40$	#3 $O = 25$ $E =$ __	80
B	#4 $O = 30$ $E = 36$	#5 $O = 71$ $E =$ __	#6 $O = 19$ $E =$ __	120
Standard	#7 $O = 35$ $E =$ __	#8 $O = 49$ $E = 50$	#9 $O = 16$ $E = 20$	100
Column Total	90	150	60	300 Sample Size

For cell 3, we have

$$E = \frac{(80)(60)}{300} = 16$$

For cell 5, we have

$$E = \frac{(120)(150)}{300} = 60$$

For cell 6, we have

$$E = \frac{(120)(60)}{300} = 24$$

For cell 7, we have

$$E = \frac{(100)(90)}{300} = 30$$

Computing the sample test statistic χ^2

Now we are ready to compute the sample statistic χ^2 for the typing students. The χ^2 value is a measure of the sum of the differences between observed frequency O and expected frequency E in each cell. These differences are listed in Table 11-4.

As you can see, if we sum the differences between the observed frequencies and the expected frequencies of the cells, we get the value zero. This total certainly does not reflect the fact that there were differences between the observed and expected frequencies. To obtain a measure whose sum does reflect the magnitude of the differences, we square the differences and work with the quantities $(O - E)^2$. But instead of using the terms $(O - E)^2$, we use the values $(O - E)^2/E$.

TABLE 11-4 Differences Between Observed and Expected Frequencies

Cell	Observed O	Expected E	Difference $(O - E)$
1	25	24	1
2	30	40	−10
3	25	16	9
4	30	36	−6
5	71	60	11
6	19	24	−5
7	35	30	5
8	49	50	−1
9	16	20	−4
			$\Sigma(O - E) = 0$

These are good points to bring to students' attention.

We use this expression because a small difference between the observed and expected frequency is not nearly as important when the expected frequency is large as it is when the expected frequency is small. For instance, for both cells 1 and 8, the squared difference $(O - E)^2$ is 1. However, this difference is more meaningful in cell 1, where the expected frequency is 24, than it is in cell 8, where the expected frequency is 50. When we divide the quantity $(O - E)^2$ by E, we take the size of the difference with respect to the size of the expected value. We use the sum of these values to form the sample statistic χ^2:

$$\chi^2 = \Sigma\frac{(O - E)^2}{E}$$

where the sum is over all cells in the contingency table.

COMMENT If you look up the word *irony* in a dictionary, you will find one of its meanings is described as "the difference between actual (or observed) results and expected results." Because irony is so prevalent in much of our human experience, it is not surprising that statisticians have incorporated a related chi-square distribution into their work.

GUIDED EXERCISE 3 *Sample χ^2*

(a) Complete Table 11-5.

TABLE 11-5 **Data of Table 11-4**

Cell	O	E	$O - E$	$(O - E)^2$	$(O - E)^2/E$
1	25	24	1	1	0.04
2	30	40	−10	100	2.50
3	25	16	9	81	5.06
4	30	36	−6	36	1.00
5	71	60	11	121	2.02
6	19	24	−5	25	1.04
7	35	30	5	25	0.83
8	49	50	____	____	____
9	16	20	____	____	____

$$\Sigma\frac{(O - E)^2}{E} = \_\_\_\_$$

→ The last two rows of Table 11-5 are

Cell	O	E	$O - E$	$(O - E)^2$	$(O - E)^2/E$
8	49	50	−1	1	0.02
9	16	20	−4	16	0.80

$$\Sigma\frac{(O - E)^2}{E} = \text{total of last column} = 13.31$$

(b) Compute the statistic χ^2 for this sample.

→ Since $\chi^2 = \Sigma\frac{(O - E)^2}{E}$, then $\chi^2 = 13.31$.

Notice that when the observed frequency and the expected frequency are very close, the quantity $(O - E)^2$ is close to zero, and so the statistic χ^2 is near zero. As the difference increases, the statistic χ^2 also increases. To determine how large the sample statistic can be before we must reject the null hypothesis of independence, we find the P-value of the statistic in the chi-square distribution, Table 5 of the Appendix, and compare it to the specified level of significance α. The P-value depends on the number of degrees of freedom. To test independence, the degrees of freedom $d.f.$ are determined by the following formula.

Degrees of freedom for test of independence

$$\text{Degrees of freedom} = (\text{Number of rows} - 1) \cdot (\text{Number of columns} - 1)$$

or

$$d.f. = (R - 1)(C - 1)$$

where R = number of cell rows

C = number of cell columns

GUIDED EXERCISE 4 **Degrees of freedom**

Determine the number of degrees of freedom in the example of keyboard arrangements (see Table 11-2). Recall that the contingency table had three rows and three columns.

$$d.f. = (R - 1)(C - 1)$$
$$= (3 - 1)(3 - 1) = (2)(2) = 4$$

Finding the P-value for tests of independence

To test the hypothesis that the letter arrangement on a keyboard and the time it takes to learn to type at 20 words per minute are independent at the $\alpha = 0.05$ level of significance, we estimate the P-value shown in Figure 11-3 on the next page for the sample test statistic $\chi^2 = 13.31$ (calculated in Guided Exercise 3). We then compare the P-value to the specified level of significance α.

For tests of independence, we always use a *right-tailed* test on the chi-square distribution. This is because we are testing to see if the χ^2 measure of the difference between the observed and expected frequencies is too large to be due to chance alone.

In Guided Exercise 4, we found that the degrees of freedom for the example of keyboard arrangements is 4. From Table 5 of the Appendix, in the row headed by $d.f. = 4$, we see that the sample $\chi^2 = 13.31$ falls between the entries 13.28 and 14.86.

FIGURE 11-3

P-value

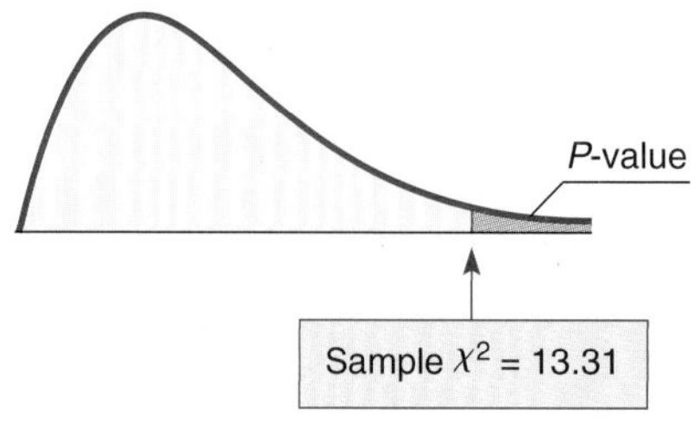

Right-tail Area	0.010	0.005
d.f. = 4	13.28	14.86
	↑ Sample χ^2 = 13.31	

The corresponding *P*-value falls between 0.005 and 0.010. From technology, we get *P*-value ≈ 0.0098.

α

0.005 0.010 0.05

Since the *P*-value is less than the level of significance $\alpha = 0.05$, we reject the null hypothesis of independence and conclude that keyboard arrangement and learning time are *not* independent.

Tests of independence for two statistical variables involve a number of steps. A summary of the procedure follows.

PROCEDURE

HOW TO TEST FOR INDEPENDENCE OF TWO STATISTICAL VARIABLES

Construct a contingency table in which the rows represent one statistical variable and the columns represent the other. Obtain a random sample of observations, which are assigned to the cells described by the rows and columns. These assignments are called the **observed values O** from the sample.

1. Set the level of significance α and use the hypotheses

   H_0: The variables are independent.

   H_1: The variables are not independent.

2. For each cell, compute the **expected frequency *E*** (do not round, but give as a decimal number).

   $$E = \frac{(\text{Row total})(\text{Column total})}{\text{Sample size}}$$

   You need a sample size large enough so that, for each cell, $E \geq 5$. Now each cell has two numbers, the observed frequency *O* from the sample and the expected frequency *E*.

   Next compute the sample *chi-square test statistic*

   $$\chi^2 = \Sigma\frac{(O - E)^2}{E} \text{ with degrees of freedom } d.f. = (R - 1)(C - 1)$$

   where the sum is over all cells in the contingency table and

   R = number of rows in contingency table

   C = number of columns in contingency table

3. Use the chi-square distribution (Table 5 of the Appendix) and a *right-tailed test* to find (or estimate) the *P-value* corresponding to the test statistic.

4. *Conclude* the test. If *P*-value $\leq \alpha$, then reject H_0. If *P*-value $> \alpha$, then do not reject H_0.

5. *Interpret your conclusion* in the context of the application.

This is a good point to emphasize. In research projects involving large contingency tables, some cells with expected frequency under 5 are permitted if the cells do not influence the model too much. Ways of analyzing such tables are left to advanced courses.

GUIDED EXERCISE 5 Testing for independence

Super Vending Machines Company is to install soda pop machines in elementary schools and high schools. The market analysts wish to know if flavor preference and school level are independent. A random sample of 200 students was taken. Their school level and soda pop preferences are given in Table 11-6. Is independence indicated at the $\alpha = 0.01$ level of significance?

STEP 1: State the null and alternate hypotheses.

→ H_0: School level and soda pop preference are independent.

H_1: School level and soda pop preference are not independent.

STEP 2:

(a) Complete the contingency Table 11-6 by filling in the required expected frequencies.

TABLE 11-6 School Level and Soda Pop Preference

Soda Pop	High School	Elementary School	Row Total
Kula Kola	$O = 33$ # 1 $E = 36$	$O = 57$ # 2 $E = 54$	90
Mountain Mist	$O = 30$ # 3 $E = 20$	$O = 20$ # 4 $E = 30$	50
Jungle Grape	$O = 5$ # 5 $E =$ _____	$O = 35$ # 6 $E =$ _____	40
Diet Pop	$O = 12$ # 7 $E =$ _____	$O = 8$ # 8 $E =$ _____	20
Column Total	80	120	200 Sample Size

→ The expected frequency

for cell 5 is $\frac{(40)(80)}{200} = 16$

for cell 6 is $\frac{(40)(120)}{200} = 24$

for cell 7 is $\frac{(20)(80)}{200} = 8$

for cell 8 is $\frac{(20)(120)}{200} = 12$

Note: In this example, the expected frequencies are all whole numbers. If the expected frequency has a decimal part, such as 8.45, do *not* round the value to the nearest whole number; rather, give the expected frequency as the decimal number.

(b) Fill in Table 11-7 and use the table to find the sample statistic χ^2.

TABLE 11-7 Computational Table for χ^2

Cell	O	E	$O - E$	$(O - E)^2$	$(O - E)^2/E$
1	33	36	−3	9	0.25
2	57	54	3	9	0.17
3	30	20	10	100	5.00
4	20	30	−10	100	3.33
5	5	16	−11	121	7.56
6	35	24	11	_____	_____
7	12	8	_____	_____	_____
8	8	12	_____	_____	_____

→ The last three rows of Table 11-7 should read as follows:

Cell	O	E	$O - E$	$(O - E)^2$	$(O - E)^2/E$
6	35	24	11	121	5.04
7	12	8	4	16	2.00
8	8	12	−4	16	1.33

χ^2 = total of last column

$$= \Sigma\frac{(O - E)^2}{E} = 24.68$$

(c) What is the size of the contingency table? Use the number of rows and the number of columns to determine the degrees of freedom.

→ The contingency table is of size 4×2. Since there are four rows and two columns,

$d.f. = (4 - 1)(2 - 1) = 3$

Continued

GUIDED EXERCISE 5 *continued*

STEP 3: Use Table 5 of the Appendix to estimate the *P*-value of the sample statistic $\chi^2 = 24.68$ with $d.f. = 3$.

Right-tail Area	0.005
d.f. = 3	12.84 ↑ Sample $\chi^2 = 24.68$

As the χ^2 values increase, the area to the right decreases, so

P-value < 0.005

STEP 4: Conclude the test by comparing the *P*-value of the sample statistic χ^2 to the level of significance $\alpha = 0.01$.

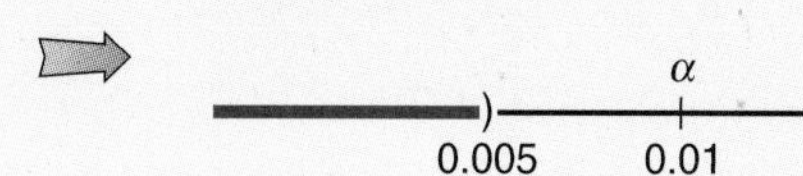

Since the *P*-value is less than α, we reject the null hypothesis of independence. Technology gives *P*-value ≈ 0.00002.

STEP 5: Interpret the test result in the context of the application.

At the 1% level of significance, we conclude that school level and soda pop preference are dependent.

TECH NOTES

The TI-84Plus and TI-83Plus calculators, Excel, and Minitab all support chi-square tests of independence. In each case, the observed data are entered in the format of the contingency table.

TI-84Plus/TI-83Plus Enter the observed data into a matrix. Set the dimension of matrix [B] to match that of the matrix of observed values. Expected values will be placed in matrix [B]. Press **STAT, TESTS,** and select option **C:χ^2-Test.** The output gives the sample χ^2 with the *P*-value.

Excel Enter the table of observed values. Use the formulas of this section to compute the expected values. Enter the corresponding table of expected values. Finally, use **paste function** (f_x) ➤ **Statistical** ➤ **Chitest.** Excel returns the *P*-value of the sample χ^2.

Minitab Enter the contingency table of observed values. Use the menu selection **Stat** ➤ **Tables** ➤ **Chi-Square Test.** The output shows the contingency table with expected values and the sample χ^2 with *P*-value.

Tests of Homogeneity

We've seen how to use contingency tables and the chi-square distribution to test for independence of two random variables. The same process enables us to determine whether several populations share the same proportions of distinct categories. Such a test is called a test of *homogeneity*.

According to the dictionary, among the definitions of the word *homogeneous* are "of the same structure" and "composed of similar parts." In statistical jargon, this translates as a test of homogeneity to see if two or more populations share specified characteristics in the same proportions.

A **test of homogeneity** tests the claim that *different populations* share the *same proportions* of specified characteristics.

The computational processes for conducting tests of independence and tests of homogeneity are the same. However, there are two main differences in the initial setup of the two types of tests, namely, the sampling method and the hypotheses.

1. **Sampling method**
   For tests of independence, we use one random sample and observe how the sample members are distributed among distinct categories.
   For tests of homogeneity, we take random samples from each different population and see how members of each population are distributed over distinct categories.

2. **Hypotheses**
   For tests of independence,
   H_0: The variables are independent.
   H_1: The variables are not independent.
   For tests of homogeneity,
   H_0: Each population shares respective characteristics in the same proportion.
   H_1: Some populations have different proportions of respective characteristics.

EXAMPLE 2 TEST OF HOMOGENEITY

Pets—who can resist a cute kitten or puppy? Tim is doing a research project involving pet preferences among students at his college. He took random samples of 300 female and 250 male students. Each sample member responded to the survey question, "If you could own only one pet, what kind would you choose?" The possible responses were: dog, cat, other pet, no pet. The results of the study follow.

Pet Preference

Gender	Dog	Cat	Other Pet	No Pet
Female	120	132	18	30
Male	135	70	20	25

Does the same proportion of males as females prefer each type of pet? Use a 1% level of significance.

We'll answer this question in several steps.

(a) First make a cluster bar graph showing the percentages of females and the percentages of males favoring each category of pet. From the graph, does it appear that the proportions are the same for males and females?

Cluster bar graphs give a visual impression of the proportions. Note that we first convert the cells to percentages from the specified population.

SOLUTION: The cluster graph shown in Figure 11-4 was created using Minitab. Looking at the graph, it appears that there are differences in the proportions of females and males preferring each type of pet. However, let's conduct a statistical test to verify our visual impression.

FIGURE 11-4

Pet Preference by Gender

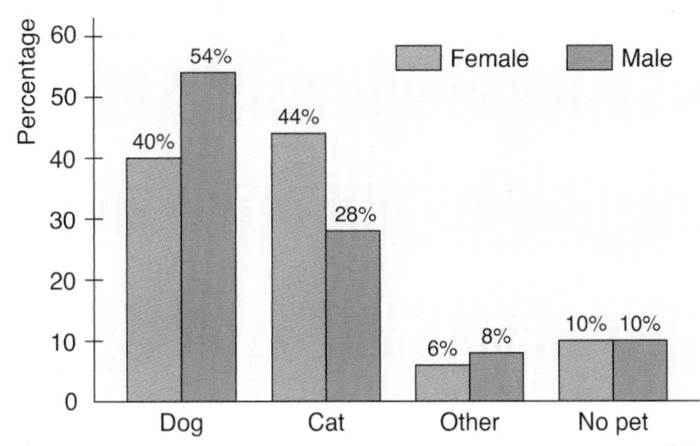

(b) Is it appropriate to use a test of homogeneity?

SOLUTION: Yes, since there are separate random samples for each designated population, male and female. We also are interested in whether each population shares the same proportion of members favoring each category of pet.

(c) State the hypotheses and conclude the test by using the Minitab printout.

H_0: The proportions of females and males naming each pet preference are the same.

H_1: The proportions of females and males naming each pet preference are not the same.

```
Chi-Square Test: Dog, Cat, Other, No Pet

Expected counts are printed below observed counts
Chi-Square contributions are printed below expected counts

            Dog       Cat      Other     No Pet    Total
1           120       132       18         30       300
         139.09    110.18    20.73      30.00
          2.620     4.320    0.359      0.000

2           135        70       20         25       250
         115.91     91.82    17.27      25.00
          3.144     5.185    0.431      0.000

Total       255       202       38         55       550

Chi-Sq = 16.059, DF = 3, P-Value = 0.001
```

Since the P-value is less than α, we reject H_0 at the 1% level of significance.

(d) Interpret the results.

SOLUTION: It appears from the sample data that male and female students at Tim's college have different preferences when it comes to selecting a pet.

PROCEDURE

HOW TO TEST FOR HOMOGENEITY OF POPULATIONS

Obtain random samples from each of the populations. For each population, determine the number of members that share a distinct specified characteristic. Make a contingency table with the different populations as the rows (or columns) and the characteristics as the columns (or rows). The values recorded in the cells of the table are the **observed values O** taken from the samples.

1. Set the level of significance and use the hypotheses

   H_0: The proportion of each population sharing specified characteristics is the same for all populations.

   H_1: The proportion of each population sharing specified characteristics is not the same for all populations.

2. Follow steps 2–5 of the procedure used to test for independence.

It is important to observe that when we reject the null hypothesis in a test of homogeneity, we don't know which proportions differ among the populations. We know only that the populations differ in some of the proportions sharing a characteristic.

VIEWPOINT Loyalty! Going, Going, Gone!

Was there a time in the past when people worked for the same company all their lives, regularly purchased the same brand names, always voted for candidates from the same political party, and loyally cheered for the same sports team? One way to look at this question is to consider tests of statistical independence. *Is customer loyalty independent of company profits? Can a company maintain its productivity independent of loyal workers? Can politicians do whatever they please independent of the voters back home? Americans may be ready to act on a pent-up desire to restore a sense of loyalty in their lives. For more information, see* American Demographics, *Vol. 19, No. 9.*

SECTION 11.1 PROBLEMS

Tables and art to accompany margin answers may be found in the back of the book.

1. Skewed right.
2. Skewness to the right decreases. Yes.
3. Right-tailed test.
4. The null hypothesis for tests of independence states that the random variables are independent. The null hypothesis for tests of homogeneity states that the proportions of each population sharing the specified characteristics are the same. For tests of independence, the alternate hypothesis is that the variables are not independent. For tests of homogeneity, the alternate hypothesis is that the proportions are not the same.

5. (a) $\alpha = 0.05$; H_0: Myers-Briggs preference and profession are independent; H_1: Myers-Briggs preference and profession are not independent.
(b) $\chi^2 = 8.649$; *d.f.* $= 2$.
(c) $0.010 < P\text{-value} < 0.025$. From TI-84, $P\text{-value} \approx 0.0132$.
(d) Reject H_0.
(e) At the 5% level of significance, there is sufficient evidence to conclude that Myers-Briggs preference and profession are not independent.

1. *Statistical Literacy* In general, are chi-square distributions symmetric or skewed? If skewed, are they skewed right or left?

2. *Statistical Literacy* For chi-square distributions, as the number of degrees of freedom increases, does any skewness increase or decrease? Do chi-square distributions become more symmetric (and normal) as the number of degrees of freedom becomes larger and larger?

3. *Statistical Literacy* For chi-square tests of independence and of homogeneity, do we use a right-tailed, left-tailed, or two-tailed test?

4. ***Critical Thinking*** In general, how do the hypotheses for chi-square tests of independence differ from those for chi-square tests of homogeneity? Explain.

For Problems 5–15, please provide the following information.

(a) What is the level of significance? State the null and alternate hypotheses.
(b) Find the value of the chi-square statistic for the sample. Are all the expected frequencies greater than 5? What sampling distribution will you use? What are the degrees of freedom?
(c) Find or estimate the *P*-value of the sample test statistic.
(d) Based on your answers in parts (a) to (c), will you reject or fail to reject the null hypothesis of independence?
(e) Interpret your conclusion in the context of the application.

Use the expected values *E* to the hundredths place.

5. *Psychology: Myers-Briggs* The following table shows the Myers-Briggs personality preferences for a random sample of 406 people in the listed professions (*Atlas of Type Tables*, by Macdaid, McCaulley, and Kainz). E refers to extroverted and I refers to introverted.

	Personality Preference Type		
Occupation	E	I	Row Total
Clergy (all denominations)	62	45	107
M.D.	68	94	162
Lawyer	56	81	137
Column Total	186	220	406

Use the chi-square test to determine if the listed occupations and personality preferences are independent at the 0.05 level of significance.

6. (a) $\alpha = 0.01$; H_0: Myers-Briggs preference and profession are independent; H_1: Myers-Briggs preference and profession are not independent.
(b) $\chi^2 = 10.26$; $d.f. = 2$.
(c) $0.005 < P\text{-value} < 0.010$. From TI-84, $P\text{-value} \approx 0.0059$.
(d) Reject H_0.
(e) At the 1% level of significance, there is sufficient evidence to conclude that Myers-Briggs preference and profession are not independent.

7. (a) $\alpha = 0.01$; H_0: Site type and pottery type are independent; H_1: Site type and pottery type are not independent.
(b) $\chi^2 = 0.5552$; $d.f. = 4$.
(c) $0.950 < P\text{-value} < 0.975$. From TI-84, $P\text{-value} \approx 0.9679$.
(d) Do not reject H_0.
(e) At the 1% level of significance, there is insufficient evidence to conclude that site type and pottery type are not independent.

8. (a) $\alpha = 0.05$; H_0: Ceremonial ranking and pottery type are independent; H_1: Ceremonial ranking and pottery type are not independent.
(b) $\chi^2 = 6.198$; $d.f. = 2$.
(c) $0.025 < P\text{-value} < 0.050$. From TI-84, $P\text{-value} \approx 0.0451$.
(d) Reject H_0.
(e) At the 5% level of significance, there is sufficient evidence to conclude that ceremonial ranking and pottery type are not independent.

6. *Psychology: Myers-Briggs* The following table shows the Myers-Briggs personality preferences for a random sample of 519 people in the listed professions (*Atlas of Type Tables,* by Macdaid, McCaulley, and Kainz). T refers to thinking and F refers to feeling.

	Personality Preference Type		
Occupation	**T**	**F**	**Row Total**
Clergy (all denominations)	57	91	148
M.D.	77	82	159
Lawyer	118	94	212
Column Total	252	267	519

Use the chi-square test to determine if the listed occupations and personality preferences are independent at the 0.01 level of significance.

7. *Archaeology: Pottery* The following table shows site type and type of pottery for a random sample of 628 sherds at a location in Sand Canyon Archaeological Project, Colorado (*The Sand Canyon Archaeological Project,* edited by Lipe).

	Pottery Type			
Site Type	**Mesa Verde Black-on-White**	**McElmo Black-on-White**	**Mancos Black-on-White**	**Row Total**
Mesa Top	75	61	53	189
Cliff-Talus	81	70	62	213
Canyon Bench	92	68	66	226
Column Total	248	199	181	628

Use a chi-square test to determine if site type and pottery type are independent at the 0.01 level of significance.

8. *Archaeology: Pottery* The following table shows ceremonial ranking and type of pottery sherd for a random sample of 434 sherds at a location in the Sand Canyon Archaeological Project, Colorado (*The Architecture of Social Integration in Prehistoric Pueblos,* edited by Lipe and Hegmon).

Ceremonial Ranking	**Cooking Jar Sherds**	**Decorated Jar Sherds (Noncooking)**	**Row Total**
A	86	49	135
B	92	53	145
C	79	75	154
Column Total	257	177	434

Use a chi-square test to determine if ceremonial ranking and pottery type are independent at the 0.05 level of significance.

9. *Ecology: Buffalo* The following table shows age distribution and location of a random sample of 166 buffalo in Yellowstone National Park (based on information from *The Bison of Yellowstone National Park,* National Park Service Scientific Monograph Series).

9. (a) $\alpha = 0.05$; H_0: Age distribution and location are independent; H_1: Age distribution and location are not independent.
(b) $\chi^2 = 0.6704$; $d.f. = 4$.
(c) $0.950 < P\text{-value} < 0.975$. From TI-84, $P\text{-value} \approx 0.9549$.
(d) Do not reject H_0.
(e) At the 5% level of significance, there is insufficient evidence to conclude that age distribution and location are not independent.

Age	Lamar District	Nez Perce District	Firehole District	Row Total
Calf	13	13	15	41
Yearling	10	11	12	33
Adult	34	28	30	92
Column Total	57	52	57	166

Use a chi-square test to determine if age distribution and location are independent at the 0.05 level of significance.

10. (a) $\alpha = 0.05$; H_0: Myers-Briggs type and area of study are independent; H_1: Myers-Briggs type and area of study are not independent.
(b) $\chi^2 = 15.6017$; $d.f. = 6$.
(c) $0.010 < P\text{-value} < 0.025$. From TI-84, $P\text{-value} \approx 0.0161$.
(d) Reject H_0.
(e) At the 5% level of significance, there is sufficient evidence to conclude that Myers-Briggs type and area of study are not independent.

10. *Psychology: Myers-Briggs* The following table shows the Myers-Briggs personality preference and area of study for a random sample of 519 college students (*Applications of the Myers-Briggs Type Indicator in Higher Education*, edited by Provost and Anchors). In the table, IN refers to introvert, intuitive; EN refers to extrovert, intuitive; IS refers to introvert, sensing; and ES refers to extrovert, sensing.

Myers-Briggs Preference	Arts & Science	Business	Allied Health	Row Total
IN	64	15	17	96
EN	82	42	30	154
IS	68	35	12	115
ES	75	42	37	154
Column Total	289	134	96	519

Use a chi-square test to determine if Myers-Briggs preference type is independent of area of study at the 0.05 level of significance.

11. (a) $\alpha = 0.05$; H_0: Age of young adult and movie preference are independent; H_1: Age of young adult and movie preference are not independent.
(b) $\chi^2 = 3.6230$; $d.f. = 4$.
(c) $0.100 < P\text{-value} < 0.900$. From TI-84, $P\text{-value} \approx 0.4594$.
(d) Do not reject H_0.
(e) At the 5% level of significance, there is insufficient evidence to conclude that age of young adult and movie preference are not independent.

11. *Sociology: Movie Preference* Mr. Acosta, a sociologist, is doing a study to see if there is a relationship between the age of a young adult (18 to 35 years old) and the type of movie preferred. A random sample of 93 adults revealed the following data. Test whether age and type of movie preferred are independent at the 0.05 level.

	Person's Age			
Movie	**18–23 yr**	**24–29 yr**	**30–35 yr**	**Row Total**
Drama	8	15	11	34
Science fiction	12	10	8	30
Comedy	9	8	12	29
Column Total	29	33	31	93

12. *Sociology: Ethnic Groups* After a large fund drive to help the Boston City Library, the following information was obtained from a random sample of contributors to the library fund. Using a 1% level of significance, test the claim that the amount contributed to the library fund is independent of ethnic group.

12. (a) $\alpha = 0.01$; H_0: Contribution level and ethnic group are independent; H_1: Contribution level and ethnic group are not independent.
(b) $\chi^2 = 13.35$; *d.f.* $= 12$.
(c) $0.100 < P\text{-value} < 0.900$. From TI-84, $P\text{-value} \approx 0.3444$.
(d) Do not reject H_0.
(e) At the 1% level of significance, there is insufficient evidence to conclude that contribution level and ethnic group are not independent.

Ethnic Group	Number of People Making Contribution					
	$1–50	$51–100	$101–150	$151–200	Over $200	Row Total
A	83	62	53	35	18	251
B	94	77	48	25	20	264
C	78	65	51	40	32	266
D	105	89	63	54	29	340
Column Total	360	293	215	154	99	1121

13. (a) $\alpha = 0.05$; H_0: Stone tool construction material and site are independent; H_1: Stone tool construction material and site are not independent.
(b) $\chi^2 = 11.15$; *d.f.* $= 3$.
(c) $0.010 < P\text{-value} < 0.025$. From TI-84, $P\text{-value} \approx 0.0110$.
(d) Reject H_0.
(e) At the 5% level of significance, there is sufficient evidence to conclude that stone tool construction material and site are not independent.

13. *Focus Problem: Archaeology* The Focus Problem at the beginning of the chapter refers to excavations at Burnt Mesa Pueblo in Bandelier National Monument. One question the archaeologists asked was: Is raw material used by prehistoric Indians for stone tool manufacture independent of the archaeological excavation site? Two different excavation sites at Burnt Mesa Pueblo gave the information in the following table. Use a chi-square test with 5% level of significance to test the claim that raw material used for construction of stone tools and excavation site are independent.

Material	Stone Tool Construction Material, Burnt Mesa Pueblo		
	Site A	Site B	Row Total
Basalt	731	584	1315
Obsidian	102	93	195
Pedernal chert	510	525	1035
Other	85	94	179
Column Total	1428	1296	2724

14. (ii) (a) $\alpha = 0.01$; H_0: The proportions of Democratic and Republican congress members spending specific amounts on home district projects are the same. H_1: The proportions of Democratic and Republican congress members spending specific amounts on home district projects are not the same.
(b) $\chi^2 = 2.18$; *d.f.* $= 2$.
(c) $0.100 < P\text{-value} < 0.900$. From TI-84, $P\text{-value} \approx 0.3370$.
(d) Do not reject H_0.
(e) At the 1% level of significance, there is insufficient evidence to conclude that party affiliation and dollars spent are not independent.

14. *Political Affiliation: Spending* Two random samples were drawn from members of the U.S. Congress. One sample was taken from members who are Democrats and the other from members who are Republicans. For each sample, the number of dollars spent on federal projects in each congressperson's home district was recorded.
(i) Make a cluster bar graph showing the percentages of Congress members from each party who spent each designated amount in their respective home districts.
(ii) Use a 1% level of significance to test whether congressional members of each political party spent designated amounts in the same proportions.

Party	Dollars Spent on Federal Projects in Home Districts			
	Less than 5 Billion	5 to 10 Billion	More than 10 Billion	Row Total
Democratic	8	15	22	45
Republican	12	19	16	47
Column Total	20	34	38	92

15. *Sociology: Methods of Communication* Random samples of people ages 15–24 and of people ages 25–34 were asked about their preferred method of (remote)

15. (ii) (a) H_0: The proportions of the different age groups having each communication preference are the same. H_1: The proportions of the different age groups having each communication preference are not the same.
(b) $\chi^2 = 9.312$; $d.f. = 3$.
(c) $0.025 < P\text{-value} < 0.050$. From TI-84, $P\text{-value} \approx 0.0254$.
(d) Reject H_0.
(e) At the 5% level of significance, there is sufficient evidence to conclude that the two age groups do not have the same proportions of communications preferences.

communication with friends. The respondents were asked to select one of the methods from the following list: cell phone, instant message, e-mail, other.

(i) Make a cluster bar graph showing the percentages in each age group who selected each method.

(ii) Test whether the two populations share the same proportions of preferences for each type of communication method. Use $\alpha = 0.05$.

	Preferred Communication Method				
Age	Cell Phone	Instant Message	E-mail	Other	Row Total
15–24	48	40	5	7	100
25–34	41	30	15	14	100
Column Total	89	70	20	21	200

SECTION 11.2 Chi-Square: Goodness of Fit

FOCUS POINTS

- Set up a test to investigate how well a sample distribution fits a given distribution.
- Use observed and expected frequencies to compute the sample χ^2 statistic.
- Find or estimate the *P*-value and complete the test.

You can present this section first or by itself if you use the overview of the χ^2 distribution at the beginning of Part I.

Last year, the labor union bargaining agents listed five categories and asked each employee to mark the *one* most important to her or him. The categories and corresponding percentages of favorable responses are shown in Table 11-8 on the next page. The bargaining agents need to determine if the *current* distribution of responses "fits" last year's distribution or if it is different.

In questions of this type, we are asking whether a population follows a specified distribution. In other words, we are testing the hypotheses

Hypotheses

H_0: The population fits the given distribution.

H_1: The population has a different distribution.

Computing sample χ^2

We use the chi-square distribution to test "goodness-of-fit" hypotheses.

Just as with tests of independence, we compute the sample statistic:

$$\chi^2 = \Sigma\frac{(O - E)^2}{E} \text{ with degrees of freedom } = k - 1$$

where E = expected frequency

O = observed frequency

$\frac{(O - E)^2}{E}$ is summed for each category in the distribution

k = number of categories in the distribution

Next we use the chi-square distribution table (Table 5 of the Appendix) to estimate the *P*-value of the sample χ^2 statistic. Finally, we compare the *P*-value to the level of significance α and conclude the test.

TABLE 11-8 Bargaining Categories (last year)

Category	Percentage of Favorable Responses
Vacation time	4%
Salary	65%
Safety regulations	13%
Health and retirement benefits	12%
Overtime policy and pay	6%

This is a good time to emphasize that although we are continuing our study of the chi-square distribution, we are shifting gears to a new application with corresponding new methods. Data Highlights (drunk drivers) can be a good topic for class discussion.

In the case of a *goodness-of-fit test,* we use the null hypothesis to compute the expected values for the categories. Let's look at the bargaining category problem to see how this is done.

In the bargaining category problem, the two hypotheses are

H_0: The present distribution of responses is the same as last year's.

H_1: The present distribution of responses is different.

The null hypothesis tells us that the *expected frequencies* of the present response distribution should follow the percentages indicated in last year's survey. To test this hypothesis, a random sample of 500 employees was taken. If the null hypothesis is true, then there should be 4%, or 20 responses, out of the 500 rating vacation time as the most important bargaining issue. Table 11-9 gives the other expected values and all the information necessary to compute the sample statistic χ^2. We see that the sample statistic is

$$\chi^2 = \Sigma\frac{(O - E)^2}{E} = 14.15$$

Larger values of the sample statistic χ^2 indicate greater differences between the proposed distribution and the distribution followed by the sample. The larger the χ^2 statistic, the stronger the evidence to reject the null hypothesis that the population distribution fits the given distribution. Consequently, goodness-of-fit tests are always *right-tailed* tests.

Type of test

For *goodness-of-fit tests,* we use a *right-tailed* test on the chi-square distribution. This is because we are testing to see if the χ^2 measure of the difference between the observed and expected frequencies is too large to be due to chance alone.

To test the hypothesis that the present distribution of responses to bargaining categories is the same as last year's, we use the chi-square distribution (Table 5

TABLE 11-9 Observed and Expected Frequencies for Bargaining Categories

Category	O	E	$(O - E)^2$	$(O - E)^2/E$
Vacation time	30	4% of 500 = 20	100	5.00
Salary	290	65% of 500 = 325	1225	3.77
Safety	70	13% of 500 = 65	25	0.38
Health and retirement	70	12% of 500 = 60	100	1.67
Overtime	40	6% of 500 = 30	100	3.33
	$\Sigma O = 500$	$\Sigma E = 500$		$\Sigma\frac{(O - E)^2}{E} = 14.15$

Degrees of freedom

of the Appendix) to estimate the *P*-value of the sample statistic $\chi^2 = 14.15$. To estimate the *P*-value, we need to know the number of degrees of freedom. In the case of a goodness-of-fit test, the degrees of freedom are found by the following formula.

This is a good time to emphasize that the degrees of freedom used in this application are quite different from those used in Section 11.1 for tests of independence.

Degrees of freedom for goodness-of-fit test

$$d.f. = k - 1$$

where k = number of categories

Notice that when we compute the expected values *E*, we must use the null hypothesis to compute all but the last one. To compute the last one, we can subtract the previous expected values from the sample size. For instance, for the bargaining issues, we could have found the number of responses for overtime policy by adding the other expected values and subtracting that sum from the sample size 500. We would again get an expected value of 30 responses. The degrees of freedom, then, is the number of *E* values that *must* be computed by using the null hypothesis.

For the bargaining issues, we have

$$d.f. = 5 - 1 = 4$$

where $k = 5$ is the number of categories.

P-value

We now have the tools necessary to use Table 5 of the Appendix to estimate the *P*-value of $\chi^2 = 14.15$. Figure 11-5 shows the *P*-value. In Table 5, we use the row headed by $d.f. = 4$. We see that $\chi^2 = 14.15$ falls between the entries 13.28 and 14.86. Therefore, the *P*-value falls between the corresponding right-tail areas 0.005 and 0.010.

To test the hypothesis that the distribution of responses to bargaining issues is the same as last year's at the 1% level of significance, we compare the *P*-value of the statistic to $\alpha = 0.01$.

α

0.005 0.010

We see that the *P*-value is less than α, so we reject the null hypothesis that the distribution of responses to bargaining issues is the same as last year's. At the 1% level of significance, we can say that the evidence supports the conclusion that this year's responses to the issues are different from last year's.

Goodness-of-fit tests involve several steps that can be summarized as follows.

FIGURE 11-5

P-value

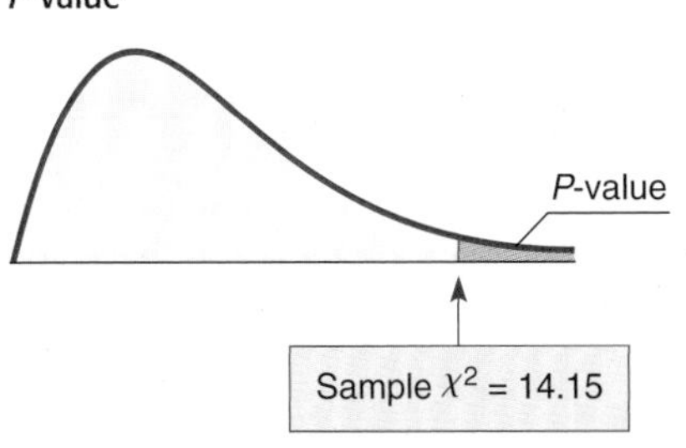

Right-tail Area	0.010	0.005
$d.f. = 4$	13.28	14.86
	↑ Sample $\chi^2 = 14.15$	

PROCEDURE

HOW TO TEST FOR GOODNESS OF FIT

First, each member of a population needs to be classified into exactly one of several different categories. Next, you need a specific (theoretical) distribution that assigns a fixed probability (or percentage) that a member of the population will fall into one of the categories. You then need a random sample size n from the population. Let O represent the *observed number* of data from the sample that fall into each category. Let E represent the *expected number* of data from the sample that, in theory, would fall into each category.

$$O = \text{observed frequency count of a category using sample data}$$
$$E = \text{expected frequency of a category}$$
$$= (\text{sample size } n)(\text{probability assigned to category})$$

The sample size n should be large enough so that $E \geq 5$ in each category.

1. Set the *level of significance* α and use the *hypotheses*

   H_0: The population fits the specified distribution of categories.

   H_1: The population has a different distribution.

2. For each category, compute $(O - E)^2/E$, then compute the sample *test statistic*

   $$\chi^2 = \Sigma\frac{(O - E)^2}{E} \quad \text{with } d.f. = k - 1$$

   where the sum is taken over all categories and k = number of categories.

3. Use the chi-square distribution (Table 5 of the Appendix) and a *right-tailed test* to find (or estimate) the *P-value* corresponding to the sample test statistic.
4. *Conclude* the test. If P-value $\leq \alpha$, then reject H_0. If P-value $> \alpha$, then do not reject H_0.
5. *Interpret your conclusion* in the context of the application.

One important application of goodness-of-fit tests is to genetics theory. Such an application is shown in Guided Exercise 6.

GUIDED EXERCISE 6 *Goodness-of-fit test*

According to genetics theory, red-green colorblindness in humans is a recessive sex-linked characteristic. In this case, the gene is carried on the X chromosome only. We will denote an X chromosome with the colorblindness gene by X_c and one without the gene by X_n. Women have two X chromosomes, and they will be red-green colorblind only if both chromosomes have the gene, designated X_cX_c. A woman can have normal vision but still carry the colorblind gene if only one of the chromosomes has the gene, designated X_cX_n. A man carries an X and a Y chromosome; if the X chromosome carries the colorblind gene (X_cY), the man is colorblind.

According to genetics theory, if a man with normal vision (X_nY) and a woman carrier (X_cX_n) have a child, the probabilities that the child will have red-green colorblindness, will have normal vision and not carry the gene, or will have normal vision and carry the gene are given by the *equally likely* events in Table 11-10.

Continued

GUIDED EXERCISE 6 *continued*

$P(\text{child has normal vision and is not a carrier}) = P(X_nY) + P(X_nX_n) = \frac{1}{2}$

$P(\text{child has normal vision and is a carrier}) = P(X_cX_n) = \frac{1}{4}$

$P(\text{child is red-green colorblind}) = P(X_cY) = \frac{1}{4}$

TABLE 11-10
Red-Green Colorblindness

	Father	
Mother	X_n	Y
X_c	X_cX_n	X_cY
X_n	X_nX_n	X_nY

To test this genetics theory, Genetics Labs took a random sample of 200 children whose mothers were carriers of the colorblind gene and whose fathers had normal vision. The results are shown in Table 11-11. We wish to test the hypothesis that the population follows the distribution predicted by the genetics theory (see Table 11-10). Use a 1% level of significance.

(a) State the null and alternate hypotheses. What is α?

H_0: The population fits the distribution predicted by genetics theory.

H_1: The population does not fit the distribution predicted by genetics theory.

$\alpha = 0.01$

(b) Fill in the rest of Table 11-11 and use the table to compute the sample statistic χ^2.

TABLE 11-11 Colorblindness Sample

Event	O	E	$(O - E)^2$	$(O - E)^2/E$
Red-green colorblind	35	50	225	4.50
Normal vision, noncarrier	105	____	____	____
Normal vision, carrier	60	____	____	____

TABLE 11-12 Completion of Table 11-11

Event	O	E	$(O - E)^2$	$(O - E)^2/E$
Red-green colorblind	35	50	225	4.50
Normal vision, noncarrier	105	100	25	0.25
Normal vision, carrier	60	50	100	2.00

The sample statistic is $\chi^2 = \Sigma\frac{(O - E)^2}{E} = 6.75$.

(c) There are $k = 3$ categories listed in Table 11-11. Use this information to compute the degrees of freedom.

$d.f. = k - 1$
$= 3 - 1 = 2$

(d) Find the P-value for $\chi^2 = 6.75$.

Using Table 5 of the Appendix and the fact that goodness-of-fit tests are right-tailed tests, we see that

Right-tail Area	0.050	0.025
$d.f. = 2$	5.99	7.38
	↑ Sample $\chi^2 = 6.75$	

$0.025 < P\text{-value} < 0.050$

(e) Conclude the test for $\alpha = 0.01$.

For $\alpha = 0.01$, we have

α
0.01 0.025 0.050

Since P-value $> \alpha$, do not reject H_0.

(f) Interpret the conclusion in the context of the application.

At the 1% level of significance, there is insufficient evidence to conclude that the population follows a distribution different from that predicted by genetics theory.

VIEWPOINT Run! Run! Run!

What description would you use for marathon runners? How about age distribution? Body weight? Length of stride? Heart rate? Blood pressure? What countries do these runners come from? What are their best running times? Make your own estimated distribution for these variables, and then consider a goodness-of-fit test for your distribution compared with available data. For more information on marathon runners, visit the Online Study Center at **www.cengage.com/statistics/Brase/UBS5e** *and find links to the Honolulu marathon site and to the* Runners World *site.*

SECTION 11.2 PROBLEMS

1. *Statistical Literacy* For a chi-square goodness-of-fit test, how are the degrees of freedom computed?

2. *Statistical Literacy* How are expected frequencies computed for goodness-of-fit tests?

3. *Statistical Literacy* Explain why goodness-of-fit tests are always right-tailed tests.

4. *Critical Thinking* When the sample evidence is sufficient to justify rejecting the null hypothesis in a goodness-of-fit test, can you tell exactly how the distribution of observed values over the specified categories differs from the expected distribution? Explain.

For Problems 5–14, please provide the following information.
(a) What is the level of significance? State the null and alternate hypotheses.
(b) Find the value of the chi-square statistic for the sample. Are all the expected frequencies greater than 5? What sampling distribution will you use? What are the degrees of freedom?
(c) Find or estimate the P-value of the sample test statistic.
(d) Based on your answers in parts (a) to (c), will you reject or fail to reject the null hypothesis that the population fits the specified distribution of categories?
(e) Interpret your conclusion in the context of the application.

5. *Census: Age* The age distribution of the Canadian population and the age distribution of a random sample of 455 residents in the Indian community of Red Lake Village (Northwest Territories) are shown below (based on *U.S. Bureau of the Census, International Data Base*).

Age (years)	Percent of Canadian Population	Observed Number in Red Lake Village
Under 5	7.2%	47
5 to 14	13.6%	75
15 to 64	67.1%	288
65 and older	12.1%	45

Use a 5% level of significance to test the claim that the age distribution of the general Canadian population fits the age distribution of the residents of Red Lake Village.

6. *Census: Type of Household* The type of household for the U.S. population and for a random sample of 411 households from the community of Dove Creek, Montana, are shown (based on *Statistical Abstract of the United States*).

1. *d.f.* = number of categories − 1.
2. Consider the sample size n of all the observed frequencies. The expected frequency for a category is computed by taking the proportion of n designated by the proposed distribution.
3. The greater the differences between the observed frequencies and the expected frequencies, the higher the sample χ^2 value. Greater χ^2 values lead to the conclusion that the differences between expected and observed frequencies are too large to be explained by chance alone.
4. No. When we reject the null hypothesis in a goodness-of-fit test, we say that the observed distribution is simply different from the expected distribution. The test does not tell us how the distributions differ in each category.
5. (a) $\alpha = 0.05$; H_0: The distributions are the same; H_1: The distributions are different.
(b) Sample $\chi^2 = 11.788$; *d.f.* = 3.
(c) $0.005 < P\text{-value} < 0.010$.
(d) Reject H_0.
(e) At the 5% level of significance, the evidence is sufficient to conclude that the age distribution of the Red Lake Village population does not fit that of the general Canadian population.

6. (a) $\alpha = 0.05$; H_0: The distributions are the same; H_1: The distributions are different.
(b) Sample $\chi^2 = 13.017$; $d.f. = 4$.
(c) $0.010 < P\text{-value} < 0.025$.
(d) Reject H_0.
(e) At the 5% level of significance, the evidence is sufficient to conclude that the Dove Creek household distribution does not fit the general U.S. household distribution.

Type of Household	Percent of U.S. Households	Observed Number of Households in Dove Creek
Married with children	26%	102
Married, no children	29%	112
Single parent	9%	33
One person	25%	96
Other (e.g., roommates, siblings)	11%	68

Use a 5% level of significance to test the claim that the distribution of U.S. households fits the Dove Creek distribution.

7. (a) $\alpha = 0.01$; H_0: The distributions are the same; H_1: The distributions are different.
(b) Sample $\chi^2 = 0.1984$; $d.f. = 4$.
(c) $P\text{-value} > 0.995$. (Note that as the χ^2 values decrease, the area in the right tail increases, so $\chi^2 < 0.207$ means that the corresponding $P\text{-value} > 0.995$.)
(d) Do not reject H_0.
(e) At the 1% level of significance, the evidence is insufficient to conclude that the regional distribution of raw materials does not fit the distribution at the current excavation site.

7. *Archaeology: Stone Tools* The types of raw materials used to construct stone tools found at the archaeological site Casa del Rito are shown below (*Bandelier Archaeological Excavation Project*, edited by Kohler and Root). A random sample of 1486 stone tools was obtained from a current excavation site.

Raw Material	Regional Percent of Stone Tools	Observed Number of Tools at Current Excavation Site
Basalt	61.3%	906
Obsidian	10.6%	162
Welded tuff	11.4%	168
Pedernal chert	13.1%	197
Other	3.6%	53

Use a 1% level of significance to test the claim that the regional distribution of raw materials fits the distribution at the current excavation site.

8. (a) $\alpha = 0.05$; H_0: The distributions are the same; H_1: The distributions are different.
(b) Sample $\chi^2 = 1.084$; $d.f. = 4$.
(c) $0.100 < P\text{-value} < 0.900$.
(d) Do not reject H_0.
(e) At the 5% level of significance, the evidence is insufficient to conclude that the natural distribution of browse does not fit the feeding pattern.

8. *Ecology: Deer* The types of browse favored by deer are shown in the following table (*The Mule Deer of Mesa Verde National Park*, edited by Mierau and Schmidt). Using binoculars, volunteers observed the feeding habits of a random sample of 320 deer.

Type of Browse	Plant Composition in Study Area	Observed Number of Deer Feeding on This Plant
Sage brush	32%	102
Rabbit brush	38.7%	125
Salt brush	12%	43
Service berry	9.3%	27
Other	8%	23

Use a 5% level of significance to test the claim that the natural distribution of browse fits the deer feeding pattern.

Students sometimes ask how to determine if a distribution is normal. There are several techniques to test whether a distribution is normal. One technique shown in Problems 9 and 10 utilizes the empirical rule to see if the observed distribution "fits" a normal distribution.

9. *Meteorology: Normal Distribution* The following problem is based on information from the *National Oceanic and Atmospheric Administration (NOAA) Environmental Data Service*. Let x be a random variable that represents the average daily temperature (in degrees Fahrenheit) in July in the town of Kit Carson, Colorado. The x distribution has a mean μ of approximately 75°F and standard deviation σ of approximately 8°F. A 20-year study (620 July days) gave the entries in the rightmost column of the following table.

9. (i) Essay.
   (ii) (a) $\alpha = 0.01$; H_0: The distributions are the same; H_1: The distributions are different.
   (b) Sample $\chi^2 = 1.5693$; $d.f. = 5$.
   (c) $0.900 < P$-value < 0.950.
   (d) Do not reject H_0.
   (e) At the 1% level of significance, the evidence is insufficient to conclude that the average daily July temperature does not follow a normal distribution.

I Region under Normal Curve	II x°F	III Expected % from Normal Curve	IV Observed Number of Days in 20 Years
$\mu - 3\sigma \le x < \mu - 2\sigma$	$51 \le x < 59$	2.35%	16
$\mu - 2\sigma \le x < \mu - \sigma$	$59 \le x < 67$	13.5%	78
$\mu - \sigma \le x < \mu$	$67 \le x < 75$	34%	212
$\mu \le x < \mu + \sigma$	$75 \le x < 83$	34%	221
$\mu + \sigma \le x < \mu + 2\sigma$	$83 \le x < 91$	13.5%	81
$\mu + 2\sigma \le x < \mu + 3\sigma$	$91 \le x < 99$	2.35%	12

(i) Remember that $\mu = 75$ and $\sigma = 8$. Examine Figure 7-3 in Chapter 7. Write a brief explanation for columns I, II, and III in the context of this problem.
(ii) Use a 1% level of significance to test the claim that the average daily July temperature follows a normal distribution with $\mu = 75$ and $\sigma = 8$.

10. (i) Essay.
   (ii) (a) $\alpha = 0.01$; H_0: The distributions are the same; H_1: The distributions are different.
   (b) Sample $\chi^2 = 0.2562$; $d.f. = 5$.
   (c) P-value > 0.995.
   (d) Do not reject H_0.
   (e) At the 1% level of significance, the evidence is insufficient to conclude that the average daily January temperature does not follow a normal distribution.

10. *Meteorology: Normal Distribution* Let x be a random variable that represents the average daily temperature (in degrees Fahrenheit) in January for the town of Hana, Maui. The x variable has a mean μ of approximately 68°F and standard deviation σ of approximately 4°F (see reference in Problem 9). A 20-year study (620 January days) gave the entries in the rightmost column of the following table.

I Region under Normal Curve	II x°F	III Expected % from Normal Curve	IV Observed Number of Days in 20 Years
$\mu - 3\sigma \le x < \mu - 2\sigma$	$56 \le x < 60$	2.35%	14
$\mu - 2\sigma \le x < \mu - \sigma$	$60 \le x < 64$	13.5%	86
$\mu - \sigma \le x < \mu$	$64 \le x < 68$	34%	207
$\mu \le x < \mu + \sigma$	$68 \le x < 72$	34%	215
$\mu + \sigma \le x < \mu + 2\sigma$	$72 \le x < 76$	13.5%	83
$\mu + 2\sigma \le x < \mu + 3\sigma$	$76 \le x < 80$	2.35%	15

(i) Remember that $\mu = 68$ and $\sigma = 4$. Examine Figure 7-3 in Chapter 7. Write a brief explanation for columns I, II, and III in the context of this problem.
(ii) Use a 1% level of significance to test the claim that the average daily January temperature follows a normal distribution with $\mu = 68$ and $\sigma = 4$.

11. (a) $\alpha = 0.05$; H_0: The distributions are the same; H_1: The distributions are different.
   (b) Sample $\chi^2 = 9.333$; $d.f. = 3$.
   (c) $0.025 < P$-value < 0.050.
   (d) Reject H_0.
   (e) At the 5% level of significance, the evidence is sufficient to conclude that the current fish distribution is different than it was 5 years ago.

11. *Ecology: Fish* The Fish and Game Department stocked Lake Lulu with fish in the following proportions: 30% catfish, 15% bass, 40% bluegill, and 15% pike. Five years later it sampled the lake to see if the distribution of fish had changed. It found that the 500 fish in the sample were distributed as follows.

Catfish	Bass	Bluegill	Pike
120	85	220	75

In the 5-year interval, did the distribution of fish change at the 0.05 level?

12. *Library: Book Circulation* The director of library services at Fairmont College did a survey of types of books (by subject) in the circulation library. Then she used library records to take a random sample of 888 books checked out last

12. (a) $\alpha = 0.05$; H_0: The distributions are the same; H_1: The distributions are different.
(b) Sample $\chi^2 = 11.92$; $d.f. = 4$.
(c) $0.010 < P\text{-value} < 0.025$.
(d) Reject H_0.
(e) At the 5% level of significance, the evidence is sufficient to conclude that the subject distribution of books in the library is different from that of books checked out by students.

term and classified the books in the sample by subject. The results are shown below.

Subject Area	Percent of Books in Circulation Library on This Subject	Number of Books in Sample on This Subject
Business	32%	268
Humanities	25%	214
Natural science	20%	215
Social science	15%	115
All other subjects	8%	76

Using a 5% level of significance, test the claim that the subject distribution of books in the library fits the distribution of books checked out by students.

13. (a) $\alpha = 0.01$; H_0: The distributions are the same; H_1: The distributions are different.
(b) Sample $\chi^2 = 13.70$; $d.f. = 5$.
(c) $0.010 < P\text{-value} < 0.025$.
(d) Do not reject H_0.
(e) At the 1% level of significance, the evidence is insufficient to conclude that the census ethnic origin distribution and the ethnic origin distribution of city residents are different.

13. *Census: California* The accuracy of a census report on a city in southern California was questioned by some government officials. A random sample of 1215 people living in the city was used to check the report, and the results are shown here:

Ethnic Origin	Census Percent	Sample Result
Black	10%	127
Asian	3%	40
Anglo	38%	480
Latino/Latina	41%	502
Native American	6%	56
All others	2%	10

Using a 1% level of significance, test the claim that the census distribution and the sample distribution agree.

14. *Accounting Records: Benford's Law* Benford's Law states that the first nonzero digits of numbers drawn at random from a large complex data file have the following probability distribution. (Reference: American Statistical Association, *Chance*, Vol. 12, No. 3, pp. 27–31; see also the Focus Problem of Chapter 9.)

First nonzero digit	1	2	3	4	5	6	7	8	9
Probability	0.301	0.176	0.125	0.097	0.079	0.067	0.058	0.051	0.046

14. (a) $\alpha = 0.01$; H_0: The distributions are the same; H_1: The distributions are different.
(b) Sample $\chi^2 = 3.559$; $d.f. = 8$.
(c) $0.100 < P\text{-value} < 0.900$.
(d) Do not reject H_0.
(e) At the 1% level of significance, the evidence is insufficient to conclude that the distribution of first nonzero digits in the accounting file does not follow Benford's Law.

Suppose that $n = 275$ numerical entries were drawn at random from a large accounting file of a major corporation. The first nonzero digits were recorded for the sample.

First nonzero digit	1	2	3	4	5	6	7	8	9
Sample frequency	83	49	32	22	25	18	13	17	16

Use a 1% level of significance to test the claim that the distribution of first nonzero digits in this accounting file follows Benford's Law.

SECTION 11.3

Testing a Single Variance or Standard Deviation

FOCUS POINTS

- Set up a test for a single variance σ^2.
- Compute the sample χ^2 statistic.
- Use the χ^2 distribution to estimate a P-value and conclude the test.

Testing σ^2

This section can be presented by itself as long as the overview of the χ^2 distribution at the beginning of Part I is used.

Many problems arise that require us to make decisions about variability. In this section, we will test hypotheses about the variance (or standard deviation) of a population. It is customary to talk about variance instead of standard deviation because our techniques employ the sample variance rather than the standard deviation. Of course, the standard deviation is just the square root of the variance, so any discussion about variance is easily converted to a similar discussion about standard deviation.

Let us consider a specific example in which we might wish to test a hypothesis about the variance. Almost everyone has had to wait in line. In a grocery store, bank, post office, or registration center, there are usually several checkout or service areas. Frequently, each service area has its own independent line. However, many businesses and government offices are adopting a "single-line" procedure.

In this section, we present more applications of the chi-square distribution.

In a single-line procedure, there is only one waiting line for everyone. As any service area becomes available, the next person in line gets served. The old independent-lines procedure has a line at each service center. An incoming customer simply picks the shortest line and hopes it will move quickly. In either procedure, the number of clerks and the rate at which they work is the same, so the average waiting time is the *same*. What is the advantage of the single-line procedure? The difference is in the *attitudes* of people who wait in the lines. A lengthy waiting line will be more acceptable if the variability of waiting times is smaller, even though the average waiting time is the same. When the variability is small, the inconvenience of waiting (although it might not be reduced) does become more predictable. This means impatience is reduced and people are happier.

To test the hypothesis that variability is less in a single-line process, we use the chi-square distribution. The next theorem tells us how to use the sample and population variance to compute values of χ^2.

THEOREM 11.1 If we have a *normal* population with variance σ^2 and a random sample of n measurements is taken from this population with sample variance s^2, then

$$\chi^2 = \frac{(n-1)s^2}{\sigma^2}$$

has a chi-square distribution with degrees of freedom $d.f. = n - 1$.

Recall that the chi-square distribution is *not* symmetrical and that there are different chi-square distributions for different degrees of freedom. Table 5 of the Appendix gives chi-square values for which the area α is to the *right* of the given chi-square value.

Table 11-13 summarizes the techniques for using the chi-square distribution (Table 5 of the Appendix) to find P-values for a right-tailed test, a left-tailed test, and a two-tailed test. Example 3 demonstrates the technique of finding P-values for a left-tailed test. Example 4 demonstrates the technique for a two-tailed test, and Guided Exercise 7 uses a right-tailed test.

TABLE 11-13 *P*-values for Chi-Square Distribution Table (Table 5 of the Appendix)

<table>
<tr><td>(a) Right-tailed test
Since the chi-square table gives right-tail probabilities, you can use the table directly to find or estimate the P-value.</td><td>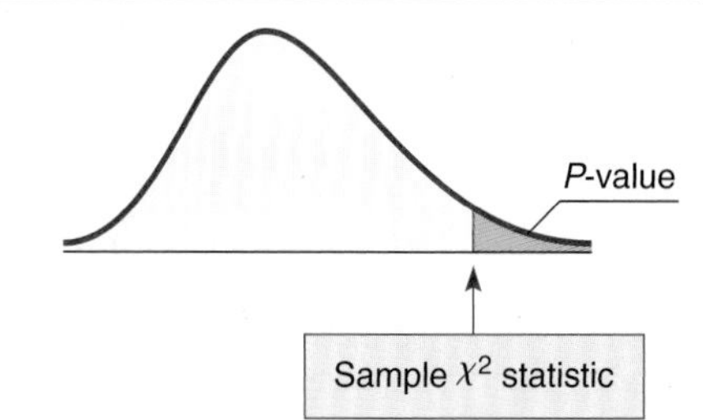
</td></tr>
<tr><td>(b) Left-tailed test
Since the chi-square table gives right-tail probabilities, you first find or estimate the quantity 1 − (P-value) from the right tail. Then subtract from 1 to get the P-value of the left-tail.</td><td>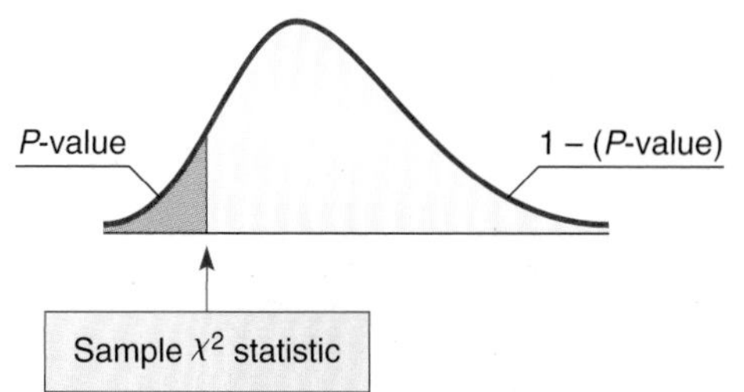
</td></tr>
<tr><td>(c) Two-tailed test
Remember that the P-value is the probability of getting a test statistic as extreme as, or more extreme than, the test statistic computed from the sample. For a two-tailed test, we need to account for corresponding equal areas in both the upper and lower tails. This means that in each tail, we have an area of P-value/2. The total P-value is then
$P\text{-value} = 2\left(\frac{P\text{-value}}{2}\right)$</td><td>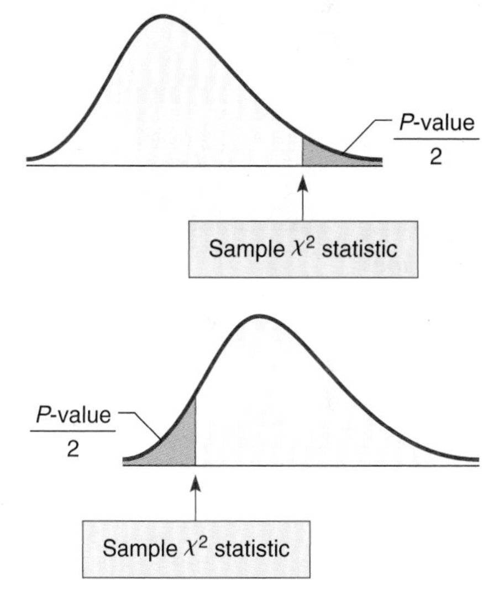

Be sure to choose the area in the appropriate tail (left or right) so that $\frac{P\text{-value}}{2} \le 0.5$.</td></tr>
</table>

Now let's use Theorem 11.1 and our knowledge of the chi-square distribution to determine if a single-line procedure has less variance of waiting times than independent lines.

EXAMPLE 3 TESTING THE VARIANCE (LEFT-TAILED TEST)

For years, a large discount store has used independent lines to check out customers. Historically the standard deviation of waiting times is 7 minutes. The manager tried a new single-line procedure. A random sample of 25 customers using the single-line procedure was monitored, and it was found that the standard deviation for waiting times was only $s = 5$ minutes. Use $\alpha = 0.05$ to test the claim that the variance in waiting times is reduced for the single-line method.

Establish H_0 and H_1

SOLUTION: As a null hypothesis, we assume that the variance of waiting times is the same as that of the former independent-lines procedure. The alternate hypothesis is that the variance for the single-line procedure is less than that for the independent-lines procedure. If we let σ be the standard deviation of waiting times for the single-line procedure, then σ^2 is the variance, and we have

Sample χ^2 value and degrees of freedom

H_0: $\sigma^2 = 49$ $\quad$ H_1: $\sigma^2 < 49$ $\quad$ (use $7^2 = 49$)

P-value

We use the chi-square distribution to test the hypotheses. Assuming that the waiting times are normally distributed, we compute our observed value of χ^2 by using Theorem 11.1, with $n = 25$.

$$s = 5 \quad \text{so} \quad s^2 = 25 \qquad \text{(observed from sample)}$$

$$\sigma = 7 \quad \text{so} \quad \sigma^2 = 49 \qquad \text{(from } H_0\text{: } \sigma^2 = 49\text{)}$$

Checkout lines

$$\chi^2 = \frac{(n-1)s^2}{\sigma^2} = \frac{(25-1)25}{49} \approx 12.24$$

$$d.f. = n - 1 = 25 - 1 = 24$$

Next we estimate the P-value for $\chi^2 = 12.24$. Since we have a left-tailed test, the P-value is the area of the chi-square distribution that lies to the *left* of $\chi^2 = 12.24$, as shown in Figure 11-6.

To estimate the P-value on the left, we consider the fact that the area of the right tail is between 0.975 and 0.990. To find an estimate for the area of the left tail, we *subtract* each right-tail endpoint from 1. The P-value (area of the left tail) is in the interval

$$1 - 0.990 < P\text{-value of left tail} < 1 - 0.975$$

$$0.010 < P\text{-value} < 0.025$$

Test conclusion

To conclude the test, we compare the P-value to the level of significance $\alpha = 0.05$.

α

0.010 $\quad$ 0.025 $\quad$ 0.05

Since the P-value is less than α, we reject H_0. At the 5% level of significance, we conclude that the variance of waiting times for a single line is less than the variance of waiting times for multiple lines.

FIGURE 11-6

P-value

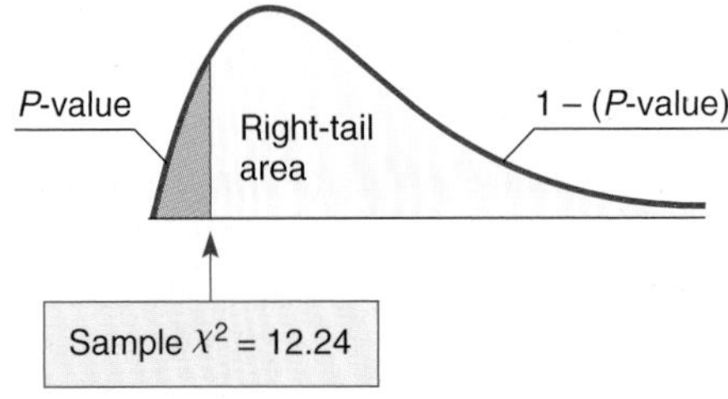

Right-tail Area	0.990	0.975
$d.f. = 24$	10.86	12.40
	↑ Sample $\chi^2 = 12.24$	

The steps used in Example 3 for testing the variance σ^2 are summarized as follows.

PROCEDURE

HOW TO TEST σ^2

You first need to know that a random variable x has a normal distribution. In testing σ^2, the normal assumption must be strictly observed (whereas in testing means, we can say "normal" or "approximately normal"). Next you need a random sample (size $n \geq 2$) of values from the x distribution for which you compute the sample variance s^2.

1. In the context of the problem, state the *null hypothesis* H_0 and the *alternate hypothesis* H_1, and set the *level of significance* α.
2. Use the value of σ^2 given in the null hypothesis H_0, the sample variance s^2, and the sample size n to compute the sample *test statistic*

$$\chi^2 = \frac{(n-1)s^2}{\sigma^2} \quad \text{with degrees of freedom } d.f. = n - 1$$

3. Use a chi-square distribution and the type of test to find or estimate the *P-value*. Use the procedures shown in Table 11-13 and Table 5 of the Appendix.
4. *Conclude* the test. If P-value $\leq \alpha$, then reject H_0. If P-value $> \alpha$, then do not reject H_0.
5. *Interpret your conclusion* in the context of the application.

EXAMPLE 4

TESTING THE VARIANCE (TWO-TAILED TEST)

Let x be a random variable that represents weight loss (in pounds) after following a certain diet for 6 months. After extensive study, it is found that x has a normal distribution with $\sigma = 5.7$ pounds. A new modification of the diet has been implemented. A random sample of $n = 21$ people use the modified diet for 6 months. For these people, the sample standard deviation of weight loss is $s = 4.1$ pounds. Does this result indicate that the variance of weight loss for the modified diet is different (either way) from the variance of weight loss for the original diet? Use $\alpha = 0.01$.

(a) What is the level of significance? State the null and alternate hypotheses.

SOLUTION: We are using $\alpha = 0.01$. The standard deviation of weight loss for the original diet is $\sigma = 5.7$ pounds, so the variance is $\sigma^2 = 32.49$. The null hypothesis is that the weight loss variance for the modified diet is the same as that for the original diet. The alternate hypothesis is that the variance is different.

$$H_0: \sigma^2 = 32.49 \qquad H_1: \sigma^2 \neq 32.49$$

(b) Compute the sample χ^2 statistic and the degrees of freedom.

SOLUTION: Using sample size $n = 21$, sample standard deviation $s = 4.1$ pounds, and $\sigma^2 = 32.49$ from the null hypothesis, we have

$$\chi^2 = \frac{(n-1)s^2}{\sigma^2} = \frac{(21-1)4.1^2}{32.49} \approx 10.35$$

with degrees of freedom $d.f. = n - 1 = 21 - 1 = 20$.

(c) Use the chi-square distribution (Table 5 of the Appendix) to estimate the P-value.

FIGURE 11-7

P-value

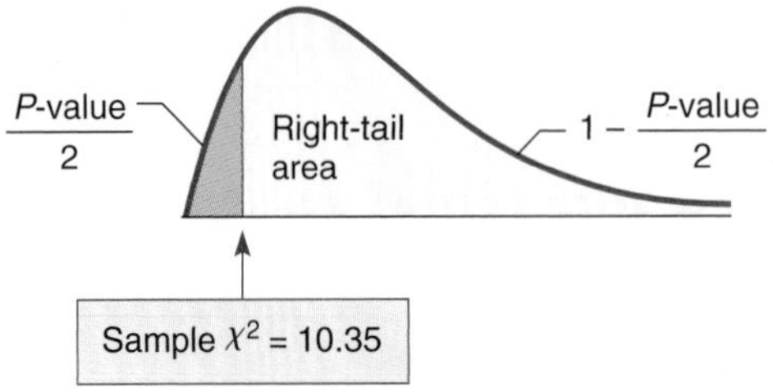

Right-tail Area	0.975	0.950
d.f. = 20	8.59	10.85
	↑ Sample $\chi^2 \approx 10.35$	

SOLUTION: For a *two-tailed* test, the area beyond the sample χ^2 represents *half* the total *P*-value or (*P*-value)/2. Figure 11-7 shows this region, which is to the left of $\chi^2 \approx 10.35$. However, Table 5 of the Appendix gives the areas in the *right tail.* We use Table 5 to find the area in the right tail and then subtract from 1 to find the corresponding area in the left tail.

From the table, we see that the right-tail area falls in the interval between 0.950 and 0.975. Subtracting each endpoint of the interval from 1 gives us an interval containing (*P*-value)/2. Multiplying by 2 gives an interval for the *P*-value.

$$1 - 0.975 < \frac{P\text{-value}}{2} < 1 - 0.950 \quad \text{Subtract right-tail-area endpoints from 1.}$$

$$0.025 < \frac{P\text{-value}}{2} < 0.050$$

$$0.05 < P\text{-value} < 0.10 \quad \text{Multiply each part by 2.}$$

(d) Conclude the test.

SOLUTION: The *P*-value is greater than $\alpha = 0.01$, so we do not reject H_0.

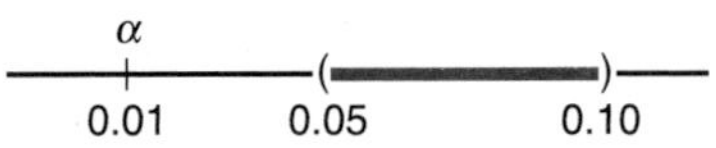

(e) Interpret the conclusion in the context of the application.

SOLUTION: At the 1% level of significance, there is insufficient evidence to conclude that the variance of weight loss using the modified diet is different from the variance of weight loss using the original diet.

GUIDED EXERCISE 7 Testing the variance (right-tailed test)

Certain industrial machines require overhaul when wear on their parts introduces too much variability to pass inspection. A government official is visiting a dentist's office to inspect the operation of an x-ray machine. If the machine emits too little radiation, clear photographs cannot be obtained. However, too much radiation can be harmful to the patient. Government regulations specify an average emission of 60 millirads with standard deviation σ of 12 millirads, and the machine has been set for these readings. After examining the machine, the inspector is satisfied that the average emission is still 60 millirads. However, there is wear on certain mechanical parts. To test variability, the inspector takes a random sample of 30 x-ray emissions and finds the sample standard deviation to be $s = 15$ millirads. Does this support the claim that the variance is too high (i.e., the machine should be overhauled)? Use a 1% level of significance.

Continued

GUIDED EXERCISE 7 *continued*

Let σ be the (population) standard deviation of emissions (in millirads) of the machine in its present condition.

(a) What is α? State H_0 and H_1.

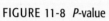

$\alpha = 0.01$. Government regulations specify that $\sigma = 12$. This means that the variance $\sigma^2 = 144$. We are to test the claim that the variance is higher than government specifications allow.

H_0: $\sigma^2 = 144$ and H_1: $\sigma^2 > 144$

(b) Compute the sample statistic χ^2 and corresponding degrees of freedom.

Using $n = 30$, $s = 15$, and $\sigma^2 = 144$ from H_0,

$$\chi^2 = \frac{(n-1)s^2}{\sigma^2} = \frac{(30-1)15^2}{144} \approx 45.3$$

Degrees of freedom $d.f. = n - 1 = 30 - 1 = 29$

(c) Estimate the P-value for the sample $\chi^2 = 45.3$ with $d.f. = 29$.

FIGURE 11-8 *P*-value

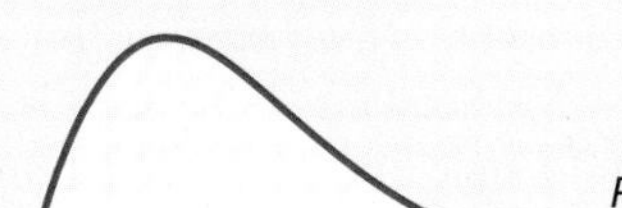

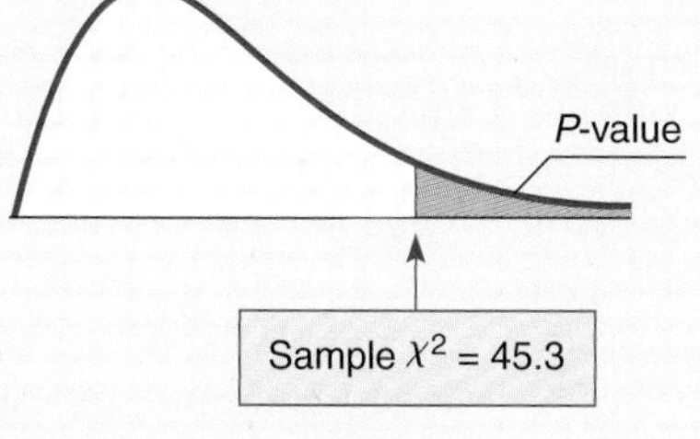

Since this is a *right-tailed* test, we look up P-values directly in the chi-square table (Table 5 of the Appendix).

Right-tail Area	0.050	0.025
d.f. = 29	42.56	45.72
	↑ Sample χ^2 = 45.3	

$0.025 < P\text{-value} < 0.050$

(d) Conclude the test.

The P-value for $\chi^2 = 45.3$ is greater than $\alpha = 0.01$.

α: 0.01 — (0.025 — 0.050)

Fail to reject H_0.

(e) Interpret the conclusion in the context of the application.

At the 1% level of significance, there is insufficient evidence to conclude that the variance of the radiation emitted by the machine is greater than that specified by government regulations. The evidence does not indicate that an adjustment is necessary at this time.

VIEWPOINT Adoption—A Good Choice!

Cuckoos are birds that are known to lay their eggs in the nests of other (host) birds. The host birds then hatch the eggs and adopt the cuckoo chicks as their own. Birds such as the meadow pipit, tree pipit, hedge sparrow, robin, and wren all have played host to cuckoo eggs and adopted their chicks. L. H. C. Tippett (1902–1985) was a pioneer in the field of statistical quality control who collected data on cuckoo eggs found in the nests of other birds. For more information and data from Tippett's study, visit the Online Study Center at **www.cengage.com/statistics/Brase/UBS5e** *and find a link to DASL, the Carnegie Mellon University Data and Story Library. Find Biology under Data Subjects, and then select the Cuckoo Egg Length Data file.*

SECTION 11.3 PROBLEMS

1. Yes. No, the chi-square test of variance requires that the x distribution be a normal distribution.
2. Use a histogram and boxplot to check for symmetry and to check that there are no outliers. Look at a normal quantile plot (generated by Minitab, SPSS, or the TI-84Plus calculator) to see if it is linear. Also, use a goodness-of-fit test to determine whether the distribution follows the empirical rule.
3. (a) $\alpha = 0.05$; H_0: $\sigma^2 = 42.3$; H_1: $\sigma^2 > 42.3$.
   (b) $\chi^2 \approx 23.98$; *d.f.* $= 22$.
   (c) $0.100 < P\text{-value} < 0.900$.
   (d) Do not reject H_0.
   (e) At the 5% level of significance, there is insufficient evidence to conclude that the variance is greater in the new section.
4. (a) $\alpha = 0.05$; H_0: $\sigma^2 = 5.1$; H_1: $\sigma^2 < 5.1$.
   (b) $\chi^2 \approx 25.88$; *d.f.* $= 40$.
   (c) Right-tail area between 0.975 and 0.950; $0.025 < P\text{-value} < 0.05$.
   (d) Reject H_0.
   (e) At the 5% level of significance, there is sufficient evidence to conclude that the current variance of age at first marriage is less than 5.1.
5. (a) $\alpha = 0.01$; H_0: $\sigma^2 = 136.2$; H_1: $\sigma^2 < 136.2$.
   (b) $\chi^2 \approx 5.92$; *d.f.* $= 7$.
   (c) Right-tailed area between 0.900 and 0.100; $0.100 < P\text{-value} < 0.900$.
   (d) Do not reject H_0.
   (e) At the 1% level of significance, there is insufficient evidence to conclude that the variance for number of mountain-climber deaths is less than 136.2.
6. (a) $\alpha = 0.05$; H_0: $\sigma^2 = 47.1$; H_1: $\sigma^2 > 47.1$.
   (b) $\chi^2 \approx 24.73$; *d.f.* $= 14$.
   (c) $0.025 < P\text{-value} < 0.050$.
   (d) Reject H_0.
   (e) At the 5% level of significance, there is sufficient evidence to conclude that the variance of annual salaries is greater in Kansas.
7. (a) $\alpha = 0.05$; H_0: $\sigma^2 = 9$; H_1: $\sigma^2 < 9$.
   (b) $\chi^2 \approx 8.82$; *d.f.* $= 22$.
   (c) Right-tail area is between 0.995 and 0.990; $0.005 < P\text{-value} < 0.010$.

1. *Statistical Literacy* Does the x distribution need to be normal in order to use the chi-square distribution to test the variance? Is it acceptable to use the chi-square distribution to test the variance if the x distribution is simply mound-shaped and more or less symmetric?

2. ***Critical Thinking*** The x distribution must be normal in order to use a chi-square distribution to test the variance. What are some methods you can use to assess whether the x distribution is normal? *Hint:* See Chapter 7 and goodness-of-fit tests.

For Problems 3–11, please provide the following information.

(a) What is the level of significance? State the null and alternate hypotheses.
(b) Find the value of the chi-square statistic for the sample. What are the degrees of freedom? What assumptions are you making about the original distribution?
(c) Find or estimate the P-value of the sample test statistic.
(d) Based on your answers in parts (a) to (c), will you reject or fail to reject the null hypothesis of independence?
(e) Interpret your conclusion in the context of the application.

In each of the following problems, assume a normal population distribution.

3. *Archaeology: Chaco Canyon* The following problem is based on information from *Archaeological Surveys of Chaco Canyon, New Mexico,* by A. Hayes, D. Brugge, and W. Judge, University of New Mexico Press. A *transect* is an archaeological study area that is 1/5 mile wide and 1 mile long. A *site* in a transect is the location of a significant archaeological find. Let x represent the number of sites per transect. In a section of Chaco Canyon, a large number of transects showed that x has a population variance $\sigma^2 = 42.3$. In a different section of Chaco Canyon, a random sample of 23 transects gave a sample variance $s^2 = 46.1$ for the number of sites per transect. Use a 5% level of significance to test the claim that the variance in the new section is greater than 42.3.

4. *Sociology: Marriage* The following problem is based on information from an article by N. Keyfitz in *The American Journal of Sociology* (Vol. 53, pp. 470–480). Let x = age in years of a rural Quebec woman at the time of her first marriage. In the year 1941, the population variance of x was approximately $\sigma^2 = 5.1$. Suppose a recent study of age at first marriage for a random sample of 41 women in rural Quebec gave a sample variance $s^2 = 3.3$. Use a 5% level of significance to test the claim that the current variance is less than 5.1.

5. *Mountain Climbing: Accidents* The following problem is based on information taken from *Accidents in North American Mountaineering* (jointly published by The American Alpine Club and The Alpine Club of Canada). Let x represent the number of mountain climbers killed each year. The long-term variance of x is approximately $\sigma^2 = 136.2$. Suppose that for the past 8 years, the variance has been $s^2 = 115.1$. Use a 1% level of significance to test the claim that the recent variance for number of mountain-climber deaths is less than 136.2.

6. *Professors: Salaries* The following problem is based on information taken from *Academe, Bulletin of the American Association of University Professors.* Let x represent the average annual salary of college and university professors (in thousands of dollars) in the United States. For all colleges and universities in the United States, the population variance of x is approximately $\sigma^2 = 47.1$. However, a random sample of 15 colleges and universities in Kansas showed that x has a sample variance $s^2 = 83.2$. Use a 5% level of significance to test the claim that the variance for colleges and universities in Kansas is greater than 47.1.

7. *Medical: Clinical Test* A new kind of typhoid shot is being developed by a medical research team. The old typhoid shot was known to protect the population for a mean time of 36 months, with a standard deviation of 3 months. To test the time variability of the new shot, a random sample of 23 people were given the

(d) Reject H_0.
(e) At the 5% level of significance, there is sufficient evidence to conclude that the variance of protection times for the new typhoid shot is less than 9.

8. (a) $\alpha = 0.01$; H_0: $\sigma^2 = 225$; H_1: $\sigma^2 > 225$.
(b) $\chi^2 \approx 23.04$; $d.f. = 9$.
(c) $0.005 < P\text{-value} < 0.010$.
(d) Reject H_0.
(e) At the 1% level of significance, there is sufficient evidence to conclude that the variance of duration times for the tranquilizer is larger than stated in the journal.

9. (a) $\alpha = 0.01$; H_0: $\sigma^2 = 0.18$; H_1: $\sigma^2 > 0.18$.
(b) $\chi^2 = 90$; $d.f. = 60$.
(c) $0.005 < P\text{-value} < 0.010$.
(d) Reject H_0.
(e) At the 1% level of significance, there is sufficient evidence to conclude that the variance of measurements for the fan blades is higher than the specified amount. The inspector is justified in claiming that the blades must be replaced.

10. (a) $\alpha = 0.01$; H_0: $\sigma^2 = 3600$; H_1: $\sigma^2 \neq 3600$.
(b) $\chi^2 = 33.12$; $d.f. = 23$.
(c) The area to the right of $\chi^2 = 33.12$ is less than 50%, so we double the right-tail area to find the *P*-value for the two-tailed test. Right-tail area is between 0.050 and 0.100. Doubling these values for a two-tailed test gives $0.100 < P\text{-value} < 0.200$.
(d) Do not reject H_0.
(e) At the 1% level of significance, there is insufficient evidence to conclude that the variance of test scores on the preliminary exam is different from 3600.

11. (a) $\alpha = 0.05$; H_0: $\sigma^2 = 23$; H_1: $\sigma^2 \neq 23$.
(b) $\chi^2 \approx 13.06$; $d.f. = 21$.
(c) The area to the left of $\chi^2 = 13.06$ is less than 50%, so we double the left-tail area to find the *P*-value for the two-tailed test. Right-tail area is between 0.950 and 0.900. Subtracting each value from 1, we find that the left-tail area is between 0.050 and 0.100. Doubling the left-tail area for a two-tailed test gives $0.100 < P\text{-value} < 0.200$.
(d) Do not reject H_0.
(e) At the 5% level of significance, there is insufficient evidence to conclude that the variance of battery lifetimes is different from 23.

new shot. Regular blood tests showed that the sample standard deviation of protection times was 1.9 months. Using a 0.05 level of significance, test the claim that the new typhoid shot has a smaller variance of protection times.

8. *Veterinary Science: Tranquilizer* Jim Mead is a veterinarian who visits a Vermont farm to examine prize bulls. In order to examine a bull, Jim first gives the animal a tranquilizer shot. The effect of the shot is supposed to last an average of 65 minutes, and it usually does. However, Jim sometimes gets chased out of the pasture by a bull that recovers too soon, and other times he becomes worried about prize bulls that take too long to recover. By reading journals, Jim has found that the tranquilizer should have a mean duration time of 65 minutes, with a standard deviation of 15 minutes. A random sample of 10 of Jim's bulls had a mean tranquilized duration time of close to 65 minutes but a standard deviation of 24 minutes. At the 1% level of significance, is Jim justified in the claim that the variance is larger than that stated in his journal?

9. *Engineering: Jet Engines* The fan blades on commercial jet engines must be replaced when wear on these parts indicates too much variability to pass inspection. If a single fan blade broke during operation, it could severely endanger a flight. A large engine contains thousands of fan blades, and safety regulations require that variability measurements on the population of all blades not exceed $\sigma^2 = 0.18$ mm^2. An engine inspector took a random sample of 61 fan blades from an engine. She measured each blade and found a sample variance of 0.27 mm^2. Using a 0.01 level of significance, is the inspector justified in claiming that all the engine fan blades must be replaced?

10. *Law: Bar Exam* A factor in determining the usefulness of an examination as a measure of demonstrated ability is the amount of spread that occurs in the grades. If the spread or variation of examination scores is very small, it usually means that the examination was either too hard or too easy. However, if the variance of scores is moderately large, then there is a definite difference in scores between "better," "average," and "poorer" students. A group of attorneys in a Midwest state has been given the task of making up this year's bar examination for the state. The examination has 500 total possible points, and from the history of past examinations, it is known that a standard deviation of around 60 points is desirable. Of course, too large or too small a standard deviation is not good. The attorneys want to test their examination to see how good it is. A preliminary version of the examination (with slight modifications to protect the integrity of the real examination) is given to a random sample of 24 newly graduated law students. Their scores give a sample standard deviation of 72 points. Using a 0.01 level of significance, test the claim that the population standard deviation for the new examination is 60 against the claim that the population standard deviation is different from 60.

11. *Engineering: Solar Batteries* A set of solar batteries is used in a research satellite. The satellite can run on only one battery, but it runs best if more than one battery is used. The variance σ^2 of lifetimes of these batteries affects the useful lifetime of the satellite before it goes dead. If the variance is too small, all the batteries will tend to die at once. Why? If the variance is too large, the batteries are simply not dependable. Why? Engineers have determined that a variance of $\sigma^2 = 23$ months (squared) is most desirable for these batteries. A random sample of 22 batteries gave a sample variance of 14.3 months (squared). Using a 0.05 level of significance, test the claim that $\sigma^2 = 23$ against the claim that σ^2 is different from 23.

PART II: INFERENCES RELATING TO LINEAR REGRESSION

SECTION 11.4 Inferences for Correlation and Regression

FOCUS POINTS

- Test the correlation coefficient ρ.
- Use sample data to compute the standard error of estimate S_e.
- Test the slope β of the least-squares line.
- Find a confidence interval for the value of y predicted for a specified value of x.

This section contains several topics: testing ρ, confidence intervals for predictions, and testing β. Testing ρ does not use the standard error of estimate S_e, but the other topics do use S_e. For this reason, testing ρ is presented first. The standard error of estimate S_e is then presented. After that, any or all of the remaining topics may be covered as you wish.

Learn more, earn more! We have probably all heard this platitude. The question is whether or not there is some truth in the statement. Do college graduates have an improved chance at a better income? Is there a trend in the general population to support the "learn more, earn more" statement?

Consider the following variables: x = percentage of the population 25 or older with at least 4 years of college and y = percentage *growth* in per capita income over the past 7 years. A random sample of six communities in Ohio gave the information (based on *Life in America's Small Cities*, by G. S. Thomas) shown in Table 11-14.

If we use what we learned in Sections 4.1 and 4.2, we can compute the correlation coefficient r and the least-squares line $\hat{y} = a + bx$ using the data of Table 11-14. However, r is only a *sample* correlation coefficient and $\hat{y} = a + bx$ is only a "*sample-based*" least-squares line. What if we used *all* possible data pairs (x, y) from *all* U.S. cities, not just the six towns in Ohio? If we accomplished this seemingly impossible task, we would have the *population* of all (x, y) pairs.

From this population of (x, y) pairs, we could (in theory) compute the *population correlation coefficient,* which we call ρ (Greek letter rho, pronounced like "row"). We could also compute the least-squares line for the entire population, which we denote as $y = \alpha + \beta x$ using more Greek letters, α (alpha) and β (beta).

This is a good time to present a brief review of the general role of samples and populations in statistics.

Sample Statistic		Population Parameter
r	→	ρ
a	→	α
b	→	β
$\hat{y} = a + bx$	→	$y = \alpha + \beta x$

Assumptions for inferences concerning linear regression

To make inferences regarding the population correlation coefficient ρ and the slope β of the population least-squares line, we need to be sure that

(a) The set (x, y) of ordered pairs is a *random sample* from the population of all possible such (x, y) pairs.

(b) For each fixed value of x, the y values have a normal distribution. All of the y distributions have the same variance, and, for a given x value, the distribution of y values has a mean that lies on the least-squares line. We also assume that for a fixed y, each x has its own normal distribution. In most cases, the results are still accurate if the distributions are simply mound-shaped and symmetric, and the y variances are approximately equal.

We say the data pairs (x, y) have a *bivariate normal distribution* when for a fixed value of x, the y values have a normal distribution and for a fixed y, the x values have a normal distribution.

We assume these conditions are met for all inferences presented in this section.

TABLE 11-14 Education and Income Growth Percentages

x	9.9	11.4	8.1	14.7	8.5	12.6
y	37.1	43.0	33.4	47.1	26.5	40.2

Testing the Correlation Coefficient

The first topic we want to study is the statistical significance of the sample correlation coefficient r. To do this, we construct a statistical test of ρ, the population correlation coefficient. The test will be based on the following theorem.

THEOREM 11.2 Let r be the sample correlation coefficient computed using data pairs (x, y). We use the null hypothesis

H_0: x and y have no linear correlation, so $\rho = 0$

The alternate hypothesis may be

$H_1: \rho > 0$ or $H_1: \rho < 0$ or $H_1: \rho \neq 0$

The conversion of r to a Student's t distribution is

$$t = \frac{r\sqrt{n-2}}{\sqrt{1-r^2}} \quad \text{with } d.f. = n - 2$$

where n is the number of sample data pairs (x, y) $(n \geq 3)$.

PROCEDURE

Problem 13 discusses how sample size might affect the significance of r.

How to test the population correlation coefficient ρ

1. Use the *null hypothesis* H_0: $\rho = 0$. In the context of the application, state the *alternate hypothesis* ($\rho > 0$ or $\rho < 0$ or $\rho \neq 0$) and set the *level of significance* α.
2. Obtain a random sample of $n \geq 3$ data pairs (x, y) and compute the sample *test statistic*

$$t = \frac{r\sqrt{n-2}}{\sqrt{1-r^2}} \quad \text{with degrees of freedom } d.f. = n - 2$$

3. Use a Student's t distribution and the type of test, one-tailed or two-tailed, to find (or estimate) the *P-value* corresponding to the test statistic.
4. *Conclude* the test. If P-value $\leq \alpha$, then reject H_0. If P-value $> \alpha$, then do not reject H_0.
5. *Interpret your conclusion* in the context of the application.

EXAMPLE 5 Testing ρ

Let's return to our data from Ohio regarding the percentage of the population with at least 4 years of college and the percentage of growth in per capita income (Table 11-14). We'll develop a test for the population correlation coefficient ρ.

SOLUTION: First, we compute the sample correlation coefficient r. Using a calculator, statistical software, or a "by-hand" calculation from Section 4.1, we find

$r \approx 0.887$

Now we test the correlation coefficient ρ. Remember that x represents percentage college graduates and y represents percentage salary increases in the general

TABLE 11-15 Excerpt from Student's t Distribution

✓one-tail area	0.010	0.005
two-tail area	0.020	0.010
$d.f.$ = 4	3.747 ↑ Sample t = 3.84	4.604

FIGURE 11-9

P-value

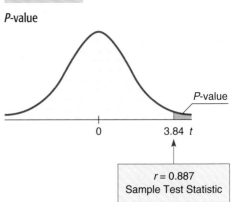

population. We suspect the population correlation is positive, $\rho > 0$. Let's use a 1% level of significance:

H_0: $\rho = 0$ (no linear correlation)

H_1: $\rho > 0$ (positive linear correlation)

Convert the sample test statistic $r = 0.887$ to t using $n = 6$.

$$t = \frac{r\sqrt{n-2}}{\sqrt{1-r^2}} = \frac{0.887\sqrt{6-2}}{\sqrt{1-0.887^2}} \approx 3.84 \qquad \text{with } d.f. = n - 2 = 6 - 2 = 4$$

The P-value for the sample test statistic $t = 3.84$ is shown in Figure 11-9. Since we have a right-tailed test, we use the one-tail area in the Student's t distribution (Table 4 of the Appendix).

From Table 11-15, we see that

$$0.005 < P\text{-value} < 0.010$$

Since the interval containing the P-value is less than the level of significance $\alpha = 0.01$, we reject H_0 and conclude that the population correlation coefficient between x and y is positive. Technology gives P-value ≈ 0.0092.

Note: Although we have shown that x and y are positively correlated, we have not shown that an increase in education *causes* an increase in earnings.

Standard Error of Estimate

Sometimes a scatter diagram clearly indicates the existence of a linear relationship between x and y, but it can happen that the points are widely scattered about the least-squares line. We need a method (besides just looking) for measuring the spread of a set of points about the least-squares line. There are three common methods of measuring the spread. One method uses the *standard error of estimate.* The others are the *coefficient of correlation* and the *coefficient of determination.*

For the standard error of estimate, we use a measure of spread that is in some ways like the standard deviation of measurements of a single variable. Let

$$\hat{y} = a + bx$$

be the predicted value of y from the least-squares line. Then $y - \hat{y}$ is the difference between the y value of the *data point* (x, y) shown on the scatter diagram (Figure 11-10) and the $\hat{y}$ value of the point on the *least-squares line* with the same

FIGURE 11-10

The Distance Between Points (x, y) and $(x, \hat{y})$

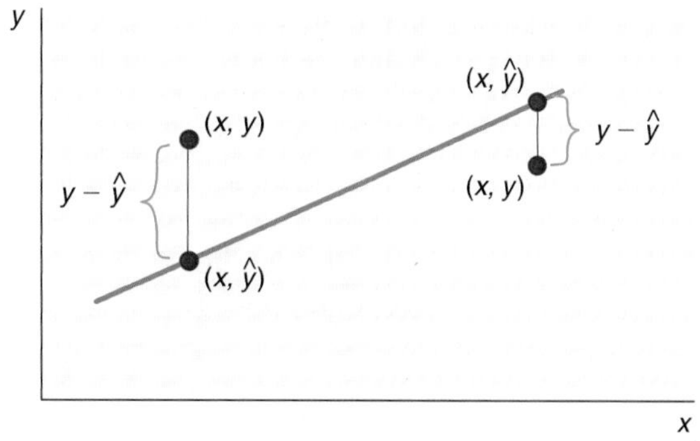

It is useful to point out that the sum of the squares of the residuals is the quantity minimized for the least-squares criterion.

Residual

x value. The quantity $y - \hat{y}$ is known as the *residual.* To avoid the difficulty of having some positive and some negative values, we square the quantity $(y - \hat{y})$. Then we sum the squares and, for technical reasons, divide this sum by $n - 2$. Finally, we take the square root to obtain the *standard error of estimate,* denoted by S_e.

$$\textbf{Standard error of estimate} = S_e = \sqrt{\frac{\Sigma(y - \hat{y})^2}{n - 2}} \qquad (1)$$

where $\hat{y} = a + bx$ and $n \geq 3$.

Note: To compute the standard error of estimate, we require that there be at least three points on the scatter diagram. If we had only two points, the line would be a perfect fit, since two points determine a line. In such a case, there would be no need to compute S_e.

The nearer the scatter points lie to the least-squares line, the smaller S_e will be. In fact, if $S_e = 0$, it follows that each $y - \hat{y}$ is also zero. This means that all the scatter points lie *on* the least-squares line if $S_e = 0$. The larger S_e becomes, the more scattered the points are.

The formula for the standard error of estimate is reminiscent of the formula for the standard deviation. It, too, is a measure of dispersion. However, the standard deviation involves differences of data values from a mean, whereas the standard error of estimate involves the differences between experimental and predicted y values for a given x (i.e., $y - \hat{y}$).

The actual computation of S_e using Equation (1) is quite long because the formula requires us to use the least-squares-line equation to compute a predicted value $\hat{y}$ for *each* x value in the data pairs. There is a computational formula that we strongly recommend you use. However, as with all the computation formulas, be careful about rounding. This formula is sensitive to rounding, and you should carry as many digits as seems reasonable for your problem. Answers will vary, depending on rounding used. We give the formula here and follow it with an example of its use.

PROCEDURE

Remind students that values for Σy, Σy^2, a, and b were already computed when finding the equation of the least-squares line.

Note that most calculators supporting two-variable statistics provide the sums Σx, Σy, Σx^2, Σy^2, and Σxy.

HOW TO FIND THE STANDARD ERROR OF ESTIMATE S_e

1. Obtain a random sample of $n \geq 3$ data pairs (x, y).
2. Use the procedures of Section 4.2 to find a and b from the sample least-squares line $\hat{y} = a + bx$.
3. The standard error of estimate is

$$S_e = \sqrt{\frac{\Sigma y^2 - a\Sigma y - b\Sigma xy}{n - 2}} \qquad (2)$$

With a considerable amount of algebra, Equations (1) and (2) can be shown to be mathematically equivalent. Equation (1) shows the strong similarity between the standard error of estimate and the standard deviation. Equation (2) is a shortcut calculation formula because it involves few subtractions. The sums Σx, Σy, Σx^2, Σy^2, and Σxy are provided directly on most calculators that support two-variable statistics.

In the next example, we show you how to compute the standard error of estimate using the computation formula.

EXAMPLE 6 LEAST-SQUARES LINE AND S_e

In this example, we find the equation of the least-squares line and the standard error of estimate for the data from Ohio regarding x = percentage of the population with at least 4 years of college and y = percentage growth in per capita income.

x	9.9	11.4	8.1	14.7	8.5	12.6
y	37.1	43.0	33.4	47.1	26.5	40.2

SOLUTION: To find the equation of the least-squares line $\hat{y} = a + bx$ and the value of S_e, we note that $n = 6$ and compute the following sums.

$$\Sigma x = 65.2;\ \Sigma y = 227.3;\ \Sigma x^2 = 740.68;\ \Sigma y^2 = 8877.67;$$
$$\Sigma xy = 2552.17$$

Using formulas (3) and (4) from Chapter 4, we have

$$b = \frac{n\Sigma xy - (\Sigma x)(\Sigma y)}{n\Sigma x^2 - (\Sigma x)^2} = \frac{6(2552.17) - (65.2)(227.3)}{6(740.68) - (65.2)^2} \approx 2.554$$

$$\bar{x} = \frac{\Sigma x}{n} = \frac{65.2}{6} \approx 10.87 \quad \text{and} \quad \bar{y} = \frac{\Sigma y}{n} = \frac{227.3}{6} \approx 37.88$$

$$a = \bar{y} - b\bar{x} \approx 37.88 - 2.554(10.87) \approx 10.12$$

The equation of the least-squares line is

$$\hat{y} \approx 10.12 + 2.554x$$

Note: The values of a and b for the least-squares line are readily available on calculators supporting two-variable statistics.

$$S_e = \sqrt{\frac{\Sigma y^2 - a\Sigma y - b\Sigma xy}{n - 2}}$$

$$\approx \sqrt{\frac{8877.67 - 10.12(227.3) - 2.554(2552.17)}{6 - 2}} \approx \sqrt{\frac{59.152}{4}} \approx 3.8$$

TECH NOTES Although many calculators that support two-variable statistics and linear regression do not provide the value of the standard error of estimate S_e directly, they do provide the sums required for the calculation of S_e. The TI-84Plus/TI-83Plus, Excel, and Minitab all provide the value of S_e.

TI-84Plus/TI-83Plus The value for S_e is given as s under STAT, TEST, option E: LinRegTTest.

Excel Use the **paste function** (fx), select **Statistical,** and choose the function **STEYX.**

Minitab Use the menu choices **Stat ➤ Regression ➤ Regression.** The value for S_e is given as s in the display.

Inferences About the Slope β

Recall that $\hat{y} = a + bx$ is the sample-based least-squares line and $y = \alpha + \beta x$ is the population least-squares line computed (in theory) from the population of all (x, y) data pairs. In many real-world applications, the slope β is very important because β measures the rate at which y changes per unit change in x. Our next topic is to develop statistical tests for β. Our work is based on the following theorem.

THEOREM 11.3 Let b be the slope of the sample least-squares line $\hat{y} = a + bx$ computed from a random sample of $n \geq 3$ data pairs (x, y). Let β be the slope of the population least-squares line $y = \alpha + \beta x$, which is in theory computed from the population of all (x, y) data pairs. Let S_e be the standard error of estimate computed from the sample. Then

$$t = \frac{b - \beta}{S_e \Big/ \sqrt{\Sigma x^2 - \frac{1}{n}(\Sigma x)^2}}$$

has a Student's t distribution with degrees of freedom $d.f. = n - 2$.

COMMENT The expression $S_e \Big/ \sqrt{\Sigma x^2 - \frac{1}{n}(\Sigma x)^2}$ is called the *standard error* for b.

Using this theorem, we can construct a procedure for statistical tests of β.

PROCEDURE

How to test β

Obtain a random sample of $n \geq 3$ data pairs (x, y). Use the procedure of Section 4.2 to find b, the slope of the sample least-squares line. Use Equation (2) of this section to find S_e, the standard error of estimate.

For a statistical test of β

1. Use the *null hypothesis* H_0: $\beta = 0$. Use an *alternate hypothesis* H_1 appropriate to your application ($\beta > 0$ or $\beta < 0$ or $\beta \neq 0$). Set the level of significance α.
2. Use the null hypothesis H_0: $\beta = 0$ and the values of S_e, n, Σx, Σx^2, and b to compute the *sample test statistic*

$$t = \frac{b}{S_e}\sqrt{\Sigma x^2 - \frac{1}{n}(\Sigma x)^2} \quad \text{with } d.f. = n - 2$$

3. Use a Student's t distribution and the type of test, one-tailed or two-tailed, to find (or estimate) the *P-value* corresponding to the test statistic.
4. *Conclude* the test. If P-value $\leq \alpha$, then reject H_0. If P-value $> \alpha$, then do not reject H_0.
5. *Interpret your conclusion* in the context of the application.

EXAMPLE 7 **TESTING β**

Returning to the sample data regarding x = percentage of the population 25 or older with at least 4 years of college and y = percentage growth in per capita income over the past 7 years (data in Table 11-14), test the claim that the slope β of the least-squares line is positive. Use $\alpha = 0.01$.

SOLUTION: In Example 6, we found the equation of the least-squares line and the standard error of estimate S_e to be

$$\hat{y} \approx 10.12 + 2.554x \quad \text{and} \quad S_e \approx 3.8$$

We also found the sums $\Sigma x^2 = 740.68$ and $\Sigma x = 65.2$. Note that the number of data pairs is $n = 6$.

To test the claim that β is positive, use the hypotheses

$$H_0: \beta = 0 \quad \text{and} \quad H_1: \beta > 0$$

Convert the sample test statistic $b = 2.554$ to t:

$$t = \frac{b}{S_e}\sqrt{\Sigma x^2 - \frac{1}{n}(\Sigma x)^2} \approx \frac{2.554}{3.8}\sqrt{740.68 - \frac{1}{6}(65.2)^2} \approx 3.81$$

with $d.f. = n - 2 = 6 - 2 = 4$.

To conclude the test, we estimate the P-value of the sample test statistic. Scanning Table 4 of the Appendix, we see that in the row with $d.f. = 4$, the sample t value 3.81 falls between the entries 3.747 and 4.604. These entries correspond to the one-tail area between 0.010 and 0.005. Therefore,

$$0.005 < P\text{-value} < 0.010$$

Since P-value $\leq \alpha$ of 0.01, we reject H_0 and conclude that the population slope of the least-squares line is positive. This means that at the 1% level of significance, the evidence indicates that the percentage growth in per capita income increases as the percentage of the population 25 or older with at least 4 years of college increases.

Both Examples 5 and 7 utilize the data of Table 11-14 regarding education levels and income growth. It is interesting to note that for the same data, the t value of the sample correlation coefficient r and the t value of the sample slope b are essentially the same. This is not an accident! Recall from Section 4.2, formula (6), that

$$b = r\left(\frac{s_y}{s_x}\right)$$ where s_y and s_x are the standard deviations of the y and x values of the data pairs, respectively

Using this relationship and some algebra, it can be shown that:

For tests of the correlation coefficient r and the slope b of the least-squares line, both b and r convert to the same t value, with $d.f. = n - 2$, where n is the number of data pairs.

In the next Guided Exercise, we take advantage of this fact.

COMPUTATION HINTS

(a) Most two-variable calculators provide the value of the correlation coefficient r. Find the t value for r. The t value for b is the same.

(b) Most computer-based statistical packages provide the t value for b. The t value for r is the same.

Problem 14 discusses the fact that for the same data, the Student's t value for r equals that for b.

GUIDED EXERCISE 8 Inference for ρ and β

How fast do puppies grow? That depends on the puppy. How about male wolf pups in the Helsinki Zoo (Finland)? Let x = age in weeks and y = weight in kilograms for a random sample of male wolf pups. The following data are based on the article *Studies of the Wolf in Finland Canis lupus L* (*Ann. Zool. Fenn.* 2: 215–259) by E. Pulliainen, University of Helsinki.

x	8	10	14	20	28	40	45
y	7	13	17	23	30	34	35

$\Sigma x = 165$; $\Sigma y = 159$; $\Sigma x^2 = 5169$; $\Sigma y^2 = 4317$; $\Sigma xy = 4659$

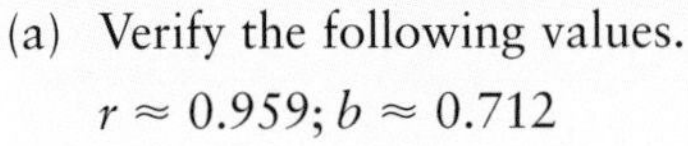

(a) Verify the following values.
$r \approx 0.959$; $b \approx 0.712$

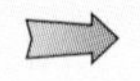

Find the values for r and b on your calculator or use the formulas of Sections 4.1 and 4.2.

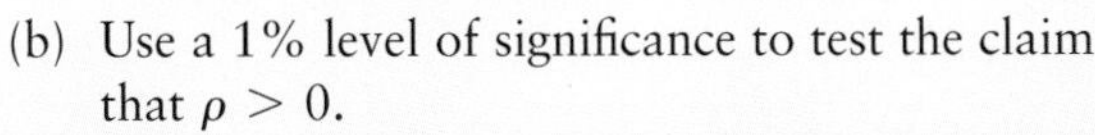

(b) Use a 1% level of significance to test the claim that $\rho > 0$.

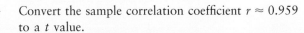

Convert the sample correlation coefficient $r \approx 0.959$ to a t value.

$$t = \frac{r\sqrt{n-2}}{\sqrt{1-r^2}} \approx \frac{0.959\sqrt{5}}{\sqrt{1-0.959^2}} \approx 7.57$$

H_0: $\rho = 0$; H_1: $\rho > 0$; $d.f. = 5$. Using the Student's t distribution, Table 4 of the Appendix, we see that the P-value corresponding to the sample t value of 7.57 is less than 0.0005. Since the P-value is less than α of 0.01, we reject H_0 and conclude that there is a positive correlation between age and weight.

(c) Use a 1% level of significance to test the claim that $\beta > 0$.

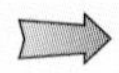

Convert $b \approx 0.712$ to a t value. Since the t value for b equals the t value for r, we use the result of part (b) and conclude that $t \approx 7.57$.

H_0: $\beta = 0$; H_1: $\beta > 0$; $d.f. = 5$. As in part (b), the P-value corresponding to the sample t value of 7.56 is less than 0.0005. We reject H_0 at the 1% level of significance and conclude that the slope of the least-squares line is positive.

TECH NOTES The t value corresponding to the correlation coefficient r is the same as the t value corresponding to b, the slope of the least-squares line. Consequently, the two tests H_0: $\rho = 0$ and H_0: $\beta = 0$ (with similar corresponding alternate hypotheses) have the same conclusions. The TI-84Plus/TI-83Plus uses this fact explicitly. Minitab and Excel show the two-tailed P-value for the slope b of the least-squares line. Excel also shows confidence intervals for β. The displays show data from Guided Exercise 8 regarding the age and weight of wolf pups.

TI-84Plus/TI-83Plus Under STAT, select TEST and use option E:LinRegTTest.

```
LinRegTTest
 y=a+bx
 β≠0 and ρ≠0
 t=7.5632
 p=6.4075E-4
 df=5.0000
↓a=5.9317
```

```
LinRegTTest
 y=a+bx
 β≠0 and ρ≠0
↑b=.7120
 s=3.3676
 r²=.9196
 r=.9590
```

Note that the value of S_e is given as s.

Excel Use the menu selection **Tools ➤ Data Analysis ➤ Regression.**

Regression Statistics	
Multiple R	0.958966516
R Square	0.919616778
Adjusted R Square	0.903540133
Standard Error	3.367628886
Observations	7

← Value of S_e (Standard Error)

	Coefficients	Standard Error	t Stat	P-value	Lower 95%	Upper 95%
Intercept	5.931681179	2.558126184	2.318760198	0.068158803	-0.644180779	12.50754314
X Variable 1	0.711989283	0.094138596	7.563202697	0.000640746	0.469998714	0.953979853

↑ b (Coefficients) ↑ for two-tailed test (P-value)

Minitab Use the menu selection **Stat ➤ Regression ➤ Regression.** The value of S_e is S; P is the P-value of a two-tailed test. For a one-tailed test, divide the P-value by 2.

```
Regression Analysis
The regression equation is
y = 5.93 + 0.712 x
Predictor        Coef        StDev        T        P
Constant        5.932        2.558     2.32    0.068
x             0.71199      0.09414     7.56    0.001
S = 3.368       R-Sq = 92.0%       R-Sq(adj) = 90.4%
```

Confidence Intervals for y

The least-squares line gives us a predicted value $\hat{y}$ for a specified x value. However, we used sample data to get the equation of the line. The line derived from the population of all data pairs is likely to have a slightly different slope, which we designate by the symbol β for population slope, and a slightly different y intercept, which we designate by the symbol α for population intercept. In addition, there is some random error ϵ, so the true y value is

$$y = \alpha + \beta x + \epsilon$$

Because of the random variable ϵ, for each x value there is a corresponding distribution of y values. The methods of linear regression were developed so that the distribution of y values for a given x would be centered on the population regression line. Furthermore, the distributions of y values corresponding to each x value all have the same standard deviation, estimated by the standard error of estimate S_e.

Using all this background, the theory tells us that for a specific x, a c *confidence interval for* y is given by the next procedure.

PROCEDURE

Remind students that this is a confidence interval for the response variable y (*not* for the mean of y values) for a given x value.

HOW TO FIND A CONFIDENCE INTERVAL FOR A PREDICTED y FROM THE LEAST-SQUARES LINE

1. Obtain a random sample of $n \geq 3$ data pairs (x, y).
2. Use the procedure of Section 4.2 to find $\hat{y} = a + bx$. You also need to find $\bar{x}$ from the sample data and the standard error of estimate S_e using Equation (2) of this section.
3. The **c confidence interval for y** for a **specified value of x** is

$$\hat{y} - E < y < \hat{y} + E$$

where

$$E = t_c S_e \sqrt{1 + \frac{1}{n} + \frac{n(x - \bar{x})^2}{n\Sigma x^2 - (\Sigma x)^2}}$$

$\hat{y} = a + bx$ is the predicted value of y from the least-squares line for a *specified* x value

c = confidence level $(0 < c < 1)$

n = number of data pairs $(n \geq 3)$

t_c = critical value from Student's t distribution for c confidence level using $d.f. = n - 2$

S_e = standard error of estimate

The formulas involved in the computation of a c confidence interval look complicated. However, they involve quantities we have already computed or values we can easily look up in tables. The next example illustrates this point.

EXAMPLE 8 CONFIDENCE INTERVAL FOR PREDICTION

June and Jim are partners in the chemistry lab. Their assignment is to determine how much copper sulfate ($CuSO_4$) will dissolve in water at 10, 20, 30, 40, 50, 60, and 70°C. Their lab results are shown in the table, where y is the weight in grams of copper sulfate that will dissolve in 100 g of water at x°C.

x	10	20	30	40	50	60	70
y	17	21	25	28	33	40	49

Find the equation of the least-squares line, and find a 95% confidence interval for the amount of copper sulfate that will dissolve in 100 g of water at 45°C.

SOLUTION: Using a calculator with appropriate formulas, we find

$$\Sigma x = 280;\ \Sigma y = 213;\ \Sigma x^2 = 14{,}000;\ \Sigma y^2 = 7229;\ \Sigma xy = 9940$$

$$\bar{x} = 40;\ \bar{y} \approx 30.429;\ b \approx 0.50714;\ a \approx 10.143;\ S_e \approx 2.35$$

Next we use the equation of the least-squares line to find $\hat{y}$ for $x = 45$°C.

$\hat{y} = a + bx$

$\hat{y} \approx 10.14 + 0.51x$

$\hat{y} \approx 10.14 + 0.51(45)$ Use 45 in place of x.

$\hat{y} \approx 33$

A 95% confidence interval is then

$$\hat{y} - E < y < \hat{y} + E$$
$$33 - E < y < 33 + E$$

where $E = t_c S_e \sqrt{1 + \frac{1}{n} + \frac{n(x - \bar{x})^2}{n\Sigma x^2 - (\Sigma x)^2}}$.

Using $n - 2 = 7 - 2 = 5$ degrees of freedom, we find from Table 4 of the Appendix that $t_{0.95} = 2.571$.

$$E \approx (2.571)(2.35)\sqrt{1 + \frac{1}{7} + \frac{7(45 - 40)^2}{7(14{,}000) - (280)^2}}$$
$$\approx (2.571)(2.35)\sqrt{1.15179} \approx 6.5$$

A 95% confidence interval for y is

$$33 - 6.5 \le y \le 33 + 6.5$$
$$26.5 \le y \le 39.5$$

This means that we are 95% sure that the interval between 26.5 g and 39.5 g is one that contains the predicted amount of copper sulfate that will dissolve in 100 g of water at 45°C. The interval is fairly wide but would decrease with more sample data.

GUIDED EXERCISE 9 Confidence interval for prediction

Let's use the data of Example 8 to compute a 95% confidence interval for y = amount of copper sulfate that will dissolve at x = 15°C.

(a) From Example 8, we have

$\hat{y} \approx 10.14 + 0.51x$

Evaluate $\hat{y}$ for $x = 15$.

→ $\hat{y} \approx 10.14 + 0.51x$
$\approx 10.14 + 0.51(15)$
≈ 17.8

(b) The bound E on the error of estimate is

$$E = t_c S_e \sqrt{1 + \frac{1}{n} + \frac{n(x - \bar{x})^2}{n\Sigma x^2 - (\Sigma x)^2}}$$

From Example 8, we know that $S_e \approx 2.35$, Σx = 280, $\Sigma x^2 = 14{,}000$, $\bar{x} = 40$, and $n = 7$. Find $t_{0.95}$ and compute E.

→ $t_{0.95} = 2.571$ for $d.f. = n - 2 = 5$

$$E \approx (2.571)(2.35)\sqrt{1 + \frac{1}{7} + \frac{7(15 - 40)^2}{7(14{,}000) - (280)^2}}$$
$$\approx (2.571)(2.35^*\sqrt{1.366071} \approx 7.1$$

(c) Find a 95% confidence interval for y.

$\hat{y} - E \le y \le \hat{y} + E$

→ The confidence interval is

$$17.8 - 7.1 \le y \le 17.8 + 7.1$$
$$10.7 \le y \le 24.9$$

As we compare the results of Guided Exercise 9 and Example 8, we notice that the 95% confidence interval of y values for x = 15°C is 7.1 units above and below the least-squares line, while the 95% confidence interval of y values for x = 45°C is only 6.5 units above and below the least-squares line. This comparison reflects the general property that confidence intervals for y are narrower the nearer we are to the mean $\bar{x}$ of the x values. As we move near the extremes of the

FIGURE 11-11

95% Confidence Band for Predicted Values $\hat{y}$

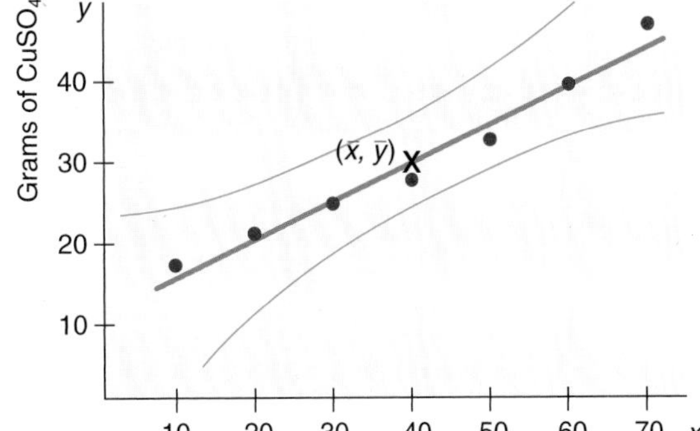

It is good to point out that the confidence intervals for forecast y values are shorter for x values near the mean $\bar{x}$ of the data values.

x distribution, the confidence intervals for y become wider. This is another reason that we should not try to use the least-squares line to predict y values for x values beyond the data extremes of the sample x distribution.

If we were to compute a 95% confidence interval for all x values in the range of the sample x values, the confidence interval band would curve away from the least-squares line, as shown in Figure 11-11.

TECH NOTES Minitab provides confidence intervals for predictions. Use the menu selection **Stat ➤ Regression ➤ Regression.** Under **Options**, enter the observed x value and set the confidence level. In the output, the confidence interval for predictions is designated by %PI.

VIEWPOINT Hawaii Island Hopping!

Suppose you want to go camping in Hawaii. Yes! Hawaii has both state and federal parks where you can enjoy camping on the beach or in the mountains. However, you will probably need to rent a car to get to the different campgrounds. How much will the car rental cost? That depends on the islands you visit. For car rental data and regression statistics that you can compute regarding costs on different Hawaiian Islands, visit the Online Study Center at **www.cengage.com/statistics/Brase/UBS5e** *and find the link to Hawaiian Islands.*

SECTION 11.4 PROBLEMS

Tables and art to accompany margin answers may be found in the back of the book.

1. ρ (Greek letter rho).
2. β (Greek letter beta).
3. As x becomes farther away from $\bar{x}$, the confidence interval for the predicted y becomes longer.
4. The t value for b equals the t value for r.

1. *Statistical Literacy* What is the symbol used for the population correlation coefficient?
2. *Statistical Literacy* What is the symbol used for the slope of the population least-squares line?
3. *Statistical Literacy* For a fixed confidence level, how does the length of the confidence interval for predicted values of y change as the corresponding x values become farther away from $\bar{x}$?
4. *Statistical Literacy* How does the t value for the sample correlation coefficient r compare to the t value for the corresponding slope b of the sample least-squares line?

Using Computer Printouts Problems 5 and 6 use the following information. Prehistoric pottery vessels are usually found as sherds (broken pieces) and are carefully reconstructed if enough sherds can be found. Information taken from *Mimbres Mogollon Archaeology* by A. I. Woosley and A. J. McIntyre (University of New Mexico Press) provides data relating x = body diameter in centimeters and y = height in centimeters of prehistoric vessels reconstructed from sherds found at a prehistoric site. The following Minitab printout provides an analysis of the data.

```
Predictor      Coef     SE Coef       T        P
Constant     -0.223      2.429     -0.09    0.929
Diameter     0.7848     0.1471      5.33    0.001

S = 4.07980       R-Sq = 80.3%
```

5. (a) Diameter.
(b) $a = -0.223$; $b = 0.7848$; $\hat{y} = -0.223 + 0.7848x$.
(c) P-value of b is 0.001. H_0: $\beta = 0$; H_1: $\beta \neq 0$. Since P-value < 0.01, reject H_0 and conclude that the slope is not zero.
(d) $r \approx 0.896$. Yes. P-value is 0.001, so we reject H_0 for $\alpha = 0.01$.

5. *Critical Thinking: Using Information from a Computer Display to Test for Significance* Refer to the Minitab printout regarding prehistoric pottery.
(a) Minitab calls the explanatory variable the predictor variable. Which is the predictor variable, the diameter of the pot or the height?
(b) For the least-squares line $\hat{y} = a + bx$, what is the value of the constant a? What is the value of the slope b? (*Note*: The slope is the coefficient of the predictor variable.) Write the equation of the least-squares line.
(c) The P-value for a two-tailed test corresponding to each coefficient is listed under P. The t value corresponding to the coefficient is listed under T. What is the P-value of the slope? What are the hypotheses for a two-tailed test of $\beta = 0$? Based on the P-value in the printout, do we reject or fail to reject the null hypothesis for $\alpha = 0.01$?
(d) Recall that the t value and resulting P-value of the slope b equal the t value and resulting P-value of the corresponding correlation coefficient r. To find the value of the sample correlation coefficient r, take the square root of the R-Sq value shown in the display. What is the value of r? Consider a two-tailed test for ρ. Based on the P-value shown in the Minitab display, is the correlation coefficient significant at the 1% level of significance?

6. (a) $S_e \approx 4.0798$.
(b) S_e slope ≈ 0.1471.

6. *Critical Thinking: Using Information in a Computer Display to Find a Confidence Interval* Refer to the Minitab printout regarding prehistoric pottery.
(a) The standard error S_e of the linear regression model is given in the printout as "S." What is the value of S_e?
(b) The standard error of the coefficient of the predictor variable is found under "SE Coef." Recall that the standard error for b is $S_e \Big/ \sqrt{\Sigma x^2 - \frac{1}{n}(\Sigma x)^2}$. From the Minitab display, what is the value of the standard error for the slope b?

In Problems 7–12, parts (a) and (b) relate to testing ρ. Part (c) requests the value of S_e. Parts (d) and (e) relate to confidence intervals for prediction. Part (f) relates to testing β. Answers may vary due to rounding.

7. (a) Use a calculator.
(b) $\alpha = 0.05$; H_0: $\rho = 0$; H_1: $\rho > 0$; sample $t \approx 2.522$; $d.f. = 4$; $0.025 < P$-value < 0.050; reject H_0. There seems to be a positive correlation between x and y. From TI-84, P-value ≈ 0.0326.
(c) Use a calculator.
(d) 45.36%.
(e) Interval from 39.05 to 51.67.
(f) $\alpha = 0.05$; H_0: $\beta = 0$; H_1: $\beta > 0$; sample $t \approx 2.522$, $d.f. = 4$; $0.025 < P$-value < 0.050; reject H_0. There seems to be a positive slope between x and y. From TI-84, P-value ≈ 0.0326.

7. *Basketball: Free Throws and Field Goals* Let x be a random variable that represents the percentage of successful free throws a professional basketball player makes in a season. Let y be a random variable that represents the percentage of successful field goals a professional basketball player makes in a season. A random sample of $n = 6$ professional basketball players gave the following information. (Reference: *The Official NBA Basketball Encyclopedia*, Villard Books.)

x	67	65	75	86	73	73
y	44	42	48	51	44	51

(a) Verify that $\Sigma x = 439$, $\Sigma y = 280$, $\Sigma x^2 = 32{,}393$, $\Sigma y^2 = 13{,}142$, $\Sigma xy = 20{,}599$, and $r \approx 0.784$.
(b) Use a 5% level of significance to test the claim that $\rho > 0$.

(c) Verify that $S_e \approx 2.6964$, $a \approx 16.542$, $b \approx 0.4117$, and $\bar{x} \approx 73.167$.
(d) Find the predicted percentage $\hat{y}$ of successful field goals for a player with $x = 70\%$ successful free throws.
(e) Find a 90% confidence interval for y when $x = 70$.
(f) Use a 5% level of significance to test the claim that $\beta > 0$.

8. (a) Use a calculator.
(b) $\alpha = 0.05$; H_0: $\rho = 0$; H_1: $\rho \neq 0$; sample $t \approx -3.931$; *d.f.* $= 4$; $0.010 < P\text{-value} < 0.020$; reject H_0. At the 5% level of significance, there seems to be a correlation between x and y. From TI-84, *P*-value ≈ 0.0171.
(c) Use a calculator.
(d) 6.72.
(e) Interval from 3.93 to 9.52.
(f) $\alpha = 0.05$; H_0: $\beta = 0$; H_1: $\beta \neq 0$; sample $t \approx -3.931$, *d.f.* $= 4$; $0.010 < P\text{-value} < 0.020$; reject H_0. At the 5% level of significance, the slope of the least-squares line is not zero. From TI-84, *P*-value ≈ 0.0171.

8. *Baseball: Batting Average and Strikeouts* Let x be a random variable that represents the batting average of a professional baseball player. Let y be a random variable that represents the percentage of strikeouts of a professional baseball player. A random sample of $n = 6$ professional baseball players gave the following information. (Reference: *The Baseball Encyclopedia,* Macmillan.)

x	0.328	0.290	0.340	0.248	0.367	0.269
y	3.2	7.6	4.0	8.6	3.1	11.1

(a) Verify that $\Sigma x = 1.842$, $\Sigma y = 37.6$, $\Sigma x^2 = 0.575838$, $\Sigma y^2 = 290.78$, $\Sigma xy = 10.87$, and $r \approx -0.891$.
(b) Use a 5% level of significance to test the claim that $\rho \neq 0$.
(c) Verify that $S_e \approx 1.6838$, $a \approx 26.247$, and $b \approx -65.081$.
(d) Find the predicted percentage of strikeouts for a player with an $x = 0.300$ batting average.
(e) Find an 80% confidence interval for y when $x = 0.300$.
(f) Use a 5% level of significance to test the claim that $\beta \neq 0$.

9. (a) Use a calculator.
(b) $\alpha = 0.01$; H_0: $\rho = 0$; H_1: $\rho < 0$; sample $t \approx -10.06$; *d.f.* $= 5$; $P\text{-value} < 0.0005$; reject H_0. The sample evidence supports a negative correlation. From TI-84, *P*-value ≈ 0.00008.
(c) Use a calculator.
(d) 2.39 hours.
(e) Interval from 2.12 to 2.66 hours.
(f) $\alpha = 0.01$; H_0: $\beta = 0$; H_1: $\beta < 0$; sample $t \approx -10.06$; *d.f.* $= 5$; $P\text{-value} < 0.0005$; reject H_0. The sample evidence supports a negative slope. From TI-84, *P*-value ≈ 0.00008.

9. *Scuba Diving: Depth* What is the optimal time for a scuba diver to be on the bottom of the ocean? That depends on the depth of the dive. The U.S. Navy has done a lot of research on this topic. The Navy defines the "optimal time" to be the time at each depth for the best balance between length of work period and decompression time after surfacing. Let x = depth of dive in meters, and let y = optimal time in hours. A random sample of divers gave the following data (based on information taken from *Medical Physiology* by A. C. Guyton, M.D.).

x	14.1	24.3	30.2	38.3	51.3	20.5	22.7
y	2.58	2.08	1.58	1.03	0.75	2.38	2.20

(a) Verify that $\Sigma x = 201.4$, $\Sigma y = 12.6$, $\Sigma x^2 = 6735.46$, $\Sigma y^2 = 25.607$, $\Sigma xy = 311.292$, and $r \approx -0.976$.
(b) Use a 1% level of significance to test the claim that $\rho < 0$.
(c) Verify that $S_e \approx 0.1660$, $a \approx 3.366$, and $b \approx -0.0544$.
(d) Find the predicted optimal time in hours for a dive depth of $x = 18$ meters.
(e) Find an 80% confidence interval for y when $x = 18$ meters.
(f) Use a 1% level of significance to test the claim that $\beta < 0$.

10. (a) Use a calculator.
(b) $\alpha = 0.01$; H_0: $\rho = 0$; H_1: $\rho > 0$; sample $t \approx 9.504$; *d.f.* $= 3$; $0.0005 < P\text{-value} < 0.005$; reject H_0. The sample evidence supports a positive correlation. From TI-84, *P*-value ≈ 0.0012.
(c) Use a calculator.
(d) 24.63 mm Hg/10.
(e) Interval from 18.1 to 31.2 mm Hg/10.
(f) $\alpha = 0.01$; H_0: $\beta = 0$; H_1: $\beta > 0$; sample $t \approx 9.504$; *d.f.* $= 3$; $0.0005 < P\text{-value} < 0.005$; reject H_0. The sample evidence supports a positive slope. From TI-84, *P*-value ≈ 0.0012.

10. *Physiology: Oxygen* Aviation and high-altitude physiology is a specialty in the study of medicine. Let x = partial pressure of oxygen in the alveoli (air cells in the lungs) when breathing naturally available air. Let y = partial pressure when breathing pure oxygen. The (x, y) data pairs correspond to elevations from 10,000 feet to 30,000 feet in 5000-foot intervals for a random sample of volunteers. Although the medical data were collected using airplanes, they apply equally well to Mt. Everest climbers (summit 29,028 feet).

x	6.7	5.1	4.2	3.3	2.1 (units: mm Hg/10)
y	43.6	32.9	26.2	16.2	13.9 (units: mm Hg/10)

(Based on information taken from *Medical Physiology* by A. C. Guyton, M.D.)
(a) Verify that $\Sigma x = 21.4$, $\Sigma y = 132.8$, $\Sigma x^2 = 103.84$, $\Sigma y^2 = 4125.46$, $\Sigma xy = 652.6$, and $r \approx 0.984$.

(b) Use a 1% level of significance to test the claim that $\rho > 0$.
(c) Verify that $S_e \approx 2.5319$, $a \approx -2.869$, and $b \approx 6.876$.
(d) Find the predicted pressure when breathing pure oxygen if the pressure from breathing available air is $x = 4.0$.
(e) Find a 90% confidence interval for y when $x = 4.0$.
(f) Use a 1% level of significance to test the claim that $\beta > 0$.

11. (a) Use a calculator.
(b) $\alpha = 0.01$; H_0: $\rho = 0$; H_1: $\rho > 0$; sample $t \approx 6.534$; $d.f. = 4$; $0.0005 < P\text{-value} < 0.005$; reject H_0. The sample evidence supports a positive correlation. From TI-84, P-value ≈ 0.0014.
(c) Use a calculator.
(d) \$12.577 thousand.
(e) Interval from 12.247 to 12.907 (thousand dollars).
(f) $\alpha = 0.01$; H_0: $\beta = 0$; H_1: $\beta > 0$; sample $t \approx 6.534$; $d.f. = 4$; $0.0005 < P\text{-value} < 0.005$; reject H_0. The sample evidence supports a positive slope. From TI-84, P-value ≈ 0.0014.

12. (a) Use a calculator.
(b) $\alpha = 0.01$; H_0: $\rho = 0$; H_1: $\rho > 0$; sample $t \approx 7.926$; $d.f. = 3$; $0.0005 < P\text{-value} < 0.005$; reject H_0. The sample evidence supports a positive correlation. From TI-84, P-value ≈ 0.0021.
(c) Use a calculator.
(d) \$36.58 (thousand).
(e) Interval from 31.2 to 41.9 (thousand dollars).
(f) $\alpha = 0.01$; H_0: $\beta = 0$; H_1: $\beta > 0$; sample $t \approx 7.926$; $d.f. = 3$; $0.0005 < P\text{-value} < 0.005$; reject H_0. The sample evidence supports a positive slope. From TI-84, P-value ≈ 0.0021.

13. (a) H_0: $\rho = 0$; H_1: $\rho \neq 0$; $d.f. = 4$; sample $t = 4.129$; $0.01 < P\text{-value} < 0.02$; do not reject H_0; r is not significant at the 0.01 level of significance.
(b) H_0: $\rho = 0$; H_1: $\rho \neq 0$; $d.f. = 8$; sample $t = 5.840$; $P\text{-value} < 0.001$; reject H_0; r is significant at the 0.01 level of significance.
(c) As n increases, the degrees of freedom increase, resulting in the t value corresponding to r also increasing, producing a smaller P-value.

11. *New Car: Negotiating Price* Suppose you are interested in buying a new Toyota Corolla. You are standing on the sales lot looking at a model with different options. The list price is on the vehicle. As a salesperson approaches, you wonder what the dealer invoice price is for this model with its options. The following data are based on information taken from *Consumer Guide* (Vol. 677). Let x be the list price (in thousands of dollars) for a random selection of Toyota Corollas of different models and options. Let y be the dealer invoice (in thousands of dollars) for the given vehicle.

x	12.6	13.0	12.8	13.6	13.4	14.2
y	11.6	12.0	11.5	12.2	12.0	12.8

(a) Verify that $\Sigma x = 79.6$, $\Sigma y = 72.1$, $\Sigma x^2 = 1057.76$, $\Sigma y^2 = 867.49$, $\Sigma xy = 957.84$, and $r \approx 0.956$.
(b) Use a 1% level of significance to test the claim that $\rho > 0$.
(c) Verify that $S_e \approx 0.1527$, $a \approx 1.965$, and $b \approx 0.758$.
(d) Find the predicted dealer invoice when the list price is $x = 14$ (thousand dollars).
(e) Find an 85% confidence interval for y when $x = 14$ (thousand dollars).
(f) Use a 1% level of significance to test the claim that $\beta > 0$.

12. *New Car: Negotiating Price* Suppose you are interested in buying a new Lincoln Navigator or Town Car. You are standing on the sales lot looking at a model with different options. The list price is on the vehicle. As a salesperson approaches, you wonder what the dealer invoice price is for this model with its options. The following data are based on information taken from *Consumer Guide* (Vol. 677). Let x be the list price (in thousands of dollars) for a random selection of these cars of different models and options. Let y be the dealer invoice (in thousands of dollars) for the given vehicle.

x	32.1	33.5	36.1	44.0	47.8
y	29.8	31.1	32.0	42.1	42.2

(a) Verify that $\Sigma x = 193.5$, $\Sigma y = 177.2$, $\Sigma x^2 = 7676.71$, $\Sigma y^2 = 6432.5$, $\Sigma xy = 7023.19$, and $r \approx 0.977$.
(b) Use a 1% level of significance to test the claim that $\rho > 0$.
(c) Verify that $S_e \approx 1.5223$, $a \approx 1.4084$, and $b \approx 0.8794$.
(d) Find the predicted dealer invoice when the list price is $x = 40$ (thousand dollars).
(e) Find a 95% confidence interval for y when $x = 40$ (thousand dollars).
(f) Use a 1% level of significance to test the claim that $\beta > 0$.

13. *Expand Your Knowledge: Sample Size and Significance of r*
(a) Suppose $n = 6$ and the sample correlation coefficient is $r = 0.90$. Is r significant at the 1% level of significance (based on a two-tailed test)?
(b) Suppose $n = 10$ and the sample correlation coefficient is $r = 0.90$. Is r significant at the 1% level of significance (based on a two-tailed test)?
(c) Explain why the test results of parts (a) and (b) are different even though the sample correlation coefficient $r = 0.90$ is the same in both parts. Does it appear that sample size plays an important role in determining the significance of a correlation coefficient? Explain.

Point out that because the t value for r equals the t value for b, the results for tests of β are identical to the results for corresponding tests of ρ.

14. (a) Yes.
(b) Yes; yes; yes.

14. *Expand Your Knowledge: Student's t Value for Sample r and for Sample b* It is not obvious from the formulas, but the values of the sample test statistic t for the correlation coefficient and for the slope of the least-squares line are equal for the same data set. This fact is based on the relation

$$b = r\frac{s_y}{s_x}$$

where s_y and s_x are the sample standard deviations of the x and y values, respectively.

(a) Many computer software packages give the t value and corresponding P-value for b. If β is significant, is ρ significant?

(b) When doing statistical tests "by hand," it is easier to compute the sample test statistic t for the sample correlation coefficient r than it is to compute the sample test statistic t for the slope b of the sample least-squares line. Compare the results of parts (b) and (f) for Problems 7–12 of this problem set. Is the sample test statistic t for r the same as the corresponding test statistic for b? If you conclude that ρ is positive, can you conclude that β is positive at the same level of significance? If you conclude that ρ is not significant, is β also not significant at the same level of significance?

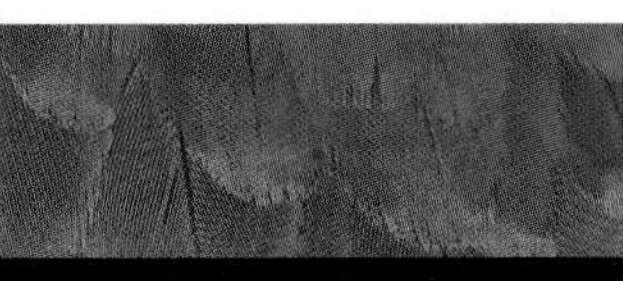

Chapter Review

SUMMARY

In this chapter, we introduced applications of the chi-square probability distribution and inferences for correlation and linear regression. In Part I, we looked at

- Properties of the chi-square distribution
- Tests of independence or homogeneity
- Tests of goodness-of-fit
- Tests of variance σ^2

In Part II, we returned to the linear regression model and linear correlation as introduced in Chapter 4. The inferences discussed were

- Testing the correlation coefficient ρ
- Testing the slope β of the least-squares line
- Confidence intervals for predicted values based on a specific value for x and the least-squares line

Procedure displays within Chapter 11 show methods and assumptions for all tests and confidence intervals discussed.

IMPORTANT WORDS & SYMBOLS

Section 11.1

Independence test
Chi-square distribution, χ^2
Degrees of freedom, $d.f. = (R - 1)(C - 1)$ for χ^2 distribution and tests of independence
Contingency table with cells
Row total
Column total
Expected frequency of a cell, E
Observed frequency of a cell, O
Homogeneity test

Section 11.2

Goodness-of-fit tests
Degrees of freedom $d.f.$ for χ^2 distribution and goodness-of-fit tests

Section 11.3

Hypotheses tests about σ^2

Section 11.4

Population correlation coefficient, ρ
Population slope β of the least-squares line
Standard error of estimate, S_e
Confidence interval for y

VIEWPOINT Movies and Money!

Young adults are the movie industry's best customers. However, going to the movies is expensive, which may explain why attendance rates increase with household income. Using what you have learned in this chapter, you can create appropriate chi-square tests to determine how good a fit exists between national percentage rates of attendance by household income and attendance rates in your demographic area. For more information and national data, see American Demographics *(Vol. 18, No. 12).*

CHAPTER REVIEW PROBLEMS

Tables and art to accompany margin answers may be found in the back of the book.

1. Chi-square.
2. Normal, Student's *t*.
3. Test of homogeneity.

Part I: Inferences Using the Chi-Square Distribution

1. *Statistical Literacy* Of the following random variables, which have only non-negative values: z, t, chi-square?
2. *Statistical Literacy* Of the following probability distributions, which are always symmetric: normal, Student's t, chi-square?
3. ***Critical Thinking*** Suppose you took random samples from three distinct age groups. Through a survey, you determined how many respondents from each age group preferred to get news from T.V., newspapers, the Internet, or another source (respondents could select only one mode). What type of test would be appropriate to determine if there is sufficient statistical evidence to claim that the proportions of each age group preferring the different modes of obtaining news are not the same? Select from tests of independence, homogeneity, and goodness-of-fit.

Before you solve Problems 4–8, first classify the problem as one of the following:

Chi-square test of independence or homogeneity
Chi-square goodness-of-fit
Chi-square for testing σ^2 or σ

Then, in each of the problems when a test is to be performed, do the following:

(i) Give the value of the level of significance. State the null and alternate hypotheses.
(ii) Find the sample test statistic.
(iii) Find or estimate the P-value of the sample test statistic.
(iv) Conclude the test.
(v) Interpret the conclusion in the context of the application.

4. Chi-square test of independence.
   (i) $\alpha = 0.01$; H_0: Time to finish a test and test score are independent. H_1: Time to finish a test and test score are not independent.
   (ii) $\chi^2 \approx 3.92$; $d.f. = 3$.
   (iii) $0.100 < P\text{-value} < 0.900$. From TI-84, P-value ≈ 0.2697.
   (iv) Do not reject H_0.
   (v) At the 1% level of significance, there is insufficient evidence to claim that time to finish a test and test results are not independent.

4. *Education: Exams* Professor Fair believes that extra time does not improve grades on exams. He randomly divided a group of 300 students into two groups and gave them all the same test. One group had exactly 1 hour in which to finish the test, and the other group could stay as long as desired. The results are shown in the following table. Test at the 0.01 level of significance that time to complete a test and test results are independent.

Time	A	B	C	F	Row Total
1 h	23	42	65	12	142
Unlimited	17	48	85	8	158
Column Total	40	90	150	20	300

5. Tires: Blowouts A consumer agency is investigating the blowout pressures of Soap Stone tires. A Soap Stone tire is said to blow out when it separates from the wheel rim due to impact forces usually caused by hitting a rock or a pothole in the road. A random sample of 30 Soap Stone tires were inflated to the recommended pressure, and then forces measured in foot-pounds were applied to each tire (1 foot-pound is the force of 1 pound dropped from a height of 1 foot). The customer complaint is that some Soap Stone tires blow out under small-impact forces, while other tires seem to be well made and don't have this fault. For the 30 test tires, the sample standard deviation of blowout forces was 1353 foot-pounds.

   Soap Stone claims its tires will blow out at an average pressure of 20,000 foot-pounds, with a standard deviation of 1020 foot-pounds. The average blowout force is not in question, but the variability of blowout forces is in question. Using a 0.01 level of significance, test the claim that the variance of blowout pressures is more than Soap Stone claims it is.

6. Packaging: Corn Flakes A machine that puts corn flakes into boxes is adjusted to put an average of 15 ounces into each box, with standard deviation of 0.25 ounce. If a random sample of 12 boxes gave a sample standard deviation of 0.38 ounce, do these data support the claim that the variance has increased and the machine needs to be brought back into adjustment? (Use a 0.01 level of significance.)

7. Teacher Ratings: Grades Professor Stone complains that student teacher ratings depend on the grade the student receives. In other words, according to Professor Stone, a teacher who gives good grades gets good ratings, and a teacher who gives bad grades gets bad ratings. To test this claim, the Student Assembly took a random sample of 300 teacher ratings on which the student's grade for the course also was indicated. The results are given in the following table. Test the hypothesis that teacher ratings and student grades are independent at the 0.01 level of significance.

Rating	A	B	C	F (or withdrawal)	Row Total
Excellent	14	18	15	3	50
Average	25	35	75	15	150
Poor	21	27	40	12	100
Column Total	60	80	130	30	300

8. Sociology: Age Distribution A sociologist is studying the age of the population in Blue Valley. Ten years ago, the population was such that 20% were under 20 years old, 15% were in the 20- to 35-year-old bracket, 30% were between 36 and 50, 25% were between 51 and 65, and 10% were over 65. A study done this year used a random sample of 210 residents. This sample showed

Under 20	20–35	36–50	51–65	Over 65
26	27	69	68	20

At the 0.01 level of significance, has the age distribution of the population of Blue Valley changed?

Part II: Inferences Relating to Linear Regression

9. Statistical Literacy What does it mean to say that the sample correlation coefficient r is significant?

10. Physiology: Children The following problem is based on information taken from the pediatrics section of *The Merck Manual* (a commonly used reference in medical schools and nursing programs). Let x be the body weight of a child (in kilograms), and let y be the metabolic rate of the child (in 100 kcal/24 h).

5. Chi-square test of σ^2.
   (i) $\alpha = 0.01$; H_0: $\sigma^2 = 1{,}040{,}400$; H_1: $\sigma^2 > 1{,}040{,}400$.
   (ii) $\chi^2 \approx 51.03$; $d.f. = 29$.
   (iii) $0.005 < P\text{-value} < 0.010$.
   (iv) Reject H_0.
   (v) At the 1% level of significance, there is sufficient evidence to conclude that the variance is greater than claimed.

6. Chi-square test of σ^2.
   (i) $\alpha = 0.01$; H_0: $\sigma^2 = 0.0625$; H_1: $\sigma^2 > 0.0625$.
   (ii) $\chi^2 \approx 25.41$; $d.f. = 11$.
   (iii) $0.005 < P\text{-value} < 0.010$.
   (iv) Reject H_0.
   (v) At the 1% level of significance, there is sufficient evidence to conclude that the variance has increased and the machine needs to be adjusted.

7. Chi-square test of independence.
   (i) $\alpha = 0.01$; H_0: Student grade and teacher rating are independent; H_1: Student grade and teacher rating are not independent.
   (ii) $\chi^2 \approx 9.80$; $d.f. = 6$.
   (iii) $0.100 < P\text{-value} < 0.900$. From TI-84, $P\text{-value} \approx 0.1337$.
   (iv) Do not reject H_0.
   (v) At the 1% level of significance, there is insufficient evidence to claim that student grade and teacher rating are not independent.

8. Chi-square test of goodness of fit.
   (i) $\alpha = 0.01$; H_0: The distributions are the same; H_1: The distributions are different.
   (ii) $\chi^2 \approx 11.93$; $d.f. = 4$.
   (iii) $0.010 < P\text{-value} < 0.025$.
   (iv) Do not reject H_0.
   (v) At the 1% level of significance, there is insufficient evidence to claim that the age distribution of the population of Blue Valley has changed.

9. We reject the null hypothesis that ρ is 0.

10. (a) Use a calculator.
    (b) (i) $\alpha = 0.01$; H_0: $\rho = 0$; H_1: $\rho > 0$.
    (ii) $t \approx 13.52$; $d.f. = 6$.
    (iii) $P\text{-value} < 0.0005$. From TI-84, $P\text{-value} \approx 0.0000$ to four decimal places.
    (iv) Reject H_0.
    (v) At the 1% level of significance, there is evidence that ρ is positive.

(c) (i) $\alpha = 0.01$; H_0: $\beta = 0$; H_1: $\beta > 0$.
(ii) $t \approx 13.52$; $d.f. = 6$.
(iii) P-value < 0.0005. From TI-84, P-value ≈ 0.0000 to four decimal places.
(iv) Reject H_0.
(v) At the 1% level of significance, there is evidence that β is positive.
(d) $\hat{y} \approx 4.876$; $E \approx 1.077$; 3.799 to 5.953.

11. (a) Use a calculator.
(b) (i) $\alpha = 0.01$; H_0: $\rho = 0$; H_1: $\rho > 0$.
(ii) $t \approx 6.665$; $d.f. = 5$.
(iii) $0.0005 < P\text{-value} < 0.005$. From TI-84, P-value ≈ 0.0006.
(iv) Reject H_0.
(v) At the 1% level of significance, there is evidence that ρ is positive.
(c) (i) $\alpha = 0.01$; H_0: $\beta = 0$; H_1: $\beta > 0$.
(ii) $t \approx 6.665$; $d.f. = 5$.
(iii) $0.0005 < P\text{-value} < 0.005$. From TI-84, P-value ≈ 0.0006.
(iv) Reject H_0.
(v) At the 1% level of significance, there is evidence that β is positive.
(d) $\hat{y} \approx 5.98$; $E \approx 1.48$; 4.498 to 7.458.

x	3.0	5.0	9.0	11.0	15.0	17.0	19.0	21.0
y	1.4	2.7	5.0	6.0	7.1	7.8	8.3	8.8

$\Sigma x = 100$; $\Sigma y = 47.1$; $\Sigma x^2 = 1552$; $\Sigma y^2 = 327.83$; $\Sigma xy = 710.3$

(a) Verify that $S_e \approx 0.518$.
(b) Verify that $r \approx 0.984$. Test that ρ is positive. Use $\alpha = 0.01$.
(c) Verify that $b \approx 0.402$. Test that β is positive. Use $\alpha = 0.01$.
(d) Verify that $\hat{y} \approx 0.856 + 0.402x$. Find a 90% confidence interval for the predicted metabolic rate for a child weighing 10 kg.

11. *Baseball: Batting Averages and Home Runs* In baseball, is there a linear correlation between batting average and home run percentage? Let x represent the batting average of a professional baseball player. Let y represent the home run percentage (number of home runs per 100 times at bat). A random sample of $n = 7$ professional baseball players gave the following information (Reference: *The Baseball Encyclopedia*, Macmillan Publishing Company).

x	0.243	0.259	0.286	0.263	0.268	0.339	0.299
y	1.4	3.6	5.5	3.8	3.5	7.3	5.0

$\Sigma x = 1.957$; $\Sigma y = 30.1$; $\Sigma x^2 \approx 0.553$; $\Sigma y^2 = 150.15$; $\Sigma xy \approx 8.753$

(a) Verify that $S_e \approx 0.647$.
(b) Verify that $r \approx 0.948$. Test that ρ is positive. Use $\alpha = 0.01$.
(c) Verify that $b \approx 55.166$. Test that β is positive. Use $\alpha = 0.01$.
(d) Verify that $\hat{y} \approx -11.123 + 55.166x$. Find a 90% confidence interval for the predicted home run percentage for a player with a batting average of 0.310.

DATA HIGHLIGHTS: GROUP PROJECTS

Break into small groups and discuss the following topics. Organize a brief outline in which you summarize the main points of your group discussion.

The *Statistical Abstract of the United States* reported information about the percentage of arrests of all drunk drivers according to age group. In the following table, the entry 3.7 in the first row means that in the entire United States, about 3.7% of all people arrested for drunk driving were in the age group 16–17 years. The Freemont County Sheriff's Office obtained data about the number of drunk drivers arrested in each age group over the past several years. In the following table, the entry 8 in the first row means that eight people in the age group 16–17 years were arrested for drunk driving in Freemont County.

Distribution of Drunk Driver Arrests by Age

Age	National Percentage	Number in Freemont County
16–17	3.7	8
18–24	18.9	35
25–29	12.9	23
30–34	10.3	19
35–39	8.5	12
40–44	7.9	14
45–49	8.0	16
50–54	7.9	13
55–59	6.8	10
60–64	5.7	9
65 and over	9.4	15
	100%	174

Use a chi-square test with 5% level of significance to test the claim that the age distribution of drunk drivers arrested in Freemont County is the same as the national age distribution of drunk drivers arrested.

(a) State the null and alternate hypotheses.
(b) Find the value of the chi-square test statistic from the sample.
(c) Find the degrees of freedom and the P-value of the test statistic.
(d) Decide whether you should reject or not reject the null hypothesis.
(e) Interpret your conclusion in the context of the problem.
(f) How could you gather data and conduct a similar test for the city or county in which you live? Explain.

LINKING CONCEPTS: WRITING PROJECTS

Discuss each of the following topics in class or review the topics on your own. Then write a brief but complete essay in which you summarize the main points. Please include formulas and graphs as appropriate.

Consider the results of a study conducted by the makers of Advil. A random sample of patients were assigned to one of two groups: One received ibuprofen and the other received a placebo. Then patients were asked if they experienced stomach upset (yes or no). The results of the study follow.

	Stomach Upset		
Group	Yes	No	Row Total
Ibuprofen	8	664	672
Placebo	6	645	651
Column total	14	1309	1323

1. In Chapter 5 on probability (Section 5.2), we considered contingency tables and the probabilities of events described by different combinations of the rows and columns. Use these techniques to compute the probability that a patient had stomach upset *given* that the patient was in the ibuprofen group. Compute the probability that a patient had stomach upset *given* that the patient was in the placebo group.
2. Are the proportions of patients having stomach upset in the two different treatment groups the same? We treated questions of this type in Section 10.3, where we applied the normal distribution to test the difference of proportions. Use such a test to determine whether or not the proportions are different at the 5% level of significance.
3. Now consider the 2×2 contingency table. We can apply techniques of tests of independence to see if the proportions of patients experiencing stomach upset in the two treatment groups are the same or not. When we apply these techniques to tests of proportions, we assume that the sample size for each treatment group is *assigned* ahead of time and is not itself a random variable. In such a case, we apply a test of homogeneity. Perform such a test.
4. Compare the results of Problems 2 and 3. Do the test conclusions agree? When testing two proportions, you can use either the normal distribution test of Section 10.3 or a chi-square test. Can you think of any advantages of one choice over the other?

USING TECHNOLOGY

Tests of Independence

A study involving people who process food gave the following information about work shift and number of sick days.

Shift	Number of Sick Days 0	1	2	3	4 or more
Day	134	44	24	10	61
Aft/ev	90	39	23	18	99
Night	107	37	21	20	82
Rotating	56	20	14	17	92

Source: United States Department of Health, Education, and Welfare, NIOSH Technical Report. Tasto, Colligan, *et al. Health Consequences of Shift Work.* Washington: GPO, 1978, 29. (*Note:* This table was adapted from Table 7 on page 25 of the source.)

Use a 1% level of significance to test the null hypothesis that work shift and number of sick days are independent against the alternate hypothesis that they are not independent. What is the sample chi-square value? What is the test conclusion?

Technology Hints

TI-84Plus/TI-83Plus

Press the **Matrix** key and enter the observed values in a matrix. Name the matrix [A]. Then enter dimension matrix [B] to the same dimensions. Matrix [B] will hold the expected values. Press the **STAT** key and under the **TESTS** menu, select option **C:χ^2-Test. Calculate** will give the sample χ^2 value and its P value. **Draw** will show the sample test statistic on the χ^2 distribution with the P-value shaded.

Excel

There are no built-in commands for executing a chi-square test. The *Technology Guide* shows a multistep process for conducting a chi-square test. The Tech Note of Section 11.1 gives a brief outline of the process.

Minitab

In Minitab, enter data for tests of independence in columns. Be sure to enter data only and not row or column totals. Then use the menu choices ➤ **Stat** ➤ **Tables** ➤ **Chisquare Test.**

SPSS

SPSS utilizes raw data to make a contingency table and then provides an option for a chi-square test of independence. For example, rather than entering the data for number of sick days versus shift as a table, in SPSS you enter all 1009 cases, where the shift variable shows the row category (day, aft/eve, night, rotating) of the entry and the sick-days variable shows the corresponding column category (number of sick days). Specifically, you would enter 134 cases with shift variable "day" and sick-day variable "0," etc. Then use the menu choices **Analyze** ➤ **Descriptive Statistics** ➤ **Crosstabs....** In the dialogue box, move the row variable and the column variable to the designated boxes. Select the Statistics option and check Chi-square. To see the expected values, select the Cells option and check Expected. The output includes a contingency table, the sample χ^2 test statistic, degrees of freedom, and the P-value of the test statistic.

Cumulative Review Problems

CHAPTERS 10–11

For all hypothesis tests, please provide the following information.

(i) What is the level of significance? State the null and alternate hypotheses.

(ii) What sampling distribution will you use? What assumptions are you making? What is the value of the sample test statistic?

(iii) Find (or estimate) the P-value. Sketch the sampling distribution and show the area corresponding to the P-value.

(iv) Based on your answers in parts (i) to (iii), will you reject or fail to reject the null hypothesis? Are the data statistically significant at level α?

(v) Interpret your conclusion in the context of the application.

1. *Inferences for Linear Regression* Plate tectonics and the spread of the ocean floor are very important in modern studies of earthquakes and earth science in general. A random sample of islands in the Indian Ocean gave the following information, where

x = age of volcanic island in the Indian Ocean (units in 10^6 years)

y = distance of the island from the center of the midoceanic ridge (units in 100 km)

x	120	83	60	50	35	30	20	17
y	30	16	15.5	14.5	22	18	12	0

Source: King, Cuchaine A.M. *Physical Geography.* Oxford: Basil Blackwell, 1980, pp. 77–86 and 196–206. Reprinted by permission of the publisher.

$\Sigma x = 415$; $\Sigma y = 128$; $\Sigma x^2 = 30{,}203$; $\Sigma y^2 = 2558.5$; $\Sigma xy = 8133$

(a) Verify that the standard error of estimate $S_e \approx 6.50$.

(b) Verify that the sample correlation coefficient $r \approx 0.709$. Use a 5% level of significance to test that ρ is positive.

(c) Verify that the equation of the least-squares line is $\hat{y} \approx 7.07 + 0.172x$. Use a 5% level of significance to test that β is positive.

(d) Given that the age of a volcanic island is 55 (units in 10^6 years), predict how far the island is from the center of the midoceanic ridge (units in 100 km). Find an 85% confidence interval for the prediction.

2. *Goodness of Fit* A recent national study gave the following information about declared majors of undergraduate college students: humanities, 15%; science, 23%; business, 29%; education, 11%; social science, 10%; all other fields, 12% (Reference: *Statistical Abstract of the United States*). A random sample of 215 college students in Colorado gave the following counts regarding college majors: humanities, 24; science, 54; business, 70; education, 16; social science, 30; all other fields, 21. Does this information indicate that the distribution of college majors for Colorado students is different from the national distribution? Use $\alpha = 0.01$.

1. (a) Use a calculator.
(b) (i) $\alpha = 0.05$; H_0: $\rho = 0$; H_1: $\rho > 0$.
(ii) Student's t, $d.f. = 6$; $t \approx 2.466$.
(iii) $0.010 < P\text{-value} < 0.025$. From TI-84, P-value ≈ 0.0244. On the t graph, shade area to the right of 2.466.
(iv) P-value interval $< \alpha = 0.05$; reject H_0.
(v) At the 5% level of significance, there is evidence of a positive correlation between age of a volcanic island in the Indian Ocean and distance of the island from the center of the midoceanic ridge.
(c) (i) $\alpha = 0.05$; H_0: $\beta = 0$; H_1: $\beta > 0$.
(ii) Student's t, $d.f. = 6$; $t \approx 2.466$.
(iii) $0.010 < P\text{-value} < 0.025$. From TI-84, P-value ≈ 0.0244. On the t graph, shade area to the right of 2.466.
(iv) P-value interval $< \alpha = 0.05$; reject H_0.
(v) At the 5% level of significance, there is evidence of a positive slope for the regression line for age of a volcanic island in the Indian Ocean and distance of the island from the center of the midoceanic ridge.
(d) $\hat{y} \approx 16.5$ (units in 100 km); $d.f. = 6$; $t_{0.85} = 1.650$; $E \approx 11.4$; 5.1 to 27.9 (units in 100 km).

3. *Test of Independence: Agriculture* Three types of fertilizer were used on 132 identical plots of maize. Each plot was harvested and the yield (in kg) was recorded (Reference: Caribbean Agricultural Research and Development Institute).

Yield (kg)	Type of Fertilizer I	II	III	Row Total
0–2.9	12	10	15	37
3.0–5.9	18	21	11	50
6.0–8.9	16	19	10	45
Column total	46	50	36	132

Use a 5% level of significance to test the hypothesis that type of fertilizer and yield of maize are independent. Interpret the results.

4. *Testing Variances: Iris* Random samples of two species of iris gave the following petal lengths (in cm) (Reference: R. A. Fisher, *Annals of Eugenics,* vol. 7).

x_1, *Iris virginica*	5.1	5.9	4.5	4.9	5.7	4.8	5.8	6.4	5.6	5.9
x_2, *Iris versicolor*	4.5	4.8	4.7	5.0	3.8	5.1	4.4	4.2		

Use a 5% level of significance to test the claim that the population standard deviation of x_1 is larger than 0.55.

5. *Testing Paired Differences* Phosphorous is a chemical that is found in many household cleaning products. Unfortunately, phosphorous also finds its way into surface water, where it can harm fish, plants, and other wildlife. Two methods of phosphorous reduction are being studied. At a random sample of 7 locations, both methods were used and the total phosphorous reduction (mg/l) was recorded. (Reference: *Environmental Protection Agency Case Study 832-R-93-005.*)

Site	1	2	3	4	5	6	7
Method I:	0.013	0.030	0.015	0.055	0.007	0.002	0.010
Method II:	0.014	0.058	0.017	0.039	0.017	0.001	0.013

Do these data indicate a difference (either way) in the average reduction of phosphorous between the two methods? Use $\alpha = 0.05$.

6. *Testing and Estimating $\mu_1 - \mu_2$, σ_1 and σ_2 Unknown* In the airline business, "on-time" flight arrival is important for connecting flights and general customer satisfaction. Is there a difference between summer and winter average on-time flight arrivals? Let x_1 be a random variable that represents percentage of on-time arrivals at major airports in the summer. Let x_2 be a random variable that represents percentage of on-time arrivals at major airports in the winter. A random sample of $n_1 = 16$ major airports showed that $\bar{x}_1 = 74.8\%$, with $s_1 = 5.2\%$. A random sample of $n_2 = 18$ major airports showed that $\bar{x}_2 = 70.1\%$, with $s_2 = 8.6\%$. (Reference: *Statistical Abstract of the United States.*)
   (a) Does this information indicate a difference (either way) in the population mean percentage of on-time arrivals for summer compared to winter? Use $\alpha = 0.05$.
   (b) Find an 95% confidence interval for $\mu_1 - \mu_2$.
   (c) What assumptions about the original populations have you made for the methods used?

2. (i) $\alpha = 0.01$; H_0: Colorado major distribution is the same as national distribution; H_1: Colorado major distribution is different from national distribution.
   (ii) Chi-square; *d.f.* = 5; $\chi^2 \approx 10.196$.
   (iii) $0.050 < P\text{-value} < 0.100$; shade region to the right of 10.196.
   (iv) *P*-value interval $> \alpha = 0.01$; fail to reject H_0.
   (v) At the 1% level of significance, the evidence is insufficient to claim that the distribution of college majors selected by Colorado students is different from the national distribution of college majors.
3. (i) $\alpha = 0.05$; H_0: Yield and fertilizer type are independent; H_1: Yield and fertilizer type are not independent.
   (ii) $\chi^2 \approx 5.005$; *d.f.* = 4.
   (iii) $0.100 < P\text{-value} < 0.900$. From TI-84, *P*-value ≈ 0.2868.
   (iv) Do not reject H_0.
   (v) At the 5% level of significance, the evidence is insufficient to conclude that fertilizer type and yield are not independent.
4. (i) $\alpha = 0.05$; H_0: $\sigma = 0.55$; H_1: $\sigma > 0.55$.
   (ii) $s \approx 0.602$; *d.f.* = 9; $\chi^2 \approx 10.78$.
   (iii) $0.100 < P\text{-value} < 0.900$. From TI-84, *P*-value ≈ 0.2868.
   (iv) Do not reject H_0.
   (v) At the 5% level of significance, there is insufficient evidence to conclude that the standard deviation of petal lengths is greater than 0.55.
5. (i) $\alpha = 0.05$; H_0: $\mu_d = 0$; H_1: $\mu_d \neq 0$.
   (ii) Student's *t*, *d.f.* = 6; $\bar{d} \approx -0.0039$; $t \approx -0.771$.
   (iii) $0.250 < P\text{-value} < 0.500$; on *t* graph, shade area to the right of 0.771 and to the left of −0.771. From TI-84, *P*-value ≈ 0.4699.
   (iv) *P*-value interval > 0.05 for α; fail to reject H_0.
   (v) At the 5% level of significance, the evidence does not show a population mean difference in phosphorous reduction between the two methods.
6. (a) (i) $\alpha = 0.05$; H_0: $\mu_1 = \mu_2$; H_1: $\mu_1 \neq \mu_2$.
   (ii) Student's *t*, *d.f.* = 15; $t \approx 1.952$.
   (iii) $0.050 < P\text{-value} < 0.100$; on *t* graph, shade area to the right of 1.952 and to the left of −1.952. From TI-84, *P*-value ≈ 0.0609.
   (iv) *P*-value interval > 0.05 for α; fail to reject H_0.
   (v) At the 5% level of significance, the evidence does not show any difference in the population mean proportion of on-time arrivals in summer versus winter.
   (b) −0.43% to 9.835%.
   (c) x_1 and x_2 distributions are approximately normal (mound-shaped and symmetric).

7. *Testing and Estimating a Difference of Proportions $p_1 - p_2$* How often do you go out dancing? This question was asked by a professional survey group on behalf of the National Arts Survey. A random sample of $n_1 = 95$ single men showed that $r_1 = 23$ went out dancing occasionally. Another random sample of $n_2 = 92$ single women showed that $r_2 = 19$ went out dancing occasionally.

(a) Do these data indicate that the proportion of single men who go out dancing occasionally is higher than the proportion of single women? Use a 5% level of significance. List the assumptions you made in solving this problem. Do you think these assumptions are realistic?

(b) Compute a 90% confidence interval for the population difference of proportions $p_1 - p_2$ of single men and single women who occasionally go out dancing.

7. (a) (i) $\alpha = 0.05$; H_0: $p_1 = p_2$; H_1: $p_1 > p_2$.
(ii) Standard normal; $\hat{p}_1 \approx 0.242$; $\hat{p}_2 \approx 0.207$; $\bar{p} \approx 0.2246$; $z \approx 0.58$.
(iii) P-value ≈ 0.2810; on standard normal curve, shade area to the right of 0.58.
(iv) P-value interval > 0.05 for α; fail to reject H_0.
(v) At the 5% level of significance, the evidence does not indicate that the population proportion of single men who go out dancing occasionally differs from the proportion of single women.

Since $n_1\bar{p}$, $n_1\bar{q}$, $n_2\bar{p}$, and $n_2\bar{q}$ are all greater than 5, the normal approximation to the binomial is justified.
(b) -0.065 to 0.139.

Appendix: Tables

1. Random Numbers
2. Binomial Probability Distribution $C_{n,r}p^r q^{n-r}$
3. Areas of a Standard Normal Distribution
4. Critical Values for Student's t Distribution
5. The χ^2 Distribution

TABLE 1 Random Numbers

92630	78240	19267	95457	53497	23894	37708	79862	76471	66418
79445	78735	71549	44843	26104	67318	00701	34986	66751	99723
59654	71966	27386	50004	05358	94031	29281	18544	52429	06080
31524	49587	76612	39789	13537	48086	59483	60680	84675	53014
06348	76938	90379	51392	55887	71015	09209	79157	24440	30244
28703	51709	94456	48396	73780	06436	86641	69239	57662	80181
68108	89266	94730	95761	75023	48464	65544	96583	18911	16391
99938	90704	93621	66330	33393	95261	95349	51769	91616	33238
91543	73196	34449	63513	83834	99411	58826	40456	69268	48562
42103	02781	73920	56297	72678	12249	25270	36678	21313	75767
17138	27584	25296	28387	51350	61664	37893	05363	44143	42677
28297	14280	54524	21618	95320	38174	60579	08089	94999	78460
09331	56712	51333	06289	75345	08811	82711	57392	25252	30333
31295	04204	93712	51287	05754	79396	87399	51773	33075	97061
36146	15560	27592	42089	99281	59640	15221	96079	09961	05371
29553	18432	13630	05529	02791	81017	49027	79031	50912	09399
23501	22642	63081	08191	89420	67800	55137	54707	32945	64522
57888	85846	67967	07835	11314	01545	48535	17142	08552	67457
55336	71264	88472	04334	63919	36394	11196	92470	70543	29776
10087	10072	55980	64688	68239	20461	89381	93809	00796	95945
34101	81277	66090	88872	37818	72142	67140	50785	21380	16703
53362	44940	60430	22834	14130	96593	23298	56203	92671	15925
82975	66158	84731	19436	55790	69229	28661	13675	99318	76873
54827	84673	22898	08094	14326	87038	42892	21127	30712	48489
25464	59098	27436	89421	80754	89924	19097	67737	80368	08795
67609	60214	41475	84950	40133	02546	09570	45682	50165	15609
44921	70924	61295	51137	47596	86735	35561	76649	18217	63446
33170	30972	98130	95828	49786	13301	36081	80761	33985	68621
84687	85445	06208	17654	51333	02878	35010	67578	61574	20749
71886	56450	36567	09395	96951	35507	17555	35212	69106	01679
00475	02224	74722	14721	40215	21351	08596	45625	83981	63748
25993	38881	68361	59560	41274	69742	40703	37993	03435	18873
92882	53178	99195	93803	56985	53089	15305	50522	55900	43026
25138	26810	07093	15677	60688	04410	24505	37890	67186	62829
84631	71882	12991	83028	82484	90339	91950	74579	03539	90122

TABLE 1 *continued*

34003	92326	12793	61453	48121	74271	28363	66561	75220	35908
53775	45749	05734	86169	42762	70175	97310	73894	88606	19994
59316	97885	72807	54966	60859	11932	35265	71601	55577	67715
20479	66557	50705	26999	09854	52591	14063	30214	19890	19292
86180	84931	25455	26044	02227	52015	21820	50599	51671	65411
21451	68001	72710	40261	61281	13172	63819	48970	51732	54113
98062	68375	80089	24135	72355	95428	11808	29740	81644	86610
01788	64429	14430	94575	75153	94576	61393	96192	03227	32258
62465	04841	43272	68702	01274	05437	22953	18946	99053	41690
94324	31089	84159	92933	99989	89500	91586	02802	69471	68274
05797	43984	21575	09908	70221	19791	51578	36432	33494	79888
10395	14289	52185	09721	25789	38562	54794	04897	59012	89251
35177	56986	25549	59730	64718	52630	31100	62384	49483	11409
25633	89619	75882	98256	02126	72099	57183	55887	09320	73463
16464	48280	94254	45777	45150	68865	11382	11782	22695	41988

Source: Reprinted from *A Million Random Digits with 100,000 Normal Deviates* by the Rand Corporation (New York: The Free Press, 1955). Copyright 1955 and 1983 by the Rand Corporation. Used by permission.

TABLE 2 Binomial Probability Distribution $C_{n,r}p^rq^{n-r}$

This table shows the probability of r successes in n independent trials, each with probability of success p.

		p																			
n	r	.01	.05	.10	.15	.20	.25	.30	.35	.40	.45	.50	.55	.60	.65	.70	.75	.80	.85	.90	.95
2	0	.980	.902	.810	.723	.640	.563	.490	.423	.360	.303	.250	.203	.160	.123	.090	.063	.040	.023	.010	.002
	1	.020	.095	.180	.255	.320	.375	.420	.455	.480	.495	.500	.495	.480	.455	.420	.375	.320	.255	.180	.095
	2	.000	.002	.010	.023	.040	.063	.090	.123	.160	.203	.250	.303	.360	.423	.490	.563	.640	.723	.810	.902
3	0	.970	.857	.729	.614	.512	.422	.343	.275	.216	.166	.125	.091	.064	.043	.027	.016	.008	.003	.001	.000
	1	.029	.135	.243	.325	.384	.422	.441	.444	.432	.408	.375	.334	.288	.239	.189	.141	.096	.057	.027	.007
	2	.000	.007	.027	.057	.096	.141	.189	.239	.288	.334	.375	.408	.432	.444	.441	.422	.384	.325	.243	.135
	3	.000	.000	.001	.003	.008	.016	.027	.043	.064	.091	.125	.166	.216	.275	.343	.422	.512	.614	.729	.857
4	0	.961	.815	.656	.522	.410	.316	.240	.179	.130	.092	.062	.041	.026	.015	.008	.004	.002	.001	.000	.000
	1	.039	.171	.292	.368	.410	.422	.412	.384	.346	.300	.250	.200	.154	.112	.076	.047	.026	.011	.004	.000
	2	.001	.014	.049	.098	.154	.211	.265	.311	.346	.368	.375	.368	.346	.311	.265	.211	.154	.098	.049	.014
	3	.000	.000	.004	.011	.026	.047	.076	.112	.154	.200	.250	.300	.346	.384	.412	.422	.410	.368	.292	.171
	4	.000	.000	.000	.001	.002	.004	.008	.015	.026	.041	.062	.092	.130	.179	.240	.316	.410	.522	.656	.815
5	0	.951	.774	.590	.444	.328	.237	.168	.116	.078	.050	.031	.019	.010	.005	.002	.001	.000	.000	.000	.000
	1	.048	.204	.328	.392	.410	.396	.360	.312	.259	.206	.156	.113	.077	.049	.028	.015	.006	.002	.000	.000
	2	.001	.021	.073	.138	.205	.264	.309	.336	.346	.337	.312	.276	.230	.181	.132	.088	.051	.024	.008	.001
	3	.000	.001	.008	.024	.051	.088	.132	.181	.230	.276	.312	.337	.346	.336	.309	.264	.205	.138	.073	.021
	4	.000	.000	.000	.002	.006	.015	.028	.049	.077	.113	.156	.206	.259	.312	.360	.396	.410	.392	.328	.204
	5	.000	.000	.000	.000	.000	.001	.002	.005	.010	.019	.031	.050	.078	.116	.168	.237	.328	.444	.590	.774
6	0	.941	.735	.531	.377	.262	.178	.118	.075	.047	.028	.016	.008	.004	.002	.001	.000	.000	.000	.000	.000
	1	.057	.232	.354	.399	.393	.356	.303	.244	.187	.136	.094	.061	.037	.020	.010	.004	.002	.000	.000	.000
	2	.001	.031	.098	.176	.246	.297	.324	.328	.311	.278	.234	.186	.138	.095	.060	.033	.015	.006	.001	.000
	3	.000	.002	.015	.042	.082	.132	.185	.236	.276	.303	.312	.303	.276	.236	.185	.132	.082	.042	.015	.002
	4	.000	.000	.001	.006	.015	.033	.060	.095	.138	.186	.234	.278	.311	.328	.324	.297	.246	.176	.098	.031
	5	.000	.000	.000	.000	.002	.004	.010	.020	.037	.061	.094	.136	.187	.244	.303	.356	.393	.399	.354	.232
	6	.000	.000	.000	.000	.000	.000	.001	.002	.004	.008	.016	.028	.047	.075	.118	.178	.262	.377	.531	.735
7	0	.932	.698	.478	.321	.210	.133	.082	.049	.028	.015	.008	.004	.002	.001	.000	.000	.000	.000	.000	.000
	1	.066	.257	.372	.396	.367	.311	.247	.185	.131	.087	.055	.032	.017	.008	.004	.001	.000	.000	.000	.000
	2	.002	.041	.124	.210	.275	.311	.318	.299	.261	.214	.164	.117	.077	.047	.025	.012	.004	.001	.000	.000
	3	.000	.004	.023	.062	.115	.173	.227	.268	.290	.292	.273	.239	.194	.144	.097	.058	.029	.011	.003	.000
	4	.000	.000	.003	.011	.029	.058	.097	.144	.194	.239	.273	.292	.290	.268	.227	.173	.115	.062	.023	.004
	5	.000	.000	.000	.001	.004	.012	.025	.047	.077	.117	.164	.214	.261	.299	.318	.311	.275	.210	.124	.041
	6	.000	.000	.000	.000	.000	.001	.004	.008	.017	.032	.055	.087	.131	.185	.247	.311	.367	.396	.372	.257
	7	.000	.000	.000	.000	.000	.000	.000	.001	.002	.004	.008	.015	.028	.049	.082	.133	.210	.321	.478	.698

TABLE 2 *continued*

		p																		
n	r	.01	.05	.10	.15	.20	.25	.30	.35	.40	.45	.50	.55	.60	.65	.70	.75	.80	.85	.90	.95
8	0	.923	.663	.430	.272	.168	.100	.058	.032	.017	.008	.004	.002	.001	.000	.000	.000	.000	.000	.000	.000
	1	.075	.279	.383	.385	.336	.267	.198	.137	.090	.055	.031	.016	.008	.003	.001	.000	.000	.000	.000	.000
	2	.003	.051	.149	.238	.294	.311	.296	.259	.209	.157	.109	.070	.041	.022	.010	.004	.001	.000	.000	.000
	3	.000	.005	.033	.084	.147	.208	.254	.279	.279	.257	.219	.172	.124	.081	.047	.023	.009	.003	.000	.000
	4	.000	.000	.005	.018	.046	.087	.136	.188	.232	.263	.273	.263	.232	.188	.136	.087	.046	.018	.005	.000
	5	.000	.000	.000	.003	.009	.023	.047	.081	.124	.172	.219	.257	.279	.279	.254	.208	.147	.084	.033	.005
	6	.000	.000	.000	.000	.001	.004	.010	.022	.041	.070	.109	.157	.209	.259	.296	.311	.294	.238	.149	.051
	7	.000	.000	.000	.000	.000	.000	.001	.003	.008	.016	.031	.055	.090	.137	.198	.267	.336	.385	.383	.279
	8	.000	.000	.000	.000	.000	.000	.000	.000	.001	.002	.004	.008	.017	.032	.058	.100	.168	.272	.430	.663
9	0	.914	.630	.387	.232	.134	.075	.040	.021	.010	.005	.002	.001	.000	.000	.000	.000	.000	.000	.000	.000
	1	.083	.299	.387	.368	.302	.225	.156	.100	.060	.034	.018	.008	.004	.001	.000	.000	.000	.000	.000	.000
	2	.003	.063	.172	.260	.302	.300	.267	.216	.161	.111	.070	.041	.021	.010	.004	.001	.000	.000	.000	.000
	3	.000	.008	.045	.107	.176	.234	.267	.272	.251	.212	.164	.116	.074	.042	.021	.009	.003	.001	.000	.000
	4	.000	.001	.007	.028	.066	.117	.172	.219	.251	.260	.246	.213	.167	.118	.074	.039	.017	.005	.001	.000
	5	.000	.000	.001	.005	.017	.039	.074	.118	.167	.213	.246	.260	.251	.219	.172	.117	.066	.028	.007	.001
	6	.000	.000	.000	.001	.003	.009	.021	.042	.074	.116	.164	.212	.251	.272	.267	.234	.176	.107	.045	.008
	7	.000	.000	.000	.000	.000	.001	.004	.010	.021	.041	.070	.111	.161	.216	.267	.300	.302	.260	.172	.063
	8	.000	.000	.000	.000	.000	.000	.000	.001	.004	.008	.018	.034	.060	.100	.156	.225	.302	.368	.387	.299
	9	.000	.000	.000	.000	.000	.000	.000	.000	.000	.001	.002	.005	.010	.021	.040	.075	.134	.232	.387	.630
10	0	.904	.599	.349	.197	.107	.056	.028	.014	.006	.003	.001	.000	.000	.000	.000	.000	.000	.000	.000	.000
	1	.091	.315	.387	.347	.268	.188	.121	.072	.040	.021	.010	.004	.002	.000	.000	.000	.000	.000	.000	.000
	2	.004	.075	.194	.276	.302	.282	.233	.176	.121	.076	.044	.023	.011	.004	.001	.000	.000	.000	.000	.000
	3	.000	.010	.057	.130	.201	.250	.267	.252	.215	.166	.117	.075	.042	.021	.009	.003	.001	.000	.000	.000
	4	.000	.001	.011	.040	.088	.146	.200	.238	.251	.238	.205	.160	.111	.069	.037	.016	.006	.001	.000	.000
	5	.000	.000	.001	.008	.026	.058	.103	.154	.201	.234	.246	.234	.201	.154	.103	.058	.026	.008	.001	.000
	6	.000	.000	.000	.001	.006	.016	.037	.069	.111	.160	.205	.238	.251	.238	.200	.146	.088	.040	.011	.001
	7	.000	.000	.000	.000	.001	.003	.009	.021	.042	.075	.117	.166	.215	.252	.267	.250	.201	.130	.057	.010
	8	.000	.000	.000	.000	.000	.000	.001	.004	.011	.023	.044	.076	.121	.176	.233	.282	.302	.276	.194	.075
	9	.000	.000	.000	.000	.000	.000	.000	.000	.002	.004	.010	.021	.040	.072	.121	.188	.268	.347	.387	.315
	10	.000	.000	.000	.000	.000	.000	.000	.000	.000	.000	.001	.003	.006	.014	.028	.056	.107	.197	.349	.599
11	0	.895	.569	.314	.167	.086	.042	.020	.009	.004	.001	.000	.000	.000	.000	.000	.000	.000	.000	.000	.000
	1	.099	.329	.384	.325	.236	.155	.093	.052	.027	.013	.005	.002	.001	.000	.000	.000	.000	.000	.000	.000
	2	.005	.087	.213	.287	.295	.258	.200	.140	.089	.051	.027	.013	.005	.002	.001	.000	.000	.000	.000	.000

TABLE 2 *continued*

n	r	.01	.05	.10	.15	.20	.25	.30	.35	.40	.45	.50	.55	.60	.65	.70	.75	.80	.85	.90	.95
		p																			
11	3	.000	.014	.071	.152	.221	.258	.257	.225	.177	.126	.081	.046	.023	.010	.004	.001	.000	.000	.000	.000
	4	.000	.001	.016	.054	.111	.172	.220	.243	.236	.206	.161	.113	.070	.038	.017	.006	.002	.000	.000	.000
	5	.000	.000	.002	.013	.039	.080	.132	.183	.221	.236	.226	.193	.147	.099	.057	.027	.010	.002	.000	.000
	6	.000	.000	.000	.002	.010	.027	.057	.099	.147	.193	.226	.236	.221	.183	.132	.080	.039	.013	.002	.000
	7	.000	.000	.000	.000	.002	.006	.017	.038	.070	.113	.161	.206	.236	.243	.220	.172	.111	.054	.016	.001
	8	.000	.000	.000	.000	.000	.001	.004	.010	.023	.046	.081	.126	.177	.225	.257	.258	.221	.152	.071	.014
	9	.000	.000	.000	.000	.000	.000	.001	.002	.005	.013	.027	.051	.089	.140	.200	.258	.295	.287	.213	.087
	10	.000	.000	.000	.000	.000	.000	.000	.000	.001	.002	.005	.013	.027	.052	.093	.155	.236	.325	.384	.329
	11	.000	.000	.000	.000	.000	.000	.000	.000	.000	.000	.000	.001	.004	.009	.020	.042	.086	.167	.314	.569
12	0	.886	.540	.282	.142	.069	.032	.014	.006	.002	.001	.000	.000	.000	.000	.000	.000	.000	.000	.000	.000
	1	.107	.341	.377	.301	.206	.127	.071	.037	.017	.008	.003	.001	.000	.000	.000	.000	.000	.000	.000	.000
	2	.006	.099	.230	.292	.283	.232	.168	.109	.064	.034	.016	.007	.002	.001	.000	.000	.000	.000	.000	.000
	3	.000	.017	.085	.172	.236	.258	.240	.195	.142	.092	.054	.028	.012	.005	.001	.000	.000	.000	.000	.000
	4	.000	.002	.021	.068	.133	.194	.231	.237	.213	.170	.121	.076	.042	.020	.008	.002	.001	.000	.000	.000
	5	.000	.000	.004	.019	.053	.103	.158	.204	.227	.223	.193	.149	.101	.059	.029	.011	.003	.001	.000	.000
	6	.000	.000	.000	.004	.016	.040	.079	.128	.177	.212	.226	.212	.177	.128	.079	.040	.016	.004	.000	.000
	7	.000	.000	.000	.001	.003	.011	.029	.059	.101	.149	.193	.223	.227	.204	.158	.103	.053	.019	.004	.000
	8	.000	.000	.000	.000	.001	.002	.008	.020	.042	.076	.121	.170	.213	.237	.231	.194	.133	.068	.021	.002
	9	.000	.000	.000	.000	.000	.000	.001	.005	.012	.028	.054	.092	.142	.195	.240	.258	.236	.172	.085	.017
	10	.000	.000	.000	.000	.000	.000	.000	.001	.002	.007	.016	.034	.064	.109	.168	.232	.283	.292	.230	.099
	11	.000	.000	.000	.000	.000	.000	.000	.000	.000	.001	.003	.008	.017	.037	.071	.127	.206	.301	.377	.341
	12	.000	.000	.000	.000	.000	.000	.000	.000	.000	.000	.000	.001	.002	.006	.014	.032	.069	.142	.282	.540
15	0	.860	.463	.206	.087	.035	.013	.005	.002	.000	.000	.000	.000	.000	.000	.000	.000	.000	.000	.000	.000
	1	.130	.366	.343	.231	.132	.067	.031	.013	.005	.002	.000	.000	.000	.000	.000	.000	.000	.000	.000	.000
	2	.009	.135	.267	.286	.231	.156	.092	.048	.022	.009	.003	.001	.000	.000	.000	.000	.000	.000	.000	.000
	3	.000	.031	.129	.218	.250	.225	.170	.111	.063	.032	.014	.005	.002	.000	.000	.000	.000	.000	.000	.000
	4	.000	.005	.043	.116	.188	.225	.219	.179	.127	.078	.042	.019	.007	.002	.001	.000	.000	.000	.000	.000
	5	.000	.001	.010	.045	.103	.165	.206	.212	.186	.140	.092	.051	.024	.010	.003	.001	.000	.000	.000	.000
	6	.000	.000	.002	.013	.043	.092	.147	.191	.207	.191	.153	.105	.061	.030	.012	.003	.001	.000	.000	.000
	7	.000	.000	.000	.003	.014	.039	.081	.132	.177	.201	.196	.165	.118	.071	.035	.013	.003	.001	.000	.000
	8	.000	.000	.000	.001	.003	.013	.035	.071	.118	.165	.196	.201	.177	.132	.081	.039	.014	.003	.000	.000
	9	.000	.000	.000	.000	.001	.003	.012	.030	.061	.105	.153	.191	.207	.191	.147	.092	.043	.013	.002	.000
	10	.000	.000	.000	.000	.000	.001	.003	.010	.024	.051	.092	.140	.186	.212	.206	.165	.103	.045	.010	.001

TABLE 2 *continued*

		p																			
n	*r*	.01	.05	.10	.15	.20	.25	.30	.35	.40	.45	.50	.55	.60	.65	.70	.75	.80	.85	.90	.95
15	11	.000	.000	.000	.000	.000	.000	.001	.002	.007	.019	.042	.078	.127	.179	.219	.225	.188	.116	.043	.005
	12	.000	.000	.000	.000	.000	.000	.000	.000	.002	.005	.014	.032	.063	.111	.170	.225	.250	.218	.129	.031
	13	.000	.000	.000	.000	.000	.000	.000	.000	.000	.001	.003	.009	.022	.048	.092	.156	.231	.286	.267	.135
	14	.000	.000	.000	.000	.000	.000	.000	.000	.000	.000	.000	.002	.005	.013	.031	.067	.132	.231	.343	.366
	15	.000	.000	.000	.000	.000	.000	.000	.000	.000	.000	.000	.000	.000	.002	.005	.013	.035	.087	.206	.463
16	0	.851	.440	.185	.074	.028	.010	.003	.001	.000	.000	.000	.000	.000	.000	.000	.000	.000	.000	.000	.000
	1	.138	.371	.329	.210	.113	.053	.023	.009	.003	.001	.000	.000	.000	.000	.000	.000	.000	.000	.000	.000
	2	.010	.146	.275	.277	.211	.134	.073	.035	.015	.006	.002	.001	.000	.000	.000	.000	.000	.000	.000	.000
	3	.000	.036	.142	.229	.246	.208	.146	.089	.047	.022	.009	.003	.001	.000	.000	.000	.000	.000	.000	.000
	4	.000	.006	.051	.131	.200	.225	.204	.155	.101	.057	.028	.011	.004	.001	.000	.000	.000	.000	.000	.000
	5	.000	.001	.014	.056	.120	.180	.210	.201	.162	.112	.067	.034	.014	.005	.001	.000	.000	.000	.000	.000
	6	.000	.000	.003	.018	.055	.110	.165	.198	.198	.168	.122	.075	.039	.017	.006	.001	.000	.000	.000	.000
	7	.000	.000	.000	.005	.020	.052	.101	.152	.189	.197	.175	.132	.084	.044	.019	.006	.001	.000	.000	.000
	8	.000	.000	.000	.001	.006	.020	.049	.092	.142	.181	.196	.181	.142	.092	.049	.020	.006	.001	.000	.000
	9	.000	.000	.000	.000	.001	.006	.019	.044	.084	.132	.175	.197	.189	.152	.101	.052	.020	.005	.000	.000
	10	.000	.000	.000	.000	.000	.001	.006	.017	.039	.075	.122	.168	.198	.198	.165	.110	.055	.018	.003	.000
	11	.000	.000	.000	.000	.000	.000	.001	.005	.014	.034	.067	.112	.162	.201	.210	.180	.120	.056	.014	.001
	12	.000	.000	.000	.000	.000	.000	.000	.001	.004	.011	.028	.057	.101	.155	.204	.225	.200	.131	.051	.006
	13	.000	.000	.000	.000	.000	.000	.000	.000	.001	.003	.009	.022	.047	.089	.146	.208	.246	.229	.142	.036
	14	.000	.000	.000	.000	.000	.000	.000	.000	.000	.001	.002	.006	.015	.035	.073	.134	.211	.277	.275	.146
	15	.000	.000	.000	.000	.000	.000	.000	.000	.000	.000	.000	.001	.003	.009	.023	.053	.113	.210	.329	.371
	16	.000	.000	.000	.000	.000	.000	.000	.000	.000	.000	.000	.000	.000	.001	.003	.010	.028	.074	.185	.440
20	0	.818	.358	.122	.039	.012	.003	.001	.000	.000	.000	.000	.000	.000	.000	.000	.000	.000	.000	.000	.000
	1	.165	.377	.270	.137	.058	.021	.007	.002	.000	.000	.000	.000	.000	.000	.000	.000	.000	.000	.000	.000
	2	.016	.189	.285	.229	.137	.067	.028	.010	.003	.001	.000	.000	.000	.000	.000	.000	.000	.000	.000	.000
	3	.001	.060	.190	.243	.205	.134	.072	.032	.012	.004	.001	.000	.000	.000	.000	.000	.000	.000	.000	.000
	4	.000	.013	.090	.182	.218	.190	.130	.074	.035	.014	.005	.001	.000	.000	.000	.000	.000	.000	.000	.000
	5	.000	.002	.032	.103	.175	.202	.179	.127	.075	.036	.015	.005	.001	.000	.000	.000	.000	.000	.000	.000
	6	.000	.000	.009	.045	.109	.169	.192	.171	.124	.075	.036	.015	.005	.001	.000	.000	.000	.000	.000	.000
	7	.000	.000	.002	.016	.055	.112	.164	.184	.166	.122	.074	.037	.015	.005	.001	.000	.000	.000	.000	.000
	8	.000	.000	.000	.005	.022	.061	.114	.161	.180	.162	.120	.073	.035	.014	.004	.001	.000	.000	.000	.000
	9	.000	.000	.000	.001	.007	.027	.065	.116	.160	.177	.160	.119	.071	.034	.012	.003	.000	.000	.000	.000

TABLE 2 *continued*

		p																			
n	*r*	.01	.05	.10	.15	.20	.25	.30	.35	.40	.45	.50	.55	.60	.65	.70	.75	.80	.85	.90	.95
20	10	.000	.000	.000	.000	.002	.010	.031	.069	.117	.159	.176	.159	.117	.069	.031	.010	.002	.000	.000	.000
	11	.000	.000	.000	.000	.000	.003	.012	.034	.071	.119	.160	.177	.160	.116	.065	.027	.007	.001	.000	.000
	12	.000	.000	.000	.000	.000	.001	.004	.014	.035	.073	.120	.162	.180	.161	.114	.061	.022	.005	.000	.000
	13	.000	.000	.000	.000	.000	.000	.001	.005	.015	.037	.074	.122	.166	.184	.164	.112	.055	.016	.002	.000
	14	.000	.000	.000	.000	.000	.000	.000	.001	.005	.015	.037	.075	.124	.171	.192	.169	.109	.045	.009	.000
	15	.000	.000	.000	.000	.000	.000	.000	.000	.001	.005	.015	.036	.075	.127	.179	.202	.175	.103	.032	.002
	16	.000	.000	.000	.000	.000	.000	.000	.000	.000	.001	.005	.014	.035	.074	.130	.190	.218	.182	.090	.013
	17	.000	.000	.000	.000	.000	.000	.000	.000	.000	.000	.001	.004	.012	.032	.072	.134	.205	.243	.190	.060
	18	.000	.000	.000	.000	.000	.000	.000	.000	.000	.000	.000	.001	.003	.010	.028	.067	.137	.229	.285	.189
	19	.000	.000	.000	.000	.000	.000	.000	.000	.000	.000	.000	.000	.000	.002	.007	.021	.058	.137	.270	.377
	20	.000	.000	.000	.000	.000	.000	.000	.000	.000	.000	.000	.000	.000	.000	.001	.003	.012	.039	.122	.358

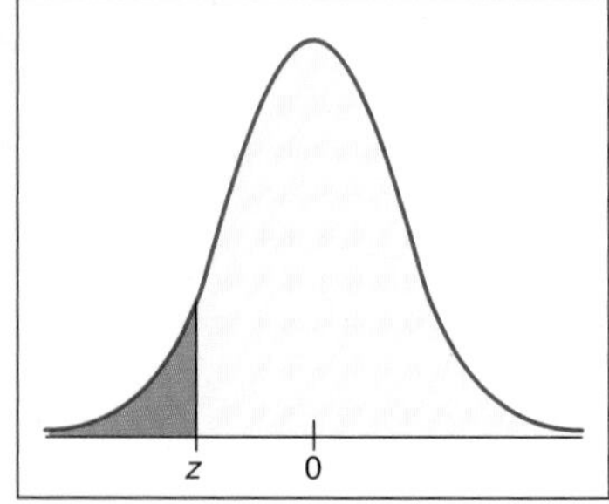

The table entry for z is the area to the left of z.

TABLE 3 Areas of a Standard Normal Distribution

(a) Table of Areas to the Left of z

z	.00	.01	.02	.03	.04	.05	.06	.07	.08	.09
−3.4	.0003	.0003	.0003	.0003	.0003	.0003	.0003	.0003	.0003	.0002
−3.3	.0005	.0005	.0005	.0004	.0004	.0004	.0004	.0004	.0004	.0003
−3.2	.0007	.0007	.0006	.0006	.0006	.0006	.0006	.0005	.0005	.0005
−3.1	.0010	.0009	.0009	.0009	.0008	.0008	.0008	.0008	.0007	.0007
−3.0	.0013	.0013	.0013	.0012	.0012	.0011	.0011	.0011	.0010	.0010
−2.9	.0019	.0018	.0018	.0017	.0016	.0016	.0015	.0015	.0014	.0014
−2.8	.0026	.0025	.0024	.0023	.0023	.0022	.0021	.0021	.0020	.0019
−2.7	.0035	.0034	.0033	.0032	.0031	.0030	.0029	.0028	.0027	.0026
−2.6	.0047	.0045	.0044	.0043	.0041	.0040	.0039	.0038	.0037	.0036
−2.5	.0062	.0060	.0059	.0057	.0055	.0054	.0052	.0051	.0049	.0048
−2.4	.0082	.0080	.0078	.0075	.0073	.0071	.0069	.0068	.0066	.0064
−2.3	.0107	.0104	.0102	.0099	.0096	.0094	.0091	.0089	.0087	.0084
−2.2	.0139	.0136	.0132	.0129	.0125	.0122	.0119	.0116	.0113	.0110
−2.1	.0179	.0174	.0170	.0166	.0162	.0158	.0154	.0150	.0146	.0143
−2.0	.0228	.0222	.0217	.0212	.0207	.0202	.0197	.0192	.0188	.0183
−1.9	.0287	.0281	.0274	.0268	.0262	.0256	.0250	.0244	.0239	.0233
−1.8	.0359	.0351	.0344	.0336	.0329	.0322	.0314	.0307	.0301	.0294
−1.7	.0446	.0436	.0427	.0418	.0409	.0401	.0392	.0384	.0375	.0367
−1.6	.0548	.0537	.0526	.0516	.0505	.0495	.0485	.0475	.0465	.0455
−1.5	.0668	.0655	.0643	.0630	.0618	.0606	.0594	.0582	.0571	.0559
−1.4	.0808	.0793	.0778	.0764	.0749	.0735	.0721	.0708	.0694	.0681
−1.3	.0968	.0951	.0934	.0918	.0901	.0885	.0869	.0853	.0838	.0823
−1.2	.1151	.1131	.1112	.1093	.1075	.1056	.1038	.1020	.1003	.0985
−1.1	.1357	.1335	.1314	.1292	.1271	.1251	.1230	.1210	.1190	.1170
−1.0	.1587	.1562	.1539	.1515	.1492	.1469	.1446	.1423	.1401	.1379
−0.9	.1841	.1814	.1788	.1762	.1736	.1711	.1685	.1660	.1635	.1611
−0.8	.2119	.2090	.2061	.2033	.2005	.1977	.1949	.1922	.1894	.1867
−0.7	.2420	.2389	.2358	.2327	.2296	.2266	.2236	.2206	.2177	.2148
−0.6	.2743	.2709	.2676	.2643	.2611	.2578	.2546	.2514	.2483	.2451
−0.5	.3085	.3050	.3015	.2981	.2946	.2912	.2877	.2843	.2810	.2776
−0.4	.3446	.3409	.3372	.3336	.3300	.3264	.3228	.3192	.3156	.3121
−0.3	.3821	.3783	.3745	.3707	.3669	.3632	.3594	.3557	.3520	.3483
−0.2	.4207	.4168	.4129	.4090	.4052	.4013	.3974	.3936	.3897	.3859
−0.1	.4602	.4562	.4522	.4483	.4443	.4404	.4364	.4325	.4286	.4247
−0.0	.5000	.4960	.4920	.4880	.4840	.4801	.4761	.4721	.4681	.4641

For values of z less than −3.49, use 0.000 to approximate the area.

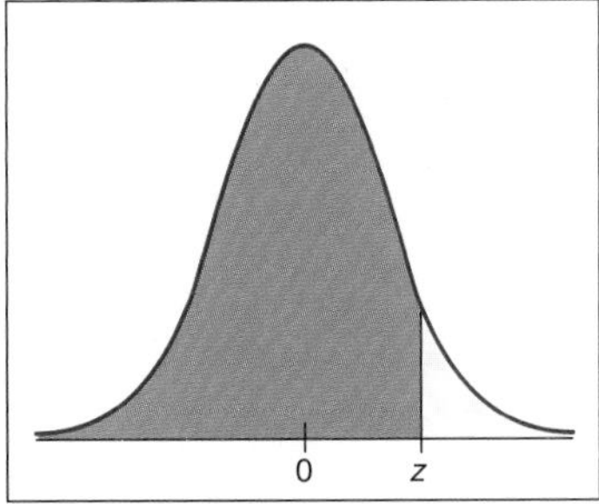

The table entry for z is the area to the left of z.

TABLE 3(a) *continued*

z	.00	.01	.02	.03	.04	.05	.06	.07	.08	.09
0.0	.5000	.5040	.5080	.5120	.5160	.5199	.5239	.5279	.5319	.5359
0.1	.5398	.5438	.5478	.5517	.5557	.5596	.5636	.5675	.5714	.5753
0.2	.5793	.5832	.5871	.5910	.5948	.5987	.6026	.6064	.6103	.6141
0.3	.6179	.6217	.6255	.6293	.6331	.6368	.6406	.6443	.6480	.6517
0.4	.6554	.6591	.6628	.6664	.6700	.6736	.6772	.6808	.6844	.6879
0.5	.6915	.6950	.6985	.7019	.7054	.7088	.7123	.7157	.7190	.7224
0.6	.7257	.7291	.7324	.7357	.7389	.7422	.7454	.7486	.7517	.7549
0.7	.7580	.7611	.7642	.7673	.7704	.7734	.7764	.7794	.7823	.7852
0.8	.7881	.7910	.7939	.7967	.7995	.8023	.8051	.8078	.8106	.8133
0.9	.8159	.8186	.8212	.8238	.8264	.8289	.8315	.8340	.8365	.8389
1.0	.8413	.8438	.8461	.8485	.8508	.8531	.8554	.8577	.8599	.8621
1.1	.8643	.8665	.8686	.8708	.8729	.8749	.8770	.8790	.8810	.8830
1.2	.8849	.8869	.8888	.8907	.8925	.8944	.8962	.8980	.8997	.9015
1.3	.9032	.9049	.9066	.9082	.9099	.9115	.9131	.9147	.9162	.9177
1.4	.9192	.9207	.9222	.9236	.9251	.9265	.9279	.9292	.9306	.9319
1.5	.9332	.9345	.9357	.9370	.9382	.9394	.9406	.9418	.9429	.9441
1.6	.9452	.9463	.9474	.9484	.9495	.9505	.9515	.9525	.9535	.9545
1.7	.9554	.9564	.9573	.9582	.9591	.9599	.9608	.9616	.9625	.9633
1.8	.9641	.9649	.9656	.9664	.9671	.9678	.9686	.9693	.9699	.9706
1.9	.9713	.9719	.9726	.9732	.9738	.9744	.9750	.9756	.9761	.9767
2.0	.9772	.9778	.9783	.9788	.9793	.9798	.9803	.9808	.9812	.9817
2.1	.9821	.9826	.9830	.9834	.9838	.9842	.9846	.9850	.9854	.9857
2.2	.9861	.9864	.9868	.9871	.9875	.9878	.9881	.9884	.9887	.9890
2.3	.9893	.9896	.9898	.9901	.9904	.9906	.9909	.9911	.9913	.9916
2.4	.9918	.9920	.9922	.9925	.9927	.9929	.9931	.9932	.9934	.9936
2.5	.9938	.9940	.9941	.9943	.9945	.9946	.9948	.9949	.9951	.9952
2.6	.9953	.9955	.9956	.9957	.9959	.9960	.9961	.9962	.9963	.9964
2.7	.9965	.9966	.9967	.9968	.9969	.9970	.9971	.9972	.9973	.9974
2.8	.9974	.9975	.9976	.9977	.9977	.9978	.9979	.9979	.9980	.9981
2.9	.9981	.9982	.9982	.9983	.9984	.9984	.9985	.9985	.9986	.9986
3.0	.9987	.9987	.9987	.9988	.9988	.9989	.9989	.9989	.9990	.9990
3.1	.9990	.9991	.9991	.9991	.9992	.9992	.9992	.9992	.9993	.9993
3.2	.9993	.9993	.9994	.9994	.9994	.9994	.9994	.9995	.9995	.9995
3.3	.9995	.9995	.9995	.9996	.9996	.9996	.9996	.9996	.9996	.9997
3.4	.9997	.9997	.9997	.9997	.9997	.9997	.9997	.9997	.9997	.9998

For z values greater than 3.49, use 1.000 to approximate the area.

TABLE 3 *continued*

(b) Confidence Interval Critical Values z_c

Level of Confidence c	Critical Value z_c
0.70, or 70%	1.04
0.75, or 75%	1.15
0.80, or 80%	1.28
0.85, or 85%	1.44
0.90, or 90%	1.645
0.95, or 95%	1.96
0.98, or 98%	2.33
0.99, or 99%	2.58

TABLE 3 *continued*

(c) Hypothesis Testing, Critical Values z_0

Level of Significance	$\alpha = 0.05$	$\alpha = 0.01$
Critical value z_0 for a left-tailed test	−1.645	−2.33
Critical value z_0 for a right-tailed test	1.645	2.33
Critical values $\pm z_0$ for a two-tailed test	±1.96	±2.58

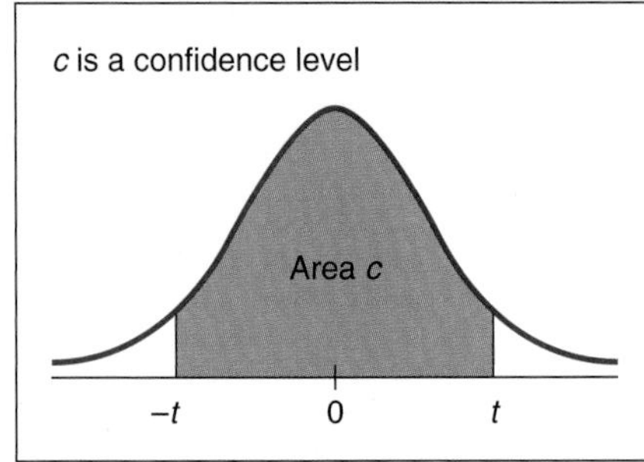

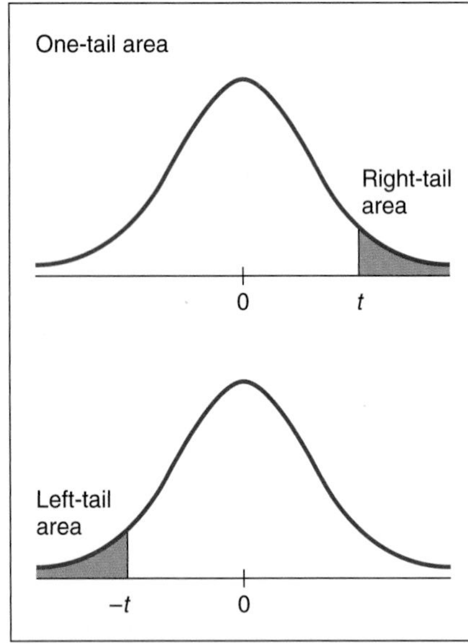

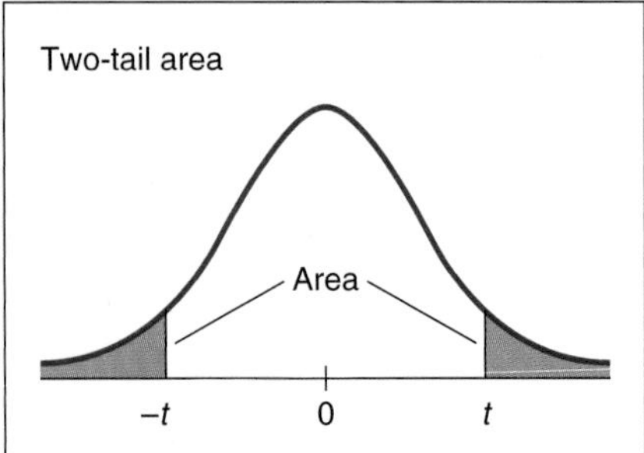

TABLE 4 Critical Values for Student's *t* Distribution

one-tail area	0.250	0.125	0.100	0.075	0.050	0.025	0.010	0.005	0.0005
two-tail area	0.500	0.250	0.200	0.150	0.100	0.050	0.020	0.010	0.0010
d.f. \ *c*	0.500	0.750	0.800	0.850	0.900	0.950	0.980	0.990	0.999
1	1.000	2.414	3.078	4.165	6.314	12.706	31.821	63.657	636.619
2	0.816	1.604	1.886	2.282	2.920	4.303	6.965	9.925	31.599
3	0.765	1.423	1.638	1.924	2.353	3.182	4.541	5.841	12.924
4	0.741	1.344	1.533	1.778	2.132	2.776	3.747	4.604	8.610
5	0.727	1.301	1.476	1.699	2.015	2.571	3.365	4.032	6.869
6	0.718	1.273	1.440	1.650	1.943	2.447	3.143	3.707	5.959
7	0.711	1.254	1.415	1.617	1.895	2.365	2.998	3.499	5.408
8	0.706	1.240	1.397	1.592	1.860	2.306	2.896	3.355	5.041
9	0.703	1.230	1.383	1.574	1.833	2.262	2.821	3.250	4.781
10	0.700	1.221	1.372	1.559	1.812	2.228	2.764	3.169	4.587
11	0.697	1.214	1.363	1.548	1.796	2.201	2.718	3.106	4.437
12	0.695	1.209	1.356	1.538	1.782	2.179	2.681	3.055	4.318
13	0.694	1.204	1.350	1.530	1.771	2.160	2.650	3.012	4.221
14	0.692	1.200	1.345	1.523	1.761	2.145	2.624	2.977	4.140
15	0.691	1.197	1.341	1.517	1.753	2.131	2.602	2.947	4.073
16	0.690	1.194	1.337	1.512	1.746	2.120	2.583	2.921	4.015
17	0.689	1.191	1.333	1.508	1.740	2.110	2.567	2.898	3.965
18	0.688	1.189	1.330	1.504	1.734	2.101	2.552	2.878	3.922
19	0.688	1.187	1.328	1.500	1.729	2.093	2.539	2.861	3.883
20	0.687	1.185	1.325	1.497	1.725	2.086	2.528	2.845	3.850
21	0.686	1.183	1.323	1.494	1.721	2.080	2.518	2.831	3.819
22	0.686	1.182	1.321	1.492	1.717	2.074	2.508	2.819	3.792
23	0.685	1.180	1.319	1.489	1.714	2.069	2.500	2.807	3.768
24	0.685	1.179	1.318	1.487	1.711	2.064	2.492	2.797	3.745
25	0.684	1.198	1.316	1.485	1.708	2.060	2.485	2.787	3.725
26	0.684	1.177	1.315	1.483	1.706	2.056	2.479	2.779	3.707
27	0.684	1.176	1.314	1.482	1.703	2.052	2.473	2.771	3.690
28	0.683	1.175	1.313	1.480	1.701	2.048	2.467	2.763	3.674
29	0.683	1.174	1.311	1.479	1.699	2.045	2.462	2.756	3.659
30	0.683	1.173	1.310	1.477	1.697	2.042	2.457	2.750	3.646
35	0.682	1.170	1.306	1.472	1.690	2.030	2.438	2.724	3.591
40	0.681	1.167	1.303	1.468	1.684	2.021	2.423	2.704	3.551
45	0.680	1.165	1.301	1.465	1.679	2.014	2.412	2.690	3.520
50	0.679	1.164	1.299	1.462	1.676	2.009	2.403	2.678	3.496
60	0.679	1.162	1.296	1.458	1.671	2.000	2.390	2.660	3.460
70	0.678	1.160	1.294	1.456	1.667	1.994	2.381	2.648	3.435
80	0.678	1.159	1.292	1.453	1.664	1.990	2.374	2.639	3.416
100	0.677	1.157	1.290	1.451	1.660	1.984	2.364	2.626	3.390
500	0.675	1.152	1.283	1.442	1.648	1.965	2.334	2.586	3.310
1000	0.675	1.151	1.282	1.441	1.646	1.962	2.330	2.581	3.300
∞	0.674	1.150	1.282	1.440	1.645	1.960	2.326	2.576	3.291

For degrees of freedom *d.f.* not in the table, use the closest *d.f.* that is *smaller.*

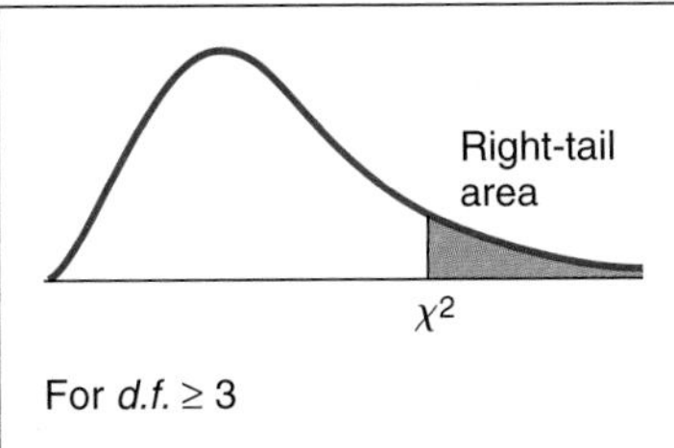

For *d.f.* ≥ 3

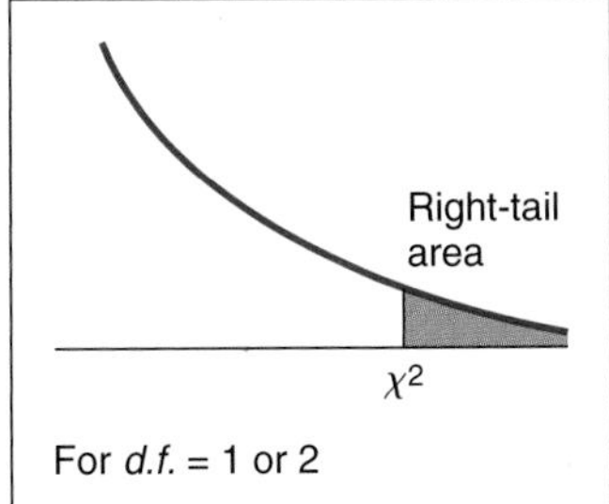

For *d.f.* = 1 or 2

TABLE 5 The χ^2 Distribution

	Right-Tail Area									
d.f.	.995	.990	.975	.950	.900	.100	.050	.025	.010	.005
1	0.0^4393	0.0^3157	0.0^3982	0.0^2393	0.0158	2.71	3.84	5.02	6.63	7.88
2	0.0100	0.0201	0.0506	0.103	0.211	4.61	5.99	7.38	9.21	10.60
3	0.072	0.115	0.216	0.352	0.584	6.25	7.81	9.35	11.34	12.84
4	0.207	0.297	0.484	0.711	1.064	7.78	9.49	11.14	13.28	14.86
5	0.412	0.554	0.831	1.145	1.61	9.24	11.07	12.83	15.09	16.75
6	0.676	0.872	1.24	1.64	2.20	10.64	12.59	14.45	16.81	18.55
7	0.989	1.24	1.69	2.17	2.83	12.02	14.07	16.01	18.48	20.28
8	1.34	1.65	2.18	2.73	3.49	13.36	15.51	17.53	20.09	21.96
9	1.73	2.09	2.70	3.33	4.17	14.68	16.92	19.02	21.67	23.59
10	2.16	2.56	3.25	3.94	4.87	15.99	18.31	20.48	23.21	25.19
11	2.60	3.05	3.82	4.57	5.58	17.28	19.68	21.92	24.72	26.76
12	3.07	3.57	4.40	5.23	6.30	18.55	21.03	23.34	26.22	28.30
13	3.57	4.11	5.01	5.89	7.04	19.81	22.36	24.74	27.69	29.82
14	4.07	4.66	5.63	6.57	7.79	21.06	23.68	26.12	29.14	31.32
15	4.60	5.23	6.26	7.26	8.55	22.31	25.00	27.49	30.58	32.80
16	5.14	5.81	6.91	7.96	9.31	23.54	26.30	28.85	32.00	34.27
17	5.70	6.41	7.56	8.67	10.09	24.77	27.59	30.19	33.41	35.72
18	6.26	7.01	8.23	9.39	10.86	25.99	28.87	31.53	34.81	37.16
19	6.84	7.63	8.91	10.12	11.65	27.20	30.14	32.85	36.19	38.58
20	7.43	8.26	8.59	10.85	12.44	28.41	31.41	34.17	37.57	40.00
21	8.03	8.90	10.28	11.59	13.24	29.62	32.67	35.48	38.93	41.40
22	8.64	9.54	10.98	12.34	14.04	30.81	33.92	36.78	40.29	42.80
23	9.26	10.20	11.69	13.09	14.85	32.01	35.17	38.08	41.64	44.18
24	9.89	10.86	12.40	13.85	15.66	33.20	36.42	39.36	42.98	45.56
25	10.52	11.52	13.12	14.61	16.47	34.38	37.65	40.65	44.31	46.93
26	11.16	12.20	13.84	15.38	17.29	35.56	38.89	41.92	45.64	48.29
27	11.81	12.88	14.57	16.15	18.11	36.74	40.11	43.19	46.96	49.64
28	12.46	13.56	15.31	16.93	18.94	37.92	41.34	44.46	48.28	50.99
29	13.21	14.26	16.05	17.71	19.77	39.09	42.56	45.72	49.59	52.34
30	13.79	14.95	16.79	18.49	20.60	40.26	43.77	46.98	50.89	53.67
40	20.71	22.16	24.43	26.51	29.05	51.80	55.76	59.34	63.69	66.77
50	27.99	29.71	32.36	34.76	37.69	63.17	67.50	71.42	76.15	79.49
60	35.53	37.48	40.48	43.19	46.46	74.40	79.08	83.30	88.38	91.95
70	43.28	45.44	48.76	51.74	55.33	85.53	90.53	95.02	100.4	104.2
80	51.17	53.54	57.15	60.39	64.28	96.58	101.9	106.6	112.3	116.3
90	59.20	61.75	65.65	69.13	73.29	107.6	113.1	118.1	124.1	128.3
100	67.33	70.06	74.22	77.93	82.36	118.5	124.3	129.6	135.8	140.2

Source: From H. L. Herter, *Biometrika*, June 1964. Printed by permission of the Biometrika Trustees.

0.0^4393 means that there are 4 0's between the decimal and 3; $0.0^4393 = 0.0000393$.

Photo Credits

Chapter 1 p. 2: (top) Paul Spinelli/MLB Photos via Getty Inages; (middle) Bettmann/Corbis; p. 3: (top) Ivan Polunin/Bruce Coleman Images; (bottom) Courtesy of the authors; p. 6: Geoffrey Bryant/Photo Researchers, Inc.; p. 13: Bay Ismoyo/Getty Images; p. 21: Tim Davis/Photo Researchers, Inc.; p. 24: Richard Lord Enterprises, Inc./Image Works.

Chapter 2 p. 34: (top) Fyodor Savintsev/ITAR-TASS/Corbis; (middle) Brown Brothers; p. 35: (top) Judy Gelles/Stock Boston; (bottom) Vandystat/Photo Researchers, Inc.; p. 37: Bob Turner/Alamy; p. 52: Myrleen Ferguson Cate/PhotoEdit; p. 57: Corbis; p. 58: Michael Doolittle/Image Works.

Chapter 3 p. 72: (top) PARAMOUNT TELEVISION / THE KOBAL COLLECTION; (middle) Imagno/Getty; p. 73: (top) Nancy Sheehan/ PhotoEdit; (bottom) Myrleen Ferguson Cate/PhotoEdit; p. 75: Skjold Photographs/PhotoEdit; p. 77: Jose Carillo/PhotoEdit; p. 84: David Young-Wolff/PhotoEdit; p. 86: Tony Freeman/PhotoEdit; p. 90: Ron Watts/Corbis; p. 92: Bob Daemmrich Photography/Image Works; p. 101: Gary Conner/PhotoEdit; p. 111: Peter Southwick/Stock Boston; p. 115: Dave G. Houser/Corbis.

Chapter 4 p. 118: (top) Getty; (middle) Archivo Iconografico, S.A./Corbis; p. 119: (top) David Young-Wolff/PhotoEdit; (bottom) Peter Menzel/Stock Boston; p. 121: Cindy Kassabi/Corbis; p. 125: David Muench/Corbis; p. 137: Joe McDonald/Corbis; p. 140: Joe McDonald/Corbis.

Chapter 5 p. 156: (top) Scot Frei/Corbis; (middle) NorthWind Picture Archives; p. 157: (top) David Young-Wolff/PhotoEdit; (bottom) John Neubauer/PhotoEdit; p. 161: Bonnie Kamin/PhotoEdit; p. 168: Philip Harvey/Corbis; p. 177: Jupiter Images.

Chapter 6 p. 202: (top) AP/Wide World Photos; (middle) National Portrait Gallery, Smithsonian Institution, Art Resource, NY; p. 203: (top) Peter Vandermark/Stock Boston; (bottom) Mitch Wojnarowicz/Image Works; p. 208: Kelly-Mooney Photography/Corbis; p. 220: Ted Curtin/Stock Boston; p. 226: Mark Richards/PhotoEdit; p. 240: Hubert Stadler/Corbis; p. 241: Jupiter Images.

Chapter 7 p. 242: (top) Picture-Desk; (middle) Stock Montage, Inc.; p. 243: (top) Dana White/PhotoEdit; (bottom) Syracuse Newspapers/Image Works; p. 252: Lois Ellen Frank/Corbis; p. 264: Pierre Arsenault/Alamy; p. 275: Philip James Corwin/Corbis; p. 280: Corbis; p. 293: William Mullins/Photo Researchers, Inc.; p. 300: Mike Mazzaschi/Stock Boston.

Chapter 8 p. 306: (top) Rusty Jarrett/Getty; (middle) The Granger Collection; p. 307: (top) Ed Bock/Corbis; (bottom) Philip James/Corbis; p. 312: Myrleen Ferguson Cate/PhotoEdit; p. 325: Francois Gohier/Photo Researchers, Inc.; p. 333: Bob Daemmrich/Stock Boston; p. 344: Judy Griesedieck/Corbis.

Chapter 9 p. 350: (top) Mary Evans Picture Library/Arthur Rackham/The Image Works; (middle) Brown Brothers; p. 351: (top) Comstock RF; (bottom) Reuters/Corbis; p. 356: Jupiter Images; p. 368: Comstock RF; p. 387: John Elk/Stock Boston; p. 401: Omni Photo/Index Stock Imagery.

Chapter 10 p. 404: (top) Printed by permission of the Norman Rockwell Family Agency Copyright © 1953 the Norman Rockwell Family Entities; (middle) John Bryson/Getty; p. 405: (top) Robert Erwin/Photo Researchers, Inc.; (bottom) Peter Southwick@Stock Boston; p. 409: Fritz Hoffman/Image Works; p. 421: Bob Winsett/Corbis; p. 440: Bob Daemmrich Photography/Image Works; p. 443: Bob Daemmrich/Stock Boston.

Chapter 11 p. 456: (top) Business Wire/Getty; (middle) Keystone Press Agency/SUMA; p. 457: (top) Nancy Richmond/Image Works; (bottom) Robert Brenner/Photo Edit; p. 4460: Tony Freeman/PhotoEdit; p. 467: Getty Images; p. 474: Skjold Photographs/PhotoEdit; p. 484: Mark Richards/PhotoEdit; p. 497: Erwin and Peggy Bauer/Animals, Animals/Earth Scenes; p. 499: Jeffrey Greenberg/Photo Researchers, Inc.; p. 511: Douglas Faulkner/Photo Researchers, Inc.; p. 513: Image 100/Royalty-Free/Corbis.

ANSWERS AND KEY STEPS TO ODD-NUMBERED PROBLEMS

CHAPTER 1

Section 1.1

1. An individual is a member of the population of interest. A variable is an aspect of an individual to be measured or observed.
3. A parameter is a numerical measurement describing data from a population. A statistic is a numerical measurement describing data from a sample.
5. (a) Response regarding frequency of eating at fast-food restaurants. (b) Qualitative. (c) Responses for *all* adults in the U.S.
7. (a) Nitrogen concentration (mg nitrogen/l water). (b) Quantitative. (c) Nitrogen concentration (mg nitrogen/l water) in the entire lake.
9. (a) Ratio. (b) Interval. (c) Nominal. (d) Ordinal. (e) Ratio. (f) Ratio.
11. (a) Nominal. (b) Ratio. (c) Interval. (d) Ordinal. (e) Ratio. (f) Interval.
13. Answers vary.
(a) For example: Use pounds. Round weights to the nearest pound. Since backpacks might weigh as much as 30 pounds, you might use a high-quality bathroom scale. (b) Some students may not allow you to weigh their backpacks for privacy reasons, etc. (c) Possibly. Some students may want to impress you with the heaviness of their backpacks, or they may be embarrassed about the "junk" they have stowed inside and thus may clean out their backpacks.

Section 1.2

1. In a stratified sample, random samples from each strata are included. In a cluster sample, the clusters to be included are selected at random and then all members of each selected cluster are included.
3. The advice is wrong. A sampling error only accounts for the difference in results based on the use of a sample rather than the entire population.
5. Use a random-number table to select four distinct numbers corresponding to people in your class.
(a) Reasons may vary. For instance, the first four students may make a special effort to get to class on time. (b) Reasons may vary. For instance, four students who come in late might all be nursing students enrolled in an anatomy and physiology class that meets the hour before in a far-away building. They may be more motivated than other students to complete a degree requirement. (c) Reasons may vary. For instance, four students sitting in the back row might be less inclined to participate in class discussions.
(d) Reasons may vary. For instance, the tallest students might all be male.
7. Answers vary. Use groups of two digits.
9. Select a starting place in the table and group the digits in groups of four. Scan the table by rows and include the first six groups with numbers between 0001 and 8615.
11. (a) Yes, when a die is rolled several times, the same number may appear more than once. Outcome on the fourth roll is 2. (b) No, for a fair die, the outcomes are random.
13. Since there are five possible outcomes for each question, read single digits from a random-number table. Select a starting place and proceed until you have 10 digits from 1 to 5. Repetition is required. The correct answer for each question will be the letter choice corresponding to the digit chosen for that question.
15. (a) Simple random sample. (b) Cluster sample. (c) Convenience sample. (d) Systematic sample. (e) Stratified sample.

Section 1.3

1. Answers vary. People with higher incomes are more likely to have high-speed Internet access and to spend more time on-line. People with high-speed Internet access might spend less time watching TV news or programming. People with higher incomes might spend less time watching TV because of access to other entertainment venues.
3. (a) Observational study. (b) Experiment. (c) Experiment. (d) Observational study.
5. (a) Use random selection to pick 10 calves to inoculate; test all calves; no placebo. (b) Use random selection to pick 9 schools to visit; survey all schools; no placebo. (c) Use random selection to pick 40 volunteers for skin patch with drug; survey all volunteers; placebo used.
7. Based on the information given, Scheme A is best because it blocks all plots bordering the river together and all plots not bordering the river together. The blocks of Scheme B do not seem to differ from each other.

Chapter 1 Review

1. (a) Stratified. (b) Students on your campus with work-study jobs. (c) Hours scheduled; quantitative; ratio. (d) Rating of applicability of work experience to future employment; qualitative; ordinal. (e) Statistic. (f) 60%; The people choosing not to respond may have certain characteristics, such as not working many hours, that would bias the study. (g) No. The sample frame is restricted to one campus.

3. Assign digits so that 3 out of the 10 digits 0 through 9 correspond to the answer "Yes" and 7 of the digits correspond to the answer "No." One assignment is digits 0, 1, and 2 correspond to "Yes" whereas digits 3, 4, 5, 6, 7, 8, and 9 correspond to "No." Starting with line 1, block 1 of Table 1, this assignment of digits gives the sequence No, Yes, No, No, Yes, No, No.
5. (a) Observational study. (b) Experiment.
7. Possible directions on survey questions: Give height in inches, give age as of last birthday, give GPA to one decimal place, and so forth. Think about the types of responses you wish to have on each question.
9. (a) Experiment, since a treatment is imposed on one colony. (b) The control group receives normal daylight/darkness conditions. The treatment group has light 24 hours per day. (c) The number of fireflies living at the end of 72 hours. (d) Ratio.

CHAPTER 2

Section 2.1

1. Class limits are possible data values. Class limits specify the span of data values that fall within a class. Class boundaries are not possible data values. They are values halfway between the upper class limit of one class and the lower class limit of the next.
3. The classes overlap so that some data values, such as 20, fall within two classes.
5. (a) Yes.
   (b) Histogram of Highway mpg

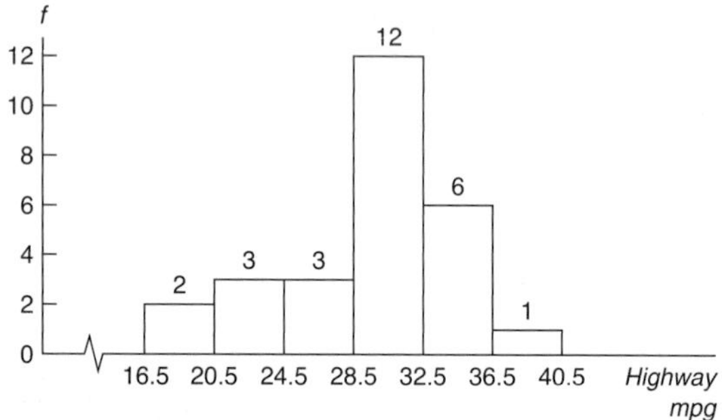

7. (a) Class width = 25.
   (b)

Class Limits	Class Boundaries	Midpoint	Frequency	Relative Frequency
236–260	235.5–260.5	248	4	0.07
261–285	260.5–285.5	273	9	0.16
286–310	285.5–310.5	298	25	0.44
311–335	310.5–335.5	323	16	0.28
336–360	335.5–360.5	348	3	0.05

   (c, d) Hours to Complete the Iditarod—Histogram, Relative-Frequency Histogram

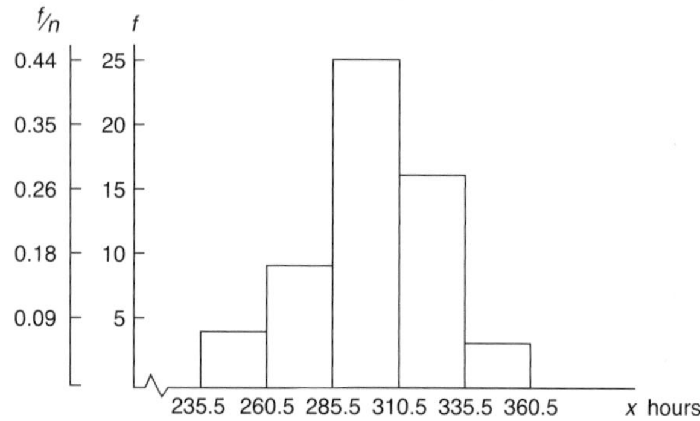

   (e) Approximately mound-shaped symmetrical.
9. (a) Class width = 12.
   (b)

Class Limits	Class Boundaries	Midpoint	Frequency	Relative Frequency
1–12	0.5–12.5	6.5	6	0.14
13–24	12.5–24.5	18.5	10	0.24
25–36	24.5–36.5	30.5	5	0.12
37–48	36.5–48.5	42.5	13	0.31
49–60	48.5–60.5	54.5	8	0.19

   (c, d) Months Before Tumor Recurrence—Histogram, Relative-Frequency Histogram

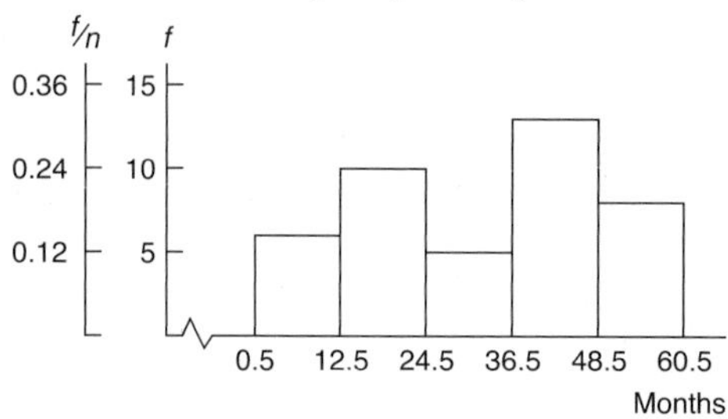

   (e) Somewhat bimodal.
11. (a) Class width = 9.
   (b)

Class Limits	Class Boundaries	Midpoint	Frequency	Relative Frequency
10–18	9.5–18.5	14	6	0.11
19–27	18.5–27.5	23	26	0.47
28–36	27.5–36.5	32	20	0.36
37–45	36.5–45.5	41	1	0.02
46–54	45.5–54.5	50	2	0.04

(c, d) Fuel Consumption (mpg)—Histogram, Relative-Frequency Histogram

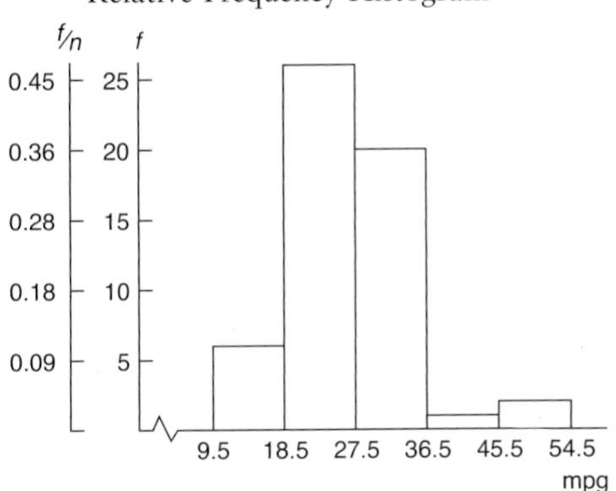

(e) Skewed slightly right.

13. (a) Clear the decimals.
(b, c) Class width = 0.40.

Class Limits	Boundaries	Midpoint	Frequency
0.46–0.85	0.455–0.855	0.655	4
0.86–1.25	0.855–1.255	1.055	5
1.26–1.65	1.255–1.655	1.455	10
1.66–2.05	1.655–2.055	1.855	5
2.06–2.45	2.055–2.455	2.255	5
2.46–2.85	2.455–2.855	2.655	3

(c) Tonnes of Wheat—Histogram

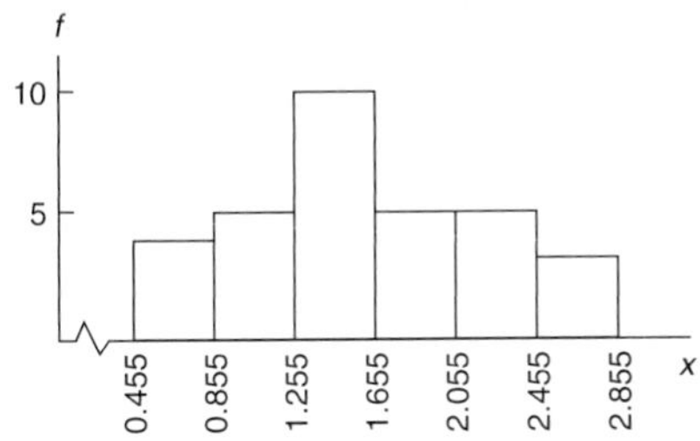

15. (a) One. (b) 5/51 or 9.8%. (c) Interval from 650 to 750.

17. Dotplot for Months Before Tumor Recurrence

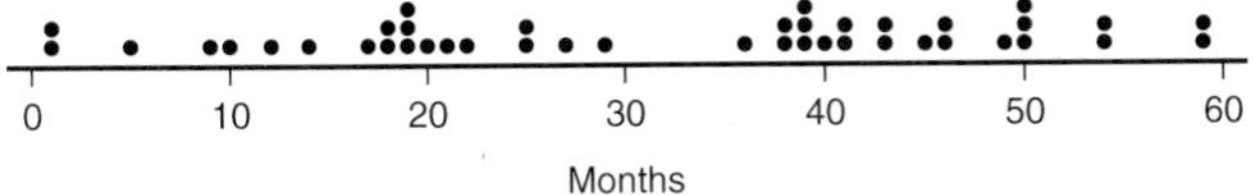

Section 2.2

1. Pareto chart, because it shows the items in order of importance to the greatest number of employees.

3. Highest Level of Education and Average Annual Household Income (in thousands of dollars)—Bar Graph

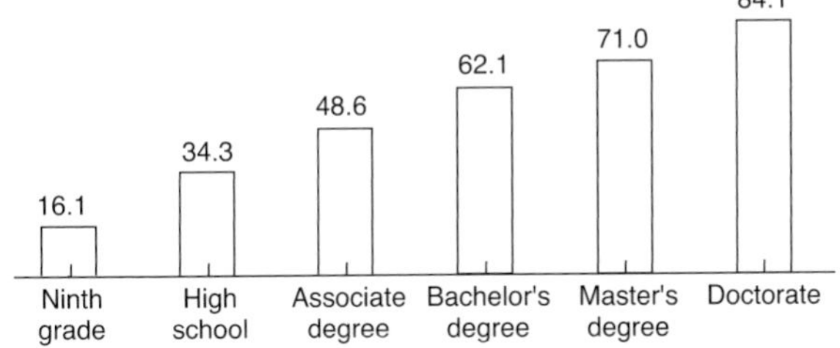

5. Annual Harvest (1000 Metric Tons)—Pareto Chart

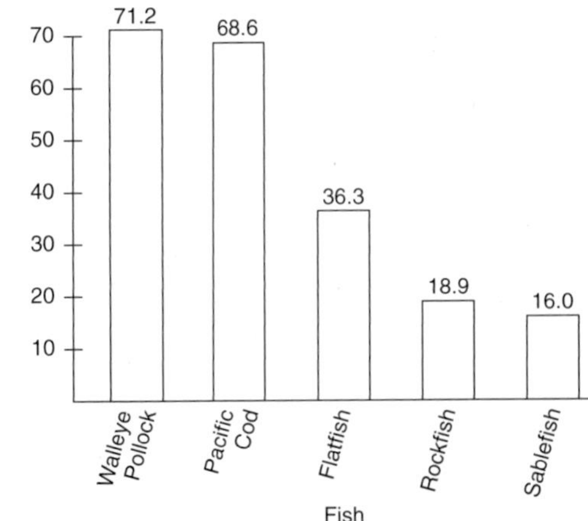

7. Where We Hide the Mess

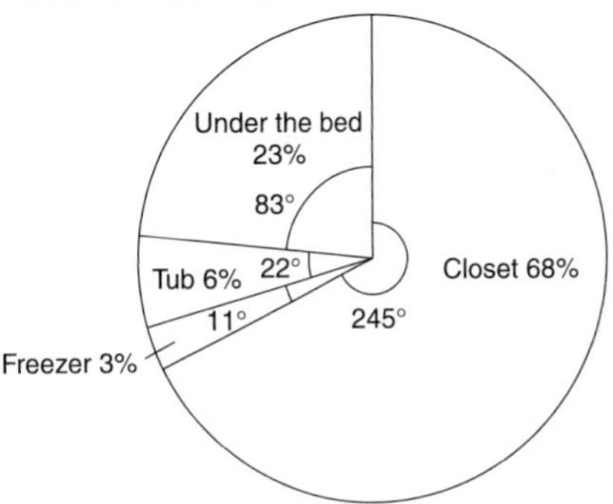

9. (a) Hawaii Crime Rate per 100,000 Population

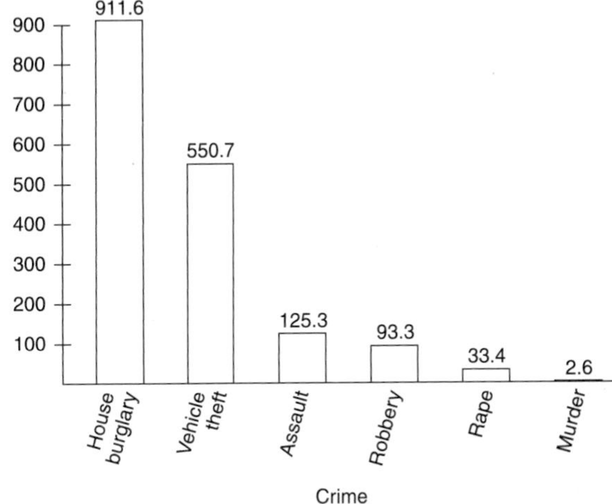

(b) A circle graph is not appropriate because the data do not reflect all types of crime. Also, the same person may have been the victim of more than one crime.

11. Elevation of Pyramid Lake Surface—Time Plot

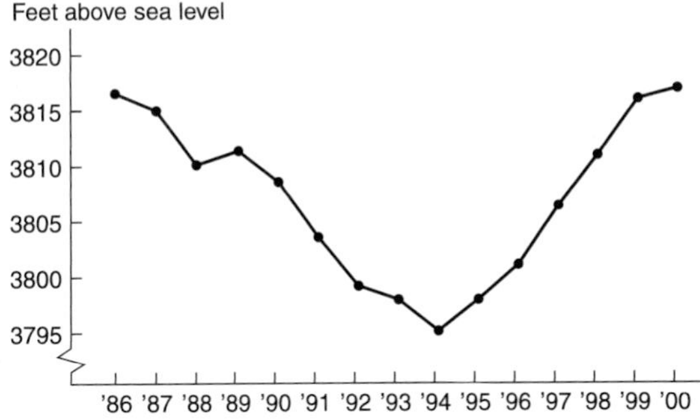

Section 2.3

1. (a) Longevity of Cowboys

4	7 = 47 years
4	7
5	2 7 8 8
6	1 6 6 8 8
7	0 2 2 3 3 5 6 7
8	4 4 4 5 6 6 7 9
9	0 1 1 2 3 7

(b) Yes, certainly these cowboys lived long lives.

3. Average Length of Hospital Stay

5	2 = 5.2 years
5	2 3 5 5 6 7
6	0 2 4 6 6 7 7 8 8 8 8 9 9
7	0 0 0 0 0 0 1 1 1 2 2 2 3 3 3 3 4 4 5 5 6 6 8
8	4 5 7
9	4 6 9
10	0 3
11	1

The distribution is skewed right.

5. (a) Minutes Beyond 2 Hours (1961–1980)

0	9 = 9 minutes past 2 hours
0	9 9
1	0 0 2 3 3 4
1	5 5 6 6 7 8 8 9
2	0 2 3 3

(b) Minutes Beyond 2 Hours (1981–2000)

0	7 = 7 minutes past 2 hours
0	7 7 7 8 8 8 8 9 9 9 9 9 9 9
1	0 0 1 1 4

(c) In more recent times, the winning times have been closer to 2 hours, with all the times between 7 and 14 minutes over 2 hours. In the earlier period, more than half the times were over 2 hours and 14 minutes.

7. Milligrams of Tar per Cigarette

1	0 = 1.0 mg tar		
1	0	11	4
2		12	0 4 8
3		13	7
4	1 5	14	1 5 9
5		15	0 1 2 8
6		16	0 6
7	3 8	17	0
8	0 6 8		
9	0		
10		29	8

The value 29.8 may be an outlier.

9. Milligrams of Nicotine per Cigarette

0	1 = 0.1 mg nicotine
0	1 4 4
0	5 6 6 6 7 7 7 8 8 9 9 9
1	0 0 0 0 0 0 0 1 2
1	
2	0

Chapter 2 Review

1. (a) Bar graph, Pareto chart, pie chart. (b) All.
3. Any large gaps between bars or between stems with leaves at the beginning or end of the data set might indicate that the extreme data values are outliers.
5. (a) Yes, with lines used instead of bars. However, because of the perspective nature of the drawing, the lengths of the bars do not represent the mileages. The scale for each bar changes. (b) Yes. The scale does not change, and the viewer is not distracted by the graphic of the highway.
7. Problems with Tax Returns

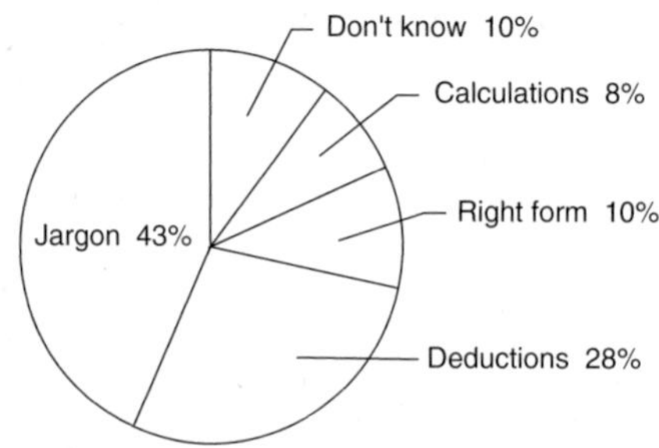

9. (a) Class width = 11.

Class Limits	Class Boundaries	Midpoint	Frequency	Relative Frequency
69–79	68.5–79.5	74	2	0.03
80–90	79.5–90.5	85	3	0.05
91–101	90.5–101.5	96	8	0.13
102–112	101.5–112.5	107	19	0.32
113–123	112.5–123.5	118	22	0.37
124–134	123.5–134.5	129	3	0.05
135–145	134.5–145.57	140	3	0.05

(b, c) Trunk Circumference (mm)—Histogram, Relative-Frequency Histogram

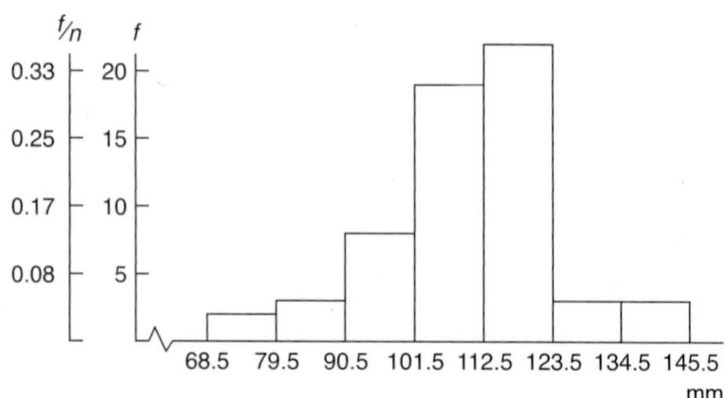

(d) Skewed slightly left.

11. (a) 1240s had 40 data values. (b) 75. (c) From 1204 to 1211. Little if any repairs or new construction.

CHAPTER 3

Section 3.1

1. Median; mode; mean.
3. Mean, median, and mode are approximately equal.
5. (a) Mode = 5; median = 4; mean = 3.8. (b) Mode. (c) Mean, median, and mode. (d) Mode, median.
7. $\bar{x} \approx 167.3$°F; median = 171°F; mode = 178°F.
9. (a) $\bar{x} \approx 3.27$; median = 3; mode = 3. (b) $\bar{x} \approx 4.21$; median = 2; mode = 1. (c) Lower Canyon mean is greater; median and mode are less. (d) Trimmed mean = 3.75 and is closer to Upper Canyon mean.
11. (a) $\bar{x}$ = \$136.15; median = \$66.50; mode = \$60. (b) 5% trimmed mean ≈ \$121.28; yes, but still higher than the median. (c) Median. The low and high prices would be useful.
13. $\Sigma wx = 85$; $\Sigma w = 10$; weighted average = 8.5.

Section 3.2

1. Mean.
3. Yes. For the sample standard deviation s, the sum $\Sigma(x - \bar{x})^2$ is divided by $n - 1$, where n is the sample size. For the population standard deviation σ, the sum $\Sigma(x - \mu)^2$ is divided by N, where N is the population size.
5. (a) (i), (ii), (iii). (b) The data change between data sets (i) and (ii) increased the squared difference sum $\Sigma(x - \bar{x})^2$ by 10, whereas the data change between data sets (ii) and (iii) increased the squared difference sum $\Sigma(x - \bar{x})^2$ by only 6.
7. (a) 15. (b) Use a calculator. (c) 37; 6.08. (d) 37; 6.08. (e) $\sigma^2 \approx 29.59$; $\sigma \approx 5.44$.
9. (a) 7.87. (b) Use a calculator. (c) $\bar{x} \approx 1.24$; $s^2 \approx 1.78$; $s \approx 1.33$. (d) $CV \approx 107\%$. The standard deviation of the time to failure is just slightly larger than the average time.
11. (a) Use a calculator. (b) $\bar{x} = 49$; $s^2 \approx 687.49$; $s \approx 26.22$. (c) $\bar{y} = 44.8$; $s^2 \approx 508.50$; $s \approx 22.55$. (d) Mallard nests, $CV \approx 53.5\%$; Canada goose nests, $CV \approx 50.3\%$. The CV gives the ratio of the standard deviation to the mean; the CV for mallard nests is slightly higher.
13. Since $CV = s/\bar{x}$, then $s = CV(\bar{x})$; $s = 0.033$.
15. Midpoints: 25.5, 35.5, 45.5; $\bar{x} \approx 35.80$; $s^2 \approx 61.1$; $s \approx 7.82$.
17. Midpoints: 10.55, 14.55, 18.55, 22.55, 26.55; $\bar{x} \approx 15.6$; $s^2 \approx 23.4$; $s \approx 4.8$.

Section 3.3

1. 82% or more of the scores were at or below Angela's score; 18% or fewer of the scores were above Angela's score.
3. No, the score 82 might have a percentile rank of less than 70.
5. Low = 2; $Q_1 = 9.5$; median = 23; $Q_3 = 28.5$; high = 42; $IQR = 19$.

Nurses' Length of Employment (months)

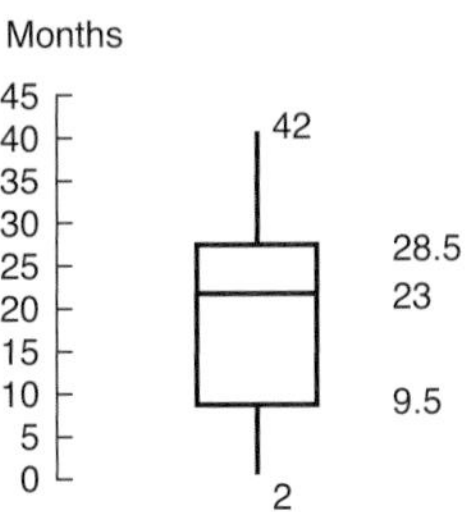

7. (a) Low = 17; $Q_1 = 22$; median = 24; $Q_3 = 27$; high = 38; $IQR = 5$. (b) Third quartile, since it is between the median and Q_3.

Bachelor's Degree Percentage by State

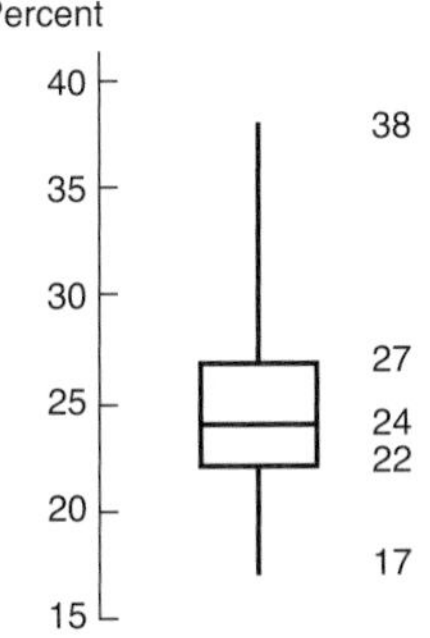

9. (a) California has the lowest premium. Pennsylvania has the highest. (b) Pennsylvania has the highest median premium. (c) California has the smallest range. Texas has the smallest interquartile range. (d) Part (a) is the five-number summary for Texas. It has the smallest IQR. Part (b) is the five-number summary for Pennsylvania. It has the largest minimum. Part (c) is the five-number summary for California. It has the lowest minimum.

Chapter 3 Review

1. (a) Variance and standard deviation. (b) Box-and-whisker plot.
3. (a) For both data sets, mean = 20 and range = 24. (b) The C1 distribution seems more symmetric because the mean and median are equal, and the median is in the center of the interquartile range. In the C2 distribution, the mean is less than the median. (c) The C1 distribution has a larger interquartile range that is symmetric about the median. The C2 distribution has a very compressed interquartile range with the median equal to Q_3.
5. (a) Low = 31; $Q_1 = 40$; median = 45; $Q_3 = 52.5$; high = 68; $IQR = 12.5$.

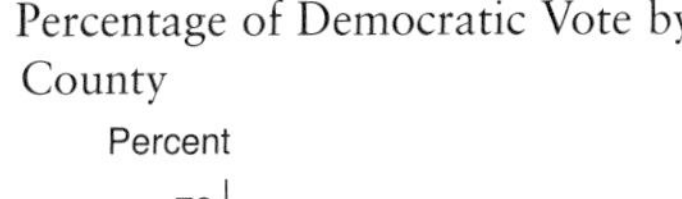
Percentage of Democratic Vote by County

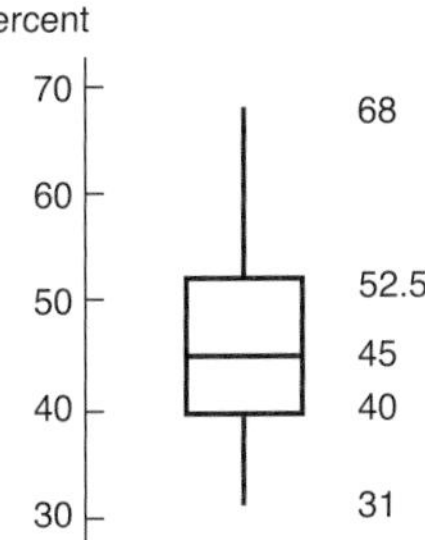

(b) Class width = 8.

Class	Midpoint	f
31–38	34.5	11
39–46	42.5	24
47–54	50.5	15
55–62	58.5	7
63–70	66.5	3

$\bar{x} \approx 46.1$; $s \approx 8.64$; 28.82 to 63.38.

(c) $\bar{x} = 46.15$; $s \approx 8.63$.

7. Mean weight = 156.25 pounds.
9. (a) No. (b) $34,206 to $68,206. (c) $10,875.
11. $\Sigma w = 16$, $\Sigma wx = 121$, average = 7.56.

CUMULATIVE REVIEW PROBLEMS

Chapters 1–3

1. (a) Median, percentile. (b) Mean, variance, standard deviation.
2. (a) Gap between first bar and rest of bars or between last bar and rest of bars. (b) Large gap between data on far-left or far-right side and rest of data. (c) Several empty stems above stem including lowest values or before stem including highest values. (d) Data beyond fences placed at $Q_1 - 1.5(IQR)$ and $Q_3 + 1.5(IQR)$.
3. (a) Same. (b) Set B has a higher mean. (c) Set B has a higher standard deviation. (d) Set B has a much longer whisker beyond Q_3.
4. (a) Set A because 86 is the relatively higher score, since a larger percentage of scores fall below it. (b) Set B because 86 is more standard deviations above the mean.
5. Assign consecutive numbers to all the wells in the study region. Then use a random number table, computer, or calculator to select 102 values that are less than or equal to the highest number assigned to a well in the study region. The sample consists of the wells with numbers corresponding to those selected.
6. Ratio.
7. 7 | 0 represents a pH level of 7.0

7	0 0 0 0 0 0 0 0 1 1 1 1 1 1 1 1 1
7	2 2 2 2 2 2 2 2 2 2 3 3 3 3 3 3 3 3 3 3
7	4 4 4 4 4 4 4 4 4 5 5 5 5 5 5 5 5
7	6 6 6 6 6 6 6 6 6 7 7 7 7 7 7
7	8 8 8 8 8 9 9 9 9 9
8	0 1 1 1 1 1 1 1
8	2 2 2 2 2 2 2
8	4 5
8	6 7
8	8 8

8. Clear the decimals. Then the highest value is 88 and the lowest is 70. The class width for the whole numbers is 4. For the actual data, the class width is 0.4.

Class Limits	Class Boundaries	Midpoint	Frequency	Relative Frequency
7.0–7.3	6.95–7.35	7.15	39	0.38
7.4–7.7	7.35–7.75	7.55	32	0.31
7.8–8.1	7.75–8.15	7.95	18	0.18
8.2–8.5	8.15–8.55	8.35	9	0.09
8.6–8.9	8.55–8.95	8.75	4	0.04

Levels of pH in West Texas Wells—Histogram, Relative-Frequency Histogram

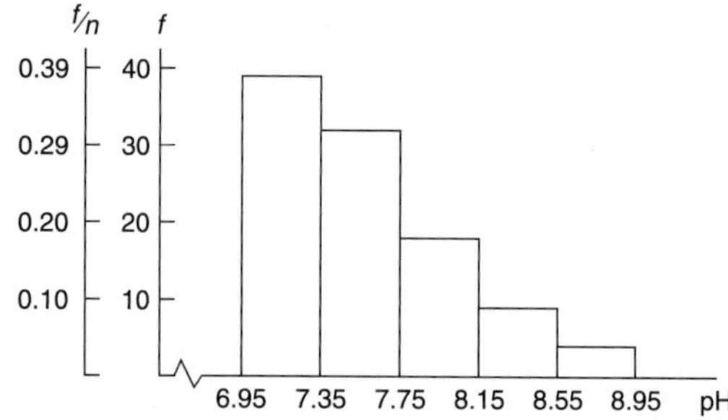

9. Range = 1.8; $\bar{x} \approx 7.58$; median = 7.5; mode = 7.3.
10. (a) Use a calculator or computer.
    (b) $s^2 \approx 0.20$; $s \approx 0.45$; $CV \approx 5.9\%$.
11. 6.68 to 8.48.
12. Levels of pH in West Texas Wells

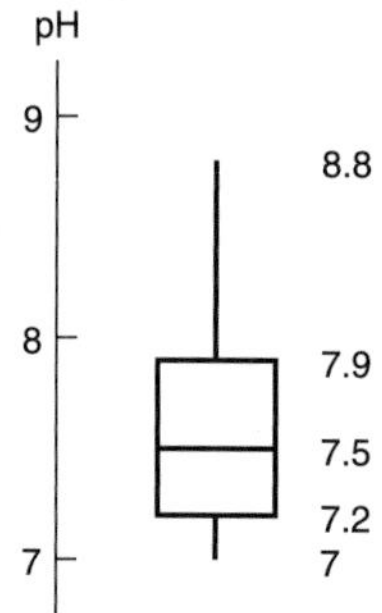

$IQR = 0.7$.

13. Skewed right. Lower values are more common.
14. No, there are no gaps in the plot, but only 6 out of 102, or about 6%, have pH levels at or above 8.4. Eight wells are neutral.
15. Half the wells have pH levels between 7.2 and 7.9. The data are skewed toward the high values, with the upper half of the pH levels spread out more than the lower half. The upper half ranges between 7.5 and 8.8, while the lower half is clustered between 7 and 7.5.
16. The report should emphasize the relatively low mean, median, and mode, and the fact that half the wells have a pH level of less than 7.5. The data are clustered at the low end of the range.

CHAPTER 4

Section 4.1

1. Explanatory variable is placed along horizontal axis, usually x axis. Response variable is placed along vertical axis, usually y axis.
3. Decreases.
5. (a) Moderate. (b) None. (c) High.
7. (a) No. (b) Increasing population might be a lurking variable causing both variables to increase.
9. (a) No. (b) One lurking variable responsible for average annual income increases is inflation. Better training might be a lurking variable responsible for shorter times to run the mile.
11. (a) Ages and Average Weights of Shetland Ponies

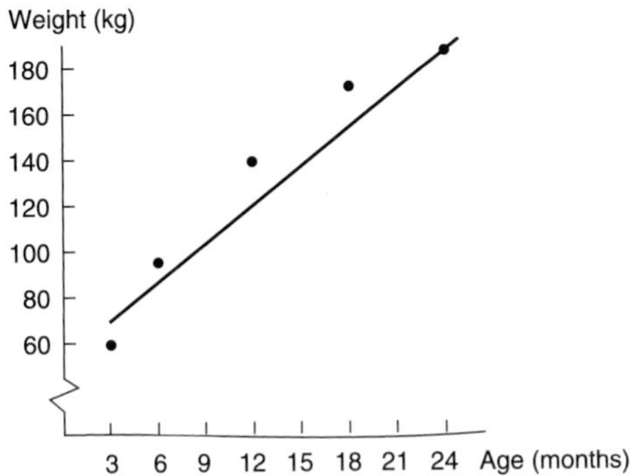

Line slopes upward.
(b) Strong; positive. (c) $r \approx 0.972$; increase.

13. (a) Lowest Barometric Pressure and Maximum Wind Speed for Tropical Cyclones

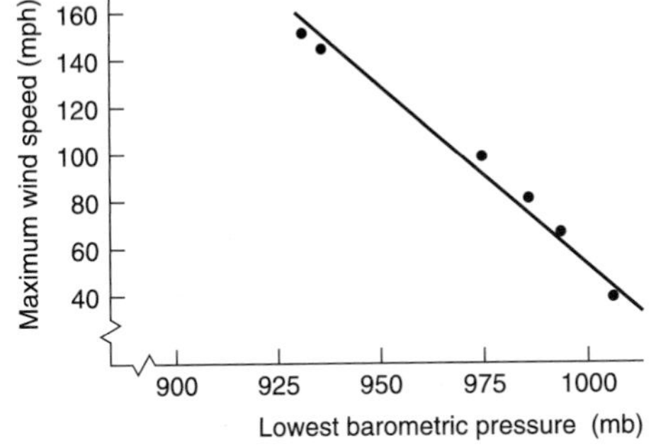

Line slopes downward.
(b) Strong; negative. (c) $r \approx -0.990$; decrease.

15. (a) Batting Average and Home Run Percentage

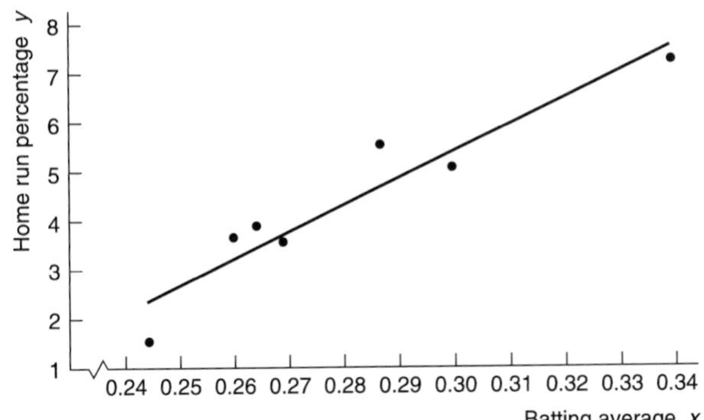

Line slopes upward.
(b) High; positive. (c) $r \approx 0.948$; increase.

17. (a) Unit Length on y Same as That on x

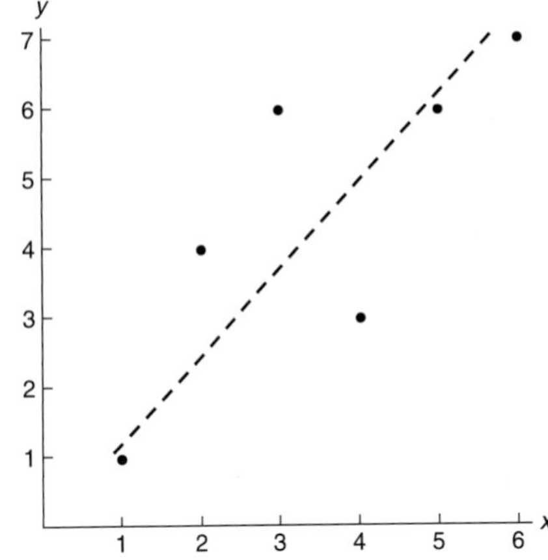

(b) Unit Length on y Twice That on x

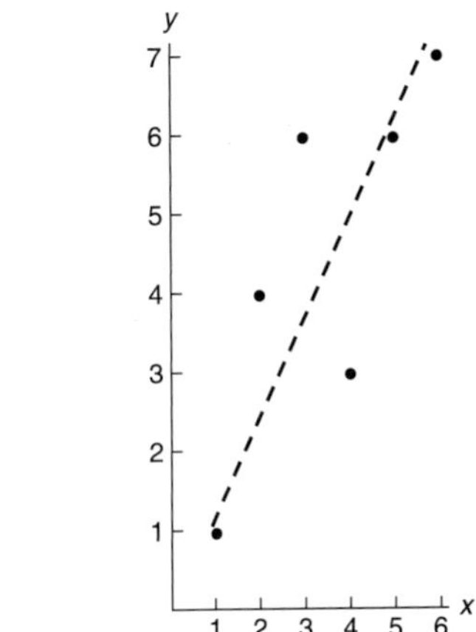

(c) Unit Length on y Half That on x

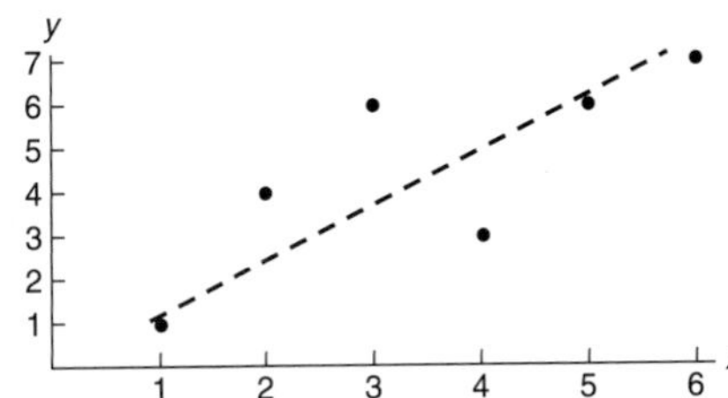

(d) The line in part b appears steeper than the line in part a, whereas the line in part c appears flatter than the line in part a. The slopes actually are all the same, but the lines look different because of the change in unit lengths on the y and x axes.

19. (a) $r \approx 0.972$ with $n = 5$ is significant for $\alpha = 0.05$. For this α, we conclude that age and weight of Shetland ponies are correlated. (b) $r \approx -0.990$ with $n = 6$ is significant for $\alpha = 0.01$. For this α, we conclude that lowest barometric pressure reading and maximum wind speed for cyclones are correlated.

Section 4.2

1. $b = -2$. When x changes by 1 unit, y decreases by 2 units.
3. Extrapolation. Extrapolation beyond the range of the data is dangerous because the relationship pattern might change.
5. (a) $\hat{y} \approx 318.16 - 30.878x$. (b) About 31 fewer frost-free days. (c) $r \approx -0.981$. Note that if the slope is negative, r is also negative.
7. (a) Total Number (in hundreds) of Jobs and Number (in hundreds) of Entry-Level Jobs

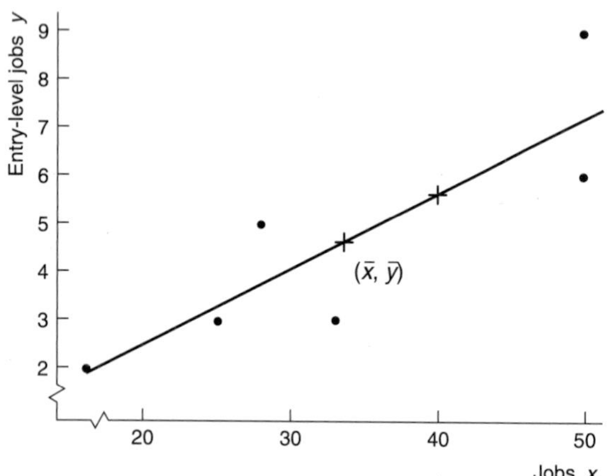

(b) Use a calculator. (c) $\bar{x} \approx 33.67$ (in hundreds) jobs; $\bar{y} \approx 4.67$ (in hundreds) entry-level jobs; $a \approx -0.748$; $b \approx 0.161$; $\hat{y} \approx -0.748 + 0.161x$. (d) See figure in part a. (e) $r^2 \approx 0.740$; 74.0% of variation explained and 26.0% unexplained. (f) 5.69 (in hundreds) jobs.

9. (a) Weight of Cars and Gasoline Mileage

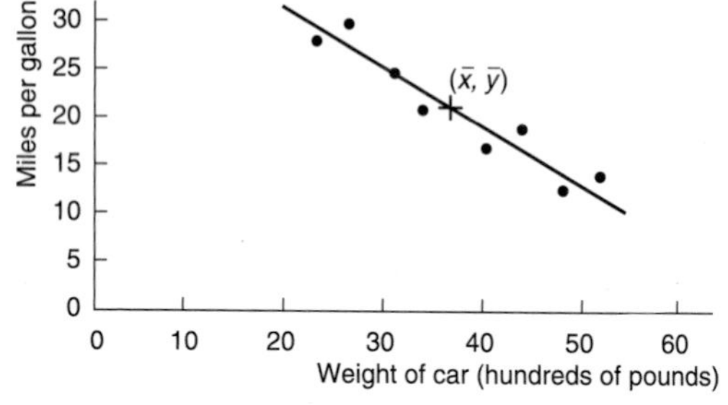

(b) Use a calculator. (c) $\bar{x} = 37.375$; $\bar{y} = 20.875$ mpg; $a \approx 43.326$; $b \approx -0.6007$; $\hat{y} \approx 43.326 - 0.6007x$. (d) See figure in part a. (e) $r^2 \approx 0.895$; 89.5% of variation explained and 10.5% unexplained. (f) 20.5 mpg.

11. (a) Age and Percentage of Fatal Accidents Due to Speeding

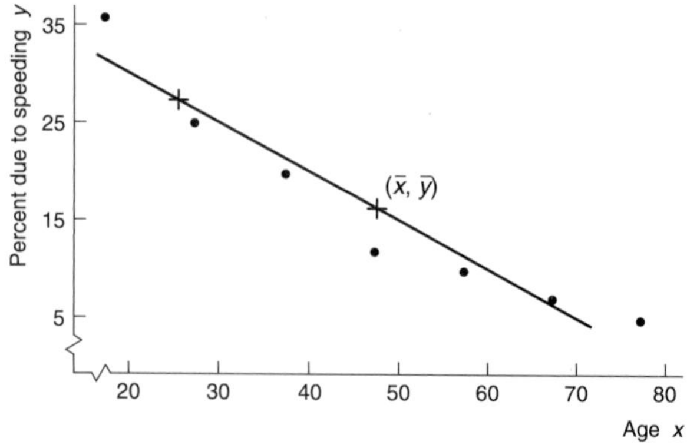

(b) Use a calculator. (c) $\bar{x} = 47$ years; $\bar{y} \approx 16.43\%$; $a \approx 39.761$; $b \approx -0.496$; $\hat{y} \approx 39.761 - 0.496x$. (d) See figure in part a. (e) $r^2 \approx 0.920$; 92.0% of variation explained and 8.0% unexplained. (f) 27.36%.

13. (a) Elevation of Archaeological Sites and Percentage of Unidentified Artifacts

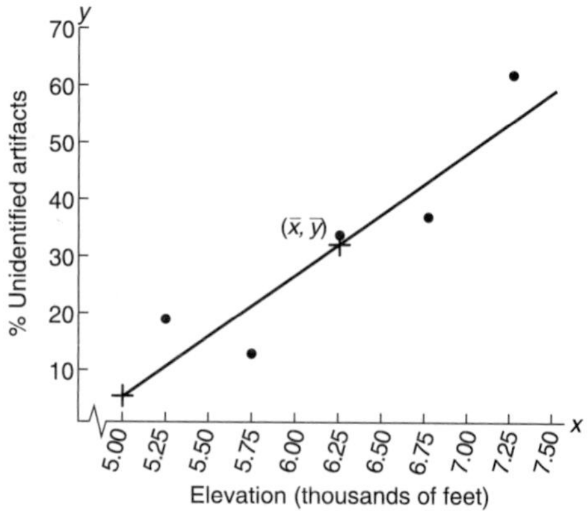

(b) Use a calculator. (c) $\bar{x} = 6.25$; $\bar{y} = 32.8$; $a = -104.7$; $b = 22$; $\hat{y} = -104.7 + 22x$. (d) See figure in part a. (e) $r^2 \approx 0.833$; 83.3% of variation explained, 16.7% unexplained. (f) 38.3.

15. (a) Yes. The pattern of residuals appears randomly scattered about the horizontal line at 0. (b) No. There do not appear to be any outliers.
17. (a) Result checks. (b) Result checks. (c) Yes. (d) The equation $x = 0.9337y - 0.1335$ does not match part b. (e) No. The least-squares equation changes depending on which variable is the explanatory variable and which is the response variable.

Chapter 4 Review

1. r will be close to 0.
3. Results are more reliable for interpolation.
5. (a) Age and Mortality Rate for Bighorn Sheep

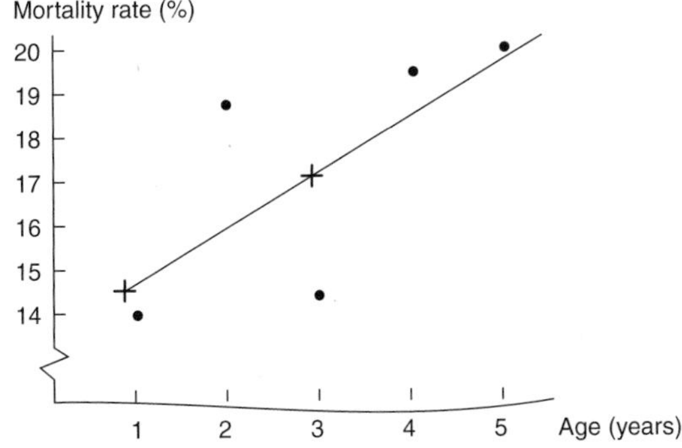

(b) $\bar{x} = 3$; $\bar{y} \approx 17.38$; $b \approx 1.27$; $\hat{y} \approx 13.57 + 1.27x$.
(c) $r \approx 0.685$; $r^2 \approx 0.469$; 46.9% explained.

7. (a) Weight of One-Year-Old versus Weight of Adult

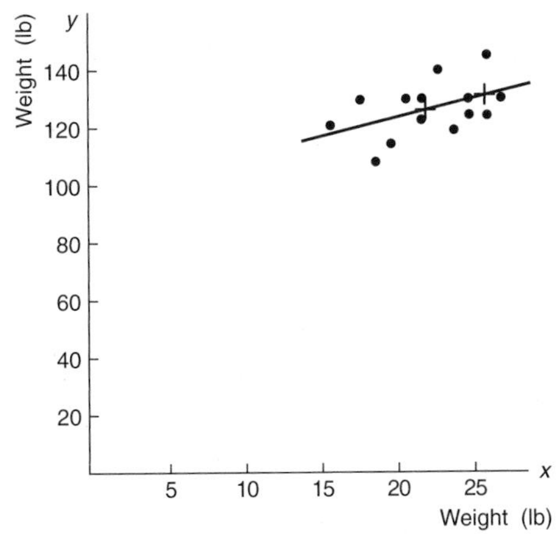

(b) $\bar{x} \approx 21.43$; $\bar{y} \approx 126.79$; $b \approx 1.285$; $\hat{y} \approx 99.25 + 1.285x$. (c) $r \approx 0.468$; $r^2 \approx 0.219$; 21.9% explained. (d) 124.95 pounds.

9. (a) Weight of Mail versus Number of Employees Required

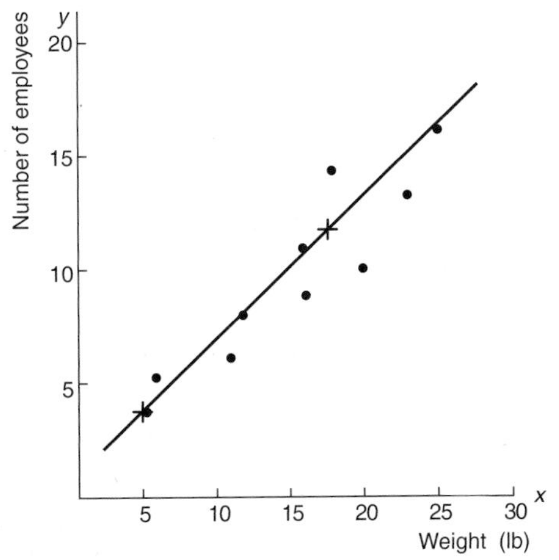

(b) $\bar{x} \approx 16.38$; $\bar{y} \approx 10.13$; $b \approx 0.554$; $\hat{y} \approx 1.051 + 0.554x$. (c) $r \approx 0.913$; $r^2 \approx 0.833$; 83.3% explained. (d) 9.36.

CHAPTER 5

Section 5.1

1. Equally likely outcomes, relative frequency, intuition.
3. (a) 1. (b) 0.
5. No. The probability of tails on the second toss is 0.50 regardless of the outcome on the first toss.
7. Answers vary. Probability as a relative frequency. One concern is whether the students in the class are more or less adept at wiggling their ears than people in the general population.
9. (a) $P(0) = 15/375$; $P(1) = 71/375$; $P(2) = 124/375$; $P(3) = 131/375$; $P(4) = 34/375$. (b) Yes. The listed numbers of similar preferences form the sample space.
11. (a) P(best idea 6 A.M.–12 noon) $= 290/966 \approx 0.30$; P(best idea 12 noon–6 P.M.) $= 135/966 \approx 0.14$; P(best idea 6 P.M.–12 midnight) $= 319/966 \approx 0.33$; P(best idea 12 midnight–6 A.M.) $= 222/966 \approx 0.23$. (b) The probabilities add up to 1. They should add up to 1 provided the intervals do not overlap and each inventor chose only one interval. The sample space is the set of four time intervals.
13. (a) P(enter if walks by) $= 58/127 \approx 0.46$. (b) P(buy if entered) $= 25/58 \approx 0.43$. (c) P(walk in and buy) $= 25/127 \approx 0.20$. (d) P(not buy) $= 1 - P$(buy) $\approx 1 - 0.43 = 0.57$.

Section 5.2

1. No. By definition, mutually exclusive events cannot occur together.
3. (a) Because the events are mutually exclusive, A cannot occur if B occurred. $P(A|B) = 0$. (b) Because $P(A|B) \neq P(A)$, the events A and B are not independent.
5. (a) $P(A \textit{ and } B)$. (b) $P(B|A)$. (c) $P(A^c|B)$. (d) $P(A \textit{ or } B)$. (e) $P(B^c \textit{ or } A)$.
7. (a) 0.2; yes. (b) 0.4; yes. (c) $1.0 - 0.2 = 0.8$.
9. (a) Yes. (b) P(5 on green *and* 3 on red) $= P(5) \cdot P(3) = (1/6)(1/6) = 1/36 \approx 0.028$. (c) P(3 on green *and* 5 on red) $= P(3) \cdot P(5) = (1/6)(1/6) = 1/36 \approx 0.028$. (d) P((5 on green *and* 3 on red) *or* (3 on green *and* 5 on red)) $= (1/36) + (1/36) = 1/18 \approx 0.056$.
11. (a) P(sum of 6) $= P$(1 *and* 5) $+ P$(2 *and* 4) $+ P$(3 *and* 3) $+ P$(4 *and* 2) $+ P$(5 *and* 1) $= (1/36) + (1/36) + (1/36) + (1/36) + (1/36) = 5/36$. (b) P(sum of 4) $= P$(1 *and* 3) $+ P$(2 *and* 2) $+ P$(3 *and* 1) $= (1/36) + (1/36) + (1/36) = 3/36$ or $1/12$. (c) P(sum of 6 *or* sum of 4) $= P$(sum of 6) $+ P$(sum of 4) $= (5/36) + (3/36) = 8/36$ or $2/9$; yes.
13. (a) No. After the first draw the sample space becomes smaller and probabilities for events on the second draw change. (b) P(ace on 1st *and* king on 2nd) $= P$(ace)$\cdot P$(king$|$ace) $= (4/52)(4/51) = 4/663$. (c) P(king on 1st *and* ace on 2nd) $= P$(king)$\cdot P$(ace$|$king) $= (4/52)(4/51) = 4/663$. (d) P(ace *and* king in either *order*) $= P$(ace on 1st *and* king on 2nd) $+ P$(king on 1st *and* ace on 2nd) $= (4/663) + (4/663) = 8/663$.
15. (a) Yes. Replacement of the card restores the sample space, and all probabilities for the second draw remain unchanged regardless of the outcome of the first card.

(b) P(ace on 1st *and* king on 2nd) = P(ace) · P(king) = (4/52)(4/52) = 1/169. (c) P(king on 1st *and* ace on 2nd) = P(king) · P(ace) = (4/52)(4/52) = 1/169.
(d) P(ace *and* king in either order) = P(ace on 1st *and* king on 2nd) + P(king on 1st *and* ace on 2nd) = (1/169) + (1/169) = 2/169.

17. (a) P(6 years old *or* older) = P(6–9) + P(10–12) + P(13 and over) = 0.27 + 0.14 + 0.22 = 0.63.
(b) P(12 years old *or* younger) = P(2 and under) + P(3–5) + P(6–9) + P(10–12) = 0.15 + 0.22 + 0.27 + 0.14 = 0.78. (c) P(between 6 and 12) = P(6–9) + P(10–12) = 0.27 + 0.14 = 0.41. (d) P(between 3 and 9) = P(3–5) + P(6–9) = 0.22 + 0.27 = 0.49. The category 13 and over contains far more ages than the group 10–12. It is not surprising that more toys are purchased for this group, since there are more children in this group.

19. The information from James Burke can be viewed as conditional probabilities. P(reports lie | person is lying) = 0.72 and P(reports lie | person is not lying) = 0.07.
(a) P(person is not lying) = 0.90; P(person is not lying *and* polygraph reports lie) = P(person is not lying) × P(reports lie | person not lying) = (0.90)(0.07) = 0.063 or 6.3%. (b) P(person is lying) = S0.10; P(person is lying *and* polygraph reports lie) = P(person is lying) × P(reports lie | person is lying) = (0.10)(0.72) = 0.072 or 7.2%. (c) P(person is not lying) = 0.5; P(person is lying) = 0.5; P(person is not lying *and* polygraph reports lie) = P(person is not lying) × P(reports lie | person not lying) = (0.50)(0.07) = 0.035 or 3.5%. P(person is lying *and* polygraph reports lie) = P(person is lying) × P(reports lie | person is lying) = (0.50)(0.72) = 0.36 or 36%. (d) P(person is not lying) = 0.15; P(person is lying) = 0.85; P(person is not lying *and* polygraph reports lie) = P(person is not lying) × P(reports lie | person is not lying) = (0.15)(0.07) = 0.0105 or 1.05%. P(person is lying *and* polygraph reports lie) = P(person is lying) × P(reports lie | person is lying) = (0.85)(0.72) = 0.612 or 61.2%.

21. (a) 72/154. (b) 82/154. (c) 79/116. (d) 37/116. (e) 72/270. (f) 82/270.

23. (a) 686/1160; 270/580; 416/580. (b) No. (c) 270/1160; 416/1160. (d) 474/1160; 310/580. (e) No. (f) 686/1160 + 580/1160 − 270/1160 = 996/1160.

Section 5.3

1. The permutations rule counts the number of different *arrangements* of r items out of n distinct items, whereas the combinations rule counts only the *number* of groups of r items out of n distinct items. The number of permutations is greater than or equal to the number of combinations.

3. (a) Use the combinations rule, since only the items in the group and not their arrangement is of concern.
(b) Use the permutations rule, since the number of arrangements within each group is of interest.

5. (a) Outcomes for Tossing a Coin Three Times

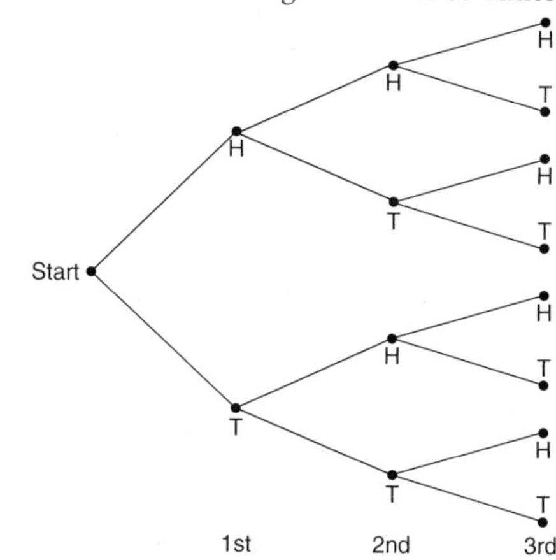

(b) 3. (c) 3/8.

7. (a) Outcomes for Drawing Two Balls (without replacement)

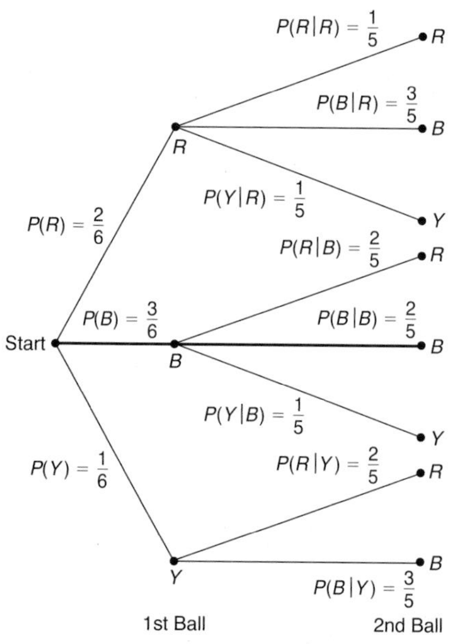

(b) P(R *and* R) = 2/6 · 1/5 = 1/15.
P(R 1st *and* B 2nd) = 2/6 · 3/5 = 1/5.
P(R 1st *and* Y 2nd) = 2/6 · 1/5 = 1/15.
P(B 1st *and* R 2nd) = 3/6 · 2/5 = 1/5.
P(B 1st *and* B 2nd) = 3/6 · 2/5 = 1/5.
P(B 1st *and* Y 2nd) = 3/6 · 1/5 = 1/10.
P(Y 1st *and* R 2nd) = 1/6 · 2/5 = 1/15.
P(Y 1st *and* B 2nd) = 1/6 · 3/5 = 1/10.

9. 4 · 3 · 2 · 1 = 24 sequences.

11. 4 · 3 · 3 = 36.

13. $P_{5,2}$ = (5!/3!) = 5 · 4 = 20.

15. $P_{7,7}$ = (7!/0!) = 7! = 5040.

17. $C_{5,2}$ = (5!/(2!3!)) = 10.

19. $C_{7,7}$ = (7!/(7!0!)) = 1.

21. $P_{15,3}$ = 2730.

23. 5 · 4 · 3 = 60.

25. $C_{15,5}$ = (15!/(5!10!)) = 3003.

27. (a) $C_{12,6} = (12!/(6!6!)) = 924$.
(b) $C_{7,6} = (7!/(6!1!)) = 7$. (c) $7/924 \approx 0.008$.

Chapter 5 Review

1. (a) The individual does not own a cell phone. (b) The individual owns a cell phone as well as a laptop computer. (c) The individual owns either a cell phone or a laptop computer, and maybe both. (d) The individual owns a cell phone, given he or she owns a laptop computer. (e) The individual owns a laptop computer, given he or she owns a cell phone.
3. (a) No. You need to know that the events are independent or you need to know the value of $P(A|B)$ or $P(B|A)$. (b) Yes. For independent events, $P(A \text{ and } B) = P(A) \cdot P(B)$.
5. $P(\text{asked}) = 24\%$; $P(\text{received}|\text{asked}) = 45\%$; $P(\text{asked } and \text{ received}) = (0.24)(0.45) = 10.8\%$.
7. (a) Drop a fixed number of tacks and count how many land flat side down. Then form the ratio of the number landing flat side down to the total number dropped. (b) Up, down. (c) $P(\text{up}) = 160/500 = 0.32$; $P(\text{down}) = 340/500 = 0.68$.
9. (a) and (b)

Outcomes x	2	3	4	5	6
$P(x)$	0.028	0.056	0.083	0.111	0.139

x	7	8	9	10	11	12
$P(x)$	0.167	0.139	0.111	0.083	0.056	0.028

11. $C_{8,2} = (8!/(2!6!)) = (8 \cdot 7/2) = 28$.
13. $4 \cdot 4 \cdot 4 \cdot 4 \cdot 4 = 1024$ choices; $P(\text{all correct}) = 1/1024 \approx 0.00098$.
15. $10 \cdot 10 \cdot 10 = 1000$.

CHAPTER 6

Section 6.1

1. (a) Discrete. (b) Continuous. (c) Continuous. (d) Discrete. (e) Continuous.
3. (a) Yes. (b) No; probabilities total to more than 1.
5. (a) Yes, 7 of the 10 digits represent "making a basket." (b) Let S represent "making a basket" and F represent "missing the shot." $F, F, S, S, S, F, F, F, S, S$. (c) Yes. Again, 7 of the 10 digits represent "making a basket." $S, S, S, S, S, S, S, S, S, S$.
7. (a) Yes, events are distinct and probabilities total to 1. (b) Income Distribution ($1000)

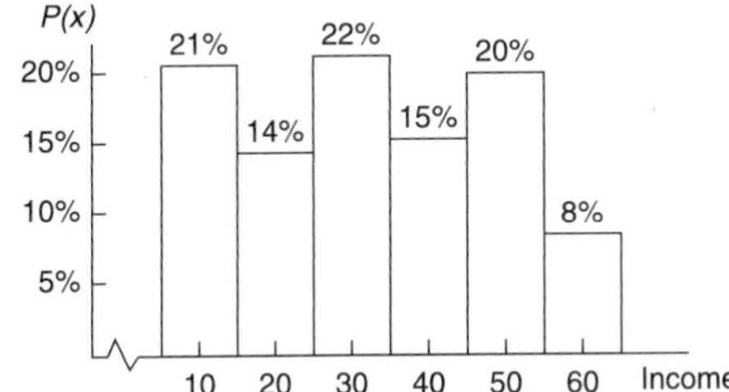

(c) 32.3 thousand dollars. (d) 16.12 thousand dollars.

9. (a) Number of Fish Caught in a 6-Hour Period at Pyramid Lake, Nevada

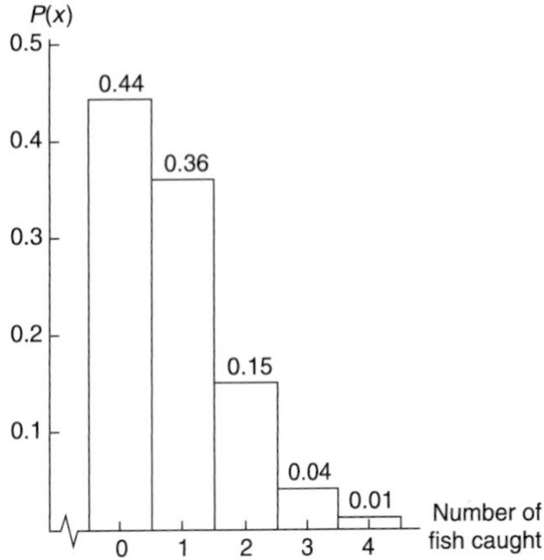

(b) 0.56. (c) 0.20. (d) 0.82. (e) 0.899.
11. (a) 15/719; 704/719. (b) $0.73; $14.27.
13. (a) 0.01191; $595.50. (b) $646; $698; $751.50; $806.50; $3497.50 total. (c) $4197.50. (d) $1502.50.

Section 6.2

1. The random variable measures the number of successes out of n trials. This text uses the letter r for the random variable.
3. Two outcomes, success or failure.
5. (a) No. A binomial probability model applies to only two outcomes per trial. (b) Yes. Assign outcome A to "success" and outcomes B and C to "failure." $p = 0.40$.
7. (a) A trial consists of looking at the class status of a randomly selected student enrolled in introductory statistics. Two outcomes are "freshman" and "not freshman." Success is freshman status; failure is any other class status. $P(\text{success}) = 0.40$. (b) Trials are not independent. With a population of only 30 students, in 5 trials without replacement, the probability of success rounded to the nearest hundredth changes for the later trials.
9. A trial is one flip of a fair quarter. Success = coin shows heads. Failure = coin shows tails. $n = 3$; $p = 0.5$; $q = 0.5$. (a) $P(r = 3 \text{ heads}) = C_{3,3}p^3q^0 = 1(0.5)^3(0.5)^0 = 0.125$. To find this value in Table 2 of the Appendix, use the group in which $n = 3$, the column headed by $p = 0.5$, and the row headed by $r = 3$. (b) $P(r = 2 \text{ heads}) = C_{3,2}p^2q^1 = 3(0.5)^2(0.5)^1 = 0.375$. To find this value in Table 2 of the Appendix, use the group in which $n = 3$, the column headed by $p = 0.5$, and the row headed by $r = 2$. (c) $P(r \text{ is 2 or more}) = P(r = 2 \text{ heads}) + P(r = 3 \text{ heads}) = 0.375 + 0.125 = 0.500$. (d) The probability of getting three tails when you toss a coin three times is the same as getting zero heads. Therefore, $P(3 \text{ tails}) = P(r = 0 \text{ heads}) = C_{3,0}p^0q^3 = 1(0.5)^0(0.5)^3 = 0.125$. To find this value in Table 2 of the Appendix, use the group in which $n = 3$, the column headed by $p = 0.5$, and the row headed by $r = 0$.
11. A trial is recording the gender of one wolf. Success = male. Failure = female. $n = 12$; $p = 0.55$; $q = 0.45$.

(a) $P(r \geq 6) = 0.740$. Six or more females means $12 - 6 = 6$ or fewer males; $P(r \leq 6) = 0.473$. Fewer than four females means more than $12 - 4 = 8$ males; $P(r > 8) = 0.135$. (b) A trial is recording the gender of one wolf. Success = male. Failure = female. $n = 12$; $p = 0.70$; $q = 0.30$. $P(r \geq 6) = 0.961$; $P(r \leq 6) = 0.117$; $P(r > 8) = 0.493$.

13. A trial consists of a woman's response regarding her mother-in-law. Success = dislike. Failure = like. $n = 6$; $p = 0.90$; $q = 0.10$. (a) $P(r = 6) = 0.531$. (b) $P(r = 0) = 0.000$ (to three digits). (c) $P(r \geq 4) = P(r = 4) + P(r = 5) + P(r = 6) = 0.098 + 0.354 + 0.531 = 0.983$. (d) $P(r \leq 3) = 1 - P(r \geq 4) \approx 1 - 0.983 = 0.017$ or 0.016 directly from table.

15. A trial is taking a polygraph exam. Success = pass. Failure = fail. $n = 9$; $p = 0.85$; $q = 0.15$. (a) $P(r = 9) = 0.232$. (b) $P(r \geq 5) = P(r = 5) + P(r = 6) + P(r = 7) + P(r = 8) + P(r = 9) = 0.028 + 0.107 + 0.260 + 0.368 + 0.232 = 0.995$. (c) $P(r \leq 4) = 1 - P(r \geq 5) \approx 1 - 0.995 = 0.005$ or 0.006 directly from table. (d) $P(r = 0) = 0.000$ (to three digits).

17. $n = 8$; $p = 0.53$; $q = 0.47$. (a) 0.812515; yes, truncated at five digits. (b) 0.187486; 0.18749; yes, rounded to five digits.

Section 6.3

1. The average number of successes.
3. (a) Yes, 120 is more than 2.5 standard deviations above the expected value. (b) Yes, 40 is less than 2.5 standard deviations below the expected value. (c) No, 70 to 90 successes is within 2.5 standard deviations of the expected value.
5. (a) Binomial Distribution
   The distribution is symmetrical.

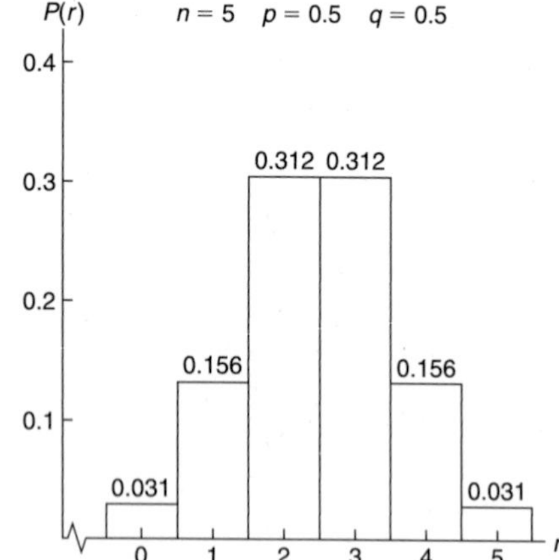

(b) Binomial Distribution
The distribution is skewed right.

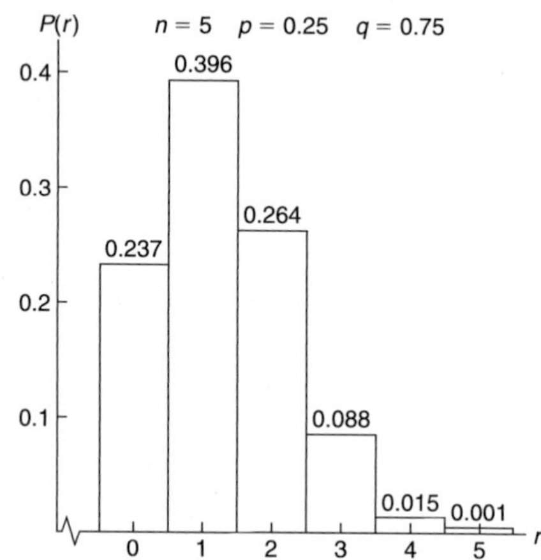

(c) Binomial Distribution
The distribution is skewed left.

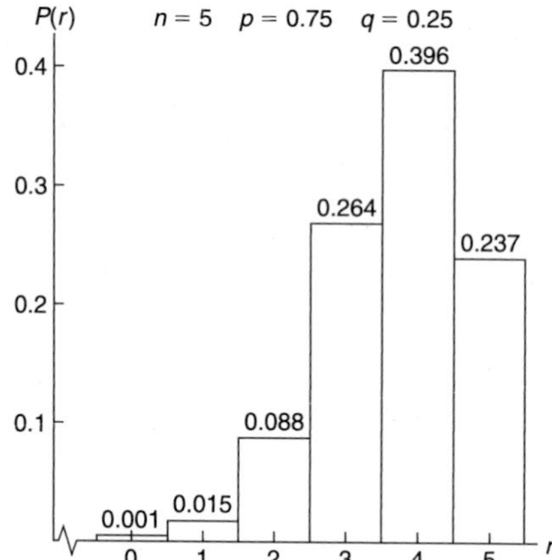

(d) The distributions are mirror images of one another.
(e) The distribution would be skewed left for $p = 0.73$ because the more likely numbers of successes are to the right of the middle.

7. (a) Binomial Distribution for Number of Illiterate People

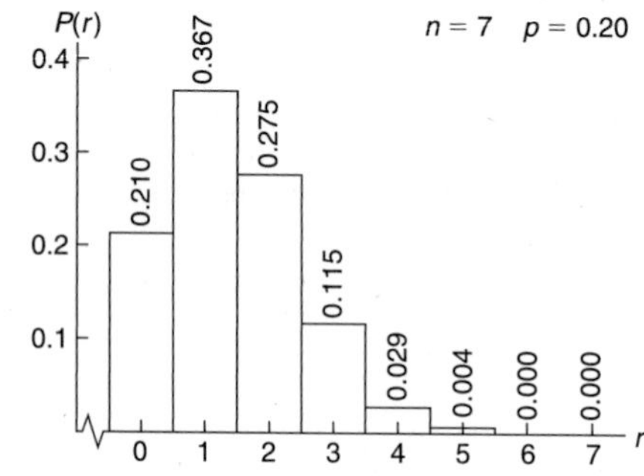

(b) $\mu = 1.4$; $\sigma \approx 1.058$.

9. (a) Binomial Distribution for Number of Gullible Consumers

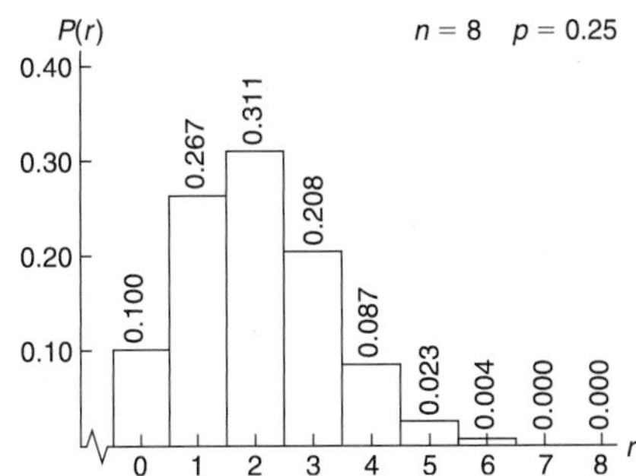

(b) $\mu = 2$; $\sigma \approx 1.225$.

11. $n = 12$; $p = 0.25$ do not serve; $p = 0.75$ serve.
(a) $P(r = 12 \text{ serve}) = 0.032$. (b) $P(r \geq 6 \text{ do not serve}) = 0.053$. (c) For serving, $\mu = 9$; $\sigma = 1.50$.

13. (a) $P(r = 7 \text{ guilty in U.S.}) = 0.028$; $P(r = 7 \text{ guilty in Japan}) = 0.698$. (b) For guilty in Japan, $\mu = 6.65$, $\sigma \approx 0.58$; for guilty in U.S., $\mu = 4.2$; $\sigma \approx 1.30$.

15. (a) Out of n trials, there can be 0 through n successes. The sum of the probabilities for all members of the sample space must be 1. (b) $r \geq 1$ consists of all members of the sample space except $r = 0$. (c) $r \geq 2$ consists of all members of the sample space except $r = 0$ and $r = 1$. (d) $r \geq m$ consists of all members of the sample space except for r values between 0 and $m - 1$.

Chapter 6 Review

1. A description of all distinct possible values of a random variable x, with a probability assignment $P(x)$ for each value or range of values. $0 \leq P(x) \leq 1$ and $\Sigma P(x) = 1$.

3. (a) Yes. $\mu = 2$ and $\sigma \approx 1.3$. Numbers of successes above 5.25 are unusual. (b) No. It would be unusual to get more than five questions correct.

5. (a) 38; 11.6.
(b) Duration of Leases in Months

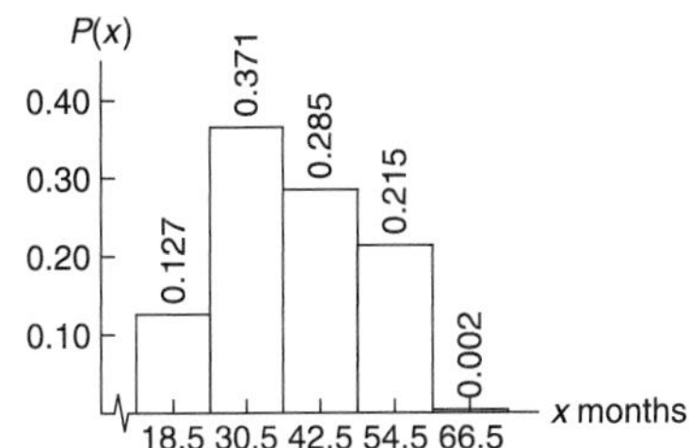

7. (a) Number of Claimants Under Age 25

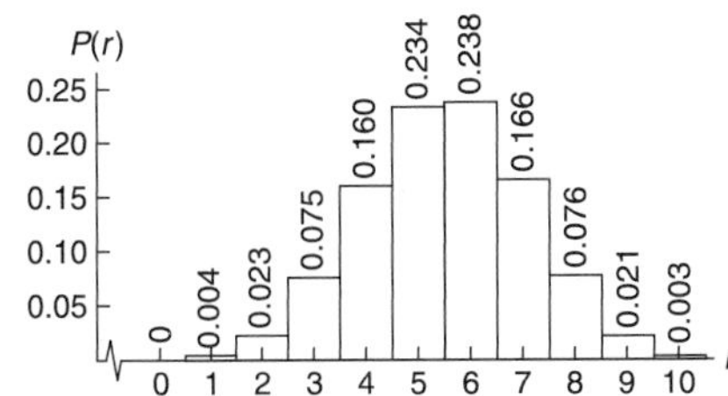

(b) $P(r \geq 6) = 0.504$. (c) $\mu = 5.5$; $\sigma \approx 1.57$.

9. (a) 0.039. (b) 0.403. (c) 8.

11. (a) Number of Good Grapefruit

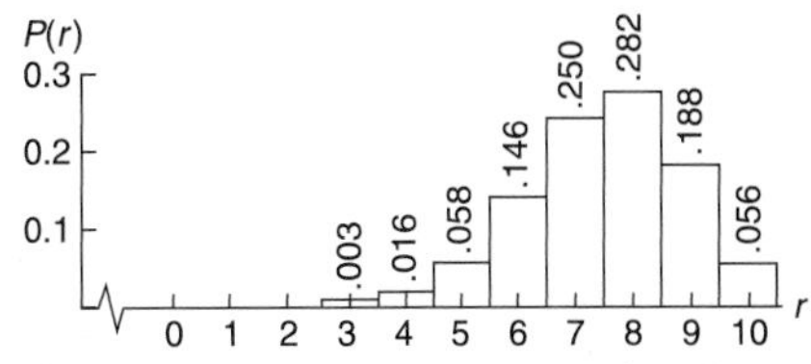

(b) 0.244, 0.999. (c) 7.5. (d) 1.37.

13. $P(r \leq 2) = 0.000$ (to three digits). The data seem to indicate that the percent favoring the increase in fees is less than 85%.

CUMULATIVE REVIEW PROBLEMS

1. The specified ranges of readings are disjoint and cover all possible readings.
2. Essay.
3. Yes; the events constitute the entire sample space.
4. (a) 0.85. (b) 0.70. (c) 0.70. (d) 0.30. (e) 0.15. (f) 0.75. (g) 0.30. (h) 0.05.
5.

x	$P(x)$
5	0.25
15	0.45
25	0.15
35	0.10
45	0.05

$\mu \approx 17.5$; $\sigma \approx 10.9$.

6. (a) $p = 0.10$. (b) $\mu = 1.2$; $\sigma \approx 1.04$. (c) 0.718. (d) 0.889.
7. (a) Blood Glucose Level

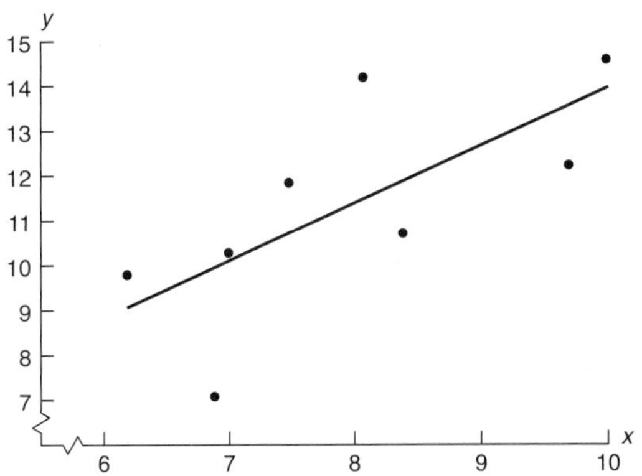

(b) $\hat{y} \approx 1.135 + 1.279x$. (c) $r \approx 0.700$; $r^2 \approx 0.490$; 49% of the variance in y is explained by the model and the variance in x. (d) 12.65.

CHAPTER 7

Section 7.1

1. (a) No, it's skewed. (b) No, it crosses the horizontal axis. (c) No, it has three peaks. (d) No, the curve is not smooth.
3. Figure 7-9 has the larger standard deviation. The mean of Figure 7-9 is $\mu = 10$. The mean of Figure 7-10 is $\mu = 4$.
5. (a) 50%. (b) 68%. (c) 99.7%.
7. (a) 50%. (b) 50%. (c) 68%. (d) 95%.
9. (a) From 1207 to 1279. (b) From 1171 to 1315. (c) From 1135 to 1351.
11. (a) From 1.70 mA to 4.60 mA. (b) From 0.25 mA to 6.05 mA.

Section 7.2

1. The number of standard deviations from the mean.
3. 0.
5. They are the same, since both are 1 standard deviation below the mean.
7. (a) Robert, Juan, and Linda each scored above the mean. (b) Joel scored on the mean. (c) Susan and Jan scored below the mean. (d) Robert, 172; Juan, 184; Susan, 110; Joel, 150; Jan, 134; Linda, 182.
9. (a) $-1.00 < z$. (b) $z < -2.00$. (c) $-2.67 < z < 2.33$. (d) $x < 4.4$. (e) $5.2 < x$. (f) $4.1 < x < 4.5$. (g) A red blood cell count of 5.9 or higher corresponds to a standard z score of 3.67. Practically no data values occur this far above the mean. Such a count would be considered unusually high for a healthy female.
11. 0.5000. 13. 0.0934. 15. 0.6736. 17. 0.0643. 19. 0.8888. 21. 0.4993. 23. 0.8953. 25. 0.3471. 27. 0.0306. 29. 0.5000. 31. 0.4483. 33. 0.8849. 35. 0.0885. 37. 0.8849. 39. 0.8808. 41. 0.3226. 43. 0.4474. 45. 0.2939. 47. 0.6704.

Section 7.3

1. 0.50.
3. Negative.
5. $P(3 \le x \le 6) = P(-0.50 \le z \le 1.00) = 0.5328$.
7. $P(50 \le x \le 70) = P(0.67 \le z \le 2.00) = 0.2286$.
9. $P(8 \le x \le 12) = P(-2.19 \le z \le -0.94) = 0.1593$.
11. $P(x \ge 30) = P(z \ge 2.94) = 0.0016$.
13. $P(x \ge 90) = P(z \ge -0.67) = 0.7486$.
15. -1.555. 17. 0.13. 19. 1.41. 21. -0.92.
23. ± 2.33.
25. (a) $P(x > 60) = P(z > -1) = 0.8413$. (b) $P(x < 110) = P(z < 1) = 0.8413$. (c) $P(60 \le x \le 110) = P(-1.00 \le z \le 1.00) = 0.8413 - 0.1587 = 0.6826$. (d) $P(x > 140) = P(z > 2.20) = 0.0139$.
27. (a) $P(x < 3.0 \text{ mm}) = P(z < -2.33) = 0.0099$. (b) $P(x > 7.0 \text{ mm}) = P(z > 2.11) = 0.0174$. (c) $P(3.0 \text{ mm} < x < 7.0 \text{ mm}) = P(-2.33 < z < 2.11) = 0.9727$.
29. (a) $P(x < 36 \text{ months}) = P(z < -1.13) = 0.1292$. The company will replace 13% of its batteries. (b) $P(z < z_0) = 10\%$ for $z_0 = -1.28$; $x = -1.28(8) + 45 = 34.76$. Guarantee the batteries for 35 months.
31. (a) According to the empirical rule, about 95% of the data lies between $\mu - 2\sigma$ and $\mu + 2\sigma$. Since this interval is 4σ wide, we have $4\sigma \approx 6$ years, so $\sigma \approx 1.5$ years. (b) $P(x > 5) = P(z > -2.00) = 0.9772$. (c) $P(x < 10) = P(z < 1.33) = 0.9082$. (d) $P(z < z_0) = 0.10$ for $z_0 = -1.28$; $x = -1.28(1.5) + 8 = 6.08$ years. Guarantee the TVs for about 6.1 years.
33. (a) $\sigma \approx 12$ beats/minute. (b) $P(x < 25) = P(z < -1.75) = 0.0401$. (c) $P(x > 60) = P(z > 1.17) = 0.1210$. (d) $P(25 \le x \le 60) = P(-1.75 \le z \le 1.17) = 0.8389$. (e) $P(z \le z_0) = 0.90$ for $z_0 = 1.28$; $x = 1.28(12) + 46 = 61.36$ beats/minute. A heart rate of 61 beats/minute corresponds to the 90% cutoff point of the distribution.
35. (a) $P(z \ge z_0) = 0.99$ for $z_0 = -2.33$; $x = -2.33(3.7) + 90 \approx 81.38$ months. Guarantee the microchips for 81 months. (b) $P(x \le 84) = P(z \le -1.62) = 0.0526$. (c) Expected loss $= (50{,}000{,}000)(0.0526) = \$2{,}630{,}000$. (d) Profit $= \$370{,}000$.

Section 7.4

1. A set of measurements or counts either existing or conceptual. For example, the population of ages of all people in Colorado; the population of weights of all students in your school; the population count of all antelope in Wyoming.
3. A numerical descriptive measure of a population, such as μ, the population mean; σ, the population standard deviation; or σ^2, the population variance.
5. A statistical inference is a conclusion about the value of a population parameter. We will do both estimation and testing.
7. They help us visualize the sampling distribution through tables and graphs that approximately represent the sampling distribution.
9. We studied the sampling distribution of mean trout lengths based on samples of size 5. Other such sampling distributions abound.

Section 7.5

Note: Answers may differ slightly depending on the number of digits carried in the standard deviation.

1. The standard deviation.
3. $\bar{x}$ is an unbiased estimator for μ; $\hat{p}$ is an unbiased estimator for p.
5. (a) 30 or more. (b) No.
7. The second. The standard error of the first is $\sigma/10$, while that of the second is $\sigma/15$, where σ is the standard deviation of the original x distribution.
9. (a) $\mu_{\bar{x}} = 15$; $\sigma_{\bar{x}} = 2.0$; $P(15 \le \bar{x} \le 17) = P(0 \le z \le 1.00) = 0.3413$. (b) $\mu_{\bar{x}} = 15$; $\sigma_{\bar{x}} = 1.75$; $P(15 \le \bar{x} \le 17) = P(0 \le z \le 1.14) = 0.3729$. (c) The standard deviation is smaller in part (b) because of the larger sample size. Therefore, the distribution about $\mu_{\bar{x}}$ is narrower in part (b).
11. (a) $P(x < 74.5) = P(z < -0.63) = 0.2643$. (b) $P(\bar{x} < 74.5) = P(z < -2.79) = 0.0026$. (c) No. If the weight of only one car were less than 74.5 tons, we could not conclude that the loader is out of

adjustment. If the mean weight for a sample of 20 cars were less than 74.5 tons, we would suspect that the loader is malfunctioning. As we see in part (b), the probability of this happening is very low if the loader is correctly adjusted.

13. (a) $P(x < 40) = P(z < -1.80) = 0.0359$. (b) Since the x distribution is approximately normal, the $\bar{x}$ distribution is approximately normal, with mean 85 and standard deviation 17.678. $P(\bar{x} < 40) = P(z < -2.55) = 0.0054$. (c) $P(\bar{x} < 40) = P(z < -3.12) = 0.0009$. (d) $P(\bar{x} < 40) = P(z < -4.02) < 0.0002$. (e) Yes; if the average value based on five tests were less than 40, the patient is almost certain to have excess insulin.
15. (a) $P(x < 54) = P(z < -1.27) = 0.1020$. (b) The expected number undernourished is 2200(0.1020), or about 224. (c) $P(\bar{x} \le 60) = P(z \le -2.99) = 0.0014$. (d) $P(\bar{x} < 64.2) = P(z < 1.20) = 0.8849$. Since the sample average is above the mean, it is quite unlikely that the doe population is undernourished.
17. (a) Since x itself represents a sample mean return based on a large (random) sample of stocks, x has a distribution that is approximately normal (central limit theorem). (b) $P(1\% \le \bar{x} \le 2\%) = P(-1.63 \le z \le 1.09) = 0.8105$. (c) $P(1\% \le \bar{x} \le 2\%) = P(-3.27 \le z \le 2.18) = 0.9849$. (d) Yes. The standard deviation decreases as the sample size increases. (e) $P(\bar{x} < 1\%) = P(z < -3.27) = 0.0005$. This is very unlikely if $\mu = 1.6\%$. One would suspect that μ has slipped below 1.6%.

Section 7.6

1. $np > 5$ and $nq > 5$, where $q = 1 - p$.
3. No, $np = 4.3$ and does not satisfy the criterion that $np > 5$.

Note: Answers may differ slightly depending on how many digits are carried in the computation of the standard deviation and z.

5. $np > 5$; $nq > 5$. (a) $P(r \ge 50) = P(x \ge 49.5) = P(z \ge -27.53) \approx 1$, or almost certain. (b) $P(r \ge 50) = P(x \ge 49.5) = P(z \ge 7.78) \approx 0$, or almost impossible for a random sample.
7. $np > 5$; $nq > 5$. (a) $P(r \ge 15) = P(x \ge 14.5) = P(z \ge -2.35) = 0.9906$. (b) $P(r \ge 30) = P(x \ge 29.5) = P(z \ge 0.62) = 0.2676$. (c) $P(25 \le r \le 35) + P(24.5 \le x \le 35.5) = P(-0.37 \le z \le 1.81) = 0.6092$. (d) $P(r > 40) = P(r \ge 41) = P(x \ge 40.5) = P(z \ge 2.80) = 0.0026$.
9. $np > 5$; $nq > 5$. (a) $P(r \ge 47) = P(x \ge 46.5) = P(z \ge -1.94) = 0.9738$. (b) $P(r \le 58) = P(x \le 58.5) = P(z \le 1.75) = 0.9599$. In parts (c) and (d), let r be the number of products that succeed, and use $p = 1 - 0.80 = 0.20$. (c) $P(r \ge 15) = P(x \ge 14.5) = P(z \ge 0.40) = 0.3446$. (d) $P(r < 10) = P(r \le 9) = P(x \le 9.5) = P(z \le -1.14) = 0.1271$.
11. $np > 5$; $nq > 5$. (a) $P(r > 180) = P(x \ge 180.5) = P(z > -1.11) = 0.8665$. (b) $P(r < 200) = P(x \le 199.5) = P(z \le 1.07) = 0.8577$. (c) P(take sample *and* buy product) $= P$(take sample) $\cdot P$(buy | take sample) $= 0.222$. (d) $P(60 \le r \le 80) = P(59.5 \le x \le 80.5) = P(-1.47 \le z \le 1.37) = 0.8439$.
13. $np > 5$; $nq > 5$. (a) 0.94. (b) $P(r \le 255)$. (c) $P(r \le 255) = P(x \le 255.5) = P(z \le 1.16) = 0.8770$.

Chapter 7 Review

1. Normal probability distributions are distributions of continuous random variables. They are symmetric about the mean and bell-shaped. Most of the data fall within 3 standard deviations of the mean. The mean and median are the same.
3. No. The probability is only about 0.025.
5. (a) A normal distribution. (b) The mean μ of the x distribution. (c) $\sigma/\sqrt{n}$, where σ is the standard deviation of the x distribution. (d) They both will be approximately normal with the same mean, but the standard deviations will be $\sigma/\sqrt{50}$ and $\sigma/\sqrt{100}$, respectively.
7. (a) 0.9821. (b) 0.3156. (c) 0.2977.
9. 1.645.
11. (a) 0.89. (b) 0. (c) 0.2514.
13. (a) 0.0166. (b) 0.975.
15. (a) 0.9772. (b) 17.3 hours.
17. (a) $P(x \ge 40) = P(z \ge 0.71) = 0.2389$. (b) $P(\bar{x} \ge 40) = P(z \ge 2.14) = 0.0162$.
19. $P(98 \le \bar{x} \le 102) = P(-1.33 \le z \le 1.33) = 0.8164$.

CHAPTER 8

Section 8.1

1. True. By definition, critical values z_c are values such that c% of the area under the normal curve falls between $-z_c$ and z_c.
3. True. By definition, the margin of error is the magnitude of the difference between $\bar{x}$ and μ.
5. False. The maximum error of estimate is $E = z_c \dfrac{\sigma}{\sqrt{n}}$. As the sample size n increases, the maximal error decreases, resulting in a shorter confidence interval for μ.
7. False. The maximal error of estimate E controls the length of the confidence interval regardless of the value of $\bar{x}$.
9. μ is either in the interval 10.1 to 12.2 or not. Therefore, the probability that μ is in this interval is either 0 or 1, not 0.95.
11. (a) 3.04 gm to 3.26 gm; 0.11 gm. (b) Distribution of weights is normal with known σ. (c) There is an 80% chance that the confidence interval is one of the intervals that contains the population average weight of Allen's hummingbirds in this region. (d) $n = 28$.
13. (a) 34.62 ml/kg to 40.38 ml/kg; 2.88 ml/kg. (b) The sample size is large (30 or more) and σ is known. (c) There is a 99% chance that the confidence interval is one of the intervals that contains the population average blood plasma level for male firefighters. (d) $n = 60$.
15. (a) 125.7 to 151.3 larceny cases; 12.8 larceny cases. (b) 123.3 to 153.7 larceny cases; 15.2 larceny cases. (c) 118.4 to 158.6 larceny cases; 20.1 larceny cases. (d) Yes. (e) Yes.
17. (a) \$53,871 to \$64,009; \$5069. (b) \$55,138 to \$62,742; \$3802. (c) \$56,175 to \$61,705; \$2765. (d) Yes. (e) Yes.

19. (a) The mean rounds to the value given. (b) Using the rounded value of part (a), the 75% interval is from 34.19 thousand to 37.81 thousand. (c) Yes. 30 thousand dollars is below the lower bound of the 75% confidence interval. We can say with 75% confidence that the mean lies between 34.19 thousand and 37.81 thousand. (d) Yes. 40 thousand is above the upper bound of the 75% confidence interval. (e) 33.41 thousand to 38.59 thousand. We can say with 90% confidence that the mean lies between 33.4 thousand and 38.6 thousand dollars. 30 thousand is below the lower bound and 40 thousand is above the upper bound.

Section 8.2

1. 2.110.
3. 1.721.
5. $t = 0$.
7. $n = 10$, with $d.f. = 9$.
9. Shorter. For $d.f. = 40$, z_c is less than t_c, and the resulting margin of error E is smaller.
11. (a) The mean and standard deviation round to the values given. (b) Using the rounded values for the mean and standard deviation given in part (a), the interval is from 1249 to 1295.
13. (a) Use a calculator. (b) 74.7 pounds to 107.3 pounds.
15. (a) The mean and standard deviation round to the given values. (b) 8.41 to 11.49. (c) Since all values in the 99.9% confidence interval are above 6, we can be almost certain that this patient no longer has a calcium deficiency.
17. (a) Boxplots differ in length of interquartile box, location of median, and length of whiskers. The boxplots come from different samples. (b) Yes; no; for 95% confidence intervals, we expect about 95% of the samples to generate intervals that contain the mean of the population.
19. (a) The mean and standard deviation round to the given values. (b) 21.6 to 28.8. (c) 19.4 to 31.0. (d) Using both confidence intervals, we can say that the P/E for Bank One is well below the population average. The P/E for AT&T Wireless is well above the population average. The P/E for Disney is within both confidence intervals. It appears that the P/E for Disney is close to the population average P/E. (e) By the central limit theorem, when n is large, the $\bar{x}$ distribution is approximately normal. In general, $n \geq 30$ is considered large.
21. (a) $d.f. = 30$; 43.58 to 46.82; 43.26 to 47.14; 42.58 to 47.82. (b) 43.63 to 46.77; 43.33 to 47.07; 42.74 to 47.66. (c) Yes; the respective intervals based on the Student's t distribution are slightly longer. (d) For Student's t, $d.f. = 80$; 44.22 to 46.18; 44.03 to 46.37; 43.65 to 46.75. For standard normal, 44.23 to 46.17; 44.05 to 46.35; 43.68 to 46.72. The intervals using the t distribution are still slightly longer than the corresponding intervals using the standard normal distribution. However, with a larger sample size, the differences between the two methods is less pronounced.

Section 8.3

1. $\hat{p} = r/n$.
3. (a) No. (b) The difference between $\hat{p}$ and p. In other words, the margin of error is the difference between results based on a random sample and results based on a population.
5. (a) $\hat{p} = 39/62 = 0.6290$. (b) 0.51 to 0.75. If this experiment were repeated many times, about 95% of the intervals would contain p. (c) Both np and nq are greater than 5. If either is less than 5, the normal curve will not necessarily give a good approximation to the binomial.
7. (a) $\hat{p} = 1619/5222 = 0.3100$. (b) 0.29 to 0.33. If we repeat the survey with many different samples of 5222 dwellings, about 99% of the intervals will contain p. (c) Both np and nq are greater than 5. If either is less than 5, the normal curve will not necessarily give a good approximation to the binomial.
9. (a) $\hat{p} = 0.5420$. (b) 0.53 to 0.56. (c) Yes. Both np and nq are greater than 5.
11. (a) $\hat{p} = 0.0304$. (b) 0.02 to 0.05. (c) Yes. Both np and nq are greater than 5.
13. (a) $\hat{p} = 0.8603$. (b) 0.84 to 0.89. (c) A recent study shows that 86% of women shoppers remained loyal to their favorite supermarket last year. The margin of error was 2.5 percentage points.
15. (a) $\hat{p} = 0.25$. (b) 0.22 to 0.28. (c) A survey of 1000 large corporations has shown that 25% will choose a nonsmoking job candidate over an equally qualified smoker. The margin of error was 2.7%.
17. (a) 208. (b) 68.
19. (a) 666. (b) 662.

Chapter 8 Review

1. See text.
3. (a) No, the probability that μ is in the interval is either 0 or 1. (b) Yes, 99% confidence intervals are constructed in such a way that 99% of all such confidence intervals based on random samples of the designated size will contain μ.
5. Interval for a mean; 176.91 to 180.49.
7. Interval for a mean.
   (a) Use a calculator. (b) 64.1 to 84.3.
9. Interval for a proportion; 0.50 to 0.54.
11. Interval for a proportion.
   (a) $\hat{p} = 0.4072$. (b) 0.333 to 0.482.

CHAPTER 9

Section 9.1

1. See text.
3. No, if we fail to reject the null hypothesis, we have not proven it beyond all doubt. We have failed only to find sufficient evidence to reject it.
5. (a) H_0: $\mu = 60$ kg. (b) H_1: $\mu < 60$ kg. (c) H_1: $\mu >$ 60 kg. (d) H_1: $\mu \neq 60$ kg. (e) For part b, the P-value area region is on the left. For part c, the P-value area is on the right. For part d, the P-value area is on both sides of the mean.
7. (a) H_0: $\mu = 16.4$ feet. (b) H_1: $\mu > 16.4$ feet. (c) H_1: $\mu < 16.4$ feet. (d) H_1: $\mu \neq 16.4$ feet. (e) For part b, the P-value area is on the right. For part c, the P-value

area is on the left. For part d, the P-value area is on both sides of the mean.

9. (a) $\alpha = 0.01$; H_0: $\mu = 4.7\%$; H_1: $\mu > 4.7\%$; right-tailed. (b) Normal; $\bar{x} = 5.38$; $z \approx 0.90$. (c) P-value $\approx$ 0.1841; on standard normal curve, shade area to the right of 0.90. (d) P-value of $0.1841 > 0.01$ for α; fail to reject H_0. (e) Insufficient evidence at the 0.01 level to reject claim that average yield for bank stocks equals average yield for all stocks.
11. (a) $\alpha = 0.01$; H_0: $\mu = 4.55$ grams; H_1: $\mu < 4.55$ grams; left-tailed. (b) Normal; $\bar{x} = 3.75$ grams; $z \approx -2.80$. (c) P-value ≈ 0.0026; on standard normal curve, shade area to the left of -2.80. (d) P-value of $0.0026 \leq 0.01$ for α; reject H_0. (e) The sample evidence is sufficient at the 0.01 level to justify rejecting H_0. It seems that the hummingbirds in the Grand Canyon region have a lower average weight.
13. (a) $\alpha = 0.01$; H_0: $\mu = 11\%$; H_1: $\mu \neq 11\%$; two-tailed. (b) Normal; $\bar{x} = 12.5\%$; $z = 1.20$. (c) P-value $= 2(0.1151) = 0.2302$; on standard normal curve, shade area to the right of 1.20 and to the left of -1.20. (d) P-value of $0.2302 > 0.01$ for α; fail to reject H_0. (e) There is insufficient evidence at the 0.01 level to reject H_0. It seems that the average hail damage to wheat crops in Weld County matches the national average.

Section 9.2

1. The P-value for a two-tailed test of μ is twice that for a one-tailed test, based on the same sample data and null hypothesis.
3. $d.f. = n - 1$.
5. Yes. When P-value < 0.01, it is also true that P-value < 0.05.
7. (a) $\alpha = 0.01$; H_0: $\mu = 16.4$ feet; H_1: $\mu > 16.4$ feet. (b) Standard normal; $z \approx 1.54$. (c) P-value ≈ 0.0618; on standard normal curve, shade area to the right of $z \approx 1.54$. (d) P-value of $0.0618 > 0.01$ for α; fail to reject H_0. (e) At the 1% level, there is insufficient evidence to say that the average storm level is increasing.
9. (a) $\alpha = 0.05$; H_0: $\mu = 41.7$; H_1: $\mu \neq 41.7$. (b) Standard normal; $z \approx -1.99$. (c) P-value $\approx 2(0.0233) \approx 0.0466$; on standard normal curve, shade area to the right of 1.99 and to the left of -1.99. (d) P-value of $0.0466 \leq 0.05$ for α; reject H_0. (e) At the 5% level, there is sufficient evidence to say that the average number of e-mails is different with the new priority system.
11. (a) $\alpha = 0.01$; H_0: $\mu = 1.75$ years; H_1: $\mu > 1.75$ years. (b) Student's t, $d.f. = 45$; $t \approx 2.481$. (c) $0.005 <$ P-value < 0.010; on t graph, shade area to the right of 2.481. From TI-84, P-value ≈ 0.0084. (d) Entire P-interval ≤ 0.01 for α; reject H_0. (e) At the 1% level of significance, the sample data indicate that the average age of the Minnesota region coyotes is higher than 1.75 years.
13. (a) $\alpha = 0.05$; H_0: $\mu = 19.4$; H_1: $\mu \neq 19.4$ (b) Student's t, $d.f. = 35$; $t \approx -1.731$. (c) $0.050 <$ P-value < 0.100; on t graph, shade area to the right of 1.731 and to the left of -1.731. From TI-84, P-value ≈ 0.0923. (d) P-value interval > 0.05 for α; fail to reject H_0. (e) At the 5% level of significance, the sample evidence does not support rejecting the claim that the average P/E of socially responsible funds is different from that of the S&P stock index.
15. i. Use a calculator. Rounded values are used in part ii.
    ii. (a) $\alpha = 0.05$; H_0: $\mu = 4.8$; H_1: $\mu < 4.8$. (b) Student's t, $d.f. = 5$; $t \approx -3.499$. (c) $0.005 <$ P-value < 0.010; on t graph, shade area to the left of -3.499. From TI-84, P-value ≈ 0.0086. (d) P-value interval ≤ 0.05 for α; reject H_0. (e) At the 5% level of significance, sample evidence supports the claim that the average RBC count for this patient is less than 4.8.
17. i. Use a calculator. Rounded values are used in part ii.
    ii. (a) $\alpha = 0.01$; H_0: $\mu = 67$; H_1: $\mu \neq 67$. (b) Student's t, $d.f. = 15$; $t \approx -1.962$. (c) $0.050 <$ P-value < 0.100; on t graph, shade area to the right of 1.962 and to the left of -1.962. From TI-84, P-value ≈ 0.0686. (d) P-value interval > 0.01; fail to reject H_0. (e) At the 1% level of significance, the sample evidence does not support the claim that the average thickness of slab avalanches in Vail is different from that in Canada.
19. i. Use a calculator. Rounded values are used in part ii.
    ii. (a) $\alpha = 0.05$; H_0: $\mu = 8.8$; H_1: $\mu \neq 8.8$. (b) Student's t, $d.f. = 13$; $t \approx -1.337$. (c) $0.200 <$ P-value < 0.250; on t graph, shade area to the right of 1.337 and to the left of -1.337. From TI-84, P-value ≈ 0.2042. (d) P-value interval $>$ 0.05; fail to reject H_0. (e) At the 5% level of significance, we cannot conclude that the average catch is different from 8.8 fish per day.
21. (a) The P-value of a one-tailed test is smaller. For a two-tailed test, the P-value is doubled because it includes the area in both tails. (b) Yes; the P-value of a one-tailed test is smaller, so it might be smaller than α, whereas the P-value of a corresponding two-tailed test may be larger than α. (c) Yes; if the two-tailed P-value is less than α, the smaller one-tail area is also less than α. (d) Yes, the conclusions can be different. The conclusion based on the two-tailed test is more conservative in the sense that the sample data must be more extreme (differ more from H_0) in order to reject H_0.
23. (a) For $\alpha = 0.01$, confidence level $c = 0.99$; interval from 20.28 to 23.72; hypothesized $\mu = 20$ is not in the interval; reject H_0. (b) H_0: $\mu = 20$; H_1: $\mu \neq 20$; $z = 3.000$; P-value ≈ 0.0026; P-value of $0.0026 \leq 0.01$ for α; reject H_0; conclusions are the same.
25. Critical value $z_0 = 2.33$; critical region is values to the right of 2.33; since the sample statistic $z = 1.54$ is not in the critical region, fail to reject H_0. At the 1% level, there is insufficient evidence to say that the average storm level is increasing. Conclusion is same as with P-value method.
27. Critical values $z_0 = \pm 1.96$; critical regions are values to the left of -1.96 together with values to the right of 1.96. Since the sample test statistic $z = -1.99$ is in the critical region, reject H_0. At the 5% level, there is

sufficient evidence to say that the average number of e-mails is different with the new priority system. Conclusion is same as with P-value method.

29. Critical value is $t_0 = 2.412$ for one-tailed test with $d.f. = 45$; critical region is values to the right of 2.412. Since the sample test statistic $t = 2.481$ is in the critical region, reject H_0. At the 1% level, the sample data indicate that the average age of Minnesota region coyotes is higher than 1.75 years. Conclusion is same as with P-value method.

Section 9.3

1. For the conditions $np > 5$ and $nq > 5$, use the value of p from H_0. Note that $q = 1 - p$.
3. Yes. The corresponding P-value for a one-tailed test is half that for a two-tailed test, so the P-value of the one-tailed test is also less than 0.01.
5. i. (a) $\alpha = 0.01$; H_0: $p = 0.301$; H_1: $p < 0.301$. (b) Standard normal; yes, $np \approx 64.7 > 5$ and $nq \approx 150.3 > 5$; $\hat{p} \approx 0.214$; $z \approx -2.78$. (c) P-value ≈ 0.0027; on standard normal curve, shade area to the left of -2.78. (d) P-value of $0.0027 \le 0.01$ for α; reject H_0. (e) At the 1% level of significance, the sample data indicate that the population proportion of numbers with a leading "1" in the revenue file is less than 0.301, predicted by Benford's Law.
   ii. Yes; the revenue data file seems to include more numbers with higher first nonzero digits than Benford's Law predicts.
   iii. We have not proved H_0 to be false. However, because our sample data led us to reject H_0 and to conclude that there are too few numbers with a leading digit of 1, more investigation is merited.
7. (a) $\alpha = 0.01$; H_0: $p = 0.70$; H_1: $p \ne 0.70$. (b) Standard normal; $\hat{p} = 0.75$; $z \approx 0.62$. (c) P-value $= 2(0.2676) = 0.5352$; on standard normal curve, shade areas to the right of 0.62 and to the left of -0.62. (d) P-value of $0.5352 > 0.01$ for α; fail to reject H_0. (e) At the 1% level of significance, we cannot say that the population proportion of arrests of males aged 15 to 34 in Rock Springs is different from 70%.
9. (a) $\alpha = 0.01$; H_0: $p = 0.77$; H_1: $p < 0.77$. (b) Standard normal; $\hat{p} \approx 0.5556$; $z \approx -2.65$. (c) P-value ≈ 0.004; on standard normal curve, shade area to the left of -2.65. (d) P-value of $0.004 \le 0.01$ for α; reject H_0. (e) At the 1% level of significance, the data show that the population proportion of driver fatalities related to alcohol is less than 77% in Kit Carson County.
11. (a) $\alpha = 0.01$; H_0: $p = 0.50$; H_1: $p < 0.50$. (b) Standard normal; $\hat{p} \approx 0.2941$; $z \approx -2.40$. (c) P-value $= 0.0082$; on standard normal curve, shade region to the left of -2.40. (d) P-value of $0.0082 \le 0.01$ for α; reject H_0. (e) At the 1% level of significance, the data indicate that the population proportion of female wolves is now less than 50% in the region.
13. (a) $\alpha = 0.01$; H_0: $p = 0.261$; H_1: $p \ne 0.261$. (b) Standard normal; $\hat{p} \approx 0.1924$; $z \approx -2.78$. (c) P-value $= 2(0.0027) = 0.0054$; on standard normal curve, shade area to the right of 2.78 and to the left of -2.78. (d) P-value of $0.0054 \le 0.01$ for α; reject H_0. (e) At the 1% level of significance, the sample data indicate that the population proportion of the five-syllable sequence is different from that of Plato's *Republic*.
15. (a) $\alpha = 0.01$; H_0: $p = 0.47$; H_1: $p > 0.47$. (b) Standard normal; $\hat{p} \approx 0.4871$; $z \approx 1.09$. (c) P-value $= 0.1379$; on standard normal curve, shade area to the right of 1.09. (d) P-value of $0.1379 > 0.01$ for α; fail to reject H_0. (e) At the 1% level of significance, there is insufficient evidence to support the claim that the population proportion of customers loyal to Chevrolet is more than 47%.
17. (a) $\alpha = 0.05$; H_0: $p = 0.092$; H_1: $p > 0.092$. (b) Standard normal; $\hat{p} \approx 0.1480$; $z \approx 2.71$. (c) P-value $= 0.0034$; on standard normal curve, shade region to the right of 2.71. (d) P-value of $0.0034 \le 0.05$ for α; reject H_0. (e) At the 5% level of significance, the data indicate that the population proportion of students with hypertension during final exams week is higher than 9.2%.
19. (a) $\alpha = 0.01$; H_0: $p = 0.82$; H_1: $p \ne 0.82$. (b) Standard normal; $\hat{p} \approx 0.7671$; $z \approx -1.18$. (c) P-value $= 2(0.1190) = 0.2380$; on standard normal curve, shade area to the right of 1.18 and to the left of -1.18. (d) P-value of $0.2380 > 0.01$ for α; fail to reject H_0. (e) At the 1% level of significance, the evidence is insufficient to indicate that the population proportion of extroverts among college student government leaders is different from 82%.
21. Critical value is $z_0 = -2.33$. The critical region consists of values less than -2.33. The sample test statistic $z = -2.65$ is in the critical region, so we reject H_0. This result is consistent with the P-value conclusion.

Chapter 9 Review

1. Look at the original x distribution. If it is normal or $n \ge 30$, and σ is known, use the standard normal distribution. If the x distribution is mound-shaped or $n \ge 30$, and σ is unknown, use the Student's t distribution. The $d.f.$ is determined by the application.
3. A larger sample size increases the $|z|$ or $|t|$ value of the sample test statistic.
5. (a) $\alpha = 0.05$; H_0: $\mu = 11.1$; H_1: $\mu \ne 11.1$. (b) Standard normal; $z = -3.00$. (c) P-value $= 0.0026$; on standard normal curve, shade area to the right of 3.00 and to the left of -3.00. (d) P-value of $0.0026 \le 0.05$ for α; reject H_0. (e) At the 5% level of significance, the evidence is sufficient to say that the miles driven per vehicle in Chicago is different from the national average.
7. (a) $\alpha = 0.01$; H_0: $\mu = 0.8$; H_1: $\mu > 0.8$. (b) Student's t, $d.f. = 8$; $t \approx 4.390$. (c) $0.0005 < P\text{-value} < 0.005$; on t graph, shade area to the right of 4.390. From TI-84, P-value ≈ 0.0012. (d) P-value interval ≤ 0.01 for α; reject H_0. (e) At the 1% level of significance, the evidence is sufficient to say that the Toylot claim of 0.8 A is too low.
9. (a) $\alpha = 0.01$; H_0: $p = 0.60$; H_1: $p < 0.60$. (b) Standard normal; $z = -3.01$. (c) P-value $= 0.0013$; on standard normal curve, shade area to the left of -3.01. (d) P-value of $0.0013 \le 0.01$ for α; reject H_0.

(e) At the 1% level of significance, the evidence is sufficient to show that the mortality rate has dropped.

11. (a) $\alpha = 0.05$; H_0: $\mu = 7$ oz; H_1: $\mu \neq 7$ oz. (b) Student's t, $d.f. = 7$; $t \approx 1.697$. (c) $0.100 < P\text{-value} < 0.150$; on t graph, shade area to the right of 1.697 and to the left of -1.697. From TI-84, P-value ≈ 0.1335. (d) P-value interval > 0.05 for α; do not reject H_0. (e) At the 5% level of significance, the evidence is insufficient to show that the population mean amount of coffee per cup is different from 7 oz.

CUMULATIVE REVIEW PROBLEMS

1. $\mu = 0$; $\sigma = 1$.
2. 95%.
3. Essay based on material from Chapter 7 and Section 1.2.
4. (a) $\sigma \approx 1.7$. (b) 0.1314. (c) 0.1075.
5. (a) Yes. Both np and nq are greater than 5.
   (b) $\mu \approx 73.5$ and $\sigma \approx 5.6$.
   (c) $P(r \geq 65) \approx P(x \geq 64.5) \approx P(z \geq -1.61) \approx 0.9463$.
6. (a) Because of the large sample size, the central limit theorem describes the $\bar{x}$ distribution (approximately).
   (b) $P(\bar{x} \leq 6820) = P(z \leq -2.75) = 0.0030$.
   (c) The probability that the average white blood cell count for 50 healthy adults is as low as or lower than 6820 is very small, 0.0030. Based on this result, it would be reasonable to gather additional facts.
7. (a) i. $\alpha = 0.01$; H_0: $\mu = 2.0$ ug/L; H_1: $\mu > 2.0$ ug/L.
   ii. Standard normal; $z = 2.53$.
   iii. P-value ≈ 0.0057; on standard normal curve, shade area to the right of 2.53.
   iv. P-value of $0.0057 \leq 0.01$ for α; reject H_0.
   v. At the 1% level of significance, the evidence is sufficient to say that the population mean discharge level of lead is higher.
   (b) 2.13 ug/L to 2.99 ug/L. (c) $n = 48$.
8. (a) Use rounded results to compute t in part (b).
   (b) i. $\alpha = 0.05$; H_0: $\mu = 10\%$; H_1: $\mu > 10\%$.
   ii. Student's t, $d.f. = 11$; $t \approx 1.248$.
   iii. $0.100 < P\text{-value} < 0.125$; on t graph, shade area to the right of 1.248. From TI-84, P-value $\approx$ 0.1190.
   iv. P-value interval > 0.05 for α; fail to reject H_0.
   v. At the 5% level of significance, the evidence does not indicate that the patient is asymptomatic.
   (c) 9.27% to 11.71%.
9. (a) i. $\alpha = 0.05$; H_0: $p = 0.10$; H_1: $p \neq 0.10$; yes, $np > 5$ and $nq > 5$; necessary to use normal approximation to the binominal.
   ii. Standard normal; $\hat{p} \approx 0.147$; $z = 1.29$.
   iii. P-value $= 2P(z > 1.29) \approx 0.1970$; on standard normal curve, shade area to the right of 1.29 and to the left of -1.29.
   iv. P-value of $0.1970 > 0.05$ for α; fail to reject H_0.
   v. At the 5% level of significance, the data do not indicate any difference from the national average for the population proportion of crime victims.
   (b) 0.063 to 0.231. (c) From sample, $p \approx \hat{p} \approx 0.147$; $n = 193$.
10. (a) Essay. (b) Outline of study.
11. Essay.

CHAPTER 10

Section 10.1

1. Paired data are dependent.
3. H_0: $\mu_d = 0$; that is, the mean of the differences is 0, so there is no difference.
5. $d.f. = n - 1$.
7. (a) $\alpha = 0.05$; H_0: $\mu_d = 0$; H_1: $\mu_d \neq 0$. (b) Student's t, $d.f. = 7$; $\bar{d} \approx 2.25$; $t \approx 0.818$. (c) $0.250 < P\text{-value} < 0.500$; on t graph, shade area to the left of -0.818 and to the right of 0.818. From TI-84, P-value ≈ 0.4402. (d) P-value interval > 0.05 for α; fail to reject H_0. (e) At the 5% level of significance, the evidence is insufficient to claim a difference in population mean percentage increases for corporate revenue and CEO salary.
9. (a) $\alpha = 0.01$; H_0: $\mu_d = 0$; H_1: $\mu_d > 0$. (b) Student's t, $d.f. = 4$; $\bar{d} \approx 12.6$; $t \approx 1.243$. (c) $0.125 < P\text{-value} < 0.250$; on t graph, shade area to the right of 1.243. From TI-84, P-value ≈ 0.1408. (d) P-value interval > 0.01 for α; fail to reject H_0. (e) At the 1% level of significance, the evidence is insufficient to claim that the average peak wind gusts are higher in January.
11. (a) $\alpha = 0.05$; H_0: $\mu_d = 0$; H_1: $\mu_d > 0$. (b) Student's t, $d.f. = 7$; $\bar{d} \approx 6.125$; $t \approx 1.762$. (c) $0.050 < P\text{-value} < 0.075$; on t graph, shade area to the right of 1.762. From TI-84, P-value ≈ 0.0607. (d) P-value interval > 0.05 for α; fail to reject H_0. (e) At the 5% level of significance, the evidence is insufficient to indicate that the population average percentage of male wolves is higher in winter.
13. (a) $\alpha = 0.05$; H_0: $\mu_d = 0$; H_1: $\mu_d > 0$. (b) Student's t, $d.f. = 8$; $\bar{d} = 2.0$; $t \approx 1.333$. (c) $0.100 < P\text{-value} < 0.125$; on t graph, shade area to the right of 1.333. From TI-84, P-value ≈ 0.1096. (d) P-value interval $>$ 0.05 for α; fail to reject H_0. (e) At the 5% level of significance, the evidence is insufficient to claim that the population score on the last round is higher than that on the first.
15. i. Use a calculator. Non-rounded results are used in part ii.
    ii. (a) $\alpha = 0.05$; H_0: $\mu_d = 0$; H_1: $\mu_d > 0$. (b) Student's t, $d.f. = 35$; $\bar{d} \approx 2.472$; $t \approx 1.223$. (c) $0.100 < P\text{-value} < 0.125$; on t graph, shade area to the right of 1.223. From TI-84, P-value ≈ 0.1147.
    (d) P-value interval > 0.05 for α; fail to reject H_0.
    (e) At the 5% level of significance, the evidence is insufficient to claim that the population mean cost of living index for housing is higher than that for groceries.
17. For a two-tailed test with $\alpha = 0.05$ and $d.f. = 7$, the critical values are $\pm t_0 = \pm 2.365$. The sample test statistic $t = 0.818$ is between -2.365 and 2.365, so we do not reject H_0. This conclusion is the same as that reached by the P-value method.

Section 10.2

1. $\bar{x}_1 - \bar{x}_2$.
3. H_0: $\mu_1 = \mu_2$ or H_0: $\mu_1 - \mu_2 = 0$.
5. Josh's, because the critical value t_c is smaller based on larger $d.f.$; Kendra's, because her value for t_c is larger.

7. (a) (i) $\alpha = 0.01$; H_0: $\mu_1 = \mu_2$; H_1: $\mu_1 > \mu_2$. (ii) Standard normal; $\bar{x}_1 - \bar{x}_2 = 0.7$; $z \approx 2.57$. (iii) P-value $= P(z > 2.57) \approx 0.0051$; on standard normal curve, shade area to the right of 2.57. (iv) P-value of $0.0051 \le 0.01$ for α; reject H_0. (v) At the 1% level of significance, the evidence is sufficient to indicate that the population mean REM sleep time for children is more than that for adults. (b) 0.07 to 1.33; Interval contains values that are all positive. At the 98% confidence level, it appears that the population mean REM sleep time for children is greater than that for adults.
9. (a) (i) $\alpha = 0.05$; H_0: $\mu_1 = \mu_2$; H_1: $\mu_1 \neq \mu_2$. (ii) Standard normal; $\bar{x}_1 - \bar{x}_2 = 0.6$; $z \approx 2.16$. (iii) P-value $= 2P(z > 2.16) \approx 2(0.0154) = 0.0308$; on standard normal curve, shade area to the right of 2.16 and to the left of -2.16. (iv) P-value of $0.0308 \le 0.05$ for α; reject H_0. (v) At the 5% level of significance, the evidence is sufficient to show that there is a difference between mean responses regarding preference for camping or fishing. (b) 0.06 to 1.14; Interval contains values that are all positive. At the 95% confidence level, it appears that the population mean response for fishing is higher than that for camping.
11. Use rounded results to compute t.
(a) (i) $\alpha = 0.01$; H_0: $\mu_1 = \mu_2$; H_1: $\mu_1 < \mu_2$. (ii) Student's t, $d.f. = 9$; $\bar{x}_1 - \bar{x}_2 = -0.36$; $t \approx -0.965$.
(iii) $0.125 < P\text{-value} < 0.250$; on t graph, shade area to the left of -0.965. For TI-84, $d.f. \approx 19.96$; P-value $\approx$ 0.1731. (iv) P-value > 0.01 for α; do not reject H_0.
(v) At the 1% level of significance, the evidence is insufficient to indicate that violent crime in the Rocky Mountain region is higher than in New England.
(b) $d.f. = 9$; $E \approx 1.05$; -1.41 to 0.69; Interval contains both negative and positive values. At the 98% confidence level, we cannot conclude that the population mean violent crime rate in the Rocky Mountain region is different from that in New England.
13. (a) (i) $\alpha = 0.05$; H_0: $\mu_1 = \mu_2$; H_1: $\mu_1 \neq \mu_2$.
(ii) Student's t, $d.f. = 29$; $\bar{x}_1 - \bar{x}_2 = -9.7$; $t \approx -0.751$.
(iii) $0.250 < P\text{-value} < 0.500$; on t graph, shade area to the right of 0.751 and to the left of -0.751. For TI-84, $d.f. \approx 57.92$; P-value ≈ 0.4556. (iv) P-value interval $>$ 0.05 for α; do not reject H_0. (v) At the 5% level of significance, the evidence is insufficient to indicate that there is a difference between the control and experimental groups in the mean score on the vocabulary portion of the test. (b) $d.f. = 29$; $E \approx 26.4$; -36.1 to 16.7; Interval contains both negative and positive values. At the 95% confidence level, we cannot conclude that the population mean vocabulary score was different between the two groups before instruction began.
15. Use rounded results to compute t.
(a) (i) $\alpha = 0.05$; H_0: $\mu_1 = \mu_2$; H_1: $\mu_1 \neq \mu_2$. (ii) Student's t, $d.f. = 14$; $\bar{x}_1 - \bar{x}_2 = 0.82$; $t \approx 0.869$.
(iii) $0.250 < P\text{-value} < 0.500$; on t graph, shade area to the right of 0.869 and to the left of -0.869. For TI-84, $d.f. \approx 28.81$; P-value ≈ 0.394. (iv) P-value interval $>$ 0.05 for α; do not reject H_0. (v) At the 5% level of significance, the evidence is insufficient to indicate that there is a difference in the mean number of cases of fox rabies between the two regions. (b) $d.f. = 14$; $E \approx 2.02$; -1.2 to 2.84; Interval contains both negative and positive values. At the 95% confidence level, we cannot conclude that there is any difference in the population mean number of fox rabies cases in the two regions.
17. Use rounded results to compute t.
(a) (i) $\alpha = 0.05$; H_0: $\mu_1 = \mu_2$; H_1: $\mu_1 \neq \mu_2$.
(ii) Student's t, $d.f. = 6$; $\bar{x}_1 - \bar{x}_2 = -1.64$; $t \approx -1.041$.
(iii) $0.250 < P\text{-value} < 0.500$; on t graph, shade area to the right of 1.041 and to the left of -1.041. For TI-84, $d.f. \approx 12.28$; P-value ≈ 0.3179. (iv) P-value interval $>$ 0.05 for α; do not reject H_0. (v) At the 5% level of significance, the evidence is insufficient to indicate that the mean time lost due to hot tempers is different from time lost due to technical workers' attitudes. (b) $d.f. = 6$; $E \approx 3.85$; -5.49 to 2.21; Interval contains both negative and positive values. At the 95% confidence level, we cannot conclude that there is any difference in the population mean time lost due to the two types of inappropriate behavior.
19. (a) $d.f. = 19.96$ (Some software will truncate this to 19.)
(b) $d.f. = 9$; the convention of using the smaller of $n_1 - 1$ and $n_2 - 1$ leads to a $d.f.$ that is always less than or equal to that computed by Satterthwaite's formula.
21. H_0: $\mu_1 = \mu_2$; H_1: $\mu_1 < \mu_2$; for $d.f. = 9$, $\alpha \approx 0.01$ in the *one-tail area* row, the critical value $t_0 = -2.821$; sample test statistic $t = -0.965$ is not in the critical region; fail to reject H_0. This result is consistent with that obtained by the P-value method.

Section 10.3

1. $\hat{p}_1 - \hat{p}_2$, where $\hat{p}_1 = r_1/n_1$ and $\hat{p}_2 = r_2/n_2$.
3. H_1: $p_1 > p_2$; H_1: $p_1 - p_2 > 0$.
5. (a) $\alpha = 0.05$; H_0: $p_1 = p_2$; H_1: $p_1 \neq p_2$. (b) Standard normal; $\bar{p} \approx 0.2911$; $\hat{p}_1 - \hat{p}_2 \approx -0.052$; $z \approx -1.13$.
(c) P-value $\approx 2P(z < -1.13) \approx 2(0.1292) = 0.2584$; on standard normal curve, shade area to the right of 1.13 and to the left of -1.13. (d) P-value of $0.2584 > 0.05$ for α; fail to reject H_0. (e) At the 5% level of significance, there is insufficient evidence to conclude that the population proportion of women favoring more tax dollars for the arts is different from the proportion of men.
7. (a) $\alpha = 0.05$; H_0: $p_1 = p_2$; H_1: $p_1 < p_2$. (b) Standard normal; $\bar{p} \approx 0.2189$; $\hat{p}_1 - \hat{p}_2 \approx -0.074$; $z \approx -2.06$.
(c) P-value $\approx P(z < -2.06) \approx 0.0197$; on standard normal curve, shade area to the left of -2.04. (d) P-value of $0.0197 \le 0.05$ for α; reject H_0. (e) At the 5% level of significance, there is sufficient evidence to conclude that the population proportion of trusting people in Chicago is higher for the older group.
9. (a) $\alpha = 0.01$; H_0: $p_1 = p_2$; H_1: $p_1 < p_2$. (b) Standard normal; $\bar{p} = 0.42$; $\hat{p}_1 - \hat{p}_2 = -0.10$; $z \approx -1.43$.
(c) P-value $\approx P(z < -1.43) \approx 0.0764$; on standard normal curve, shade area to the left of -1.43. (d) P-value of $0.0764 > 0.01$ for α; fail to reject H_0. (e) At the 1% level of significance, there is insufficient evidence to conclude that the population proportion of adults who believe in extraterrestrials and who attended college is higher than the proportion who did not attend college.

11. For a two-tailed test with $\alpha = 0.05$, the critical values are $\pm z_0 = \pm 1.96$. The sample test statistic $z = -1.13$ is between -1.96 and 1.96, so we do not reject H_0. This conclusion is the same as that reached by the *P*-value method.
13. (a) $\hat{\sigma} = 0.0232$; $E = 0.0599$; the interval is from 0.67 to 0.79. (b) The confidence interval contains values that are all positive, so we can be 99% sure that $p_1 > p_2$.
15. (a) $\hat{p}_1 = 0.3095$; $\hat{p}_2 = 0.1184$; $\hat{\sigma} = 0.0413$; interval from 0.085 to 0.297. (b) The interval contains numbers that are all positive. At the 99% confidence level, a greater proportion of hogans occur in Fort Defiance.
17. (a) Based on the same data, a 99% confidence interval is longer than a 95% confidence interval. Therefore, if the 95% confidence interval has both positive and negative values, so will the 99% confidence interval. However, for the same data, a 90% confidence interval is shorter than a 95% confidence interval. The 90% confidence interval might contain only positive or only negative values even if the 95% interval contains both. (b) Based on the same data, a 99% confidence interval is longer than a 95% confidence interval. Even if the 95% confidence interval contains values that are all positive, the longer 99% interval could contain both positive and negative values. Since, for the same data, a 90% confidence interval is shorter than a 95% confidence interval, if the 95% confidence interval contains only positive values, so will the 90% confidence interval.

Chapter 10 Review

1. Two random samples are independent if the selection of sample data from one population is completely unrelated to the selection of sample data from the other population.
3. Difference of means.
(a) Use a calculator. (b) $d.f. \approx 71$; to use Table 4, round down to $d.f. \approx 70$; $E \approx 0.83$; interval from -0.06 to 1.6. (c) Because the interval contains both positive and negative values, we cannot conclude at the 95% confidence level that there is any difference in soil water content in the two fields. (d) Student's *t* distribution, because σ_1 and σ_2 are unknown. Both samples are large, so no assumptions about the original distributions are needed. (e) (i) $\alpha = 0.01$; H_0: $\mu_1 = \mu_2$; H_1: $\mu_1 > \mu_2$. (ii) Student's *t*; $d.f. = 71$ (use $d.f. = 70$ in Table 4 of the Appendix); $t \approx 1.841$. (iii) $0.025 < P\text{-value} < 0.050$; on *t* graph, shade area to the right of 1.841. For TI-84, $d.f. \approx 140.50$; $P\text{-value} \approx 0.034$. (iv) $P\text{-value} > 0.01$ for α; fail to reject H_0. (v) At the 1% level of significance, the evidence does not show that the population mean soil water content of the first field is higher than that of the second.
5. Difference of means.
(a) $d.f. \approx 17$; $E \approx 2.5$; interval from 5.5 to 10.5 lb.
(b) Yes. The interval contains values that are all positive. At the 75% level of confidence, it appears that the average weight of adult male wolves from the Northwest Territories is greater. (c) (i) $\alpha = 0.01$; H_0: $\mu_1 = \mu_2$; H_1: $\mu_1 \neq \mu_2$. (ii) Student's *t*; $d.f. = 17$; $t \approx 3.743$.
(iii) $0.001 < P\text{-value} < 0.010$; on *t* graph, shade area to the right of 3.743 and to the left of -3.743. (iv) $P\text{-value} \leq 0.01$ for α; reject H_0. (v) At the 1% level of significance, the evidence is sufficient to conclude that the average weight of adult male wolves in the Northwest Territories is different from that of Alaska wolves.
7. Difference of proportions.
(a) $\hat{p}_1 = 0.8495$; $\hat{p}_2 = 0.8916$; -0.1409 to 0.0567.
(b) No. The interval contains both negative and positive numbers. We do not detect a difference in the proportions at the 95% confidence level. (c) (i) $\alpha = 0.05$; H_0: $p_1 = p_2$; H_1: $p_1 \neq p_2$. (ii) Normal distribution; $z \approx -0.83$. (iii) $P\text{-value} = 2(0.2033) = 0.4066$; on the normal graph, shade area to the left of -0.83 and to the right of 0.83. (iv) *P*-value of $0.4066 > \alpha = 0.05$; fail to reject H_0. (v) At the 5% level of significance, there is insufficient evidence to conclude that the proportion of accurate responses from face-to-face interviews differs from the proportion for telephone interviews.
9. (i) $\alpha = 0.05$; H_0: $\mu_d = 0$; H_1: $\mu_d < 0$. (ii) Student's *t*, $d.f. = 4$; $\bar{d} \approx -4.94$; $t = -2.832$. (iii) $0.010 < P\text{-value} < 0.025$; on *t* graph, shade area to the left of -2.832. For TI-84, $P\text{-value} \approx 0.0236$. (iv) $P\text{-value} \leq 0.05$ for α; reject H_0. (v) At the 5% level of significance, there is sufficient evidence to claim that the population average net sales improved.

CHAPTER 11

Section 11.1

1. Skewed right.
3. Right-tailed test.
5. (a) $\alpha = 0.05$; H_0: Myers-Briggs preference and profession are independent; H_1: Myers-Briggs preference and profession are not independent. (b) $\chi^2 = 8.649$; $d.f. = 2$. (c) $0.010 < P\text{-value} < 0.025$. From TI-84, $P\text{-value} \approx 0.0132$. (d) Reject H_0. (e) At the 5% level of significance, there is sufficient evidence to conclude that Myers-Briggs preference and profession are not independent.
7. (a) $\alpha = 0.01$; H_0: Site type and pottery type are independent; H_1: Site type and pottery type are not independent. (b) $\chi^2 = 0.5552$; $d.f. = 4$. (c) $0.950 < P\text{-value} < 0.975$. From TI-84, $P\text{-value} \approx 0.9679$.
(d) Do not reject H_0. (e) At the 1% level of significance, there is insufficient evidence to conclude that site type and pottery type are not independent.
9. (a) $\alpha = 0.05$; H_0: Age distribution and location are independent; H_1: Age distribution and location are not independent. (b) $\chi^2 = 0.6704$; $d.f. = 4$. (c) $0.950 < P\text{-value} < 0.975$. From TI-84, $P\text{-value} \approx 0.9549$.
(d) Do not reject H_0. (e) At the 5% level of significance, there is insufficient evidence to conclude that age distribution and location are not independent.
11. (a) $\alpha = 0.05$; H_0: Age of young adult and movie preference are independent; H_1: Age of young adult and movie preference are not independent. (b) $\chi^2 = 3.6230$; $d.f. = 4$. (c) $0.100 < P\text{-value} < 0.900$. From TI-84, $P\text{-value} \approx 0.4594$. (d) Do not reject H_0. (e) At the 5% level of significance, there is insufficient evidence to conclude that age of young adult and movie preference are not independent.

13. (a) $\alpha = 0.05$; H_0: Stone tool construction material and site are independent; H_1: Stone tool construction material and site are not independent. (b) $\chi^2 = 11.15$; $d.f. = 3$. (c) $0.010 < P\text{-value} < 0.025$. From TI-84, $P\text{-value} \approx 0.0110$. (d) Reject H_0. (e) At the 5% level of significance, there is sufficient evidence to conclude that stone tool construction material and site are not independent.
15. (i) Communication Preference by Percentage of Age Group

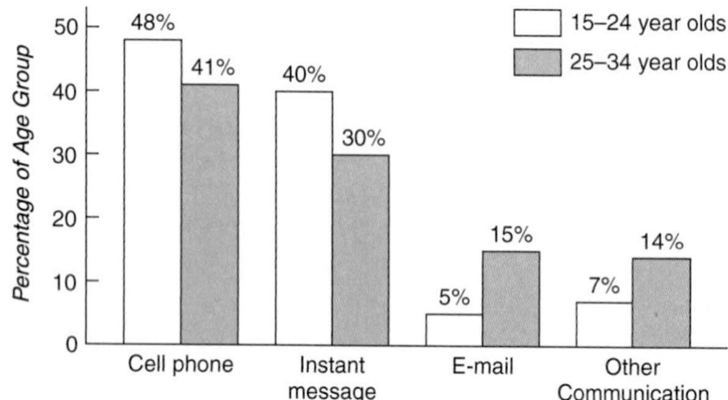

(ii) (a) H_0: The proportions of the different age groups having each communication preference are the same. H_1: The proportions of the different age groups having each communication preference are not the same. (b) $\chi^2 = 9.312$; $d.f. = 3$. (c) $0.025 < P\text{-value} < 0.050$. From TI-84, $P\text{-value} \approx 0.0254$. (d) Reject H_0. (e) At the 5% level of significance, there is sufficient evidence to conclude that the two age groups do not have the same proportions of communications preferences.

Section 11.2

1. $d.f.$ = number of categories − 1.
3. The greater the differences between the observed frequencies and the expected frequencies, the higher the sample χ^2 value. Greater χ^2 values lead to the conclusion that the differences between expected and observed frequencies are too large to be explained by chance alone.
5. (a) $\alpha = 0.05$; H_0: The distributions are the same; H_1: The distributions are different. (b) Sample $\chi^2 = 11.788$; $d.f. = 3$. (c) $0.005 < P\text{-value} < 0.010$. (d) Reject H_0. (e) At the 5% level of significance, the evidence is sufficient to conclude that the age distribution of the Red Lake Village population does not fit the age distribution of the general Canadian population.
7. (a) $\alpha = 0.01$; H_0: The distributions are the same; H_1: The distributions are different. (b) Sample $\chi^2 = 0.1984$; $d.f. = 4$. (c) $P\text{-value} > 0.995$. (Note that as the χ^2 values decrease, the area in the right tail increases, so $\chi^2 < 0.207$ means that the corresponding $P\text{-value} > 0.995$.) (d) Do not reject H_0. (e) At the 1% level of significance, the evidence is insufficient to conclude that the regional distribution of raw materials does not fit the distribution at the current excavation site.
9. (i) Essay. (ii) (a) $\alpha = 0.01$; H_0: The distributions are the same; H_1: The distributions are different. (b) Sample $\chi^2 = 1.5693$; $d.f. = 5$. (c) $0.900 < P\text{-value} < 0.950$. (d) Do not reject H_0. (e) At the 1% level of significance, the evidence is insufficient to conclude that the average daily July temperature does not follow a normal distribution.
11. (a) $\alpha = 0.05$; H_0: The distributions are the same; H_1: The distributions are different. (b) Sample $\chi^2 = 9.333$; $d.f. = 3$. (c) $0.025 < P\text{-value} < 0.050$. (d) Reject H_0. (e) At the 5% level of significance, the evidence is sufficient to conclude that the current fish distribution is different than it was 5 years ago.
13. (a) $\alpha = 0.01$; H_0: The distributions are the same; H_1: The distributions are different. (b) Sample $\chi^2 = 13.70$; $d.f. = 5$. (c) $0.010 < P\text{-value} < 0.025$. (d) Do not reject H_0. (e) At the 1% level of significance, the evidence is insufficient to conclude that the census ethnic origin distribution and the ethnic origin distribution of city residents are different.

Section 11.3

1. Yes. No, the chi-square test of variance requires that the x distribution be a normal distribution.
3. (a) $\alpha = 0.05$; H_0: $\sigma^2 = 42.3$; H_1: $\sigma^2 > 42.3$. (b) $\chi^2 \approx 23.98$; $d.f. = 22$. (c) $0.100 < P\text{-value} < 0.900$. (d) Do not reject H_0. (e) At the 5% level of significance, there is insufficient evidence to conclude that the variance is greater in the new section.
5. (a) $\alpha = 0.01$; H_0: $\sigma^2 = 136.2$; H_1: $\sigma^2 < 136.2$. (b) $\chi^2 \approx 5.92$; $d.f. = 7$. (c) Right-tailed area between 0.900 and 0.100; $0.100 < P\text{-value} < 0.900$. (d) Do not reject H_0. (e) At the 1% level of significance, there is insufficient evidence to conclude that the variance for number of mountain-climber deaths is less than 136.2.
7. (a) $\alpha = 0.05$; H_0: $\sigma^2 = 9$; H_1: $\sigma^2 < 9$. (b) $\chi^2 \approx 8.82$; $d.f. = 22$. (c) Right-tail area is between 0.995 and 0.990; $0.005 < P\text{-value} < 0.010$. (d) Reject H_0. (e) At the 5% level of significance, there is sufficient evidence to conclude that the variance of protection times for the new typhoid shot is less than 9.
9. (a) $\alpha = 0.01$; H_0: $\sigma^2 = 0.18$; H_1: $\sigma^2 > 0.18$. (b) $\chi^2 = 90$; $d.f. = 60$. (c) $0.005 < P\text{-value} < 0.010$. (d) Reject H_0. (e) At the 1% level of significance, there is sufficient evidence to conclude that the variance of measurements for the fan blades is higher than the specified amount. The inspector is justified in claiming that the blades must be replaced.
11. (a) $\alpha = 0.05$; H_0: $\sigma^2 = 23$; H_1: $\sigma^2 \neq 23$. (b) $\chi^2 \approx 13.06$; $d.f. = 21$. (c) The area to the left of $\chi^2 = 13.06$ is less than 50%, so we double the left-tail area to find the P-value for the two-tailed test. Right-tail area is between 0.950 and 0.900. Subtracting each value from 1, we find that the left-tail area is between 0.050 and 0.100. Doubling the left-tail area for a two-tailed test gives $0.100 < P\text{-value} < 0.200$. (d) Do not reject H_0. (e) At the 5% level of significance, there is insufficient evidence to conclude that the variance of battery lifetimes is different from 23.

Section 11.4

1. ρ (Greek letter rho).
3. As x becomes farther away from $\bar{x}$, the confidence interval for the predicted y becomes longer.

5. (a) Diameter. (b) $a = -0.223$; $b = 0.7848$; $\hat{y} = -0.223 + 0.7848x$. (c) P-value of b is 0.001. H_0: $\beta = 0$; H_1: $\beta \neq 0$. Since P-value < 0.01, reject H_0 and conclude that the slope is not zero. (d) $r \approx 0.896$. Yes. P-value is 0.001, so we reject H_0 for $\alpha = 0.01$.
7. (a) Use a calculator. (b) $\alpha = 0.05$; H_0: $\rho = 0$; H_1: $\rho > 0$; sample $t \approx 2.522$; $d.f. = 4$; $0.025 <$ P-value < 0.050; reject H_0. There seems to be a positive correlation between x and y. From TI-84, P-value $\approx$ 0.0326. (c) Use a calculator. (d) 45.36%. (e) Interval from 39.05 to 51.67. (f) $\alpha = 0.05$; H_0: $\beta = 0$; H_1: $\beta > 0$; sample $t \approx 2.522$; $d.f. = 4$; $0.025 <$ P-value < 0.050; reject H_0. There seems to be a positive slope between x and y. From TI-84, P-value ≈ 0.0326.
9. (a) Use a calculator. (b) $\alpha = 0.01$; H_0: $\rho = 0$; H_1: $\rho < 0$; sample $t \approx -10.06$; $d.f. = 5$; P-value $<$ 0.0005; reject H_0. The sample evidence supports a negative correlation. From TI-84, P-value ≈ 0.00008. (c) Use a calculator. (d) 2.39 hours. (e) Interval from 2.12 to 2.66 hours. (f) $\alpha = 0.01$; H_0: $\beta = 0$; H_1: $\beta < 0$; sample $t \approx -10.06$; $d.f. = 5$; P-value < 0.0005; reject H_0. The sample evidence supports a negative slope. From TI-84, P-value ≈ 0.00008.
11. (a) Use a calculator. (b) $\alpha = 0.01$; H_0: $\rho = 0$; H_1: $\rho > 0$; sample $t \approx 6.534$; $d.f. = 4$; $0.0005 <$ P-value $<$ 0.005; reject H_0. The sample evidence supports a positive correlation. From TI-84, P-value ≈ 0.0014. (c) Use a calculator. (d) \$12.577 thousand. (e) Interval from 12.247 to 12.907 (thousand dollars). (f) $\alpha = 0.01$; H_0: $\beta = 0$; H_1: $\beta > 0$; sample $t \approx 6.534$; $d.f. = 4$; $0.0005 <$ P-value < 0.005; reject H_0. The sample evidence supports a positive slope. From TI-84, P-value ≈ 0.0014.
13. (a) H_0: $\rho = 0$; H_1: $\rho \neq 0$; $d.f. = 4$; sample $t = 4.129$; $0.01 <$ P-value < 0.02; do not reject H_0; r is not significant at the 0.01 level of significance. (b) H_0: $\rho = 0$; H_1: $\rho \neq 0$; $d.f. = 8$; sample $t = 5.840$; P-value $<$ 0.001; reject H_0; r is significant at the 0.01 level of significance. (c) As n increases, the t value corresponding to r also increases, resulting in a smaller P-value.

Chapter 11 Review

1. Chi-square.
3. Test of homogeneity.
5. Chi-square test of σ^2. (i) $\alpha = 0.01$; H_0: $\sigma^2 = 1{,}040{,}400$; H_1: $\sigma^2 > 1{,}040{,}400$. (ii) $\chi^2 \approx 51.03$; $d.f. = 29$. (iii) $0.005 <$ P-value < 0.010. (iv) Reject H_0. (v) At the 1% level of significance, there is sufficient evidence to conclude that the variance is greater than claimed.
7. Chi-square test of independence. (i) $\alpha = 0.01$; H_0: Student grade and teacher rating are independent; H_1: Student grade and teacher rating are not independent. (ii) $\chi^2 \approx 9.80$; $d.f. = 6$. (iii) $0.100 <$ P-value < 0.900. From TI-84, P-value ≈ 0.1337. (iv) Do not reject H_0. (v) At the 1% level of significance, there is insufficient evidence to claim that student grade and teacher rating are not independent.
9. We reject the null hypothesis that ρ is zero.
11. (a) Use a calculator. (b) (i) $\alpha = 0.01$; H_0: $\rho = 0$; H_1: $\rho > 0$. (ii) $t \approx 6.665$; $d.f. = 5$. (iii) $0.0005 <$ P-value < 0.005. From TI-84, P-value ≈ 0.0006. (iv) Reject H_0. (v) At the 1% level of significance, there is evidence that ρ is positive. (c) (i) $\alpha = 0.01$; H_0: $\beta = 0$; H_1: $\beta > 0$. (ii) $t \approx 6.665$; $d.f. = 5$. (iii) $0.0005 <$ P-value < 0.005. From TI-84, P-value $\approx$ 0.0006. (iv) Reject H_0. (v) At the 1% level of significance, there is evidence that β is positive. (d) $\hat{y} \approx 5.98$; $E \approx 1.48$; 4.498 to 7.458.

CUMULATIVE REVIEW PROBLEMS CHAPTERS 10–11

1. (a) Use a calculator. (b) (i) $\alpha = 0.05$; H_0: $\rho = 0$; H_1: $\rho > 0$. (ii) Student's t, $d.f. = 6$; $t \approx 2.466$. (iii) $0.010 <$ P-value < 0.025. On the t graph, shade area to the right of 2.466. From TI-84, P-value ≈ 0.0244. (iv) P-value interval $< \alpha = 0.05$; reject H_0. (v) At the 5% level of significance, there is evidence of a positive correlation between age of a volcanic island in the Indian Ocean and distance of the island from the center of the mid-oceanic ridge. (c) (i) $\alpha = 0.05$; H_0: $\beta = 0$; H_1: $\beta > 0$. (ii) Student's t, $d.f. = 6$; $t \approx 2.466$. (iii) $0.010 <$ P-value < 0.025. On the t graph, shade area to the right of 2.466. From TI-84, P-value ≈ 0.0244. (iv) P-value interval $< \alpha = 0.05$; reject H_0. (v) At the 5% level of significance, there is evidence of a positive slope for the regression line for age of a volcanic island in the Indian Ocean and distance of the island from the center of the midoceanic ridge. (d) $\hat{y} \approx 16.5$ (units in 100 km); $d.f. = 6$; $t_{0.85} = 1.650$; $E \approx 11.4$; 5.1 to 27.9 (units in 100 km).
2. (i) $\alpha = 0.01$; H_0: Colorado major distribution is the same as national distribution; H_1: Colorado major distribution is different from national distribution. (ii) Chi-square; $d.f. = 5$; $\chi^2 \approx 10.196$. (iii) $0.050 <$ P-value $<$ 0.100; shade region to the right of 10.196. (iv) P-value interval $> \alpha = 0.01$; fail to reject H_0. (v) At the 1% level of significance, the evidence is insufficient to claim that the distribution of college majors selected by Colorado students is different from the national distribution of college majors.
3. (i) $\alpha = 0.05$; H_0: Yield and fertilizer type are independent; H_1: Yield and fertilizer type are not independent. (ii) Chi-square distribution $\chi^2 \approx 5.005$; $d.f. = 4$. (iii) $0.100 <$ P-value < 0.900. From TI-84, P-value $\approx$ 0.2868. (iv) Do not reject H_0. (v) At the 5% level of significance, the evidence is insufficient to conclude that fertilizer type and yield are not independent.
4. (i) $\alpha = 0.05$; H_0: $\sigma = 0.55$; H_1: $\sigma > 0.55$. (ii) Chi-square distribution $s \approx 0.602$; $d.f. = 9$; $\chi^2 \approx 10.78$. (iii) $0.100 <$ P-value < 0.900. (iv) Do not reject H_0. (v) At the 5% level of significance, there is insufficient evidence to conclude that the standard deviation of petal lengths is greater than 0.55.
5. (i) $\alpha = 0.05$; H_0: $\mu_d = 0$; H_1: $\mu_d \neq 0$. (ii) Student's t, $d.f. = 6$; $\bar{d} \approx -0.00390$; $t \approx -0.771$. (iii) $0.250 <$ P-value < 0.500; on t graph, shade area to the right of

0.771 and to the left of −0.771. From TI-84, P-value ≈ 0.4699. (iv) P-value interval > 0.05 for α; fail to reject H_0. (v) At the 5% level of significance, the evidence does not show a population mean difference in phosphorous reduction between the two methods.

6. (a) (i) $\alpha = 0.05$; H_0: $\mu_1 = \mu_2$; H_1: $\mu_1 \neq \mu_2$. (ii) Student's t, $d.f. = 15$; $t \approx 1.952$. (iii) 0.050 < P-value < 0.100; on t graph, shade area to the right of 1.952 and to the left of −0.1952. From TI-84, P-value ≈ 0.0609. (iv) P-value interval > 0.05 for α; fail to reject H_0. (v) At the 5% level of significance, the evidence does not show any difference in the population mean proportion of on-time arrivals in summer versus winter. (b) −0.43% to 9.835%. (c) x_1 and x_2 distributions are approximately normal (mound-shaped and symmetric).

7. (a) (i) $\alpha = 0.05$; H_0: $p_1 = p_2$; H_1: $p_1 > p_2$. (ii) Standard normal; $\hat{p}_1 \approx 0.242$; $\hat{p}_2 \approx 0.207$; $\bar{p} \approx 0.2246$; $z \approx 0.58$. (iii) P-value ≈ 0.2810; on standard normal curve, shade area to the right of 0.58. (iv) P-value interval > 0.05 for α; fail to reject H_0. (v) At the 5% level of significance, the evidence does not indicate that the population proportion of single men who go out dancing occasionally differs from the proportion of single women. Since $n_1\bar{p}$, $n_1\bar{q}$, $n_2\bar{p}$, and $n_2\bar{q}$ are all greater than 5, the normal approximation to the binomial is justified. (b) −0.065 to 0.139.

Answers to Selected Even-Numbered Problems

CHAPTER 2

Even-numbered answers not included here appear in the margins of the chapters, next to the problems.

Section 2.1

6. (a) Employee Salaries—Histogram

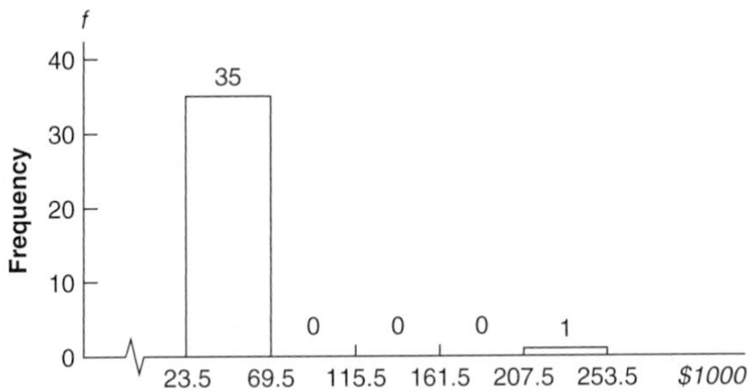

(c) Employee Salaries—Histogram

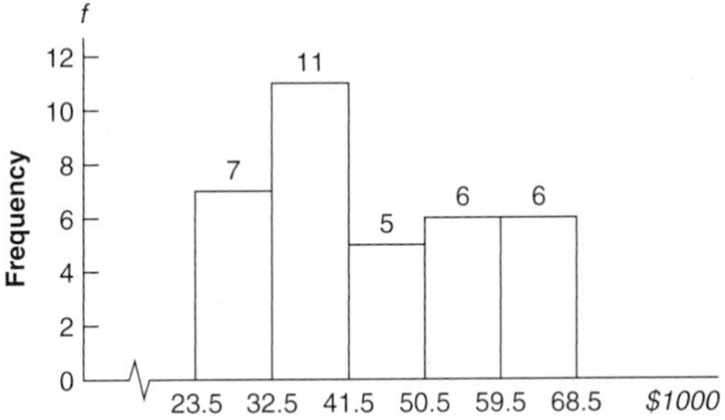

8. (a) Class width = 11.
(b)

Class Limits	Class Boundaries	Midpoint	Frequency	Relative Frequency
45–55	44.5–55.5	50	3	0.04
56–66	55.5–66.5	61	7	0.10
67–77	66.5–77.5	72	22	0.31
78–88	77.5–88.5	83	26	0.37
89–99	88.5–99.5	94	9	0.13
100–110	99.5–110.5	103	3	0.04

(c, d) Glucose Level (mg/100 ml)—Histogram, Relative-Frequency Histogram

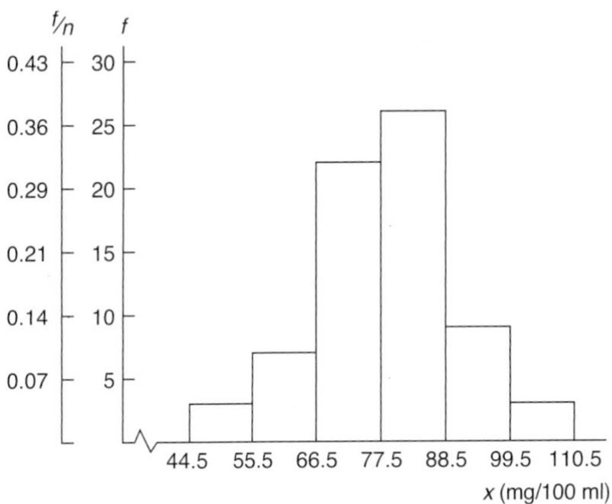

10. (a) Class width = 28.
(b)

Class Limits	Class Boundaries	Midpoint	Frequency	Relative Frequency
10–37	9.5–37.5	23.5	7	0.10
38–65	37.5–65.5	51.5	25	0.34
66–93	65.5–93.5	79.5	26	0.36
94–121	93.5–121.5	107.5	9	0.12
122–149	121.5–149.5	135.5	5	0.07
150–177	149.5–177.5	163.5	0	0.00
178–205	177.5–205.5	191.5	1	0.01

(c, d) Depth of Artifacts (cm)—Histogram, Relative-Frequency Histogram

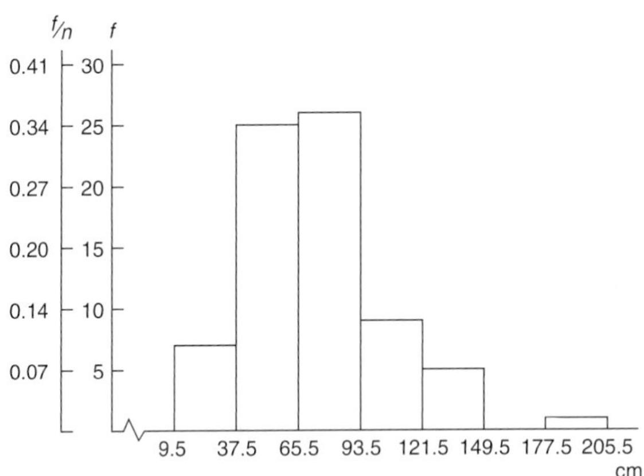

12. (a) Class width = 6.
(b)

Words of Three Syllables or More

Class Limits	Class Boundaries	Midpoint	Frequency	Relative Frequency
0–5	−0.5–5.5	2.5	13	0.24
6–11	5.5–11.5	8.5	15	0.27
12–17	11.5–17.5	14.5	11	0.20
18–23	17.5–23.5	20.5	3	0.05
24–29	23.5–29.5	26.5	6	0.11
30–35	29.5–35.5	32.5	4	0.07
36–41	35.5–41.5	38.5	2	0.04
42–47	41.5–47.5	44.5	1	0.02

(c, d) Words of Three Syllables or More—Histogram, Relative-Frequency Histogram

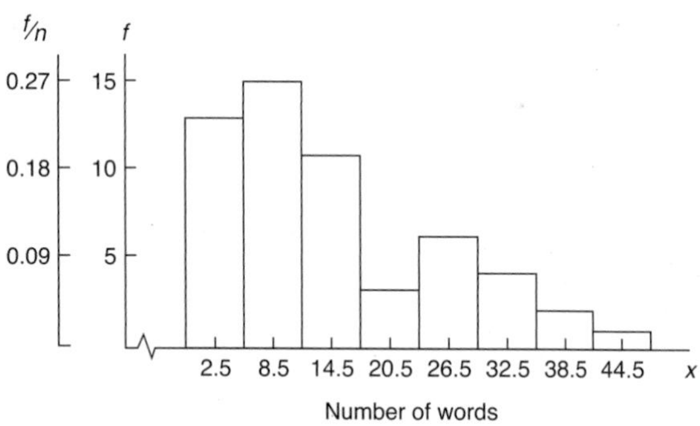

14. (b)

Baseball Batting Averages (class width = 0.043)

Class Limits	Class Boundaries	Midpoint	Frequency
0.107–0.149	0.1065–0.1495	0.128	3
0.150–0.192	0.1495–0.1925	0.171	4
0.193–0.235	0.1925–0.2355	0.214	3
0.236–0.278	0.2355–0.2785	0.257	10
0.279–0.321	0.2785–0.3215	0.3	6

(b, c) Baseball Batting Averages—Histogram

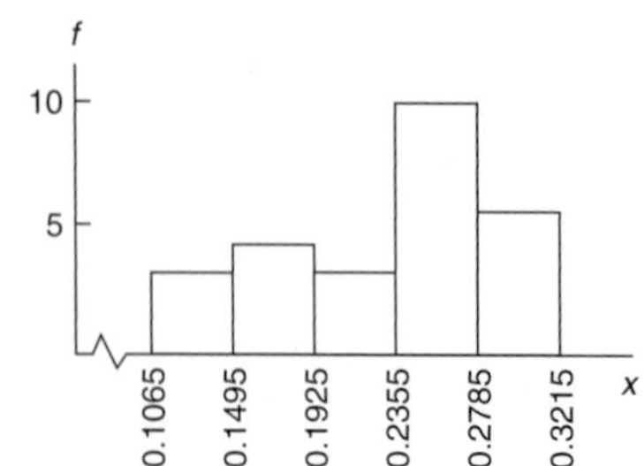

16. Dotplot for Iditarod Finish Time (in hours)

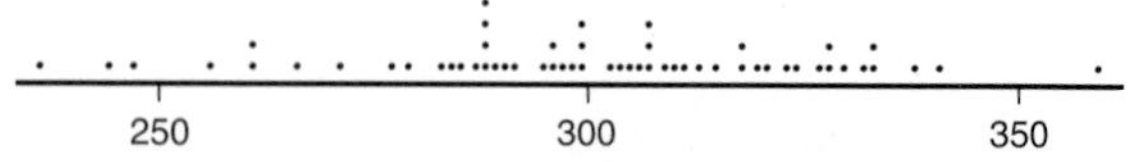

Section 2.2

4. Number of Kids Killed by Injury (per 100,000 children)—Pareto Chart

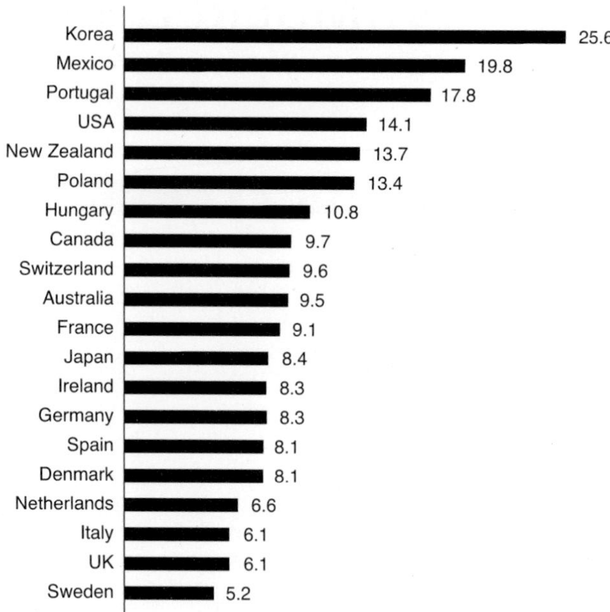

6. (a) Number of Spearheads—Pareto Chart

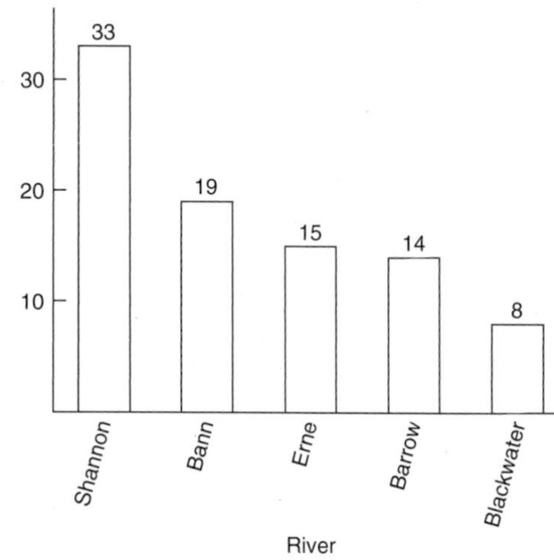

(b) Number of Spearheads—Circle Graph

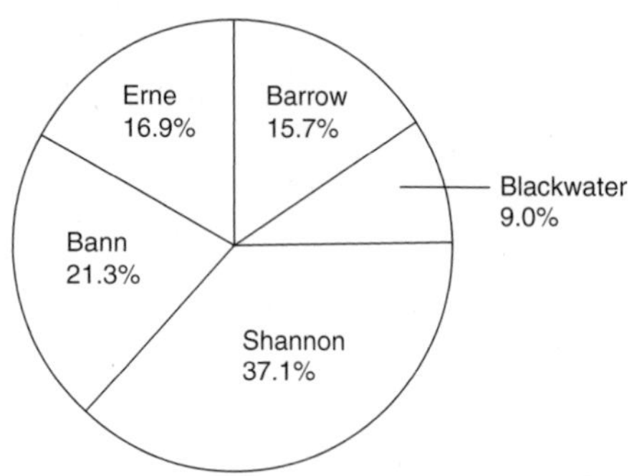

8. How College Professors Spend Their Time—Circle Graph

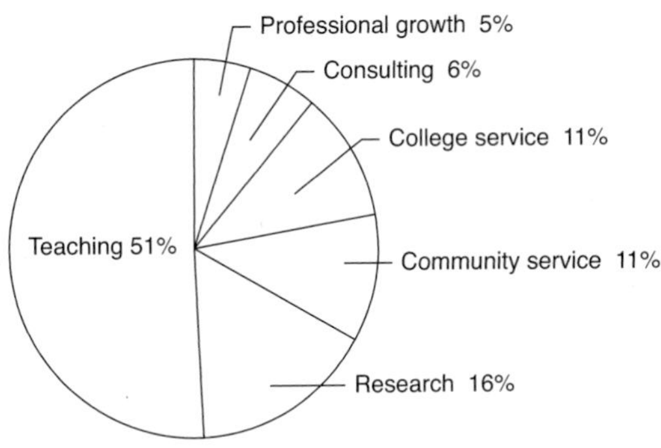

10. Driving Complaints—Pareto Chart

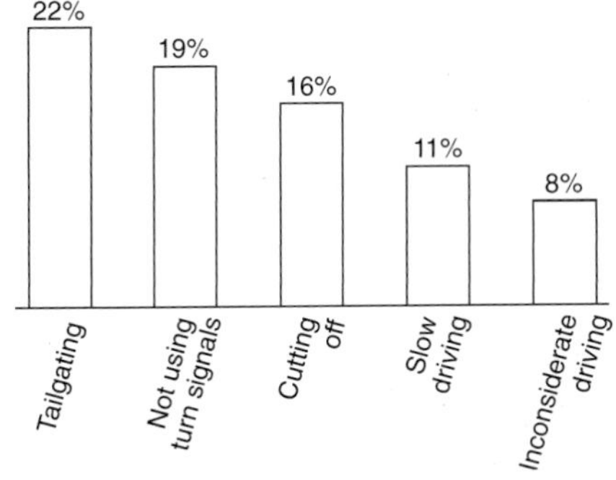

No. The total is not 100%, and it is not clear if respondents could mark more than one complaint.

12. Changes in Boys' Heights with Age—Time-Series Graph

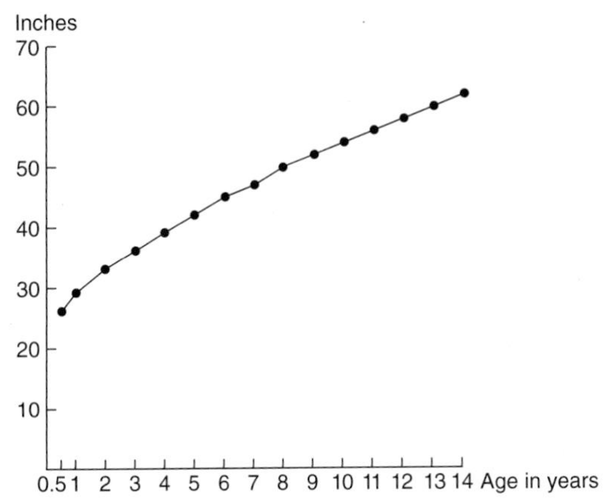

Chapter 2 Review

8. (a)

Age of DUI Arrests

1	6 = 16 years
1	6 8
2	0 1 1 2 2 2 3 4 4 5 6 6 6 7 7 7 9
3	0 0 1 1 2 3 4 4 5 5 6 7 8 9
4	0 0 1 3 5 6 7 7 9 9
5	1 3 5 6 8
6	3 4

(b) Class width = 7.

Age Distribution of DUI Arrests

Class Limits	Class Boundaries	Midpoint	Frequency	Relative Frequency
16–22	15.5–22.5	19	8	0.16
23–29	22.5–29.5	26	11	0.22
30–36	29.5–36.5	33	11	0.22
37–43	36.5–43.5	40	7	0.14
44–50	43.5–50.5	47	6	0.12
51–57	50.5–57.5	54	4	0.08
58–64	57.5–64.5	61	3	0.06

(c) Age Distribution of DUI Arrests—Histogram

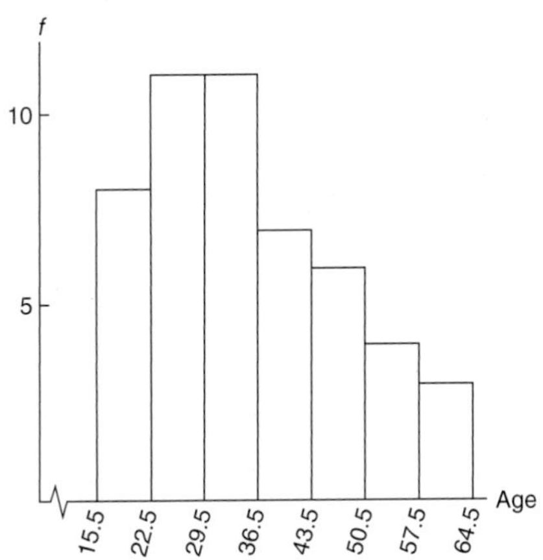

10. (a) Distribution of Civil Justice Caseloads Involving Businesses—Pareto Chart

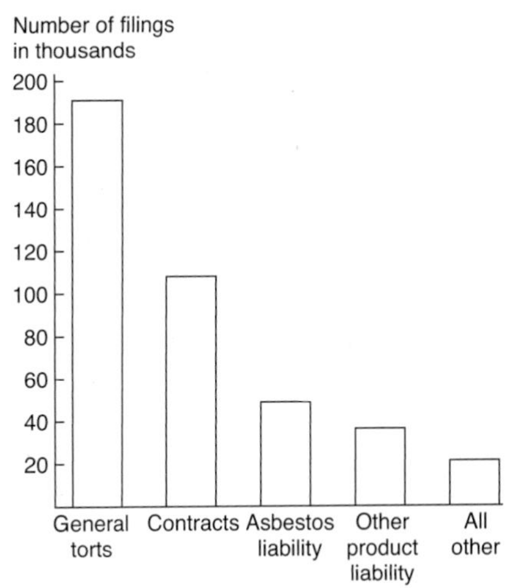

(b) Distribution of Civil Justice Caseloads Involving Businesses—Pie Chart

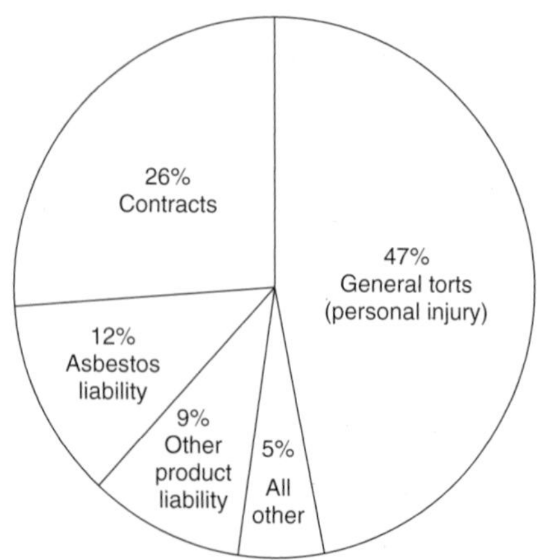

10. (a) Low value = 4; $Q_1 = 61.5$; median = 65.5; $Q_3 = 71.5$; high value = 80. (b) $IQR = 10$. (c) Lower limit = 46.5; upper limit = 86.5. (d) Yes, the value 4 is below the lower limit and is probably an error. Our guess is that one of the students is 4 feet tall and listed height in feet instead of inches. There are no values above the upper limit.

Students' Heights (inches)

CHAPTER 3

Section 3.3

6. (a) Low = 3; $Q_1 = 16$; median = 23; $Q_3 = 30$; high = 72; $IQR = 14$.

Clerical Staff Length of Employment (months)

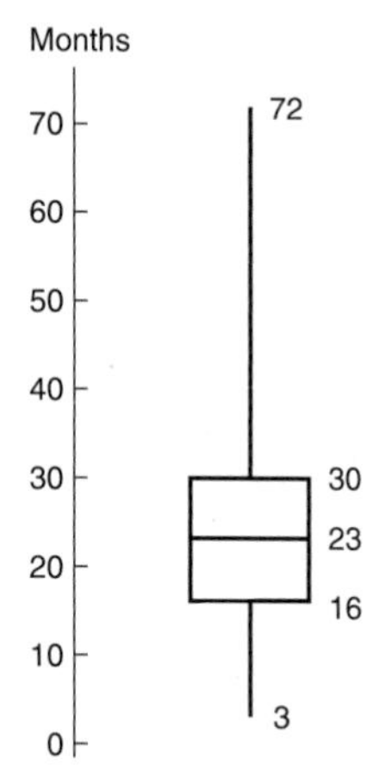

8. (a) Low = 5; $Q_1 = 9$; median = 10; $Q_3 = 12$; high = 15; $IQR = 3$. (b) First quartile, since it is below Q_1.

High-School Dropout Percentage by State

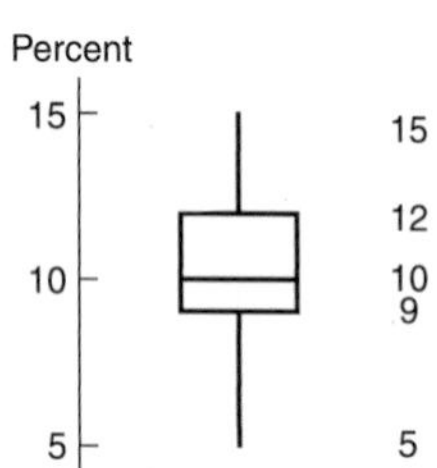

Chapter 3 Review

8. (a) Low = 7.8; $Q_1 = 14.2$ (kilograms); median = 20.25; $Q_3 = 23.8$; high = 29.5. (b) $IQR = 9.6$ kilograms. (d) Yes, the lower half shows slightly more spread.

Maize Harvest

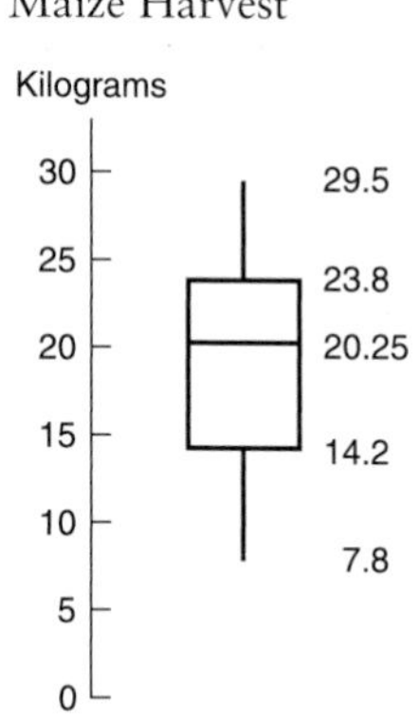

10. (a) Low = 6; $Q_1 = 10$; median = 11; $Q_3 = 13$; high = 16; $IQR = 3$.

Soil Water Content

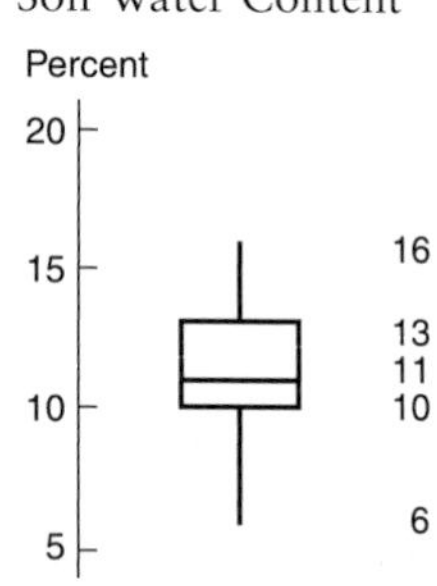

CHAPTER 4

Section 4.1

12. (a) Group Health Insurance Plans: Average Number of Employees versus Administrative Costs as a Percentage of Claims

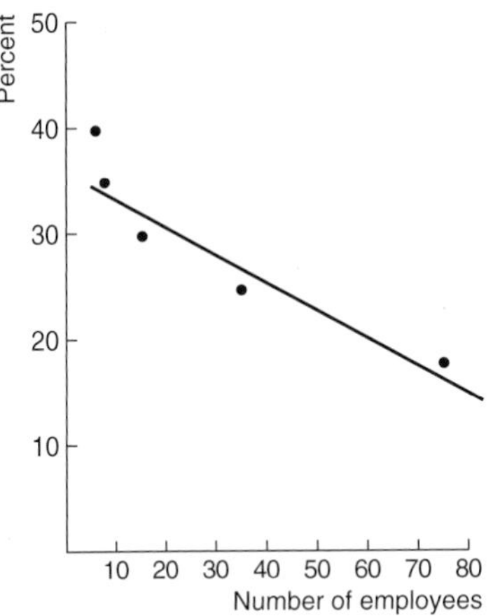

14. (a) Magnitude (Richter Scale) and Depth (km) of Earthquakes

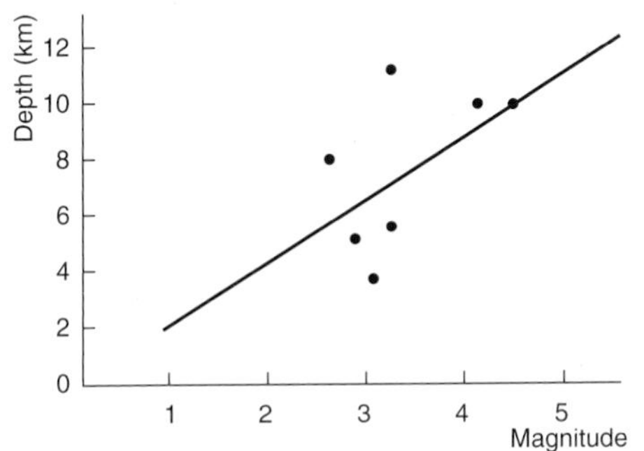

16. (a) Student Enrollment (in thousands) versus Number of Burglaries

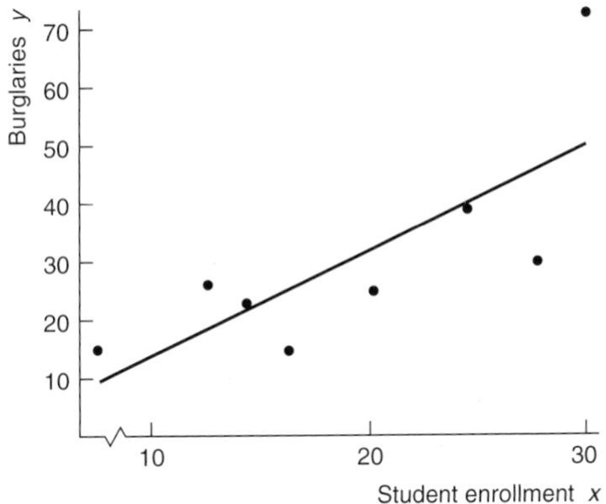

Section 4.2

8. (a) Percent Change in Rate of Violent Crime and Percent Change in Rate of Imprisonment in U.S. Population

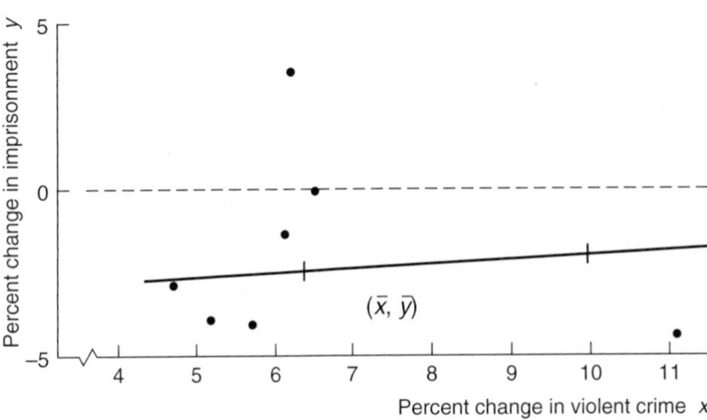

10. (a) Fouls and Basketball Wins

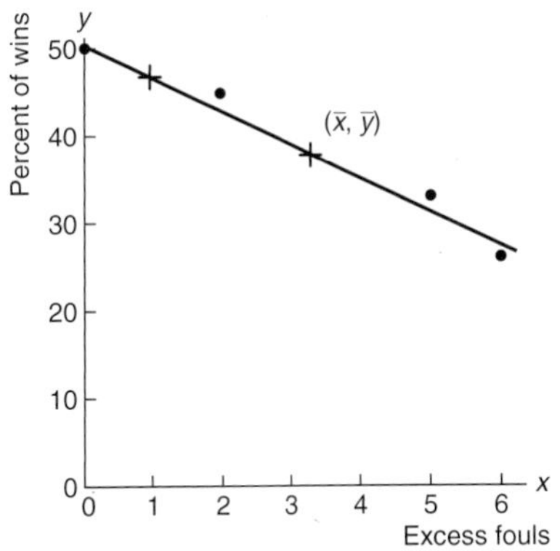

12. (a) Age and Percentage of Fatal Accidents Due to Failure to Yield

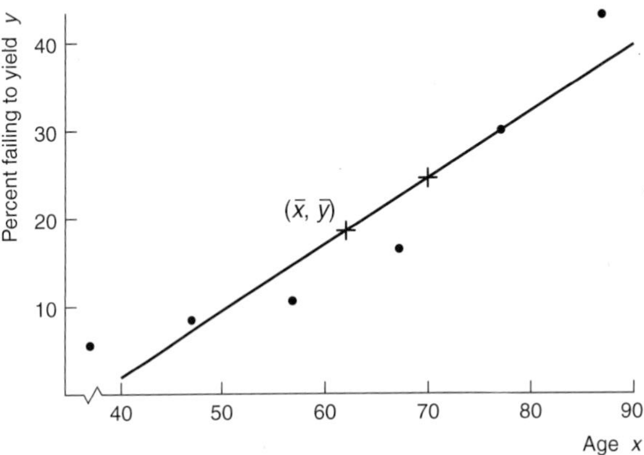

14. (a) Chirps per Second and Temperature (°F)

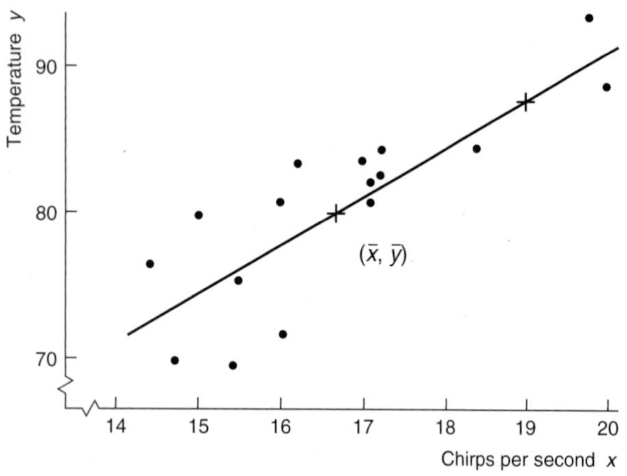

16. (a) Residuals: 2.9, 2.1, −0.1, −2.1, −0.5, −2.3, −1.9, 1.9.
Residual Plot

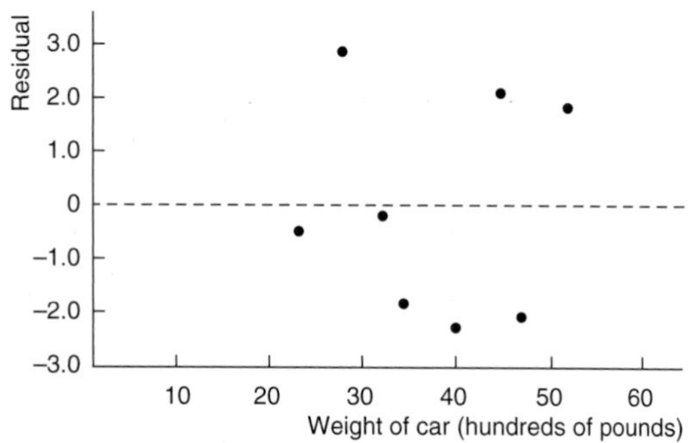

Chapter 4 Review

6. (a) Annual Salary (thousands) and Number of Job Changes

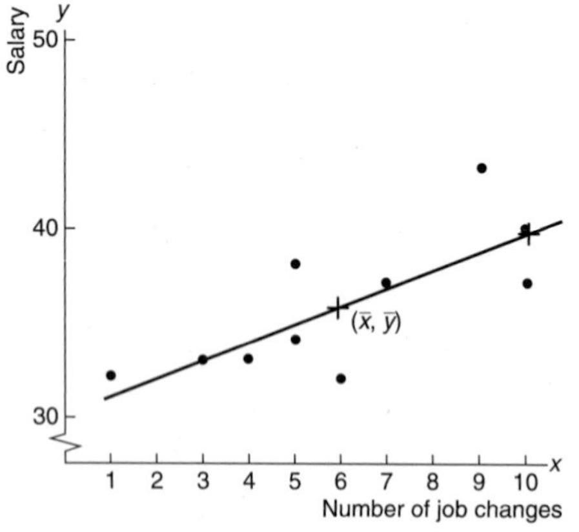

8. (a) Number of Insurance Sales and Number of Visits

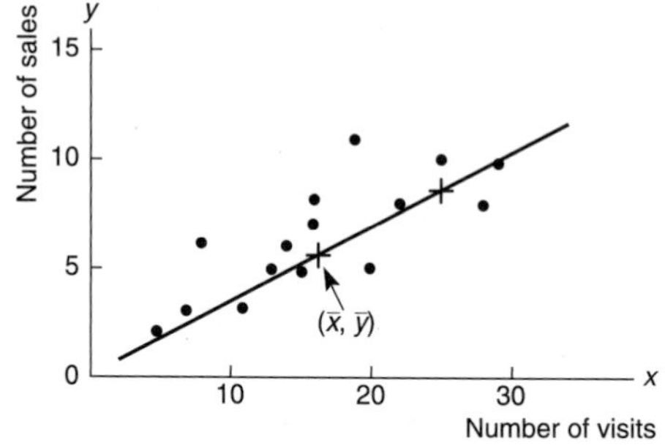

10. (a) Percent Population Change and Crime Rate

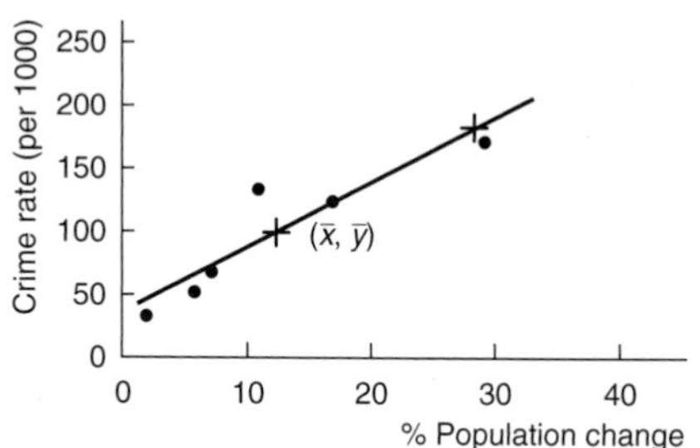

CHAPTER 5

Section 5.3

6. (a) Outcomes of Tossing a Coin and Throwing a Die

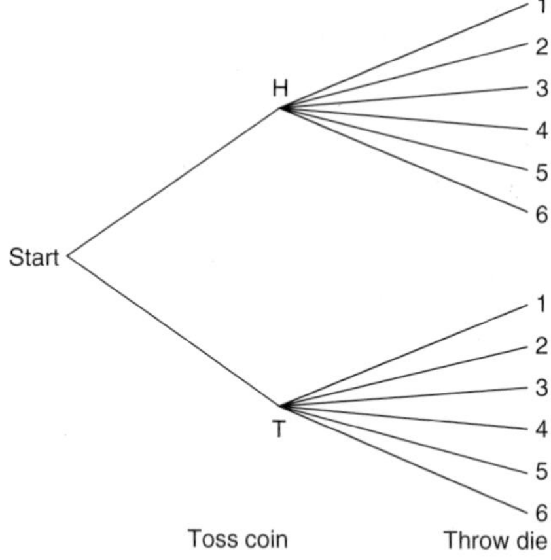

8. (a) Outcomes of Answering Three Multiple-Choice Questions

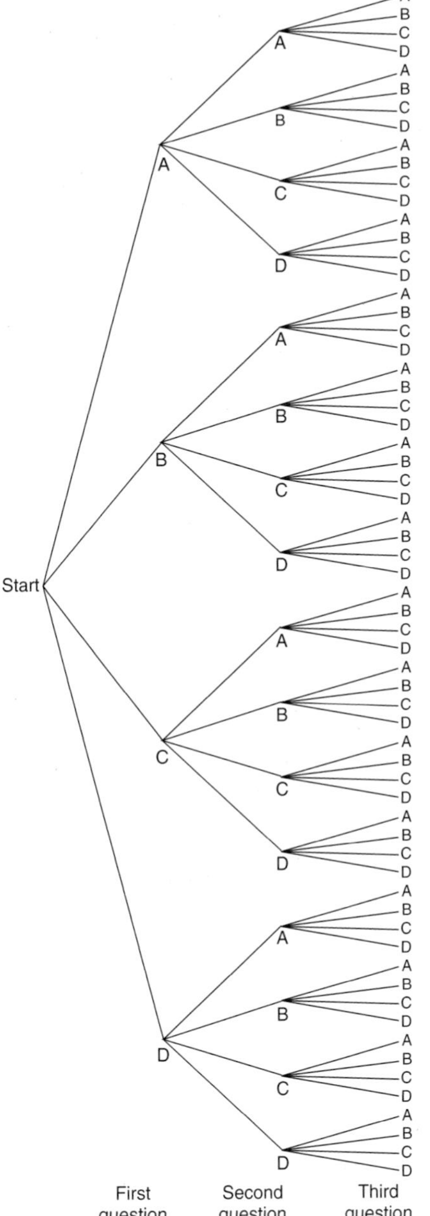

Chapter 5 Review

14. Ways to Satisfy Literature, Social Science, and Philosophy Requirements

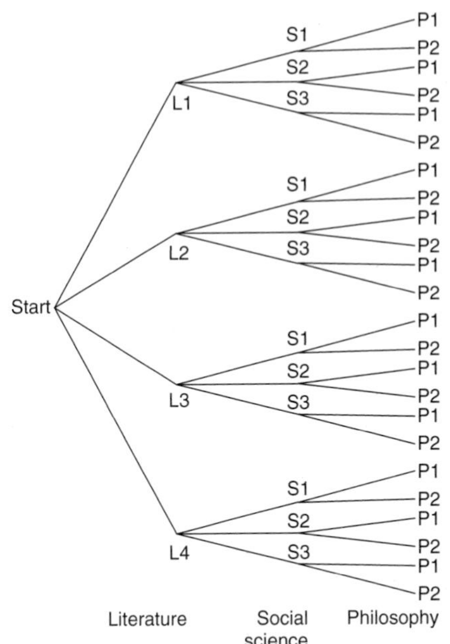

CHAPTER 6

Section 6.1

6. (b) Ages of Promotion-Sensitive Shoppers

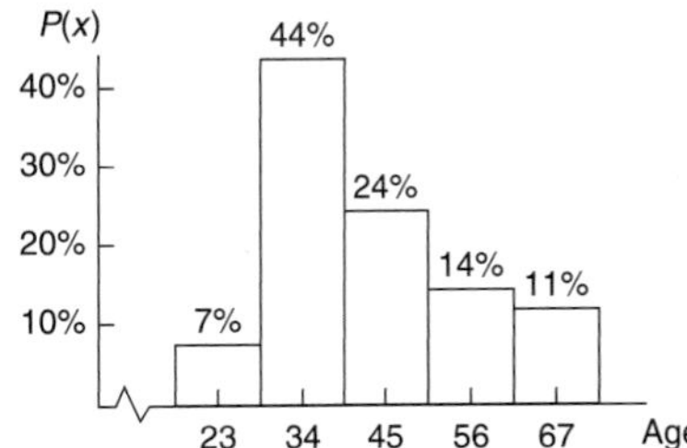

8. (b) Ages of Nurses

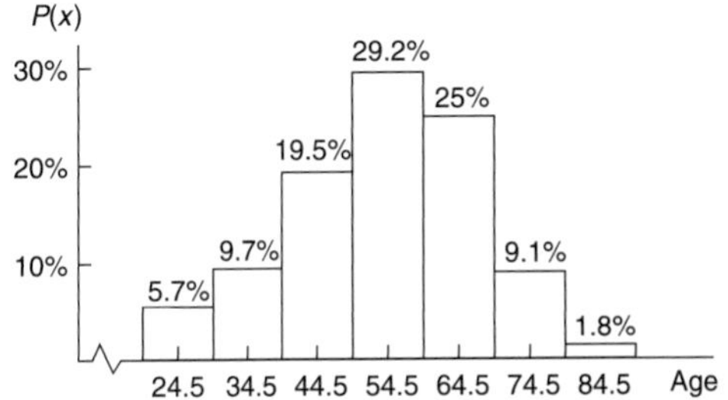

Section 6.3

6. (a) Binomial Distribution for Number of Defective Syringes

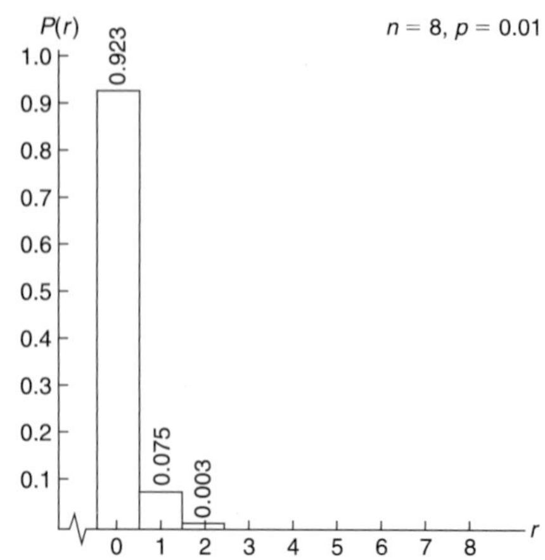

8. (a) Binomial Distribution for Number of Automobile Damage Claims by People Under Age 25

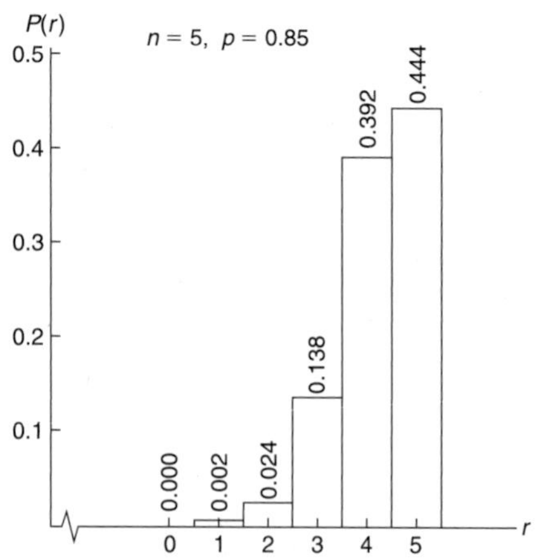

10. (b) Binomial Distribution for Number of Parolees Who Do Not Become Repeat Offenders

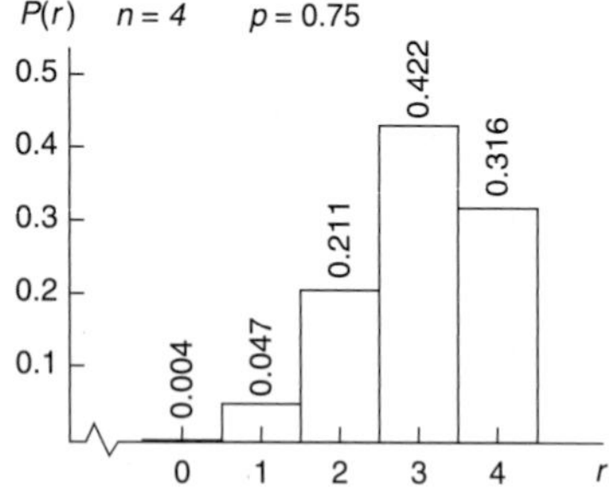

CHAPTER 7

Section 7.1

4. (a) Normal Curve

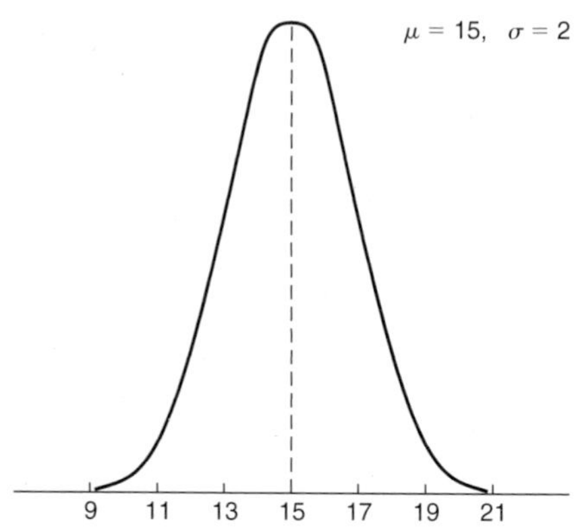

(b) Normal Curve

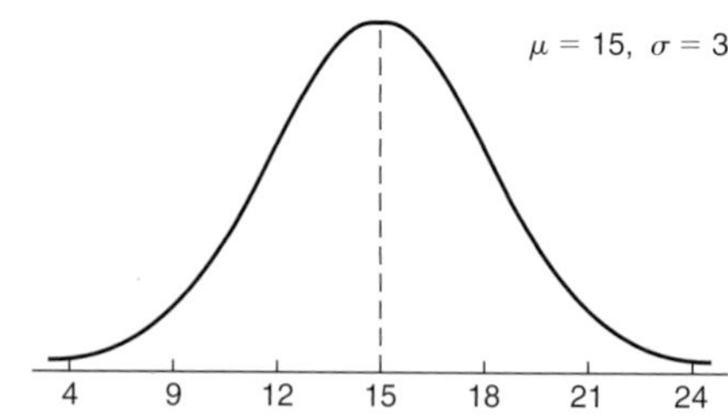

(c) Normal Curve

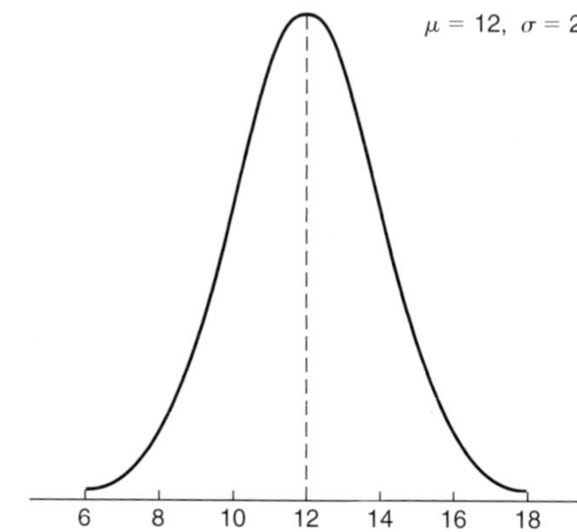

(d) Normal Curve

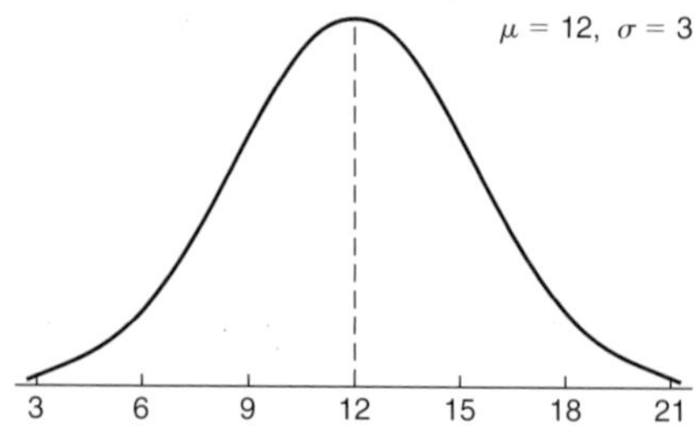

INDEX

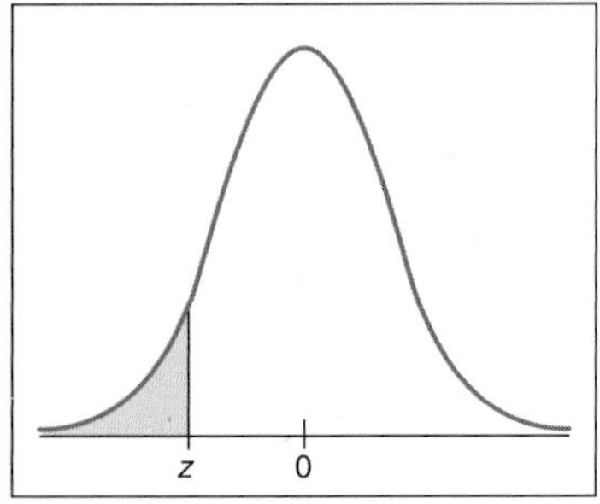

The table entry for z is the area to the left of z.

Areas of a Standard Normal Distribution

(a) Table of Areas to the Left of z

z	.00	.01	.02	.03	.04	.05	.06	.07	.08	.09
−3.4	.0003	.0003	.0003	.0003	.0003	.0003	.0003	.0003	.0003	.0002
−3.3	.0005	.0005	.0005	.0004	.0004	.0004	.0004	.0004	.0004	.0003
−3.2	.0007	.0007	.0006	.0006	.0006	.0006	.0006	.0005	.0005	.0005
−3.1	.0010	.0009	.0009	.0009	.0008	.0008	.0008	.0008	.0007	.0007
−3.0	.0013	.0013	.0013	.0012	.0012	.0011	.0011	.0011	.0010	.0010
−2.9	.0019	.0018	.0018	.0017	.0016	.0016	.0015	.0015	.0014	.0014
−2.8	.0026	.0025	.0024	.0023	.0023	.0022	.0021	.0021	.0020	.0019
−2.7	.0035	.0034	.0033	.0032	.0031	.0030	.0029	.0028	.0027	.0026
−2.6	.0047	.0045	.0044	.0043	.0041	.0040	.0039	.0038	.0037	.0036
−2.5	.0062	.0060	.0059	.0057	.0055	.0054	.0052	.0051	.0049	.0048
−2.4	.0082	.0080	.0078	.0075	.0073	.0071	.0069	.0068	.0066	.0064
−2.3	.0107	.0104	.0102	.0099	.0096	.0094	.0091	.0089	.0087	.0084
−2.2	.0139	.0136	.0132	.0129	.0125	.0122	.0119	.0116	.0113	.0110
−2.1	.0179	.0174	.0170	.0166	.0162	.0158	.0154	.0150	.0146	.0143
−2.0	.0228	.0222	.0217	.0212	.0207	.0202	.0197	.0192	.0188	.0183
−1.9	.0287	.0281	.0274	.0268	.0262	.0256	.0250	.0244	.0239	.0233
−1.8	.0359	.0351	.0344	.0336	.0329	.0322	.0314	.0307	.0301	.0294
−1.7	.0446	.0436	.0427	.0418	.0409	.0401	.0392	.0384	.0375	.0367
−1.6	.0548	.0537	.0526	.0516	.0505	.0495	.0485	.0475	.0465	.0455
−1.5	.0668	.0655	.0643	.0630	.0618	.0606	.0594	.0582	.0571	.0559
−1.4	.0808	.0793	.0778	.0764	.0749	.0735	.0721	.0708	.0694	.0681
−1.3	.0968	.0951	.0934	.0918	.0901	.0885	.0869	.0853	.0838	.0823
−1.2	.1151	.1131	.1112	.1093	.1075	.1056	.1038	.1020	.1003	.0985
−1.1	.1357	.1335	.1314	.1292	.1271	.1251	.1230	.1210	.1190	.1170
−1.0	.1587	.1562	.1539	.1515	.1492	.1469	.1446	.1423	.1401	.1379
−0.9	.1841	.1814	.1788	.1762	.1736	.1711	.1685	.1660	.1635	.1611
−0.8	.2119	.2090	.2061	.2033	.2005	.1977	.1949	.1922	.1894	.1867
−0.7	.2420	.2389	.2358	.2327	.2296	.2266	.2236	.2206	.2177	.2148
−0.6	.2743	.2709	.2676	.2643	.2611	.2578	.2546	.2514	.2483	.2451
−0.5	.3085	.3050	.3015	.2981	.2946	.2912	.2877	.2843	.2810	.2776
−0.4	.3446	.3409	.3372	.3336	.3300	.3264	.3228	.3192	.3156	.3121
−0.3	.3821	.3783	.3745	.3707	.3669	.3632	.3594	.3557	.3520	.3483
−0.2	.4207	.4168	.4129	.4090	.4052	.4013	.3974	.3936	.3897	.3859
−0.1	.4602	.4562	.4522	.4483	.4443	.4404	.4364	.4325	.4286	.4247
−0.0	.5000	.4960	.4920	.4880	.4840	.4801	.4761	.4721	.4681	.4641

For values of z less than −3.49, use 0.000 to approximate the area.